CRIME STATE RANKINGS
1996

Crime in the 50 United States

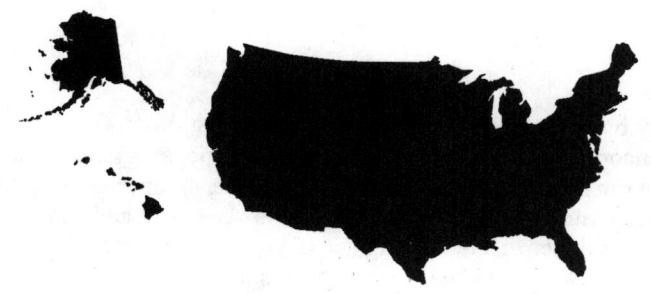

Editors:

Kathleen O'Leary Morgan, Scott Morgan and Neal Quitno

Morgan Quitno Press
© Copyright 1996, All Rights Reserved

512 East 9th Street, P.O. Box 1656, Lawrence, KS 66044
800-457-0742 or 913-841-3534

Third Edition

ISBN:
1-56692-311-5
ISSN:
1077-4408

Crime State Rankings 1996 sells for $49.95 and is only available in sewn, hardcover binding. For those who prefer ranking information tailored to a particular state, we also offer Crime State Perspectives, state-specific reports for each of the 50 states. These individual guides provide information on a state's data and rank for each of the categories featured in the national Crime State Rankings volume. Perspectives sell for $19.00 or $9.50 if ordered with Crime State Rankings. If you are interested in city and metropolitan crime data, we offer City Crime Rankings, 2nd Edition for $34.95 (hardcover). If health statistics are your interest, please ask about our annual Health Care State Rankings ($49.95 hardcover). If you are interested in a general view of the states, please ask about our annual State Rankings ($49.95 hardcover). We also offer the data in our books on diskette.

Third Edition
Printed in the United States of America
June 1996

PREFACE

Juvenile and adult arrests, corrections, law enforcement personnel and expenditures, offenses, crime clearances, courts, drug and alcohol prevention and treatment programs. In all, more than 500 tables of state statistics covering a broad range of crime-related categories are included in *Crime State Rankings 1996*. Now in its third edition, this comprehensive reference volume presents a huge collection of state crime information in a straightforward, easy-to-understand format.

Important Notes About *Crime State Rankings 1996*

This third edition of Crime State Rankings is the product of months of research designed to bring the best possible information to our readers. With each new volume, we thoroughly review the previous year's book, examining each table, updating most of them, removing others that are no longer pertinent and adding new data of interest. *Crime State Rankings 1996* is the result of that review process, and with 502 tables of state crime comparisons, it is our largest volume yet.

While there are many changes and updates, many of the features that have made this book so popular with both reviewers and researchers have not changed. Data are presented in both alphabetical and rank order so that readers may quickly find information for a particular state and then just as quickly learn which states rank above and below that state. Source information and other pertinent footnotes are clearly shown at the bottom of each page and national totals, rates and percentages are prominently displayed at the top of each table. Every other line is shaded in gray for easier reading. In addition, numerous information finding tools are provided: a thorough table of contents, table listings at the beginning of each chapter, a detailed index and a chapter thumb index. Also included is a roster of sources, with addresses, phone numbers and now internet homepage sites as well.

As in all of our reference books, the numbers shown in Crime State Rankings 1996 are "complete" numbers, meaning that no additional calculations are required to convert them from thousands, millions, etc. All states are ranked on a high to low basis. Any ties among states are shown alphabetically for a given ranking. Numbers reported in parentheses "( )" are negative numbers. For tables with national totals (as opposed to rates, per capita's, etc.) we include a separate column showing what percent of the national total each individual state's total represents. This column is headed by "% of USA." This percentage figure is particularly interesting when compared with a state's share of the nation's population for a particular year. The appendix contains population tables to aid in these comparisons.

For those interested in focusing on crime information for just one state, we once again are offering our *Crime State Perspective* series of publications. These 21-page, comb-bound reports feature data and ranking information for an individual state, pulled from *Crime State Rankings 1996*. (For example, *New York Crime in Perspective* contains crime information about the state of New York only.) When purchased individually, *Crime State Perspectives* sell for $19. When purchased with a copy of *Crime State Rankings 1995*, these handy quick reference guides are just $9.50.

Crime State Rankings proved to be so popular that we have since launched a companion volume of crime data, *City Crime Rankings*. Now in its second edition, this reference book was created in response to the large number of requests we received for crime data broken down by city and metropolitan area. *City Crime Rankings* ranks all cities of 100,000 population or more and all metropolitan areas (some as small as 65,000 population) in 40 categories of crime each. Numbers of crimes, crime rates, changes in crime rates over one and five years are presented for all major crime categories reported by the FBI. This book sells for $34.95 (hardcover; s/h included.)

Our company also continues to offer two other publications, *State Rankings* and *Health Care State Rankings*. In its seventh edition in 1996, *State Rankings* provides a general view of the states by featuring state statistics in categories ranging from agriculture to transportation, taxes to education and social welfare to health. This book has received great acclaim for its ease of use and simple presentation of state data. Also continued this year is *Health Care State Rankings*, a series now in its fourth edition. Following the same format as the book you are holding, *Health Care State Rankings* focuses on state health issues instead of crime. Included in this volume are data on health care facilities, providers, insurance and finance, incidence of disease, mortality, physical fitness, natality and reproductive health. Both *State Rankings* and *Health Care State Rankings* sell for $49.95 (hardcover) each including shipping. *State Perspectives* are also available for each of these books, selling for $19 individually or $9.50 if purchased with their corresponding national volume. We also offer the data in our books on diskette (.dbf format). If you would like a brochure or further information, please call us at 1-800-457-0742.

Finally, many thanks to all of the hard working librarians and government workers who so willingly helped us in developing, designing and producing this book. Most of all, thanks to you, our readers. We enjoy doing this and appreciate your writing or calling us with your suggestions.

THE EDITORS

WHICH STATE IS THE MOST DANGEROUS?

Las Vegas is easily one of the most popular vacation destinations in America. But with that popularity comes at least some trouble. With "help" from Las Vegas, the whole state of Nevada knocks Louisiana out of the unenviable position as our 1996 Most Dangerous State. In the more eagerly sought category of Safest State, Vermont surged back into first, replacing Maine (which pushed Vermont out last year).

Using 14 basic criteria (listed below) the "Most Dangerous State" was determined by comparing state crime rates, juvenile crime statistics, corrections data, police protection and expenditures. These factors provide a statistical basis for comparing states' abilities to keep their streets safe for the average citizen.

Our methodology was fairly simple. Once the 14 factors were determined, we averaged each state's ranking for all 14 categories. Based on this composite number (the "AVG" in the table to the right), states were then ranked from "most dangerous" (lowest average ranking) to "safest" (highest average ranking). States with no data available for a given category were ranked only on the remaining factors.

Morgan Quitno Press prides itself on presenting facts in a nonbiased, objective manner. A central theme of our books is our clear presentation of data, with the analysis left to our readers. However, with each new edition, we incorporate what we determine to be the most critical statistical measurements into our computer program and present an "award" based on the results. Annually since 1991 we have named the "Most Livable State" based on data from our *State Rankings* series. In 1993, we began the "Healthiest State" award based on data from our *Health Care State Rankings* series. With the debut of our third series of books in 1994, *Crime State Rankings*, we designated the "Most Dangerous State." In 1995, we began two new awards, "Safest City" and "Safest Metropolitan Area" based on our newest reference book, *City Crime Rankings*.

1996 MOST DANGEROUS STATE

RANK	STATE	AVG	'95	RANK	STATE	AVG	'95
1	Nevada	7.00	3	26	Kansas	25.25	23
2	Louisiana	9.07	1	27	Hawaii	26.14	30
3	Florida	10.50	4	28	Indiana	26.43	31
4	Maryland	11.57	2	30	Ohio	26.43	29
5	Arizona	12.64	7	30	Connecticut	27.36	36
6	California	15.07	8	31	Massachusetts	27.86	28
7	New Mexico	15.79	9	32	Virginia	28.64	32
8	Illinois	16.36	5	33	Delaware	28.79	12
9	Missouri	16.43	17	34	Kentucky	29.21	44
10	South Carolina	17.21	10	35	Utah	30.07	33
11	Texas	17.57	6	36	Minnesota	30.29	42
12	Alaska	19.14	14	37	Wisconsin	30.71	34
13	Michigan	19.57	13	38	Idaho	30.86	35
14	New York	19.71	11	38	Pennsylvania	31.57	38
15	Georgia	20.00	21	40	Wyoming	32.00	40
16	Oklahoma	20.21	15	41	Montana	32.08	38
17	North Carolina	20.57	19	42	Nebraska	32.36	43
18	Tennessee	20.64	16	43	South Dakota	33.07	37
19	Oregon	21.43	24	44	Rhode Island	33.43	41
20	Mississippi	22.00	25	45	Iowa	39.29	45
21	Colorado	22.21	18	46	West Virginia	40.93	48
22	New Jersey	23.00	22	47	New Hampshire	41.00	47
23	Alabama	23.86	20	48	North Dakota	42.50	46
24	Washington	24.50	27	49	Maine	43.50	50
25	Arkansas	25.14	26	50	Vermont	46.43	49

FACTORS CONSIDERED:
1. Crime Rate (Table 310)
2. Violent Crime Rate (Table 316)
3. Murder Rate (Table 325)
4. Rape Rate (Table 344)
5. Robbery Rate (Table 350)
6. Aggravated Assault Rate (Table 365)
7. Property Crime Rate (Table 380)
8. Percent Change in Crime Rate: 1990 to 1994 (Table 466)
9. Percent Change in Violent Crime Rate: 1990 to 1994 (Table 470)
10. State Prisoner Incarceration Rate (Table 102)
11. Reported Juvenile Arrest Rate (Table 38)
12. Reported Juvenile Arrest Rate for Violent Crime (Table 44)
13. State-Local Government Expenditures for Police Protection as a Percent of All Direct Expenditures (Table 230)
14. Full-Time Sworn Officers in Law Enforcement Agencies per 10,000 Population (Table 268)

Being named the "Most Dangerous State" is never met with much enthusiasm. Nevada can correctly point out that crimes committed by out-of-state visitors are only divided by its resident population. However, the fact remains that relative to its sister states, Nevada does have a crime problem. Our intent is not to anger, but rather to provoke and facilitate a productive discussion among state leaders and citizens about a problem of great concern to us all.

THE EDITORS

TABLE OF CONTENTS

I. Arrests

TABLE OF CONTENTS (continued)

II. Corrections

TABLE OF CONTENTS (continued)

TABLE OF CONTENTS (continued)

III. Drugs and Alcohol

IV. Finance

TABLE OF CONTENTS (continued)

V. Law Enforcement

TABLE OF CONTENTS (continued)

VI. Offenses

TABLE OF CONTENTS (continued)

Urban/Rural Crime

TABLE OF CONTENTS (continued)

TABLE OF CONTENTS (continued)

1990 Crimes

VII. Appendix

VIII. Sources

IX. Index

I. ARRESTS

1   Reported Arrests in 1994
2   Reported Arrest Rate in 1994
3   Reported Arrests for Crime Index Offenses in 1994
4   Reported Arrest Rate for Crime Index Offenses in 1994
5   Reported Arrests for Violent Crime in 1994
6   Reported Arrest Rate for Violent Crime in 1994
7   Reported Arrests for Murder in 1994
8   Reported Arrest Rate for Murder in 1994
9   Reported Arrests for Rape in 1994
10   Reported Arrest Rate for Rape in 1994
11   Reported Arrests for Robbery in 1994
12   Reported Arrest Rate for Robbery in 1994
13   Reported Arrests for Aggravated Assault in 1994
14   Reported Arrest Rate for Aggravated Assault in 1994
15   Reported Arrests for Property Crime in 1994
16   Reported Arrest Rate for Property Crime in 1994
17   Reported Arrests for Burglary in 1994
18   Reported Arrest Rate for Burglary in 1994
19   Reported Arrests for Larceny and Theft in 1994
20   Reported Arrest Rate for Larceny and Theft in 1994
21   Reported Arrests for Motor Vehicle Theft in 1994
22   Reported Arrest Rate for Motor Vehicle Theft in 1994
23   Reported Arrests for Arson in 1994
24   Reported Arrest Rate for Arson in 1994
25   Reported Arrests for Weapons Violations in 1994
26   Reported Arrest Rate for Weapons Violations in 1994
27   Reported Arrests for Driving Under the Influence in 1994
28   Reported Arrest Rate for Driving Under the Influence in 1994
29   Reported Arrests for Drug Abuse Violations in 1994
30   Reported Arrest Rate for Drug Abuse Violations in 1994
31   Reported Arrests for Sex Offenses in 1994
32   Reported Arrest Rate for Sex Offenses in 1994
33   Reported Arrests for Prostitution and Commercialized Vice in 1994
34   Reported Arrest Rate for Prostitution and Commercialized Vice in 1994
35   Reported Arrests for Offenses Against Families and Children in 1994
36   Reported Arrest Rate for Offenses Against Families and Children in 1994

Juvenile Arrests

37   Reported Arrests of Juveniles in 1994
38   Reported Juvenile Arrest Rate in 1994
39   Reported Arrests of Juveniles as a Percent of All Arrests in 1994
40   Reported Arrests of Juveniles for Crime Index Offenses in 1994
41   Reported Juvenile Arrest Rate for Crime Index Offenses in 1994
42   Reported Arrests of Juveniles for Crime Index Offenses as a Percent of All Such Arrests in 1994
43   Reported Arrests of Juveniles for Violent Crime in 1994
44   Reported Juvenile Arrest Rate for Violent Crime in 1994
45   Reported Arrests of Juveniles for Violent Crime as a Percent of All Such Arrests in 1994
46   Reported Arrests of Juveniles for Murder in 1994
47   Reported Juvenile Arrest Rate for Murder in 1994
48   Reported Arrests of Juveniles for Murder as a Percent of All Such Arrests in 1994
49   Reported Arrests of Juveniles for Rape in 1994
50   Reported Juvenile Arrest Rate for Rape in 1994
51   Reported Arrests of Juveniles for Rape as a Percent of All Such Arrests in 1994
52   Reported Arrests of Juveniles for Robbery in 1994
53   Reported Juvenile Arrest Rate for Robbery in 1994
54   Reported Arrests of Juveniles for Robbery as a Percent of All Such Arrests in 1994
55   Reported Arrests of Juveniles for Aggravated Assault in 1994
56   Reported Juvenile Arrest Rate for Aggravated Assault in 1994
57   Reported Arrests of Juveniles for Aggravated Assault as a Percent of All Such Arrests in 1994

I. ARRESTS (continued)

Important Note Regarding Juvenile Arrest Rates

The juvenile arrest rates shown in tables 38 to 89 were calculated by the editors as follows:

    The state arrest numbers reported by the FBI are only from those law enforcement agencies that submitted complete arrests reports for 12 months in 1994. Included in the FBI report are population totals of these reporting jurisdictions by state. Using these FBI population figures, we first determined what percentage the FBI numbers represented of each state's total resident population. Next, using 1994 US Census Bureau state estimates for 10 to 17 year olds, we multiplied the percentages derived from the FBI population figures into the Census Bureau's total juvenile population estimates. The resulting juvenile population is the base that was used to determine juvenile arrests per 100,000 juvenile population. The national rate was calculated in the same manner.

    Reports from law enforcement agencies in Illinois, Mississippi, New Mexico and Tennessee represented less than half of their state populations. Thus the rates for these states may be somewhat skewed.

Reported Arrests in 1994

National Total = 11,877,188 Reported Arrests*

ALPHA ORDER

RANK	STATE	ARRESTS	% of USA
20	Alabama	199,303	1.68%
41	Alaska	38,417	0.32%
15	Arizona	271,026	2.28%
23	Arkansas	175,692	1.48%
1	California	1,616,563	13.61%
17	Colorado	217,438	1.83%
22	Connecticut	182,873	1.54%
47	Delaware	9,729	0.08%
4	Florida	756,362	6.37%
12	Georgia	286,256	2.41%
35	Hawaii	68,990	0.58%
36	Idaho	63,762	0.54%
33	Illinois	83,693	0.70%
25	Indiana	150,746	1.27%
32	Iowa	87,257	0.73%
NA	Kansas**	NA	NA
29	Kentucky	113,630	0.96%
21	Louisiana	189,392	1.59%
39	Maine	46,627	0.39%
14	Maryland	273,198	2.30%
27	Massachusetts	138,524	1.17%
10	Michigan	352,288	2.97%
18	Minnesota	203,786	1.72%
37	Mississippi	61,676	0.52%
13	Missouri	278,583	2.35%
NA	Montana**	NA	NA
34	Nebraska	80,346	0.68%
31	Nevada	106,315	0.90%
46	New Hampshire	24,625	0.21%
8	New Jersey	377,146	3.18%
44	New Mexico	26,072	0.22%
2	New York	1,171,999	9.87%
5	North Carolina	437,063	3.68%
45	North Dakota	25,296	0.21%
9	Ohio	369,112	3.11%
26	Oklahoma	148,542	1.25%
24	Oregon	157,775	1.33%
11	Pennsylvania	347,930	2.93%
40	Rhode Island	41,135	0.35%
19	South Carolina	202,609	1.71%
42	South Dakota	29,766	0.25%
28	Tennessee	138,239	1.16%
3	Texas	1,035,601	8.72%
30	Utah	112,226	0.94%
48	Vermont	3,702	0.03%
7	Virginia	387,065	3.26%
16	Washington	230,280	1.94%
38	West Virginia	59,828	0.50%
6	Wisconsin	420,676	3.54%
43	Wyoming	29,527	0.25%

RANK ORDER

RANK	STATE	ARRESTS	% of USA
1	California	1,616,563	13.61%
2	New York	1,171,999	9.87%
3	Texas	1,035,601	8.72%
4	Florida	756,362	6.37%
5	North Carolina	437,063	3.68%
6	Wisconsin	420,676	3.54%
7	Virginia	387,065	3.26%
8	New Jersey	377,146	3.18%
9	Ohio	369,112	3.11%
10	Michigan	352,288	2.97%
11	Pennsylvania	347,930	2.93%
12	Georgia	286,256	2.41%
13	Missouri	278,583	2.35%
14	Maryland	273,198	2.30%
15	Arizona	271,026	2.28%
16	Washington	230,280	1.94%
17	Colorado	217,438	1.83%
18	Minnesota	203,786	1.72%
19	South Carolina	202,609	1.71%
20	Alabama	199,303	1.68%
21	Louisiana	189,392	1.59%
22	Connecticut	182,873	1.54%
23	Arkansas	175,692	1.48%
24	Oregon	157,775	1.33%
25	Indiana	150,746	1.27%
26	Oklahoma	148,542	1.25%
27	Massachusetts	138,524	1.17%
28	Tennessee	138,239	1.16%
29	Kentucky	113,630	0.96%
30	Utah	112,226	0.94%
31	Nevada	106,315	0.90%
32	Iowa	87,257	0.73%
33	Illinois	83,693	0.70%
34	Nebraska	80,346	0.68%
35	Hawaii	68,990	0.58%
36	Idaho	63,762	0.54%
37	Mississippi	61,676	0.52%
38	West Virginia	59,828	0.50%
39	Maine	46,627	0.39%
40	Rhode Island	41,135	0.35%
41	Alaska	38,417	0.32%
42	South Dakota	29,766	0.25%
43	Wyoming	29,527	0.25%
44	New Mexico	26,072	0.22%
45	North Dakota	25,296	0.21%
46	New Hampshire	24,625	0.21%
47	Delaware	9,729	0.08%
48	Vermont	3,702	0.03%
NA	Kansas**	NA	NA
NA	Montana**	NA	NA
	District of Columbia	48,502	0.41%

Source: Federal Bureau of Investigation
"Crime in the United States 1994" (Uniform Crime Reports, November 19, 1995)
*By law enforcement agencies submitting complete reports to the F.B.I. for 12 months in 1994. The F.B.I. estimates 14,648,700 reported and unreported arrests occurred in 1994.
**Not available.

Reported Arrest Rate in 1994

National Rate = 5,720.6 Reported Arrests per 100,000 Population*

ALPHA ORDER			RANK ORDER		
RANK	STATE	RATE	RANK	STATE	RATE
32	Alabama	5,122.2	1	Colorado	8,584.2
11	Alaska	6,751.7	2	Missouri	8,488.2
9	Arizona	6,942.3	3	Wisconsin	8,447.3
8	Arkansas	7,272.0	4	Nevada	7,910.3
31	California	5,155.8	5	Mississippi	7,797.2
1	Colorado	8,584.2	6	New York	7,359.5
14	Connecticut	6,606.7	7	South Dakota	7,277.8
47	Delaware	2,560.3	8	Arkansas	7,272.0
26	Florida	5,509.2	9	Arizona	6,942.3
10	Georgia	6,841.7	10	Georgia	6,841.7
21	Hawaii	5,851.6	11	Alaska	6,751.7
22	Idaho	5,780.8	12	Tennessee	6,723.7
35	Illinois	4,712.4	13	New Mexico	6,651.0
37	Indiana	4,668.5	14	Connecticut	6,606.7
43	Iowa	3,598.2	15	Utah	6,559.1
NA	Kansas**	NA	16	Wyoming	6,532.5
23	Kentucky	5,603.1	17	North Carolina	6,384.2
19	Louisiana	6,250.6	18	Texas	6,376.9
41	Maine	3,866.3	19	Louisiana	6,250.6
28	Maryland	5,471.6	20	Virginia	5,976.0
45	Massachusetts	3,386.9	21	Hawaii	5,851.6
36	Michigan	4,682.2	22	Idaho	5,780.8
34	Minnesota	4,784.8	23	Kentucky	5,603.1
5	Mississippi	7,797.2	24	Washington	5,555.6
2	Missouri	8,488.2	25	South Carolina	5,537.3
NA	Montana**	NA	26	Florida	5,509.2
29	Nebraska	5,447.2	27	Ohio	5,475.6
4	Nevada	7,910.3	28	Maryland	5,471.6
44	New Hampshire	3,458.6	29	Nebraska	5,447.2
33	New Jersey	4,928.1	30	Oregon	5,207.1
13	New Mexico	6,651.0	31	California	5,155.8
6	New York	7,359.5	32	Alabama	5,122.2
17	North Carolina	6,384.2	33	New Jersey	4,928.1
39	North Dakota	4,582.6	34	Minnesota	4,784.8
27	Ohio	5,475.6	35	Illinois	4,712.4
38	Oklahoma	4,624.6	36	Michigan	4,682.2
30	Oregon	5,207.1	37	Indiana	4,668.5
42	Pennsylvania	3,748.0	38	Oklahoma	4,624.6
40	Rhode Island	4,125.9	39	North Dakota	4,582.6
25	South Carolina	5,537.3	40	Rhode Island	4,125.9
7	South Dakota	7,277.8	41	Maine	3,866.3
12	Tennessee	6,723.7	42	Pennsylvania	3,748.0
18	Texas	6,376.9	43	Iowa	3,598.2
15	Utah	6,559.1	44	New Hampshire	3,458.6
48	Vermont	1,242.3	45	Massachusetts	3,386.9
20	Virginia	5,976.0	46	West Virginia	3,287.3
24	Washington	5,555.6	47	Delaware	2,560.3
46	West Virginia	3,287.3	48	Vermont	1,242.3
3	Wisconsin	8,447.3	NA	Kansas**	NA
16	Wyoming	6,532.5	NA	Montana**	NA
				District of Columbia	8,509.1

Source: Morgan Quitno Press using data from Federal Bureau of Investigation
"Crime in the United States 1994" (Uniform Crime Reports, November 19, 1995)
By law enforcement agencies submitting complete reports to the F.B.I. for 12 months in 1994. These rates based on population estimates for areas under the jurisdiction of those agencies reporting. Arrest rate based on the F.B.I. estimate of total arrests is 5,626.7 reported and unreported arrests per 100,000 population.
**Not available.*

Reported Arrests for Crime Index Offenses in 1994

National Total = 2,384,244 Reported Arrests*

ALPHA ORDER

RANK	STATE	ARRESTS	% of USA
22	Alabama	38,153	1.60%
40	Alaska	8,186	0.34%
14	Arizona	56,110	2.35%
29	Arkansas	23,444	0.98%
1	California	409,015	17.15%
19	Colorado	42,166	1.77%
21	Connecticut	39,103	1.64%
47	Delaware	2,357	0.10%
2	Florida	202,506	8.49%
13	Georgia	56,659	2.38%
35	Hawaii	13,032	0.55%
37	Idaho	11,861	0.50%
33	Illinois	14,440	0.61%
25	Indiana	29,073	1.22%
32	Iowa	15,523	0.65%
NA	Kansas**	NA	NA
30	Kentucky	22,019	0.92%
17	Louisiana	45,515	1.91%
38	Maine	9,940	0.42%
10	Maryland	64,086	2.69%
23	Massachusetts	34,363	1.44%
9	Michigan	68,272	2.86%
20	Minnesota	39,743	1.67%
36	Mississippi	11,945	0.50%
16	Missouri	50,909	2.14%
NA	Montana**	NA	NA
34	Nebraska	13,487	0.57%
31	Nevada	17,354	0.73%
45	New Hampshire	3,901	0.16%
7	New Jersey	74,350	3.12%
44	New Mexico	3,907	0.16%
4	New York	169,805	7.12%
5	North Carolina	84,504	3.54%
43	North Dakota	4,082	0.17%
12	Ohio	59,295	2.49%
26	Oklahoma	28,663	1.20%
18	Oregon	42,539	1.78%
6	Pennsylvania	77,393	3.25%
41	Rhode Island	8,155	0.34%
24	South Carolina	34,220	1.44%
42	South Dakota	4,912	0.21%
27	Tennessee	28,281	1.19%
3	Texas	184,035	7.72%
28	Utah	26,282	1.10%
48	Vermont	637	0.03%
11	Virginia	62,340	2.61%
15	Washington	55,492	2.33%
39	West Virginia	9,234	0.39%
8	Wisconsin	68,479	2.87%
46	Wyoming	3,819	0.16%

RANK ORDER

RANK	STATE	ARRESTS	% of USA
1	California	409,015	17.15%
2	Florida	202,506	8.49%
3	Texas	184,035	7.72%
4	New York	169,805	7.12%
5	North Carolina	84,504	3.54%
6	Pennsylvania	77,393	3.25%
7	New Jersey	74,350	3.12%
8	Wisconsin	68,479	2.87%
9	Michigan	68,272	2.86%
10	Maryland	64,086	2.69%
11	Virginia	62,340	2.61%
12	Ohio	59,295	2.49%
13	Georgia	56,659	2.38%
14	Arizona	56,110	2.35%
15	Washington	55,492	2.33%
16	Missouri	50,909	2.14%
17	Louisiana	45,515	1.91%
18	Oregon	42,539	1.78%
19	Colorado	42,166	1.77%
20	Minnesota	39,743	1.67%
21	Connecticut	39,103	1.64%
22	Alabama	38,153	1.60%
23	Massachusetts	34,363	1.44%
24	South Carolina	34,220	1.44%
25	Indiana	29,073	1.22%
26	Oklahoma	28,663	1.20%
27	Tennessee	28,281	1.19%
28	Utah	26,282	1.10%
29	Arkansas	23,444	0.98%
30	Kentucky	22,019	0.92%
31	Nevada	17,354	0.73%
32	Iowa	15,523	0.65%
33	Illinois	14,440	0.61%
34	Nebraska	13,487	0.57%
35	Hawaii	13,032	0.55%
36	Mississippi	11,945	0.50%
37	Idaho	11,861	0.50%
38	Maine	9,940	0.42%
39	West Virginia	9,234	0.39%
40	Alaska	8,186	0.34%
41	Rhode Island	8,155	0.34%
42	South Dakota	4,912	0.21%
43	North Dakota	4,082	0.17%
44	New Mexico	3,907	0.16%
45	New Hampshire	3,901	0.16%
46	Wyoming	3,819	0.16%
47	Delaware	2,357	0.10%
48	Vermont	637	0.03%
NA	Kansas**	NA	NA
NA	Montana**	NA	NA
	District of Columbia	10,658	0.45%

Source: Federal Bureau of Investigation
    "Crime in the United States 1994" (Uniform Crime Reports, November 19, 1995)
By law enforcement agencies submitting complete reports to the F.B.I. for 12 months in 1994. The F.B.I. estimates 2,910,400 reported and unreported arrests for crime index offenses occurred in 1994. Crime index offenses consist of murder, forcible rape, robbery, aggravated assault, burglary, larceny-theft, motor vehicle theft and arson.
**Not available.*

3

Reported Arrest Rate for Crime Index Offenses in 1994

National Rate = 1,148.4 Reported Arrests per 100,000 Population*

RANK	STATE	RATE
26	Alabama	980.5
7	Alaska	1,438.7
8	Arizona	1,437.2
28	Arkansas	970.4
15	California	1,304.5
1	Colorado	1,664.7
9	Connecticut	1,412.7
45	Delaware	620.3
6	Florida	1,475.0
13	Georgia	1,354.2
21	Hawaii	1,105.3
23	Idaho	1,075.3
42	Illinois	813.1
34	Indiana	900.4
44	Iowa	640.1
NA	Kansas**	NA
22	Kentucky	1,085.7
5	Louisiana	1,502.1
40	Maine	824.2
17	Maryland	1,283.5
38	Massachusetts	840.2
33	Michigan	907.4
31	Minnesota	933.2
4	Mississippi	1,510.1
2	Missouri	1,551.2
NA	Montana**	NA
32	Nebraska	914.4
16	Nevada	1,291.2
46	New Hampshire	547.9
27	New Jersey	971.5
25	New Mexico	996.7
24	New York	1,066.3
18	North Carolina	1,234.4
43	North Dakota	739.5
36	Ohio	879.6
35	Oklahoma	892.4
10	Oregon	1,403.9
39	Pennsylvania	833.7
41	Rhode Island	818.0
30	South Carolina	935.2
19	South Dakota	1,201.0
11	Tennessee	1,375.5
20	Texas	1,133.2
3	Utah	1,536.1
48	Vermont	213.8
29	Virginia	962.5
14	Washington	1,338.8
47	West Virginia	507.4
12	Wisconsin	1,375.1
37	Wyoming	844.9

RANK	STATE	RATE
1	Colorado	1,664.7
2	Missouri	1,551.2
3	Utah	1,536.1
4	Mississippi	1,510.1
5	Louisiana	1,502.1
6	Florida	1,475.0
7	Alaska	1,438.7
8	Arizona	1,437.2
9	Connecticut	1,412.7
10	Oregon	1,403.9
11	Tennessee	1,375.5
12	Wisconsin	1,375.1
13	Georgia	1,354.2
14	Washington	1,338.8
15	California	1,304.5
16	Nevada	1,291.2
17	Maryland	1,283.5
18	North Carolina	1,234.4
19	South Dakota	1,201.0
20	Texas	1,133.2
21	Hawaii	1,105.3
22	Kentucky	1,085.7
23	Idaho	1,075.3
24	New York	1,066.3
25	New Mexico	996.7
26	Alabama	980.5
27	New Jersey	971.5
28	Arkansas	970.4
29	Virginia	962.5
30	South Carolina	935.2
31	Minnesota	933.2
32	Nebraska	914.4
33	Michigan	907.4
34	Indiana	900.4
35	Oklahoma	892.4
36	Ohio	879.6
37	Wyoming	844.9
38	Massachusetts	840.2
39	Pennsylvania	833.7
40	Maine	824.2
41	Rhode Island	818.0
42	Illinois	813.1
43	North Dakota	739.5
44	Iowa	640.1
45	Delaware	620.3
46	New Hampshire	547.9
47	West Virginia	507.4
48	Vermont	213.8
NA	Kansas**	NA
NA	Montana**	NA
	District of Columbia	1,869.8

Source: Morgan Quitno Press using data from Federal Bureau of Investigation
"Crime in the United States 1994" (Uniform Crime Reports, November 19, 1995)
By law enforcement agencies submitting complete reports to the F.B.I. for 12 months in 1994. These rates based on population estimates for areas under the jurisdiction of those agencies reporting. Arrest rate based on the F.B.I. estimate of reported and unreported arrests for crime index offenses is 1,117.9 arrests per 100,000 population.
Not available.

Reported Arrests for Violent Crime in 1994

National Total = 644,983 Reported Arrests*

ALPHA ORDER

RANK	STATE	ARRESTS	% of USA
15	Alabama	12,419	1.93%
36	Alaska	1,611	0.25%
18	Arizona	9,554	1.48%
28	Arkansas	5,091	0.79%
1	California	150,531	23.34%
22	Colorado	8,084	1.25%
21	Connecticut	8,665	1.34%
43	Delaware	738	0.11%
3	Florida	58,609	9.09%
9	Georgia	15,246	2.36%
40	Hawaii	1,323	0.21%
39	Idaho	1,392	0.22%
33	Illinois	2,357	0.37%
25	Indiana	6,950	1.08%
30	Iowa	3,300	0.51%
NA	Kansas**	NA	NA
20	Kentucky	9,127	1.42%
16	Louisiana	11,868	1.84%
41	Maine	827	0.13%
13	Maryland	13,594	2.11%
10	Massachusetts	14,975	2.32%
6	Michigan	22,243	3.45%
26	Minnesota	6,923	1.07%
35	Mississippi	1,976	0.31%
12	Missouri	13,944	2.16%
NA	Montana**	NA	NA
38	Nebraska	1,467	0.23%
31	Nevada	3,277	0.51%
46	New Hampshire	481	0.07%
8	New Jersey	20,591	3.19%
42	New Mexico	798	0.12%
2	New York	66,881	10.37%
5	North Carolina	25,828	4.00%
47	North Dakota	189	0.03%
11	Ohio	14,490	2.25%
27	Oklahoma	6,157	0.95%
29	Oregon	4,994	0.77%
7	Pennsylvania	20,804	3.23%
34	Rhode Island	2,322	0.36%
17	South Carolina	10,160	1.58%
44	South Dakota	609	0.09%
24	Tennessee	7,296	1.13%
4	Texas	37,165	5.76%
32	Utah	2,564	0.40%
48	Vermont	89	0.01%
14	Virginia	13,289	2.06%
23	Washington	7,862	1.22%
37	West Virginia	1,490	0.23%
19	Wisconsin	9,247	1.43%
45	Wyoming	528	0.08%

RANK ORDER

RANK	STATE	ARRESTS	% of USA
1	California	150,531	23.34%
2	New York	66,881	10.37%
3	Florida	58,609	9.09%
4	Texas	37,165	5.76%
5	North Carolina	25,828	4.00%
6	Michigan	22,243	3.45%
7	Pennsylvania	20,804	3.23%
8	New Jersey	20,591	3.19%
9	Georgia	15,246	2.36%
10	Massachusetts	14,975	2.32%
11	Ohio	14,490	2.25%
12	Missouri	13,944	2.16%
13	Maryland	13,594	2.11%
14	Virginia	13,289	2.06%
15	Alabama	12,419	1.93%
16	Louisiana	11,868	1.84%
17	South Carolina	10,160	1.58%
18	Arizona	9,554	1.48%
19	Wisconsin	9,247	1.43%
20	Kentucky	9,127	1.42%
21	Connecticut	8,665	1.34%
22	Colorado	8,084	1.25%
23	Washington	7,862	1.22%
24	Tennessee	7,296	1.13%
25	Indiana	6,950	1.08%
26	Minnesota	6,923	1.07%
27	Oklahoma	6,157	0.95%
28	Arkansas	5,091	0.79%
29	Oregon	4,994	0.77%
30	Iowa	3,300	0.51%
31	Nevada	3,277	0.51%
32	Utah	2,564	0.40%
33	Illinois	2,357	0.37%
34	Rhode Island	2,322	0.36%
35	Mississippi	1,976	0.31%
36	Alaska	1,611	0.25%
37	West Virginia	1,490	0.23%
38	Nebraska	1,467	0.23%
39	Idaho	1,392	0.22%
40	Hawaii	1,323	0.21%
41	Maine	827	0.13%
42	New Mexico	798	0.12%
43	Delaware	738	0.11%
44	South Dakota	609	0.09%
45	Wyoming	528	0.08%
46	New Hampshire	481	0.07%
47	North Dakota	189	0.03%
48	Vermont	89	0.01%
NA	Kansas**	NA	NA
NA	Montana**	NA	NA
	District of Columbia	5,058	0.78%

Source: Federal Bureau of Investigation
"Crime in the United States 1994" (Uniform Crime Reports, November 19, 1995)
*By law enforcement agencies submitting complete reports to the F.B.I. for 12 months in 1994. The F.B.I. estimates 778,730 reported and unreported arrests for violent crimes occurred in 1994. Violent crimes are offenses of murder, forcible rape, robbery and aggravated assault.
**Not available.

Reported Arrest Rate for Violent Crime in 1994

National Rate = 310.7 Reported Arrests per 100,000 Population*

ALPHA ORDER				RANK ORDER		
RANK	STATE	RATE		RANK	STATE	RATE
11	Alabama	319.2		1	California	480.1
15	Alaska	283.1		2	Kentucky	450.0
20	Arizona	244.7		3	Florida	426.9
27	Arkansas	210.7		4	Missouri	424.9
1	California	480.1		5	New York	420.0
12	Colorado	319.1		6	Louisiana	391.7
13	Connecticut	313.0		7	North Carolina	377.3
30	Delaware	194.2		8	Massachusetts	366.1
3	Florida	426.9		9	Georgia	364.4
9	Georgia	364.4		10	Tennessee	354.9
42	Hawaii	112.2		11	Alabama	319.2
40	Idaho	126.2		12	Colorado	319.1
39	Illinois	132.7		13	Connecticut	313.0
25	Indiana	215.2		14	Michigan	295.6
38	Iowa	136.1		15	Alaska	283.1
NA	Kansas**	NA		16	South Carolina	277.7
2	Kentucky	450.0		17	Maryland	272.3
6	Louisiana	391.7		18	New Jersey	269.1
45	Maine	68.6		19	Mississippi	249.8
17	Maryland	272.3		20	Arizona	244.7
8	Massachusetts	366.1		21	Nevada	243.8
14	Michigan	295.6		22	Rhode Island	232.9
35	Minnesota	162.5		23	Texas	228.8
19	Mississippi	249.8		24	Pennsylvania	224.1
4	Missouri	424.9		25	Indiana	215.2
NA	Montana**	NA		26	Ohio	215.0
43	Nebraska	99.5		27	Arkansas	210.7
21	Nevada	243.8		28	Virginia	205.2
46	New Hampshire	67.6		29	New Mexico	203.6
18	New Jersey	269.1		30	Delaware	194.2
29	New Mexico	203.6		31	Oklahoma	191.7
5	New York	420.0		32	Washington	189.7
7	North Carolina	377.3		33	Wisconsin	185.7
47	North Dakota	34.2		34	Oregon	164.8
26	Ohio	215.0		35	Minnesota	162.5
31	Oklahoma	191.7		36	Utah	149.9
34	Oregon	164.8		37	South Dakota	148.9
24	Pennsylvania	224.1		38	Iowa	136.1
22	Rhode Island	232.9		39	Illinois	132.7
16	South Carolina	277.7		40	Idaho	126.2
37	South Dakota	148.9		41	Wyoming	116.8
10	Tennessee	354.9		42	Hawaii	112.2
23	Texas	228.8		43	Nebraska	99.5
36	Utah	149.9		44	West Virginia	81.9
48	Vermont	29.9		45	Maine	68.6
28	Virginia	205.2		46	New Hampshire	67.6
32	Washington	189.7		47	North Dakota	34.2
44	West Virginia	81.9		48	Vermont	29.9
33	Wisconsin	185.7		NA	Kansas**	NA
41	Wyoming	116.8		NA	Montana**	NA
					District of Columbia	887.4

Source: Morgan Quitno Press using data from Federal Bureau of Investigation
    "Crime in the United States 1994" (Uniform Crime Reports, November 19, 1995)
*By law enforcement agencies submitting complete reports to the F.B.I. for 12 months in 1994. These rates based on population estimates for areas under the jurisdiction of those agencies reporting. Arrest rate based on the F.B.I. estimate of reported and unreported arrests for violent crimes is 299.1 arrests per 100,000 population.
**Not available.

Reported Arrests for Murder in 1994

National Total = 18,497 Reported Arrests*

ALPHA ORDER					RANK ORDER			
RANK	STATE	ARRESTS	% of USA		RANK	STATE	ARRESTS	% of USA
13	Alabama	469	2.54%		1	California	2,973	16.07%
38	Alaska	35	0.19%		2	Michigan	1,649	8.91%
17	Arizona	327	1.77%		3	New York	1,564	8.46%
19	Arkansas	299	1.62%		4	Texas	1,532	8.28%
1	California	2,973	16.07%		5	Florida	1,196	6.47%
29	Colorado	162	0.88%		6	North Carolina	754	4.08%
23	Connecticut	193	1.04%		7	Missouri	594	3.21%
45	Delaware	6	0.03%		8	Maryland	587	3.17%
5	Florida	1,196	6.47%		9	Pennsylvania	576	3.11%
14	Georgia	429	2.32%		10	Louisiana	500	2.70%
34	Hawaii	62	0.34%		11	Ohio	493	2.67%
37	Idaho	36	0.19%		12	Virginia	476	2.57%
32	Illinois	112	0.61%		13	Alabama	469	2.54%
30	Indiana	158	0.85%		14	Georgia	429	2.32%
41	Iowa	26	0.14%		15	Wisconsin	418	2.26%
NA	Kansas**	NA	NA		16	South Carolina	344	1.86%
25	Kentucky	182	0.98%		17	Arizona	327	1.77%
10	Louisiana	500	2.70%		18	New Jersey	319	1.72%
42	Maine	12	0.06%		19	Arkansas	299	1.62%
8	Maryland	587	3.17%		20	Oklahoma	239	1.29%
31	Massachusetts	123	0.66%		21	Oregon	205	1.11%
2	Michigan	1,649	8.91%		22	Tennessee	199	1.08%
26	Minnesota	170	0.92%		23	Connecticut	193	1.04%
28	Mississippi	166	0.90%		24	Washington	189	1.02%
7	Missouri	594	3.21%		25	Kentucky	182	0.98%
NA	Montana**	NA	NA		26	Minnesota	170	0.92%
35	Nebraska	44	0.24%		27	Nevada	169	0.91%
27	Nevada	169	0.91%		28	Mississippi	166	0.90%
46	New Hampshire	5	0.03%		29	Colorado	162	0.88%
18	New Jersey	319	1.72%		30	Indiana	158	0.85%
39	New Mexico	32	0.17%		31	Massachusetts	123	0.66%
3	New York	1,564	8.46%		32	Illinois	112	0.61%
6	North Carolina	754	4.08%		33	West Virginia	104	0.56%
47	North Dakota	2	0.01%		34	Hawaii	62	0.34%
11	Ohio	493	2.67%		35	Nebraska	44	0.24%
20	Oklahoma	239	1.29%		36	Utah	39	0.21%
21	Oregon	205	1.11%		37	Idaho	36	0.19%
9	Pennsylvania	576	3.11%		38	Alaska	35	0.19%
40	Rhode Island	31	0.17%		39	New Mexico	32	0.17%
16	South Carolina	344	1.86%		40	Rhode Island	31	0.17%
44	South Dakota	7	0.04%		41	Iowa	26	0.14%
22	Tennessee	199	1.08%		42	Maine	12	0.06%
4	Texas	1,532	8.28%		42	Wyoming	12	0.06%
36	Utah	39	0.21%		44	South Dakota	7	0.04%
48	Vermont	1	0.01%		45	Delaware	6	0.03%
12	Virginia	476	2.57%		46	New Hampshire	5	0.03%
24	Washington	189	1.02%		47	North Dakota	2	0.01%
33	West Virginia	104	0.56%		48	Vermont	1	0.01%
15	Wisconsin	418	2.26%		NA	Kansas**	NA	NA
42	Wyoming	12	0.06%		NA	Montana**	NA	NA
						District of Columbia	277	1.50%

Source: Federal Bureau of Investigation
    "Crime in the United States 1994" (Uniform Crime Reports, November 19, 1995)
*By law enforcement agencies submitting complete reports to the F.B.I. for 12 months in 1994. The F.B.I. estimates 22,100 reported and unreported arrests for murder occurred in 1994. Murder includes nonnegligent manslaughter.
**Not available.

Reported Arrest Rate for Murder in 1994

National Rate = 8.9 Reported Arrests per 100,000 Population*

ALPHA ORDER RANK	STATE	RATE	RANK ORDER RANK	STATE	RATE
7	Alabama	12.1	1	Michigan	21.9
28	Alaska	6.2	2	Mississippi	21.0
18	Arizona	8.4	3	Missouri	18.1
6	Arkansas	12.4	4	Louisiana	16.5
13	California	9.5	5	Nevada	12.6
26	Colorado	6.4	6	Arkansas	12.4
24	Connecticut	7.0	7	Alabama	12.1
43	Delaware	1.6	8	Maryland	11.8
17	Florida	8.7	9	North Carolina	11.0
10	Georgia	10.3	10	Georgia	10.3
31	Hawaii	5.3	11	New York	9.8
36	Idaho	3.3	12	Tennessee	9.7
27	Illinois	6.3	13	California	9.5
32	Indiana	4.9	14	South Carolina	9.4
44	Iowa	1.1	14	Texas	9.4
NA	Kansas**	NA	16	Kentucky	9.0
16	Kentucky	9.0	17	Florida	8.7
4	Louisiana	16.5	18	Arizona	8.4
45	Maine	1.0	18	Wisconsin	8.4
8	Maryland	11.8	20	New Mexico	8.2
38	Massachusetts	3.0	21	Oklahoma	7.4
1	Michigan	21.9	22	Ohio	7.3
35	Minnesota	4.0	22	Virginia	7.3
2	Mississippi	21.0	24	Connecticut	7.0
3	Missouri	18.1	25	Oregon	6.8
NA	Montana**	NA	26	Colorado	6.4
38	Nebraska	3.0	27	Illinois	6.3
5	Nevada	12.6	28	Alaska	6.2
46	New Hampshire	0.7	28	Pennsylvania	6.2
34	New Jersey	4.2	30	West Virginia	5.7
20	New Mexico	8.2	31	Hawaii	5.3
11	New York	9.8	32	Indiana	4.9
9	North Carolina	11.0	33	Washington	4.6
47	North Dakota	0.4	34	New Jersey	4.2
22	Ohio	7.3	35	Minnesota	4.0
21	Oklahoma	7.4	36	Idaho	3.3
25	Oregon	6.8	37	Rhode Island	3.1
28	Pennsylvania	6.2	38	Massachusetts	3.0
37	Rhode Island	3.1	38	Nebraska	3.0
14	South Carolina	9.4	40	Wyoming	2.7
42	South Dakota	1.7	41	Utah	2.3
12	Tennessee	9.7	42	South Dakota	1.7
14	Texas	9.4	43	Delaware	1.6
41	Utah	2.3	44	Iowa	1.1
48	Vermont	0.3	45	Maine	1.0
22	Virginia	7.3	46	New Hampshire	0.7
33	Washington	4.6	47	North Dakota	0.4
30	West Virginia	5.7	48	Vermont	0.3
18	Wisconsin	8.4	NA	Kansas**	NA
40	Wyoming	2.7	NA	Montana**	NA
				District of Columbia	48.6

Source: Morgan Quitno Press using data from Federal Bureau of Investigation
    "Crime in the United States 1994" (Uniform Crime Reports, November 19, 1995)
*By law enforcement agencies submitting complete reports to the F.B.I. for 12 months in 1994. These rates based
on population estimates for areas under the jurisdiction of those agencies reporting. Arrest rate based on the F.B.I.
estimate of reported and unreported arrests for murder is 8.5 arrests per 100,000 population.
**Not available.

Reported Arrests for Rape in 1994

National Total = 29,791 Reported Arrests*

ALPHA ORDER					RANK ORDER			
RANK	STATE		ARRESTS	% of USA	RANK	STATE	ARRESTS	% of USA
19	Alabama		485	1.63%	1	California	3,303	11.09%
38	Alaska		118	0.40%	2	Texas	2,505	8.41%
29	Arizona		246	0.83%	3	Florida	2,366	7.94%
22	Arkansas		457	1.53%	4	New York	1,940	6.51%
1	California		3,303	11.09%	5	Michigan	1,883	6.32%
21	Colorado		467	1.57%	6	Ohio	1,239	4.16%
27	Connecticut		380	1.28%	7	Pennsylvania	1,177	3.95%
39	Delaware		102	0.34%	8	New Jersey	1,061	3.56%
3	Florida		2,366	7.94%	9	Minnesota	1,045	3.51%
18	Georgia		575	1.93%	10	Washington	925	3.10%
34	Hawaii		149	0.50%	11	Maryland	910	3.05%
44	Idaho		68	0.23%	12	Virginia	808	2.71%
31	Illinois		210	0.70%	13	North Carolina	795	2.67%
35	Indiana		140	0.47%	14	Wisconsin	687	2.31%
37	Iowa		135	0.45%	15	South Carolina	669	2.25%
NA	Kansas**		NA	NA	16	Missouri	665	2.23%
24	Kentucky		408	1.37%	17	Massachusetts	618	2.07%
20	Louisiana		479	1.61%	18	Georgia	575	1.93%
40	Maine		94	0.32%	19	Alabama	485	1.63%
11	Maryland		910	3.05%	20	Louisiana	479	1.61%
17	Massachusetts		618	2.07%	21	Colorado	467	1.57%
5	Michigan		1,883	6.32%	22	Arkansas	457	1.53%
9	Minnesota		1,045	3.51%	23	Oklahoma	447	1.50%
32	Mississippi		180	0.60%	24	Kentucky	408	1.37%
16	Missouri		665	2.23%	25	Tennessee	391	1.31%
NA	Montana**		NA	NA	26	Oregon	384	1.29%
30	Nebraska		215	0.72%	27	Connecticut	380	1.28%
28	Nevada		281	0.94%	28	Nevada	281	0.94%
43	New Hampshire		71	0.24%	29	Arizona	246	0.83%
8	New Jersey		1,061	3.56%	30	Nebraska	215	0.72%
45	New Mexico		54	0.18%	31	Illinois	210	0.70%
4	New York		1,940	6.51%	32	Mississippi	180	0.60%
13	North Carolina		795	2.67%	33	Utah	164	0.55%
47	North Dakota		36	0.12%	34	Hawaii	149	0.50%
6	Ohio		1,239	4.16%	35	Indiana	140	0.47%
23	Oklahoma		447	1.50%	36	West Virginia	139	0.47%
26	Oregon		384	1.29%	37	Iowa	135	0.45%
7	Pennsylvania		1,177	3.95%	38	Alaska	118	0.40%
41	Rhode Island		84	0.28%	39	Delaware	102	0.34%
15	South Carolina		669	2.25%	40	Maine	94	0.32%
42	South Dakota		73	0.25%	41	Rhode Island	84	0.28%
25	Tennessee		391	1.31%	42	South Dakota	73	0.25%
2	Texas		2,505	8.41%	43	New Hampshire	71	0.24%
33	Utah		164	0.55%	44	Idaho	68	0.23%
48	Vermont		27	0.09%	45	New Mexico	54	0.18%
12	Virginia		808	2.71%	46	Wyoming	41	0.14%
10	Washington		925	3.10%	47	North Dakota	36	0.12%
36	West Virginia		139	0.47%	48	Vermont	27	0.09%
14	Wisconsin		687	2.31%	NA	Kansas**	NA	NA
46	Wyoming		41	0.14%	NA	Montana**	NA	NA
						District of Columbia	95	0.32%

Source: Federal Bureau of Investigation
     "Crime in the United States 1994" (Uniform Crime Reports, November 19, 1995)
*By law enforcement agencies submitting complete reports to the F.B.I. for 12 months in 1994. The F.B.I. estimates 36,610 reported and unreported arrests for rape occurred in 1994. Forcible rape is the carnal knowledge of a female forcibly and against her will. Assaults or attempts to commit rape by force or threat of force are included.
**Not available.

Reported Arrest Rate for Rape in 1994

National Rate = 14.3 Reported Arrests per 100,000 Population*

ALPHA ORDER

RANK	STATE	RATE
31	Alabama	12.5
7	Alaska	20.7
45	Arizona	6.3
11	Arkansas	18.9
36	California	10.5
12	Colorado	18.4
26	Connecticut	13.7
1	Delaware	26.8
17	Florida	17.2
26	Georgia	13.7
30	Hawaii	12.6
46	Idaho	6.2
34	Illinois	11.8
48	Indiana	4.3
47	Iowa	5.6
NA	Kansas**	NA
9	Kentucky	20.1
18	Louisiana	15.8
42	Maine	7.8
15	Maryland	18.2
20	Massachusetts	15.1
2	Michigan	25.0
3	Minnesota	24.5
4	Mississippi	22.8
8	Missouri	20.3
NA	Montana**	NA
21	Nebraska	14.6
6	Nevada	20.9
37	New Hampshire	10.0
22	New Jersey	13.9
24	New Mexico	13.8
33	New York	12.2
35	North Carolina	11.6
44	North Dakota	6.5
12	Ohio	18.4
22	Oklahoma	13.9
28	Oregon	12.7
28	Pennsylvania	12.7
41	Rhode Island	8.4
14	South Carolina	18.3
16	South Dakota	17.8
10	Tennessee	19.0
19	Texas	15.4
38	Utah	9.6
39	Vermont	9.1
31	Virginia	12.5
5	Washington	22.3
43	West Virginia	7.6
24	Wisconsin	13.8
39	Wyoming	9.1

RANK ORDER

RANK	STATE	RATE
1	Delaware	26.8
2	Michigan	25.0
3	Minnesota	24.5
4	Mississippi	22.8
5	Washington	22.3
6	Nevada	20.9
7	Alaska	20.7
8	Missouri	20.3
9	Kentucky	20.1
10	Tennessee	19.0
11	Arkansas	18.9
12	Colorado	18.4
12	Ohio	18.4
14	South Carolina	18.3
15	Maryland	18.2
16	South Dakota	17.8
17	Florida	17.2
18	Louisiana	15.8
19	Texas	15.4
20	Massachusetts	15.1
21	Nebraska	14.6
22	New Jersey	13.9
22	Oklahoma	13.9
24	New Mexico	13.8
24	Wisconsin	13.8
26	Connecticut	13.7
26	Georgia	13.7
28	Oregon	12.7
28	Pennsylvania	12.7
30	Hawaii	12.6
31	Alabama	12.5
31	Virginia	12.5
33	New York	12.2
34	Illinois	11.8
35	North Carolina	11.6
36	California	10.5
37	New Hampshire	10.0
38	Utah	9.6
39	Vermont	9.1
39	Wyoming	9.1
41	Rhode Island	8.4
42	Maine	7.8
43	West Virginia	7.6
44	North Dakota	6.5
45	Arizona	6.3
46	Idaho	6.2
47	Iowa	5.6
48	Indiana	4.3
NA	Kansas**	NA
NA	Montana**	NA
	District of Columbia	16.7

Source: Morgan Quitno Press using data from Federal Bureau of Investigation
    "Crime in the United States 1994" (Uniform Crime Reports, November 19, 1995)
*By law enforcement agencies submitting complete reports to the F.B.I. for 12 months in 1994. These rates based on population estimates for areas under the jurisdiction of those agencies reporting. Arrest rate based on the F.B.I. estimate of reported and unreported arrests for rape is 14.1 arrests per 100,000 population.
**Not available.

Reported Arrests for Robbery in 1994

National Total = 146,979 Reported Arrests*

RANK	STATE	ARRESTS	% of USA
17	Alabama	2,085	1.42%
39	Alaska	184	0.13%
21	Arizona	1,519	1.03%
28	Arkansas	992	0.67%
2	California	27,978	19.04%
26	Colorado	1,064	0.72%
16	Connecticut	2,181	1.48%
42	Delaware	98	0.07%
3	Florida	11,254	7.66%
11	Georgia	3,160	2.15%
33	Hawaii	459	0.31%
41	Idaho	100	0.07%
32	Illinois	548	0.37%
30	Indiana	819	0.56%
36	Iowa	289	0.20%
NA	Kansas**	NA	NA
29	Kentucky	930	0.63%
18	Louisiana	1,722	1.17%
40	Maine	122	0.08%
7	Maryland	4,584	3.12%
14	Massachusetts	2,298	1.56%
8	Michigan	4,553	3.10%
23	Minnesota	1,462	0.99%
31	Mississippi	559	0.38%
12	Missouri	2,849	1.94%
NA	Montana**	NA	NA
35	Nebraska	320	0.22%
25	Nevada	1,211	0.82%
43	New Hampshire	76	0.05%
6	New Jersey	5,981	4.07%
44	New Mexico	74	0.05%
1	New York	29,339	19.96%
10	North Carolina	3,839	2.61%
47	North Dakota	31	0.02%
9	Ohio	4,493	3.06%
27	Oklahoma	1,032	0.70%
22	Oregon	1,479	1.01%
5	Pennsylvania	7,188	4.89%
38	Rhode Island	237	0.16%
20	South Carolina	1,543	1.05%
45	South Dakota	51	0.03%
24	Tennessee	1,214	0.83%
4	Texas	8,729	5.94%
34	Utah	407	0.28%
48	Vermont	1	0.00%
13	Virginia	2,580	1.76%
19	Washington	1,625	1.11%
37	West Virginia	247	0.17%
15	Wisconsin	2,251	1.53%
46	Wyoming	49	0.03%

RANK	STATE	ARRESTS	% of USA
1	New York	29,339	19.96%
2	California	27,978	19.04%
3	Florida	11,254	7.66%
4	Texas	8,729	5.94%
5	Pennsylvania	7,188	4.89%
6	New Jersey	5,981	4.07%
7	Maryland	4,584	3.12%
8	Michigan	4,553	3.10%
9	Ohio	4,493	3.06%
10	North Carolina	3,839	2.61%
11	Georgia	3,160	2.15%
12	Missouri	2,849	1.94%
13	Virginia	2,580	1.76%
14	Massachusetts	2,298	1.56%
15	Wisconsin	2,251	1.53%
16	Connecticut	2,181	1.48%
17	Alabama	2,085	1.42%
18	Louisiana	1,722	1.17%
19	Washington	1,625	1.11%
20	South Carolina	1,543	1.05%
21	Arizona	1,519	1.03%
22	Oregon	1,479	1.01%
23	Minnesota	1,462	0.99%
24	Tennessee	1,214	0.83%
25	Nevada	1,211	0.82%
26	Colorado	1,064	0.72%
27	Oklahoma	1,032	0.70%
28	Arkansas	992	0.67%
29	Kentucky	930	0.63%
30	Indiana	819	0.56%
31	Mississippi	559	0.38%
32	Illinois	548	0.37%
33	Hawaii	459	0.31%
34	Utah	407	0.28%
35	Nebraska	320	0.22%
36	Iowa	289	0.20%
37	West Virginia	247	0.17%
38	Rhode Island	237	0.16%
39	Alaska	184	0.13%
40	Maine	122	0.08%
41	Idaho	100	0.07%
42	Delaware	98	0.07%
43	New Hampshire	76	0.05%
44	New Mexico	74	0.05%
45	South Dakota	51	0.03%
46	Wyoming	49	0.03%
47	North Dakota	31	0.02%
48	Vermont	1	0.00%
NA	Kansas**	NA	NA
NA	Montana**	NA	NA
	District of Columbia	1,173	0.80%

Source: Federal Bureau of Investigation
   "Crime in the United States 1994" (Uniform Crime Reports, November 19, 1995)
*By law enforcement agencies submitting complete reports to the F.B.I. for 12 months in 1994. The F.B.I. estimates 172,290 reported and unreported arrests for robbery occurred in 1994. Robbery is the taking or attempting to take anything of value by force or threat of force.
**Not available.

Reported Arrest Rate for Robbery in 1994

National Rate = 70.8 Reported Arrests per 100,000 Population*

ALPHA ORDER

RANK	STATE	RATE
19	Alabama	53.6
31	Alaska	32.3
28	Arizona	38.9
25	Arkansas	41.1
4	California	89.2
24	Colorado	42.0
7	Connecticut	78.8
34	Delaware	25.8
6	Florida	82.0
10	Georgia	75.5
28	Hawaii	38.9
46	Idaho	9.1
33	Illinois	30.9
35	Indiana	25.4
42	Iowa	11.9
NA	Kansas**	NA
21	Kentucky	45.9
15	Louisiana	56.8
45	Maine	10.1
2	Maryland	91.8
16	Massachusetts	56.2
13	Michigan	60.5
30	Minnesota	34.3
11	Mississippi	70.7
5	Missouri	86.8
NA	Montana**	NA
38	Nebraska	21.7
3	Nevada	90.1
44	New Hampshire	10.7
8	New Jersey	78.2
39	New Mexico	18.9
1	New York	184.2
17	North Carolina	56.1
47	North Dakota	5.6
12	Ohio	66.7
32	Oklahoma	32.1
20	Oregon	48.8
9	Pennsylvania	77.4
36	Rhode Island	23.8
23	South Carolina	42.2
41	South Dakota	12.5
14	Tennessee	59.0
18	Texas	53.8
36	Utah	23.8
48	Vermont	0.3
26	Virginia	39.8
27	Washington	39.2
40	West Virginia	13.6
22	Wisconsin	45.2
43	Wyoming	10.8

RANK ORDER

RANK	STATE	RATE
1	New York	184.2
2	Maryland	91.8
3	Nevada	90.1
4	California	89.2
5	Missouri	86.8
6	Florida	82.0
7	Connecticut	78.8
8	New Jersey	78.2
9	Pennsylvania	77.4
10	Georgia	75.5
11	Mississippi	70.7
12	Ohio	66.7
13	Michigan	60.5
14	Tennessee	59.0
15	Louisiana	56.8
16	Massachusetts	56.2
17	North Carolina	56.1
18	Texas	53.8
19	Alabama	53.6
20	Oregon	48.8
21	Kentucky	45.9
22	Wisconsin	45.2
23	South Carolina	42.2
24	Colorado	42.0
25	Arkansas	41.1
26	Virginia	39.8
27	Washington	39.2
28	Arizona	38.9
28	Hawaii	38.9
30	Minnesota	34.3
31	Alaska	32.3
32	Oklahoma	32.1
33	Illinois	30.9
34	Delaware	25.8
35	Indiana	25.4
36	Rhode Island	23.8
36	Utah	23.8
38	Nebraska	21.7
39	New Mexico	18.9
40	West Virginia	13.6
41	South Dakota	12.5
42	Iowa	11.9
43	Wyoming	10.8
44	New Hampshire	10.7
45	Maine	10.1
46	Idaho	9.1
47	North Dakota	5.6
48	Vermont	0.3
NA	Kansas**	NA
NA	Montana**	NA
	District of Columbia	205.8

Source: Morgan Quitno Press using data from Federal Bureau of Investigation
"Crime in the United States 1994" (Uniform Crime Reports, November 19, 1995)
*By law enforcement agencies submitting complete reports to the F.B.I. for 12 months in 1994. These rates based
on population estimates for areas under the jurisdiction of those agencies reporting. Arrest rate based on the F.B.I.
estimate of reported and unreported arrests for robbery is 66.2 arrests per 100,000 population.
**Not available.

Reported Arrests for Aggravated Assault in 1994

National Total = 449,716 Reported Arrests*

ALPHA ORDER

RANK	STATE	ARRESTS	% of USA
13	Alabama	9,380	2.09%
35	Alaska	1,274	0.28%
19	Arizona	7,462	1.66%
28	Arkansas	3,343	0.74%
1	California	116,277	25.86%
20	Colorado	6,391	1.42%
21	Connecticut	5,911	1.31%
43	Delaware	532	0.12%
2	Florida	43,793	9.74%
10	Georgia	11,082	2.46%
40	Hawaii	653	0.15%
36	Idaho	1,188	0.26%
34	Illinois	1,487	0.33%
23	Indiana	5,833	1.30%
30	Iowa	2,850	0.63%
NA	Kansas**	NA	NA
16	Kentucky	7,607	1.69%
14	Louisiana	9,167	2.04%
42	Maine	599	0.13%
18	Maryland	7,513	1.67%
8	Massachusetts	11,936	2.65%
6	Michigan	14,158	3.15%
27	Minnesota	4,246	0.94%
37	Mississippi	1,071	0.24%
11	Missouri	9,836	2.19%
NA	Montana**	NA	NA
39	Nebraska	888	0.20%
33	Nevada	1,616	0.36%
46	New Hampshire	329	0.07%
7	New Jersey	13,230	2.94%
41	New Mexico	638	0.14%
3	New York	34,038	7.57%
5	North Carolina	20,440	4.55%
47	North Dakota	120	0.03%
15	Ohio	8,265	1.84%
26	Oklahoma	4,439	0.99%
29	Oregon	2,926	0.65%
9	Pennsylvania	11,863	2.64%
31	Rhode Island	1,970	0.44%
17	South Carolina	7,604	1.69%
44	South Dakota	478	0.11%
24	Tennessee	5,492	1.22%
4	Texas	24,399	5.43%
32	Utah	1,954	0.43%
48	Vermont	60	0.01%
12	Virginia	9,425	2.10%
25	Washington	5,123	1.14%
38	West Virginia	1,000	0.22%
22	Wisconsin	5,891	1.31%
45	Wyoming	426	0.09%

RANK ORDER

RANK	STATE	ARRESTS	% of USA
1	California	116,277	25.86%
2	Florida	43,793	9.74%
3	New York	34,038	7.57%
4	Texas	24,399	5.43%
5	North Carolina	20,440	4.55%
6	Michigan	14,158	3.15%
7	New Jersey	13,230	2.94%
8	Massachusetts	11,936	2.65%
9	Pennsylvania	11,863	2.64%
10	Georgia	11,082	2.46%
11	Missouri	9,836	2.19%
12	Virginia	9,425	2.10%
13	Alabama	9,380	2.09%
14	Louisiana	9,167	2.04%
15	Ohio	8,265	1.84%
16	Kentucky	7,607	1.69%
17	South Carolina	7,604	1.69%
18	Maryland	7,513	1.67%
19	Arizona	7,462	1.66%
20	Colorado	6,391	1.42%
21	Connecticut	5,911	1.31%
22	Wisconsin	5,891	1.31%
23	Indiana	5,833	1.30%
24	Tennessee	5,492	1.22%
25	Washington	5,123	1.14%
26	Oklahoma	4,439	0.99%
27	Minnesota	4,246	0.94%
28	Arkansas	3,343	0.74%
29	Oregon	2,926	0.65%
30	Iowa	2,850	0.63%
31	Rhode Island	1,970	0.44%
32	Utah	1,954	0.43%
33	Nevada	1,616	0.36%
34	Illinois	1,487	0.33%
35	Alaska	1,274	0.28%
36	Idaho	1,188	0.26%
37	Mississippi	1,071	0.24%
38	West Virginia	1,000	0.22%
39	Nebraska	888	0.20%
40	Hawaii	653	0.15%
41	New Mexico	638	0.14%
42	Maine	599	0.13%
43	Delaware	532	0.12%
44	South Dakota	478	0.11%
45	Wyoming	426	0.09%
46	New Hampshire	329	0.07%
47	North Dakota	120	0.03%
48	Vermont	60	0.01%
NA	Kansas**	NA	NA
NA	Montana**	NA	NA
	District of Columbia	3,513	0.78%

Source: Federal Bureau of Investigation
      "Crime in the United States 1994" (Uniform Crime Reports, November 19, 1995)
*By law enforcement agencies submitting complete reports to the F.B.I. for 12 months in 1994. The F.B.I. estimates 547,760 reported and unreported arrests for aggravated assault occurred in 1994. Aggravated assault is an attack for the purpose of inflicting severe bodily injury.
**Not available.

Reported Arrest Rate for Aggravated Assault in 1994

National Rate = 216.6 Reported Arrests per 100,000 Population*

ALPHA ORDER

RANK	STATE	RATE
11	Alabama	241.1
12	Alaska	223.9
17	Arizona	191.1
26	Arkansas	138.4
2	California	370.9
10	Colorado	252.3
14	Connecticut	213.5
25	Delaware	140.0
3	Florida	319.0
9	Georgia	264.9
43	Hawaii	55.4
37	Idaho	107.7
41	Illinois	83.7
19	Indiana	180.6
34	Iowa	117.5
NA	Kansas**	NA
1	Kentucky	375.1
4	Louisiana	302.5
45	Maine	49.7
22	Maryland	150.5
7	Massachusetts	291.8
18	Michigan	188.2
38	Minnesota	99.7
28	Mississippi	135.4
5	Missouri	299.7
NA	Montana**	NA
42	Nebraska	60.2
32	Nevada	120.2
46	New Hampshire	46.2
20	New Jersey	172.9
21	New Mexico	162.8
13	New York	213.7
6	North Carolina	298.6
47	North Dakota	21.7
31	Ohio	122.6
27	Oklahoma	138.2
39	Oregon	96.6
29	Pennsylvania	127.8
16	Rhode Island	197.6
15	South Carolina	207.8
35	South Dakota	116.9
8	Tennessee	267.1
23	Texas	150.2
36	Utah	114.2
48	Vermont	20.1
24	Virginia	145.5
30	Washington	123.6
44	West Virginia	54.9
33	Wisconsin	118.3
40	Wyoming	94.2

RANK ORDER

RANK	STATE	RATE
1	Kentucky	375.1
2	California	370.9
3	Florida	319.0
4	Louisiana	302.5
5	Missouri	299.7
6	North Carolina	298.6
7	Massachusetts	291.8
8	Tennessee	267.1
9	Georgia	264.9
10	Colorado	252.3
11	Alabama	241.1
12	Alaska	223.9
13	New York	213.7
14	Connecticut	213.5
15	South Carolina	207.8
16	Rhode Island	197.6
17	Arizona	191.1
18	Michigan	188.2
19	Indiana	180.6
20	New Jersey	172.9
21	New Mexico	162.8
22	Maryland	150.5
23	Texas	150.2
24	Virginia	145.5
25	Delaware	140.0
26	Arkansas	138.4
27	Oklahoma	138.2
28	Mississippi	135.4
29	Pennsylvania	127.8
30	Washington	123.6
31	Ohio	122.6
32	Nevada	120.2
33	Wisconsin	118.3
34	Iowa	117.5
35	South Dakota	116.9
36	Utah	114.2
37	Idaho	107.7
38	Minnesota	99.7
39	Oregon	96.6
40	Wyoming	94.2
41	Illinois	83.7
42	Nebraska	60.2
43	Hawaii	55.4
44	West Virginia	54.9
45	Maine	49.7
46	New Hampshire	46.2
47	North Dakota	21.7
48	Vermont	20.1
NA	Kansas**	NA
NA	Montana**	NA
	District of Columbia	616.3

Source: Morgan Quitno Press using data from Federal Bureau of Investigation
"Crime in the United States 1994" (Uniform Crime Reports, November 19, 1995)
By law enforcement agencies submitting complete reports to the F.B.I. for 12 months in 1994. These rates based on population estimates for areas under the jurisdiction of those agencies reporting. Arrest rate based on the F.B.I. estimate of reported and unreported arrests for aggravated assault is 210.4 arrests per 100,000 population.
**Not available.*

Reported Arrests for Property Crime in 1994

National Total = 1,739,261 Reported Arrests*

ALPHA ORDER

RANK	STATE	ARRESTS	% of USA
22	Alabama	25,734	1.48%
40	Alaska	6,575	0.38%
12	Arizona	46,556	2.68%
29	Arkansas	18,353	1.06%
1	California	258,484	14.86%
18	Colorado	34,082	1.96%
21	Connecticut	30,438	1.75%
47	Delaware	1,619	0.09%
3	Florida	143,897	8.27%
15	Georgia	41,413	2.38%
35	Hawaii	11,709	0.67%
36	Idaho	10,469	0.60%
33	Illinois	12,083	0.69%
26	Indiana	22,123	1.27%
32	Iowa	12,223	0.70%
NA	Kansas**	NA	NA
31	Kentucky	12,892	0.74%
19	Louisiana	33,647	1.93%
38	Maine	9,113	0.52%
9	Maryland	50,492	2.90%
28	Massachusetts	19,388	1.11%
13	Michigan	46,029	2.65%
20	Minnesota	32,820	1.89%
37	Mississippi	9,969	0.57%
17	Missouri	36,965	2.13%
NA	Montana**	NA	NA
34	Nebraska	12,020	0.69%
30	Nevada	14,077	0.81%
44	New Hampshire	3,420	0.20%
8	New Jersey	53,759	3.09%
46	New Mexico	3,109	0.18%
4	New York	102,924	5.92%
6	North Carolina	58,676	3.37%
43	North Dakota	3,893	0.22%
14	Ohio	44,805	2.58%
25	Oklahoma	22,506	1.29%
16	Oregon	37,545	2.16%
7	Pennsylvania	56,589	3.25%
41	Rhode Island	5,833	0.34%
23	South Carolina	24,060	1.38%
42	South Dakota	4,303	0.25%
27	Tennessee	20,985	1.21%
2	Texas	146,870	8.44%
24	Utah	23,718	1.36%
48	Vermont	548	0.03%
10	Virginia	49,051	2.82%
11	Washington	47,630	2.74%
39	West Virginia	7,744	0.45%
5	Wisconsin	59,232	3.41%
45	Wyoming	3,291	0.19%

RANK ORDER

RANK	STATE	ARRESTS	% of USA
1	California	258,484	14.86%
2	Texas	146,870	8.44%
3	Florida	143,897	8.27%
4	New York	102,924	5.92%
5	Wisconsin	59,232	3.41%
6	North Carolina	58,676	3.37%
7	Pennsylvania	56,589	3.25%
8	New Jersey	53,759	3.09%
9	Maryland	50,492	2.90%
10	Virginia	49,051	2.82%
11	Washington	47,630	2.74%
12	Arizona	46,556	2.68%
13	Michigan	46,029	2.65%
14	Ohio	44,805	2.58%
15	Georgia	41,413	2.38%
16	Oregon	37,545	2.16%
17	Missouri	36,965	2.13%
18	Colorado	34,082	1.96%
19	Louisiana	33,647	1.93%
20	Minnesota	32,820	1.89%
21	Connecticut	30,438	1.75%
22	Alabama	25,734	1.48%
23	South Carolina	24,060	1.38%
24	Utah	23,718	1.36%
25	Oklahoma	22,506	1.29%
26	Indiana	22,123	1.27%
27	Tennessee	20,985	1.21%
28	Massachusetts	19,388	1.11%
29	Arkansas	18,353	1.06%
30	Nevada	14,077	0.81%
31	Kentucky	12,892	0.74%
32	Iowa	12,223	0.70%
33	Illinois	12,083	0.69%
34	Nebraska	12,020	0.69%
35	Hawaii	11,709	0.67%
36	Idaho	10,469	0.60%
37	Mississippi	9,969	0.57%
38	Maine	9,113	0.52%
39	West Virginia	7,744	0.45%
40	Alaska	6,575	0.38%
41	Rhode Island	5,833	0.34%
42	South Dakota	4,303	0.25%
43	North Dakota	3,893	0.22%
44	New Hampshire	3,420	0.20%
45	Wyoming	3,291	0.19%
46	New Mexico	3,109	0.18%
47	Delaware	1,619	0.09%
48	Vermont	548	0.03%
NA	Kansas**	NA	NA
NA	Montana**	NA	NA
	District of Columbia	5,600	0.32%

Source: Federal Bureau of Investigation
    "Crime in the United States 1994" (Uniform Crime Reports, November 19, 1995)
*By law enforcement agencies submitting complete reports to the F.B.I. for 12 months in 1994. The F.B.I. estimates 2,131,700 reported and unreported arrests for property crime occurred in 1994. Property crimes are offenses of burglary, larceny-theft, motor vehicle theft and arson.
**Not available.

Reported Arrest Rate for Property Crime in 1994

National Rate = 837.7 Reported Arrests per 100,000 Population*

ALPHA ORDER

RANK	STATE	RATE
36	Alabama	661.4
7	Alaska	1,155.5
5	Arizona	1,192.5
26	Arkansas	759.6
22	California	824.4
2	Colorado	1,345.5
11	Connecticut	1,099.6
46	Delaware	426.1
13	Florida	1,048.1
18	Georgia	989.8
17	Hawaii	993.1
19	Idaho	949.1
34	Illinois	680.3
33	Indiana	685.1
43	Iowa	504.0
NA	Kansas**	NA
39	Kentucky	635.7
10	Louisiana	1,110.5
28	Maine	755.6
16	Maryland	1,011.3
45	Massachusetts	474.0
40	Michigan	611.8
25	Minnesota	770.6
3	Mississippi	1,260.3
9	Missouri	1,126.3
NA	Montana**	NA
23	Nebraska	814.9
14	Nevada	1,047.4
44	New Hampshire	480.3
31	New Jersey	702.5
24	New Mexico	793.1
38	New York	646.3
21	North Carolina	857.1
30	North Dakota	705.3
35	Ohio	664.7
32	Oklahoma	700.7
4	Oregon	1,239.1
41	Pennsylvania	609.6
42	Rhode Island	585.1
37	South Carolina	657.6
12	South Dakota	1,052.1
15	Tennessee	1,020.7
20	Texas	904.4
1	Utah	1,386.2
48	Vermont	183.9
27	Virginia	757.3
8	Washington	1,149.1
47	West Virginia	425.5
6	Wisconsin	1,189.4
29	Wyoming	728.1

RANK ORDER

RANK	STATE	RATE
1	Utah	1,386.2
2	Colorado	1,345.5
3	Mississippi	1,260.3
4	Oregon	1,239.1
5	Arizona	1,192.5
6	Wisconsin	1,189.4
7	Alaska	1,155.5
8	Washington	1,149.1
9	Missouri	1,126.3
10	Louisiana	1,110.5
11	Connecticut	1,099.6
12	South Dakota	1,052.1
13	Florida	1,048.1
14	Nevada	1,047.4
15	Tennessee	1,020.7
16	Maryland	1,011.3
17	Hawaii	993.1
18	Georgia	989.8
19	Idaho	949.1
20	Texas	904.4
21	North Carolina	857.1
22	California	824.4
23	Nebraska	814.9
24	New Mexico	793.1
25	Minnesota	770.6
26	Arkansas	759.6
27	Virginia	757.3
28	Maine	755.6
29	Wyoming	728.1
30	North Dakota	705.3
31	New Jersey	702.5
32	Oklahoma	700.7
33	Indiana	685.1
34	Illinois	680.3
35	Ohio	664.7
36	Alabama	661.4
37	South Carolina	657.6
38	New York	646.3
39	Kentucky	635.7
40	Michigan	611.8
41	Pennsylvania	609.6
42	Rhode Island	585.1
43	Iowa	504.0
44	New Hampshire	480.3
45	Massachusetts	474.0
46	Delaware	426.1
47	West Virginia	425.5
48	Vermont	183.9
NA	Kansas**	NA
NA	Montana**	NA
	District of Columbia	982.5

Source: Morgan Quitno Press using data from Federal Bureau of Investigation
"Crime in the United States 1994" (Uniform Crime Reports, November 19, 1995)
*By law enforcement agencies submitting complete reports to the F.B.I. for 12 months in 1994. These rates based on population estimates for areas under the jurisdiction of those agencies reporting. Arrest rate based on the F.B.I. estimate of reported and unreported arrests for property crime is 818.8 arrests per 100,000 population.
**Not available.

Reported Arrests for Burglary in 1994

National Total = 319,926 Reported Arrests*

ALPHA ORDER

RANK	STATE	ARRESTS	% of USA
23	Alabama	4,053	1.27%
41	Alaska	952	0.30%
14	Arizona	6,459	2.02%
26	Arkansas	3,393	1.06%
1	California	69,363	21.68%
25	Colorado	3,472	1.09%
18	Connecticut	5,294	1.65%
44	Delaware	401	0.13%
2	Florida	29,290	9.16%
12	Georgia	6,785	2.12%
36	Hawaii	1,527	0.48%
38	Idaho	1,271	0.40%
37	Illinois	1,360	0.43%
28	Indiana	2,863	0.89%
33	Iowa	1,836	0.57%
NA	Kansas**	NA	NA
29	Kentucky	2,853	0.89%
15	Louisiana	6,439	2.01%
34	Maine	1,820	0.57%
6	Maryland	10,288	3.22%
20	Massachusetts	4,660	1.46%
9	Michigan	8,805	2.75%
22	Minnesota	4,276	1.34%
32	Mississippi	1,960	0.61%
17	Missouri	5,496	1.72%
NA	Montana**	NA	NA
39	Nebraska	1,221	0.38%
27	Nevada	3,355	1.05%
46	New Hampshire	399	0.12%
8	New Jersey	9,505	2.97%
42	New Mexico	606	0.19%
4	New York	18,771	5.87%
5	North Carolina	16,321	5.10%
47	North Dakota	382	0.12%
10	Ohio	8,285	2.59%
24	Oklahoma	4,026	1.26%
21	Oregon	4,474	1.40%
7	Pennsylvania	9,831	3.07%
40	Rhode Island	1,071	0.33%
19	South Carolina	5,038	1.57%
43	South Dakota	553	0.17%
30	Tennessee	2,849	0.89%
3	Texas	22,884	7.15%
31	Utah	2,262	0.71%
48	Vermont	171	0.05%
11	Virginia	7,077	2.21%
16	Washington	6,175	1.93%
35	West Virginia	1,604	0.50%
13	Wisconsin	6,659	2.08%
44	Wyoming	401	0.13%

RANK ORDER

RANK	STATE	ARRESTS	% of USA
1	California	69,363	21.68%
2	Florida	29,290	9.16%
3	Texas	22,884	7.15%
4	New York	18,771	5.87%
5	North Carolina	16,321	5.10%
6	Maryland	10,288	3.22%
7	Pennsylvania	9,831	3.07%
8	New Jersey	9,505	2.97%
9	Michigan	8,805	2.75%
10	Ohio	8,285	2.59%
11	Virginia	7,077	2.21%
12	Georgia	6,785	2.12%
13	Wisconsin	6,659	2.08%
14	Arizona	6,459	2.02%
15	Louisiana	6,439	2.01%
16	Washington	6,175	1.93%
17	Missouri	5,496	1.72%
18	Connecticut	5,294	1.65%
19	South Carolina	5,038	1.57%
20	Massachusetts	4,660	1.46%
21	Oregon	4,474	1.40%
22	Minnesota	4,276	1.34%
23	Alabama	4,053	1.27%
24	Oklahoma	4,026	1.26%
25	Colorado	3,472	1.09%
26	Arkansas	3,393	1.06%
27	Nevada	3,355	1.05%
28	Indiana	2,863	0.89%
29	Kentucky	2,853	0.89%
30	Tennessee	2,849	0.89%
31	Utah	2,262	0.71%
32	Mississippi	1,960	0.61%
33	Iowa	1,836	0.57%
34	Maine	1,820	0.57%
35	West Virginia	1,604	0.50%
36	Hawaii	1,527	0.48%
37	Illinois	1,360	0.43%
38	Idaho	1,271	0.40%
39	Nebraska	1,221	0.38%
40	Rhode Island	1,071	0.33%
41	Alaska	952	0.30%
42	New Mexico	606	0.19%
43	South Dakota	553	0.17%
44	Delaware	401	0.13%
44	Wyoming	401	0.13%
46	New Hampshire	399	0.12%
47	North Dakota	382	0.12%
48	Vermont	171	0.05%
NA	Kansas**	NA	NA
NA	Montana**	NA	NA
	District of Columbia	1,090	0.34%

Source: Federal Bureau of Investigation
    "Crime in the United States 1994" (Uniform Crime Reports, November 19, 1995)
*By law enforcement agencies submitting complete reports to the F.B.I. for 12 months in 1994. The F.B.I. estimates 396,100 reported and unreported arrests for burglary occurred in 1993. Burglary is the unlawful entry of a structure to commit a felony or theft. Attempts are included.
**Not available.

Reported Arrest Rate for Burglary in 1994

National Rate = 154.1 Reported Arrests per 100,000 Population*

ALPHA ORDER

RANK	STATE	RATE
38	Alabama	104.2
10	Alaska	167.3
11	Arizona	165.4
19	Arkansas	140.4
4	California	221.2
22	Colorado	137.1
8	Connecticut	191.3
37	Delaware	105.5
5	Florida	213.3
12	Georgia	162.2
26	Hawaii	129.5
32	Idaho	115.2
44	Illinois	76.6
40	Indiana	88.7
45	Iowa	75.7
NA	Kansas**	NA
18	Kentucky	140.7
6	Louisiana	212.5
14	Maine	150.9
7	Maryland	206.0
33	Massachusetts	113.9
31	Michigan	117.0
39	Minnesota	100.4
2	Mississippi	247.8
9	Missouri	167.5
NA	Montana**	NA
43	Nebraska	82.8
1	Nevada	249.6
48	New Hampshire	56.0
28	New Jersey	124.2
13	New Mexico	154.6
30	New York	117.9
3	North Carolina	238.4
46	North Dakota	69.2
29	Ohio	122.9
27	Oklahoma	125.3
16	Oregon	147.7
36	Pennsylvania	105.9
35	Rhode Island	107.4
21	South Carolina	137.7
23	South Dakota	135.2
20	Tennessee	138.6
17	Texas	140.9
25	Utah	132.2
47	Vermont	57.4
34	Virginia	109.3
15	Washington	149.0
42	West Virginia	88.1
24	Wisconsin	133.7
40	Wyoming	88.7

RANK ORDER

RANK	STATE	RATE
1	Nevada	249.6
2	Mississippi	247.8
3	North Carolina	238.4
4	California	221.2
5	Florida	213.3
6	Louisiana	212.5
7	Maryland	206.0
8	Connecticut	191.3
9	Missouri	167.5
10	Alaska	167.3
11	Arizona	165.4
12	Georgia	162.2
13	New Mexico	154.6
14	Maine	150.9
15	Washington	149.0
16	Oregon	147.7
17	Texas	140.9
18	Kentucky	140.7
19	Arkansas	140.4
20	Tennessee	138.6
21	South Carolina	137.7
22	Colorado	137.1
23	South Dakota	135.2
24	Wisconsin	133.7
25	Utah	132.2
26	Hawaii	129.5
27	Oklahoma	125.3
28	New Jersey	124.2
29	Ohio	122.9
30	New York	117.9
31	Michigan	117.0
32	Idaho	115.2
33	Massachusetts	113.9
34	Virginia	109.3
35	Rhode Island	107.4
36	Pennsylvania	105.9
37	Delaware	105.5
38	Alabama	104.2
39	Minnesota	100.4
40	Indiana	88.7
40	Wyoming	88.7
42	West Virginia	88.1
43	Nebraska	82.8
44	Illinois	76.6
45	Iowa	75.7
46	North Dakota	69.2
47	Vermont	57.4
48	New Hampshire	56.0
NA	Kansas**	NA
NA	Montana**	NA
	District of Columbia	191.2

Source: Morgan Quitno Press using data from Federal Bureau of Investigation
   "Crime in the United States 1994" (Uniform Crime Reports, November 19, 1995)
*By law enforcement agencies submitting complete reports to the F.B.I. for 12 months in 1994. These rates based
on population estimates for areas under the jurisdiction of those agencies reporting. Arrest rate based on the F.B.I.
estimate of reported and unreported arrests for burglary is 152.1 arrests per 100,000 population.
**Not available.

Reported Arrests for Larceny and Theft in 1994

National Total = 1,236,311 Reported Arrests*

ALPHA ORDER

RANK	STATE	ARRESTS	% of USA
22	Alabama	19,900	1.61%
40	Alaska	4,943	0.40%
11	Arizona	36,261	2.93%
28	Arkansas	14,139	1.14%
1	California	145,135	11.74%
16	Colorado	28,355	2.29%
21	Connecticut	22,245	1.80%
47	Delaware	1,099	0.09%
3	Florida	99,633	8.06%
15	Georgia	31,113	2.52%
36	Hawaii	8,377	0.68%
35	Idaho	8,426	0.68%
30	Illinois	10,368	0.84%
25	Indiana	17,024	1.38%
33	Iowa	9,521	0.77%
NA	Kansas**	NA	NA
34	Kentucky	8,560	0.69%
19	Louisiana	25,460	2.06%
38	Maine	6,648	0.54%
13	Maryland	32,107	2.60%
29	Massachusetts	12,594	1.02%
12	Michigan	33,052	2.67%
20	Minnesota	24,658	1.99%
37	Mississippi	6,976	0.56%
18	Missouri	27,452	2.22%
NA	Montana**	NA	NA
31	Nebraska	10,178	0.82%
32	Nevada	9,805	0.79%
44	New Hampshire	2,829	0.23%
6	New Jersey	41,236	3.34%
46	New Mexico	2,273	0.18%
4	New York	73,177	5.92%
7	North Carolina	39,485	3.19%
43	North Dakota	3,192	0.26%
14	Ohio	31,806	2.57%
27	Oklahoma	15,841	1.28%
17	Oregon	28,223	2.28%
9	Pennsylvania	37,976	3.07%
41	Rhode Island	4,153	0.34%
24	South Carolina	17,763	1.44%
42	South Dakota	3,488	0.28%
26	Tennessee	16,317	1.32%
2	Texas	110,175	8.91%
23	Utah	19,702	1.59%
48	Vermont	348	0.03%
10	Virginia	37,674	3.05%
8	Washington	38,556	3.12%
39	West Virginia	5,548	0.45%
5	Wisconsin	46,952	3.80%
45	Wyoming	2,708	0.22%

RANK ORDER

RANK	STATE	ARRESTS	% of USA
1	California	145,135	11.74%
2	Texas	110,175	8.91%
3	Florida	99,633	8.06%
4	New York	73,177	5.92%
5	Wisconsin	46,952	3.80%
6	New Jersey	41,236	3.34%
7	North Carolina	39,485	3.19%
8	Washington	38,556	3.12%
9	Pennsylvania	37,976	3.07%
10	Virginia	37,674	3.05%
11	Arizona	36,261	2.93%
12	Michigan	33,052	2.67%
13	Maryland	32,107	2.60%
14	Ohio	31,806	2.57%
15	Georgia	31,113	2.52%
16	Colorado	28,355	2.29%
17	Oregon	28,223	2.28%
18	Missouri	27,452	2.22%
19	Louisiana	25,460	2.06%
20	Minnesota	24,658	1.99%
21	Connecticut	22,245	1.80%
22	Alabama	19,900	1.61%
23	Utah	19,702	1.59%
24	South Carolina	17,763	1.44%
25	Indiana	17,024	1.38%
26	Tennessee	16,317	1.32%
27	Oklahoma	15,841	1.28%
28	Arkansas	14,139	1.14%
29	Massachusetts	12,594	1.02%
30	Illinois	10,368	0.84%
31	Nebraska	10,178	0.82%
32	Nevada	9,805	0.79%
33	Iowa	9,521	0.77%
34	Kentucky	8,560	0.69%
35	Idaho	8,426	0.68%
36	Hawaii	8,377	0.68%
37	Mississippi	6,976	0.56%
38	Maine	6,648	0.54%
39	West Virginia	5,548	0.45%
40	Alaska	4,943	0.40%
41	Rhode Island	4,153	0.34%
42	South Dakota	3,488	0.28%
43	North Dakota	3,192	0.26%
44	New Hampshire	2,829	0.23%
45	Wyoming	2,708	0.22%
46	New Mexico	2,273	0.18%
47	Delaware	1,099	0.09%
48	Vermont	348	0.03%
NA	Kansas**	NA	NA
NA	Montana**	NA	NA
	District of Columbia	2,860	0.23%

Source: Federal Bureau of Investigation
   "Crime in the United States 1994" (Uniform Crime Reports, November 19, 1995)
*By law enforcement agencies submitting complete reports to the F.B.I. for 12 months in 1994. The F.B.I. estimates
1,514,500 reported and unreported arrests for larceny and theft occurred in 1994. Larceny and theft is the unlawful
taking of property without use of force, violence or fraud. Attempts are included. Motor vehicle thefts are excluded.
**Not available.

Reported Arrest Rate for Larceny and Theft in 1994

National Rate = 595.5 Reported Arrests per 100,000 Population*

ALPHA ORDER

RANK	STATE	RATE
33	Alabama	511.4
8	Alaska	868.7
6	Arizona	928.8
23	Arkansas	585.2
37	California	462.9
2	Colorado	1,119.4
12	Connecticut	803.6
47	Delaware	289.2
17	Florida	725.7
15	Georgia	743.6
18	Hawaii	710.5
14	Idaho	763.9
24	Illinois	583.8
32	Indiana	527.2
44	Iowa	392.6
NA	Kansas**	NA
40	Kentucky	422.1
10	Louisiana	840.3
30	Maine	551.2
21	Maryland	643.0
45	Massachusetts	307.9
39	Michigan	439.3
27	Minnesota	579.0
7	Mississippi	881.9
11	Missouri	836.4
NA	Montana**	NA
19	Nebraska	690.0
16	Nevada	729.5
43	New Hampshire	397.3
31	New Jersey	538.8
26	New Mexico	579.8
38	New York	459.5
29	North Carolina	576.8
28	North Dakota	578.3
36	Ohio	471.8
34	Oklahoma	493.2
4	Oregon	931.5
42	Pennsylvania	409.1
41	Rhode Island	416.5
35	South Carolina	485.5
9	South Dakota	852.8
13	Tennessee	793.6
20	Texas	678.4
1	Utah	1,151.5
48	Vermont	116.8
25	Virginia	581.7
5	Washington	930.2
46	West Virginia	304.8
3	Wisconsin	942.8
22	Wyoming	599.1

RANK ORDER

RANK	STATE	RATE
1	Utah	1,151.5
2	Colorado	1,119.4
3	Wisconsin	942.8
4	Oregon	931.5
5	Washington	930.2
6	Arizona	928.8
7	Mississippi	881.9
8	Alaska	868.7
9	South Dakota	852.8
10	Louisiana	840.3
11	Missouri	836.4
12	Connecticut	803.6
13	Tennessee	793.6
14	Idaho	763.9
15	Georgia	743.6
16	Nevada	729.5
17	Florida	725.7
18	Hawaii	710.5
19	Nebraska	690.0
20	Texas	678.4
21	Maryland	643.0
22	Wyoming	599.1
23	Arkansas	585.2
24	Illinois	583.8
25	Virginia	581.7
26	New Mexico	579.8
27	Minnesota	579.0
28	North Dakota	578.3
29	North Carolina	576.8
30	Maine	551.2
31	New Jersey	538.8
32	Indiana	527.2
33	Alabama	511.4
34	Oklahoma	493.2
35	South Carolina	485.5
36	Ohio	471.8
37	California	462.9
38	New York	459.5
39	Michigan	439.3
40	Kentucky	422.1
41	Rhode Island	416.5
42	Pennsylvania	409.1
43	New Hampshire	397.3
44	Iowa	392.6
45	Massachusetts	307.9
46	West Virginia	304.8
47	Delaware	289.2
48	Vermont	116.8
NA	Kansas**	NA
NA	Montana**	NA

District of Columbia   501.8

Source: Morgan Quitno Press using data from Federal Bureau of Investigation
"Crime in the United States 1994" (Uniform Crime Reports, November 19, 1995)
*By law enforcement agencies submitting complete reports to the F.B.I. for 12 months in 1994. These rates based on population estimates for areas under the jurisdiction of those agencies reporting. Arrest rate based on the F.B.I. estimate of reported and unreported arrests for larceny and theft is 581.7 arrests per 100,000 population.
**Not available.

Reported Arrests for Motor Vehicle Theft in 1994

National Total = 166,260 Reported Arrests*

ALPHA ORDER

RANK	STATE	ARRESTS	% of USA
26	Alabama	1,655	1.00%
36	Alaska	646	0.39%
14	Arizona	3,408	2.05%
33	Arkansas	690	0.42%
1	California	41,415	24.91%
23	Colorado	1,883	1.13%
16	Connecticut	2,615	1.57%
47	Delaware	104	0.06%
2	Florida	14,281	8.59%
15	Georgia	3,130	1.88%
24	Hawaii	1,742	1.05%
35	Idaho	649	0.39%
42	Illinois	260	0.16%
21	Indiana	2,050	1.23%
34	Iowa	683	0.41%
NA	Kansas**	NA	NA
29	Kentucky	1,251	0.75%
28	Louisiana	1,524	0.92%
37	Maine	512	0.31%
6	Maryland	7,472	4.49%
22	Massachusetts	1,950	1.17%
13	Michigan	3,501	2.11%
12	Minnesota	3,542	2.13%
31	Mississippi	949	0.57%
11	Missouri	3,565	2.14%
NA	Montana**	NA	NA
38	Nebraska	499	0.30%
32	Nevada	840	0.51%
46	New Hampshire	119	0.07%
18	New Jersey	2,455	1.48%
43	New Mexico	175	0.11%
4	New York	10,155	6.11%
19	North Carolina	2,345	1.41%
41	North Dakota	298	0.18%
9	Ohio	4,042	2.43%
20	Oklahoma	2,191	1.32%
8	Oregon	4,298	2.59%
5	Pennsylvania	8,011	4.82%
39	Rhode Island	491	0.30%
30	South Carolina	1,047	0.63%
44	South Dakota	146	0.09%
25	Tennessee	1,687	1.01%
3	Texas	12,875	7.74%
27	Utah	1,581	0.95%
48	Vermont	15	0.01%
10	Virginia	3,771	2.27%
17	Washington	2,489	1.50%
40	West Virginia	483	0.29%
7	Wisconsin	5,012	3.01%
45	Wyoming	135	0.08%

RANK ORDER

RANK	STATE	ARRESTS	% of USA
1	California	41,415	24.91%
2	Florida	14,281	8.59%
3	Texas	12,875	7.74%
4	New York	10,155	6.11%
5	Pennsylvania	8,011	4.82%
6	Maryland	7,472	4.49%
7	Wisconsin	5,012	3.01%
8	Oregon	4,298	2.59%
9	Ohio	4,042	2.43%
10	Virginia	3,771	2.27%
11	Missouri	3,565	2.14%
12	Minnesota	3,542	2.13%
13	Michigan	3,501	2.11%
14	Arizona	3,408	2.05%
15	Georgia	3,130	1.88%
16	Connecticut	2,615	1.57%
17	Washington	2,489	1.50%
18	New Jersey	2,455	1.48%
19	North Carolina	2,345	1.41%
20	Oklahoma	2,191	1.32%
21	Indiana	2,050	1.23%
22	Massachusetts	1,950	1.17%
23	Colorado	1,883	1.13%
24	Hawaii	1,742	1.05%
25	Tennessee	1,687	1.01%
26	Alabama	1,655	1.00%
27	Utah	1,581	0.95%
28	Louisiana	1,524	0.92%
29	Kentucky	1,251	0.75%
30	South Carolina	1,047	0.63%
31	Mississippi	949	0.57%
32	Nevada	840	0.51%
33	Arkansas	690	0.42%
34	Iowa	683	0.41%
35	Idaho	649	0.39%
36	Alaska	646	0.39%
37	Maine	512	0.31%
38	Nebraska	499	0.30%
39	Rhode Island	491	0.30%
40	West Virginia	483	0.29%
41	North Dakota	298	0.18%
42	Illinois	260	0.16%
43	New Mexico	175	0.11%
44	South Dakota	146	0.09%
45	Wyoming	135	0.08%
46	New Hampshire	119	0.07%
47	Delaware	104	0.06%
48	Vermont	15	0.01%
NA	Kansas**	NA	NA
NA	Montana**	NA	NA
	District of Columbia	1,623	0.98%

Source: Federal Bureau of Investigation
   "Crime in the United States 1994" (Uniform Crime Reports, November 19, 1995)
*By law enforcement agencies submitting complete reports to the F.B.I. for 12 months in 1993. The F.B.I. estimates 200,200 reported and unreported arrests for motor vehicle theft occurred in 1994. Motor vehicle theft includes the theft or attempted theft of a self-propelled vehicle. Excludes motorboats, construction equipment, airplanes and farming equipment. **Not available.*

Reported Arrest Rate for Motor Vehicle Theft in 1994

National Rate = 80.1 Reported Arrests per 100,000 Population*

ALPHA ORDER

RANK	STATE	RATE
34	Alabama	42.5
6	Alaska	113.5
12	Arizona	87.3
41	Arkansas	28.6
4	California	132.1
18	Colorado	74.3
10	Connecticut	94.5
44	Delaware	27.4
8	Florida	104.0
17	Georgia	74.8
2	Hawaii	147.8
26	Idaho	58.8
47	Illinois	14.6
21	Indiana	63.5
43	Iowa	28.2
NA	Kansas**	NA
23	Kentucky	61.7
29	Louisiana	50.3
34	Maine	42.5
1	Maryland	149.6
31	Massachusetts	47.7
32	Michigan	46.5
14	Minnesota	83.2
5	Mississippi	120.0
7	Missouri	108.6
NA	Montana**	NA
38	Nebraska	33.8
22	Nevada	62.5
46	New Hampshire	16.7
39	New Jersey	32.1
33	New Mexico	44.6
20	New York	63.8
37	North Carolina	34.3
28	North Dakota	54.0
24	Ohio	60.0
19	Oklahoma	68.2
3	Oregon	141.8
13	Pennsylvania	86.3
30	Rhode Island	49.2
41	South Carolina	28.6
36	South Dakota	35.7
15	Tennessee	82.1
16	Texas	79.3
11	Utah	92.4
48	Vermont	5.0
27	Virginia	58.2
24	Washington	60.0
45	West Virginia	26.5
9	Wisconsin	100.6
40	Wyoming	29.9

RANK ORDER

RANK	STATE	RATE
1	Maryland	149.6
2	Hawaii	147.8
3	Oregon	141.8
4	California	132.1
5	Mississippi	120.0
6	Alaska	113.5
7	Missouri	108.6
8	Florida	104.0
9	Wisconsin	100.6
10	Connecticut	94.5
11	Utah	92.4
12	Arizona	87.3
13	Pennsylvania	86.3
14	Minnesota	83.2
15	Tennessee	82.1
16	Texas	79.3
17	Georgia	74.8
18	Colorado	74.3
19	Oklahoma	68.2
20	New York	63.8
21	Indiana	63.5
22	Nevada	62.5
23	Kentucky	61.7
24	Ohio	60.0
24	Washington	60.0
26	Idaho	58.8
27	Virginia	58.2
28	North Dakota	54.0
29	Louisiana	50.3
30	Rhode Island	49.2
31	Massachusetts	47.7
32	Michigan	46.5
33	New Mexico	44.6
34	Alabama	42.5
34	Maine	42.5
36	South Dakota	35.7
37	North Carolina	34.3
38	Nebraska	33.8
39	New Jersey	32.1
40	Wyoming	29.9
41	Arkansas	28.6
41	South Carolina	28.6
43	Iowa	28.2
44	Delaware	27.4
45	West Virginia	26.5
46	New Hampshire	16.7
47	Illinois	14.6
48	Vermont	5.0
NA	Kansas**	NA
NA	Montana**	NA

District of Columbia	284.7

Source: Morgan Quitno Press using data from Federal Bureau of Investigation
   "Crime in the United States 1994" (Uniform Crime Reports, November 19, 1995)
*By law enforcement agencies submitting complete reports to the F.B.I. for 12 months in 1994. These rates based
on population estimates for areas under the jurisdiction of those agencies reporting. Arrest rate based on the F.B.I.
estimate of reported and unreported arrests for motor vehicle theft is 76.9 arrests per 100,000 population.
**Not available.

Reported Arrests for Arson in 1994

National Total = 16,764 Reported Arrests*

<table>
<tr><td colspan="4">ALPHA ORDER</td><td colspan="4">RANK ORDER</td></tr>
<tr><td>RANK</td><td>STATE</td><td>ARRESTS</td><td>% of USA</td><td>RANK</td><td>STATE</td><td>ARRESTS</td><td>% of USA</td></tr>
<tr><td>32</td><td>Alabama</td><td>126</td><td>0.75%</td><td>1</td><td>California</td><td>2,571</td><td>15.34%</td></tr>
<tr><td>45</td><td>Alaska</td><td>34</td><td>0.20%</td><td>2</td><td>Texas</td><td>936</td><td>5.58%</td></tr>
<tr><td>16</td><td>Arizona</td><td>428</td><td>2.55%</td><td>3</td><td>New York</td><td>821</td><td>4.90%</td></tr>
<tr><td>31</td><td>Arkansas</td><td>131</td><td>0.78%</td><td>4</td><td>Pennsylvania</td><td>771</td><td>4.60%</td></tr>
<tr><td>1</td><td>California</td><td>2,571</td><td>15.34%</td><td>5</td><td>Florida</td><td>693</td><td>4.13%</td></tr>
<tr><td>19</td><td>Colorado</td><td>372</td><td>2.22%</td><td>6</td><td>Ohio</td><td>672</td><td>4.01%</td></tr>
<tr><td>21</td><td>Connecticut</td><td>284</td><td>1.69%</td><td>7</td><td>Michigan</td><td>671</td><td>4.00%</td></tr>
<tr><td>47</td><td>Delaware</td><td>15</td><td>0.09%</td><td>8</td><td>Maryland</td><td>625</td><td>3.73%</td></tr>
<tr><td>5</td><td>Florida</td><td>693</td><td>4.13%</td><td>9</td><td>Wisconsin</td><td>609</td><td>3.63%</td></tr>
<tr><td>18</td><td>Georgia</td><td>385</td><td>2.30%</td><td>10</td><td>New Jersey</td><td>563</td><td>3.36%</td></tr>
<tr><td>42</td><td>Hawaii</td><td>63</td><td>0.38%</td><td>11</td><td>Oregon</td><td>550</td><td>3.28%</td></tr>
<tr><td>33</td><td>Idaho</td><td>123</td><td>0.73%</td><td>12</td><td>Virginia</td><td>529</td><td>3.16%</td></tr>
<tr><td>38</td><td>Illinois</td><td>95</td><td>0.57%</td><td>13</td><td>North Carolina</td><td>525</td><td>3.13%</td></tr>
<tr><td>25</td><td>Indiana</td><td>186</td><td>1.11%</td><td>14</td><td>Missouri</td><td>452</td><td>2.70%</td></tr>
<tr><td>27</td><td>Iowa</td><td>183</td><td>1.09%</td><td>15</td><td>Oklahoma</td><td>448</td><td>2.67%</td></tr>
<tr><td>NA</td><td>Kansas**</td><td>NA</td><td>NA</td><td>16</td><td>Arizona</td><td>428</td><td>2.55%</td></tr>
<tr><td>22</td><td>Kentucky</td><td>228</td><td>1.36%</td><td>17</td><td>Washington</td><td>410</td><td>2.45%</td></tr>
<tr><td>23</td><td>Louisiana</td><td>224</td><td>1.34%</td><td>18</td><td>Georgia</td><td>385</td><td>2.30%</td></tr>
<tr><td>29</td><td>Maine</td><td>133</td><td>0.79%</td><td>19</td><td>Colorado</td><td>372</td><td>2.22%</td></tr>
<tr><td>8</td><td>Maryland</td><td>625</td><td>3.73%</td><td>20</td><td>Minnesota</td><td>344</td><td>2.05%</td></tr>
<tr><td>26</td><td>Massachusetts</td><td>184</td><td>1.10%</td><td>21</td><td>Connecticut</td><td>284</td><td>1.69%</td></tr>
<tr><td>7</td><td>Michigan</td><td>671</td><td>4.00%</td><td>22</td><td>Kentucky</td><td>228</td><td>1.36%</td></tr>
<tr><td>20</td><td>Minnesota</td><td>344</td><td>2.05%</td><td>23</td><td>Louisiana</td><td>224</td><td>1.34%</td></tr>
<tr><td>39</td><td>Mississippi</td><td>84</td><td>0.50%</td><td>24</td><td>South Carolina</td><td>212</td><td>1.26%</td></tr>
<tr><td>14</td><td>Missouri</td><td>452</td><td>2.70%</td><td>25</td><td>Indiana</td><td>186</td><td>1.11%</td></tr>
<tr><td>NA</td><td>Montana**</td><td>NA</td><td>NA</td><td>26</td><td>Massachusetts</td><td>184</td><td>1.10%</td></tr>
<tr><td>34</td><td>Nebraska</td><td>122</td><td>0.73%</td><td>27</td><td>Iowa</td><td>183</td><td>1.09%</td></tr>
<tr><td>40</td><td>Nevada</td><td>77</td><td>0.46%</td><td>28</td><td>Utah</td><td>173</td><td>1.03%</td></tr>
<tr><td>41</td><td>New Hampshire</td><td>73</td><td>0.44%</td><td>29</td><td>Maine</td><td>133</td><td>0.79%</td></tr>
<tr><td>10</td><td>New Jersey</td><td>563</td><td>3.36%</td><td>30</td><td>Tennessee</td><td>132</td><td>0.79%</td></tr>
<tr><td>43</td><td>New Mexico</td><td>55</td><td>0.33%</td><td>31</td><td>Arkansas</td><td>131</td><td>0.78%</td></tr>
<tr><td>3</td><td>New York</td><td>821</td><td>4.90%</td><td>32</td><td>Alabama</td><td>126</td><td>0.75%</td></tr>
<tr><td>13</td><td>North Carolina</td><td>525</td><td>3.13%</td><td>33</td><td>Idaho</td><td>123</td><td>0.73%</td></tr>
<tr><td>46</td><td>North Dakota</td><td>21</td><td>0.13%</td><td>34</td><td>Nebraska</td><td>122</td><td>0.73%</td></tr>
<tr><td>6</td><td>Ohio</td><td>672</td><td>4.01%</td><td>35</td><td>Rhode Island</td><td>118</td><td>0.70%</td></tr>
<tr><td>15</td><td>Oklahoma</td><td>448</td><td>2.67%</td><td>36</td><td>South Dakota</td><td>116</td><td>0.69%</td></tr>
<tr><td>11</td><td>Oregon</td><td>550</td><td>3.28%</td><td>37</td><td>West Virginia</td><td>109</td><td>0.65%</td></tr>
<tr><td>4</td><td>Pennsylvania</td><td>771</td><td>4.60%</td><td>38</td><td>Illinois</td><td>95</td><td>0.57%</td></tr>
<tr><td>35</td><td>Rhode Island</td><td>118</td><td>0.70%</td><td>39</td><td>Mississippi</td><td>84</td><td>0.50%</td></tr>
<tr><td>24</td><td>South Carolina</td><td>212</td><td>1.26%</td><td>40</td><td>Nevada</td><td>77</td><td>0.46%</td></tr>
<tr><td>36</td><td>South Dakota</td><td>116</td><td>0.69%</td><td>41</td><td>New Hampshire</td><td>73</td><td>0.44%</td></tr>
<tr><td>30</td><td>Tennessee</td><td>132</td><td>0.79%</td><td>42</td><td>Hawaii</td><td>63</td><td>0.38%</td></tr>
<tr><td>2</td><td>Texas</td><td>936</td><td>5.58%</td><td>43</td><td>New Mexico</td><td>55</td><td>0.33%</td></tr>
<tr><td>28</td><td>Utah</td><td>173</td><td>1.03%</td><td>44</td><td>Wyoming</td><td>47</td><td>0.28%</td></tr>
<tr><td>48</td><td>Vermont</td><td>14</td><td>0.08%</td><td>45</td><td>Alaska</td><td>34</td><td>0.20%</td></tr>
<tr><td>12</td><td>Virginia</td><td>529</td><td>3.16%</td><td>46</td><td>North Dakota</td><td>21</td><td>0.13%</td></tr>
<tr><td>17</td><td>Washington</td><td>410</td><td>2.45%</td><td>47</td><td>Delaware</td><td>15</td><td>0.09%</td></tr>
<tr><td>37</td><td>West Virginia</td><td>109</td><td>0.65%</td><td>48</td><td>Vermont</td><td>14</td><td>0.08%</td></tr>
<tr><td>9</td><td>Wisconsin</td><td>609</td><td>3.63%</td><td>NA</td><td>Kansas**</td><td>NA</td><td>NA</td></tr>
<tr><td>44</td><td>Wyoming</td><td>47</td><td>0.28%</td><td>NA</td><td>Montana**</td><td>NA</td><td>NA</td></tr>
<tr><td colspan="4"></td><td colspan="2">District of Columbia</td><td>27</td><td>0.16%</td></tr>
</table>

Source: Federal Bureau of Investigation
   "Crime in the United States 1994" (Uniform Crime Reports, November 19, 1995)
*By law enforcement agencies submitting complete reports to the F.B.I. for 12 months in 1994. The F.B.I. estimates 20,900 reported and unreported arrests for arson occurred in 1994. Arson is the willful burning of or attempt to burn a building, vehicle or another's personal property.
**Not available.

Reported Arrest Rate for Arson in 1994

National Rate = 8.1 Reported Arrests per 100,000 Population*

ALPHA ORDER

RANK	STATE	RATE
48	Alabama	3.2
33	Alaska	6.0
12	Arizona	11.0
39	Arkansas	5.4
25	California	8.2
3	Colorado	14.7
16	Connecticut	10.3
46	Delaware	3.9
43	Florida	5.0
21	Georgia	9.2
40	Hawaii	5.3
10	Idaho	11.2
40	Illinois	5.3
35	Indiana	5.8
29	Iowa	7.5
NA	Kansas**	NA
10	Kentucky	11.2
30	Louisiana	7.4
12	Maine	11.0
7	Maryland	12.5
45	Massachusetts	4.5
22	Michigan	8.9
27	Minnesota	8.1
14	Mississippi	10.6
6	Missouri	13.8
NA	Montana**	NA
23	Nebraska	8.3
38	Nevada	5.7
16	New Hampshire	10.3
30	New Jersey	7.4
4	New Mexico	14.0
42	New York	5.2
28	North Carolina	7.7
47	North Dakota	3.8
19	Ohio	10.0
5	Oklahoma	13.9
2	Oregon	18.2
23	Pennsylvania	8.3
9	Rhode Island	11.8
35	South Carolina	5.8
1	South Dakota	28.4
32	Tennessee	6.4
35	Texas	5.8
18	Utah	10.1
44	Vermont	4.7
25	Virginia	8.2
20	Washington	9.9
33	West Virginia	6.0
8	Wisconsin	12.2
15	Wyoming	10.4

RANK ORDER

RANK	STATE	RATE
1	South Dakota	28.4
2	Oregon	18.2
3	Colorado	14.7
4	New Mexico	14.0
5	Oklahoma	13.9
6	Missouri	13.8
7	Maryland	12.5
8	Wisconsin	12.2
9	Rhode Island	11.8
10	Idaho	11.2
10	Kentucky	11.2
12	Arizona	11.0
12	Maine	11.0
14	Mississippi	10.6
15	Wyoming	10.4
16	Connecticut	10.3
16	New Hampshire	10.3
18	Utah	10.1
19	Ohio	10.0
20	Washington	9.9
21	Georgia	9.2
22	Michigan	8.9
23	Nebraska	8.3
23	Pennsylvania	8.3
25	California	8.2
25	Virginia	8.2
27	Minnesota	8.1
28	North Carolina	7.7
29	Iowa	7.5
30	Louisiana	7.4
30	New Jersey	7.4
32	Tennessee	6.4
33	Alaska	6.0
33	West Virginia	6.0
35	Indiana	5.8
35	South Carolina	5.8
35	Texas	5.8
38	Nevada	5.7
39	Arkansas	5.4
40	Hawaii	5.3
40	Illinois	5.3
42	New York	5.2
43	Florida	5.0
44	Vermont	4.7
45	Massachusetts	4.5
46	Delaware	3.9
47	North Dakota	3.8
48	Alabama	3.2
NA	Kansas**	NA
NA	Montana**	NA
	District of Columbia	4.7

Source: Morgan Quitno Press using data from Federal Bureau of Investigation
   "Crime in the United States 1994" (Uniform Crime Reports, November 19, 1995)
*By law enforcement agencies submitting complete reports to the F.B.I. for 12 months in 1994. These rates based on population estimates for areas under the jurisdiction of those agencies reporting. Arrest rate based on the F.B.I. estimate of reported and unreported arrests for arson is 8.0 arrests per 100,000 population.
**Not available.

Reported Arrests for Weapons Violations in 1994

National Total = 213,494 Reported Arrests*

ALPHA ORDER

RANK	STATE	ARRESTS	% of USA
25	Alabama	2,799	1.31%
39	Alaska	633	0.30%
15	Arizona	4,497	2.11%
21	Arkansas	2,985	1.40%
1	California	41,564	19.47%
17	Colorado	4,045	1.89%
22	Connecticut	2,978	1.39%
46	Delaware	101	0.05%
4	Florida	9,154	4.29%
12	Georgia	5,872	2.75%
38	Hawaii	685	0.32%
36	Idaho	893	0.42%
29	Illinois	1,720	0.81%
28	Indiana	1,866	0.87%
37	Iowa	718	0.34%
NA	Kansas**	NA	NA
34	Kentucky	1,331	0.62%
19	Louisiana	3,078	1.44%
41	Maine	333	0.16%
13	Maryland	4,926	2.31%
31	Massachusetts	1,453	0.68%
8	Michigan	7,018	3.29%
24	Minnesota	2,847	1.33%
35	Mississippi	940	0.44%
11	Missouri	6,595	3.09%
NA	Montana**	NA	NA
33	Nebraska	1,333	0.62%
27	Nevada	2,268	1.06%
47	New Hampshire	94	0.04%
9	New Jersey	6,890	3.23%
42	New Mexico	306	0.14%
3	New York	15,126	7.08%
6	North Carolina	8,362	3.92%
45	North Dakota	146	0.07%
10	Ohio	6,698	3.14%
20	Oklahoma	3,051	1.43%
18	Oregon	3,139	1.47%
14	Pennsylvania	4,579	2.14%
40	Rhode Island	577	0.27%
16	South Carolina	4,166	1.95%
44	South Dakota	200	0.09%
26	Tennessee	2,705	1.27%
2	Texas	20,729	9.71%
30	Utah	1,557	0.73%
48	Vermont	3	0.00%
5	Virginia	8,418	3.94%
23	Washington	2,949	1.38%
32	West Virginia	1,340	0.63%
7	Wisconsin	7,910	3.71%
43	Wyoming	260	0.12%

RANK ORDER

RANK	STATE	ARRESTS	% of USA
1	California	41,564	19.47%
2	Texas	20,729	9.71%
3	New York	15,126	7.08%
4	Florida	9,154	4.29%
5	Virginia	8,418	3.94%
6	North Carolina	8,362	3.92%
7	Wisconsin	7,910	3.71%
8	Michigan	7,018	3.29%
9	New Jersey	6,890	3.23%
10	Ohio	6,698	3.14%
11	Missouri	6,595	3.09%
12	Georgia	5,872	2.75%
13	Maryland	4,926	2.31%
14	Pennsylvania	4,579	2.14%
15	Arizona	4,497	2.11%
16	South Carolina	4,166	1.95%
17	Colorado	4,045	1.89%
18	Oregon	3,139	1.47%
19	Louisiana	3,078	1.44%
20	Oklahoma	3,051	1.43%
21	Arkansas	2,985	1.40%
22	Connecticut	2,978	1.39%
23	Washington	2,949	1.38%
24	Minnesota	2,847	1.33%
25	Alabama	2,799	1.31%
26	Tennessee	2,705	1.27%
27	Nevada	2,268	1.06%
28	Indiana	1,866	0.87%
29	Illinois	1,720	0.81%
30	Utah	1,557	0.73%
31	Massachusetts	1,453	0.68%
32	West Virginia	1,340	0.63%
33	Nebraska	1,333	0.62%
34	Kentucky	1,331	0.62%
35	Mississippi	940	0.44%
36	Idaho	893	0.42%
37	Iowa	718	0.34%
38	Hawaii	685	0.32%
39	Alaska	633	0.30%
40	Rhode Island	577	0.27%
41	Maine	333	0.16%
42	New Mexico	306	0.14%
43	Wyoming	260	0.12%
44	South Dakota	200	0.09%
45	North Dakota	146	0.07%
46	Delaware	101	0.05%
47	New Hampshire	94	0.04%
48	Vermont	3	0.00%
NA	Kansas**	NA	NA
NA	Montana**	NA	NA
	District of Columbia	1,657	0.78%

Source: Federal Bureau of Investigation
   "Crime in the United States 1994" (Uniform Crime Reports, November 19, 1995)
*By law enforcement agencies submitting complete reports to the F.B.I. for 12 months in 1994. The F.B.I. estimates
259,400 reported and unreported arrests for weapons violations occurred in 1994. Weapons violations include
illegal carrying and possession.
**Not available.

Reported Arrest Rate for Weapons Violations in 1994

National Rate = 102.8 Reported Arrests per 100,000 Population*

ALPHA ORDER

RANK	STATE	RATE
31	Alabama	71.9
15	Alaska	111.2
13	Arizona	115.2
10	Arkansas	123.6
6	California	132.6
3	Colorado	159.7
16	Connecticut	107.6
45	Delaware	26.6
34	Florida	66.7
5	Georgia	140.3
36	Hawaii	58.1
28	Idaho	81.0
21	Illinois	96.8
38	Indiana	57.8
43	Iowa	29.6
NA	Kansas**	NA
35	Kentucky	65.6
18	Louisiana	101.6
44	Maine	27.6
20	Maryland	98.7
42	Massachusetts	35.5
24	Michigan	93.3
33	Minnesota	66.8
12	Mississippi	118.8
1	Missouri	200.9
NA	Montana**	NA
26	Nebraska	90.4
2	Nevada	168.8
47	New Hampshire	13.2
27	New Jersey	90.0
29	New Mexico	78.1
22	New York	95.0
11	North Carolina	122.1
46	North Dakota	26.4
19	Ohio	99.4
22	Oklahoma	95.0
17	Oregon	103.6
40	Pennsylvania	49.3
37	Rhode Island	57.9
14	South Carolina	113.9
41	South Dakota	48.9
7	Tennessee	131.6
9	Texas	127.6
25	Utah	91.0
48	Vermont	1.0
8	Virginia	130.0
32	Washington	71.1
30	West Virginia	73.6
4	Wisconsin	158.8
39	Wyoming	57.5

RANK ORDER

RANK	STATE	RATE
1	Missouri	200.9
2	Nevada	168.8
3	Colorado	159.7
4	Wisconsin	158.8
5	Georgia	140.3
6	California	132.6
7	Tennessee	131.6
8	Virginia	130.0
9	Texas	127.6
10	Arkansas	123.6
11	North Carolina	122.1
12	Mississippi	118.8
13	Arizona	115.2
14	South Carolina	113.9
15	Alaska	111.2
16	Connecticut	107.6
17	Oregon	103.6
18	Louisiana	101.6
19	Ohio	99.4
20	Maryland	98.7
21	Illinois	96.8
22	New York	95.0
22	Oklahoma	95.0
24	Michigan	93.3
25	Utah	91.0
26	Nebraska	90.4
27	New Jersey	90.0
28	Idaho	81.0
29	New Mexico	78.1
30	West Virginia	73.6
31	Alabama	71.9
32	Washington	71.1
33	Minnesota	66.8
34	Florida	66.7
35	Kentucky	65.6
36	Hawaii	58.1
37	Rhode Island	57.9
38	Indiana	57.8
39	Wyoming	57.5
40	Pennsylvania	49.3
41	South Dakota	48.9
42	Massachusetts	35.5
43	Iowa	29.6
44	Maine	27.6
45	Delaware	26.6
46	North Dakota	26.4
47	New Hampshire	13.2
48	Vermont	1.0
NA	Kansas**	NA
NA	Montana**	NA

District of Columbia 290.7

Source: Morgan Quitno Press using data from Federal Bureau of Investigation
    "Crime in the United States 1994" (Uniform Crime Reports, November 19, 1995)
*By law enforcement agencies submitting complete reports to the F.B.I. for 12 months in 1994. These rates based on population estimates for areas under the jurisdiction of those agencies reporting. Arrest rate based on the F.B.I. estimate of reported and unreported arrests for weapons violations is 99.6 arrests per 100,000 population.
**Not available.

26

Reported Arrests for Driving Under the Influence in 1994

National Total = 1,079,533 Reported Arrests*

ALPHA ORDER

RANK	STATE	ARRESTS	% of USA
22	Alabama	18,220	1.69%
39	Alaska	4,891	0.45%
13	Arizona	26,548	2.46%
20	Arkansas	18,688	1.73%
1	California	206,508	19.13%
16	Colorado	21,439	1.99%
31	Connecticut	9,417	0.87%
48	Delaware	1	0.00%
3	Florida	51,182	4.74%
6	Georgia	34,732	3.22%
43	Hawaii	4,311	0.40%
30	Idaho	10,091	0.93%
34	Illinois	6,975	0.65%
24	Indiana	16,416	1.52%
26	Iowa	13,897	1.29%
NA	Kansas**	NA	NA
32	Kentucky	9,139	0.85%
27	Louisiana	13,667	1.27%
35	Maine	6,938	0.64%
17	Maryland	21,210	1.96%
29	Massachusetts	12,209	1.13%
5	Michigan	41,235	3.82%
9	Minnesota	31,048	2.88%
38	Mississippi	5,397	0.50%
18	Missouri	21,193	1.96%
NA	Montana**	NA	NA
28	Nebraska	12,604	1.17%
37	Nevada	6,074	0.56%
42	New Hampshire	4,321	0.40%
14	New Jersey	23,620	2.19%
40	New Mexico	4,775	0.44%
4	New York	48,620	4.50%
11	North Carolina	29,860	2.77%
45	North Dakota	2,780	0.26%
12	Ohio	28,628	2.65%
15	Oklahoma	22,643	2.10%
21	Oregon	18,437	1.71%
10	Pennsylvania	30,346	2.81%
46	Rhode Island	1,972	0.18%
23	South Carolina	17,252	1.60%
44	South Dakota	4,088	0.38%
25	Tennessee	15,889	1.47%
2	Texas	90,876	8.42%
36	Utah	6,515	0.60%
47	Vermont	1,465	0.14%
8	Virginia	32,982	3.06%
19	Washington	19,457	1.80%
33	West Virginia	8,555	0.79%
7	Wisconsin	34,551	3.20%
41	Wyoming	4,516	0.42%

RANK ORDER

RANK	STATE	ARRESTS	% of USA
1	California	206,508	19.13%
2	Texas	90,876	8.42%
3	Florida	51,182	4.74%
4	New York	48,620	4.50%
5	Michigan	41,235	3.82%
6	Georgia	34,732	3.22%
7	Wisconsin	34,551	3.20%
8	Virginia	32,982	3.06%
9	Minnesota	31,048	2.88%
10	Pennsylvania	30,346	2.81%
11	North Carolina	29,860	2.77%
12	Ohio	28,628	2.65%
13	Arizona	26,548	2.46%
14	New Jersey	23,620	2.19%
15	Oklahoma	22,643	2.10%
16	Colorado	21,439	1.99%
17	Maryland	21,210	1.96%
18	Missouri	21,193	1.96%
19	Washington	19,457	1.80%
20	Arkansas	18,688	1.73%
21	Oregon	18,437	1.71%
22	Alabama	18,220	1.69%
23	South Carolina	17,252	1.60%
24	Indiana	16,416	1.52%
25	Tennessee	15,889	1.47%
26	Iowa	13,897	1.29%
27	Louisiana	13,667	1.27%
28	Nebraska	12,604	1.17%
29	Massachusetts	12,209	1.13%
30	Idaho	10,091	0.93%
31	Connecticut	9,417	0.87%
32	Kentucky	9,139	0.85%
33	West Virginia	8,555	0.79%
34	Illinois	6,975	0.65%
35	Maine	6,938	0.64%
36	Utah	6,515	0.60%
37	Nevada	6,074	0.56%
38	Mississippi	5,397	0.50%
39	Alaska	4,891	0.45%
40	New Mexico	4,775	0.44%
41	Wyoming	4,516	0.42%
42	New Hampshire	4,321	0.40%
43	Hawaii	4,311	0.40%
44	South Dakota	4,088	0.38%
45	North Dakota	2,780	0.26%
46	Rhode Island	1,972	0.18%
47	Vermont	1,465	0.14%
48	Delaware	1	0.00%
NA	Kansas**	NA	NA
NA	Montana**	NA	NA
	District of Columbia	3,355	0.31%

Source: Federal Bureau of Investigation
   "Crime in the United States 1994" (Uniform Crime Reports, November 19, 1995)
*By law enforcement agencies submitting complete reports to the F.B.I. for 12 months in 1994. The F.B.I. estimates 1,384,600 reported and unreported arrests for driving under the influence occurred in 1994. Includes driving any vehicle while drunk or under the influence of liquor or narcotics.
**Not available.

Reported Arrest Rate for Driving Under the Influence in 1994

National Rate = 520.0 Reported Arrests per 100,000 Population*

ALPHA ORDER

RANK	STATE	RATE
31	Alabama	468.3
5	Alaska	859.6
15	Arizona	680.0
9	Arkansas	773.5
16	California	658.6
7	Colorado	846.4
42	Connecticut	340.2
48	Delaware	0.3
40	Florida	372.8
8	Georgia	830.1
41	Hawaii	365.6
4	Idaho	914.9
38	Illinois	392.7
25	Indiana	508.4
21	Iowa	573.1
NA	Kansas**	NA
34	Kentucky	450.6
33	Louisiana	451.1
20	Maine	575.3
36	Maryland	424.8
46	Massachusetts	298.5
23	Michigan	548.0
11	Minnesota	729.0
14	Mississippi	682.3
17	Missouri	645.7
NA	Montana**	NA
6	Nebraska	854.5
32	Nevada	451.9
19	New Hampshire	606.9
44	New Jersey	308.6
1	New Mexico	1,218.1
45	New York	305.3
35	North Carolina	436.2
26	North Dakota	503.6
37	Ohio	424.7
12	Oklahoma	705.0
18	Oregon	608.5
43	Pennsylvania	326.9
47	Rhode Island	197.8
28	South Carolina	471.5
2	South Dakota	999.5
10	Tennessee	772.8
22	Texas	559.6
39	Utah	380.8
27	Vermont	491.6
24	Virginia	509.2
30	Washington	469.4
29	West Virginia	470.1
13	Wisconsin	693.8
3	Wyoming	999.1

RANK ORDER

RANK	STATE	RATE
1	New Mexico	1,218.1
2	South Dakota	999.5
3	Wyoming	999.1
4	Idaho	914.9
5	Alaska	859.6
6	Nebraska	854.5
7	Colorado	846.4
8	Georgia	830.1
9	Arkansas	773.5
10	Tennessee	772.8
11	Minnesota	729.0
12	Oklahoma	705.0
13	Wisconsin	693.8
14	Mississippi	682.3
15	Arizona	680.0
16	California	658.6
17	Missouri	645.7
18	Oregon	608.5
19	New Hampshire	606.9
20	Maine	575.3
21	Iowa	573.1
22	Texas	559.6
23	Michigan	548.0
24	Virginia	509.2
25	Indiana	508.4
26	North Dakota	503.6
27	Vermont	491.6
28	South Carolina	471.5
29	West Virginia	470.1
30	Washington	469.4
31	Alabama	468.3
32	Nevada	451.9
33	Louisiana	451.1
34	Kentucky	450.6
35	North Carolina	436.2
36	Maryland	424.8
37	Ohio	424.7
38	Illinois	392.7
39	Utah	380.8
40	Florida	372.8
41	Hawaii	365.6
42	Connecticut	340.2
43	Pennsylvania	326.9
44	New Jersey	308.6
45	New York	305.3
46	Massachusetts	298.5
47	Rhode Island	197.8
48	Delaware	0.3
NA	Kansas**	NA
NA	Montana**	NA

District of Columbia 588.6

Source: Morgan Quitno Press using data from Federal Bureau of Investigation
    "Crime in the United States 1994" (Uniform Crime Reports, November 19, 1995)
*By law enforcement agencies submitting complete reports to the F.B.I. for 12 months in 1994. These rates based on population estimates for areas under the jurisdiction of those agencies reporting. Arrest rate based on the F.B.I. estimate of reported and unreported arrests for driving under the influence is 531.8 arrests per 100,000 population.
**Not available.

Reported Arrests for Drug Abuse Violations in 1994

National Total = 1,118,346 Reported Arrests*

ALPHA ORDER

RANK	STATE	ARRESTS	% of USA
25	Alabama	11,027	0.99%
42	Alaska	1,436	0.13%
13	Arizona	21,352	1.91%
27	Arkansas	9,212	0.82%
1	California	270,792	24.21%
24	Colorado	12,101	1.08%
15	Connecticut	19,909	1.78%
47	Delaware	619	0.06%
3	Florida	79,951	7.15%
11	Georgia	24,979	2.23%
37	Hawaii	3,694	0.33%
38	Idaho	3,030	0.27%
33	Illinois	4,856	0.43%
31	Indiana	7,529	0.67%
35	Iowa	4,524	0.40%
NA	Kansas**	NA	NA
29	Kentucky	8,867	0.79%
19	Louisiana	14,735	1.32%
40	Maine	2,639	0.24%
6	Maryland	37,858	3.39%
14	Massachusetts	20,100	1.80%
10	Michigan	29,221	2.61%
22	Minnesota	12,612	1.13%
34	Mississippi	4,752	0.42%
17	Missouri	17,826	1.59%
NA	Montana**	NA	NA
32	Nebraska	5,286	0.47%
28	Nevada	9,186	0.82%
41	New Hampshire	2,067	0.18%
5	New Jersey	49,102	4.39%
44	New Mexico	1,121	0.10%
2	New York	130,860	11.70%
8	North Carolina	29,987	2.68%
46	North Dakota	652	0.06%
7	Ohio	31,575	2.82%
23	Oklahoma	12,234	1.09%
20	Oregon	14,008	1.25%
9	Pennsylvania	29,705	2.66%
36	Rhode Island	3,985	0.36%
16	South Carolina	17,835	1.59%
45	South Dakota	1,020	0.09%
26	Tennessee	10,012	0.90%
4	Texas	72,000	6.44%
30	Utah	8,254	0.74%
48	Vermont	214	0.02%
12	Virginia	24,102	2.16%
21	Washington	13,848	1.24%
39	West Virginia	2,640	0.24%
18	Wisconsin	16,688	1.49%
43	Wyoming	1,171	0.10%

RANK ORDER

RANK	STATE	ARRESTS	% of USA
1	California	270,792	24.21%
2	New York	130,860	11.70%
3	Florida	79,951	7.15%
4	Texas	72,000	6.44%
5	New Jersey	49,102	4.39%
6	Maryland	37,858	3.39%
7	Ohio	31,575	2.82%
8	North Carolina	29,987	2.68%
9	Pennsylvania	29,705	2.66%
10	Michigan	29,221	2.61%
11	Georgia	24,979	2.23%
12	Virginia	24,102	2.16%
13	Arizona	21,352	1.91%
14	Massachusetts	20,100	1.80%
15	Connecticut	19,909	1.78%
16	South Carolina	17,835	1.59%
17	Missouri	17,826	1.59%
18	Wisconsin	16,688	1.49%
19	Louisiana	14,735	1.32%
20	Oregon	14,008	1.25%
21	Washington	13,848	1.24%
22	Minnesota	12,612	1.13%
23	Oklahoma	12,234	1.09%
24	Colorado	12,101	1.08%
25	Alabama	11,027	0.99%
26	Tennessee	10,012	0.90%
27	Arkansas	9,212	0.82%
28	Nevada	9,186	0.82%
29	Kentucky	8,867	0.79%
30	Utah	8,254	0.74%
31	Indiana	7,529	0.67%
32	Nebraska	5,286	0.47%
33	Illinois	4,856	0.43%
34	Mississippi	4,752	0.42%
35	Iowa	4,524	0.40%
36	Rhode Island	3,985	0.36%
37	Hawaii	3,694	0.33%
38	Idaho	3,030	0.27%
39	West Virginia	2,640	0.24%
40	Maine	2,639	0.24%
41	New Hampshire	2,067	0.18%
42	Alaska	1,436	0.13%
43	Wyoming	1,171	0.10%
44	New Mexico	1,121	0.10%
45	South Dakota	1,020	0.09%
46	North Dakota	652	0.06%
47	Delaware	619	0.06%
48	Vermont	214	0.02%
NA	Kansas**	NA	NA
NA	Montana**	NA	NA
	District of Columbia	7,173	0.64%

Source: Federal Bureau of Investigation
   "Crime in the United States 1994" (Uniform Crime Reports, November 19, 1995)
*By law enforcement agencies submitting complete reports to the F.B.I. for 12 months in 1994. The F.B.I. estimates 1,351,400 reported and unreported arrests for drug abuse violations occurred in 1994. Includes offenses relating to possession, sale, use, growing and manufacturing of narcotic drugs.
**Not available.

29

Reported Arrest Rate for Drug Abuse Violations in 1994

National Rate = 538.6 Reported Arrests per 100,000 Population*

ALPHA ORDER				RANK ORDER		
RANK	STATE	RATE		RANK	STATE	RATE
36	Alabama	283.4		1	California	863.7
40	Alaska	252.4		2	New York	821.7
10	Arizona	546.9		3	Maryland	758.2
25	Arkansas	381.3		4	Connecticut	719.3
1	California	863.7		5	Nevada	683.5
17	Colorado	477.7		6	New Jersey	641.6
4	Connecticut	719.3		7	Mississippi	600.8
45	Delaware	162.9		8	Georgia	597.0
9	Florida	582.4		9	Florida	582.4
8	Georgia	597.0		10	Arizona	546.9
32	Hawaii	313.3		11	Missouri	543.1
37	Idaho	274.7		12	Massachusetts	491.4
38	Illinois	273.4		13	South Carolina	487.4
42	Indiana	233.2		14	Tennessee	487.0
44	Iowa	186.6		15	Louisiana	486.3
NA	Kansas**	NA		16	Utah	482.4
22	Kentucky	437.2		17	Colorado	477.7
15	Louisiana	486.3		18	Ohio	468.4
43	Maine	218.8		19	Oregon	462.3
3	Maryland	758.2		20	Texas	443.3
12	Massachusetts	491.4		21	North Carolina	438.0
24	Michigan	388.4		22	Kentucky	437.2
33	Minnesota	296.1		23	Rhode Island	399.7
7	Mississippi	600.8		24	Michigan	388.4
11	Missouri	543.1		25	Arkansas	381.3
NA	Montana**	NA		26	Oklahoma	380.9
28	Nebraska	358.4		27	Virginia	372.1
5	Nevada	683.5		28	Nebraska	358.4
34	New Hampshire	290.3		29	Wisconsin	335.1
6	New Jersey	641.6		30	Washington	334.1
35	New Mexico	286.0		31	Pennsylvania	320.0
2	New York	821.7		32	Hawaii	313.3
21	North Carolina	438.0		33	Minnesota	296.1
47	North Dakota	118.1		34	New Hampshire	290.3
18	Ohio	468.4		35	New Mexico	286.0
26	Oklahoma	380.9		36	Alabama	283.4
19	Oregon	462.3		37	Idaho	274.7
31	Pennsylvania	320.0		38	Illinois	273.4
23	Rhode Island	399.7		39	Wyoming	259.1
13	South Carolina	487.4		40	Alaska	252.4
41	South Dakota	249.4		41	South Dakota	249.4
14	Tennessee	487.0		42	Indiana	233.2
20	Texas	443.3		43	Maine	218.8
16	Utah	482.4		44	Iowa	186.6
48	Vermont	71.8		45	Delaware	162.9
27	Virginia	372.1		46	West Virginia	145.1
30	Washington	334.1		47	North Dakota	118.1
46	West Virginia	145.1		48	Vermont	71.8
29	Wisconsin	335.1		NA	Kansas**	NA
39	Wyoming	259.1		NA	Montana**	NA

| | | | | | District of Columbia | 1,258.4 |

Source: Morgan Quitno Press using data from Federal Bureau of Investigation
"Crime in the United States 1994" (Uniform Crime Reports, November 19, 1995)
*By law enforcement agencies submitting complete reports to the F.B.I. for 12 months in 1994. These rates based on population estimates for areas under the jurisdiction of those agencies reporting. Arrest rate based on the F.B.I. estimate of reported and unreported arrests for drug abuse violations is 519.1 arrests per 100,000 population.
**Not available.

Reported Arrests for Sex Offenses in 1994

National Total = 81,887 Reported Arrests*

ALPHA ORDER

RANK	STATE	ARRESTS	% of USA
35	Alabama	396	0.48%
37	Alaska	390	0.48%
15	Arizona	2,055	2.51%
30	Arkansas	504	0.62%
1	California	15,995	19.53%
16	Colorado	1,672	2.04%
27	Connecticut	843	1.03%
45	Delaware	86	0.11%
4	Florida	4,779	5.84%
6	Georgia	2,991	3.65%
33	Hawaii	448	0.55%
39	Idaho	280	0.34%
34	Illinois	411	0.50%
21	Indiana	1,137	1.39%
40	Iowa	279	0.34%
NA	Kansas**	NA	NA
19	Kentucky	1,364	1.67%
20	Louisiana	1,149	1.40%
31	Maine	474	0.58%
17	Maryland	1,657	2.02%
24	Massachusetts	931	1.14%
11	Michigan	2,320	2.83%
26	Minnesota	852	1.04%
41	Mississippi	172	0.21%
12	Missouri	2,273	2.78%
NA	Montana**	NA	NA
28	Nebraska	797	0.97%
25	Nevada	913	1.11%
42	New Hampshire	168	0.21%
14	New Jersey	2,166	2.65%
47	New Mexico	63	0.08%
2	New York	6,360	7.77%
8	North Carolina	2,591	3.16%
46	North Dakota	72	0.09%
9	Ohio	2,427	2.96%
23	Oklahoma	988	1.21%
18	Oregon	1,556	1.90%
13	Pennsylvania	2,262	2.76%
36	Rhode Island	393	0.48%
29	South Carolina	691	0.84%
43	South Dakota	126	0.15%
32	Tennessee	462	0.56%
3	Texas	5,597	6.84%
22	Utah	1,113	1.36%
48	Vermont	16	0.02%
7	Virginia	2,926	3.57%
10	Washington	2,341	2.86%
38	West Virginia	309	0.38%
5	Wisconsin	3,851	4.70%
44	Wyoming	125	0.15%

RANK ORDER

RANK	STATE	ARRESTS	% of USA
1	California	15,995	19.53%
2	New York	6,360	7.77%
3	Texas	5,597	6.84%
4	Florida	4,779	5.84%
5	Wisconsin	3,851	4.70%
6	Georgia	2,991	3.65%
7	Virginia	2,926	3.57%
8	North Carolina	2,591	3.16%
9	Ohio	2,427	2.96%
10	Washington	2,341	2.86%
11	Michigan	2,320	2.83%
12	Missouri	2,273	2.78%
13	Pennsylvania	2,262	2.76%
14	New Jersey	2,166	2.65%
15	Arizona	2,055	2.51%
16	Colorado	1,672	2.04%
17	Maryland	1,657	2.02%
18	Oregon	1,556	1.90%
19	Kentucky	1,364	1.67%
20	Louisiana	1,149	1.40%
21	Indiana	1,137	1.39%
22	Utah	1,113	1.36%
23	Oklahoma	988	1.21%
24	Massachusetts	931	1.14%
25	Nevada	913	1.11%
26	Minnesota	852	1.04%
27	Connecticut	843	1.03%
28	Nebraska	797	0.97%
29	South Carolina	691	0.84%
30	Arkansas	504	0.62%
31	Maine	474	0.58%
32	Tennessee	462	0.56%
33	Hawaii	448	0.55%
34	Illinois	411	0.50%
35	Alabama	396	0.48%
36	Rhode Island	393	0.48%
37	Alaska	390	0.48%
38	West Virginia	309	0.38%
39	Idaho	280	0.34%
40	Iowa	279	0.34%
41	Mississippi	172	0.21%
42	New Hampshire	168	0.21%
43	South Dakota	126	0.15%
44	Wyoming	125	0.15%
45	Delaware	86	0.11%
46	North Dakota	72	0.09%
47	New Mexico	63	0.08%
48	Vermont	16	0.02%
NA	Kansas**	NA	NA
NA	Montana**	NA	NA
	District of Columbia	116	0.14%

Source: Federal Bureau of Investigation
"Crime in the United States 1994" (Uniform Crime Reports, November 19, 1995)
By law enforcement agencies submitting complete reports to the F.B.I. for 12 months in 1994. The F.B.I. estimates 100,700 reported and unreported arrests for sex offenses occurred in 1994. Excludes forcible rape, prostitution and commercialized vice. Includes statutory rape and offenses against chastity, common decency, morals and the like.
***Not available.*

Reported Arrest Rate for Sex Offenses in 1994

National Rate = 39.4 Reported Arrests per 100,000 Population*

ALPHA ORDER

RANK ORDER

RANK	STATE	RATE
47	Alabama	10.2
4	Alaska	68.5
11	Arizona	52.6
40	Arkansas	20.9
13	California	51.0
7	Colorado	66.0
29	Connecticut	30.5
37	Delaware	22.6
23	Florida	34.8
2	Georgia	71.5
18	Hawaii	38.0
32	Idaho	25.4
35	Illinois	23.1
22	Indiana	35.2
46	Iowa	11.5
NA	Kansas**	NA
6	Kentucky	67.3
19	Louisiana	37.9
17	Maine	39.3
25	Maryland	33.2
36	Massachusetts	22.8
26	Michigan	30.8
41	Minnesota	20.0
39	Mississippi	21.7
3	Missouri	69.3
NA	Montana**	NA
10	Nebraska	54.0
5	Nevada	67.9
34	New Hampshire	23.6
30	New Jersey	28.3
44	New Mexico	16.1
15	New York	39.9
20	North Carolina	37.8
45	North Dakota	13.0
21	Ohio	36.0
26	Oklahoma	30.8
12	Oregon	51.4
33	Pennsylvania	24.4
16	Rhode Island	39.4
42	South Carolina	18.9
26	South Dakota	30.8
38	Tennessee	22.5
24	Texas	34.5
8	Utah	65.0
48	Vermont	5.4
14	Virginia	45.2
9	Washington	56.5
43	West Virginia	17.0
1	Wisconsin	77.3
31	Wyoming	27.7

RANK	STATE	RATE
1	Wisconsin	77.3
2	Georgia	71.5
3	Missouri	69.3
4	Alaska	68.5
5	Nevada	67.9
6	Kentucky	67.3
7	Colorado	66.0
8	Utah	65.0
9	Washington	56.5
10	Nebraska	54.0
11	Arizona	52.6
12	Oregon	51.4
13	California	51.0
14	Virginia	45.2
15	New York	39.9
16	Rhode Island	39.4
17	Maine	39.3
18	Hawaii	38.0
19	Louisiana	37.9
20	North Carolina	37.8
21	Ohio	36.0
22	Indiana	35.2
23	Florida	34.8
24	Texas	34.5
25	Maryland	33.2
26	Michigan	30.8
26	Oklahoma	30.8
26	South Dakota	30.8
29	Connecticut	30.5
30	New Jersey	28.3
31	Wyoming	27.7
32	Idaho	25.4
33	Pennsylvania	24.4
34	New Hampshire	23.6
35	Illinois	23.1
36	Massachusetts	22.8
37	Delaware	22.6
38	Tennessee	22.5
39	Mississippi	21.7
40	Arkansas	20.9
41	Minnesota	20.0
42	South Carolina	18.9
43	West Virginia	17.0
44	New Mexico	16.1
45	North Dakota	13.0
46	Iowa	11.5
47	Alabama	10.2
48	Vermont	5.4
NA	Kansas**	NA
NA	Montana**	NA
	District of Columbia	20.4

Source: Morgan Quitno Press using data from Federal Bureau of Investigation
"Crime in the United States 1994" (Uniform Crime Reports, November 19, 1995)
*By law enforcement agencies submitting complete reports to the F.B.I. for 12 months in 1994. These rates based on population estimates for areas under the jurisdiction of those agencies reporting. Arrest rate based on the F.B.I. estimate of reported and unreported arrests for sex offenses is 38.7 arrests per 100,000 population.
**Not available.

Reported Arrests for Prostitution and Commercialized Vice in 1994

National Total = 86,818 Reported Arrests*

ALPHA ORDER

RANK	STATE	ARRESTS	% of USA
36	Alabama	245	0.28%
37	Alaska	149	0.17%
12	Arizona	1,755	2.02%
31	Arkansas	320	0.37%
1	California	18,032	20.77%
16	Colorado	1,425	1.64%
23	Connecticut	846	0.97%
42	Delaware	11	0.01%
4	Florida	7,149	8.23%
14	Georgia	1,501	1.73%
28	Hawaii	455	0.52%
41	Idaho	18	0.02%
35	Illinois	258	0.30%
21	Indiana	1,008	1.16%
34	Iowa	260	0.30%
NA	Kansas**	NA	NA
27	Kentucky	510	0.59%
29	Louisiana	350	0.40%
39	Maine	68	0.08%
15	Maryland	1,431	1.65%
11	Massachusetts	2,342	2.70%
7	Michigan	2,853	3.29%
17	Minnesota	1,313	1.51%
40	Mississippi	38	0.04%
6	Missouri	3,101	3.57%
NA	Montana**	NA	NA
33	Nebraska	266	0.31%
8	Nevada	2,735	3.15%
43	New Hampshire	10	0.01%
9	New Jersey	2,516	2.90%
47	New Mexico	0	0.00%
2	New York	12,307	14.18%
22	North Carolina	980	1.13%
46	North Dakota	1	0.00%
5	Ohio	3,665	4.22%
32	Oklahoma	289	0.33%
24	Oregon	769	0.89%
10	Pennsylvania	2,454	2.83%
30	Rhode Island	327	0.38%
25	South Carolina	663	0.76%
45	South Dakota	4	0.00%
20	Tennessee	1,109	1.28%
3	Texas	7,153	8.24%
26	Utah	566	0.65%
47	Vermont	0	0.00%
19	Virginia	1,215	1.40%
18	Washington	1,234	1.42%
38	West Virginia	124	0.14%
13	Wisconsin	1,701	1.96%
44	Wyoming	6	0.01%

RANK ORDER

RANK	STATE	ARRESTS	% of USA
1	California	18,032	20.77%
2	New York	12,307	14.18%
3	Texas	7,153	8.24%
4	Florida	7,149	8.23%
5	Ohio	3,665	4.22%
6	Missouri	3,101	3.57%
7	Michigan	2,853	3.29%
8	Nevada	2,735	3.15%
9	New Jersey	2,516	2.90%
10	Pennsylvania	2,454	2.83%
11	Massachusetts	2,342	2.70%
12	Arizona	1,755	2.02%
13	Wisconsin	1,701	1.96%
14	Georgia	1,501	1.73%
15	Maryland	1,431	1.65%
16	Colorado	1,425	1.64%
17	Minnesota	1,313	1.51%
18	Washington	1,234	1.42%
19	Virginia	1,215	1.40%
20	Tennessee	1,109	1.28%
21	Indiana	1,008	1.16%
22	North Carolina	980	1.13%
23	Connecticut	846	0.97%
24	Oregon	769	0.89%
25	South Carolina	663	0.76%
26	Utah	566	0.65%
27	Kentucky	510	0.59%
28	Hawaii	455	0.52%
29	Louisiana	350	0.40%
30	Rhode Island	327	0.38%
31	Arkansas	320	0.37%
32	Oklahoma	289	0.33%
33	Nebraska	266	0.31%
34	Iowa	260	0.30%
35	Illinois	258	0.30%
36	Alabama	245	0.28%
37	Alaska	149	0.17%
38	West Virginia	124	0.14%
39	Maine	68	0.08%
40	Mississippi	38	0.04%
41	Idaho	18	0.02%
42	Delaware	11	0.01%
43	New Hampshire	10	0.01%
44	Wyoming	6	0.01%
45	South Dakota	4	0.00%
46	North Dakota	1	0.00%
47	New Mexico	0	0.00%
47	Vermont	0	0.00%
NA	Kansas**	NA	NA
NA	Montana**	NA	NA
	District of Columbia	1,286	1.48%

Source: Federal Bureau of Investigation
   "Crime in the United States 1994" (Uniform Crime Reports, November 19, 1995)
*By law enforcement agencies submitting complete reports to the F.B.I. for 12 months in 1994. The F.B.I. estimates
98,800 reported and unreported arrests for prostitution and commercialized vice occurred in 1994. Includes keeping
a bawdy house, procuring or transporting women for immoral purposes. Attempts are included.
**Not available.

Reported Arrest Rate for Prostitution and Commercialized Vice in 1994

National Rate = 41.8 Reported Arrests per 100,000 Population*

ALPHA ORDER

RANK	STATE	RATE
38	Alabama	6.3
25	Alaska	26.2
10	Arizona	45.0
33	Arkansas	13.2
4	California	57.5
6	Colorado	56.3
21	Connecticut	30.6
41	Delaware	2.9
9	Florida	52.1
14	Georgia	35.9
12	Hawaii	38.6
42	Idaho	1.6
31	Illinois	14.5
19	Indiana	31.2
35	Iowa	10.7
NA	Kansas**	NA
27	Kentucky	25.1
34	Louisiana	11.6
39	Maine	5.6
23	Maryland	28.7
5	Massachusetts	57.3
13	Michigan	37.9
20	Minnesota	30.8
40	Mississippi	4.8
2	Missouri	94.5
NA	Montana**	NA
30	Nebraska	18.0
1	Nevada	203.5
43	New Hampshire	1.4
17	New Jersey	32.9
47	New Mexico	0.0
3	New York	77.3
32	North Carolina	14.3
46	North Dakota	0.2
7	Ohio	54.4
36	Oklahoma	9.0
26	Oregon	25.4
24	Pennsylvania	26.4
18	Rhode Island	32.8
29	South Carolina	18.1
45	South Dakota	1.0
8	Tennessee	53.9
11	Texas	44.0
16	Utah	33.1
47	Vermont	0.0
28	Virginia	18.8
22	Washington	29.8
37	West Virginia	6.8
15	Wisconsin	34.2
44	Wyoming	1.3

RANK ORDER

RANK	STATE	RATE
1	Nevada	203.5
2	Missouri	94.5
3	New York	77.3
4	California	57.5
5	Massachusetts	57.3
6	Colorado	56.3
7	Ohio	54.4
8	Tennessee	53.9
9	Florida	52.1
10	Arizona	45.0
11	Texas	44.0
12	Hawaii	38.6
13	Michigan	37.9
14	Georgia	35.9
15	Wisconsin	34.2
16	Utah	33.1
17	New Jersey	32.9
18	Rhode Island	32.8
19	Indiana	31.2
20	Minnesota	30.8
21	Connecticut	30.6
22	Washington	29.8
23	Maryland	28.7
24	Pennsylvania	26.4
25	Alaska	26.2
26	Oregon	25.4
27	Kentucky	25.1
28	Virginia	18.8
29	South Carolina	18.1
30	Nebraska	18.0
31	Illinois	14.5
32	North Carolina	14.3
33	Arkansas	13.2
34	Louisiana	11.6
35	Iowa	10.7
36	Oklahoma	9.0
37	West Virginia	6.8
38	Alabama	6.3
39	Maine	5.6
40	Mississippi	4.8
41	Delaware	2.9
42	Idaho	1.6
43	New Hampshire	1.4
44	Wyoming	1.3
45	South Dakota	1.0
46	North Dakota	0.2
47	New Mexico	0.0
47	Vermont	0.0
NA	Kansas**	NA
NA	Montana**	NA
	District of Columbia	225.6

Source: Morgan Quitno Press using data from Federal Bureau of Investigation
   "Crime in the United States 1994" (Uniform Crime Reports, November 19, 1995)
*By law enforcement agencies submitting complete reports to the F.B.I. for 12 months in 1994. These rates based
on population estimates for areas under the jurisdiction of those agencies reporting. Arrest rate based on the F.B.I.
estimate of reported and unreported arrests for prostitution and commercialized vice is 38.0 arrests per 100,000
population. **Not available.

Reported Arrests for Offenses Against Families and Children in 1994

National Total = 92,108 Reported Arrests*

<table>
<tr><td colspan="4"><u>ALPHA ORDER</u></td><td colspan="4"><u>RANK ORDER</u></td></tr>
<tr><td>RANK</td><td>STATE</td><td>ARRESTS</td><td>% of USA</td><td>RANK</td><td>STATE</td><td>ARRESTS</td><td>% of USA</td></tr>
<tr><td>22</td><td>Alabama</td><td>1,060</td><td>1.15%</td><td>1</td><td>New Jersey</td><td>16,503</td><td>17.92%</td></tr>
<tr><td>45</td><td>Alaska</td><td>100</td><td>0.11%</td><td>2</td><td>Ohio</td><td>13,069</td><td>14.19%</td></tr>
<tr><td>12</td><td>Arizona</td><td>2,025</td><td>2.20%</td><td>3</td><td>Texas</td><td>7,451</td><td>8.09%</td></tr>
<tr><td>25</td><td>Arkansas</td><td>908</td><td>0.99%</td><td>4</td><td>North Carolina</td><td>6,240</td><td>6.77%</td></tr>
<tr><td>31</td><td>California</td><td>686</td><td>0.74%</td><td>5</td><td>Wisconsin</td><td>5,153</td><td>5.59%</td></tr>
<tr><td>18</td><td>Colorado</td><td>1,373</td><td>1.49%</td><td>6</td><td>Massachusetts</td><td>3,088</td><td>3.35%</td></tr>
<tr><td>10</td><td>Connecticut</td><td>2,386</td><td>2.59%</td><td>7</td><td>Georgia</td><td>2,751</td><td>2.99%</td></tr>
<tr><td>46</td><td>Delaware</td><td>63</td><td>0.07%</td><td>8</td><td>Missouri</td><td>2,646</td><td>2.87%</td></tr>
<tr><td>16</td><td>Florida</td><td>1,447</td><td>1.57%</td><td>9</td><td>Michigan</td><td>2,600</td><td>2.82%</td></tr>
<tr><td>7</td><td>Georgia</td><td>2,751</td><td>2.99%</td><td>10</td><td>Connecticut</td><td>2,386</td><td>2.59%</td></tr>
<tr><td>13</td><td>Hawaii</td><td>1,939</td><td>2.11%</td><td>11</td><td>Virginia</td><td>2,051</td><td>2.23%</td></tr>
<tr><td>38</td><td>Idaho</td><td>240</td><td>0.26%</td><td>12</td><td>Arizona</td><td>2,025</td><td>2.20%</td></tr>
<tr><td>39</td><td>Illinois</td><td>239</td><td>0.26%</td><td>13</td><td>Hawaii</td><td>1,939</td><td>2.11%</td></tr>
<tr><td>21</td><td>Indiana</td><td>1,167</td><td>1.27%</td><td>14</td><td>Kentucky</td><td>1,697</td><td>1.84%</td></tr>
<tr><td>42</td><td>Iowa</td><td>208</td><td>0.23%</td><td>15</td><td>Maryland</td><td>1,659</td><td>1.80%</td></tr>
<tr><td>NA</td><td>Kansas**</td><td>NA</td><td>NA</td><td>16</td><td>Florida</td><td>1,447</td><td>1.57%</td></tr>
<tr><td>14</td><td>Kentucky</td><td>1,697</td><td>1.84%</td><td>17</td><td>Nebraska</td><td>1,418</td><td>1.54%</td></tr>
<tr><td>19</td><td>Louisiana</td><td>1,288</td><td>1.40%</td><td>18</td><td>Colorado</td><td>1,373</td><td>1.49%</td></tr>
<tr><td>37</td><td>Maine</td><td>262</td><td>0.28%</td><td>19</td><td>Louisiana</td><td>1,288</td><td>1.40%</td></tr>
<tr><td>15</td><td>Maryland</td><td>1,659</td><td>1.80%</td><td>20</td><td>South Carolina</td><td>1,169</td><td>1.27%</td></tr>
<tr><td>6</td><td>Massachusetts</td><td>3,088</td><td>3.35%</td><td>21</td><td>Indiana</td><td>1,167</td><td>1.27%</td></tr>
<tr><td>9</td><td>Michigan</td><td>2,600</td><td>2.82%</td><td>22</td><td>Alabama</td><td>1,060</td><td>1.15%</td></tr>
<tr><td>32</td><td>Minnesota</td><td>656</td><td>0.71%</td><td>23</td><td>Washington</td><td>984</td><td>1.07%</td></tr>
<tr><td>30</td><td>Mississippi</td><td>702</td><td>0.76%</td><td>24</td><td>Tennessee</td><td>936</td><td>1.02%</td></tr>
<tr><td>8</td><td>Missouri</td><td>2,646</td><td>2.87%</td><td>25</td><td>Arkansas</td><td>908</td><td>0.99%</td></tr>
<tr><td>NA</td><td>Montana**</td><td>NA</td><td>NA</td><td>26</td><td>New Mexico</td><td>903</td><td>0.98%</td></tr>
<tr><td>17</td><td>Nebraska</td><td>1,418</td><td>1.54%</td><td>27</td><td>Oklahoma</td><td>887</td><td>0.96%</td></tr>
<tr><td>28</td><td>Nevada</td><td>822</td><td>0.89%</td><td>28</td><td>Nevada</td><td>822</td><td>0.89%</td></tr>
<tr><td>47</td><td>New Hampshire</td><td>34</td><td>0.04%</td><td>29</td><td>Pennsylvania</td><td>765</td><td>0.83%</td></tr>
<tr><td>1</td><td>New Jersey</td><td>16,503</td><td>17.92%</td><td>30</td><td>Mississippi</td><td>702</td><td>0.76%</td></tr>
<tr><td>26</td><td>New Mexico</td><td>903</td><td>0.98%</td><td>31</td><td>California</td><td>686</td><td>0.74%</td></tr>
<tr><td>48</td><td>New York</td><td>0</td><td>0.00%</td><td>32</td><td>Minnesota</td><td>656</td><td>0.71%</td></tr>
<tr><td>4</td><td>North Carolina</td><td>6,240</td><td>6.77%</td><td>33</td><td>Utah</td><td>569</td><td>0.62%</td></tr>
<tr><td>40</td><td>North Dakota</td><td>230</td><td>0.25%</td><td>34</td><td>Rhode Island</td><td>471</td><td>0.51%</td></tr>
<tr><td>2</td><td>Ohio</td><td>13,069</td><td>14.19%</td><td>35</td><td>West Virginia</td><td>444</td><td>0.48%</td></tr>
<tr><td>27</td><td>Oklahoma</td><td>887</td><td>0.96%</td><td>36</td><td>Oregon</td><td>329</td><td>0.36%</td></tr>
<tr><td>36</td><td>Oregon</td><td>329</td><td>0.36%</td><td>37</td><td>Maine</td><td>262</td><td>0.28%</td></tr>
<tr><td>29</td><td>Pennsylvania</td><td>765</td><td>0.83%</td><td>38</td><td>Idaho</td><td>240</td><td>0.26%</td></tr>
<tr><td>34</td><td>Rhode Island</td><td>471</td><td>0.51%</td><td>39</td><td>Illinois</td><td>239</td><td>0.26%</td></tr>
<tr><td>20</td><td>South Carolina</td><td>1,169</td><td>1.27%</td><td>40</td><td>North Dakota</td><td>230</td><td>0.25%</td></tr>
<tr><td>41</td><td>South Dakota</td><td>209</td><td>0.23%</td><td>41</td><td>South Dakota</td><td>209</td><td>0.23%</td></tr>
<tr><td>24</td><td>Tennessee</td><td>936</td><td>1.02%</td><td>42</td><td>Iowa</td><td>208</td><td>0.23%</td></tr>
<tr><td>3</td><td>Texas</td><td>7,451</td><td>8.09%</td><td>43</td><td>Vermont</td><td>140</td><td>0.15%</td></tr>
<tr><td>33</td><td>Utah</td><td>569</td><td>0.62%</td><td>44</td><td>Wyoming</td><td>129</td><td>0.14%</td></tr>
<tr><td>43</td><td>Vermont</td><td>140</td><td>0.15%</td><td>45</td><td>Alaska</td><td>100</td><td>0.11%</td></tr>
<tr><td>11</td><td>Virginia</td><td>2,051</td><td>2.23%</td><td>46</td><td>Delaware</td><td>63</td><td>0.07%</td></tr>
<tr><td>23</td><td>Washington</td><td>984</td><td>1.07%</td><td>47</td><td>New Hampshire</td><td>34</td><td>0.04%</td></tr>
<tr><td>35</td><td>West Virginia</td><td>444</td><td>0.48%</td><td>48</td><td>New York</td><td>0</td><td>0.00%</td></tr>
<tr><td>5</td><td>Wisconsin</td><td>5,153</td><td>5.59%</td><td>NA</td><td>Kansas**</td><td>NA</td><td>NA</td></tr>
<tr><td>44</td><td>Wyoming</td><td>129</td><td>0.14%</td><td>NA</td><td>Montana**</td><td>NA</td><td>NA</td></tr>
<tr><td></td><td></td><td></td><td></td><td></td><td>District of Columbia</td><td>12</td><td>0.01%</td></tr>
</table>

Source: Federal Bureau of Investigation
   "Crime in the United States 1994" (Uniform Crime Reports, November 19, 1995)
*By law enforcement agencies submitting complete reports to the F.B.I. for 12 months in 1994. The F.B.I. estimates 117,200 reported and unreported arrests for offenses against families and children occurred in 1994. Includes nonsupport, neglect, desertion or abuse of family and children.
**Not available.

Reported Arrest Rate for Offenses Against Families and Children in 1994

National Rate = 44.4 Reported Arrests per 100,000 Population*

ALPHA ORDER				RANK ORDER		
RANK	STATE	RATE		RANK	STATE	RATE
33	Alabama	27.2		1	New Mexico	230.4
38	Alaska	17.6		2	New Jersey	215.6
16	Arizona	51.9		3	Ohio	193.9
24	Arkansas	37.6		4	Hawaii	164.5
47	California	2.2		5	Wisconsin	103.5
15	Colorado	54.2		6	Nebraska	96.1
9	Connecticut	86.2		7	North Carolina	91.1
39	Delaware	16.6		8	Mississippi	88.7
43	Florida	10.5		9	Connecticut	86.2
13	Georgia	65.8		10	Kentucky	83.7
4	Hawaii	164.5		11	Missouri	80.6
36	Idaho	21.8		12	Massachusetts	75.5
41	Illinois	13.5		13	Georgia	65.8
25	Indiana	36.1		14	Nevada	61.2
44	Iowa	8.6		15	Colorado	54.2
NA	Kansas**	NA		16	Arizona	51.9
10	Kentucky	83.7		17	South Dakota	51.1
22	Louisiana	42.5		18	Rhode Island	47.2
37	Maine	21.7		19	Vermont	47.0
28	Maryland	33.2		20	Texas	45.9
12	Massachusetts	75.5		21	Tennessee	45.5
26	Michigan	34.6		22	Louisiana	42.5
40	Minnesota	15.4		23	North Dakota	41.7
8	Mississippi	88.7		24	Arkansas	37.6
11	Missouri	80.6		25	Indiana	36.1
NA	Montana**	NA		26	Michigan	34.6
6	Nebraska	96.1		27	Utah	33.3
14	Nevada	61.2		28	Maryland	33.2
46	New Hampshire	4.8		29	South Carolina	31.9
2	New Jersey	215.6		30	Virginia	31.7
1	New Mexico	230.4		31	Wyoming	28.5
48	New York	0.0		32	Oklahoma	27.6
7	North Carolina	91.1		33	Alabama	27.2
23	North Dakota	41.7		34	West Virginia	24.4
3	Ohio	193.9		35	Washington	23.7
32	Oklahoma	27.6		36	Idaho	21.8
42	Oregon	10.9		37	Maine	21.7
45	Pennsylvania	8.2		38	Alaska	17.6
18	Rhode Island	47.2		39	Delaware	16.6
29	South Carolina	31.9		40	Minnesota	15.4
17	South Dakota	51.1		41	Illinois	13.5
21	Tennessee	45.5		42	Oregon	10.9
20	Texas	45.9		43	Florida	10.5
27	Utah	33.3		44	Iowa	8.6
19	Vermont	47.0		45	Pennsylvania	8.2
30	Virginia	31.7		46	New Hampshire	4.8
35	Washington	23.7		47	California	2.2
34	West Virginia	24.4		48	New York	0.0
5	Wisconsin	103.5		NA	Kansas**	NA
31	Wyoming	28.5		NA	Montana**	NA
					District of Columbia	2.1

Source: Morgan Quitno Press using data from Federal Bureau of Investigation
"Crime in the United States 1994" (Uniform Crime Reports, November 19, 1995)
*By law enforcement agencies submitting complete reports to the F.B.I. for 12 months in 1994. These rates based on population estimates for areas under the jurisdiction of those agencies reporting. Arrest rate based on the F.B.I. estimate of reported and unreported arrests for offenses against families and children is 45.0 arrests per 100,000 population. **Not available.

Reported Arrests of Juveniles in 1994

National Total = 2,209,675 Reported Arrests*

ALPHA ORDER

RANK	STATE	ARRESTS	% of USA
34	Alabama	17,018	0.77%
43	Alaska	6,737	0.30%
9	Arizona	64,452	2.92%
31	Arkansas	18,730	0.85%
1	California	257,389	11.65%
14	Colorado	51,163	2.32%
23	Connecticut	32,154	1.46%
47	Delaware	1,796	0.08%
4	Florida	154,569	7.00%
21	Georgia	37,514	1.70%
26	Hawaii	20,648	0.93%
27	Idaho	20,034	0.91%
29	Illinois	19,671	0.89%
18	Indiana	38,756	1.75%
35	Iowa	16,940	0.77%
NA	Kansas**	NA	NA
36	Kentucky	11,644	0.53%
22	Louisiana	33,997	1.54%
37	Maine	10,295	0.47%
16	Maryland	48,295	2.19%
30	Massachusetts	19,530	0.88%
11	Michigan	55,254	2.50%
10	Minnesota	58,900	2.67%
39	Mississippi	9,225	0.42%
20	Missouri	38,141	1.73%
NA	Montana**	NA	NA
33	Nebraska	17,065	0.77%
32	Nevada	18,186	0.82%
45	New Hampshire	5,951	0.27%
6	New Jersey	87,875	3.98%
46	New Mexico	5,619	0.25%
3	New York	163,723	7.41%
15	North Carolina	49,086	2.22%
41	North Dakota	7,569	0.34%
8	Ohio	76,423	3.46%
24	Oklahoma	27,632	1.25%
17	Oregon	44,750	2.03%
7	Pennsylvania	87,748	3.97%
38	Rhode Island	9,664	0.44%
25	South Carolina	26,381	1.19%
40	South Dakota	8,959	0.41%
28	Tennessee	19,923	0.90%
2	Texas	212,326	9.61%
19	Utah	38,697	1.75%
48	Vermont	467	0.02%
12	Virginia	53,533	2.42%
13	Washington	52,993	2.40%
42	West Virginia	6,869	0.31%
5	Wisconsin	134,941	6.11%
44	Wyoming	6,710	0.30%

RANK ORDER

RANK	STATE	ARRESTS	% of USA
1	California	257,389	11.65%
2	Texas	212,326	9.61%
3	New York	163,723	7.41%
4	Florida	154,569	7.00%
5	Wisconsin	134,941	6.11%
6	New Jersey	87,875	3.98%
7	Pennsylvania	87,748	3.97%
8	Ohio	76,423	3.46%
9	Arizona	64,452	2.92%
10	Minnesota	58,900	2.67%
11	Michigan	55,254	2.50%
12	Virginia	53,533	2.42%
13	Washington	52,993	2.40%
14	Colorado	51,163	2.32%
15	North Carolina	49,086	2.22%
16	Maryland	48,295	2.19%
17	Oregon	44,750	2.03%
18	Indiana	38,756	1.75%
19	Utah	38,697	1.75%
20	Missouri	38,141	1.73%
21	Georgia	37,514	1.70%
22	Louisiana	33,997	1.54%
23	Connecticut	32,154	1.46%
24	Oklahoma	27,632	1.25%
25	South Carolina	26,381	1.19%
26	Hawaii	20,648	0.93%
27	Idaho	20,034	0.91%
28	Tennessee	19,923	0.90%
29	Illinois	19,671	0.89%
30	Massachusetts	19,530	0.88%
31	Arkansas	18,730	0.85%
32	Nevada	18,186	0.82%
33	Nebraska	17,065	0.77%
34	Alabama	17,018	0.77%
35	Iowa	16,940	0.77%
36	Kentucky	11,644	0.53%
37	Maine	10,295	0.47%
38	Rhode Island	9,664	0.44%
39	Mississippi	9,225	0.42%
40	South Dakota	8,959	0.41%
41	North Dakota	7,569	0.34%
42	West Virginia	6,869	0.31%
43	Alaska	6,737	0.30%
44	Wyoming	6,710	0.30%
45	New Hampshire	5,951	0.27%
46	New Mexico	5,619	0.25%
47	Delaware	1,796	0.08%
48	Vermont	467	0.02%
NA	Kansas**	NA	NA
NA	Montana**	NA	NA
	District of Columbia	3,733	0.17%

Source: Federal Bureau of Investigation
    "Crime in the United States 1994" (Uniform Crime Reports, November 19, 1995)
*Arrests of youths 17 years and younger by law enforcement agencies submitting complete reports to the F.B.I. for 12 months in 1994.
**Not available.

Reported Juvenile Arrest Rate in 1994

National Rate = 9,414.0 Reported Arrests per 100,000 Juvenile Population*

ALPHA ORDER

RANK	STATE	RATE
46	Alabama	3,774.0
27	Alaska	8,969.2
5	Arizona	14,094.2
39	Arkansas	6,433.0
36	California	7,504.3
2	Colorado	17,344.4
10	Connecticut	11,600.4
45	Delaware	4,482.2
11	Florida	11,405.7
33	Georgia	7,706.4
3	Hawaii	16,340.0
9	Idaho	12,712.5
23	Illinois	9,826.9
19	Indiana	10,342.6
42	Iowa	5,750.9
NA	Kansas**	NA
44	Kentucky	4,873.5
31	Louisiana	8,590.1
35	Maine	7,509.2
25	Maryland	9,271.8
43	Massachusetts	4,889.7
41	Michigan	6,244.4
12	Minnesota	11,264.9
28	Mississippi	8,907.0
21	Missouri	9,872.9
NA	Montana**	NA
26	Nebraska	9,243.7
8	Nevada	12,748.0
34	New Hampshire	7,538.5
13	New Jersey	11,222.3
16	New Mexico	10,747.1
20	New York	9,960.4
38	North Carolina	6,684.1
15	North Dakota	10,767.2
22	Ohio	9,828.7
37	Oklahoma	6,947.5
7	Oregon	12,765.7
29	Pennsylvania	8,877.2
24	Rhode Island	9,551.8
40	South Carolina	6,300.4
4	South Dakota	16,299.2
30	Tennessee	8,655.0
17	Texas	10,510.5
6	Utah	13,756.7
48	Vermont	1,384.4
32	Virginia	7,898.0
14	Washington	11,026.6
47	West Virginia	3,258.7
1	Wisconsin	22,275.1
18	Wyoming	10,494.5

RANK ORDER

RANK	STATE	RATE
1	Wisconsin	22,275.1
2	Colorado	17,344.4
3	Hawaii	16,340.0
4	South Dakota	16,299.2
5	Arizona	14,094.2
6	Utah	13,756.7
7	Oregon	12,765.7
8	Nevada	12,748.0
9	Idaho	12,712.5
10	Connecticut	11,600.4
11	Florida	11,405.7
12	Minnesota	11,264.9
13	New Jersey	11,222.3
14	Washington	11,026.6
15	North Dakota	10,767.2
16	New Mexico	10,747.1
17	Texas	10,510.5
18	Wyoming	10,494.5
19	Indiana	10,342.6
20	New York	9,960.4
21	Missouri	9,872.9
22	Ohio	9,828.7
23	Illinois	9,826.9
24	Rhode Island	9,551.8
25	Maryland	9,271.8
26	Nebraska	9,243.7
27	Alaska	8,969.2
28	Mississippi	8,907.0
29	Pennsylvania	8,877.2
30	Tennessee	8,655.0
31	Louisiana	8,590.1
32	Virginia	7,898.0
33	Georgia	7,706.4
34	New Hampshire	7,538.5
35	Maine	7,509.2
36	California	7,504.3
37	Oklahoma	6,947.5
38	North Carolina	6,684.1
39	Arkansas	6,433.0
40	South Carolina	6,300.4
41	Michigan	6,244.4
42	Iowa	5,750.9
43	Massachusetts	4,889.7
44	Kentucky	4,873.5
45	Delaware	4,482.2
46	Alabama	3,774.0
47	West Virginia	3,258.7
48	Vermont	1,384.4
NA	Kansas**	NA
NA	Montana**	NA

District of Columbia   8,580.4

Source: Morgan Quitno Press using data from Federal Bureau of Investigation
   "Crime in the United States 1994" (Uniform Crime Reports, November 19, 1995)
*By law enforcement agencies submitting complete reports to the F.B.I. for 12 months in 1994. Arrests of youths 17
years and younger divided into population of 10 to 17 year olds. See important note at beginning of this chapter.
**Not available.

Reported Arrests of Juveniles as a Percent of All Arrests in 1994

National Percent = 18.60% of Reported Arrests*

ALPHA ORDER				RANK ORDER		
RANK	STATE	PERCENT		RANK	STATE	PERCENT
48	Alabama	8.54		1	Utah	34.48
31	Alaska	17.54		2	Wisconsin	32.08
12	Arizona	23.78		3	Idaho	31.42
46	Arkansas	10.66		4	South Dakota	30.10
33	California	15.92		5	Hawaii	29.93
13	Colorado	23.53		6	North Dakota	29.92
30	Connecticut	17.58		7	Minnesota	28.90
27	Delaware	18.46		8	Oregon	28.36
24	Florida	20.44		9	Indiana	25.71
41	Georgia	13.11		10	Pennsylvania	25.22
5	Hawaii	29.93		11	New Hampshire	24.17
3	Idaho	31.42		12	Arizona	23.78
14	Illinois	23.50		13	Colorado	23.53
9	Indiana	25.71		14	Illinois	23.50
25	Iowa	19.41		15	Rhode Island	23.49
NA	Kansas**	NA		16	New Jersey	23.30
47	Kentucky	10.25		17	Washington	23.01
28	Louisiana	17.95		18	Wyoming	22.72
19	Maine	22.08		19	Maine	22.08
29	Maryland	17.68		20	New Mexico	21.55
37	Massachusetts	14.10		21	Nebraska	21.24
34	Michigan	15.68		22	Ohio	20.70
7	Minnesota	28.90		23	Texas	20.50
35	Mississippi	14.96		24	Florida	20.44
40	Missouri	13.69		25	Iowa	19.41
NA	Montana**	NA		26	Oklahoma	18.60
21	Nebraska	21.24		27	Delaware	18.46
32	Nevada	17.11		28	Louisiana	17.95
11	New Hampshire	24.17		29	Maryland	17.68
16	New Jersey	23.30		30	Connecticut	17.58
20	New Mexico	21.55		31	Alaska	17.54
38	New York	13.97		32	Nevada	17.11
45	North Carolina	11.23		33	California	15.92
6	North Dakota	29.92		34	Michigan	15.68
22	Ohio	20.70		35	Mississippi	14.96
26	Oklahoma	18.60		36	Tennessee	14.41
8	Oregon	28.36		37	Massachusetts	14.10
10	Pennsylvania	25.22		38	New York	13.97
15	Rhode Island	23.49		39	Virginia	13.83
42	South Carolina	13.02		40	Missouri	13.69
4	South Dakota	30.10		41	Georgia	13.11
36	Tennessee	14.41		42	South Carolina	13.02
23	Texas	20.50		43	Vermont	12.61
1	Utah	34.48		44	West Virginia	11.48
43	Vermont	12.61		45	North Carolina	11.23
39	Virginia	13.83		46	Arkansas	10.66
17	Washington	23.01		47	Kentucky	10.25
44	West Virginia	11.48		48	Alabama	8.54
2	Wisconsin	32.08		NA	Kansas**	NA
18	Wyoming	22.72		NA	Montana**	NA
					District of Columbia	7.70

Source: Morgan Quitno Press using data from Federal Bureau of Investigation
    "Crime in the United States 1994" (Uniform Crime Reports, November 19, 1995)
*Arrests of youths 17 years and younger by law enforcement agencies submitting complete reports to the F.B.I. for 12 months in 1994.
**Not available.

Reported Arrests of Juveniles for Crime Index Offenses in 1994

National Total = 735,648 Reported Arrests*

ALPHA ORDER					RANK ORDER			
RANK	STATE	ARRESTS	% of USA		RANK	STATE	ARRESTS	% of USA
26	Alabama	7,500	1.02%		1	California	104,372	14.19%
38	Alaska	3,279	0.45%		2	Texas	66,566	9.05%
13	Arizona	18,397	2.50%		3	Florida	64,531	8.77%
29	Arkansas	6,382	0.87%		4	New York	43,761	5.95%
1	California	104,372	14.19%		5	Wisconsin	32,443	4.41%
17	Colorado	15,278	2.08%		6	Pennsylvania	24,729	3.36%
24	Connecticut	9,939	1.35%		7	Washington	24,394	3.32%
47	Delaware	759	0.10%		8	New Jersey	23,492	3.19%
3	Florida	64,531	8.77%		9	Michigan	21,776	2.96%
19	Georgia	13,648	1.86%		10	Ohio	19,904	2.71%
36	Hawaii	4,664	0.63%		11	Maryland	19,641	2.67%
27	Idaho	6,733	0.92%		12	Minnesota	19,302	2.62%
33	Illinois	5,266	0.72%		13	Arizona	18,397	2.50%
23	Indiana	11,308	1.54%		14	North Carolina	16,969	2.31%
31	Iowa	6,003	0.82%		15	Virginia	16,363	2.22%
NA	Kansas**	NA	NA		16	Oregon	15,591	2.12%
35	Kentucky	4,727	0.64%		17	Colorado	15,278	2.08%
22	Louisiana	11,899	1.62%		18	Utah	14,515	1.97%
37	Maine	4,567	0.62%		19	Georgia	13,648	1.86%
11	Maryland	19,641	2.67%		20	Oklahoma	12,281	1.67%
28	Massachusetts	6,673	0.91%		21	Missouri	12,081	1.64%
9	Michigan	21,776	2.96%		22	Louisiana	11,899	1.62%
12	Minnesota	19,302	2.62%		23	Indiana	11,308	1.54%
39	Mississippi	3,137	0.43%		24	Connecticut	9,939	1.35%
21	Missouri	12,081	1.64%		25	South Carolina	9,210	1.25%
NA	Montana**	NA	NA		26	Alabama	7,500	1.02%
32	Nebraska	5,974	0.81%		27	Idaho	6,733	0.92%
34	Nevada	4,776	0.65%		28	Massachusetts	6,673	0.91%
45	New Hampshire	1,622	0.22%		29	Arkansas	6,382	0.87%
8	New Jersey	23,492	3.19%		30	Tennessee	6,117	0.83%
44	New Mexico	1,633	0.22%		31	Iowa	6,003	0.82%
4	New York	43,761	5.95%		32	Nebraska	5,974	0.81%
14	North Carolina	16,969	2.31%		33	Illinois	5,266	0.72%
43	North Dakota	2,235	0.30%		34	Nevada	4,776	0.65%
10	Ohio	19,904	2.71%		35	Kentucky	4,727	0.64%
20	Oklahoma	12,281	1.67%		36	Hawaii	4,664	0.63%
16	Oregon	15,591	2.12%		37	Maine	4,567	0.62%
6	Pennsylvania	24,729	3.36%		38	Alaska	3,279	0.45%
40	Rhode Island	2,967	0.40%		39	Mississippi	3,137	0.43%
25	South Carolina	9,210	1.25%		40	Rhode Island	2,967	0.40%
41	South Dakota	2,542	0.35%		41	South Dakota	2,542	0.35%
30	Tennessee	6,117	0.83%		42	West Virginia	2,526	0.34%
2	Texas	66,566	9.05%		43	North Dakota	2,235	0.30%
18	Utah	14,515	1.97%		44	New Mexico	1,633	0.22%
48	Vermont	214	0.03%		45	New Hampshire	1,622	0.22%
15	Virginia	16,363	2.22%		46	Wyoming	1,609	0.22%
7	Washington	24,394	3.32%		47	Delaware	759	0.10%
42	West Virginia	2,526	0.34%		48	Vermont	214	0.03%
5	Wisconsin	32,443	4.41%		NA	Kansas**	NA	NA
46	Wyoming	1,609	0.22%		NA	Montana**	NA	NA
						District of Columbia	1,353	0.18%

Source: Federal Bureau of Investigation
   "Crime in the United States 1994" (Uniform Crime Reports, November 19, 1995)
*Arrests of youths 17 years and younger by law enforcement agencies submitting complete reports to the F.B.I. for 12 months in 1994. Crime index offenses consist of murder, forcible rape, robbery, aggravated assault, burglary, larceny-theft, motor vehicle theft and arson.
**Not available.

Reported Juvenile Arrest Rate for Crime Index Offenses in 1994

National Rate = 3,134.1 Reported Arrests per 100,000 Juvenile Population*

ALPHA ORDER

RANK	STATE	RATE
46	Alabama	1,663.3
8	Alaska	4,365.4
10	Arizona	4,023.0
40	Arkansas	2,191.9
23	California	3,043.0
2	Colorado	5,179.3
14	Connecticut	3,585.8
44	Delaware	1,894.2
5	Florida	4,761.8
29	Georgia	2,803.7
13	Hawaii	3,690.9
9	Idaho	4,272.4
32	Illinois	2,630.7
25	Indiana	3,017.7
42	Iowa	2,037.9
NA	Kansas**	NA
43	Kentucky	1,978.4
26	Louisiana	3,006.5
16	Maine	3,331.2
11	Maryland	3,770.7
45	Massachusetts	1,670.7
36	Michigan	2,461.0
12	Minnesota	3,691.6
24	Mississippi	3,028.9
20	Missouri	3,127.2
NA	Montana**	NA
18	Nebraska	3,236.0
15	Nevada	3,347.9
41	New Hampshire	2,054.7
27	New Jersey	3,000.1
21	New Mexico	3,123.3
30	New York	2,662.3
38	North Carolina	2,310.7
19	North Dakota	3,179.4
33	Ohio	2,559.8
22	Oklahoma	3,087.8
7	Oregon	4,447.6
35	Pennsylvania	2,501.7
28	Rhode Island	2,932.5
39	South Carolina	2,199.6
6	South Dakota	4,624.7
31	Tennessee	2,657.4
17	Texas	3,295.1
3	Utah	5,160.0
48	Vermont	634.4
37	Virginia	2,414.1
4	Washington	5,075.8
47	West Virginia	1,198.4
1	Wisconsin	5,355.5
34	Wyoming	2,516.5

RANK ORDER

RANK	STATE	RATE
1	Wisconsin	5,355.5
2	Colorado	5,179.3
3	Utah	5,160.0
4	Washington	5,075.8
5	Florida	4,761.8
6	South Dakota	4,624.7
7	Oregon	4,447.6
8	Alaska	4,365.4
9	Idaho	4,272.4
10	Arizona	4,023.0
11	Maryland	3,770.7
12	Minnesota	3,691.6
13	Hawaii	3,690.9
14	Connecticut	3,585.8
15	Nevada	3,347.9
16	Maine	3,331.2
17	Texas	3,295.1
18	Nebraska	3,236.0
19	North Dakota	3,179.4
20	Missouri	3,127.2
21	New Mexico	3,123.3
22	Oklahoma	3,087.8
23	California	3,043.0
24	Mississippi	3,028.9
25	Indiana	3,017.7
26	Louisiana	3,006.5
27	New Jersey	3,000.1
28	Rhode Island	2,932.5
29	Georgia	2,803.7
30	New York	2,662.3
31	Tennessee	2,657.4
32	Illinois	2,630.7
33	Ohio	2,559.8
34	Wyoming	2,516.5
35	Pennsylvania	2,501.7
36	Michigan	2,461.0
37	Virginia	2,414.1
38	North Carolina	2,310.7
39	South Carolina	2,199.6
40	Arkansas	2,191.9
41	New Hampshire	2,054.7
42	Iowa	2,037.9
43	Kentucky	1,978.4
44	Delaware	1,894.2
45	Massachusetts	1,670.7
46	Alabama	1,663.3
47	West Virginia	1,198.4
48	Vermont	634.4
NA	Kansas**	NA
NA	Montana**	NA
	District of Columbia	3,109.9

Source: Morgan Quitno Press using data from Federal Bureau of Investigation
    "Crime in the United States 1994" (Uniform Crime Reports, November 19, 1995)
*By law enforcement agencies submitting complete reports to the F.B.I. for 12 months in 1993. Arrests of youths 17 years and younger divided into population of 10 to 17 year olds. See important note at beginning of this chapter. Crime index offenses consist of murder, forcible rape, robbery, aggravated assault, burglary, larceny-theft, motor vehicle theft and arson.   **Not available.

41

Reported Arrests of Juveniles for Crime Index Offenses
As a Percent of All Such Arrests in 1994
National Percent = 30.85% of Reported Arrests for Crime Index Offenses*

ALPHA ORDER

RANK	STATE	PERCENT
47	Alabama	19.66
14	Alaska	40.06
25	Arizona	32.79
34	Arkansas	27.22
40	California	25.52
20	Colorado	36.23
41	Connecticut	25.42
26	Delaware	32.20
29	Florida	31.87
42	Georgia	24.09
22	Hawaii	35.79
1	Idaho	56.77
18	Illinois	36.47
15	Indiana	38.90
16	Iowa	38.67
NA	Kansas**	NA
45	Kentucky	21.47
38	Louisiana	26.14
7	Maine	45.95
31	Maryland	30.65
48	Massachusetts	19.42
28	Michigan	31.90
5	Minnesota	48.57
36	Mississippi	26.26
43	Missouri	23.73
NA	Montana**	NA
8	Nebraska	44.29
32	Nevada	27.52
13	New Hampshire	41.58
30	New Jersey	31.60
12	New Mexico	41.80
39	New York	25.77
46	North Carolina	20.08
3	North Dakota	54.75
24	Ohio	33.57
10	Oklahoma	42.85
17	Oregon	36.65
27	Pennsylvania	31.95
19	Rhode Island	36.38
35	South Carolina	26.91
4	South Dakota	51.75
44	Tennessee	21.63
21	Texas	36.17
2	Utah	55.23
23	Vermont	33.59
37	Virginia	26.25
9	Washington	43.96
33	West Virginia	27.36
6	Wisconsin	47.38
11	Wyoming	42.13

RANK ORDER

RANK	STATE	PERCENT
1	Idaho	56.77
2	Utah	55.23
3	North Dakota	54.75
4	South Dakota	51.75
5	Minnesota	48.57
6	Wisconsin	47.38
7	Maine	45.95
8	Nebraska	44.29
9	Washington	43.96
10	Oklahoma	42.85
11	Wyoming	42.13
12	New Mexico	41.80
13	New Hampshire	41.58
14	Alaska	40.06
15	Indiana	38.90
16	Iowa	38.67
17	Oregon	36.65
18	Illinois	36.47
19	Rhode Island	36.38
20	Colorado	36.23
21	Texas	36.17
22	Hawaii	35.79
23	Vermont	33.59
24	Ohio	33.57
25	Arizona	32.79
26	Delaware	32.20
27	Pennsylvania	31.95
28	Michigan	31.90
29	Florida	31.87
30	New Jersey	31.60
31	Maryland	30.65
32	Nevada	27.52
33	West Virginia	27.36
34	Arkansas	27.22
35	South Carolina	26.91
36	Mississippi	26.26
37	Virginia	26.25
38	Louisiana	26.14
39	New York	25.77
40	California	25.52
41	Connecticut	25.42
42	Georgia	24.09
43	Missouri	23.73
44	Tennessee	21.63
45	Kentucky	21.47
46	North Carolina	20.08
47	Alabama	19.66
48	Massachusetts	19.42
NA	Kansas**	NA
NA	Montana**	NA

District of Columbia   12.69

Source: Morgan Quitno Press using data from Federal Bureau of Investigation
"Crime in the United States 1994" (Uniform Crime Reports, November 19, 1995)
*Arrests of youths 17 years and younger by law enforcement agencies submitting complete reports to the F.B.I. for 12 months in 1994. Crime index offenses consist of murder, forcible rape, robbery, aggravated assault, burglary, larceny-theft, motor vehicle theft and arson.
**Not available.

Reported Arrests of Juveniles for Violent Crime in 1994

National Total = 125,085 Reported Arrests*

ALPHA ORDER

RANK	STATE	ARRESTS	% of USA
24	Alabama	1,392	1.11%
39	Alaska	288	0.23%
13	Arizona	2,266	1.81%
28	Arkansas	927	0.74%
1	California	22,053	17.63%
23	Colorado	1,554	1.24%
22	Connecticut	1,608	1.29%
43	Delaware	149	0.12%
3	Florida	11,604	9.28%
14	Georgia	2,262	1.81%
38	Hawaii	326	0.26%
35	Idaho	412	0.33%
31	Illinois	755	0.60%
20	Indiana	1,734	1.39%
32	Iowa	742	0.59%
NA	Kansas**	NA	NA
29	Kentucky	772	0.62%
18	Louisiana	2,002	1.60%
41	Maine	174	0.14%
8	Maryland	3,562	2.85%
12	Massachusetts	2,381	1.90%
7	Michigan	4,126	3.30%
16	Minnesota	2,159	1.73%
36	Mississippi	337	0.27%
17	Missouri	2,062	1.65%
NA	Montana**	NA	NA
36	Nebraska	337	0.27%
33	Nevada	553	0.44%
45	New Hampshire	83	0.07%
5	New Jersey	5,737	4.59%
40	New Mexico	206	0.16%
2	New York	17,177	13.73%
10	North Carolina	3,213	2.57%
47	North Dakota	54	0.04%
9	Ohio	3,235	2.59%
25	Oklahoma	1,361	1.09%
26	Oregon	1,253	1.00%
6	Pennsylvania	5,359	4.28%
34	Rhode Island	500	0.40%
21	South Carolina	1,612	1.29%
42	South Dakota	153	0.12%
29	Tennessee	772	0.62%
4	Texas	9,151	7.32%
27	Utah	998	0.80%
48	Vermont	8	0.01%
19	Virginia	1,757	1.40%
15	Washington	2,205	1.76%
43	West Virginia	149	0.12%
11	Wisconsin	2,799	2.24%
46	Wyoming	77	0.06%

RANK ORDER

RANK	STATE	ARRESTS	% of USA
1	California	22,053	17.63%
2	New York	17,177	13.73%
3	Florida	11,604	9.28%
4	Texas	9,151	7.32%
5	New Jersey	5,737	4.59%
6	Pennsylvania	5,359	4.28%
7	Michigan	4,126	3.30%
8	Maryland	3,562	2.85%
9	Ohio	3,235	2.59%
10	North Carolina	3,213	2.57%
11	Wisconsin	2,799	2.24%
12	Massachusetts	2,381	1.90%
13	Arizona	2,266	1.81%
14	Georgia	2,262	1.81%
15	Washington	2,205	1.76%
16	Minnesota	2,159	1.73%
17	Missouri	2,062	1.65%
18	Louisiana	2,002	1.60%
19	Virginia	1,757	1.40%
20	Indiana	1,734	1.39%
21	South Carolina	1,612	1.29%
22	Connecticut	1,608	1.29%
23	Colorado	1,554	1.24%
24	Alabama	1,392	1.11%
25	Oklahoma	1,361	1.09%
26	Oregon	1,253	1.00%
27	Utah	998	0.80%
28	Arkansas	927	0.74%
29	Kentucky	772	0.62%
29	Tennessee	772	0.62%
31	Illinois	755	0.60%
32	Iowa	742	0.59%
33	Nevada	553	0.44%
34	Rhode Island	500	0.40%
35	Idaho	412	0.33%
36	Mississippi	337	0.27%
36	Nebraska	337	0.27%
38	Hawaii	326	0.26%
39	Alaska	288	0.23%
40	New Mexico	206	0.16%
41	Maine	174	0.14%
42	South Dakota	153	0.12%
43	Delaware	149	0.12%
43	West Virginia	149	0.12%
45	New Hampshire	83	0.07%
46	Wyoming	77	0.06%
47	North Dakota	54	0.04%
48	Vermont	8	0.01%
NA	Kansas**	NA	NA
NA	Montana**	NA	NA
	District of Columbia	689	0.55%

Source: Federal Bureau of Investigation
  "Crime in the United States 1994" (Uniform Crime Reports, November 19, 1995)
*Arrests of youths 17 years and younger by law enforcement agencies submitting complete reports to the F.B.I. for 12 months in 1994. Violent crimes are offenses of murder, forcible rape, robbery and aggravated assault.
**Not available.

Reported Juvenile Arrest Rate for Violent Crime in 1994

National Rate = 532.9 Reported Arrests per 100,000 Juvenile Population*

ALPHA ORDER

RANK	STATE	RATE
36	Alabama	308.7
26	Alaska	383.4
12	Arizona	495.5
35	Arkansas	318.4
5	California	643.0
10	Colorado	526.8
7	Connecticut	580.1
28	Delaware	371.8
2	Florida	856.3
15	Georgia	464.7
40	Hawaii	258.0
38	Idaho	261.4
27	Illinois	377.2
16	Indiana	462.7
41	Iowa	251.9
NA	Kansas**	NA
34	Kentucky	323.1
11	Louisiana	505.8
43	Maine	126.9
4	Maryland	683.8
6	Massachusetts	596.1
14	Michigan	466.3
22	Minnesota	412.9
33	Mississippi	325.4
9	Missouri	533.8
NA	Montana**	NA
42	Nebraska	182.5
24	Nevada	387.6
45	New Hampshire	105.1
3	New Jersey	732.7
23	New Mexico	394.0
1	New York	1,045.0
20	North Carolina	437.5
46	North Dakota	76.8
21	Ohio	416.1
31	Oklahoma	342.2
29	Oregon	357.4
8	Pennsylvania	542.2
13	Rhode Island	494.2
25	South Carolina	385.0
37	South Dakota	278.4
32	Tennessee	335.4
19	Texas	453.0
30	Utah	354.8
48	Vermont	23.7
39	Virginia	259.2
18	Washington	458.8
47	West Virginia	70.7
17	Wisconsin	462.0
44	Wyoming	120.4

RANK ORDER

RANK	STATE	RATE
1	New York	1,045.0
2	Florida	856.3
3	New Jersey	732.7
4	Maryland	683.8
5	California	643.0
6	Massachusetts	596.1
7	Connecticut	580.1
8	Pennsylvania	542.2
9	Missouri	533.8
10	Colorado	526.8
11	Louisiana	505.8
12	Arizona	495.5
13	Rhode Island	494.2
14	Michigan	466.3
15	Georgia	464.7
16	Indiana	462.7
17	Wisconsin	462.0
18	Washington	458.8
19	Texas	453.0
20	North Carolina	437.5
21	Ohio	416.1
22	Minnesota	412.9
23	New Mexico	394.0
24	Nevada	387.6
25	South Carolina	385.0
26	Alaska	383.4
27	Illinois	377.2
28	Delaware	371.8
29	Oregon	357.4
30	Utah	354.8
31	Oklahoma	342.2
32	Tennessee	335.4
33	Mississippi	325.4
34	Kentucky	323.1
35	Arkansas	318.4
36	Alabama	308.7
37	South Dakota	278.4
38	Idaho	261.4
39	Virginia	259.2
40	Hawaii	258.0
41	Iowa	251.9
42	Nebraska	182.5
43	Maine	126.9
44	Wyoming	120.4
45	New Hampshire	105.1
46	North Dakota	76.8
47	West Virginia	70.7
48	Vermont	23.7
NA	Kansas**	NA
NA	Montana**	NA
	District of Columbia	1,583.7

Source: Morgan Quitno Press using data from Federal Bureau of Investigation
   "Crime in the United States 1994" (Uniform Crime Reports, November 19, 1995)
*By law enforcement agencies submitting complete reports to the F.B.I. for 12 months in 1993. Arrests of youths 17 years and younger divided into population of 10 to 17 year olds. See important note at beginning of this chapter. Violent crimes are offenses of murder, forcible rape, robbery and aggravated assault.
**Not available.

Reported Arrests of Juveniles for Violent Crime
As a Percent of All Such Arrests in 1994
National Percent = 19.39% of Reported Arrests for Violent Crime*

ALPHA ORDER

RANK	STATE	PERCENT
44	Alabama	11.21
31	Alaska	17.88
18	Arizona	23.72
30	Arkansas	18.21
40	California	14.65
27	Colorado	19.22
28	Connecticut	18.56
25	Delaware	20.19
26	Florida	19.80
38	Georgia	14.84
16	Hawaii	24.64
5	Idaho	29.60
2	Illinois	32.03
15	Indiana	24.95
20	Iowa	22.48
NA	Kansas**	NA
48	Kentucky	8.46
35	Louisiana	16.87
24	Maine	21.04
9	Maryland	26.20
36	Massachusetts	15.90
29	Michigan	18.55
3	Minnesota	31.19
33	Mississippi	17.05
39	Missouri	14.79
NA	Montana**	NA
19	Nebraska	22.97
34	Nevada	16.88
32	New Hampshire	17.26
8	New Jersey	27.86
10	New Mexico	25.81
12	New York	25.68
43	North Carolina	12.44
6	North Dakota	28.57
21	Ohio	22.33
22	Oklahoma	22.10
14	Oregon	25.09
11	Pennsylvania	25.76
23	Rhode Island	21.53
37	South Carolina	15.87
13	South Dakota	25.12
45	Tennessee	10.58
17	Texas	24.62
1	Utah	38.92
47	Vermont	8.99
42	Virginia	13.22
7	Washington	28.05
46	West Virginia	10.00
4	Wisconsin	30.27
41	Wyoming	14.58

RANK ORDER

RANK	STATE	PERCENT
1	Utah	38.92
2	Illinois	32.03
3	Minnesota	31.19
4	Wisconsin	30.27
5	Idaho	29.60
6	North Dakota	28.57
7	Washington	28.05
8	New Jersey	27.86
9	Maryland	26.20
10	New Mexico	25.81
11	Pennsylvania	25.76
12	New York	25.68
13	South Dakota	25.12
14	Oregon	25.09
15	Indiana	24.95
16	Hawaii	24.64
17	Texas	24.62
18	Arizona	23.72
19	Nebraska	22.97
20	Iowa	22.48
21	Ohio	22.33
22	Oklahoma	22.10
23	Rhode Island	21.53
24	Maine	21.04
25	Delaware	20.19
26	Florida	19.80
27	Colorado	19.22
28	Connecticut	18.56
29	Michigan	18.55
30	Arkansas	18.21
31	Alaska	17.88
32	New Hampshire	17.26
33	Mississippi	17.05
34	Nevada	16.88
35	Louisiana	16.87
36	Massachusetts	15.90
37	South Carolina	15.87
38	Georgia	14.84
39	Missouri	14.79
40	California	14.65
41	Wyoming	14.58
42	Virginia	13.22
43	North Carolina	12.44
44	Alabama	11.21
45	Tennessee	10.58
46	West Virginia	10.00
47	Vermont	8.99
48	Kentucky	8.46
NA	Kansas**	NA
NA	Montana**	NA
	District of Columbia	13.62

Source: Morgan Quitno Press using data from Federal Bureau of Investigation
"Crime in the United States 1994" (Uniform Crime Reports, November 19, 1995)
*Arrests of youths 17 years and younger by law enforcement agencies submitting complete reports to the F.B.I. for 12 months in 1994. Violent crimes are offenses of murder, forcible rape, robbery and aggravated assault.
**Not available.

Reported Arrests of Juveniles for Murder in 1994

National Total = 3,102 Reported Arrests*

ALPHA ORDER

RANK	STATE	ARRESTS	% of USA
14	Alabama	68	2.19%
33	Alaska	12	0.39%
13	Arizona	69	2.22%
18	Arkansas	51	1.64%
1	California	545	17.57%
31	Colorado	14	0.45%
23	Connecticut	34	1.10%
40	Delaware	2	0.06%
5	Florida	197	6.35%
16	Georgia	60	1.93%
36	Hawaii	8	0.26%
38	Idaho	6	0.19%
28	Illinois	20	0.64%
29	Indiana	18	0.58%
40	Iowa	2	0.06%
NA	Kansas**	NA	NA
32	Kentucky	13	0.42%
12	Louisiana	75	2.42%
43	Maine	1	0.03%
7	Maryland	103	3.32%
30	Massachusetts	16	0.52%
4	Michigan	224	7.22%
23	Minnesota	34	1.10%
26	Mississippi	28	0.90%
6	Missouri	110	3.55%
NA	Montana**	NA	NA
34	Nebraska	10	0.32%
27	Nevada	22	0.71%
46	New Hampshire	0	0.00%
18	New Jersey	51	1.64%
36	New Mexico	8	0.26%
3	New York	266	8.58%
10	North Carolina	82	2.64%
46	North Dakota	0	0.00%
8	Ohio	101	3.26%
17	Oklahoma	52	1.68%
22	Oregon	35	1.13%
11	Pennsylvania	77	2.48%
40	Rhode Island	2	0.06%
20	South Carolina	48	1.55%
43	South Dakota	1	0.03%
25	Tennessee	32	1.03%
2	Texas	368	11.86%
35	Utah	9	0.29%
46	Vermont	0	0.00%
15	Virginia	66	2.13%
21	Washington	36	1.16%
38	West Virginia	6	0.19%
9	Wisconsin	93	3.00%
43	Wyoming	1	0.03%

RANK ORDER

RANK	STATE	ARRESTS	% of USA
1	California	545	17.57%
2	Texas	368	11.86%
3	New York	266	8.58%
4	Michigan	224	7.22%
5	Florida	197	6.35%
6	Missouri	110	3.55%
7	Maryland	103	3.32%
8	Ohio	101	3.26%
9	Wisconsin	93	3.00%
10	North Carolina	82	2.64%
11	Pennsylvania	77	2.48%
12	Louisiana	75	2.42%
13	Arizona	69	2.22%
14	Alabama	68	2.19%
15	Virginia	66	2.13%
16	Georgia	60	1.93%
17	Oklahoma	52	1.68%
18	Arkansas	51	1.64%
18	New Jersey	51	1.64%
20	South Carolina	48	1.55%
21	Washington	36	1.16%
22	Oregon	35	1.13%
23	Connecticut	34	1.10%
23	Minnesota	34	1.10%
25	Tennessee	32	1.03%
26	Mississippi	28	0.90%
27	Nevada	22	0.71%
28	Illinois	20	0.64%
29	Indiana	18	0.58%
30	Massachusetts	16	0.52%
31	Colorado	14	0.45%
32	Kentucky	13	0.42%
33	Alaska	12	0.39%
34	Nebraska	10	0.32%
35	Utah	9	0.29%
36	Hawaii	8	0.26%
36	New Mexico	8	0.26%
38	Idaho	6	0.19%
38	West Virginia	6	0.19%
40	Delaware	2	0.06%
40	Iowa	2	0.06%
40	Rhode Island	2	0.06%
43	Maine	1	0.03%
43	South Dakota	1	0.03%
43	Wyoming	1	0.03%
46	New Hampshire	0	0.00%
46	North Dakota	0	0.00%
46	Vermont	0	0.00%
NA	Kansas**	NA	NA
NA	Montana**	NA	NA
	District of Columbia	26	0.84%

Source: Federal Bureau of Investigation
   "Crime in the United States 1994" (Uniform Crime Reports, November 19, 1995)
*Arrests of youths 17 years and younger by law enforcement agencies submitting complete reports to the F.B.I. for 12 months in 1994. Includes nonnegligent manslaughter.
**Not available.

Reported Juvenile Arrest Rate for Murder in 1994

National Rate = 13.2 Reported Arrests per 100,000 Juvenile Population*

<table>
<tr><td colspan="3">ALPHA ORDER</td><td colspan="3">RANK ORDER</td></tr>
<tr><td>RANK</td><td>STATE</td><td>RATE</td><td>RANK</td><td>STATE</td><td>RATE</td></tr>
<tr><td>14</td><td>Alabama</td><td>15.1</td><td>1</td><td>Missouri</td><td>28.5</td></tr>
<tr><td>9</td><td>Alaska</td><td>16.0</td><td>2</td><td>Mississippi</td><td>27.0</td></tr>
<tr><td>14</td><td>Arizona</td><td>15.1</td><td>3</td><td>Michigan</td><td>25.3</td></tr>
<tr><td>7</td><td>Arkansas</td><td>17.5</td><td>4</td><td>Maryland</td><td>19.8</td></tr>
<tr><td>10</td><td>California</td><td>15.9</td><td>5</td><td>Louisiana</td><td>19.0</td></tr>
<tr><td>36</td><td>Colorado</td><td>4.7</td><td>6</td><td>Texas</td><td>18.2</td></tr>
<tr><td>20</td><td>Connecticut</td><td>12.3</td><td>7</td><td>Arkansas</td><td>17.5</td></tr>
<tr><td>34</td><td>Delaware</td><td>5.0</td><td>8</td><td>New York</td><td>16.2</td></tr>
<tr><td>16</td><td>Florida</td><td>14.5</td><td>9</td><td>Alaska</td><td>16.0</td></tr>
<tr><td>20</td><td>Georgia</td><td>12.3</td><td>10</td><td>California</td><td>15.9</td></tr>
<tr><td>31</td><td>Hawaii</td><td>6.3</td><td>11</td><td>Nevada</td><td>15.4</td></tr>
<tr><td>38</td><td>Idaho</td><td>3.8</td><td>11</td><td>Wisconsin</td><td>15.4</td></tr>
<tr><td>24</td><td>Illinois</td><td>10.0</td><td>13</td><td>New Mexico</td><td>15.3</td></tr>
<tr><td>35</td><td>Indiana</td><td>4.8</td><td>14</td><td>Alabama</td><td>15.1</td></tr>
<tr><td>44</td><td>Iowa</td><td>0.7</td><td>14</td><td>Arizona</td><td>15.1</td></tr>
<tr><td>NA</td><td>Kansas**</td><td>NA</td><td>16</td><td>Florida</td><td>14.5</td></tr>
<tr><td>32</td><td>Kentucky</td><td>5.4</td><td>17</td><td>Tennessee</td><td>13.9</td></tr>
<tr><td>5</td><td>Louisiana</td><td>19.0</td><td>18</td><td>Oklahoma</td><td>13.1</td></tr>
<tr><td>44</td><td>Maine</td><td>0.7</td><td>19</td><td>Ohio</td><td>13.0</td></tr>
<tr><td>4</td><td>Maryland</td><td>19.8</td><td>20</td><td>Connecticut</td><td>12.3</td></tr>
<tr><td>37</td><td>Massachusetts</td><td>4.0</td><td>20</td><td>Georgia</td><td>12.3</td></tr>
<tr><td>3</td><td>Michigan</td><td>25.3</td><td>22</td><td>South Carolina</td><td>11.5</td></tr>
<tr><td>29</td><td>Minnesota</td><td>6.5</td><td>23</td><td>North Carolina</td><td>11.2</td></tr>
<tr><td>2</td><td>Mississippi</td><td>27.0</td><td>24</td><td>Illinois</td><td>10.0</td></tr>
<tr><td>1</td><td>Missouri</td><td>28.5</td><td>24</td><td>Oregon</td><td>10.0</td></tr>
<tr><td>NA</td><td>Montana**</td><td>NA</td><td>26</td><td>Virginia</td><td>9.7</td></tr>
<tr><td>32</td><td>Nebraska</td><td>5.4</td><td>27</td><td>Pennsylvania</td><td>7.8</td></tr>
<tr><td>11</td><td>Nevada</td><td>15.4</td><td>28</td><td>Washington</td><td>7.5</td></tr>
<tr><td>46</td><td>New Hampshire</td><td>0.0</td><td>29</td><td>Minnesota</td><td>6.5</td></tr>
<tr><td>29</td><td>New Jersey</td><td>6.5</td><td>29</td><td>New Jersey</td><td>6.5</td></tr>
<tr><td>13</td><td>New Mexico</td><td>15.3</td><td>31</td><td>Hawaii</td><td>6.3</td></tr>
<tr><td>8</td><td>New York</td><td>16.2</td><td>32</td><td>Kentucky</td><td>5.4</td></tr>
<tr><td>23</td><td>North Carolina</td><td>11.2</td><td>32</td><td>Nebraska</td><td>5.4</td></tr>
<tr><td>46</td><td>North Dakota</td><td>0.0</td><td>34</td><td>Delaware</td><td>5.0</td></tr>
<tr><td>19</td><td>Ohio</td><td>13.0</td><td>35</td><td>Indiana</td><td>4.8</td></tr>
<tr><td>18</td><td>Oklahoma</td><td>13.1</td><td>36</td><td>Colorado</td><td>4.7</td></tr>
<tr><td>24</td><td>Oregon</td><td>10.0</td><td>37</td><td>Massachusetts</td><td>4.0</td></tr>
<tr><td>27</td><td>Pennsylvania</td><td>7.8</td><td>38</td><td>Idaho</td><td>3.8</td></tr>
<tr><td>41</td><td>Rhode Island</td><td>2.0</td><td>39</td><td>Utah</td><td>3.2</td></tr>
<tr><td>22</td><td>South Carolina</td><td>11.5</td><td>40</td><td>West Virginia</td><td>2.8</td></tr>
<tr><td>42</td><td>South Dakota</td><td>1.8</td><td>41</td><td>Rhode Island</td><td>2.0</td></tr>
<tr><td>17</td><td>Tennessee</td><td>13.9</td><td>42</td><td>South Dakota</td><td>1.8</td></tr>
<tr><td>6</td><td>Texas</td><td>18.2</td><td>43</td><td>Wyoming</td><td>1.6</td></tr>
<tr><td>39</td><td>Utah</td><td>3.2</td><td>44</td><td>Iowa</td><td>0.7</td></tr>
<tr><td>46</td><td>Vermont</td><td>0.0</td><td>44</td><td>Maine</td><td>0.7</td></tr>
<tr><td>26</td><td>Virginia</td><td>9.7</td><td>46</td><td>New Hampshire</td><td>0.0</td></tr>
<tr><td>28</td><td>Washington</td><td>7.5</td><td>46</td><td>North Dakota</td><td>0.0</td></tr>
<tr><td>40</td><td>West Virginia</td><td>2.8</td><td>46</td><td>Vermont</td><td>0.0</td></tr>
<tr><td>11</td><td>Wisconsin</td><td>15.4</td><td>NA</td><td>Kansas**</td><td>NA</td></tr>
<tr><td>43</td><td>Wyoming</td><td>1.6</td><td>NA</td><td>Montana**</td><td>NA</td></tr>
<tr><td></td><td></td><td></td><td></td><td>District of Columbia</td><td>59.8</td></tr>
</table>

Source: Morgan Quitno Press using data from Federal Bureau of Investigation
"Crime in the United States 1994" (Uniform Crime Reports, November 19, 1995)
*By law enforcement agencies submitting complete reports to the F.B.I. for 12 months in 1994. Includes nonnegligent manslaughter. Arrests of youths 17 years and younger divided into population of 10 to 17 year olds. See important note at beginning of this chapter.
**Not available.

Reported Arrests of Juveniles for Murder
As a Percent of All Such Arrests in 1994
National Percent = 16.77% of Reported Arrests for Murder*

ALPHA ORDER

RANK	STATE	PERCENT
27	Alabama	14.50
1	Alaska	34.29
9	Arizona	21.10
19	Arkansas	17.06
14	California	18.33
39	Colorado	8.64
16	Connecticut	17.62
2	Delaware	33.33
23	Florida	16.47
29	Georgia	13.99
36	Hawaii	12.90
22	Idaho	16.67
15	Illinois	17.86
37	Indiana	11.39
42	Iowa	7.69
NA	Kansas**	NA
43	Kentucky	7.14
26	Louisiana	15.00
40	Maine	8.33
17	Maryland	17.55
35	Massachusetts	13.01
32	Michigan	13.58
11	Minnesota	20.00
21	Mississippi	16.87
13	Missouri	18.52
NA	Montana**	NA
6	Nebraska	22.73
34	Nevada	13.02
46	New Hampshire	0.00
25	New Jersey	15.99
3	New Mexico	25.00
20	New York	17.01
38	North Carolina	10.88
46	North Dakota	0.00
10	Ohio	20.49
8	Oklahoma	21.76
18	Oregon	17.07
33	Pennsylvania	13.37
44	Rhode Island	6.45
30	South Carolina	13.95
28	South Dakota	14.29
24	Tennessee	16.08
4	Texas	24.02
5	Utah	23.08
46	Vermont	0.00
31	Virginia	13.87
12	Washington	19.05
45	West Virginia	5.77
7	Wisconsin	22.25
40	Wyoming	8.33

RANK ORDER

RANK	STATE	PERCENT
1	Alaska	34.29
2	Delaware	33.33
3	New Mexico	25.00
4	Texas	24.02
5	Utah	23.08
6	Nebraska	22.73
7	Wisconsin	22.25
8	Oklahoma	21.76
9	Arizona	21.10
10	Ohio	20.49
11	Minnesota	20.00
12	Washington	19.05
13	Missouri	18.52
14	California	18.33
15	Illinois	17.86
16	Connecticut	17.62
17	Maryland	17.55
18	Oregon	17.07
19	Arkansas	17.06
20	New York	17.01
21	Mississippi	16.87
22	Idaho	16.67
23	Florida	16.47
24	Tennessee	16.08
25	New Jersey	15.99
26	Louisiana	15.00
27	Alabama	14.50
28	South Dakota	14.29
29	Georgia	13.99
30	South Carolina	13.95
31	Virginia	13.87
32	Michigan	13.58
33	Pennsylvania	13.37
34	Nevada	13.02
35	Massachusetts	13.01
36	Hawaii	12.90
37	Indiana	11.39
38	North Carolina	10.88
39	Colorado	8.64
40	Maine	8.33
40	Wyoming	8.33
42	Iowa	7.69
43	Kentucky	7.14
44	Rhode Island	6.45
45	West Virginia	5.77
46	New Hampshire	0.00
46	North Dakota	0.00
46	Vermont	0.00
NA	Kansas**	NA
NA	Montana**	NA
	District of Columbia	9.39

Source: Morgan Quitno Press using data from Federal Bureau of Investigation
"Crime in the United States 1994" (Uniform Crime Reports, November 19, 1995)
*Arrests of youths 17 years and younger by law enforcement agencies submitting complete reports to the F.B.I. for 12 months in 1994. Includes nonnegligent manslaughter.
**Not available.

Reported Arrests of Juveniles for Rape in 1994

National Total = 4,859 Reported Arrests*

ALPHA ORDER

RANK	STATE	ARRESTS	% of USA
30	Alabama	34	0.70%
35	Alaska	30	0.62%
30	Arizona	34	0.70%
23	Arkansas	56	1.15%
1	California	459	9.45%
22	Colorado	62	1.28%
23	Connecticut	56	1.15%
37	Delaware	25	0.51%
2	Florida	395	8.13%
15	Georgia	95	1.96%
36	Hawaii	26	0.54%
45	Idaho	6	0.12%
20	Illinois	69	1.42%
41	Indiana	11	0.23%
32	Iowa	32	0.66%
NA	Kansas**	NA	NA
28	Kentucky	43	0.88%
18	Louisiana	71	1.46%
39	Maine	18	0.37%
11	Maryland	165	3.40%
20	Massachusetts	69	1.42%
4	Michigan	286	5.89%
10	Minnesota	216	4.45%
33	Mississippi	31	0.64%
14	Missouri	99	2.04%
NA	Montana**	NA	NA
29	Nebraska	39	0.80%
33	Nevada	31	0.64%
40	New Hampshire	17	0.35%
8	New Jersey	232	4.77%
47	New Mexico	3	0.06%
6	New York	269	5.54%
16	North Carolina	94	1.93%
41	North Dakota	11	0.23%
5	Ohio	281	5.78%
18	Oklahoma	71	1.46%
26	Oregon	50	1.03%
7	Pennsylvania	266	5.47%
38	Rhode Island	22	0.45%
13	South Carolina	114	2.35%
43	South Dakota	8	0.16%
27	Tennessee	44	0.91%
3	Texas	394	8.11%
25	Utah	51	1.05%
48	Vermont	1	0.02%
17	Virginia	92	1.89%
9	Washington	224	4.61%
43	West Virginia	8	0.16%
12	Wisconsin	136	2.80%
46	Wyoming	4	0.08%

RANK ORDER

RANK	STATE	ARRESTS	% of USA
1	California	459	9.45%
2	Florida	395	8.13%
3	Texas	394	8.11%
4	Michigan	286	5.89%
5	Ohio	281	5.78%
6	New York	269	5.54%
7	Pennsylvania	266	5.47%
8	New Jersey	232	4.77%
9	Washington	224	4.61%
10	Minnesota	216	4.45%
11	Maryland	165	3.40%
12	Wisconsin	136	2.80%
13	South Carolina	114	2.35%
14	Missouri	99	2.04%
15	Georgia	95	1.96%
16	North Carolina	94	1.93%
17	Virginia	92	1.89%
18	Louisiana	71	1.46%
18	Oklahoma	71	1.46%
20	Illinois	69	1.42%
20	Massachusetts	69	1.42%
22	Colorado	62	1.28%
23	Arkansas	56	1.15%
23	Connecticut	56	1.15%
25	Utah	51	1.05%
26	Oregon	50	1.03%
27	Tennessee	44	0.91%
28	Kentucky	43	0.88%
29	Nebraska	39	0.80%
30	Alabama	34	0.70%
30	Arizona	34	0.70%
32	Iowa	32	0.66%
33	Mississippi	31	0.64%
33	Nevada	31	0.64%
35	Alaska	30	0.62%
36	Hawaii	26	0.54%
37	Delaware	25	0.51%
38	Rhode Island	22	0.45%
39	Maine	18	0.37%
40	New Hampshire	17	0.35%
41	Indiana	11	0.23%
41	North Dakota	11	0.23%
43	South Dakota	8	0.16%
43	West Virginia	8	0.16%
45	Idaho	6	0.12%
46	Wyoming	4	0.08%
47	New Mexico	3	0.06%
48	Vermont	1	0.02%
NA	Kansas**	NA	NA
NA	Montana**	NA	NA
	District of Columbia	9	0.19%

Source: Federal Bureau of Investigation
   "Crime in the United States 1994" (Uniform Crime Reports, November 19, 1995)
*Arrests of youths 17 years and younger by law enforcement agencies submitting complete reports to the F.B.I. for 12 months in 1994. Forcible rape is the carnal knowledge of a female forcibly and against her will. Assaults or attempts to commit rape by force or threat of force are included. However, statutory rape without force and other sex offenses are excluded. **Not available.

Reported Juvenile Arrest Rate for Rape in 1994

National Rate = 20.7 Arrests per 100,000 Juvenile Population*

ALPHA ORDER

RANK ORDER

RANK	STATE	RATE
41	Alabama	7.5
4	Alaska	39.9
42	Arizona	7.4
25	Arkansas	19.2
37	California	13.4
20	Colorado	21.0
22	Connecticut	20.2
1	Delaware	62.4
11	Florida	29.1
23	Georgia	19.5
21	Hawaii	20.6
45	Idaho	3.8
6	Illinois	34.5
48	Indiana	2.9
40	Iowa	10.9
NA	Kansas**	NA
28	Kentucky	18.0
29	Louisiana	17.9
38	Maine	13.1
8	Maryland	31.7
31	Massachusetts	17.3
7	Michigan	32.3
3	Minnesota	41.3
9	Mississippi	29.9
14	Missouri	25.6
NA	Montana**	NA
19	Nebraska	21.1
16	Nevada	21.7
18	New Hampshire	21.5
10	New Jersey	29.6
44	New Mexico	5.7
32	New York	16.4
39	North Carolina	12.8
33	North Dakota	15.6
5	Ohio	36.1
29	Oklahoma	17.9
35	Oregon	14.3
13	Pennsylvania	26.9
16	Rhode Island	21.7
12	South Carolina	27.2
34	South Dakota	14.6
26	Tennessee	19.1
23	Texas	19.5
27	Utah	18.1
47	Vermont	3.0
36	Virginia	13.6
2	Washington	46.6
45	West Virginia	3.8
15	Wisconsin	22.4
43	Wyoming	6.3

RANK	STATE	RATE
1	Delaware	62.4
2	Washington	46.6
3	Minnesota	41.3
4	Alaska	39.9
5	Ohio	36.1
6	Illinois	34.5
7	Michigan	32.3
8	Maryland	31.7
9	Mississippi	29.9
10	New Jersey	29.6
11	Florida	29.1
12	South Carolina	27.2
13	Pennsylvania	26.9
14	Missouri	25.6
15	Wisconsin	22.4
16	Nevada	21.7
16	Rhode Island	21.7
18	New Hampshire	21.5
19	Nebraska	21.1
20	Colorado	21.0
21	Hawaii	20.6
22	Connecticut	20.2
23	Georgia	19.5
23	Texas	19.5
25	Arkansas	19.2
26	Tennessee	19.1
27	Utah	18.1
28	Kentucky	18.0
29	Louisiana	17.9
29	Oklahoma	17.9
31	Massachusetts	17.3
32	New York	16.4
33	North Dakota	15.6
34	South Dakota	14.6
35	Oregon	14.3
36	Virginia	13.6
37	California	13.4
38	Maine	13.1
39	North Carolina	12.8
40	Iowa	10.9
41	Alabama	7.5
42	Arizona	7.4
43	Wyoming	6.3
44	New Mexico	5.7
45	Idaho	3.8
45	West Virginia	3.8
47	Vermont	3.0
48	Indiana	2.9
NA	Kansas**	NA
NA	Montana**	NA

District of Columbia   20.7

Source: Morgan Quitno Press using data from Federal Bureau of Investigation
"Crime in the United States 1994" (Uniform Crime Reports, November 19, 1995)
*By law enforcement agencies submitting complete reports to the F.B.I. for 12 months in 1994. Arrests of youths 17 years and younger divided into population of 10 to 17 year olds. See important note at beginning of this chapter. Forcible rape is the carnal knowledge of a female forcibly and against her will. Assaults or attempts to commit rape by force or threat of force are included. **Not available.

Reported Arrests of Juveniles for Rape
As a Percent of All Such Arrests in 1994
National Percent = 16.31% of Arrests for Rape*

ALPHA ORDER

RANK STATE | PERCENT

RANK	STATE	PERCENT
45	Alabama	7.01
5	Alaska	25.42
31	Arizona	13.82
34	Arkansas	12.25
29	California	13.90
32	Colorado	13.28
28	Connecticut	14.74
6	Delaware	24.51
21	Florida	16.69
22	Georgia	16.52
18	Hawaii	17.45
43	Idaho	8.82
1	Illinois	32.86
44	Indiana	7.86
9	Iowa	23.70
NA	Kansas**	NA
41	Kentucky	10.54
27	Louisiana	14.82
15	Maine	19.15
17	Maryland	18.13
38	Massachusetts	11.17
25	Michigan	15.19
13	Minnesota	20.67
19	Mississippi	17.22
26	Missouri	14.89
NA	Montana**	NA
16	Nebraska	18.14
39	Nevada	11.03
8	New Hampshire	23.94
12	New Jersey	21.87
47	New Mexico	5.56
30	New York	13.87
35	North Carolina	11.82
3	North Dakota	30.56
10	Ohio	22.68
23	Oklahoma	15.88
33	Oregon	13.02
11	Pennsylvania	22.60
4	Rhode Island	26.19
20	South Carolina	17.04
40	South Dakota	10.96
37	Tennessee	11.25
24	Texas	15.73
2	Utah	31.10
48	Vermont	3.70
36	Virginia	11.39
7	Washington	24.22
46	West Virginia	5.76
14	Wisconsin	19.80
42	Wyoming	9.76

RANK ORDER

RANK	STATE	PERCENT
1	Illinois	32.86
2	Utah	31.10
3	North Dakota	30.56
4	Rhode Island	26.19
5	Alaska	25.42
6	Delaware	24.51
7	Washington	24.22
8	New Hampshire	23.94
9	Iowa	23.70
10	Ohio	22.68
11	Pennsylvania	22.60
12	New Jersey	21.87
13	Minnesota	20.67
14	Wisconsin	19.80
15	Maine	19.15
16	Nebraska	18.14
17	Maryland	18.13
18	Hawaii	17.45
19	Mississippi	17.22
20	South Carolina	17.04
21	Florida	16.69
22	Georgia	16.52
23	Oklahoma	15.88
24	Texas	15.73
25	Michigan	15.19
26	Missouri	14.89
27	Louisiana	14.82
28	Connecticut	14.74
29	California	13.90
30	New York	13.87
31	Arizona	13.82
32	Colorado	13.28
33	Oregon	13.02
34	Arkansas	12.25
35	North Carolina	11.82
36	Virginia	11.39
37	Tennessee	11.25
38	Massachusetts	11.17
39	Nevada	11.03
40	South Dakota	10.96
41	Kentucky	10.54
42	Wyoming	9.76
43	Idaho	8.82
44	Indiana	7.86
45	Alabama	7.01
46	West Virginia	5.76
47	New Mexico	5.56
48	Vermont	3.70
NA	Kansas**	NA
NA	Montana**	NA
	District of Columbia	9.47

Source: Morgan Quitno Press using data from Federal Bureau of Investigation
    "Crime in the United States 1994" (Uniform Crime Reports, November 19, 1995)
*Arrests of youths 17 years and younger by law enforcement agencies submitting complete reports to the F.B.I. for 12 months in 1994. Forcible rape is the carnal knowledge of a female forcibly and against her will. Assaults or attempts to commit rape by force or threat of force are included. However, statutory rape without force and other sex offenses are excluded. **Not available.

Reported Arrests of Juveniles for Robbery in 1994

National Total = 47,094 Reported Arrests*

ALPHA ORDER

RANK	STATE	ARRESTS	% of USA
21	Alabama	422	0.90%
38	Alaska	59	0.13%
19	Arizona	435	0.92%
26	Arkansas	267	0.57%
2	California	8,946	19.00%
23	Colorado	380	0.81%
18	Connecticut	559	1.19%
42	Delaware	26	0.06%
3	Florida	3,693	7.84%
13	Georgia	688	1.46%
33	Hawaii	144	0.31%
41	Idaho	40	0.08%
29	Illinois	209	0.44%
28	Indiana	239	0.51%
36	Iowa	98	0.21%
NA	Kansas**	NA	NA
32	Kentucky	160	0.34%
20	Louisiana	423	0.90%
40	Maine	50	0.11%
9	Maryland	1,230	2.61%
16	Massachusetts	621	1.32%
8	Michigan	1,231	2.61%
14	Minnesota	656	1.39%
35	Mississippi	107	0.23%
12	Missouri	731	1.55%
NA	Montana**	NA	NA
34	Nebraska	126	0.27%
27	Nevada	253	0.54%
46	New Hampshire	15	0.03%
5	New Jersey	2,225	4.72%
42	New Mexico	26	0.06%
1	New York	11,092	23.55%
11	North Carolina	795	1.69%
47	North Dakota	8	0.02%
7	Ohio	1,463	3.11%
25	Oklahoma	374	0.79%
22	Oregon	421	0.89%
6	Pennsylvania	2,189	4.65%
37	Rhode Island	93	0.20%
24	South Carolina	377	0.80%
45	South Dakota	18	0.04%
30	Tennessee	200	0.42%
4	Texas	3,321	7.05%
31	Utah	194	0.41%
48	Vermont	0	0.00%
17	Virginia	597	1.27%
15	Washington	641	1.36%
39	West Virginia	51	0.11%
10	Wisconsin	924	1.96%
44	Wyoming	21	0.04%

RANK ORDER

RANK	STATE	ARRESTS	% of USA
1	New York	11,092	23.55%
2	California	8,946	19.00%
3	Florida	3,693	7.84%
4	Texas	3,321	7.05%
5	New Jersey	2,225	4.72%
6	Pennsylvania	2,189	4.65%
7	Ohio	1,463	3.11%
8	Michigan	1,231	2.61%
9	Maryland	1,230	2.61%
10	Wisconsin	924	1.96%
11	North Carolina	795	1.69%
12	Missouri	731	1.55%
13	Georgia	688	1.46%
14	Minnesota	656	1.39%
15	Washington	641	1.36%
16	Massachusetts	621	1.32%
17	Virginia	597	1.27%
18	Connecticut	559	1.19%
19	Arizona	435	0.92%
20	Louisiana	423	0.90%
21	Alabama	422	0.90%
22	Oregon	421	0.89%
23	Colorado	380	0.81%
24	South Carolina	377	0.80%
25	Oklahoma	374	0.79%
26	Arkansas	267	0.57%
27	Nevada	253	0.54%
28	Indiana	239	0.51%
29	Illinois	209	0.44%
30	Tennessee	200	0.42%
31	Utah	194	0.41%
32	Kentucky	160	0.34%
33	Hawaii	144	0.31%
34	Nebraska	126	0.27%
35	Mississippi	107	0.23%
36	Iowa	98	0.21%
37	Rhode Island	93	0.20%
38	Alaska	59	0.13%
39	West Virginia	51	0.11%
40	Maine	50	0.11%
41	Idaho	40	0.08%
42	Delaware	26	0.06%
42	New Mexico	26	0.06%
44	Wyoming	21	0.04%
45	South Dakota	18	0.04%
46	New Hampshire	15	0.03%
47	North Dakota	8	0.02%
48	Vermont	0	0.00%
NA	Kansas**	NA	NA
NA	Montana**	NA	NA
	District of Columbia	256	0.54%

Source: Federal Bureau of Investigation
   "Crime in the United States 1994" (Uniform Crime Reports, November 19, 1995)
*Arrests of youths 17 years and younger by law enforcement agencies submitting complete reports to the F.B.I. for 12 months in 1994. Robbery is the taking or attempting to take anything of value by force or threat of force.
**Not available.

Reported Juvenile Arrest Rate for Robbery in 1994

National Rate = 200.6 Reported Arrests per 100,000 Juvenile Population*

ALPHA ORDER

RANK	STATE	RATE
27	Alabama	93.6
33	Alaska	78.5
25	Arizona	95.1
29	Arkansas	91.7
4	California	260.8
17	Colorado	128.8
7	Connecticut	201.7
37	Delaware	64.9
3	Florida	272.5
14	Georgia	141.3
20	Hawaii	114.0
44	Idaho	25.4
23	Illinois	104.4
38	Indiana	63.8
41	Iowa	33.3
NA	Kansas**	NA
36	Kentucky	67.0
22	Louisiana	106.9
40	Maine	36.5
5	Maryland	236.1
12	Massachusetts	155.5
15	Michigan	139.1
18	Minnesota	125.5
24	Mississippi	103.3
8	Missouri	189.2
NA	Montana**	NA
35	Nebraska	68.3
10	Nevada	177.3
46	New Hampshire	19.0
2	New Jersey	284.2
39	New Mexico	49.7
1	New York	674.8
21	North Carolina	108.3
47	North Dakota	11.4
9	Ohio	188.2
26	Oklahoma	94.0
19	Oregon	120.1
6	Pennsylvania	221.5
28	Rhode Island	91.9
30	South Carolina	90.0
43	South Dakota	32.7
32	Tennessee	86.9
11	Texas	164.4
34	Utah	69.0
48	Vermont	0.0
31	Virginia	88.1
16	Washington	133.4
45	West Virginia	24.2
13	Wisconsin	152.5
42	Wyoming	32.8

RANK ORDER

RANK	STATE	RATE
1	New York	674.8
2	New Jersey	284.2
3	Florida	272.5
4	California	260.8
5	Maryland	236.1
6	Pennsylvania	221.5
7	Connecticut	201.7
8	Missouri	189.2
9	Ohio	188.2
10	Nevada	177.3
11	Texas	164.4
12	Massachusetts	155.5
13	Wisconsin	152.5
14	Georgia	141.3
15	Michigan	139.1
16	Washington	133.4
17	Colorado	128.8
18	Minnesota	125.5
19	Oregon	120.1
20	Hawaii	114.0
21	North Carolina	108.3
22	Louisiana	106.9
23	Illinois	104.4
24	Mississippi	103.3
25	Arizona	95.1
26	Oklahoma	94.0
27	Alabama	93.6
28	Rhode Island	91.9
29	Arkansas	91.7
30	South Carolina	90.0
31	Virginia	88.1
32	Tennessee	86.9
33	Alaska	78.5
34	Utah	69.0
35	Nebraska	68.3
36	Kentucky	67.0
37	Delaware	64.9
38	Indiana	63.8
39	New Mexico	49.7
40	Maine	36.5
41	Iowa	33.3
42	Wyoming	32.8
43	South Dakota	32.7
44	Idaho	25.4
45	West Virginia	24.2
46	New Hampshire	19.0
47	North Dakota	11.4
48	Vermont	0.0
NA	Kansas**	NA
NA	Montana**	NA

District of Columbia 588.4

Source: Morgan Quitno Press using data from Federal Bureau of Investigation
"Crime in the United States 1994" (Uniform Crime Reports, November 19, 1995)
*By law enforcement agencies submitting complete reports to the F.B.I. for 12 months in 1994. Arrests of youths 17 years and younger divided into population of 10 to 17 year olds. See important note at beginning of this chapter. Robbery is the taking or attempting to take anything of value by force or threat of force.
**Not available.

Reported Arrests of Juveniles for Robbery
As a Percent of All Such Arrests in 1994
National Percent = 32.04% of Reported Arrests for Robbery*

RANK	STATE	PERCENT
43	Alabama	20.24
21	Alaska	32.07
26	Arizona	28.64
30	Arkansas	26.92
22	California	31.98
15	Colorado	35.71
35	Connecticut	25.63
32	Delaware	26.53
19	Florida	32.81
39	Georgia	21.77
23	Hawaii	31.37
6	Idaho	40.00
10	Illinois	38.14
25	Indiana	29.18
18	Iowa	33.91
NA	Kansas**	NA
46	Kentucky	17.20
36	Louisiana	24.56
5	Maine	40.98
31	Maryland	26.83
29	Massachusetts	27.02
28	Michigan	27.04
2	Minnesota	44.87
45	Mississippi	19.14
34	Missouri	25.66
NA	Montana**	NA
8	Nebraska	39.38
40	Nevada	20.89
44	New Hampshire	19.74
13	New Jersey	37.20
17	New Mexico	35.14
12	New York	37.81
41	North Carolina	20.71
33	North Dakota	25.81
20	Ohio	32.56
14	Oklahoma	36.24
27	Oregon	28.47
24	Pennsylvania	30.45
9	Rhode Island	39.24
37	South Carolina	24.43
16	South Dakota	35.29
47	Tennessee	16.47
11	Texas	38.05
1	Utah	47.67
48	Vermont	0.00
38	Virginia	23.14
7	Washington	39.45
42	West Virginia	20.65
4	Wisconsin	41.05
3	Wyoming	42.86

RANK	STATE	PERCENT
1	Utah	47.67
2	Minnesota	44.87
3	Wyoming	42.86
4	Wisconsin	41.05
5	Maine	40.98
6	Idaho	40.00
7	Washington	39.45
8	Nebraska	39.38
9	Rhode Island	39.24
10	Illinois	38.14
11	Texas	38.05
12	New York	37.81
13	New Jersey	37.20
14	Oklahoma	36.24
15	Colorado	35.71
16	South Dakota	35.29
17	New Mexico	35.14
18	Iowa	33.91
19	Florida	32.81
20	Ohio	32.56
21	Alaska	32.07
22	California	31.98
23	Hawaii	31.37
24	Pennsylvania	30.45
25	Indiana	29.18
26	Arizona	28.64
27	Oregon	28.47
28	Michigan	27.04
29	Massachusetts	27.02
30	Arkansas	26.92
31	Maryland	26.83
32	Delaware	26.53
33	North Dakota	25.81
34	Missouri	25.66
35	Connecticut	25.63
36	Louisiana	24.56
37	South Carolina	24.43
38	Virginia	23.14
39	Georgia	21.77
40	Nevada	20.89
41	North Carolina	20.71
42	West Virginia	20.65
43	Alabama	20.24
44	New Hampshire	19.74
45	Mississippi	19.14
46	Kentucky	17.20
47	Tennessee	16.47
48	Vermont	0.00
NA	Kansas**	NA
NA	Montana**	NA
	District of Columbia	21.82

Source: Morgan Quitno Press using data from Federal Bureau of Investigation
"Crime in the United States 1994" (Uniform Crime Reports, November 19, 1995)
Arrests of youths 17 years and younger by law enforcement agencies submitting complete reports to the F.B.I. for 12 months in 1994. Robbery is the taking or attempting to take anything of value by force or threat of force.
**Not available.*

Reported Arrests of Juveniles for Aggravated Assault in 1994

National total = 70,030 Reported Arrests*

ALPHA ORDER

RANK	STATE	ARRESTS	% of USA
24	Alabama	868	1.24%
36	Alaska	187	0.27%
10	Arizona	1,728	2.47%
30	Arkansas	553	0.79%
1	California	12,103	17.28%
20	Colorado	1,098	1.57%
23	Connecticut	959	1.37%
43	Delaware	96	0.14%
2	Florida	7,319	10.45%
15	Georgia	1,419	2.03%
40	Hawaii	148	0.21%
34	Idaho	360	0.51%
32	Illinois	457	0.65%
13	Indiana	1,466	2.09%
28	Iowa	610	0.87%
NA	Kansas**	NA	NA
29	Kentucky	556	0.79%
14	Louisiana	1,433	2.05%
42	Maine	105	0.15%
9	Maryland	2,064	2.95%
11	Massachusetts	1,675	2.39%
7	Michigan	2,385	3.41%
18	Minnesota	1,253	1.79%
37	Mississippi	171	0.24%
19	Missouri	1,122	1.60%
NA	Montana**	NA	NA
39	Nebraska	162	0.23%
35	Nevada	247	0.35%
45	New Hampshire	51	0.07%
5	New Jersey	3,229	4.61%
38	New Mexico	169	0.24%
3	New York	5,550	7.93%
8	North Carolina	2,242	3.20%
47	North Dakota	35	0.05%
16	Ohio	1,390	1.98%
25	Oklahoma	864	1.23%
26	Oregon	747	1.07%
6	Pennsylvania	2,827	4.04%
33	Rhode Island	383	0.55%
21	South Carolina	1,073	1.53%
41	South Dakota	126	0.18%
31	Tennessee	496	0.71%
4	Texas	5,068	7.24%
27	Utah	744	1.06%
48	Vermont	7	0.01%
22	Virginia	1,002	1.43%
17	Washington	1,304	1.86%
44	West Virginia	84	0.12%
12	Wisconsin	1,646	2.35%
45	Wyoming	51	0.07%

RANK ORDER

RANK	STATE	ARRESTS	% of USA
1	California	12,103	17.28%
2	Florida	7,319	10.45%
3	New York	5,550	7.93%
4	Texas	5,068	7.24%
5	New Jersey	3,229	4.61%
6	Pennsylvania	2,827	4.04%
7	Michigan	2,385	3.41%
8	North Carolina	2,242	3.20%
9	Maryland	2,064	2.95%
10	Arizona	1,728	2.47%
11	Massachusetts	1,675	2.39%
12	Wisconsin	1,646	2.35%
13	Indiana	1,466	2.09%
14	Louisiana	1,433	2.05%
15	Georgia	1,419	2.03%
16	Ohio	1,390	1.98%
17	Washington	1,304	1.86%
18	Minnesota	1,253	1.79%
19	Missouri	1,122	1.60%
20	Colorado	1,098	1.57%
21	South Carolina	1,073	1.53%
22	Virginia	1,002	1.43%
23	Connecticut	959	1.37%
24	Alabama	868	1.24%
25	Oklahoma	864	1.23%
26	Oregon	747	1.07%
27	Utah	744	1.06%
28	Iowa	610	0.87%
29	Kentucky	556	0.79%
30	Arkansas	553	0.79%
31	Tennessee	496	0.71%
32	Illinois	457	0.65%
33	Rhode Island	383	0.55%
34	Idaho	360	0.51%
35	Nevada	247	0.35%
36	Alaska	187	0.27%
37	Mississippi	171	0.24%
38	New Mexico	169	0.24%
39	Nebraska	162	0.23%
40	Hawaii	148	0.21%
41	South Dakota	126	0.18%
42	Maine	105	0.15%
43	Delaware	96	0.14%
44	West Virginia	84	0.12%
45	New Hampshire	51	0.07%
45	Wyoming	51	0.07%
47	North Dakota	35	0.05%
48	Vermont	7	0.01%
NA	Kansas**	NA	NA
NA	Montana**	NA	NA
	District of Columbia	398	0.57%

Source: Federal Bureau of Investigation
   "Crime in the United States 1994" (Uniform Crime Reports, November 19, 1995)
*Arrests of youths 17 years and younger by law enforcement agencies submitting complete reports to the F.B.I. for 12 months in 1994. Aggravated assault is an attack for the purpose of inflicting severe bodily injury.
**Not available.

Reported Juvenile Arrest Rate for Aggravated Assault in 1994

National Rate = 298.4 Reported Arrests per 100,000 Juvenile Population*

ALPHA ORDER

RANK	STATE	RATE
35	Alabama	192.5
24	Alaska	249.0
7	Arizona	377.9
36	Arkansas	189.9
10	California	352.9
8	Colorado	372.2
11	Connecticut	346.0
25	Delaware	239.6
1	Florida	540.1
15	Georgia	291.5
41	Hawaii	117.1
29	Idaho	228.4
30	Illinois	228.3
5	Indiana	391.2
34	Iowa	207.1
NA	Kansas**	NA
27	Kentucky	232.7
9	Louisiana	362.1
44	Maine	76.6
4	Maryland	396.3
2	Massachusetts	419.4
20	Michigan	269.5
25	Minnesota	239.6
39	Mississippi	165.1
16	Missouri	290.4
NA	Montana**	NA
42	Nebraska	87.8
38	Nevada	173.1
45	New Hampshire	64.6
3	New Jersey	412.4
13	New Mexico	323.2
12	New York	337.6
14	North Carolina	305.3
46	North Dakota	49.8
37	Ohio	178.8
31	Oklahoma	217.2
33	Oregon	213.1
17	Pennsylvania	286.0
6	Rhode Island	378.6
22	South Carolina	256.3
28	South Dakota	229.2
32	Tennessee	215.5
23	Texas	250.9
21	Utah	264.5
48	Vermont	20.8
40	Virginia	147.8
19	Washington	271.3
47	West Virginia	39.9
18	Wisconsin	271.7
43	Wyoming	79.8

RANK ORDER

RANK	STATE	RATE
1	Florida	540.1
2	Massachusetts	419.4
3	New Jersey	412.4
4	Maryland	396.3
5	Indiana	391.2
6	Rhode Island	378.6
7	Arizona	377.9
8	Colorado	372.2
9	Louisiana	362.1
10	California	352.9
11	Connecticut	346.0
12	New York	337.6
13	New Mexico	323.2
14	North Carolina	305.3
15	Georgia	291.5
16	Missouri	290.4
17	Pennsylvania	286.0
18	Wisconsin	271.7
19	Washington	271.3
20	Michigan	269.5
21	Utah	264.5
22	South Carolina	256.3
23	Texas	250.9
24	Alaska	249.0
25	Delaware	239.6
25	Minnesota	239.6
27	Kentucky	232.7
28	South Dakota	229.2
29	Idaho	228.4
30	Illinois	228.3
31	Oklahoma	217.2
32	Tennessee	215.5
33	Oregon	213.1
34	Iowa	207.1
35	Alabama	192.5
36	Arkansas	189.9
37	Ohio	178.8
38	Nevada	173.1
39	Mississippi	165.1
40	Virginia	147.8
41	Hawaii	117.1
42	Nebraska	87.8
43	Wyoming	79.8
44	Maine	76.6
45	New Hampshire	64.6
46	North Dakota	49.8
47	West Virginia	39.9
48	Vermont	20.8
NA	Kansas**	NA
NA	Montana**	NA
	District of Columbia	914.8

*Source: Morgan Quitno Press using data from Federal Bureau of Investigation
"Crime in the United States 1994" (Uniform Crime Reports, November 19, 1995)*
By law enforcement agencies submitting complete reports to the F.B.I. for 12 months in 1994. Arrests of youths 17 years and younger divided into population of 10 to 17 year olds. See important note at beginning of this chapter. Aggravated assault is an attack for the purpose of inflicting severe bodily injury.
***Not available.*

Reported Arrests of Juveniles for Aggravated Assault
As a Percent of All Such Arrests in 1994
National Percent = 15.57% of Reported Arrests for Aggravated Assault*

ALPHA ORDER

RANK	STATE	PERCENT
45	Alabama	9.25
35	Alaska	14.68
15	Arizona	23.16
28	Arkansas	16.54
44	California	10.41
24	Colorado	17.18
30	Connecticut	16.22
22	Delaware	18.05
27	Florida	16.71
38	Georgia	12.80
16	Hawaii	22.66
3	Idaho	30.30
2	Illinois	30.73
12	Indiana	25.13
17	Iowa	21.40
NA	Kansas**	NA
48	Kentucky	7.31
32	Louisiana	15.63
23	Maine	17.53
7	Maryland	27.47
37	Massachusetts	14.03
25	Michigan	16.85
4	Minnesota	29.51
31	Mississippi	15.97
41	Missouri	11.41
NA	Montana**	NA
21	Nebraska	18.24
34	Nevada	15.28
33	New Hampshire	15.50
13	New Jersey	24.41
8	New Mexico	26.49
29	New York	16.31
42	North Carolina	10.97
5	North Dakota	29.17
26	Ohio	16.82
19	Oklahoma	19.46
10	Oregon	25.53
14	Pennsylvania	23.83
20	Rhode Island	19.44
36	South Carolina	14.11
9	South Dakota	26.36
46	Tennessee	9.03
18	Texas	20.77
1	Utah	38.08
40	Vermont	11.67
43	Virginia	10.63
11	Washington	25.45
47	West Virginia	8.40
6	Wisconsin	27.94
39	Wyoming	11.97

RANK ORDER

RANK	STATE	PERCENT
1	Utah	38.08
2	Illinois	30.73
3	Idaho	30.30
4	Minnesota	29.51
5	North Dakota	29.17
6	Wisconsin	27.94
7	Maryland	27.47
8	New Mexico	26.49
9	South Dakota	26.36
10	Oregon	25.53
11	Washington	25.45
12	Indiana	25.13
13	New Jersey	24.41
14	Pennsylvania	23.83
15	Arizona	23.16
16	Hawaii	22.66
17	Iowa	21.40
18	Texas	20.77
19	Oklahoma	19.46
20	Rhode Island	19.44
21	Nebraska	18.24
22	Delaware	18.05
23	Maine	17.53
24	Colorado	17.18
25	Michigan	16.85
26	Ohio	16.82
27	Florida	16.71
28	Arkansas	16.54
29	New York	16.31
30	Connecticut	16.22
31	Mississippi	15.97
32	Louisiana	15.63
33	New Hampshire	15.50
34	Nevada	15.28
35	Alaska	14.68
36	South Carolina	14.11
37	Massachusetts	14.03
38	Georgia	12.80
39	Wyoming	11.97
40	Vermont	11.67
41	Missouri	11.41
42	North Carolina	10.97
43	Virginia	10.63
44	California	10.41
45	Alabama	9.25
46	Tennessee	9.03
47	West Virginia	8.40
48	Kentucky	7.31
NA	Kansas**	NA
NA	Montana**	NA
	District of Columbia	11.33

Source: Morgan Quitno Press using data from Federal Bureau of Investigation
   "Crime in the United States 1994" (Uniform Crime Reports, November 19, 1995)
*Arrests of youths 17 years and younger by law enforcement agencies submitting complete reports to the F.B.I. for
12 months in 1994. Aggravated assault is an attack for the purpose of inflicting severe bodily injury.
**Not available.

Reported Arrests of Juveniles for Property Crime in 1994

National Total = 610,563 Reported Arrests*

ALPHA ORDER

RANK ORDER

RANK	STATE	ARRESTS	% of USA		RANK	STATE	ARRESTS	% of USA
27	Alabama	6,108	1.00%		1	California	82,319	13.48%
38	Alaska	2,991	0.49%		2	Texas	57,415	9.40%
12	Arizona	16,131	2.64%		3	Florida	52,927	8.67%
29	Arkansas	5,455	0.89%		4	Wisconsin	29,644	4.86%
1	California	82,319	13.48%		5	New York	26,584	4.35%
17	Colorado	13,724	2.25%		6	Washington	22,189	3.63%
24	Connecticut	8,331	1.36%		7	Pennsylvania	19,370	3.17%
47	Delaware	610	0.10%		8	New Jersey	17,755	2.91%
3	Florida	52,927	8.67%		9	Michigan	17,650	2.89%
19	Georgia	11,386	1.86%		10	Minnesota	17,143	2.81%
34	Hawaii	4,338	0.71%		11	Ohio	16,669	2.73%
26	Idaho	6,321	1.04%		12	Arizona	16,131	2.64%
32	Illinois	4,511	0.74%		13	Maryland	16,079	2.63%
23	Indiana	9,574	1.57%		14	Virginia	14,606	2.39%
31	Iowa	5,261	0.86%		15	Oregon	14,338	2.35%
NA	Kansas**	NA	NA		16	North Carolina	13,756	2.25%
37	Kentucky	3,955	0.65%		17	Colorado	13,724	2.25%
22	Louisiana	9,897	1.62%		18	Utah	13,517	2.21%
33	Maine	4,393	0.72%		19	Georgia	11,386	1.86%
13	Maryland	16,079	2.63%		20	Oklahoma	10,920	1.79%
35	Massachusetts	4,292	0.70%		21	Missouri	10,019	1.64%
9	Michigan	17,650	2.89%		22	Louisiana	9,897	1.62%
10	Minnesota	17,143	2.81%		23	Indiana	9,574	1.57%
39	Mississippi	2,800	0.46%		24	Connecticut	8,331	1.36%
21	Missouri	10,019	1.64%		25	South Carolina	7,598	1.24%
NA	Montana**	NA	NA		26	Idaho	6,321	1.04%
28	Nebraska	5,637	0.92%		27	Alabama	6,108	1.00%
36	Nevada	4,223	0.69%		28	Nebraska	5,637	0.92%
44	New Hampshire	1,539	0.25%		29	Arkansas	5,455	0.89%
8	New Jersey	17,755	2.91%		30	Tennessee	5,345	0.88%
46	New Mexico	1,427	0.23%		31	Iowa	5,261	0.86%
5	New York	26,584	4.35%		32	Illinois	4,511	0.74%
16	North Carolina	13,756	2.25%		33	Maine	4,393	0.72%
43	North Dakota	2,181	0.36%		34	Hawaii	4,338	0.71%
11	Ohio	16,669	2.73%		35	Massachusetts	4,292	0.70%
20	Oklahoma	10,920	1.79%		36	Nevada	4,223	0.69%
15	Oregon	14,338	2.35%		37	Kentucky	3,955	0.65%
7	Pennsylvania	19,370	3.17%		38	Alaska	2,991	0.49%
40	Rhode Island	2,467	0.40%		39	Mississippi	2,800	0.46%
25	South Carolina	7,598	1.24%		40	Rhode Island	2,467	0.40%
41	South Dakota	2,389	0.39%		41	South Dakota	2,389	0.39%
30	Tennessee	5,345	0.88%		42	West Virginia	2,377	0.39%
2	Texas	57,415	9.40%		43	North Dakota	2,181	0.36%
18	Utah	13,517	2.21%		44	New Hampshire	1,539	0.25%
48	Vermont	206	0.03%		45	Wyoming	1,532	0.25%
14	Virginia	14,606	2.39%		46	New Mexico	1,427	0.23%
6	Washington	22,189	3.63%		47	Delaware	610	0.10%
42	West Virginia	2,377	0.39%		48	Vermont	206	0.03%
4	Wisconsin	29,644	4.86%		NA	Kansas**	NA	NA
45	Wyoming	1,532	0.25%		NA	Montana**	NA	NA
						District of Columbia	664	0.11%

Source: Federal Bureau of Investigation
   "Crime in the United States 1994" (Uniform Crime Reports, November 19, 1995)
*Arrests of youths 17 years and younger by law enforcement agencies submitting complete reports to the F.B.I. for 12 months in 1994. Property crimes are offenses of burglary, larceny-theft, motor vehicle theft and arson.
**Not available.

Reported Juvenile Arrest Rate for Property Crime in 1994

National Rate = 2,601.2 Reported Arrests per 100,000 Juvenile Population*

ALPHA ORDER

RANK	STATE	RATE
45	Alabama	1,354.6
8	Alaska	3,982.0
10	Arizona	3,527.5
38	Arkansas	1,873.6
27	California	2,400.1
3	Colorado	4,652.5
17	Connecticut	3,005.6
44	Delaware	1,522.3
9	Florida	3,905.5
29	Georgia	2,339.0
11	Hawaii	3,432.9
7	Idaho	4,011.0
32	Illinois	2,253.5
24	Indiana	2,555.0
41	Iowa	1,786.0
NA	Kansas**	NA
42	Kentucky	1,655.3
25	Louisiana	2,500.7
13	Maine	3,204.3
15	Maryland	3,086.9
47	Massachusetts	1,074.6
35	Michigan	1,994.7
12	Minnesota	3,278.7
22	Mississippi	2,703.5
23	Missouri	2,593.4
NA	Montana**	NA
16	Nebraska	3,053.4
18	Nevada	2,960.2
37	New Hampshire	1,949.6
31	New Jersey	2,267.5
21	New Mexico	2,729.3
43	New York	1,617.3
39	North Carolina	1,873.2
14	North Dakota	3,102.6
34	Ohio	2,143.8
20	Oklahoma	2,745.6
6	Oregon	4,090.1
36	Pennsylvania	1,959.6
26	Rhode Island	2,438.3
40	South Carolina	1,814.6
5	South Dakota	4,346.3
30	Tennessee	2,322.0
19	Texas	2,842.1
2	Utah	4,805.3
48	Vermont	610.7
33	Virginia	2,154.9
4	Washington	4,617.0
46	West Virginia	1,127.7
1	Wisconsin	4,893.4
28	Wyoming	2,396.1

RANK ORDER

RANK	STATE	RATE
1	Wisconsin	4,893.4
2	Utah	4,805.3
3	Colorado	4,652.5
4	Washington	4,617.0
5	South Dakota	4,346.3
6	Oregon	4,090.1
7	Idaho	4,011.0
8	Alaska	3,982.0
9	Florida	3,905.5
10	Arizona	3,527.5
11	Hawaii	3,432.9
12	Minnesota	3,278.7
13	Maine	3,204.3
14	North Dakota	3,102.6
15	Maryland	3,086.9
16	Nebraska	3,053.4
17	Connecticut	3,005.6
18	Nevada	2,960.2
19	Texas	2,842.1
20	Oklahoma	2,745.6
21	New Mexico	2,729.3
22	Mississippi	2,703.5
23	Missouri	2,593.4
24	Indiana	2,555.0
25	Louisiana	2,500.7
26	Rhode Island	2,438.3
27	California	2,400.1
28	Wyoming	2,396.1
29	Georgia	2,339.0
30	Tennessee	2,322.0
31	New Jersey	2,267.5
32	Illinois	2,253.5
33	Virginia	2,154.9
34	Ohio	2,143.8
35	Michigan	1,994.7
36	Pennsylvania	1,959.6
37	New Hampshire	1,949.6
38	Arkansas	1,873.6
39	North Carolina	1,873.2
40	South Carolina	1,814.6
41	Iowa	1,786.0
42	Kentucky	1,655.3
43	New York	1,617.3
44	Delaware	1,522.3
45	Alabama	1,354.6
46	West Virginia	1,127.7
47	Massachusetts	1,074.6
48	Vermont	610.7
NA	Kansas**	NA
NA	Montana**	NA
	District of Columbia	1,526.2

Source: Morgan Quitno Press using data from Federal Bureau of Investigation
    "Crime in the United States 1994" (Uniform Crime Reports, November 19, 1995)
*By law enforcement agencies submitting complete reports to the F.B.I. for 12 months in 1994. Arrests of youths 17 years and younger divided into population of 10 to 17 year olds. See important note at beginning of this chapter.
Property crimes are offenses of burglary, larceny-theft, motor vehicle theft and arson.
**Not available.

Reported Arrests of Juveniles for Property Crime
As a Percent of All Such Arrests in 1994
National Percent = 35.10% of Reported Arrests for Property Crime*

ALPHA ORDER

RANK	STATE	PERCENT
46	Alabama	23.74
13	Alaska	45.49
28	Arizona	34.65
38	Arkansas	29.72
31	California	31.85
18	Colorado	40.27
42	Connecticut	27.37
22	Delaware	37.68
27	Florida	36.78
41	Georgia	27.49
26	Hawaii	37.05
1	Idaho	60.38
24	Illinois	37.33
15	Indiana	43.28
16	Iowa	43.04
NA	Kansas**	NA
35	Kentucky	30.68
39	Louisiana	29.41
8	Maine	48.21
32	Maryland	31.84
48	Massachusetts	22.14
20	Michigan	38.35
5	Minnesota	52.23
40	Mississippi	28.09
43	Missouri	27.10
NA	Montana**	NA
9	Nebraska	46.90
36	Nevada	30.00
14	New Hampshire	45.00
30	New Jersey	33.03
12	New Mexico	45.90
44	New York	25.83
47	North Carolina	23.44
3	North Dakota	56.02
25	Ohio	37.20
7	Oklahoma	48.52
21	Oregon	38.19
29	Pennsylvania	34.23
17	Rhode Island	42.29
33	South Carolina	31.58
4	South Dakota	55.52
45	Tennessee	25.47
19	Texas	39.09
2	Utah	56.99
23	Vermont	37.59
37	Virginia	29.78
10	Washington	46.59
34	West Virginia	30.69
6	Wisconsin	50.05
11	Wyoming	46.55

RANK ORDER

RANK	STATE	PERCENT
1	Idaho	60.38
2	Utah	56.99
3	North Dakota	56.02
4	South Dakota	55.52
5	Minnesota	52.23
6	Wisconsin	50.05
7	Oklahoma	48.52
8	Maine	48.21
9	Nebraska	46.90
10	Washington	46.59
11	Wyoming	46.55
12	New Mexico	45.90
13	Alaska	45.49
14	New Hampshire	45.00
15	Indiana	43.28
16	Iowa	43.04
17	Rhode Island	42.29
18	Colorado	40.27
19	Texas	39.09
20	Michigan	38.35
21	Oregon	38.19
22	Delaware	37.68
23	Vermont	37.59
24	Illinois	37.33
25	Ohio	37.20
26	Hawaii	37.05
27	Florida	36.78
28	Arizona	34.65
29	Pennsylvania	34.23
30	New Jersey	33.03
31	California	31.85
32	Maryland	31.84
33	South Carolina	31.58
34	West Virginia	30.69
35	Kentucky	30.68
36	Nevada	30.00
37	Virginia	29.78
38	Arkansas	29.72
39	Louisiana	29.41
40	Mississippi	28.09
41	Georgia	27.49
42	Connecticut	27.37
43	Missouri	27.10
44	New York	25.83
45	Tennessee	25.47
46	Alabama	23.74
47	North Carolina	23.44
48	Massachusetts	22.14
NA	Kansas**	NA
NA	Montana**	NA

District of Columbia   11.86

Source: Morgan Quitno Press using data from Federal Bureau of Investigation
    "Crime in the United States 1994" (Uniform Crime Reports, November 19, 1995)
*Arrests of youths 17 years and younger by law enforcement agencies submitting complete reports to the F.B.I. for
12 months in 1994. Property crimes are offenses of burglary, larceny-theft, motor vehicle theft and arson.
**Not available.

Reported Arrests of Juveniles for Burglary in 1994

National Total = 115,681 Reported Arrests*

<u>ALPHA ORDER</u>

RANK	STATE	ARRESTS	% of USA
28	Alabama	1,002	0.87%
38	Alaska	586	0.51%
12	Arizona	2,879	2.49%
26	Arkansas	1,195	1.03%
1	California	22,110	19.11%
21	Colorado	1,617	1.40%
22	Connecticut	1,585	1.37%
46	Delaware	175	0.15%
2	Florida	12,048	10.41%
16	Georgia	2,089	1.81%
37	Hawaii	632	0.55%
34	Idaho	725	0.63%
36	Illinois	670	0.58%
25	Indiana	1,250	1.08%
29	Iowa	924	0.80%
NA	Kansas**	NA	NA
33	Kentucky	809	0.70%
17	Louisiana	2,083	1.80%
30	Maine	894	0.77%
12	Maryland	2,879	2.49%
27	Massachusetts	1,192	1.03%
11	Michigan	3,178	2.75%
15	Minnesota	2,136	1.85%
35	Mississippi	710	0.61%
23	Missouri	1,574	1.36%
NA	Montana**	NA	NA
39	Nebraska	534	0.46%
31	Nevada	862	0.75%
45	New Hampshire	177	0.15%
8	New Jersey	3,370	2.91%
42	New Mexico	317	0.27%
4	New York	5,124	4.43%
5	North Carolina	3,825	3.31%
44	North Dakota	183	0.16%
9	Ohio	3,215	2.78%
20	Oklahoma	1,747	1.51%
18	Oregon	1,939	1.68%
7	Pennsylvania	3,563	3.08%
41	Rhode Island	452	0.39%
19	South Carolina	1,889	1.63%
43	South Dakota	306	0.26%
31	Tennessee	862	0.75%
3	Texas	10,993	9.50%
24	Utah	1,401	1.21%
48	Vermont	72	0.06%
14	Virginia	2,413	2.09%
10	Washington	3,203	2.77%
40	West Virginia	515	0.45%
6	Wisconsin	3,590	3.10%
47	Wyoming	135	0.12%

<u>RANK ORDER</u>

RANK	STATE	ARRESTS	% of USA
1	California	22,110	19.11%
2	Florida	12,048	10.41%
3	Texas	10,993	9.50%
4	New York	5,124	4.43%
5	North Carolina	3,825	3.31%
6	Wisconsin	3,590	3.10%
7	Pennsylvania	3,563	3.08%
8	New Jersey	3,370	2.91%
9	Ohio	3,215	2.78%
10	Washington	3,203	2.77%
11	Michigan	3,178	2.75%
12	Arizona	2,879	2.49%
12	Maryland	2,879	2.49%
14	Virginia	2,413	2.09%
15	Minnesota	2,136	1.85%
16	Georgia	2,089	1.81%
17	Louisiana	2,083	1.80%
18	Oregon	1,939	1.68%
19	South Carolina	1,889	1.63%
20	Oklahoma	1,747	1.51%
21	Colorado	1,617	1.40%
22	Connecticut	1,585	1.37%
23	Missouri	1,574	1.36%
24	Utah	1,401	1.21%
25	Indiana	1,250	1.08%
26	Arkansas	1,195	1.03%
27	Massachusetts	1,192	1.03%
28	Alabama	1,002	0.87%
29	Iowa	924	0.80%
30	Maine	894	0.77%
31	Nevada	862	0.75%
31	Tennessee	862	0.75%
33	Kentucky	809	0.70%
34	Idaho	725	0.63%
35	Mississippi	710	0.61%
36	Illinois	670	0.58%
37	Hawaii	632	0.55%
38	Alaska	586	0.51%
39	Nebraska	534	0.46%
40	West Virginia	515	0.45%
41	Rhode Island	452	0.39%
42	New Mexico	317	0.27%
43	South Dakota	306	0.26%
44	North Dakota	183	0.16%
45	New Hampshire	177	0.15%
46	Delaware	175	0.15%
47	Wyoming	135	0.12%
48	Vermont	72	0.06%
NA	Kansas**	NA	NA
NA	Montana**	NA	NA
	District of Columbia	52	0.04%

Source: Federal Bureau of Investigation
"Crime in the United States 1994" (Uniform Crime Reports, November 19, 1995)
Arrests of youths 17 years and younger by law enforcement agencies submitting complete reports to the F.B.I. for 12 months in 1994. Burglary is the unlawful entry of a structure to commit a felony or theft. Attempts are included.
**Not available.*

Reported Juvenile Arrest Rate for Burglary in 1994

National Rate = 492.8 Reported Arrests per 100,000 Juvenile Population*

ALPHA ORDER

RANK ORDER

RANK	STATE	RATE		RANK	STATE	RATE
46	Alabama	222.2		1	Florida	889.0
2	Alaska	780.2		2	Alaska	780.2
7	Arizona	629.6		3	Mississippi	685.5
29	Arkansas	410.4		4	Washington	666.5
6	California	644.6		5	Maine	652.1
15	Colorado	548.2		6	California	644.6
11	Connecticut	571.8		7	Arizona	629.6
25	Delaware	436.7		8	New Mexico	606.3
1	Florida	889.0		9	Nevada	604.2
27	Georgia	429.1		10	Wisconsin	592.6
19	Hawaii	500.1		11	Connecticut	571.8
21	Idaho	460.0		12	South Dakota	556.7
37	Illinois	334.7		13	Oregon	553.1
38	Indiana	333.6		14	Maryland	552.7
39	Iowa	313.7		15	Colorado	548.2
NA	Kansas**	NA		16	Texas	544.2
36	Kentucky	338.6		17	Louisiana	526.3
17	Louisiana	526.3		18	North Carolina	520.9
5	Maine	652.1		19	Hawaii	500.1
14	Maryland	552.7		20	Utah	498.1
41	Massachusetts	298.4		21	Idaho	460.0
34	Michigan	359.2		22	South Carolina	451.1
30	Minnesota	408.5		23	Rhode Island	446.8
3	Mississippi	685.5		24	Oklahoma	439.2
31	Missouri	407.4		25	Delaware	436.7
NA	Montana**	NA		26	New Jersey	430.4
42	Nebraska	289.3		27	Georgia	429.1
9	Nevada	604.2		28	Ohio	413.5
45	New Hampshire	224.2		29	Arkansas	410.4
26	New Jersey	430.4		30	Minnesota	408.5
8	New Mexico	606.3		31	Missouri	407.4
40	New York	311.7		32	Tennessee	374.5
18	North Carolina	520.9		33	Pennsylvania	360.5
43	North Dakota	260.3		34	Michigan	359.2
28	Ohio	413.5		35	Virginia	356.0
24	Oklahoma	439.2		36	Kentucky	338.6
13	Oregon	553.1		37	Illinois	334.7
33	Pennsylvania	360.5		38	Indiana	333.6
23	Rhode Island	446.8		39	Iowa	313.7
22	South Carolina	451.1		40	New York	311.7
12	South Dakota	556.7		41	Massachusetts	298.4
32	Tennessee	374.5		42	Nebraska	289.3
16	Texas	544.2		43	North Dakota	260.3
20	Utah	498.1		44	West Virginia	244.3
47	Vermont	213.4		45	New Hampshire	224.2
35	Virginia	356.0		46	Alabama	222.2
4	Washington	666.5		47	Vermont	213.4
44	West Virginia	244.3		48	Wyoming	211.1
10	Wisconsin	592.6		NA	Kansas**	NA
48	Wyoming	211.1		NA	Montana**	NA
					District of Columbia	119.5

Source: Morgan Quitno Press using data from Federal Bureau of Investigation
"Crime in the United States 1994" (Uniform Crime Reports, November 19, 1995)
*By law enforcement agencies submitting complete reports to the F.B.I. for 12 months in 1994. Arrests of youths 17 years and younger divided into population of 10 to 17 year olds. See important note at beginning of this chapter. Burglary is the unlawful entry of a structure to commit a felony or theft. Attempts are included.
**Not available.

Reported Arrests of Juveniles for Burglary
As a Percent of All Such Arrests in 1994
National Percent = 36.16% of Reported Burglary Arrests*

ALPHA ORDER

RANK	STATE	PERCENT
47	Alabama	24.72
2	Alaska	61.55
15	Arizona	44.57
32	Arkansas	35.22
37	California	31.88
14	Colorado	46.57
40	Connecticut	29.94
19	Delaware	43.64
25	Florida	41.13
38	Georgia	30.79
24	Hawaii	41.39
3	Idaho	57.04
10	Illinois	49.26
18	Indiana	43.66
8	Iowa	50.33
NA	Kansas**	NA
42	Kentucky	28.36
35	Louisiana	32.35
11	Maine	49.12
43	Maryland	27.98
46	Massachusetts	25.58
30	Michigan	36.09
9	Minnesota	49.95
29	Mississippi	36.22
41	Missouri	28.64
NA	Montana**	NA
17	Nebraska	43.73
45	Nevada	25.69
16	New Hampshire	44.36
31	New Jersey	35.46
6	New Mexico	52.31
44	New York	27.30
48	North Carolina	23.44
13	North Dakota	47.91
26	Ohio	38.81
20	Oklahoma	43.39
21	Oregon	43.34
28	Pennsylvania	36.24
22	Rhode Island	42.20
27	South Carolina	37.50
4	South Dakota	55.33
39	Tennessee	30.26
12	Texas	48.04
1	Utah	61.94
23	Vermont	42.11
33	Virginia	34.10
7	Washington	51.87
36	West Virginia	32.11
5	Wisconsin	53.91
34	Wyoming	33.67

RANK ORDER

RANK	STATE	PERCENT
1	Utah	61.94
2	Alaska	61.55
3	Idaho	57.04
4	South Dakota	55.33
5	Wisconsin	53.91
6	New Mexico	52.31
7	Washington	51.87
8	Iowa	50.33
9	Minnesota	49.95
10	Illinois	49.26
11	Maine	49.12
12	Texas	48.04
13	North Dakota	47.91
14	Colorado	46.57
15	Arizona	44.57
16	New Hampshire	44.36
17	Nebraska	43.73
18	Indiana	43.66
19	Delaware	43.64
20	Oklahoma	43.39
21	Oregon	43.34
22	Rhode Island	42.20
23	Vermont	42.11
24	Hawaii	41.39
25	Florida	41.13
26	Ohio	38.81
27	South Carolina	37.50
28	Pennsylvania	36.24
29	Mississippi	36.22
30	Michigan	36.09
31	New Jersey	35.46
32	Arkansas	35.22
33	Virginia	34.10
34	Wyoming	33.67
35	Louisiana	32.35
36	West Virginia	32.11
37	California	31.88
38	Georgia	30.79
39	Tennessee	30.26
40	Connecticut	29.94
41	Missouri	28.64
42	Kentucky	28.36
43	Maryland	27.98
44	New York	27.30
45	Nevada	25.69
46	Massachusetts	25.58
47	Alabama	24.72
48	North Carolina	23.44
NA	Kansas**	NA
NA	Montana**	NA
	District of Columbia	4.77

Source: Morgan Quitno Press using data from Federal Bureau of Investigation
   "Crime in the United States 1994" (Uniform Crime Reports, November 19, 1995)
*Arrests of youths 17 years and younger by law enforcement agencies submitting complete reports to the F.B.I. for
12 months in 1994. Burglary is the unlawful entry of a structure to commit a felony or theft. Attempts are included.
**Not available.

Reported Arrests of Juveniles for Larceny and Theft in 1994

National Total = 412,349 Reported Arrests*

ALPHA ORDER

RANK ORDER

RANK	STATE	ARRESTS	% of USA	RANK	STATE	ARRESTS	% of USA
28	Alabama	4,632	1.12%	1	California	43,212	10.48%
38	Alaska	2,084	0.51%	2	Texas	39,450	9.57%
11	Arizona	11,346	2.75%	3	Florida	33,540	8.13%
29	Arkansas	3,952	0.96%	4	Wisconsin	22,462	5.45%
1	California	43,212	10.48%	5	New York	18,365	4.45%
12	Colorado	11,090	2.69%	6	Washington	17,098	4.15%
24	Connecticut	5,266	1.28%	7	New Jersey	12,716	3.08%
47	Delaware	335	0.08%	8	Minnesota	12,637	3.06%
3	Florida	33,540	8.13%	9	Michigan	12,422	3.01%
19	Georgia	7,829	1.90%	10	Pennsylvania	11,905	2.89%
33	Hawaii	3,271	0.79%	11	Arizona	11,346	2.75%
25	Idaho	5,077	1.23%	12	Colorado	11,090	2.69%
32	Illinois	3,660	0.89%	13	Ohio	10,929	2.65%
21	Indiana	7,164	1.74%	14	Utah	10,861	2.63%
30	Iowa	3,818	0.93%	15	Oregon	10,446	2.53%
NA	Kansas**	NA	NA	16	Virginia	10,188	2.47%
36	Kentucky	2,544	0.62%	17	North Carolina	8,927	2.16%
22	Louisiana	7,123	1.73%	18	Maryland	8,822	2.14%
34	Maine	3,121	0.76%	19	Georgia	7,829	1.90%
18	Maryland	8,822	2.14%	20	Oklahoma	7,722	1.87%
37	Massachusetts	2,367	0.57%	21	Indiana	7,164	1.74%
9	Michigan	12,422	3.01%	22	Louisiana	7,123	1.73%
8	Minnesota	12,637	3.06%	23	Missouri	6,955	1.69%
42	Mississippi	1,699	0.41%	24	Connecticut	5,266	1.28%
23	Missouri	6,955	1.69%	25	Idaho	5,077	1.23%
NA	Montana**	NA	NA	25	South Carolina	5,077	1.23%
27	Nebraska	4,746	1.15%	27	Nebraska	4,746	1.15%
35	Nevada	2,903	0.70%	28	Alabama	4,632	1.12%
45	New Hampshire	1,247	0.30%	29	Arkansas	3,952	0.96%
7	New Jersey	12,716	3.08%	30	Iowa	3,818	0.93%
46	New Mexico	1,011	0.25%	31	Tennessee	3,781	0.92%
5	New York	18,365	4.45%	32	Illinois	3,660	0.89%
17	North Carolina	8,927	2.16%	33	Hawaii	3,271	0.79%
40	North Dakota	1,776	0.43%	34	Maine	3,121	0.76%
13	Ohio	10,929	2.65%	35	Nevada	2,903	0.70%
20	Oklahoma	7,722	1.87%	36	Kentucky	2,544	0.62%
15	Oregon	10,446	2.53%	37	Massachusetts	2,367	0.57%
10	Pennsylvania	11,905	2.89%	38	Alaska	2,084	0.51%
41	Rhode Island	1,723	0.42%	39	South Dakota	1,879	0.46%
25	South Carolina	5,077	1.23%	40	North Dakota	1,776	0.43%
39	South Dakota	1,879	0.46%	41	Rhode Island	1,723	0.42%
31	Tennessee	3,781	0.92%	42	Mississippi	1,699	0.41%
2	Texas	39,450	9.57%	43	West Virginia	1,595	0.39%
14	Utah	10,861	2.63%	44	Wyoming	1,308	0.32%
48	Vermont	124	0.03%	45	New Hampshire	1,247	0.30%
16	Virginia	10,188	2.47%	46	New Mexico	1,011	0.25%
6	Washington	17,098	4.15%	47	Delaware	335	0.08%
43	West Virginia	1,595	0.39%	48	Vermont	124	0.03%
4	Wisconsin	22,462	5.45%	NA	Kansas**	NA	NA
44	Wyoming	1,308	0.32%	NA	Montana**	NA	NA
					District of Columbia	144	0.03%

Source: Federal Bureau of Investigation
     "Crime in the United States 1994" (Uniform Crime Reports, November 19, 1995)
*Arrests of youths 17 years and younger by law enforcement agencies submitting complete reports to the F.B.I. for
12 months in 1994. Larceny and theft is the unlawful taking of property without use of force, violence or fraud.
Attempts are included. Motor vehicle thefts are excluded.
**Not available.

Reported Arrest Rate of Juveniles for Larceny and Theft in 1994

National Rate = 1,756.7 Arrests per 100,000 Juvenile Population*

ALPHA ORDER

RANK	STATE	RATE
44	Alabama	1,027.2
8	Alaska	2,774.5
12	Arizona	2,481.1
36	Arkansas	1,357.3
38	California	1,259.9
2	Colorado	3,759.5
22	Connecticut	1,899.8
45	Delaware	836.0
13	Florida	2,474.9
31	Georgia	1,608.3
9	Hawaii	2,588.5
6	Idaho	3,221.6
23	Illinois	1,828.4
21	Indiana	1,911.8
37	Iowa	1,296.2
NA	Kansas**	NA
43	Kentucky	1,064.8
25	Louisiana	1,799.8
15	Maine	2,276.5
27	Maryland	1,693.7
47	Massachusetts	592.6
35	Michigan	1,403.9
14	Minnesota	2,416.9
29	Mississippi	1,640.4
24	Missouri	1,800.3
NA	Montana**	NA
10	Nebraska	2,570.8
17	Nevada	2,034.9
32	New Hampshire	1,579.7
30	New Jersey	1,623.9
20	New Mexico	1,933.7
42	New York	1,117.3
39	North Carolina	1,215.6
11	North Dakota	2,526.4
34	Ohio	1,405.6
19	Oklahoma	1,941.5
7	Oregon	2,979.9
41	Pennsylvania	1,204.4
26	Rhode Island	1,703.0
40	South Carolina	1,212.5
5	South Dakota	3,418.5
28	Tennessee	1,642.6
18	Texas	1,952.8
1	Utah	3,861.1
48	Vermont	367.6
33	Virginia	1,503.1
4	Washington	3,557.7
46	West Virginia	756.7
3	Wisconsin	3,707.9
16	Wyoming	2,045.7

RANK ORDER

RANK	STATE	RATE
1	Utah	3,861.1
2	Colorado	3,759.5
3	Wisconsin	3,707.9
4	Washington	3,557.7
5	South Dakota	3,418.5
6	Idaho	3,221.6
7	Oregon	2,979.9
8	Alaska	2,774.5
9	Hawaii	2,588.5
10	Nebraska	2,570.8
11	North Dakota	2,526.4
12	Arizona	2,481.1
13	Florida	2,474.9
14	Minnesota	2,416.9
15	Maine	2,276.5
16	Wyoming	2,045.7
17	Nevada	2,034.9
18	Texas	1,952.8
19	Oklahoma	1,941.5
20	New Mexico	1,933.7
21	Indiana	1,911.8
22	Connecticut	1,899.8
23	Illinois	1,828.4
24	Missouri	1,800.3
25	Louisiana	1,799.8
26	Rhode Island	1,703.0
27	Maryland	1,693.7
28	Tennessee	1,642.6
29	Mississippi	1,640.4
30	New Jersey	1,623.9
31	Georgia	1,608.3
32	New Hampshire	1,579.7
33	Virginia	1,503.1
34	Ohio	1,405.6
35	Michigan	1,403.9
36	Arkansas	1,357.3
37	Iowa	1,296.2
38	California	1,259.9
39	North Carolina	1,215.6
40	South Carolina	1,212.5
41	Pennsylvania	1,204.4
42	New York	1,117.3
43	Kentucky	1,064.8
44	Alabama	1,027.2
45	Delaware	836.0
46	West Virginia	756.7
47	Massachusetts	592.6
48	Vermont	367.6
NA	Kansas**	NA
NA	Montana**	NA
	District of Columbia	331.0

Source: Morgan Quitno Press using data from Federal Bureau of Investigation
"Crime in the United States 1994" (Uniform Crime Reports, November 19, 1995)
*By law enforcement agencies submitting complete reports to the F.B.I. for 12 months in 1994. Arrests of youths 17 years and younger divided into population of 10 to 17 year olds. See important note at beginning of this chapter. Larceny and theft is the unlawful taking of property without use of force, violence or fraud. Attempts are included. Motor vehicle thefts are excluded. **Not available.

Reported Arrests of Juveniles for Larceny and Theft
As a Percent of All Such Arrests in 1994
National Percent = 33.35% of Reported Larceny and Theft Arrests*

ALPHA ORDER

RANK	STATE	PERCENT
45	Alabama	23.28
14	Alaska	42.16
28	Arizona	31.29
37	Arkansas	27.95
31	California	29.77
18	Colorado	39.11
44	Connecticut	23.67
30	Delaware	30.48
26	Florida	33.66
41	Georgia	25.16
19	Hawaii	39.05
1	Idaho	60.25
24	Illinois	35.30
15	Indiana	42.08
17	Iowa	40.10
NA	Kansas**	NA
32	Kentucky	29.72
36	Louisiana	27.98
9	Maine	46.95
38	Maryland	27.48
48	Massachusetts	18.79
20	Michigan	37.58
5	Minnesota	51.25
43	Mississippi	24.35
40	Missouri	25.34
NA	Montana**	NA
10	Nebraska	46.63
33	Nevada	29.61
13	New Hampshire	44.08
29	New Jersey	30.84
11	New Mexico	44.48
42	New York	25.10
47	North Carolina	22.61
2	North Dakota	55.64
25	Ohio	34.36
6	Oklahoma	48.75
21	Oregon	37.01
27	Pennsylvania	31.35
16	Rhode Island	41.49
35	South Carolina	28.58
4	South Dakota	53.87
46	Tennessee	23.17
22	Texas	35.81
3	Utah	55.13
23	Vermont	35.63
39	Virginia	27.04
12	Washington	44.35
34	West Virginia	28.75
8	Wisconsin	47.84
7	Wyoming	48.30

RANK ORDER

RANK	STATE	PERCENT
1	Idaho	60.25
2	North Dakota	55.64
3	Utah	55.13
4	South Dakota	53.87
5	Minnesota	51.25
6	Oklahoma	48.75
7	Wyoming	48.30
8	Wisconsin	47.84
9	Maine	46.95
10	Nebraska	46.63
11	New Mexico	44.48
12	Washington	44.35
13	New Hampshire	44.08
14	Alaska	42.16
15	Indiana	42.08
16	Rhode Island	41.49
17	Iowa	40.10
18	Colorado	39.11
19	Hawaii	39.05
20	Michigan	37.58
21	Oregon	37.01
22	Texas	35.81
23	Vermont	35.63
24	Illinois	35.30
25	Ohio	34.36
26	Florida	33.66
27	Pennsylvania	31.35
28	Arizona	31.29
29	New Jersey	30.84
30	Delaware	30.48
31	California	29.77
32	Kentucky	29.72
33	Nevada	29.61
34	West Virginia	28.75
35	South Carolina	28.58
36	Louisiana	27.98
37	Arkansas	27.95
38	Maryland	27.48
39	Virginia	27.04
40	Missouri	25.34
41	Georgia	25.16
42	New York	25.10
43	Mississippi	24.35
44	Connecticut	23.67
45	Alabama	23.28
46	Tennessee	23.17
47	North Carolina	22.61
48	Massachusetts	18.79
NA	Kansas**	NA
NA	Montana**	NA

District of Columbia 5.03

Source: Morgan Quitno Press using data from Federal Bureau of Investigation
  "Crime in the United States 1994" (Uniform Crime Reports, November 19, 1995)
*Arrests of youths 17 years and younger by law enforcement agencies submitting complete reports to the F.B.I. for
12 months in 1994. Larceny and theft is the unlawful taking of property without use of force, violence or fraud.
Attempts are included. Motor vehicle thefts are excluded.
**Not available.

Reported Arrests of Juveniles for Motor Vehicle Theft in 1994

National Total = 73,265 Reported Arrests*

ALPHA ORDER

RANK	STATE	ARRESTS	% of USA
29	Alabama	448	0.61%
35	Alaska	303	0.41%
13	Arizona	1,604	2.19%
37	Arkansas	281	0.38%
1	California	15,377	20.99%
22	Colorado	802	1.09%
17	Connecticut	1,331	1.82%
44	Delaware	88	0.12%
2	Florida	7,023	9.59%
16	Georgia	1,351	1.84%
32	Hawaii	401	0.55%
30	Idaho	428	0.58%
42	Illinois	132	0.18%
21	Indiana	1,062	1.45%
33	Iowa	392	0.54%
NA	Kansas**	NA	NA
28	Kentucky	501	0.68%
26	Louisiana	590	0.81%
36	Maine	293	0.40%
4	Maryland	3,996	5.45%
24	Massachusetts	655	0.89%
10	Michigan	1,795	2.45%
9	Minnesota	2,127	2.90%
34	Mississippi	357	0.49%
18	Missouri	1,304	1.78%
NA	Montana**	NA	NA
38	Nebraska	270	0.37%
31	Nevada	422	0.58%
46	New Hampshire	61	0.08%
15	New Jersey	1,353	1.85%
45	New Mexico	77	0.11%
7	New York	2,730	3.73%
23	North Carolina	772	1.05%
40	North Dakota	204	0.28%
8	Ohio	2,142	2.92%
19	Oklahoma	1,182	1.61%
14	Oregon	1,549	2.11%
5	Pennsylvania	3,474	4.74%
41	Rhode Island	200	0.27%
27	South Carolina	561	0.77%
43	South Dakota	100	0.14%
25	Tennessee	650	0.89%
3	Texas	6,460	8.82%
20	Utah	1,111	1.52%
48	Vermont	8	0.01%
11	Virginia	1,754	2.39%
12	Washington	1,614	2.20%
39	West Virginia	224	0.31%
6	Wisconsin	3,183	4.34%
47	Wyoming	59	0.08%

RANK ORDER

RANK	STATE	ARRESTS	% of USA
1	California	15,377	20.99%
2	Florida	7,023	9.59%
3	Texas	6,460	8.82%
4	Maryland	3,996	5.45%
5	Pennsylvania	3,474	4.74%
6	Wisconsin	3,183	4.34%
7	New York	2,730	3.73%
8	Ohio	2,142	2.92%
9	Minnesota	2,127	2.90%
10	Michigan	1,795	2.45%
11	Virginia	1,754	2.39%
12	Washington	1,614	2.20%
13	Arizona	1,604	2.19%
14	Oregon	1,549	2.11%
15	New Jersey	1,353	1.85%
16	Georgia	1,351	1.84%
17	Connecticut	1,331	1.82%
18	Missouri	1,304	1.78%
19	Oklahoma	1,182	1.61%
20	Utah	1,111	1.52%
21	Indiana	1,062	1.45%
22	Colorado	802	1.09%
23	North Carolina	772	1.05%
24	Massachusetts	655	0.89%
25	Tennessee	650	0.89%
26	Louisiana	590	0.81%
27	South Carolina	561	0.77%
28	Kentucky	501	0.68%
29	Alabama	448	0.61%
30	Idaho	428	0.58%
31	Nevada	422	0.58%
32	Hawaii	401	0.55%
33	Iowa	392	0.54%
34	Mississippi	357	0.49%
35	Alaska	303	0.41%
36	Maine	293	0.40%
37	Arkansas	281	0.38%
38	Nebraska	270	0.37%
39	West Virginia	224	0.31%
40	North Dakota	204	0.28%
41	Rhode Island	200	0.27%
42	Illinois	132	0.18%
43	South Dakota	100	0.14%
44	Delaware	88	0.12%
45	New Mexico	77	0.11%
46	New Hampshire	61	0.08%
47	Wyoming	59	0.08%
48	Vermont	8	0.01%
NA	Kansas**	NA	NA
NA	Montana**	NA	NA
	District of Columbia	464	0.63%

Source: Federal Bureau of Investigation
   "Crime in the United States 1994" (Uniform Crime Reports, November 19, 1995)
*Arrests of youths 17 years and younger by law enforcement agencies submitting complete reports to the F.B.I. for 12 months in 1994. Motor vehicle theft includes the theft or attempted theft of a self-propelled vehicle. Excludes motorboats, construction equipment, airplanes and farming equipment.
**Not available.

Reported Arrest Rate of Juveniles for Motor Vehicle Theft in 1994

National Rate = 312.1 Reported Arrests per 100,000 Juvenile Population*

ALPHA ORDER

RANK ORDER

RANK	STATE	RATE		RANK	STATE	RATE
43	Alabama	99.4		1	Maryland	767.2
8	Alaska	403.4		2	Wisconsin	525.4
11	Arizona	350.8		3	Florida	518.2
44	Arkansas	96.5		4	Connecticut	480.2
5	California	448.3		5	California	448.3
24	Colorado	271.9		6	Oregon	441.9
4	Connecticut	480.2		7	Minnesota	406.8
27	Delaware	219.6		8	Alaska	403.4
3	Florida	518.2		9	Utah	395.0
22	Georgia	277.5		10	Pennsylvania	351.5
16	Hawaii	317.3		11	Arizona	350.8
25	Idaho	271.6		12	Mississippi	344.7
47	Illinois	65.9		13	Missouri	337.5
20	Indiana	283.4		14	Washington	335.8
40	Iowa	133.1		15	Texas	319.8
NA	Kansas**	NA		16	Hawaii	317.3
29	Kentucky	209.7		17	Oklahoma	297.2
36	Louisiana	149.1		18	Nevada	295.8
28	Maine	213.7		19	North Dakota	290.2
1	Maryland	767.2		20	Indiana	283.4
35	Massachusetts	164.0		21	Tennessee	282.4
30	Michigan	202.9		22	Georgia	277.5
7	Minnesota	406.8		23	Ohio	275.5
12	Mississippi	344.7		24	Colorado	271.9
13	Missouri	337.5		25	Idaho	271.6
NA	Montana**	NA		26	Virginia	258.8
38	Nebraska	146.3		27	Delaware	219.6
18	Nevada	295.8		28	Maine	213.7
46	New Hampshire	77.3		29	Kentucky	209.7
33	New Jersey	172.8		30	Michigan	202.9
37	New Mexico	147.3		31	Rhode Island	197.7
34	New York	166.1		32	South Dakota	181.9
42	North Carolina	105.1		33	New Jersey	172.8
19	North Dakota	290.2		34	New York	166.1
23	Ohio	275.5		35	Massachusetts	164.0
17	Oklahoma	297.2		36	Louisiana	149.1
6	Oregon	441.9		37	New Mexico	147.3
10	Pennsylvania	351.5		38	Nebraska	146.3
31	Rhode Island	197.7		39	South Carolina	134.0
39	South Carolina	134.0		40	Iowa	133.1
32	South Dakota	181.9		41	West Virginia	106.3
21	Tennessee	282.4		42	North Carolina	105.1
15	Texas	319.8		43	Alabama	99.4
9	Utah	395.0		44	Arkansas	96.5
48	Vermont	23.7		45	Wyoming	92.3
26	Virginia	258.8		46	New Hampshire	77.3
14	Washington	335.8		47	Illinois	65.9
41	West Virginia	106.3		48	Vermont	23.7
2	Wisconsin	525.4		NA	Kansas**	NA
45	Wyoming	92.3		NA	Montana**	NA
					District of Columbia	1,066.5

Source: Morgan Quitno Press using data from Federal Bureau of Investigation
"Crime in the United States 1994" (Uniform Crime Reports, November 19, 1995)
*By law enforcement agencies submitting complete reports to the F.B.I. for 12 months in 1994. Arrests of youths 17 years and younger divided into population of 10 to 17 year olds. See important note at beginning of this chapter. Motor vehicle theft includes the theft or attempted theft of a self-propelled vehicle. Excludes motorboats, construction equipment, airplanes and farming equipment. **Not available.

Reported Arrests of Juveniles for Motor Vehicle Theft
As a Percent of All Such Arrests in 1994
National Percent = 44.07% of Reported Motor Vehicle Theft Arrests*

ALPHA ORDER

RANK	STATE	PERCENT
46	Alabama	27.07
27	Alaska	46.90
26	Arizona	47.07
36	Arkansas	40.72
41	California	37.13
34	Colorado	42.59
21	Connecticut	50.90
1	Delaware	84.62
25	Florida	49.18
33	Georgia	43.16
48	Hawaii	23.02
5	Idaho	65.95
22	Illinois	50.77
18	Indiana	51.80
9	Iowa	57.39
NA	Kansas**	NA
37	Kentucky	40.05
38	Louisiana	38.71
10	Maine	57.23
15	Maryland	53.48
44	Massachusetts	33.59
19	Michigan	51.27
8	Minnesota	60.05
40	Mississippi	37.62
42	Missouri	36.58
NA	Montana**	NA
12	Nebraska	54.11
23	Nevada	50.24
20	New Hampshire	51.26
11	New Jersey	55.11
30	New Mexico	44.00
47	New York	26.88
45	North Carolina	32.92
4	North Dakota	68.46
17	Ohio	52.99
13	Oklahoma	53.95
43	Oregon	36.04
32	Pennsylvania	43.37
35	Rhode Island	40.73
14	South Carolina	53.58
3	South Dakota	68.49
39	Tennessee	38.53
24	Texas	50.17
2	Utah	70.27
16	Vermont	53.33
28	Virginia	46.51
6	Washington	64.85
29	West Virginia	46.38
7	Wisconsin	63.51
31	Wyoming	43.70

RANK ORDER

RANK	STATE	PERCENT
1	Delaware	84.62
2	Utah	70.27
3	South Dakota	68.49
4	North Dakota	68.46
5	Idaho	65.95
6	Washington	64.85
7	Wisconsin	63.51
8	Minnesota	60.05
9	Iowa	57.39
10	Maine	57.23
11	New Jersey	55.11
12	Nebraska	54.11
13	Oklahoma	53.95
14	South Carolina	53.58
15	Maryland	53.48
16	Vermont	53.33
17	Ohio	52.99
18	Indiana	51.80
19	Michigan	51.27
20	New Hampshire	51.26
21	Connecticut	50.90
22	Illinois	50.77
23	Nevada	50.24
24	Texas	50.17
25	Florida	49.18
26	Arizona	47.07
27	Alaska	46.90
28	Virginia	46.51
29	West Virginia	46.38
30	New Mexico	44.00
31	Wyoming	43.70
32	Pennsylvania	43.37
33	Georgia	43.16
34	Colorado	42.59
35	Rhode Island	40.73
36	Arkansas	40.72
37	Kentucky	40.05
38	Louisiana	38.71
39	Tennessee	38.53
40	Mississippi	37.62
41	California	37.13
42	Missouri	36.58
43	Oregon	36.04
44	Massachusetts	33.59
45	North Carolina	32.92
46	Alabama	27.07
47	New York	26.88
48	Hawaii	23.02
NA	Kansas**	NA
NA	Montana**	NA
	District of Columbia	28.59

Source: Morgan Quitno Press using data from Federal Bureau of Investigation
"Crime in the United States 1994" (Uniform Crime Reports, November 19, 1995)
Arrests of youths 17 years and younger by law enforcement agencies submitting complete reports to the F.B.I. for 12 months in 1994. Motor vehicle theft includes the theft or attempted theft of a self-propelled vehicle. Excludes motorboats, construction equipment, airplanes and farming equipment.
**Not available.*

Reported Arrests of Juveniles for Arson in 1994

National Total = 9,268 Reported Arrests*

ALPHA ORDER					RANK ORDER			
RANK	STATE		ARRESTS	% of USA	RANK	STATE	ARRESTS	% of USA
43	Alabama		26	0.28%	1	California	1,620	17.48%
45	Alaska		18	0.19%	2	Texas	512	5.52%
11	Arizona		302	3.26%	3	Pennsylvania	428	4.62%
42	Arkansas		27	0.29%	4	Wisconsin	409	4.41%
1	California		1,620	17.48%	5	Oregon	404	4.36%
18	Colorado		215	2.32%	6	Ohio	383	4.13%
20	Connecticut		149	1.61%	7	Maryland	382	4.12%
47	Delaware		12	0.13%	8	New York	365	3.94%
9	Florida		316	3.41%	9	Florida	316	3.41%
23	Georgia		117	1.26%	9	New Jersey	316	3.41%
39	Hawaii		34	0.37%	11	Arizona	302	3.26%
29	Idaho		91	0.98%	12	Washington	274	2.96%
36	Illinois		49	0.53%	13	Oklahoma	269	2.90%
27	Indiana		98	1.06%	14	Michigan	255	2.75%
22	Iowa		127	1.37%	15	Virginia	251	2.71%
NA	Kansas**		NA	NA	16	Minnesota	243	2.62%
25	Kentucky		101	1.09%	17	North Carolina	232	2.50%
25	Louisiana		101	1.09%	18	Colorado	215	2.32%
31	Maine		85	0.92%	19	Missouri	186	2.01%
7	Maryland		382	4.12%	20	Connecticut	149	1.61%
32	Massachusetts		78	0.84%	21	Utah	144	1.55%
14	Michigan		255	2.75%	22	Iowa	127	1.37%
16	Minnesota		243	2.62%	23	Georgia	117	1.26%
39	Mississippi		34	0.37%	24	South Dakota	104	1.12%
19	Missouri		186	2.01%	25	Kentucky	101	1.09%
NA	Montana**		NA	NA	25	Louisiana	101	1.09%
30	Nebraska		87	0.94%	27	Indiana	98	1.06%
38	Nevada		36	0.39%	28	Rhode Island	92	0.99%
34	New Hampshire		54	0.58%	29	Idaho	91	0.98%
9	New Jersey		316	3.41%	30	Nebraska	87	0.94%
44	New Mexico		22	0.24%	31	Maine	85	0.92%
8	New York		365	3.94%	32	Massachusetts	78	0.84%
17	North Carolina		232	2.50%	33	South Carolina	71	0.77%
45	North Dakota		18	0.19%	34	New Hampshire	54	0.58%
6	Ohio		383	4.13%	35	Tennessee	52	0.56%
13	Oklahoma		269	2.90%	36	Illinois	49	0.53%
5	Oregon		404	4.36%	37	West Virginia	43	0.46%
3	Pennsylvania		428	4.62%	38	Nevada	36	0.39%
28	Rhode Island		92	0.99%	39	Hawaii	34	0.37%
33	South Carolina		71	0.77%	39	Mississippi	34	0.37%
24	South Dakota		104	1.12%	41	Wyoming	30	0.32%
35	Tennessee		52	0.56%	42	Arkansas	27	0.29%
2	Texas		512	5.52%	43	Alabama	26	0.28%
21	Utah		144	1.55%	44	New Mexico	22	0.24%
48	Vermont		2	0.02%	45	Alaska	18	0.19%
15	Virginia		251	2.71%	45	North Dakota	18	0.19%
12	Washington		274	2.96%	47	Delaware	12	0.13%
37	West Virginia		43	0.46%	48	Vermont	2	0.02%
4	Wisconsin		409	4.41%	NA	Kansas**	NA	NA
41	Wyoming		30	0.32%	NA	Montana**	NA	NA
						District of Columbia	4	0.04%

Source: Federal Bureau of Investigation
   "Crime in the United States 1994" (Uniform Crime Reports, November 19, 1995)
*Arrests of youths 17 years and younger by law enforcement agencies submitting complete reports to the F.B.I. for 12 months in 1994. Arson is the willful burning of or attempt to burn a building, vehicle or another's personal property.
**Not available.

Reported Juvenile Arrest Rate for Arson in 1994

National Rate = 39.5 Reported Arrests per 100,000 Juvenile Population*

ALPHA ORDER				RANK ORDER		
RANK	STATE	RATE		RANK	STATE	RATE
48	Alabama	5.8		1	South Dakota	189.2
38	Alaska	24.0		2	Oregon	115.2
9	Arizona	66.0		3	Rhode Island	90.9
46	Arkansas	9.3		4	Maryland	73.3
17	California	47.2		5	Colorado	72.9
5	Colorado	72.9		6	New Hampshire	68.4
13	Connecticut	53.8		7	Oklahoma	67.6
29	Delaware	29.9		8	Wisconsin	67.5
40	Florida	23.3		9	Arizona	66.0
38	Georgia	24.0		10	Maine	62.0
31	Hawaii	26.9		11	Idaho	57.7
11	Idaho	57.7		12	Washington	57.0
37	Illinois	24.5		13	Connecticut	53.8
32	Indiana	26.2		14	Utah	51.2
22	Iowa	43.1		15	Ohio	49.3
NA	Kansas**	NA		16	Missouri	48.1
23	Kentucky	42.3		17	California	47.2
34	Louisiana	25.5		18	Nebraska	47.1
10	Maine	62.0		19	Wyoming	46.9
4	Maryland	73.3		20	Minnesota	46.5
44	Massachusetts	19.5		21	Pennsylvania	43.3
30	Michigan	28.8		22	Iowa	43.1
20	Minnesota	46.5		23	Kentucky	42.3
27	Mississippi	32.8		24	New Mexico	42.1
16	Missouri	48.1		25	New Jersey	40.4
NA	Montana**	NA		26	Virginia	37.0
18	Nebraska	47.1		27	Mississippi	32.8
36	Nevada	25.2		28	North Carolina	31.6
6	New Hampshire	68.4		29	Delaware	29.9
25	New Jersey	40.4		30	Michigan	28.8
24	New Mexico	42.1		31	Hawaii	26.9
42	New York	22.2		32	Indiana	26.2
28	North Carolina	31.6		33	North Dakota	25.6
33	North Dakota	25.6		34	Louisiana	25.5
15	Ohio	49.3		35	Texas	25.3
7	Oklahoma	67.6		36	Nevada	25.2
2	Oregon	115.2		37	Illinois	24.5
21	Pennsylvania	43.3		38	Alaska	24.0
3	Rhode Island	90.9		38	Georgia	24.0
45	South Carolina	17.0		40	Florida	23.3
1	South Dakota	189.2		41	Tennessee	22.6
41	Tennessee	22.6		42	New York	22.2
35	Texas	25.3		43	West Virginia	20.4
14	Utah	51.2		44	Massachusetts	19.5
47	Vermont	5.9		45	South Carolina	17.0
26	Virginia	37.0		46	Arkansas	9.3
12	Washington	57.0		47	Vermont	5.9
43	West Virginia	20.4		48	Alabama	5.8
8	Wisconsin	67.5		NA	Kansas**	NA
19	Wyoming	46.9		NA	Montana**	NA
					District of Columbia	9.2

Source: Morgan Quitno Press using data from Federal Bureau of Investigation
   "Crime in the United States 1994" (Uniform Crime Reports, November 19, 1995)
*By law enforcement agencies submitting complete reports to the F.B.I. for 12 months in 1994. Arrests of youths 17
years and younger divided into population of 10 to 17 year olds. See important note at beginning of this chapter.
Arson is the willful burning of or attempt to burn a building, vehicle or another's personal property.
**Not available.

Reported Arrests of Juveniles for Arson
As a Percent of All Such Arrests in 1994
National Percent = 55.29% of Reported Arson Arrests*

ALPHA ORDER

RANK ORDER

RANK	STATE	PERCENT		RANK	STATE	PERCENT
46	Alabama	20.63		1	South Dakota	89.66
26	Alaska	52.94		2	North Dakota	85.71
11	Arizona	70.56		3	Utah	83.24
47	Arkansas	20.61		4	Delaware	80.00
17	California	63.01		5	Rhode Island	77.97
20	Colorado	57.80		6	Idaho	73.98
28	Connecticut	52.46		7	New Hampshire	73.97
4	Delaware	80.00		8	Oregon	73.45
32	Florida	45.60		9	Nebraska	71.31
45	Georgia	30.39		10	Minnesota	70.64
25	Hawaii	53.97		11	Arizona	70.56
6	Idaho	73.98		12	Iowa	69.40
29	Illinois	51.58		13	Wisconsin	67.16
27	Indiana	52.69		14	Washington	66.83
12	Iowa	69.40		15	Maine	63.91
NA	Kansas**	NA		16	Wyoming	63.83
35	Kentucky	44.30		17	California	63.01
33	Louisiana	45.09		18	Maryland	61.12
15	Maine	63.91		19	Oklahoma	60.04
18	Maryland	61.12		20	Colorado	57.80
37	Massachusetts	42.39		21	Ohio	56.99
43	Michigan	38.00		22	New Jersey	56.13
10	Minnesota	70.64		23	Pennsylvania	55.51
39	Mississippi	40.48		24	Texas	54.70
38	Missouri	41.15		25	Hawaii	53.97
NA	Montana**	NA		26	Alaska	52.94
9	Nebraska	71.31		27	Indiana	52.69
31	Nevada	46.75		28	Connecticut	52.46
7	New Hampshire	73.97		29	Illinois	51.58
22	New Jersey	56.13		30	Virginia	47.45
40	New Mexico	40.00		31	Nevada	46.75
34	New York	44.46		32	Florida	45.60
36	North Carolina	44.19		33	Louisiana	45.09
2	North Dakota	85.71		34	New York	44.46
21	Ohio	56.99		35	Kentucky	44.30
19	Oklahoma	60.04		36	North Carolina	44.19
8	Oregon	73.45		37	Massachusetts	42.39
23	Pennsylvania	55.51		38	Missouri	41.15
5	Rhode Island	77.97		39	Mississippi	40.48
44	South Carolina	33.49		40	New Mexico	40.00
1	South Dakota	89.66		41	West Virginia	39.45
42	Tennessee	39.39		42	Tennessee	39.39
24	Texas	54.70		43	Michigan	38.00
3	Utah	83.24		44	South Carolina	33.49
48	Vermont	14.29		45	Georgia	30.39
30	Virginia	47.45		46	Alabama	20.63
14	Washington	66.83		47	Arkansas	20.61
41	West Virginia	39.45		48	Vermont	14.29
13	Wisconsin	67.16		NA	Kansas**	NA
16	Wyoming	63.83		NA	Montana**	NA

| | District of Columbia | 14.81 |

Source: Morgan Quitno Press using data from Federal Bureau of Investigation
   "Crime in the United States 1994" (Uniform Crime Reports, November 19, 1995)
*Arrests of youths 17 years and younger by law enforcement agencies submitting complete reports to the F.B.I. for 12 months in 1994. Arson is the willful burning of or attempt to burn a building, vehicle or another's personal property.
**Not available.

Reported Arrests of Juveniles for Weapons Violations in 1994

National Total = 52,200 Reported Arrests*

ALPHA ORDER

RANK	STATE	ARRESTS	% of USA
25	Alabama	584	1.12%
38	Alaska	148	0.28%
19	Arizona	950	1.82%
29	Arkansas	406	0.78%
1	California	10,499	20.11%
16	Colorado	1,007	1.93%
20	Connecticut	872	1.67%
46	Delaware	33	0.06%
6	Florida	2,136	4.09%
14	Georgia	1,145	2.19%
41	Hawaii	112	0.21%
31	Idaho	313	0.60%
26	Illinois	537	1.03%
30	Indiana	397	0.76%
38	Iowa	148	0.28%
NA	Kansas**	NA	NA
36	Kentucky	159	0.30%
22	Louisiana	720	1.38%
43	Maine	91	0.17%
13	Maryland	1,231	2.36%
33	Massachusetts	301	0.58%
10	Michigan	1,518	2.91%
12	Minnesota	1,258	2.41%
34	Mississippi	224	0.43%
17	Missouri	1,000	1.92%
NA	Montana**	NA	NA
32	Nebraska	307	0.59%
27	Nevada	529	1.01%
47	New Hampshire	26	0.05%
5	New Jersey	2,583	4.95%
42	New Mexico	110	0.21%
3	New York	3,460	6.63%
8	North Carolina	1,629	3.12%
45	North Dakota	53	0.10%
11	Ohio	1,466	2.81%
24	Oklahoma	623	1.19%
23	Oregon	709	1.36%
7	Pennsylvania	1,681	3.22%
35	Rhode Island	210	0.40%
18	South Carolina	988	1.89%
44	South Dakota	90	0.17%
28	Tennessee	518	0.99%
2	Texas	4,841	9.27%
21	Utah	818	1.57%
48	Vermont	2	0.00%
9	Virginia	1,554	2.98%
15	Washington	1,026	1.97%
37	West Virginia	152	0.29%
4	Wisconsin	2,699	5.17%
40	Wyoming	138	0.26%

RANK ORDER

RANK	STATE	ARRESTS	% of USA
1	California	10,499	20.11%
2	Texas	4,841	9.27%
3	New York	3,460	6.63%
4	Wisconsin	2,699	5.17%
5	New Jersey	2,583	4.95%
6	Florida	2,136	4.09%
7	Pennsylvania	1,681	3.22%
8	North Carolina	1,629	3.12%
9	Virginia	1,554	2.98%
10	Michigan	1,518	2.91%
11	Ohio	1,466	2.81%
12	Minnesota	1,258	2.41%
13	Maryland	1,231	2.36%
14	Georgia	1,145	2.19%
15	Washington	1,026	1.97%
16	Colorado	1,007	1.93%
17	Missouri	1,000	1.92%
18	South Carolina	988	1.89%
19	Arizona	950	1.82%
20	Connecticut	872	1.67%
21	Utah	818	1.57%
22	Louisiana	720	1.38%
23	Oregon	709	1.36%
24	Oklahoma	623	1.19%
25	Alabama	584	1.12%
26	Illinois	537	1.03%
27	Nevada	529	1.01%
28	Tennessee	518	0.99%
29	Arkansas	406	0.78%
30	Indiana	397	0.76%
31	Idaho	313	0.60%
32	Nebraska	307	0.59%
33	Massachusetts	301	0.58%
34	Mississippi	224	0.43%
35	Rhode Island	210	0.40%
36	Kentucky	159	0.30%
37	West Virginia	152	0.29%
38	Alaska	148	0.28%
38	Iowa	148	0.28%
40	Wyoming	138	0.26%
41	Hawaii	112	0.21%
42	New Mexico	110	0.21%
43	Maine	91	0.17%
44	South Dakota	90	0.17%
45	North Dakota	53	0.10%
46	Delaware	33	0.06%
47	New Hampshire	26	0.05%
48	Vermont	2	0.00%
NA	Kansas**	NA	NA
NA	Montana**	NA	NA
	District of Columbia	199	0.38%

Source: Federal Bureau of Investigation
    "Crime in the United States 1994" (Uniform Crime Reports, November 19, 1995)
*Arrests of youths 17 years and younger by law enforcement agencies submitting complete reports to the F.B.I. for 12 months in 1994. Weapons violations include illegal carrying and possession.
**Not available.

Reported Arrest Rate of Juveniles for Weapons Violations in 1994

National Rate = 222.4 Reported Arrests per 100,000 Juvenile Population*

ALPHA ORDER

RANK	STATE	RATE
37	Alabama	129.5
27	Alaska	197.0
23	Arizona	207.7
36	Arkansas	139.4
6	California	306.1
3	Colorado	341.4
5	Connecticut	314.6
40	Delaware	82.4
34	Florida	157.6
14	Georgia	235.2
39	Hawaii	88.6
26	Idaho	198.6
8	Illinois	268.3
38	Indiana	105.9
46	Iowa	50.2
NA	Kansas**	NA
44	Kentucky	66.5
29	Louisiana	181.9
45	Maine	66.4
12	Maryland	236.3
41	Massachusetts	75.4
30	Michigan	171.6
10	Minnesota	240.6
18	Mississippi	216.3
9	Missouri	258.9
NA	Montana**	NA
32	Nebraska	166.3
2	Nevada	370.8
47	New Hampshire	32.9
4	New Jersey	329.9
22	New Mexico	210.4
21	New York	210.5
17	North Carolina	221.8
41	North Dakota	75.4
28	Ohio	188.5
35	Oklahoma	156.6
25	Oregon	202.3
31	Pennsylvania	170.1
24	Rhode Island	207.6
13	South Carolina	236.0
33	South Dakota	163.7
16	Tennessee	225.0
11	Texas	239.6
7	Utah	290.8
48	Vermont	5.9
15	Virginia	229.3
20	Washington	213.5
43	West Virginia	72.1
1	Wisconsin	445.5
19	Wyoming	215.8

RANK ORDER

RANK	STATE	RATE
1	Wisconsin	445.5
2	Nevada	370.8
3	Colorado	341.4
4	New Jersey	329.9
5	Connecticut	314.6
6	California	306.1
7	Utah	290.8
8	Illinois	268.3
9	Missouri	258.9
10	Minnesota	240.6
11	Texas	239.6
12	Maryland	236.3
13	South Carolina	236.0
14	Georgia	235.2
15	Virginia	229.3
16	Tennessee	225.0
17	North Carolina	221.8
18	Mississippi	216.3
19	Wyoming	215.8
20	Washington	213.5
21	New York	210.5
22	New Mexico	210.4
23	Arizona	207.7
24	Rhode Island	207.6
25	Oregon	202.3
26	Idaho	198.6
27	Alaska	197.0
28	Ohio	188.5
29	Louisiana	181.9
30	Michigan	171.6
31	Pennsylvania	170.1
32	Nebraska	166.3
33	South Dakota	163.7
34	Florida	157.6
35	Oklahoma	156.6
36	Arkansas	139.4
37	Alabama	129.5
38	Indiana	105.9
39	Hawaii	88.6
40	Delaware	82.4
41	Massachusetts	75.4
41	North Dakota	75.4
43	West Virginia	72.1
44	Kentucky	66.5
45	Maine	66.4
46	Iowa	50.2
47	New Hampshire	32.9
48	Vermont	5.9
NA	Kansas**	NA
NA	Montana**	NA
	District of Columbia	457.4

Source: Morgan Quitno Press using data from Federal Bureau of Investigation
    "Crime in the United States 1994" (Uniform Crime Reports, November 19, 1995)
*By law enforcement agencies submitting complete reports to the F.B.I. for 12 months in 1994. Arrests of youths 17 years and younger divided into population of 10 to 17 year olds. See important note at beginning of this chapter. Weapons violations include illegal carrying and possession.
**Not available.

Reported Arrests of Juveniles for Weapons Violations
As a Percent of All Such Arrests in 1994
National Percent = 24.45% of Reported Arrests for Weapons Violations*

ALPHA ORDER

RANK	STATE	PERCENT
36	Alabama	20.86
25	Alaska	23.38
35	Arizona	21.13
46	Arkansas	13.60
19	California	25.26
21	Colorado	24.89
16	Connecticut	29.28
14	Delaware	32.67
27	Florida	23.33
40	Georgia	19.50
44	Hawaii	16.35
11	Idaho	35.05
15	Illinois	31.22
34	Indiana	21.28
38	Iowa	20.61
NA	Kansas**	NA
47	Kentucky	11.95
24	Louisiana	23.39
18	Maine	27.33
20	Maryland	24.99
37	Massachusetts	20.72
33	Michigan	21.63
5	Minnesota	44.19
22	Mississippi	23.83
45	Missouri	15.16
NA	Montana**	NA
29	Nebraska	23.03
28	Nevada	23.32
17	New Hampshire	27.66
6	New Jersey	37.49
10	New Mexico	35.95
30	New York	22.87
41	North Carolina	19.48
9	North Dakota	36.30
32	Ohio	21.89
39	Oklahoma	20.42
31	Oregon	22.59
7	Pennsylvania	36.71
8	Rhode Island	36.40
23	South Carolina	23.72
4	South Dakota	45.00
42	Tennessee	19.15
26	Texas	23.35
3	Utah	52.54
1	Vermont	66.67
43	Virginia	18.46
12	Washington	34.79
48	West Virginia	11.34
13	Wisconsin	34.12
2	Wyoming	53.08

RANK ORDER

RANK	STATE	PERCENT
1	Vermont	66.67
2	Wyoming	53.08
3	Utah	52.54
4	South Dakota	45.00
5	Minnesota	44.19
6	New Jersey	37.49
7	Pennsylvania	36.71
8	Rhode Island	36.40
9	North Dakota	36.30
10	New Mexico	35.95
11	Idaho	35.05
12	Washington	34.79
13	Wisconsin	34.12
14	Delaware	32.67
15	Illinois	31.22
16	Connecticut	29.28
17	New Hampshire	27.66
18	Maine	27.33
19	California	25.26
20	Maryland	24.99
21	Colorado	24.89
22	Mississippi	23.83
23	South Carolina	23.72
24	Louisiana	23.39
25	Alaska	23.38
26	Texas	23.35
27	Florida	23.33
28	Nevada	23.32
29	Nebraska	23.03
30	New York	22.87
31	Oregon	22.59
32	Ohio	21.89
33	Michigan	21.63
34	Indiana	21.28
35	Arizona	21.13
36	Alabama	20.86
37	Massachusetts	20.72
38	Iowa	20.61
39	Oklahoma	20.42
40	Georgia	19.50
41	North Carolina	19.48
42	Tennessee	19.15
43	Virginia	18.46
44	Hawaii	16.35
45	Missouri	15.16
46	Arkansas	13.60
47	Kentucky	11.95
48	West Virginia	11.34
NA	Kansas**	NA
NA	Montana**	NA
	District of Columbia	12.01

Source: Morgan Quitno Press using data from Federal Bureau of Investigation
    "Crime in the United States 1994" (Uniform Crime Reports, November 19, 1995)
*Arrests of youths 17 years and younger by law enforcement agencies submitting complete reports to the F.B.I. for
12 months in 1994. Weapons violations include illegal carrying and possession.
**Not available.

Reported Arrests of Juveniles for Driving Under the Influence in 1994

National Total = 10,573 Reported Arrests*

ALPHA ORDER

RANK	STATE	ARRESTS	% of USA
29	Alabama	112	1.06%
40	Alaska	57	0.54%
12	Arizona	280	2.65%
14	Arkansas	253	2.39%
1	California	1,780	16.84%
13	Colorado	271	2.56%
28	Connecticut	121	1.14%
48	Delaware	0	0.00%
16	Florida	234	2.21%
8	Georgia	352	3.33%
43	Hawaii	44	0.42%
25	Idaho	151	1.43%
40	Illinois	57	0.54%
33	Indiana	94	0.89%
20	Iowa	184	1.74%
NA	Kansas**	NA	NA
30	Kentucky	109	1.03%
27	Louisiana	133	1.26%
33	Maine	94	0.89%
22	Maryland	180	1.70%
35	Massachusetts	89	0.84%
4	Michigan	453	4.28%
6	Minnesota	367	3.47%
37	Mississippi	63	0.60%
17	Missouri	208	1.97%
NA	Montana**	NA	NA
11	Nebraska	293	2.77%
44	Nevada	40	0.38%
39	New Hampshire	58	0.55%
24	New Jersey	159	1.50%
32	New Mexico	101	0.96%
10	New York	296	2.80%
3	North Carolina	485	4.59%
40	North Dakota	57	0.54%
9	Ohio	346	3.27%
15	Oklahoma	249	2.36%
19	Oregon	189	1.79%
17	Pennsylvania	208	1.97%
46	Rhode Island	21	0.20%
21	South Carolina	182	1.72%
45	South Dakota	32	0.30%
31	Tennessee	107	1.01%
2	Texas	792	7.49%
26	Utah	147	1.39%
46	Vermont	21	0.20%
7	Virginia	357	3.38%
23	Washington	177	1.67%
36	West Virginia	72	0.68%
5	Wisconsin	439	4.15%
38	Wyoming	59	0.56%

RANK ORDER

RANK	STATE	ARRESTS	% of USA
1	California	1,780	16.84%
2	Texas	792	7.49%
3	North Carolina	485	4.59%
4	Michigan	453	4.28%
5	Wisconsin	439	4.15%
6	Minnesota	367	3.47%
7	Virginia	357	3.38%
8	Georgia	352	3.33%
9	Ohio	346	3.27%
10	New York	296	2.80%
11	Nebraska	293	2.77%
12	Arizona	280	2.65%
13	Colorado	271	2.56%
14	Arkansas	253	2.39%
15	Oklahoma	249	2.36%
16	Florida	234	2.21%
17	Missouri	208	1.97%
17	Pennsylvania	208	1.97%
19	Oregon	189	1.79%
20	Iowa	184	1.74%
21	South Carolina	182	1.72%
22	Maryland	180	1.70%
23	Washington	177	1.67%
24	New Jersey	159	1.50%
25	Idaho	151	1.43%
26	Utah	147	1.39%
27	Louisiana	133	1.26%
28	Connecticut	121	1.14%
29	Alabama	112	1.06%
30	Kentucky	109	1.03%
31	Tennessee	107	1.01%
32	New Mexico	101	0.96%
33	Indiana	94	0.89%
33	Maine	94	0.89%
35	Massachusetts	89	0.84%
36	West Virginia	72	0.68%
37	Mississippi	63	0.60%
38	Wyoming	59	0.56%
39	New Hampshire	58	0.55%
40	Alaska	57	0.54%
40	Illinois	57	0.54%
40	North Dakota	57	0.54%
43	Hawaii	44	0.42%
44	Nevada	40	0.38%
45	South Dakota	32	0.30%
46	Rhode Island	21	0.20%
46	Vermont	21	0.20%
48	Delaware	0	0.00%
NA	Kansas**	NA	NA
NA	Montana**	NA	NA
	District of Columbia	0	0.00%

Source: Federal Bureau of Investigation
   "Crime in the United States 1994" (Uniform Crime Reports, November 19, 1995)
Arrests of youths 17 years and younger by law enforcement agencies submitting complete reports to the F.B.I. for 12 months in 1994. Includes driving any vehicle while drunk or under the influence of liquor or narcotics.
**Not available.*

Reported Juvenile Arrest Rate for Driving Under the Influence in 1994

National Rate = 45.0 Reported Arrests per 100,000 Juvenile Population*

ALPHA ORDER

RANK ORDER

RANK	STATE	RATE
41	Alabama	24.8
8	Alaska	75.9
18	Arizona	61.2
6	Arkansas	86.9
25	California	51.9
5	Colorado	91.9
30	Connecticut	43.7
48	Delaware	0.0
47	Florida	17.3
11	Georgia	72.3
34	Hawaii	34.8
3	Idaho	95.8
38	Illinois	28.5
40	Indiana	25.1
16	Iowa	62.5
NA	Kansas**	NA
28	Kentucky	45.6
37	Louisiana	33.6
13	Maine	68.6
35	Maryland	34.6
42	Massachusetts	22.3
26	Michigan	51.2
12	Minnesota	70.2
19	Mississippi	60.8
22	Missouri	53.8
NA	Montana**	NA
2	Nebraska	158.7
39	Nevada	28.0
9	New Hampshire	73.5
45	New Jersey	20.3
1	New Mexico	193.2
46	New York	18.0
14	North Carolina	66.0
7	North Dakota	81.1
29	Ohio	44.5
15	Oklahoma	62.6
21	Oregon	53.9
43	Pennsylvania	21.0
44	Rhode Island	20.8
31	South Carolina	43.5
20	South Dakota	58.2
27	Tennessee	46.5
32	Texas	39.2
24	Utah	52.3
17	Vermont	62.3
23	Virginia	52.7
33	Washington	36.8
36	West Virginia	34.2
10	Wisconsin	72.5
4	Wyoming	92.3

RANK	STATE	RATE
1	New Mexico	193.2
2	Nebraska	158.7
3	Idaho	95.8
4	Wyoming	92.3
5	Colorado	91.9
6	Arkansas	86.9
7	North Dakota	81.1
8	Alaska	75.9
9	New Hampshire	73.5
10	Wisconsin	72.5
11	Georgia	72.3
12	Minnesota	70.2
13	Maine	68.6
14	North Carolina	66.0
15	Oklahoma	62.6
16	Iowa	62.5
17	Vermont	62.3
18	Arizona	61.2
19	Mississippi	60.8
20	South Dakota	58.2
21	Oregon	53.9
22	Missouri	53.8
23	Virginia	52.7
24	Utah	52.3
25	California	51.9
26	Michigan	51.2
27	Tennessee	46.5
28	Kentucky	45.6
29	Ohio	44.5
30	Connecticut	43.7
31	South Carolina	43.5
32	Texas	39.2
33	Washington	36.8
34	Hawaii	34.8
35	Maryland	34.6
36	West Virginia	34.2
37	Louisiana	33.6
38	Illinois	28.5
39	Nevada	28.0
40	Indiana	25.1
41	Alabama	24.8
42	Massachusetts	22.3
43	Pennsylvania	21.0
44	Rhode Island	20.8
45	New Jersey	20.3
46	New York	18.0
47	Florida	17.3
48	Delaware	0.0
NA	Kansas**	NA
NA	Montana**	NA

District of Columbia   0.0

Source: Morgan Quitno Press using data from Federal Bureau of Investigation
  "Crime in the United States 1994" (Uniform Crime Reports, November 19, 1995)
By law enforcement agencies submitting complete reports to the F.B.I. for 12 months in 1994. Arrests of youths 17
years and younger divided into population of 10 to 17 year olds. See important note at beginning of this chapter.
Includes driving any vehicle while drunk or under the influence of liquor or narcotics.
***Not available.*

Reported Arrests of Juveniles for Driving Under the Influence
As a Percent of All Such Arrests in 1994
National Percent = 0.98% of Reported Arrests for Driving Under the Influence*

ALPHA ORDER

RANK	STATE	PERCENT
44	Alabama	0.61
19	Alaska	1.17
25	Arizona	1.05
8	Arkansas	1.35
34	California	0.86
15	Colorado	1.26
13	Connecticut	1.28
48	Delaware	0.00
47	Florida	0.46
29	Georgia	1.01
28	Hawaii	1.02
6	Idaho	1.50
37	Illinois	0.82
46	Indiana	0.57
11	Iowa	1.32
NA	Kansas**	NA
17	Kentucky	1.19
31	Louisiana	0.97
8	Maine	1.35
35	Maryland	0.85
39	Massachusetts	0.73
21	Michigan	1.10
18	Minnesota	1.18
19	Mississippi	1.17
30	Missouri	0.98
NA	Montana**	NA
1	Nebraska	2.32
43	Nevada	0.66
10	New Hampshire	1.34
41	New Jersey	0.67
3	New Mexico	2.12
44	New York	0.61
5	North Carolina	1.62
4	North Dakota	2.05
16	Ohio	1.21
21	Oklahoma	1.10
27	Oregon	1.03
40	Pennsylvania	0.69
24	Rhode Island	1.06
25	South Carolina	1.05
38	South Dakota	0.78
41	Tennessee	0.67
33	Texas	0.87
2	Utah	2.26
7	Vermont	1.43
23	Virginia	1.08
32	Washington	0.91
36	West Virginia	0.84
14	Wisconsin	1.27
12	Wyoming	1.31

RANK ORDER

RANK	STATE	PERCENT
1	Nebraska	2.32
2	Utah	2.26
3	New Mexico	2.12
4	North Dakota	2.05
5	North Carolina	1.62
6	Idaho	1.50
7	Vermont	1.43
8	Arkansas	1.35
8	Maine	1.35
10	New Hampshire	1.34
11	Iowa	1.32
12	Wyoming	1.31
13	Connecticut	1.28
14	Wisconsin	1.27
15	Colorado	1.26
16	Ohio	1.21
17	Kentucky	1.19
18	Minnesota	1.18
19	Alaska	1.17
19	Mississippi	1.17
21	Michigan	1.10
21	Oklahoma	1.10
23	Virginia	1.08
24	Rhode Island	1.06
25	Arizona	1.05
25	South Carolina	1.05
27	Oregon	1.03
28	Hawaii	1.02
29	Georgia	1.01
30	Missouri	0.98
31	Louisiana	0.97
32	Washington	0.91
33	Texas	0.87
34	California	0.86
35	Maryland	0.85
36	West Virginia	0.84
37	Illinois	0.82
38	South Dakota	0.78
39	Massachusetts	0.73
40	Pennsylvania	0.69
41	New Jersey	0.67
41	Tennessee	0.67
43	Nevada	0.66
44	Alabama	0.61
44	New York	0.61
46	Indiana	0.57
47	Florida	0.46
48	Delaware	0.00
NA	Kansas**	NA
NA	Montana**	NA
	District of Columbia	0.00

Source: Morgan Quitno Press using data from Federal Bureau of Investigation
"Crime in the United States 1994" (Uniform Crime Reports, November 19, 1995)
Arrests of youths 17 years and younger by law enforcement agencies submitting complete reports to the F.B.I. for 12 months in 1994. Includes driving any vehicle while drunk or under the influence of liquor or narcotics.
**Not available.*

Reported Arrests of Juveniles for Drug Abuse Violations in 1994

National Total = 131,220 Reported Arrests*

RANK	STATE	ARRESTS	% of USA
29	Alabama	945	0.72%
43	Alaska	286	0.22%
8	Arizona	3,886	2.96%
32	Arkansas	771	0.59%
1	California	22,809	17.38%
18	Colorado	2,197	1.67%
11	Connecticut	3,110	2.37%
46	Delaware	93	0.07%
4	Florida	8,644	6.59%
17	Georgia	2,308	1.76%
33	Hawaii	664	0.51%
37	Idaho	504	0.38%
27	Illinois	1,086	0.83%
25	Indiana	1,203	0.92%
39	Iowa	368	0.28%
NA	Kansas**	NA	NA
31	Kentucky	825	0.63%
22	Louisiana	1,668	1.27%
38	Maine	384	0.29%
6	Maryland	6,246	4.76%
16	Massachusetts	2,382	1.82%
10	Michigan	3,361	2.56%
15	Minnesota	2,553	1.95%
35	Mississippi	569	0.43%
19	Missouri	2,124	1.62%
NA	Montana**	NA	NA
36	Nebraska	534	0.41%
30	Nevada	878	0.67%
40	New Hampshire	356	0.27%
5	New Jersey	8,189	6.24%
41	New Mexico	310	0.24%
2	New York	13,048	9.94%
13	North Carolina	3,003	2.29%
47	North Dakota	78	0.06%
9	Ohio	3,849	2.93%
26	Oklahoma	1,166	0.89%
24	Oregon	1,645	1.25%
7	Pennsylvania	4,405	3.36%
34	Rhode Island	593	0.45%
20	South Carolina	2,061	1.57%
44	South Dakota	205	0.16%
28	Tennessee	1,044	0.80%
3	Texas	10,592	8.07%
23	Utah	1,648	1.26%
48	Vermont	27	0.02%
14	Virginia	2,562	1.95%
21	Washington	1,884	1.44%
42	West Virginia	306	0.23%
12	Wisconsin	3,076	2.34%
45	Wyoming	188	0.14%

RANK	STATE	ARRESTS	% of USA
1	California	22,809	17.38%
2	New York	13,048	9.94%
3	Texas	10,592	8.07%
4	Florida	8,644	6.59%
5	New Jersey	8,189	6.24%
6	Maryland	6,246	4.76%
7	Pennsylvania	4,405	3.36%
8	Arizona	3,886	2.96%
9	Ohio	3,849	2.93%
10	Michigan	3,361	2.56%
11	Connecticut	3,110	2.37%
12	Wisconsin	3,076	2.34%
13	North Carolina	3,003	2.29%
14	Virginia	2,562	1.95%
15	Minnesota	2,553	1.95%
16	Massachusetts	2,382	1.82%
17	Georgia	2,308	1.76%
18	Colorado	2,197	1.67%
19	Missouri	2,124	1.62%
20	South Carolina	2,061	1.57%
21	Washington	1,884	1.44%
22	Louisiana	1,668	1.27%
23	Utah	1,648	1.26%
24	Oregon	1,645	1.25%
25	Indiana	1,203	0.92%
26	Oklahoma	1,166	0.89%
27	Illinois	1,086	0.83%
28	Tennessee	1,044	0.80%
29	Alabama	945	0.72%
30	Nevada	878	0.67%
31	Kentucky	825	0.63%
32	Arkansas	771	0.59%
33	Hawaii	664	0.51%
34	Rhode Island	593	0.45%
35	Mississippi	569	0.43%
36	Nebraska	534	0.41%
37	Idaho	504	0.38%
38	Maine	384	0.29%
39	Iowa	368	0.28%
40	New Hampshire	356	0.27%
41	New Mexico	310	0.24%
42	West Virginia	306	0.23%
43	Alaska	286	0.22%
44	South Dakota	205	0.16%
45	Wyoming	188	0.14%
46	Delaware	93	0.07%
47	North Dakota	78	0.06%
48	Vermont	27	0.02%
NA	Kansas**	NA	NA
NA	Montana**	NA	NA
	District of Columbia	587	0.45%

Source: Federal Bureau of Investigation
"Crime in the United States 1994" (Uniform Crime Reports, November 19, 1995)
*Arrests of youths 17 years and younger by law enforcement agencies submitting complete reports to the F.B.I. for 12 months in 1994. Includes offenses relating to possession, sale, use, growing and manufacturing of narcotic drugs.
**Not available.

Reported Arrest Rate of Juveniles for Drug Abuse Violations in 1994

National Rate = 559.0 Reported Arrests per 100,000 Juvenile Population*

ALPHA ORDER

RANK ORDER

RANK	STATE	RATE		RANK	STATE	RATE
44	Alabama	209.6		1	Maryland	1,199.1
31	Alaska	380.8		2	Connecticut	1,122.0
4	Arizona	849.8		3	New Jersey	1,045.8
42	Arkansas	264.8		4	Arizona	849.8
7	California	665.0		5	New York	793.8
6	Colorado	744.8		6	Colorado	744.8
2	Connecticut	1,122.0		7	California	665.0
43	Delaware	232.1		8	Florida	637.8
8	Florida	637.8		9	Nevada	615.5
23	Georgia	474.1		10	Massachusetts	596.4
17	Hawaii	525.5		11	New Mexico	592.9
37	Idaho	319.8		12	Rhode Island	586.1
16	Illinois	542.5		13	Utah	585.9
36	Indiana	321.0		14	Missouri	549.8
46	Iowa	124.9		15	Mississippi	549.4
NA	Kansas**	NA		16	Illinois	542.5
35	Kentucky	345.3		17	Hawaii	525.5
28	Louisiana	421.5		18	Texas	524.3
41	Maine	280.1		19	Wisconsin	507.8
1	Maryland	1,199.1		20	Ohio	495.0
10	Massachusetts	596.4		21	South Carolina	492.2
32	Michigan	379.8		22	Minnesota	488.3
22	Minnesota	488.3		23	Georgia	474.1
15	Mississippi	549.4		24	Oregon	469.3
14	Missouri	549.8		25	Tennessee	453.5
NA	Montana**	NA		26	New Hampshire	451.0
40	Nebraska	289.3		27	Pennsylvania	445.6
9	Nevada	615.5		28	Louisiana	421.5
26	New Hampshire	451.0		29	North Carolina	408.9
3	New Jersey	1,045.8		30	Washington	392.0
11	New Mexico	592.9		31	Alaska	380.8
5	New York	793.8		32	Michigan	379.8
29	North Carolina	408.9		33	Virginia	378.0
47	North Dakota	111.0		34	South Dakota	373.0
20	Ohio	495.0		35	Kentucky	345.3
39	Oklahoma	293.2		36	Indiana	321.0
24	Oregon	469.3		37	Idaho	319.8
27	Pennsylvania	445.6		38	Wyoming	294.0
12	Rhode Island	586.1		39	Oklahoma	293.2
21	South Carolina	492.2		40	Nebraska	289.3
34	South Dakota	373.0		41	Maine	280.1
25	Tennessee	453.5		42	Arkansas	264.8
18	Texas	524.3		43	Delaware	232.1
13	Utah	585.9		44	Alabama	209.6
48	Vermont	80.0		45	West Virginia	145.2
33	Virginia	378.0		46	Iowa	124.9
30	Washington	392.0		47	North Dakota	111.0
45	West Virginia	145.2		48	Vermont	80.0
19	Wisconsin	507.8		NA	Kansas**	NA
38	Wyoming	294.0		NA	Montana**	NA
					District of Columbia	1,349.2

Source: Morgan Quitno Press using data from Federal Bureau of Investigation
   "Crime in the United States 1994" (Uniform Crime Reports, November 19, 1995)
*By law enforcement agencies submitting complete reports to the F.B.I. for 12 months in 1994. Arrests of youths 17 years and younger divided into population of 10 to 17 year olds. See important note at beginning of this chapter. Includes offenses relating to possession, sale, use, growing and manufacturing of narcotic drugs.
**Not available.

Reported Arrests of Juveniles for Drug Abuse Violations
As a Percent of All Such Arrests in 1994
National Percent = 11.73% of Reported Drug Abuse Violation Arrests*

ALPHA ORDER

RANK	STATE	PERCENT
45	Alabama	8.57
6	Alaska	19.92
8	Arizona	18.20
47	Arkansas	8.37
46	California	8.42
9	Colorado	18.16
17	Connecticut	15.62
18	Delaware	15.02
35	Florida	10.81
44	Georgia	9.24
10	Hawaii	17.98
13	Idaho	16.63
2	Illinois	22.36
16	Indiana	15.98
48	Iowa	8.13
NA	Kansas**	NA
43	Kentucky	9.30
34	Louisiana	11.32
22	Maine	14.55
14	Maryland	16.50
29	Massachusetts	11.85
33	Michigan	11.50
3	Minnesota	20.24
26	Mississippi	11.97
28	Missouri	11.92
NA	Montana**	NA
38	Nebraska	10.10
41	Nevada	9.56
11	New Hampshire	17.22
12	New Jersey	16.68
1	New Mexico	27.65
40	New York	9.97
39	North Carolina	10.01
27	North Dakota	11.96
25	Ohio	12.19
42	Oklahoma	9.53
30	Oregon	11.74
20	Pennsylvania	14.83
19	Rhode Island	14.88
32	South Carolina	11.56
4	South Dakota	20.10
37	Tennessee	10.43
21	Texas	14.71
5	Utah	19.97
24	Vermont	12.62
36	Virginia	10.63
23	Washington	13.60
31	West Virginia	11.59
7	Wisconsin	18.43
15	Wyoming	16.05

RANK ORDER

RANK	STATE	PERCENT
1	New Mexico	27.65
2	Illinois	22.36
3	Minnesota	20.24
4	South Dakota	20.10
5	Utah	19.97
6	Alaska	19.92
7	Wisconsin	18.43
8	Arizona	18.20
9	Colorado	18.16
10	Hawaii	17.98
11	New Hampshire	17.22
12	New Jersey	16.68
13	Idaho	16.63
14	Maryland	16.50
15	Wyoming	16.05
16	Indiana	15.98
17	Connecticut	15.62
18	Delaware	15.02
19	Rhode Island	14.88
20	Pennsylvania	14.83
21	Texas	14.71
22	Maine	14.55
23	Washington	13.60
24	Vermont	12.62
25	Ohio	12.19
26	Mississippi	11.97
27	North Dakota	11.96
28	Missouri	11.92
29	Massachusetts	11.85
30	Oregon	11.74
31	West Virginia	11.59
32	South Carolina	11.56
33	Michigan	11.50
34	Louisiana	11.32
35	Florida	10.81
36	Virginia	10.63
37	Tennessee	10.43
38	Nebraska	10.10
39	North Carolina	10.01
40	New York	9.97
41	Nevada	9.56
42	Oklahoma	9.53
43	Kentucky	9.30
44	Georgia	9.24
45	Alabama	8.57
46	California	8.42
47	Arkansas	8.37
48	Iowa	8.13
NA	Kansas**	NA
NA	Montana**	NA
	District of Columbia	8.18

Source: Morgan Quitno Press using data from Federal Bureau of Investigation
     "Crime in the United States 1994" (Uniform Crime Reports, November 19, 1995)
*Arrests of youths 17 years and younger by law enforcement agencies submitting complete reports to the F.B.I. for 12 months in 1994. Includes offenses relating to possession, sale, use, growing and manufacturing of narcotic drugs.
**Not available.

Reported Arrests of Juveniles for Sex Offenses in 1994

National Total = 14,418 Reported Arrests*

ALPHA ORDER

RANK	STATE	ARRESTS	% of USA
41	Alabama	29	0.20%
33	Alaska	76	0.53%
18	Arizona	306	2.12%
37	Arkansas	50	0.35%
1	California	2,245	15.57%
14	Colorado	368	2.55%
23	Connecticut	166	1.15%
45	Delaware	12	0.08%
6	Florida	584	4.05%
17	Georgia	329	2.28%
28	Hawaii	111	0.77%
32	Idaho	83	0.58%
33	Illinois	76	0.53%
21	Indiana	190	1.32%
35	Iowa	70	0.49%
NA	Kansas**	NA	NA
25	Kentucky	131	0.91%
22	Louisiana	168	1.17%
26	Maine	128	0.89%
11	Maryland	414	2.87%
29	Massachusetts	93	0.65%
9	Michigan	441	3.06%
20	Minnesota	245	1.70%
44	Mississippi	21	0.15%
16	Missouri	333	2.31%
NA	Montana**	NA	NA
27	Nebraska	114	0.79%
30	Nevada	91	0.63%
40	New Hampshire	31	0.22%
8	New Jersey	470	3.26%
46	New Mexico	9	0.06%
3	New York	1,257	8.72%
19	North Carolina	248	1.72%
42	North Dakota	25	0.17%
13	Ohio	380	2.64%
31	Oklahoma	86	0.60%
15	Oregon	360	2.50%
7	Pennsylvania	500	3.47%
36	Rhode Island	57	0.40%
24	South Carolina	151	1.05%
43	South Dakota	24	0.17%
38	Tennessee	34	0.24%
4	Texas	993	6.89%
12	Utah	404	2.80%
48	Vermont	5	0.03%
10	Virginia	436	3.02%
5	Washington	609	4.22%
39	West Virginia	33	0.23%
2	Wisconsin	1,411	9.79%
47	Wyoming	7	0.05%

RANK ORDER

RANK	STATE	ARRESTS	% of USA
1	California	2,245	15.57%
2	Wisconsin	1,411	9.79%
3	New York	1,257	8.72%
4	Texas	993	6.89%
5	Washington	609	4.22%
6	Florida	584	4.05%
7	Pennsylvania	500	3.47%
8	New Jersey	470	3.26%
9	Michigan	441	3.06%
10	Virginia	436	3.02%
11	Maryland	414	2.87%
12	Utah	404	2.80%
13	Ohio	380	2.64%
14	Colorado	368	2.55%
15	Oregon	360	2.50%
16	Missouri	333	2.31%
17	Georgia	329	2.28%
18	Arizona	306	2.12%
19	North Carolina	248	1.72%
20	Minnesota	245	1.70%
21	Indiana	190	1.32%
22	Louisiana	168	1.17%
23	Connecticut	166	1.15%
24	South Carolina	151	1.05%
25	Kentucky	131	0.91%
26	Maine	128	0.89%
27	Nebraska	114	0.79%
28	Hawaii	111	0.77%
29	Massachusetts	93	0.65%
30	Nevada	91	0.63%
31	Oklahoma	86	0.60%
32	Idaho	83	0.58%
33	Alaska	76	0.53%
33	Illinois	76	0.53%
35	Iowa	70	0.49%
36	Rhode Island	57	0.40%
37	Arkansas	50	0.35%
38	Tennessee	34	0.24%
39	West Virginia	33	0.23%
40	New Hampshire	31	0.22%
41	Alabama	29	0.20%
42	North Dakota	25	0.17%
43	South Dakota	24	0.17%
44	Mississippi	21	0.15%
45	Delaware	12	0.08%
46	New Mexico	9	0.06%
47	Wyoming	7	0.05%
48	Vermont	5	0.03%
NA	Kansas**	NA	NA
NA	Montana**	NA	NA
	District of Columbia	14	0.10%

Source: Federal Bureau of Investigation
   "Crime in the United States 1994" (Uniform Crime Reports, November 19, 1995)
Arrests of youths 17 years and younger by law enforcement agencies submitting complete reports to the F.B.I. for 12 months in 1994. Excludes forcible rape, prostitution and commercialized vice. Includes statutory rape and offenses against chastity, common decency, morals and the like.
**Not available.*

Reported Arrest Rate of Juveniles for Sex Offenses in 1994

National Rate = 61.4 Reported Arrests per 100,000 Juvenile Population*

ALPHA ORDER				RANK ORDER		
RANK	STATE	RATE		RANK	STATE	RATE
48	Alabama	6.4		1	Wisconsin	232.9
6	Alaska	101.2		2	Utah	143.6
13	Arizona	66.9		3	Washington	126.7
42	Arkansas	17.2		4	Colorado	124.8
14	California	65.5		5	Oregon	102.7
4	Colorado	124.8		6	Alaska	101.2
19	Connecticut	59.9		7	Maine	93.4
37	Delaware	29.9		8	Hawaii	87.8
30	Florida	43.1		9	Missouri	86.2
12	Georgia	67.6		10	Maryland	79.5
8	Hawaii	87.8		11	New York	76.5
22	Idaho	52.7		12	Georgia	67.6
33	Illinois	38.0		13	Arizona	66.9
23	Indiana	50.7		14	California	65.5
38	Iowa	23.8		15	Virginia	64.3
NA	Kansas**	NA		16	Nevada	63.8
21	Kentucky	54.8		17	Nebraska	61.8
31	Louisiana	42.4		18	New Jersey	60.0
7	Maine	93.4		19	Connecticut	59.9
10	Maryland	79.5		20	Rhode Island	56.3
39	Massachusetts	23.3		21	Kentucky	54.8
25	Michigan	49.8		22	Idaho	52.7
28	Minnesota	46.9		23	Indiana	50.7
41	Mississippi	20.3		24	Pennsylvania	50.6
9	Missouri	86.2		25	Michigan	49.8
NA	Montana**	NA		26	Texas	49.2
17	Nebraska	61.8		27	Ohio	48.9
16	Nevada	63.8		28	Minnesota	46.9
32	New Hampshire	39.3		29	South Dakota	43.7
18	New Jersey	60.0		30	Florida	43.1
42	New Mexico	17.2		31	Louisiana	42.4
11	New York	76.5		32	New Hampshire	39.3
36	North Carolina	33.8		33	Illinois	38.0
35	North Dakota	35.6		34	South Carolina	36.1
27	Ohio	48.9		35	North Dakota	35.6
40	Oklahoma	21.6		36	North Carolina	33.8
5	Oregon	102.7		37	Delaware	29.9
24	Pennsylvania	50.6		38	Iowa	23.8
20	Rhode Island	56.3		39	Massachusetts	23.3
34	South Carolina	36.1		40	Oklahoma	21.6
29	South Dakota	43.7		41	Mississippi	20.3
45	Tennessee	14.8		42	Arkansas	17.2
26	Texas	49.2		42	New Mexico	17.2
2	Utah	143.6		44	West Virginia	15.7
45	Vermont	14.8		45	Tennessee	14.8
15	Virginia	64.3		45	Vermont	14.8
3	Washington	126.7		47	Wyoming	10.9
44	West Virginia	15.7		48	Alabama	6.4
1	Wisconsin	232.9		NA	Kansas**	NA
47	Wyoming	10.9		NA	Montana**	NA
					District of Columbia	32.2

Source: Morgan Quitno Press using data from Federal Bureau of Investigation
   "Crime in the United States 1994" (Uniform Crime Reports, November 19, 1995)
*By law enforcement agencies submitting complete reports to the F.B.I. for 12 months in 1994. Arrests of youths 17 years and younger divided into population of 10 to 17 year olds. See important note at beginning of this chapter. Excludes forcible rape, prostitution and commercialized vice. Includes statutory rape and offenses against chastity, common decency, morals and the like. **Not available.

Reported Arrests of Juveniles for Sex Offenses
As a Percent of All Such Arrests in 1994
National Percent = 17.61% of Reported Sex Offense Arrests*

ALPHA ORDER

RANK ORDER

RANK	STATE	PERCENT	RANK	STATE	PERCENT
47	Alabama	7.32	1	Wisconsin	36.64
19	Alaska	19.49	2	Utah	36.30
28	Arizona	14.89	3	North Dakota	34.72
42	Arkansas	9.92	4	Vermont	31.25
34	California	14.04	5	Idaho	29.64
14	Colorado	22.01	6	Minnesota	28.76
18	Connecticut	19.69	7	Maine	27.00
35	Delaware	13.95	8	Washington	26.01
36	Florida	12.22	9	Iowa	25.09
38	Georgia	11.00	10	Maryland	24.98
11	Hawaii	24.78	11	Hawaii	24.78
5	Idaho	29.64	12	Oregon	23.14
22	Illinois	18.49	13	Pennsylvania	22.10
25	Indiana	16.71	14	Colorado	22.01
9	Iowa	25.09	15	South Carolina	21.85
NA	Kansas**	NA	16	New Jersey	21.70
43	Kentucky	9.60	17	New York	19.76
30	Louisiana	14.62	18	Connecticut	19.69
7	Maine	27.00	19	Alaska	19.49
10	Maryland	24.98	20	South Dakota	19.05
40	Massachusetts	9.99	21	Michigan	19.01
21	Michigan	19.01	22	Illinois	18.49
6	Minnesota	28.76	23	New Hampshire	18.45
37	Mississippi	12.21	24	Texas	17.74
29	Missouri	14.65	25	Indiana	16.71
NA	Montana**	NA	26	Ohio	15.66
32	Nebraska	14.30	27	Virginia	14.90
41	Nevada	9.97	28	Arizona	14.89
23	New Hampshire	18.45	29	Missouri	14.65
16	New Jersey	21.70	30	Louisiana	14.62
33	New Mexico	14.29	31	Rhode Island	14.50
17	New York	19.76	32	Nebraska	14.30
44	North Carolina	9.57	33	New Mexico	14.29
3	North Dakota	34.72	34	California	14.04
26	Ohio	15.66	35	Delaware	13.95
45	Oklahoma	8.70	36	Florida	12.22
12	Oregon	23.14	37	Mississippi	12.21
13	Pennsylvania	22.10	38	Georgia	11.00
31	Rhode Island	14.50	39	West Virginia	10.68
15	South Carolina	21.85	40	Massachusetts	9.99
20	South Dakota	19.05	41	Nevada	9.97
46	Tennessee	7.36	42	Arkansas	9.92
24	Texas	17.74	43	Kentucky	9.60
2	Utah	36.30	44	North Carolina	9.57
4	Vermont	31.25	45	Oklahoma	8.70
27	Virginia	14.90	46	Tennessee	7.36
8	Washington	26.01	47	Alabama	7.32
39	West Virginia	10.68	48	Wyoming	5.60
1	Wisconsin	36.64	NA	Kansas**	NA
48	Wyoming	5.60	NA	Montana**	NA

District of Columbia 12.07

Source: Morgan Quitno Press using data from Federal Bureau of Investigation
"Crime in the United States 1994" (Uniform Crime Reports, November 19, 1995)
*Arrests of youths 17 years and younger by law enforcement agencies submitting complete reports to the F.B.I. for 12 months in 1994. Excludes forcible rape, prostitution and commercialized vice. Includes statutory rape and offenses against chastity, common decency, morals and the like.
**Not available.

Reported Arrests of Juveniles for Prostitution and Commercialized Vice in 1994

National Total = 1,013 Reported Arrests*

ALPHA ORDER

RANK	STATE	ARRESTS	% of USA
37	Alabama	2	0.20%
27	Alaska	7	0.69%
14	Arizona	20	1.97%
30	Arkansas	6	0.59%
1	California	202	19.94%
21	Colorado	12	1.18%
12	Connecticut	22	2.17%
43	Delaware	0	0.00%
2	Florida	103	10.17%
14	Georgia	20	1.97%
23	Hawaii	11	1.09%
37	Idaho	2	0.20%
32	Illinois	4	0.39%
18	Indiana	14	1.38%
32	Iowa	4	0.39%
NA	Kansas**	NA	NA
27	Kentucky	7	0.69%
32	Louisiana	4	0.39%
42	Maine	1	0.10%
21	Maryland	12	1.18%
23	Massachusetts	11	1.09%
11	Michigan	25	2.47%
8	Minnesota	35	3.46%
32	Mississippi	4	0.39%
5	Missouri	43	4.24%
NA	Montana**	NA	NA
27	Nebraska	7	0.69%
31	Nevada	5	0.49%
37	New Hampshire	2	0.20%
10	New Jersey	27	2.67%
43	New Mexico	0	0.00%
4	New York	84	8.29%
25	North Carolina	10	0.99%
43	North Dakota	0	0.00%
5	Ohio	43	4.24%
19	Oklahoma	13	1.28%
19	Oregon	13	1.28%
12	Pennsylvania	22	2.17%
32	Rhode Island	4	0.39%
16	South Carolina	17	1.68%
43	South Dakota	0	0.00%
37	Tennessee	2	0.20%
3	Texas	94	9.28%
26	Utah	9	0.89%
43	Vermont	0	0.00%
17	Virginia	15	1.48%
7	Washington	42	4.15%
37	West Virginia	2	0.20%
9	Wisconsin	31	3.06%
43	Wyoming	0	0.00%

RANK ORDER

RANK	STATE	ARRESTS	% of USA
1	California	202	19.94%
2	Florida	103	10.17%
3	Texas	94	9.28%
4	New York	84	8.29%
5	Missouri	43	4.24%
5	Ohio	43	4.24%
7	Washington	42	4.15%
8	Minnesota	35	3.46%
9	Wisconsin	31	3.06%
10	New Jersey	27	2.67%
11	Michigan	25	2.47%
12	Connecticut	22	2.17%
12	Pennsylvania	22	2.17%
14	Arizona	20	1.97%
14	Georgia	20	1.97%
16	South Carolina	17	1.68%
17	Virginia	15	1.48%
18	Indiana	14	1.38%
19	Oklahoma	13	1.28%
19	Oregon	13	1.28%
21	Colorado	12	1.18%
21	Maryland	12	1.18%
23	Hawaii	11	1.09%
23	Massachusetts	11	1.09%
25	North Carolina	10	0.99%
26	Utah	9	0.89%
27	Alaska	7	0.69%
27	Kentucky	7	0.69%
27	Nebraska	7	0.69%
30	Arkansas	6	0.59%
31	Nevada	5	0.49%
32	Illinois	4	0.39%
32	Iowa	4	0.39%
32	Louisiana	4	0.39%
32	Mississippi	4	0.39%
32	Rhode Island	4	0.39%
37	Alabama	2	0.20%
37	Idaho	2	0.20%
37	New Hampshire	2	0.20%
37	Tennessee	2	0.20%
37	West Virginia	2	0.20%
42	Maine	1	0.10%
43	Delaware	0	0.00%
43	New Mexico	0	0.00%
43	North Dakota	0	0.00%
43	South Dakota	0	0.00%
43	Vermont	0	0.00%
43	Wyoming	0	0.00%
NA	Kansas**	NA	NA
NA	Montana**	NA	NA
	District of Columbia	0	0.00%

Source: Federal Bureau of Investigation
   "Crime in the United States 1994" (Uniform Crime Reports, November 19, 1995)
*Arrests of youths 17 years and younger by law enforcement agencies submitting complete reports to the F.B.I. for 12 months in 1994. Includes keeping a bawdy house, procuring or transporting women for immoral purposes. Attempts are included.
**Not available.

Reported Juvenile Arrest Rate for Prostitution and Commercialized Vice in 1994

National Rate = 4.3 Reported Arrests per 100,000 Population*

ALPHA ORDER

RANK	STATE	RATE
42	Alabama	0.4
2	Alaska	9.3
13	Arizona	4.4
33	Arkansas	2.1
8	California	5.9
14	Colorado	4.1
5	Connecticut	7.9
43	Delaware	0.0
6	Florida	7.6
14	Georgia	4.1
3	Hawaii	8.7
37	Idaho	1.3
34	Illinois	2.0
20	Indiana	3.7
35	Iowa	1.4
NA	Kansas**	NA
26	Kentucky	2.9
38	Louisiana	1.0
41	Maine	0.7
30	Maryland	2.3
27	Massachusetts	2.8
27	Michigan	2.8
7	Minnesota	6.7
18	Mississippi	3.9
1	Missouri	11.1
NA	Montana**	NA
19	Nebraska	3.8
22	Nevada	3.5
29	New Hampshire	2.5
23	New Jersey	3.4
43	New Mexico	0.0
10	New York	5.1
35	North Carolina	1.4
43	North Dakota	0.0
9	Ohio	5.5
24	Oklahoma	3.3
20	Oregon	3.7
31	Pennsylvania	2.2
17	Rhode Island	4.0
14	South Carolina	4.1
43	South Dakota	0.0
39	Tennessee	0.9
12	Texas	4.7
25	Utah	3.2
43	Vermont	0.0
31	Virginia	2.2
3	Washington	8.7
39	West Virginia	0.9
10	Wisconsin	5.1
43	Wyoming	0.0

RANK ORDER

RANK	STATE	RATE
1	Missouri	11.1
2	Alaska	9.3
3	Hawaii	8.7
3	Washington	8.7
5	Connecticut	7.9
6	Florida	7.6
7	Minnesota	6.7
8	California	5.9
9	Ohio	5.5
10	New York	5.1
10	Wisconsin	5.1
12	Texas	4.7
13	Arizona	4.4
14	Colorado	4.1
14	Georgia	4.1
14	South Carolina	4.1
17	Rhode Island	4.0
18	Mississippi	3.9
19	Nebraska	3.8
20	Indiana	3.7
20	Oregon	3.7
22	Nevada	3.5
23	New Jersey	3.4
24	Oklahoma	3.3
25	Utah	3.2
26	Kentucky	2.9
27	Massachusetts	2.8
27	Michigan	2.8
29	New Hampshire	2.5
30	Maryland	2.3
31	Pennsylvania	2.2
31	Virginia	2.2
33	Arkansas	2.1
34	Illinois	2.0
35	Iowa	1.4
35	North Carolina	1.4
37	Idaho	1.3
38	Louisiana	1.0
39	Tennessee	0.9
39	West Virginia	0.9
41	Maine	0.7
42	Alabama	0.4
43	Delaware	0.0
43	New Mexico	0.0
43	North Dakota	0.0
43	South Dakota	0.0
43	Vermont	0.0
43	Wyoming	0.0
NA	Kansas**	NA
NA	Montana**	NA
	District of Columbia	0.0

Source: Morgan Quitno Press using data from Federal Bureau of Investigation
  "Crime in the United States 1994" (Uniform Crime Reports, November 19, 1995)
*By law enforcement agencies submitting complete reports to the F.B.I. for 12 months in 1994. Arrests of youths 17 years and younger divided into population of 10 to 17 year olds. See important note at beginning of this chapter. Includes keeping a bawdy house, procuring or transporting women for immoral purposes. Attempts are included.
**Not available.

Reported Arrests of Juveniles for Prostitution and Commercialized Vice As a Percent of All Such Arrests in 1994
National Percent = 1.17% of Reported Prostitution/Commercialized Vice Arrests*

<table>
<tr><td colspan="3">ALPHA ORDER</td><td colspan="3">RANK ORDER</td></tr>
<tr><td>RANK</td><td>STATE</td><td>PERCENT</td><td>RANK</td><td>STATE</td><td>PERCENT</td></tr>
<tr><td>38</td><td>Alabama</td><td>0.82</td><td>1</td><td>New Hampshire</td><td>20.00</td></tr>
<tr><td>4</td><td>Alaska</td><td>4.70</td><td>2</td><td>Idaho</td><td>11.11</td></tr>
<tr><td>29</td><td>Arizona</td><td>1.14</td><td>3</td><td>Mississippi</td><td>10.53</td></tr>
<tr><td>12</td><td>Arkansas</td><td>1.88</td><td>4</td><td>Alaska</td><td>4.70</td></tr>
<tr><td>31</td><td>California</td><td>1.12</td><td>5</td><td>Oklahoma</td><td>4.50</td></tr>
<tr><td>36</td><td>Colorado</td><td>0.84</td><td>6</td><td>Washington</td><td>3.40</td></tr>
<tr><td>9</td><td>Connecticut</td><td>2.60</td><td>7</td><td>Minnesota</td><td>2.67</td></tr>
<tr><td>43</td><td>Delaware</td><td>0.00</td><td>8</td><td>Nebraska</td><td>2.63</td></tr>
<tr><td>20</td><td>Florida</td><td>1.44</td><td>9</td><td>Connecticut</td><td>2.60</td></tr>
<tr><td>24</td><td>Georgia</td><td>1.33</td><td>10</td><td>South Carolina</td><td>2.56</td></tr>
<tr><td>11</td><td>Hawaii</td><td>2.42</td><td>11</td><td>Hawaii</td><td>2.42</td></tr>
<tr><td>2</td><td>Idaho</td><td>11.11</td><td>12</td><td>Arkansas</td><td>1.88</td></tr>
<tr><td>17</td><td>Illinois</td><td>1.55</td><td>13</td><td>Wisconsin</td><td>1.82</td></tr>
<tr><td>21</td><td>Indiana</td><td>1.39</td><td>14</td><td>Oregon</td><td>1.69</td></tr>
<tr><td>18</td><td>Iowa</td><td>1.54</td><td>15</td><td>West Virginia</td><td>1.61</td></tr>
<tr><td>NA</td><td>Kansas**</td><td>NA</td><td>16</td><td>Utah</td><td>1.59</td></tr>
<tr><td>23</td><td>Kentucky</td><td>1.37</td><td>17</td><td>Illinois</td><td>1.55</td></tr>
<tr><td>29</td><td>Louisiana</td><td>1.14</td><td>18</td><td>Iowa</td><td>1.54</td></tr>
<tr><td>19</td><td>Maine</td><td>1.47</td><td>19</td><td>Maine</td><td>1.47</td></tr>
<tr><td>36</td><td>Maryland</td><td>0.84</td><td>20</td><td>Florida</td><td>1.44</td></tr>
<tr><td>40</td><td>Massachusetts</td><td>0.47</td><td>21</td><td>Indiana</td><td>1.39</td></tr>
<tr><td>35</td><td>Michigan</td><td>0.88</td><td>21</td><td>Missouri</td><td>1.39</td></tr>
<tr><td>7</td><td>Minnesota</td><td>2.67</td><td>23</td><td>Kentucky</td><td>1.37</td></tr>
<tr><td>3</td><td>Mississippi</td><td>10.53</td><td>24</td><td>Georgia</td><td>1.33</td></tr>
<tr><td>21</td><td>Missouri</td><td>1.39</td><td>25</td><td>Texas</td><td>1.31</td></tr>
<tr><td>NA</td><td>Montana**</td><td>NA</td><td>26</td><td>Virginia</td><td>1.23</td></tr>
<tr><td>8</td><td>Nebraska</td><td>2.63</td><td>27</td><td>Rhode Island</td><td>1.22</td></tr>
<tr><td>41</td><td>Nevada</td><td>0.18</td><td>28</td><td>Ohio</td><td>1.17</td></tr>
<tr><td>1</td><td>New Hampshire</td><td>20.00</td><td>29</td><td>Arizona</td><td>1.14</td></tr>
<tr><td>32</td><td>New Jersey</td><td>1.07</td><td>29</td><td>Louisiana</td><td>1.14</td></tr>
<tr><td>43</td><td>New Mexico</td><td>0.00</td><td>31</td><td>California</td><td>1.12</td></tr>
<tr><td>39</td><td>New York</td><td>0.68</td><td>32</td><td>New Jersey</td><td>1.07</td></tr>
<tr><td>33</td><td>North Carolina</td><td>1.02</td><td>33</td><td>North Carolina</td><td>1.02</td></tr>
<tr><td>43</td><td>North Dakota</td><td>0.00</td><td>34</td><td>Pennsylvania</td><td>0.90</td></tr>
<tr><td>28</td><td>Ohio</td><td>1.17</td><td>35</td><td>Michigan</td><td>0.88</td></tr>
<tr><td>5</td><td>Oklahoma</td><td>4.50</td><td>36</td><td>Colorado</td><td>0.84</td></tr>
<tr><td>14</td><td>Oregon</td><td>1.69</td><td>36</td><td>Maryland</td><td>0.84</td></tr>
<tr><td>34</td><td>Pennsylvania</td><td>0.90</td><td>38</td><td>Alabama</td><td>0.82</td></tr>
<tr><td>27</td><td>Rhode Island</td><td>1.22</td><td>39</td><td>New York</td><td>0.68</td></tr>
<tr><td>10</td><td>South Carolina</td><td>2.56</td><td>40</td><td>Massachusetts</td><td>0.47</td></tr>
<tr><td>43</td><td>South Dakota</td><td>0.00</td><td>41</td><td>Nevada</td><td>0.18</td></tr>
<tr><td>41</td><td>Tennessee</td><td>0.18</td><td>41</td><td>Tennessee</td><td>0.18</td></tr>
<tr><td>25</td><td>Texas</td><td>1.31</td><td>43</td><td>Delaware</td><td>0.00</td></tr>
<tr><td>16</td><td>Utah</td><td>1.59</td><td>43</td><td>New Mexico</td><td>0.00</td></tr>
<tr><td>43</td><td>Vermont</td><td>0.00</td><td>43</td><td>North Dakota</td><td>0.00</td></tr>
<tr><td>26</td><td>Virginia</td><td>1.23</td><td>43</td><td>South Dakota</td><td>0.00</td></tr>
<tr><td>6</td><td>Washington</td><td>3.40</td><td>43</td><td>Vermont</td><td>0.00</td></tr>
<tr><td>15</td><td>West Virginia</td><td>1.61</td><td>43</td><td>Wyoming</td><td>0.00</td></tr>
<tr><td>13</td><td>Wisconsin</td><td>1.82</td><td>NA</td><td>Kansas**</td><td>NA</td></tr>
<tr><td>43</td><td>Wyoming</td><td>0.00</td><td>NA</td><td>Montana**</td><td>NA</td></tr>
<tr><td></td><td></td><td></td><td></td><td>District of Columbia</td><td>0.00</td></tr>
</table>

Source: Morgan Quitno Press using data from Federal Bureau of Investigation
"Crime in the United States 1994" (Uniform Crime Reports, November 19, 1995)
*Arrests of youths 17 years and younger by law enforcement agencies submitting complete reports to the F.B.I. for 12 months in 1994. Includes keeping a bawdy house, procuring or transporting women for immoral purposes. Attempts are included.
**Not available.

Reported Arrests of Juveniles for Offenses Against Families & Children in 1994

National Total = 4,232 Reported Arrests*

ALPHA ORDER

RANK	STATE	ARRESTS	% of USA
37	Alabama	6	0.14%
42	Alaska	1	0.02%
44	Arizona	0	0.00%
15	Arkansas	59	1.39%
31	California	11	0.26%
22	Colorado	24	0.57%
8	Connecticut	112	2.65%
40	Delaware	3	0.07%
28	Florida	17	0.40%
16	Georgia	52	1.23%
5	Hawaii	132	3.12%
39	Idaho	4	0.09%
42	Illinois	1	0.02%
13	Indiana	69	1.63%
34	Iowa	9	0.21%
NA	Kansas**	NA	NA
36	Kentucky	8	0.19%
9	Louisiana	107	2.53%
34	Maine	9	0.21%
26	Maryland	20	0.47%
4	Massachusetts	156	3.69%
44	Michigan	0	0.00%
21	Minnesota	27	0.64%
31	Mississippi	11	0.26%
7	Missouri	116	2.74%
NA	Montana**	NA	NA
24	Nebraska	23	0.54%
25	Nevada	22	0.52%
44	New Hampshire	0	0.00%
22	New Jersey	24	0.57%
11	New Mexico	90	2.13%
44	New York	0	0.00%
6	North Carolina	120	2.84%
10	North Dakota	100	2.36%
1	Ohio	1,500	35.44%
13	Oklahoma	69	1.63%
37	Oregon	6	0.14%
18	Pennsylvania	39	0.92%
18	Rhode Island	39	0.92%
12	South Carolina	82	1.94%
27	South Dakota	19	0.45%
30	Tennessee	14	0.33%
2	Texas	506	11.96%
28	Utah	17	0.40%
44	Vermont	0	0.00%
20	Virginia	37	0.87%
17	Washington	51	1.21%
40	West Virginia	3	0.07%
2	Wisconsin	506	11.96%
31	Wyoming	11	0.26%

RANK ORDER

RANK	STATE	ARRESTS	% of USA
1	Ohio	1,500	35.44%
2	Texas	506	11.96%
2	Wisconsin	506	11.96%
4	Massachusetts	156	3.69%
5	Hawaii	132	3.12%
6	North Carolina	120	2.84%
7	Missouri	116	2.74%
8	Connecticut	112	2.65%
9	Louisiana	107	2.53%
10	North Dakota	100	2.36%
11	New Mexico	90	2.13%
12	South Carolina	82	1.94%
13	Indiana	69	1.63%
13	Oklahoma	69	1.63%
15	Arkansas	59	1.39%
16	Georgia	52	1.23%
17	Washington	51	1.21%
18	Pennsylvania	39	0.92%
18	Rhode Island	39	0.92%
20	Virginia	37	0.87%
21	Minnesota	27	0.64%
22	Colorado	24	0.57%
22	New Jersey	24	0.57%
24	Nebraska	23	0.54%
25	Nevada	22	0.52%
26	Maryland	20	0.47%
27	South Dakota	19	0.45%
28	Florida	17	0.40%
28	Utah	17	0.40%
30	Tennessee	14	0.33%
31	California	11	0.26%
31	Mississippi	11	0.26%
31	Wyoming	11	0.26%
34	Iowa	9	0.21%
34	Maine	9	0.21%
36	Kentucky	8	0.19%
37	Alabama	6	0.14%
37	Oregon	6	0.14%
39	Idaho	4	0.09%
40	Delaware	3	0.07%
40	West Virginia	3	0.07%
42	Alaska	1	0.02%
42	Illinois	1	0.02%
44	Arizona	0	0.00%
44	Michigan	0	0.00%
44	New Hampshire	0	0.00%
44	New York	0	0.00%
44	Vermont	0	0.00%
NA	Kansas**	NA	NA
NA	Montana**	NA	NA
	District of Columbia	0	0.00%

Source: Federal Bureau of Investigation
   "Crime in the United States 1994" (Uniform Crime Reports, November 19, 1995)
*Arrests of youths 17 years and younger by law enforcement agencies submitting complete reports to the F.B.I. for 12 months in 1994. Includes nonsupport, neglect, desertion or abuse of family and children.
**Not available.

Reported Juvenile Arrest Rate for Offenses Against Families & Children in 1994

National Rate = 18.0 Reported Arrests per 100,000 Juvenile Population*

ALPHA ORDER

RANK ORDER

RANK	STATE	RATE		RANK	STATE	RATE
39	Alabama	1.3		1	Ohio	192.9
39	Alaska	1.3		2	New Mexico	172.1
44	Arizona	0.0		3	North Dakota	142.3
13	Arkansas	20.3		4	Hawaii	104.5
43	California	0.3		5	Wisconsin	83.5
24	Colorado	8.1		6	Connecticut	40.4
6	Connecticut	40.4		7	Massachusetts	39.1
25	Delaware	7.5		8	Rhode Island	38.5
39	Florida	1.3		9	South Dakota	34.6
21	Georgia	10.7		10	Missouri	30.0
4	Hawaii	104.5		11	Louisiana	27.0
36	Idaho	2.5		12	Texas	25.0
42	Illinois	0.5		13	Arkansas	20.3
15	Indiana	18.4		14	South Carolina	19.6
34	Iowa	3.1		15	Indiana	18.4
NA	Kansas**	NA		16	Oklahoma	17.3
33	Kentucky	3.3		17	Wyoming	17.2
11	Louisiana	27.0		18	North Carolina	16.3
26	Maine	6.6		19	Nevada	15.4
32	Maryland	3.8		20	Nebraska	12.5
7	Massachusetts	39.1		21	Georgia	10.7
44	Michigan	0.0		22	Mississippi	10.6
30	Minnesota	5.2		22	Washington	10.6
22	Mississippi	10.6		24	Colorado	8.1
10	Missouri	30.0		25	Delaware	7.5
NA	Montana**	NA		26	Maine	6.6
20	Nebraska	12.5		27	Tennessee	6.1
19	Nevada	15.4		28	Utah	6.0
44	New Hampshire	0.0		29	Virginia	5.5
34	New Jersey	3.1		30	Minnesota	5.2
2	New Mexico	172.1		31	Pennsylvania	3.9
44	New York	0.0		32	Maryland	3.8
18	North Carolina	16.3		33	Kentucky	3.3
3	North Dakota	142.3		34	Iowa	3.1
1	Ohio	192.9		34	New Jersey	3.1
16	Oklahoma	17.3		36	Idaho	2.5
37	Oregon	1.7		37	Oregon	1.7
31	Pennsylvania	3.9		38	West Virginia	1.4
8	Rhode Island	38.5		39	Alabama	1.3
14	South Carolina	19.6		39	Alaska	1.3
9	South Dakota	34.6		39	Florida	1.3
27	Tennessee	6.1		42	Illinois	0.5
12	Texas	25.0		43	California	0.3
28	Utah	6.0		44	Arizona	0.0
44	Vermont	0.0		44	Michigan	0.0
29	Virginia	5.5		44	New Hampshire	0.0
22	Washington	10.6		44	New York	0.0
38	West Virginia	1.4		44	Vermont	0.0
5	Wisconsin	83.5		NA	Kansas**	NA
17	Wyoming	17.2		NA	Montana**	NA
					District of Columbia	0.0

Source: Morgan Quitno Press using data from Federal Bureau of Investigation
    "Crime in the United States 1994" (Uniform Crime Reports, November 19, 1995)
*By law enforcement agencies submitting complete reports to the F.B.I. for 12 months in 1994. Arrests of youths 17
years and younger divided into population of 10 to 17 year olds. See important note at beginning of this chapter.
Includes nonsupport, neglect, desertion or abuse of family and children.
**Not available.

Reported Arrests of Juveniles for Offenses Against Families and Children
As a Percent of All Such Arrests in 1994
National Percent = 4.59% of Offenses Against Families and Children Arrests*

ALPHA ORDER

RANK ORDER

RANK	STATE	PERCENT		RANK	STATE	PERCENT
40	Alabama	0.57		1	North Dakota	43.48
38	Alaska	1.00		2	Ohio	11.48
44	Arizona	0.00		3	New Mexico	9.97
13	Arkansas	6.50		4	Wisconsin	9.82
33	California	1.60		5	South Dakota	9.09
30	Colorado	1.75		6	Wyoming	8.53
19	Connecticut	4.69		7	Louisiana	8.31
18	Delaware	4.76		8	Rhode Island	8.28
37	Florida	1.17		9	Oklahoma	7.78
27	Georgia	1.89		10	South Carolina	7.01
11	Hawaii	6.81		11	Hawaii	6.81
31	Idaho	1.67		12	Texas	6.79
42	Illinois	0.42		13	Arkansas	6.50
14	Indiana	5.91		14	Indiana	5.91
21	Iowa	4.33		15	Washington	5.18
NA	Kansas**	NA		16	Pennsylvania	5.10
41	Kentucky	0.47		17	Massachusetts	5.05
7	Louisiana	8.31		18	Delaware	4.76
23	Maine	3.44		19	Connecticut	4.69
36	Maryland	1.21		20	Missouri	4.38
17	Massachusetts	5.05		21	Iowa	4.33
44	Michigan	0.00		22	Minnesota	4.12
22	Minnesota	4.12		23	Maine	3.44
34	Mississippi	1.57		24	Utah	2.99
20	Missouri	4.38		25	Nevada	2.68
NA	Montana**	NA		26	North Carolina	1.92
32	Nebraska	1.62		27	Georgia	1.89
25	Nevada	2.68		28	Oregon	1.82
44	New Hampshire	0.00		29	Virginia	1.80
43	New Jersey	0.15		30	Colorado	1.75
3	New Mexico	9.97		31	Idaho	1.67
44	New York	0.00		32	Nebraska	1.62
26	North Carolina	1.92		33	California	1.60
1	North Dakota	43.48		34	Mississippi	1.57
2	Ohio	11.48		35	Tennessee	1.50
9	Oklahoma	7.78		36	Maryland	1.21
28	Oregon	1.82		37	Florida	1.17
16	Pennsylvania	5.10		38	Alaska	1.00
8	Rhode Island	8.28		39	West Virginia	0.68
10	South Carolina	7.01		40	Alabama	0.57
5	South Dakota	9.09		41	Kentucky	0.47
35	Tennessee	1.50		42	Illinois	0.42
12	Texas	6.79		43	New Jersey	0.15
24	Utah	2.99		44	Arizona	0.00
44	Vermont	0.00		44	Michigan	0.00
29	Virginia	1.80		44	New Hampshire	0.00
15	Washington	5.18		44	New York	0.00
39	West Virginia	0.68		44	Vermont	0.00
4	Wisconsin	9.82		NA	Kansas**	NA
6	Wyoming	8.53		NA	Montana**	NA
					District of Columbia	0.00

Source: Morgan Quitno Press using data from Federal Bureau of Investigation
   "Crime in the United States 1994" (Uniform Crime Reports, November 19, 1995)
*Arrests of youths 17 years and younger by law enforcement agencies submitting complete reports to the F.B.I. for
12 months in 1994. Includes nonsupport, neglect, desertion or abuse of family and children.
**Not available.

Percent of Crimes Cleared in 1994

National Percent = 21.5% Cleared*

<u>ALPHA ORDER</u>

<u>RANK ORDER</u>

RANK	STATE	PERCENT	RANK	STATE	PERCENT
NA	Alabama**	NA	1	South Dakota	32.1
5	Alaska	27.3	2	Wyoming	28.9
40	Arizona	18.3	3	Maine	28.5
4	Arkansas	27.5	4	Arkansas	27.5
33	California	20.2	5	Alaska	27.3
15	Colorado	24.3	6	Wisconsin	26.7
32	Connecticut	20.3	7	Kentucky	25.8
10	Delaware	25.6	7	Nebraska	25.8
30	Florida	21.2	7	Utah	25.8
23	Georgia	22.4	10	Delaware	25.6
45	Hawaii	15.4	11	Virginia	25.5
12	Idaho	24.9	12	Idaho	24.9
25	Illinois	22.3	12	Pennsylvania	24.9
41	Indiana	18.1	14	Louisiana	24.5
42	Iowa	18.0	15	Colorado	24.3
NA	Kansas**	NA	16	North Dakota	23.7
7	Kentucky	25.8	17	Minnesota	23.5
14	Louisiana	24.5	18	Tennessee	23.3
3	Maine	28.5	19	Massachusetts	23.0
29	Maryland	21.3	19	Texas	23.0
19	Massachusetts	23.0	21	Missouri	22.9
46	Michigan	13.6	22	Oregon	22.6
17	Minnesota	23.5	23	Georgia	22.4
37	Mississippi	19.5	23	Washington	22.4
21	Missouri	22.9	25	Illinois	22.3
NA	Montana**	NA	25	South Carolina	22.3
7	Nebraska	25.8	27	North Carolina	22.2
43	Nevada	17.0	28	Ohio	21.8
39	New Hampshire	18.6	29	Maryland	21.3
38	New Jersey	19.4	30	Florida	21.2
31	New Mexico	21.1	31	New Mexico	21.1
36	New York	20.0	32	Connecticut	20.3
27	North Carolina	22.2	33	California	20.2
16	North Dakota	23.7	33	Oklahoma	20.2
28	Ohio	21.8	33	West Virginia	20.2
33	Oklahoma	20.2	36	New York	20.0
22	Oregon	22.6	37	Mississippi	19.5
12	Pennsylvania	24.9	38	New Jersey	19.4
44	Rhode Island	16.8	39	New Hampshire	18.6
25	South Carolina	22.3	40	Arizona	18.3
1	South Dakota	32.1	41	Indiana	18.1
18	Tennessee	23.3	42	Iowa	18.0
19	Texas	23.0	43	Nevada	17.0
7	Utah	25.8	44	Rhode Island	16.8
47	Vermont	3.9	45	Hawaii	15.4
11	Virginia	25.5	46	Michigan	13.6
23	Washington	22.4	47	Vermont	3.9
33	West Virginia	20.2	NA	Alabama**	NA
6	Wisconsin	26.7	NA	Kansas**	NA
2	Wyoming	28.9	NA	Montana**	NA
				District of Columbia	16.3

Source: Federal Bureau of Investigation (unpublished data)
*Includes murder, rape, robbery, aggravated assault, burglary, larceny-theft and motor vehicle theft. A crime is considered cleared when at least one person is arrested, charged and turned over to the court for prosecution. Clearances recorded in 1994 may be for crimes which occurred in prior years. Several crimes may be cleared by the arrest of one person while the arrest of many persons may clear only one crime.
**Not available.

Percent of Violent Crimes Cleared in 1994

National Percent = 45.4% Cleared*

ALPHA ORDER

RANK	STATE	PERCENT
NA	Alabama**	NA
10	Alaska	55.0
38	Arizona	41.9
12	Arkansas	54.1
30	California	46.5
9	Colorado	55.6
33	Connecticut	44.7
1	Delaware	68.1
27	Florida	47.6
36	Georgia	43.7
40	Hawaii	40.7
6	Idaho	57.2
44	Illinois	35.8
42	Indiana	38.0
28	Iowa	47.5
NA	Kansas**	NA
8	Kentucky	56.7
24	Louisiana	48.0
5	Maine	61.0
37	Maryland	42.7
11	Massachusetts	54.3
45	Michigan	28.9
18	Minnesota	51.1
43	Mississippi	36.2
35	Missouri	44.5
NA	Montana**	NA
4	Nebraska	61.5
46	Nevada	28.2
26	New Hampshire	47.7
39	New Jersey	41.4
34	New Mexico	44.6
41	New York	38.9
16	North Carolina	51.8
22	North Dakota	48.7
32	Ohio	45.2
23	Oklahoma	48.5
31	Oregon	45.4
25	Pennsylvania	47.8
21	Rhode Island	49.1
19	South Carolina	50.8
2	South Dakota	64.7
14	Tennessee	53.6
20	Texas	50.1
17	Utah	51.3
47	Vermont	23.1
7	Virginia	57.0
15	Washington	52.3
29	West Virginia	47.0
12	Wisconsin	54.1
3	Wyoming	64.0

RANK ORDER

RANK	STATE	PERCENT
1	Delaware	68.1
2	South Dakota	64.7
3	Wyoming	64.0
4	Nebraska	61.5
5	Maine	61.0
6	Idaho	57.2
7	Virginia	57.0
8	Kentucky	56.7
9	Colorado	55.6
10	Alaska	55.0
11	Massachusetts	54.3
12	Arkansas	54.1
12	Wisconsin	54.1
14	Tennessee	53.6
15	Washington	52.3
16	North Carolina	51.8
17	Utah	51.3
18	Minnesota	51.1
19	South Carolina	50.8
20	Texas	50.1
21	Rhode Island	49.1
22	North Dakota	48.7
23	Oklahoma	48.5
24	Louisiana	48.0
25	Pennsylvania	47.8
26	New Hampshire	47.7
27	Florida	47.6
28	Iowa	47.5
29	West Virginia	47.0
30	California	46.5
31	Oregon	45.4
32	Ohio	45.2
33	Connecticut	44.7
34	New Mexico	44.6
35	Missouri	44.5
36	Georgia	43.7
37	Maryland	42.7
38	Arizona	41.9
39	New Jersey	41.4
40	Hawaii	40.7
41	New York	38.9
42	Indiana	38.0
43	Mississippi	36.2
44	Illinois	35.8
45	Michigan	28.9
46	Nevada	28.2
47	Vermont	23.1
NA	Alabama**	NA
NA	Kansas**	NA
NA	Montana**	NA

District of Columbia 36.5

Source: Federal Bureau of Investigation (unpublished data)
*Includes murder, rape, robbery and aggravated assault. A crime is considered cleared when at least one person is arrested, charged and turned over to the court for prosecution. Clearances recorded in 1994 may be for crimes which occurred in prior years. Several crimes may be cleared by the arrest of one person while the arrest of many persons may clear only one crime.
**Not available.

Percent of Murders Cleared in 1994

National Percent = 64.6% Cleared*

RANK	STATE	PERCENT
NA	Alabama**	NA
4	Alaska	89.2
34	Arizona	65.5
9	Arkansas	81.0
42	California	56.5
41	Colorado	60.1
27	Connecticut	69.0
43	Delaware	55.6
30	Florida	67.6
18	Georgia	74.8
28	Hawaii	68.0
6	Idaho	85.0
47	Illinois	5.8
45	Indiana	43.2
37	Iowa	63.6
NA	Kansas**	NA
17	Kentucky	74.9
40	Louisiana	60.5
20	Maine	74.1
31	Maryland	66.5
39	Massachusetts	61.1
33	Michigan	65.6
25	Minnesota	71.2
12	Mississippi	79.1
8	Missouri	83.6
NA	Montana**	NA
21	Nebraska	74.0
44	Nevada	46.7
11	New Hampshire	80.0
29	New Jersey	67.9
19	New Mexico	74.3
35	New York	65.1
10	North Carolina	80.8
1	North Dakota	100.0
14	Ohio	76.7
3	Oklahoma	89.8
7	Oregon	83.8
16	Pennsylvania	75.6
32	Rhode Island	65.9
15	South Carolina	75.9
13	South Dakota	77.8
36	Tennessee	64.4
24	Texas	72.1
23	Utah	73.2
46	Vermont	20.0
22	Virginia	73.3
26	Washington	70.5
2	West Virginia	92.9
5	Wisconsin	86.8
38	Wyoming	62.5

RANK	STATE	PERCENT
1	North Dakota	100.0
2	West Virginia	92.9
3	Oklahoma	89.8
4	Alaska	89.2
5	Wisconsin	86.8
6	Idaho	85.0
7	Oregon	83.8
8	Missouri	83.6
9	Arkansas	81.0
10	North Carolina	80.8
11	New Hampshire	80.0
12	Mississippi	79.1
13	South Dakota	77.8
14	Ohio	76.7
15	South Carolina	75.9
16	Pennsylvania	75.6
17	Kentucky	74.9
18	Georgia	74.8
19	New Mexico	74.3
20	Maine	74.1
21	Nebraska	74.0
22	Virginia	73.3
23	Utah	73.2
24	Texas	72.1
25	Minnesota	71.2
26	Washington	70.5
27	Connecticut	69.0
28	Hawaii	68.0
29	New Jersey	67.9
30	Florida	67.6
31	Maryland	66.5
32	Rhode Island	65.9
33	Michigan	65.6
34	Arizona	65.5
35	New York	65.1
36	Tennessee	64.4
37	Iowa	63.6
38	Wyoming	62.5
39	Massachusetts	61.1
40	Louisiana	60.5
41	Colorado	60.1
42	California	56.5
43	Delaware	55.6
44	Nevada	46.7
45	Indiana	43.2
46	Vermont	20.0
47	Illinois	5.8
NA	Alabama**	NA
NA	Kansas**	NA
NA	Montana**	NA
	District of Columbia	57.9

Source: Federal Bureau of Investigation (unpublished data)
*Includes nonnegligent manslaughter. A crime is considered cleared when at least one person is arrested, charged and turned over to the court for prosecution. Clearances recorded in 1994 may be for crimes which occurred in prior years. Several crimes may be cleared by the arrest of one person while the arrest of many persons may clear only one crime.
**Not available.

Percent of Rapes Cleared in 1994

National Percent = 51.9% Cleared*

ALPHA ORDER

RANK	STATE	PERCENT	RANK	STATE	PERCENT
NA	Alabama**	NA	1	Virginia	71.6
33	Alaska	43.9	2	Tennessee	66.1
43	Arizona	31.1	3	Delaware	64.5
13	Arkansas	56.7	4	Wisconsin	62.1
19	California	53.1	5	Pennsylvania	61.9
23	Colorado	52.0	6	Massachusetts	61.1
30	Connecticut	47.2	7	Nebraska	60.4
3	Delaware	64.5	8	Texas	60.0
16	Florida	55.0	9	Hawaii	59.6
17	Georgia	54.9	10	Maryland	58.7
9	Hawaii	59.6	11	Oklahoma	58.6
38	Idaho	38.7	12	Missouri	58.4
NA	Illinois**	NA	13	Arkansas	56.7
36	Indiana	41.6	14	Minnesota	56.5
39	Iowa	37.6	15	New Jersey	56.3
NA	Kansas**	NA	16	Florida	55.0
26	Kentucky	49.8	17	Georgia	54.9
29	Louisiana	47.8	18	North Carolina	53.9
27	Maine	49.4	19	California	53.1
10	Maryland	58.7	20	New York	52.7
6	Massachusetts	61.1	20	South Dakota	52.7
44	Michigan	28.3	22	South Carolina	52.6
14	Minnesota	56.5	23	Colorado	52.0
25	Mississippi	51.3	24	Ohio	51.7
12	Missouri	58.4	25	Mississippi	51.3
NA	Montana**	NA	26	Kentucky	49.8
7	Nebraska	60.4	27	Maine	49.4
45	Nevada	22.1	28	Washington	49.0
34	New Hampshire	42.2	29	Louisiana	47.8
15	New Jersey	56.3	30	Connecticut	47.2
41	New Mexico	36.8	31	West Virginia	46.8
20	New York	52.7	32	Wyoming	46.6
18	North Carolina	53.9	33	Alaska	43.9
40	North Dakota	37.3	34	New Hampshire	42.2
24	Ohio	51.7	35	Utah	41.8
11	Oklahoma	58.6	36	Indiana	41.6
37	Oregon	39.5	37	Oregon	39.5
5	Pennsylvania	61.9	38	Idaho	38.7
42	Rhode Island	33.0	39	Iowa	37.6
22	South Carolina	52.6	40	North Dakota	37.3
20	South Dakota	52.7	41	New Mexico	36.8
2	Tennessee	66.1	42	Rhode Island	33.0
8	Texas	60.0	43	Arizona	31.1
35	Utah	41.8	44	Michigan	28.3
46	Vermont	16.6	45	Nevada	22.1
1	Virginia	71.6	46	Vermont	16.6
28	Washington	49.0	NA	Alabama**	NA
31	West Virginia	46.8	NA	Illinois**	NA
4	Wisconsin	62.1	NA	Kansas**	NA
32	Wyoming	46.6	NA	Montana**	NA
				District of Columbia	48.2

Source: Federal Bureau of Investigation (unpublished data)
*Forcible rape including attempts. However, statutory rape without force and other sex offenses are excluded. A crime is considered cleared when at least one person is arrested, charged and turned over to the court for prosecution. Clearances recorded in 1994 may be for crimes which occurred in prior years. Several crimes may be cleared by the arrest of one person while the arrest of many persons may clear only one crime.
**Not available.

Percent of Robberies Cleared in 1994

National Percent = 24.4% Cleared*

ALPHA ORDER				RANK ORDER		
RANK	STATE	PERCENT		RANK	STATE	PERCENT
NA	Alabama**	NA		1	South Dakota	51.6
43	Alaska	16.5		2	Idaho	38.6
31	Arizona	24.3		2	Maine	38.6
16	Arkansas	30.6		4	North Dakota	38.0
34	California	23.3		5	Virginia	36.6
21	Colorado	28.4		6	New Hampshire	35.9
28	Connecticut	25.0		7	Wyoming	35.4
8	Delaware	33.6		8	Delaware	33.6
30	Florida	24.5		9	Wisconsin	33.0
24	Georgia	27.7		10	North Carolina	32.9
33	Hawaii	23.8		11	Kentucky	32.5
2	Idaho	38.6		12	Nebraska	32.4
45	Illinois	15.8		13	Oklahoma	31.7
40	Indiana	20.0		14	South Carolina	31.5
38	Iowa	21.3		15	Oregon	31.1
NA	Kansas**	NA		16	Arkansas	30.6
11	Kentucky	32.5		17	Ohio	29.8
37	Louisiana	22.2		18	Tennessee	29.4
2	Maine	38.6		18	Texas	29.4
39	Maryland	20.7		20	Utah	29.2
21	Massachusetts	28.4		21	Colorado	28.4
47	Michigan	10.9		21	Massachusetts	28.4
26	Minnesota	26.6		23	Washington	28.2
40	Mississippi	20.0		24	Georgia	27.7
31	Missouri	24.3		25	Pennsylvania	27.4
NA	Montana**	NA		26	Minnesota	26.6
12	Nebraska	32.4		27	West Virginia	26.1
42	Nevada	17.3		28	Connecticut	25.0
6	New Hampshire	35.9		28	New York	25.0
35	New Jersey	23.0		30	Florida	24.5
44	New Mexico	15.9		31	Arizona	24.3
28	New York	25.0		31	Missouri	24.3
10	North Carolina	32.9		33	Hawaii	23.8
4	North Dakota	38.0		34	California	23.3
17	Ohio	29.8		35	New Jersey	23.0
13	Oklahoma	31.7		36	Rhode Island	22.4
15	Oregon	31.1		37	Louisiana	22.2
25	Pennsylvania	27.4		38	Iowa	21.3
36	Rhode Island	22.4		39	Maryland	20.7
14	South Carolina	31.5		40	Indiana	20.0
1	South Dakota	51.6		40	Mississippi	20.0
18	Tennessee	29.4		42	Nevada	17.3
18	Texas	29.4		43	Alaska	16.5
20	Utah	29.2		44	New Mexico	15.9
46	Vermont	14.9		45	Illinois	15.8
5	Virginia	36.6		46	Vermont	14.9
23	Washington	28.2		47	Michigan	10.9
27	West Virginia	26.1		NA	Alabama**	NA
9	Wisconsin	33.0		NA	Kansas**	NA
7	Wyoming	35.4		NA	Montana**	NA
					District of Columbia	15.0

Source: Federal Bureau of Investigation (unpublished data)
*Robbery is the taking of anything of value by force or threat of force. Attempts are included. A crime is considered cleared when at least one person is arrested, charged and turned over to the court for prosecution. Clearances recorded in 1994 may be for crimes which occurred in prior years. Several crimes may be cleared by the arrest of one person while the arrest of many persons may clear only one crime.
**Not available.

Percent of Aggravated Assaults Cleared in 1994

National Percent = 56.4% Cleared*

ALPHA ORDER

RANK ORDER

RANK	STATE	PERCENT		RANK	STATE	PERCENT
NA	Alabama**	NA		1	Delaware	77.2
8	Alaska	66.6		2	Maine	70.7
42	Arizona	47.9		3	Wisconsin	69.9
18	Arkansas	60.3		4	South Dakota	69.5
20	California	59.4		5	Nebraska	69.3
11	Colorado	64.4		6	Wyoming	68.9
21	Connecticut	59.3		7	Virginia	68.5
1	Delaware	77.2		8	Alaska	66.6
27	Florida	56.9		9	Minnesota	65.1
39	Georgia	51.2		10	Pennsylvania	64.8
41	Hawaii	49.3		11	Colorado	64.4
16	Idaho	60.4		12	Tennessee	64.2
34	Illinois	52.6		13	Massachusetts	63.1
43	Indiana	45.4		14	Washington	62.2
32	Iowa	53.4		15	Kentucky	61.8
NA	Kansas**	NA		16	Idaho	60.4
15	Kentucky	61.8		16	Utah	60.4
22	Louisiana	58.8		18	Arkansas	60.3
2	Maine	70.7		19	Rhode Island	59.6
22	Maryland	58.8		20	California	59.4
13	Massachusetts	63.1		21	Connecticut	59.3
45	Michigan	37.5		22	Louisiana	58.8
9	Minnesota	65.1		22	Maryland	58.8
44	Mississippi	44.5		24	North Carolina	58.6
33	Missouri	53.3		25	Texas	58.0
NA	Montana**	NA		26	New Jersey	57.7
5	Nebraska	69.3		27	Florida	56.9
46	Nevada	35.3		27	North Dakota	56.9
29	New Hampshire	56.6		29	New Hampshire	56.6
26	New Jersey	57.7		30	Ohio	55.9
39	New Mexico	51.2		31	South Carolina	55.0
35	New York	52.4		32	Iowa	53.4
24	North Carolina	58.6		33	Missouri	53.3
27	North Dakota	56.9		34	Illinois	52.6
30	Ohio	55.9		35	New York	52.4
37	Oklahoma	51.4		36	Oregon	51.5
36	Oregon	51.5		37	Oklahoma	51.4
10	Pennsylvania	64.8		38	West Virginia	51.3
19	Rhode Island	59.6		39	Georgia	51.2
31	South Carolina	55.0		39	New Mexico	51.2
4	South Dakota	69.5		41	Hawaii	49.3
12	Tennessee	64.2		42	Arizona	47.9
25	Texas	58.0		43	Indiana	45.4
16	Utah	60.4		44	Mississippi	44.5
47	Vermont	28.2		45	Michigan	37.5
7	Virginia	68.5		46	Nevada	35.3
14	Washington	62.2		47	Vermont	28.2
38	West Virginia	51.3		NA	Alabama**	NA
3	Wisconsin	69.9		NA	Kansas**	NA
6	Wyoming	68.9		NA	Montana**	NA

District of Columbia 51.6

Source: Federal Bureau of Investigation (unpublished data)

*Aggravated assault is an attack for the purpose of inflicting severe bodily injury. A crime is considered cleared when at least one person is arrested, charged and turned over to the court for prosecution. Clearances recorded in 1994 may be for crimes which occurred in prior years. Several crimes may be cleared by the arrest of one person while the arrest of many persons may clear only one crime.

**Not available.

Percent of Property Crimes Cleared in 1994

National Percent = 17.7% Cleared*

ALPHA ORDER				RANK ORDER		
RANK	STATE	PERCENT		RANK	STATE	PERCENT
NA	Alabama**	NA		1	South Dakota	29.5
7	Alaska	23.0		2	Maine	27.2
37	Arizona	16.0		3	Wyoming	26.6
6	Arkansas	23.7		4	Wisconsin	24.7
43	California	15.0		5	Utah	24.3
13	Colorado	21.0		6	Arkansas	23.7
27	Connecticut	17.6		7	Alaska	23.0
17	Delaware	19.8		7	North Dakota	23.0
33	Florida	16.9		9	Idaho	22.5
18	Georgia	19.7		9	Virginia	22.5
44	Hawaii	14.4		11	Nebraska	22.3
9	Idaho	22.5		12	Pennsylvania	21.5
24	Illinois	18.5		13	Colorado	21.0
39	Indiana	15.4		13	Minnesota	21.0
41	Iowa	15.2		15	Louisiana	20.5
NA	Kansas**	NA		15	Oregon	20.5
20	Kentucky	19.3		17	Delaware	19.8
15	Louisiana	20.5		18	Georgia	19.7
2	Maine	27.2		19	Washington	19.4
30	Maryland	17.4		20	Kentucky	19.3
34	Massachusetts	16.8		20	Missouri	19.3
46	Michigan	11.0		20	Texas	19.3
13	Minnesota	21.0		23	Ohio	18.7
27	Mississippi	17.6		24	Illinois	18.5
20	Missouri	19.3		25	North Carolina	18.3
NA	Montana**	NA		26	Tennessee	17.8
11	Nebraska	22.3		27	Connecticut	17.6
42	Nevada	15.1		27	Mississippi	17.6
31	New Hampshire	17.3		27	West Virginia	17.6
37	New Jersey	16.0		30	Maryland	17.4
32	New Mexico	17.1		31	New Hampshire	17.3
40	New York	15.3		32	New Mexico	17.1
25	North Carolina	18.3		33	Florida	16.9
7	North Dakota	23.0		34	Massachusetts	16.8
23	Ohio	18.7		35	Oklahoma	16.4
35	Oklahoma	16.4		36	South Carolina	16.3
15	Oregon	20.5		37	Arizona	16.0
12	Pennsylvania	21.5		37	New Jersey	16.0
45	Rhode Island	13.6		39	Indiana	15.4
36	South Carolina	16.3		40	New York	15.3
1	South Dakota	29.5		41	Iowa	15.2
26	Tennessee	17.8		42	Nevada	15.1
20	Texas	19.3		43	California	15.0
5	Utah	24.3		44	Hawaii	14.4
47	Vermont	3.3		45	Rhode Island	13.6
9	Virginia	22.5		46	Michigan	11.0
19	Washington	19.4		47	Vermont	3.3
27	West Virginia	17.6		NA	Alabama**	NA
4	Wisconsin	24.7		NA	Kansas**	NA
3	Wyoming	26.6		NA	Montana**	NA
				District of Columbia		9.9

Source: Federal Bureau of Investigation (unpublished data)
*Property crimes are offenses of burglary, larceny-theft and motor vehicle theft. A crime is considered cleared when at least one person is arrested, charged and turned over to the court for prosecution. Clearances recorded in 1994 may be for crimes which occurred in prior years. Several crimes may be cleared by the arrest of one person while the arrest of many persons may clear only one crime.
**Not available.

Percent of Burglaries Cleared in 1994

National Percent = 13.4% Cleared*

ALPHA ORDER

RANK	STATE	PERCENT
NA	Alabama**	NA
6	Alaska	17.4
43	Arizona	9.3
8	Arkansas	17.0
33	California	12.2
28	Colorado	13.3
31	Connecticut	12.4
5	Delaware	18.5
17	Florida	14.9
26	Georgia	13.7
40	Hawaii	10.1
23	Idaho	14.0
41	Illinois	9.8
42	Indiana	9.7
45	Iowa	8.7
NA	Kansas**	NA
15	Kentucky	15.0
11	Louisiana	15.7
3	Maine	20.9
14	Maryland	15.1
20	Massachusetts	14.7
46	Michigan	7.4
30	Minnesota	12.8
36	Mississippi	11.4
17	Missouri	14.9
NA	Montana**	NA
12	Nebraska	15.3
37	Nevada	11.2
39	New Hampshire	10.4
32	New Jersey	12.3
44	New Mexico	9.2
33	New York	12.2
10	North Carolina	15.9
19	North Dakota	14.8
22	Ohio	14.3
27	Oklahoma	13.4
29	Oregon	13.2
8	Pennsylvania	17.0
38	Rhode Island	10.5
23	South Carolina	14.0
2	South Dakota	21.4
12	Tennessee	15.3
23	Texas	14.0
15	Utah	15.0
47	Vermont	3.7
1	Virginia	22.1
35	Washington	11.9
21	West Virginia	14.6
6	Wisconsin	17.4
4	Wyoming	20.3

RANK ORDER

RANK	STATE	PERCENT
1	Virginia	22.1
2	South Dakota	21.4
3	Maine	20.9
4	Wyoming	20.3
5	Delaware	18.5
6	Alaska	17.4
6	Wisconsin	17.4
8	Arkansas	17.0
8	Pennsylvania	17.0
10	North Carolina	15.9
11	Louisiana	15.7
12	Nebraska	15.3
12	Tennessee	15.3
14	Maryland	15.1
15	Kentucky	15.0
15	Utah	15.0
17	Florida	14.9
17	Missouri	14.9
19	North Dakota	14.8
20	Massachusetts	14.7
21	West Virginia	14.6
22	Ohio	14.3
23	Idaho	14.0
23	South Carolina	14.0
23	Texas	14.0
26	Georgia	13.7
27	Oklahoma	13.4
28	Colorado	13.3
29	Oregon	13.2
30	Minnesota	12.8
31	Connecticut	12.4
32	New Jersey	12.3
33	California	12.2
33	New York	12.2
35	Washington	11.9
36	Mississippi	11.4
37	Nevada	11.2
38	Rhode Island	10.5
39	New Hampshire	10.4
40	Hawaii	10.1
41	Illinois	9.8
42	Indiana	9.7
43	Arizona	9.3
44	New Mexico	9.2
45	Iowa	8.7
46	Michigan	7.4
47	Vermont	3.7
NA	Alabama**	NA
NA	Kansas**	NA
NA	Montana**	NA

District of Columbia 11.8

Source: Federal Bureau of Investigation (unpublished data)
*Burglary is the unlawful entry of a structure to commit a felony or theft. Attempts are included. A crime is considered cleared when at least one person is arrested, charged and turned over to the court for prosecution. Clearances recorded in 1994 may be for crimes which occurred in prior years. Several crimes may be cleared by the arrest of one person while the arrest of many persons may clear only one crime.
**Not available.

Percent of Larcenies and Thefts Cleared in 1994

National Percent = 19.9% Cleared*

ALPHA ORDER			RANK ORDER		
RANK	STATE	PERCENT	RANK	STATE	PERCENT
NA	Alabama**	NA	1	South Dakota	30.8
7	Alaska	24.7	2	Maine	28.2
31	Arizona	19.1	3	Wyoming	27.3
6	Arkansas	25.6	4	Wisconsin	26.9
38	California	17.9	5	Utah	25.7
13	Colorado	23.2	6	Arkansas	25.6
22	Connecticut	21.1	7	Alaska	24.7
20	Delaware	21.2	8	Pennsylvania	24.3
36	Florida	18.2	9	Idaho	24.2
23	Georgia	21.0	10	Nebraska	24.0
45	Hawaii	15.6	11	North Dakota	23.6
9	Idaho	24.2	12	Louisiana	23.4
16	Illinois	22.7	13	Colorado	23.2
41	Indiana	17.4	14	Oregon	23.0
43	Iowa	16.8	15	Minnesota	22.8
NA	Kansas**	NA	16	Illinois	22.7
27	Kentucky	20.3	17	Virginia	21.9
12	Louisiana	23.4	18	Washington	21.8
2	Maine	28.2	19	Texas	21.4
33	Maryland	18.8	20	Delaware	21.2
39	Massachusetts	17.6	20	Missouri	21.2
46	Michigan	12.6	22	Connecticut	21.1
15	Minnesota	22.8	23	Georgia	21.0
25	Mississippi	20.7	23	New Mexico	21.0
20	Missouri	21.2	25	Mississippi	20.7
NA	Montana**	NA	26	New Jersey	20.4
10	Nebraska	24.0	27	Kentucky	20.3
37	Nevada	18.1	28	Ohio	19.9
30	New Hampshire	19.4	29	Tennessee	19.5
26	New Jersey	20.4	30	New Hampshire	19.4
23	New Mexico	21.0	31	Arizona	19.1
34	New York	18.6	32	West Virginia	18.9
35	North Carolina	18.4	33	Maryland	18.8
11	North Dakota	23.6	34	New York	18.6
28	Ohio	19.9	35	North Carolina	18.4
39	Oklahoma	17.6	36	Florida	18.2
14	Oregon	23.0	37	Nevada	18.1
8	Pennsylvania	24.3	38	California	17.9
44	Rhode Island	16.0	39	Massachusetts	17.6
42	South Carolina	17.2	39	Oklahoma	17.6
1	South Dakota	30.8	41	Indiana	17.4
29	Tennessee	19.5	42	South Carolina	17.2
19	Texas	21.4	43	Iowa	16.8
5	Utah	25.7	44	Rhode Island	16.0
47	Vermont	3.1	45	Hawaii	15.6
17	Virginia	21.9	46	Michigan	12.6
18	Washington	21.8	47	Vermont	3.1
32	West Virginia	18.9	NA	Alabama**	NA
4	Wisconsin	26.9	NA	Kansas**	NA
3	Wyoming	27.3	NA	Montana**	NA
			District of Columbia		8.9

Source: Federal Bureau of Investigation (unpublished data)
*Larceny and theft is the unlawful taking of property without use of force, violence or fraud. Attempts are included. Motor vehicle thefts are excluded. A crime is considered cleared when at least one person is arrested, charged and turned over to the court for prosecution. Clearances recorded in 1994 may be for crimes which occurred in prior years. Several crimes may be cleared by the arrest of one person while the arrest of many persons may clear only one crime. **Not available.

Percent of Motor Vehicle Thefts Cleared in 1994

National Percent = 14.0% Cleared*

ALPHA ORDER

RANK	STATE	PERCENT
NA	Alabama**	NA
17	Alaska	20.0
38	Arizona	11.3
6	Arkansas	30.2
41	California	10.0
15	Colorado	20.4
40	Connecticut	10.3
34	Delaware	13.7
32	Florida	14.2
12	Georgia	23.9
36	Hawaii	12.9
8	Idaho	29.2
33	Illinois	14.0
31	Indiana	14.4
19	Iowa	17.8
NA	Kansas**	NA
11	Kentucky	24.8
37	Louisiana	12.7
1	Maine	43.0
29	Maryland	14.8
21	Massachusetts	17.1
42	Michigan	9.0
10	Minnesota	25.4
26	Mississippi	15.9
22	Missouri	17.0
NA	Montana**	NA
14	Nebraska	21.4
45	Nevada	7.9
35	New Hampshire	13.0
47	New Jersey	4.9
39	New Mexico	10.8
44	New York	8.2
9	North Carolina	28.3
4	North Dakota	31.6
16	Ohio	20.3
23	Oklahoma	16.5
20	Oregon	17.6
27	Pennsylvania	15.8
43	Rhode Island	8.3
25	South Carolina	16.1
2	South Dakota	42.6
29	Tennessee	14.8
18	Texas	18.2
5	Utah	31.0
46	Vermont	5.1
7	Virginia	29.6
27	Washington	15.8
24	West Virginia	16.4
13	Wisconsin	22.0
3	Wyoming	36.1

RANK ORDER

RANK	STATE	PERCENT
1	Maine	43.0
2	South Dakota	42.6
3	Wyoming	36.1
4	North Dakota	31.6
5	Utah	31.0
6	Arkansas	30.2
7	Virginia	29.6
8	Idaho	29.2
9	North Carolina	28.3
10	Minnesota	25.4
11	Kentucky	24.8
12	Georgia	23.9
13	Wisconsin	22.0
14	Nebraska	21.4
15	Colorado	20.4
16	Ohio	20.3
17	Alaska	20.0
18	Texas	18.2
19	Iowa	17.8
20	Oregon	17.6
21	Massachusetts	17.1
22	Missouri	17.0
23	Oklahoma	16.5
24	West Virginia	16.4
25	South Carolina	16.1
26	Mississippi	15.9
27	Pennsylvania	15.8
27	Washington	15.8
29	Maryland	14.8
29	Tennessee	14.8
31	Indiana	14.4
32	Florida	14.2
33	Illinois	14.0
34	Delaware	13.7
35	New Hampshire	13.0
36	Hawaii	12.9
37	Louisiana	12.7
38	Arizona	11.3
39	New Mexico	10.8
40	Connecticut	10.3
41	California	10.0
42	Michigan	9.0
43	Rhode Island	8.3
44	New York	8.2
45	Nevada	7.9
46	Vermont	5.1
47	New Jersey	4.9
NA	Alabama**	NA
NA	Kansas**	NA
NA	Montana**	NA
	District of Columbia	10.8

Source: Federal Bureau of Investigation (unpublished data)
*Motor vehicle theft includes the theft or attempted theft of a self-propelled vehicle. Excludes motorboats, construction equipment, airplanes and farming equipment. A crime is considered cleared when at least one person is arrested, charged and turned over to the court for prosecution. Clearances recorded in 1994 may be for crimes which occurred in prior years. Several crimes may be cleared by the arrest of one person while the arrest of many persons may clear only one crime. **Not available.

II. CORRECTIONS

II. CORRECTIONS (continued)

Prisoners in State Correctional Institutions in 1995

National Total = 1,004,608 State Prisoners*

RANK	STATE	PRISONERS	% of USA	RANK	STATE	PRISONERS	% of USA
16	Alabama	20,082	2.00%	1	California	131,342	13.07%
41	Alaska	3,031	0.30%	2	Texas	127,092	12.65%
15	Arizona	20,907	2.08%	3	New York	68,526	6.82%
29	Arkansas	8,825	0.88%	4	Florida	61,992	6.17%
1	California	131,342	13.07%	5	Ohio	43,158	4.30%
27	Colorado	10,757	1.07%	6	Michigan	41,377	4.12%
21	Connecticut	15,005	1.49%	7	Illinois	37,790	3.76%
35	Delaware	4,651	0.46%	8	Georgia	34,111	3.40%
4	Florida	61,992	6.17%	9	Pennsylvania	29,844	2.97%
8	Georgia	34,111	3.40%	10	Virginia	27,310	2.72%
37	Hawaii	3,583	0.36%	11	North Carolina	26,818	2.67%
39	Idaho	3,240	0.32%	12	New Jersey	25,626	2.55%
7	Illinois	37,790	3.76%	13	Louisiana	24,840	2.47%
20	Indiana	15,699	1.56%	14	Maryland	21,441	2.13%
33	Iowa	5,692	0.57%	15	Arizona	20,907	2.08%
32	Kansas	6,927	0.69%	16	Alabama	20,082	2.00%
24	Kentucky	11,949	1.19%	17	South Carolina	19,481	1.94%
13	Louisiana	24,840	2.47%	18	Missouri	18,940	1.89%
47	Maine	1,459	0.15%	19	Oklahoma	17,605	1.75%
14	Maryland	21,441	2.13%	20	Indiana	15,699	1.56%
25	Massachusetts	11,469	1.14%	21	Connecticut	15,005	1.49%
6	Michigan	41,377	4.12%	22	Tennessee	14,933	1.49%
34	Minnesota	4,764	0.47%	23	Mississippi	12,446	1.24%
23	Mississippi	12,446	1.24%	24	Kentucky	11,949	1.19%
18	Missouri	18,940	1.89%	25	Massachusetts	11,469	1.14%
45	Montana	1,801	0.18%	26	Washington	11,402	1.13%
42	Nebraska	2,801	0.28%	27	Colorado	10,757	1.07%
31	Nevada	7,487	0.75%	28	Wisconsin	10,632	1.06%
44	New Hampshire	2,065	0.21%	29	Arkansas	8,825	0.88%
12	New Jersey	25,626	2.55%	30	Oregon	7,505	0.75%
36	New Mexico	4,121	0.41%	31	Nevada	7,487	0.75%
3	New York	68,526	6.82%	32	Kansas	6,927	0.69%
11	North Carolina	26,818	2.67%	33	Iowa	5,692	0.57%
50	North Dakota	610	0.06%	34	Minnesota	4,764	0.47%
5	Ohio	43,158	4.30%	35	Delaware	4,651	0.46%
19	Oklahoma	17,605	1.75%	36	New Mexico	4,121	0.41%
30	Oregon	7,505	0.75%	37	Hawaii	3,583	0.36%
9	Pennsylvania	29,844	2.97%	38	Utah	3,272	0.33%
40	Rhode Island	3,132	0.31%	39	Idaho	3,240	0.32%
17	South Carolina	19,481	1.94%	40	Rhode Island	3,132	0.31%
46	South Dakota	1,780	0.18%	41	Alaska	3,031	0.30%
22	Tennessee	14,933	1.49%	42	Nebraska	2,801	0.28%
2	Texas	127,092	12.65%	43	West Virginia	2,438	0.24%
38	Utah	3,272	0.33%	44	New Hampshire	2,065	0.21%
49	Vermont	1,058	0.11%	45	Montana	1,801	0.18%
10	Virginia	27,310	2.72%	46	South Dakota	1,780	0.18%
26	Washington	11,402	1.13%	47	Maine	1,459	0.15%
43	West Virginia	2,438	0.24%	48	Wyoming	1,308	0.13%
28	Wisconsin	10,632	1.06%	49	Vermont	1,058	0.11%
48	Wyoming	1,308	0.13%	50	North Dakota	610	0.06%
					District of Columbia	10,484	1.04%

Source: U.S. Department of Justice, Bureau of Justice Statistics
Press Release (December 3, 1995)

*As of June 30, 1995. Totals include inmates sentenced to more than one year and those sentenced to a year or less or with no sentence. Does not include 99,466 prisoners under federal jurisdiction. State and federal prisoners combined total 1,104,074.

State Prisoner Incarceration Rate in 1995

National Rate = 372 State Prisoners per 100,000 Population*

ALPHA ORDER				RANK ORDER		
RANK	STATE	RATE		RANK	STATE	RATE
8	Alabama	459		1	Texas	659
25	Alaska	293		2	Louisiana	573
5	Arizona	473		3	Oklahoma	536
20	Arkansas	349		4	South Carolina	510
14	California	402		5	Arizona	473
26	Colorado	287		6	Georgia	468
21	Connecticut	325		6	Nevada	468
13	Delaware	406		8	Alabama	459
10	Florida	437		9	Mississippi	447
6	Georgia	468		10	Florida	437
35	Hawaii	218		11	Michigan	434
28	Idaho	278		12	Virginia	412
23	Illinois	320		13	Delaware	406
30	Indiana	270		14	California	402
38	Iowa	201		15	Maryland	398
31	Kansas	269		16	Ohio	387
24	Kentucky	310		17	New York	377
2	Louisiana	573		18	North Carolina	357
48	Maine	112		19	Missouri	356
15	Maryland	398		20	Arkansas	349
42	Massachusetts	180		21	Connecticut	325
11	Michigan	434		22	New Jersey	323
49	Minnesota	103		23	Illinois	320
9	Mississippi	447		24	Kentucky	310
19	Missouri	356		25	Alaska	293
37	Montana	207		26	Colorado	287
44	Nebraska	168		27	Tennessee	284
6	Nevada	468		28	Idaho	278
42	New Hampshire	180		29	Wyoming	271
22	New Jersey	323		30	Indiana	270
34	New Mexico	234		31	Kansas	269
17	New York	377		32	Pennsylvania	247
18	North Carolina	357		33	South Dakota	245
50	North Dakota	90		34	New Mexico	234
16	Ohio	387		35	Hawaii	218
3	Oklahoma	536		36	Washington	210
39	Oregon	199		37	Montana	207
32	Pennsylvania	247		38	Iowa	201
41	Rhode Island	190		39	Oregon	199
4	South Carolina	510		40	Wisconsin	196
33	South Dakota	245		41	Rhode Island	190
27	Tennessee	284		42	Massachusetts	180
1	Texas	659		42	New Hampshire	180
45	Utah	166		44	Nebraska	168
46	Vermont	135		45	Utah	166
12	Virginia	412		46	Vermont	135
36	Washington	210		47	West Virginia	134
47	West Virginia	134		48	Maine	112
40	Wisconsin	196		49	Minnesota	103
29	Wyoming	271		50	North Dakota	90

District of Columbia 1,722

Source: U.S. Department of Justice, Bureau of Justice Statistics
   Press Release (December 3, 1995)
*As of June 30, 1995. Includes only inmates sentenced to more than one year. Does not include federal incarceration rate of 31 prisoners per 100,000 population. State and federal combined incarceration rate is 403 prisoners per 100,000 population.

Prisoners in State Correctional Institutions in 1994

National Total = 920,650 State Prisoners*

ALPHA ORDER

RANK	STATE	PRISONERS	% of USA
16	Alabama	19,098	2.07%
38	Alaska	3,128	0.34%
17	Arizona	18,830	2.05%
29	Arkansas	8,916	0.97%
1	California	124,813	13.56%
27	Colorado	9,954	1.08%
21	Connecticut	14,427	1.57%
35	Delaware	4,324	0.47%
4	Florida	56,052	6.09%
8	Georgia	30,292	3.29%
37	Hawaii	3,246	0.35%
41	Idaho	2,861	0.31%
7	Illinois	35,614	3.87%
20	Indiana	14,826	1.61%
33	Iowa	5,090	0.55%
32	Kansas	6,090	0.66%
24	Kentucky	10,724	1.16%
12	Louisiana	23,333	2.53%
47	Maine	1,468	0.16%
14	Maryland	20,887	2.27%
23	Massachusetts	11,166	1.21%
6	Michigan	40,220	4.37%
34	Minnesota	4,573	0.50%
26	Mississippi	10,631	1.15%
18	Missouri	16,957	1.84%
45	Montana	1,654	0.18%
42	Nebraska	2,449	0.27%
30	Nevada	6,745	0.73%
44	New Hampshire	1,895	0.21%
11	New Jersey	24,471	2.66%
36	New Mexico	3,704	0.40%
3	New York	65,962	7.16%
13	North Carolina	22,650	2.46%
50	North Dakota	522	0.06%
5	Ohio	41,156	4.47%
19	Oklahoma	16,306	1.77%
31	Oregon	6,723	0.73%
9	Pennsylvania	27,082	2.94%
39	Rhode Island	3,049	0.33%
15	South Carolina	19,646	2.13%
46	South Dakota	1,636	0.18%
22	Tennessee	14,397	1.56%
2	Texas	100,136	10.88%
40	Utah	2,948	0.32%
48	Vermont	1,182	0.13%
10	Virginia	24,822	2.70%
25	Washington	10,650	1.16%
43	West Virginia	1,941	0.21%
28	Wisconsin	9,206	1.00%
49	Wyoming	1,174	0.13%

RANK ORDER

RANK	STATE	PRISONERS	% of USA
1	California	124,813	13.56%
2	Texas	100,136	10.88%
3	New York	65,962	7.16%
4	Florida	56,052	6.09%
5	Ohio	41,156	4.47%
6	Michigan	40,220	4.37%
7	Illinois	35,614	3.87%
8	Georgia	30,292	3.29%
9	Pennsylvania	27,082	2.94%
10	Virginia	24,822	2.70%
11	New Jersey	24,471	2.66%
12	Louisiana	23,333	2.53%
13	North Carolina	22,650	2.46%
14	Maryland	20,887	2.27%
15	South Carolina	19,646	2.13%
16	Alabama	19,098	2.07%
17	Arizona	18,830	2.05%
18	Missouri	16,957	1.84%
19	Oklahoma	16,306	1.77%
20	Indiana	14,826	1.61%
21	Connecticut	14,427	1.57%
22	Tennessee	14,397	1.56%
23	Massachusetts	11,166	1.21%
24	Kentucky	10,724	1.16%
25	Washington	10,650	1.16%
26	Mississippi	10,631	1.15%
27	Colorado	9,954	1.08%
28	Wisconsin	9,206	1.00%
29	Arkansas	8,916	0.97%
30	Nevada	6,745	0.73%
31	Oregon	6,723	0.73%
32	Kansas	6,090	0.66%
33	Iowa	5,090	0.55%
34	Minnesota	4,573	0.50%
35	Delaware	4,324	0.47%
36	New Mexico	3,704	0.40%
37	Hawaii	3,246	0.35%
38	Alaska	3,128	0.34%
39	Rhode Island	3,049	0.33%
40	Utah	2,948	0.32%
41	Idaho	2,861	0.31%
42	Nebraska	2,449	0.27%
43	West Virginia	1,941	0.21%
44	New Hampshire	1,895	0.21%
45	Montana	1,654	0.18%
46	South Dakota	1,636	0.18%
47	Maine	1,468	0.16%
48	Vermont	1,182	0.13%
49	Wyoming	1,174	0.13%
50	North Dakota	522	0.06%
	District of Columbia	11,033	1.20%

Source: U.S. Department of Justice, Bureau of Justice Statistics
Press Release (December 3, 1995)

*As of June 30, 1994. Totals include inmates sentenced to more than one year and those sentenced to a year or less or with no sentence. Does not include 93,708 prisoners under federal jurisdiction. State and federal prisoners combined total 1,014,367.

Percent Change in Number of State Prisoners: 1994 to 1995

National Percent Change = 9.1% Increase*

ALPHA ORDER				RANK ORDER		
RANK	**STATE**	**PERCENT CHANGE**		**RANK**	**STATE**	**PERCENT CHANGE**
34	Alabama	5.2		1	Texas	26.9
49	Alaska	(3.1)		2	North Carolina	18.4
16	Arizona	11.0		3	Mississippi	17.1
48	Arkansas	(1.0)		4	North Dakota	16.9
34	California	5.2		5	Wisconsin	15.5
27	Colorado	8.1		6	Nebraska	14.4
39	Connecticut	4.0		7	Kansas	13.7
29	Delaware	7.6		8	Idaho	13.2
19	Florida	10.6		9	Georgia	12.6
9	Georgia	12.6		10	Iowa	11.8
20	Hawaii	10.4		11	Missouri	11.7
8	Idaho	13.2		12	Oregon	11.6
32	Illinois	6.1		13	Kentucky	11.4
33	Indiana	5.9		13	Wyoming	11.4
10	Iowa	11.8		15	New Mexico	11.3
7	Kansas	13.7		16	Arizona	11.0
13	Kentucky	11.4		16	Nevada	11.0
31	Louisiana	6.5		16	Utah	11.0
46	Maine	(0.6)		19	Florida	10.6
43	Maryland	2.7		20	Hawaii	10.4
43	Massachusetts	2.7		21	Pennsylvania	10.2
42	Michigan	2.9		22	Virginia	10.0
38	Minnesota	4.2		23	New Hampshire	9.0
3	Mississippi	17.1		24	Montana	8.9
11	Missouri	11.7		25	South Dakota	8.8
24	Montana	8.9		26	West Virginia	8.6
6	Nebraska	14.4		27	Colorado	8.1
16	Nevada	11.0		28	Oklahoma	8.0
23	New Hampshire	9.0		29	Delaware	7.6
37	New Jersey	4.7		30	Washington	7.1
15	New Mexico	11.3		31	Louisiana	6.5
40	New York	3.9		32	Illinois	6.1
2	North Carolina	18.4		33	Indiana	5.9
4	North Dakota	16.9		34	Alabama	5.2
36	Ohio	4.9		34	California	5.2
28	Oklahoma	8.0		36	Ohio	4.9
12	Oregon	11.6		37	New Jersey	4.7
21	Pennsylvania	10.2		38	Minnesota	4.2
43	Rhode Island	2.7		39	Connecticut	4.0
47	South Carolina	(0.8)		40	New York	3.9
25	South Dakota	8.8		41	Tennessee	3.7
41	Tennessee	3.7		42	Michigan	2.9
1	Texas	26.9		43	Maryland	2.7
16	Utah	11.0		43	Massachusetts	2.7
NA	Vermont**	NA		43	Rhode Island	2.7
22	Virginia	10.0		46	Maine	(0.6)
30	Washington	7.1		47	South Carolina	(0.8)
26	West Virginia	8.6		48	Arkansas	(1.0)
5	Wisconsin	15.5		49	Alaska	(3.1)
13	Wyoming	11.4		NA	Vermont**	NA
					District of Columbia	(5.0)

Source: U.S. Department of Justice, Bureau of Justice Statistics
    Press Release (December 3, 1995)
*From June 30, 1994 to June 30, 1995. Includes inmates sentenced to more than one year and those sentenced to a year or less or with no sentence. The percent change in number of prisoners under federal jurisdiction during the same period was a 6.1% increase. The combined state and federal increase was 8.8%.
**Previous year's data are not comparable.

State Prison Population as a Percent of Highest Capacity in 1994

National Percent = 117% of Highest Capacity*

ALPHA ORDER				RANK ORDER		
RANK	STATE	PERCENT		RANK	STATE	PERCENT
20	Alabama	109		1	California	184
21	Alaska	108		2	Ohio	171
34	Arizona	100		3	Iowa	167
29	Arkansas	103		4	Massachusetts	148
1	California	184		5	Michigan	146
16	Colorado	114		6	Virginia	145
39	Connecticut	98		7	New Jersey	142
26	Delaware	105		8	Illinois	138
34	Florida	100		8	Pennsylvania	138
32	Georgia	102		10	Wisconsin	133
12	Hawaii	128		11	Nebraska	131
26	Idaho	105		12	Hawaii	128
8	Illinois	138		13	Montana	125
44	Indiana	96		14	Oklahoma	122
3	Iowa	167		15	South Dakota	117
44	Kansas	96		16	Colorado	114
29	Kentucky	103		16	Maine	114
42	Louisiana	97		16	South Carolina	114
16	Maine	114		19	Minnesota	110
34	Maryland	100		20	Alabama	109
4	Massachusetts	148		21	Alaska	108
5	Michigan	146		21	New Hampshire	108
19	Minnesota	110		21	Wyoming	108
34	Mississippi	100		24	Nevada	106
38	Missouri	99		24	Oregon	106
13	Montana	125		26	Delaware	105
11	Nebraska	131		26	Idaho	105
24	Nevada	106		28	New York	104
21	New Hampshire	108		29	Arkansas	103
7	New Jersey	142		29	Kentucky	103
47	New Mexico	95		29	Washington	103
28	New York	104		32	Georgia	102
44	North Carolina	96		32	West Virginia	102
48	North Dakota	89		34	Arizona	100
2	Ohio	171		34	Florida	100
14	Oklahoma	122		34	Maryland	100
24	Oregon	106		34	Mississippi	100
8	Pennsylvania	138		38	Missouri	99
49	Rhode Island	85		39	Connecticut	98
16	South Carolina	114		39	Tennessee	98
15	South Dakota	117		39	Vermont	98
39	Tennessee	98		42	Louisiana	97
42	Texas	97		42	Texas	97
50	Utah	84		44	Indiana	96
39	Vermont	98		44	Kansas	96
6	Virginia	145		44	North Carolina	96
29	Washington	103		47	New Mexico	95
32	West Virginia	102		48	North Dakota	89
10	Wisconsin	133		49	Rhode Island	85
21	Wyoming	108		50	Utah	84
					District of Columbia	99

Source: U.S. Department of Justice, Bureau of Justice Statistics
"Prisoners in 1994" (Bulletin, August 1995, NCJ-151654)
*As of December 31, 1994. Federal prison population is at 125% of highest rated capacity.

Prisoners in State Correctional Institutions: Year End 1994

National Total = 959,637 State Prisoners*

<table>
<tr><td colspan="4">ALPHA ORDER</td><td colspan="4">RANK ORDER</td></tr>
<tr><th>RANK</th><th>STATE</th><th>PRISONERS</th><th>% of USA</th><th>RANK</th><th>STATE</th><th>PRISONERS</th><th>% of USA</th></tr>
<tr><td>16</td><td>Alabama</td><td>19,573</td><td>2.04%</td><td>1</td><td>California</td><td>125,605</td><td>13.09%</td></tr>
<tr><td>38</td><td>Alaska</td><td>3,292</td><td>0.34%</td><td>2</td><td>Texas</td><td>118,195</td><td>12.32%</td></tr>
<tr><td>15</td><td>Arizona</td><td>19,746</td><td>2.06%</td><td>3</td><td>New York</td><td>66,750</td><td>6.96%</td></tr>
<tr><td>29</td><td>Arkansas</td><td>8,643</td><td>0.90%</td><td>4</td><td>Florida</td><td>57,168</td><td>5.96%</td></tr>
<tr><td>1</td><td>California</td><td>125,605</td><td>13.09%</td><td>5</td><td>Ohio</td><td>43,074</td><td>4.49%</td></tr>
<tr><td>27</td><td>Colorado</td><td>10,717</td><td>1.12%</td><td>6</td><td>Michigan</td><td>40,631</td><td>4.23%</td></tr>
<tr><td>22</td><td>Connecticut</td><td>14,380</td><td>1.50%</td><td>7</td><td>Illinois</td><td>36,531</td><td>3.81%</td></tr>
<tr><td>35</td><td>Delaware</td><td>4,466</td><td>0.47%</td><td>8</td><td>Georgia</td><td>33,425</td><td>3.48%</td></tr>
<tr><td>4</td><td>Florida</td><td>57,168</td><td>5.96%</td><td>9</td><td>Pennsylvania</td><td>28,302</td><td>2.95%</td></tr>
<tr><td>8</td><td>Georgia</td><td>33,425</td><td>3.48%</td><td>10</td><td>Virginia</td><td>26,968</td><td>2.81%</td></tr>
<tr><td>37</td><td>Hawaii</td><td>3,333</td><td>0.35%</td><td>11</td><td>New Jersey</td><td>24,632</td><td>2.57%</td></tr>
<tr><td>41</td><td>Idaho</td><td>2,811</td><td>0.29%</td><td>12</td><td>Louisiana</td><td>24,063</td><td>2.51%</td></tr>
<tr><td>7</td><td>Illinois</td><td>36,531</td><td>3.81%</td><td>13</td><td>North Carolina</td><td>23,648</td><td>2.46%</td></tr>
<tr><td>20</td><td>Indiana</td><td>15,014</td><td>1.56%</td><td>14</td><td>Maryland</td><td>20,998</td><td>2.19%</td></tr>
<tr><td>33</td><td>Iowa</td><td>5,437</td><td>0.57%</td><td>15</td><td>Arizona</td><td>19,746</td><td>2.06%</td></tr>
<tr><td>32</td><td>Kansas</td><td>6,371</td><td>0.66%</td><td>16</td><td>Alabama</td><td>19,573</td><td>2.04%</td></tr>
<tr><td>24</td><td>Kentucky</td><td>11,066</td><td>1.15%</td><td>17</td><td>South Carolina</td><td>18,999</td><td>1.98%</td></tr>
<tr><td>12</td><td>Louisiana</td><td>24,063</td><td>2.51%</td><td>18</td><td>Missouri</td><td>17,898</td><td>1.87%</td></tr>
<tr><td>47</td><td>Maine</td><td>1,474</td><td>0.15%</td><td>19</td><td>Oklahoma</td><td>16,631</td><td>1.73%</td></tr>
<tr><td>14</td><td>Maryland</td><td>20,998</td><td>2.19%</td><td>20</td><td>Indiana</td><td>15,014</td><td>1.56%</td></tr>
<tr><td>23</td><td>Massachusetts</td><td>11,293</td><td>1.18%</td><td>21</td><td>Tennessee</td><td>14,401</td><td>1.50%</td></tr>
<tr><td>6</td><td>Michigan</td><td>40,631</td><td>4.23%</td><td>22</td><td>Connecticut</td><td>14,380</td><td>1.50%</td></tr>
<tr><td>34</td><td>Minnesota</td><td>4,575</td><td>0.48%</td><td>23</td><td>Massachusetts</td><td>11,293</td><td>1.18%</td></tr>
<tr><td>25</td><td>Mississippi</td><td>10,930</td><td>1.14%</td><td>24</td><td>Kentucky</td><td>11,066</td><td>1.15%</td></tr>
<tr><td>18</td><td>Missouri</td><td>17,898</td><td>1.87%</td><td>25</td><td>Mississippi</td><td>10,930</td><td>1.14%</td></tr>
<tr><td>45</td><td>Montana</td><td>1,764</td><td>0.18%</td><td>26</td><td>Washington</td><td>10,833</td><td>1.13%</td></tr>
<tr><td>42</td><td>Nebraska</td><td>2,711</td><td>0.28%</td><td>27</td><td>Colorado</td><td>10,717</td><td>1.12%</td></tr>
<tr><td>30</td><td>Nevada</td><td>6,993</td><td>0.73%</td><td>28</td><td>Wisconsin</td><td>10,022</td><td>1.04%</td></tr>
<tr><td>43</td><td>New Hampshire</td><td>2,021</td><td>0.21%</td><td>29</td><td>Arkansas</td><td>8,643</td><td>0.90%</td></tr>
<tr><td>11</td><td>New Jersey</td><td>24,632</td><td>2.57%</td><td>30</td><td>Nevada</td><td>6,993</td><td>0.73%</td></tr>
<tr><td>36</td><td>New Mexico</td><td>3,712</td><td>0.39%</td><td>31</td><td>Oregon</td><td>6,936</td><td>0.72%</td></tr>
<tr><td>3</td><td>New York</td><td>66,750</td><td>6.96%</td><td>32</td><td>Kansas</td><td>6,371</td><td>0.66%</td></tr>
<tr><td>13</td><td>North Carolina</td><td>23,648</td><td>2.46%</td><td>33</td><td>Iowa</td><td>5,437</td><td>0.57%</td></tr>
<tr><td>50</td><td>North Dakota</td><td>536</td><td>0.06%</td><td>34</td><td>Minnesota</td><td>4,575</td><td>0.48%</td></tr>
<tr><td>5</td><td>Ohio</td><td>43,074</td><td>4.49%</td><td>35</td><td>Delaware</td><td>4,466</td><td>0.47%</td></tr>
<tr><td>19</td><td>Oklahoma</td><td>16,631</td><td>1.73%</td><td>36</td><td>New Mexico</td><td>3,712</td><td>0.39%</td></tr>
<tr><td>31</td><td>Oregon</td><td>6,936</td><td>0.72%</td><td>37</td><td>Hawaii</td><td>3,333</td><td>0.35%</td></tr>
<tr><td>9</td><td>Pennsylvania</td><td>28,302</td><td>2.95%</td><td>38</td><td>Alaska</td><td>3,292</td><td>0.34%</td></tr>
<tr><td>40</td><td>Rhode Island</td><td>2,919</td><td>0.30%</td><td>39</td><td>Utah</td><td>3,045</td><td>0.32%</td></tr>
<tr><td>17</td><td>South Carolina</td><td>18,999</td><td>1.98%</td><td>40</td><td>Rhode Island</td><td>2,919</td><td>0.30%</td></tr>
<tr><td>46</td><td>South Dakota</td><td>1,708</td><td>0.18%</td><td>41</td><td>Idaho</td><td>2,811</td><td>0.29%</td></tr>
<tr><td>21</td><td>Tennessee</td><td>14,401</td><td>1.50%</td><td>42</td><td>Nebraska</td><td>2,711</td><td>0.28%</td></tr>
<tr><td>2</td><td>Texas</td><td>118,195</td><td>12.32%</td><td>43</td><td>New Hampshire</td><td>2,021</td><td>0.21%</td></tr>
<tr><td>39</td><td>Utah</td><td>3,045</td><td>0.32%</td><td>44</td><td>West Virginia</td><td>1,930</td><td>0.20%</td></tr>
<tr><td>48</td><td>Vermont</td><td>1,301</td><td>0.14%</td><td>45</td><td>Montana</td><td>1,764</td><td>0.18%</td></tr>
<tr><td>10</td><td>Virginia</td><td>26,968</td><td>2.81%</td><td>46</td><td>South Dakota</td><td>1,708</td><td>0.18%</td></tr>
<tr><td>26</td><td>Washington</td><td>10,833</td><td>1.13%</td><td>47</td><td>Maine</td><td>1,474</td><td>0.15%</td></tr>
<tr><td>44</td><td>West Virginia</td><td>1,930</td><td>0.20%</td><td>48</td><td>Vermont</td><td>1,301</td><td>0.14%</td></tr>
<tr><td>28</td><td>Wisconsin</td><td>10,022</td><td>1.04%</td><td>49</td><td>Wyoming</td><td>1,217</td><td>0.13%</td></tr>
<tr><td>49</td><td>Wyoming</td><td>1,217</td><td>0.13%</td><td>50</td><td>North Dakota</td><td>536</td><td>0.06%</td></tr>
<tr><td></td><td></td><td></td><td></td><td></td><td>District of Columbia</td><td>10,949</td><td>1.14%</td></tr>
</table>

Source: U.S. Department of Justice, Bureau of Justice Statistics
Press Release (December 3, 1995)

As of December 31, 1994. Totals reflect all prisoners, including those sentenced to a year or less and those unsentenced. National total does not include 95,034 prisoners under federal jurisdiction. State and federal prisoners combined total 1,054,671.

Projected State Prisoner Population in 2000

National Total = 1,038,965*

ALPHA ORDER

RANK	STATE	PRISONERS	% of USA
11	Alabama	25,359	2.44%
24	Alaska	5,623	0.54%
NA	Arizona**	NA	NA
23	Arkansas	12,119	1.17%
1	California	232,770	22.40%
16	Colorado	15,455	1.49%
NA	Connecticut**	NA	NA
27	Delaware	5,088	0.49%
NA	Florida**	NA	NA
NA	Georgia**	NA	NA
30	Hawaii	2,105	0.20%
28	Idaho	3,712	0.36%
4	Illinois	51,216	4.93%
15	Indiana	16,086	1.55%
NA	Iowa**	NA	NA
NA	Kansas**	NA	NA
17	Kentucky	15,227	1.47%
7	Louisiana	34,000	3.27%
NA	Maine**	NA	NA
10	Maryland	25,599	2.46%
20	Massachusetts	13,403	1.29%
NA	Michigan**	NA	NA
25	Minnesota	5,558	0.53%
22	Mississippi	12,973	1.25%
12	Missouri	23,432	2.26%
NA	Montana**	NA	NA
NA	Nebraska**	NA	NA
NA	Nevada**	NA	NA
NA	New Hampshire**	NA	NA
NA	New Jersey**	NA	NA
26	New Mexico	5,199	0.50%
3	New York	77,750	7.48%
8	North Carolina	30,761	2.96%
34	North Dakota	589	0.06%
5	Ohio	46,483	4.47%
13	Oklahoma	20,223	1.95%
21	Oregon	13,116	1.26%
9	Pennsylvania	27,686	2.66%
29	Rhode Island	3,337	0.32%
NA	South Carolina**	NA	NA
31	South Dakota	1,822	0.18%
14	Tennessee	19,961	1.92%
2	Texas	206,162	19.84%
NA	Utah**	NA	NA
32	Vermont	1,640	0.16%
6	Virginia	40,984	3.94%
19	Washington	14,121	1.36%
NA	West Virginia**	NA	NA
18	Wisconsin	15,012	1.44%
33	Wyoming*	1,269	0.12%

RANK ORDER

RANK	STATE	PRISONERS	% of USA
1	California	232,770	22.40%
2	Texas	206,162	19.84%
3	New York	77,750	7.48%
4	Illinois	51,216	4.93%
5	Ohio	46,483	4.47%
6	Virginia	40,984	3.94%
7	Louisiana	34,000	3.27%
8	North Carolina	30,761	2.96%
9	Pennsylvania	27,686	2.66%
10	Maryland	25,599	2.46%
11	Alabama	25,359	2.44%
12	Missouri	23,432	2.26%
13	Oklahoma	20,223	1.95%
14	Tennessee	19,961	1.92%
15	Indiana	16,086	1.55%
16	Colorado	15,455	1.49%
17	Kentucky	15,227	1.47%
18	Wisconsin	15,012	1.44%
19	Washington	14,121	1.36%
20	Massachusetts	13,403	1.29%
21	Oregon	13,116	1.26%
22	Mississippi	12,973	1.25%
23	Arkansas	12,119	1.17%
24	Alaska	5,623	0.54%
25	Minnesota	5,558	0.53%
26	New Mexico	5,199	0.50%
27	Delaware	5,088	0.49%
28	Idaho	3,712	0.36%
29	Rhode Island	3,337	0.32%
30	Hawaii	2,105	0.20%
31	South Dakota	1,822	0.18%
32	Vermont	1,640	0.16%
33	Wyoming*	1,269	0.12%
34	North Dakota	589	0.06%
NA	Arizona**	NA	NA
NA	Connecticut**	NA	NA
NA	Florida**	NA	NA
NA	Georgia**	NA	NA
NA	Iowa**	NA	NA
NA	Kansas**	NA	NA
NA	Maine**	NA	NA
NA	Michigan**	NA	NA
NA	Montana**	NA	NA
NA	Nebraska**	NA	NA
NA	Nevada**	NA	NA
NA	New Hampshire**	NA	NA
NA	New Jersey**	NA	NA
NA	South Carolina**	NA	NA
NA	Utah**	NA	NA
NA	West Virginia**	NA	NA
	District of Columbia	13,125	1.26%

Source: CEGA Publishing (Lincoln, NE)
"Corrections Compendium" (March 1995, Volume XX, No.3)
*The national total does not include states not shown separately. Nor does it include 133,534 prisoners projected to be under federal jurisdiction. The national percent increase based on current and projected prison population of reporting states is 50.82% from 1994 to 2000. Wyoming's figure is for men only.
**Not available.

Projected State Prisoner Incarceration Rate in 2000

National Projected Rate = 501 Prisoners per 100,000 Population*

ALPHA ORDER

RANK	STATE	RATE
8	Alabama	565
2	Alaska	803
NA	Arizona**	NA
11	Arkansas	470
5	California	667
19	Colorado	381
NA	Connecticut**	NA
4	Delaware	670
NA	Florida**	NA
NA	Georgia**	NA
32	Hawaii	159
22	Idaho	288
14	Illinois	421
26	Indiana	266
NA	Iowa**	NA
NA	Kansas**	NA
18	Kentucky	382
3	Louisiana	759
NA	Maine**	NA
9	Maryland	481
30	Massachusetts	225
NA	Michigan**	NA
33	Minnesota	115
10	Mississippi	472
12	Missouri	431
NA	Montana**	NA
NA	Nebraska**	NA
NA	Nevada**	NA
NA	New Hampshire**	NA
NA	New Jersey**	NA
23	New Mexico	285
13	New York	426
16	North Carolina	404
34	North Dakota	92
15	Ohio	406
6	Oklahoma	598
17	Oregon	385
30	Pennsylvania	225
21	Rhode Island	334
NA	South Carolina**	NA
28	South Dakota	236
20	Tennessee	361
1	Texas	1,029
NA	Utah**	NA
25	Vermont	277
7	Virginia	582
29	Washington	233
NA	West Virginia**	NA
24	Wisconsin	279
27	Wyoming	243

RANK ORDER

RANK	STATE	RATE
1	Texas	1,029
2	Alaska	803
3	Louisiana	759
4	Delaware	670
5	California	667
6	Oklahoma	598
7	Virginia	582
8	Alabama	565
9	Maryland	481
10	Mississippi	472
11	Arkansas	470
12	Missouri	431
13	New York	426
14	Illinois	421
15	Ohio	406
16	North Carolina	404
17	Oregon	385
18	Kentucky	382
19	Colorado	381
20	Tennessee	361
21	Rhode Island	334
22	Idaho	288
23	New Mexico	285
24	Wisconsin	279
25	Vermont	277
26	Indiana	266
27	Wyoming	243
28	South Dakota	236
29	Washington	233
30	Massachusetts	225
30	Pennsylvania	225
32	Hawaii	159
33	Minnesota	115
34	North Dakota	92
NA	Arizona**	NA
NA	Connecticut**	NA
NA	Florida**	NA
NA	Georgia**	NA
NA	Iowa**	NA
NA	Kansas**	NA
NA	Maine**	NA
NA	Michigan**	NA
NA	Montana**	NA
NA	Nebraska**	NA
NA	Nevada**	NA
NA	New Hampshire**	NA
NA	New Jersey**	NA
NA	South Carolina**	NA
NA	Utah**	NA
NA	West Virginia**	NA

District of Columbia	2,444

Source: Morgan Quitno Press using data from CEGA Publishing (Lincoln, NE)
"Corrections Compendium" (March 1995, Volume XX, No.3)
The national rate does not include states not shown separately. Nor does it include prisoners projected to be under federal jurisdiction.
**Not available.*

State Prisoners Sentenced to More than One Year in 1994

National Total = 932,668 State Prisoners*

ALPHA ORDER

RANK	STATE	PRISONERS	% of USA	RANK	STATE	PRISONERS	% of USA
15	Alabama	19,074	2.05%	1	California	121,084	12.98%
42	Alaska	1,934	0.21%	2	Texas	118,094	12.66%
16	Arizona	19,005	2.04%	3	New York	66,750	7.16%
29	Arkansas	8,711	0.93%	4	Florida	57,129	6.13%
1	California	121,084	12.98%	5	Ohio	41,913	4.49%
25	Colorado	10,717	1.15%	6	Michigan	40,775	4.37%
26	Connecticut	10,500	1.13%	7	Illinois	36,531	3.92%
38	Delaware	2,788	0.30%	8	Georgia	32,523	3.49%
4	Florida	57,129	6.13%	9	Pennsylvania	28,301	3.03%
8	Georgia	32,523	3.49%	10	Virginia	26,016	2.79%
40	Hawaii	2,392	0.26%	11	New Jersey	24,544	2.63%
37	Idaho	2,964	0.32%	12	North Carolina	22,983	2.46%
7	Illinois	36,531	3.92%	13	Louisiana	22,956	2.46%
20	Indiana	14,925	1.60%	14	Maryland	19,854	2.13%
33	Iowa	5,437	0.58%	15	Alabama	19,074	2.05%
31	Kansas	6,373	0.68%	16	Arizona	19,005	2.04%
22	Kentucky	11,066	1.19%	17	South Carolina	18,168	1.95%
13	Louisiana	22,956	2.46%	18	Missouri	17,898	1.92%
47	Maine	1,484	0.16%	19	Oklahoma	16,631	1.78%
14	Maryland	19,854	2.13%	20	Indiana	14,925	1.60%
27	Massachusetts	10,340	1.11%	21	Tennessee	14,474	1.55%
6	Michigan	40,775	4.37%	22	Kentucky	11,066	1.19%
34	Minnesota	4,572	0.49%	23	Mississippi	10,950	1.17%
23	Mississippi	10,950	1.17%	24	Washington	10,833	1.16%
18	Missouri	17,898	1.92%	25	Colorado	10,717	1.15%
46	Montana	1,680	0.18%	26	Connecticut	10,500	1.13%
39	Nebraska	2,590	0.28%	27	Massachusetts	10,340	1.11%
30	Nevada	6,877	0.74%	28	Wisconsin	9,519	1.02%
41	New Hampshire	2,021	0.22%	29	Arkansas	8,711	0.93%
11	New Jersey	24,544	2.63%	30	Nevada	6,877	0.74%
35	New Mexico	3,679	0.39%	31	Kansas	6,373	0.68%
3	New York	66,750	7.16%	32	Oregon	5,458	0.59%
12	North Carolina	22,983	2.46%	33	Iowa	5,437	0.58%
50	North Dakota	501	0.05%	34	Minnesota	4,572	0.49%
5	Ohio	41,913	4.49%	35	New Mexico	3,679	0.39%
19	Oklahoma	16,631	1.78%	36	Utah	2,997	0.32%
32	Oregon	5,458	0.59%	37	Idaho	2,964	0.32%
9	Pennsylvania	28,301	3.03%	38	Delaware	2,788	0.30%
44	Rhode Island	1,853	0.20%	39	Nebraska	2,590	0.28%
17	South Carolina	18,168	1.95%	40	Hawaii	2,392	0.26%
45	South Dakota	1,734	0.19%	41	New Hampshire	2,021	0.22%
21	Tennessee	14,474	1.55%	42	Alaska	1,934	0.21%
2	Texas	118,094	12.66%	43	West Virginia	1,930	0.21%
36	Utah	2,997	0.32%	44	Rhode Island	1,853	0.20%
49	Vermont	981	0.11%	45	South Dakota	1,734	0.19%
10	Virginia	26,016	2.79%	46	Montana	1,680	0.18%
24	Washington	10,833	1.16%	47	Maine	1,484	0.16%
43	West Virginia	1,930	0.21%	48	Wyoming	1,217	0.13%
28	Wisconsin	9,519	1.02%	49	Vermont	981	0.11%
48	Wyoming	1,217	0.13%	50	North Dakota	501	0.05%
					District of Columbia	8,962	0.96%

Source: U.S. Department of Justice, Bureau of Justice Statistics
    "Prisoners in 1994" (Bulletin, August 1995, NCJ-151654)
Advance figures as of December 31, 1994. Does not include 79,795 prisoners under federal jurisdiction sentenced
to more than one year. State and federal prisoners sentenced to more than one year total 1,012,463.

Female Prisoners in State Correctional Institutions in 1994

National Total = 57,263 State Female Prisoners*

ALPHA ORDER

RANK	STATE	PRISONERS	% of USA
14	Alabama	1,214	2.12%
38	Alaska	218	0.38%
13	Arizona	1,273	2.22%
27	Arkansas	597	1.04%
2	California	8,215	14.35%
25	Colorado	670	1.17%
20	Connecticut	999	1.74%
34	Delaware	279	0.49%
4	Florida	3,064	5.35%
7	Georgia	2,012	3.51%
35	Hawaii	257	0.45%
39	Idaho	177	0.31%
8	Illinois	1,813	3.17%
21	Indiana	826	1.44%
32	Iowa	351	0.61%
33	Kansas	344	0.60%
26	Kentucky	637	1.11%
12	Louisiana	1,287	2.25%
47	Maine	65	0.11%
18	Maryland	1,039	1.81%
24	Massachusetts	680	1.19%
6	Michigan	2,023	3.53%
36	Minnesota	232	0.41%
23	Mississippi	686	1.20%
17	Missouri	1,042	1.82%
48	Montana	55	0.10%
40	Nebraska	157	0.27%
29	Nevada	478	0.83%
43	New Hampshire	110	0.19%
16	New Jersey	1,168	2.04%
37	New Mexico	225	0.39%
3	New York	3,575	6.24%
15	North Carolina	1,186	2.07%
50	North Dakota	16	0.03%
5	Ohio	2,595	4.53%
9	Oklahoma	1,607	2.81%
31	Oregon	379	0.66%
11	Pennsylvania	1,322	2.31%
41	Rhode Island	150	0.26%
19	South Carolina	1,022	1.78%
44	South Dakota	108	0.19%
27	Tennessee	597	1.04%
1	Texas	8,839	15.44%
42	Utah	129	0.23%
49	Vermont	49	0.09%
10	Virginia	1,527	2.67%
22	Washington	698	1.22%
45	West Virginia	91	0.16%
30	Wisconsin	412	0.72%
46	Wyoming	82	0.14%

RANK ORDER

RANK	STATE	PRISONERS	% of USA
1	Texas	8,839	15.44%
2	California	8,215	14.35%
3	New York	3,575	6.24%
4	Florida	3,064	5.35%
5	Ohio	2,595	4.53%
6	Michigan	2,023	3.53%
7	Georgia	2,012	3.51%
8	Illinois	1,813	3.17%
9	Oklahoma	1,607	2.81%
10	Virginia	1,527	2.67%
11	Pennsylvania	1,322	2.31%
12	Louisiana	1,287	2.25%
13	Arizona	1,273	2.22%
14	Alabama	1,214	2.12%
15	North Carolina	1,186	2.07%
16	New Jersey	1,168	2.04%
17	Missouri	1,042	1.82%
18	Maryland	1,039	1.81%
19	South Carolina	1,022	1.78%
20	Connecticut	999	1.74%
21	Indiana	826	1.44%
22	Washington	698	1.22%
23	Mississippi	686	1.20%
24	Massachusetts	680	1.19%
25	Colorado	670	1.17%
26	Kentucky	637	1.11%
27	Arkansas	597	1.04%
27	Tennessee	597	1.04%
29	Nevada	478	0.83%
30	Wisconsin	412	0.72%
31	Oregon	379	0.66%
32	Iowa	351	0.61%
33	Kansas	344	0.60%
34	Delaware	279	0.49%
35	Hawaii	257	0.45%
36	Minnesota	232	0.41%
37	New Mexico	225	0.39%
38	Alaska	218	0.38%
39	Idaho	177	0.31%
40	Nebraska	157	0.27%
41	Rhode Island	150	0.26%
42	Utah	129	0.23%
43	New Hampshire	110	0.19%
44	South Dakota	108	0.19%
45	West Virginia	91	0.16%
46	Wyoming	82	0.14%
47	Maine	65	0.11%
48	Montana	55	0.10%
49	Vermont	49	0.09%
50	North Dakota	16	0.03%
	District of Columbia	686	1.20%

Source: U.S. Department of Justice, Bureau of Justice Statistics
"Prisoners in 1994" (Bulletin, August 1995, NCJ-151654)
Advance figures as of December 31, 1994. Does not include 7,140 female prisoners under federal jurisdiction.
State and federal female prisoners total 64,403.

Female State Prisoner Incarceration Rate in 1994

National Rate = 40 State Female Prisoners per 100,000 Female Population*

ALPHA ORDER

RANK	STATE	RATE
6	Alabama	53
18	Alaska	37
4	Arizona	57
11	Arkansas	45
9	California	47
21	Colorado	36
18	Connecticut	37
18	Delaware	37
14	Florida	42
7	Georgia	52
26	Hawaii	30
25	Idaho	31
26	Illinois	30
31	Indiana	27
34	Iowa	24
32	Kansas	26
24	Kentucky	32
5	Louisiana	54
49	Maine	9
22	Maryland	34
44	Massachusetts	11
15	Michigan	41
46	Minnesota	10
10	Mississippi	46
16	Missouri	38
41	Montana	13
39	Nebraska	18
3	Nevada	61
38	New Hampshire	19
30	New Jersey	28
37	New Mexico	20
16	New York	38
26	North Carolina	30
50	North Dakota	5
11	Ohio	45
1	Oklahoma	96
43	Oregon	12
36	Pennsylvania	21
46	Rhode Island	10
8	South Carolina	48
29	South Dakota	29
35	Tennessee	22
2	Texas	94
41	Utah	13
44	Vermont	11
11	Virginia	45
32	Washington	26
46	West Virginia	10
40	Wisconsin	15
22	Wyoming	34

RANK ORDER

RANK	STATE	RATE
1	Oklahoma	96
2	Texas	94
3	Nevada	61
4	Arizona	57
5	Louisiana	54
6	Alabama	53
7	Georgia	52
8	South Carolina	48
9	California	47
10	Mississippi	46
11	Arkansas	45
11	Ohio	45
11	Virginia	45
14	Florida	42
15	Michigan	41
16	Missouri	38
16	New York	38
18	Alaska	37
18	Connecticut	37
18	Delaware	37
21	Colorado	36
22	Maryland	34
22	Wyoming	34
24	Kentucky	32
25	Idaho	31
26	Hawaii	30
26	Illinois	30
26	North Carolina	30
29	South Dakota	29
30	New Jersey	28
31	Indiana	27
32	Kansas	26
32	Washington	26
34	Iowa	24
35	Tennessee	22
36	Pennsylvania	21
37	New Mexico	20
38	New Hampshire	19
39	Nebraska	18
40	Wisconsin	15
41	Montana	13
41	Utah	13
43	Oregon	12
44	Massachusetts	11
44	Vermont	11
46	Minnesota	10
46	Rhode Island	10
46	West Virginia	10
49	Maine	9
50	North Dakota	5

| | District of Columbia | 159 |

Source: U.S. Department of Justice, Bureau of Justice Statistics
   "Prisoners in 1994" (Bulletin, August 1995, NCJ-151654)

*As of December 31, 1994. Rate is for female prisoners sentenced to more than one year. National rate does not include federal female inmates. Federal female incarceration rate is four federal female prisoners per 100,000 female population. The combined federal/state female incarceration rate is 45 female prisoners per 100,000 female population.

Female Prisoners in State Correctional Institutions As a Percent of All State Prisoners in 1994
National Percent = 6.0% of State Prisoners are Female*

ALPHA ORDER

RANK	STATE	PERCENT
15	Alabama	6.2
8	Alaska	6.6
11	Arizona	6.4
5	Arkansas	6.8
9	California	6.5
13	Colorado	6.3
4	Connecticut	6.9
13	Delaware	6.3
29	Florida	5.4
19	Georgia	6.0
2	Hawaii	7.7
19	Idaho	6.0
37	Illinois	5.0
27	Indiana	5.5
9	Iowa	6.5
29	Kansas	5.4
23	Kentucky	5.8
34	Louisiana	5.3
45	Maine	4.2
40	Maryland	4.9
19	Massachusetts	6.0
37	Michigan	5.0
35	Minnesota	5.1
18	Mississippi	6.1
23	Missouri	5.8
49	Montana	3.3
19	Nebraska	6.0
6	Nevada	6.7
29	New Hampshire	5.4
41	New Jersey	4.7
23	New Mexico	5.8
29	New York	5.4
37	North Carolina	5.0
50	North Dakota	3.0
15	Ohio	6.2
1	Oklahoma	9.7
27	Oregon	5.5
41	Pennsylvania	4.7
35	Rhode Island	5.1
29	South Carolina	5.4
15	South Dakota	6.2
46	Tennessee	4.1
3	Texas	7.5
44	Utah	4.3
48	Vermont	3.8
23	Virginia	5.8
11	Washington	6.4
41	West Virginia	4.7
46	Wisconsin	4.1
6	Wyoming	6.7

RANK ORDER

RANK	STATE	PERCENT
1	Oklahoma	9.7
2	Hawaii	7.7
3	Texas	7.5
4	Connecticut	6.9
5	Arkansas	6.8
6	Nevada	6.7
6	Wyoming	6.7
8	Alaska	6.6
9	California	6.5
9	Iowa	6.5
11	Arizona	6.4
11	Washington	6.4
13	Colorado	6.3
13	Delaware	6.3
15	Alabama	6.2
15	Ohio	6.2
15	South Dakota	6.2
18	Mississippi	6.1
19	Georgia	6.0
19	Idaho	6.0
19	Massachusetts	6.0
19	Nebraska	6.0
23	Kentucky	5.8
23	Missouri	5.8
23	New Mexico	5.8
23	Virginia	5.8
27	Indiana	5.5
27	Oregon	5.5
29	Florida	5.4
29	Kansas	5.4
29	New Hampshire	5.4
29	New York	5.4
29	South Carolina	5.4
34	Louisiana	5.3
35	Minnesota	5.1
35	Rhode Island	5.1
37	Illinois	5.0
37	Michigan	5.0
37	North Carolina	5.0
40	Maryland	4.9
41	New Jersey	4.7
41	Pennsylvania	4.7
41	West Virginia	4.7
44	Utah	4.3
45	Maine	4.2
46	Tennessee	4.1
46	Wisconsin	4.1
48	Vermont	3.8
49	Montana	3.3
50	North Dakota	3.0
	District of Columbia	6.3

Source: U.S. Department of Justice, Bureau of Justice Statistics
    "Prisoners in 1994" (Bulletin, August 1995, NCJ-151654)
*As of December 31, 1994.   Rate does not include federal female inmates. Federal female inmates constitute 7.5% of federal inmates. The federal/state combined rate is 6.1%.

Percent Change in Female State Prisoner Population: 1993 to 1994

National Percent Change = 11.5% Increase*

ALPHA ORDER

RANK	STATE	PERCENT CHANGE
32	Alabama	7.3
1	Alaska	37.1
12	Arizona	22.8
15	Arkansas	20.6
30	California	8.4
11	Colorado	23.6
44	Connecticut	0.5
29	Delaware	8.6
23	Florida	13.5
22	Georgia	14.3
8	Hawaii	24.8
16	Idaho	19.6
31	Illinois	7.4
35	Indiana	6.2
7	Iowa	24.9
6	Kansas	25.1
18	Kentucky	16.9
20	Louisiana	15.5
2	Maine	30.0
33	Maryland	6.5
39	Massachusetts	4.1
25	Michigan	12.5
14	Minnesota	20.8
18	Mississippi	16.9
24	Missouri	13.3
49	Montana	(17.9)
47	Nebraska	(7.1)
8	Nevada	24.8
3	New Hampshire	27.9
40	New Jersey	3.1
28	New Mexico	9.2
43	New York	1.3
36	North Carolina	5.9
50	North Dakota	(23.8)
45	Ohio	0.4
42	Oklahoma	1.6
26	Oregon	11.5
27	Pennsylvania	10.7
46	Rhode Island	(3.2)
48	South Carolina	(7.5)
13	South Dakota	22.7
17	Tennessee	17.5
4	Texas	27.2
37	Utah	4.9
41	Vermont	2.1
5	Virginia	25.3
38	Washington	4.8
21	West Virginia	15.2
33	Wisconsin	6.5
10	Wyoming	24.2

RANK ORDER

RANK	STATE	PERCENT CHANGE
1	Alaska	37.1
2	Maine	30.0
3	New Hampshire	27.9
4	Texas	27.2
5	Virginia	25.3
6	Kansas	25.1
7	Iowa	24.9
8	Hawaii	24.8
8	Nevada	24.8
10	Wyoming	24.2
11	Colorado	23.6
12	Arizona	22.8
13	South Dakota	22.7
14	Minnesota	20.8
15	Arkansas	20.6
16	Idaho	19.6
17	Tennessee	17.5
18	Kentucky	16.9
18	Mississippi	16.9
20	Louisiana	15.5
21	West Virginia	15.2
22	Georgia	14.3
23	Florida	13.5
24	Missouri	13.3
25	Michigan	12.5
26	Oregon	11.5
27	Pennsylvania	10.7
28	New Mexico	9.2
29	Delaware	8.6
30	California	8.4
31	Illinois	7.4
32	Alabama	7.3
33	Maryland	6.5
33	Wisconsin	6.5
35	Indiana	6.2
36	North Carolina	5.9
37	Utah	4.9
38	Washington	4.8
39	Massachusetts	4.1
40	New Jersey	3.1
41	Vermont	2.1
42	Oklahoma	1.6
43	New York	1.3
44	Connecticut	0.5
45	Ohio	0.4
46	Rhode Island	(3.2)
47	Nebraska	(7.1)
48	South Carolina	(7.5)
49	Montana	(17.9)
50	North Dakota	(23.8)

District of Columbia	(0.1)

Source: U.S. Department of Justice, Bureau of Justice Statistics
    "Prisoners in 1994" (Bulletin, August 1995, NCJ-151654)
*As of December 31, 1994.   Rate does not include federal female inmates. Federal female inmates increased by 3.6%. The combined federal/state female population grew by 10.6%.

White Prisoners in State Correctional Institutions in 1993

National Total = 375,244 White State Prisoners*

ALPHA ORDER

RANK	STATE	PRISONERS	% of USA
21	Alabama	6,411	1.71%
43	Alaska	1,385	0.37%
7	Arizona	13,936	3.71%
29	Arkansas	3,653	0.97%
1	California	75,761	20.19%
18	Colorado	6,802	1.81%
28	Connecticut	3,672	0.98%
44	Delaware	1,326	0.35%
3	Florida	21,029	5.60%
10	Georgia	8,761	2.33%
49	Hawaii	637	0.17%
36	Idaho	2,371	0.63%
11	Illinois	8,569	2.28%
12	Indiana	8,506	2.27%
31	Iowa	3,458	0.92%
32	Kansas	3,392	0.90%
17	Kentucky	6,923	1.84%
23	Louisiana	5,221	1.39%
42	Maine	1,414	0.38%
26	Maryland	4,662	1.24%
25	Massachusetts	4,808	1.28%
6	Michigan	16,243	4.33%
37	Minnesota	2,209	0.59%
34	Mississippi	2,496	0.67%
13	Missouri	8,403	2.24%
45	Montana	1,256	0.33%
40	Nebraska	1,568	0.42%
30	Nevada	3,544	0.94%
39	New Hampshire	1,691	0.45%
19	New Jersey	6,639	1.77%
33	New Mexico	2,943	0.78%
2	New York	26,954	7.18%
16	North Carolina	7,223	1.92%
50	North Dakota	392	0.10%
4	Ohio	18,415	4.91%
8	Oklahoma	9,042	2.41%
24	Oregon	4,814	1.28%
9	Pennsylvania	8,892	2.37%
38	Rhode Island	1,882	0.50%
22	South Carolina	5,736	1.53%
47	South Dakota	1,148	0.31%
20	Tennessee	6,595	1.76%
5	Texas	18,359	4.89%
35	Utah	2,450	0.65%
46	Vermont	1,223	0.33%
14	Virginia	7,815	2.08%
15	Washington	7,471	1.99%
41	West Virginia	1,534	0.41%
27	Wisconsin	4,442	1.18%
48	Wyoming	1,006	0.27%

RANK ORDER

RANK	STATE	PRISONERS	% of USA
1	California	75,761	20.19%
2	New York	26,954	7.18%
3	Florida	21,029	5.60%
4	Ohio	18,415	4.91%
5	Texas	18,359	4.89%
6	Michigan	16,243	4.33%
7	Arizona	13,936	3.71%
8	Oklahoma	9,042	2.41%
9	Pennsylvania	8,892	2.37%
10	Georgia	8,761	2.33%
11	Illinois	8,569	2.28%
12	Indiana	8,506	2.27%
13	Missouri	8,403	2.24%
14	Virginia	7,815	2.08%
15	Washington	7,471	1.99%
16	North Carolina	7,223	1.92%
17	Kentucky	6,923	1.84%
18	Colorado	6,802	1.81%
19	New Jersey	6,639	1.77%
20	Tennessee	6,595	1.76%
21	Alabama	6,411	1.71%
22	South Carolina	5,736	1.53%
23	Louisiana	5,221	1.39%
24	Oregon	4,814	1.28%
25	Massachusetts	4,808	1.28%
26	Maryland	4,662	1.24%
27	Wisconsin	4,442	1.18%
28	Connecticut	3,672	0.98%
29	Arkansas	3,653	0.97%
30	Nevada	3,544	0.94%
31	Iowa	3,458	0.92%
32	Kansas	3,392	0.90%
33	New Mexico	2,943	0.78%
34	Mississippi	2,496	0.67%
35	Utah	2,450	0.65%
36	Idaho	2,371	0.63%
37	Minnesota	2,209	0.59%
38	Rhode Island	1,882	0.50%
39	New Hampshire	1,691	0.45%
40	Nebraska	1,568	0.42%
41	West Virginia	1,534	0.41%
42	Maine	1,414	0.38%
43	Alaska	1,385	0.37%
44	Delaware	1,326	0.35%
45	Montana	1,256	0.33%
46	Vermont	1,223	0.33%
47	South Dakota	1,148	0.31%
48	Wyoming	1,006	0.27%
49	Hawaii	637	0.17%
50	North Dakota	392	0.10%
	District of Columbia	162	0.04%

Source: U.S. Department of Justice, Bureau of Justice Statistics
   "Correctional Populations in the United States, 1993" (October 1995, NCJ 156241)
*As of December 31, 1993. National total does not include 56,536 white federal prisoners.

White State Prisoner Incarceration Rate in 1993

National Rate = 172 White State Prisoners per 100,000 White Population*

ALPHA ORDER

RANK	STATE	RATE
11	Alabama	204
4	Alaska	290
1	Arizona	386
21	Arkansas	178
3	California	295
15	Colorado	198
38	Connecticut	126
6	Delaware	233
22	Florida	177
23	Georgia	174
37	Hawaii	127
10	Idaho	212
45	Illinois	89
26	Indiana	161
39	Iowa	125
33	Kansas	143
16	Kentucky	196
20	Louisiana	179
40	Maine	116
35	Maryland	133
46	Massachusetts	88
11	Michigan	204
50	Minnesota	51
32	Mississippi	148
19	Missouri	182
27	Montana	158
43	Nebraska	101
5	Nevada	277
28	New Hampshire	153
42	New Jersey	104
14	New Mexico	202
17	New York	192
34	North Carolina	134
49	North Dakota	65
18	Ohio	188
2	Oklahoma	335
25	Oregon	164
48	Pennsylvania	83
13	Rhode Island	203
7	South Carolina	224
24	South Dakota	173
29	Tennessee	152
40	Texas	116
35	Utah	133
8	Vermont	215
29	Virginia	152
29	Washington	152
47	West Virginia	87
44	Wisconsin	93
8	Wyoming	215

RANK ORDER

RANK	STATE	RATE
1	Arizona	386
2	Oklahoma	335
3	California	295
4	Alaska	290
5	Nevada	277
6	Delaware	233
7	South Carolina	224
8	Vermont	215
8	Wyoming	215
10	Idaho	212
11	Alabama	204
11	Michigan	204
13	Rhode Island	203
14	New Mexico	202
15	Colorado	198
16	Kentucky	196
17	New York	192
18	Ohio	188
19	Missouri	182
20	Louisiana	179
21	Arkansas	178
22	Florida	177
23	Georgia	174
24	South Dakota	173
25	Oregon	164
26	Indiana	161
27	Montana	158
28	New Hampshire	153
29	Tennessee	152
29	Virginia	152
29	Washington	152
32	Mississippi	148
33	Kansas	143
34	North Carolina	134
35	Maryland	133
35	Utah	133
37	Hawaii	127
38	Connecticut	126
39	Iowa	125
40	Maine	116
40	Texas	116
42	New Jersey	104
43	Nebraska	101
44	Wisconsin	93
45	Illinois	89
46	Massachusetts	88
47	West Virginia	87
48	Pennsylvania	83
49	North Dakota	65
50	Minnesota	51

| | District of Columbia | 92 |

Source: Morgan Quitno Press using data from U.S. Department of Justice, Bureau of Justice Statistics
"Correctional Populations in the United States, 1993" (October 1995, NCJ 156241)
*As of December 31, 1993. White population estimates are for 1995. National rate does not include 56,536 white federal prisoners.

White Prisoners in State Correctional Institutions
As a Percent of All Prisoners in 1993
National Percent = 43.77% White*

ALPHA ORDER

RANK	STATE	PERCENT
36	Alabama	34.42
28	Alaska	51.24
11	Arizona	78.24
32	Arkansas	42.35
19	California	63.16
14	Colorado	71.89
44	Connecticut	26.82
41	Delaware	31.50
35	Florida	39.64
40	Georgia	31.53
50	Hawaii	20.36
4	Idaho	90.98
47	Illinois	24.84
22	Indiana	58.78
16	Iowa	70.60
21	Kansas	59.23
18	Kentucky	66.31
48	Louisiana	23.24
2	Maine	96.26
49	Maryland	23.01
30	Massachusetts	47.92
34	Michigan	41.31
25	Minnesota	52.60
46	Mississippi	25.19
26	Missouri	51.94
9	Montana	81.51
20	Nebraska	62.27
23	Nevada	57.74
3	New Hampshire	95.27
43	New Jersey	27.86
8	New Mexico	84.13
33	New York	41.74
39	North Carolina	32.99
10	North Dakota	78.71
31	Ohio	45.31
24	Oklahoma	55.10
13	Oregon	73.42
38	Pennsylvania	34.13
17	Rhode Island	67.62
42	South Carolina	30.67
12	South Dakota	73.92
27	Tennessee	51.43
45	Texas	26.18
7	Utah	84.83
1	Vermont	100.00
37	Virginia	34.20
15	Washington	71.71
6	West Virginia	84.99
29	Wisconsin	50.59
5	Wyoming	89.11

RANK ORDER

RANK	STATE	PERCENT
1	Vermont	100.00
2	Maine	96.26
3	New Hampshire	95.27
4	Idaho	90.98
5	Wyoming	89.11
6	West Virginia	84.99
7	Utah	84.83
8	New Mexico	84.13
9	Montana	81.51
10	North Dakota	78.71
11	Arizona	78.24
12	South Dakota	73.92
13	Oregon	73.42
14	Colorado	71.89
15	Washington	71.71
16	Iowa	70.60
17	Rhode Island	67.62
18	Kentucky	66.31
19	California	63.16
20	Nebraska	62.27
21	Kansas	59.23
22	Indiana	58.78
23	Nevada	57.74
24	Oklahoma	55.10
25	Minnesota	52.60
26	Missouri	51.94
27	Tennessee	51.43
28	Alaska	51.24
29	Wisconsin	50.59
30	Massachusetts	47.92
31	Ohio	45.31
32	Arkansas	42.35
33	New York	41.74
34	Michigan	41.31
35	Florida	39.64
36	Alabama	34.42
37	Virginia	34.20
38	Pennsylvania	34.13
39	North Carolina	32.99
40	Georgia	31.53
41	Delaware	31.50
42	South Carolina	30.67
43	New Jersey	27.86
44	Connecticut	26.82
45	Texas	26.18
46	Mississippi	25.19
47	Illinois	24.84
48	Louisiana	23.24
49	Maryland	23.01
50	Hawaii	20.36

District of Columbia 1.49

Source: Morgan Quitno Press using data from U.S. Department of Justice, Bureau of Justice Statistics
   "Correctional Populations in the United States, 1993" (October 1995, NCJ 156241)
*As of December 31, 1993. National percent does not include white federal prisoners. Federal prison population
is 63.11% white. Combined state and federal percentage is 45.60% white.

Black Prisoners in State Correctional Institutions in 1993

National Total = 426,401 Black State Prisoners*

ALPHA ORDER					RANK ORDER			
RANK	STATE		PRISONERS	% of USA	RANK	STATE	PRISONERS	% of USA
16	Alabama		12,179	2.86%	1	California	39,104	9.17%
39	Alaska		336	0.08%	2	New York	35,275	8.27%
26	Arizona		3,087	0.72%	3	Texas	31,277	7.34%
23	Arkansas		4,925	1.16%	4	Florida	30,997	7.27%
1	California		39,104	9.17%	5	Illinois	22,535	5.28%
29	Colorado		2,327	0.55%	6	Ohio	22,226	5.21%
19	Connecticut		6,310	1.48%	7	Michigan	22,099	5.18%
28	Delaware		2,800	0.66%	8	Georgia	18,855	4.42%
4	Florida		30,997	7.27%	9	Louisiana	17,201	4.03%
8	Georgia		18,855	4.42%	10	New Jersey	15,671	3.68%
42	Hawaii		163	0.04%	11	Maryland	15,539	3.64%
45	Idaho		49	0.01%	12	Virginia	14,886	3.49%
5	Illinois		22,535	5.28%	13	Pennsylvania	14,706	3.45%
21	Indiana		5,906	1.39%	14	North Carolina	13,977	3.28%
34	Iowa		1,221	0.29%	15	South Carolina	12,890	3.02%
31	Kansas		2,223	0.52%	16	Alabama	12,179	2.86%
25	Kentucky		3,503	0.82%	17	Missouri	7,728	1.81%
9	Louisiana		17,201	4.03%	18	Mississippi	7,341	1.72%
47	Maine		37	0.01%	19	Connecticut	6,310	1.48%
11	Maryland		15,539	3.64%	20	Tennessee	6,182	1.45%
27	Massachusetts		3,022	0.71%	21	Indiana	5,906	1.39%
7	Michigan		22,099	5.18%	22	Oklahoma	5,784	1.36%
33	Minnesota		1,404	0.33%	23	Arkansas	4,925	1.16%
18	Mississippi		7,341	1.72%	24	Wisconsin	4,111	0.96%
17	Missouri		7,728	1.81%	25	Kentucky	3,503	0.82%
48	Montana		27	0.01%	26	Arizona	3,087	0.72%
35	Nebraska		874	0.20%	27	Massachusetts	3,022	0.71%
32	Nevada		1,823	0.43%	28	Delaware	2,800	0.66%
43	New Hampshire		76	0.02%	29	Colorado	2,327	0.55%
10	New Jersey		15,671	3.68%	30	Washington	2,271	0.53%
38	New Mexico		395	0.09%	31	Kansas	2,223	0.52%
2	New York		35,275	8.27%	32	Nevada	1,823	0.43%
14	North Carolina		13,977	3.28%	33	Minnesota	1,404	0.33%
49	North Dakota		12	0.00%	34	Iowa	1,221	0.29%
6	Ohio		22,226	5.21%	35	Nebraska	874	0.20%
22	Oklahoma		5,784	1.36%	35	Rhode Island	874	0.20%
37	Oregon		872	0.20%	37	Oregon	872	0.20%
13	Pennsylvania		14,706	3.45%	38	New Mexico	395	0.09%
35	Rhode Island		874	0.20%	39	Alaska	336	0.08%
15	South Carolina		12,890	3.02%	40	West Virginia	269	0.06%
46	South Dakota		47	0.01%	41	Utah	243	0.06%
20	Tennessee		6,182	1.45%	42	Hawaii	163	0.04%
3	Texas		31,277	7.34%	43	New Hampshire	76	0.02%
41	Utah		243	0.06%	44	Wyoming	59	0.01%
50	Vermont		0	0.00%	45	Idaho	49	0.01%
12	Virginia		14,886	3.49%	46	South Dakota	47	0.01%
30	Washington		2,271	0.53%	47	Maine	37	0.01%
40	West Virginia		269	0.06%	48	Montana	27	0.01%
24	Wisconsin		4,111	0.96%	49	North Dakota	12	0.00%
44	Wyoming		59	0.01%	50	Vermont	0	0.00%
						District of Columbia	10,683	2.51%

Source: U.S. Department of Justice, Bureau of Justice Statistics
"Correctional Populations in the United States, 1993" (October 1995, NCJ 156241)
*As of December 31, 1993. National total does not include 30,169 black federal prisoners.

Black State Prisoner Incarceration Rate in 1993

National Rate = 1,287 Black State Prisoners per 100,000 Black Population*

ALPHA ORDER

RANK	STATE	RATE
37	Alabama	1,125
25	Alaska	1,292
1	Arizona	2,510
26	Arkansas	1,273
13	California	1,557
14	Colorado	1,501
3	Connecticut	2,146
4	Delaware	2,121
15	Florida	1,495
40	Georgia	964
48	Hawaii	453
39	Idaho	980
33	Illinois	1,222
30	Indiana	1,241
5	Iowa	2,105
20	Kansas	1,389
32	Kentucky	1,225
29	Louisiana	1,255
41	Maine	925
36	Maryland	1,136
43	Massachusetts	889
12	Michigan	1,561
23	Minnesota	1,350
45	Mississippi	771
24	Missouri	1,328
42	Montana	900
21	Nebraska	1,366
7	Nevada	1,823
27	New Hampshire	1,267
22	New Jersey	1,357
31	New Mexico	1,234
38	New York	1,086
44	North Carolina	877
49	North Dakota	300
8	Ohio	1,774
2	Oklahoma	2,370
10	Oregon	1,615
28	Pennsylvania	1,259
6	Rhode Island	1,942
35	South Carolina	1,140
11	South Dakota	1,567
46	Tennessee	732
19	Texas	1,390
9	Utah	1,736
50	Vermont	0
34	Virginia	1,159
18	Washington	1,393
47	West Virginia	489
17	Wisconsin	1,432
16	Wyoming	1,475

RANK ORDER

RANK	STATE	RATE
1	Arizona	2,510
2	Oklahoma	2,370
3	Connecticut	2,146
4	Delaware	2,121
5	Iowa	2,105
6	Rhode Island	1,942
7	Nevada	1,823
8	Ohio	1,774
9	Utah	1,736
10	Oregon	1,615
11	South Dakota	1,567
12	Michigan	1,561
13	California	1,557
14	Colorado	1,501
15	Florida	1,495
16	Wyoming	1,475
17	Wisconsin	1,432
18	Washington	1,393
19	Texas	1,390
20	Kansas	1,389
21	Nebraska	1,366
22	New Jersey	1,357
23	Minnesota	1,350
24	Missouri	1,328
25	Alaska	1,292
26	Arkansas	1,273
27	New Hampshire	1,267
28	Pennsylvania	1,259
29	Louisiana	1,255
30	Indiana	1,241
31	New Mexico	1,234
32	Kentucky	1,225
33	Illinois	1,222
34	Virginia	1,159
35	South Carolina	1,140
36	Maryland	1,136
37	Alabama	1,125
38	New York	1,086
39	Idaho	980
40	Georgia	964
41	Maine	925
42	Montana	900
43	Massachusetts	889
44	North Carolina	877
45	Mississippi	771
46	Tennessee	732
47	West Virginia	489
48	Hawaii	453
49	North Dakota	300
50	Vermont	0

	District of Columbia	2,895

Source: Morgan Quitno Press using data from U.S. Department of Justice, Bureau of Justice Statistics
"Correctional Populations in the United States, 1993" (October 1995, NCJ 156241)
*As of December 31, 1993. Black population estimates are for 1995. National rate does not include 30,169 black federal prisoners.

Black Prisoners in State Correctional Institutions
As a Percent of All Prisoners in 1993
National Percent = 49.73% Black*

ALPHA ORDER

RANK	STATE	PERCENT
8	Alabama	65.39
39	Alaska	12.43
36	Arizona	17.33
13	Arkansas	57.10
29	California	32.60
34	Colorado	24.59
21	Connecticut	46.09
6	Delaware	66.51
12	Florida	58.43
5	Georgia	67.87
43	Hawaii	5.21
48	Idaho	1.88
9	Illinois	65.33
23	Indiana	40.82
33	Iowa	24.93
24	Kansas	38.82
27	Kentucky	33.55
2	Louisiana	76.56
46	Maine	2.52
1	Maryland	76.68
31	Massachusetts	30.12
15	Michigan	56.21
28	Minnesota	33.43
3	Mississippi	74.10
19	Missouri	47.77
49	Montana	1.75
26	Nebraska	34.71
32	Nevada	29.70
44	New Hampshire	4.28
7	New Jersey	65.76
40	New Mexico	11.29
17	New York	54.63
11	North Carolina	63.85
47	North Dakota	2.41
16	Ohio	54.69
25	Oklahoma	35.25
38	Oregon	13.30
14	Pennsylvania	56.45
30	Rhode Island	31.40
4	South Carolina	68.92
45	South Dakota	3.03
18	Tennessee	48.21
22	Texas	44.60
41	Utah	8.41
50	Vermont	0.00
10	Virginia	65.15
35	Washington	21.80
37	West Virginia	14.90
20	Wisconsin	46.82
42	Wyoming	5.23

RANK ORDER

RANK	STATE	PERCENT
1	Maryland	76.68
2	Louisiana	76.56
3	Mississippi	74.10
4	South Carolina	68.92
5	Georgia	67.87
6	Delaware	66.51
7	New Jersey	65.76
8	Alabama	65.39
9	Illinois	65.33
10	Virginia	65.15
11	North Carolina	63.85
12	Florida	58.43
13	Arkansas	57.10
14	Pennsylvania	56.45
15	Michigan	56.21
16	Ohio	54.69
17	New York	54.63
18	Tennessee	48.21
19	Missouri	47.77
20	Wisconsin	46.82
21	Connecticut	46.09
22	Texas	44.60
23	Indiana	40.82
24	Kansas	38.82
25	Oklahoma	35.25
26	Nebraska	34.71
27	Kentucky	33.55
28	Minnesota	33.43
29	California	32.60
30	Rhode Island	31.40
31	Massachusetts	30.12
32	Nevada	29.70
33	Iowa	24.93
34	Colorado	24.59
35	Washington	21.80
36	Arizona	17.33
37	West Virginia	14.90
38	Oregon	13.30
39	Alaska	12.43
40	New Mexico	11.29
41	Utah	8.41
42	Wyoming	5.23
43	Hawaii	5.21
44	New Hampshire	4.28
45	South Dakota	3.03
46	Maine	2.52
47	North Dakota	2.41
48	Idaho	1.88
49	Montana	1.75
50	Vermont	0.00

District of Columbia	98.51

Source: Morgan Quitno Press using data from U.S. Department of Justice, Bureau of Justice Statistics
    "Correctional Populations in the United States, 1993" (October 1995, NCJ 156241)
*As of December 31, 1993. National percent does not include black federal prisoners. Federal prison population
is 33.68% black. Combined state and federal percentage is 48.21% black.

Average Annual Operating Expenditures per State Prison Inmate in 1990

National Average = $15,586 per Inmate*

ALPHA ORDER				RANK ORDER		
RANK	STATE	AVG EXPENDITURE		RANK	STATE	AVG EXPENDITURE
48	Alabama	$8,718		1	Alaska	$28,214
1	Alaska	28,214		2	Minnesota	26,661
41	Arizona	10,311		3	Maine	22,656
50	Arkansas	7,557		4	California	21,816
4	California	21,816		5	New Jersey	20,703
29	Colorado	14,180		6	Tennessee	20,048
15	Connecticut	17,002		7	Washington	19,742
37	Delaware	11,208		8	Hawaii	19,542
30	Florida	13,902		9	Wisconsin	18,965
33	Georgia	12,930		10	New York	18,670
8	Hawaii	19,542		11	North Carolina	18,486
45	Idaho	9,450		12	Iowa	18,304
20	Illinois	15,980		13	Maryland	17,214
25	Indiana	14,822		14	New Hampshire	17,208
12	Iowa	18,304		15	Connecticut	17,002
26	Kansas	14,670		16	New Mexico	16,711
38	Kentucky	11,118		17	Michigan	16,649
46	Louisiana	9,337		18	Rhode Island	16,497
3	Maine	22,656		19	Virginia	16,145
13	Maryland	17,214		20	Illinois	15,980
24	Massachusetts	15,152		21	Vermont	15,905
17	Michigan	16,649		22	Pennsylvania	15,438
2	Minnesota	26,661		23	Utah	15,251
47	Mississippi	9,133		24	Massachusetts	15,152
44	Missouri	9,766		25	Indiana	14,822
27	Montana	14,590		26	Kansas	14,670
31	Nebraska	13,012		27	Montana	14,590
49	Nevada	8,630		28	North Dakota	14,581
14	New Hampshire	17,208		29	Colorado	14,180
5	New Jersey	20,703		30	Florida	13,902
16	New Mexico	16,711		31	Nebraska	13,012
10	New York	18,670		32	Texas	12,988
11	North Carolina	18,486		33	Georgia	12,930
28	North Dakota	14,581		34	Wyoming	12,151
39	Ohio	11,028		35	West Virginia	11,699
43	Oklahoma	9,919		36	Oregon	11,516
36	Oregon	11,516		37	Delaware	11,208
22	Pennsylvania	15,438		38	Kentucky	11,118
18	Rhode Island	16,497		39	Ohio	11,028
42	South Carolina	10,268		40	South Dakota	10,859
40	South Dakota	10,859		41	Arizona	10,311
6	Tennessee	20,048		42	South Carolina	10,268
32	Texas	12,988		43	Oklahoma	9,919
23	Utah	15,251		44	Missouri	9,766
21	Vermont	15,905		45	Idaho	9,450
19	Virginia	16,145		46	Louisiana	9,337
7	Washington	19,742		47	Mississippi	9,133
35	West Virginia	11,699		48	Alabama	8,718
9	Wisconsin	18,965		49	Nevada	8,630
34	Wyoming	12,151		50	Arkansas	7,557
					District of Columbia	13,894

Source: U.S. Department of Justice, Bureau of Justice Statistics
  "Census of State and Federal Correctional Facilities, 1990" (1992, NCJ-137003)
For fiscal year 1990. Determined by dividing the amount spent on salaries, wages, supplies, utilities,
transportation, contractual services and other current operating items by the average daily inmate population.
Federal average is $14,456, combined federal/state average is $15,496. This census is done every five years.

Percent of Sentence Served by Violent Offenders in 1994

National Average = 46% of Sentence Served*

<u>ALPHA ORDER</u>

RANK	STATE	PERCENT
NA	Alabama**	NA
6	Alaska	65
7	Arizona	62
34	Arkansas	36
1	California	85
14	Colorado	52
NA	Connecticut**	NA
8	Delaware	59
18	Florida	47
17	Georgia	48
24	Hawaii	42
4	Idaho	67
23	Illinois	43
NA	Indiana**	NA
37	Iowa	32
NA	Kansas**	NA
29	Kentucky	38
9	Louisiana	57
NA	Maine**	NA
11	Maryland	54
2	Massachusetts	77
NA	Michigan**	NA
3	Minnesota	73
27	Mississippi	40
15	Missouri	51
31	Montana	37
21	Nebraska	45
NA	Nevada**	NA
26	New Hampshire	41
31	New Jersey	37
NA	New Mexico**	NA
11	New York	54
38	North Carolina	30
20	North Dakota	46
39	Ohio	17
34	Oklahoma	36
24	Oregon	42
16	Pennsylvania	49
NA	Rhode Island**	NA
31	South Carolina	37
NA	South Dakota**	NA
36	Tennessee	35
28	Texas	39
21	Utah	45
10	Vermont	56
NA	Virginia**	NA
4	Washington	67
11	West Virginia	54
29	Wisconsin	38
18	Wyoming	47

<u>RANK ORDER</u>

RANK	STATE	PERCENT
1	California	85
2	Massachusetts	77
3	Minnesota	73
4	Idaho	67
4	Washington	67
6	Alaska	65
7	Arizona	62
8	Delaware	59
9	Louisiana	57
10	Vermont	56
11	Maryland	54
11	New York	54
11	West Virginia	54
14	Colorado	52
15	Missouri	51
16	Pennsylvania	49
17	Georgia	48
18	Florida	47
18	Wyoming	47
20	North Dakota	46
21	Nebraska	45
21	Utah	45
23	Illinois	43
24	Hawaii	42
24	Oregon	42
26	New Hampshire	41
27	Mississippi	40
28	Texas	39
29	Kentucky	38
29	Wisconsin	38
31	Montana	37
31	New Jersey	37
31	South Carolina	37
34	Arkansas	36
34	Oklahoma	36
36	Tennessee	35
37	Iowa	32
38	North Carolina	30
39	Ohio	17
NA	Alabama**	NA
NA	Connecticut**	NA
NA	Indiana**	NA
NA	Kansas**	NA
NA	Maine**	NA
NA	Michigan**	NA
NA	Nevada**	NA
NA	New Mexico**	NA
NA	Rhode Island**	NA
NA	South Dakota**	NA
NA	Virginia**	NA
	District of Columbia	67

Source: U.S. Department of Justice, Bureau of Justice Statistics
"Violent Offenders in State Prison: Sentences and Timed Served" (Selected Findings, July 1995, NCJ-154632)
*National figure is for reporting states. "Time served" includes time served in jail and prison before release.
**Not available.

Prisoners Under Sentence of Death in 1994

National Total = 2,884 State Prisoners*

ALPHA ORDER

RANK	STATE	PRISONERS	% of USA
7	Alabama	135	4.68%
NA	Alaska**	NA	NA
9	Arizona	121	4.20%
20	Arkansas	36	1.25%
2	California	381	13.21%
32	Colorado	3	0.10%
31	Connecticut	4	0.14%
24	Delaware	14	0.49%
3	Florida	342	11.86%
12	Georgia	96	3.33%
NA	Hawaii**	NA	NA
22	Idaho	19	0.66%
5	Illinois	155	5.37%
18	Indiana	47	1.63%
NA	Iowa**	NA	NA
NA	Kansas**	NA	NA
21	Kentucky	29	1.01%
18	Louisiana	47	1.63%
NA	Maine**	NA	NA
25	Maryland	13	0.45%
NA	Massachusetts**	NA	NA
NA	Michigan**	NA	NA
NA	Minnesota**	NA	NA
17	Mississippi	50	1.73%
13	Missouri	88	3.05%
30	Montana	8	0.28%
26	Nebraska	10	0.35%
14	Nevada	66	2.29%
35	New Hampshire	0	0.00%
29	New Jersey	9	0.31%
33	New Mexico	2	0.07%
NA	New York**	NA	NA
10	North Carolina	111	3.85%
NA	North Dakota**	NA	NA
6	Ohio	140	4.85%
8	Oklahoma	129	4.47%
23	Oregon	17	0.59%
4	Pennsylvania	182	6.31%
NA	Rhode Island**	NA	NA
15	South Carolina	59	2.05%
33	South Dakota	2	0.07%
11	Tennessee	100	3.47%
1	Texas	394	13.66%
26	Utah	10	0.35%
NA	Vermont**	NA	NA
16	Virginia	55	1.91%
26	Washington	10	0.35%
NA	West Virginia**	NA	NA
NA	Wisconsin**	NA	NA
35	Wyoming	0	0.00%

RANK ORDER

RANK	STATE	PRISONERS	% of USA
1	Texas	394	13.66%
2	California	381	13.21%
3	Florida	342	11.86%
4	Pennsylvania	182	6.31%
5	Illinois	155	5.37%
6	Ohio	140	4.85%
7	Alabama	135	4.68%
8	Oklahoma	129	4.47%
9	Arizona	121	4.20%
10	North Carolina	111	3.85%
11	Tennessee	100	3.47%
12	Georgia	96	3.33%
13	Missouri	88	3.05%
14	Nevada	66	2.29%
15	South Carolina	59	2.05%
16	Virginia	55	1.91%
17	Mississippi	50	1.73%
18	Indiana	47	1.63%
18	Louisiana	47	1.63%
20	Arkansas	36	1.25%
21	Kentucky	29	1.01%
22	Idaho	19	0.66%
23	Oregon	17	0.59%
24	Delaware	14	0.49%
25	Maryland	13	0.45%
26	Nebraska	10	0.35%
26	Utah	10	0.35%
26	Washington	10	0.35%
29	New Jersey	9	0.31%
30	Montana	8	0.28%
31	Connecticut	4	0.14%
32	Colorado	3	0.10%
33	New Mexico	2	0.07%
33	South Dakota	2	0.07%
35	New Hampshire	0	0.00%
35	Wyoming	0	0.00%
NA	Alaska**	NA	NA
NA	Hawaii**	NA	NA
NA	Iowa**	NA	NA
NA	Kansas**	NA	NA
NA	Maine**	NA	NA
NA	Massachusetts**	NA	NA
NA	Michigan**	NA	NA
NA	Minnesota**	NA	NA
NA	New York**	NA	NA
NA	North Dakota**	NA	NA
NA	Rhode Island**	NA	NA
NA	Vermont**	NA	NA
NA	West Virginia**	NA	NA
NA	Wisconsin**	NA	NA
	District of Columbia**	NA	NA

Source: U.S. Department of Justice, Bureau of Justice Statistics
   "Capital Punishment 1994" (Bulletin, February 1996, NCJ-158023)
*As of December 31, 1994. Does not includes six federal prisoners under sentence of death. There were 31 executions in 1994.
**No death penalty as of 12/31/94.

Male Prisoners Under Sentence of Death in 1994

National Total = 2,843 Male State Prisoners*

ALPHA ORDER

RANK	STATE	PRISONERS	% of USA
7	Alabama	130	4.57%
NA	Alaska**	NA	NA
9	Arizona	120	4.22%
20	Arkansas	36	1.27%
2	California	375	13.19%
32	Colorado	3	0.11%
31	Connecticut	4	0.14%
24	Delaware	14	0.49%
3	Florida	338	11.89%
12	Georgia	96	3.38%
NA	Hawaii**	NA	NA
22	Idaho	18	0.63%
5	Illinois	150	5.28%
18	Indiana	47	1.65%
NA	Iowa**	NA	NA
NA	Kansas**	NA	NA
21	Kentucky	29	1.02%
18	Louisiana	47	1.65%
NA	Maine**	NA	NA
25	Maryland	13	0.46%
NA	Massachusetts**	NA	NA
NA	Michigan**	NA	NA
NA	Minnesota**	NA	NA
17	Mississippi	49	1.72%
13	Missouri	86	3.02%
30	Montana	8	0.28%
26	Nebraska	10	0.35%
14	Nevada	65	2.29%
35	New Hampshire	0	0.00%
29	New Jersey	9	0.32%
33	New Mexico	2	0.07%
NA	New York**	NA	NA
10	North Carolina	109	3.83%
NA	North Dakota**	NA	NA
6	Ohio	140	4.92%
8	Oklahoma	125	4.40%
23	Oregon	17	0.60%
4	Pennsylvania	178	6.26%
NA	Rhode Island**	NA	NA
15	South Carolina	59	2.08%
33	South Dakota	2	0.07%
11	Tennessee	99	3.48%
1	Texas	390	13.72%
26	Utah	10	0.35%
NA	Vermont**	NA	NA
16	Virginia	55	1.93%
26	Washington	10	0.35%
NA	West Virginia**	NA	NA
NA	Wisconsin**	NA	NA
35	Wyoming	0	0.00%

RANK ORDER

RANK	STATE	PRISONERS	% of USA
1	Texas	390	13.72%
2	California	375	13.19%
3	Florida	338	11.89%
4	Pennsylvania	178	6.26%
5	Illinois	150	5.28%
6	Ohio	140	4.92%
7	Alabama	130	4.57%
8	Oklahoma	125	4.40%
9	Arizona	120	4.22%
10	North Carolina	109	3.83%
11	Tennessee	99	3.48%
12	Georgia	96	3.38%
13	Missouri	86	3.02%
14	Nevada	65	2.29%
15	South Carolina	59	2.08%
16	Virginia	55	1.93%
17	Mississippi	49	1.72%
18	Indiana	47	1.65%
18	Louisiana	47	1.65%
20	Arkansas	36	1.27%
21	Kentucky	29	1.02%
22	Idaho	18	0.63%
23	Oregon	17	0.60%
24	Delaware	14	0.49%
25	Maryland	13	0.46%
26	Nebraska	10	0.35%
26	Utah	10	0.35%
26	Washington	10	0.35%
29	New Jersey	9	0.32%
30	Montana	8	0.28%
31	Connecticut	4	0.14%
32	Colorado	3	0.11%
33	New Mexico	2	0.07%
33	South Dakota	2	0.07%
35	New Hampshire	0	0.00%
35	Wyoming	0	0.00%
NA	Alaska**	NA	NA
NA	Hawaii**	NA	NA
NA	Iowa**	NA	NA
NA	Kansas**	NA	NA
NA	Maine**	NA	NA
NA	Massachusetts**	NA	NA
NA	Michigan**	NA	NA
NA	Minnesota**	NA	NA
NA	New York**	NA	NA
NA	North Dakota**	NA	NA
NA	Rhode Island**	NA	NA
NA	Vermont**	NA	NA
NA	West Virginia**	NA	NA
NA	Wisconsin**	NA	NA
	District of Columbia**	NA	NA

Source: Morgan Quitno Press using data from U.S. Department of Justice, Bureau of Justice Statistics
   "Capital Punishment 1994" (Bulletin, February 1996, NCJ-158023)
*As of December 31, 1994. Does not includes six male federal prisoners under sentence of death. There were 31 executions in 1994. All were male.
**No death penalty as of 12/31/94.

Female Prisoners Under Sentence of Death in 1994

National Total = 41 Female State Prisoners*

RANK	STATE	PRISONERS	% of USA
2	Alabama	5	12.20%
NA	Alaska**	NA	NA
10	Arizona	1	2.44%
15	Arkansas	0	0.00%
1	California	6	14.63%
15	Colorado	0	0.00%
15	Connecticut	0	0.00%
15	Delaware	0	0.00%
4	Florida	4	9.76%
15	Georgia	0	0.00%
NA	Hawaii**	NA	NA
10	Idaho	1	2.44%
2	Illinois	5	12.20%
15	Indiana	0	0.00%
NA	Iowa**	NA	NA
NA	Kansas**	NA	NA
15	Kentucky	0	0.00%
15	Louisiana	0	0.00%
NA	Maine**	NA	NA
15	Maryland	0	0.00%
NA	Massachusetts**	NA	NA
NA	Michigan**	NA	NA
NA	Minnesota**	NA	NA
10	Mississippi	1	2.44%
8	Missouri	2	4.88%
15	Montana	0	0.00%
15	Nebraska	0	0.00%
10	Nevada	1	2.44%
15	New Hampshire	0	0.00%
15	New Jersey	0	0.00%
15	New Mexico	0	0.00%
NA	New York**	NA	NA
8	North Carolina	2	4.88%
NA	North Dakota**	NA	NA
15	Ohio	0	0.00%
4	Oklahoma	4	9.76%
15	Oregon	0	0.00%
4	Pennsylvania	4	9.76%
NA	Rhode Island**	NA	NA
15	South Carolina	0	0.00%
15	South Dakota	0	0.00%
10	Tennessee	1	2.44%
4	Texas	4	9.76%
15	Utah	0	0.00%
NA	Vermont**	NA	NA
15	Virginia	0	0.00%
15	Washington	0	0.00%
NA	West Virginia**	NA	NA
NA	Wisconsin**	NA	NA
15	Wyoming	0	0.00%

RANK	STATE	PRISONERS	% of USA
1	California	6	14.63%
2	Alabama	5	12.20%
2	Illinois	5	12.20%
4	Florida	4	9.76%
4	Oklahoma	4	9.76%
4	Pennsylvania	4	9.76%
4	Texas	4	9.76%
8	Missouri	2	4.88%
8	North Carolina	2	4.88%
10	Arizona	1	2.44%
10	Idaho	1	2.44%
10	Mississippi	1	2.44%
10	Nevada	1	2.44%
10	Tennessee	1	2.44%
15	Arkansas	0	0.00%
15	Colorado	0	0.00%
15	Connecticut	0	0.00%
15	Delaware	0	0.00%
15	Georgia	0	0.00%
15	Indiana	0	0.00%
15	Kentucky	0	0.00%
15	Louisiana	0	0.00%
15	Maryland	0	0.00%
15	Montana	0	0.00%
15	Nebraska	0	0.00%
15	New Hampshire	0	0.00%
15	New Jersey	0	0.00%
15	New Mexico	0	0.00%
15	Ohio	0	0.00%
15	Oregon	0	0.00%
15	South Carolina	0	0.00%
15	South Dakota	0	0.00%
15	Utah	0	0.00%
15	Virginia	0	0.00%
15	Washington	0	0.00%
15	Wyoming	0	0.00%
NA	Alaska**	NA	NA
NA	Hawaii**	NA	NA
NA	Iowa**	NA	NA
NA	Kansas**	NA	NA
NA	Maine**	NA	NA
NA	Massachusetts**	NA	NA
NA	Michigan**	NA	NA
NA	Minnesota**	NA	NA
NA	New York**	NA	NA
NA	North Dakota**	NA	NA
NA	Rhode Island**	NA	NA
NA	Vermont**	NA	NA
NA	West Virginia**	NA	NA
NA	Wisconsin**	NA	NA
	District of Columbia**	NA	NA

Source: U.S. Department of Justice, Bureau of Justice Statistics
   "Capital Punishment 1994" (Bulletin, February 1996, NCJ-158023)
*As of December 31, 1994. There were no federal female prisoners under sentence of death. There were 31 executions in 1994, none of whom were female.
**No death penalty as of 12/31/94.

Percent of Prisoners Under Sentence of Death Who Are Female: 1994

National Percent = 1.42% of State Death Sentence Prisoners*

Source: Morgan Quitno Press using data from U.S. Department of Justice, Bureau of Justice Statistics
    "Capital Punishment 1994" (Bulletin, February 1996, NCJ-158023)
*As of December 31, 1994. There were no federal female prisoners under sentence of death. There were 31
executions in 1994, none of whom were female.
**No death penalty as of 12/31/94.

White Prisoners Under Sentence of Death in 1994

National Total = 1,642 White State Prisoners*

ALPHA ORDER

RANK	STATE	PRISONERS	% of USA
6	Alabama	74	4.51%
NA	Alaska**	NA	NA
4	Arizona	100	6.09%
19	Arkansas	21	1.28%
2	California	226	13.76%
30	Colorado	3	0.18%
31	Connecticut	2	0.12%
25	Delaware	7	0.43%
3	Florida	214	13.03%
12	Georgia	53	3.23%
NA	Hawaii**	NA	NA
21	Idaho	19	1.16%
10	Illinois	57	3.47%
15	Indiana	31	1.89%
NA	Iowa**	NA	NA
NA	Kansas**	NA	NA
18	Kentucky	23	1.40%
22	Louisiana	16	0.97%
NA	Maine**	NA	NA
31	Maryland	2	0.12%
NA	Massachusetts**	NA	NA
NA	Michigan**	NA	NA
NA	Minnesota**	NA	NA
20	Mississippi	20	1.22%
13	Missouri	51	3.11%
28	Montana	6	0.37%
25	Nebraska	7	0.43%
14	Nevada	45	2.74%
35	New Hampshire	0	0.00%
29	New Jersey	4	0.24%
31	New Mexico	2	0.12%
NA	New York**	NA	NA
11	North Carolina	55	3.35%
NA	North Dakota**	NA	NA
7	Ohio	69	4.20%
5	Oklahoma	79	4.81%
23	Oregon	15	0.91%
8	Pennsylvania	66	4.02%
NA	Rhode Island**	NA	NA
15	South Carolina	31	1.89%
31	South Dakota	2	0.12%
8	Tennessee	66	4.02%
1	Texas	235	14.31%
24	Utah	8	0.49%
NA	Vermont**	NA	NA
17	Virginia	26	1.58%
25	Washington	7	0.43%
NA	West Virginia**	NA	NA
35	Wisconsin	0	0.00%
35	Wyoming	0	0.00%

RANK ORDER

RANK	STATE	PRISONERS	% of USA
1	Texas	235	14.31%
2	California	226	13.76%
3	Florida	214	13.03%
4	Arizona	100	6.09%
5	Oklahoma	79	4.81%
6	Alabama	74	4.51%
7	Ohio	69	4.20%
8	Pennsylvania	66	4.02%
8	Tennessee	66	4.02%
10	Illinois	57	3.47%
11	North Carolina	55	3.35%
12	Georgia	53	3.23%
13	Missouri	51	3.11%
14	Nevada	45	2.74%
15	Indiana	31	1.89%
15	South Carolina	31	1.89%
17	Virginia	26	1.58%
18	Kentucky	23	1.40%
19	Arkansas	21	1.28%
20	Mississippi	20	1.22%
21	Idaho	19	1.16%
22	Louisiana	16	0.97%
23	Oregon	15	0.91%
24	Utah	8	0.49%
25	Delaware	7	0.43%
25	Nebraska	7	0.43%
25	Washington	7	0.43%
28	Montana	6	0.37%
29	New Jersey	4	0.24%
30	Colorado	3	0.18%
31	Connecticut	2	0.12%
31	Maryland	2	0.12%
31	New Mexico	2	0.12%
31	South Dakota	2	0.12%
35	New Hampshire	0	0.00%
35	Wisconsin	0	0.00%
35	Wyoming	0	0.00%
NA	Alaska**	NA	NA
NA	Hawaii**	NA	NA
NA	Iowa**	NA	NA
NA	Kansas**	NA	NA
NA	Maine**	NA	NA
NA	Massachusetts**	NA	NA
NA	Michigan**	NA	NA
NA	Minnesota**	NA	NA
NA	New York**	NA	NA
NA	North Dakota**	NA	NA
NA	Rhode Island**	NA	NA
NA	Vermont**	NA	NA
NA	West Virginia**	NA	NA
	District of Columbia**	NA	NA

Source: U.S. Department of Justice, Bureau of Justice Statistics
    "Capital Punishment 1994" (Bulletin, February 1996, NCJ-158023)
*As of December 31, 1994. Does not includes three white federal prisoners under sentence of death. There were
31 executions in 1994, 20 of whom were white prisoners.
**No death penalty as of 12/31/94.

Percent of Prisoners Under Sentence of Death Who Are White: 1994

National Percent = 56.93% of Death Sentence Prisoners*

<table>
<tr><td colspan="3"><u>ALPHA ORDER</u></td><td colspan="3"><u>RANK ORDER</u></td></tr>
<tr><td>RANK</td><td>STATE</td><td>PERCENT</td><td>RANK</td><td>STATE</td><td>PERCENT</td></tr>
<tr><td>22</td><td>Alabama</td><td>54.81</td><td>1</td><td>Colorado</td><td>100.00</td></tr>
<tr><td>NA</td><td>Alaska**</td><td>NA</td><td>1</td><td>Idaho</td><td>100.00</td></tr>
<tr><td>6</td><td>Arizona</td><td>82.64</td><td>1</td><td>New Mexico</td><td>100.00</td></tr>
<tr><td>19</td><td>Arkansas</td><td>58.33</td><td>1</td><td>South Dakota</td><td>100.00</td></tr>
<tr><td>18</td><td>California</td><td>59.32</td><td>5</td><td>Oregon</td><td>88.24</td></tr>
<tr><td>1</td><td>Colorado</td><td>100.00</td><td>6</td><td>Arizona</td><td>82.64</td></tr>
<tr><td>24</td><td>Connecticut</td><td>50.00</td><td>7</td><td>Utah</td><td>80.00</td></tr>
<tr><td>24</td><td>Delaware</td><td>50.00</td><td>8</td><td>Kentucky</td><td>79.31</td></tr>
<tr><td>15</td><td>Florida</td><td>62.57</td><td>9</td><td>Montana</td><td>75.00</td></tr>
<tr><td>21</td><td>Georgia</td><td>55.21</td><td>10</td><td>Nebraska</td><td>70.00</td></tr>
<tr><td>NA</td><td>Hawaii**</td><td>NA</td><td>10</td><td>Washington</td><td>70.00</td></tr>
<tr><td>1</td><td>Idaho</td><td>100.00</td><td>12</td><td>Nevada</td><td>68.18</td></tr>
<tr><td>31</td><td>Illinois</td><td>36.77</td><td>13</td><td>Tennessee</td><td>66.00</td></tr>
<tr><td>14</td><td>Indiana</td><td>65.96</td><td>14</td><td>Indiana</td><td>65.96</td></tr>
<tr><td>NA</td><td>Iowa**</td><td>NA</td><td>15</td><td>Florida</td><td>62.57</td></tr>
<tr><td>NA</td><td>Kansas**</td><td>NA</td><td>16</td><td>Oklahoma</td><td>61.24</td></tr>
<tr><td>8</td><td>Kentucky</td><td>79.31</td><td>17</td><td>Texas</td><td>59.64</td></tr>
<tr><td>33</td><td>Louisiana</td><td>34.04</td><td>18</td><td>California</td><td>59.32</td></tr>
<tr><td>NA</td><td>Maine**</td><td>NA</td><td>19</td><td>Arkansas</td><td>58.33</td></tr>
<tr><td>34</td><td>Maryland</td><td>15.38</td><td>20</td><td>Missouri</td><td>57.95</td></tr>
<tr><td>NA</td><td>Massachusetts**</td><td>NA</td><td>21</td><td>Georgia</td><td>55.21</td></tr>
<tr><td>NA</td><td>Michigan**</td><td>NA</td><td>22</td><td>Alabama</td><td>54.81</td></tr>
<tr><td>NA</td><td>Minnesota**</td><td>NA</td><td>23</td><td>South Carolina</td><td>52.54</td></tr>
<tr><td>30</td><td>Mississippi</td><td>40.00</td><td>24</td><td>Connecticut</td><td>50.00</td></tr>
<tr><td>20</td><td>Missouri</td><td>57.95</td><td>24</td><td>Delaware</td><td>50.00</td></tr>
<tr><td>9</td><td>Montana</td><td>75.00</td><td>26</td><td>North Carolina</td><td>49.55</td></tr>
<tr><td>10</td><td>Nebraska</td><td>70.00</td><td>27</td><td>Ohio</td><td>49.29</td></tr>
<tr><td>12</td><td>Nevada</td><td>68.18</td><td>28</td><td>Virginia</td><td>47.27</td></tr>
<tr><td>35</td><td>New Hampshire</td><td>0.00</td><td>29</td><td>New Jersey</td><td>44.44</td></tr>
<tr><td>29</td><td>New Jersey</td><td>44.44</td><td>30</td><td>Mississippi</td><td>40.00</td></tr>
<tr><td>1</td><td>New Mexico</td><td>100.00</td><td>31</td><td>Illinois</td><td>36.77</td></tr>
<tr><td>NA</td><td>New York**</td><td>NA</td><td>32</td><td>Pennsylvania</td><td>36.26</td></tr>
<tr><td>26</td><td>North Carolina</td><td>49.55</td><td>33</td><td>Louisiana</td><td>34.04</td></tr>
<tr><td>NA</td><td>North Dakota**</td><td>NA</td><td>34</td><td>Maryland</td><td>15.38</td></tr>
<tr><td>27</td><td>Ohio</td><td>49.29</td><td>35</td><td>New Hampshire</td><td>0.00</td></tr>
<tr><td>16</td><td>Oklahoma</td><td>61.24</td><td>35</td><td>Wyoming</td><td>0.00</td></tr>
<tr><td>5</td><td>Oregon</td><td>88.24</td><td>NA</td><td>Alaska**</td><td>NA</td></tr>
<tr><td>32</td><td>Pennsylvania</td><td>36.26</td><td>NA</td><td>Hawaii**</td><td>NA</td></tr>
<tr><td>NA</td><td>Rhode Island**</td><td>NA</td><td>NA</td><td>Iowa**</td><td>NA</td></tr>
<tr><td>23</td><td>South Carolina</td><td>52.54</td><td>NA</td><td>Kansas**</td><td>NA</td></tr>
<tr><td>1</td><td>South Dakota</td><td>100.00</td><td>NA</td><td>Maine**</td><td>NA</td></tr>
<tr><td>13</td><td>Tennessee</td><td>66.00</td><td>NA</td><td>Massachusetts**</td><td>NA</td></tr>
<tr><td>17</td><td>Texas</td><td>59.64</td><td>NA</td><td>Michigan**</td><td>NA</td></tr>
<tr><td>7</td><td>Utah</td><td>80.00</td><td>NA</td><td>Minnesota**</td><td>NA</td></tr>
<tr><td>NA</td><td>Vermont**</td><td>NA</td><td>NA</td><td>New York**</td><td>NA</td></tr>
<tr><td>28</td><td>Virginia</td><td>47.27</td><td>NA</td><td>North Dakota**</td><td>NA</td></tr>
<tr><td>10</td><td>Washington</td><td>70.00</td><td>NA</td><td>Rhode Island**</td><td>NA</td></tr>
<tr><td>NA</td><td>West Virginia**</td><td>NA</td><td>NA</td><td>Vermont**</td><td>NA</td></tr>
<tr><td>NA</td><td>Wisconsin**</td><td>NA</td><td>NA</td><td>West Virginia**</td><td>NA</td></tr>
<tr><td>35</td><td>Wyoming</td><td>0.00</td><td>NA</td><td>Wisconsin**</td><td>NA</td></tr>
<tr><td></td><td></td><td></td><td></td><td>District of Columbia**</td><td>NA</td></tr>
</table>

Source: Morgan Quitno Press using data from U.S. Department of Justice, Bureau of Justice Statistics
"Capital Punishment 1994" (Bulletin, February 1996, NCJ-158023)
*As of December 31, 1994. Does not includes three white federal prisoners under sentence of death. There were
31 executions in 1994, 20 of whom were white prisoners.
**No death penalty as of 12/31/94.

Black Prisoners Under Sentence of Death in 1994

National Total = 1,194 Black State Prisoners*

ALPHA ORDER

RANK	STATE	PRISONERS	% of USA
7	Alabama	59	4.94%
NA	Alaska**	NA	NA
19	Arizona	15	1.26%
19	Arkansas	15	1.26%
2	California	147	12.31%
30	Colorado	0	0.00%
26	Connecticut	2	0.17%
22	Delaware	7	0.59%
3	Florida	128	10.72%
9	Georgia	43	3.60%
NA	Hawaii**	NA	NA
30	Idaho	0	0.00%
5	Illinois	98	8.21%
18	Indiana	16	1.34%
NA	Iowa**	NA	NA
NA	Kansas**	NA	NA
23	Kentucky	6	0.50%
13	Louisiana	31	2.60%
NA	Maine**	NA	NA
21	Maryland	11	0.92%
NA	Massachusetts**	NA	NA
NA	Michigan**	NA	NA
NA	Minnesota**	NA	NA
14	Mississippi	30	2.51%
11	Missouri	37	3.10%
30	Montana	0	0.00%
26	Nebraska	2	0.17%
17	Nevada	21	1.76%
30	New Hampshire	0	0.00%
24	New Jersey	5	0.42%
30	New Mexico	0	0.00%
NA	New York**	NA	NA
8	North Carolina	54	4.52%
NA	North Dakota**	NA	NA
6	Ohio	70	5.86%
10	Oklahoma	40	3.35%
29	Oregon	1	0.08%
4	Pennsylvania	109	9.13%
NA	Rhode Island**	NA	NA
16	South Carolina	28	2.35%
30	South Dakota	0	0.00%
12	Tennessee	32	2.68%
1	Texas	153	12.81%
26	Utah	2	0.17%
NA	Vermont**	NA	NA
15	Virginia	29	2.43%
25	Washington	3	0.25%
NA	West Virginia**	NA	NA
NA	Wisconsin**	NA	NA
30	Wyoming	0	0.00%

RANK ORDER

RANK	STATE	PRISONERS	% of USA
1	Texas	153	12.81%
2	California	147	12.31%
3	Florida	128	10.72%
4	Pennsylvania	109	9.13%
5	Illinois	98	8.21%
6	Ohio	70	5.86%
7	Alabama	59	4.94%
8	North Carolina	54	4.52%
9	Georgia	43	3.60%
10	Oklahoma	40	3.35%
11	Missouri	37	3.10%
12	Tennessee	32	2.68%
13	Louisiana	31	2.60%
14	Mississippi	30	2.51%
15	Virginia	29	2.43%
16	South Carolina	28	2.35%
17	Nevada	21	1.76%
18	Indiana	16	1.34%
19	Arizona	15	1.26%
19	Arkansas	15	1.26%
21	Maryland	11	0.92%
22	Delaware	7	0.59%
23	Kentucky	6	0.50%
24	New Jersey	5	0.42%
25	Washington	3	0.25%
26	Connecticut	2	0.17%
26	Nebraska	2	0.17%
26	Utah	2	0.17%
29	Oregon	1	0.08%
30	Colorado	0	0.00%
30	Idaho	0	0.00%
30	Montana	0	0.00%
30	New Hampshire	0	0.00%
30	New Mexico	0	0.00%
30	South Dakota	0	0.00%
30	Wyoming	0	0.00%
NA	Alaska**	NA	NA
NA	Hawaii**	NA	NA
NA	Iowa**	NA	NA
NA	Kansas**	NA	NA
NA	Maine**	NA	NA
NA	Massachusetts**	NA	NA
NA	Michigan**	NA	NA
NA	Minnesota**	NA	NA
NA	New York**	NA	NA
NA	North Dakota**	NA	NA
NA	Rhode Island**	NA	NA
NA	Vermont**	NA	NA
NA	West Virginia**	NA	NA
NA	Wisconsin**	NA	NA
	District of Columbia**	NA	NA

*Source: U.S. Department of Justice, Bureau of Justice Statistics
"Capital Punishment 1994" (Bulletin, February 1996, NCJ-158023)*
*As of December 31, 1994. Does not includes three black federal prisoners under sentence of death. There were
31 executions in 1994, 11 of whom were black prisoners.
**No death penalty as of 12/31/94.

Percent of Prisoners Under Sentence of Death Who Are Black: 1994

National Percent = 41.40% of Death Sentence Prisoners*

ALPHA ORDER

RANK	STATE	PERCENT
14	Alabama	43.70
NA	Alaska**	NA
28	Arizona	12.40
16	Arkansas	41.67
18	California	38.58
30	Colorado	0.00
8	Connecticut	50.00
8	Delaware	50.00
19	Florida	37.43
13	Georgia	44.79
NA	Hawaii**	NA
30	Idaho	0.00
3	Illinois	63.23
20	Indiana	34.04
NA	Iowa**	NA
NA	Kansas**	NA
25	Kentucky	20.69
2	Louisiana	65.96
NA	Maine**	NA
1	Maryland	84.62
NA	Massachusetts**	NA
NA	Michigan**	NA
NA	Minnesota**	NA
4	Mississippi	60.00
15	Missouri	42.05
30	Montana	0.00
26	Nebraska	20.00
22	Nevada	31.82
30	New Hampshire	0.00
6	New Jersey	55.56
30	New Mexico	0.00
NA	New York**	NA
11	North Carolina	48.65
NA	North Dakota**	NA
8	Ohio	50.00
23	Oklahoma	31.01
29	Oregon	5.88
5	Pennsylvania	59.89
NA	Rhode Island**	NA
12	South Carolina	47.46
30	South Dakota	0.00
21	Tennessee	32.00
17	Texas	38.83
26	Utah	20.00
NA	Vermont**	NA
7	Virginia	52.73
24	Washington	30.00
NA	West Virginia**	NA
NA	Wisconsin**	NA
30	Wyoming	0.00

RANK ORDER

RANK	STATE	PERCENT
1	Maryland	84.62
2	Louisiana	65.96
3	Illinois	63.23
4	Mississippi	60.00
5	Pennsylvania	59.89
6	New Jersey	55.56
7	Virginia	52.73
8	Connecticut	50.00
8	Delaware	50.00
8	Ohio	50.00
11	North Carolina	48.65
12	South Carolina	47.46
13	Georgia	44.79
14	Alabama	43.70
15	Missouri	42.05
16	Arkansas	41.67
17	Texas	38.83
18	California	38.58
19	Florida	37.43
20	Indiana	34.04
21	Tennessee	32.00
22	Nevada	31.82
23	Oklahoma	31.01
24	Washington	30.00
25	Kentucky	20.69
26	Nebraska	20.00
26	Utah	20.00
28	Arizona	12.40
29	Oregon	5.88
30	Colorado	0.00
30	Idaho	0.00
30	Montana	0.00
30	New Hampshire	0.00
30	New Mexico	0.00
30	South Dakota	0.00
30	Wyoming	0.00
NA	Alaska**	NA
NA	Hawaii**	NA
NA	Iowa**	NA
NA	Kansas**	NA
NA	Maine**	NA
NA	Massachusetts**	NA
NA	Michigan**	NA
NA	Minnesota**	NA
NA	New York**	NA
NA	North Dakota**	NA
NA	Rhode Island**	NA
NA	Vermont**	NA
NA	West Virginia**	NA
NA	Wisconsin**	NA
	District of Columbia**	NA

Source: Morgan Quitno Press using data from U.S. Department of Justice, Bureau of Justice Statistics
    "Capital Punishment 1994" (Bulletin, February 1996, NCJ-158023)
*As of December 31, 1994. Does not includes three black federal prisoners under sentence of death. There were
31 executions in 1994, 11 of whom were black prisoners.
**No death penalty as of 12/31/94.

Prisoners Executed: 1930 to 1994

National Total = 4,116 Prisoners*

ALPHA ORDER					RANK ORDER			

RANK	STATE	EXECUTIONS	% of USA		RANK	STATE	EXECUTIONS	% of USA
12	Alabama	145	3.52%		1	Georgia	384	9.33%
43	Alaska	0	0.00%		2	Texas	382	9.28%
25	Arizona	41	1.00%		3	New York	329	7.99%
13	Arkansas	127	3.09%		4	California	294	7.14%
4	California	294	7.14%		5	North Carolina	269	6.54%
23	Colorado	47	1.14%		6	Florida	203	4.93%
29	Connecticut	21	0.51%		7	Ohio	172	4.18%
33	Delaware	16	0.39%		8	South Carolina	166	4.03%
6	Florida	203	4.93%		9	Mississippi	158	3.84%
1	Georgia	384	9.33%		10	Louisiana	154	3.74%
43	Hawaii	0	0.00%		11	Pennsylvania	152	3.69%
39	Idaho	4	0.10%		12	Alabama	145	3.52%
17	Illinois	92	2.24%		13	Arkansas	127	3.09%
24	Indiana	44	1.07%		14	Virginia	116	2.82%
31	Iowa	18	0.44%		15	Kentucky	103	2.50%
34	Kansas	15	0.36%		16	Tennessee	93	2.26%
15	Kentucky	103	2.50%		17	Illinois	92	2.24%
10	Louisiana	154	3.74%		18	New Jersey	74	1.80%
43	Maine	0	0.00%		19	Missouri	73	1.77%
20	Maryland	69	1.68%		20	Maryland	69	1.68%
28	Massachusetts	27	0.66%		21	Oklahoma	63	1.53%
43	Michigan	0	0.00%		22	Washington	49	1.19%
43	Minnesota	0	0.00%		23	Colorado	47	1.14%
9	Mississippi	158	3.84%		24	Indiana	44	1.07%
19	Missouri	73	1.77%		25	Arizona	41	1.00%
37	Montana	6	0.15%		26	West Virginia	40	0.97%
38	Nebraska	5	0.12%		27	Nevada	34	0.83%
27	Nevada	34	0.83%		28	Massachusetts	27	0.66%
41	New Hampshire	1	0.02%		29	Connecticut	21	0.51%
18	New Jersey	74	1.80%		30	Oregon	19	0.46%
35	New Mexico	8	0.19%		31	Iowa	18	0.44%
3	New York	329	7.99%		32	Utah	17	0.41%
5	North Carolina	269	6.54%		33	Delaware	16	0.39%
43	North Dakota	0	0.00%		34	Kansas	15	0.36%
7	Ohio	172	4.18%		35	New Mexico	8	0.19%
21	Oklahoma	63	1.53%		35	Wyoming	8	0.19%
30	Oregon	19	0.46%		37	Montana	6	0.15%
11	Pennsylvania	152	3.69%		38	Nebraska	5	0.12%
43	Rhode Island	0	0.00%		39	Idaho	4	0.10%
8	South Carolina	166	4.03%		39	Vermont	4	0.10%
41	South Dakota	1	0.02%		41	New Hampshire	1	0.02%
16	Tennessee	93	2.26%		41	South Dakota	1	0.02%
2	Texas	382	9.28%		43	Alaska	0	0.00%
32	Utah	17	0.41%		43	Hawaii	0	0.00%
39	Vermont	4	0.10%		43	Maine	0	0.00%
14	Virginia	116	2.82%		43	Michigan	0	0.00%
22	Washington	49	1.19%		43	Minnesota	0	0.00%
26	West Virginia	40	0.97%		43	North Dakota	0	0.00%
43	Wisconsin	0	0.00%		43	Rhode Island	0	0.00%
35	Wyoming	8	0.19%		43	Wisconsin	0	0.00%
					District of Columbia	40	0.97%

Source: U.S. Department of Justice, Bureau of Justice Statistics
   "Capital Punishment 1994" (Bulletin, February 1996, NCJ-158023)
*Includes 33 executions by the federal government. Does not include 160 executions carried out under military authority. There were no executions from 1968 to 1976. Of the total, 3,560 were executed for murder, 455 for rape and 70 for other offenses (armed robbery (25), kidnapping (20), burglary (11), sabotage (6), aggravated assault (6) and espionage (2)).

Prisoners Executed: 1977 to 1994

National Total = 257 Prisoners*

ALPHA ORDER

RANK	STATE	EXECUTIONS	% of USA
7	Alabama	10	3.89%
25	Alaska	0	0.00%
15	Arizona	3	1.17%
8	Arkansas	9	3.50%
18	California	2	0.78%
25	Colorado	0	0.00%
25	Connecticut	0	0.00%
11	Delaware	4	1.56%
2	Florida	33	12.84%
5	Georgia	18	7.00%
25	Hawaii	0	0.00%
21	Idaho	1	0.39%
18	Illinois	2	0.78%
15	Indiana	3	1.17%
25	Iowa	0	0.00%
25	Kansas	0	0.00%
25	Kentucky	0	0.00%
4	Louisiana	21	8.17%
25	Maine	0	0.00%
21	Maryland	1	0.39%
25	Massachusetts	0	0.00%
25	Michigan	0	0.00%
25	Minnesota	0	0.00%
11	Mississippi	4	1.56%
6	Missouri	11	4.28%
25	Montana	0	0.00%
21	Nebraska	1	0.39%
10	Nevada	5	1.95%
25	New Hampshire	0	0.00%
25	New Jersey	0	0.00%
25	New Mexico	0	0.00%
25	New York	0	0.00%
9	North Carolina	6	2.33%
25	North Dakota	0	0.00%
25	Ohio	0	0.00%
15	Oklahoma	3	1.17%
25	Oregon	0	0.00%
25	Pennsylvania	0	0.00%
25	Rhode Island	0	0.00%
11	South Carolina	4	1.56%
25	South Dakota	0	0.00%
25	Tennessee	0	0.00%
1	Texas	85	33.07%
11	Utah	4	1.56%
25	Vermont	0	0.00%
3	Virginia	24	9.34%
18	Washington	2	0.78%
25	West Virginia	0	0.00%
25	Wisconsin	0	0.00%
21	Wyoming	1	0.39%

RANK ORDER

RANK	STATE	EXECUTIONS	% of USA
1	Texas	85	33.07%
2	Florida	33	12.84%
3	Virginia	24	9.34%
4	Louisiana	21	8.17%
5	Georgia	18	7.00%
6	Missouri	11	4.28%
7	Alabama	10	3.89%
8	Arkansas	9	3.50%
9	North Carolina	6	2.33%
10	Nevada	5	1.95%
11	Delaware	4	1.56%
11	Mississippi	4	1.56%
11	South Carolina	4	1.56%
11	Utah	4	1.56%
15	Arizona	3	1.17%
15	Indiana	3	1.17%
15	Oklahoma	3	1.17%
18	California	2	0.78%
18	Illinois	2	0.78%
18	Washington	2	0.78%
21	Idaho	1	0.39%
21	Maryland	1	0.39%
21	Nebraska	1	0.39%
21	Wyoming	1	0.39%
25	Alaska	0	0.00%
25	Colorado	0	0.00%
25	Connecticut	0	0.00%
25	Hawaii	0	0.00%
25	Iowa	0	0.00%
25	Kansas	0	0.00%
25	Kentucky	0	0.00%
25	Maine	0	0.00%
25	Massachusetts	0	0.00%
25	Michigan	0	0.00%
25	Minnesota	0	0.00%
25	Montana	0	0.00%
25	New Hampshire	0	0.00%
25	New Jersey	0	0.00%
25	New Mexico	0	0.00%
25	New York	0	0.00%
25	North Dakota	0	0.00%
25	Ohio	0	0.00%
25	Oregon	0	0.00%
25	Pennsylvania	0	0.00%
25	Rhode Island	0	0.00%
25	South Dakota	0	0.00%
25	Tennessee	0	0.00%
25	Vermont	0	0.00%
25	West Virginia	0	0.00%
25	Wisconsin	0	0.00%
	District of Columbia	0	0.00%

Source: U.S. Department of Justice, Bureau of Justice Statistics
"Capital Punishment 1994" (Bulletin, February 1996, NCJ-158023)
As of December 31, 1994. All executions since 1977 have been for murder.

Prisoners Sentenced to Death: 1973 to 1994

National Total = 5,273 Death Sentences*

ALPHA ORDER					RANK ORDER			
RANK	STATE	SENTENCES	% of USA		RANK	STATE	SENTENCES	% of USA
9	Alabama	227	4.30%		1	Florida	702	13.31%
NA	Alaska**	NA	NA		2	Texas	624	11.83%
11	Arizona	191	3.62%		3	California	534	10.13%
20	Arkansas	73	1.38%		4	North Carolina	364	6.90%
3	California	534	10.13%		5	Ohio	280	5.31%
31	Colorado	14	0.27%		6	Georgia	246	4.67%
34	Connecticut	5	0.09%		7	Pennsylvania	244	4.63%
26	Delaware	31	0.59%		8	Oklahoma	236	4.48%
1	Florida	702	13.31%		9	Alabama	227	4.30%
6	Georgia	246	4.67%		10	Illinois	223	4.23%
NA	Hawaii**	NA	NA		11	Arizona	191	3.62%
25	Idaho	32	0.61%		12	Tennessee	163	3.09%
10	Illinois	223	4.23%		13	Louisiana	142	2.69%
19	Indiana	80	1.52%		14	Mississippi	132	2.50%
NA	Iowa**	NA	NA		15	South Carolina	129	2.45%
NA	Kansas**	NA	NA		16	Missouri	117	2.22%
21	Kentucky	58	1.10%		17	Virginia	96	1.82%
13	Louisiana	142	2.69%		18	Nevada	95	1.80%
NA	Maine**	NA	NA		19	Indiana	80	1.52%
23	Maryland	37	0.70%		20	Arkansas	73	1.38%
35	Massachusetts	4	0.08%		21	Kentucky	58	1.10%
NA	Michigan**	NA	NA		22	New Jersey	38	0.72%
NA	Minnesota**	NA	NA		23	Maryland	37	0.70%
14	Mississippi	132	2.50%		24	Oregon	35	0.66%
16	Missouri	117	2.22%		25	Idaho	32	0.61%
32	Montana	13	0.25%		26	Delaware	31	0.59%
30	Nebraska	21	0.40%		27	Washington	25	0.47%
18	Nevada	95	1.80%		28	New Mexico	23	0.44%
39	New Hampshire	0	0.00%		28	Utah	23	0.44%
22	New Jersey	38	0.72%		30	Nebraska	21	0.40%
28	New Mexico	23	0.44%		31	Colorado	14	0.27%
36	New York	3	0.06%		32	Montana	13	0.25%
4	North Carolina	364	6.90%		33	Wyoming	9	0.17%
NA	North Dakota**	NA	NA		34	Connecticut	5	0.09%
5	Ohio	280	5.31%		35	Massachusetts	4	0.08%
8	Oklahoma	236	4.48%		36	New York	3	0.06%
24	Oregon	35	0.66%		37	Rhode Island	2	0.04%
7	Pennsylvania	244	4.63%		37	South Dakota	2	0.04%
37	Rhode Island	2	0.04%		39	New Hampshire	0	0.00%
15	South Carolina	129	2.45%		NA	Alaska**	NA	NA
37	South Dakota	2	0.04%		NA	Hawaii**	NA	NA
12	Tennessee	163	3.09%		NA	Iowa**	NA	NA
2	Texas	624	11.83%		NA	Kansas**	NA	NA
28	Utah	23	0.44%		NA	Maine**	NA	NA
NA	Vermont**	NA	NA		NA	Michigan**	NA	NA
17	Virginia	96	1.82%		NA	Minnesota**	NA	NA
27	Washington	25	0.47%		NA	North Dakota**	NA	NA
NA	West Virginia**	NA	NA		NA	Vermont**	NA	NA
NA	Wisconsin**	NA	NA		NA	West Virginia**	NA	NA
33	Wyoming	9	0.17%		NA	Wisconsin**	NA	NA
						District of Columbia**	NA	NA

Source: U.S. Department of Justice, Bureau of Justice Statistics
   "Capital Punishment 1994" (Bulletin, February 1996, NCJ-158023)
*As of December 31, 1994. Does not includes seven federal prisoners sentenced to death.
**No death penalty as of 12/31/94.

Death Sentences Overturned or Commuted: 1973 to 1994

National Total = 1,979 Sentences*

ALPHA ORDER				RANK ORDER			
RANK	STATE	SENTENCES	% of USA	RANK	STATE	SENTENCES	% of USA
8	Alabama	78	3.94%	1	Florida	307	15.51%
NA	Alaska**	NA	NA	2	North Carolina	243	12.28%
12	Arizona	61	3.08%	3	Ohio	135	6.82%
17	Arkansas	27	1.36%	4	Texas	133	6.72%
5	California	129	6.52%	5	California	129	6.52%
29	Colorado	10	0.51%	6	Georgia	124	6.27%
37	Connecticut	1	0.05%	7	Oklahoma	100	5.05%
25	Delaware	13	0.66%	8	Alabama	78	3.94%
1	Florida	307	15.51%	9	Mississippi	74	3.74%
6	Georgia	124	6.27%	10	Louisiana	70	3.54%
NA	Hawaii**	NA	NA	11	South Carolina	63	3.18%
28	Idaho	11	0.56%	12	Arizona	61	3.08%
15	Illinois	53	2.68%	13	Tennessee	57	2.88%
17	Indiana	27	1.36%	14	Pennsylvania	55	2.78%
NA	Iowa**	NA	NA	15	Illinois	53	2.68%
NA	Kansas**	NA	NA	16	Kentucky	28	1.41%
16	Kentucky	28	1.41%	17	Arkansas	27	1.36%
10	Louisiana	70	3.54%	17	Indiana	27	1.36%
NA	Maine**	NA	NA	19	Maryland	22	1.11%
19	Maryland	22	1.11%	20	Nevada	21	1.06%
34	Massachusetts	4	0.20%	20	New Mexico	21	1.06%
NA	Michigan**	NA	NA	22	New Jersey	20	1.01%
NA	Minnesota**	NA	NA	23	Oregon	18	0.91%
9	Mississippi	74	3.74%	24	Missouri	14	0.71%
24	Missouri	14	0.71%	25	Delaware	13	0.66%
33	Montana	5	0.25%	25	Virginia	13	0.66%
31	Nebraska	8	0.40%	27	Washington	12	0.61%
20	Nevada	21	1.06%	28	Idaho	11	0.56%
38	New Hampshire	0	0.00%	29	Colorado	10	0.51%
22	New Jersey	20	1.01%	30	Utah	9	0.45%
20	New Mexico	21	1.06%	31	Nebraska	8	0.40%
35	New York	3	0.15%	32	Wyoming	7	0.35%
2	North Carolina	243	12.28%	33	Montana	5	0.25%
NA	North Dakota**	NA	NA	34	Massachusetts	4	0.20%
3	Ohio	135	6.82%	35	New York	3	0.15%
7	Oklahoma	100	5.05%	36	Rhode Island	2	0.10%
23	Oregon	18	0.91%	37	Connecticut	1	0.05%
14	Pennsylvania	55	2.78%	38	New Hampshire	0	0.00%
36	Rhode Island	2	0.10%	38	South Dakota	0	0.00%
11	South Carolina	63	3.18%	NA	Alaska**	NA	NA
38	South Dakota	0	0.00%	NA	Hawaii**	NA	NA
13	Tennessee	57	2.88%	NA	Iowa**	NA	NA
4	Texas	133	6.72%	NA	Kansas**	NA	NA
30	Utah	9	0.45%	NA	Maine**	NA	NA
NA	Vermont**	NA	NA	NA	Michigan**	NA	NA
25	Virginia	13	0.66%	NA	Minnesota**	NA	NA
27	Washington	12	0.61%	NA	North Dakota**	NA	NA
NA	West Virginia**	NA	NA	NA	Vermont**	NA	NA
NA	Wisconsin**	NA	NA	NA	West Virginia**	NA	NA
32	Wyoming	7	0.35%	NA	Wisconsin**	NA	NA
					District of Columbia**	NA	NA

*Source: Morgan Quitno Press using data from U.S. Department of Justice, Bureau of Justice Statistics
"Capital Punishment 1994" (Bulletin, February 1996, NCJ-158023)*
As of December 31, 1994. Does not include one federal prisoner whose sentence was overturned.
**No death penalty as of 12/31/94.*

Percent of Death Penalty Sentences Overturned or Commuted: 1973 to 1994

National Percent = 37.48% of Sentences*

ALPHA ORDER

RANK	STATE	PERCENT
27	Alabama	34.36
NA	Alaska**	NA
29	Arizona	31.94
24	Arkansas	36.99
30	California	24.16
6	Colorado	71.43
35	Connecticut	20.00
20	Delaware	41.94
18	Florida	43.73
12	Georgia	50.41
NA	Hawaii**	NA
26	Idaho	34.38
31	Illinois	23.77
28	Indiana	33.75
NA	Iowa**	NA
NA	Kansas**	NA
15	Kentucky	48.28
13	Louisiana	49.30
NA	Maine**	NA
8	Maryland	59.46
1	Massachusetts	100.00
NA	Michigan**	NA
NA	Minnesota**	NA
9	Mississippi	56.06
37	Missouri	11.97
22	Montana	38.46
23	Nebraska	38.10
33	Nevada	22.11
38	New Hampshire	0.00
10	New Jersey	52.63
4	New Mexico	91.30
1	New York	100.00
7	North Carolina	66.76
NA	North Dakota**	NA
16	Ohio	48.21
19	Oklahoma	42.37
11	Oregon	51.43
32	Pennsylvania	22.54
1	Rhode Island	100.00
14	South Carolina	48.84
38	South Dakota	0.00
25	Tennessee	34.97
34	Texas	21.31
21	Utah	39.13
NA	Vermont**	NA
36	Virginia	13.54
17	Washington	48.00
NA	West Virginia**	NA
NA	Wisconsin**	NA
5	Wyoming	77.78

RANK ORDER

RANK	STATE	PERCENT
1	Massachusetts	100.00
1	New York	100.00
1	Rhode Island	100.00
4	New Mexico	91.30
5	Wyoming	77.78
6	Colorado	71.43
7	North Carolina	66.76
8	Maryland	59.46
9	Mississippi	56.06
10	New Jersey	52.63
11	Oregon	51.43
12	Georgia	50.41
13	Louisiana	49.30
14	South Carolina	48.84
15	Kentucky	48.28
16	Ohio	48.21
17	Washington	48.00
18	Florida	43.73
19	Oklahoma	42.37
20	Delaware	41.94
21	Utah	39.13
22	Montana	38.46
23	Nebraska	38.10
24	Arkansas	36.99
25	Tennessee	34.97
26	Idaho	34.38
27	Alabama	34.36
28	Indiana	33.75
29	Arizona	31.94
30	California	24.16
31	Illinois	23.77
32	Pennsylvania	22.54
33	Nevada	22.11
34	Texas	21.31
35	Connecticut	20.00
36	Virginia	13.54
37	Missouri	11.97
38	New Hampshire	0.00
38	South Dakota	0.00
NA	Alaska**	NA
NA	Hawaii**	NA
NA	Iowa**	NA
NA	Kansas**	NA
NA	Maine**	NA
NA	Michigan**	NA
NA	Minnesota**	NA
NA	North Dakota**	NA
NA	Vermont**	NA
NA	West Virginia**	NA
NA	Wisconsin**	NA
	District of Columbia**	NA

Source: Morgan Quitno Press using data from U.S. Department of Justice, Bureau of Justice Statistics "Capital Punishment 1994" (Bulletin, February 1996, NCJ-158023)
As of December 31, 1994. Does not include one federal prisoner whose sentence was overturned.
**No death penalty as of 12/31/94.*

Sentenced Prisoners Admitted to State Correctional Institutions in 1993

National Total = 493,160 Prisoners Admitted*

ALPHA ORDER

RANK ORDER

RANK	STATE	ADMISSIONS	% of USA	RANK	STATE	ADMISSIONS	% of USA
16	Alabama	8,740	1.77%	1	California	99,189	20.11%
35	Alaska	2,613	0.53%	2	New York	35,802	7.26%
18	Arizona	8,171	1.66%	3	Florida	32,269	6.54%
30	Arkansas	3,836	0.78%	4	Texas	29,916	6.07%
1	California	99,189	20.11%	5	North Carolina	25,577	5.19%
28	Colorado	4,510	0.91%	6	Ohio	22,583	4.58%
19	Connecticut	7,538	1.53%	7	Illinois	21,717	4.40%
41	Delaware	1,327	0.27%	8	Georgia	15,264	3.10%
3	Florida	32,269	6.54%	9	New Jersey	12,679	2.57%
8	Georgia	15,264	3.10%	10	Michigan	12,590	2.55%
38	Hawaii	1,823	0.37%	11	Virginia	12,489	2.53%
39	Idaho	1,770	0.36%	12	Louisiana	11,977	2.43%
7	Illinois	21,717	4.40%	13	Pennsylvania	9,893	2.01%
21	Indiana	6,830	1.38%	14	Missouri	9,812	1.99%
31	Iowa	3,611	0.73%	15	Maryland	8,800	1.78%
29	Kansas	3,853	0.78%	16	Alabama	8,740	1.77%
23	Kentucky	5,825	1.18%	17	South Carolina	8,189	1.66%
12	Louisiana	11,977	2.43%	18	Arizona	8,171	1.66%
46	Maine	757	0.15%	19	Connecticut	7,538	1.53%
15	Maryland	8,800	1.78%	20	Oklahoma	7,049	1.43%
26	Massachusetts	4,862	0.99%	21	Indiana	6,830	1.38%
10	Michigan	12,590	2.55%	22	Tennessee	6,695	1.36%
34	Minnesota	3,035	0.62%	23	Kentucky	5,825	1.18%
27	Mississippi	4,768	0.97%	24	Wisconsin	5,814	1.18%
14	Missouri	9,812	1.99%	25	Washington	5,425	1.10%
47	Montana	680	0.14%	26	Massachusetts	4,862	0.99%
40	Nebraska	1,468	0.30%	27	Mississippi	4,768	0.97%
33	Nevada	3,202	0.65%	28	Colorado	4,510	0.91%
42	New Hampshire	957	0.19%	29	Kansas	3,853	0.78%
9	New Jersey	12,679	2.57%	30	Arkansas	3,836	0.78%
36	New Mexico	2,334	0.47%	31	Iowa	3,611	0.73%
2	New York	35,802	7.26%	32	Oregon	3,599	0.73%
5	North Carolina	25,577	5.19%	33	Nevada	3,202	0.65%
50	North Dakota	352	0.07%	34	Minnesota	3,035	0.62%
6	Ohio	22,583	4.58%	35	Alaska	2,613	0.53%
20	Oklahoma	7,049	1.43%	36	New Mexico	2,334	0.47%
32	Oregon	3,599	0.73%	37	Utah	1,924	0.39%
13	Pennsylvania	9,893	2.01%	38	Hawaii	1,823	0.37%
44	Rhode Island	875	0.18%	39	Idaho	1,770	0.36%
17	South Carolina	8,189	1.66%	40	Nebraska	1,468	0.30%
45	South Dakota	820	0.17%	41	Delaware	1,327	0.27%
22	Tennessee	6,695	1.36%	42	New Hampshire	957	0.19%
4	Texas	29,916	6.07%	43	West Virginia	882	0.18%
37	Utah	1,924	0.39%	44	Rhode Island	875	0.18%
49	Vermont	497	0.10%	45	South Dakota	820	0.17%
11	Virginia	12,489	2.53%	46	Maine	757	0.15%
25	Washington	5,425	1.10%	47	Montana	680	0.14%
43	West Virginia	882	0.18%	48	Wyoming	513	0.10%
24	Wisconsin	5,814	1.18%	49	Vermont	497	0.10%
48	Wyoming	513	0.10%	50	North Dakota	352	0.07%
					District of Columbia	7,459	1.51%

Source: U.S. Department of Justice, Bureau of Justice Statistics
   "Correctional Populations in the United States, 1993" (October 1995, NCJ 156241)
*Includes sentenced prisoners admitted because of new court commitments, parole violators returned, escapees returned and others. Does not include 25,402 new federal commitments.

Sentenced Prisoners Admitted to State Correctional Institutions Through New Court Commitments in 1993
National Total = 318,069 New Prisoners*

ALPHA ORDER

RANK	STATE	PRISONERS	% of USA
16	Alabama	6,491	2.04%
38	Alaska	1,068	0.34%
15	Arizona	6,606	2.08%
28	Arkansas	2,737	0.86%
1	California	43,149	13.57%
26	Colorado	3,131	0.98%
27	Connecticut	3,007	0.95%
40	Delaware	975	0.31%
2	Florida	25,296	7.95%
8	Georgia	10,905	3.43%
39	Hawaii	1,010	0.32%
35	Idaho	1,327	0.42%
6	Illinois	16,796	5.28%
18	Indiana	6,217	1.95%
32	Iowa	2,144	0.67%
33	Kansas	2,055	0.65%
23	Kentucky	4,163	1.31%
11	Louisiana	8,326	2.62%
46	Maine	484	0.15%
13	Maryland	7,123	2.24%
30	Massachusetts	2,429	0.76%
12	Michigan	7,564	2.38%
31	Minnesota	2,191	0.69%
22	Mississippi	4,476	1.41%
14	Missouri	6,914	2.17%
49	Montana	304	0.10%
37	Nebraska	1,122	0.35%
29	Nevada	2,573	0.81%
43	New Hampshire	720	0.23%
10	New Jersey	8,563	2.69%
36	New Mexico	1,263	0.40%
3	New York	24,897	7.83%
4	North Carolina	20,688	6.50%
50	North Dakota	275	0.09%
5	Ohio	18,492	5.81%
17	Oklahoma	6,285	1.98%
34	Oregon	1,649	0.52%
20	Pennsylvania	5,953	1.87%
45	Rhode Island	596	0.19%
19	South Carolina	6,120	1.92%
44	South Dakota	642	0.20%
25	Tennessee	3,969	1.25%
7	Texas	15,524	4.88%
41	Utah	907	0.29%
48	Vermont	322	0.10%
9	Virginia	9,971	3.13%
21	Washington	4,699	1.48%
42	West Virginia	753	0.24%
24	Wisconsin	4,130	1.30%
47	Wyoming	417	0.13%

RANK ORDER

RANK	STATE	PRISONERS	% of USA
1	California	43,149	13.57%
2	Florida	25,296	7.95%
3	New York	24,897	7.83%
4	North Carolina	20,688	6.50%
5	Ohio	18,492	5.81%
6	Illinois	16,796	5.28%
7	Texas	15,524	4.88%
8	Georgia	10,905	3.43%
9	Virginia	9,971	3.13%
10	New Jersey	8,563	2.69%
11	Louisiana	8,326	2.62%
12	Michigan	7,564	2.38%
13	Maryland	7,123	2.24%
14	Missouri	6,914	2.17%
15	Arizona	6,606	2.08%
16	Alabama	6,491	2.04%
17	Oklahoma	6,285	1.98%
18	Indiana	6,217	1.95%
19	South Carolina	6,120	1.92%
20	Pennsylvania	5,953	1.87%
21	Washington	4,699	1.48%
22	Mississippi	4,476	1.41%
23	Kentucky	4,163	1.31%
24	Wisconsin	4,130	1.30%
25	Tennessee	3,969	1.25%
26	Colorado	3,131	0.98%
27	Connecticut	3,007	0.95%
28	Arkansas	2,737	0.86%
29	Nevada	2,573	0.81%
30	Massachusetts	2,429	0.76%
31	Minnesota	2,191	0.69%
32	Iowa	2,144	0.67%
33	Kansas	2,055	0.65%
34	Oregon	1,649	0.52%
35	Idaho	1,327	0.42%
36	New Mexico	1,263	0.40%
37	Nebraska	1,122	0.35%
38	Alaska	1,068	0.34%
39	Hawaii	1,010	0.32%
40	Delaware	975	0.31%
41	Utah	907	0.29%
42	West Virginia	753	0.24%
43	New Hampshire	720	0.23%
44	South Dakota	642	0.20%
45	Rhode Island	596	0.19%
46	Maine	484	0.15%
47	Wyoming	417	0.13%
48	Vermont	322	0.10%
49	Montana	304	0.10%
50	North Dakota	275	0.09%
	District of Columbia	651	0.20%

Source: U.S. Department of Justice, Bureau of Justice Statistics
"Correctional Populations in the United States, 1993" (October 1995, NCJ 156241)
*Does not include 23,653 new federal court commitments.

Parole Violators Returned to State Prison in 1993

National Total = 146,366 Prisoners*

ALPHA ORDER

RANK	STATE	PRISONERS	% of USA
18	Alabama	1,784	1.22%
35	Alaska	433	0.30%
22	Arizona	1,444	0.99%
26	Arkansas	992	0.68%
1	California	55,011	37.58%
28	Colorado	984	0.67%
9	Connecticut	3,698	2.53%
44	Delaware	119	0.08%
3	Florida	6,470	4.42%
6	Georgia	4,161	2.84%
31	Hawaii	805	0.55%
37	Idaho	416	0.28%
7	Illinois	4,095	2.80%
32	Indiana	581	0.40%
29	Iowa	889	0.61%
19	Kansas	1,747	1.19%
21	Kentucky	1,503	1.03%
12	Louisiana	3,316	2.27%
40	Maine	260	0.18%
20	Maryland	1,546	1.06%
23	Massachusetts	1,097	0.75%
10	Michigan	3,619	2.47%
30	Minnesota	844	0.58%
45	Mississippi	115	0.08%
14	Missouri	2,270	1.55%
45	Montana	115	0.08%
39	Nebraska	335	0.23%
33	Nevada	561	0.38%
41	New Hampshire	221	0.15%
11	New Jersey	3,478	2.38%
25	New Mexico	997	0.68%
4	New York	6,355	4.34%
5	North Carolina	4,665	3.19%
49	North Dakota	75	0.05%
8	Ohio	3,906	2.67%
38	Oklahoma	340	0.23%
17	Oregon	1,831	1.25%
36	Pennsylvania	418	0.29%
42	Rhode Island	215	0.15%
16	South Carolina	1,946	1.33%
43	South Dakota	153	0.10%
13	Tennessee	2,609	1.78%
2	Texas	13,455	9.19%
24	Utah	1,008	0.69%
47	Vermont	114	0.08%
15	Virginia	1,964	1.34%
34	Washington	533	0.36%
48	West Virginia	89	0.06%
27	Wisconsin	987	0.67%
50	Wyoming	52	0.04%

RANK ORDER

RANK	STATE	PRISONERS	% of USA
1	California	55,011	37.58%
2	Texas	13,455	9.19%
3	Florida	6,470	4.42%
4	New York	6,355	4.34%
5	North Carolina	4,665	3.19%
6	Georgia	4,161	2.84%
7	Illinois	4,095	2.80%
8	Ohio	3,906	2.67%
9	Connecticut	3,698	2.53%
10	Michigan	3,619	2.47%
11	New Jersey	3,478	2.38%
12	Louisiana	3,316	2.27%
13	Tennessee	2,609	1.78%
14	Missouri	2,270	1.55%
15	Virginia	1,964	1.34%
16	South Carolina	1,946	1.33%
17	Oregon	1,831	1.25%
18	Alabama	1,784	1.22%
19	Kansas	1,747	1.19%
20	Maryland	1,546	1.06%
21	Kentucky	1,503	1.03%
22	Arizona	1,444	0.99%
23	Massachusetts	1,097	0.75%
24	Utah	1,008	0.69%
25	New Mexico	997	0.68%
26	Arkansas	992	0.68%
27	Wisconsin	987	0.67%
28	Colorado	984	0.67%
29	Iowa	889	0.61%
30	Minnesota	844	0.58%
31	Hawaii	805	0.55%
32	Indiana	581	0.40%
33	Nevada	561	0.38%
34	Washington	533	0.36%
35	Alaska	433	0.30%
36	Pennsylvania	418	0.29%
37	Idaho	416	0.28%
38	Oklahoma	340	0.23%
39	Nebraska	335	0.23%
40	Maine	260	0.18%
41	New Hampshire	221	0.15%
42	Rhode Island	215	0.15%
43	South Dakota	153	0.10%
44	Delaware	119	0.08%
45	Mississippi	115	0.08%
45	Montana	115	0.08%
47	Vermont	114	0.08%
48	West Virginia	89	0.06%
49	North Dakota	75	0.05%
50	Wyoming	52	0.04%
	District of Columbia	1,745	1.19%

Source: U.S. Department of Justice, Bureau of Justice Statistics
"Correctional Populations in the United States, 1993" (October 1995, NCJ 156241)
*Includes other conditional release violators. Does not include 1,346 federal parole violators.

Escapees Returned to State Prison in 1993

National Total = 12,872 Prisoners*

ALPHA ORDER

RANK	STATE	PRISONERS	% of USA
11	Alabama	238	1.85%
45	Alaska	4	0.03%
21	Arizona	79	0.61%
36	Arkansas	12	0.09%
5	California	624	4.85%
9	Colorado	372	2.89%
3	Connecticut	827	6.42%
18	Delaware	112	0.87%
10	Florida	253	1.97%
19	Georgia	107	0.83%
41	Hawaii	8	0.06%
35	Idaho	13	0.10%
4	Illinois	764	5.94%
36	Indiana	12	0.09%
8	Iowa	384	2.98%
29	Kansas	25	0.19%
16	Kentucky	123	0.96%
24	Louisiana	71	0.55%
41	Maine	8	0.06%
15	Maryland	127	0.99%
23	Massachusetts	74	0.57%
2	Michigan	1,177	9.14%
NA	Minnesota**	NA	NA
28	Mississippi	41	0.32%
6	Missouri	600	4.66%
NA	Montana**	NA	NA
38	Nebraska	11	0.09%
25	Nevada	68	0.53%
32	New Hampshire	16	0.12%
13	New Jersey	155	1.20%
27	New Mexico	48	0.37%
1	New York	3,749	29.13%
12	North Carolina	205	1.59%
46	North Dakota	2	0.02%
40	Ohio	9	0.07%
7	Oklahoma	424	3.29%
22	Oregon	75	0.58%
41	Pennsylvania	8	0.06%
26	Rhode Island	51	0.40%
17	South Carolina	116	0.90%
32	South Dakota	16	0.12%
20	Tennessee	89	0.69%
NA	Texas**	NA	NA
44	Utah	5	0.04%
38	Vermont	11	0.09%
30	Virginia	20	0.16%
14	Washington	144	1.12%
31	West Virginia	19	0.15%
NA	Wisconsin**	NA	NA
32	Wyoming	16	0.12%

RANK ORDER

RANK	STATE	PRISONERS	% of USA
1	New York	3,749	29.13%
2	Michigan	1,177	9.14%
3	Connecticut	827	6.42%
4	Illinois	764	5.94%
5	California	624	4.85%
6	Missouri	600	4.66%
7	Oklahoma	424	3.29%
8	Iowa	384	2.98%
9	Colorado	372	2.89%
10	Florida	253	1.97%
11	Alabama	238	1.85%
12	North Carolina	205	1.59%
13	New Jersey	155	1.20%
14	Washington	144	1.12%
15	Maryland	127	0.99%
16	Kentucky	123	0.96%
17	South Carolina	116	0.90%
18	Delaware	112	0.87%
19	Georgia	107	0.83%
20	Tennessee	89	0.69%
21	Arizona	79	0.61%
22	Oregon	75	0.58%
23	Massachusetts	74	0.57%
24	Louisiana	71	0.55%
25	Nevada	68	0.53%
26	Rhode Island	51	0.40%
27	New Mexico	48	0.37%
28	Mississippi	41	0.32%
29	Kansas	25	0.19%
30	Virginia	20	0.16%
31	West Virginia	19	0.15%
32	New Hampshire	16	0.12%
32	South Dakota	16	0.12%
32	Wyoming	16	0.12%
35	Idaho	13	0.10%
36	Arkansas	12	0.09%
36	Indiana	12	0.09%
38	Nebraska	11	0.09%
38	Vermont	11	0.09%
40	Ohio	9	0.07%
41	Hawaii	8	0.06%
41	Maine	8	0.06%
41	Pennsylvania	8	0.06%
44	Utah	5	0.04%
45	Alaska	4	0.03%
46	North Dakota	2	0.02%
NA	Minnesota**	NA	NA
NA	Montana**	NA	NA
NA	Texas**	NA	NA
NA	Wisconsin**	NA	NA
	District of Columbia	1,560	12.12%

Source: U.S. Department of Justice, Bureau of Justice Statistics
    "Correctional Populations in the United States, 1993" (October 1995, NCJ 156241)
*Includes AWOLs returned.
**Not available.

Prisoners Released from State Correctional Institutions in 1993

National Total = 437,099 Prisoners*

RANK	STATE	PRISONERS	% of USA
17	Alabama	7,508	1.72%
36	Alaska	1,854	0.42%
18	Arizona	6,863	1.57%
28	Arkansas	4,047	0.93%
1	California	89,083	20.38%
29	Colorado	4,045	0.93%
20	Connecticut	5,824	1.33%
41	Delaware	1,251	0.29%
3	Florida	27,688	6.33%
8	Georgia	12,801	2.93%
38	Hawaii	1,715	0.39%
40	Idaho	1,420	0.32%
7	Illinois	18,862	4.32%
19	Indiana	6,257	1.43%
32	Iowa	3,231	0.74%
27	Kansas	4,154	0.95%
21	Kentucky	5,749	1.32%
12	Louisiana	10,405	2.38%
44	Maine	803	0.18%
15	Maryland	8,487	1.94%
24	Massachusetts	5,253	1.20%
9	Michigan	12,385	2.83%
34	Minnesota	2,657	0.61%
30	Mississippi	3,885	0.89%
13	Missouri	9,821	2.25%
47	Montana	687	0.16%
39	Nebraska	1,436	0.33%
33	Nevada	3,113	0.71%
42	New Hampshire	959	0.22%
10	New Jersey	11,501	2.63%
35	New Mexico	2,115	0.48%
2	New York	32,969	7.54%
4	North Carolina	24,175	5.53%
50	North Dakota	334	0.08%
5	Ohio	20,320	4.65%
23	Oklahoma	5,461	1.25%
31	Oregon	3,724	0.85%
14	Pennsylvania	8,814	2.02%
43	Rhode Island	866	0.20%
16	South Carolina	7,905	1.81%
45	South Dakota	754	0.17%
22	Tennessee	5,720	1.31%
6	Texas	20,256	4.63%
37	Utah	1,740	0.40%
48	Vermont	469	0.11%
11	Virginia	10,843	2.48%
25	Washington	4,965	1.14%
46	West Virginia	751	0.17%
26	Wisconsin	4,646	1.06%
49	Wyoming	449	0.10%

RANK	STATE	PRISONERS	% of USA
1	California	89,083	20.38%
2	New York	32,969	7.54%
3	Florida	27,688	6.33%
4	North Carolina	24,175	5.53%
5	Ohio	20,320	4.65%
6	Texas	20,256	4.63%
7	Illinois	18,862	4.32%
8	Georgia	12,801	2.93%
9	Michigan	12,385	2.83%
10	New Jersey	11,501	2.63%
11	Virginia	10,843	2.48%
12	Louisiana	10,405	2.38%
13	Missouri	9,821	2.25%
14	Pennsylvania	8,814	2.02%
15	Maryland	8,487	1.94%
16	South Carolina	7,905	1.81%
17	Alabama	7,508	1.72%
18	Arizona	6,863	1.57%
19	Indiana	6,257	1.43%
20	Connecticut	5,824	1.33%
21	Kentucky	5,749	1.32%
22	Tennessee	5,720	1.31%
23	Oklahoma	5,461	1.25%
24	Massachusetts	5,253	1.20%
25	Washington	4,965	1.14%
26	Wisconsin	4,646	1.06%
27	Kansas	4,154	0.95%
28	Arkansas	4,047	0.93%
29	Colorado	4,045	0.93%
30	Mississippi	3,885	0.89%
31	Oregon	3,724	0.85%
32	Iowa	3,231	0.74%
33	Nevada	3,113	0.71%
34	Minnesota	2,657	0.61%
35	New Mexico	2,115	0.48%
36	Alaska	1,854	0.42%
37	Utah	1,740	0.40%
38	Hawaii	1,715	0.39%
39	Nebraska	1,436	0.33%
40	Idaho	1,420	0.32%
41	Delaware	1,251	0.29%
42	New Hampshire	959	0.22%
43	Rhode Island	866	0.20%
44	Maine	803	0.18%
45	South Dakota	754	0.17%
46	West Virginia	751	0.17%
47	Montana	687	0.16%
48	Vermont	469	0.11%
49	Wyoming	449	0.10%
50	North Dakota	334	0.08%
	District of Columbia	6,079	1.39%

Source: U.S. Department of Justice, Bureau of Justice Statistics
    "Correctional Populations in the United States, 1993" (October 1995, NCJ 156241)
*Includes conditional releases, unconditional releases, escapees, out on appeal, deaths and other releases. Does not include 19,309 federal prisoners released.

State Prisoners Released with Conditions in 1993

National Total = 350,031 Prisoners*

ALPHA ORDER

RANK	STATE	PRISONERS	% of USA
19	Alabama	4,752	1.36%
35	Alaska	1,470	0.42%
16	Arizona	6,184	1.77%
26	Arkansas	3,093	0.88%
1	California	82,526	23.58%
31	Colorado	2,383	0.68%
24	Connecticut	3,529	1.01%
45	Delaware	505	0.14%
4	Florida	19,568	5.59%
7	Georgia	10,526	3.01%
36	Hawaii	1,458	0.42%
39	Idaho	1,195	0.34%
6	Illinois	17,457	4.99%
17	Indiana	5,632	1.61%
28	Iowa	2,803	0.80%
22	Kansas	4,003	1.14%
25	Kentucky	3,364	0.96%
10	Louisiana	9,484	2.71%
47	Maine	442	0.13%
14	Maryland	7,403	2.11%
38	Massachusetts	1,408	0.40%
9	Michigan	9,847	2.81%
30	Minnesota	2,396	0.68%
32	Mississippi	2,207	0.63%
12	Missouri	8,656	2.47%
44	Montana	538	0.15%
40	Nebraska	841	0.24%
33	Nevada	1,648	0.47%
42	New Hampshire	669	0.19%
11	New Jersey	9,242	2.64%
37	New Mexico	1,448	0.41%
2	New York	25,825	7.38%
3	North Carolina	23,579	6.74%
50	North Dakota	230	0.07%
13	Ohio	7,990	2.28%
29	Oklahoma	2,709	0.77%
23	Oregon	3,584	1.02%
15	Pennsylvania	6,738	1.92%
41	Rhode Island	782	0.22%
18	South Carolina	5,452	1.56%
46	South Dakota	475	0.14%
20	Tennessee	4,554	1.30%
5	Texas	19,461	5.56%
34	Utah	1,545	0.44%
48	Vermont	290	0.08%
8	Virginia	9,890	2.83%
27	Washington	3,075	0.88%
43	West Virginia	592	0.17%
21	Wisconsin	4,162	1.19%
49	Wyoming	255	0.07%

RANK ORDER

RANK	STATE	PRISONERS	% of USA
1	California	82,526	23.58%
2	New York	25,825	7.38%
3	North Carolina	23,579	6.74%
4	Florida	19,568	5.59%
5	Texas	19,461	5.56%
6	Illinois	17,457	4.99%
7	Georgia	10,526	3.01%
8	Virginia	9,890	2.83%
9	Michigan	9,847	2.81%
10	Louisiana	9,484	2.71%
11	New Jersey	9,242	2.64%
12	Missouri	8,656	2.47%
13	Ohio	7,990	2.28%
14	Maryland	7,403	2.11%
15	Pennsylvania	6,738	1.92%
16	Arizona	6,184	1.77%
17	Indiana	5,632	1.61%
18	South Carolina	5,452	1.56%
19	Alabama	4,752	1.36%
20	Tennessee	4,554	1.30%
21	Wisconsin	4,162	1.19%
22	Kansas	4,003	1.14%
23	Oregon	3,584	1.02%
24	Connecticut	3,529	1.01%
25	Kentucky	3,364	0.96%
26	Arkansas	3,093	0.88%
27	Washington	3,075	0.88%
28	Iowa	2,803	0.80%
29	Oklahoma	2,709	0.77%
30	Minnesota	2,396	0.68%
31	Colorado	2,383	0.68%
32	Mississippi	2,207	0.63%
33	Nevada	1,648	0.47%
34	Utah	1,545	0.44%
35	Alaska	1,470	0.42%
36	Hawaii	1,458	0.42%
37	New Mexico	1,448	0.41%
38	Massachusetts	1,408	0.40%
39	Idaho	1,195	0.34%
40	Nebraska	841	0.24%
41	Rhode Island	782	0.22%
42	New Hampshire	669	0.19%
43	West Virginia	592	0.17%
44	Montana	538	0.15%
45	Delaware	505	0.14%
46	South Dakota	475	0.14%
47	Maine	442	0.13%
48	Vermont	290	0.08%
49	Wyoming	255	0.07%
50	North Dakota	230	0.07%
	District of Columbia	2,166	0.62%

Source: U.S. Department of Justice, Bureau of Justice Statistics
   "Correctional Populations in the United States, 1993" (October 1995, NCJ 156241)
*Released on parole, probation, supervised mandatory release or other conditions. Does not include 5,742 federal prisoners released with condition.

State Prisoners Released Conditionally as a Percent of All Releases in 1993

National Percent = 80.08% of Prisoners Released*

<table>
<tr><td colspan="3">ALPHA ORDER</td><td colspan="3">RANK ORDER</td></tr>
<tr><td>RANK</td><td>STATE</td><td>PERCENT</td><td>RANK</td><td>STATE</td><td>PERCENT</td></tr>
<tr><td>35</td><td>Alabama</td><td>63.29</td><td>1</td><td>North Carolina</td><td>97.53</td></tr>
<tr><td>24</td><td>Alaska</td><td>79.29</td><td>2</td><td>Kansas</td><td>96.36</td></tr>
<tr><td>11</td><td>Arizona</td><td>90.11</td><td>3</td><td>Oregon</td><td>96.24</td></tr>
<tr><td>29</td><td>Arkansas</td><td>76.43</td><td>4</td><td>Texas</td><td>96.08</td></tr>
<tr><td>5</td><td>California</td><td>92.64</td><td>5</td><td>California</td><td>92.64</td></tr>
<tr><td>40</td><td>Colorado</td><td>58.91</td><td>6</td><td>Illinois</td><td>92.55</td></tr>
<tr><td>39</td><td>Connecticut</td><td>60.59</td><td>7</td><td>Virginia</td><td>91.21</td></tr>
<tr><td>48</td><td>Delaware</td><td>40.37</td><td>8</td><td>Louisiana</td><td>91.15</td></tr>
<tr><td>30</td><td>Florida</td><td>70.67</td><td>9</td><td>Rhode Island</td><td>90.30</td></tr>
<tr><td>20</td><td>Georgia</td><td>82.23</td><td>10</td><td>Minnesota</td><td>90.18</td></tr>
<tr><td>18</td><td>Hawaii</td><td>85.01</td><td>11</td><td>Arizona</td><td>90.11</td></tr>
<tr><td>19</td><td>Idaho</td><td>84.15</td><td>12</td><td>Indiana</td><td>90.01</td></tr>
<tr><td>6</td><td>Illinois</td><td>92.55</td><td>13</td><td>Wisconsin</td><td>89.58</td></tr>
<tr><td>12</td><td>Indiana</td><td>90.01</td><td>14</td><td>Utah</td><td>88.79</td></tr>
<tr><td>17</td><td>Iowa</td><td>86.75</td><td>15</td><td>Missouri</td><td>88.14</td></tr>
<tr><td>2</td><td>Kansas</td><td>96.36</td><td>16</td><td>Maryland</td><td>87.23</td></tr>
<tr><td>42</td><td>Kentucky</td><td>58.51</td><td>17</td><td>Iowa</td><td>86.75</td></tr>
<tr><td>8</td><td>Louisiana</td><td>91.15</td><td>18</td><td>Hawaii</td><td>85.01</td></tr>
<tr><td>45</td><td>Maine</td><td>55.04</td><td>19</td><td>Idaho</td><td>84.15</td></tr>
<tr><td>16</td><td>Maryland</td><td>87.23</td><td>20</td><td>Georgia</td><td>82.23</td></tr>
<tr><td>50</td><td>Massachusetts</td><td>26.80</td><td>21</td><td>New Jersey</td><td>80.36</td></tr>
<tr><td>23</td><td>Michigan</td><td>79.51</td><td>22</td><td>Tennessee</td><td>79.62</td></tr>
<tr><td>10</td><td>Minnesota</td><td>90.18</td><td>23</td><td>Michigan</td><td>79.51</td></tr>
<tr><td>43</td><td>Mississippi</td><td>56.81</td><td>24</td><td>Alaska</td><td>79.29</td></tr>
<tr><td>15</td><td>Missouri</td><td>88.14</td><td>25</td><td>West Virginia</td><td>78.83</td></tr>
<tr><td>27</td><td>Montana</td><td>78.31</td><td>26</td><td>New York</td><td>78.33</td></tr>
<tr><td>41</td><td>Nebraska</td><td>58.57</td><td>27</td><td>Montana</td><td>78.31</td></tr>
<tr><td>46</td><td>Nevada</td><td>52.94</td><td>28</td><td>Pennsylvania</td><td>76.45</td></tr>
<tr><td>31</td><td>New Hampshire</td><td>69.76</td><td>29</td><td>Arkansas</td><td>76.43</td></tr>
<tr><td>21</td><td>New Jersey</td><td>80.36</td><td>30</td><td>Florida</td><td>70.67</td></tr>
<tr><td>34</td><td>New Mexico</td><td>68.46</td><td>31</td><td>New Hampshire</td><td>69.76</td></tr>
<tr><td>26</td><td>New York</td><td>78.33</td><td>32</td><td>South Carolina</td><td>68.97</td></tr>
<tr><td>1</td><td>North Carolina</td><td>97.53</td><td>33</td><td>North Dakota</td><td>68.86</td></tr>
<tr><td>33</td><td>North Dakota</td><td>68.86</td><td>34</td><td>New Mexico</td><td>68.46</td></tr>
<tr><td>49</td><td>Ohio</td><td>39.32</td><td>35</td><td>Alabama</td><td>63.29</td></tr>
<tr><td>47</td><td>Oklahoma</td><td>49.61</td><td>36</td><td>South Dakota</td><td>63.00</td></tr>
<tr><td>3</td><td>Oregon</td><td>96.24</td><td>37</td><td>Washington</td><td>61.93</td></tr>
<tr><td>28</td><td>Pennsylvania</td><td>76.45</td><td>38</td><td>Vermont</td><td>61.83</td></tr>
<tr><td>9</td><td>Rhode Island</td><td>90.30</td><td>39</td><td>Connecticut</td><td>60.59</td></tr>
<tr><td>32</td><td>South Carolina</td><td>68.97</td><td>40</td><td>Colorado</td><td>58.91</td></tr>
<tr><td>36</td><td>South Dakota</td><td>63.00</td><td>41</td><td>Nebraska</td><td>58.57</td></tr>
<tr><td>22</td><td>Tennessee</td><td>79.62</td><td>42</td><td>Kentucky</td><td>58.51</td></tr>
<tr><td>4</td><td>Texas</td><td>96.08</td><td>43</td><td>Mississippi</td><td>56.81</td></tr>
<tr><td>14</td><td>Utah</td><td>88.79</td><td>44</td><td>Wyoming</td><td>56.79</td></tr>
<tr><td>38</td><td>Vermont</td><td>61.83</td><td>45</td><td>Maine</td><td>55.04</td></tr>
<tr><td>7</td><td>Virginia</td><td>91.21</td><td>46</td><td>Nevada</td><td>52.94</td></tr>
<tr><td>37</td><td>Washington</td><td>61.93</td><td>47</td><td>Oklahoma</td><td>49.61</td></tr>
<tr><td>25</td><td>West Virginia</td><td>78.83</td><td>48</td><td>Delaware</td><td>40.37</td></tr>
<tr><td>13</td><td>Wisconsin</td><td>89.58</td><td>49</td><td>Ohio</td><td>39.32</td></tr>
<tr><td>44</td><td>Wyoming</td><td>56.79</td><td>50</td><td>Massachusetts</td><td>26.80</td></tr>
<tr><td></td><td></td><td></td><td></td><td>District of Columbia</td><td>35.63</td></tr>
</table>

Source: Morgan Quitno Press using data from U.S. Department of Justice, Bureau of Justice Statistics
"Correctional Populations in the United States, 1993" (October 1995, NCJ 156241)
*Released on parole, probation, supervised mandatory release or other conditions. Does not include federal prisoners released with condition. Federal percent is 29.74% of releases. The combined state and federal percent is 77.95% of prisoners released are released with conditions.

State Prisoners Released on Parole in 1993

National Total = 162,185 Prisoners*

ALPHA ORDER

RANK	STATE	PRISONERS	% of USA
17	Alabama	2,728	1.68%
45	Alaska	47	0.03%
28	Arizona	981	0.60%
19	Arkansas	2,390	1.47%
50	California	0	0.00%
20	Colorado	2,231	1.38%
35	Connecticut	482	0.30%
44	Delaware	104	0.06%
41	Florida	223	0.14%
5	Georgia	9,613	5.93%
30	Hawaii	778	0.48%
34	Idaho	514	0.32%
46	Illinois	38	0.02%
48	Indiana	5	0.00%
23	Iowa	1,635	1.01%
16	Kansas	3,163	1.95%
18	Kentucky	2,674	1.65%
21	Louisiana	1,752	1.08%
49	Maine	4	0.00%
12	Maryland	3,913	2.41%
25	Massachusetts	1,408	0.87%
4	Michigan	9,847	6.07%
47	Minnesota	19	0.01%
26	Mississippi	1,366	0.84%
8	Missouri	6,245	3.85%
38	Montana	419	0.26%
29	Nebraska	841	0.52%
22	Nevada	1,648	1.02%
32	New Hampshire	607	0.37%
6	New Jersey	8,947	5.52%
27	New Mexico	1,249	0.77%
2	New York	22,451	13.84%
1	North Carolina	23,560	14.53%
43	North Dakota	115	0.07%
10	Ohio	4,831	2.98%
31	Oklahoma	749	0.46%
14	Oregon	3,584	2.21%
7	Pennsylvania	6,738	4.15%
36	Rhode Island	468	0.29%
11	South Carolina	4,049	2.50%
37	South Dakota	427	0.26%
15	Tennessee	3,176	1.96%
3	Texas	12,469	7.69%
24	Utah	1,545	0.95%
40	Vermont	239	0.15%
9	Virginia	5,266	3.25%
39	Washington	347	0.21%
33	West Virginia	566	0.35%
13	Wisconsin	3,586	2.21%
42	Wyoming	145	0.09%

RANK ORDER

RANK	STATE	PRISONERS	% of USA
1	North Carolina	23,560	14.53%
2	New York	22,451	13.84%
3	Texas	12,469	7.69%
4	Michigan	9,847	6.07%
5	Georgia	9,613	5.93%
6	New Jersey	8,947	5.52%
7	Pennsylvania	6,738	4.15%
8	Missouri	6,245	3.85%
9	Virginia	5,266	3.25%
10	Ohio	4,831	2.98%
11	South Carolina	4,049	2.50%
12	Maryland	3,913	2.41%
13	Wisconsin	3,586	2.21%
14	Oregon	3,584	2.21%
15	Tennessee	3,176	1.96%
16	Kansas	3,163	1.95%
17	Alabama	2,728	1.68%
18	Kentucky	2,674	1.65%
19	Arkansas	2,390	1.47%
20	Colorado	2,231	1.38%
21	Louisiana	1,752	1.08%
22	Nevada	1,648	1.02%
23	Iowa	1,635	1.01%
24	Utah	1,545	0.95%
25	Massachusetts	1,408	0.87%
26	Mississippi	1,366	0.84%
27	New Mexico	1,249	0.77%
28	Arizona	981	0.60%
29	Nebraska	841	0.52%
30	Hawaii	778	0.48%
31	Oklahoma	749	0.46%
32	New Hampshire	607	0.37%
33	West Virginia	566	0.35%
34	Idaho	514	0.32%
35	Connecticut	482	0.30%
36	Rhode Island	468	0.29%
37	South Dakota	427	0.26%
38	Montana	419	0.26%
39	Washington	347	0.21%
40	Vermont	239	0.15%
41	Florida	223	0.14%
42	Wyoming	145	0.09%
43	North Dakota	115	0.07%
44	Delaware	104	0.06%
45	Alaska	47	0.03%
46	Illinois	38	0.02%
47	Minnesota	19	0.01%
48	Indiana	5	0.00%
49	Maine	4	0.00%
50	California	0	0.00%
	District of Columbia	2,003	1.24%

Source: U.S. Department of Justice, Bureau of Justice Statistics
   "Correctional Populations in the United States, 1993" (October 1995, NCJ 156241)
*Does not include 3,009 federal prisoners released on parole.

State Prisoners Released on Probation in 1993

National Total = 23,094 Prisoners*

ALPHA ORDER

RANK	STATE	PRISONERS	% of USA
3	Alabama	2,024	8.76%
11	Alaska	718	3.11%
20	Arizona	224	0.97%
31	Arkansas	0	0.00%
31	California	0	0.00%
21	Colorado	152	0.66%
31	Connecticut	0	0.00%
31	Delaware	0	0.00%
6	Florida	1,709	7.40%
28	Georgia	32	0.14%
13	Hawaii	658	2.85%
14	Idaho	644	2.79%
31	Illinois	0	0.00%
2	Indiana	2,638	11.42%
18	Iowa	341	1.48%
15	Kansas	532	2.30%
12	Kentucky	690	2.99%
17	Louisiana	371	1.61%
16	Maine	425	1.84%
31	Maryland	0	0.00%
31	Massachusetts	0	0.00%
31	Michigan	0	0.00%
31	Minnesota	0	0.00%
10	Mississippi	841	3.64%
5	Missouri	1,727	7.48%
22	Montana	119	0.52%
31	Nebraska	0	0.00%
31	Nevada	0	0.00%
25	New Hampshire	62	0.27%
31	New Jersey	0	0.00%
31	New Mexico	0	0.00%
31	New York	0	0.00%
30	North Carolina	19	0.08%
23	North Dakota	101	0.44%
1	Ohio	3,159	13.68%
4	Oklahoma	1,799	7.79%
31	Oregon	0	0.00%
31	Pennsylvania	0	0.00%
19	Rhode Island	314	1.36%
7	South Carolina	1,397	6.05%
27	South Dakota	48	0.21%
9	Tennessee	1,076	4.66%
8	Texas	1,097	4.75%
31	Utah	0	0.00%
26	Vermont	51	0.22%
31	Virginia	0	0.00%
31	Washington	0	0.00%
29	West Virginia	26	0.11%
31	Wisconsin	0	0.00%
24	Wyoming	100	0.43%

RANK ORDER

RANK	STATE	PRISONERS	% of USA
1	Ohio	3,159	13.68%
2	Indiana	2,638	11.42%
3	Alabama	2,024	8.76%
4	Oklahoma	1,799	7.79%
5	Missouri	1,727	7.48%
6	Florida	1,709	7.40%
7	South Carolina	1,397	6.05%
8	Texas	1,097	4.75%
9	Tennessee	1,076	4.66%
10	Mississippi	841	3.64%
11	Alaska	718	3.11%
12	Kentucky	690	2.99%
13	Hawaii	658	2.85%
14	Idaho	644	2.79%
15	Kansas	532	2.30%
16	Maine	425	1.84%
17	Louisiana	371	1.61%
18	Iowa	341	1.48%
19	Rhode Island	314	1.36%
20	Arizona	224	0.97%
21	Colorado	152	0.66%
22	Montana	119	0.52%
23	North Dakota	101	0.44%
24	Wyoming	100	0.43%
25	New Hampshire	62	0.27%
26	Vermont	51	0.22%
27	South Dakota	48	0.21%
28	Georgia	32	0.14%
29	West Virginia	26	0.11%
30	North Carolina	19	0.08%
31	Arkansas	0	0.00%
31	California	0	0.00%
31	Connecticut	0	0.00%
31	Delaware	0	0.00%
31	Illinois	0	0.00%
31	Maryland	0	0.00%
31	Massachusetts	0	0.00%
31	Michigan	0	0.00%
31	Minnesota	0	0.00%
31	Nebraska	0	0.00%
31	Nevada	0	0.00%
31	New Jersey	0	0.00%
31	New Mexico	0	0.00%
31	New York	0	0.00%
31	Oregon	0	0.00%
31	Pennsylvania	0	0.00%
31	Utah	0	0.00%
31	Virginia	0	0.00%
31	Washington	0	0.00%
31	Wisconsin	0	0.00%
	District of Columbia	0	0.00%

Source: U.S. Department of Justice, Bureau of Justice Statistics
    "Correctional Populations in the United States, 1993" (October 1995, NCJ 156241)
*Does not include 15 federal prisoners released on probation. Of states showing no prisoners released on
probation, only Utah has a probation program.

State Prisoners Released on Supervised Mandatory Release in 1993

National Total = 132,061 Prisoners*

RANK STATE	PRISONERS	% of USA	RANK STATE	PRISONERS	% of USA
ALPHA ORDER			**RANK ORDER**		
15 Alabama	0	0.00%	1 California	82,526	62.49%
13 Alaska	251	0.19%	2 Illinois	17,419	13.19%
14 Arizona	147	0.11%	3 Louisiana	7,361	5.57%
15 Arkansas	0	0.00%	4 Virginia	4,624	3.50%
1 California	82,526	62.49%	5 Texas	4,153	3.14%
15 Colorado	0	0.00%	6 Maryland	3,490	2.64%
15 Connecticut	0	0.00%	7 New York	3,374	2.55%
12 Delaware	401	0.30%	8 Indiana	2,989	2.26%
15 Florida	0	0.00%	9 Washington	2,728	2.07%
15 Georgia	0	0.00%	10 Minnesota	1,859	1.41%
15 Hawaii	0	0.00%	11 Wisconsin	576	0.44%
15 Idaho	0	0.00%	12 Delaware	401	0.30%
2 Illinois	17,419	13.19%	13 Alaska	251	0.19%
8 Indiana	2,989	2.26%	14 Arizona	147	0.11%
15 Iowa	0	0.00%	15 Alabama	0	0.00%
15 Kansas	0	0.00%	15 Arkansas	0	0.00%
15 Kentucky	0	0.00%	15 Colorado	0	0.00%
3 Louisiana	7,361	5.57%	15 Connecticut	0	0.00%
15 Maine	0	0.00%	15 Florida	0	0.00%
6 Maryland	3,490	2.64%	15 Georgia	0	0.00%
15 Massachusetts	0	0.00%	15 Hawaii	0	0.00%
15 Michigan	0	0.00%	15 Idaho	0	0.00%
10 Minnesota	1,859	1.41%	15 Iowa	0	0.00%
15 Mississippi	0	0.00%	15 Kansas	0	0.00%
15 Missouri	0	0.00%	15 Kentucky	0	0.00%
15 Montana	0	0.00%	15 Maine	0	0.00%
15 Nebraska	0	0.00%	15 Massachusetts	0	0.00%
15 Nevada	0	0.00%	15 Michigan	0	0.00%
15 New Hampshire	0	0.00%	15 Mississippi	0	0.00%
15 New Jersey	0	0.00%	15 Missouri	0	0.00%
15 New Mexico	0	0.00%	15 Montana	0	0.00%
7 New York	3,374	2.55%	15 Nebraska	0	0.00%
15 North Carolina	0	0.00%	15 Nevada	0	0.00%
15 North Dakota	0	0.00%	15 New Hampshire	0	0.00%
15 Ohio	0	0.00%	15 New Jersey	0	0.00%
15 Oklahoma	0	0.00%	15 New Mexico	0	0.00%
15 Oregon	0	0.00%	15 North Carolina	0	0.00%
15 Pennsylvania	0	0.00%	15 North Dakota	0	0.00%
15 Rhode Island	0	0.00%	15 Ohio	0	0.00%
15 South Carolina	0	0.00%	15 Oklahoma	0	0.00%
15 South Dakota	0	0.00%	15 Oregon	0	0.00%
15 Tennessee	0	0.00%	15 Pennsylvania	0	0.00%
5 Texas	4,153	3.14%	15 Rhode Island	0	0.00%
15 Utah	0	0.00%	15 South Carolina	0	0.00%
15 Vermont	0	0.00%	15 South Dakota	0	0.00%
4 Virginia	4,624	3.50%	15 Tennessee	0	0.00%
9 Washington	2,728	2.07%	15 Utah	0	0.00%
15 West Virginia	0	0.00%	15 Vermont	0	0.00%
11 Wisconsin	576	0.44%	15 West Virginia	0	0.00%
15 Wyoming	0	0.00%	15 Wyoming	0	0.00%
			District of Columbia	163	0.12%

Source: U.S. Department of Justice, Bureau of Justice Statistics
   "Correctional Populations in the United States, 1993" (October 1995, NCJ 156241)
*Does not include 2,718 federal prisoners on supervised mandatory release. Of states showing no prisoners
released on supervised mandatory release, only Hawaii, Maine, Missouri, Montana, South Carolina and Utah have
such a program.

State Prisoners Released Unconditionally in 1993

National Total = 56,835 Prisoners*

ALPHA ORDER

RANK	STATE	PRISONERS	% of USA
3	Alabama	2,351	4.14%
32	Alaska	331	0.58%
31	Arizona	359	0.63%
18	Arkansas	880	1.55%
16	California	1,038	1.83%
14	Colorado	1,073	1.89%
11	Connecticut	1,579	2.78%
29	Delaware	453	0.80%
2	Florida	7,227	12.72%
12	Georgia	1,538	2.71%
38	Hawaii	223	0.39%
40	Idaho	158	0.28%
35	Illinois	286	0.50%
25	Indiana	584	1.03%
34	Iowa	306	0.54%
46	Kansas	100	0.18%
7	Kentucky	2,158	3.80%
28	Louisiana	519	0.91%
32	Maine	331	0.58%
20	Maryland	867	1.53%
4	Massachusetts	2,263	3.98%
22	Michigan	779	1.37%
36	Minnesota	256	0.45%
10	Mississippi	1,583	2.79%
24	Missouri	589	1.04%
47	Montana	97	0.17%
26	Nebraska	574	1.01%
13	Nevada	1,379	2.43%
41	New Hampshire	152	0.27%
8	New Jersey	1,885	3.32%
23	New Mexico	600	1.06%
15	New York	1,051	1.85%
30	North Carolina	365	0.64%
45	North Dakota	101	0.18%
1	Ohio	12,012	21.13%
6	Oklahoma	2,222	3.91%
50	Oregon	16	0.03%
21	Pennsylvania	821	1.44%
49	Rhode Island	17	0.03%
5	South Carolina	2,245	3.95%
37	South Dakota	241	0.42%
17	Tennessee	908	1.60%
27	Texas	541	0.95%
39	Utah	170	0.30%
44	Vermont	105	0.18%
19	Virginia	874	1.54%
9	Washington	1,694	2.98%
43	West Virginia	108	0.19%
48	Wisconsin	92	0.16%
42	Wyoming	143	0.25%

RANK ORDER

RANK	STATE	PRISONERS	% of USA
1	Ohio	12,012	21.13%
2	Florida	7,227	12.72%
3	Alabama	2,351	4.14%
4	Massachusetts	2,263	3.98%
5	South Carolina	2,245	3.95%
6	Oklahoma	2,222	3.91%
7	Kentucky	2,158	3.80%
8	New Jersey	1,885	3.32%
9	Washington	1,694	2.98%
10	Mississippi	1,583	2.79%
11	Connecticut	1,579	2.78%
12	Georgia	1,538	2.71%
13	Nevada	1,379	2.43%
14	Colorado	1,073	1.89%
15	New York	1,051	1.85%
16	California	1,038	1.83%
17	Tennessee	908	1.60%
18	Arkansas	880	1.55%
19	Virginia	874	1.54%
20	Maryland	867	1.53%
21	Pennsylvania	821	1.44%
22	Michigan	779	1.37%
23	New Mexico	600	1.06%
24	Missouri	589	1.04%
25	Indiana	584	1.03%
26	Nebraska	574	1.01%
27	Texas	541	0.95%
28	Louisiana	519	0.91%
29	Delaware	453	0.80%
30	North Carolina	365	0.64%
31	Arizona	359	0.63%
32	Alaska	331	0.58%
32	Maine	331	0.58%
34	Iowa	306	0.54%
35	Illinois	286	0.50%
36	Minnesota	256	0.45%
37	South Dakota	241	0.42%
38	Hawaii	223	0.39%
39	Utah	170	0.30%
40	Idaho	158	0.28%
41	New Hampshire	152	0.27%
42	Wyoming	143	0.25%
43	West Virginia	108	0.19%
44	Vermont	105	0.18%
45	North Dakota	101	0.18%
46	Kansas	100	0.18%
47	Montana	97	0.17%
48	Wisconsin	92	0.16%
49	Rhode Island	17	0.03%
50	Oregon	16	0.03%
	District of Columbia	591	1.04%

Source: U.S. Department of Justice, Bureau of Justice Statistics
"Correctional Populations in the United States, 1993" (October 1995, NCJ 156241)
*Does not include 12,801 federal prisoners released without conditions.

State Prisoners Released Unconditionally as a Percent of All Releases in 1993

National Percent = 13.00% of Released Prisoners*

ALPHA ORDER				RANK ORDER		
RANK	STATE	PERCENT		RANK	STATE	PERCENT
13	Alabama	31.31		1	Ohio	59.11
22	Alaska	17.85		2	Nevada	44.30
40	Arizona	5.23		3	Massachusetts	43.08
21	Arkansas	21.74		4	Maine	41.22
49	California	1.17		5	Mississippi	40.75
18	Colorado	26.53		6	Oklahoma	40.69
17	Connecticut	27.11		7	Nebraska	39.97
9	Delaware	36.21		8	Kentucky	37.54
19	Florida	26.10		9	Delaware	36.21
29	Georgia	12.01		10	Washington	34.12
28	Hawaii	13.00		11	South Dakota	31.96
30	Idaho	11.13		12	Wyoming	31.85
47	Illinois	1.52		13	Alabama	31.31
35	Indiana	9.33		14	North Dakota	30.24
34	Iowa	9.47		15	South Carolina	28.40
44	Kansas	2.41		16	New Mexico	28.37
8	Kentucky	37.54		17	Connecticut	27.11
41	Louisiana	4.99		18	Colorado	26.53
4	Maine	41.22		19	Florida	26.10
31	Maryland	10.22		20	Vermont	22.39
3	Massachusetts	43.08		21	Arkansas	21.74
38	Michigan	6.29		22	Alaska	17.85
33	Minnesota	9.63		23	New Jersey	16.39
5	Mississippi	40.75		24	Tennessee	15.87
39	Missouri	6.00		25	New Hampshire	15.85
27	Montana	14.12		26	West Virginia	14.38
7	Nebraska	39.97		27	Montana	14.12
2	Nevada	44.30		28	Hawaii	13.00
25	New Hampshire	15.85		29	Georgia	12.01
23	New Jersey	16.39		30	Idaho	11.13
16	New Mexico	28.37		31	Maryland	10.22
42	New York	3.19		32	Utah	9.77
48	North Carolina	1.51		33	Minnesota	9.63
14	North Dakota	30.24		34	Iowa	9.47
1	Ohio	59.11		35	Indiana	9.33
6	Oklahoma	40.69		36	Pennsylvania	9.31
50	Oregon	0.43		37	Virginia	8.06
36	Pennsylvania	9.31		38	Michigan	6.29
46	Rhode Island	1.96		39	Missouri	6.00
15	South Carolina	28.40		40	Arizona	5.23
11	South Dakota	31.96		41	Louisiana	4.99
24	Tennessee	15.87		42	New York	3.19
43	Texas	2.67		43	Texas	2.67
32	Utah	9.77		44	Kansas	2.41
20	Vermont	22.39		45	Wisconsin	1.98
37	Virginia	8.06		46	Rhode Island	1.96
10	Washington	34.12		47	Illinois	1.52
26	West Virginia	14.38		48	North Carolina	1.51
45	Wisconsin	1.98		49	California	1.17
12	Wyoming	31.85		50	Oregon	0.43
					District of Columbia	9.72

Source: Morgan Quitno Press using data from U.S. Department of Justice, Bureau of Justice Statistics
   "Correctional Populations in the United States, 1993" (October 1995, NCJ 156241)
*Does not include federal prisoners released without conditions. Federal percent is 66.30% of releases. The
combined state and federal percent is 15.26% of prisoners released are released without conditions.

State Prisoners Released on Appeal or Bond in 1993

National Total = 1,090 Prisoners*

ALPHA ORDER

RANK	STATE	PRISONERS	% of USA
3	Alabama	72	6.61%
20	Alaska	8	0.73%
29	Arizona	0	0.00%
12	Arkansas	24	2.20%
NA	California**	NA	NA
14	Colorado	16	1.47%
1	Connecticut	317	29.08%
29	Delaware	0	0.00%
NA	Florida**	NA	NA
NA	Georgia**	NA	NA
29	Hawaii	0	0.00%
25	Idaho	4	0.37%
11	Illinois	29	2.66%
NA	Indiana**	NA	NA
10	Iowa	30	2.75%
20	Kansas	8	0.73%
NA	Kentucky**	NA	NA
4	Louisiana	70	6.42%
22	Maine	7	0.64%
NA	Maryland**	NA	NA
29	Massachusetts	0	0.00%
6	Michigan	47	4.31%
NA	Minnesota**	NA	NA
NA	Mississippi**	NA	NA
14	Missouri	16	1.47%
29	Montana	0	0.00%
NA	Nebraska**	NA	NA
27	Nevada	3	0.28%
23	New Hampshire	6	0.55%
5	New Jersey	56	5.14%
25	New Mexico	4	0.37%
2	New York	181	16.61%
29	North Carolina	0	0.00%
NA	North Dakota**	NA	NA
7	Ohio	45	4.13%
29	Oklahoma	0	0.00%
13	Oregon	17	1.56%
8	Pennsylvania	36	3.30%
19	Rhode Island	12	1.10%
17	South Carolina	13	1.19%
28	South Dakota	2	0.18%
NA	Tennessee**	NA	NA
NA	Texas**	NA	NA
14	Utah	16	1.47%
NA	Vermont**	NA	NA
17	Virginia	13	1.19%
9	Washington	31	2.84%
29	West Virginia	0	0.00%
NA	Wisconsin**	NA	NA
23	Wyoming	6	0.55%

RANK ORDER

RANK	STATE	PRISONERS	% of USA
1	Connecticut	317	29.08%
2	New York	181	16.61%
3	Alabama	72	6.61%
4	Louisiana	70	6.42%
5	New Jersey	56	5.14%
6	Michigan	47	4.31%
7	Ohio	45	4.13%
8	Pennsylvania	36	3.30%
9	Washington	31	2.84%
10	Iowa	30	2.75%
11	Illinois	29	2.66%
12	Arkansas	24	2.20%
13	Oregon	17	1.56%
14	Colorado	16	1.47%
14	Missouri	16	1.47%
14	Utah	16	1.47%
17	South Carolina	13	1.19%
17	Virginia	13	1.19%
19	Rhode Island	12	1.10%
20	Alaska	8	0.73%
20	Kansas	8	0.73%
22	Maine	7	0.64%
23	New Hampshire	6	0.55%
23	Wyoming	6	0.55%
25	Idaho	4	0.37%
25	New Mexico	4	0.37%
27	Nevada	3	0.28%
28	South Dakota	2	0.18%
29	Arizona	0	0.00%
29	Delaware	0	0.00%
29	Hawaii	0	0.00%
29	Massachusetts	0	0.00%
29	Montana	0	0.00%
29	North Carolina	0	0.00%
29	Oklahoma	0	0.00%
29	West Virginia	0	0.00%
NA	California**	NA	NA
NA	Florida**	NA	NA
NA	Georgia**	NA	NA
NA	Indiana**	NA	NA
NA	Kentucky**	NA	NA
NA	Maryland**	NA	NA
NA	Minnesota**	NA	NA
NA	Mississippi**	NA	NA
NA	Nebraska**	NA	NA
NA	North Dakota**	NA	NA
NA	Tennessee**	NA	NA
NA	Texas**	NA	NA
NA	Vermont**	NA	NA
NA	Wisconsin**	NA	NA
	District of Columbia**	NA	NA

Source: U.S. Department of Justice, Bureau of Justice Statistics
   "Correctional Populations in the United States, 1993" (October 1995, NCJ 156241)
*Does not include 16 federal prisoners released on appeal or bond.
**Not available or applicable.

State Prisoners Escaped in 1993

National Total = 14,035 Prisoners*

ALPHA ORDER					RANK ORDER			
RANK	STATE		PRISONERS	% of USA	RANK	STATE	PRISONERS	% of USA
10	Alabama		206	1.47%	1	New York	4,844	34.51%
31	Alaska		24	0.17%	2	Michigan	1,511	10.77%
30	Arizona		25	0.18%	3	California	1,104	7.87%
38	Arkansas		11	0.08%	4	Illinois	888	6.33%
3	California		1,104	7.87%	5	Missouri	515	3.67%
7	Colorado		343	2.44%	6	Oklahoma	474	3.38%
9	Connecticut		236	1.68%	7	Colorado	343	2.44%
18	Delaware		102	0.73%	8	Florida	269	1.92%
8	Florida		269	1.92%	9	Connecticut	236	1.68%
14	Georgia		141	1.00%	10	Alabama	206	1.47%
44	Hawaii		8	0.06%	11	North Carolina	190	1.35%
36	Idaho		15	0.11%	12	Maryland	164	1.17%
4	Illinois		888	6.33%	13	New Jersey	160	1.14%
38	Indiana		11	0.08%	14	Georgia	141	1.00%
45	Iowa		7	0.05%	14	Washington	141	1.00%
29	Kansas		30	0.21%	16	South Carolina	132	0.94%
17	Kentucky		111	0.79%	17	Kentucky	111	0.79%
22	Louisiana		67	0.48%	18	Delaware	102	0.73%
42	Maine		9	0.06%	19	Oregon	98	0.70%
12	Maryland		164	1.17%	20	Tennessee	95	0.68%
24	Massachusetts		59	0.42%	21	Nevada	73	0.52%
2	Michigan		1,511	10.77%	22	Louisiana	67	0.48%
NA	Minnesota**		NA	NA	23	Vermont	64	0.46%
31	Mississippi		24	0.17%	24	Massachusetts	59	0.42%
5	Missouri		515	3.67%	25	Montana	49	0.35%
25	Montana		49	0.35%	26	Rhode Island	48	0.34%
40	Nebraska		10	0.07%	27	New Mexico	36	0.26%
21	Nevada		73	0.52%	28	West Virginia	31	0.22%
34	New Hampshire		20	0.14%	29	Kansas	30	0.21%
13	New Jersey		160	1.14%	30	Arizona	25	0.18%
27	New Mexico		36	0.26%	31	Alaska	24	0.17%
1	New York		4,844	34.51%	31	Mississippi	24	0.17%
11	North Carolina		190	1.35%	33	Wyoming	22	0.16%
47	North Dakota		2	0.01%	34	New Hampshire	20	0.14%
37	Ohio		13	0.09%	35	South Dakota	18	0.13%
6	Oklahoma		474	3.38%	36	Idaho	15	0.11%
19	Oregon		98	0.70%	37	Ohio	13	0.09%
42	Pennsylvania		9	0.06%	38	Arkansas	11	0.08%
26	Rhode Island		48	0.34%	38	Indiana	11	0.08%
16	South Carolina		132	0.94%	40	Nebraska	10	0.07%
35	South Dakota		18	0.13%	40	Texas	10	0.07%
20	Tennessee		95	0.68%	42	Maine	9	0.06%
40	Texas		10	0.07%	42	Pennsylvania	9	0.06%
45	Utah		7	0.05%	44	Hawaii	8	0.06%
23	Vermont		64	0.46%	45	Iowa	7	0.05%
NA	Virginia**		NA	NA	45	Utah	7	0.05%
14	Washington		141	1.00%	47	North Dakota	2	0.01%
28	West Virginia		31	0.22%	NA	Minnesota**	NA	NA
NA	Wisconsin**		NA	NA	NA	Virginia**	NA	NA
33	Wyoming		22	0.16%	NA	Wisconsin**	NA	NA
						District of Columbia	1,608	11.46%

Source: U.S. Department of Justice, Bureau of Justice Statistics
   "Correctional Populations in the United States, 1993" (October 1995, NCJ 156241)
*Includes AWOLs.
**Not available.

State Prisoner Deaths in 1993

National Total = 2,477 Prisoners

ALPHA ORDER

RANK	STATE	DEATHS	% of USA
15	Alabama	55	2.22%
28	Alaska	15	0.61%
18	Arizona	43	1.74%
30	Arkansas	10	0.40%
2	California	245	9.89%
28	Colorado	15	0.61%
8	Connecticut	91	3.67%
35	Delaware	8	0.32%
4	Florida	167	6.74%
9	Georgia	81	3.27%
46	Hawaii	2	0.08%
35	Idaho	8	0.32%
7	Illinois	103	4.16%
21	Indiana	30	1.21%
38	Iowa	7	0.28%
30	Kansas	10	0.40%
24	Kentucky	26	1.05%
12	Louisiana	63	2.54%
40	Maine	5	0.20%
17	Maryland	46	1.86%
23	Massachusetts	29	1.17%
6	Michigan	106	4.28%
40	Minnesota	5	0.20%
25	Mississippi	24	0.97%
18	Missouri	43	1.74%
44	Montana	3	0.12%
35	Nebraska	8	0.32%
30	Nevada	10	0.40%
43	New Hampshire	4	0.16%
5	New Jersey	121	4.88%
39	New Mexico	6	0.24%
1	New York	377	15.22%
20	North Carolina	41	1.66%
49	North Dakota	0	0.00%
10	Ohio	80	3.23%
14	Oklahoma	56	2.26%
33	Oregon	9	0.36%
11	Pennsylvania	79	3.19%
44	Rhode Island	3	0.12%
12	South Carolina	63	2.54%
33	South Dakota	9	0.36%
21	Tennessee	30	1.21%
3	Texas	244	9.85%
46	Utah	2	0.08%
49	Vermont	0	0.00%
16	Virginia	50	2.02%
26	Washington	20	0.81%
48	West Virginia	1	0.04%
27	Wisconsin	19	0.77%
40	Wyoming	5	0.20%

RANK ORDER

RANK	STATE	DEATHS	% of USA
1	New York	377	15.22%
2	California	245	9.89%
3	Texas	244	9.85%
4	Florida	167	6.74%
5	New Jersey	121	4.88%
6	Michigan	106	4.28%
7	Illinois	103	4.16%
8	Connecticut	91	3.67%
9	Georgia	81	3.27%
10	Ohio	80	3.23%
11	Pennsylvania	79	3.19%
12	Louisiana	63	2.54%
12	South Carolina	63	2.54%
14	Oklahoma	56	2.26%
15	Alabama	55	2.22%
16	Virginia	50	2.02%
17	Maryland	46	1.86%
18	Arizona	43	1.74%
18	Missouri	43	1.74%
20	North Carolina	41	1.66%
21	Indiana	30	1.21%
21	Tennessee	30	1.21%
23	Massachusetts	29	1.17%
24	Kentucky	26	1.05%
25	Mississippi	24	0.97%
26	Washington	20	0.81%
27	Wisconsin	19	0.77%
28	Alaska	15	0.61%
28	Colorado	15	0.61%
30	Arkansas	10	0.40%
30	Kansas	10	0.40%
30	Nevada	10	0.40%
33	Oregon	9	0.36%
33	South Dakota	9	0.36%
35	Delaware	8	0.32%
35	Idaho	8	0.32%
35	Nebraska	8	0.32%
38	Iowa	7	0.28%
39	New Mexico	6	0.24%
40	Maine	5	0.20%
40	Minnesota	5	0.20%
40	Wyoming	5	0.20%
43	New Hampshire	4	0.16%
44	Montana	3	0.12%
44	Rhode Island	3	0.12%
46	Hawaii	2	0.08%
46	Utah	2	0.08%
48	West Virginia	1	0.04%
49	North Dakota	0	0.00%
49	Vermont	0	0.00%
	District of Columbia*	NA	NA

Source: U.S. Department of Justice, Bureau of Justice Statistics
"HIV in U.S. Prisons and Jails, 1993" (Bulletin, August 1995, NCJ-152765)
*Not available.

Death Rate of State Prisoners in 1993

National Rate = 290 State Prisoner Deaths per 100,000 Inmates

ALPHA ORDER

RANK	STATE	RATE
15	Alabama	300
5	Alaska	512
22	Arizona	253
44	Arkansas	114
30	California	212
38	Colorado	163
1	Connecticut	754
36	Delaware	187
10	Florida	330
15	Georgia	300
47	Hawaii	65
14	Idaho	307
12	Illinois	311
31	Indiana	211
41	Iowa	149
39	Kansas	161
24	Kentucky	247
19	Louisiana	287
8	Maine	340
27	Maryland	228
17	Massachusetts	291
20	Michigan	266
43	Minnesota	117
23	Mississippi	250
21	Missouri	260
32	Montana	208
11	Nebraska	314
40	Nevada	154
28	New Hampshire	227
4	New Jersey	530
37	New Mexico	174
2	New York	590
34	North Carolina	194
49	North Dakota	0
33	Ohio	201
7	Oklahoma	357
42	Oregon	136
13	Pennsylvania	309
45	Rhode Island	106
9	South Carolina	333
3	South Dakota	585
25	Tennessee	239
18	Texas	289
46	Utah	71
49	Vermont	0
26	Virginia	229
35	Washington	193
48	West Virginia	54
29	Wisconsin	226
6	Wyoming	472

RANK ORDER

RANK	STATE	RATE
1	Connecticut	754
2	New York	590
3	South Dakota	585
4	New Jersey	530
5	Alaska	512
6	Wyoming	472
7	Oklahoma	357
8	Maine	340
9	South Carolina	333
10	Florida	330
11	Nebraska	314
12	Illinois	311
13	Pennsylvania	309
14	Idaho	307
15	Alabama	300
15	Georgia	300
17	Massachusetts	291
18	Texas	289
19	Louisiana	287
20	Michigan	266
21	Missouri	260
22	Arizona	253
23	Mississippi	250
24	Kentucky	247
25	Tennessee	239
26	Virginia	229
27	Maryland	228
28	New Hampshire	227
29	Wisconsin	226
30	California	212
31	Indiana	211
32	Montana	208
33	Ohio	201
34	North Carolina	194
35	Washington	193
36	Delaware	187
37	New Mexico	174
38	Colorado	163
39	Kansas	161
40	Nevada	154
41	Iowa	149
42	Oregon	136
43	Minnesota	117
44	Arkansas	114
45	Rhode Island	106
46	Utah	71
47	Hawaii	65
48	West Virginia	54
49	North Dakota	0
49	Vermont	0
	District of Columbia*	NA

Source: U.S. Department of Justice, Bureau of Justice Statistics
  "HIV in U.S. Prisons and Jails, 1993" (Bulletin, August 1995, NCJ-152765)
Not available.

State Prisoner Deaths by Illness or Other Natural Causes in 1993

National Total = 1,188 Deaths*

ALPHA ORDER

RANK	STATE	DEATHS	% of USA
NA	Alabama**	NA	NA
37	Alaska	3	0.25%
12	Arizona	34	2.86%
26	Arkansas	9	0.76%
4	California	95	8.00%
25	Colorado	10	0.84%
NA	Connecticut**	NA	NA
31	Delaware	6	0.51%
5	Florida	76	6.40%
13	Georgia	32	2.69%
40	Hawaii	2	0.17%
37	Idaho	3	0.25%
7	Illinois	63	5.30%
14	Indiana	26	2.19%
29	Iowa	7	0.59%
28	Kansas	8	0.67%
18	Kentucky	21	1.77%
NA	Louisiana**	NA	NA
34	Maine	4	0.34%
18	Maryland	21	1.77%
24	Massachusetts	12	1.01%
2	Michigan	98	8.25%
34	Minnesota	4	0.34%
21	Mississippi	18	1.52%
14	Missouri	26	2.19%
37	Montana	3	0.25%
31	Nebraska	6	0.51%
29	Nevada	7	0.59%
41	New Hampshire	1	0.08%
10	New Jersey	38	3.20%
NA	New Mexico**	NA	NA
3	New York	97	8.16%
16	North Carolina	24	2.02%
45	North Dakota	0	0.00%
8	Ohio	57	4.80%
11	Oklahoma	37	3.11%
31	Oregon	6	0.51%
6	Pennsylvania	65	5.47%
41	Rhode Island	1	0.08%
9	South Carolina	46	3.87%
26	South Dakota	9	0.76%
20	Tennessee	20	1.68%
1	Texas	129	10.86%
41	Utah	1	0.08%
45	Vermont	0	0.00%
16	Virginia	24	2.02%
21	Washington	18	1.52%
41	West Virginia	1	0.08%
23	Wisconsin	16	1.35%
34	Wyoming	4	0.34%

RANK ORDER

RANK	STATE	DEATHS	% of USA
1	Texas	129	10.86%
2	Michigan	98	8.25%
3	New York	97	8.16%
4	California	95	8.00%
5	Florida	76	6.40%
6	Pennsylvania	65	5.47%
7	Illinois	63	5.30%
8	Ohio	57	4.80%
9	South Carolina	46	3.87%
10	New Jersey	38	3.20%
11	Oklahoma	37	3.11%
12	Arizona	34	2.86%
13	Georgia	32	2.69%
14	Indiana	26	2.19%
14	Missouri	26	2.19%
16	North Carolina	24	2.02%
16	Virginia	24	2.02%
18	Kentucky	21	1.77%
18	Maryland	21	1.77%
20	Tennessee	20	1.68%
21	Mississippi	18	1.52%
21	Washington	18	1.52%
23	Wisconsin	16	1.35%
24	Massachusetts	12	1.01%
25	Colorado	10	0.84%
26	Arkansas	9	0.76%
26	South Dakota	9	0.76%
28	Kansas	8	0.67%
29	Iowa	7	0.59%
29	Nevada	7	0.59%
31	Delaware	6	0.51%
31	Nebraska	6	0.51%
31	Oregon	6	0.51%
34	Maine	4	0.34%
34	Minnesota	4	0.34%
34	Wyoming	4	0.34%
37	Alaska	3	0.25%
37	Idaho	3	0.25%
37	Montana	3	0.25%
40	Hawaii	2	0.17%
41	New Hampshire	1	0.08%
41	Rhode Island	1	0.08%
41	Utah	1	0.08%
41	West Virginia	1	0.08%
45	North Dakota	0	0.00%
45	Vermont	0	0.00%
NA	Alabama**	NA	NA
NA	Connecticut**	NA	NA
NA	Louisiana**	NA	NA
NA	New Mexico**	NA	NA
	District of Columbia**	NA	NA

Source: U.S. Department of Justice, Bureau of Justice Statistics
  "Correctional Populations in the United States, 1993" (October 1995, NCJ 156241)
*Excludes AIDS.
**Not available.

Deaths of State Prisoners by Illness or Other Natural Causes
As a Percent of All Prison Deaths in 1993
National Percent = 48.85% of Deaths*

ALPHA ORDER

RANK	STATE	PERCENT
NA	Alabama**	NA
44	Alaska	20.00
17	Arizona	75.56
7	Arkansas	90.00
34	California	47.50
24	Colorado	66.67
NA	Connecticut**	NA
18	Delaware	75.00
36	Florida	45.51
38	Georgia	39.51
1	Hawaii	100.00
39	Idaho	37.50
28	Illinois	61.17
9	Indiana	86.67
1	Iowa	100.00
13	Kansas	80.00
12	Kentucky	80.77
NA	Louisiana**	NA
13	Maine	80.00
35	Maryland	45.65
37	Massachusetts	41.38
6	Michigan	92.45
13	Minnesota	80.00
18	Mississippi	75.00
29	Missouri	60.47
1	Montana	100.00
18	Nebraska	75.00
23	Nevada	70.00
43	New Hampshire	25.00
41	New Jersey	31.40
NA	New Mexico**	NA
42	New York	25.73
30	North Carolina	58.54
45	North Dakota	0.00
22	Ohio	72.15
27	Oklahoma	66.07
24	Oregon	66.67
11	Pennsylvania	82.28
40	Rhode Island	33.33
21	South Carolina	73.02
1	South Dakota	100.00
24	Tennessee	66.67
31	Texas	52.87
32	Utah	50.00
45	Vermont	0.00
33	Virginia	48.00
7	Washington	90.00
1	West Virginia	100.00
10	Wisconsin	84.21
13	Wyoming	80.00

RANK ORDER

RANK	STATE	PERCENT
1	Hawaii	100.00
1	Iowa	100.00
1	Montana	100.00
1	South Dakota	100.00
1	West Virginia	100.00
6	Michigan	92.45
7	Arkansas	90.00
7	Washington	90.00
9	Indiana	86.67
10	Wisconsin	84.21
11	Pennsylvania	82.28
12	Kentucky	80.77
13	Kansas	80.00
13	Maine	80.00
13	Minnesota	80.00
13	Wyoming	80.00
17	Arizona	75.56
18	Delaware	75.00
18	Mississippi	75.00
18	Nebraska	75.00
21	South Carolina	73.02
22	Ohio	72.15
23	Nevada	70.00
24	Colorado	66.67
24	Oregon	66.67
24	Tennessee	66.67
27	Oklahoma	66.07
28	Illinois	61.17
29	Missouri	60.47
30	North Carolina	58.54
31	Texas	52.87
32	Utah	50.00
33	Virginia	48.00
34	California	47.50
35	Maryland	45.65
36	Florida	45.51
37	Massachusetts	41.38
38	Georgia	39.51
39	Idaho	37.50
40	Rhode Island	33.33
41	New Jersey	31.40
42	New York	25.73
43	New Hampshire	25.00
44	Alaska	20.00
45	North Dakota	0.00
45	Vermont	0.00
NA	Alabama**	NA
NA	Connecticut**	NA
NA	Louisiana**	NA
NA	New Mexico**	NA

District of Columbia**　　　　NA

*Source: Morgan Quitno Press using data from U.S. Department of Justice, Bureau of Justice Statistics
"Correctional Populations in the United States, 1993" (October 1995, NCJ 156241)*
Excludes AIDS.
**Not available.*

Deaths of State Prisoners by AIDS in 1993

National Total = 761 Deaths

<u>ALPHA ORDER</u>				<u>RANK ORDER</u>			
RANK	STATE	DEATHS	% of USA	RANK	STATE	DEATHS	% of USA
15	Alabama	8	1.05%	1	New York	220	28.91%
29	Alaska	0	0.00%	2	California	83	10.91%
29	Arizona	0	0.00%	3	Florida	79	10.38%
29	Arkansas	0	0.00%	3	Texas	79	10.38%
2	California	83	10.91%	5	New Jersey	70	9.20%
23	Colorado	1	0.13%	6	Connecticut	45	5.91%
6	Connecticut	45	5.91%	7	Georgia	40	5.26%
29	Delaware	0	0.00%	8	Illinois	23	3.02%
3	Florida	79	10.38%	9	Maryland	20	2.63%
7	Georgia	40	5.26%	10	North Carolina	15	1.97%
29	Hawaii	0	0.00%	11	Massachusetts	14	1.84%
23	Idaho	1	0.13%	11	South Carolina	14	1.84%
8	Illinois	23	3.02%	11	Virginia	14	1.84%
23	Indiana	1	0.13%	14	Pennsylvania	9	1.18%
29	Iowa	0	0.00%	15	Alabama	8	1.05%
29	Kansas	0	0.00%	16	Ohio	6	0.79%
19	Kentucky	2	0.26%	17	Tennessee	5	0.66%
NA	Louisiana*	NA	NA	18	Mississippi	3	0.39%
29	Maine	0	0.00%	19	Kentucky	2	0.26%
9	Maryland	20	2.63%	19	Missouri	2	0.26%
11	Massachusetts	14	1.84%	19	Oklahoma	2	0.26%
NA	Michigan*	NA	NA	19	Rhode Island	2	0.26%
23	Minnesota	1	0.13%	23	Colorado	1	0.13%
18	Mississippi	3	0.39%	23	Idaho	1	0.13%
19	Missouri	2	0.26%	23	Indiana	1	0.13%
29	Montana	0	0.00%	23	Minnesota	1	0.13%
29	Nebraska	0	0.00%	23	Nevada	1	0.13%
23	Nevada	1	0.13%	23	New Hampshire	1	0.13%
23	New Hampshire	1	0.13%	29	Alaska	0	0.00%
5	New Jersey	70	9.20%	29	Arizona	0	0.00%
NA	New Mexico*	NA	NA	29	Arkansas	0	0.00%
1	New York	220	28.91%	29	Delaware	0	0.00%
10	North Carolina	15	1.97%	29	Hawaii	0	0.00%
29	North Dakota	0	0.00%	29	Iowa	0	0.00%
16	Ohio	6	0.79%	29	Kansas	0	0.00%
19	Oklahoma	2	0.26%	29	Maine	0	0.00%
29	Oregon	0	0.00%	29	Montana	0	0.00%
14	Pennsylvania	9	1.18%	29	Nebraska	0	0.00%
19	Rhode Island	2	0.26%	29	North Dakota	0	0.00%
11	South Carolina	14	1.84%	29	Oregon	0	0.00%
NA	South Dakota*	NA	NA	29	Utah	0	0.00%
17	Tennessee	5	0.66%	29	Vermont	0	0.00%
3	Texas	79	10.38%	29	Washington	0	0.00%
29	Utah	0	0.00%	29	West Virginia	0	0.00%
29	Vermont	0	0.00%	29	Wisconsin	0	0.00%
11	Virginia	14	1.84%	29	Wyoming	0	0.00%
29	Washington	0	0.00%	NA	Louisiana*	NA	NA
29	West Virginia	0	0.00%	NA	Michigan*	NA	NA
29	Wisconsin	0	0.00%	NA	New Mexico*	NA	NA
29	Wyoming	0	0.00%	NA	South Dakota*	NA	NA
					District of Columbia*	NA	NA

Source: U.S. Department of Justice, Bureau of Justice Statistics
   "HIV in U.S. Prisons and Jails, 1993" (Bulletin, August 1995, NCJ-152765)
*Not available.

AIDS-Related Death Rate of State Prisoners in 1993

National Rate = 89 State Prisoner Deaths per 100,000 Inmates

ALPHA ORDER				RANK ORDER		
RANK	STATE	RATE		RANK	STATE	RATE
16	Alabama	44		1	Connecticut	373
29	Alaska	0		2	New York	344
29	Arizona	0		3	New Jersey	307
29	Arkansas	0		4	Florida	156
10	California	72		5	Georgia	148
27	Colorado	11		6	Massachusetts	141
1	Connecticut	373		7	Maryland	99
29	Delaware	0		8	Texas	93
4	Florida	156		9	South Carolina	74
5	Georgia	148		10	California	72
29	Hawaii	0		11	North Carolina	71
18	Idaho	38		11	Rhode Island	71
13	Illinois	70		13	Illinois	70
28	Indiana	7		14	Virginia	64
29	Iowa	0		15	New Hampshire	57
29	Kansas	0		16	Alabama	44
22	Kentucky	19		17	Tennessee	40
NA	Louisiana*	NA		18	Idaho	38
29	Maine	0		19	Pennsylvania	35
7	Maryland	99		20	Mississippi	31
6	Massachusetts	141		21	Minnesota	23
NA	Michigan*	NA		22	Kentucky	19
21	Minnesota	23		23	Nevada	15
20	Mississippi	31		23	Ohio	15
26	Missouri	12		25	Oklahoma	13
29	Montana	0		26	Missouri	12
29	Nebraska	0		27	Colorado	11
23	Nevada	15		28	Indiana	7
15	New Hampshire	57		29	Alaska	0
3	New Jersey	307		29	Arizona	0
NA	New Mexico*	NA		29	Arkansas	0
2	New York	344		29	Delaware	0
11	North Carolina	71		29	Hawaii	0
29	North Dakota	0		29	Iowa	0
23	Ohio	15		29	Kansas	0
25	Oklahoma	13		29	Maine	0
29	Oregon	0		29	Montana	0
19	Pennsylvania	35		29	Nebraska	0
11	Rhode Island	71		29	North Dakota	0
9	South Carolina	74		29	Oregon	0
NA	South Dakota*	NA		29	Utah	0
17	Tennessee	40		29	Vermont	0
8	Texas	93		29	Washington	0
29	Utah	0		29	West Virginia	0
29	Vermont	0		29	Wisconsin	0
14	Virginia	64		29	Wyoming	0
29	Washington	0		NA	Louisiana*	NA
29	West Virginia	0		NA	Michigan*	NA
29	Wisconsin	0		NA	New Mexico*	NA
29	Wyoming	0		NA	South Dakota*	NA
					District of Columbia*	NA

Source: U.S. Department of Justice, Bureau of Justice Statistics
   "HIV in U.S. Prisons and Jails, 1993" (Bulletin, August 1995, NCJ-152765)
*Not available.

Deaths of State Prisoners by AIDS as a Percent of All Prison Deaths in 1993

National Percent = 33.2% of Deaths

<table>
<tr><td colspan="3">ALPHA ORDER</td><td colspan="3">RANK ORDER</td></tr>
<tr><th>RANK</th><th>STATE</th><th>PERCENT</th><th>RANK</th><th>STATE</th><th>PERCENT</th></tr>
<tr><td>18</td><td>Alabama</td><td>14.5</td><td>1</td><td>Rhode Island*</td><td>66.7</td></tr>
<tr><td>29</td><td>Alaska</td><td>0.0</td><td>2</td><td>New York</td><td>58.4</td></tr>
<tr><td>29</td><td>Arizona</td><td>0.0</td><td>3</td><td>New Jersey</td><td>57.9</td></tr>
<tr><td>29</td><td>Arkansas</td><td>0.0</td><td>4</td><td>Connecticut</td><td>49.5</td></tr>
<tr><td>10</td><td>California</td><td>34.0</td><td>5</td><td>Georgia</td><td>49.4</td></tr>
<tr><td>25</td><td>Colorado</td><td>6.7</td><td>6</td><td>Massachusetts</td><td>48.3</td></tr>
<tr><td>4</td><td>Connecticut</td><td>49.5</td><td>7</td><td>Florida</td><td>47.3</td></tr>
<tr><td>29</td><td>Delaware*</td><td>0.0</td><td>8</td><td>Maryland</td><td>43.5</td></tr>
<tr><td>7</td><td>Florida</td><td>47.3</td><td>9</td><td>North Carolina</td><td>36.6</td></tr>
<tr><td>5</td><td>Georgia</td><td>49.4</td><td>10</td><td>California</td><td>34.0</td></tr>
<tr><td>29</td><td>Hawaii*</td><td>0.0</td><td>11</td><td>Texas</td><td>32.4</td></tr>
<tr><td>19</td><td>Idaho*</td><td>12.5</td><td>12</td><td>Virginia</td><td>28.0</td></tr>
<tr><td>14</td><td>Illinois</td><td>22.3</td><td>13</td><td>New Hampshire*</td><td>25.0</td></tr>
<tr><td>28</td><td>Indiana</td><td>3.3</td><td>14</td><td>Illinois</td><td>22.3</td></tr>
<tr><td>29</td><td>Iowa*</td><td>0.0</td><td>15</td><td>South Carolina</td><td>22.2</td></tr>
<tr><td>29</td><td>Kansas</td><td>0.0</td><td>16</td><td>Minnesota*</td><td>20.0</td></tr>
<tr><td>23</td><td>Kentucky</td><td>7.7</td><td>17</td><td>Tennessee</td><td>16.7</td></tr>
<tr><td>NA</td><td>Louisiana**</td><td>NA</td><td>18</td><td>Alabama</td><td>14.5</td></tr>
<tr><td>29</td><td>Maine*</td><td>0.0</td><td>19</td><td>Idaho*</td><td>12.5</td></tr>
<tr><td>8</td><td>Maryland</td><td>43.5</td><td>19</td><td>Mississippi</td><td>12.5</td></tr>
<tr><td>6</td><td>Massachusetts</td><td>48.3</td><td>21</td><td>Pennsylvania</td><td>11.4</td></tr>
<tr><td>NA</td><td>Michigan**</td><td>NA</td><td>22</td><td>Nevada</td><td>10.0</td></tr>
<tr><td>16</td><td>Minnesota*</td><td>20.0</td><td>23</td><td>Kentucky</td><td>7.7</td></tr>
<tr><td>19</td><td>Mississippi</td><td>12.5</td><td>24</td><td>Ohio</td><td>7.5</td></tr>
<tr><td>26</td><td>Missouri</td><td>4.7</td><td>25</td><td>Colorado</td><td>6.7</td></tr>
<tr><td>29</td><td>Montana*</td><td>0.0</td><td>26</td><td>Missouri</td><td>4.7</td></tr>
<tr><td>29</td><td>Nebraska*</td><td>0.0</td><td>27</td><td>Oklahoma</td><td>3.6</td></tr>
<tr><td>22</td><td>Nevada</td><td>10.0</td><td>28</td><td>Indiana</td><td>3.3</td></tr>
<tr><td>13</td><td>New Hampshire*</td><td>25.0</td><td>29</td><td>Alaska</td><td>0.0</td></tr>
<tr><td>3</td><td>New Jersey</td><td>57.9</td><td>29</td><td>Arizona</td><td>0.0</td></tr>
<tr><td>NA</td><td>New Mexico**</td><td>NA</td><td>29</td><td>Arkansas</td><td>0.0</td></tr>
<tr><td>2</td><td>New York</td><td>58.4</td><td>29</td><td>Delaware*</td><td>0.0</td></tr>
<tr><td>9</td><td>North Carolina</td><td>36.6</td><td>29</td><td>Hawaii*</td><td>0.0</td></tr>
<tr><td>29</td><td>North Dakota*</td><td>0.0</td><td>29</td><td>Iowa*</td><td>0.0</td></tr>
<tr><td>24</td><td>Ohio</td><td>7.5</td><td>29</td><td>Kansas</td><td>0.0</td></tr>
<tr><td>27</td><td>Oklahoma</td><td>3.6</td><td>29</td><td>Maine*</td><td>0.0</td></tr>
<tr><td>29</td><td>Oregon*</td><td>0.0</td><td>29</td><td>Montana*</td><td>0.0</td></tr>
<tr><td>21</td><td>Pennsylvania</td><td>11.4</td><td>29</td><td>Nebraska*</td><td>0.0</td></tr>
<tr><td>1</td><td>Rhode Island*</td><td>66.7</td><td>29</td><td>North Dakota*</td><td>0.0</td></tr>
<tr><td>15</td><td>South Carolina</td><td>22.2</td><td>29</td><td>Oregon*</td><td>0.0</td></tr>
<tr><td>NA</td><td>South Dakota**</td><td>NA</td><td>29</td><td>Utah*</td><td>0.0</td></tr>
<tr><td>17</td><td>Tennessee</td><td>16.7</td><td>29</td><td>Vermont*</td><td>0.0</td></tr>
<tr><td>11</td><td>Texas</td><td>32.4</td><td>29</td><td>Washington</td><td>0.0</td></tr>
<tr><td>29</td><td>Utah*</td><td>0.0</td><td>29</td><td>West Virginia*</td><td>0.0</td></tr>
<tr><td>29</td><td>Vermont*</td><td>0.0</td><td>29</td><td>Wisconsin</td><td>0.0</td></tr>
<tr><td>12</td><td>Virginia</td><td>28.0</td><td>29</td><td>Wyoming*</td><td>0.0</td></tr>
<tr><td>29</td><td>Washington</td><td>0.0</td><td>NA</td><td>Louisiana**</td><td>NA</td></tr>
<tr><td>29</td><td>West Virginia*</td><td>0.0</td><td>NA</td><td>Michigan**</td><td>NA</td></tr>
<tr><td>29</td><td>Wisconsin</td><td>0.0</td><td>NA</td><td>New Mexico**</td><td>NA</td></tr>
<tr><td>29</td><td>Wyoming*</td><td>0.0</td><td>NA</td><td>South Dakota**</td><td>NA</td></tr>
<tr><td></td><td></td><td></td><td></td><td>District of Columbia**</td><td>NA</td></tr>
</table>

Source: U.S. Department of Justice, Bureau of Justice Statistics
    "HIV in U.S. Prisons and Jails, 1993" (Bulletin, August 1995, NCJ-152765)
*Rates calculated by the editors for these states with fewer than ten AIDS-related deaths.
**Not available.

State Prisoners Known to be Positive for HIV Infection/AIDS in 1993

National Total = 20,579 Inmates*

<table>
<tr><td colspan="4"><u>ALPHA ORDER</u></td><td colspan="4"><u>RANK ORDER</u></td></tr>
<tr><td>RANK</td><td>STATE</td><td>INMATES</td><td>% of USA</td><td>RANK</td><td>STATE</td><td>INMATES</td><td>% of USA</td></tr>
<tr><td>18</td><td>Alabama</td><td>194</td><td>0.94%</td><td>1</td><td>New York</td><td>8,000</td><td>38.87%</td></tr>
<tr><td>NA</td><td>Alaska**</td><td>NA</td><td>NA</td><td>2</td><td>Florida</td><td>1,780</td><td>8.65%</td></tr>
<tr><td>24</td><td>Arizona</td><td>89</td><td>0.43%</td><td>3</td><td>Texas</td><td>1,212</td><td>5.89%</td></tr>
<tr><td>27</td><td>Arkansas</td><td>80</td><td>0.39%</td><td>4</td><td>California</td><td>1,048</td><td>5.09%</td></tr>
<tr><td>4</td><td>California</td><td>1,048</td><td>5.09%</td><td>5</td><td>Connecticut</td><td>886</td><td>4.31%</td></tr>
<tr><td>28</td><td>Colorado</td><td>74</td><td>0.36%</td><td>6</td><td>New Jersey</td><td>881</td><td>4.28%</td></tr>
<tr><td>5</td><td>Connecticut</td><td>886</td><td>4.31%</td><td>7</td><td>Maryland</td><td>769</td><td>3.74%</td></tr>
<tr><td>22</td><td>Delaware</td><td>113</td><td>0.55%</td><td>8</td><td>Georgia</td><td>745</td><td>3.62%</td></tr>
<tr><td>2</td><td>Florida</td><td>1,780</td><td>8.65%</td><td>9</td><td>Illinois</td><td>591</td><td>2.87%</td></tr>
<tr><td>8</td><td>Georgia</td><td>745</td><td>3.62%</td><td>10</td><td>North Carolina</td><td>485</td><td>2.36%</td></tr>
<tr><td>37</td><td>Hawaii</td><td>21</td><td>0.10%</td><td>11</td><td>South Carolina</td><td>452</td><td>2.20%</td></tr>
<tr><td>35</td><td>Idaho</td><td>26</td><td>0.13%</td><td>12</td><td>Michigan</td><td>434</td><td>2.11%</td></tr>
<tr><td>9</td><td>Illinois</td><td>591</td><td>2.87%</td><td>13</td><td>Pennsylvania</td><td>409</td><td>1.99%</td></tr>
<tr><td>NA</td><td>Indiana**</td><td>NA</td><td>NA</td><td>14</td><td>Massachusetts</td><td>394</td><td>1.91%</td></tr>
<tr><td>40</td><td>Iowa</td><td>11</td><td>0.05%</td><td>15</td><td>Ohio</td><td>355</td><td>1.73%</td></tr>
<tr><td>32</td><td>Kansas</td><td>39</td><td>0.19%</td><td>16</td><td>Louisiana</td><td>262</td><td>1.27%</td></tr>
<tr><td>31</td><td>Kentucky</td><td>42</td><td>0.20%</td><td>17</td><td>Virginia</td><td>207</td><td>1.01%</td></tr>
<tr><td>16</td><td>Louisiana</td><td>262</td><td>1.27%</td><td>18</td><td>Alabama</td><td>194</td><td>0.94%</td></tr>
<tr><td>42</td><td>Maine</td><td>8</td><td>0.04%</td><td>19</td><td>Nevada</td><td>163</td><td>0.79%</td></tr>
<tr><td>7</td><td>Maryland</td><td>769</td><td>3.74%</td><td>20</td><td>Missouri</td><td>136</td><td>0.66%</td></tr>
<tr><td>14</td><td>Massachusetts</td><td>394</td><td>1.91%</td><td>21</td><td>Mississippi</td><td>118</td><td>0.57%</td></tr>
<tr><td>12</td><td>Michigan</td><td>434</td><td>2.11%</td><td>22</td><td>Delaware</td><td>113</td><td>0.55%</td></tr>
<tr><td>33</td><td>Minnesota</td><td>30</td><td>0.15%</td><td>23</td><td>Oklahoma</td><td>102</td><td>0.50%</td></tr>
<tr><td>21</td><td>Mississippi</td><td>118</td><td>0.57%</td><td>24</td><td>Arizona</td><td>89</td><td>0.43%</td></tr>
<tr><td>20</td><td>Missouri</td><td>136</td><td>0.66%</td><td>24</td><td>Rhode Island</td><td>89</td><td>0.43%</td></tr>
<tr><td>46</td><td>Montana</td><td>5</td><td>0.02%</td><td>26</td><td>Tennessee</td><td>88</td><td>0.43%</td></tr>
<tr><td>38</td><td>Nebraska</td><td>17</td><td>0.08%</td><td>27</td><td>Arkansas</td><td>80</td><td>0.39%</td></tr>
<tr><td>19</td><td>Nevada</td><td>163</td><td>0.79%</td><td>28</td><td>Colorado</td><td>74</td><td>0.36%</td></tr>
<tr><td>38</td><td>New Hampshire</td><td>17</td><td>0.08%</td><td>29</td><td>Washington</td><td>63</td><td>0.31%</td></tr>
<tr><td>6</td><td>New Jersey</td><td>881</td><td>4.28%</td><td>30</td><td>Wisconsin</td><td>56</td><td>0.27%</td></tr>
<tr><td>40</td><td>New Mexico</td><td>11</td><td>0.05%</td><td>31</td><td>Kentucky</td><td>42</td><td>0.20%</td></tr>
<tr><td>1</td><td>New York</td><td>8,000</td><td>38.87%</td><td>32</td><td>Kansas</td><td>39</td><td>0.19%</td></tr>
<tr><td>10</td><td>North Carolina</td><td>485</td><td>2.36%</td><td>33</td><td>Minnesota</td><td>30</td><td>0.15%</td></tr>
<tr><td>47</td><td>North Dakota</td><td>2</td><td>0.01%</td><td>34</td><td>Oregon</td><td>29</td><td>0.14%</td></tr>
<tr><td>15</td><td>Ohio</td><td>355</td><td>1.73%</td><td>35</td><td>Idaho</td><td>26</td><td>0.13%</td></tr>
<tr><td>23</td><td>Oklahoma</td><td>102</td><td>0.50%</td><td>35</td><td>Utah</td><td>26</td><td>0.13%</td></tr>
<tr><td>34</td><td>Oregon</td><td>29</td><td>0.14%</td><td>37</td><td>Hawaii</td><td>21</td><td>0.10%</td></tr>
<tr><td>13</td><td>Pennsylvania</td><td>409</td><td>1.99%</td><td>38</td><td>Nebraska</td><td>17</td><td>0.08%</td></tr>
<tr><td>24</td><td>Rhode Island</td><td>89</td><td>0.43%</td><td>38</td><td>New Hampshire</td><td>17</td><td>0.08%</td></tr>
<tr><td>11</td><td>South Carolina</td><td>452</td><td>2.20%</td><td>40</td><td>Iowa</td><td>11</td><td>0.05%</td></tr>
<tr><td>NA</td><td>South Dakota**</td><td>NA</td><td>NA</td><td>40</td><td>New Mexico</td><td>11</td><td>0.05%</td></tr>
<tr><td>26</td><td>Tennessee</td><td>88</td><td>0.43%</td><td>42</td><td>Maine</td><td>8</td><td>0.04%</td></tr>
<tr><td>3</td><td>Texas</td><td>1,212</td><td>5.89%</td><td>42</td><td>West Virginia</td><td>8</td><td>0.04%</td></tr>
<tr><td>35</td><td>Utah</td><td>26</td><td>0.13%</td><td>44</td><td>Vermont</td><td>6</td><td>0.03%</td></tr>
<tr><td>44</td><td>Vermont</td><td>6</td><td>0.03%</td><td>44</td><td>Wyoming</td><td>6</td><td>0.03%</td></tr>
<tr><td>17</td><td>Virginia</td><td>207</td><td>1.01%</td><td>46</td><td>Montana</td><td>5</td><td>0.02%</td></tr>
<tr><td>29</td><td>Washington</td><td>63</td><td>0.31%</td><td>47</td><td>North Dakota</td><td>2</td><td>0.01%</td></tr>
<tr><td>42</td><td>West Virginia</td><td>8</td><td>0.04%</td><td>NA</td><td>Alaska**</td><td>NA</td><td>NA</td></tr>
<tr><td>30</td><td>Wisconsin</td><td>56</td><td>0.27%</td><td>NA</td><td>Indiana**</td><td>NA</td><td>NA</td></tr>
<tr><td>44</td><td>Wyoming</td><td>6</td><td>0.03%</td><td>NA</td><td>South Dakota**</td><td>NA</td><td>NA</td></tr>
<tr><td></td><td></td><td></td><td></td><td></td><td>District of Columbia**</td><td>NA</td><td>NA</td></tr>
</table>

Source: U.S. Department of Justice, Bureau of Justice Statistics
   "HIV in U.S. Prisons and Jails, 1993" (Bulletin, August 1995, NCJ-152765)
Does not include 959 positive federal inmates.
**Not available.*

State Prisoners Known to be Positive for HIV Infection/AIDS As a Percent of Total Prison Population in 1993 National Percent = 2.6% of State Prisoners*

ALPHA ORDER

RANK	STATE	PERCENT
18	Alabama	1.1
NA	Alaska**	NA
38	Arizona	0.5
21	Arkansas	1.0
23	California	0.9
27	Colorado	0.8
2	Connecticut	6.6
8	Delaware	2.7
6	Florida	3.4
8	Georgia	2.7
31	Hawaii	0.7
21	Idaho	1.0
13	Illinois	1.7
NA	Indiana**	NA
47	Iowa	0.2
31	Kansas	0.7
38	Kentucky	0.5
15	Louisiana	1.6
35	Maine	0.6
4	Maryland	3.8
3	Massachusetts	3.9
18	Michigan	1.1
31	Minnesota	0.7
17	Mississippi	1.4
27	Missouri	0.8
44	Montana	0.3
31	Nebraska	0.7
11	Nevada	2.6
23	New Hampshire	0.9
5	New Jersey	3.7
44	New Mexico	0.3
1	New York	12.4
12	North Carolina	2.2
44	North Dakota	0.3
23	Ohio	0.9
27	Oklahoma	0.8
42	Oregon	0.4
15	Pennsylvania	1.6
6	Rhode Island	3.4
8	South Carolina	2.7
NA	South Dakota**	NA
27	Tennessee	0.8
13	Texas	1.7
23	Utah	0.9
38	Vermont	0.5
18	Virginia	1.1
35	Washington	0.6
42	West Virginia	0.4
35	Wisconsin	0.6
38	Wyoming	0.5

RANK ORDER

RANK	STATE	PERCENT
1	New York	12.4
2	Connecticut	6.6
3	Massachusetts	3.9
4	Maryland	3.8
5	New Jersey	3.7
6	Florida	3.4
6	Rhode Island	3.4
8	Delaware	2.7
8	Georgia	2.7
8	South Carolina	2.7
11	Nevada	2.6
12	North Carolina	2.2
13	Illinois	1.7
13	Texas	1.7
15	Louisiana	1.6
15	Pennsylvania	1.6
17	Mississippi	1.4
18	Alabama	1.1
18	Michigan	1.1
18	Virginia	1.1
21	Arkansas	1.0
21	Idaho	1.0
23	California	0.9
23	New Hampshire	0.9
23	Ohio	0.9
23	Utah	0.9
27	Colorado	0.8
27	Missouri	0.8
27	Oklahoma	0.8
27	Tennessee	0.8
31	Hawaii	0.7
31	Kansas	0.7
31	Minnesota	0.7
31	Nebraska	0.7
35	Maine	0.6
35	Washington	0.6
35	Wisconsin	0.6
38	Arizona	0.5
38	Kentucky	0.5
38	Vermont	0.5
38	Wyoming	0.5
42	Oregon	0.4
42	West Virginia	0.4
44	Montana	0.3
44	New Mexico	0.3
44	North Dakota	0.3
47	Iowa	0.2
NA	Alaska**	NA
NA	Indiana**	NA
NA	South Dakota**	NA
	District of Columbia**	NA

Source: U.S. Department of Justice, Bureau of Justice Statistics
    "HIV in U.S. Prisons and Jails, 1993" (Bulletin, August 1995, NCJ-152765)
Federal rate is 1.2%, combined state and federal rate is 2.4%.
**Not available.*

Deaths of State Prisoners by Suicide in 1993

National Total = 145 Suicides

ALPHA ORDER

RANK	STATE	SUICIDES	% of USA
NA	Alabama*	NA	NA
12	Alaska	3	2.07%
7	Arizona	5	3.45%
26	Arkansas	1	0.69%
1	California	28	19.31%
19	Colorado	2	1.38%
26	Connecticut	1	0.69%
36	Delaware	0	0.00%
7	Florida	5	3.45%
12	Georgia	3	2.07%
36	Hawaii	0	0.00%
9	Idaho	4	2.76%
9	Illinois	4	2.76%
19	Indiana	2	1.38%
36	Iowa	0	0.00%
36	Kansas	0	0.00%
19	Kentucky	2	1.38%
NA	Louisiana*	NA	NA
26	Maine	1	0.69%
19	Maryland	2	1.38%
19	Massachusetts	2	1.38%
6	Michigan	7	4.83%
36	Minnesota	0	0.00%
19	Mississippi	2	1.38%
26	Missouri	1	0.69%
36	Montana	0	0.00%
26	Nebraska	1	0.69%
26	Nevada	1	0.69%
26	New Hampshire	1	0.69%
12	New Jersey	3	2.07%
NA	New Mexico*	NA	NA
3	New York	10	6.90%
19	North Carolina	2	1.38%
36	North Dakota	0	0.00%
4	Ohio	8	5.52%
4	Oklahoma	8	5.52%
12	Oregon	3	2.07%
12	Pennsylvania	3	2.07%
36	Rhode Island	0	0.00%
26	South Carolina	1	0.69%
36	South Dakota	0	0.00%
12	Tennessee	3	2.07%
2	Texas	17	11.72%
26	Utah	1	0.69%
36	Vermont	0	0.00%
9	Virginia	4	2.76%
36	Washington	0	0.00%
36	West Virginia	0	0.00%
12	Wisconsin	3	2.07%
26	Wyoming	1	0.69%

RANK ORDER

RANK	STATE	SUICIDES	% of USA
1	California	28	19.31%
2	Texas	17	11.72%
3	New York	10	6.90%
4	Ohio	8	5.52%
4	Oklahoma	8	5.52%
6	Michigan	7	4.83%
7	Arizona	5	3.45%
7	Florida	5	3.45%
9	Idaho	4	2.76%
9	Illinois	4	2.76%
9	Virginia	4	2.76%
12	Alaska	3	2.07%
12	Georgia	3	2.07%
12	New Jersey	3	2.07%
12	Oregon	3	2.07%
12	Pennsylvania	3	2.07%
12	Tennessee	3	2.07%
12	Wisconsin	3	2.07%
19	Colorado	2	1.38%
19	Indiana	2	1.38%
19	Kentucky	2	1.38%
19	Maryland	2	1.38%
19	Massachusetts	2	1.38%
19	Mississippi	2	1.38%
19	North Carolina	2	1.38%
26	Arkansas	1	0.69%
26	Connecticut	1	0.69%
26	Maine	1	0.69%
26	Missouri	1	0.69%
26	Nebraska	1	0.69%
26	Nevada	1	0.69%
26	New Hampshire	1	0.69%
26	South Carolina	1	0.69%
26	Utah	1	0.69%
26	Wyoming	1	0.69%
36	Delaware	0	0.00%
36	Hawaii	0	0.00%
36	Iowa	0	0.00%
36	Kansas	0	0.00%
36	Minnesota	0	0.00%
36	Montana	0	0.00%
36	North Dakota	0	0.00%
36	Rhode Island	0	0.00%
36	South Dakota	0	0.00%
36	Vermont	0	0.00%
36	Washington	0	0.00%
36	West Virginia	0	0.00%
NA	Alabama*	NA	NA
NA	Louisiana*	NA	NA
NA	New Mexico*	NA	NA
	District of Columbia*	NA	NA

Source: U.S. Department of Justice, Bureau of Justice Statistics
"Correctional Populations in the United States, 1993" (October 1995, NCJ 156241)
*Not available.

Deaths of State Prisoners by Suicide as a Percent of All Prison Deaths in 1993

National Percent = 5.96% of Deaths

RANK	STATE	PERCENT
NA	Alabama*	NA
5	Alaska	20.00
13	Arizona	11.11
15	Arkansas	10.00
10	California	14.00
11	Colorado	13.33
35	Connecticut	1.10
36	Delaware	0.00
30	Florida	2.99
29	Georgia	3.70
36	Hawaii	0.00
1	Idaho	50.00
27	Illinois	3.88
23	Indiana	6.67
36	Iowa	0.00
36	Kansas	0.00
20	Kentucky	7.69
NA	Louisiana*	NA
5	Maine	20.00
26	Maryland	4.35
22	Massachusetts	6.90
24	Michigan	6.60
36	Minnesota	0.00
18	Mississippi	8.33
33	Missouri	2.33
36	Montana	0.00
12	Nebraska	12.50
15	Nevada	10.00
4	New Hampshire	25.00
32	New Jersey	2.48
NA	New Mexico*	NA
31	New York	2.65
25	North Carolina	4.88
36	North Dakota	0.00
14	Ohio	10.13
9	Oklahoma	14.29
3	Oregon	33.33
28	Pennsylvania	3.80
36	Rhode Island	0.00
34	South Carolina	1.59
36	South Dakota	0.00
15	Tennessee	10.00
21	Texas	6.97
1	Utah	50.00
36	Vermont	0.00
19	Virginia	8.00
36	Washington	0.00
36	West Virginia	0.00
8	Wisconsin	15.79
5	Wyoming	20.00

RANK	STATE	PERCENT
1	Idaho	50.00
1	Utah	50.00
3	Oregon	33.33
4	New Hampshire	25.00
5	Alaska	20.00
5	Maine	20.00
5	Wyoming	20.00
8	Wisconsin	15.79
9	Oklahoma	14.29
10	California	14.00
11	Colorado	13.33
12	Nebraska	12.50
13	Arizona	11.11
14	Ohio	10.13
15	Arkansas	10.00
15	Nevada	10.00
15	Tennessee	10.00
18	Mississippi	8.33
19	Virginia	8.00
20	Kentucky	7.69
21	Texas	6.97
22	Massachusetts	6.90
23	Indiana	6.67
24	Michigan	6.60
25	North Carolina	4.88
26	Maryland	4.35
27	Illinois	3.88
28	Pennsylvania	3.80
29	Georgia	3.70
30	Florida	2.99
31	New York	2.65
32	New Jersey	2.48
33	Missouri	2.33
34	South Carolina	1.59
35	Connecticut	1.10
36	Delaware	0.00
36	Hawaii	0.00
36	Iowa	0.00
36	Kansas	0.00
36	Minnesota	0.00
36	Montana	0.00
36	North Dakota	0.00
36	Rhode Island	0.00
36	South Dakota	0.00
36	Vermont	0.00
36	Washington	0.00
36	West Virginia	0.00
NA	Alabama*	NA
NA	Louisiana*	NA
NA	New Mexico*	NA
	District of Columbia*	NA

Source: U.S. Department of Justice, Bureau of Justice Statistics
   "Correctional Populations in the United States, 1993" (October 1995, NCJ 156241)
*Not available.

Adults Under State Correctional Supervision in 1993

National Total = 4,711,500 Adults*

ALPHA ORDER

RANK	STATE	ADULTS	% of USA
22	Alabama	66,400	1.41%
47	Alaska	6,600	0.14%
24	Arizona	65,700	1.39%
30	Arkansas	31,900	0.68%
2	California	557,000	11.82%
27	Colorado	53,400	1.13%
25	Connecticut	64,900	1.38%
35	Delaware	20,600	0.44%
3	Florida	302,800	6.43%
5	Georgia	216,400	4.59%
39	Hawaii	14,500	0.31%
43	Idaho	9,600	0.20%
10	Illinois	148,700	3.16%
14	Indiana	108,400	2.30%
33	Iowa	22,800	0.48%
29	Kansas	39,700	0.84%
31	Kentucky	31,000	0.66%
16	Louisiana	78,800	1.67%
41	Maine	10,800	0.23%
13	Maryland	123,300	2.62%
18	Massachusetts	69,400	1.47%
7	Michigan	205,400	4.36%
15	Minnesota	83,900	1.78%
32	Mississippi	25,000	0.53%
20	Missouri	67,700	1.44%
46	Montana	7,000	0.15%
37	Nebraska	19,500	0.41%
34	Nevada	21,400	0.45%
45	New Hampshire	7,700	0.16%
8	New Jersey	180,600	3.83%
38	New Mexico	15,400	0.33%
4	New York	301,400	6.40%
12	North Carolina	134,400	2.85%
50	North Dakota	2,900	0.06%
9	Ohio	157,100	3.33%
28	Oklahoma	44,300	0.94%
26	Oregon	61,900	1.31%
6	Pennsylvania	205,500	4.36%
36	Rhode Island	19,700	0.42%
21	South Carolina	67,103	1.42%
47	South Dakota	6,600	0.14%
17	Tennessee	78,000	1.66%
1	Texas	620,000	13.16%
39	Utah	14,500	0.31%
44	Vermont	7,800	0.17%
19	Virginia	67,900	1.44%
11	Washington	135,600	2.88%
42	West Virginia	10,600	0.22%
23	Wisconsin	66,300	1.41%
49	Wyoming	4,900	0.10%

RANK ORDER

RANK	STATE	ADULTS	% of USA
1	Texas	620,000	13.16%
2	California	557,000	11.82%
3	Florida	302,800	6.43%
4	New York	301,400	6.40%
5	Georgia	216,400	4.59%
6	Pennsylvania	205,500	4.36%
7	Michigan	205,400	4.36%
8	New Jersey	180,600	3.83%
9	Ohio	157,100	3.33%
10	Illinois	148,700	3.16%
11	Washington	135,600	2.88%
12	North Carolina	134,400	2.85%
13	Maryland	123,300	2.62%
14	Indiana	108,400	2.30%
15	Minnesota	83,900	1.78%
16	Louisiana	78,800	1.67%
17	Tennessee	78,000	1.66%
18	Massachusetts	69,400	1.47%
19	Virginia	67,900	1.44%
20	Missouri	67,700	1.44%
21	South Carolina	67,103	1.42%
22	Alabama	66,400	1.41%
23	Wisconsin	66,300	1.41%
24	Arizona	65,700	1.39%
25	Connecticut	64,900	1.38%
26	Oregon	61,900	1.31%
27	Colorado	53,400	1.13%
28	Oklahoma	44,300	0.94%
29	Kansas	39,700	0.84%
30	Arkansas	31,900	0.68%
31	Kentucky	31,000	0.66%
32	Mississippi	25,000	0.53%
33	Iowa	22,800	0.48%
34	Nevada	21,400	0.45%
35	Delaware	20,600	0.44%
36	Rhode Island	19,700	0.42%
37	Nebraska	19,500	0.41%
38	New Mexico	15,400	0.33%
39	Hawaii	14,500	0.31%
39	Utah	14,500	0.31%
41	Maine	10,800	0.23%
42	West Virginia	10,600	0.22%
43	Idaho	9,600	0.20%
44	Vermont	7,800	0.17%
45	New Hampshire	7,700	0.16%
46	Montana	7,000	0.15%
47	Alaska	6,600	0.14%
47	South Dakota	6,600	0.14%
49	Wyoming	4,900	0.10%
50	North Dakota	2,900	0.06%
	District of Columbia	29,000	0.62%

Source: U.S. Department of Justice, Bureau of Justice Statistics
   "Correctional Populations in the United States, 1993" (October 1995, NCJ 156241)
*Includes adults in prison or jail, on probation or parole. Does not include 168,000 adults under federal
correctional supervision.

Percent of Population Under State Correctional Supervision in 1993

National Percent = 2.5% of Adult Population*

ALPHA ORDER   RANK ORDER

RANK	STATE	PERCENT		RANK	STATE	PERCENT
22	Alabama	2.1		1	Texas	4.8
35	Alaska	1.6		2	Georgia	4.3
18	Arizona	2.3		3	Delaware	3.9
28	Arkansas	1.8		4	Washington	3.5
16	California	2.5		5	Maryland	3.3
24	Colorado	2.0		6	Michigan	3.0
10	Connecticut	2.6		6	New Jersey	3.0
3	Delaware	3.9		8	Florida	2.9
8	Florida	2.9		9	Oregon	2.8
2	Georgia	4.3		10	Connecticut	2.6
32	Hawaii	1.7		10	Indiana	2.6
40	Idaho	1.3		10	Louisiana	2.6
32	Illinois	1.7		10	Minnesota	2.6
10	Indiana	2.6		10	North Carolina	2.6
46	Iowa	1.1		10	Rhode Island	2.6
19	Kansas	2.2		16	California	2.5
46	Kentucky	1.1		16	South Carolina	2.5
10	Louisiana	2.6		18	Arizona	2.3
43	Maine	1.2		19	Kansas	2.2
5	Maryland	3.3		19	New York	2.2
36	Massachusetts	1.5		19	Pennsylvania	2.2
6	Michigan	3.0		22	Alabama	2.1
10	Minnesota	2.6		22	Nevada	2.1
40	Mississippi	1.3		24	Colorado	2.0
28	Missouri	1.8		24	Tennessee	2.0
43	Montana	1.2		26	Ohio	1.9
32	Nebraska	1.7		26	Oklahoma	1.9
22	Nevada	2.1		28	Arkansas	1.8
48	New Hampshire	0.9		28	Missouri	1.8
6	New Jersey	3.0		28	Vermont	1.8
38	New Mexico	1.4		28	Wisconsin	1.8
19	New York	2.2		32	Hawaii	1.7
10	North Carolina	2.6		32	Illinois	1.7
50	North Dakota	0.6		32	Nebraska	1.7
26	Ohio	1.9		35	Alaska	1.6
26	Oklahoma	1.9		36	Massachusetts	1.5
9	Oregon	2.8		36	Wyoming	1.5
19	Pennsylvania	2.2		38	New Mexico	1.4
10	Rhode Island	2.6		38	Virginia	1.4
16	South Carolina	2.5		40	Idaho	1.3
40	South Dakota	1.3		40	Mississippi	1.3
24	Tennessee	2.0		40	South Dakota	1.3
1	Texas	4.8		43	Maine	1.2
43	Utah	1.2		43	Montana	1.2
28	Vermont	1.8		43	Utah	1.2
38	Virginia	1.4		46	Iowa	1.1
4	Washington	3.5		46	Kentucky	1.1
49	West Virginia	0.8		48	New Hampshire	0.9
28	Wisconsin	1.8		49	West Virginia	0.8
36	Wyoming	1.5		50	North Dakota	0.6

District of Columbia   6.3

Source: U.S. Department of Justice, Bureau of Justice Statistics
"Correctional Populations in the United States, 1993" (October 1995, NCJ 156241)
*Includes adults in prison or jail, on probation or parole. Does not include adults under federal correctional supervision. Federal percent is 0.1% making a combined state and federal percent of 2.6% of adult population is under state or federal correctional supervision.

Adults on State Probation in 1994

National Total = 2,917,119 Adults*

ALPHA ORDER

RANK	STATE	ADULTS	% of USA
24	Alabama	36,024	1.23%
49	Alaska	3,173	0.11%
21	Arizona	36,916	1.27%
30	Arkansas	18,598	0.64%
2	California	285,105	9.77%
22	Colorado	36,430	1.25%
16	Connecticut	53,453	1.83%
33	Delaware	15,507	0.53%
3	Florida	239,108	8.20%
6	Georgia	140,684	4.82%
35	Hawaii	12,515	0.43%
45	Idaho	5,153	0.18%
14	Illinois	79,466	2.72%
12	Indiana	82,804	2.84%
34	Iowa	15,502	0.53%
28	Kansas	24,102	0.83%
36	Kentucky	11,417	0.39%
26	Louisiana	33,604	1.15%
40	Maine	8,669	0.30%
15	Maryland	76,940	2.64%
17	Massachusetts	46,672	1.60%
5	Michigan	143,178	4.91%
13	Minnesota	81,972	2.81%
38	Mississippi	9,041	0.31%
23	Missouri	36,295	1.24%
44	Montana	5,641	0.19%
32	Nebraska	17,554	0.60%
37	Nevada	9,410	0.32%
46	New Hampshire	4,323	0.15%
8	New Jersey	106,921	3.67%
39	New Mexico	8,670	0.30%
4	New York	164,569	5.64%
11	North Carolina	89,889	3.08%
50	North Dakota	2,006	0.07%
9	Ohio	105,953	3.63%
27	Oklahoma	26,484	0.91%
20	Oregon	38,086	1.31%
10	Pennsylvania	99,524	3.41%
31	Rhode Island	18,179	0.62%
19	South Carolina	40,456	1.39%
47	South Dakota	3,410	0.12%
25	Tennessee	35,727	1.22%
1	Texas	394,578	13.53%
41	Utah	7,638	0.26%
42	Vermont	6,676	0.23%
29	Virginia	24,089	0.83%
7	Washington	111,450	3.82%
43	West Virginia	5,950	0.20%
18	Wisconsin	45,901	1.57%
48	Wyoming	3,382	0.12%

RANK ORDER

RANK	STATE	ADULTS	% of USA
1	Texas	394,578	13.53%
2	California	285,105	9.77%
3	Florida	239,108	8.20%
4	New York	164,569	5.64%
5	Michigan	143,178	4.91%
6	Georgia	140,684	4.82%
7	Washington	111,450	3.82%
8	New Jersey	106,921	3.67%
9	Ohio	105,953	3.63%
10	Pennsylvania	99,524	3.41%
11	North Carolina	89,889	3.08%
12	Indiana	82,804	2.84%
13	Minnesota	81,972	2.81%
14	Illinois	79,466	2.72%
15	Maryland	76,940	2.64%
16	Connecticut	53,453	1.83%
17	Massachusetts	46,672	1.60%
18	Wisconsin	45,901	1.57%
19	South Carolina	40,456	1.39%
20	Oregon	38,086	1.31%
21	Arizona	36,916	1.27%
22	Colorado	36,430	1.25%
23	Missouri	36,295	1.24%
24	Alabama	36,024	1.23%
25	Tennessee	35,727	1.22%
26	Louisiana	33,604	1.15%
27	Oklahoma	26,484	0.91%
28	Kansas	24,102	0.83%
29	Virginia	24,089	0.83%
30	Arkansas	18,598	0.64%
31	Rhode Island	18,179	0.62%
32	Nebraska	17,554	0.60%
33	Delaware	15,507	0.53%
34	Iowa	15,502	0.53%
35	Hawaii	12,515	0.43%
36	Kentucky	11,417	0.39%
37	Nevada	9,410	0.32%
38	Mississippi	9,041	0.31%
39	New Mexico	8,670	0.30%
40	Maine	8,669	0.30%
41	Utah	7,638	0.26%
42	Vermont	6,676	0.23%
43	West Virginia	5,950	0.20%
44	Montana	5,641	0.19%
45	Idaho	5,153	0.18%
46	New Hampshire	4,323	0.15%
47	South Dakota	3,410	0.12%
48	Wyoming	3,382	0.12%
49	Alaska	3,173	0.11%
50	North Dakota	2,006	0.07%
	District of Columbia	8,325	0.29%

Source: U.S. Department of Justice, Bureau of Justice Statistics
   "The Nation's Correctional Population Tops 5 Million" (Press Release, August 27, 1995, NCJ-1564432)
*As of December 31, 1994. Does not include 45,047 adults on federal probation.

Rate of Adults on State Probation in 1994

National Rate = 1,517 Adults on Probation per 100,000 Adult Population*

ALPHA ORDER

RANK	STATE	RATE
26	Alabama	1,148
39	Alaska	766
22	Arizona	1,257
30	Arkansas	1,026
23	California	1,253
19	Colorado	1,350
8	Connecticut	2,149
2	Delaware	2,920
7	Florida	2,237
4	Georgia	2,725
18	Hawaii	1,430
43	Idaho	649
36	Illinois	917
11	Indiana	1,935
41	Iowa	738
20	Kansas	1,293
50	Kentucky	400
28	Louisiana	1,091
34	Maine	928
9	Maryland	2,056
31	Massachusetts	1,011
10	Michigan	2,054
5	Minnesota	2,465
47	Mississippi	473
33	Missouri	931
37	Montana	913
17	Nebraska	1,486
38	Nevada	870
45	New Hampshire	512
12	New Jersey	1,790
40	New Mexico	750
25	New York	1,205
13	North Carolina	1,692
48	North Dakota	430
21	Ohio	1,285
27	Oklahoma	1,114
14	Oregon	1,654
29	Pennsylvania	1,087
6	Rhode Island	2,401
16	South Carolina	1,492
42	South Dakota	665
35	Tennessee	921
1	Texas	3,017
44	Utah	618
15	Vermont	1,538
46	Virginia	487
3	Washington	2,832
49	West Virginia	427
24	Wisconsin	1,229
32	Wyoming	998

RANK ORDER

RANK	STATE	RATE
1	Texas	3,017
2	Delaware	2,920
3	Washington	2,832
4	Georgia	2,725
5	Minnesota	2,465
6	Rhode Island	2,401
7	Florida	2,237
8	Connecticut	2,149
9	Maryland	2,056
10	Michigan	2,054
11	Indiana	1,935
12	New Jersey	1,790
13	North Carolina	1,692
14	Oregon	1,654
15	Vermont	1,538
16	South Carolina	1,492
17	Nebraska	1,486
18	Hawaii	1,430
19	Colorado	1,350
20	Kansas	1,293
21	Ohio	1,285
22	Arizona	1,257
23	California	1,253
24	Wisconsin	1,229
25	New York	1,205
26	Alabama	1,148
27	Oklahoma	1,114
28	Louisiana	1,091
29	Pennsylvania	1,087
30	Arkansas	1,026
31	Massachusetts	1,011
32	Wyoming	998
33	Missouri	931
34	Maine	928
35	Tennessee	921
36	Illinois	917
37	Montana	913
38	Nevada	870
39	Alaska	766
40	New Mexico	750
41	Iowa	738
42	South Dakota	665
43	Idaho	649
44	Utah	618
45	New Hampshire	512
46	Virginia	487
47	Mississippi	473
48	North Dakota	430
49	West Virginia	427
50	Kentucky	400
	District of Columbia	1,846

Source: U.S. Department of Justice, Bureau of Justice Statistics
   "The Nation's Correctional Population Tops 5 Million" (Press Release, August 27, 1995, NCJ-1564432)
*As of December 31, 1994. Federal rate is 23 adults on probation per 100,000 adult population.

Adults on State Parole in 1994

National Total = 628,729 Adults*

ALPHA ORDER

RANK	STATE	ADULTS	% of USA
19	Alabama	6,760	1.08%
43	Alaska	678	0.11%
25	Arizona	4,351	0.69%
22	Arkansas	4,915	0.78%
2	California	85,084	13.53%
30	Colorado	2,463	0.39%
38	Connecticut	1,200	0.19%
39	Delaware	1,029	0.16%
8	Florida	19,089	3.04%
9	Georgia	17,505	2.78%
33	Hawaii	1,663	0.26%
40	Idaho	862	0.14%
6	Illinois	26,695	4.25%
27	Indiana	3,296	0.52%
28	Iowa	2,972	0.47%
20	Kansas	6,291	1.00%
24	Kentucky	4,380	0.70%
10	Louisiana	17,112	2.72%
50	Maine	40	0.01%
11	Maryland	14,795	2.35%
23	Massachusetts	4,533	0.72%
13	Michigan	12,922	2.06%
32	Minnesota	1,904	0.30%
35	Mississippi	1,517	0.24%
14	Missouri	12,592	2.00%
45	Montana	636	0.10%
42	Nebraska	771	0.12%
26	Nevada	3,529	0.56%
41	New Hampshire	835	0.13%
5	New Jersey	41,820	6.65%
36	New Mexico	1,505	0.24%
4	New York	53,832	8.56%
7	North Carolina	21,027	3.34%
49	North Dakota	93	0.01%
17	Ohio	7,180	1.14%
29	Oklahoma	2,604	0.41%
12	Oregon	14,264	2.27%
3	Pennsylvania	70,355	11.19%
47	Rhode Island	528	0.08%
21	South Carolina	6,029	0.96%
44	South Dakota	661	0.11%
15	Tennessee	10,260	1.63%
1	Texas	108,563	17.27%
31	Utah	2,438	0.39%
46	Vermont	592	0.09%
16	Virginia	9,649	1.53%
34	Washington	1,650	0.26%
37	West Virginia	1,259	0.20%
18	Wisconsin	7,065	1.12%
48	Wyoming	362	0.06%

RANK ORDER

RANK	STATE	ADULTS	% of USA
1	Texas	108,563	17.27%
2	California	85,084	13.53%
3	Pennsylvania	70,355	11.19%
4	New York	53,832	8.56%
5	New Jersey	41,820	6.65%
6	Illinois	26,695	4.25%
7	North Carolina	21,027	3.34%
8	Florida	19,089	3.04%
9	Georgia	17,505	2.78%
10	Louisiana	17,112	2.72%
11	Maryland	14,795	2.35%
12	Oregon	14,264	2.27%
13	Michigan	12,922	2.06%
14	Missouri	12,592	2.00%
15	Tennessee	10,260	1.63%
16	Virginia	9,649	1.53%
17	Ohio	7,180	1.14%
18	Wisconsin	7,065	1.12%
19	Alabama	6,760	1.08%
20	Kansas	6,291	1.00%
21	South Carolina	6,029	0.96%
22	Arkansas	4,915	0.78%
23	Massachusetts	4,533	0.72%
24	Kentucky	4,380	0.70%
25	Arizona	4,351	0.69%
26	Nevada	3,529	0.56%
27	Indiana	3,296	0.52%
28	Iowa	2,972	0.47%
29	Oklahoma	2,604	0.41%
30	Colorado	2,463	0.39%
31	Utah	2,438	0.39%
32	Minnesota	1,904	0.30%
33	Hawaii	1,663	0.26%
34	Washington	1,650	0.26%
35	Mississippi	1,517	0.24%
36	New Mexico	1,505	0.24%
37	West Virginia	1,259	0.20%
38	Connecticut	1,200	0.19%
39	Delaware	1,029	0.16%
40	Idaho	862	0.14%
41	New Hampshire	835	0.13%
42	Nebraska	771	0.12%
43	Alaska	678	0.11%
44	South Dakota	661	0.11%
45	Montana	636	0.10%
46	Vermont	592	0.09%
47	Rhode Island	528	0.08%
48	Wyoming	362	0.06%
49	North Dakota	93	0.01%
50	Maine	40	0.01%
	District of Columbia	6,574	1.05%

Source: U.S. Department of Justice, Bureau of Justice Statistics
"The Nation's Correctional Population Tops 5 Million" (Press Release, August 27, 1995, NCJ-1564432)
*As of December 31, 1994. Does not include 61,430 adults on federal parole.

Rate of Adults on State Parole in 1994

National Rate = 327 Adults on State Parole per 100,000 Population*

ALPHA ORDER

RANK	STATE	RATE
18	Alabama	215
26	Alaska	164
28	Arizona	148
15	Arkansas	271
9	California	374
39	Colorado	92
47	Connecticut	48
21	Delaware	194
25	Florida	179
10	Georgia	339
22	Hawaii	190
34	Idaho	109
14	Illinois	308
43	Indiana	77
29	Iowa	142
11	Kansas	338
27	Kentucky	153
5	Louisiana	556
50	Maine	4
7	Maryland	395
38	Massachusetts	98
24	Michigan	185
46	Minnesota	57
42	Mississippi	79
13	Missouri	323
36	Montana	103
45	Nebraska	65
12	Nevada	326
37	New Hampshire	99
3	New Jersey	700
31	New Mexico	130
8	New York	394
6	North Carolina	396
49	North Dakota	20
41	Ohio	87
33	Oklahoma	110
4	Oregon	619
2	Pennsylvania	769
44	Rhode Island	70
17	South Carolina	222
32	South Dakota	129
16	Tennessee	265
1	Texas	830
19	Utah	197
30	Vermont	136
20	Virginia	195
48	Washington	42
40	West Virginia	90
23	Wisconsin	189
35	Wyoming	107

RANK ORDER

RANK	STATE	RATE
1	Texas	830
2	Pennsylvania	769
3	New Jersey	700
4	Oregon	619
5	Louisiana	556
6	North Carolina	396
7	Maryland	395
8	New York	394
9	California	374
10	Georgia	339
11	Kansas	338
12	Nevada	326
13	Missouri	323
14	Illinois	308
15	Arkansas	271
16	Tennessee	265
17	South Carolina	222
18	Alabama	215
19	Utah	197
20	Virginia	195
21	Delaware	194
22	Hawaii	190
23	Wisconsin	189
24	Michigan	185
25	Florida	179
26	Alaska	164
27	Kentucky	153
28	Arizona	148
29	Iowa	142
30	Vermont	136
31	New Mexico	130
32	South Dakota	129
33	Oklahoma	110
34	Idaho	109
35	Wyoming	107
36	Montana	103
37	New Hampshire	99
38	Massachusetts	98
39	Colorado	92
40	West Virginia	90
41	Ohio	87
42	Mississippi	79
43	Indiana	77
44	Rhode Island	70
45	Nebraska	65
46	Minnesota	57
47	Connecticut	48
48	Washington	42
49	North Dakota	20
50	Maine	4
	District of Columbia	1,458

Source: U.S. Department of Justice, Bureau of Justice Statistics
   "The Nation's Correctional Population Tops 5 Million" (Press Release, August 27, 1995, NCJ-1564432)
*As of December 31, 1994. Federal rate is 32 adults on parole per 100,000 adult population.

State and Local Government Employees in Corrections in 1992

National Total = 533,569 Employees*

ALPHA ORDER

RANK	STATE	EMPLOYEES	% of USA
25	Alabama	5,869	1.10%
45	Alaska	1,273	0.24%
15	Arizona	10,123	1.90%
31	Arkansas	3,805	0.71%
1	California	60,854	11.41%
24	Colorado	6,183	1.16%
28	Connecticut	5,418	1.02%
41	Delaware	1,675	0.31%
4	Florida	41,785	7.83%
7	Georgia	18,796	3.52%
38	Hawaii	2,026	0.38%
42	Idaho	1,654	0.31%
5	Illinois	19,614	3.68%
18	Indiana	9,408	1.76%
36	Iowa	2,781	0.52%
30	Kansas	4,890	0.92%
23	Kentucky	6,807	1.28%
16	Louisiana	9,801	1.84%
39	Maine	1,868	0.35%
13	Maryland	10,921	2.05%
17	Massachusetts	9,630	1.80%
6	Michigan	19,403	3.64%
27	Minnesota	5,533	1.04%
34	Mississippi	3,525	0.66%
21	Missouri	8,610	1.61%
46	Montana	1,265	0.24%
37	Nebraska	2,550	0.48%
33	Nevada	3,571	0.67%
44	New Hampshire	1,376	0.26%
9	New Jersey	18,158	3.40%
32	New Mexico	3,736	0.70%
2	New York	58,988	11.06%
11	North Carolina	15,099	2.83%
50	North Dakota	674	0.13%
10	Ohio	16,722	3.13%
26	Oklahoma	5,641	1.06%
29	Oregon	5,370	1.01%
8	Pennsylvania	18,653	3.50%
40	Rhode Island	1,821	0.34%
20	South Carolina	8,651	1.62%
47	South Dakota	820	0.15%
14	Tennessee	10,579	1.98%
3	Texas	46,440	8.70%
35	Utah	2,815	0.53%
49	Vermont	697	0.13%
12	Virginia	13,988	2.62%
19	Washington	9,121	1.71%
43	West Virginia	1,414	0.27%
22	Wisconsin	7,329	1.37%
48	Wyoming	779	0.15%

RANK ORDER

RANK	STATE	EMPLOYEES	% of USA
1	California	60,854	11.41%
2	New York	58,988	11.06%
3	Texas	46,440	8.70%
4	Florida	41,785	7.83%
5	Illinois	19,614	3.68%
6	Michigan	19,403	3.64%
7	Georgia	18,796	3.52%
8	Pennsylvania	18,653	3.50%
9	New Jersey	18,158	3.40%
10	Ohio	16,722	3.13%
11	North Carolina	15,099	2.83%
12	Virginia	13,988	2.62%
13	Maryland	10,921	2.05%
14	Tennessee	10,579	1.98%
15	Arizona	10,123	1.90%
16	Louisiana	9,801	1.84%
17	Massachusetts	9,630	1.80%
18	Indiana	9,408	1.76%
19	Washington	9,121	1.71%
20	South Carolina	8,651	1.62%
21	Missouri	8,610	1.61%
22	Wisconsin	7,329	1.37%
23	Kentucky	6,807	1.28%
24	Colorado	6,183	1.16%
25	Alabama	5,869	1.10%
26	Oklahoma	5,641	1.06%
27	Minnesota	5,533	1.04%
28	Connecticut	5,418	1.02%
29	Oregon	5,370	1.01%
30	Kansas	4,890	0.92%
31	Arkansas	3,805	0.71%
32	New Mexico	3,736	0.70%
33	Nevada	3,571	0.67%
34	Mississippi	3,525	0.66%
35	Utah	2,815	0.53%
36	Iowa	2,781	0.52%
37	Nebraska	2,550	0.48%
38	Hawaii	2,026	0.38%
39	Maine	1,868	0.35%
40	Rhode Island	1,821	0.34%
41	Delaware	1,675	0.31%
42	Idaho	1,654	0.31%
43	West Virginia	1,414	0.27%
44	New Hampshire	1,376	0.26%
45	Alaska	1,273	0.24%
46	Montana	1,265	0.24%
47	South Dakota	820	0.15%
48	Wyoming	779	0.15%
49	Vermont	697	0.13%
50	North Dakota	674	0.13%
	District of Columbia	5,060	0.95%

Source: U.S. Bureau of the Census
      "Public Employment: 1992" (September 1994, GE/92-1)
*Full-time equivalent as of October 1992.

166

State and Local Government Employees in Corrections
As a Percent of All State and Local Government Employees in 1992
National Percent = 3.99% of Employees*

ALPHA ORDER

RANK	STATE	EMPLOYEES
41	Alabama	2.49
37	Alaska	2.77
4	Arizona	5.08
34	Arkansas	2.96
11	California	4.26
26	Colorado	3.34
20	Connecticut	3.58
8	Delaware	4.44
1	Florida	6.29
5	Georgia	4.73
29	Hawaii	3.14
38	Idaho	2.75
23	Illinois	3.46
28	Indiana	3.16
49	Iowa	1.79
30	Kansas	3.11
23	Kentucky	3.46
16	Louisiana	3.93
35	Maine	2.87
7	Maryland	4.56
22	Massachusetts	3.47
12	Michigan	4.21
43	Minnesota	2.31
45	Mississippi	2.27
21	Missouri	3.48
42	Montana	2.33
40	Nebraska	2.56
2	Nevada	5.41
39	New Hampshire	2.66
9	New Jersey	4.35
19	New Mexico	3.65
3	New York	5.12
14	North Carolina	4.09
48	North Dakota	1.80
31	Ohio	3.10
33	Oklahoma	3.00
23	Oregon	3.46
18	Pennsylvania	3.66
17	Rhode Island	3.82
10	South Carolina	4.29
47	South Dakota	2.09
13	Tennessee	4.17
6	Texas	4.70
32	Utah	3.03
44	Vermont	2.28
15	Virginia	4.05
27	Washington	3.31
50	West Virginia	1.53
36	Wisconsin	2.80
46	Wyoming	2.13

RANK ORDER

RANK	STATE	EMPLOYEES
1	Florida	6.29
2	Nevada	5.41
3	New York	5.12
4	Arizona	5.08
5	Georgia	4.73
6	Texas	4.70
7	Maryland	4.56
8	Delaware	4.44
9	New Jersey	4.35
10	South Carolina	4.29
11	California	4.26
12	Michigan	4.21
13	Tennessee	4.17
14	North Carolina	4.09
15	Virginia	4.05
16	Louisiana	3.93
17	Rhode Island	3.82
18	Pennsylvania	3.66
19	New Mexico	3.65
20	Connecticut	3.58
21	Missouri	3.48
22	Massachusetts	3.47
23	Illinois	3.46
23	Kentucky	3.46
23	Oregon	3.46
26	Colorado	3.34
27	Washington	3.31
28	Indiana	3.16
29	Hawaii	3.14
30	Kansas	3.11
31	Ohio	3.10
32	Utah	3.03
33	Oklahoma	3.00
34	Arkansas	2.96
35	Maine	2.87
36	Wisconsin	2.80
37	Alaska	2.77
38	Idaho	2.75
39	New Hampshire	2.66
40	Nebraska	2.56
41	Alabama	2.49
42	Montana	2.33
43	Minnesota	2.31
44	Vermont	2.28
45	Mississippi	2.27
46	Wyoming	2.13
47	South Dakota	2.09
48	North Dakota	1.80
49	Iowa	1.79
50	West Virginia	1.53

District of Columbia — 9.26

Source: Morgan Quitno Press using data from U.S. Bureau of the Census
"Public Employment: 1992" (September 1994, GE/92-1)
*Full-time equivalent as of October 1992.

State Government Employees in Corrections in 1993

National Total = 362,689 Employees*

ALPHA ORDER

RANK	STATE	EMPLOYEES	% of USA
26	Alabama	4,240	1.17%
41	Alaska	1,234	0.34%
20	Arizona	6,350	1.75%
31	Arkansas	2,868	0.79%
1	California	37,341	10.30%
28	Colorado	3,769	1.04%
22	Connecticut	6,186	1.71%
40	Delaware	1,481	0.41%
4	Florida	29,069	8.01%
6	Georgia	14,835	4.09%
36	Hawaii	2,121	0.58%
42	Idaho	1,194	0.33%
7	Illinois	12,669	3.49%
21	Indiana	6,233	1.72%
34	Iowa	2,184	0.60%
29	Kansas	3,460	0.95%
25	Kentucky	5,026	1.39%
18	Louisiana	6,585	1.82%
43	Maine	1,110	0.31%
12	Maryland	9,421	2.60%
23	Massachusetts	5,719	1.58%
5	Michigan	15,114	4.17%
33	Minnesota	2,585	0.71%
30	Mississippi	3,131	0.86%
17	Missouri	6,593	1.82%
46	Montana	781	0.22%
39	Nebraska	1,766	0.49%
37	Nevada	2,120	0.58%
44	New Hampshire	988	0.27%
13	New Jersey	9,405	2.59%
27	New Mexico	3,795	1.05%
2	New York	34,147	9.41%
8	North Carolina	12,367	3.41%
49	North Dakota	499	0.14%
9	Ohio	11,261	3.10%
19	Oklahoma	6,389	1.76%
32	Oregon	2,675	0.74%
11	Pennsylvania	9,562	2.64%
38	Rhode Island	1,814	0.50%
14	South Carolina	7,423	2.05%
48	South Dakota	641	0.18%
16	Tennessee	6,892	1.90%
3	Texas	31,632	8.72%
35	Utah	2,157	0.59%
47	Vermont	737	0.20%
10	Virginia	10,790	2.98%
15	Washington	7,415	2.04%
45	West Virginia	801	0.22%
24	Wisconsin	5,641	1.56%
50	Wyoming	473	0.13%

RANK ORDER

RANK	STATE	EMPLOYEES	% of USA
1	California	37,341	10.30%
2	New York	34,147	9.41%
3	Texas	31,632	8.72%
4	Florida	29,069	8.01%
5	Michigan	15,114	4.17%
6	Georgia	14,835	4.09%
7	Illinois	12,669	3.49%
8	North Carolina	12,367	3.41%
9	Ohio	11,261	3.10%
10	Virginia	10,790	2.98%
11	Pennsylvania	9,562	2.64%
12	Maryland	9,421	2.60%
13	New Jersey	9,405	2.59%
14	South Carolina	7,423	2.05%
15	Washington	7,415	2.04%
16	Tennessee	6,892	1.90%
17	Missouri	6,593	1.82%
18	Louisiana	6,585	1.82%
19	Oklahoma	6,389	1.76%
20	Arizona	6,350	1.75%
21	Indiana	6,233	1.72%
22	Connecticut	6,186	1.71%
23	Massachusetts	5,719	1.58%
24	Wisconsin	5,641	1.56%
25	Kentucky	5,026	1.39%
26	Alabama	4,240	1.17%
27	New Mexico	3,795	1.05%
28	Colorado	3,769	1.04%
29	Kansas	3,460	0.95%
30	Mississippi	3,131	0.86%
31	Arkansas	2,868	0.79%
32	Oregon	2,675	0.74%
33	Minnesota	2,585	0.71%
34	Iowa	2,184	0.60%
35	Utah	2,157	0.59%
36	Hawaii	2,121	0.58%
37	Nevada	2,120	0.58%
38	Rhode Island	1,814	0.50%
39	Nebraska	1,766	0.49%
40	Delaware	1,481	0.41%
41	Alaska	1,234	0.34%
42	Idaho	1,194	0.33%
43	Maine	1,110	0.31%
44	New Hampshire	988	0.27%
45	West Virginia	801	0.22%
46	Montana	781	0.22%
47	Vermont	737	0.20%
48	South Dakota	641	0.18%
49	North Dakota	499	0.14%
50	Wyoming	473	0.13%
	District of Columbia**	NA	NA

Source: U.S. Bureau of the Census
   "Public Employment: 1993" (http://www.census.gov)
Full-time equivalent as of October 1993.
***Not applicable.*

State Government Employees in Corrections
As a Percent of All State Government Employees in 1993
National Percent = 9.32% of Employees*

ALPHA ORDER

RANK	STATE	PERCENT
42	Alabama	5.12
39	Alaska	5.65
6	Arizona	11.20
33	Arkansas	6.15
10	California	10.86
30	Colorado	6.91
11	Connecticut	10.31
25	Delaware	7.25
1	Florida	17.40
4	Georgia	12.52
47	Hawaii	4.10
36	Idaho	5.81
12	Illinois	9.61
27	Indiana	7.10
46	Iowa	4.28
25	Kansas	7.25
29	Kentucky	7.01
24	Louisiana	7.28
40	Maine	5.21
5	Maryland	11.23
27	Massachusetts	7.10
8	Michigan	11.12
48	Minnesota	3.85
32	Mississippi	6.56
20	Missouri	8.36
44	Montana	4.50
34	Nebraska	6.06
8	Nevada	11.12
35	New Hampshire	5.85
19	New Jersey	8.54
18	New Mexico	8.85
3	New York	12.77
7	North Carolina	11.18
49	North Dakota	3.18
22	Ohio	7.97
14	Oklahoma	9.37
38	Oregon	5.67
31	Pennsylvania	6.60
15	Rhode Island	9.15
13	South Carolina	9.53
43	South Dakota	4.61
17	Tennessee	8.92
2	Texas	12.78
41	Utah	5.13
36	Vermont	5.81
16	Virginia	9.14
23	Washington	7.69
50	West Virginia	2.40
21	Wisconsin	8.11
45	Wyoming	4.35

RANK ORDER

RANK	STATE	PERCENT
1	Florida	17.40
2	Texas	12.78
3	New York	12.77
4	Georgia	12.52
5	Maryland	11.23
6	Arizona	11.20
7	North Carolina	11.18
8	Michigan	11.12
8	Nevada	11.12
10	California	10.86
11	Connecticut	10.31
12	Illinois	9.61
13	South Carolina	9.53
14	Oklahoma	9.37
15	Rhode Island	9.15
16	Virginia	9.14
17	Tennessee	8.92
18	New Mexico	8.85
19	New Jersey	8.54
20	Missouri	8.36
21	Wisconsin	8.11
22	Ohio	7.97
23	Washington	7.69
24	Louisiana	7.28
25	Delaware	7.25
25	Kansas	7.25
27	Indiana	7.10
27	Massachusetts	7.10
29	Kentucky	7.01
30	Colorado	6.91
31	Pennsylvania	6.60
32	Mississippi	6.56
33	Arkansas	6.15
34	Nebraska	6.06
35	New Hampshire	5.85
36	Idaho	5.81
36	Vermont	5.81
38	Oregon	5.67
39	Alaska	5.65
40	Maine	5.21
41	Utah	5.13
42	Alabama	5.12
43	South Dakota	4.61
44	Montana	4.50
45	Wyoming	4.35
46	Iowa	4.28
47	Hawaii	4.10
48	Minnesota	3.85
49	North Dakota	3.18
50	West Virginia	2.40
	District of Columbia**	NA

Source: Morgan Quitno Press using data from U.S. Bureau of the Census
     "Public Employment: 1993" (http://www.census.gov)
Full-time equivalent as of October 1993.
**Not applicable.*

State Correctional Officers in 1994

National Total = 195,205 Officers*

ALPHA ORDER					RANK ORDER			
RANK	STATE		OFFICERS	% of USA	RANK	STATE	OFFICERS	% of USA
23	Alabama		2,508	1.28%	1	New York	20,099	10.30%
40	Alaska		779	0.40%	2	Texas	20,019	10.26%
15	Arizona		4,218	2.16%	3	California	17,938	9.19%
27	Arkansas		1,793	0.92%	4	Florida	14,226	7.29%
3	California		17,938	9.19%	5	Michigan	9,145	4.68%
25	Colorado		2,001	1.03%	6	Georgia	7,932	4.06%
13	Connecticut		4,794	2.46%	7	Illinois	7,321	3.75%
38	Delaware		911	0.47%	8	North Carolina	6,693	3.43%
4	Florida		14,226	7.29%	9	Ohio	6,072	3.11%
6	Georgia		7,932	4.06%	10	Virginia	5,595	2.87%
36	Hawaii		956	0.49%	11	Pennsylvania	5,447	2.79%
41	Idaho		669	0.34%	12	New Jersey	5,367	2.75%
7	Illinois		7,321	3.75%	13	Connecticut	4,794	2.46%
16	Indiana		4,006	2.05%	14	Maryland	4,219	2.16%
32	Iowa		1,236	0.63%	15	Arizona	4,218	2.16%
28	Kansas		1,773	0.91%	16	Indiana	4,006	2.05%
30	Kentucky		1,681	0.86%	17	Louisiana	3,809	1.95%
17	Louisiana		3,809	1.95%	18	South Carolina	3,471	1.78%
42	Maine		611	0.31%	19	Massachusetts	3,271	1.68%
14	Maryland		4,219	2.16%	20	Tennessee	3,122	1.60%
19	Massachusetts		3,271	1.68%	21	Missouri	2,799	1.43%
5	Michigan		9,145	4.68%	22	Washington	2,702	1.38%
31	Minnesota		1,418	0.73%	23	Alabama	2,508	1.28%
26	Mississippi		1,810	0.93%	24	Wisconsin	2,421	1.24%
21	Missouri		2,799	1.43%	25	Colorado	2,001	1.03%
49	Montana		222	0.11%	26	Mississippi	1,810	0.93%
43	Nebraska		600	0.31%	27	Arkansas	1,793	0.92%
35	Nevada		1,088	0.56%	28	Kansas	1,773	0.91%
45	New Hampshire		478	0.24%	29	Oklahoma	1,711	0.88%
12	New Jersey		5,367	2.75%	30	Kentucky	1,681	0.86%
33	New Mexico		1,178	0.60%	31	Minnesota	1,418	0.73%
1	New York		20,099	10.30%	32	Iowa	1,236	0.63%
8	North Carolina		6,693	3.43%	33	New Mexico	1,178	0.60%
50	North Dakota		118	0.06%	34	Oregon	1,091	0.56%
9	Ohio		6,072	3.11%	35	Nevada	1,088	0.56%
29	Oklahoma		1,711	0.88%	36	Hawaii	956	0.49%
34	Oregon		1,091	0.56%	37	Utah	938	0.48%
11	Pennsylvania		5,447	2.79%	38	Delaware	911	0.47%
39	Rhode Island		907	0.46%	39	Rhode Island	907	0.46%
18	South Carolina		3,471	1.78%	40	Alaska	779	0.40%
47	South Dakota		318	0.16%	41	Idaho	669	0.34%
20	Tennessee		3,122	1.60%	42	Maine	611	0.31%
2	Texas		20,019	10.26%	43	Nebraska	600	0.31%
37	Utah		938	0.48%	44	West Virginia	545	0.28%
46	Vermont		407	0.21%	45	New Hampshire	478	0.24%
10	Virginia		5,595	2.87%	46	Vermont	407	0.21%
22	Washington		2,702	1.38%	47	South Dakota	318	0.16%
44	West Virginia		545	0.28%	48	Wyoming	241	0.12%
24	Wisconsin		2,421	1.24%	49	Montana	222	0.11%
48	Wyoming		241	0.12%	50	North Dakota	118	0.06%
						District of Columbia	2,531	1.30%

Source: American Correctional Association (Lanham, MD)
"1995 Directory of Juvenile and Adult Correctional Departments, Institutions, Agencies and Paroling Authorities"
As of June 30, 1994. Total does not include 10,238 federal correctional officers.

Male Correctional Officers in Adult Systems in 1994

National Total = 160,058 Male Officers*

ALPHA ORDER

RANK	STATE	OFFICERS	% of USA
23	Alabama	1,948	1.22%
39	Alaska	632	0.39%
14	Arizona	3,393	2.12%
27	Arkansas	1,426	0.89%
3	California	14,574	9.11%
24	Colorado	1,618	1.01%
13	Connecticut	3,776	2.36%
37	Delaware	783	0.49%
4	Florida	10,513	6.57%
6	Georgia	6,472	4.04%
36	Hawaii	830	0.52%
40	Idaho	569	0.36%
7	Illinois	6,423	4.01%
16	Indiana	3,098	1.94%
32	Iowa	1,056	0.66%
25	Kansas	1,502	0.94%
28	Kentucky	1,400	0.87%
17	Louisiana	2,970	1.86%
41	Maine	547	0.34%
15	Maryland	3,315	2.07%
NA	Massachusetts**	NA	NA
5	Michigan	7,261	4.54%
30	Minnesota	1,082	0.68%
29	Mississippi	1,090	0.68%
20	Missouri	2,400	1.50%
47	Montana	200	0.12%
43	Nebraska	488	0.30%
34	Nevada	910	0.57%
44	New Hampshire	438	0.27%
11	New Jersey	4,675	2.92%
31	New Mexico	1,073	0.67%
1	New York	18,600	11.62%
8	North Carolina	5,672	3.54%
49	North Dakota	107	0.07%
10	Ohio	4,985	3.11%
26	Oklahoma	1,494	0.93%
33	Oregon	937	0.59%
9	Pennsylvania	5,002	3.13%
35	Rhode Island	834	0.52%
18	South Carolina	2,506	1.57%
46	South Dakota	257	0.16%
19	Tennessee	2,501	1.56%
2	Texas	15,270	9.54%
38	Utah	770	0.48%
45	Vermont	367	0.23%
12	Virginia	4,410	2.76%
21	Washington	2,171	1.36%
42	West Virginia	493	0.31%
22	Wisconsin	1,968	1.23%
47	Wyoming	200	0.12%

RANK ORDER

RANK	STATE	OFFICERS	% of USA
1	New York	18,600	11.62%
2	Texas	15,270	9.54%
3	California	14,574	9.11%
4	Florida	10,513	6.57%
5	Michigan	7,261	4.54%
6	Georgia	6,472	4.04%
7	Illinois	6,423	4.01%
8	North Carolina	5,672	3.54%
9	Pennsylvania	5,002	3.13%
10	Ohio	4,985	3.11%
11	New Jersey	4,675	2.92%
12	Virginia	4,410	2.76%
13	Connecticut	3,776	2.36%
14	Arizona	3,393	2.12%
15	Maryland	3,315	2.07%
16	Indiana	3,098	1.94%
17	Louisiana	2,970	1.86%
18	South Carolina	2,506	1.57%
19	Tennessee	2,501	1.56%
20	Missouri	2,400	1.50%
21	Washington	2,171	1.36%
22	Wisconsin	1,968	1.23%
23	Alabama	1,948	1.22%
24	Colorado	1,618	1.01%
25	Kansas	1,502	0.94%
26	Oklahoma	1,494	0.93%
27	Arkansas	1,426	0.89%
28	Kentucky	1,400	0.87%
29	Mississippi	1,090	0.68%
30	Minnesota	1,082	0.68%
31	New Mexico	1,073	0.67%
32	Iowa	1,056	0.66%
33	Oregon	937	0.59%
34	Nevada	910	0.57%
35	Rhode Island	834	0.52%
36	Hawaii	830	0.52%
37	Delaware	783	0.49%
38	Utah	770	0.48%
39	Alaska	632	0.39%
40	Idaho	569	0.36%
41	Maine	547	0.34%
42	West Virginia	493	0.31%
43	Nebraska	488	0.30%
44	New Hampshire	438	0.27%
45	Vermont	367	0.23%
46	South Dakota	257	0.16%
47	Montana	200	0.12%
47	Wyoming	200	0.12%
49	North Dakota	107	0.07%
NA	Massachusetts**	NA	NA
	District of Columbia	1,781	1.11%

Source: American Correctional Association (Lanham, MD)
"1995 Directory of Juvenile and Adult Correctional Departments, Institutions, Agencies and Paroling Authorities"
As of June 30, 1994. Total does not include 9,117 male federal correctional officers.

Female Correctional Officers in Adult Systems in 1994

National Total = 35,147 Female Officers*

ALPHA ORDER					RANK ORDER			
RANK	STATE		OFFICERS	% of USA	RANK	STATE	OFFICERS	% of USA
20	Alabama		560	1.59%	1	Texas	4,749	13.51%
35	Alaska		147	0.42%	2	Florida	3,713	10.56%
16	Arizona		825	2.35%	3	California	3,364	9.57%
26	Arkansas		367	1.04%	4	Michigan	1,884	5.36%
3	California		3,364	9.57%	5	New York	1,499	4.26%
25	Colorado		383	1.09%	6	Georgia	1,460	4.15%
10	Connecticut		1,018	2.90%	7	Virginia	1,185	3.37%
36	Delaware		128	0.36%	8	Ohio	1,087	3.09%
2	Florida		3,713	10.56%	9	North Carolina	1,021	2.90%
6	Georgia		1,460	4.15%	10	Connecticut	1,018	2.90%
37	Hawaii		126	0.36%	11	South Carolina	965	2.75%
40	Idaho		100	0.28%	12	Indiana	908	2.58%
14	Illinois		898	2.55%	13	Maryland	904	2.57%
12	Indiana		908	2.58%	14	Illinois	898	2.55%
31	Iowa		180	0.51%	15	Louisiana	839	2.39%
29	Kansas		271	0.77%	16	Arizona	825	2.35%
28	Kentucky		281	0.80%	17	Mississippi	720	2.05%
15	Louisiana		839	2.39%	18	New Jersey	692	1.97%
42	Maine		64	0.18%	19	Tennessee	621	1.77%
13	Maryland		904	2.57%	20	Alabama	560	1.59%
NA	Massachusetts**		NA	NA	21	Washington	531	1.51%
4	Michigan		1,884	5.36%	22	Wisconsin	453	1.29%
27	Minnesota		336	0.96%	23	Pennsylvania	445	1.27%
17	Mississippi		720	2.05%	24	Missouri	399	1.14%
24	Missouri		399	1.14%	25	Colorado	383	1.09%
48	Montana		22	0.06%	26	Arkansas	367	1.04%
38	Nebraska		112	0.32%	27	Minnesota	336	0.96%
32	Nevada		178	0.51%	28	Kentucky	281	0.80%
46	New Hampshire		40	0.11%	29	Kansas	271	0.77%
18	New Jersey		692	1.97%	30	Oklahoma	217	0.62%
39	New Mexico		105	0.30%	31	Iowa	180	0.51%
5	New York		1,499	4.26%	32	Nevada	178	0.51%
9	North Carolina		1,021	2.90%	33	Utah	168	0.48%
49	North Dakota		11	0.03%	34	Oregon	154	0.44%
8	Ohio		1,087	3.09%	35	Alaska	147	0.42%
30	Oklahoma		217	0.62%	36	Delaware	128	0.36%
34	Oregon		154	0.44%	37	Hawaii	126	0.36%
23	Pennsylvania		445	1.27%	38	Nebraska	112	0.32%
41	Rhode Island		73	0.21%	39	New Mexico	105	0.30%
11	South Carolina		965	2.75%	40	Idaho	100	0.28%
43	South Dakota		61	0.17%	41	Rhode Island	73	0.21%
19	Tennessee		621	1.77%	42	Maine	64	0.18%
1	Texas		4,749	13.51%	43	South Dakota	61	0.17%
33	Utah		168	0.48%	44	West Virginia	52	0.15%
46	Vermont		40	0.11%	45	Wyoming	41	0.12%
7	Virginia		1,185	3.37%	46	New Hampshire	40	0.11%
21	Washington		531	1.51%	46	Vermont	40	0.11%
44	West Virginia		52	0.15%	48	Montana	22	0.06%
22	Wisconsin		453	1.29%	49	North Dakota	11	0.03%
45	Wyoming		41	0.12%	NA	Massachusetts**	NA	NA
						District of Columbia	750	2.13%

Source: American Correctional Association (Lanham, MD)
   "1995 Directory of Juvenile and Adult Correctional Departments, Institutions, Agencies and Paroling Authorities"
*As of June 30, 1994. Total does not include 1,131 female federal correctional officers.

State Prisoners per Correctional Officer in 1994

National Rate = 4.25 Prisoners per Officer*

ALPHA ORDER

RANK	STATE	RATE
7	Alabama	6.80
42	Alaska	3.00
26	Arizona	4.25
16	Arkansas	5.00
5	California	7.33
29	Colorado	4.07
22	Connecticut	4.50
28	Delaware	4.19
14	Florida	5.60
24	Georgia	4.30
48	Hawaii	2.50
16	Idaho	5.00
23	Illinois	4.40
30	Indiana	4.00
1	Iowa	12.23
39	Kansas	3.40
4	Kentucky	7.90
37	Louisiana	3.50
50	Maine	2.30
9	Maryland	5.90
40	Massachusetts	3.36
16	Michigan	5.00
41	Minnesota	3.10
12	Mississippi	5.75
8	Missouri	6.04
2	Montana	10.76
24	Nebraska	4.30
36	Nevada	3.60
30	New Hampshire	4.00
35	New Jersey	3.66
47	New Mexico	2.90
42	New York	3.00
42	North Carolina	3.00
16	North Dakota	5.00
3	Ohio	8.70
6	Oklahoma	7.08
9	Oregon	5.90
20	Pennsylvania	4.90
42	Rhode Island	3.00
15	South Carolina	5.10
21	South Dakota	4.64
30	Tennessee	4.00
34	Texas	3.87
11	Utah	5.80
49	Vermont	2.40
38	Virginia	3.41
27	Washington	4.20
42	West Virginia	3.00
30	Wisconsin	4.00
13	Wyoming	5.65

RANK ORDER

RANK	STATE	RATE
1	Iowa	12.23
2	Montana	10.76
3	Ohio	8.70
4	Kentucky	7.90
5	California	7.33
6	Oklahoma	7.08
7	Alabama	6.80
8	Missouri	6.04
9	Maryland	5.90
9	Oregon	5.90
11	Utah	5.80
12	Mississippi	5.75
13	Wyoming	5.65
14	Florida	5.60
15	South Carolina	5.10
16	Arkansas	5.00
16	Idaho	5.00
16	Michigan	5.00
16	North Dakota	5.00
20	Pennsylvania	4.90
21	South Dakota	4.64
22	Connecticut	4.50
23	Illinois	4.40
24	Georgia	4.30
24	Nebraska	4.30
26	Arizona	4.25
27	Washington	4.20
28	Delaware	4.19
29	Colorado	4.07
30	Indiana	4.00
30	New Hampshire	4.00
30	Tennessee	4.00
30	Wisconsin	4.00
34	Texas	3.87
35	New Jersey	3.66
36	Nevada	3.60
37	Louisiana	3.50
38	Virginia	3.41
39	Kansas	3.40
40	Massachusetts	3.36
41	Minnesota	3.10
42	Alaska	3.00
42	New York	3.00
42	North Carolina	3.00
42	Rhode Island	3.00
42	West Virginia	3.00
47	New Mexico	2.90
48	Hawaii	2.50
49	Vermont	2.40
50	Maine	2.30

	District of Columbia	3.91

Source: American Correctional Association (Lanham, MD)
"1995 Directory of Juvenile and Adult Correctional Departments, Institutions, Agencies and Paroling Authorities"
*As of June 30, 1994. National rate does not include federal or District of Columbia prisoner to officer rate.
Federal rate is eight prisoners per officer.

Turnover Rate of Correctional Officers in Adult Systems in 1994

National Rate = 11.00%*

ALPHA ORDER		
RANK	STATE	TURNOVER RATE
36	Alabama	7.00
17	Alaska	13.00
1	Arizona	28.50
2	Arkansas	25.00
43	California	4.50
43	Colorado	4.50
31	Connecticut	9.00
47	Delaware	4.20
26	Florida	10.70
7	Georgia	20.00
40	Hawaii	5.00
20	Idaho	11.50
43	Illinois	4.50
11	Indiana	16.26
23	Iowa	11.00
12	Kansas	15.10
5	Kentucky	22.00
8	Louisiana	19.00
13	Maine	15.00
28	Maryland	10.00
9	Massachusetts	17.00
40	Michigan	5.00
31	Minnesota	9.00
39	Mississippi	5.40
16	Missouri	13.50
28	Montana	10.00
20	Nebraska	11.50
20	Nevada	11.50
23	New Hampshire	11.00
34	New Jersey	8.40
6	New Mexico	20.50
50	New York	2.30
23	North Carolina	11.00
49	North Dakota	3.00
18	Ohio	12.80
27	Oklahoma	10.60
31	Oregon	9.00
48	Pennsylvania	4.00
38	Rhode Island	6.00
4	South Carolina	23.20
3	South Dakota	24.30
14	Tennessee	14.00
30	Texas	9.60
43	Utah	4.50
18	Vermont	12.80
14	Virginia	14.00
37	Washington	6.40
40	West Virginia	5.00
35	Wisconsin	7.10
9	Wyoming	17.00

RANK ORDER		
RANK	STATE	TURNOVER RATE
1	Arizona	28.50
2	Arkansas	25.00
3	South Dakota	24.30
4	South Carolina	23.20
5	Kentucky	22.00
6	New Mexico	20.50
7	Georgia	20.00
8	Louisiana	19.00
9	Massachusetts	17.00
9	Wyoming	17.00
11	Indiana	16.26
12	Kansas	15.10
13	Maine	15.00
14	Tennessee	14.00
14	Virginia	14.00
16	Missouri	13.50
17	Alaska	13.00
18	Ohio	12.80
18	Vermont	12.80
20	Idaho	11.50
20	Nebraska	11.50
20	Nevada	11.50
23	Iowa	11.00
23	New Hampshire	11.00
23	North Carolina	11.00
26	Florida	10.70
27	Oklahoma	10.60
28	Maryland	10.00
28	Montana	10.00
30	Texas	9.60
31	Connecticut	9.00
31	Minnesota	9.00
31	Oregon	9.00
34	New Jersey	8.40
35	Wisconsin	7.10
36	Alabama	7.00
37	Washington	6.40
38	Rhode Island	6.00
39	Mississippi	5.40
40	Hawaii	5.00
40	Michigan	5.00
40	West Virginia	5.00
43	California	4.50
43	Colorado	4.50
43	Illinois	4.50
43	Utah	4.50
47	Delaware	4.20
48	Pennsylvania	4.00
49	North Dakota	3.00
50	New York	2.30
	District of Columbia	9.90

Source: American Correctional Association (Lanham, MD)
    "1995 Directory of Juvenile and Adult Correctional Departments, Institutions, Agencies and Paroling Authorities"
*As of June 30, 1994. National rate does not include federal or District of Columbia turnover rate. Federal turnover rate is 5.3%.

Average Annual Salary of State Corrections Officers in 1992

National Average = $24,239*

ALPHA ORDER

RANK	STATE	SALARY
14	Alabama	$25,240
1	Alaska	41,215
26	Arizona	20,250
45	Arkansas	16,458
2	California	38,604
11	Colorado	26,220
5	Connecticut	29,000
35	Delaware	18,902
34	Florida	18,987
28	Georgia	20,171
17	Hawaii	24,701
25	Idaho	20,363
13	Illinois	25,440
NA	Indiana**	NA
12	Iowa	25,800
18	Kansas	24,144
40	Kentucky	17,796
27	Louisiana	20,184
31	Maine	19,427
NA	Maryland**	NA
16	Massachusetts	25,000
7	Michigan	28,870
10	Minnesota	27,000
37	Mississippi	18,000
36	Missouri	18,015
41	Montana	17,506
30	Nebraska	19,902
9	Nevada	27,622
20	New Hampshire	23,897
3	New Jersey	34,984
42	New Mexico	17,325
4	New York	29,128
32	North Carolina	19,236
46	North Dakota	16,000
22	Ohio	23,046
33	Oklahoma	19,038
6	Oregon	28,944
8	Pennsylvania	28,479
19	Rhode Island	24,136
44	South Carolina	16,498
47	South Dakota	15,548
37	Tennessee	18,000
21	Texas	23,385
NA	Utah**	NA
23	Vermont	21,653
24	Virginia	21,534
15	Washington	25,098
37	West Virginia	18,000
29	Wisconsin	20,006
43	Wyoming	17,249

RANK ORDER

RANK	STATE	SALARY
1	Alaska	$41,215
2	California	38,604
3	New Jersey	34,984
4	New York	29,128
5	Connecticut	29,000
6	Oregon	28,944
7	Michigan	28,870
8	Pennsylvania	28,479
9	Nevada	27,622
10	Minnesota	27,000
11	Colorado	26,220
12	Iowa	25,800
13	Illinois	25,440
14	Alabama	25,240
15	Washington	25,098
16	Massachusetts	25,000
17	Hawaii	24,701
18	Kansas	24,144
19	Rhode Island	24,136
20	New Hampshire	23,897
21	Texas	23,385
22	Ohio	23,046
23	Vermont	21,653
24	Virginia	21,534
25	Idaho	20,363
26	Arizona	20,250
27	Louisiana	20,184
28	Georgia	20,171
29	Wisconsin	20,006
30	Nebraska	19,902
31	Maine	19,427
32	North Carolina	19,236
33	Oklahoma	19,038
34	Florida	18,987
35	Delaware	18,902
36	Missouri	18,015
37	Mississippi	18,000
37	Tennessee	18,000
37	West Virginia	18,000
40	Kentucky	17,796
41	Montana	17,506
42	New Mexico	17,325
43	Wyoming	17,249
44	South Carolina	16,498
45	Arkansas	16,458
46	North Dakota	16,000
47	South Dakota	15,548
NA	Indiana**	NA
NA	Maryland**	NA
NA	Utah**	NA
	District of Columbia	35,027

Source: Contact Publications (Lincoln, NE)
"Corrections Compendium" (October 1992)
**The national average was calculated by Morgan Quitno Press by using a weighted average of the 48 state averages.*
***Not available.*

Jail and Detention Centers in 1993

National Total = 3,304 Jails*

ALPHA ORDER

RANK	STATE	JAILS	% of USA
4	Alabama	129	3.90%
45	Alaska	5	0.15%
34	Arizona	33	1.00%
19	Arkansas	83	2.51%
3	California	136	4.12%
26	Colorado	61	1.85%
NA	Connecticut**	NA	NA
NA	Delaware**	NA	NA
9	Florida	100	3.03%
2	Georgia	202	6.11%
NA	Hawaii**	NA	NA
32	Idaho	39	1.18%
14	Illinois	93	2.81%
18	Indiana	88	2.66%
16	Iowa	90	2.72%
11	Kansas	96	2.91%
20	Kentucky	81	2.45%
11	Louisiana	96	2.91%
43	Maine	15	0.45%
34	Maryland	33	1.00%
41	Massachusetts	20	0.61%
17	Michigan	89	2.69%
23	Minnesota	75	2.27%
13	Mississippi	95	2.88%
5	Missouri	127	3.84%
29	Montana	44	1.33%
25	Nebraska	64	1.94%
41	Nevada	20	0.61%
44	New Hampshire	11	0.33%
37	New Jersey	25	0.76%
33	New Mexico	34	1.03%
22	New York	78	2.36%
8	North Carolina	104	3.15%
37	North Dakota	25	0.76%
6	Ohio	120	3.63%
9	Oklahoma	100	3.03%
30	Oregon	43	1.30%
21	Pennsylvania	79	2.39%
NA	Rhode Island**	NA	NA
28	South Carolina	55	1.66%
36	South Dakota	28	0.85%
7	Tennessee	111	3.36%
1	Texas	267	8.08%
37	Utah	25	0.76%
NA	Vermont**	NA	NA
14	Virginia	93	2.81%
27	Washington	56	1.69%
31	West Virginia	41	1.24%
24	Wisconsin	72	2.18%
40	Wyoming	22	0.67%

RANK ORDER

RANK	STATE	JAILS	% of USA
1	Texas	267	8.08%
2	Georgia	202	6.11%
3	California	136	4.12%
4	Alabama	129	3.90%
5	Missouri	127	3.84%
6	Ohio	120	3.63%
7	Tennessee	111	3.36%
8	North Carolina	104	3.15%
9	Florida	100	3.03%
9	Oklahoma	100	3.03%
11	Kansas	96	2.91%
11	Louisiana	96	2.91%
13	Mississippi	95	2.88%
14	Illinois	93	2.81%
14	Virginia	93	2.81%
16	Iowa	90	2.72%
17	Michigan	89	2.69%
18	Indiana	88	2.66%
19	Arkansas	83	2.51%
20	Kentucky	81	2.45%
21	Pennsylvania	79	2.39%
22	New York	78	2.36%
23	Minnesota	75	2.27%
24	Wisconsin	72	2.18%
25	Nebraska	64	1.94%
26	Colorado	61	1.85%
27	Washington	56	1.69%
28	South Carolina	55	1.66%
29	Montana	44	1.33%
30	Oregon	43	1.30%
31	West Virginia	41	1.24%
32	Idaho	39	1.18%
33	New Mexico	34	1.03%
34	Arizona	33	1.00%
34	Maryland	33	1.00%
36	South Dakota	28	0.85%
37	New Jersey	25	0.76%
37	North Dakota	25	0.76%
37	Utah	25	0.76%
40	Wyoming	22	0.67%
41	Massachusetts	20	0.61%
41	Nevada	20	0.61%
43	Maine	15	0.45%
44	New Hampshire	11	0.33%
45	Alaska	5	0.15%
NA	Connecticut**	NA	NA
NA	Delaware**	NA	NA
NA	Hawaii**	NA	NA
NA	Rhode Island**	NA	NA
NA	Vermont**	NA	NA
	District of Columbia	1	0.03%

Source: U.S. Department of Justice, Bureau of Justice Statistics
"Jail and Jail Inmates 1993-94" (Bulletin, April 1995, NCJ-151651)
As of July 1, 1993. Jails are locally operated correctional facilities that confine persons before or after adjudication. Inmates sentenced to jail usually have a sentence of a year or less.
**These states have combined state and local jail systems and are excluded from this count.*

Local Jail Populations as a Percent of Highest Capacity in 1993

National Percent = 96.8% of Highest Capacity*

ALPHA ORDER				RANK ORDER		
RANK	STATE	PERCENT		RANK	STATE	PERCENT
36	Alabama	76.0		1	Virginia	160.4
44	Alaska	47.7		2	South Carolina	123.8
11	Arizona	97.8		3	New Jersey	119.8
29	Arkansas	83.4		4	Texas	114.9
5	California	112.8		5	California	112.8
14	Colorado	93.5		6	Massachusetts	105.8
NA	Connecticut**	NA		7	Washington	101.6
NA	Delaware**	NA		8	Pennsylvania	100.9
28	Florida	84.0		9	Maryland	98.9
19	Georgia	89.7		10	Ohio	98.0
NA	Hawaii**	NA		11	Arizona	97.8
24	Idaho	88.1		12	Indiana	97.1
13	Illinois	96.1		13	Illinois	96.1
12	Indiana	97.1		14	Colorado	93.5
35	Iowa	76.4		15	New Mexico	91.3
30	Kansas	82.7		16	Michigan	90.8
18	Kentucky	90.3		17	Mississippi	90.6
31	Louisiana	81.7		18	Kentucky	90.3
38	Maine	71.4		19	Georgia	89.7
9	Maryland	98.9		20	Wisconsin	89.5
6	Massachusetts	105.8		21	Tennessee	89.4
16	Michigan	90.8		22	West Virginia	88.4
32	Minnesota	78.3		23	North Carolina	88.3
17	Mississippi	90.6		24	Idaho	88.1
34	Missouri	77.4		25	New York	85.7
41	Montana	59.7		26	Utah	84.8
40	Nebraska	64.0		27	Oregon	84.3
33	Nevada	78.2		28	Florida	84.0
39	New Hampshire	67.2		29	Arkansas	83.4
3	New Jersey	119.8		30	Kansas	82.7
15	New Mexico	91.3		31	Louisiana	81.7
25	New York	85.7		32	Minnesota	78.3
23	North Carolina	88.3		33	Nevada	78.2
45	North Dakota	42.8		34	Missouri	77.4
10	Ohio	98.0		35	Iowa	76.4
37	Oklahoma	74.9		36	Alabama	76.0
27	Oregon	84.3		37	Oklahoma	74.9
8	Pennsylvania	100.9		38	Maine	71.4
NA	Rhode Island**	NA		39	New Hampshire	67.2
2	South Carolina	123.8		40	Nebraska	64.0
42	South Dakota	53.9		41	Montana	59.7
21	Tennessee	89.4		42	South Dakota	53.9
4	Texas	114.9		43	Wyoming	51.5
26	Utah	84.8		44	Alaska	47.7
NA	Vermont**	NA		45	North Dakota	42.8
1	Virginia	160.4		NA	Connecticut**	NA
7	Washington	101.6		NA	Delaware**	NA
22	West Virginia	88.4		NA	Hawaii**	NA
20	Wisconsin	89.5		NA	Rhode Island**	NA
43	Wyoming	51.5		NA	Vermont**	NA
					District of Columbia	121.2

Source: U.S. Department of Justice, Bureau of Justice Statistics
    "Jail and Jail Inmates 1993-94" (Bulletin, April 1995, NCJ-151651)
*As of July 1, 1993. Jails are locally operated correctional facilities that confine persons before or after
adjudication. Inmates sentenced to jail usually have a sentence of a year or less.
**These states have combined state and local jail systems and are excluded from this count.

Inmates in Local Jails in 1993

National Total = 459,804 Inmates*

ALPHA ORDER					RANK ORDER			
RANK	**STATE**		**INMATES**	**% of USA**	**RANK**	**STATE**	**INMATES**	**% of USA**
21	Alabama		7,072	1.54%	1	California	69,298	15.07%
45	Alaska		31	0.01%	2	Texas	55,395	12.05%
20	Arizona		7,231	1.57%	3	Florida	34,183	7.43%
32	Arkansas		2,846	0.62%	4	New York	29,809	6.48%
1	California		69,298	15.07%	5	Georgia	22,663	4.93%
23	Colorado		6,316	1.37%	6	Pennsylvania	19,231	4.18%
NA	Connecticut**		NA	NA	7	Louisiana	16,208	3.52%
NA	Delaware**		NA	NA	8	New Jersey	15,122	3.29%
3	Florida		34,183	7.43%	9	Virginia	14,623	3.18%
5	Georgia		22,663	4.93%	10	Illinois	14,549	3.16%
NA	Hawaii**		NA	NA	11	Tennessee	14,375	3.13%
38	Idaho		1,485	0.32%	12	Michigan	12,479	2.71%
10	Illinois		14,549	3.16%	13	Ohio	11,695	2.54%
16	Indiana		8,297	1.80%	14	Maryland	9,358	2.04%
37	Iowa		1,602	0.35%	15	North Carolina	8,939	1.94%
33	Kansas		2,797	0.61%	16	Indiana	8,297	1.80%
22	Kentucky		6,813	1.48%	17	Wisconsin	7,879	1.71%
7	Louisiana		16,208	3.52%	18	Massachusetts	7,878	1.71%
40	Maine		704	0.15%	19	Washington	7,435	1.62%
14	Maryland		9,358	2.04%	20	Arizona	7,231	1.57%
18	Massachusetts		7,878	1.71%	21	Alabama	7,072	1.54%
12	Michigan		12,479	2.71%	22	Kentucky	6,813	1.48%
29	Minnesota		3,654	0.79%	23	Colorado	6,316	1.37%
26	Mississippi		4,851	1.06%	24	South Carolina	5,713	1.24%
25	Missouri		5,030	1.09%	25	Missouri	5,030	1.09%
41	Montana		680	0.15%	26	Mississippi	4,851	1.06%
36	Nebraska		1,680	0.37%	27	Oklahoma	4,102	0.89%
31	Nevada		2,987	0.65%	28	Oregon	3,777	0.82%
39	New Hampshire		1,127	0.25%	29	Minnesota	3,654	0.79%
8	New Jersey		15,122	3.29%	30	New Mexico	3,058	0.67%
30	New Mexico		3,058	0.67%	31	Nevada	2,987	0.65%
4	New York		29,809	6.48%	32	Arkansas	2,846	0.62%
15	North Carolina		8,939	1.94%	33	Kansas	2,797	0.61%
44	North Dakota		361	0.08%	34	Utah	1,895	0.41%
13	Ohio		11,695	2.54%	35	West Virginia	1,771	0.39%
27	Oklahoma		4,102	0.89%	36	Nebraska	1,680	0.37%
28	Oregon		3,777	0.82%	37	Iowa	1,602	0.35%
6	Pennsylvania		19,231	4.18%	38	Idaho	1,485	0.32%
NA	Rhode Island**		NA	NA	39	New Hampshire	1,127	0.25%
24	South Carolina		5,713	1.24%	40	Maine	704	0.15%
42	South Dakota		623	0.14%	41	Montana	680	0.15%
11	Tennessee		14,375	3.13%	42	South Dakota	623	0.14%
2	Texas		55,395	12.05%	43	Wyoming	495	0.11%
34	Utah		1,895	0.41%	44	North Dakota	361	0.08%
NA	Vermont**		NA	NA	45	Alaska	31	0.01%
9	Virginia		14,623	3.18%	NA	Connecticut**	NA	NA
19	Washington		7,435	1.62%	NA	Delaware**	NA	NA
35	West Virginia		1,771	0.39%	NA	Hawaii**	NA	NA
17	Wisconsin		7,879	1.71%	NA	Rhode Island**	NA	NA
43	Wyoming		495	0.11%	NA	Vermont**	NA	NA
						District of Columbia	1,687	0.37%

Source: U.S. Department of Justice, Bureau of Justice Statistics
   "Jail and Jail Inmates 1993-94" (Bulletin, April 1995, NCJ-151651)
*As of July 1, 1993. Jails are locally operated correctional facilities that confine persons before or after
adjudication. Inmates sentenced to jail usually have a sentence of a year or less.
**These states have combined state and local jail systems and are excluded from this count.

Operating Costs per Inmate in Local Jails: 1993

National Average = $14,667 Per Inmate*

ALPHA ORDER

RANK ORDER

RANK	STATE	PER INMATE		RANK	STATE	PER INMATE
42	Alabama	$8,297		1	New York	$29,297
NA	Alaska**	NA		2	Massachusetts	27,531
39	Arizona	8,552		3	Oregon	24,345
34	Arkansas	11,201		4	Minnesota	24,238
25	California	14,134		5	Nevada	23,367
9	Colorado	19,177		6	New Hampshire	22,993
NA	Connecticut**	NA		7	Maine	21,200
NA	Delaware**	NA		8	Wyoming	20,130
13	Florida	17,530		9	Colorado	19,177
35	Georgia	10,259		10	Kansas	18,972
NA	Hawaii**	NA		11	Ohio	18,152
31	Idaho	11,676		12	North Dakota	17,607
26	Illinois	13,766		13	Florida	17,530
36	Indiana	10,255		14	Iowa	17,399
14	Iowa	17,399		15	New Jersey	17,259
10	Kansas	18,972		16	Maryland	16,812
33	Kentucky	11,416		17	Michigan	16,451
41	Louisiana	8,404		18	Pennsylvania	16,448
7	Maine	21,200		19	Utah	16,129
16	Maryland	16,812		20	Virginia	15,872
2	Massachusetts	27,531		21	Washington	15,331
17	Michigan	16,451		22	Nebraska	15,198
4	Minnesota	24,238		23	Wisconsin	15,057
44	Mississippi	7,014		24	Missouri	14,575
24	Missouri	14,575		25	California	14,134
28	Montana	13,121		26	Illinois	13,766
22	Nebraska	15,198		27	New Mexico	13,273
5	Nevada	23,367		28	Montana	13,121
6	New Hampshire	22,993		29	South Dakota	13,109
15	New Jersey	17,259		30	North Carolina	12,620
27	New Mexico	13,273		31	Idaho	11,676
1	New York	29,297		32	West Virginia	11,474
30	North Carolina	12,620		33	Kentucky	11,416
12	North Dakota	17,607		34	Arkansas	11,201
11	Ohio	18,152		35	Georgia	10,259
37	Oklahoma	9,397		36	Indiana	10,255
3	Oregon	24,345		37	Oklahoma	9,397
18	Pennsylvania	16,448		38	Texas	9,304
NA	Rhode Island**	NA		39	Arizona	8,552
40	South Carolina	8,438		40	South Carolina	8,438
29	South Dakota	13,109		41	Louisiana	8,404
43	Tennessee	7,675		42	Alabama	8,297
38	Texas	9,304		43	Tennessee	7,675
19	Utah	16,129		44	Mississippi	7,014
NA	Vermont**	NA		NA	Alaska**	NA
20	Virginia	15,872		NA	Connecticut**	NA
21	Washington	15,331		NA	Delaware**	NA
32	West Virginia	11,474		NA	Hawaii**	NA
23	Wisconsin	15,057		NA	Rhode Island**	NA
8	Wyoming	20,130		NA	Vermont**	NA
					District of Columbia**	NA

Source: U.S. Department of Justice, Bureau of Justice Statistics
    "Jail and Jail Inmates 1993-94" (Bulletin, April 1995, NCJ-151651)
*As of July 1, 1993.   The cost (excluding capital outlays) to keep one jail inmate incarcerated for a year. Jails are locally operated correctional facilities that confine persons before or after adjudication. Inmates sentenced to jail usually have a sentence of a year or less.
**These states have combined state and local jail systems and are excluded from this count.

Male Inmates in Local Jails in 1993

National Total = 415,161 Male Inmates*

ALPHA ORDER					RANK ORDER			
RANK	STATE	INMATES	% of USA		RANK	STATE	INMATES	% of USA
20	Alabama	6,485	1.56%		1	California	61,646	14.85%
45	Alaska	30	0.01%		2	Texas	48,806	11.76%
21	Arizona	6,471	1.56%		3	Florida	30,500	7.35%
31	Arkansas	2,632	0.63%		4	New York	27,156	6.54%
1	California	61,646	14.85%		5	Georgia	20,943	5.04%
23	Colorado	5,787	1.39%		6	Pennsylvania	17,597	4.24%
NA	Connecticut**	NA	NA		7	Louisiana	14,800	3.56%
NA	Delaware**	NA	NA		8	New Jersey	14,035	3.38%
3	Florida	30,500	7.35%		9	Illinois	13,482	3.25%
5	Georgia	20,943	5.04%		10	Tennessee	13,048	3.14%
NA	Hawaii**	NA	NA		11	Virginia	13,042	3.14%
38	Idaho	1,383	0.33%		12	Michigan	11,395	2.74%
9	Illinois	13,482	3.25%		13	Ohio	10,332	2.49%
16	Indiana	7,653	1.84%		14	Maryland	8,524	2.05%
37	Iowa	1,477	0.36%		15	North Carolina	7,800	1.88%
33	Kansas	2,520	0.61%		16	Indiana	7,653	1.84%
22	Kentucky	6,198	1.49%		17	Massachusetts	7,522	1.81%
7	Louisiana	14,800	3.56%		18	Wisconsin	7,169	1.73%
40	Maine	658	0.16%		19	Washington	6,663	1.60%
14	Maryland	8,524	2.05%		20	Alabama	6,485	1.56%
17	Massachusetts	7,522	1.81%		21	Arizona	6,471	1.56%
12	Michigan	11,395	2.74%		22	Kentucky	6,198	1.49%
29	Minnesota	3,395	0.82%		23	Colorado	5,787	1.39%
26	Mississippi	4,459	1.07%		24	South Carolina	5,242	1.26%
25	Missouri	4,572	1.10%		25	Missouri	4,572	1.10%
41	Montana	604	0.15%		26	Mississippi	4,459	1.07%
36	Nebraska	1,545	0.37%		27	Oklahoma	3,589	0.86%
32	Nevada	2,593	0.62%		28	Oregon	3,441	0.83%
39	New Hampshire	990	0.24%		29	Minnesota	3,395	0.82%
8	New Jersey	14,035	3.38%		30	New Mexico	2,772	0.67%
30	New Mexico	2,772	0.67%		31	Arkansas	2,632	0.63%
4	New York	27,156	6.54%		32	Nevada	2,593	0.62%
15	North Carolina	7,800	1.88%		33	Kansas	2,520	0.61%
44	North Dakota	327	0.08%		34	Utah	1,715	0.41%
13	Ohio	10,332	2.49%		35	West Virginia	1,653	0.40%
27	Oklahoma	3,589	0.86%		36	Nebraska	1,545	0.37%
28	Oregon	3,441	0.83%		37	Iowa	1,477	0.36%
6	Pennsylvania	17,597	4.24%		38	Idaho	1,383	0.33%
NA	Rhode Island**	NA	NA		39	New Hampshire	990	0.24%
24	South Carolina	5,242	1.26%		40	Maine	658	0.16%
42	South Dakota	557	0.13%		41	Montana	604	0.15%
10	Tennessee	13,048	3.14%		42	South Dakota	557	0.13%
2	Texas	48,806	11.76%		43	Wyoming	444	0.11%
34	Utah	1,715	0.41%		44	North Dakota	327	0.08%
NA	Vermont**	NA	NA		45	Alaska	30	0.01%
11	Virginia	13,042	3.14%		NA	Connecticut**	NA	NA
19	Washington	6,663	1.60%		NA	Delaware**	NA	NA
35	West Virginia	1,653	0.40%		NA	Hawaii**	NA	NA
18	Wisconsin	7,169	1.73%		NA	Rhode Island**	NA	NA
43	Wyoming	444	0.11%		NA	Vermont**	NA	NA
						District of Columbia	1,509	0.36%

Source: U.S. Department of Justice, Bureau of Justice Statistics
"Correctional Populations in the United States, 1993" (October 1995, NCJ-156241)
*As of July 1, 1993. Jails are locally operated correctional facilities that confine persons before or after adjudication. Inmates sentenced to jail usually have a sentence of a year or less.
**These states have combined state and local jail systems and are excluded from this count.

Female Inmates in Local Jails in 1993

National Total = 44,184 Female Inmates*

ALPHA ORDER					RANK ORDER			
RANK	STATE	INMATES	% of USA		RANK	STATE	INMATES	% of USA
20	Alabama	587	1.33%		1	California	7,652	17.32%
45	Alaska	1	0.00%		2	Texas	6,589	14.91%
16	Arizona	760	1.72%		3	Florida	3,683	8.34%
33	Arkansas	214	0.48%		4	New York	2,653	6.00%
1	California	7,652	17.32%		5	Georgia	1,720	3.89%
22	Colorado	529	1.20%		6	Pennsylvania	1,634	3.70%
NA	Connecticut**	NA	NA		7	Virginia	1,581	3.58%
NA	Delaware**	NA	NA		8	Louisiana	1,408	3.19%
3	Florida	3,683	8.34%		9	Ohio	1,363	3.08%
5	Georgia	1,720	3.89%		10	Tennessee	1,327	3.00%
NA	Hawaii**	NA	NA		11	New Jersey	1,087	2.46%
39	Idaho	102	0.23%		12	Michigan	1,084	2.45%
13	Illinois	1,067	2.41%		13	Illinois	1,067	2.41%
19	Indiana	644	1.46%		14	Maryland	834	1.89%
37	Iowa	125	0.28%		15	Washington	772	1.75%
31	Kansas	277	0.63%		16	Arizona	760	1.72%
21	Kentucky	547	1.24%		17	North Carolina	748	1.69%
8	Louisiana	1,408	3.19%		18	Wisconsin	710	1.61%
43	Maine	46	0.10%		19	Indiana	644	1.46%
14	Maryland	834	1.89%		20	Alabama	587	1.33%
28	Massachusetts	356	0.81%		21	Kentucky	547	1.24%
12	Michigan	1,084	2.45%		22	Colorado	529	1.20%
32	Minnesota	259	0.59%		23	Oklahoma	513	1.16%
27	Mississippi	392	0.89%		24	South Carolina	471	1.07%
25	Missouri	458	1.04%		25	Missouri	458	1.04%
40	Montana	76	0.17%		26	Nevada	394	0.89%
36	Nebraska	135	0.31%		27	Mississippi	392	0.89%
26	Nevada	394	0.89%		28	Massachusetts	356	0.81%
35	New Hampshire	137	0.31%		29	Oregon	336	0.76%
11	New Jersey	1,087	2.46%		30	New Mexico	286	0.65%
30	New Mexico	286	0.65%		31	Kansas	277	0.63%
4	New York	2,653	6.00%		32	Minnesota	259	0.59%
17	North Carolina	748	1.69%		33	Arkansas	214	0.48%
44	North Dakota	34	0.08%		34	Utah	180	0.41%
9	Ohio	1,363	3.08%		35	New Hampshire	137	0.31%
23	Oklahoma	513	1.16%		36	Nebraska	135	0.31%
29	Oregon	336	0.76%		37	Iowa	125	0.28%
6	Pennsylvania	1,634	3.70%		38	West Virginia	118	0.27%
NA	Rhode Island**	NA	NA		39	Idaho	102	0.23%
24	South Carolina	471	1.07%		40	Montana	76	0.17%
41	South Dakota	66	0.15%		41	South Dakota	66	0.15%
10	Tennessee	1,327	3.00%		42	Wyoming	51	0.12%
2	Texas	6,589	14.91%		43	Maine	46	0.10%
34	Utah	180	0.41%		44	North Dakota	34	0.08%
NA	Vermont**	NA	NA		45	Alaska	1	0.00%
7	Virginia	1,581	3.58%		NA	Connecticut**	NA	NA
15	Washington	772	1.75%		NA	Delaware**	NA	NA
38	West Virginia	118	0.27%		NA	Hawaii**	NA	NA
18	Wisconsin	710	1.61%		NA	Rhode Island**	NA	NA
42	Wyoming	51	0.12%		NA	Vermont**	NA	NA
						District of Columbia	178	0.40%

Source: U.S. Department of Justice, Bureau of Justice Statistics
   "Correctional Populations in the United States, 1993" (October 1995, NCJ-156241)
*As of July 1, 1993. Jails are locally operated correctional facilities that confine persons before or after adjudication. Inmates sentenced to jail usually have a sentence of a year or less.
**These states have combined state and local jail systems and are excluded from this count.

White Inmates in Local Jails in 1993

National Total = 153,999 White Inmates*

ALPHA ORDER					RANK ORDER			

RANK	STATE	INMATES	% of USA		RANK	STATE	INMATES	% of USA
24	Alabama	2,147	1.39%		1	California	18,471	11.99%
45	Alaska	15	0.01%		2	Texas	16,863	10.95%
18	Arizona	2,980	1.94%		3	Florida	14,030	9.11%
29	Arkansas	1,379	0.90%		4	Pennsylvania	8,054	5.23%
1	California	18,471	11.99%		5	New York	6,419	4.17%
23	Colorado	2,299	1.49%		6	Michigan	5,424	3.52%
NA	Connecticut**	NA	NA		7	Georgia	5,368	3.49%
NA	Delaware**	NA	NA		8	Tennessee	5,296	3.44%
3	Florida	14,030	9.11%		9	Washington	4,735	3.07%
7	Georgia	5,368	3.49%		10	Indiana	4,718	3.06%
NA	Hawaii**	NA	NA		11	Virginia	4,659	3.03%
37	Idaho	832	0.54%		12	Ohio	4,126	2.68%
15	Illinois	3,800	2.47%		13	Wisconsin	3,915	2.54%
10	Indiana	4,718	3.06%		14	Kentucky	3,812	2.48%
34	Iowa	1,016	0.66%		15	Illinois	3,800	2.47%
28	Kansas	1,497	0.97%		16	Massachusetts	3,099	2.01%
14	Kentucky	3,812	2.48%		17	Maryland	3,000	1.95%
19	Louisiana	2,654	1.72%		18	Arizona	2,980	1.94%
39	Maine	577	0.37%		19	Louisiana	2,654	1.72%
17	Maryland	3,000	1.95%		20	North Carolina	2,494	1.62%
16	Massachusetts	3,099	2.01%		21	New Jersey	2,471	1.60%
6	Michigan	5,424	3.52%		22	Oregon	2,350	1.53%
24	Minnesota	2,147	1.39%		23	Colorado	2,299	1.49%
35	Mississippi	972	0.63%		24	Alabama	2,147	1.39%
26	Missouri	2,039	1.32%		24	Minnesota	2,147	1.39%
41	Montana	408	0.26%		26	Missouri	2,039	1.32%
36	Nebraska	928	0.60%		27	Oklahoma	1,899	1.23%
33	Nevada	1,209	0.79%		28	Kansas	1,497	0.97%
38	New Hampshire	594	0.39%		29	Arkansas	1,379	0.90%
21	New Jersey	2,471	1.60%		30	West Virginia	1,325	0.86%
40	New Mexico	479	0.31%		31	Utah	1,264	0.82%
5	New York	6,419	4.17%		32	South Carolina	1,248	0.81%
20	North Carolina	2,494	1.62%		33	Nevada	1,209	0.79%
44	North Dakota	241	0.16%		34	Iowa	1,016	0.66%
12	Ohio	4,126	2.68%		35	Mississippi	972	0.63%
27	Oklahoma	1,899	1.23%		36	Nebraska	928	0.60%
22	Oregon	2,350	1.53%		37	Idaho	832	0.54%
4	Pennsylvania	8,054	5.23%		38	New Hampshire	594	0.39%
NA	Rhode Island**	NA	NA		39	Maine	577	0.37%
32	South Carolina	1,248	0.81%		40	New Mexico	479	0.31%
42	South Dakota	376	0.24%		41	Montana	408	0.26%
8	Tennessee	5,296	3.44%		42	South Dakota	376	0.24%
2	Texas	16,863	10.95%		43	Wyoming	364	0.24%
31	Utah	1,264	0.82%		44	North Dakota	241	0.16%
NA	Vermont**	NA	NA		45	Alaska	15	0.01%
11	Virginia	4,659	3.03%		NA	Connecticut**	NA	NA
9	Washington	4,735	3.07%		NA	Delaware**	NA	NA
30	West Virginia	1,325	0.86%		NA	Hawaii**	NA	NA
13	Wisconsin	3,915	2.54%		NA	Rhode Island**	NA	NA
43	Wyoming	364	0.24%		NA	Vermont**	NA	NA
						District of Columbia***	NA	NA

Source: U.S. Department of Justice, Bureau of Justice Statistics
   "Correctional Populations in the United States, 1993" (October 1995, NCJ-156241)
*As of July 1, 1993. Jails are locally operated correctional facilities that confine persons before or after
adjudication. Inmates sentenced to jail usually have a sentence of a year or less.
**These states have combined state and local jail systems and are excluded from this count.
***Not available.

White Inmates in Local Jails as a Percent of All Inmates in 1993

National Percent = 33.49% of Inmates*

ALPHA ORDER

RANK	STATE	PERCENT
35	Alabama	30.36
20	Alaska	48.39
24	Arizona	41.21
19	Arkansas	48.45
37	California	26.65
30	Colorado	36.40
NA	Connecticut**	NA
NA	Delaware**	NA
25	Florida	41.04
39	Georgia	23.69
NA	Hawaii**	NA
13	Idaho	56.03
38	Illinois	26.12
12	Indiana	56.86
7	Iowa	63.42
16	Kansas	53.52
14	Kentucky	55.95
43	Louisiana	16.37
1	Maine	81.96
32	Maryland	32.06
28	Massachusetts	39.34
22	Michigan	43.47
11	Minnesota	58.76
42	Mississippi	20.04
26	Missouri	40.54
10	Montana	60.00
15	Nebraska	55.24
27	Nevada	40.48
17	New Hampshire	52.71
44	New Jersey	16.34
45	New Mexico	15.66
41	New York	21.53
36	North Carolina	27.90
4	North Dakota	66.76
31	Ohio	35.28
21	Oklahoma	46.29
8	Oregon	62.22
23	Pennsylvania	41.88
NA	Rhode Island**	NA
40	South Carolina	21.84
9	South Dakota	60.35
29	Tennessee	36.84
34	Texas	30.44
5	Utah	66.70
NA	Vermont**	NA
33	Virginia	31.86
6	Washington	63.69
2	West Virginia	74.82
18	Wisconsin	49.69
3	Wyoming	73.54

RANK ORDER

RANK	STATE	PERCENT
1	Maine	81.96
2	West Virginia	74.82
3	Wyoming	73.54
4	North Dakota	66.76
5	Utah	66.70
6	Washington	63.69
7	Iowa	63.42
8	Oregon	62.22
9	South Dakota	60.35
10	Montana	60.00
11	Minnesota	58.76
12	Indiana	56.86
13	Idaho	56.03
14	Kentucky	55.95
15	Nebraska	55.24
16	Kansas	53.52
17	New Hampshire	52.71
18	Wisconsin	49.69
19	Arkansas	48.45
20	Alaska	48.39
21	Oklahoma	46.29
22	Michigan	43.47
23	Pennsylvania	41.88
24	Arizona	41.21
25	Florida	41.04
26	Missouri	40.54
27	Nevada	40.48
28	Massachusetts	39.34
29	Tennessee	36.84
30	Colorado	36.40
31	Ohio	35.28
32	Maryland	32.06
33	Virginia	31.86
34	Texas	30.44
35	Alabama	30.36
36	North Carolina	27.90
37	California	26.65
38	Illinois	26.12
39	Georgia	23.69
40	South Carolina	21.84
41	New York	21.53
42	Mississippi	20.04
43	Louisiana	16.37
44	New Jersey	16.34
45	New Mexico	15.66
NA	Connecticut**	NA
NA	Delaware**	NA
NA	Hawaii**	NA
NA	Rhode Island**	NA
NA	Vermont**	NA
	District of Columbia***	NA

Source: Morgan Quitno Press using data from U.S. Department of Justice, Bureau of Justice Statistics
    "Correctional Populations in the United States, 1993" (October 1995, NCJ-156241)
*As of July 1, 1993. Jails are locally operated correctional facilities that confine persons before or after adjudication. Inmates sentenced to jail usually have a sentence of a year or less.
**These states have combined state and local jail systems and are excluded from this count.
***Not available.

Black Inmates in Local Jails in 1993

National Total = 173,193 Black Inmates*

ALPHA ORDER					RANK ORDER			
RANK	STATE	INMATES	% of USA		RANK	STATE	INMATES	% of USA
15	Alabama	3,922	2.26%		1	Texas	20,925	12.08%
45	Alaska	0	0.00%		2	Florida	16,426	9.48%
27	Arizona	921	0.53%		3	California	13,887	8.02%
25	Arkansas	1,246	0.72%		4	Georgia	12,764	7.37%
3	California	13,887	8.02%		5	New York	12,114	6.99%
31	Colorado	473	0.27%		6	Illinois	8,822	5.09%
NA	Connecticut**	NA	NA		7	Tennessee	8,590	4.96%
NA	Delaware**	NA	NA		8	Pennsylvania	8,511	4.91%
2	Florida	16,426	9.48%		9	Virginia	8,183	4.72%
4	Georgia	12,764	7.37%		10	Louisiana	6,435	3.72%
NA	Hawaii**	NA	NA		11	Maryland	6,165	3.56%
41	Idaho	13	0.01%		12	New Jersey	5,656	3.27%
6	Illinois	8,822	5.09%		13	North Carolina	5,443	3.14%
23	Indiana	1,650	0.95%		14	Michigan	4,658	2.69%
34	Iowa	306	0.18%		15	Alabama	3,922	2.26%
28	Kansas	792	0.46%		16	Ohio	3,548	2.05%
22	Kentucky	1,810	1.05%		17	South Carolina	3,331	1.92%
10	Louisiana	6,435	3.72%		18	Mississippi	2,650	1.53%
42	Maine	11	0.01%		19	Wisconsin	2,587	1.49%
11	Maryland	6,165	3.56%		20	Massachusetts	2,246	1.30%
20	Massachusetts	2,246	1.30%		21	Missouri	2,208	1.27%
14	Michigan	4,658	2.69%		22	Kentucky	1,810	1.05%
29	Minnesota	783	0.45%		23	Indiana	1,650	0.95%
18	Mississippi	2,650	1.53%		24	Washington	1,299	0.75%
21	Missouri	2,208	1.27%		25	Arkansas	1,246	0.72%
40	Montana	14	0.01%		26	Oklahoma	1,151	0.66%
32	Nebraska	415	0.24%		27	Arizona	921	0.53%
30	Nevada	636	0.37%		28	Kansas	792	0.46%
42	New Hampshire	11	0.01%		29	Minnesota	783	0.45%
12	New Jersey	5,656	3.27%		30	Nevada	636	0.37%
37	New Mexico	142	0.08%		31	Colorado	473	0.27%
5	New York	12,114	6.99%		32	Nebraska	415	0.24%
13	North Carolina	5,443	3.14%		33	Oregon	389	0.22%
44	North Dakota	10	0.01%		34	Iowa	306	0.18%
16	Ohio	3,548	2.05%		35	West Virginia	217	0.13%
26	Oklahoma	1,151	0.66%		36	Utah	148	0.09%
33	Oregon	389	0.22%		37	New Mexico	142	0.08%
8	Pennsylvania	8,511	4.91%		38	South Dakota	22	0.01%
NA	Rhode Island**	NA	NA		39	Wyoming	20	0.01%
17	South Carolina	3,331	1.92%		40	Montana	14	0.01%
38	South Dakota	22	0.01%		41	Idaho	13	0.01%
7	Tennessee	8,590	4.96%		42	Maine	11	0.01%
1	Texas	20,925	12.08%		42	New Hampshire	11	0.01%
36	Utah	148	0.09%		44	North Dakota	10	0.01%
NA	Vermont**	NA	NA		45	Alaska	0	0.00%
9	Virginia	8,183	4.72%		NA	Connecticut**	NA	NA
24	Washington	1,299	0.75%		NA	Delaware**	NA	NA
35	West Virginia	217	0.13%		NA	Hawaii**	NA	NA
19	Wisconsin	2,587	1.49%		NA	Rhode Island**	NA	NA
39	Wyoming	20	0.01%		NA	Vermont**	NA	NA
						District of Columbia***	NA	NA

Source: U.S. Department of Justice, Bureau of Justice Statistics
   "Correctional Populations in the United States, 1993" (October 1995, NCJ-156241)
*As of July 1, 1993.   Jails are locally operated correctional facilities that confine persons before or after adjudication. Inmates sentenced to jail usually have a sentence of a year or less.
**These states have combined state and local jail systems and are excluded from this count.
***Not available.

Black Inmates in Local Jails as a Percent of All Inmates in 1993

National Percent = 37.67% of Inmates*

ALPHA ORDER			RANK ORDER		
RANK	STATE	PERCENT	RANK	STATE	PERCENT
8	Alabama	55.46	1	Maryland	65.88
45	Alaska	0.00	2	North Carolina	60.89
32	Arizona	12.74	3	Illinois	60.64
13	Arkansas	43.78	4	Tennessee	59.76
28	California	20.04	5	South Carolina	58.31
36	Colorado	7.49	6	Georgia	56.32
NA	Connecticut**	NA	7	Virginia	55.96
NA	Delaware**	NA	8	Alabama	55.46
10	Florida	48.05	9	Mississippi	54.63
6	Georgia	56.32	10	Florida	48.05
NA	Hawaii**	NA	11	Pennsylvania	44.26
44	Idaho	0.88	12	Missouri	43.90
3	Illinois	60.64	13	Arkansas	43.78
29	Indiana	19.89	14	New York	40.64
30	Iowa	19.10	15	Louisiana	39.70
22	Kansas	28.32	16	Texas	37.77
24	Kentucky	26.57	17	New Jersey	37.40
15	Louisiana	39.70	18	Michigan	37.33
42	Maine	1.56	19	Wisconsin	32.83
1	Maryland	65.88	20	Ohio	30.34
21	Massachusetts	28.51	21	Massachusetts	28.51
18	Michigan	37.33	22	Kansas	28.32
26	Minnesota	21.43	23	Oklahoma	28.06
9	Mississippi	54.63	24	Kentucky	26.57
12	Missouri	43.90	25	Nebraska	24.70
41	Montana	2.06	26	Minnesota	21.43
25	Nebraska	24.70	27	Nevada	21.29
27	Nevada	21.29	28	California	20.04
43	New Hampshire	0.98	29	Indiana	19.89
17	New Jersey	37.40	30	Iowa	19.10
37	New Mexico	4.64	31	Washington	17.47
14	New York	40.64	32	Arizona	12.74
2	North Carolina	60.89	33	West Virginia	12.25
40	North Dakota	2.77	34	Oregon	10.30
20	Ohio	30.34	35	Utah	7.81
23	Oklahoma	28.06	36	Colorado	7.49
34	Oregon	10.30	37	New Mexico	4.64
11	Pennsylvania	44.26	38	Wyoming	4.04
NA	Rhode Island**	NA	39	South Dakota	3.53
5	South Carolina	58.31	40	North Dakota	2.77
39	South Dakota	3.53	41	Montana	2.06
4	Tennessee	59.76	42	Maine	1.56
16	Texas	37.77	43	New Hampshire	0.98
35	Utah	7.81	44	Idaho	0.88
NA	Vermont**	NA	45	Alaska	0.00
7	Virginia	55.96	NA	Connecticut**	NA
31	Washington	17.47	NA	Delaware**	NA
33	West Virginia	12.25	NA	Hawaii**	NA
19	Wisconsin	32.83	NA	Rhode Island**	NA
38	Wyoming	4.04	NA	Vermont**	NA
				District of Columbia***	NA

Source: Morgan Quitno Press using data from U.S. Department of Justice, Bureau of Justice Statistics
   "Correctional Populations in the United States, 1993" (October 1995, NCJ-156241)
*As of July 1, 1993. Jails are locally operated correctional facilities that confine persons before or after
adjudication. Inmates sentenced to jail usually have a sentence of a year or less.
**These states have combined state and local jail systems and are excluded from this count.
***Not available.

Hispanic Inmates in Local Jails in 1993

National Total = 58,947 Hispanic Inmates*

ALPHA ORDER

RANK	STATE	INMATES	% of USA
35	Alabama	47	0.08%
45	Alaska	3	0.01%
5	Arizona	1,872	3.18%
39	Arkansas	31	0.05%
1	California	22,110	37.51%
12	Colorado	860	1.46%
NA	Connecticut**	NA	NA
NA	Delaware**	NA	NA
4	Florida	2,764	4.69%
20	Georgia	254	0.43%
NA	Hawaii**	NA	NA
18	Idaho	262	0.44%
9	Illinois	1,274	2.16%
28	Indiana	162	0.27%
32	Iowa	71	0.12%
23	Kansas	204	0.35%
30	Kentucky	80	0.14%
24	Louisiana	190	0.32%
43	Maine	7	0.01%
24	Maryland	190	0.32%
8	Massachusetts	1,324	2.25%
13	Michigan	577	0.98%
27	Minnesota	166	0.28%
37	Mississippi	41	0.07%
31	Missouri	75	0.13%
38	Montana	40	0.07%
26	Nebraska	176	0.30%
21	Nevada	252	0.43%
40	New Hampshire	23	0.04%
6	New Jersey	1,809	3.07%
10	New Mexico	1,229	2.08%
3	New York	6,483	11.00%
29	North Carolina	150	0.25%
40	North Dakota	23	0.04%
22	Ohio	221	0.37%
19	Oklahoma	260	0.44%
14	Oregon	413	0.70%
7	Pennsylvania	1,596	2.71%
NA	Rhode Island**	NA	NA
36	South Carolina	43	0.07%
44	South Dakota	6	0.01%
34	Tennessee	56	0.10%
2	Texas	11,729	19.90%
15	Utah	351	0.60%
NA	Vermont**	NA	NA
16	Virginia	287	0.49%
11	Washington	891	1.51%
42	West Virginia	11	0.02%
17	Wisconsin	272	0.46%
33	Wyoming	58	0.10%

RANK ORDER

RANK	STATE	INMATES	% of USA
1	California	22,110	37.51%
2	Texas	11,729	19.90%
3	New York	6,483	11.00%
4	Florida	2,764	4.69%
5	Arizona	1,872	3.18%
6	New Jersey	1,809	3.07%
7	Pennsylvania	1,596	2.71%
8	Massachusetts	1,324	2.25%
9	Illinois	1,274	2.16%
10	New Mexico	1,229	2.08%
11	Washington	891	1.51%
12	Colorado	860	1.46%
13	Michigan	577	0.98%
14	Oregon	413	0.70%
15	Utah	351	0.60%
16	Virginia	287	0.49%
17	Wisconsin	272	0.46%
18	Idaho	262	0.44%
19	Oklahoma	260	0.44%
20	Georgia	254	0.43%
21	Nevada	252	0.43%
22	Ohio	221	0.37%
23	Kansas	204	0.35%
24	Louisiana	190	0.32%
24	Maryland	190	0.32%
26	Nebraska	176	0.30%
27	Minnesota	166	0.28%
28	Indiana	162	0.27%
29	North Carolina	150	0.25%
30	Kentucky	80	0.14%
31	Missouri	75	0.13%
32	Iowa	71	0.12%
33	Wyoming	58	0.10%
34	Tennessee	56	0.10%
35	Alabama	47	0.08%
36	South Carolina	43	0.07%
37	Mississippi	41	0.07%
38	Montana	40	0.07%
39	Arkansas	31	0.05%
40	New Hampshire	23	0.04%
40	North Dakota	23	0.04%
42	West Virginia	11	0.02%
43	Maine	7	0.01%
44	South Dakota	6	0.01%
45	Alaska	3	0.01%
NA	Connecticut**	NA	NA
NA	Delaware**	NA	NA
NA	Hawaii**	NA	NA
NA	Rhode Island**	NA	NA
NA	Vermont**	NA	NA
	District of Columbia***	NA	NA

Source: U.S. Department of Justice, Bureau of Justice Statistics
    "Correctional Populations in the United States, 1993" (October 1995, NCJ-156241)
As of July 1, 1993. Jails are locally operated correctional facilities that confine persons before or after adjudication. Inmates sentenced to jail usually have a sentence of a year or less.
**These states have combined state and local jail systems and are excluded from this count.*
***Not available.*

Hispanic Inmates in Local Jails as a Percent of All Inmates in 1993

National Percent = 12.82% of Inmates*

ALPHA ORDER

RANK ORDER

RANK	STATE	PERCENT	RANK	STATE	PERCENT
43	Alabama	0.66	1	New Mexico	40.19
15	Alaska	9.68	2	California	31.91
3	Arizona	25.89	3	Arizona	25.89
38	Arkansas	1.09	4	New York	21.75
2	California	31.91	5	Texas	21.17
9	Colorado	13.62	6	Utah	18.52
NA	Connecticut**	NA	7	Idaho	17.64
NA	Delaware**	NA	8	Massachusetts	16.81
19	Florida	8.09	9	Colorado	13.62
37	Georgia	1.12	10	Washington	11.98
NA	Hawaii**	NA	11	New Jersey	11.96
7	Idaho	17.64	12	Wyoming	11.72
16	Illinois	8.76	13	Oregon	10.93
31	Indiana	1.95	14	Nebraska	10.48
26	Iowa	4.43	15	Alaska	9.68
20	Kansas	7.29	16	Illinois	8.76
35	Kentucky	1.17	17	Nevada	8.44
35	Louisiana	1.17	18	Pennsylvania	8.30
39	Maine	0.99	19	Florida	8.09
29	Maryland	2.03	20	Kansas	7.29
8	Massachusetts	16.81	21	North Dakota	6.37
24	Michigan	4.62	22	Oklahoma	6.34
25	Minnesota	4.54	23	Montana	5.88
41	Mississippi	0.85	24	Michigan	4.62
34	Missouri	1.49	25	Minnesota	4.54
23	Montana	5.88	26	Iowa	4.43
14	Nebraska	10.48	27	Wisconsin	3.45
17	Nevada	8.44	28	New Hampshire	2.04
28	New Hampshire	2.04	29	Maryland	2.03
11	New Jersey	11.96	30	Virginia	1.96
1	New Mexico	40.19	31	Indiana	1.95
4	New York	21.75	32	Ohio	1.89
33	North Carolina	1.68	33	North Carolina	1.68
21	North Dakota	6.37	34	Missouri	1.49
32	Ohio	1.89	35	Kentucky	1.17
22	Oklahoma	6.34	35	Louisiana	1.17
13	Oregon	10.93	37	Georgia	1.12
18	Pennsylvania	8.30	38	Arkansas	1.09
NA	Rhode Island**	NA	39	Maine	0.99
42	South Carolina	0.75	40	South Dakota	0.96
40	South Dakota	0.96	41	Mississippi	0.85
45	Tennessee	0.39	42	South Carolina	0.75
5	Texas	21.17	43	Alabama	0.66
6	Utah	18.52	44	West Virginia	0.62
NA	Vermont**	NA	45	Tennessee	0.39
30	Virginia	1.96	NA	Connecticut**	NA
10	Washington	11.98	NA	Delaware**	NA
44	West Virginia	0.62	NA	Hawaii**	NA
27	Wisconsin	3.45	NA	Rhode Island**	NA
12	Wyoming	11.72	NA	Vermont**	NA
				District of Columbia***	NA

Source: Morgan Quitno Press using data from U.S. Department of Justice, Bureau of Justice Statistics
"Correctional Populations in the United States, 1993" (October 1995, NCJ-156241)
*As of July 1, 1993. Jails are locally operated correctional facilities that confine persons before or after adjudication. Inmates sentenced to jail usually have a sentence of a year or less.
**These states have combined state and local jail systems and are excluded from this count.
***Not available.

Correctional Officers in Local Jails in 1993

National Total = 117,900 Officers*

ALPHA ORDER					RANK ORDER			

RANK	STATE	OFFICERS	% of USA		RANK	STATE	OFFICERS	% of USA
23	Alabama	1,301	1.10%		1	New York	12,824	10.88%
45	Alaska	24	0.02%		2	Texas	11,304	9.59%
21	Arizona	1,489	1.26%		3	California	10,389	8.81%
29	Arkansas	854	0.72%		4	Florida	8,547	7.25%
3	California	10,389	8.81%		5	Pennsylvania	4,937	4.19%
17	Colorado	1,843	1.56%		6	Illinois	3,843	3.26%
NA	Connecticut**	NA	NA		7	Georgia	3,815	3.24%
NA	Delaware**	NA	NA		8	Ohio	3,557	3.02%
4	Florida	8,547	7.25%		9	Tennessee	3,258	2.76%
7	Georgia	3,815	3.24%		10	Virginia	3,103	2.63%
NA	Hawaii**	NA	NA		11	New Jersey	3,065	2.60%
39	Idaho	410	0.35%		12	Michigan	2,939	2.49%
6	Illinois	3,843	3.26%		13	Massachusetts	2,851	2.42%
18	Indiana	1,582	1.34%		14	Maryland	2,272	1.93%
31	Iowa	812	0.69%		15	Louisiana	2,132	1.81%
28	Kansas	977	0.83%		16	North Carolina	2,123	1.80%
22	Kentucky	1,412	1.20%		17	Colorado	1,843	1.56%
15	Louisiana	2,132	1.81%		18	Indiana	1,582	1.34%
37	Maine	490	0.42%		19	Washington	1,581	1.34%
14	Maryland	2,272	1.93%		20	Wisconsin	1,545	1.31%
13	Massachusetts	2,851	2.42%		21	Arizona	1,489	1.26%
12	Michigan	2,939	2.49%		22	Kentucky	1,412	1.20%
24	Minnesota	1,248	1.06%		23	Alabama	1,301	1.10%
33	Mississippi	753	0.64%		24	Minnesota	1,248	1.06%
25	Missouri	1,093	0.93%		25	Missouri	1,093	0.93%
44	Montana	208	0.18%		26	South Carolina	1,046	0.89%
34	Nebraska	709	0.60%		27	Oregon	1,019	0.86%
35	Nevada	549	0.47%		28	Kansas	977	0.83%
40	New Hampshire	259	0.22%		29	Arkansas	854	0.72%
11	New Jersey	3,065	2.60%		30	Oklahoma	820	0.70%
32	New Mexico	786	0.67%		31	Iowa	812	0.69%
1	New York	12,824	10.88%		32	New Mexico	786	0.67%
16	North Carolina	2,123	1.80%		33	Mississippi	753	0.64%
41	North Dakota	233	0.20%		34	Nebraska	709	0.60%
8	Ohio	3,557	3.02%		35	Nevada	549	0.47%
30	Oklahoma	820	0.70%		36	Utah	499	0.42%
27	Oregon	1,019	0.86%		37	Maine	490	0.42%
5	Pennsylvania	4,937	4.19%		38	West Virginia	483	0.41%
NA	Rhode Island**	NA	NA		39	Idaho	410	0.35%
26	South Carolina	1,046	0.89%		40	New Hampshire	259	0.22%
43	South Dakota	220	0.19%		41	North Dakota	233	0.20%
9	Tennessee	3,258	2.76%		42	Wyoming	223	0.19%
2	Texas	11,304	9.59%		43	South Dakota	220	0.19%
36	Utah	499	0.42%		44	Montana	208	0.18%
NA	Vermont**	NA	NA		45	Alaska	24	0.02%
10	Virginia	3,103	2.63%		NA	Connecticut**	NA	NA
19	Washington	1,581	1.34%		NA	Delaware**	NA	NA
38	West Virginia	483	0.41%		NA	Hawaii**	NA	NA
20	Wisconsin	1,545	1.31%		NA	Rhode Island**	NA	NA
42	Wyoming	223	0.19%		NA	Vermont**	NA	NA
						District of Columbia	512	0.43%

Source: U.S. Department of Justice, Bureau of Justice Statistics
   "Correctional Populations in the United States, 1993" (October 1995, NCJ 156241)
*National total includes estimates for units that did not provide data. Includes 113,300 full-time and 4,600 part-time officers.
**These states have combined state and local jail systems and are excluded from this count.

Number of Local Jail Inmates per Correctional Officer in 1993

National Rate = 3.9 Inmates per Officer*

ALPHA ORDER

RANK	STATE	RATE
6	Alabama	4.8
NA	Alaska**	NA
7	Arizona	4.7
28	Arkansas	3.2
1	California	6.6
33	Colorado	2.8
NA	Connecticut**	NA
NA	Delaware**	NA
22	Florida	3.5
4	Georgia	5.1
NA	Hawaii**	NA
24	Idaho	3.4
20	Illinois	3.6
4	Indiana	5.1
41	Iowa	2.0
34	Kansas	2.7
14	Kentucky	4.2
9	Louisiana	4.6
44	Maine	1.4
16	Maryland	4.1
38	Massachusetts	2.5
18	Michigan	3.9
34	Minnesota	2.7
2	Mississippi	5.7
25	Missouri	3.3
32	Montana	2.9
39	Nebraska	2.2
3	Nevada	5.3
36	New Hampshire	2.6
22	New Jersey	3.5
25	New Mexico	3.3
41	New York	2.0
17	North Carolina	4.0
43	North Dakota	1.5
30	Ohio	3.1
20	Oklahoma	3.6
25	Oregon	3.3
31	Pennsylvania	3.0
NA	Rhode Island**	NA
12	South Carolina	4.3
36	South Dakota	2.6
14	Tennessee	4.2
9	Texas	4.6
19	Utah	3.8
NA	Vermont**	NA
12	Virginia	4.3
7	Washington	4.7
28	West Virginia	3.2
9	Wisconsin	4.6
39	Wyoming	2.2

RANK ORDER

RANK	STATE	RATE
1	California	6.6
2	Mississippi	5.7
3	Nevada	5.3
4	Georgia	5.1
4	Indiana	5.1
6	Alabama	4.8
7	Arizona	4.7
7	Washington	4.7
9	Louisiana	4.6
9	Texas	4.6
9	Wisconsin	4.6
12	South Carolina	4.3
12	Virginia	4.3
14	Kentucky	4.2
14	Tennessee	4.2
16	Maryland	4.1
17	North Carolina	4.0
18	Michigan	3.9
19	Utah	3.8
20	Illinois	3.6
20	Oklahoma	3.6
22	Florida	3.5
22	New Jersey	3.5
24	Idaho	3.4
25	Missouri	3.3
25	New Mexico	3.3
25	Oregon	3.3
28	Arkansas	3.2
28	West Virginia	3.2
30	Ohio	3.1
31	Pennsylvania	3.0
32	Montana	2.9
33	Colorado	2.8
34	Kansas	2.7
34	Minnesota	2.7
36	New Hampshire	2.6
36	South Dakota	2.6
38	Massachusetts	2.5
39	Nebraska	2.2
39	Wyoming	2.2
41	Iowa	2.0
41	New York	2.0
43	North Dakota	1.5
44	Maine	1.4
NA	Alaska**	NA
NA	Connecticut**	NA
NA	Delaware**	NA
NA	Hawaii**	NA
NA	Rhode Island**	NA
NA	Vermont**	NA

District of Columbia   3.3

Source: U.S. Department of Justice, Bureau of Justice Statistics
"Correctional Populations in the United States, 1993" (October 1995, NCJ 156241)
*Inmate-to-staff ratios were calculated by dividing the reported number of inmates by the reported number of staff.
**These states have combined state and local jail systems and are excluded from this count.

Juvenile Offenders in Custody in 1993

National Total = 36,374 Juveniles*

RANK	STATE	JUVENILES	% of USA
NA	Alabama**	NA	NA
NA	Alaska**	NA	NA
22	Arizona	537	1.48%
35	Arkansas	200	0.55%
1	California	7,694	21.15%
9	Colorado	1,005	2.76%
32	Connecticut	237	0.65%
NA	Delaware**	NA	NA
7	Florida	1,272	3.50%
13	Georgia	742	2.04%
43	Hawaii	62	0.17%
NA	Idaho**	NA	NA
6	Illinois	1,403	3.86%
12	Indiana	812	2.23%
34	Iowa	210	0.58%
27	Kansas	385	1.06%
18	Kentucky	576	1.58%
10	Louisiana	981	2.70%
33	Maine	234	0.64%
16	Maryland	639	1.76%
5	Massachusetts	1,747	4.80%
15	Michigan	689	1.89%
39	Minnesota	165	0.45%
26	Mississippi	451	1.24%
24	Missouri	470	1.29%
42	Montana	105	0.29%
30	Nebraska	262	0.72%
29	Nevada	267	0.73%
36	New Hampshire	183	0.50%
20	New Jersey	560	1.54%
28	New Mexico	308	0.85%
2	New York	3,349	9.21%
11	North Carolina	862	2.37%
31	North Dakota	251	0.69%
3	Ohio	2,123	5.84%
25	Oklahoma	467	1.28%
21	Oregon	552	1.52%
19	Pennsylvania	572	1.57%
40	Rhode Island	160	0.44%
8	South Carolina	1,174	3.23%
37	South Dakota	182	0.50%
17	Tennessee	617	1.70%
4	Texas	1,967	5.41%
23	Utah	474	1.30%
44	Vermont	28	0.08%
NA	Virginia**	NA	NA
NA	Washington**	NA	NA
41	West Virginia	109	0.30%
14	Wisconsin	740	2.03%
38	Wyoming	171	0.47%

RANK	STATE	JUVENILES	% of USA
1	California	7,694	21.15%
2	New York	3,349	9.21%
3	Ohio	2,123	5.84%
4	Texas	1,967	5.41%
5	Massachusetts	1,747	4.80%
6	Illinois	1,403	3.86%
7	Florida	1,272	3.50%
8	South Carolina	1,174	3.23%
9	Colorado	1,005	2.76%
10	Louisiana	981	2.70%
11	North Carolina	862	2.37%
12	Indiana	812	2.23%
13	Georgia	742	2.04%
14	Wisconsin	740	2.03%
15	Michigan	689	1.89%
16	Maryland	639	1.76%
17	Tennessee	617	1.70%
18	Kentucky	576	1.58%
19	Pennsylvania	572	1.57%
20	New Jersey	560	1.54%
21	Oregon	552	1.52%
22	Arizona	537	1.48%
23	Utah	474	1.30%
24	Missouri	470	1.29%
25	Oklahoma	467	1.28%
26	Mississippi	451	1.24%
27	Kansas	385	1.06%
28	New Mexico	308	0.85%
29	Nevada	267	0.73%
30	Nebraska	262	0.72%
31	North Dakota	251	0.69%
32	Connecticut	237	0.65%
33	Maine	234	0.64%
34	Iowa	210	0.58%
35	Arkansas	200	0.55%
36	New Hampshire	183	0.50%
37	South Dakota	182	0.50%
38	Wyoming	171	0.47%
39	Minnesota	165	0.45%
40	Rhode Island	160	0.44%
41	West Virginia	109	0.30%
42	Montana	105	0.29%
43	Hawaii	62	0.17%
44	Vermont	28	0.08%
NA	Alabama**	NA	NA
NA	Alaska**	NA	NA
NA	Delaware**	NA	NA
NA	Idaho**	NA	NA
NA	Virginia**	NA	NA
NA	Washington**	NA	NA
	District of Columbia	380	1.04%

Source: Contact Publications (Lincoln, NE)
        "Corrections Compendium" (December 1993)
*National total is only for states shown. This information was collected through a survey mailed to the departments
of juvenile corrections in the 50 states, the District of Columbia and the Federal Bureau of Prisons. Alabama and
Alaska were unable to participate and Delaware, Idaho, Virginia and Washington did not respond.
**Not available.*

Juvenile Custody Rate in 1993

National Rate = 58 Juveniles per 100,000 Juveniles*

ALPHA ORDER

RANK ORDER

RANK	STATE	RATE		RANK	STATE	RATE
NA	Alabama**	NA		1	North Dakota	146
NA	Alaska**	NA		2	Massachusetts	125
27	Arizona	50		3	Wyoming	124
35	Arkansas	31		4	South Carolina	123
6	California	90		5	Colorado	107
5	Colorado	107		6	California	90
35	Connecticut	31		7	South Dakota	88
NA	Delaware**	NA		8	Louisiana	79
31	Florida	40		9	Maine	76
31	Georgia	40		9	Nevada	76
41	Hawaii	21		11	New York	75
NA	Idaho**	NA		12	Ohio	74
29	Illinois	46		13	Oregon	71
22	Indiana	55		13	Utah	71
38	Iowa	29		15	Rhode Island	68
21	Kansas	56		16	New Hampshire	65
19	Kentucky	59		17	New Mexico	64
8	Louisiana	79		18	Nebraska	60
9	Maine	76		19	Kentucky	59
25	Maryland	51		19	Mississippi	59
2	Massachusetts	125		21	Kansas	56
39	Michigan	27		22	Indiana	55
44	Minnesota	13		22	Wisconsin	55
19	Mississippi	59		24	Oklahoma	54
34	Missouri	34		25	Maryland	51
30	Montana	45		25	North Carolina	51
18	Nebraska	60		27	Arizona	50
9	Nevada	76		28	Tennessee	49
16	New Hampshire	65		29	Illinois	46
37	New Jersey	30		30	Montana	45
17	New Mexico	64		31	Florida	40
11	New York	75		31	Georgia	40
25	North Carolina	51		33	Texas	38
1	North Dakota	146		34	Missouri	34
12	Ohio	74		35	Arkansas	31
24	Oklahoma	54		35	Connecticut	31
13	Oregon	71		37	New Jersey	30
42	Pennsylvania	20		38	Iowa	29
15	Rhode Island	68		39	Michigan	27
4	South Carolina	123		40	West Virginia	25
7	South Dakota	88		41	Hawaii	21
28	Tennessee	49		42	Pennsylvania	20
33	Texas	38		43	Vermont	19
13	Utah	71		44	Minnesota	13
43	Vermont	19		NA	Alabama**	NA
NA	Virginia**	NA		NA	Alaska**	NA
NA	Washington**	NA		NA	Delaware**	NA
40	West Virginia	25		NA	Idaho**	NA
22	Wisconsin	55		NA	Virginia**	NA
3	Wyoming	124		NA	Washington**	NA

District of Columbia   330

Source: Morgan Quitno Press using data from Contact Publications (Lincoln, NE)
    "Corrections Compendium" (December 1993)
*National rate is only for states shown. This information was collected through a survey mailed to the departments
of juvenile corrections in the 50 states, the District of Columbia and the Federal Bureau of Prisons. Alabama and
Alaska were unable to participate and Delaware, Idaho, Virginia and Washington did not respond.
**Not available.

Juveniles in Custody at Public Facilities Administered
By State and Local Governments in 1991
National Total = 57,542 Juveniles

ALPHA ORDER

RANK	STATE	JUVENILES	% of USA
20	Alabama	846	1.47%
39	Alaska	217	0.38%
16	Arizona	947	1.65%
35	Arkansas	285	0.50%
1	California	15,904	27.64%
24	Colorado	687	1.19%
34	Connecticut	290	0.50%
45	Delaware	130	0.23%
6	Florida	2,008	3.49%
10	Georgia	1,566	2.72%
48	Hawaii	84	0.15%
44	Idaho	143	0.25%
5	Illinois	2,029	3.53%
12	Indiana	1,395	2.42%
30	Iowa	418	0.73%
25	Kansas	667	1.16%
26	Kentucky	666	1.16%
14	Louisiana	1,122	1.95%
37	Maine	249	0.43%
21	Maryland	831	1.44%
41	Massachusetts	180	0.31%
7	Michigan	1,968	3.42%
27	Minnesota	645	1.12%
30	Mississippi	418	0.73%
15	Missouri	1,060	1.84%
38	Montana	230	0.40%
33	Nebraska	293	0.51%
28	Nevada	555	0.96%
47	New Hampshire	108	0.19%
8	New Jersey	1,719	2.99%
29	New Mexico	527	0.92%
4	New York	2,648	4.60%
19	North Carolina	893	1.55%
49	North Dakota	75	0.13%
2	Ohio	3,696	6.42%
32	Oklahoma	336	0.58%
23	Oregon	723	1.26%
13	Pennsylvania	1,289	2.24%
43	Rhode Island	161	0.28%
17	South Carolina	926	1.61%
39	South Dakota	217	0.38%
22	Tennessee	755	1.31%
3	Texas	2,661	4.62%
36	Utah	273	0.47%
50	Vermont	17	0.03%
9	Virginia	1,712	2.98%
11	Washington	1,418	2.46%
42	West Virginia	166	0.29%
18	Wisconsin	896	1.56%
46	Wyoming	113	0.20%

RANK ORDER

RANK	STATE	JUVENILES	% of USA
1	California	15,904	27.64%
2	Ohio	3,696	6.42%
3	Texas	2,661	4.62%
4	New York	2,648	4.60%
5	Illinois	2,029	3.53%
6	Florida	2,008	3.49%
7	Michigan	1,968	3.42%
8	New Jersey	1,719	2.99%
9	Virginia	1,712	2.98%
10	Georgia	1,566	2.72%
11	Washington	1,418	2.46%
12	Indiana	1,395	2.42%
13	Pennsylvania	1,289	2.24%
14	Louisiana	1,122	1.95%
15	Missouri	1,060	1.84%
16	Arizona	947	1.65%
17	South Carolina	926	1.61%
18	Wisconsin	896	1.56%
19	North Carolina	893	1.55%
20	Alabama	846	1.47%
21	Maryland	831	1.44%
22	Tennessee	755	1.31%
23	Oregon	723	1.26%
24	Colorado	687	1.19%
25	Kansas	667	1.16%
26	Kentucky	666	1.16%
27	Minnesota	645	1.12%
28	Nevada	555	0.96%
29	New Mexico	527	0.92%
30	Iowa	418	0.73%
30	Mississippi	418	0.73%
32	Oklahoma	336	0.58%
33	Nebraska	293	0.51%
34	Connecticut	290	0.50%
35	Arkansas	285	0.50%
36	Utah	273	0.47%
37	Maine	249	0.43%
38	Montana	230	0.40%
39	Alaska	217	0.38%
39	South Dakota	217	0.38%
41	Massachusetts	180	0.31%
42	West Virginia	166	0.29%
43	Rhode Island	161	0.28%
44	Idaho	143	0.25%
45	Delaware	130	0.23%
46	Wyoming	113	0.20%
47	New Hampshire	108	0.19%
48	Hawaii	84	0.15%
49	North Dakota	75	0.13%
50	Vermont	17	0.03%
	District of Columbia	380	0.66%

Source: U.S. Department of Justice, Office of Juvenile Justice and Delinquency Prevention
"Children in Custody 1991: Public Facilities" (Fact Sheet #5, September 1993)

Custody Rate of Juveniles in Public Facilities Administered
By State and Local Governments in 1991
National Rate = 221 Juveniles in Custody per 100,000 Juveniles

ALPHA ORDER

RANK ORDER

RANK	STATE	RATE		RANK	STATE	RATE
25	Alabama	174		1	California	492
3	Alaska	312		2	Nevada	427
14	Arizona	226		3	Alaska	312
41	Arkansas	100		4	Ohio	300
1	California	492		5	New Mexico	268
22	Colorado	186		6	Virginia	264
38	Connecticut	123		7	South Carolina	257
21	Delaware	187		8	Washington	256
30	Florida	161		9	Louisiana	251
11	Georgia	235		10	South Dakota	246
48	Hawaii	71		11	Georgia	235
43	Idaho	98		12	Kansas	232
24	Illinois	181		13	Montana	230
17	Indiana	214		14	Arizona	226
36	Iowa	128		15	New Jersey	222
12	Kansas	232		16	Oregon	220
33	Kentucky	151		17	Indiana	214
9	Louisiana	251		18	Michigan	209
23	Maine	185		19	Missouri	206
26	Maryland	172		20	New York	192
49	Massachusetts	37		21	Delaware	187
18	Michigan	209		22	Colorado	186
36	Minnesota	128		23	Maine	185
38	Mississippi	123		24	Illinois	181
19	Missouri	206		25	Alabama	174
13	Montana	230		26	Maryland	172
32	Nebraska	155		27	North Carolina	168
2	Nevada	427		27	Rhode Island	168
44	New Hampshire	95		29	Wyoming	164
15	New Jersey	222		30	Florida	161
5	New Mexico	268		31	Wisconsin	157
20	New York	192		32	Nebraska	155
27	North Carolina	168		33	Kentucky	151
42	North Dakota	99		34	Texas	144
4	Ohio	300		35	Tennessee	138
46	Oklahoma	90		36	Iowa	128
16	Oregon	220		36	Minnesota	128
40	Pennsylvania	106		38	Connecticut	123
27	Rhode Island	168		38	Mississippi	123
7	South Carolina	257		40	Pennsylvania	106
10	South Dakota	246		41	Arkansas	100
35	Tennessee	138		42	North Dakota	99
34	Texas	144		43	Idaho	98
44	Utah	95		44	New Hampshire	95
50	Vermont	28		44	Utah	95
6	Virginia	264		46	Oklahoma	90
8	Washington	256		47	West Virginia	77
47	West Virginia	77		48	Hawaii	71
31	Wisconsin	157		49	Massachusetts	37
29	Wyoming	164		50	Vermont	28

District of Columbia   826

*Source: U.S. Department of Justice, Office of Juvenile Justice and Delinquency Prevention
"Children in Custody 1991: Public Facilities" (Fact Sheet #5, September 1993)*

Public Juvenile Facilities Administered by State and Local Governments in 1991

National Total = 1,076 Facilities

ALPHA ORDER

RANK	STATE	FACILITIES	% of USA
16	Alabama	22	2.04%
38	Alaska	5	0.46%
21	Arizona	16	1.49%
31	Arkansas	10	0.93%
1	California	106	9.85%
32	Colorado	9	0.84%
40	Connecticut	4	0.37%
42	Delaware	3	0.28%
7	Florida	51	4.74%
14	Georgia	28	2.60%
45	Hawaii	2	0.19%
42	Idaho	3	0.28%
18	Illinois	20	1.86%
12	Indiana	33	3.07%
27	Iowa	12	1.12%
27	Kansas	12	1.12%
11	Kentucky	34	3.16%
23	Louisiana	15	1.39%
49	Maine	1	0.09%
23	Maryland	15	1.39%
32	Massachusetts	9	0.84%
8	Michigan	46	4.28%
19	Minnesota	19	1.77%
35	Mississippi	8	0.74%
9	Missouri	42	3.90%
38	Montana	5	0.46%
40	Nebraska	4	0.37%
32	Nevada	9	0.84%
45	New Hampshire	2	0.19%
6	New Jersey	53	4.93%
26	New Mexico	14	1.30%
2	New York	78	7.25%
15	North Carolina	24	2.23%
42	North Dakota	3	0.28%
3	Ohio	64	5.95%
21	Oklahoma	16	1.49%
23	Oregon	15	1.39%
10	Pennsylvania	35	3.25%
45	Rhode Island	2	0.19%
29	South Carolina	11	1.02%
36	South Dakota	6	0.56%
16	Tennessee	22	2.04%
5	Texas	56	5.20%
20	Utah	17	1.58%
49	Vermont	1	0.09%
4	Virginia	61	5.67%
13	Washington	30	2.79%
36	West Virginia	6	0.56%
29	Wisconsin	11	1.02%
45	Wyoming	2	0.19%

RANK ORDER

RANK	STATE	FACILITIES	% of USA
1	California	106	9.85%
2	New York	78	7.25%
3	Ohio	64	5.95%
4	Virginia	61	5.67%
5	Texas	56	5.20%
6	New Jersey	53	4.93%
7	Florida	51	4.74%
8	Michigan	46	4.28%
9	Missouri	42	3.90%
10	Pennsylvania	35	3.25%
11	Kentucky	34	3.16%
12	Indiana	33	3.07%
13	Washington	30	2.79%
14	Georgia	28	2.60%
15	North Carolina	24	2.23%
16	Alabama	22	2.04%
16	Tennessee	22	2.04%
18	Illinois	20	1.86%
19	Minnesota	19	1.77%
20	Utah	17	1.58%
21	Arizona	16	1.49%
21	Oklahoma	16	1.49%
23	Louisiana	15	1.39%
23	Maryland	15	1.39%
23	Oregon	15	1.39%
26	New Mexico	14	1.30%
27	Iowa	12	1.12%
27	Kansas	12	1.12%
29	South Carolina	11	1.02%
29	Wisconsin	11	1.02%
31	Arkansas	10	0.93%
32	Colorado	9	0.84%
32	Massachusetts	9	0.84%
32	Nevada	9	0.84%
35	Mississippi	8	0.74%
36	South Dakota	6	0.56%
36	West Virginia	6	0.56%
38	Alaska	5	0.46%
38	Montana	5	0.46%
40	Connecticut	4	0.37%
40	Nebraska	4	0.37%
42	Delaware	3	0.28%
42	Idaho	3	0.28%
42	North Dakota	3	0.28%
45	Hawaii	2	0.19%
45	New Hampshire	2	0.19%
45	Rhode Island	2	0.19%
45	Wyoming	2	0.19%
49	Maine	1	0.09%
49	Vermont	1	0.09%
	District of Columbia	4	0.37%

Source: U.S. Department of Justice, Office of Juvenile Justice and Delinquency Prevention
"Children in Custody 1991: Public Facilities" (Fact Sheet #5, September 1993)

Juveniles Admitted to Public Juvenile Facilities in 1990

National Total = 683,636 Juveniles

ALPHA ORDER

RANK	STATE	JUVENILES	% of USA
21	Alabama	10,217	1.49%
41	Alaska	1,482	0.22%
13	Arizona	15,857	2.32%
33	Arkansas	4,555	0.67%
1	California	170,462	24.93%
17	Colorado	13,691	2.00%
36	Connecticut	2,960	0.43%
42	Delaware	1,424	0.21%
3	Florida	40,276	5.89%
11	Georgia	17,343	2.54%
40	Hawaii	1,555	0.23%
43	Idaho	1,235	0.18%
6	Illinois	22,412	3.28%
12	Indiana	16,363	2.39%
34	Iowa	3,861	0.56%
30	Kansas	5,921	0.87%
31	Kentucky	5,526	0.81%
27	Louisiana	6,307	0.92%
47	Maine	572	0.08%
22	Maryland	9,482	1.39%
35	Massachusetts	3,254	0.48%
9	Michigan	17,816	2.61%
19	Minnesota	10,878	1.59%
28	Mississippi	6,190	0.91%
18	Missouri	10,945	1.60%
44	Montana	1,084	0.16%
37	Nebraska	2,911	0.43%
8	Nevada	19,665	2.88%
48	New Hampshire	516	0.08%
15	New Jersey	15,130	2.21%
25	New Mexico	7,115	1.04%
16	New York	15,109	2.21%
26	North Carolina	6,977	1.02%
45	North Dakota	664	0.10%
2	Ohio	48,035	7.03%
29	Oklahoma	5,963	0.87%
20	Oregon	10,354	1.51%
14	Pennsylvania	15,249	2.23%
46	Rhode Island	589	0.09%
32	South Carolina	4,742	0.69%
38	South Dakota	2,837	0.41%
7	Tennessee	21,349	3.12%
4	Texas	38,398	5.62%
24	Utah	8,559	1.25%
50	Vermont	308	0.05%
10	Virginia	17,411	2.55%
5	Washington	23,166	3.39%
39	West Virginia	1,611	0.24%
23	Wisconsin	9,269	1.36%
49	Wyoming	353	0.05%

RANK ORDER

RANK	STATE	JUVENILES	% of USA
1	California	170,462	24.93%
2	Ohio	48,035	7.03%
3	Florida	40,276	5.89%
4	Texas	38,398	5.62%
5	Washington	23,166	3.39%
6	Illinois	22,412	3.28%
7	Tennessee	21,349	3.12%
8	Nevada	19,665	2.88%
9	Michigan	17,816	2.61%
10	Virginia	17,411	2.55%
11	Georgia	17,343	2.54%
12	Indiana	16,363	2.39%
13	Arizona	15,857	2.32%
14	Pennsylvania	15,249	2.23%
15	New Jersey	15,130	2.21%
16	New York	15,109	2.21%
17	Colorado	13,691	2.00%
18	Missouri	10,945	1.60%
19	Minnesota	10,878	1.59%
20	Oregon	10,354	1.51%
21	Alabama	10,217	1.49%
22	Maryland	9,482	1.39%
23	Wisconsin	9,269	1.36%
24	Utah	8,559	1.25%
25	New Mexico	7,115	1.04%
26	North Carolina	6,977	1.02%
27	Louisiana	6,307	0.92%
28	Mississippi	6,190	0.91%
29	Oklahoma	5,963	0.87%
30	Kansas	5,921	0.87%
31	Kentucky	5,526	0.81%
32	South Carolina	4,742	0.69%
33	Arkansas	4,555	0.67%
34	Iowa	3,861	0.56%
35	Massachusetts	3,254	0.48%
36	Connecticut	2,960	0.43%
37	Nebraska	2,911	0.43%
38	South Dakota	2,837	0.41%
39	West Virginia	1,611	0.24%
40	Hawaii	1,555	0.23%
41	Alaska	1,482	0.22%
42	Delaware	1,424	0.21%
43	Idaho	1,235	0.18%
44	Montana	1,084	0.16%
45	North Dakota	664	0.10%
46	Rhode Island	589	0.09%
47	Maine	572	0.08%
48	New Hampshire	516	0.08%
49	Wyoming	353	0.05%
50	Vermont	308	0.05%
	District of Columbia	5,688	0.83%

Source: U.S. Department of Justice, Bureau of Justice Statistics
"Sourcebook of Criminal Justice Statistics 1993" (September 1994, NCJ-148211)

Juveniles Discharged from Public Juvenile Facilities in 1990

National Total = 674,597 Juveniles

ALPHA ORDER

RANK ORDER

RANK	STATE	JUVENILES	% of USA		RANK	STATE	JUVENILES	% of USA
20	Alabama	10,322	1.53%		1	California	168,252	24.94%
41	Alaska	1,472	0.22%		2	Ohio	47,264	7.01%
13	Arizona	15,520	2.30%		3	Florida	40,133	5.95%
33	Arkansas	4,521	0.67%		4	Texas	37,816	5.61%
1	California	168,252	24.94%		5	Washington	22,683	3.36%
17	Colorado	13,593	2.01%		6	Illinois	22,443	3.33%
36	Connecticut	2,948	0.44%		7	Tennessee	21,447	3.18%
42	Delaware	1,432	0.21%		8	Nevada	19,585	2.90%
3	Florida	40,133	5.95%		9	Michigan	17,550	2.60%
10	Georgia	17,382	2.58%		10	Georgia	17,382	2.58%
40	Hawaii	1,562	0.23%		11	Virginia	16,894	2.50%
43	Idaho	1,221	0.18%		12	Indiana	15,933	2.36%
6	Illinois	22,443	3.33%		13	Arizona	15,520	2.30%
12	Indiana	15,933	2.36%		14	Pennsylvania	14,909	2.21%
34	Iowa	3,872	0.57%		15	New York	14,791	2.19%
29	Kansas	5,851	0.87%		16	New Jersey	14,611	2.17%
31	Kentucky	5,445	0.81%		17	Colorado	13,593	2.01%
30	Louisiana	5,814	0.86%		18	Minnesota	10,814	1.60%
48	Maine	386	0.06%		19	Missouri	10,779	1.60%
22	Maryland	9,494	1.41%		20	Alabama	10,322	1.53%
35	Massachusetts	3,229	0.48%		21	Oregon	10,204	1.51%
9	Michigan	17,550	2.60%		22	Maryland	9,494	1.41%
18	Minnesota	10,814	1.60%		23	Wisconsin	9,124	1.35%
27	Mississippi	6,206	0.92%		24	Utah	8,402	1.25%
19	Missouri	10,779	1.60%		25	New Mexico	6,984	1.04%
44	Montana	966	0.14%		26	North Carolina	6,736	1.00%
37	Nebraska	2,937	0.44%		27	Mississippi	6,206	0.92%
8	Nevada	19,585	2.90%		28	Oklahoma	5,943	0.88%
47	New Hampshire	562	0.08%		29	Kansas	5,851	0.87%
16	New Jersey	14,611	2.17%		30	Louisiana	5,814	0.86%
25	New Mexico	6,984	1.04%		31	Kentucky	5,445	0.81%
15	New York	14,791	2.19%		32	South Carolina	4,543	0.67%
26	North Carolina	6,736	1.00%		33	Arkansas	4,521	0.67%
46	North Dakota	580	0.09%		34	Iowa	3,872	0.57%
2	Ohio	47,264	7.01%		35	Massachusetts	3,229	0.48%
28	Oklahoma	5,943	0.88%		36	Connecticut	2,948	0.44%
21	Oregon	10,204	1.51%		37	Nebraska	2,937	0.44%
14	Pennsylvania	14,909	2.21%		38	South Dakota	2,842	0.42%
45	Rhode Island	607	0.09%		39	West Virginia	1,597	0.24%
32	South Carolina	4,543	0.67%		40	Hawaii	1,562	0.23%
38	South Dakota	2,842	0.42%		41	Alaska	1,472	0.22%
7	Tennessee	21,447	3.18%		42	Delaware	1,432	0.21%
4	Texas	37,816	5.61%		43	Idaho	1,221	0.18%
24	Utah	8,402	1.25%		44	Montana	966	0.14%
50	Vermont	308	0.05%		45	Rhode Island	607	0.09%
11	Virginia	16,894	2.50%		46	North Dakota	580	0.09%
5	Washington	22,683	3.36%		47	New Hampshire	562	0.08%
39	West Virginia	1,597	0.24%		48	Maine	386	0.06%
23	Wisconsin	9,124	1.35%		49	Wyoming	344	0.05%
49	Wyoming	344	0.05%		50	Vermont	308	0.05%
						District of Columbia	5,744	0.85%

Source: U.S. Department of Justice, Bureau of Justice Statistics
"Sourcebook of Criminal Justice Statistics 1993" (September 1994, NCJ-148211)

Boot Camp and Shock Incarceration Camps Participants in 1993

National Total = 5,937 Participants*

ALPHA ORDER				RANK ORDER			
RANK	STATE	PARTICIPANTS	% of USA	RANK	STATE	PARTICIPANTS	% of USA
14	Alabama	113	1.90%	1	New York	1,492	25.13%
NA	Alaska**	NA	NA	2	Georgia	1,273	21.44%
11	Arizona	131	2.21%	3	Illinois	405	6.82%
8	Arkansas	150	2.53%	4	Oklahoma	368	6.20%
10	California	133	2.24%	5	Texas	301	5.07%
13	Colorado	114	1.92%	6	Michigan	300	5.05%
NA	Connecticut**	NA	NA	7	Mississippi	238	4.01%
NA	Delaware**	NA	NA	8	Arkansas	150	2.53%
16	Florida	97	1.63%	9	Massachusetts	137	2.31%
2	Georgia	1,273	21.44%	10	California	133	2.24%
NA	Hawaii**	NA	NA	11	Arizona	131	2.21%
NA	Idaho**	NA	NA	12	Louisiana	120	2.02%
3	Illinois	405	6.82%	13	Colorado	114	1.92%
NA	Indiana**	NA	NA	14	Alabama	113	1.90%
NA	Iowa**	NA	NA	15	Tennessee	100	1.68%
18	Kansas	78	1.31%	16	Florida	97	1.63%
25	Kentucky	20	0.34%	17	North Carolina	84	1.41%
12	Louisiana	120	2.02%	18	Kansas	78	1.31%
NA	Maine**	NA	NA	19	Nevada	77	1.30%
NA	Maryland**	NA	NA	20	Virginia	54	0.91%
9	Massachusetts	137	2.31%	21	Pennsylvania	48	0.81%
6	Michigan	300	5.05%	22	Minnesota	38	0.64%
22	Minnesota	38	0.64%	22	Wisconsin	38	0.64%
7	Mississippi	238	4.01%	24	New Hampshire	28	0.47%
NA	Missouri**	NA	NA	25	Kentucky	20	0.34%
NA	Montana**	NA	NA	NA	Alaska**	NA	NA
NA	Nebraska**	NA	NA	NA	Connecticut**	NA	NA
19	Nevada	77	1.30%	NA	Delaware**	NA	NA
24	New Hampshire	28	0.47%	NA	Hawaii**	NA	NA
NA	New Jersey**	NA	NA	NA	Idaho**	NA	NA
NA	New Mexico**	NA	NA	NA	Indiana**	NA	NA
1	New York	1,492	25.13%	NA	Iowa**	NA	NA
17	North Carolina	84	1.41%	NA	Maine**	NA	NA
NA	North Dakota**	NA	NA	NA	Maryland**	NA	NA
NA	Ohio**	NA	NA	NA	Missouri**	NA	NA
4	Oklahoma	368	6.20%	NA	Montana**	NA	NA
NA	Oregon**	NA	NA	NA	Nebraska**	NA	NA
21	Pennsylvania	48	0.81%	NA	New Jersey**	NA	NA
NA	Rhode Island**	NA	NA	NA	New Mexico**	NA	NA
NA	South Carolina**	NA	NA	NA	North Dakota**	NA	NA
NA	South Dakota**	NA	NA	NA	Ohio**	NA	NA
15	Tennessee	100	1.68%	NA	Oregon**	NA	NA
5	Texas	301	5.07%	NA	Rhode Island**	NA	NA
NA	Utah**	NA	NA	NA	South Carolina**	NA	NA
NA	Vermont**	NA	NA	NA	South Dakota**	NA	NA
20	Virginia	54	0.91%	NA	Utah**	NA	NA
NA	Washington**	NA	NA	NA	Vermont**	NA	NA
NA	West Virginia**	NA	NA	NA	Washington**	NA	NA
22	Wisconsin	38	0.64%	NA	West Virginia**	NA	NA
NA	Wyoming**	NA	NA	NA	Wyoming**	NA	NA
					District of Columbia**	NA	NA

Source: Contact Publications (Lincoln, NE)
     "Corrections Compendium" (September 1993)
*National total is only for states shown. This information was collected through a survey mailed to the departments
of juvenile corrections in the 50 states, the District of Columbia and the Federal Bureau of Prisons.
**Either no program or did not respond to survey.

III. DRUGS AND ALCOHOL

Alcohol and Other Drug Treatment Units in 1993

National Total = 7,679 Units*

ALPHA ORDER					RANK ORDER			

RANK	STATE	UNITS	% of USA		RANK	STATE	UNITS	% of USA
39	Alabama	38	0.49%		1	California	861	11.21%
28	Alaska	56	0.73%		2	New York	747	9.73%
26	Arizona	66	0.86%		3	Florida	511	6.65%
44	Arkansas	29	0.38%		4	Ohio	441	5.74%
1	California	861	11.21%		5	Pennsylvania	399	5.20%
17	Colorado	124	1.61%		6	Massachusetts	385	5.01%
16	Connecticut	129	1.68%		7	Minnesota	371	4.83%
46	Delaware	23	0.30%		8	Texas	343	4.47%
3	Florida	511	6.65%		8	Wisconsin	343	4.47%
30	Georgia	55	0.72%		10	Illinois	296	3.85%
47	Hawaii	22	0.29%		11	Michigan	249	3.24%
24	Idaho	78	1.02%		12	Virginia	182	2.37%
10	Illinois	296	3.85%		13	Kentucky	180	2.34%
33	Indiana	51	0.66%		14	New Jersey	176	2.29%
43	Iowa	31	0.40%		15	Oregon	131	1.71%
31	Kansas	54	0.70%		16	Connecticut	129	1.68%
13	Kentucky	180	2.34%		17	Colorado	124	1.61%
23	Louisiana	86	1.12%		18	Maryland	121	1.58%
34	Maine	45	0.59%		18	Washington	121	1.58%
18	Maryland	121	1.58%		20	Nebraska	107	1.39%
6	Massachusetts	385	5.01%		21	Missouri	102	1.33%
11	Michigan	249	3.24%		22	Tennessee	100	1.30%
7	Minnesota	371	4.83%		23	Louisiana	86	1.12%
25	Mississippi	77	1.00%		24	Idaho	78	1.02%
21	Missouri	102	1.33%		25	Mississippi	77	1.00%
45	Montana	24	0.31%		26	Arizona	66	0.86%
20	Nebraska	107	1.39%		27	Utah	60	0.78%
41	Nevada	35	0.46%		28	Alaska	56	0.73%
41	New Hampshire	35	0.46%		28	West Virginia	56	0.73%
14	New Jersey	176	2.29%		30	Georgia	55	0.72%
34	New Mexico	45	0.59%		31	Kansas	54	0.70%
2	New York	747	9.73%		31	Oklahoma	54	0.70%
36	North Carolina	44	0.57%		33	Indiana	51	0.66%
49	North Dakota	8	0.10%		34	Maine	45	0.59%
4	Ohio	441	5.74%		34	New Mexico	45	0.59%
31	Oklahoma	54	0.70%		36	North Carolina	44	0.57%
15	Oregon	131	1.71%		36	Rhode Island	44	0.57%
5	Pennsylvania	399	5.20%		38	South Dakota	43	0.56%
36	Rhode Island	44	0.57%		39	Alabama	38	0.49%
39	South Carolina	38	0.49%		39	South Carolina	38	0.49%
38	South Dakota	43	0.56%		41	Nevada	35	0.46%
22	Tennessee	100	1.30%		41	New Hampshire	35	0.46%
8	Texas	343	4.47%		43	Iowa	31	0.40%
27	Utah	60	0.78%		44	Arkansas	29	0.38%
48	Vermont	16	0.21%		45	Montana	24	0.31%
12	Virginia	182	2.37%		46	Delaware	23	0.30%
18	Washington	121	1.58%		47	Hawaii	22	0.29%
28	West Virginia	56	0.73%		48	Vermont	16	0.21%
8	Wisconsin	343	4.47%		49	North Dakota	8	0.10%
NA	Wyoming**	NA	NA		NA	Wyoming**	NA	NA
						District of Columbia	47	0.61%

Source: U.S. Department of Health and Human Services, Substance Abuse and Mental Health Services Administration "State Resources and Services Related to Alcohol and Other Drug Problems-Fiscal Year 1993" (January 1995)
Does not include 92 units in U.S. territories. Data are only from treatment units that received at least some funds administered by a state's alcohol/drug agency in fiscal year 1993.
**Not available.*

Alcohol and Other Drug Treatment Admissions in 1993

National Total = 1,806,973 Admissions*

<u>ALPHA ORDER</u>

RANK	STATE	ADMISSIONS	% of USA
30	Alabama	15,530	0.86%
40	Alaska	8,260	0.46%
27	Arizona	21,258	1.18%
33	Arkansas	13,879	0.77%
2	California	142,881	7.91%
9	Colorado	68,899	3.81%
17	Connecticut	32,674	1.81%
45	Delaware	6,105	0.34%
4	Florida	95,860	5.31%
11	Georgia	62,254	3.45%
49	Hawaii	3,758	0.21%
48	Idaho	4,593	0.25%
5	Illinois	92,331	5.11%
26	Indiana	21,666	1.20%
34	Iowa	13,126	0.73%
28	Kansas	16,887	0.93%
21	Kentucky	27,826	1.54%
22	Louisiana	27,677	1.53%
32	Maine	14,149	0.78%
18	Maryland	32,139	1.78%
6	Massachusetts	88,925	4.92%
7	Michigan	75,105	4.16%
20	Minnesota	28,362	1.57%
39	Mississippi	10,779	0.60%
19	Missouri	30,221	1.67%
41	Montana	7,318	0.40%
25	Nebraska	22,791	1.26%
46	Nevada	5,307	0.29%
43	New Hampshire	6,441	0.36%
13	New Jersey	54,411	3.01%
38	New Mexico	11,477	0.64%
1	New York	148,185	8.20%
14	North Carolina	48,194	2.67%
47	North Dakota	4,815	0.27%
8	Ohio	71,000	3.93%
42	Oklahoma	6,452	0.36%
16	Oregon	33,708	1.87%
10	Pennsylvania	64,965	3.60%
37	Rhode Island	11,587	0.64%
23	South Carolina	26,681	1.48%
35	South Dakota	12,896	0.71%
36	Tennessee	12,078	0.67%
12	Texas	58,338	3.23%
31	Utah	14,672	0.81%
44	Vermont	6,395	0.35%
24	Virginia	26,560	1.47%
15	Washington	40,312	2.23%
29	West Virginia	16,013	0.89%
3	Wisconsin	124,921	6.91%
NA	Wyoming**	NA	NA

<u>RANK ORDER</u>

RANK	STATE	ADMISSIONS	% of USA
1	New York	148,185	8.20%
2	California	142,881	7.91%
3	Wisconsin	124,921	6.91%
4	Florida	95,860	5.31%
5	Illinois	92,331	5.11%
6	Massachusetts	88,925	4.92%
7	Michigan	75,105	4.16%
8	Ohio	71,000	3.93%
9	Colorado	68,899	3.81%
10	Pennsylvania	64,965	3.60%
11	Georgia	62,254	3.45%
12	Texas	58,338	3.23%
13	New Jersey	54,411	3.01%
14	North Carolina	48,194	2.67%
15	Washington	40,312	2.23%
16	Oregon	33,708	1.87%
17	Connecticut	32,674	1.81%
18	Maryland	32,139	1.78%
19	Missouri	30,221	1.67%
20	Minnesota	28,362	1.57%
21	Kentucky	27,826	1.54%
22	Louisiana	27,677	1.53%
23	South Carolina	26,681	1.48%
24	Virginia	26,560	1.47%
25	Nebraska	22,791	1.26%
26	Indiana	21,666	1.20%
27	Arizona	21,258	1.18%
28	Kansas	16,887	0.93%
29	West Virginia	16,013	0.89%
30	Alabama	15,530	0.86%
31	Utah	14,672	0.81%
32	Maine	14,149	0.78%
33	Arkansas	13,879	0.77%
34	Iowa	13,126	0.73%
35	South Dakota	12,896	0.71%
36	Tennessee	12,078	0.67%
37	Rhode Island	11,587	0.64%
38	New Mexico	11,477	0.64%
39	Mississippi	10,779	0.60%
40	Alaska	8,260	0.46%
41	Montana	7,318	0.40%
42	Oklahoma	6,452	0.36%
43	New Hampshire	6,441	0.36%
44	Vermont	6,395	0.35%
45	Delaware	6,105	0.34%
46	Nevada	5,307	0.29%
47	North Dakota	4,815	0.27%
48	Idaho	4,593	0.25%
49	Hawaii	3,758	0.21%
NA	Wyoming**	NA	NA
	District of Columbia	16,312	0.90%

Source: U.S. Department of Health and Human Services, Substance Abuse and Mental Health Services Administration
"State Resources and Services Related to Alcohol and Other Drug Problems-Fiscal Year 1993" (January 1995)
*Does not include 22,829 admissions in U.S. territories. Data are only from treatment units that received at least some funds administered by a state's alcohol/drug agency in fiscal year 1993.
**Not available.

Male Admissions to Alcohol and Other Drug Treatment Programs in 1993

National Total = 1,273,158 Admissions*

ALPHA ORDER					RANK ORDER			

RANK	STATE	ADMISSIONS	% of USA		RANK	STATE	ADMISSIONS	% of USA
31	Alabama	11,440	0.90%		1	New York	110,822	8.70%
40	Alaska	5,991	0.47%		2	California	93,551	7.35%
27	Arizona	15,341	1.20%		3	Wisconsin	91,563	7.19%
33	Arkansas	11,255	0.88%		4	Illinois	65,274	5.13%
2	California	93,551	7.35%		5	Massachusetts	64,379	5.06%
6	Colorado	55,099	4.33%		6	Colorado	55,099	4.33%
16	Connecticut	24,700	1.94%		7	Michigan	51,013	4.01%
45	Delaware	4,461	0.35%		8	Ohio	47,973	3.77%
12	Florida	41,052	3.22%		9	Pennsylvania	47,050	3.70%
10	Georgia	45,586	3.58%		10	Georgia	45,586	3.58%
49	Hawaii	2,515	0.20%		11	Texas	42,870	3.37%
48	Idaho	3,341	0.26%		12	Florida	41,052	3.22%
4	Illinois	65,274	5.13%		13	New Jersey	38,759	3.04%
25	Indiana	16,248	1.28%		14	North Carolina	35,751	2.81%
34	Iowa	9,832	0.77%		15	Washington	28,040	2.20%
28	Kansas	12,742	1.00%		16	Connecticut	24,700	1.94%
20	Kentucky	21,088	1.66%		17	Maryland	22,593	1.77%
23	Louisiana	19,498	1.53%		18	Missouri	22,171	1.74%
30	Maine	11,608	0.91%		19	Oregon	21,678	1.70%
17	Maryland	22,593	1.77%		20	Kentucky	21,088	1.66%
5	Massachusetts	64,379	5.06%		21	Minnesota	20,137	1.58%
7	Michigan	51,013	4.01%		22	South Carolina	19,720	1.55%
21	Minnesota	20,137	1.58%		23	Louisiana	19,498	1.53%
38	Mississippi	8,532	0.67%		24	Nebraska	17,586	1.38%
18	Missouri	22,171	1.74%		25	Indiana	16,248	1.28%
41	Montana	5,269	0.41%		26	Virginia	15,425	1.21%
24	Nebraska	17,586	1.38%		27	Arizona	15,341	1.20%
46	Nevada	3,669	0.29%		28	Kansas	12,742	1.00%
43	New Hampshire	4,779	0.38%		29	West Virginia	12,472	0.98%
13	New Jersey	38,759	3.04%		30	Maine	11,608	0.91%
37	New Mexico	8,705	0.68%		31	Alabama	11,440	0.90%
1	New York	110,822	8.70%		32	Utah	11,289	0.89%
14	North Carolina	35,751	2.81%		33	Arkansas	11,255	0.88%
47	North Dakota	3,401	0.27%		34	Iowa	9,832	0.77%
8	Ohio	47,973	3.77%		35	South Dakota	9,313	0.73%
44	Oklahoma	4,739	0.37%		36	Tennessee	8,851	0.70%
19	Oregon	21,678	1.70%		37	New Mexico	8,705	0.68%
9	Pennsylvania	47,050	3.70%		38	Mississippi	8,532	0.67%
39	Rhode Island	8,109	0.64%		39	Rhode Island	8,109	0.64%
22	South Carolina	19,720	1.55%		40	Alaska	5,991	0.47%
35	South Dakota	9,313	0.73%		41	Montana	5,269	0.41%
36	Tennessee	8,851	0.70%		42	Vermont	4,877	0.38%
11	Texas	42,870	3.37%		43	New Hampshire	4,779	0.38%
32	Utah	11,289	0.89%		44	Oklahoma	4,739	0.37%
42	Vermont	4,877	0.38%		45	Delaware	4,461	0.35%
26	Virginia	15,425	1.21%		46	Nevada	3,669	0.29%
15	Washington	28,040	2.20%		47	North Dakota	3,401	0.27%
29	West Virginia	12,472	0.98%		48	Idaho	3,341	0.26%
3	Wisconsin	91,563	7.19%		49	Hawaii	2,515	0.20%
NA	Wyoming**	NA	NA		NA	Wyoming**	NA	NA
						District of Columbia	11,001	0.86%

Source: U.S. Department of Health and Human Services, Substance Abuse and Mental Health Services Administration "State Resources and Services Related to Alcohol and Other Drug Problems-Fiscal Year 1993" (January 1995)
Does not include 20,568 admissions in U.S. territories. Data are only from treatment units that received at least some funds administered by a state's alcohol/drug agency in fiscal year 1993. An additional 39,433 admissions were not reported by sex.
**Not available.*

Male Admissions to Alcohol and Other Drug Treatment Programs
As a Percent of All Admissions in 1993
National Percent = 70.46% Males*

ALPHA ORDER

RANK ORDER

RANK	STATE	PERCENT		RANK	STATE	PERCENT
19	Alabama	73.66		1	Maine	82.04
28	Alaska	72.53		2	Arkansas	81.09
32	Arizona	72.17		3	Colorado	79.97
2	Arkansas	81.09		4	Mississippi	79.15
46	California	65.47		5	West Virginia	77.89
3	Colorado	79.97		6	Nebraska	77.16
11	Connecticut	75.60		7	Utah	76.94
26	Delaware	73.07		8	Vermont	76.26
49	Florida	42.82		9	New Mexico	75.85
25	Georgia	73.23		10	Kentucky	75.79
45	Hawaii	66.92		11	Connecticut	75.60
27	Idaho	72.74		12	Kansas	75.45
36	Illinois	70.70		13	Indiana	74.99
13	Indiana	74.99		14	Iowa	74.90
14	Iowa	74.90		15	New York	74.79
12	Kansas	75.45		16	New Hampshire	74.20
10	Kentucky	75.79		17	North Carolina	74.18
38	Louisiana	70.45		18	South Carolina	73.91
1	Maine	82.04		19	Alabama	73.66
39	Maryland	70.30		20	Texas	73.49
30	Massachusetts	72.40		21	Oklahoma	73.45
43	Michigan	67.92		22	Missouri	73.36
35	Minnesota	71.00		23	Wisconsin	73.30
4	Mississippi	79.15		24	Tennessee	73.28
22	Missouri	73.36		25	Georgia	73.23
33	Montana	72.00		26	Delaware	73.07
6	Nebraska	77.16		27	Idaho	72.74
42	Nevada	69.14		28	Alaska	72.53
16	New Hampshire	74.20		29	Pennsylvania	72.42
34	New Jersey	71.23		30	Massachusetts	72.40
9	New Mexico	75.85		31	South Dakota	72.22
15	New York	74.79		32	Arizona	72.17
17	North Carolina	74.18		33	Montana	72.00
37	North Dakota	70.63		34	New Jersey	71.23
44	Ohio	67.57		35	Minnesota	71.00
21	Oklahoma	73.45		36	Illinois	70.70
47	Oregon	64.31		37	North Dakota	70.63
29	Pennsylvania	72.42		38	Louisiana	70.45
40	Rhode Island	69.98		39	Maryland	70.30
18	South Carolina	73.91		40	Rhode Island	69.98
31	South Dakota	72.22		41	Washington	69.56
24	Tennessee	73.28		42	Nevada	69.14
20	Texas	73.49		43	Michigan	67.92
7	Utah	76.94		44	Ohio	67.57
8	Vermont	76.26		45	Hawaii	66.92
48	Virginia	58.08		46	California	65.47
41	Washington	69.56		47	Oregon	64.31
5	West Virginia	77.89		48	Virginia	58.08
23	Wisconsin	73.30		49	Florida	42.82
NA	Wyoming**	NA		NA	Wyoming**	NA
					District of Columbia	67.44

Source: Morgan Quitno Press using data from U.S. Department of Health and Human Services, Substance Abuse and Mental Health Services Administration
"State Resources and Services Related to Alcohol and Other Drug Problems-Fiscal Year 1993" (January 1995)
*Does not include admissions in U.S. territories. Data are only from treatment units that received at least some funds administered by a state's alcohol/drug agency in fiscal year 1993. An additional 39,433 admissions were not reported by sex. **Not available.*

Female Admissions to Alcohol and Other Drug Treatment Programs in 1993

National Total = 494,331 Female Admissions*

ALPHA ORDER

RANK ORDER

RANK	STATE	ADMISSIONS	% of USA	RANK	STATE	ADMISSIONS	% of USA
29	Alabama	4,090	0.83%	1	California	49,330	9.98%
39	Alaska	2,269	0.46%	2	New York	37,363	7.56%
25	Arizona	5,917	1.20%	3	Wisconsin	33,358	6.75%
37	Arkansas	2,624	0.53%	4	Illinois	27,057	5.47%
1	California	49,330	9.98%	5	Massachusetts	24,546	4.97%
13	Colorado	13,800	2.79%	6	Michigan	23,909	4.84%
22	Connecticut	7,974	1.61%	7	Ohio	23,027	4.66%
44	Delaware	1,644	0.33%	8	Pennsylvania	17,915	3.62%
10	Florida	16,395	3.32%	9	Georgia	16,668	3.37%
9	Georgia	16,668	3.37%	10	Florida	16,395	3.32%
49	Hawaii	1,192	0.24%	11	New Jersey	15,652	3.17%
48	Idaho	1,252	0.25%	12	Texas	15,468	3.13%
4	Illinois	27,057	5.47%	13	Colorado	13,800	2.79%
26	Indiana	5,418	1.10%	14	North Carolina	12,443	2.52%
34	Iowa	3,294	0.67%	15	Washington	12,272	2.48%
28	Kansas	4,145	0.84%	16	Oregon	12,030	2.43%
24	Kentucky	6,738	1.36%	17	Virginia	10,498	2.12%
20	Louisiana	8,179	1.65%	18	Maryland	9,539	1.93%
38	Maine	2,541	0.51%	19	Minnesota	8,214	1.66%
18	Maryland	9,539	1.93%	20	Louisiana	8,179	1.65%
5	Massachusetts	24,546	4.97%	21	Missouri	8,050	1.63%
6	Michigan	23,909	4.84%	22	Connecticut	7,974	1.61%
19	Minnesota	8,214	1.66%	23	South Carolina	6,961	1.41%
40	Mississippi	2,247	0.45%	24	Kentucky	6,738	1.36%
21	Missouri	8,050	1.63%	25	Arizona	5,917	1.20%
41	Montana	2,049	0.41%	26	Indiana	5,418	1.10%
27	Nebraska	5,205	1.05%	27	Nebraska	5,205	1.05%
45	Nevada	1,638	0.33%	28	Kansas	4,145	0.84%
43	New Hampshire	1,662	0.34%	29	Alabama	4,090	0.83%
11	New Jersey	15,652	3.17%	30	South Dakota	3,583	0.72%
36	New Mexico	2,772	0.56%	31	West Virginia	3,541	0.72%
2	New York	37,363	7.56%	32	Rhode Island	3,478	0.70%
14	North Carolina	12,443	2.52%	33	Utah	3,325	0.67%
47	North Dakota	1,414	0.29%	34	Iowa	3,294	0.67%
7	Ohio	23,027	4.66%	35	Tennessee	3,227	0.65%
42	Oklahoma	1,713	0.35%	36	New Mexico	2,772	0.56%
16	Oregon	12,030	2.43%	37	Arkansas	2,624	0.53%
8	Pennsylvania	17,915	3.62%	38	Maine	2,541	0.51%
32	Rhode Island	3,478	0.70%	39	Alaska	2,269	0.46%
23	South Carolina	6,961	1.41%	40	Mississippi	2,247	0.45%
30	South Dakota	3,583	0.72%	41	Montana	2,049	0.41%
35	Tennessee	3,227	0.65%	42	Oklahoma	1,713	0.35%
12	Texas	15,468	3.13%	43	New Hampshire	1,662	0.34%
33	Utah	3,325	0.67%	44	Delaware	1,644	0.33%
46	Vermont	1,497	0.30%	45	Nevada	1,638	0.33%
17	Virginia	10,498	2.12%	46	Vermont	1,497	0.30%
15	Washington	12,272	2.48%	47	North Dakota	1,414	0.29%
31	West Virginia	3,541	0.72%	48	Idaho	1,252	0.25%
3	Wisconsin	33,358	6.75%	49	Hawaii	1,192	0.24%
NA	Wyoming**	NA	NA	NA	Wyoming**	NA	NA
					District of Columbia	5,209	1.05%

*Source: U.S. Department of Health and Human Services, Substance Abuse and Mental Health Services Administration
"State Resources and Services Related to Alcohol and Other Drug Problems-Fiscal Year 1993" (January 1995)
*Does not include 2,261 admissions in U.S. territories. Data are only from treatment units that received at least
some funds administered by a state's alcohol/drug agency in fiscal year 1993. An additional 39,433 admissions
were not reported by sex.
**Not available.*

Female Admissions to Alcohol and Other Drug Treatment Programs
As a Percent of All Admissions in 1993
National Percent = 27.36% Female*

ALPHA ORDER

RANK	STATE	PERCENT
30	Alabama	26.34
21	Alaska	27.47
17	Arizona	27.83
47	Arkansas	18.91
3	California	34.53
46	Colorado	20.03
38	Connecticut	24.40
23	Delaware	26.93
49	Florida	17.10
24	Georgia	26.77
6	Hawaii	31.72
22	Idaho	27.26
13	Illinois	29.30
36	Indiana	25.01
35	Iowa	25.10
37	Kansas	24.55
39	Kentucky	24.21
11	Louisiana	29.55
48	Maine	17.96
10	Maryland	29.68
19	Massachusetts	27.60
5	Michigan	31.83
14	Minnesota	28.96
45	Mississippi	20.85
27	Missouri	26.64
16	Montana	28.00
42	Nebraska	22.84
7	Nevada	30.86
33	New Hampshire	25.80
15	New Jersey	28.77
40	New Mexico	24.15
34	New York	25.21
32	North Carolina	25.82
12	North Dakota	29.37
4	Ohio	32.43
28	Oklahoma	26.55
2	Oregon	35.69
20	Pennsylvania	27.58
9	Rhode Island	30.02
31	South Carolina	26.09
18	South Dakota	27.78
25	Tennessee	26.72
29	Texas	26.51
43	Utah	22.66
41	Vermont	23.41
1	Virginia	39.53
8	Washington	30.44
44	West Virginia	22.11
26	Wisconsin	26.70
NA	Wyoming**	NA

RANK ORDER

RANK	STATE	PERCENT
1	Virginia	39.53
2	Oregon	35.69
3	California	34.53
4	Ohio	32.43
5	Michigan	31.83
6	Hawaii	31.72
7	Nevada	30.86
8	Washington	30.44
9	Rhode Island	30.02
10	Maryland	29.68
11	Louisiana	29.55
12	North Dakota	29.37
13	Illinois	29.30
14	Minnesota	28.96
15	New Jersey	28.77
16	Montana	28.00
17	Arizona	27.83
18	South Dakota	27.78
19	Massachusetts	27.60
20	Pennsylvania	27.58
21	Alaska	27.47
22	Idaho	27.26
23	Delaware	26.93
24	Georgia	26.77
25	Tennessee	26.72
26	Wisconsin	26.70
27	Missouri	26.64
28	Oklahoma	26.55
29	Texas	26.51
30	Alabama	26.34
31	South Carolina	26.09
32	North Carolina	25.82
33	New Hampshire	25.80
34	New York	25.21
35	Iowa	25.10
36	Indiana	25.01
37	Kansas	24.55
38	Connecticut	24.40
39	Kentucky	24.21
40	New Mexico	24.15
41	Vermont	23.41
42	Nebraska	22.84
43	Utah	22.66
44	West Virginia	22.11
45	Mississippi	20.85
46	Colorado	20.03
47	Arkansas	18.91
48	Maine	17.96
49	Florida	17.10
NA	Wyoming**	NA
	District of Columbia	31.93

Source: Morgan Quitno Press using data from U.S. Department of Health and Human Services, Substance Abuse and Mental Health Services Administration

"State Resources and Services Related to Alcohol and Other Drug Problems-Fiscal Year 1993" (January 1995)
*Does not include admissions in U.S. territories. Data are only from treatment units that received at least some funds administered by a state's alcohol/drug agency in fiscal year 1993. An additional 39,433 admissions were not reported by sex. **Not available.*

White Admissions to Alcohol and Other Drug Treatment Programs in 1993

National Total = 1,077,768 White Admissions*

ALPHA ORDER

RANK	STATE	ADMISSIONS	% of USA
35	Alabama	8,844	0.82%
47	Alaska	3,358	0.31%
29	Arizona	12,407	1.15%
34	Arkansas	8,904	0.83%
2	California	74,864	6.95%
7	Colorado	41,502	3.85%
20	Connecticut	17,728	1.64%
46	Delaware	3,422	0.32%
10	Florida	33,174	3.08%
11	Georgia	32,268	2.99%
49	Hawaii	1,639	0.15%
43	Idaho	4,014	0.37%
8	Illinois	41,295	3.83%
24	Indiana	15,602	1.45%
30	Iowa	11,815	1.10%
31	Kansas	11,793	1.09%
17	Kentucky	23,026	2.14%
28	Louisiana	12,458	1.16%
27	Maine	13,458	1.25%
22	Maryland	16,356	1.52%
4	Massachusetts	61,672	5.72%
5	Michigan	49,460	4.59%
18	Minnesota	20,928	1.94%
41	Mississippi	4,865	0.45%
19	Missouri	20,524	1.90%
40	Montana	5,930	0.55%
21	Nebraska	16,905	1.57%
44	Nevada	3,902	0.36%
39	New Hampshire	6,108	0.57%
13	New Jersey	27,457	2.55%
48	New Mexico	3,247	0.30%
3	New York	73,390	6.81%
14	North Carolina	26,277	2.44%
45	North Dakota	3,611	0.34%
6	Ohio	48,364	4.49%
42	Oklahoma	4,319	0.40%
15	Oregon	25,738	2.39%
9	Pennsylvania	37,664	3.49%
33	Rhode Island	9,014	0.84%
23	South Carolina	15,946	1.48%
37	South Dakota	8,189	0.76%
36	Tennessee	8,756	0.81%
16	Texas	23,743	2.20%
32	Utah	10,689	0.99%
38	Vermont	6,171	0.57%
25	Virginia	15,559	1.44%
12	Washington	29,359	2.72%
26	West Virginia	14,898	1.38%
1	Wisconsin	106,532	9.88%
NA	Wyoming**	NA	NA

RANK ORDER

RANK	STATE	ADMISSIONS	% of USA
1	Wisconsin	106,532	9.88%
2	California	74,864	6.95%
3	New York	73,390	6.81%
4	Massachusetts	61,672	5.72%
5	Michigan	49,460	4.59%
6	Ohio	48,364	4.49%
7	Colorado	41,502	3.85%
8	Illinois	41,295	3.83%
9	Pennsylvania	37,664	3.49%
10	Florida	33,174	3.08%
11	Georgia	32,268	2.99%
12	Washington	29,359	2.72%
13	New Jersey	27,457	2.55%
14	North Carolina	26,277	2.44%
15	Oregon	25,738	2.39%
16	Texas	23,743	2.20%
17	Kentucky	23,026	2.14%
18	Minnesota	20,928	1.94%
19	Missouri	20,524	1.90%
20	Connecticut	17,728	1.64%
21	Nebraska	16,905	1.57%
22	Maryland	16,356	1.52%
23	South Carolina	15,946	1.48%
24	Indiana	15,602	1.45%
25	Virginia	15,559	1.44%
26	West Virginia	14,898	1.38%
27	Maine	13,458	1.25%
28	Louisiana	12,458	1.16%
29	Arizona	12,407	1.15%
30	Iowa	11,815	1.10%
31	Kansas	11,793	1.09%
32	Utah	10,689	0.99%
33	Rhode Island	9,014	0.84%
34	Arkansas	8,904	0.83%
35	Alabama	8,844	0.82%
36	Tennessee	8,756	0.81%
37	South Dakota	8,189	0.76%
38	Vermont	6,171	0.57%
39	New Hampshire	6,108	0.57%
40	Montana	5,930	0.55%
41	Mississippi	4,865	0.45%
42	Oklahoma	4,319	0.40%
43	Idaho	4,014	0.37%
44	Nevada	3,902	0.36%
45	North Dakota	3,611	0.34%
46	Delaware	3,422	0.32%
47	Alaska	3,358	0.31%
48	New Mexico	3,247	0.30%
49	Hawaii	1,639	0.15%
NA	Wyoming**	NA	NA
	District of Columbia	624	0.06%

Source: U.S. Department of Health and Human Services, Substance Abuse and Mental Health Services Administration "State Resources and Services Related to Alcohol and Other Drug Problems-Fiscal Year 1993" (January 1995)
*Does not include 43 white admissions in U.S. territories. Data are only from treatment units that received at least some funds administered by a state's alcohol/drug agency in fiscal year 1993. An additional 49,100 admissions were not reported by race.
**Not available.

White Admissions to Alcohol and Other Drug Treatment Programs
As a Percent of All Admissions in 1993
National Percent = 59.64% of Admissions*

ALPHA ORDER

RANK ORDER

RANK	STATE	PERCENT
33	Alabama	56.95
47	Alaska	40.65
31	Arizona	58.36
26	Arkansas	64.15
37	California	52.40
28	Colorado	60.24
36	Connecticut	54.26
34	Delaware	56.05
48	Florida	34.61
38	Georgia	51.83
45	Hawaii	43.61
6	Idaho	87.39
44	Illinois	44.72
19	Indiana	72.01
5	Iowa	90.01
20	Kansas	69.83
8	Kentucky	82.75
43	Louisiana	45.01
2	Maine	95.12
39	Maryland	50.89
21	Massachusetts	69.35
25	Michigan	65.85
14	Minnesota	73.79
42	Mississippi	45.13
23	Missouri	67.91
9	Montana	81.03
13	Nebraska	74.17
15	Nevada	73.53
3	New Hampshire	94.83
40	New Jersey	50.46
49	New Mexico	28.29
41	New York	49.53
35	North Carolina	54.52
12	North Dakota	74.99
22	Ohio	68.12
24	Oklahoma	66.94
11	Oregon	76.36
32	Pennsylvania	57.98
10	Rhode Island	77.79
29	South Carolina	59.77
27	South Dakota	63.50
18	Tennessee	72.50
46	Texas	40.70
16	Utah	72.85
1	Vermont	96.50
30	Virginia	58.58
17	Washington	72.83
4	West Virginia	93.04
7	Wisconsin	85.28
NA	Wyoming**	NA

RANK	STATE	PERCENT
1	Vermont	96.50
2	Maine	95.12
3	New Hampshire	94.83
4	West Virginia	93.04
5	Iowa	90.01
6	Idaho	87.39
7	Wisconsin	85.28
8	Kentucky	82.75
9	Montana	81.03
10	Rhode Island	77.79
11	Oregon	76.36
12	North Dakota	74.99
13	Nebraska	74.17
14	Minnesota	73.79
15	Nevada	73.53
16	Utah	72.85
17	Washington	72.83
18	Tennessee	72.50
19	Indiana	72.01
20	Kansas	69.83
21	Massachusetts	69.35
22	Ohio	68.12
23	Missouri	67.91
24	Oklahoma	66.94
25	Michigan	65.85
26	Arkansas	64.15
27	South Dakota	63.50
28	Colorado	60.24
29	South Carolina	59.77
30	Virginia	58.58
31	Arizona	58.36
32	Pennsylvania	57.98
33	Alabama	56.95
34	Delaware	56.05
35	North Carolina	54.52
36	Connecticut	54.26
37	California	52.40
38	Georgia	51.83
39	Maryland	50.89
40	New Jersey	50.46
41	New York	49.53
42	Mississippi	45.13
43	Louisiana	45.01
44	Illinois	44.72
45	Hawaii	43.61
46	Texas	40.70
47	Alaska	40.65
48	Florida	34.61
49	New Mexico	28.29
NA	Wyoming**	NA

District of Columbia 3.83

Source: Morgan Quitno Press using data from U.S. Department of Health and Human Services, Substance Abuse and Mental Health Services Administration
"State Resources and Services Related to Alcohol and Other Drug Problems-Fiscal Year 1993" (January 1995)
*Does not include admissions in U.S. territories. Data are only from treatment units that received at least some funds administered by a state's alcohol/drug agency in fiscal year 1993. An additional 49,100 admissions were not reported by race. **Not available.

Black Admissions to Alcohol and Other Drug Treatment Programs in 1993

National Total = 470,239 Black Admissions*

ALPHA ORDER					RANK ORDER			
RANK	STATE		ADMISSIONS	% of USA	RANK	STATE	ADMISSIONS	% of USA
20	Alabama		6,541	1.39%	1	New York	52,561	11.18%
40	Alaska		350	0.07%	2	Illinois	43,698	9.29%
33	Arizona		1,582	0.34%	3	California	29,734	6.32%
24	Arkansas		4,828	1.03%	4	Georgia	29,597	6.29%
3	California		29,734	6.32%	5	Pennsylvania	23,716	5.04%
21	Colorado		6,350	1.35%	6	Michigan	21,611	4.60%
19	Connecticut		9,210	1.96%	7	Ohio	20,694	4.40%
31	Delaware		2,480	0.53%	8	North Carolina	20,562	4.37%
11	Florida		16,151	3.43%	9	New Jersey	19,484	4.14%
4	Georgia		29,597	6.29%	10	Texas	19,344	4.11%
43	Hawaii		130	0.03%	11	Florida	16,151	3.43%
49	Idaho		16	0.00%	12	Massachusetts	15,223	3.24%
2	Illinois		43,698	9.29%	13	Maryland	15,186	3.23%
23	Indiana		5,323	1.13%	14	Louisiana	14,971	3.18%
37	Iowa		739	0.16%	15	Wisconsin	12,016	2.56%
29	Kansas		3,116	0.66%	16	South Carolina	10,315	2.19%
28	Kentucky		3,193	0.68%	17	Virginia	10,030	2.13%
14	Louisiana		14,971	3.18%	18	Missouri	9,241	1.97%
42	Maine		136	0.03%	19	Connecticut	9,210	1.96%
13	Maryland		15,186	3.23%	20	Alabama	6,541	1.39%
12	Massachusetts		15,223	3.24%	21	Colorado	6,350	1.35%
6	Michigan		21,611	4.60%	22	Mississippi	5,356	1.14%
26	Minnesota		3,817	0.81%	23	Indiana	5,323	1.13%
22	Mississippi		5,356	1.14%	24	Arkansas	4,828	1.03%
18	Missouri		9,241	1.97%	25	Washington	4,311	0.92%
47	Montana		50	0.01%	26	Minnesota	3,817	0.81%
32	Nebraska		2,128	0.45%	27	Tennessee	3,201	0.68%
38	Nevada		675	0.14%	28	Kentucky	3,193	0.68%
45	New Hampshire		123	0.03%	29	Kansas	3,116	0.66%
9	New Jersey		19,484	4.14%	30	Oregon	2,753	0.59%
41	New Mexico		283	0.06%	31	Delaware	2,480	0.53%
1	New York		52,561	11.18%	32	Nebraska	2,128	0.45%
8	North Carolina		20,562	4.37%	33	Arizona	1,582	0.34%
48	North Dakota		28	0.01%	34	Rhode Island	1,367	0.29%
7	Ohio		20,694	4.40%	35	Oklahoma	1,101	0.23%
35	Oklahoma		1,101	0.23%	36	West Virginia	983	0.21%
30	Oregon		2,753	0.59%	37	Iowa	739	0.16%
5	Pennsylvania		23,716	5.04%	38	Nevada	675	0.14%
34	Rhode Island		1,367	0.29%	39	Utah	529	0.11%
16	South Carolina		10,315	2.19%	40	Alaska	350	0.07%
44	South Dakota		127	0.03%	41	New Mexico	283	0.06%
27	Tennessee		3,201	0.68%	42	Maine	136	0.03%
10	Texas		19,344	4.11%	43	Hawaii	130	0.03%
39	Utah		529	0.11%	44	South Dakota	127	0.03%
46	Vermont		65	0.01%	45	New Hampshire	123	0.03%
17	Virginia		10,030	2.13%	46	Vermont	65	0.01%
25	Washington		4,311	0.92%	47	Montana	50	0.01%
36	West Virginia		983	0.21%	48	North Dakota	28	0.01%
15	Wisconsin		12,016	2.56%	49	Idaho	16	0.00%
NA	Wyoming**		NA	NA	NA	Wyoming**	NA	NA
						District of Columbia	15,214	3.24%

Source: U.S. Department of Health and Human Services, Substance Abuse and Mental Health Services Administration
"State Resources and Services Related to Alcohol and Other Drug Problems-Fiscal Year 1993" (January 1995)
*Does not include 5 black admissions in U.S. territories. Data are only from treatment units that received at least some funds administered by a state's alcohol/drug agency in fiscal year 1993. An additional 49,100 admissions were not reported by race.
**Not available.

Black Admissions to Alcohol and Other Drug Treatment Programs
As a Percent of All Admissions in 1993
National Percent = 26.02% of Admissions*

ALPHA ORDER

RANK	STATE	PERCENT
7	Alabama	42.12
39	Alaska	4.24
36	Arizona	7.44
14	Arkansas	34.79
22	California	20.81
34	Colorado	9.22
19	Connecticut	28.19
8	Delaware	40.62
26	Florida	16.85
3	Georgia	47.54
41	Hawaii	3.46
49	Idaho	0.35
4	Illinois	47.33
21	Indiana	24.57
38	Iowa	5.63
23	Kansas	18.45
30	Kentucky	11.47
1	Louisiana	54.09
46	Maine	0.96
5	Maryland	47.25
24	Massachusetts	17.12
18	Michigan	28.77
27	Minnesota	13.46
2	Mississippi	49.69
16	Missouri	30.58
47	Montana	0.68
33	Nebraska	9.34
28	Nevada	12.72
43	New Hampshire	1.91
12	New Jersey	35.81
42	New Mexico	2.47
13	New York	35.47
6	North Carolina	42.67
48	North Dakota	0.58
17	Ohio	29.15
25	Oklahoma	17.06
35	Oregon	8.17
11	Pennsylvania	36.51
29	Rhode Island	11.80
9	South Carolina	38.66
45	South Dakota	0.98
20	Tennessee	26.50
15	Texas	33.16
40	Utah	3.61
44	Vermont	1.02
10	Virginia	37.76
31	Washington	10.69
37	West Virginia	6.14
32	Wisconsin	9.62
NA	Wyoming**	NA

RANK ORDER

RANK	STATE	PERCENT
1	Louisiana	54.09
2	Mississippi	49.69
3	Georgia	47.54
4	Illinois	47.33
5	Maryland	47.25
6	North Carolina	42.67
7	Alabama	42.12
8	Delaware	40.62
9	South Carolina	38.66
10	Virginia	37.76
11	Pennsylvania	36.51
12	New Jersey	35.81
13	New York	35.47
14	Arkansas	34.79
15	Texas	33.16
16	Missouri	30.58
17	Ohio	29.15
18	Michigan	28.77
19	Connecticut	28.19
20	Tennessee	26.50
21	Indiana	24.57
22	California	20.81
23	Kansas	18.45
24	Massachusetts	17.12
25	Oklahoma	17.06
26	Florida	16.85
27	Minnesota	13.46
28	Nevada	12.72
29	Rhode Island	11.80
30	Kentucky	11.47
31	Washington	10.69
32	Wisconsin	9.62
33	Nebraska	9.34
34	Colorado	9.22
35	Oregon	8.17
36	Arizona	7.44
37	West Virginia	6.14
38	Iowa	5.63
39	Alaska	4.24
40	Utah	3.61
41	Hawaii	3.46
42	New Mexico	2.47
43	New Hampshire	1.91
44	Vermont	1.02
45	South Dakota	0.98
46	Maine	0.96
47	Montana	0.68
48	North Dakota	0.58
49	Idaho	0.35
NA	Wyoming**	NA

District of Columbia   93.27

Source: Morgan Quitno Press using data from U.S. Department of Health and Human Services, Substance Abuse and Mental Health Services Administration
"State Resources and Services Related to Alcohol and Other Drug Problems-Fiscal Year 1993" (January 1995)
*Does not include admissions in U.S. territories. Data are only from treatment units that received at least some funds administered by a state's alcohol/drug agency in fiscal year 1993. An additional 49,100 admissions were not reported by race. **Not available.

Hispanic Admissions to Alcohol and Other Drug Treatment Programs in 1993

National Total = 145,457 Hispanic Admissions*

ALPHA ORDER

RANK	STATE	ADMISSIONS	% of USA
37	Alabama	14	0.01%
35	Alaska	50	0.03%
11	Arizona	4,663	3.21%
33	Arkansas	84	0.06%
1	California	32,086	22.06%
3	Colorado	16,936	11.64%
9	Connecticut	5,516	3.79%
29	Delaware	136	0.09%
7	Florida	5,943	4.09%
27	Georgia	205	0.14%
38	Hawaii	0	0.00%
38	Idaho	0	0.00%
8	Illinois	5,832	4.01%
23	Indiana	327	0.22%
25	Iowa	282	0.19%
16	Kansas	1,547	1.06%
30	Kentucky	119	0.08%
NA	Louisiana**	NA	NA
38	Maine	0	0.00%
22	Maryland	334	0.23%
5	Massachusetts	9,801	6.74%
14	Michigan	2,304	1.58%
38	Minnesota	0	0.00%
38	Mississippi	0	0.00%
38	Missouri	0	0.00%
28	Montana	147	0.10%
18	Nebraska	1,389	0.95%
21	Nevada	427	0.29%
36	New Hampshire	34	0.02%
6	New Jersey	6,838	4.70%
10	New Mexico	5,231	3.60%
2	New York	18,357	12.62%
24	North Carolina	300	0.21%
38	North Dakota	0	0.00%
19	Ohio	1,386	0.95%
38	Oklahoma	0	0.00%
15	Oregon	2,165	1.49%
38	Pennsylvania	0	0.00%
20	Rhode Island	778	0.53%
26	South Carolina	273	0.19%
31	South Dakota	110	0.08%
38	Tennessee	0	0.00%
4	Texas	14,703	10.11%
17	Utah	1,458	1.00%
34	Vermont	66	0.05%
38	Virginia	0	0.00%
13	Washington	2,410	1.66%
32	West Virginia	101	0.07%
12	Wisconsin	2,807	1.93%
NA	Wyoming**	NA	NA

RANK ORDER

RANK	STATE	ADMISSIONS	% of USA
1	California	32,086	22.06%
2	New York	18,357	12.62%
3	Colorado	16,936	11.64%
4	Texas	14,703	10.11%
5	Massachusetts	9,801	6.74%
6	New Jersey	6,838	4.70%
7	Florida	5,943	4.09%
8	Illinois	5,832	4.01%
9	Connecticut	5,516	3.79%
10	New Mexico	5,231	3.60%
11	Arizona	4,663	3.21%
12	Wisconsin	2,807	1.93%
13	Washington	2,410	1.66%
14	Michigan	2,304	1.58%
15	Oregon	2,165	1.49%
16	Kansas	1,547	1.06%
17	Utah	1,458	1.00%
18	Nebraska	1,389	0.95%
19	Ohio	1,386	0.95%
20	Rhode Island	778	0.53%
21	Nevada	427	0.29%
22	Maryland	334	0.23%
23	Indiana	327	0.22%
24	North Carolina	300	0.21%
25	Iowa	282	0.19%
26	South Carolina	273	0.19%
27	Georgia	205	0.14%
28	Montana	147	0.10%
29	Delaware	136	0.09%
30	Kentucky	119	0.08%
31	South Dakota	110	0.08%
32	West Virginia	101	0.07%
33	Arkansas	84	0.06%
34	Vermont	66	0.05%
35	Alaska	50	0.03%
36	New Hampshire	34	0.02%
37	Alabama	14	0.01%
38	Hawaii	0	0.00%
38	Idaho	0	0.00%
38	Maine	0	0.00%
38	Minnesota	0	0.00%
38	Mississippi	0	0.00%
38	Missouri	0	0.00%
38	North Dakota	0	0.00%
38	Oklahoma	0	0.00%
38	Pennsylvania	0	0.00%
38	Tennessee	0	0.00%
38	Virginia	0	0.00%
NA	Louisiana**	NA	NA
NA	Wyoming**	NA	NA
	District of Columbia	298	0.20%

Source: U.S. Department of Health and Human Services, Substance Abuse and Mental Health Services Administration
"State Resources and Services Related to Alcohol and Other Drug Problems-Fiscal Year 1993" (January 1995)
*Does not include 22,581 Hispanic admissions in U.S. territories. Data are only from treatment units that received at least some funds administered by a state's alcohol/drug agency in fiscal year 1993. An additional 49,100 admissions were not reported by race.
**Not available.

Hispanic Admissions to Alcohol and Other Drug Treatment Programs
As a Percent of All Admissions in 1993
National Percent = 8.05% of Admissions*

ALPHA ORDER

RANK ORDER

RANK	STATE	PERCENT
37	Alabama	0.09
32	Alaska	0.61
5	Arizona	21.94
32	Arkansas	0.61
4	California	22.46
3	Colorado	24.58
6	Connecticut	16.88
21	Delaware	2.23
16	Florida	6.20
36	Georgia	0.33
38	Hawaii	0.00
38	Idaho	0.00
15	Illinois	6.32
25	Indiana	1.51
22	Iowa	2.15
11	Kansas	9.16
35	Kentucky	0.43
NA	Louisiana**	NA
38	Maine	0.00
26	Maryland	1.04
9	Massachusetts	11.02
19	Michigan	3.07
38	Minnesota	0.00
38	Mississippi	0.00
38	Missouri	0.00
23	Montana	2.01
17	Nebraska	6.09
12	Nevada	8.05
34	New Hampshire	0.53
7	New Jersey	12.57
1	New Mexico	45.58
8	New York	12.39
31	North Carolina	0.62
38	North Dakota	0.00
24	Ohio	1.95
38	Oklahoma	0.00
14	Oregon	6.42
38	Pennsylvania	0.00
13	Rhode Island	6.71
28	South Carolina	1.02
29	South Dakota	0.85
38	Tennessee	0.00
2	Texas	25.20
10	Utah	9.94
27	Vermont	1.03
38	Virginia	0.00
18	Washington	5.98
30	West Virginia	0.63
20	Wisconsin	2.25
NA	Wyoming**	NA

RANK	STATE	PERCENT
1	New Mexico	45.58
2	Texas	25.20
3	Colorado	24.58
4	California	22.46
5	Arizona	21.94
6	Connecticut	16.88
7	New Jersey	12.57
8	New York	12.39
9	Massachusetts	11.02
10	Utah	9.94
11	Kansas	9.16
12	Nevada	8.05
13	Rhode Island	6.71
14	Oregon	6.42
15	Illinois	6.32
16	Florida	6.20
17	Nebraska	6.09
18	Washington	5.98
19	Michigan	3.07
20	Wisconsin	2.25
21	Delaware	2.23
22	Iowa	2.15
23	Montana	2.01
24	Ohio	1.95
25	Indiana	1.51
26	Maryland	1.04
27	Vermont	1.03
28	South Carolina	1.02
29	South Dakota	0.85
30	West Virginia	0.63
31	North Carolina	0.62
32	Alaska	0.61
32	Arkansas	0.61
34	New Hampshire	0.53
35	Kentucky	0.43
36	Georgia	0.33
37	Alabama	0.09
38	Hawaii	0.00
38	Idaho	0.00
38	Maine	0.00
38	Minnesota	0.00
38	Mississippi	0.00
38	Missouri	0.00
38	North Dakota	0.00
38	Oklahoma	0.00
38	Pennsylvania	0.00
38	Tennessee	0.00
38	Virginia	0.00
NA	Louisiana**	NA
NA	Wyoming**	NA

District of Columbia 1.83

Source: Morgan Quitno Press using data from U.S. Department of Health and Human Services, Substance Abuse
and Mental Health Services Administration
"State Resources and Services Related to Alcohol and Other Drug Problems-Fiscal Year 1993" (January 1995)
*Does not include admissions in U.S. territories. Data are only from treatment units that received at least some
funds administered by a state's alcohol/drug agency in fiscal year 1993. An additional 49,100 admissions were not
reported by race. **Not available.

Admissions of Juveniles in Alcohol and Other Drug Treatment Programs in 1993

National Total = 107,416 Juvenile Admissions*

ALPHA ORDER

RANK	STATE	ADMISSIONS	% of USA
29	Alabama	1,115	1.04%
38	Alaska	582	0.54%
36	Arizona	689	0.64%
34	Arkansas	834	0.78%
3	California	7,769	7.23%
12	Colorado	3,261	3.04%
41	Connecticut	476	0.44%
49	Delaware	11	0.01%
4	Florida	6,077	5.66%
23	Georgia	1,619	1.51%
31	Hawaii	997	0.93%
32	Idaho	983	0.92%
2	Illinois	7,983	7.43%
35	Indiana	717	0.67%
30	Iowa	1,045	0.97%
33	Kansas	955	0.89%
15	Kentucky	1,992	1.85%
21	Louisiana	1,695	1.58%
39	Maine	543	0.51%
13	Maryland	2,985	2.78%
19	Massachusetts	1,781	1.66%
8	Michigan	4,785	4.45%
24	Minnesota	1,518	1.41%
48	Mississippi	143	0.13%
26	Missouri	1,374	1.28%
42	Montana	385	0.36%
17	Nebraska	1,914	1.78%
47	Nevada	211	0.20%
43	New Hampshire	339	0.32%
16	New Jersey	1,974	1.84%
37	New Mexico	675	0.63%
7	New York	5,757	5.36%
18	North Carolina	1,820	1.69%
46	North Dakota	215	0.20%
1	Ohio	8,001	7.45%
44	Oklahoma	300	0.28%
5	Oregon	6,061	5.64%
9	Pennsylvania	4,260	3.97%
40	Rhode Island	535	0.50%
14	South Carolina	2,172	2.02%
22	South Dakota	1,666	1.55%
28	Tennessee	1,171	1.09%
10	Texas	3,668	3.41%
20	Utah	1,769	1.65%
45	Vermont	293	0.27%
25	Virginia	1,467	1.37%
11	Washington	3,568	3.32%
27	West Virginia	1,256	1.17%
6	Wisconsin	5,867	5.46%
NA	Wyoming**	NA	NA

RANK ORDER

RANK	STATE	ADMISSIONS	% of USA
1	Ohio	8,001	7.45%
2	Illinois	7,983	7.43%
3	California	7,769	7.23%
4	Florida	6,077	5.66%
5	Oregon	6,061	5.64%
6	Wisconsin	5,867	5.46%
7	New York	5,757	5.36%
8	Michigan	4,785	4.45%
9	Pennsylvania	4,260	3.97%
10	Texas	3,668	3.41%
11	Washington	3,568	3.32%
12	Colorado	3,261	3.04%
13	Maryland	2,985	2.78%
14	South Carolina	2,172	2.02%
15	Kentucky	1,992	1.85%
16	New Jersey	1,974	1.84%
17	Nebraska	1,914	1.78%
18	North Carolina	1,820	1.69%
19	Massachusetts	1,781	1.66%
20	Utah	1,769	1.65%
21	Louisiana	1,695	1.58%
22	South Dakota	1,666	1.55%
23	Georgia	1,619	1.51%
24	Minnesota	1,518	1.41%
25	Virginia	1,467	1.37%
26	Missouri	1,374	1.28%
27	West Virginia	1,256	1.17%
28	Tennessee	1,171	1.09%
29	Alabama	1,115	1.04%
30	Iowa	1,045	0.97%
31	Hawaii	997	0.93%
32	Idaho	983	0.92%
33	Kansas	955	0.89%
34	Arkansas	834	0.78%
35	Indiana	717	0.67%
36	Arizona	689	0.64%
37	New Mexico	675	0.63%
38	Alaska	582	0.54%
39	Maine	543	0.51%
40	Rhode Island	535	0.50%
41	Connecticut	476	0.44%
42	Montana	385	0.36%
43	New Hampshire	339	0.32%
44	Oklahoma	300	0.28%
45	Vermont	293	0.27%
46	North Dakota	215	0.20%
47	Nevada	211	0.20%
48	Mississippi	143	0.13%
49	Delaware	11	0.01%
NA	Wyoming**	NA	NA
	District of Columbia	143	0.13%

Source: U.S. Department of Health and Human Services, Substance Abuse and Mental Health Services Administration
"State Resources and Services Related to Alcohol and Other Drug Problems-Fiscal Year 1993" (January 1995)
*Youths 17 years and younger. Does not include 1,040 admissions of juveniles in U.S. territories. Data are only from treatment units that received at least some funds administered by a state's alcohol/drug agency in fiscal year 1993. An additional 41,229 admissions were not reported by age.
**Not available.

Admissions of Juveniles in Alcohol and Other Drug Treatment Programs As a Percent of All Admissions in 1993
National Percent = 5.94% of Admissions*

ALPHA ORDER

RANK	STATE	PERCENT
15	Alabama	7.18
17	Alaska	7.05
44	Arizona	3.24
23	Arkansas	6.01
27	California	5.44
31	Colorado	4.73
47	Connecticut	1.46
49	Delaware	0.18
20	Florida	6.34
45	Georgia	2.60
1	Hawaii	26.53
2	Idaho	21.40
10	Illinois	8.65
43	Indiana	3.31
13	Iowa	7.96
25	Kansas	5.66
16	Kentucky	7.16
22	Louisiana	6.12
40	Maine	3.84
8	Maryland	9.29
46	Massachusetts	2.00
19	Michigan	6.37
28	Minnesota	5.35
48	Mississippi	1.33
36	Missouri	4.55
29	Montana	5.26
11	Nebraska	8.40
38	Nevada	3.98
29	New Hampshire	5.26
42	New Jersey	3.63
24	New Mexico	5.88
39	New York	3.89
41	North Carolina	3.78
37	North Dakota	4.47
6	Ohio	11.27
33	Oklahoma	4.65
3	Oregon	17.98
18	Pennsylvania	6.56
34	Rhode Island	4.62
12	South Carolina	8.14
4	South Dakota	12.92
7	Tennessee	9.70
21	Texas	6.29
5	Utah	12.06
35	Vermont	4.58
26	Virginia	5.52
9	Washington	8.85
14	West Virginia	7.84
32	Wisconsin	4.70
NA	Wyoming**	NA

RANK ORDER

RANK	STATE	PERCENT
1	Hawaii	26.53
2	Idaho	21.40
3	Oregon	17.98
4	South Dakota	12.92
5	Utah	12.06
6	Ohio	11.27
7	Tennessee	9.70
8	Maryland	9.29
9	Washington	8.85
10	Illinois	8.65
11	Nebraska	8.40
12	South Carolina	8.14
13	Iowa	7.96
14	West Virginia	7.84
15	Alabama	7.18
16	Kentucky	7.16
17	Alaska	7.05
18	Pennsylvania	6.56
19	Michigan	6.37
20	Florida	6.34
21	Texas	6.29
22	Louisiana	6.12
23	Arkansas	6.01
24	New Mexico	5.88
25	Kansas	5.66
26	Virginia	5.52
27	California	5.44
28	Minnesota	5.35
29	Montana	5.26
29	New Hampshire	5.26
31	Colorado	4.73
32	Wisconsin	4.70
33	Oklahoma	4.65
34	Rhode Island	4.62
35	Vermont	4.58
36	Missouri	4.55
37	North Dakota	4.47
38	Nevada	3.98
39	New York	3.89
40	Maine	3.84
41	North Carolina	3.78
42	New Jersey	3.63
43	Indiana	3.31
44	Arizona	3.24
45	Georgia	2.60
46	Massachusetts	2.00
47	Connecticut	1.46
48	Mississippi	1.33
49	Delaware	0.18
NA	Wyoming**	NA
	District of Columbia	0.88

Source: Morgan Quitno Press using data from U.S. Department of Health and Human Services, Substance Abuse and Mental Health Services Administration
"State Resources and Services Related to Alcohol and Other Drug Problems-Fiscal Year 1993" (January 1995)
*Youths 17 years and younger. Does not include admissions in U.S. territories. Data are only from treatment units that received at least some funds administered by a state's alcohol/drug agency in fiscal year 1993. An additional 41,229 admissions were not reported by race. **Not available.

Expenditures for State-Supported Alcohol and Other Drug Abuse Services: 1993

National Total = $3,632,987,042*

ALPHA ORDER

RANK	STATE	EXPENDITURES	% of USA
33	Alabama	$18,065,495	0.50%
28	Alaska	28,088,225	0.77%
25	Arizona	32,838,245	0.90%
41	Arkansas	11,238,381	0.31%
2	California	500,943,954	13.79%
22	Colorado	44,279,464	1.22%
10	Connecticut	92,837,713	2.56%
45	Delaware	7,180,556	0.20%
4	Florida	147,674,947	4.06%
17	Georgia	69,606,260	1.92%
36	Hawaii	14,603,823	0.40%
47	Idaho	6,139,141	0.17%
5	Illinois	147,117,555	4.05%
20	Indiana	46,636,000	1.28%
24	Iowa	34,965,359	0.96%
35	Kansas	14,631,292	0.40%
30	Kentucky	24,549,699	0.68%
26	Louisiana	30,362,624	0.84%
43	Maine	10,798,553	0.30%
12	Maryland	78,812,460	2.17%
15	Massachusetts	71,421,389	1.97%
8	Michigan	138,369,618	3.81%
18	Minnesota	63,530,790	1.75%
42	Mississippi	11,019,744	0.30%
23	Missouri	43,948,561	1.21%
39	Montana	12,940,582	0.36%
37	Nebraska	13,715,995	0.38%
44	Nevada	10,096,652	0.28%
48	New Hampshire	5,282,449	0.15%
11	New Jersey	85,449,000	2.35%
34	New Mexico	15,677,542	0.43%
1	New York	760,185,867	20.92%
19	North Carolina	53,052,660	1.46%
49	North Dakota	4,084,000	0.11%
6	Ohio	140,371,415	3.86%
32	Oklahoma	22,392,837	0.62%
13	Oregon	73,458,228	2.02%
7	Pennsylvania	139,904,395	3.85%
31	Rhode Island	23,111,047	0.64%
21	South Carolina	44,527,001	1.23%
38	South Dakota	13,067,239	0.36%
27	Tennessee	29,025,397	0.80%
9	Texas	126,393,813	3.48%
29	Utah	26,288,652	0.72%
46	Vermont	6,768,140	0.19%
14	Virginia	73,444,483	2.02%
16	Washington	70,778,272	1.95%
40	West Virginia	11,670,728	0.32%
3	Wisconsin	148,144,800	4.08%
NA	Wyoming**	NA	NA

RANK ORDER

RANK	STATE	EXPENDITURES	% of USA
1	New York	$760,185,867	20.92%
2	California	500,943,954	13.79%
3	Wisconsin	148,144,800	4.08%
4	Florida	147,674,947	4.06%
5	Illinois	147,117,555	4.05%
6	Ohio	140,371,415	3.86%
7	Pennsylvania	139,904,395	3.85%
8	Michigan	138,369,618	3.81%
9	Texas	126,393,813	3.48%
10	Connecticut	92,837,713	2.56%
11	New Jersey	85,449,000	2.35%
12	Maryland	78,812,460	2.17%
13	Oregon	73,458,228	2.02%
14	Virginia	73,444,483	2.02%
15	Massachusetts	71,421,389	1.97%
16	Washington	70,778,272	1.95%
17	Georgia	69,606,260	1.92%
18	Minnesota	63,530,790	1.75%
19	North Carolina	53,052,660	1.46%
20	Indiana	46,636,000	1.28%
21	South Carolina	44,527,001	1.23%
22	Colorado	44,279,464	1.22%
23	Missouri	43,948,561	1.21%
24	Iowa	34,965,359	0.96%
25	Arizona	32,838,245	0.90%
26	Louisiana	30,362,624	0.84%
27	Tennessee	29,025,397	0.80%
28	Alaska	28,088,225	0.77%
29	Utah	26,288,652	0.72%
30	Kentucky	24,549,699	0.68%
31	Rhode Island	23,111,047	0.64%
32	Oklahoma	22,392,837	0.62%
33	Alabama	18,065,495	0.50%
34	New Mexico	15,677,542	0.43%
35	Kansas	14,631,292	0.40%
36	Hawaii	14,603,823	0.40%
37	Nebraska	13,715,995	0.38%
38	South Dakota	13,067,239	0.36%
39	Montana	12,940,582	0.36%
40	West Virginia	11,670,728	0.32%
41	Arkansas	11,238,381	0.31%
42	Mississippi	11,019,744	0.30%
43	Maine	10,798,553	0.30%
44	Nevada	10,096,652	0.28%
45	Delaware	7,180,556	0.20%
46	Vermont	6,768,140	0.19%
47	Idaho	6,139,141	0.17%
48	New Hampshire	5,282,449	0.15%
49	North Dakota	4,084,000	0.11%
NA	Wyoming**	NA	NA
	District of Columbia	33,496,000	0.92%

Source: U.S. Department of Health and Human Services, Substance Abuse and Mental Health Services Administration
"State Resources and Services Related to Alcohol and Other Drug Problems-Fiscal Year 1993" (January 1995)
*Funds for treatment and prevention programs as well as "other" costs (e.g. administration, capital construction and research.) Total does not include $56,242,585 in Puerto Rico and $1,096,784 in Guam.
**Not available.

Per Capita Expenditures for State-Supported Alcohol and Other Drug Abuse Services in 1993
National Per Capita = $14.09*

ALPHA ORDER

RANK	STATE	PER CAPITA
48	Alabama	$4.32
1	Alaska	46.97
33	Arizona	8.33
47	Arkansas	4.63
8	California	16.05
18	Colorado	12.41
4	Connecticut	28.32
27	Delaware	10.27
26	Florida	10.76
28	Georgia	10.09
17	Hawaii	12.52
45	Idaho	5.58
16	Illinois	12.58
34	Indiana	8.17
19	Iowa	12.39
43	Kansas	5.78
40	Kentucky	6.47
37	Louisiana	7.08
30	Maine	8.72
9	Maryland	15.92
21	Massachusetts	11.87
11	Michigan	14.63
13	Minnesota	14.04
49	Mississippi	4.18
32	Missouri	8.40
10	Montana	15.39
31	Nebraska	8.50
36	Nevada	7.29
46	New Hampshire	4.70
25	New Jersey	10.87
29	New Mexico	9.70
2	New York	41.88
35	North Carolina	7.63
42	North Dakota	6.41
15	Ohio	12.69
39	Oklahoma	6.93
5	Oregon	24.20
23	Pennsylvania	11.63
6	Rhode Island	23.13
20	South Carolina	12.28
7	South Dakota	18.22
44	Tennessee	5.70
38	Texas	7.00
12	Utah	14.13
22	Vermont	11.75
24	Virginia	11.34
14	Washington	13.47
41	West Virginia	6.42
3	Wisconsin	29.37
NA	Wyoming**	NA

RANK ORDER

RANK	STATE	PER CAPITA
1	Alaska	$46.97
2	New York	41.88
3	Wisconsin	29.37
4	Connecticut	28.32
5	Oregon	24.20
6	Rhode Island	23.13
7	South Dakota	18.22
8	California	16.05
9	Maryland	15.92
10	Montana	15.39
11	Michigan	14.63
12	Utah	14.13
13	Minnesota	14.04
14	Washington	13.47
15	Ohio	12.69
16	Illinois	12.58
17	Hawaii	12.52
18	Colorado	12.41
19	Iowa	12.39
20	South Carolina	12.28
21	Massachusetts	11.87
22	Vermont	11.75
23	Pennsylvania	11.63
24	Virginia	11.34
25	New Jersey	10.87
26	Florida	10.76
27	Delaware	10.27
28	Georgia	10.09
29	New Mexico	9.70
30	Maine	8.72
31	Nebraska	8.50
32	Missouri	8.40
33	Arizona	8.33
34	Indiana	8.17
35	North Carolina	7.63
36	Nevada	7.29
37	Louisiana	7.08
38	Texas	7.00
39	Oklahoma	6.93
40	Kentucky	6.47
41	West Virginia	6.42
42	North Dakota	6.41
43	Kansas	5.78
44	Tennessee	5.70
45	Idaho	5.58
46	New Hampshire	4.70
47	Arkansas	4.63
48	Alabama	4.32
49	Mississippi	4.18
NA	Wyoming**	NA
	District of Columbia	57.95

Source: Morgan Quitno Press using data from U.S. Department of Health and Human Services, Substance Abuse and Mental Health Services Administration
   "State Resources and Services Related to Alcohol and Other Drug Problems-Fiscal Year 1993" (January 1995)
*Funds for treatment and prevention programs as well as "other" costs (e.g. administration, capital construction and research.) National per capita does not include expenditures in Puerto Rico and Guam.
**Not available.

Expenditures for State-Supported Alcohol and Other Drug Abuse Treatment Programs in 1993
National Total = $2,786,794,358*

ALPHA ORDER					RANK ORDER			
RANK	STATE	EXPENDITURES	% of USA		RANK	STATE	EXPENDITURES	% of USA
33	Alabama	$13,914,820	0.50%		1	New York	$581,346,997	20.86%
27	Alaska	23,673,849	0.85%		2	California	359,145,246	12.89%
24	Arizona	28,196,140	1.01%		3	Florida	127,199,647	4.56%
42	Arkansas	8,354,884	0.30%		4	Illinois	122,761,788	4.41%
2	California	359,145,246	12.89%		5	Michigan	109,769,760	3.94%
22	Colorado	34,717,361	1.25%		6	Ohio	103,309,948	3.71%
10	Connecticut	78,531,396	2.82%		7	Wisconsin	98,786,191	3.54%
45	Delaware	6,279,543	0.23%		8	Pennsylvania	98,464,813	3.53%
3	Florida	127,199,647	4.56%		9	Texas	89,986,626	3.23%
12	Georgia	65,603,184	2.35%		10	Connecticut	78,531,396	2.82%
36	Hawaii	11,803,822	0.42%		11	New Jersey	73,222,000	2.63%
47	Idaho	4,327,021	0.16%		12	Georgia	65,603,184	2.35%
4	Illinois	122,761,788	4.41%		13	Massachusetts	63,562,272	2.28%
19	Indiana	38,011,610	1.36%		14	Virginia	62,617,643	2.25%
25	Iowa	27,798,901	1.00%		15	Maryland	60,112,328	2.16%
38	Kansas	11,109,663	0.40%		16	Minnesota	56,812,963	2.04%
29	Kentucky	18,755,816	0.67%		17	Washington	49,520,213	1.78%
26	Louisiana	26,572,183	0.95%		18	North Carolina	38,267,641	1.37%
41	Maine	8,800,816	0.32%		19	Indiana	38,011,610	1.36%
15	Maryland	60,112,328	2.16%		20	Missouri	37,972,360	1.36%
13	Massachusetts	63,562,272	2.28%		21	Oregon	35,638,552	1.28%
5	Michigan	109,769,760	3.94%		22	Colorado	34,717,361	1.25%
16	Minnesota	56,812,963	2.04%		23	South Carolina	28,410,310	1.02%
43	Mississippi	7,613,128	0.27%		24	Arizona	28,196,140	1.01%
20	Missouri	37,972,360	1.36%		25	Iowa	27,798,901	1.00%
37	Montana	11,256,224	0.40%		26	Louisiana	26,572,183	0.95%
39	Nebraska	10,741,702	0.39%		27	Alaska	23,673,849	0.85%
44	Nevada	6,971,957	0.25%		28	Tennessee	20,272,958	0.73%
49	New Hampshire	3,624,395	0.13%		29	Kentucky	18,755,816	0.67%
11	New Jersey	73,222,000	2.63%		30	Utah	18,527,888	0.66%
35	New Mexico	11,874,839	0.43%		31	Oklahoma	18,451,906	0.66%
1	New York	581,346,997	20.86%		32	Rhode Island	16,172,384	0.58%
18	North Carolina	38,267,641	1.37%		33	Alabama	13,914,820	0.50%
48	North Dakota	3,656,000	0.13%		34	South Dakota	11,930,201	0.43%
6	Ohio	103,309,948	3.71%		35	New Mexico	11,874,839	0.43%
31	Oklahoma	18,451,906	0.66%		36	Hawaii	11,803,822	0.42%
21	Oregon	35,638,552	1.28%		37	Montana	11,256,224	0.40%
8	Pennsylvania	98,464,813	3.53%		38	Kansas	11,109,663	0.40%
32	Rhode Island	16,172,384	0.58%		39	Nebraska	10,741,702	0.39%
23	South Carolina	28,410,310	1.02%		40	West Virginia	10,236,665	0.37%
34	South Dakota	11,930,201	0.43%		41	Maine	8,800,816	0.32%
28	Tennessee	20,272,958	0.73%		42	Arkansas	8,354,884	0.30%
9	Texas	89,986,626	3.23%		43	Mississippi	7,613,128	0.27%
30	Utah	18,527,888	0.66%		44	Nevada	6,971,957	0.25%
46	Vermont	4,420,804	0.16%		45	Delaware	6,279,543	0.23%
14	Virginia	62,617,643	2.25%		46	Vermont	4,420,804	0.16%
17	Washington	49,520,213	1.78%		47	Idaho	4,327,021	0.16%
40	West Virginia	10,236,665	0.37%		48	North Dakota	3,656,000	0.13%
7	Wisconsin	98,786,191	3.54%		49	New Hampshire	3,624,395	0.13%
NA	Wyoming**	NA	NA		NA	Wyoming**	NA	NA
						District of Columbia	27,685,000	0.99%

Source: U.S. Department of Health and Human Services, Substance Abuse and Mental Health Services Administration
"State Resources and Services Related to Alcohol and Other Drug Problems-Fiscal Year 1993" (January 1995)
*Total does not include $33,374,152 in Puerto Rico or $709,754 in Guam.
**Not available.

Expenditures per Alcohol and Other Drug Treatment Admission in 1993

National Rate = $1,542 in Treatment Expenditures per Admission*

ALPHA ORDER				RANK ORDER		
RANK	STATE	RATE		RANK	STATE	RATE
35	Alabama	$896		1	New York	$3,923
3	Alaska	2,866		2	Hawaii	3,141
22	Arizona	1,326		3	Alaska	2,866
46	Arkansas	602		4	Oklahoma	2,860
5	California	2,514		5	California	2,514
48	Colorado	504		6	Connecticut	2,403
6	Connecticut	2,403		7	Virginia	2,358
31	Delaware	1,029		8	Iowa	2,118
21	Florida	1,327		9	Minnesota	2,003
29	Georgia	1,054		10	Maryland	1,870
2	Hawaii	3,141		11	Indiana	1,754
33	Idaho	942		12	Tennessee	1,679
20	Illinois	1,330		13	Texas	1,543
11	Indiana	1,754		14	Montana	1,538
8	Iowa	2,118		15	Pennsylvania	1,516
43	Kansas	658		16	Michigan	1,462
42	Kentucky	674		17	Ohio	1,455
32	Louisiana	960		18	Rhode Island	1,396
45	Maine	622		19	New Jersey	1,346
10	Maryland	1,870		20	Illinois	1,330
39	Massachusetts	715		21	Florida	1,327
16	Michigan	1,462		22	Arizona	1,326
9	Minnesota	2,003		23	Nevada	1,314
40	Mississippi	706		24	Utah	1,263
25	Missouri	1,256		25	Missouri	1,256
14	Montana	1,538		26	Washington	1,228
49	Nebraska	471		27	South Carolina	1,065
23	Nevada	1,314		28	Oregon	1,057
47	New Hampshire	563		29	Georgia	1,054
19	New Jersey	1,346		30	New Mexico	1,035
30	New Mexico	1,035		31	Delaware	1,029
1	New York	3,923		32	Louisiana	960
36	North Carolina	794		33	Idaho	942
38	North Dakota	759		34	South Dakota	925
17	Ohio	1,455		35	Alabama	896
4	Oklahoma	2,860		36	North Carolina	794
28	Oregon	1,057		37	Wisconsin	791
15	Pennsylvania	1,516		38	North Dakota	759
18	Rhode Island	1,396		39	Massachusetts	715
27	South Carolina	1,065		40	Mississippi	706
34	South Dakota	925		41	Vermont	691
12	Tennessee	1,679		42	Kentucky	674
13	Texas	1,543		43	Kansas	658
24	Utah	1,263		44	West Virginia	639
41	Vermont	691		45	Maine	622
7	Virginia	2,358		46	Arkansas	602
26	Washington	1,228		47	New Hampshire	563
44	West Virginia	639		48	Colorado	504
37	Wisconsin	791		49	Nebraska	471
NA	Wyoming**	NA		NA	Wyoming**	NA
				District of Columbia		1,697

Source: Morgan Quitno Press using data from U.S. Department of Health and Human Services, Substance Abuse
and Mental Health Services Administration
   "State Resources and Services Related to Alcohol and Other Drug Problems-Fiscal Year 1993" (January 1995)
*Does not include admissions in U.S. territories. Data are only from treatment units that received at least some
funds administered by a state's alcohol/drug agency in fiscal year 1993.
**Not available.

Per Capita Expenditures for State-Supported Alcohol and Other Drug Abuse Treatment Programs in 1993
National Per Capita = $10.81*

ALPHA ORDER

RANK	STATE	PER CAPITA
47	Alabama	$3.33
1	Alaska	39.59
31	Arizona	7.15
46	Arkansas	3.45
12	California	11.50
18	Colorado	9.73
3	Connecticut	23.96
25	Delaware	8.98
24	Florida	9.27
20	Georgia	9.51
15	Hawaii	10.12
45	Idaho	3.93
14	Illinois	10.50
33	Indiana	6.66
17	Iowa	9.85
43	Kansas	4.39
42	Kentucky	4.94
35	Louisiana	6.20
32	Maine	7.10
9	Maryland	12.14
13	Massachusetts	10.56
11	Michigan	11.61
8	Minnesota	12.56
49	Mississippi	2.88
30	Missouri	7.25
7	Montana	13.38
33	Nebraska	6.66
40	Nevada	5.03
48	New Hampshire	3.23
23	New Jersey	9.32
29	New Mexico	7.35
2	New York	32.02
39	North Carolina	5.50
36	North Dakota	5.74
22	Ohio	9.34
37	Oklahoma	5.71
10	Oregon	11.74
26	Pennsylvania	8.18
6	Rhode Island	16.19
27	South Carolina	7.83
5	South Dakota	16.64
44	Tennessee	3.98
41	Texas	4.99
16	Utah	9.96
28	Vermont	7.68
19	Virginia	9.67
21	Washington	9.42
38	West Virginia	5.63
4	Wisconsin	19.58
NA	Wyoming**	NA

RANK ORDER

RANK	STATE	PER CAPITA
1	Alaska	$39.59
2	New York	32.02
3	Connecticut	23.96
4	Wisconsin	19.58
5	South Dakota	16.64
6	Rhode Island	16.19
7	Montana	13.38
8	Minnesota	12.56
9	Maryland	12.14
10	Oregon	11.74
11	Michigan	11.61
12	California	11.50
13	Massachusetts	10.56
14	Illinois	10.50
15	Hawaii	10.12
16	Utah	9.96
17	Iowa	9.85
18	Colorado	9.73
19	Virginia	9.67
20	Georgia	9.51
21	Washington	9.42
22	Ohio	9.34
23	New Jersey	9.32
24	Florida	9.27
25	Delaware	8.98
26	Pennsylvania	8.18
27	South Carolina	7.83
28	Vermont	7.68
29	New Mexico	7.35
30	Missouri	7.25
31	Arizona	7.15
32	Maine	7.10
33	Indiana	6.66
33	Nebraska	6.66
35	Louisiana	6.20
36	North Dakota	5.74
37	Oklahoma	5.71
38	West Virginia	5.63
39	North Carolina	5.50
40	Nevada	5.03
41	Texas	4.99
42	Kentucky	4.94
43	Kansas	4.39
44	Tennessee	3.98
45	Idaho	3.93
46	Arkansas	3.45
47	Alabama	3.33
48	New Hampshire	3.23
49	Mississippi	2.88
NA	Wyoming**	NA

District of Columbia   47.90

Source: Morgan Quitno Press using data from U.S. Department of Health and Human Services, Substance Abuse and Mental Health Services Administration
"State Resources and Services Related to Alcohol and Other Drug Problems-Fiscal Year 1993" (January 1995)
*National per capita does not include expenditures in Puerto Rico and Guam.
**Not available.

Expenditures for State-Supported Alcohol and
Other Drug Abuse Prevention Programs in 1993
National Total = $531,791,347*

ALPHA ORDER

RANK	STATE	EXPENDITURES	% of USA
32	Alabama	$3,047,099	0.57%
30	Alaska	3,939,936	0.74%
29	Arizona	3,990,055	0.75%
37	Arkansas	2,108,103	0.40%
2	California	66,713,683	12.55%
18	Colorado	6,688,501	1.26%
16	Connecticut	8,757,207	1.65%
48	Delaware	654,662	0.12%
10	Florida	16,885,958	3.18%
27	Georgia	4,003,076	0.75%
40	Hawaii	1,401,352	0.26%
46	Idaho	882,335	0.17%
9	Illinois	17,006,074	3.20%
17	Indiana	7,734,086	1.45%
20	Iowa	6,256,738	1.18%
36	Kansas	2,532,304	0.48%
24	Kentucky	5,793,883	1.09%
34	Louisiana	2,868,915	0.54%
45	Maine	1,076,522	0.20%
13	Maryland	10,166,912	1.91%
25	Massachusetts	5,759,117	1.08%
7	Michigan	19,518,081	3.67%
26	Minnesota	4,282,635	0.81%
41	Mississippi	1,390,210	0.26%
28	Missouri	4,001,578	0.75%
43	Montana	1,234,296	0.23%
35	Nebraska	2,544,202	0.48%
38	Nevada	1,952,659	0.37%
42	New Hampshire	1,246,957	0.23%
15	New Jersey	9,800,000	1.84%
31	New Mexico	3,802,703	0.72%
1	New York	97,311,581	18.30%
12	North Carolina	12,163,561	2.29%
49	North Dakota	428,000	0.08%
4	Ohio	29,984,945	5.64%
33	Oklahoma	2,979,071	0.56%
8	Oregon	17,776,054	3.34%
6	Pennsylvania	28,009,427	5.27%
19	Rhode Island	6,328,072	1.19%
11	South Carolina	14,908,432	2.80%
47	South Dakota	876,716	0.16%
21	Tennessee	6,173,667	1.16%
3	Texas	30,649,235	5.76%
22	Utah	6,131,834	1.15%
39	Vermont	1,776,113	0.33%
14	Virginia	9,952,233	1.87%
23	Washington	5,947,298	1.12%
44	West Virginia	1,077,460	0.20%
5	Wisconsin	28,581,809	5.37%
NA	Wyoming**	NA	NA

RANK ORDER

RANK	STATE	EXPENDITURES	% of USA
1	New York	$97,311,581	18.30%
2	California	66,713,683	12.55%
3	Texas	30,649,235	5.76%
4	Ohio	29,984,945	5.64%
5	Wisconsin	28,581,809	5.37%
6	Pennsylvania	28,009,427	5.27%
7	Michigan	19,518,081	3.67%
8	Oregon	17,776,054	3.34%
9	Illinois	17,006,074	3.20%
10	Florida	16,885,958	3.18%
11	South Carolina	14,908,432	2.80%
12	North Carolina	12,163,561	2.29%
13	Maryland	10,166,912	1.91%
14	Virginia	9,952,233	1.87%
15	New Jersey	9,800,000	1.84%
16	Connecticut	8,757,207	1.65%
17	Indiana	7,734,086	1.45%
18	Colorado	6,688,501	1.26%
19	Rhode Island	6,328,072	1.19%
20	Iowa	6,256,738	1.18%
21	Tennessee	6,173,667	1.16%
22	Utah	6,131,834	1.15%
23	Washington	5,947,298	1.12%
24	Kentucky	5,793,883	1.09%
25	Massachusetts	5,759,117	1.08%
26	Minnesota	4,282,635	0.81%
27	Georgia	4,003,076	0.75%
28	Missouri	4,001,578	0.75%
29	Arizona	3,990,055	0.75%
30	Alaska	3,939,936	0.74%
31	New Mexico	3,802,703	0.72%
32	Alabama	3,047,099	0.57%
33	Oklahoma	2,979,071	0.56%
34	Louisiana	2,868,915	0.54%
35	Nebraska	2,544,202	0.48%
36	Kansas	2,532,304	0.48%
37	Arkansas	2,108,103	0.40%
38	Nevada	1,952,659	0.37%
39	Vermont	1,776,113	0.33%
40	Hawaii	1,401,352	0.26%
41	Mississippi	1,390,210	0.26%
42	New Hampshire	1,246,957	0.23%
43	Montana	1,234,296	0.23%
44	West Virginia	1,077,460	0.20%
45	Maine	1,076,522	0.20%
46	Idaho	882,335	0.17%
47	South Dakota	876,716	0.16%
48	Delaware	654,662	0.12%
49	North Dakota	428,000	0.08%
NA	Wyoming**	NA	NA
	District of Columbia	2,696,000	0.51%

Source: U.S. Department of Health and Human Services, Substance Abuse and Mental Health Services Administration
"State Resources and Services Related to Alcohol and Other Drug Problems-Fiscal Year 1993" (January 1995)
*Total does not include $8,405,235 in Puerto Rico or $361,294 in Guam.
**Not available.

Per Capita Expenditures for State-Supported Alcohol and Other Drug Abuse Prevention Programs in 1993
National Per Capita = $2.06*

ALPHA ORDER				RANK ORDER		
RANK	STATE	PER CAPITA		RANK	STATE	PER CAPITA
44	Alabama	$0.73		1	Alaska	$6.59
1	Alaska	6.59		2	Rhode Island	6.33
34	Arizona	1.01		3	Oregon	5.86
40	Arkansas	0.87		4	Wisconsin	5.67
14	California	2.14		5	New York	5.36
17	Colorado	1.87		6	South Carolina	4.11
10	Connecticut	2.67		7	Utah	3.30
38	Delaware	0.94		8	Vermont	3.08
28	Florida	1.23		9	Ohio	2.71
48	Georgia	0.58		10	Connecticut	2.67
31	Hawaii	1.20		11	New Mexico	2.35
42	Idaho	0.80		12	Pennsylvania	2.33
24	Illinois	1.45		13	Iowa	2.22
26	Indiana	1.36		14	California	2.14
13	Iowa	2.22		15	Michigan	2.06
35	Kansas	1.00		16	Maryland	2.05
22	Kentucky	1.53		17	Colorado	1.87
45	Louisiana	0.67		18	North Carolina	1.75
40	Maine	0.87		19	Texas	1.70
16	Maryland	2.05		20	Nebraska	1.58
36	Massachusetts	0.96		21	Virginia	1.54
15	Michigan	2.06		22	Kentucky	1.53
37	Minnesota	0.95		23	Montana	1.47
49	Mississippi	0.53		24	Illinois	1.45
43	Missouri	0.76		25	Nevada	1.41
23	Montana	1.47		26	Indiana	1.36
20	Nebraska	1.58		27	New Jersey	1.25
25	Nevada	1.41		28	Florida	1.23
33	New Hampshire	1.11		29	South Dakota	1.22
27	New Jersey	1.25		30	Tennessee	1.21
11	New Mexico	2.35		31	Hawaii	1.20
5	New York	5.36		32	Washington	1.13
18	North Carolina	1.75		33	New Hampshire	1.11
45	North Dakota	0.67		34	Arizona	1.01
9	Ohio	2.71		35	Kansas	1.00
39	Oklahoma	0.92		36	Massachusetts	0.96
3	Oregon	5.86		37	Minnesota	0.95
12	Pennsylvania	2.33		38	Delaware	0.94
2	Rhode Island	6.33		39	Oklahoma	0.92
6	South Carolina	4.11		40	Arkansas	0.87
29	South Dakota	1.22		40	Maine	0.87
30	Tennessee	1.21		42	Idaho	0.80
19	Texas	1.70		43	Missouri	0.76
7	Utah	3.30		44	Alabama	0.73
8	Vermont	3.08		45	Louisiana	0.67
21	Virginia	1.54		45	North Dakota	0.67
32	Washington	1.13		47	West Virginia	0.59
47	West Virginia	0.59		48	Georgia	0.58
4	Wisconsin	5.67		49	Mississippi	0.53
NA	Wyoming**	NA		NA	Wyoming**	NA
					District of Columbia	4.66

Source: Morgan Quitno Press using data from U.S. Department of Health and Human Services, Substance Abuse and Mental Health Services Administration
  "State Resources and Services Related to Alcohol and Other Drug Problems-Fiscal Year 1993" (January 1995)
*National per capita does not include expenditures in Puerto Rico and Guam.
**Not available.

IV. FINANCE

State and Local Government Expenditures for Justice Activities in 1993

National Total = $82,714,296,000*

ALPHA ORDER

RANK	STATE	EXPENDITURES	% of USA
27	Alabama	$860,307,000	1.04%
37	Alaska	380,730,000	0.46%
17	Arizona	1,392,547,000	1.68%
36	Arkansas	410,689,000	0.50%
1	California	14,100,087,000	17.05%
23	Colorado	1,076,010,000	1.30%
21	Connecticut	1,119,803,000	1.35%
43	Delaware	244,656,000	0.30%
3	Florida	5,403,959,000	6.53%
10	Georgia	2,014,025,000	2.43%
34	Hawaii	435,355,000	0.53%
42	Idaho	252,798,000	0.31%
5	Illinois	3,406,251,000	4.12%
22	Indiana	1,109,647,000	1.34%
32	Iowa	584,189,000	0.71%
31	Kansas	630,535,000	0.76%
28	Kentucky	754,667,000	0.91%
19	Louisiana	1,192,508,000	1.44%
44	Maine	228,824,000	0.28%
14	Maryland	1,734,302,000	2.10%
11	Massachusetts	1,884,605,000	2.28%
8	Michigan	2,998,924,000	3.63%
18	Minnesota	1,210,654,000	1.46%
38	Mississippi	368,599,000	0.45%
24	Missouri	1,050,092,000	1.27%
46	Montana	194,559,000	0.24%
39	Nebraska	340,629,000	0.41%
30	Nevada	640,867,000	0.77%
41	New Hampshire	281,787,000	0.34%
9	New Jersey	2,979,615,000	3.60%
33	New Mexico	508,241,000	0.61%
2	New York	9,003,153,000	10.88%
12	North Carolina	1,825,844,000	2.21%
50	North Dakota	90,307,000	0.11%
6	Ohio	3,062,938,000	3.70%
29	Oklahoma	663,550,000	0.80%
25	Oregon	909,431,000	1.10%
7	Pennsylvania	3,056,141,000	3.69%
40	Rhode Island	323,063,000	0.39%
26	South Carolina	871,362,000	1.05%
48	South Dakota	132,894,000	0.16%
20	Tennessee	1,157,659,000	1.40%
4	Texas	5,063,009,000	6.12%
35	Utah	420,020,000	0.51%
49	Vermont	126,908,000	0.15%
13	Virginia	1,805,053,000	2.18%
15	Washington	1,725,482,000	2.09%
45	West Virginia	223,203,000	0.27%
16	Wisconsin	1,592,277,000	1.93%
47	Wyoming	144,937,000	0.18%

RANK ORDER

RANK	STATE	EXPENDITURES	% of USA
1	California	$14,100,087,000	17.05%
2	New York	9,003,153,000	10.88%
3	Florida	5,403,959,000	6.53%
4	Texas	5,063,009,000	6.12%
5	Illinois	3,406,251,000	4.12%
6	Ohio	3,062,938,000	3.70%
7	Pennsylvania	3,056,141,000	3.69%
8	Michigan	2,998,924,000	3.63%
9	New Jersey	2,979,615,000	3.60%
10	Georgia	2,014,025,000	2.43%
11	Massachusetts	1,884,605,000	2.28%
12	North Carolina	1,825,844,000	2.21%
13	Virginia	1,805,053,000	2.18%
14	Maryland	1,734,302,000	2.10%
15	Washington	1,725,482,000	2.09%
16	Wisconsin	1,592,277,000	1.93%
17	Arizona	1,392,547,000	1.68%
18	Minnesota	1,210,654,000	1.46%
19	Louisiana	1,192,508,000	1.44%
20	Tennessee	1,157,659,000	1.40%
21	Connecticut	1,119,803,000	1.35%
22	Indiana	1,109,647,000	1.34%
23	Colorado	1,076,010,000	1.30%
24	Missouri	1,050,092,000	1.27%
25	Oregon	909,431,000	1.10%
26	South Carolina	871,362,000	1.05%
27	Alabama	860,307,000	1.04%
28	Kentucky	754,667,000	0.91%
29	Oklahoma	663,550,000	0.80%
30	Nevada	640,867,000	0.77%
31	Kansas	630,535,000	0.76%
32	Iowa	584,189,000	0.71%
33	New Mexico	508,241,000	0.61%
34	Hawaii	435,355,000	0.53%
35	Utah	420,020,000	0.51%
36	Arkansas	410,689,000	0.50%
37	Alaska	380,730,000	0.46%
38	Mississippi	368,599,000	0.45%
39	Nebraska	340,629,000	0.41%
40	Rhode Island	323,063,000	0.39%
41	New Hampshire	281,787,000	0.34%
42	Idaho	252,798,000	0.31%
43	Delaware	244,656,000	0.30%
44	Maine	228,824,000	0.28%
45	West Virginia	223,203,000	0.27%
46	Montana	194,559,000	0.24%
47	Wyoming	144,937,000	0.18%
48	South Dakota	132,894,000	0.16%
49	Vermont	126,908,000	0.15%
50	North Dakota	90,307,000	0.11%
	District of Columbia	726,604,000	0.88%

Source: Morgan Quitno Press using data from U.S. Bureau of the Census
"Government Finances: 1992-1993" (http://www.census.gov)
*Direct Expenditures. Includes Police Protection, Corrections and Judicial and Legal Services.

Per Capita State & Local Government Expenditures for Justice Activities: 1993

National Per Capita = $320.85*

ALPHA ORDER

RANK ORDER

RANK	STATE	PER CAPITA		RANK	STATE	PER CAPITA
40	Alabama	$205.77		1	Alaska	$636.67
1	Alaska	636.67		2	New York	495.96
8	Arizona	353.08		3	Nevada	462.72
47	Arkansas	169.36		4	California	451.64
4	California	451.64		5	Florida	393.82
19	Colorado	301.57		6	New Jersey	379.13
11	Connecticut	341.61		7	Hawaii	373.37
10	Delaware	350.01		8	Arizona	353.08
5	Florida	393.82		9	Maryland	350.22
21	Georgia	291.85		10	Delaware	350.01
7	Hawaii	373.37		11	Connecticut	341.61
34	Idaho	229.61		12	Washington	328.35
22	Illinois	291.38		13	Rhode Island	323.39
44	Indiana	194.44		14	Michigan	317.11
39	Iowa	207.01		15	Wisconsin	315.68
31	Kansas	249.03		16	New Mexico	314.51
43	Kentucky	198.96		17	Massachusetts	313.16
25	Louisiana	278.04		18	Wyoming	308.38
46	Maine	184.68		19	Colorado	301.57
9	Maryland	350.22		20	Oregon	299.65
17	Massachusetts	313.16		21	Georgia	291.85
14	Michigan	317.11		22	Illinois	291.38
27	Minnesota	267.61		23	Texas	280.51
49	Mississippi	139.67		24	Virginia	278.77
42	Missouri	200.59		25	Louisiana	278.04
33	Montana	231.34		26	Ohio	276.91
38	Nebraska	211.05		27	Minnesota	267.61
3	Nevada	462.72		28	North Carolina	262.60
30	New Hampshire	250.92		29	Pennsylvania	254.02
6	New Jersey	379.13		30	New Hampshire	250.92
16	New Mexico	314.51		31	Kansas	249.03
2	New York	495.96		32	South Carolina	240.24
28	North Carolina	262.60		33	Montana	231.34
48	North Dakota	141.77		34	Idaho	229.61
26	Ohio	276.91		35	Tennessee	227.30
41	Oklahoma	205.31		36	Utah	225.82
20	Oregon	299.65		37	Vermont	220.33
29	Pennsylvania	254.02		38	Nebraska	211.05
13	Rhode Island	323.39		39	Iowa	207.01
32	South Carolina	240.24		40	Alabama	205.77
45	South Dakota	185.35		41	Oklahoma	205.31
35	Tennessee	227.30		42	Missouri	200.59
23	Texas	280.51		43	Kentucky	198.96
36	Utah	225.82		44	Indiana	194.44
37	Vermont	220.33		45	South Dakota	185.35
24	Virginia	278.77		46	Maine	184.68
12	Washington	328.35		47	Arkansas	169.36
50	West Virginia	122.77		48	North Dakota	141.77
15	Wisconsin	315.68		49	Mississippi	139.67
18	Wyoming	308.38		50	West Virginia	122.77

District of Columbia 1,257.10

Source: Morgan Quitno Press using data from U.S. Bureau of the Census
"Government Finances: 1992-1993" (http://www.census.gov)
*Direct Expenditures. Includes Police Protection, Corrections and Judicial and Legal Services.

State and Local Government Expenditures for Justice Activities
As a Percent of All Direct Expenditures in 1993
National Percent = 6.85% of Direct Expenditures*

ALPHA ORDER

RANK	STATE	PERCENT
36	Alabama	5.38
33	Alaska	5.58
4	Arizona	8.23
40	Arkansas	5.12
3	California	8.50
19	Colorado	6.38
24	Connecticut	6.16
7	Delaware	7.15
2	Florida	9.43
8	Georgia	7.13
25	Hawaii	6.10
17	Idaho	6.50
14	Illinois	6.77
41	Indiana	5.09
45	Iowa	4.87
22	Kansas	6.22
39	Kentucky	5.35
18	Louisiana	6.45
47	Maine	4.26
5	Maryland	8.15
28	Massachusetts	5.95
12	Michigan	7.01
43	Minnesota	4.99
48	Mississippi	4.04
27	Missouri	6.06
30	Montana	5.72
46	Nebraska	4.46
1	Nevada	9.55
25	New Hampshire	6.10
9	New Jersey	7.11
10	New Mexico	7.10
13	New York	6.99
16	North Carolina	6.66
49	North Dakota	3.18
20	Ohio	6.34
34	Oklahoma	5.57
21	Oregon	6.26
31	Pennsylvania	5.68
23	Rhode Island	6.17
29	South Carolina	5.87
42	South Dakota	5.04
32	Tennessee	5.65
11	Texas	7.06
37	Utah	5.36
44	Vermont	4.93
6	Virginia	7.36
35	Washington	5.54
50	West Virginia	2.95
15	Wisconsin	6.73
37	Wyoming	5.36

RANK ORDER

RANK	STATE	PERCENT
1	Nevada	9.55
2	Florida	9.43
3	California	8.50
4	Arizona	8.23
5	Maryland	8.15
6	Virginia	7.36
7	Delaware	7.15
8	Georgia	7.13
9	New Jersey	7.11
10	New Mexico	7.10
11	Texas	7.06
12	Michigan	7.01
13	New York	6.99
14	Illinois	6.77
15	Wisconsin	6.73
16	North Carolina	6.66
17	Idaho	6.50
18	Louisiana	6.45
19	Colorado	6.38
20	Ohio	6.34
21	Oregon	6.26
22	Kansas	6.22
23	Rhode Island	6.17
24	Connecticut	6.16
25	Hawaii	6.10
25	New Hampshire	6.10
27	Missouri	6.06
28	Massachusetts	5.95
29	South Carolina	5.87
30	Montana	5.72
31	Pennsylvania	5.68
32	Tennessee	5.65
33	Alaska	5.58
34	Oklahoma	5.57
35	Washington	5.54
36	Alabama	5.38
37	Utah	5.36
37	Wyoming	5.36
39	Kentucky	5.35
40	Arkansas	5.12
41	Indiana	5.09
42	South Dakota	5.04
43	Minnesota	4.99
44	Vermont	4.93
45	Iowa	4.87
46	Nebraska	4.46
47	Maine	4.26
48	Mississippi	4.04
49	North Dakota	3.18
50	West Virginia	2.95

| | District of Columbia | 11.80 |

Source: Morgan Quitno Press using data from U.S. Bureau of the Census
"Government Finances: 1992-1993" (http://www.census.gov)
*Direct Expenditures. Includes Police Protection, Corrections and Judicial and Legal Services.

State Government Expenditures for Justice Activities in 1993

National Total = $30,695,903,000*

ALPHA ORDER

RANK ORDER

RANK	STATE	EXPENDITURES	% of USA
26	Alabama	$383,143,000	1.25%
32	Alaska	281,387,000	0.92%
18	Arizona	475,000,000	1.55%
38	Arkansas	184,949,000	0.60%
1	California	4,012,080,000	13.07%
23	Colorado	427,195,000	1.39%
15	Connecticut	709,339,000	2.31%
39	Delaware	171,215,000	0.56%
4	Florida	1,703,591,000	5.55%
14	Georgia	740,623,000	2.41%
34	Hawaii	231,049,000	0.75%
43	Idaho	116,274,000	0.38%
8	Illinois	1,039,805,000	3.39%
19	Indiana	461,436,000	1.50%
31	Iowa	282,151,000	0.92%
30	Kansas	289,084,000	0.94%
24	Kentucky	417,590,000	1.36%
22	Louisiana	453,583,000	1.48%
44	Maine	108,118,000	0.35%
12	Maryland	936,062,000	3.05%
11	Massachusetts	965,454,000	3.15%
5	Michigan	1,242,159,000	4.05%
28	Minnesota	348,399,000	1.14%
41	Mississippi	145,447,000	0.47%
27	Missouri	382,754,000	1.25%
47	Montana	91,659,000	0.30%
40	Nebraska	145,704,000	0.47%
37	Nevada	200,165,000	0.65%
42	New Hampshire	140,189,000	0.46%
7	New Jersey	1,066,561,000	3.47%
33	New Mexico	259,297,000	0.84%
2	New York	3,082,320,000	10.04%
9	North Carolina	1,004,179,000	3.27%
50	North Dakota	32,792,000	0.11%
10	Ohio	987,355,000	3.22%
29	Oklahoma	334,757,000	1.09%
25	Oregon	389,282,000	1.27%
6	Pennsylvania	1,076,544,000	3.51%
35	Rhode Island	206,369,000	0.67%
20	South Carolina	459,255,000	1.50%
48	South Dakota	66,722,000	0.22%
21	Tennessee	458,428,000	1.49%
3	Texas	1,799,207,000	5.86%
36	Utah	202,075,000	0.66%
46	Vermont	97,051,000	0.32%
13	Virginia	755,684,000	2.46%
16	Washington	648,246,000	2.11%
45	West Virginia	106,485,000	0.35%
17	Wisconsin	521,133,000	1.70%
49	Wyoming	56,557,000	0.18%

RANK	STATE	EXPENDITURES	% of USA
1	California	$4,012,080,000	13.07%
2	New York	3,082,320,000	10.04%
3	Texas	1,799,207,000	5.86%
4	Florida	1,703,591,000	5.55%
5	Michigan	1,242,159,000	4.05%
6	Pennsylvania	1,076,544,000	3.51%
7	New Jersey	1,066,561,000	3.47%
8	Illinois	1,039,805,000	3.39%
9	North Carolina	1,004,179,000	3.27%
10	Ohio	987,355,000	3.22%
11	Massachusetts	965,454,000	3.15%
12	Maryland	936,062,000	3.05%
13	Virginia	755,684,000	2.46%
14	Georgia	740,623,000	2.41%
15	Connecticut	709,339,000	2.31%
16	Washington	648,246,000	2.11%
17	Wisconsin	521,133,000	1.70%
18	Arizona	475,000,000	1.55%
19	Indiana	461,436,000	1.50%
20	South Carolina	459,255,000	1.50%
21	Tennessee	458,428,000	1.49%
22	Louisiana	453,583,000	1.48%
23	Colorado	427,195,000	1.39%
24	Kentucky	417,590,000	1.36%
25	Oregon	389,282,000	1.27%
26	Alabama	383,143,000	1.25%
27	Missouri	382,754,000	1.25%
28	Minnesota	348,399,000	1.14%
29	Oklahoma	334,757,000	1.09%
30	Kansas	289,084,000	0.94%
31	Iowa	282,151,000	0.92%
32	Alaska	281,387,000	0.92%
33	New Mexico	259,297,000	0.84%
34	Hawaii	231,049,000	0.75%
35	Rhode Island	206,369,000	0.67%
36	Utah	202,075,000	0.66%
37	Nevada	200,165,000	0.65%
38	Arkansas	184,949,000	0.60%
39	Delaware	171,215,000	0.56%
40	Nebraska	145,704,000	0.47%
41	Mississippi	145,447,000	0.47%
42	New Hampshire	140,189,000	0.46%
43	Idaho	116,274,000	0.38%
44	Maine	108,118,000	0.35%
45	West Virginia	106,485,000	0.35%
46	Vermont	97,051,000	0.32%
47	Montana	91,659,000	0.30%
48	South Dakota	66,722,000	0.22%
49	Wyoming	56,557,000	0.18%
50	North Dakota	32,792,000	0.11%
	District of Columbia**	NA	NA

*Source: Morgan Quitno Press using data from U.S. Bureau of the Census
"Government Finances: 1992-1993" (http://www.census.gov)*
*Direct Expenditures. Includes Police Protection, Corrections and Judicial and Legal Services.
**Not applicable.*

Per Capita State Government Expenditures for Justice Activities in 1993

National Per Capita = $119.07*

ALPHA ORDER

RANK	STATE	PER CAPITA
37	Alabama	$91.64
1	Alaska	470.55
21	Arizona	120.44
46	Arkansas	76.27
15	California	128.51
23	Colorado	119.73
3	Connecticut	216.39
2	Delaware	244.94
19	Florida	124.15
29	Georgia	107.32
5	Hawaii	198.16
31	Idaho	105.61
42	Illinois	88.95
44	Indiana	80.85
34	Iowa	99.98
25	Kansas	114.17
26	Kentucky	110.09
30	Louisiana	105.75
43	Maine	87.26
6	Maryland	189.03
10	Massachusetts	160.43
14	Michigan	131.35
45	Minnesota	77.01
49	Mississippi	55.11
47	Missouri	73.11
27	Montana	108.99
38	Nebraska	90.28
11	Nevada	144.52
18	New Hampshire	124.83
13	New Jersey	135.71
9	New Mexico	160.46
7	New York	169.80
12	North Carolina	144.42
50	North Dakota	51.48
41	Ohio	89.26
32	Oklahoma	103.58
16	Oregon	128.26
40	Pennsylvania	89.48
4	Rhode Island	206.58
17	South Carolina	126.62
36	South Dakota	93.06
39	Tennessee	90.01
35	Texas	99.68
28	Utah	108.64
8	Vermont	168.49
24	Virginia	116.71
20	Washington	123.36
48	West Virginia	58.57
33	Wisconsin	103.32
22	Wyoming	120.33

RANK ORDER

RANK	STATE	PER CAPITA
1	Alaska	$470.55
2	Delaware	244.94
3	Connecticut	216.39
4	Rhode Island	206.58
5	Hawaii	198.16
6	Maryland	189.03
7	New York	169.80
8	Vermont	168.49
9	New Mexico	160.46
10	Massachusetts	160.43
11	Nevada	144.52
12	North Carolina	144.42
13	New Jersey	135.71
14	Michigan	131.35
15	California	128.51
16	Oregon	128.26
17	South Carolina	126.62
18	New Hampshire	124.83
19	Florida	124.15
20	Washington	123.36
21	Arizona	120.44
22	Wyoming	120.33
23	Colorado	119.73
24	Virginia	116.71
25	Kansas	114.17
26	Kentucky	110.09
27	Montana	108.99
28	Utah	108.64
29	Georgia	107.32
30	Louisiana	105.75
31	Idaho	105.61
32	Oklahoma	103.58
33	Wisconsin	103.32
34	Iowa	99.98
35	Texas	99.68
36	South Dakota	93.06
37	Alabama	91.64
38	Nebraska	90.28
39	Tennessee	90.01
40	Pennsylvania	89.48
41	Ohio	89.26
42	Illinois	88.95
43	Maine	87.26
44	Indiana	80.85
45	Minnesota	77.01
46	Arkansas	76.27
47	Missouri	73.11
48	West Virginia	58.57
49	Mississippi	55.11
50	North Dakota	51.48

District of Columbia**   NA

Source: Morgan Quitno Press using data from U.S. Bureau of the Census
"Government Finances: 1992-1993" (http://www.census.gov)
*Direct Expenditures. Includes Police Protection, Corrections and Judicial and Legal Services.
**Not applicable.

223

State Government Expenditures for Justice Activities
As a Percent of All Direct Expenditures in 1993
National Percent = 5.80% of Direct Expenditures*

ALPHA ORDER

RANK	STATE	PERCENT
36	Alabama	4.77
14	Alaska	6.49
5	Arizona	7.24
45	Arkansas	4.10
11	California	6.64
10	Colorado	6.79
9	Connecticut	6.82
4	Delaware	7.98
3	Florida	8.19
12	Georgia	6.62
43	Hawaii	4.22
19	Idaho	5.90
33	Illinois	4.95
37	Indiana	4.73
31	Iowa	5.15
6	Kansas	7.10
30	Kentucky	5.21
41	Louisiana	4.50
47	Maine	3.47
2	Maryland	8.64
22	Massachusetts	5.59
15	Michigan	6.42
46	Minnesota	3.67
48	Mississippi	3.39
35	Missouri	4.79
39	Montana	4.57
29	Nebraska	5.22
7	Nevada	6.94
28	New Hampshire	5.40
32	New Jersey	5.12
13	New Mexico	6.59
18	New York	6.11
1	North Carolina	8.73
50	North Dakota	1.92
42	Ohio	4.23
24	Oklahoma	5.56
21	Oregon	5.76
44	Pennsylvania	4.14
19	Rhode Island	5.90
26	South Carolina	5.54
34	South Dakota	4.81
25	Tennessee	5.55
16	Texas	6.27
23	Utah	5.58
16	Vermont	6.27
8	Virginia	6.89
37	Washington	4.73
49	West Virginia	2.26
27	Wisconsin	5.42
40	Wyoming	4.53

RANK ORDER

RANK	STATE	PERCENT
1	North Carolina	8.73
2	Maryland	8.64
3	Florida	8.19
4	Delaware	7.98
5	Arizona	7.24
6	Kansas	7.10
7	Nevada	6.94
8	Virginia	6.89
9	Connecticut	6.82
10	Colorado	6.79
11	California	6.64
12	Georgia	6.62
13	New Mexico	6.59
14	Alaska	6.49
15	Michigan	6.42
16	Texas	6.27
16	Vermont	6.27
18	New York	6.11
19	Idaho	5.90
19	Rhode Island	5.90
21	Oregon	5.76
22	Massachusetts	5.59
23	Utah	5.58
24	Oklahoma	5.56
25	Tennessee	5.55
26	South Carolina	5.54
27	Wisconsin	5.42
28	New Hampshire	5.40
29	Nebraska	5.22
30	Kentucky	5.21
31	Iowa	5.15
32	New Jersey	5.12
33	Illinois	4.95
34	South Dakota	4.81
35	Missouri	4.79
36	Alabama	4.77
37	Indiana	4.73
37	Washington	4.73
39	Montana	4.57
40	Wyoming	4.53
41	Louisiana	4.50
42	Ohio	4.23
43	Hawaii	4.22
44	Pennsylvania	4.14
45	Arkansas	4.10
46	Minnesota	3.67
47	Maine	3.47
48	Mississippi	3.39
49	West Virginia	2.26
50	North Dakota	1.92

District of Columbia** — NA

Source: Morgan Quitno Press using data from U.S. Bureau of the Census
   "Government Finances: 1992-1993" (http://www.census.gov)
*Direct Expenditures. Includes Police Protection, Corrections and Judicial and Legal Services.
**Not applicable.

Local Government Expenditures for Justice Activities in 1993

National Total = $52,018,393,000*

ALPHA ORDER

ALPHA ORDER

RANK	STATE	EXPENDITURES	% of USA
25	Alabama	$477,164,000	0.92%
45	Alaska	99,343,000	0.19%
15	Arizona	917,547,000	1.76%
34	Arkansas	225,740,000	0.43%
1	California	10,088,007,000	19.39%
22	Colorado	648,815,000	1.25%
28	Connecticut	410,464,000	0.79%
47	Delaware	73,441,000	0.14%
3	Florida	3,700,368,000	7.11%
10	Georgia	1,273,402,000	2.45%
37	Hawaii	204,306,000	0.39%
40	Idaho	136,524,000	0.26%
5	Illinois	2,366,446,000	4.55%
23	Indiana	648,211,000	1.25%
32	Iowa	302,038,000	0.58%
29	Kansas	341,451,000	0.66%
30	Kentucky	337,077,000	0.65%
19	Louisiana	738,925,000	1.42%
41	Maine	120,706,000	0.23%
18	Maryland	798,240,000	1.53%
14	Massachusetts	919,151,000	1.77%
9	Michigan	1,756,765,000	3.38%
16	Minnesota	862,255,000	1.66%
35	Mississippi	223,152,000	0.43%
21	Missouri	667,338,000	1.28%
44	Montana	102,900,000	0.20%
38	Nebraska	194,925,000	0.37%
26	Nevada	440,702,000	0.85%
39	New Hampshire	141,598,000	0.27%
8	New Jersey	1,913,054,000	3.68%
33	New Mexico	248,944,000	0.48%
2	New York	5,920,833,000	11.38%
17	North Carolina	821,665,000	1.58%
49	North Dakota	57,515,000	0.11%
6	Ohio	2,075,583,000	3.99%
31	Oklahoma	328,793,000	0.63%
24	Oregon	520,149,000	1.00%
7	Pennsylvania	1,979,597,000	3.81%
43	Rhode Island	116,694,000	0.22%
27	South Carolina	412,107,000	0.79%
48	South Dakota	66,172,000	0.13%
20	Tennessee	699,231,000	1.34%
4	Texas	3,263,802,000	6.27%
36	Utah	217,945,000	0.42%
50	Vermont	29,857,000	0.06%
13	Virginia	1,049,369,000	2.02%
11	Washington	1,077,236,000	2.07%
42	West Virginia	116,718,000	0.22%
12	Wisconsin	1,071,144,000	2.06%
46	Wyoming	88,380,000	0.17%

RANK ORDER

RANK	STATE	EXPENDITURES	% of USA
1	California	$10,088,007,000	19.39%
2	New York	5,920,833,000	11.38%
3	Florida	3,700,368,000	7.11%
4	Texas	3,263,802,000	6.27%
5	Illinois	2,366,446,000	4.55%
6	Ohio	2,075,583,000	3.99%
7	Pennsylvania	1,979,597,000	3.81%
8	New Jersey	1,913,054,000	3.68%
9	Michigan	1,756,765,000	3.38%
10	Georgia	1,273,402,000	2.45%
11	Washington	1,077,236,000	2.07%
12	Wisconsin	1,071,144,000	2.06%
13	Virginia	1,049,369,000	2.02%
14	Massachusetts	919,151,000	1.77%
15	Arizona	917,547,000	1.76%
16	Minnesota	862,255,000	1.66%
17	North Carolina	821,665,000	1.58%
18	Maryland	798,240,000	1.53%
19	Louisiana	738,925,000	1.42%
20	Tennessee	699,231,000	1.34%
21	Missouri	667,338,000	1.28%
22	Colorado	648,815,000	1.25%
23	Indiana	648,211,000	1.25%
24	Oregon	520,149,000	1.00%
25	Alabama	477,164,000	0.92%
26	Nevada	440,702,000	0.85%
27	South Carolina	412,107,000	0.79%
28	Connecticut	410,464,000	0.79%
29	Kansas	341,451,000	0.66%
30	Kentucky	337,077,000	0.65%
31	Oklahoma	328,793,000	0.63%
32	Iowa	302,038,000	0.58%
33	New Mexico	248,944,000	0.48%
34	Arkansas	225,740,000	0.43%
35	Mississippi	223,152,000	0.43%
36	Utah	217,945,000	0.42%
37	Hawaii	204,306,000	0.39%
38	Nebraska	194,925,000	0.37%
39	New Hampshire	141,598,000	0.27%
40	Idaho	136,524,000	0.26%
41	Maine	120,706,000	0.23%
42	West Virginia	116,718,000	0.22%
43	Rhode Island	116,694,000	0.22%
44	Montana	102,900,000	0.20%
45	Alaska	99,343,000	0.19%
46	Wyoming	88,380,000	0.17%
47	Delaware	73,441,000	0.14%
48	South Dakota	66,172,000	0.13%
49	North Dakota	57,515,000	0.11%
50	Vermont	29,857,000	0.06%
	District of Columbia	726,604,000	1.40%

Source: Morgan Quitno Press using data from U.S. Bureau of the Census
   "Government Finances: 1992-1993" (http://www.census.gov)
*Direct Expenditures. Includes Police Protection, Corrections and Judicial and Legal Services.

Per Capita Local Government Expenditures for Justice Activities in 1993

National Per Capita = $201.78*

ALPHA ORDER

RANK	STATE	PER CAPITA
37	Alabama	$114.13
20	Alaska	166.13
6	Arizona	232.64
44	Arkansas	93.09
2	California	323.13
15	Colorado	181.84
30	Connecticut	125.22
41	Delaware	105.07
4	Florida	269.67
14	Georgia	184.52
17	Hawaii	175.22
31	Idaho	124.00
9	Illinois	202.43
39	Indiana	113.58
40	Iowa	107.03
27	Kansas	134.85
47	Kentucky	88.87
18	Louisiana	172.28
43	Maine	97.42
23	Maryland	161.20
25	Massachusetts	152.73
13	Michigan	185.76
10	Minnesota	190.60
48	Mississippi	84.56
28	Missouri	127.48
32	Montana	122.35
33	Nebraska	120.77
3	Nevada	318.20
29	New Hampshire	126.09
5	New Jersey	243.42
24	New Mexico	154.05
1	New York	326.16
34	North Carolina	118.17
46	North Dakota	90.29
12	Ohio	187.65
42	Oklahoma	101.73
19	Oregon	171.38
21	Pennsylvania	164.54
36	Rhode Island	116.81
38	South Carolina	113.62
45	South Dakota	92.29
26	Tennessee	137.29
16	Texas	180.83
35	Utah	117.17
50	Vermont	51.84
22	Virginia	162.06
8	Washington	204.99
49	West Virginia	64.20
7	Wisconsin	212.36
11	Wyoming	188.04

RANK ORDER

RANK	STATE	PER CAPITA
1	New York	$326.16
2	California	323.13
3	Nevada	318.20
4	Florida	269.67
5	New Jersey	243.42
6	Arizona	232.64
7	Wisconsin	212.36
8	Washington	204.99
9	Illinois	202.43
10	Minnesota	190.60
11	Wyoming	188.04
12	Ohio	187.65
13	Michigan	185.76
14	Georgia	184.52
15	Colorado	181.84
16	Texas	180.83
17	Hawaii	175.22
18	Louisiana	172.28
19	Oregon	171.38
20	Alaska	166.13
21	Pennsylvania	164.54
22	Virginia	162.06
23	Maryland	161.20
24	New Mexico	154.05
25	Massachusetts	152.73
26	Tennessee	137.29
27	Kansas	134.85
28	Missouri	127.48
29	New Hampshire	126.09
30	Connecticut	125.22
31	Idaho	124.00
32	Montana	122.35
33	Nebraska	120.77
34	North Carolina	118.17
35	Utah	117.17
36	Rhode Island	116.81
37	Alabama	114.13
38	South Carolina	113.62
39	Indiana	113.58
40	Iowa	107.03
41	Delaware	105.07
42	Oklahoma	101.73
43	Maine	97.42
44	Arkansas	93.09
45	South Dakota	92.29
46	North Dakota	90.29
47	Kentucky	88.87
48	Mississippi	84.56
49	West Virginia	64.20
50	Vermont	51.84

District of Columbia   1,257.10

Source: Morgan Quitno Press using data from U.S. Bureau of the Census
"Government Finances: 1992-1993" (http://www.census.gov)
*Direct Expenditures. Includes Police Protection, Corrections and Judicial and Legal Services.

Local Government Expenditures for Justice Activities
As a Percent of All Direct Expenditures in 1993
National Percent = 7.67% of Direct Expenditures*

ALPHA ORDER

RANK	STATE	PERCENT
31	Alabama	6.00
49	Alaska	4.00
6	Arizona	8.86
25	Arkansas	6.43
4	California	9.56
29	Colorado	6.14
41	Connecticut	5.28
33	Delaware	5.76
3	Florida	10.13
17	Georgia	7.47
1	Hawaii	12.28
21	Idaho	7.11
9	Illinois	8.07
38	Indiana	5.38
45	Iowa	4.63
35	Kansas	5.62
37	Kentucky	5.53
7	Louisiana	8.79
39	Maine	5.34
12	Maryland	7.64
26	Massachusetts	6.39
16	Michigan	7.51
32	Minnesota	5.84
46	Mississippi	4.62
19	Missouri	7.14
18	Montana	7.37
48	Nebraska	4.02
2	Nevada	11.51
22	New Hampshire	7.00
5	New Jersey	9.07
11	New Mexico	7.72
15	New York	7.56
42	North Carolina	5.17
44	North Dakota	5.09
8	Ohio	8.32
36	Oklahoma	5.57
24	Oregon	6.70
20	Pennsylvania	7.12
23	Rhode Island	6.71
27	South Carolina	6.29
40	South Dakota	5.30
34	Tennessee	5.72
14	Texas	7.59
42	Utah	5.17
50	Vermont	2.90
10	Virginia	7.73
28	Washington	6.18
47	West Virginia	4.08
13	Wisconsin	7.63
30	Wyoming	6.07

RANK ORDER

RANK	STATE	PERCENT
1	Hawaii	12.28
2	Nevada	11.51
3	Florida	10.13
4	California	9.56
5	New Jersey	9.07
6	Arizona	8.86
7	Louisiana	8.79
8	Ohio	8.32
9	Illinois	8.07
10	Virginia	7.73
11	New Mexico	7.72
12	Maryland	7.64
13	Wisconsin	7.63
14	Texas	7.59
15	New York	7.56
16	Michigan	7.51
17	Georgia	7.47
18	Montana	7.37
19	Missouri	7.14
20	Pennsylvania	7.12
21	Idaho	7.11
22	New Hampshire	7.00
23	Rhode Island	6.71
24	Oregon	6.70
25	Arkansas	6.43
26	Massachusetts	6.39
27	South Carolina	6.29
28	Washington	6.18
29	Colorado	6.14
30	Wyoming	6.07
31	Alabama	6.00
32	Minnesota	5.84
33	Delaware	5.76
34	Tennessee	5.72
35	Kansas	5.62
36	Oklahoma	5.57
37	Kentucky	5.53
38	Indiana	5.38
39	Maine	5.34
40	South Dakota	5.30
41	Connecticut	5.28
42	North Carolina	5.17
42	Utah	5.17
44	North Dakota	5.09
45	Iowa	4.63
46	Mississippi	4.62
47	West Virginia	4.08
48	Nebraska	4.02
49	Alaska	4.00
50	Vermont	2.90

District of Columbia   11.80

Source: Morgan Quitno Press using data from U.S. Bureau of the Census
"Government Finances: 1992-1993" (http://www.census.gov)
*Direct Expenditures. Includes Police Protection, Corrections and Judicial and Legal Services.

State and Local Government Expenditures for Police Protection in 1993

National Total = $36,146,000,000*

ALPHA ORDER

RANK	STATE	EXPENDITURES	% of USA
25	Alabama	$403,181,000	1.12%
39	Alaska	138,173,000	0.38%
18	Arizona	582,674,000	1.61%
37	Arkansas	181,502,000	0.50%
1	California	5,996,920,000	16.59%
23	Colorado	474,503,000	1.31%
24	Connecticut	467,224,000	1.29%
44	Delaware	100,660,000	0.28%
3	Florida	2,528,443,000	7.00%
11	Georgia	810,995,000	2.24%
36	Hawaii	181,684,000	0.50%
42	Idaho	120,476,000	0.33%
5	Illinois	1,800,898,000	4.98%
22	Indiana	478,449,000	1.32%
31	Iowa	276,207,000	0.76%
30	Kansas	290,256,000	0.80%
28	Kentucky	318,302,000	0.88%
17	Louisiana	586,490,000	1.62%
43	Maine	101,285,000	0.28%
15	Maryland	704,031,000	1.95%
10	Massachusetts	834,870,000	2.31%
9	Michigan	1,201,374,000	3.32%
19	Minnesota	562,711,000	1.56%
34	Mississippi	193,535,000	0.54%
20	Missouri	548,040,000	1.52%
46	Montana	82,242,000	0.23%
38	Nebraska	161,448,000	0.45%
32	Nevada	268,672,000	0.74%
41	New Hampshire	131,844,000	0.36%
6	New Jersey	1,410,423,000	3.90%
33	New Mexico	223,524,000	0.62%
2	New York	3,786,053,000	10.47%
13	North Carolina	763,475,000	2.11%
50	North Dakota	43,908,000	0.12%
7	Ohio	1,351,479,000	3.74%
29	Oklahoma	316,441,000	0.88%
26	Oregon	392,133,000	1.08%
8	Pennsylvania	1,248,804,000	3.45%
40	Rhode Island	136,139,000	0.38%
27	South Carolina	334,990,000	0.93%
48	South Dakota	60,388,000	0.17%
21	Tennessee	484,461,000	1.34%
4	Texas	2,127,049,000	5.88%
35	Utah	187,786,000	0.52%
49	Vermont	54,885,000	0.15%
12	Virginia	807,381,000	2.23%
16	Washington	698,680,000	1.93%
45	West Virginia	96,185,000	0.27%
14	Wisconsin	758,373,000	2.10%
47	Wyoming	69,732,000	0.19%

RANK ORDER

RANK	STATE	EXPENDITURES	% of USA
1	California	$5,996,920,000	16.59%
2	New York	3,786,053,000	10.47%
3	Florida	2,528,443,000	7.00%
4	Texas	2,127,049,000	5.88%
5	Illinois	1,800,898,000	4.98%
6	New Jersey	1,410,423,000	3.90%
7	Ohio	1,351,479,000	3.74%
8	Pennsylvania	1,248,804,000	3.45%
9	Michigan	1,201,374,000	3.32%
10	Massachusetts	834,870,000	2.31%
11	Georgia	810,995,000	2.24%
12	Virginia	807,381,000	2.23%
13	North Carolina	763,475,000	2.11%
14	Wisconsin	758,373,000	2.10%
15	Maryland	704,031,000	1.95%
16	Washington	698,680,000	1.93%
17	Louisiana	586,490,000	1.62%
18	Arizona	582,674,000	1.61%
19	Minnesota	562,711,000	1.56%
20	Missouri	548,040,000	1.52%
21	Tennessee	484,461,000	1.34%
22	Indiana	478,449,000	1.32%
23	Colorado	474,503,000	1.31%
24	Connecticut	467,224,000	1.29%
25	Alabama	403,181,000	1.12%
26	Oregon	392,133,000	1.08%
27	South Carolina	334,990,000	0.93%
28	Kentucky	318,302,000	0.88%
29	Oklahoma	316,441,000	0.88%
30	Kansas	290,256,000	0.80%
31	Iowa	276,207,000	0.76%
32	Nevada	268,672,000	0.74%
33	New Mexico	223,524,000	0.62%
34	Mississippi	193,535,000	0.54%
35	Utah	187,786,000	0.52%
36	Hawaii	181,684,000	0.50%
37	Arkansas	181,502,000	0.50%
38	Nebraska	161,448,000	0.45%
39	Alaska	138,173,000	0.38%
40	Rhode Island	136,139,000	0.38%
41	New Hampshire	131,844,000	0.36%
42	Idaho	120,476,000	0.33%
43	Maine	101,285,000	0.28%
44	Delaware	100,660,000	0.28%
45	West Virginia	96,185,000	0.27%
46	Montana	82,242,000	0.23%
47	Wyoming	69,732,000	0.19%
48	South Dakota	60,388,000	0.17%
49	Vermont	54,885,000	0.15%
50	North Dakota	43,908,000	0.12%
	District of Columbia	266,622,000	0.74%

Source: U.S. Bureau of the Census
"Government Finances: 1992-1993" (http://www.census.gov)
*Direct Expenditures.

Per Capita State & Local Government Expenditures for Police Protection: 1993

National Per Capita = $140.21*

ALPHA ORDER

RANK	STATE	PER CAPITA
39	Alabama	$96.43
1	Alaska	231.06
11	Arizona	147.74
47	Arkansas	74.85
4	California	192.09
19	Colorado	132.99
13	Connecticut	142.53
12	Delaware	144.01
5	Florida	184.26
27	Georgia	117.52
7	Hawaii	155.82
31	Idaho	109.42
8	Illinois	154.05
45	Indiana	83.84
37	Iowa	97.88
29	Kansas	114.64
44	Kentucky	83.92
17	Louisiana	136.74
46	Maine	81.75
14	Maryland	142.17
15	Massachusetts	138.73
22	Michigan	127.04
24	Minnesota	124.38
48	Mississippi	73.34
32	Missouri	104.69
38	Montana	97.79
35	Nebraska	100.03
3	Nevada	193.99
28	New Hampshire	117.40
6	New Jersey	179.47
16	New Mexico	138.32
2	New York	208.56
30	North Carolina	109.81
49	North Dakota	68.93
25	Ohio	122.18
36	Oklahoma	97.91
21	Oregon	129.20
33	Pennsylvania	103.80
18	Rhode Island	136.28
42	South Carolina	92.36
43	South Dakota	84.22
41	Tennessee	95.12
26	Texas	117.85
34	Utah	100.96
40	Vermont	95.29
23	Virginia	124.69
20	Washington	132.96
50	West Virginia	52.91
9	Wisconsin	150.35
10	Wyoming	148.37

RANK ORDER

RANK	STATE	PER CAPITA
1	Alaska	$231.06
2	New York	208.56
3	Nevada	193.99
4	California	192.09
5	Florida	184.26
6	New Jersey	179.47
7	Hawaii	155.82
8	Illinois	154.05
9	Wisconsin	150.35
10	Wyoming	148.37
11	Arizona	147.74
12	Delaware	144.01
13	Connecticut	142.53
14	Maryland	142.17
15	Massachusetts	138.73
16	New Mexico	138.32
17	Louisiana	136.74
18	Rhode Island	136.28
19	Colorado	132.99
20	Washington	132.96
21	Oregon	129.20
22	Michigan	127.04
23	Virginia	124.69
24	Minnesota	124.38
25	Ohio	122.18
26	Texas	117.85
27	Georgia	117.52
28	New Hampshire	117.40
29	Kansas	114.64
30	North Carolina	109.81
31	Idaho	109.42
32	Missouri	104.69
33	Pennsylvania	103.80
34	Utah	100.96
35	Nebraska	100.03
36	Oklahoma	97.91
37	Iowa	97.88
38	Montana	97.79
39	Alabama	96.43
40	Vermont	95.29
41	Tennessee	95.12
42	South Carolina	92.36
43	South Dakota	84.22
44	Kentucky	83.92
45	Indiana	83.84
46	Maine	81.75
47	Arkansas	74.85
48	Mississippi	73.34
49	North Dakota	68.93
50	West Virginia	52.91
	District of Columbia	461.28

Source: Morgan Quitno Press using data from U.S. Bureau of the Census
   "Government Finances: 1992-1993" (http://www.census.gov)
*Direct Expenditures.

State and Local Government Expenditures for Police Protection
As a Percent of All Direct Expenditures in 1993
National Percent = 2.99% of Direct Expenditures*

ALPHA ORDER

RANK	STATE	PERCENT
31	Alabama	2.52
47	Alaska	2.03
5	Arizona	3.44
39	Arkansas	2.26
3	California	3.61
20	Colorado	2.81
29	Connecticut	2.57
15	Delaware	2.94
1	Florida	4.41
17	Georgia	2.87
30	Hawaii	2.55
13	Idaho	3.10
4	Illinois	3.58
43	Indiana	2.20
37	Iowa	2.30
18	Kansas	2.86
39	Kentucky	2.26
10	Louisiana	3.17
48	Maine	1.88
7	Maryland	3.31
26	Massachusetts	2.64
20	Michigan	2.81
35	Minnesota	2.32
45	Mississippi	2.12
11	Missouri	3.16
32	Montana	2.42
46	Nebraska	2.11
2	Nevada	4.00
19	New Hampshire	2.85
6	New Jersey	3.36
12	New Mexico	3.12
15	New York	2.94
23	North Carolina	2.79
49	North Dakota	1.55
22	Ohio	2.80
25	Oklahoma	2.65
24	Oregon	2.70
35	Pennsylvania	2.32
27	Rhode Island	2.60
39	South Carolina	2.26
38	South Dakota	2.29
34	Tennessee	2.37
14	Texas	2.97
33	Utah	2.40
44	Vermont	2.13
8	Virginia	3.29
42	Washington	2.24
50	West Virginia	1.27
9	Wisconsin	3.21
28	Wyoming	2.58

RANK ORDER

RANK	STATE	PERCENT
1	Florida	4.41
2	Nevada	4.00
3	California	3.61
4	Illinois	3.58
5	Arizona	3.44
6	New Jersey	3.36
7	Maryland	3.31
8	Virginia	3.29
9	Wisconsin	3.21
10	Louisiana	3.17
11	Missouri	3.16
12	New Mexico	3.12
13	Idaho	3.10
14	Texas	2.97
15	Delaware	2.94
15	New York	2.94
17	Georgia	2.87
18	Kansas	2.86
19	New Hampshire	2.85
20	Colorado	2.81
20	Michigan	2.81
22	Ohio	2.80
23	North Carolina	2.79
24	Oregon	2.70
25	Oklahoma	2.65
26	Massachusetts	2.64
27	Rhode Island	2.60
28	Wyoming	2.58
29	Connecticut	2.57
30	Hawaii	2.55
31	Alabama	2.52
32	Montana	2.42
33	Utah	2.40
34	Tennessee	2.37
35	Minnesota	2.32
35	Pennsylvania	2.32
37	Iowa	2.30
38	South Dakota	2.29
39	Arkansas	2.26
39	Kentucky	2.26
39	South Carolina	2.26
42	Washington	2.24
43	Indiana	2.20
44	Vermont	2.13
45	Mississippi	2.12
46	Nebraska	2.11
47	Alaska	2.03
48	Maine	1.88
49	North Dakota	1.55
50	West Virginia	1.27
	District of Columbia	4.33

Source: Morgan Quitno Press using data from U.S. Bureau of the Census
"Government Finances: 1992-1993" (http://www.census.gov)
*Direct Expenditures.

State Government Expenditures for Police Protection in 1993

National Total = $4,960,517,000*

ALPHA ORDER

RANK	STATE	EXPENDITURES	% of USA
24	Alabama	$66,109,000	1.33%
29	Alaska	47,111,000	0.95%
18	Arizona	96,792,000	1.95%
33	Arkansas	39,673,000	0.80%
1	California	718,108,000	14.48%
32	Colorado	43,012,000	0.87%
21	Connecticut	84,223,000	1.70%
37	Delaware	34,296,000	0.69%
7	Florida	197,814,000	3.99%
16	Georgia	105,723,000	2.13%
49	Hawaii	7,820,000	0.16%
40	Idaho	28,890,000	0.58%
4	Illinois	219,884,000	4.43%
15	Indiana	108,196,000	2.18%
28	Iowa	48,327,000	0.97%
34	Kansas	38,941,000	0.79%
19	Kentucky	88,769,000	1.79%
17	Louisiana	99,295,000	2.00%
44	Maine	23,784,000	0.48%
12	Maryland	141,180,000	2.85%
11	Massachusetts	157,180,000	3.17%
8	Michigan	190,547,000	3.84%
26	Minnesota	62,559,000	1.26%
36	Mississippi	35,878,000	0.72%
22	Missouri	79,913,000	1.61%
46	Montana	18,045,000	0.36%
38	Nebraska	32,570,000	0.66%
39	Nevada	30,457,000	0.61%
43	New Hampshire	25,734,000	0.52%
5	New Jersey	213,862,000	4.31%
31	New Mexico	46,404,000	0.94%
3	New York	285,257,000	5.75%
10	North Carolina	158,619,000	3.20%
50	North Dakota	7,295,000	0.15%
9	Ohio	162,242,000	3.27%
30	Oklahoma	46,597,000	0.94%
23	Oregon	73,284,000	1.48%
2	Pennsylvania	300,216,000	6.05%
41	Rhode Island	26,520,000	0.53%
20	South Carolina	87,685,000	1.77%
47	South Dakota	14,229,000	0.29%
25	Tennessee	65,537,000	1.32%
6	Texas	212,293,000	4.28%
35	Utah	36,005,000	0.73%
42	Vermont	26,350,000	0.53%
13	Virginia	134,429,000	2.71%
14	Washington	109,247,000	2.20%
45	West Virginia	23,540,000	0.47%
27	Wisconsin	50,916,000	1.03%
48	Wyoming	9,160,000	0.18%

RANK ORDER

RANK	STATE	EXPENDITURES	% of USA
1	California	$718,108,000	14.48%
2	Pennsylvania	300,216,000	6.05%
3	New York	285,257,000	5.75%
4	Illinois	219,884,000	4.43%
5	New Jersey	213,862,000	4.31%
6	Texas	212,293,000	4.28%
7	Florida	197,814,000	3.99%
8	Michigan	190,547,000	3.84%
9	Ohio	162,242,000	3.27%
10	North Carolina	158,619,000	3.20%
11	Massachusetts	157,180,000	3.17%
12	Maryland	141,180,000	2.85%
13	Virginia	134,429,000	2.71%
14	Washington	109,247,000	2.20%
15	Indiana	108,196,000	2.18%
16	Georgia	105,723,000	2.13%
17	Louisiana	99,295,000	2.00%
18	Arizona	96,792,000	1.95%
19	Kentucky	88,769,000	1.79%
20	South Carolina	87,685,000	1.77%
21	Connecticut	84,223,000	1.70%
22	Missouri	79,913,000	1.61%
23	Oregon	73,284,000	1.48%
24	Alabama	66,109,000	1.33%
25	Tennessee	65,537,000	1.32%
26	Minnesota	62,559,000	1.26%
27	Wisconsin	50,916,000	1.03%
28	Iowa	48,327,000	0.97%
29	Alaska	47,111,000	0.95%
30	Oklahoma	46,597,000	0.94%
31	New Mexico	46,404,000	0.94%
32	Colorado	43,012,000	0.87%
33	Arkansas	39,673,000	0.80%
34	Kansas	38,941,000	0.79%
35	Utah	36,005,000	0.73%
36	Mississippi	35,878,000	0.72%
37	Delaware	34,296,000	0.69%
38	Nebraska	32,570,000	0.66%
39	Nevada	30,457,000	0.61%
40	Idaho	28,890,000	0.58%
41	Rhode Island	26,520,000	0.53%
42	Vermont	26,350,000	0.53%
43	New Hampshire	25,734,000	0.52%
44	Maine	23,784,000	0.48%
45	West Virginia	23,540,000	0.47%
46	Montana	18,045,000	0.36%
47	South Dakota	14,229,000	0.29%
48	Wyoming	9,160,000	0.18%
49	Hawaii	7,820,000	0.16%
50	North Dakota	7,295,000	0.15%
	District of Columbia**	NA	NA

Source: U.S. Bureau of the Census
"Government Finances: 1992-1993" (http://www.census.gov)
*Direct Expenditures.
**Not applicable.

Per Capita State Government Expenditures for Police Protection in 1993

National Per Capita = $19.24*

ALPHA ORDER

RANK	STATE	PER CAPITA
34	Alabama	$15.81
1	Alaska	78.78
12	Arizona	24.54
33	Arkansas	16.36
17	California	23.00
46	Colorado	12.05
10	Connecticut	25.69
2	Delaware	49.06
40	Florida	14.42
37	Georgia	15.32
50	Hawaii	6.71
8	Idaho	26.24
31	Illinois	18.81
30	Indiana	18.96
32	Iowa	17.13
36	Kansas	15.38
15	Kentucky	23.40
16	Louisiana	23.15
29	Maine	19.20
5	Maryland	28.51
9	Massachusetts	26.12
25	Michigan	20.15
42	Minnesota	13.83
43	Mississippi	13.60
38	Missouri	15.27
21	Montana	21.46
24	Nebraska	20.18
20	Nevada	21.99
18	New Hampshire	22.92
6	New Jersey	27.21
4	New Mexico	28.72
35	New York	15.71
19	North Carolina	22.81
48	North Dakota	11.45
39	Ohio	14.67
40	Oklahoma	14.42
14	Oregon	24.15
11	Pennsylvania	24.95
7	Rhode Island	26.55
13	South Carolina	24.18
26	South Dakota	19.85
45	Tennessee	12.87
47	Texas	11.76
28	Utah	19.36
3	Vermont	45.75
23	Virginia	20.76
22	Washington	20.79
44	West Virginia	12.95
49	Wisconsin	10.09
27	Wyoming	19.49

RANK ORDER

RANK	STATE	PER CAPITA
1	Alaska	$78.78
2	Delaware	49.06
3	Vermont	45.75
4	New Mexico	28.72
5	Maryland	28.51
6	New Jersey	27.21
7	Rhode Island	26.55
8	Idaho	26.24
9	Massachusetts	26.12
10	Connecticut	25.69
11	Pennsylvania	24.95
12	Arizona	24.54
13	South Carolina	24.18
14	Oregon	24.15
15	Kentucky	23.40
16	Louisiana	23.15
17	California	23.00
18	New Hampshire	22.92
19	North Carolina	22.81
20	Nevada	21.99
21	Montana	21.46
22	Washington	20.79
23	Virginia	20.76
24	Nebraska	20.18
25	Michigan	20.15
26	South Dakota	19.85
27	Wyoming	19.49
28	Utah	19.36
29	Maine	19.20
30	Indiana	18.96
31	Illinois	18.81
32	Iowa	17.13
33	Arkansas	16.36
34	Alabama	15.81
35	New York	15.71
36	Kansas	15.38
37	Georgia	15.32
38	Missouri	15.27
39	Ohio	14.67
40	Florida	14.42
40	Oklahoma	14.42
42	Minnesota	13.83
43	Mississippi	13.60
44	West Virginia	12.95
45	Tennessee	12.87
46	Colorado	12.05
47	Texas	11.76
48	North Dakota	11.45
49	Wisconsin	10.09
50	Hawaii	6.71
	District of Columbia**	NA

Source: Morgan Quitno Press using data from U.S. Bureau of the Census "Government Finances: 1992-1993" (http://www.census.gov)
Direct Expenditures.
**Not applicable.*

State Government Expenditures for Police Protection
As a Percent of All Direct Expenditures in 1993
National Percent = 0.94% of Direct Expenditures*

ALPHA ORDER

RANK	STATE	PERCENT
34	Alabama	0.82
14	Alaska	1.09
3	Arizona	1.47
31	Arkansas	0.88
8	California	1.19
44	Colorado	0.68
35	Connecticut	0.81
2	Delaware	1.60
27	Florida	0.95
27	Georgia	0.95
50	Hawaii	0.14
3	Idaho	1.47
18	Illinois	1.05
12	Indiana	1.11
31	Iowa	0.88
26	Kansas	0.96
12	Kentucky	1.11
24	Louisiana	0.98
39	Maine	0.76
6	Maryland	1.30
29	Massachusetts	0.91
24	Michigan	0.98
45	Minnesota	0.66
33	Mississippi	0.84
21	Missouri	1.00
30	Montana	0.90
10	Nebraska	1.17
16	Nevada	1.06
22	New Hampshire	0.99
19	New Jersey	1.03
9	New Mexico	1.18
46	New York	0.57
5	North Carolina	1.38
49	North Dakota	0.43
43	Ohio	0.69
38	Oklahoma	0.77
15	Oregon	1.08
11	Pennsylvania	1.16
39	Rhode Island	0.76
16	South Carolina	1.06
19	South Dakota	1.03
37	Tennessee	0.79
41	Texas	0.74
22	Utah	0.99
1	Vermont	1.70
7	Virginia	1.23
36	Washington	0.80
48	West Virginia	0.50
47	Wisconsin	0.53
42	Wyoming	0.73

RANK ORDER

RANK	STATE	PERCENT
1	Vermont	1.70
2	Delaware	1.60
3	Arizona	1.47
3	Idaho	1.47
5	North Carolina	1.38
6	Maryland	1.30
7	Virginia	1.23
8	California	1.19
9	New Mexico	1.18
10	Nebraska	1.17
11	Pennsylvania	1.16
12	Indiana	1.11
12	Kentucky	1.11
14	Alaska	1.09
15	Oregon	1.08
16	Nevada	1.06
16	South Carolina	1.06
18	Illinois	1.05
19	New Jersey	1.03
19	South Dakota	1.03
21	Missouri	1.00
22	New Hampshire	0.99
22	Utah	0.99
24	Louisiana	0.98
24	Michigan	0.98
26	Kansas	0.96
27	Florida	0.95
27	Georgia	0.95
29	Massachusetts	0.91
30	Montana	0.90
31	Arkansas	0.88
31	Iowa	0.88
33	Mississippi	0.84
34	Alabama	0.82
35	Connecticut	0.81
36	Washington	0.80
37	Tennessee	0.79
38	Oklahoma	0.77
39	Maine	0.76
39	Rhode Island	0.76
41	Texas	0.74
42	Wyoming	0.73
43	Ohio	0.69
44	Colorado	0.68
45	Minnesota	0.66
46	New York	0.57
47	Wisconsin	0.53
48	West Virginia	0.50
49	North Dakota	0.43
50	Hawaii	0.14

District of Columbia**   NA

Source: Morgan Quitno Press using data from U.S. Bureau of the Census
    "Government Finances: 1992-1993" (http://www.census.gov)
*Direct Expenditures.
**Not applicable.

Local Government Expenditures for Police Protection in 1993

National Total = $31,185,483,000*

ALPHA ORDER

RANK	STATE	EXPENDITURES	% of USA
25	Alabama	$337,072,000	1.08%
42	Alaska	91,062,000	0.29%
19	Arizona	485,882,000	1.56%
37	Arkansas	141,829,000	0.45%
1	California	5,278,812,000	16.93%
21	Colorado	431,491,000	1.38%
23	Connecticut	383,001,000	1.23%
45	Delaware	66,364,000	0.21%
3	Florida	2,330,629,000	7.47%
11	Georgia	705,272,000	2.26%
34	Hawaii	173,864,000	0.56%
41	Idaho	91,586,000	0.29%
5	Illinois	1,581,014,000	5.07%
24	Indiana	370,253,000	1.19%
32	Iowa	227,880,000	0.73%
28	Kansas	251,315,000	0.81%
31	Kentucky	229,533,000	0.74%
18	Louisiana	487,195,000	1.56%
43	Maine	77,501,000	0.25%
16	Maryland	562,851,000	1.80%
12	Massachusetts	677,690,000	2.17%
8	Michigan	1,010,827,000	3.24%
17	Minnesota	500,152,000	1.60%
35	Mississippi	157,657,000	0.51%
20	Missouri	468,127,000	1.50%
46	Montana	64,197,000	0.21%
38	Nebraska	128,878,000	0.41%
30	Nevada	238,215,000	0.76%
40	New Hampshire	106,110,000	0.34%
6	New Jersey	1,196,561,000	3.84%
33	New Mexico	177,120,000	0.57%
2	New York	3,500,796,000	11.23%
14	North Carolina	604,856,000	1.94%
49	North Dakota	36,613,000	0.12%
7	Ohio	1,189,237,000	3.81%
27	Oklahoma	269,844,000	0.87%
26	Oregon	318,849,000	1.02%
9	Pennsylvania	948,588,000	3.04%
39	Rhode Island	109,619,000	0.35%
29	South Carolina	247,305,000	0.79%
48	South Dakota	46,159,000	0.15%
22	Tennessee	418,924,000	1.34%
4	Texas	1,914,756,000	6.14%
36	Utah	151,781,000	0.49%
50	Vermont	28,535,000	0.09%
13	Virginia	672,952,000	2.16%
15	Washington	589,433,000	1.89%
44	West Virginia	72,645,000	0.23%
10	Wisconsin	707,457,000	2.27%
47	Wyoming	60,572,000	0.19%

RANK ORDER

RANK	STATE	EXPENDITURES	% of USA
1	California	$5,278,812,000	16.93%
2	New York	3,500,796,000	11.23%
3	Florida	2,330,629,000	7.47%
4	Texas	1,914,756,000	6.14%
5	Illinois	1,581,014,000	5.07%
6	New Jersey	1,196,561,000	3.84%
7	Ohio	1,189,237,000	3.81%
8	Michigan	1,010,827,000	3.24%
9	Pennsylvania	948,588,000	3.04%
10	Wisconsin	707,457,000	2.27%
11	Georgia	705,272,000	2.26%
12	Massachusetts	677,690,000	2.17%
13	Virginia	672,952,000	2.16%
14	North Carolina	604,856,000	1.94%
15	Washington	589,433,000	1.89%
16	Maryland	562,851,000	1.80%
17	Minnesota	500,152,000	1.60%
18	Louisiana	487,195,000	1.56%
19	Arizona	485,882,000	1.56%
20	Missouri	468,127,000	1.50%
21	Colorado	431,491,000	1.38%
22	Tennessee	418,924,000	1.34%
23	Connecticut	383,001,000	1.23%
24	Indiana	370,253,000	1.19%
25	Alabama	337,072,000	1.08%
26	Oregon	318,849,000	1.02%
27	Oklahoma	269,844,000	0.87%
28	Kansas	251,315,000	0.81%
29	South Carolina	247,305,000	0.79%
30	Nevada	238,215,000	0.76%
31	Kentucky	229,533,000	0.74%
32	Iowa	227,880,000	0.73%
33	New Mexico	177,120,000	0.57%
34	Hawaii	173,864,000	0.56%
35	Mississippi	157,657,000	0.51%
36	Utah	151,781,000	0.49%
37	Arkansas	141,829,000	0.45%
38	Nebraska	128,878,000	0.41%
39	Rhode Island	109,619,000	0.35%
40	New Hampshire	106,110,000	0.34%
41	Idaho	91,586,000	0.29%
42	Alaska	91,062,000	0.29%
43	Maine	77,501,000	0.25%
44	West Virginia	72,645,000	0.23%
45	Delaware	66,364,000	0.21%
46	Montana	64,197,000	0.21%
47	Wyoming	60,572,000	0.19%
48	South Dakota	46,159,000	0.15%
49	North Dakota	36,613,000	0.12%
50	Vermont	28,535,000	0.09%
	District of Columbia	266,622,000	0.85%

Source: U.S. Bureau of the Census
"Government Finances: 1992-1993" (http://www.census.gov)
Direct Expenditures.

Per Capita Local Government Expenditures for Police Protection in 1993

National Per Capita = $120.97*

ALPHA ORDER

RANK	STATE	PER CAPITA
37	Alabama	$80.62
5	Alaska	152.28
11	Arizona	123.20
47	Arkansas	58.49
4	California	169.08
12	Colorado	120.93
13	Connecticut	116.84
28	Delaware	94.94
3	Florida	169.85
26	Georgia	102.20
7	Hawaii	149.11
33	Idaho	83.18
9	Illinois	135.24
42	Indiana	64.88
36	Iowa	80.75
27	Kansas	99.26
45	Kentucky	60.51
15	Louisiana	113.59
44	Maine	62.55
14	Maryland	113.66
16	Massachusetts	112.61
22	Michigan	106.89
18	Minnesota	110.56
46	Mississippi	59.74
30	Missouri	89.42
40	Montana	76.33
38	Nebraska	79.85
2	Nevada	172.00
29	New Hampshire	94.49
6	New Jersey	152.25
20	New Mexico	109.60
1	New York	192.85
31	North Carolina	86.99
48	North Dakota	57.48
21	Ohio	107.52
32	Oklahoma	83.49
24	Oregon	105.06
39	Pennsylvania	78.85
19	Rhode Island	109.73
41	South Carolina	68.18
43	South Dakota	64.38
34	Tennessee	82.25
23	Texas	106.09
35	Utah	81.60
49	Vermont	49.54
25	Virginia	103.93
17	Washington	112.17
50	West Virginia	39.96
8	Wisconsin	140.26
10	Wyoming	128.88

RANK ORDER

RANK	STATE	PER CAPITA
1	New York	$192.85
2	Nevada	172.00
3	Florida	169.85
4	California	169.08
5	Alaska	152.28
6	New Jersey	152.25
7	Hawaii	149.11
8	Wisconsin	140.26
9	Illinois	135.24
10	Wyoming	128.88
11	Arizona	123.20
12	Colorado	120.93
13	Connecticut	116.84
14	Maryland	113.66
15	Louisiana	113.59
16	Massachusetts	112.61
17	Washington	112.17
18	Minnesota	110.56
19	Rhode Island	109.73
20	New Mexico	109.60
21	Ohio	107.52
22	Michigan	106.89
23	Texas	106.09
24	Oregon	105.06
25	Virginia	103.93
26	Georgia	102.20
27	Kansas	99.26
28	Delaware	94.94
29	New Hampshire	94.49
30	Missouri	89.42
31	North Carolina	86.99
32	Oklahoma	83.49
33	Idaho	83.18
34	Tennessee	82.25
35	Utah	81.60
36	Iowa	80.75
37	Alabama	80.62
38	Nebraska	79.85
39	Pennsylvania	78.85
40	Montana	76.33
41	South Carolina	68.18
42	Indiana	64.88
43	South Dakota	64.38
44	Maine	62.55
45	Kentucky	60.51
46	Mississippi	59.74
47	Arkansas	58.49
48	North Dakota	57.48
49	Vermont	49.54
50	West Virginia	39.96
	District of Columbia	461.28

Source: Morgan Quitno Press using data from U.S. Bureau of the Census
"Government Finances: 1992-1993" (http://www.census.gov)
*Direct Expenditures.

Local Government Expenditures for Police Protection
As a Percent of All Direct Expenditures in 1993
National Percent = 4.60% of Direct Expenditures*

ALPHA ORDER

RANK ORDER

RANK	STATE	PERCENT		RANK	STATE	PERCENT
26	Alabama	4.24		1	Hawaii	10.45
37	Alaska	3.66		2	Florida	6.38
20	Arizona	4.69		3	Rhode Island	6.30
32	Arkansas	4.04		4	Nevada	6.22
14	California	5.00		5	Louisiana	5.80
31	Colorado	4.08		6	New Jersey	5.67
16	Connecticut	4.93		7	New Mexico	5.49
11	Delaware	5.21		8	Illinois	5.39
2	Florida	6.38		9	Maryland	5.38
28	Georgia	4.14		10	New Hampshire	5.24
1	Hawaii	10.45		11	Delaware	5.21
17	Idaho	4.77		12	Wisconsin	5.04
8	Illinois	5.39		13	Missouri	5.01
47	Indiana	3.08		14	California	5.00
39	Iowa	3.49		15	Virginia	4.96
28	Kansas	4.14		16	Connecticut	4.93
34	Kentucky	3.77		17	Idaho	4.77
5	Louisiana	5.80		17	Ohio	4.77
40	Maine	3.43		19	Massachusetts	4.71
9	Maryland	5.38		20	Arizona	4.69
19	Massachusetts	4.71		21	Montana	4.60
25	Michigan	4.32		22	Oklahoma	4.57
43	Minnesota	3.39		23	New York	4.47
45	Mississippi	3.27		24	Texas	4.45
13	Missouri	5.01		25	Michigan	4.32
21	Montana	4.60		26	Alabama	4.24
49	Nebraska	2.66		27	Wyoming	4.16
4	Nevada	6.22		28	Georgia	4.14
10	New Hampshire	5.24		28	Kansas	4.14
6	New Jersey	5.67		30	Oregon	4.11
7	New Mexico	5.49		31	Colorado	4.08
23	New York	4.47		32	Arkansas	4.04
33	North Carolina	3.80		33	North Carolina	3.80
46	North Dakota	3.24		34	Kentucky	3.77
17	Ohio	4.77		34	South Carolina	3.77
22	Oklahoma	4.57		36	South Dakota	3.70
30	Oregon	4.11		37	Alaska	3.66
42	Pennsylvania	3.41		38	Utah	3.60
3	Rhode Island	6.30		39	Iowa	3.49
34	South Carolina	3.77		40	Maine	3.43
36	South Dakota	3.70		40	Tennessee	3.43
40	Tennessee	3.43		42	Pennsylvania	3.41
24	Texas	4.45		43	Minnesota	3.39
38	Utah	3.60		44	Washington	3.38
48	Vermont	2.77		45	Mississippi	3.27
15	Virginia	4.96		46	North Dakota	3.24
44	Washington	3.38		47	Indiana	3.08
50	West Virginia	2.54		48	Vermont	2.77
12	Wisconsin	5.04		49	Nebraska	2.66
27	Wyoming	4.16		50	West Virginia	2.54
					District of Columbia	4.33

Source: Morgan Quitno Press using data from U.S. Bureau of the Census
   "Government Finances: 1992-1993" (http://www.census.gov)
*Direct Expenditures.

State and Local Government Expenditures for Corrections in 1993

National Total = $29,614,412,000*

ALPHA ORDER

RANK	STATE	EXPENDITURES	% of USA
28	Alabama	$257,972,000	0.87%
36	Alaska	131,527,000	0.44%
17	Arizona	490,161,000	1.66%
33	Arkansas	158,428,000	0.53%
1	California	4,832,709,000	16.32%
22	Colorado	384,358,000	1.30%
19	Connecticut	443,980,000	1.50%
41	Delaware	89,902,000	0.30%
4	Florida	1,837,231,000	6.20%
10	Georgia	909,510,000	3.07%
38	Hawaii	112,541,000	0.38%
43	Idaho	78,936,000	0.27%
8	Illinois	980,938,000	3.31%
20	Indiana	415,999,000	1.40%
34	Iowa	152,052,000	0.51%
31	Kansas	207,966,000	0.70%
27	Kentucky	273,957,000	0.93%
23	Louisiana	380,279,000	1.28%
42	Maine	88,511,000	0.30%
14	Maryland	693,291,000	2.34%
13	Massachusetts	693,691,000	2.34%
5	Michigan	1,168,107,000	3.94%
24	Minnesota	358,743,000	1.21%
40	Mississippi	106,120,000	0.36%
25	Missouri	311,073,000	1.05%
46	Montana	49,191,000	0.17%
37	Nebraska	113,505,000	0.38%
29	Nevada	245,343,000	0.83%
44	New Hampshire	72,629,000	0.25%
9	New Jersey	937,165,000	3.16%
32	New Mexico	198,924,000	0.67%
2	New York	3,472,632,000	11.73%
11	North Carolina	771,998,000	2.61%
50	North Dakota	24,311,000	0.08%
7	Ohio	999,411,000	3.37%
30	Oklahoma	214,646,000	0.72%
26	Oregon	306,038,000	1.03%
6	Pennsylvania	1,093,143,000	3.69%
39	Rhode Island	107,217,000	0.36%
21	South Carolina	414,864,000	1.40%
47	South Dakota	43,643,000	0.15%
18	Tennessee	458,870,000	1.55%
3	Texas	2,015,875,000	6.81%
35	Utah	140,696,000	0.48%
48	Vermont	41,810,000	0.14%
12	Virginia	707,854,000	2.39%
15	Washington	679,409,000	2.29%
45	West Virginia	58,732,000	0.20%
16	Wisconsin	531,092,000	1.79%
49	Wyoming	39,407,000	0.13%

RANK ORDER

RANK	STATE	EXPENDITURES	% of USA
1	California	$4,832,709,000	16.32%
2	New York	3,472,632,000	11.73%
3	Texas	2,015,875,000	6.81%
4	Florida	1,837,231,000	6.20%
5	Michigan	1,168,107,000	3.94%
6	Pennsylvania	1,093,143,000	3.69%
7	Ohio	999,411,000	3.37%
8	Illinois	980,938,000	3.31%
9	New Jersey	937,165,000	3.16%
10	Georgia	909,510,000	3.07%
11	North Carolina	771,998,000	2.61%
12	Virginia	707,854,000	2.39%
13	Massachusetts	693,691,000	2.34%
14	Maryland	693,291,000	2.34%
15	Washington	679,409,000	2.29%
16	Wisconsin	531,092,000	1.79%
17	Arizona	490,161,000	1.66%
18	Tennessee	458,870,000	1.55%
19	Connecticut	443,980,000	1.50%
20	Indiana	415,999,000	1.40%
21	South Carolina	414,864,000	1.40%
22	Colorado	384,358,000	1.30%
23	Louisiana	380,279,000	1.28%
24	Minnesota	358,743,000	1.21%
25	Missouri	311,073,000	1.05%
26	Oregon	306,038,000	1.03%
27	Kentucky	273,957,000	0.93%
28	Alabama	257,972,000	0.87%
29	Nevada	245,343,000	0.83%
30	Oklahoma	214,646,000	0.72%
31	Kansas	207,966,000	0.70%
32	New Mexico	198,924,000	0.67%
33	Arkansas	158,428,000	0.53%
34	Iowa	152,052,000	0.51%
35	Utah	140,696,000	0.48%
36	Alaska	131,527,000	0.44%
37	Nebraska	113,505,000	0.38%
38	Hawaii	112,541,000	0.38%
39	Rhode Island	107,217,000	0.36%
40	Mississippi	106,120,000	0.36%
41	Delaware	89,902,000	0.30%
42	Maine	88,511,000	0.30%
43	Idaho	78,936,000	0.27%
44	New Hampshire	72,629,000	0.25%
45	West Virginia	58,732,000	0.20%
46	Montana	49,191,000	0.17%
47	South Dakota	43,643,000	0.15%
48	Vermont	41,810,000	0.14%
49	Wyoming	39,407,000	0.13%
50	North Dakota	24,311,000	0.08%
	District of Columbia	318,025,000	1.07%

Source: U.S. Bureau of the Census
"Government Finances: 1992-1993" (http://www.census.gov)
*Direct Expenditures.

Per Capita State and Local Government Expenditures for Corrections in 1993

National Per Capita = $114.87*

ALPHA ORDER

RANK	STATE	PER CAPITA
43	Alabama	$61.70
1	Alaska	219.94
11	Arizona	124.28
41	Arkansas	65.33
4	California	154.80
20	Colorado	107.72
6	Connecticut	135.44
10	Delaware	128.62
7	Florida	133.89
8	Georgia	131.79
24	Hawaii	96.52
37	Idaho	71.69
29	Illinois	83.91
34	Indiana	72.89
47	Iowa	53.88
31	Kansas	82.14
36	Kentucky	72.23
28	Louisiana	88.66
38	Maine	71.44
5	Maryland	140.00
15	Massachusetts	115.27
12	Michigan	123.52
32	Minnesota	79.30
48	Mississippi	40.21
45	Missouri	59.42
46	Montana	58.49
39	Nebraska	70.33
3	Nevada	177.14
42	New Hampshire	64.67
14	New Jersey	119.25
13	New Mexico	123.10
2	New York	191.30
18	North Carolina	111.03
49	North Dakota	38.16
26	Ohio	90.35
40	Oklahoma	66.41
23	Oregon	100.84
25	Pennsylvania	90.86
21	Rhode Island	107.32
16	South Carolina	114.38
44	South Dakota	60.87
27	Tennessee	90.10
17	Texas	111.69
33	Utah	75.64
35	Vermont	72.59
19	Virginia	109.32
9	Washington	129.29
50	West Virginia	32.31
22	Wisconsin	105.29
30	Wyoming	83.84

RANK ORDER

RANK	STATE	PER CAPITA
1	Alaska	$219.94
2	New York	191.30
3	Nevada	177.14
4	California	154.80
5	Maryland	140.00
6	Connecticut	135.44
7	Florida	133.89
8	Georgia	131.79
9	Washington	129.29
10	Delaware	128.62
11	Arizona	124.28
12	Michigan	123.52
13	New Mexico	123.10
14	New Jersey	119.25
15	Massachusetts	115.27
16	South Carolina	114.38
17	Texas	111.69
18	North Carolina	111.03
19	Virginia	109.32
20	Colorado	107.72
21	Rhode Island	107.32
22	Wisconsin	105.29
23	Oregon	100.84
24	Hawaii	96.52
25	Pennsylvania	90.86
26	Ohio	90.35
27	Tennessee	90.10
28	Louisiana	88.66
29	Illinois	83.91
30	Wyoming	83.84
31	Kansas	82.14
32	Minnesota	79.30
33	Utah	75.64
34	Indiana	72.89
35	Vermont	72.59
36	Kentucky	72.23
37	Idaho	71.69
38	Maine	71.44
39	Nebraska	70.33
40	Oklahoma	66.41
41	Arkansas	65.33
42	New Hampshire	64.67
43	Alabama	61.70
44	South Dakota	60.87
45	Missouri	59.42
46	Montana	58.49
47	Iowa	53.88
48	Mississippi	40.21
49	North Dakota	38.16
50	West Virginia	32.31
	District of Columbia	550.22

Source: Morgan Quitno Press using data from U.S. Bureau of the Census
"Government Finances: 1992-1993" (http://www.census.gov)
*Direct Expenditures.

State and Local Government Expenditures for Corrections
As a Percent of All Direct Expenditures in 1993
National Percent = 2.45% of Direct Expenditures*

ALPHA ORDER

RANK ORDER

RANK	STATE	PERCENT		RANK	STATE	PERCENT
40	Alabama	1.61		1	Nevada	3.65
32	Alaska	1.93		2	Maryland	3.26
6	Arizona	2.90		3	Georgia	3.22
29	Arkansas	1.98		4	Florida	3.20
5	California	2.91		5	California	2.91
16	Colorado	2.28		6	Arizona	2.90
15	Connecticut	2.44		7	Virginia	2.88
14	Delaware	2.63		8	North Carolina	2.82
4	Florida	3.20		9	Texas	2.81
3	Georgia	3.22		10	South Carolina	2.80
41	Hawaii	1.58		11	New Mexico	2.78
27	Idaho	2.03		12	Michigan	2.73
30	Illinois	1.95		13	New York	2.70
33	Indiana	1.91		14	Delaware	2.63
47	Iowa	1.27		15	Connecticut	2.44
25	Kansas	2.05		16	Colorado	2.28
31	Kentucky	1.94		17	Wisconsin	2.25
24	Louisiana	2.06		18	New Jersey	2.24
38	Maine	1.65		18	Tennessee	2.24
2	Maryland	3.26		20	Massachusetts	2.19
20	Massachusetts	2.19		21	Washington	2.18
12	Michigan	2.73		22	Oregon	2.11
43	Minnesota	1.48		23	Ohio	2.07
48	Mississippi	1.16		24	Louisiana	2.06
36	Missouri	1.79		25	Kansas	2.05
46	Montana	1.45		25	Rhode Island	2.05
43	Nebraska	1.48		27	Idaho	2.03
1	Nevada	3.65		27	Pennsylvania	2.03
42	New Hampshire	1.57		29	Arkansas	1.98
18	New Jersey	2.24		30	Illinois	1.95
11	New Mexico	2.78		31	Kentucky	1.94
13	New York	2.70		32	Alaska	1.93
8	North Carolina	2.82		33	Indiana	1.91
49	North Dakota	0.86		34	Oklahoma	1.80
23	Ohio	2.07		34	Utah	1.80
34	Oklahoma	1.80		36	Missouri	1.79
22	Oregon	2.11		37	South Dakota	1.66
27	Pennsylvania	2.03		38	Maine	1.65
25	Rhode Island	2.05		39	Vermont	1.62
10	South Carolina	2.80		40	Alabama	1.61
37	South Dakota	1.66		41	Hawaii	1.58
18	Tennessee	2.24		42	New Hampshire	1.57
9	Texas	2.81		43	Minnesota	1.48
34	Utah	1.80		43	Nebraska	1.48
39	Vermont	1.62		45	Wyoming	1.46
7	Virginia	2.88		46	Montana	1.45
21	Washington	2.18		47	Iowa	1.27
50	West Virginia	0.78		48	Mississippi	1.16
17	Wisconsin	2.25		49	North Dakota	0.86
45	Wyoming	1.46		50	West Virginia	0.78
					District of Columbia	5.17

Source: Morgan Quitno Press using data from U.S. Bureau of the Census
     "Government Finances: 1992-1993" (http://www.census.gov)
*Direct Expenditures.

State Government Expenditures for Corrections in 1993

National Total = $19,091,342,000*

ALPHA ORDER					RANK ORDER			
RANK	STATE	EXPENDITURES	% of USA		RANK	STATE	EXPENDITURES	% of USA
27	Alabama	$178,491,000	0.93%		1	California	$2,842,662,000	14.89%
33	Alaska	131,527,000	0.69%		2	New York	1,782,186,000	9.34%
19	Arizona	311,285,000	1.63%		3	Texas	1,317,035,000	6.90%
35	Arkansas	115,407,000	0.60%		4	Florida	1,072,471,000	5.62%
1	California	2,842,662,000	14.89%		5	Michigan	897,632,000	4.70%
22	Colorado	263,716,000	1.38%		6	Ohio	706,381,000	3.70%
16	Connecticut	443,979,000	2.33%		7	Illinois	624,722,000	3.27%
39	Delaware	89,881,000	0.47%		8	New Jersey	605,386,000	3.17%
4	Florida	1,072,471,000	5.62%		9	Pennsylvania	596,770,000	3.13%
12	Georgia	582,339,000	3.05%		10	North Carolina	594,814,000	3.12%
36	Hawaii	112,541,000	0.59%		11	Maryland	584,014,000	3.06%
42	Idaho	61,151,000	0.32%		12	Georgia	582,339,000	3.05%
7	Illinois	624,722,000	3.27%		13	Massachusetts	500,734,000	2.62%
21	Indiana	299,948,000	1.57%		14	Washington	482,216,000	2.53%
34	Iowa	120,521,000	0.63%		15	Virginia	465,248,000	2.44%
29	Kansas	165,939,000	0.87%		16	Connecticut	443,979,000	2.33%
26	Kentucky	191,262,000	1.00%		17	Wisconsin	337,239,000	1.77%
23	Louisiana	258,713,000	1.36%		18	South Carolina	331,370,000	1.74%
43	Maine	52,834,000	0.28%		19	Arizona	311,285,000	1.63%
11	Maryland	584,014,000	3.06%		20	Tennessee	304,081,000	1.59%
13	Massachusetts	500,734,000	2.62%		21	Indiana	299,948,000	1.57%
5	Michigan	897,632,000	4.70%		22	Colorado	263,716,000	1.38%
28	Minnesota	177,948,000	0.93%		23	Louisiana	258,713,000	1.36%
40	Mississippi	86,329,000	0.45%		24	Missouri	207,407,000	1.09%
24	Missouri	207,407,000	1.09%		25	Oklahoma	198,167,000	1.04%
46	Montana	39,912,000	0.21%		26	Kentucky	191,262,000	1.00%
41	Nebraska	83,767,000	0.44%		27	Alabama	178,491,000	0.93%
31	Nevada	152,384,000	0.80%		28	Minnesota	177,948,000	0.93%
44	New Hampshire	49,533,000	0.26%		29	Kansas	165,939,000	0.87%
8	New Jersey	605,386,000	3.17%		30	Oregon	165,360,000	0.87%
32	New Mexico	136,703,000	0.72%		31	Nevada	152,384,000	0.80%
2	New York	1,782,186,000	9.34%		32	New Mexico	136,703,000	0.72%
10	North Carolina	594,814,000	3.12%		33	Alaska	131,527,000	0.69%
50	North Dakota	16,408,000	0.09%		34	Iowa	120,521,000	0.63%
6	Ohio	706,381,000	3.70%		35	Arkansas	115,407,000	0.60%
25	Oklahoma	198,167,000	1.04%		36	Hawaii	112,541,000	0.59%
30	Oregon	165,360,000	0.87%		37	Rhode Island	107,217,000	0.56%
9	Pennsylvania	596,770,000	3.13%		38	Utah	105,701,000	0.55%
37	Rhode Island	107,217,000	0.56%		39	Delaware	89,881,000	0.47%
18	South Carolina	331,370,000	1.74%		40	Mississippi	86,329,000	0.45%
48	South Dakota	33,517,000	0.18%		41	Nebraska	83,767,000	0.44%
20	Tennessee	304,081,000	1.59%		42	Idaho	61,151,000	0.32%
3	Texas	1,317,035,000	6.90%		43	Maine	52,834,000	0.28%
38	Utah	105,701,000	0.55%		44	New Hampshire	49,533,000	0.26%
45	Vermont	41,794,000	0.22%		45	Vermont	41,794,000	0.22%
15	Virginia	465,248,000	2.44%		46	Montana	39,912,000	0.21%
14	Washington	482,216,000	2.53%		47	West Virginia	37,450,000	0.20%
47	West Virginia	37,450,000	0.20%		48	South Dakota	33,517,000	0.18%
17	Wisconsin	337,239,000	1.77%		49	Wyoming	27,250,000	0.14%
49	Wyoming	27,250,000	0.14%		50	North Dakota	16,408,000	0.09%
					District of Columbia**		NA	NA

Source: U.S. Bureau of the Census
    "Government Finances: 1992-1993" (http://www.census.gov)
*Direct Expenditures.
**Not applicable.

Per Capita State Government Expenditures for Corrections in 1993

National Per Capita = $74.05*

ALPHA ORDER

RANK	STATE	PER CAPITA
44	Alabama	$42.69
1	Alaska	219.94
17	Arizona	78.93
39	Arkansas	47.59
12	California	91.05
20	Colorado	73.91
2	Connecticut	135.44
3	Delaware	128.59
18	Florida	78.16
15	Georgia	84.38
8	Hawaii	96.52
32	Idaho	55.54
34	Illinois	53.44
35	Indiana	52.56
43	Iowa	42.71
25	Kansas	65.54
37	Kentucky	50.42
28	Louisiana	60.32
45	Maine	42.64
4	Maryland	117.93
16	Massachusetts	83.21
9	Michigan	94.92
47	Minnesota	39.33
48	Mississippi	32.71
46	Missouri	39.62
40	Montana	47.46
36	Nebraska	51.90
5	Nevada	110.02
42	New Hampshire	44.11
19	New Jersey	77.03
14	New Mexico	84.59
7	New York	98.18
13	North Carolina	85.55
49	North Dakota	25.76
26	Ohio	63.86
27	Oklahoma	61.31
33	Oregon	54.48
38	Pennsylvania	49.60
6	Rhode Island	107.32
11	South Carolina	91.36
41	South Dakota	46.75
29	Tennessee	59.71
21	Texas	72.97
31	Utah	56.83
22	Vermont	72.56
23	Virginia	71.85
10	Washington	91.76
50	West Virginia	20.60
24	Wisconsin	66.86
30	Wyoming	57.98

RANK ORDER

RANK	STATE	PER CAPITA
1	Alaska	$219.94
2	Connecticut	135.44
3	Delaware	128.59
4	Maryland	117.93
5	Nevada	110.02
6	Rhode Island	107.32
7	New York	98.18
8	Hawaii	96.52
9	Michigan	94.92
10	Washington	91.76
11	South Carolina	91.36
12	California	91.05
13	North Carolina	85.55
14	New Mexico	84.59
15	Georgia	84.38
16	Massachusetts	83.21
17	Arizona	78.93
18	Florida	78.16
19	New Jersey	77.03
20	Colorado	73.91
21	Texas	72.97
22	Vermont	72.56
23	Virginia	71.85
24	Wisconsin	66.86
25	Kansas	65.54
26	Ohio	63.86
27	Oklahoma	61.31
28	Louisiana	60.32
29	Tennessee	59.71
30	Wyoming	57.98
31	Utah	56.83
32	Idaho	55.54
33	Oregon	54.48
34	Illinois	53.44
35	Indiana	52.56
36	Nebraska	51.90
37	Kentucky	50.42
38	Pennsylvania	49.60
39	Arkansas	47.59
40	Montana	47.46
41	South Dakota	46.75
42	New Hampshire	44.11
43	Iowa	42.71
44	Alabama	42.69
45	Maine	42.64
46	Missouri	39.62
47	Minnesota	39.33
48	Mississippi	32.71
49	North Dakota	25.76
50	West Virginia	20.60
	District of Columbia**	NA

Source: Morgan Quitno Press using data from U.S. Bureau of the Census
"Government Finances: 1992-1993" (http://www.census.gov)
*Direct Expenditures.
**Not applicable.

State Government Expenditures for Corrections
As a Percent of All Direct Expenditures in 1993
National Percent = 3.61% of Direct Expenditures*

ALPHA ORDER

RANK ORDER

RANK	STATE	PERCENT	RANK	STATE	PERCENT
40	Alabama	2.22	1	Maryland	5.39
25	Alaska	3.03	2	Nevada	5.28
6	Arizona	4.74	3	Georgia	5.21
34	Arkansas	2.56	4	North Carolina	5.17
7	California	4.71	5	Florida	5.16
12	Colorado	4.19	6	Arizona	4.74
10	Connecticut	4.27	7	California	4.71
12	Delaware	4.19	8	Michigan	4.64
5	Florida	5.16	9	Texas	4.59
3	Georgia	5.21	10	Connecticut	4.27
43	Hawaii	2.06	11	Virginia	4.24
22	Idaho	3.11	12	Colorado	4.19
28	Illinois	2.98	12	Delaware	4.19
23	Indiana	3.08	14	Kansas	4.08
41	Iowa	2.20	15	South Carolina	4.00
14	Kansas	4.08	16	Tennessee	3.68
38	Kentucky	2.38	17	New York	3.53
34	Louisiana	2.56	18	Washington	3.52
48	Maine	1.70	19	Wisconsin	3.51
1	Maryland	5.39	20	New Mexico	3.48
31	Massachusetts	2.90	21	Oklahoma	3.29
8	Michigan	4.64	22	Idaho	3.11
47	Minnesota	1.87	23	Indiana	3.08
44	Mississippi	2.01	24	Rhode Island	3.07
33	Missouri	2.60	25	Alaska	3.03
45	Montana	1.99	25	Ohio	3.03
27	Nebraska	3.00	27	Nebraska	3.00
2	Nevada	5.28	28	Illinois	2.98
46	New Hampshire	1.91	29	Utah	2.92
30	New Jersey	2.91	30	New Jersey	2.91
20	New Mexico	3.48	31	Massachusetts	2.90
17	New York	3.53	32	Vermont	2.70
4	North Carolina	5.17	33	Missouri	2.60
49	North Dakota	0.96	34	Arkansas	2.56
25	Ohio	3.03	34	Louisiana	2.56
21	Oklahoma	3.29	36	Oregon	2.45
36	Oregon	2.45	37	South Dakota	2.42
39	Pennsylvania	2.30	38	Kentucky	2.38
24	Rhode Island	3.07	39	Pennsylvania	2.30
15	South Carolina	4.00	40	Alabama	2.22
37	South Dakota	2.42	41	Iowa	2.20
16	Tennessee	3.68	42	Wyoming	2.18
9	Texas	4.59	43	Hawaii	2.06
29	Utah	2.92	44	Mississippi	2.01
32	Vermont	2.70	45	Montana	1.99
11	Virginia	4.24	46	New Hampshire	1.91
18	Washington	3.52	47	Minnesota	1.87
50	West Virginia	0.79	48	Maine	1.70
19	Wisconsin	3.51	49	North Dakota	0.96
42	Wyoming	2.18	50	West Virginia	0.79
				District of Columbia**	NA

Source: Morgan Quitno Press using data from U.S. Bureau of the Census
   "Government Finances: 1992-1993" (http://www.census.gov)
*Direct Expenditures.
**Not applicable.

Local Government Expenditures for Corrections in 1993

National Total = $10,523,070,000*

ALPHA ORDER

RANK	STATE	EXPENDITURES	% of USA
28	Alabama	$79,481,000	0.76%
48	Alaska	0	0.00%
16	Arizona	178,876,000	1.70%
30	Arkansas	43,021,000	0.41%
1	California	1,990,047,000	18.91%
21	Colorado	120,642,000	1.15%
47	Connecticut	1,000	0.00%
45	Delaware	21,000	0.00%
3	Florida	764,760,000	7.27%
8	Georgia	327,171,000	3.11%
48	Hawaii	0	0.00%
39	Idaho	17,785,000	0.17%
6	Illinois	356,216,000	3.39%
22	Indiana	116,051,000	1.10%
34	Iowa	31,531,000	0.30%
31	Kansas	42,027,000	0.40%
27	Kentucky	82,695,000	0.79%
20	Louisiana	121,566,000	1.16%
32	Maine	35,677,000	0.34%
23	Maryland	109,277,000	1.04%
14	Massachusetts	192,957,000	1.83%
10	Michigan	270,475,000	2.57%
15	Minnesota	180,795,000	1.72%
38	Mississippi	19,791,000	0.19%
24	Missouri	103,666,000	0.99%
43	Montana	9,279,000	0.09%
35	Nebraska	29,738,000	0.28%
25	Nevada	92,959,000	0.88%
36	New Hampshire	23,096,000	0.22%
7	New Jersey	331,779,000	3.15%
29	New Mexico	62,221,000	0.59%
2	New York	1,690,446,000	16.06%
17	North Carolina	177,184,000	1.68%
44	North Dakota	7,903,000	0.08%
9	Ohio	293,030,000	2.78%
40	Oklahoma	16,479,000	0.16%
19	Oregon	140,678,000	1.34%
5	Pennsylvania	496,373,000	4.72%
48	Rhode Island	0	0.00%
26	South Carolina	83,494,000	0.79%
42	South Dakota	10,126,000	0.10%
18	Tennessee	154,789,000	1.47%
4	Texas	698,840,000	6.64%
33	Utah	34,995,000	0.33%
46	Vermont	16,000	0.00%
11	Virginia	242,606,000	2.31%
12	Washington	197,193,000	1.87%
37	West Virginia	21,282,000	0.20%
13	Wisconsin	193,853,000	1.84%
41	Wyoming	12,157,000	0.12%

RANK ORDER

RANK	STATE	EXPENDITURES	% of USA
1	California	$1,990,047,000	18.91%
2	New York	1,690,446,000	16.06%
3	Florida	764,760,000	7.27%
4	Texas	698,840,000	6.64%
5	Pennsylvania	496,373,000	4.72%
6	Illinois	356,216,000	3.39%
7	New Jersey	331,779,000	3.15%
8	Georgia	327,171,000	3.11%
9	Ohio	293,030,000	2.78%
10	Michigan	270,475,000	2.57%
11	Virginia	242,606,000	2.31%
12	Washington	197,193,000	1.87%
13	Wisconsin	193,853,000	1.84%
14	Massachusetts	192,957,000	1.83%
15	Minnesota	180,795,000	1.72%
16	Arizona	178,876,000	1.70%
17	North Carolina	177,184,000	1.68%
18	Tennessee	154,789,000	1.47%
19	Oregon	140,678,000	1.34%
20	Louisiana	121,566,000	1.16%
21	Colorado	120,642,000	1.15%
22	Indiana	116,051,000	1.10%
23	Maryland	109,277,000	1.04%
24	Missouri	103,666,000	0.99%
25	Nevada	92,959,000	0.88%
26	South Carolina	83,494,000	0.79%
27	Kentucky	82,695,000	0.79%
28	Alabama	79,481,000	0.76%
29	New Mexico	62,221,000	0.59%
30	Arkansas	43,021,000	0.41%
31	Kansas	42,027,000	0.40%
32	Maine	35,677,000	0.34%
33	Utah	34,995,000	0.33%
34	Iowa	31,531,000	0.30%
35	Nebraska	29,738,000	0.28%
36	New Hampshire	23,096,000	0.22%
37	West Virginia	21,282,000	0.20%
38	Mississippi	19,791,000	0.19%
39	Idaho	17,785,000	0.17%
40	Oklahoma	16,479,000	0.16%
41	Wyoming	12,157,000	0.12%
42	South Dakota	10,126,000	0.10%
43	Montana	9,279,000	0.09%
44	North Dakota	7,903,000	0.08%
45	Delaware	21,000	0.00%
46	Vermont	16,000	0.00%
47	Connecticut	1,000	0.00%
48	Alaska	0	0.00%
48	Hawaii	0	0.00%
48	Rhode Island	0	0.00%
	District of Columbia	318,025,000	3.02%

Source: U.S. Bureau of the Census
"Government Finances: 1992-1993" (http://www.census.gov)
*Direct Expenditures.

Per Capita Local Government Expenditures for Corrections in 1993

National Per Capita = $40.82*

ALPHA ORDER

RANK ORDER

RANK	STATE	PER CAPITA		RANK	STATE	PER CAPITA
32	Alabama	$19.01		1	New York	$93.12
47	Alaska	0.00		2	Nevada	67.12
7	Arizona	45.35		3	California	63.74
35	Arkansas	17.74		4	Florida	55.73
3	California	63.74		5	Georgia	47.41
16	Colorado	33.81		6	Oregon	46.35
47	Connecticut	0.00		7	Arizona	45.35
45	Delaware	0.03		8	New Jersey	42.22
4	Florida	55.73		9	Pennsylvania	41.26
5	Georgia	47.41		10	Minnesota	39.96
47	Hawaii	0.00		11	Texas	38.72
37	Idaho	16.15		12	New Mexico	38.50
18	Illinois	30.47		13	Wisconsin	38.43
30	Indiana	20.33		14	Washington	37.52
41	Iowa	11.17		15	Virginia	37.47
36	Kansas	16.60		16	Colorado	33.81
28	Kentucky	21.80		17	Massachusetts	32.06
22	Louisiana	28.34		18	Illinois	30.47
20	Maine	28.79		19	Tennessee	30.39
27	Maryland	22.07		20	Maine	28.79
17	Massachusetts	32.06		21	Michigan	28.60
21	Michigan	28.60		22	Louisiana	28.34
10	Minnesota	39.96		23	Ohio	26.49
43	Mississippi	7.50		24	Wyoming	25.87
31	Missouri	19.80		25	North Carolina	25.48
42	Montana	11.03		26	South Carolina	23.02
34	Nebraska	18.43		27	Maryland	22.07
2	Nevada	67.12		28	Kentucky	21.80
29	New Hampshire	20.57		29	New Hampshire	20.57
8	New Jersey	42.22		30	Indiana	20.33
12	New Mexico	38.50		31	Missouri	19.80
1	New York	93.12		32	Alabama	19.01
25	North Carolina	25.48		33	Utah	18.81
39	North Dakota	12.41		34	Nebraska	18.43
23	Ohio	26.49		35	Arkansas	17.74
44	Oklahoma	5.10		36	Kansas	16.60
6	Oregon	46.35		37	Idaho	16.15
9	Pennsylvania	41.26		38	South Dakota	14.12
47	Rhode Island	0.00		39	North Dakota	12.41
26	South Carolina	23.02		40	West Virginia	11.71
38	South Dakota	14.12		41	Iowa	11.17
19	Tennessee	30.39		42	Montana	11.03
11	Texas	38.72		43	Mississippi	7.50
33	Utah	18.81		44	Oklahoma	5.10
45	Vermont	0.03		45	Delaware	0.03
15	Virginia	37.47		45	Vermont	0.03
14	Washington	37.52		47	Alaska	0.00
40	West Virginia	11.71		47	Connecticut	0.00
13	Wisconsin	38.43		47	Hawaii	0.00
24	Wyoming	25.87		47	Rhode Island	0.00
					District of Columbia	550.22

Source: Morgan Quitno Press using data from U.S. Bureau of the Census
        "Government Finances: 1992-1993" (http://www.census.gov)
*Direct Expenditures.

Local Government Expenditures for Corrections
As a Percent of All Direct Expenditures in 1993
National Percent = 1.55% of Direct Expenditures*

ALPHA ORDER

RANK	STATE	PERCENT
31	Alabama	1.00
45	Alaska	0.00
10	Arizona	1.73
20	Arkansas	1.23
6	California	1.89
25	Colorado	1.14
45	Connecticut	0.00
45	Delaware	0.00
3	Florida	2.09
5	Georgia	1.92
45	Hawaii	0.00
33	Idaho	0.93
22	Illinois	1.21
32	Indiana	0.96
42	Iowa	0.48
39	Kansas	0.69
16	Kentucky	1.36
14	Louisiana	1.45
12	Maine	1.58
30	Maryland	1.05
17	Massachusetts	1.34
24	Michigan	1.16
21	Minnesota	1.22
43	Mississippi	0.41
28	Missouri	1.11
40	Montana	0.66
41	Nebraska	0.61
1	Nevada	2.43
25	New Hampshire	1.14
13	New Jersey	1.57
4	New Mexico	1.93
2	New York	2.16
28	North Carolina	1.11
38	North Dakota	0.70
23	Ohio	1.17
44	Oklahoma	0.28
7	Oregon	1.81
8	Pennsylvania	1.79
45	Rhode Island	0.00
18	South Carolina	1.27
36	South Dakota	0.81
18	Tennessee	1.27
11	Texas	1.63
35	Utah	0.83
45	Vermont	0.00
8	Virginia	1.79
27	Washington	1.13
37	West Virginia	0.74
15	Wisconsin	1.38
34	Wyoming	0.84

RANK ORDER

RANK	STATE	PERCENT
1	Nevada	2.43
2	New York	2.16
3	Florida	2.09
4	New Mexico	1.93
5	Georgia	1.92
6	California	1.89
7	Oregon	1.81
8	Pennsylvania	1.79
8	Virginia	1.79
10	Arizona	1.73
11	Texas	1.63
12	Maine	1.58
13	New Jersey	1.57
14	Louisiana	1.45
15	Wisconsin	1.38
16	Kentucky	1.36
17	Massachusetts	1.34
18	South Carolina	1.27
18	Tennessee	1.27
20	Arkansas	1.23
21	Minnesota	1.22
22	Illinois	1.21
23	Ohio	1.17
24	Michigan	1.16
25	Colorado	1.14
25	New Hampshire	1.14
27	Washington	1.13
28	Missouri	1.11
28	North Carolina	1.11
30	Maryland	1.05
31	Alabama	1.00
32	Indiana	0.96
33	Idaho	0.93
34	Wyoming	0.84
35	Utah	0.83
36	South Dakota	0.81
37	West Virginia	0.74
38	North Dakota	0.70
39	Kansas	0.69
40	Montana	0.66
41	Nebraska	0.61
42	Iowa	0.48
43	Mississippi	0.41
44	Oklahoma	0.28
45	Alaska	0.00
45	Connecticut	0.00
45	Delaware	0.00
45	Hawaii	0.00
45	Rhode Island	0.00
45	Vermont	0.00

District of Columbia   5.17

Source: Morgan Quitno Press using data from U.S. Bureau of the Census
"Government Finances: 1992-1993" (http://www.census.gov)
*Direct Expenditures.

State and Local Government Expenditures for Judicial and Legal Services: 1993

National Total = $16,953,884,000*

ALPHA ORDER

RANK	STATE	EXPENDITURES	% of USA
25	Alabama	$199,154,000	1.17%
34	Alaska	111,030,000	0.65%
13	Arizona	319,712,000	1.89%
39	Arkansas	70,759,000	0.42%
1	California	3,270,458,000	19.29%
20	Colorado	217,149,000	1.28%
24	Connecticut	208,599,000	1.23%
44	Delaware	54,094,000	0.32%
3	Florida	1,038,285,000	6.12%
15	Georgia	293,520,000	1.73%
29	Hawaii	141,130,000	0.83%
45	Idaho	53,386,000	0.31%
9	Illinois	624,415,000	3.68%
21	Indiana	215,199,000	1.27%
28	Iowa	155,930,000	0.92%
31	Kansas	132,313,000	0.78%
27	Kentucky	162,408,000	0.96%
19	Louisiana	225,739,000	1.33%
46	Maine	39,028,000	0.23%
12	Maryland	336,980,000	1.99%
10	Massachusetts	356,044,000	2.10%
8	Michigan	629,443,000	3.71%
18	Minnesota	289,200,000	1.71%
40	Mississippi	68,944,000	0.41%
26	Missouri	190,979,000	1.13%
43	Montana	63,126,000	0.37%
42	Nebraska	65,676,000	0.39%
32	Nevada	126,852,000	0.75%
38	New Hampshire	77,314,000	0.46%
7	New Jersey	632,027,000	3.73%
36	New Mexico	85,793,000	0.51%
2	New York	1,744,468,000	10.29%
16	North Carolina	290,371,000	1.71%
50	North Dakota	22,088,000	0.13%
6	Ohio	712,048,000	4.20%
30	Oklahoma	132,463,000	0.78%
23	Oregon	211,260,000	1.25%
5	Pennsylvania	714,194,000	4.21%
37	Rhode Island	79,707,000	0.47%
33	South Carolina	121,508,000	0.72%
49	South Dakota	28,863,000	0.17%
22	Tennessee	214,328,000	1.26%
4	Texas	920,085,000	5.43%
35	Utah	91,538,000	0.54%
48	Vermont	30,213,000	0.18%
17	Virginia	289,818,000	1.71%
11	Washington	347,393,000	2.05%
41	West Virginia	68,286,000	0.40%
14	Wisconsin	302,812,000	1.79%
47	Wyoming	35,798,000	0.21%

RANK ORDER

RANK	STATE	EXPENDITURES	% of USA
1	California	$3,270,458,000	19.29%
2	New York	1,744,468,000	10.29%
3	Florida	1,038,285,000	6.12%
4	Texas	920,085,000	5.43%
5	Pennsylvania	714,194,000	4.21%
6	Ohio	712,048,000	4.20%
7	New Jersey	632,027,000	3.73%
8	Michigan	629,443,000	3.71%
9	Illinois	624,415,000	3.68%
10	Massachusetts	356,044,000	2.10%
11	Washington	347,393,000	2.05%
12	Maryland	336,980,000	1.99%
13	Arizona	319,712,000	1.89%
14	Wisconsin	302,812,000	1.79%
15	Georgia	293,520,000	1.73%
16	North Carolina	290,371,000	1.71%
17	Virginia	289,818,000	1.71%
18	Minnesota	289,200,000	1.71%
19	Louisiana	225,739,000	1.33%
20	Colorado	217,149,000	1.28%
21	Indiana	215,199,000	1.27%
22	Tennessee	214,328,000	1.26%
23	Oregon	211,260,000	1.25%
24	Connecticut	208,599,000	1.23%
25	Alabama	199,154,000	1.17%
26	Missouri	190,979,000	1.13%
27	Kentucky	162,408,000	0.96%
28	Iowa	155,930,000	0.92%
29	Hawaii	141,130,000	0.83%
30	Oklahoma	132,463,000	0.78%
31	Kansas	132,313,000	0.78%
32	Nevada	126,852,000	0.75%
33	South Carolina	121,508,000	0.72%
34	Alaska	111,030,000	0.65%
35	Utah	91,538,000	0.54%
36	New Mexico	85,793,000	0.51%
37	Rhode Island	79,707,000	0.47%
38	New Hampshire	77,314,000	0.46%
39	Arkansas	70,759,000	0.42%
40	Mississippi	68,944,000	0.41%
41	West Virginia	68,286,000	0.40%
42	Nebraska	65,676,000	0.39%
43	Montana	63,126,000	0.37%
44	Delaware	54,094,000	0.32%
45	Idaho	53,386,000	0.31%
46	Maine	39,028,000	0.23%
47	Wyoming	35,798,000	0.21%
48	Vermont	30,213,000	0.18%
49	South Dakota	28,863,000	0.17%
50	North Dakota	22,088,000	0.13%
	District of Columbia	141,957,000	0.84%

Source: U.S. Bureau of the Census
"Government Finances: 1992-1993" (http://www.census.gov)
*Direct expenditures. Includes Courts, Prosecution and Legal Services and Public Defense.

Per Capita State and Local Government Expenditures
For Judicial and Legal Services in 1993
National Per Capita = $65.76*

ALPHA ORDER

RANK	STATE	PER CAPITA
34	Alabama	$47.63
1	Alaska	185.67
6	Arizona	81.06
49	Arkansas	29.18
3	California	104.76
21	Colorado	60.86
20	Connecticut	63.64
9	Delaware	77.39
11	Florida	75.67
37	Georgia	42.53
2	Hawaii	121.04
33	Idaho	48.49
26	Illinois	53.41
43	Indiana	37.71
25	Iowa	55.26
30	Kansas	52.26
36	Kentucky	42.82
28	Louisiana	52.63
48	Maine	31.50
15	Maryland	68.05
24	Massachusetts	59.16
16	Michigan	66.56
19	Minnesota	63.93
50	Mississippi	26.13
45	Missouri	36.48
12	Montana	75.06
41	Nebraska	40.69
5	Nevada	91.59
14	New Hampshire	68.85
7	New Jersey	80.42
27	New Mexico	53.09
4	New York	96.10
39	North Carolina	41.76
46	North Dakota	34.68
18	Ohio	64.37
40	Oklahoma	40.98
13	Oregon	69.61
23	Pennsylvania	59.36
8	Rhode Island	79.79
47	South Carolina	33.50
42	South Dakota	40.26
38	Tennessee	42.08
31	Texas	50.98
32	Utah	49.21
29	Vermont	52.45
35	Virginia	44.76
17	Washington	66.11
44	West Virginia	37.56
22	Wisconsin	60.03
10	Wyoming	76.17

RANK ORDER

RANK	STATE	PER CAPITA
1	Alaska	$185.67
2	Hawaii	121.04
3	California	104.76
4	New York	96.10
5	Nevada	91.59
6	Arizona	81.06
7	New Jersey	80.42
8	Rhode Island	79.79
9	Delaware	77.39
10	Wyoming	76.17
11	Florida	75.67
12	Montana	75.06
13	Oregon	69.61
14	New Hampshire	68.85
15	Maryland	68.05
16	Michigan	66.56
17	Washington	66.11
18	Ohio	64.37
19	Minnesota	63.93
20	Connecticut	63.64
21	Colorado	60.86
22	Wisconsin	60.03
23	Pennsylvania	59.36
24	Massachusetts	59.16
25	Iowa	55.26
26	Illinois	53.41
27	New Mexico	53.09
28	Louisiana	52.63
29	Vermont	52.45
30	Kansas	52.26
31	Texas	50.98
32	Utah	49.21
33	Idaho	48.49
34	Alabama	47.63
35	Virginia	44.76
36	Kentucky	42.82
37	Georgia	42.53
38	Tennessee	42.08
39	North Carolina	41.76
40	Oklahoma	40.98
41	Nebraska	40.69
42	South Dakota	40.26
43	Indiana	37.71
44	West Virginia	37.56
45	Missouri	36.48
46	North Dakota	34.68
47	South Carolina	33.50
48	Maine	31.50
49	Arkansas	29.18
50	Mississippi	26.13
	District of Columbia	245.60

Source: Morgan Quitno Press using data from U.S. Bureau of the Census
    "Government Finances: 1992-1993" (http://www.census.gov)
*Direct expenditures. Includes Courts, Prosecution and Legal Services and Public Defense.

State and Local Government Expenditures for Judicial and Legal Services As a Percent of All Direct Expenditures in 1993
National Percent = 1.40% of Direct Expenditures*

ALPHA ORDER

RANK	STATE	PERCENT
25	Alabama	1.25
8	Alaska	1.63
3	Arizona	1.89
45	Arkansas	0.88
2	California	1.97
22	Colorado	1.29
33	Connecticut	1.15
9	Delaware	1.58
6	Florida	1.81
42	Georgia	1.04
1	Hawaii	1.98
16	Idaho	1.37
26	Illinois	1.24
43	Indiana	0.99
20	Iowa	1.30
20	Kansas	1.30
33	Kentucky	1.15
27	Louisiana	1.22
50	Maine	0.73
9	Maryland	1.58
35	Massachusetts	1.12
13	Michigan	1.47
29	Minnesota	1.19
49	Mississippi	0.76
38	Missouri	1.10
5	Montana	1.86
46	Nebraska	0.86
3	Nevada	1.89
7	New Hampshire	1.67
12	New Jersey	1.51
28	New Mexico	1.20
17	New York	1.36
40	North Carolina	1.06
48	North Dakota	0.78
13	Ohio	1.47
37	Oklahoma	1.11
15	Oregon	1.46
18	Pennsylvania	1.33
11	Rhode Island	1.52
47	South Carolina	0.82
38	South Dakota	1.10
41	Tennessee	1.05
23	Texas	1.28
31	Utah	1.17
31	Vermont	1.17
30	Virginia	1.18
35	Washington	1.12
44	West Virginia	0.90
23	Wisconsin	1.28
19	Wyoming	1.32

RANK ORDER

RANK	STATE	PERCENT
1	Hawaii	1.98
2	California	1.97
3	Arizona	1.89
3	Nevada	1.89
5	Montana	1.86
6	Florida	1.81
7	New Hampshire	1.67
8	Alaska	1.63
9	Delaware	1.58
9	Maryland	1.58
11	Rhode Island	1.52
12	New Jersey	1.51
13	Michigan	1.47
13	Ohio	1.47
15	Oregon	1.46
16	Idaho	1.37
17	New York	1.36
18	Pennsylvania	1.33
19	Wyoming	1.32
20	Iowa	1.30
20	Kansas	1.30
22	Colorado	1.29
23	Texas	1.28
23	Wisconsin	1.28
25	Alabama	1.25
26	Illinois	1.24
27	Louisiana	1.22
28	New Mexico	1.20
29	Minnesota	1.19
30	Virginia	1.18
31	Utah	1.17
31	Vermont	1.17
33	Connecticut	1.15
33	Kentucky	1.15
35	Massachusetts	1.12
35	Washington	1.12
37	Oklahoma	1.11
38	Missouri	1.10
38	South Dakota	1.10
40	North Carolina	1.06
41	Tennessee	1.05
42	Georgia	1.04
43	Indiana	0.99
44	West Virginia	0.90
45	Arkansas	0.88
46	Nebraska	0.86
47	South Carolina	0.82
48	North Dakota	0.78
49	Mississippi	0.76
50	Maine	0.73

District of Columbia   2.31

Source: Morgan Quitno Press using data from U.S. Bureau of the Census
     "Government Finances: 1992-1993" (http://www.census.gov)
*Direct expenditures. Includes Courts, Prosecution and Legal Services and Public Defense.

State Government Expenditures for Judicial and Legal Services in 1993

National Total = $6,644,044,000*

ALPHA ORDER

RANK	STATE	EXPENDITURES	% of USA
15	Alabama	$138,543,000	2.09%
23	Alaska	102,749,000	1.55%
31	Arizona	66,923,000	1.01%
42	Arkansas	29,869,000	0.45%
2	California	451,310,000	6.79%
18	Colorado	120,467,000	1.81%
10	Connecticut	181,137,000	2.73%
37	Delaware	47,038,000	0.71%
3	Florida	433,306,000	6.52%
36	Georgia	52,561,000	0.79%
21	Hawaii	110,688,000	1.67%
45	Idaho	26,233,000	0.39%
9	Illinois	195,199,000	2.94%
35	Indiana	53,292,000	0.80%
20	Iowa	113,303,000	1.71%
28	Kansas	84,204,000	1.27%
16	Kentucky	137,559,000	2.07%
24	Louisiana	95,575,000	1.44%
41	Maine	31,500,000	0.47%
8	Maryland	210,868,000	3.17%
4	Massachusetts	307,540,000	4.63%
13	Michigan	153,980,000	2.32%
22	Minnesota	107,892,000	1.62%
46	Mississippi	23,240,000	0.35%
25	Missouri	95,434,000	1.44%
40	Montana	33,702,000	0.51%
43	Nebraska	29,367,000	0.44%
49	Nevada	17,324,000	0.26%
32	New Hampshire	64,922,000	0.98%
7	New Jersey	247,313,000	3.72%
29	New Mexico	76,190,000	1.15%
1	New York	1,014,877,000	15.27%
6	North Carolina	250,746,000	3.77%
50	North Dakota	9,089,000	0.14%
19	Ohio	118,732,000	1.79%
26	Oklahoma	89,993,000	1.35%
14	Oregon	150,638,000	2.27%
11	Pennsylvania	179,558,000	2.70%
30	Rhode Island	72,632,000	1.09%
39	South Carolina	40,200,000	0.61%
48	South Dakota	18,976,000	0.29%
27	Tennessee	88,810,000	1.34%
5	Texas	269,879,000	4.06%
33	Utah	60,369,000	0.91%
44	Vermont	28,907,000	0.44%
12	Virginia	156,007,000	2.35%
34	Washington	56,783,000	0.85%
38	West Virginia	45,495,000	0.68%
17	Wisconsin	132,978,000	2.00%
47	Wyoming	20,147,000	0.30%

RANK ORDER

RANK	STATE	EXPENDITURES	% of USA
1	New York	$1,014,877,000	15.27%
2	California	451,310,000	6.79%
3	Florida	433,306,000	6.52%
4	Massachusetts	307,540,000	4.63%
5	Texas	269,879,000	4.06%
6	North Carolina	250,746,000	3.77%
7	New Jersey	247,313,000	3.72%
8	Maryland	210,868,000	3.17%
9	Illinois	195,199,000	2.94%
10	Connecticut	181,137,000	2.73%
11	Pennsylvania	179,558,000	2.70%
12	Virginia	156,007,000	2.35%
13	Michigan	153,980,000	2.32%
14	Oregon	150,638,000	2.27%
15	Alabama	138,543,000	2.09%
16	Kentucky	137,559,000	2.07%
17	Wisconsin	132,978,000	2.00%
18	Colorado	120,467,000	1.81%
19	Ohio	118,732,000	1.79%
20	Iowa	113,303,000	1.71%
21	Hawaii	110,688,000	1.67%
22	Minnesota	107,892,000	1.62%
23	Alaska	102,749,000	1.55%
24	Louisiana	95,575,000	1.44%
25	Missouri	95,434,000	1.44%
26	Oklahoma	89,993,000	1.35%
27	Tennessee	88,810,000	1.34%
28	Kansas	84,204,000	1.27%
29	New Mexico	76,190,000	1.15%
30	Rhode Island	72,632,000	1.09%
31	Arizona	66,923,000	1.01%
32	New Hampshire	64,922,000	0.98%
33	Utah	60,369,000	0.91%
34	Washington	56,783,000	0.85%
35	Indiana	53,292,000	0.80%
36	Georgia	52,561,000	0.79%
37	Delaware	47,038,000	0.71%
38	West Virginia	45,495,000	0.68%
39	South Carolina	40,200,000	0.61%
40	Montana	33,702,000	0.51%
41	Maine	31,500,000	0.47%
42	Arkansas	29,869,000	0.45%
43	Nebraska	29,367,000	0.44%
44	Vermont	28,907,000	0.44%
45	Idaho	26,233,000	0.39%
46	Mississippi	23,240,000	0.35%
47	Wyoming	20,147,000	0.30%
48	South Dakota	18,976,000	0.29%
49	Nevada	17,324,000	0.26%
50	North Dakota	9,089,000	0.14%
	District of Columbia**	NA	NA

Source: U.S. Bureau of the Census
    "Government Finances: 1992-1993" (http://www.census.gov)
*Direct expenditures. Includes Courts, Prosecution and Legal Services and Public Defense.
**Not applicable.

Per Capita State Government Expenditures for Judicial and Legal Services: 1993

National Per Capita = $25.77*

ALPHA ORDER				RANK ORDER		
RANK	STATE	PER CAPITA		RANK	STATE	PER CAPITA
20	Alabama	$33.14		1	Alaska	$171.82
1	Alaska	171.82		2	Hawaii	94.93
36	Arizona	16.97		3	Rhode Island	72.70
44	Arkansas	12.32		4	Delaware	67.29
41	California	14.46		5	New Hampshire	57.81
18	Colorado	33.76		6	New York	55.91
7	Connecticut	55.26		7	Connecticut	55.26
4	Delaware	67.29		8	Massachusetts	51.10
22	Florida	31.58		9	Vermont	50.19
50	Georgia	7.62		10	Oregon	49.63
2	Hawaii	94.93		11	New Mexico	47.15
31	Idaho	23.83		12	Wyoming	42.87
37	Illinois	16.70		13	Maryland	42.58
48	Indiana	9.34		14	Iowa	40.15
14	Iowa	40.15		15	Montana	40.07
19	Kansas	33.26		16	Kentucky	36.27
16	Kentucky	36.27		17	North Carolina	36.06
32	Louisiana	22.28		18	Colorado	33.76
27	Maine	25.42		19	Kansas	33.26
13	Maryland	42.58		20	Alabama	33.14
8	Massachusetts	51.10		21	Utah	32.46
38	Michigan	16.28		22	Florida	31.58
30	Minnesota	23.85		23	New Jersey	31.47
49	Mississippi	8.81		24	Oklahoma	27.84
33	Missouri	18.23		25	South Dakota	26.47
15	Montana	40.07		26	Wisconsin	26.36
34	Nebraska	18.20		27	Maine	25.42
43	Nevada	12.51		28	West Virginia	25.02
5	New Hampshire	57.81		29	Virginia	24.09
23	New Jersey	31.47		30	Minnesota	23.85
11	New Mexico	47.15		31	Idaho	23.83
6	New York	55.91		32	Louisiana	22.28
17	North Carolina	36.06		33	Missouri	18.23
42	North Dakota	14.27		34	Nebraska	18.20
47	Ohio	10.73		35	Tennessee	17.44
24	Oklahoma	27.84		36	Arizona	16.97
10	Oregon	49.63		37	Illinois	16.70
40	Pennsylvania	14.92		38	Michigan	16.28
3	Rhode Island	72.70		39	Texas	14.95
45	South Carolina	11.08		40	Pennsylvania	14.92
25	South Dakota	26.47		41	California	14.46
35	Tennessee	17.44		42	North Dakota	14.27
39	Texas	14.95		43	Nevada	12.51
21	Utah	32.46		44	Arkansas	12.32
9	Vermont	50.19		45	South Carolina	11.08
29	Virginia	24.09		46	Washington	10.81
46	Washington	10.81		47	Ohio	10.73
28	West Virginia	25.02		48	Indiana	9.34
26	Wisconsin	26.36		49	Mississippi	8.81
12	Wyoming	42.87		50	Georgia	7.62
					District of Columbia**	NA

Source: Morgan Quitno Press using data from U.S. Bureau of the Census
"Government Finances: 1992-1993" (http://www.census.gov)
*Direct expenditures. Includes Courts, Prosecution and Legal Services and Public Defense.
**Not applicable.

State Government Expenditures for Judicial and Legal Services
As a Percent of All Direct Expenditures in 1993
National Percent = 1.26% of Direct Expenditures*

ALPHA ORDER

RANK	STATE	PERCENT
18	Alabama	1.73
2	Alaska	2.37
33	Arizona	1.02
42	Arkansas	0.66
40	California	0.75
14	Colorado	1.91
17	Connecticut	1.74
4	Delaware	2.19
6	Florida	2.08
49	Georgia	0.47
10	Hawaii	2.02
27	Idaho	1.33
38	Illinois	0.93
44	Indiana	0.55
8	Iowa	2.07
8	Kansas	2.07
19	Kentucky	1.71
36	Louisiana	0.95
34	Maine	1.01
12	Maryland	1.95
16	Massachusetts	1.78
39	Michigan	0.80
30	Minnesota	1.14
45	Mississippi	0.54
28	Missouri	1.20
20	Montana	1.68
32	Nebraska	1.05
43	Nevada	0.60
1	New Hampshire	2.50
29	New Jersey	1.19
13	New Mexico	1.94
11	New York	2.01
5	North Carolina	2.18
46	North Dakota	0.53
47	Ohio	0.51
23	Oklahoma	1.50
3	Oregon	2.23
41	Pennsylvania	0.69
6	Rhode Island	2.08
48	South Carolina	0.48
26	South Dakota	1.37
31	Tennessee	1.08
37	Texas	0.94
21	Utah	1.67
15	Vermont	1.87
24	Virginia	1.42
50	Washington	0.41
35	West Virginia	0.96
25	Wisconsin	1.38
22	Wyoming	1.61

RANK ORDER

RANK	STATE	PERCENT
1	New Hampshire	2.50
2	Alaska	2.37
3	Oregon	2.23
4	Delaware	2.19
5	North Carolina	2.18
6	Florida	2.08
6	Rhode Island	2.08
8	Iowa	2.07
8	Kansas	2.07
10	Hawaii	2.02
11	New York	2.01
12	Maryland	1.95
13	New Mexico	1.94
14	Colorado	1.91
15	Vermont	1.87
16	Massachusetts	1.78
17	Connecticut	1.74
18	Alabama	1.73
19	Kentucky	1.71
20	Montana	1.68
21	Utah	1.67
22	Wyoming	1.61
23	Oklahoma	1.50
24	Virginia	1.42
25	Wisconsin	1.38
26	South Dakota	1.37
27	Idaho	1.33
28	Missouri	1.20
29	New Jersey	1.19
30	Minnesota	1.14
31	Tennessee	1.08
32	Nebraska	1.05
33	Arizona	1.02
34	Maine	1.01
35	West Virginia	0.96
36	Louisiana	0.95
37	Texas	0.94
38	Illinois	0.93
39	Michigan	0.80
40	California	0.75
41	Pennsylvania	0.69
42	Arkansas	0.66
43	Nevada	0.60
44	Indiana	0.55
45	Mississippi	0.54
46	North Dakota	0.53
47	Ohio	0.51
48	South Carolina	0.48
49	Georgia	0.47
50	Washington	0.41
	District of Columbia**	NA

Source: Morgan Quitno Press using data from U.S. Bureau of the Census
"Government Finances: 1992-1993" (http://www.census.gov)
*Direct expenditures. Includes Courts, Prosecution and Legal Services and Public Defense.
**Not applicable.

Local Government Expenditures for Judicial and Legal Services in 1993

National Total = $10,309,840,000*

ALPHA ORDER

ALPHA ORDER / RANK ORDER

RANK	STATE	EXPENDITURES	% of USA	RANK	STATE	EXPENDITURES	% of USA
25	Alabama	$60,611,000	0.59%	1	California	$2,819,148,000	27.34%
46	Alaska	8,281,000	0.08%	2	New York	729,591,000	7.08%
11	Arizona	252,789,000	2.45%	3	Texas	650,206,000	6.31%
31	Arkansas	40,890,000	0.40%	4	Florida	604,979,000	5.87%
1	California	2,819,148,000	27.34%	5	Ohio	593,316,000	5.75%
21	Colorado	96,682,000	0.94%	6	Pennsylvania	534,636,000	5.19%
37	Connecticut	27,462,000	0.27%	7	Michigan	475,463,000	4.61%
49	Delaware	7,056,000	0.07%	8	Illinois	429,216,000	4.16%
4	Florida	604,979,000	5.87%	9	New Jersey	384,714,000	3.73%
12	Georgia	240,959,000	2.34%	10	Washington	290,610,000	2.82%
35	Hawaii	30,442,000	0.30%	11	Arizona	252,789,000	2.45%
38	Idaho	27,153,000	0.26%	12	Georgia	240,959,000	2.34%
8	Illinois	429,216,000	4.16%	13	Minnesota	181,308,000	1.76%
15	Indiana	161,907,000	1.57%	14	Wisconsin	169,834,000	1.65%
29	Iowa	42,627,000	0.41%	15	Indiana	161,907,000	1.57%
27	Kansas	48,109,000	0.47%	16	Virginia	133,811,000	1.30%
39	Kentucky	24,849,000	0.24%	17	Louisiana	130,164,000	1.26%
17	Louisiana	130,164,000	1.26%	18	Maryland	126,112,000	1.22%
47	Maine	7,528,000	0.07%	19	Tennessee	125,518,000	1.22%
18	Maryland	126,112,000	1.22%	20	Nevada	109,528,000	1.06%
26	Massachusetts	48,504,000	0.47%	21	Colorado	96,682,000	0.94%
7	Michigan	475,463,000	4.61%	22	Missouri	95,545,000	0.93%
13	Minnesota	181,308,000	1.76%	23	South Carolina	81,308,000	0.79%
28	Mississippi	45,704,000	0.44%	24	Oregon	60,622,000	0.59%
22	Missouri	95,545,000	0.93%	25	Alabama	60,611,000	0.59%
36	Montana	29,424,000	0.29%	26	Massachusetts	48,504,000	0.47%
33	Nebraska	36,309,000	0.35%	27	Kansas	48,109,000	0.47%
20	Nevada	109,528,000	1.06%	28	Mississippi	45,704,000	0.44%
43	New Hampshire	12,392,000	0.12%	29	Iowa	42,627,000	0.41%
9	New Jersey	384,714,000	3.73%	30	Oklahoma	42,470,000	0.41%
45	New Mexico	9,603,000	0.09%	31	Arkansas	40,890,000	0.40%
2	New York	729,591,000	7.08%	32	North Carolina	39,625,000	0.38%
32	North Carolina	39,625,000	0.38%	33	Nebraska	36,309,000	0.35%
42	North Dakota	12,999,000	0.13%	34	Utah	31,169,000	0.30%
5	Ohio	593,316,000	5.75%	35	Hawaii	30,442,000	0.30%
30	Oklahoma	42,470,000	0.41%	36	Montana	29,424,000	0.29%
24	Oregon	60,622,000	0.59%	37	Connecticut	27,462,000	0.27%
6	Pennsylvania	534,636,000	5.19%	38	Idaho	27,153,000	0.26%
48	Rhode Island	7,075,000	0.07%	39	Kentucky	24,849,000	0.24%
23	South Carolina	81,308,000	0.79%	40	West Virginia	22,791,000	0.22%
44	South Dakota	9,887,000	0.10%	41	Wyoming	15,651,000	0.15%
19	Tennessee	125,518,000	1.22%	42	North Dakota	12,999,000	0.13%
3	Texas	650,206,000	6.31%	43	New Hampshire	12,392,000	0.12%
34	Utah	31,169,000	0.30%	44	South Dakota	9,887,000	0.10%
50	Vermont	1,306,000	0.01%	45	New Mexico	9,603,000	0.09%
16	Virginia	133,811,000	1.30%	46	Alaska	8,281,000	0.08%
10	Washington	290,610,000	2.82%	47	Maine	7,528,000	0.07%
40	West Virginia	22,791,000	0.22%	48	Rhode Island	7,075,000	0.07%
14	Wisconsin	169,834,000	1.65%	49	Delaware	7,056,000	0.07%
41	Wyoming	15,651,000	0.15%	50	Vermont	1,306,000	0.01%
					District of Columbia	141,957,000	1.38%

Source: U.S. Bureau of the Census
   "Government Finances: 1992-1993" (http://www.census.gov)
*Direct expenditures. Includes Courts, Prosecution and Legal Services and Public Defense.

Per Capita Local Government Expenditures for Judicial & Legal Services: 1993

National Per Capita = $39.99*

ALPHA ORDER			RANK ORDER		
RANK	STATE	PER CAPITA	RANK	STATE	PER CAPITA
36	Alabama	$14.50	1	California	$90.30
37	Alaska	13.85	2	Nevada	79.08
3	Arizona	64.09	3	Arizona	64.09
33	Arkansas	16.86	4	Washington	55.30
1	California	90.30	5	Ohio	53.64
20	Colorado	27.10	6	Michigan	50.28
43	Connecticut	8.38	7	New Jersey	48.95
42	Delaware	10.09	8	Pennsylvania	44.44
9	Florida	44.09	9	Florida	44.09
15	Georgia	34.92	10	New York	40.19
21	Hawaii	26.11	11	Minnesota	40.08
23	Idaho	24.66	12	Illinois	36.72
12	Illinois	36.72	13	Texas	36.02
19	Indiana	28.37	14	Montana	34.99
35	Iowa	15.11	15	Georgia	34.92
30	Kansas	19.00	16	Wisconsin	33.67
46	Kentucky	6.55	17	Wyoming	33.30
18	Louisiana	30.35	18	Louisiana	30.35
47	Maine	6.08	19	Indiana	28.37
22	Maryland	25.47	20	Colorado	27.10
44	Massachusetts	8.06	21	Hawaii	26.11
6	Michigan	50.28	22	Maryland	25.47
11	Minnesota	40.08	23	Idaho	24.66
32	Mississippi	17.32	24	Tennessee	24.65
31	Missouri	18.25	25	Nebraska	22.50
14	Montana	34.99	26	South Carolina	22.42
25	Nebraska	22.50	27	Virginia	20.67
2	Nevada	79.08	28	North Dakota	20.41
41	New Hampshire	11.03	29	Oregon	19.97
7	New Jersey	48.95	30	Kansas	19.00
48	New Mexico	5.94	31	Missouri	18.25
10	New York	40.19	32	Mississippi	17.32
49	North Carolina	5.70	33	Arkansas	16.86
28	North Dakota	20.41	34	Utah	16.76
5	Ohio	53.64	35	Iowa	15.11
39	Oklahoma	13.14	36	Alabama	14.50
29	Oregon	19.97	37	Alaska	13.85
8	Pennsylvania	44.44	38	South Dakota	13.79
45	Rhode Island	7.08	39	Oklahoma	13.14
26	South Carolina	22.42	40	West Virginia	12.54
38	South Dakota	13.79	41	New Hampshire	11.03
24	Tennessee	24.65	42	Delaware	10.09
13	Texas	36.02	43	Connecticut	8.38
34	Utah	16.76	44	Massachusetts	8.06
50	Vermont	2.27	45	Rhode Island	7.08
27	Virginia	20.67	46	Kentucky	6.55
4	Washington	55.30	47	Maine	6.08
40	West Virginia	12.54	48	New Mexico	5.94
16	Wisconsin	33.67	49	North Carolina	5.70
17	Wyoming	33.30	50	Vermont	2.27
				District of Columbia	245.60

Source: Morgan Quitno Press using data from U.S. Bureau of the Census
    "Government Finances: 1992-1993" (http://www.census.gov)
*Direct expenditures. Includes Courts, Prosecution and Legal Services and Public Defense.

Local Government Expenditures for Judicial and Legal Services As a Percent of All Direct Expenditures in 1993
National Percent = 1.52% of Direct Expenditures*

ALPHA ORDER

RANK ORDER

RANK	STATE	PERCENT		RANK	STATE	PERCENT
35	Alabama	0.76		1	Nevada	2.86
46	Alaska	0.33		2	California	2.67
3	Arizona	2.44		3	Arizona	2.44
22	Arkansas	1.17		4	Ohio	2.38
2	California	2.67		5	Montana	2.11
30	Colorado	0.91		6	Michigan	2.03
44	Connecticut	0.35		7	Pennsylvania	1.92
41	Delaware	0.55		8	Hawaii	1.83
11	Florida	1.66		9	New Jersey	1.82
15	Georgia	1.41		10	Washington	1.67
8	Hawaii	1.83		11	Florida	1.66
15	Idaho	1.41		12	Louisiana	1.55
14	Illinois	1.46		13	Texas	1.51
17	Indiana	1.34		14	Illinois	1.46
39	Iowa	0.65		15	Georgia	1.41
32	Kansas	0.79		15	Idaho	1.41
42	Kentucky	0.41		17	Indiana	1.34
12	Louisiana	1.55		18	South Carolina	1.24
46	Maine	0.33		19	Minnesota	1.23
20	Maryland	1.21		20	Maryland	1.21
45	Massachusetts	0.34		20	Wisconsin	1.21
6	Michigan	2.03		22	Arkansas	1.17
19	Minnesota	1.23		23	North Dakota	1.15
28	Mississippi	0.95		24	Wyoming	1.08
26	Missouri	1.02		25	Tennessee	1.03
5	Montana	2.11		26	Missouri	1.02
36	Nebraska	0.75		27	Virginia	0.99
1	Nevada	2.86		28	Mississippi	0.95
40	New Hampshire	0.61		29	New York	0.93
9	New Jersey	1.82		30	Colorado	0.91
48	New Mexico	0.30		31	West Virginia	0.80
29	New York	0.93		32	Kansas	0.79
49	North Carolina	0.25		32	South Dakota	0.79
23	North Dakota	1.15		34	Oregon	0.78
4	Ohio	2.38		35	Alabama	0.76
38	Oklahoma	0.72		36	Nebraska	0.75
34	Oregon	0.78		37	Utah	0.74
7	Pennsylvania	1.92		38	Oklahoma	0.72
42	Rhode Island	0.41		39	Iowa	0.65
18	South Carolina	1.24		40	New Hampshire	0.61
32	South Dakota	0.79		41	Delaware	0.55
25	Tennessee	1.03		42	Kentucky	0.41
13	Texas	1.51		42	Rhode Island	0.41
37	Utah	0.74		44	Connecticut	0.35
50	Vermont	0.13		45	Massachusetts	0.34
27	Virginia	0.99		46	Alaska	0.33
10	Washington	1.67		46	Maine	0.33
31	West Virginia	0.80		48	New Mexico	0.30
20	Wisconsin	1.21		49	North Carolina	0.25
24	Wyoming	1.08		50	Vermont	0.13
					District of Columbia	2.31

Source: Morgan Quitno Press using data from U.S. Bureau of the Census
    "Government Finances: 1992-1993" (http://www.census.gov)
*Direct expenditures. Includes Courts, Prosecution and Legal Services and Public Defense.

State and Local Government Judicial and Legal Payroll in 1992

National Total = $832,108,000*

ALPHA ORDER

RANK	STATE	PAYROLL	% of USA
25	Alabama	$9,508,000	1.14%
35	Alaska	4,423,000	0.53%
12	Arizona	17,024,000	2.05%
40	Arkansas	3,418,000	0.41%
1	California	133,094,000	15.99%
19	Colorado	12,953,000	1.56%
23	Connecticut	10,709,000	1.29%
39	Delaware	3,450,000	0.41%
3	Florida	48,121,000	5.78%
13	Georgia	16,311,000	1.96%
28	Hawaii	7,932,000	0.95%
43	Idaho	2,776,000	0.33%
6	Illinois	34,995,000	4.21%
24	Indiana	10,016,000	1.20%
29	Iowa	7,599,000	0.91%
31	Kansas	6,630,000	0.80%
27	Kentucky	8,737,000	1.05%
21	Louisiana	11,300,000	1.36%
45	Maine	1,893,000	0.23%
10	Maryland	18,067,000	2.17%
14	Massachusetts	15,867,000	1.91%
9	Michigan	28,990,000	3.48%
17	Minnesota	13,450,000	1.62%
36	Mississippi	4,300,000	0.52%
20	Missouri	11,513,000	1.38%
47	Montana	1,674,000	0.20%
38	Nebraska	3,644,000	0.44%
32	Nevada	6,612,000	0.79%
44	New Hampshire	2,296,000	0.28%
4	New Jersey	46,455,000	5.58%
34	New Mexico	4,729,000	0.57%
2	New York	96,616,000	11.61%
16	North Carolina	14,009,000	1.68%
48	North Dakota	1,645,000	0.20%
7	Ohio	34,683,000	4.17%
30	Oklahoma	6,664,000	0.80%
26	Oregon	9,088,000	1.09%
8	Pennsylvania	34,513,000	4.15%
41	Rhode Island	3,122,000	0.38%
33	South Carolina	5,813,000	0.70%
46	South Dakota	1,715,000	0.21%
22	Tennessee	10,756,000	1.29%
5	Texas	43,180,000	5.19%
37	Utah	4,288,000	0.52%
50	Vermont	1,460,000	0.18%
15	Virginia	14,796,000	1.78%
11	Washington	17,601,000	2.12%
42	West Virginia	3,111,000	0.37%
18	Wisconsin	13,072,000	1.57%
49	Wyoming	1,574,000	0.19%

RANK ORDER

RANK	STATE	PAYROLL	% of USA
1	California	$133,094,000	15.99%
2	New York	96,616,000	11.61%
3	Florida	48,121,000	5.78%
4	New Jersey	46,455,000	5.58%
5	Texas	43,180,000	5.19%
6	Illinois	34,995,000	4.21%
7	Ohio	34,683,000	4.17%
8	Pennsylvania	34,513,000	4.15%
9	Michigan	28,990,000	3.48%
10	Maryland	18,067,000	2.17%
11	Washington	17,601,000	2.12%
12	Arizona	17,024,000	2.05%
13	Georgia	16,311,000	1.96%
14	Massachusetts	15,867,000	1.91%
15	Virginia	14,796,000	1.78%
16	North Carolina	14,009,000	1.68%
17	Minnesota	13,450,000	1.62%
18	Wisconsin	13,072,000	1.57%
19	Colorado	12,953,000	1.56%
20	Missouri	11,513,000	1.38%
21	Louisiana	11,300,000	1.36%
22	Tennessee	10,756,000	1.29%
23	Connecticut	10,709,000	1.29%
24	Indiana	10,016,000	1.20%
25	Alabama	9,508,000	1.14%
26	Oregon	9,088,000	1.09%
27	Kentucky	8,737,000	1.05%
28	Hawaii	7,932,000	0.95%
29	Iowa	7,599,000	0.91%
30	Oklahoma	6,664,000	0.80%
31	Kansas	6,630,000	0.80%
32	Nevada	6,612,000	0.79%
33	South Carolina	5,813,000	0.70%
34	New Mexico	4,729,000	0.57%
35	Alaska	4,423,000	0.53%
36	Mississippi	4,300,000	0.52%
37	Utah	4,288,000	0.52%
38	Nebraska	3,644,000	0.44%
39	Delaware	3,450,000	0.41%
40	Arkansas	3,418,000	0.41%
41	Rhode Island	3,122,000	0.38%
42	West Virginia	3,111,000	0.37%
43	Idaho	2,776,000	0.33%
44	New Hampshire	2,296,000	0.28%
45	Maine	1,893,000	0.23%
46	South Dakota	1,715,000	0.21%
47	Montana	1,674,000	0.20%
48	North Dakota	1,645,000	0.20%
49	Wyoming	1,574,000	0.19%
50	Vermont	1,460,000	0.18%
	District of Columbia	5,914,000	0.71%

Source: U.S. Bureau of the Census
   "Public Employment: 1992" (September 1994, GE/92-1)
*Includes court and court related activities (except probation and parole which are part of corrections), court activities of sheriff's offices, prosecuting attorneys' and public defenders' offices, legal departments and attorneys providing governmentwide legal service.

State and Local Government Police Protection Payroll in 1992

National Total = $2,061,157,000*

RANK	STATE	PAYROLL	% of USA
24	Alabama	$23,009,000	1.12%
42	Alaska	6,225,000	0.30%
18	Arizona	32,647,000	1.58%
35	Arkansas	10,006,000	0.49%
1	California	326,715,000	15.85%
23	Colorado	26,053,000	1.26%
19	Connecticut	31,041,000	1.51%
45	Delaware	5,503,000	0.27%
3	Florida	127,130,000	6.17%
13	Georgia	39,849,000	1.93%
33	Hawaii	11,857,000	0.58%
43	Idaho	6,172,000	0.30%
4	Illinois	120,889,000	5.87%
20	Indiana	27,941,000	1.36%
31	Iowa	15,168,000	0.74%
30	Kansas	15,687,000	0.76%
29	Kentucky	16,189,000	0.79%
25	Louisiana	22,383,000	1.09%
41	Maine	6,719,000	0.33%
11	Maryland	43,439,000	2.11%
10	Massachusetts	55,287,000	2.68%
9	Michigan	63,433,000	3.08%
21	Minnesota	27,538,000	1.34%
34	Mississippi	10,345,000	0.50%
17	Missouri	33,626,000	1.63%
46	Montana	4,137,000	0.20%
36	Nebraska	9,551,000	0.46%
32	Nevada	14,535,000	0.71%
40	New Hampshire	8,007,000	0.39%
6	New Jersey	101,253,000	4.91%
37	New Mexico	9,420,000	0.46%
2	New York	254,441,000	12.34%
14	North Carolina	38,070,000	1.85%
50	North Dakota	2,702,000	0.13%
8	Ohio	72,250,000	3.51%
27	Oklahoma	18,103,000	0.88%
26	Oregon	19,653,000	0.95%
7	Pennsylvania	82,363,000	4.00%
39	Rhode Island	8,102,000	0.39%
28	South Carolina	17,574,000	0.85%
49	South Dakota	3,000,000	0.15%
22	Tennessee	26,083,000	1.27%
5	Texas	117,654,000	5.71%
38	Utah	9,010,000	0.44%
48	Vermont	3,266,000	0.16%
12	Virginia	40,527,000	1.97%
15	Washington	35,917,000	1.74%
44	West Virginia	5,848,000	0.28%
16	Wisconsin	34,881,000	1.69%
47	Wyoming	3,325,000	0.16%

RANK	STATE	PAYROLL	% of USA
1	California	$326,715,000	15.85%
2	New York	254,441,000	12.34%
3	Florida	127,130,000	6.17%
4	Illinois	120,889,000	5.87%
5	Texas	117,654,000	5.71%
6	New Jersey	101,253,000	4.91%
7	Pennsylvania	82,363,000	4.00%
8	Ohio	72,250,000	3.51%
9	Michigan	63,433,000	3.08%
10	Massachusetts	55,287,000	2.68%
11	Maryland	43,439,000	2.11%
12	Virginia	40,527,000	1.97%
13	Georgia	39,849,000	1.93%
14	North Carolina	38,070,000	1.85%
15	Washington	35,917,000	1.74%
16	Wisconsin	34,881,000	1.69%
17	Missouri	33,626,000	1.63%
18	Arizona	32,647,000	1.58%
19	Connecticut	31,041,000	1.51%
20	Indiana	27,941,000	1.36%
21	Minnesota	27,538,000	1.34%
22	Tennessee	26,083,000	1.27%
23	Colorado	26,053,000	1.26%
24	Alabama	23,009,000	1.12%
25	Louisiana	22,383,000	1.09%
26	Oregon	19,653,000	0.95%
27	Oklahoma	18,103,000	0.88%
28	South Carolina	17,574,000	0.85%
29	Kentucky	16,189,000	0.79%
30	Kansas	15,687,000	0.76%
31	Iowa	15,168,000	0.74%
32	Nevada	14,535,000	0.71%
33	Hawaii	11,857,000	0.58%
34	Mississippi	10,345,000	0.50%
35	Arkansas	10,006,000	0.49%
36	Nebraska	9,551,000	0.46%
37	New Mexico	9,420,000	0.46%
38	Utah	9,010,000	0.44%
39	Rhode Island	8,102,000	0.39%
40	New Hampshire	8,007,000	0.39%
41	Maine	6,719,000	0.33%
42	Alaska	6,225,000	0.30%
43	Idaho	6,172,000	0.30%
44	West Virginia	5,848,000	0.28%
45	Delaware	5,503,000	0.27%
46	Montana	4,137,000	0.20%
47	Wyoming	3,325,000	0.16%
48	Vermont	3,266,000	0.16%
49	South Dakota	3,000,000	0.15%
50	North Dakota	2,702,000	0.13%
	District of Columbia	16,635,000	0.81%

Source: U.S. Bureau of the Census
    "Public Employment: 1992" (September 1994, GE/92-1)
*All activities concerned with the enforcement of law and order, including coroner's offices, police training academies, investigation bureaus and local jails.

State and Local Government Corrections Payroll in 1992

National Total = $1,307,814,000*

ALPHA ORDER

RANK ORDER

RANK	STATE	PAYROLL	% of USA	RANK	STATE	PAYROLL	% of USA
28	Alabama	$11,992,000	0.92%	1	California	$205,551,000	15.72%
39	Alaska	4,672,000	0.36%	2	New York	192,737,000	14.74%
16	Arizona	20,516,000	1.57%	3	Texas	89,725,000	6.86%
34	Arkansas	6,124,000	0.47%	4	Florida	85,184,000	6.51%
1	California	205,551,000	15.72%	5	Michigan	57,333,000	4.38%
22	Colorado	16,041,000	1.23%	6	New Jersey	52,508,000	4.01%
18	Connecticut	18,123,000	1.39%	7	Illinois	47,493,000	3.63%
42	Delaware	3,685,000	0.28%	8	Pennsylvania	43,444,000	3.32%
4	Florida	85,184,000	6.51%	9	Ohio	39,925,000	3.05%
11	Georgia	28,857,000	2.21%	10	North Carolina	29,753,000	2.28%
40	Hawaii	4,581,000	0.35%	11	Georgia	28,857,000	2.21%
44	Idaho	3,242,000	0.25%	12	Virginia	27,844,000	2.13%
7	Illinois	47,493,000	3.63%	13	Maryland	27,579,000	2.11%
21	Indiana	16,862,000	1.29%	14	Massachusetts	25,706,000	1.97%
33	Iowa	6,714,000	0.51%	15	Washington	23,257,000	1.78%
29	Kansas	10,861,000	0.83%	16	Arizona	20,516,000	1.57%
27	Kentucky	12,154,000	0.93%	17	Tennessee	19,496,000	1.49%
19	Louisiana	18,092,000	1.38%	18	Connecticut	18,123,000	1.39%
41	Maine	3,983,000	0.30%	19	Louisiana	18,092,000	1.38%
13	Maryland	27,579,000	2.11%	20	Wisconsin	17,361,000	1.33%
14	Massachusetts	25,706,000	1.97%	21	Indiana	16,862,000	1.29%
5	Michigan	57,333,000	4.38%	22	Colorado	16,041,000	1.23%
23	Minnesota	15,430,000	1.18%	23	Minnesota	15,430,000	1.18%
37	Mississippi	5,236,000	0.40%	24	South Carolina	15,220,000	1.16%
25	Missouri	14,761,000	1.13%	25	Missouri	14,761,000	1.13%
45	Montana	2,464,000	0.19%	26	Oregon	13,810,000	1.06%
38	Nebraska	4,781,000	0.37%	27	Kentucky	12,154,000	0.93%
30	Nevada	10,324,000	0.79%	28	Alabama	11,992,000	0.92%
43	New Hampshire	3,452,000	0.26%	29	Kansas	10,861,000	0.83%
6	New Jersey	52,508,000	4.01%	30	Nevada	10,324,000	0.79%
32	New Mexico	7,085,000	0.54%	31	Oklahoma	9,605,000	0.73%
2	New York	192,737,000	14.74%	32	New Mexico	7,085,000	0.54%
10	North Carolina	29,753,000	2.28%	33	Iowa	6,714,000	0.51%
50	North Dakota	1,249,000	0.10%	34	Arkansas	6,124,000	0.47%
9	Ohio	39,925,000	3.05%	35	Rhode Island	5,973,000	0.46%
31	Oklahoma	9,605,000	0.73%	36	Utah	5,792,000	0.44%
26	Oregon	13,810,000	1.06%	37	Mississippi	5,236,000	0.40%
8	Pennsylvania	43,444,000	3.32%	38	Nebraska	4,781,000	0.37%
35	Rhode Island	5,973,000	0.46%	39	Alaska	4,672,000	0.36%
24	South Carolina	15,220,000	1.16%	40	Hawaii	4,581,000	0.35%
48	South Dakota	1,436,000	0.11%	41	Maine	3,983,000	0.30%
17	Tennessee	19,496,000	1.49%	42	Delaware	3,685,000	0.28%
3	Texas	89,725,000	6.86%	43	New Hampshire	3,452,000	0.26%
36	Utah	5,792,000	0.44%	44	Idaho	3,242,000	0.25%
47	Vermont	1,643,000	0.13%	45	Montana	2,464,000	0.19%
12	Virginia	27,844,000	2.13%	46	West Virginia	1,932,000	0.15%
15	Washington	23,257,000	1.78%	47	Vermont	1,643,000	0.13%
46	West Virginia	1,932,000	0.15%	48	South Dakota	1,436,000	0.11%
20	Wisconsin	17,361,000	1.33%	49	Wyoming	1,344,000	0.10%
49	Wyoming	1,344,000	0.10%	50	North Dakota	1,249,000	0.10%
					District of Columbia	14,884,000	1.14%

Source: U.S. Bureau of the Census
    "Public Employment: 1992" (September 1994, GE/92-1)
All activities pertaining to the confinement and correction of adults and minors accused or convicted of criminal offenses. Includes any pardon, probation or parole activity.

Base Salary for Justices of States' Highest Courts in 1995

National Average = $91,093

<table>
<tr><td colspan="3">ALPHA ORDER</td><td colspan="3">RANK ORDER</td></tr>
<tr><th>RANK</th><th>STATE</th><th>SALARY</th><th>RANK</th><th>STATE</th><th>SALARY</th></tr>
<tr><td>3</td><td>Alabama</td><td>$115,695</td><td>1</td><td>California</td><td>$131,085</td></tr>
<tr><td>14</td><td>Alaska</td><td>104,472</td><td>2</td><td>New York</td><td>125,000</td></tr>
<tr><td>21</td><td>Arizona</td><td>96,314</td><td>3</td><td>Alabama</td><td>115,695</td></tr>
<tr><td>26</td><td>Arkansas</td><td>95,216</td><td>4</td><td>New Jersey</td><td>115,000</td></tr>
<tr><td>1</td><td>California</td><td>131,085</td><td>5</td><td>Illinois</td><td>112,124</td></tr>
<tr><td>40</td><td>Colorado</td><td>84,000</td><td>6</td><td>Michigan</td><td>111,941</td></tr>
<tr><td>12</td><td>Connecticut</td><td>106,533</td><td>7</td><td>Pennsylvania</td><td>110,963</td></tr>
<tr><td>10</td><td>Delaware</td><td>108,300</td><td>8</td><td>Florida</td><td>109,664</td></tr>
<tr><td>8</td><td>Florida</td><td>109,664</td><td>9</td><td>Georgia</td><td>109,459</td></tr>
<tr><td>9</td><td>Georgia</td><td>109,459</td><td>10</td><td>Delaware</td><td>108,300</td></tr>
<tr><td>31</td><td>Hawaii</td><td>93,780</td><td>11</td><td>Washington</td><td>107,200</td></tr>
<tr><td>46</td><td>Idaho</td><td>79,183</td><td>12</td><td>Connecticut</td><td>106,533</td></tr>
<tr><td>5</td><td>Illinois</td><td>112,124</td><td>13</td><td>Virginia</td><td>105,111</td></tr>
<tr><td>44</td><td>Indiana</td><td>81,000</td><td>14</td><td>Alaska</td><td>104,472</td></tr>
<tr><td>30</td><td>Iowa</td><td>93,900</td><td>15</td><td>Rhode Island</td><td>104,403</td></tr>
<tr><td>35</td><td>Kansas</td><td>87,876</td><td>16</td><td>Maryland</td><td>102,000</td></tr>
<tr><td>41</td><td>Kentucky</td><td>83,752</td><td>17</td><td>Ohio</td><td>101,150</td></tr>
<tr><td>29</td><td>Louisiana</td><td>94,300</td><td>18</td><td>Tennessee</td><td>99,240</td></tr>
<tr><td>43</td><td>Maine</td><td>83,616</td><td>19</td><td>Wisconsin</td><td>97,756</td></tr>
<tr><td>16</td><td>Maryland</td><td>102,000</td><td>20</td><td>South Carolina</td><td>97,040</td></tr>
<tr><td>24</td><td>Massachusetts</td><td>95,808</td><td>21</td><td>Arizona</td><td>96,314</td></tr>
<tr><td>6</td><td>Michigan</td><td>111,941</td><td>22</td><td>North Carolina</td><td>96,000</td></tr>
<tr><td>28</td><td>Minnesota</td><td>94,395</td><td>23</td><td>Missouri</td><td>95,897</td></tr>
<tr><td>33</td><td>Mississippi</td><td>90,800</td><td>24</td><td>Massachusetts</td><td>95,808</td></tr>
<tr><td>23</td><td>Missouri</td><td>95,897</td><td>25</td><td>New Hampshire</td><td>95,623</td></tr>
<tr><td>50</td><td>Montana</td><td>64,452</td><td>26</td><td>Arkansas</td><td>95,216</td></tr>
<tr><td>34</td><td>Nebraska</td><td>88,157</td><td>27</td><td>Texas</td><td>94,686</td></tr>
<tr><td>37</td><td>Nevada</td><td>85,000</td><td>28</td><td>Minnesota</td><td>94,395</td></tr>
<tr><td>25</td><td>New Hampshire</td><td>95,623</td><td>29</td><td>Louisiana</td><td>94,300</td></tr>
<tr><td>4</td><td>New Jersey</td><td>115,000</td><td>30</td><td>Iowa</td><td>93,900</td></tr>
<tr><td>45</td><td>New Mexico</td><td>79,567</td><td>31</td><td>Hawaii</td><td>93,780</td></tr>
<tr><td>2</td><td>New York</td><td>125,000</td><td>32</td><td>Utah</td><td>92,000</td></tr>
<tr><td>22</td><td>North Carolina</td><td>96,000</td><td>33</td><td>Mississippi</td><td>90,800</td></tr>
<tr><td>49</td><td>North Dakota</td><td>71,555</td><td>34</td><td>Nebraska</td><td>88,157</td></tr>
<tr><td>17</td><td>Ohio</td><td>101,150</td><td>35</td><td>Kansas</td><td>87,876</td></tr>
<tr><td>36</td><td>Oklahoma</td><td>87,700</td><td>36</td><td>Oklahoma</td><td>87,700</td></tr>
<tr><td>42</td><td>Oregon</td><td>83,700</td><td>37</td><td>Nevada</td><td>85,000</td></tr>
<tr><td>7</td><td>Pennsylvania</td><td>110,963</td><td>37</td><td>West Virginia</td><td>85,000</td></tr>
<tr><td>15</td><td>Rhode Island</td><td>104,403</td><td>37</td><td>Wyoming</td><td>85,000</td></tr>
<tr><td>20</td><td>South Carolina</td><td>97,040</td><td>40</td><td>Colorado</td><td>84,000</td></tr>
<tr><td>48</td><td>South Dakota</td><td>74,241</td><td>41</td><td>Kentucky</td><td>83,752</td></tr>
<tr><td>18</td><td>Tennessee</td><td>99,240</td><td>42</td><td>Oregon</td><td>83,700</td></tr>
<tr><td>27</td><td>Texas</td><td>94,686</td><td>43</td><td>Maine</td><td>83,616</td></tr>
<tr><td>32</td><td>Utah</td><td>92,000</td><td>44</td><td>Indiana</td><td>81,000</td></tr>
<tr><td>47</td><td>Vermont</td><td>76,365</td><td>45</td><td>New Mexico</td><td>79,567</td></tr>
<tr><td>13</td><td>Virginia</td><td>105,111</td><td>46</td><td>Idaho</td><td>79,183</td></tr>
<tr><td>11</td><td>Washington</td><td>107,200</td><td>47</td><td>Vermont</td><td>76,365</td></tr>
<tr><td>37</td><td>West Virginia</td><td>85,000</td><td>48</td><td>South Dakota</td><td>74,241</td></tr>
<tr><td>19</td><td>Wisconsin</td><td>97,756</td><td>49</td><td>North Dakota</td><td>71,555</td></tr>
<tr><td>37</td><td>Wyoming</td><td>85,000</td><td>50</td><td>Montana</td><td>64,452</td></tr>
<tr><td></td><td></td><td></td><td></td><td>District of Columbia</td><td>141,700</td></tr>
</table>

Source: National Center for State Courts
"Survey of Judicial Salaries-Winter 1995" (State Court Report, Winter 1995, Volume 1, Number 2)

Base Salary of Judges of Intermediate Appellate Courts in 1995

National Average = $93,970

ALPHA ORDER

RANK	STATE	SALARY
3	Alabama	$114,615
13	Alaska	98,688
17	Arizona	94,021
18	Arkansas	92,205
1	California	122,893
34	Colorado	79,500
12	Connecticut	99,077
NA	Delaware*	NA
9	Florida	104,181
4	Georgia	108,765
24	Hawaii	89,780
37	Idaho	78,183
8	Illinois	105,528
38	Indiana	76,500
22	Iowa	90,300
30	Kansas	84,739
33	Kentucky	80,333
26	Louisiana	89,300
NA	Maine*	NA
14	Maryland	95,300
28	Massachusetts	88,730
6	Michigan	107,463
27	Minnesota	88,945
31	Mississippi	84,000
25	Missouri	89,558
NA	Montana*	NA
32	Nebraska	83,749
NA	Nevada*	NA
NA	New Hampshire*	NA
5	New Jersey	108,000
39	New Mexico	75,589
2	New York	115,500
21	North Carolina	92,000
40	North Dakota	67,551
16	Ohio	94,200
35	Oklahoma	78,660
36	Oregon	78,600
7	Pennsylvania	107,264
NA	Rhode Island*	NA
19	South Carolina	92,190
NA	South Dakota*	NA
15	Tennessee	94,620
23	Texas	89,952
29	Utah	87,850
NA	Vermont*	NA
11	Virginia	99,760
10	Washington	101,900
NA	West Virginia*	NA
20	Wisconsin	92,041
NA	Wyoming*	NA

RANK ORDER

RANK	STATE	SALARY
1	California	$122,893
2	New York	115,500
3	Alabama	114,615
4	Georgia	108,765
5	New Jersey	108,000
6	Michigan	107,463
7	Pennsylvania	107,264
8	Illinois	105,528
9	Florida	104,181
10	Washington	101,900
11	Virginia	99,760
12	Connecticut	99,077
13	Alaska	98,688
14	Maryland	95,300
15	Tennessee	94,620
16	Ohio	94,200
17	Arizona	94,021
18	Arkansas	92,205
19	South Carolina	92,190
20	Wisconsin	92,041
21	North Carolina	92,000
22	Iowa	90,300
23	Texas	89,952
24	Hawaii	89,780
25	Missouri	89,558
26	Louisiana	89,300
27	Minnesota	88,945
28	Massachusetts	88,730
29	Utah	87,850
30	Kansas	84,739
31	Mississippi	84,000
32	Nebraska	83,749
33	Kentucky	80,333
34	Colorado	79,500
35	Oklahoma	78,660
36	Oregon	78,600
37	Idaho	78,183
38	Indiana	76,500
39	New Mexico	75,589
40	North Dakota	67,551
NA	Delaware*	NA
NA	Maine*	NA
NA	Montana*	NA
NA	Nevada*	NA
NA	New Hampshire*	NA
NA	Rhode Island*	NA
NA	South Dakota*	NA
NA	Vermont*	NA
NA	West Virginia*	NA
NA	Wyoming*	NA
	District of Columbia*	NA

Source: National Center for State Courts
"Survey of Judicial Salaries-Winter 1995" (State Court Report, Winter 1995, Volume 1, Number 2)
*No intermediate court.

Base Salaries of Judges of General Trial Courts in 1995

National Average = $85,699

ALPHA ORDER				RANK ORDER		
RANK	STATE	SALARY		RANK	STATE	SALARY
32	Alabama	$78,300		1	New York	$113,000
7	Alaska	96,600		2	California	107,390
25	Arizona	82,555		3	Delaware	102,900
15	Arkansas	89,188		4	New Jersey	100,000
2	California	107,390		5	Florida	98,698
39	Colorado	75,000		6	Virginia	97,485
10	Connecticut	94,647		7	Alaska	96,600
3	Delaware	102,900		7	Washington	96,600
5	Florida	98,698		9	Pennsylvania	95,111
31	Georgia	78,564		10	Connecticut	94,647
18	Hawaii	86,780		11	South Carolina	92,190
42	Idaho	74,214		12	Maryland	91,700
14	Illinois	90,242		13	Tennessee	90,540
49	Indiana	61,740		14	Illinois	90,242
41	Iowa	74,800		15	Arkansas	89,188
35	Kansas	76,395		16	Rhode Island	88,131
34	Kentucky	76,916		17	North Carolina	87,000
22	Louisiana	84,300		18	Hawaii	86,780
29	Maine	79,073		19	Wisconsin	86,289
12	Maryland	91,700		20	Texas	85,217
21	Massachusetts	85,180		21	Massachusetts	85,180
50	Michigan	61,565		22	Louisiana	84,300
24	Minnesota	83,494		23	Utah	83,650
27	Mississippi	81,200		24	Minnesota	83,494
43	Missouri	73,134		25	Arizona	82,555
47	Montana	63,178		26	Nebraska	81,546
26	Nebraska	81,546		27	Mississippi	81,200
30	Nevada	79,000		28	West Virginia	80,000
48	New Hampshire	62,753		29	Maine	79,073
4	New Jersey	100,000		30	Nevada	79,000
44	New Mexico	71,810		31	Georgia	78,564
1	New York	113,000		32	Alabama	78,300
17	North Carolina	87,000		33	Wyoming	77,000
46	North Dakota	65,970		34	Kentucky	76,916
37	Ohio	76,150		35	Kansas	76,395
39	Oklahoma	75,000		36	Oregon	76,200
36	Oregon	76,200		37	Ohio	76,150
9	Pennsylvania	95,111		38	Vermont	75,539
16	Rhode Island	88,131		39	Colorado	75,000
11	South Carolina	92,190		39	Oklahoma	75,000
45	South Dakota	69,333		41	Iowa	74,800
13	Tennessee	90,540		42	Idaho	74,214
20	Texas	85,217		43	Missouri	73,134
23	Utah	83,650		44	New Mexico	71,810
38	Vermont	75,539		45	South Dakota	69,333
6	Virginia	97,485		46	North Dakota	65,970
7	Washington	96,600		47	Montana	63,178
28	West Virginia	80,000		48	New Hampshire	62,753
19	Wisconsin	86,289		49	Indiana	61,740
33	Wyoming	77,000		50	Michigan	61,565
					District of Columbia	133,600

Source: National Center for State Courts
"Survey of Judicial Salaries-Winter 1995" (State Court Report, Winter 1995, Volume 1, Number 2)

V. LAW ENFORCEMENT

Federal Law Enforcement Officers in 1993

National Total = 68,825 Officers*

ALPHA ORDER

RANK	STATE	OFFICERS	% of USA
20	Alabama	888	1.29%
41	Alaska	234	0.34%
7	Arizona	2,103	3.06%
42	Arkansas	227	0.33%
1	California	9,006	13.09%
14	Colorado	1,084	1.58%
30	Connecticut	451	0.66%
49	Delaware	81	0.12%
4	Florida	4,362	6.34%
8	Georgia	1,866	2.71%
28	Hawaii	483	0.70%
43	Idaho	178	0.26%
6	Illinois	2,365	3.44%
27	Indiana	585	0.85%
46	Iowa	123	0.18%
31	Kansas	441	0.64%
21	Kentucky	829	1.20%
12	Louisiana	1,254	1.82%
36	Maine	303	0.44%
19	Maryland	892	1.30%
17	Massachusetts	989	1.44%
10	Michigan	1,523	2.21%
22	Minnesota	734	1.07%
40	Mississippi	236	0.34%
16	Missouri	1,014	1.47%
35	Montana	306	0.44%
44	Nebraska	172	0.25%
33	Nevada	344	0.50%
50	New Hampshire	55	0.08%
9	New Jersey	1,755	2.55%
24	New Mexico	633	0.92%
3	New York	6,305	9.16%
23	North Carolina	721	1.05%
38	North Dakota	251	0.36%
18	Ohio	903	1.31%
25	Oklahoma	608	0.88%
26	Oregon	596	0.87%
5	Pennsylvania	2,820	4.10%
47	Rhode Island	114	0.17%
29	South Carolina	461	0.67%
45	South Dakota	158	0.23%
13	Tennessee	1,211	1.76%
2	Texas	7,761	11.28%
39	Utah	249	0.36%
37	Vermont	269	0.39%
11	Virginia	1,274	1.85%
15	Washington	1,058	1.54%
33	West Virginia	344	0.50%
32	Wisconsin	410	0.60%
48	Wyoming	93	0.14%

RANK ORDER

RANK	STATE	OFFICERS	% of USA
1	California	9,006	13.09%
2	Texas	7,761	11.28%
3	New York	6,305	9.16%
4	Florida	4,362	6.34%
5	Pennsylvania	2,820	4.10%
6	Illinois	2,365	3.44%
7	Arizona	2,103	3.06%
8	Georgia	1,866	2.71%
9	New Jersey	1,755	2.55%
10	Michigan	1,523	2.21%
11	Virginia	1,274	1.85%
12	Louisiana	1,254	1.82%
13	Tennessee	1,211	1.76%
14	Colorado	1,084	1.58%
15	Washington	1,058	1.54%
16	Missouri	1,014	1.47%
17	Massachusetts	989	1.44%
18	Ohio	903	1.31%
19	Maryland	892	1.30%
20	Alabama	888	1.29%
21	Kentucky	829	1.20%
22	Minnesota	734	1.07%
23	North Carolina	721	1.05%
24	New Mexico	633	0.92%
25	Oklahoma	608	0.88%
26	Oregon	596	0.87%
27	Indiana	585	0.85%
28	Hawaii	483	0.70%
29	South Carolina	461	0.67%
30	Connecticut	451	0.66%
31	Kansas	441	0.64%
32	Wisconsin	410	0.60%
33	Nevada	344	0.50%
33	West Virginia	344	0.50%
35	Montana	306	0.44%
36	Maine	303	0.44%
37	Vermont	269	0.39%
38	North Dakota	251	0.36%
39	Utah	249	0.36%
40	Mississippi	236	0.34%
41	Alaska	234	0.34%
42	Arkansas	227	0.33%
43	Idaho	178	0.26%
44	Nebraska	172	0.25%
45	South Dakota	158	0.23%
46	Iowa	123	0.18%
47	Rhode Island	114	0.17%
48	Wyoming	93	0.14%
49	Delaware	81	0.12%
50	New Hampshire	55	0.08%
	District of Columbia	6,133	8.91%

Source: U.S. Department of Justice, Bureau of Justice Statistics
"Federal Law Enforcement Officers, 1993" (NCJ-151166, December 1994)
*Full-time officers authorized to carry firearms and make arrests. National total includes 1,570 officers whose state was not available. Includes F.B.I., Customs Service, Immigration and Naturalization Serv, I.R.S., Postal Inspection, Drug Enf. Admn, Secret Service, Nat'l Park Service, Bur of Alcohol, Tobacco and Firearms, Capitol Police, U.S. Courts, Fed Bureau of Prisons, Tenn Valley Auth, and U.S. Forest Service.

Rate of Federal Law Enforcement Officers in 1993

National Rate = 2.7 Officers per 10,000 Population*

ALPHA ORDER

RANK	STATE	RATE
22	Alabama	2.1
6	Alaska	3.9
1	Arizona	5.3
45	Arkansas	0.9
12	California	2.9
11	Colorado	3.0
37	Connecticut	1.4
40	Delaware	1.2
10	Florida	3.2
14	Georgia	2.7
4	Hawaii	4.1
33	Idaho	1.6
23	Illinois	2.0
43	Indiana	1.0
50	Iowa	0.4
32	Kansas	1.7
19	Kentucky	2.2
12	Louisiana	2.9
16	Maine	2.4
31	Maryland	1.8
33	Massachusetts	1.6
33	Michigan	1.6
33	Minnesota	1.6
45	Mississippi	0.9
28	Missouri	1.9
8	Montana	3.6
41	Nebraska	1.1
15	Nevada	2.5
49	New Hampshire	0.5
19	New Jersey	2.2
6	New Mexico	3.9
9	New York	3.5
43	North Carolina	1.0
5	North Dakota	4.0
47	Ohio	0.8
28	Oklahoma	1.9
23	Oregon	2.0
18	Pennsylvania	2.3
41	Rhode Island	1.1
38	South Carolina	1.3
19	South Dakota	2.2
16	Tennessee	2.4
3	Texas	4.3
38	Utah	1.3
2	Vermont	4.7
23	Virginia	2.0
23	Washington	2.0
28	West Virginia	1.9
47	Wisconsin	0.8
23	Wyoming	2.0

RANK ORDER

RANK	STATE	RATE
1	Arizona	5.3
2	Vermont	4.7
3	Texas	4.3
4	Hawaii	4.1
5	North Dakota	4.0
6	Alaska	3.9
6	New Mexico	3.9
8	Montana	3.6
9	New York	3.5
10	Florida	3.2
11	Colorado	3.0
12	California	2.9
12	Louisiana	2.9
14	Georgia	2.7
15	Nevada	2.5
16	Maine	2.4
16	Tennessee	2.4
18	Pennsylvania	2.3
19	Kentucky	2.2
19	New Jersey	2.2
19	South Dakota	2.2
22	Alabama	2.1
23	Illinois	2.0
23	Oregon	2.0
23	Virginia	2.0
23	Washington	2.0
23	Wyoming	2.0
28	Missouri	1.9
28	Oklahoma	1.9
28	West Virginia	1.9
31	Maryland	1.8
32	Kansas	1.7
33	Idaho	1.6
33	Massachusetts	1.6
33	Michigan	1.6
33	Minnesota	1.6
37	Connecticut	1.4
38	South Carolina	1.3
38	Utah	1.3
40	Delaware	1.2
41	Nebraska	1.1
41	Rhode Island	1.1
43	Indiana	1.0
43	North Carolina	1.0
45	Arkansas	0.9
45	Mississippi	0.9
47	Ohio	0.8
47	Wisconsin	0.8
49	New Hampshire	0.5
50	Iowa	0.4
	District of Columbia	106.1

Source: U.S. Department of Justice, Bureau of Justice Statistics
   "Federal Law Enforcement Officers, 1993" (NCJ-151166, December 1994)
*Full-time officers authorized to carry firearms and make arrests. National total includes officers whose state was not available. Includes F.B.I., Customs Service, Immigration and Naturalization Serv, I.R.S., Postal Inspection, Drug Enf. Admn, Secret Service, Nat'l Park Service, Bur of Alcohol, Tobacco and Firearms, Capitol Police, U.S. Courts, Fed Bureau of Prisons, Tenn Valley Auth, and U.S. Forest Service.

Law Enforcement Agencies in 1992

National Total = 17,358 Agencies*

RANK	STATE	AGENCIES	% of USA
18	Alabama	377	2.17%
46	Alaska	48	0.28%
43	Arizona	102	0.59%
26	Arkansas	277	1.60%
11	California	493	2.84%
32	Colorado	218	1.26%
37	Connecticut	133	0.77%
48	Delaware	42	0.24%
20	Florida	371	2.14%
8	Georgia	540	3.11%
50	Hawaii	6	0.03%
42	Idaho	112	0.65%
4	Illinois	894	5.15%
14	Indiana	448	2.58%
15	Iowa	427	2.46%
22	Kansas	345	1.99%
18	Kentucky	377	2.17%
21	Louisiana	348	2.00%
35	Maine	142	0.82%
39	Maryland	124	0.71%
17	Massachusetts	388	2.24%
6	Michigan	578	3.33%
13	Minnesota	456	2.63%
25	Mississippi	297	1.71%
5	Missouri	594	3.42%
40	Montana	119	0.69%
29	Nebraska	247	1.42%
49	Nevada	35	0.20%
30	New Hampshire	228	1.31%
9	New Jersey	534	3.08%
41	New Mexico	115	0.66%
6	New York	578	3.33%
12	North Carolina	458	2.64%
36	North Dakota	134	0.77%
3	Ohio	908	5.23%
16	Oklahoma	410	2.36%
33	Oregon	183	1.05%
2	Pennsylvania	1,167	6.72%
46	Rhode Island	48	0.28%
27	South Carolina	255	1.47%
34	South Dakota	171	0.99%
24	Tennessee	326	1.88%
1	Texas	1,712	9.86%
38	Utah	127	0.73%
45	Vermont	73	0.42%
23	Virginia	327	1.88%
28	Washington	252	1.45%
30	West Virginia	228	1.31%
10	Wisconsin	506	2.92%
44	Wyoming	77	0.44%

RANK	STATE	AGENCIES	% of USA
1	Texas	1,712	9.86%
2	Pennsylvania	1,167	6.72%
3	Ohio	908	5.23%
4	Illinois	894	5.15%
5	Missouri	594	3.42%
6	Michigan	578	3.33%
6	New York	578	3.33%
8	Georgia	540	3.11%
9	New Jersey	534	3.08%
10	Wisconsin	506	2.92%
11	California	493	2.84%
12	North Carolina	458	2.64%
13	Minnesota	456	2.63%
14	Indiana	448	2.58%
15	Iowa	427	2.46%
16	Oklahoma	410	2.36%
17	Massachusetts	388	2.24%
18	Alabama	377	2.17%
18	Kentucky	377	2.17%
20	Florida	371	2.14%
21	Louisiana	348	2.00%
22	Kansas	345	1.99%
23	Virginia	327	1.88%
24	Tennessee	326	1.88%
25	Mississippi	297	1.71%
26	Arkansas	277	1.60%
27	South Carolina	255	1.47%
28	Washington	252	1.45%
29	Nebraska	247	1.42%
30	New Hampshire	228	1.31%
30	West Virginia	228	1.31%
32	Colorado	218	1.26%
33	Oregon	183	1.05%
34	South Dakota	171	0.99%
35	Maine	142	0.82%
36	North Dakota	134	0.77%
37	Connecticut	133	0.77%
38	Utah	127	0.73%
39	Maryland	124	0.71%
40	Montana	119	0.69%
41	New Mexico	115	0.66%
42	Idaho	112	0.65%
43	Arizona	102	0.59%
44	Wyoming	77	0.44%
45	Vermont	73	0.42%
46	Alaska	48	0.28%
46	Rhode Island	48	0.28%
48	Delaware	42	0.24%
49	Nevada	35	0.20%
50	Hawaii	6	0.03%
	District of Columbia	3	0.02%

Source: U.S. Department of Justice, Bureau of Justice Statistics
"Census of State and Local Law Enforcement Agencies, 1992" (Bulletin, July 1993, NCJ-142972)
*Includes state and local police, sheriffs' departments and special police agencies.

Population per Law Enforcement Agency in 1992

National Rate = 14,695 Population per Agency*

ALPHA ORDER

RANK ORDER

RANK	STATE	RATE
29	Alabama	10,971
27	Alaska	12,229
5	Arizona	37,569
39	Arkansas	8,661
2	California	62,611
15	Colorado	15,917
8	Connecticut	24,669
12	Delaware	16,405
6	Florida	36,356
25	Georgia	12,502
1	Hawaii	193,333
35	Idaho	9,527
23	Illinois	13,010
24	Indiana	12,638
45	Iowa	6,585
43	Kansas	7,313
32	Kentucky	9,960
26	Louisiana	12,319
38	Maine	8,697
3	Maryland	39,581
16	Massachusetts	15,459
13	Michigan	16,327
34	Minnesota	9,825
36	Mississippi	8,801
37	Missouri	8,742
44	Montana	6,924
46	Nebraska	6,502
4	Nevada	37,914
48	New Hampshire	4,873
19	New Jersey	14,586
22	New Mexico	13,748
7	New York	31,348
18	North Carolina	14,941
49	North Dakota	4,746
28	Ohio	12,132
41	Oklahoma	7,834
14	Oregon	16,268
31	Pennsylvania	10,290
9	Rhode Island	20,938
21	South Carolina	14,129
50	South Dakota	4,158
17	Tennessee	15,411
30	Texas	10,313
20	Utah	14,276
42	Vermont	7,808
11	Virginia	19,502
10	Washington	20,381
40	West Virginia	7,947
33	Wisconsin	9,895
47	Wyoming	6,052

RANK	STATE	RATE
1	Hawaii	193,333
2	California	62,611
3	Maryland	39,581
4	Nevada	37,914
5	Arizona	37,569
6	Florida	36,356
7	New York	31,348
8	Connecticut	24,669
9	Rhode Island	20,938
10	Washington	20,381
11	Virginia	19,502
12	Delaware	16,405
13	Michigan	16,327
14	Oregon	16,268
15	Colorado	15,917
16	Massachusetts	15,459
17	Tennessee	15,411
18	North Carolina	14,941
19	New Jersey	14,586
20	Utah	14,276
21	South Carolina	14,129
22	New Mexico	13,748
23	Illinois	13,010
24	Indiana	12,638
25	Georgia	12,502
26	Louisiana	12,319
27	Alaska	12,229
28	Ohio	12,132
29	Alabama	10,971
30	Texas	10,313
31	Pennsylvania	10,290
32	Kentucky	9,960
33	Wisconsin	9,895
34	Minnesota	9,825
35	Idaho	9,527
36	Mississippi	8,801
37	Missouri	8,742
38	Maine	8,697
39	Arkansas	8,661
40	West Virginia	7,947
41	Oklahoma	7,834
42	Vermont	7,808
43	Kansas	7,313
44	Montana	6,924
45	Iowa	6,585
46	Nebraska	6,502
47	Wyoming	6,052
48	New Hampshire	4,873
49	North Dakota	4,746
50	South Dakota	4,158

District of Columbia   196,333

Source: Morgan Quitno Press using data from U.S. Department of Justice, Bureau of Justice Statistics "Census of State and Local Law Enforcement Agencies, 1992" (Bulletin, July 1993, NCJ-142972)
*Includes state and local police, sheriffs' departments and special police agencies.

Law Enforcement Agencies per 1,000 Square Miles in 1992

National Rate = 4.58 Agencies per 1,000 Square Miles*

ALPHA ORDER

RANK	STATE	RATE
24	Alabama	7.19
50	Alaska	0.07
45	Arizona	0.89
32	Arkansas	5.21
37	California	3.01
39	Colorado	2.09
6	Connecticut	23.99
8	Delaware	16.87
30	Florida	5.64
15	Georgia	9.08
48	Hawaii	0.55
43	Idaho	1.34
9	Illinois	15.44
10	Indiana	12.30
22	Iowa	7.59
33	Kansas	4.19
14	Kentucky	9.33
25	Louisiana	6.71
34	Maine	4.01
12	Maryland	9.99
2	Massachusetts	36.76
28	Michigan	5.97
31	Minnesota	5.24
27	Mississippi	6.13
16	Missouri	8.52
46	Montana	0.81
36	Nebraska	3.19
49	Nevada	0.32
5	New Hampshire	24.38
1	New Jersey	61.22
44	New Mexico	0.95
11	New York	10.61
17	North Carolina	8.51
40	North Dakota	1.90
7	Ohio	20.26
29	Oklahoma	5.87
41	Oregon	1.86
4	Pennsylvania	25.34
3	Rhode Island	31.07
18	South Carolina	7.97
38	South Dakota	2.22
19	Tennessee	7.74
26	Texas	6.37
42	Utah	1.50
22	Vermont	7.59
21	Virginia	7.65
35	Washington	3.53
13	West Virginia	9.41
20	Wisconsin	7.72
47	Wyoming	0.79

RANK ORDER

RANK	STATE	RATE
1	New Jersey	61.22
2	Massachusetts	36.76
3	Rhode Island	31.07
4	Pennsylvania	25.34
5	New Hampshire	24.38
6	Connecticut	23.99
7	Ohio	20.26
8	Delaware	16.87
9	Illinois	15.44
10	Indiana	12.30
11	New York	10.61
12	Maryland	9.99
13	West Virginia	9.41
14	Kentucky	9.33
15	Georgia	9.08
16	Missouri	8.52
17	North Carolina	8.51
18	South Carolina	7.97
19	Tennessee	7.74
20	Wisconsin	7.72
21	Virginia	7.65
22	Iowa	7.59
22	Vermont	7.59
24	Alabama	7.19
25	Louisiana	6.71
26	Texas	6.37
27	Mississippi	6.13
28	Michigan	5.97
29	Oklahoma	5.87
30	Florida	5.64
31	Minnesota	5.24
32	Arkansas	5.21
33	Kansas	4.19
34	Maine	4.01
35	Washington	3.53
36	Nebraska	3.19
37	California	3.01
38	South Dakota	2.22
39	Colorado	2.09
40	North Dakota	1.90
41	Oregon	1.86
42	Utah	1.50
43	Idaho	1.34
44	New Mexico	0.95
45	Arizona	0.89
46	Montana	0.81
47	Wyoming	0.79
48	Hawaii	0.55
49	Nevada	0.32
50	Alaska	0.07
	District of Columbia**	NA

Source: Morgan Quitno Press using data from U.S. Department of Justice, Bureau of Justice Statistics
"Census of State and Local Law Enforcement Agencies, 1992" (Bulletin, July 1993, NCJ-142972)
*Includes state and local police, sheriffs' departments and special police agencies.
**The District of Columbia has three agencies for its 68 square miles.

Full-Time Sworn Officers in Law Enforcement Agencies in 1992

National Total = 603,954 Officers*

<table>
<thead>
<tr><th colspan="4">ALPHA ORDER</th><th colspan="4">RANK ORDER</th></tr>
<tr><th>RANK</th><th>STATE</th><th>OFFICERS</th><th>% of USA</th><th>RANK</th><th>STATE</th><th>OFFICERS</th><th>% of USA</th></tr>
</thead>
<tbody>
<tr><td>20</td><td>Alabama</td><td>8,771</td><td>1.45%</td><td>1</td><td>New York</td><td>68,208</td><td>11.29%</td></tr>
<tr><td>49</td><td>Alaska</td><td>1,057</td><td>0.18%</td><td>2</td><td>California</td><td>65,797</td><td>10.89%</td></tr>
<tr><td>23</td><td>Arizona</td><td>7,900</td><td>1.31%</td><td>3</td><td>Texas</td><td>41,349</td><td>6.85%</td></tr>
<tr><td>33</td><td>Arkansas</td><td>4,475</td><td>0.74%</td><td>4</td><td>Illinois</td><td>35,674</td><td>5.91%</td></tr>
<tr><td>2</td><td>California</td><td>65,797</td><td>10.89%</td><td>5</td><td>Florida</td><td>32,879</td><td>5.44%</td></tr>
<tr><td>21</td><td>Colorado</td><td>8,726</td><td>1.44%</td><td>6</td><td>New Jersey</td><td>26,688</td><td>4.42%</td></tr>
<tr><td>25</td><td>Connecticut</td><td>7,639</td><td>1.26%</td><td>7</td><td>Pennsylvania</td><td>23,700</td><td>3.92%</td></tr>
<tr><td>44</td><td>Delaware</td><td>1,572</td><td>0.26%</td><td>8</td><td>Ohio</td><td>20,929</td><td>3.47%</td></tr>
<tr><td>5</td><td>Florida</td><td>32,879</td><td>5.44%</td><td>9</td><td>Michigan</td><td>19,642</td><td>3.25%</td></tr>
<tr><td>10</td><td>Georgia</td><td>16,792</td><td>2.78%</td><td>10</td><td>Georgia</td><td>16,792</td><td>2.78%</td></tr>
<tr><td>38</td><td>Hawaii</td><td>2,783</td><td>0.46%</td><td>11</td><td>Virginia</td><td>16,365</td><td>2.71%</td></tr>
<tr><td>42</td><td>Idaho</td><td>2,157</td><td>0.36%</td><td>12</td><td>Massachusetts</td><td>16,014</td><td>2.65%</td></tr>
<tr><td>4</td><td>Illinois</td><td>35,674</td><td>5.91%</td><td>13</td><td>Louisiana</td><td>15,049</td><td>2.49%</td></tr>
<tr><td>19</td><td>Indiana</td><td>10,038</td><td>1.66%</td><td>14</td><td>North Carolina</td><td>14,586</td><td>2.42%</td></tr>
<tr><td>31</td><td>Iowa</td><td>4,703</td><td>0.78%</td><td>15</td><td>Maryland</td><td>12,601</td><td>2.09%</td></tr>
<tr><td>29</td><td>Kansas</td><td>5,631</td><td>0.93%</td><td>16</td><td>Wisconsin</td><td>11,594</td><td>1.92%</td></tr>
<tr><td>28</td><td>Kentucky</td><td>6,085</td><td>1.01%</td><td>17</td><td>Missouri</td><td>11,266</td><td>1.87%</td></tr>
<tr><td>13</td><td>Louisiana</td><td>15,049</td><td>2.49%</td><td>18</td><td>Tennessee</td><td>10,379</td><td>1.72%</td></tr>
<tr><td>41</td><td>Maine</td><td>2,267</td><td>0.38%</td><td>19</td><td>Indiana</td><td>10,038</td><td>1.66%</td></tr>
<tr><td>15</td><td>Maryland</td><td>12,601</td><td>2.09%</td><td>20</td><td>Alabama</td><td>8,771</td><td>1.45%</td></tr>
<tr><td>12</td><td>Massachusetts</td><td>16,014</td><td>2.65%</td><td>21</td><td>Colorado</td><td>8,726</td><td>1.44%</td></tr>
<tr><td>9</td><td>Michigan</td><td>19,642</td><td>3.25%</td><td>22</td><td>Washington</td><td>8,192</td><td>1.36%</td></tr>
<tr><td>26</td><td>Minnesota</td><td>7,365</td><td>1.22%</td><td>23</td><td>Arizona</td><td>7,900</td><td>1.31%</td></tr>
<tr><td>32</td><td>Mississippi</td><td>4,675</td><td>0.77%</td><td>24</td><td>South Carolina</td><td>7,752</td><td>1.28%</td></tr>
<tr><td>17</td><td>Missouri</td><td>11,266</td><td>1.87%</td><td>25</td><td>Connecticut</td><td>7,639</td><td>1.26%</td></tr>
<tr><td>45</td><td>Montana</td><td>1,410</td><td>0.23%</td><td>26</td><td>Minnesota</td><td>7,365</td><td>1.22%</td></tr>
<tr><td>35</td><td>Nebraska</td><td>3,084</td><td>0.51%</td><td>27</td><td>Oklahoma</td><td>6,458</td><td>1.07%</td></tr>
<tr><td>36</td><td>Nevada</td><td>3,052</td><td>0.51%</td><td>28</td><td>Kentucky</td><td>6,085</td><td>1.01%</td></tr>
<tr><td>43</td><td>New Hampshire</td><td>2,139</td><td>0.35%</td><td>29</td><td>Kansas</td><td>5,631</td><td>0.93%</td></tr>
<tr><td>6</td><td>New Jersey</td><td>26,688</td><td>4.42%</td><td>30</td><td>Oregon</td><td>5,495</td><td>0.91%</td></tr>
<tr><td>34</td><td>New Mexico</td><td>3,420</td><td>0.57%</td><td>31</td><td>Iowa</td><td>4,703</td><td>0.78%</td></tr>
<tr><td>1</td><td>New York</td><td>68,208</td><td>11.29%</td><td>32</td><td>Mississippi</td><td>4,675</td><td>0.77%</td></tr>
<tr><td>14</td><td>North Carolina</td><td>14,586</td><td>2.42%</td><td>33</td><td>Arkansas</td><td>4,475</td><td>0.74%</td></tr>
<tr><td>48</td><td>North Dakota</td><td>1,060</td><td>0.18%</td><td>34</td><td>New Mexico</td><td>3,420</td><td>0.57%</td></tr>
<tr><td>8</td><td>Ohio</td><td>20,929</td><td>3.47%</td><td>35</td><td>Nebraska</td><td>3,084</td><td>0.51%</td></tr>
<tr><td>27</td><td>Oklahoma</td><td>6,458</td><td>1.07%</td><td>36</td><td>Nevada</td><td>3,052</td><td>0.51%</td></tr>
<tr><td>30</td><td>Oregon</td><td>5,495</td><td>0.91%</td><td>37</td><td>Utah</td><td>2,979</td><td>0.49%</td></tr>
<tr><td>7</td><td>Pennsylvania</td><td>23,700</td><td>3.92%</td><td>38</td><td>Hawaii</td><td>2,783</td><td>0.46%</td></tr>
<tr><td>40</td><td>Rhode Island</td><td>2,389</td><td>0.40%</td><td>39</td><td>West Virginia</td><td>2,622</td><td>0.43%</td></tr>
<tr><td>24</td><td>South Carolina</td><td>7,752</td><td>1.28%</td><td>40</td><td>Rhode Island</td><td>2,389</td><td>0.40%</td></tr>
<tr><td>47</td><td>South Dakota</td><td>1,145</td><td>0.19%</td><td>41</td><td>Maine</td><td>2,267</td><td>0.38%</td></tr>
<tr><td>18</td><td>Tennessee</td><td>10,379</td><td>1.72%</td><td>42</td><td>Idaho</td><td>2,157</td><td>0.36%</td></tr>
<tr><td>3</td><td>Texas</td><td>41,349</td><td>6.85%</td><td>43</td><td>New Hampshire</td><td>2,139</td><td>0.35%</td></tr>
<tr><td>37</td><td>Utah</td><td>2,979</td><td>0.49%</td><td>44</td><td>Delaware</td><td>1,572</td><td>0.26%</td></tr>
<tr><td>50</td><td>Vermont</td><td>978</td><td>0.16%</td><td>45</td><td>Montana</td><td>1,410</td><td>0.23%</td></tr>
<tr><td>11</td><td>Virginia</td><td>16,365</td><td>2.71%</td><td>46</td><td>Wyoming</td><td>1,210</td><td>0.20%</td></tr>
<tr><td>22</td><td>Washington</td><td>8,192</td><td>1.36%</td><td>47</td><td>South Dakota</td><td>1,145</td><td>0.19%</td></tr>
<tr><td>39</td><td>West Virginia</td><td>2,622</td><td>0.43%</td><td>48</td><td>North Dakota</td><td>1,060</td><td>0.18%</td></tr>
<tr><td>16</td><td>Wisconsin</td><td>11,594</td><td>1.92%</td><td>49</td><td>Alaska</td><td>1,057</td><td>0.18%</td></tr>
<tr><td>46</td><td>Wyoming</td><td>1,210</td><td>0.20%</td><td>50</td><td>Vermont</td><td>978</td><td>0.16%</td></tr>
<tr><td></td><td></td><td></td><td></td><td></td><td>District of Columbia</td><td>5,213</td><td>0.86%</td></tr>
</tbody>
</table>

Source: U.S. Department of Justice, Bureau of Justice Statistics
   "Census of State and Local Law Enforcement Agencies, 1992" (Bulletin, July 1993, NCJ-142972)
*Includes state and local police, sheriffs' departments and special police agencies.

Percent of Full-Time Law Enforcement Agency Employees
Who are Sworn Officers: 1992
National Rate = 71.81% of Employees are Sworn Officers*

ALPHA ORDER

RANK	STATE	PERCENT
29	Alabama	70.07
44	Alaska	64.26
50	Arizona	59.65
40	Arkansas	65.59
41	California	65.42
31	Colorado	69.48
4	Connecticut	82.35
8	Delaware	78.36
48	Florida	60.87
33	Georgia	68.49
7	Hawaii	80.02
20	Idaho	73.82
9	Illinois	77.23
36	Indiana	67.21
15	Iowa	75.16
27	Kansas	71.90
11	Kentucky	76.55
1	Louisiana	86.64
34	Maine	68.43
16	Maryland	74.69
14	Massachusetts	75.61
17	Michigan	74.47
25	Minnesota	72.41
30	Mississippi	69.89
23	Missouri	73.30
38	Montana	66.48
22	Nebraska	73.53
47	Nevada	61.13
19	New Hampshire	73.91
5	New Jersey	81.40
32	New Mexico	68.99
6	New York	80.08
18	North Carolina	74.29
24	North Dakota	73.15
28	Ohio	70.43
35	Oklahoma	67.59
39	Oregon	66.13
2	Pennsylvania	83.67
3	Rhode Island	82.64
10	South Carolina	76.76
26	South Dakota	71.92
45	Tennessee	63.48
42	Texas	64.36
46	Utah	61.64
21	Vermont	73.59
12	Virginia	76.28
43	Washington	64.34
37	West Virginia	67.02
13	Wisconsin	75.88
49	Wyoming	60.02

RANK ORDER

RANK	STATE	PERCENT
1	Louisiana	86.64
2	Pennsylvania	83.67
3	Rhode Island	82.64
4	Connecticut	82.35
5	New Jersey	81.40
6	New York	80.08
7	Hawaii	80.02
8	Delaware	78.36
9	Illinois	77.23
10	South Carolina	76.76
11	Kentucky	76.55
12	Virginia	76.28
13	Wisconsin	75.88
14	Massachusetts	75.61
15	Iowa	75.16
16	Maryland	74.69
17	Michigan	74.47
18	North Carolina	74.29
19	New Hampshire	73.91
20	Idaho	73.82
21	Vermont	73.59
22	Nebraska	73.53
23	Missouri	73.30
24	North Dakota	73.15
25	Minnesota	72.41
26	South Dakota	71.92
27	Kansas	71.90
28	Ohio	70.43
29	Alabama	70.07
30	Mississippi	69.89
31	Colorado	69.48
32	New Mexico	68.99
33	Georgia	68.49
34	Maine	68.43
35	Oklahoma	67.59
36	Indiana	67.21
37	West Virginia	67.02
38	Montana	66.48
39	Oregon	66.13
40	Arkansas	65.59
41	California	65.42
42	Texas	64.36
43	Washington	64.34
44	Alaska	64.26
45	Tennessee	63.48
46	Utah	61.64
47	Nevada	61.13
48	Florida	60.87
49	Wyoming	60.02
50	Arizona	59.65

| | District of Columbia | 84.43 |

Source: Morgan Quitno Press using data from U.S. Department of Justice, Bureau of Justice Statistics
"Census of State and Local Law Enforcement Agencies, 1992" (Bulletin, July 1993, NCJ-142972)
*Includes state and local police, sheriffs' departments and special police agencies.

Rate of Full-Time Sworn Officers in Law Enforcement Agencies in 1992

National Rate = 23.68 Officers per 10,000 Population*

ALPHA ORDER

RANK ORDER

RANK	STATE	RATE	RANK	STATE	RATE
25	Alabama	21.21	1	New York	37.64
38	Alaska	18.01	2	Louisiana	35.10
28	Arizona	20.62	3	New Jersey	34.26
35	Arkansas	18.65	4	Illinois	30.67
23	California	21.32	5	Massachusetts	26.70
9	Colorado	25.15	6	Wyoming	25.97
15	Connecticut	23.28	7	Maryland	25.67
18	Delaware	22.82	8	Virginia	25.66
11	Florida	24.38	9	Colorado	25.15
10	Georgia	24.87	10	Georgia	24.87
12	Hawaii	23.99	11	Florida	24.38
29	Idaho	20.22	12	Hawaii	23.99
4	Illinois	30.67	13	Rhode Island	23.77
40	Indiana	17.73	14	Texas	23.42
43	Iowa	16.72	15	Connecticut	23.28
19	Kansas	22.32	16	Wisconsin	23.16
47	Kentucky	16.21	17	Nevada	23.00
2	Louisiana	35.10	18	Delaware	22.82
37	Maine	18.36	19	Kansas	22.32
7	Maryland	25.67	20	Missouri	21.69
5	Massachusetts	26.70	21	New Mexico	21.63
26	Michigan	20.81	22	South Carolina	21.52
45	Minnesota	16.44	23	California	21.32
39	Mississippi	17.88	23	North Carolina	21.32
20	Missouri	21.69	25	Alabama	21.21
42	Montana	17.11	26	Michigan	20.81
33	Nebraska	19.20	27	Tennessee	20.66
17	Nevada	23.00	28	Arizona	20.62
32	New Hampshire	19.25	29	Idaho	20.22
3	New Jersey	34.26	30	Oklahoma	20.11
21	New Mexico	21.63	31	Pennsylvania	19.74
1	New York	37.64	32	New Hampshire	19.25
23	North Carolina	21.32	33	Nebraska	19.20
44	North Dakota	16.67	34	Ohio	19.00
34	Ohio	19.00	35	Arkansas	18.65
30	Oklahoma	20.11	36	Oregon	18.46
36	Oregon	18.46	37	Maine	18.36
31	Pennsylvania	19.74	38	Alaska	18.01
13	Rhode Island	23.77	39	Mississippi	17.88
22	South Carolina	21.52	40	Indiana	17.73
48	South Dakota	16.10	41	Vermont	17.16
27	Tennessee	20.66	42	Montana	17.11
14	Texas	23.42	43	Iowa	16.72
46	Utah	16.43	44	North Dakota	16.67
41	Vermont	17.16	45	Minnesota	16.44
8	Virginia	25.66	46	Utah	16.43
49	Washington	15.95	47	Kentucky	16.21
50	West Virginia	14.47	48	South Dakota	16.10
16	Wisconsin	23.16	49	Washington	15.95
6	Wyoming	25.97	50	West Virginia	14.47
				District of Columbia	88.51

Source: Morgan Quitno Press using data from U.S. Department of Justice, Bureau of Justice Statistics
"Census of State and Local Law Enforcement Agencies, 1992" (Bulletin, July 1993, NCJ-142972)
*Includes state and local police, sheriffs' departments and special police agencies.

Full-Time Sworn Law Enforcement Officers per 1,000 Square Miles in 1992

National Rate - 159 Officers per 1,000 Square Miles*

ALPHA ORDER

RANK ORDER

RANK	STATE	RATE
24	Alabama	167
50	Alaska	2
37	Arizona	69
34	Arkansas	84
12	California	402
34	Colorado	84
4	Connecticut	1,378
7	Delaware	632
10	Florida	500
15	Georgia	282
18	Hawaii	255
45	Idaho	26
8	Illinois	616
16	Indiana	276
34	Iowa	84
38	Kansas	68
27	Kentucky	151
14	Louisiana	290
39	Maine	64
6	Maryland	1,016
3	Massachusetts	1,517
22	Michigan	203
33	Minnesota	85
31	Mississippi	97
25	Missouri	162
49	Montana	10
41	Nebraska	40
43	Nevada	28
21	New Hampshire	229
1	New Jersey	3,060
43	New Mexico	28
5	New York	1,252
17	North Carolina	271
46	North Dakota	15
11	Ohio	467
32	Oklahoma	92
40	Oregon	56
9	Pennsylvania	515
2	Rhode Island	1,546
20	South Carolina	242
46	South Dakota	15
19	Tennessee	246
26	Texas	154
42	Utah	35
30	Vermont	102
13	Virginia	383
28	Washington	115
29	West Virginia	108
23	Wisconsin	177
48	Wyoming	12

RANK	STATE	RATE
1	New Jersey	3,060
2	Rhode Island	1,546
3	Massachusetts	1,517
4	Connecticut	1,378
5	New York	1,252
6	Maryland	1,016
7	Delaware	632
8	Illinois	616
9	Pennsylvania	515
10	Florida	500
11	Ohio	467
12	California	402
13	Virginia	383
14	Louisiana	290
15	Georgia	282
16	Indiana	276
17	North Carolina	271
18	Hawaii	255
19	Tennessee	246
20	South Carolina	242
21	New Hampshire	229
22	Michigan	203
23	Wisconsin	177
24	Alabama	167
25	Missouri	162
26	Texas	154
27	Kentucky	151
28	Washington	115
29	West Virginia	108
30	Vermont	102
31	Mississippi	97
32	Oklahoma	92
33	Minnesota	85
34	Arkansas	84
34	Colorado	84
34	Iowa	84
37	Arizona	69
38	Kansas	68
39	Maine	64
40	Oregon	56
41	Nebraska	40
42	Utah	35
43	Nevada	28
43	New Mexico	28
45	Idaho	26
46	North Dakota	15
46	South Dakota	15
48	Wyoming	12
49	Montana	10
50	Alaska	2

District of Columbia** — NA

Source: Morgan Quitno Press using data from U.S. Department of Justice, Bureau of Justice Statistics
"Census of State and Local Law Enforcement Agencies, 1992" (Bulletin, July 1993, NCJ-142972)
*Includes state and local police, sheriffs' departments and special police agencies.
**The District of Columbia has 5,213 sworn officers for its 68 square miles.

Full-Time Employees in Law Enforcement Agencies in 1992

National Total = 841,099 Employees*

ALPHA ORDER

RANK	STATE	EMPLOYEES	% of USA
23	Alabama	12,517	1.49%
47	Alaska	1,645	0.20%
20	Arizona	13,243	1.57%
31	Arkansas	6,823	0.81%
1	California	100,582	11.96%
22	Colorado	12,559	1.49%
27	Connecticut	9,276	1.10%
46	Delaware	2,006	0.24%
4	Florida	54,011	6.42%
10	Georgia	24,516	2.91%
39	Hawaii	3,478	0.41%
41	Idaho	2,922	0.35%
5	Illinois	46,189	5.49%
19	Indiana	14,935	1.78%
33	Iowa	6,257	0.74%
30	Kansas	7,832	0.93%
29	Kentucky	7,949	0.95%
14	Louisiana	17,370	2.07%
40	Maine	3,313	0.39%
15	Maryland	16,871	2.01%
12	Massachusetts	21,181	2.52%
9	Michigan	26,375	3.14%
24	Minnesota	10,171	1.21%
32	Mississippi	6,689	0.80%
17	Missouri	15,370	1.83%
44	Montana	2,121	0.25%
37	Nebraska	4,194	0.50%
34	Nevada	4,993	0.59%
42	New Hampshire	2,894	0.34%
6	New Jersey	32,785	3.90%
35	New Mexico	4,957	0.59%
2	New York	85,177	10.13%
13	North Carolina	19,633	2.33%
49	North Dakota	1,449	0.17%
7	Ohio	29,718	3.53%
26	Oklahoma	9,554	1.14%
28	Oregon	8,310	0.99%
8	Pennsylvania	28,326	3.37%
43	Rhode Island	2,891	0.34%
25	South Carolina	10,099	1.20%
48	South Dakota	1,592	0.19%
16	Tennessee	16,349	1.94%
3	Texas	64,247	7.64%
36	Utah	4,833	0.57%
50	Vermont	1,329	0.16%
11	Virginia	21,454	2.55%
21	Washington	12,733	1.51%
38	West Virginia	3,912	0.47%
18	Wisconsin	15,279	1.82%
45	Wyoming	2,016	0.24%

RANK ORDER

RANK	STATE	EMPLOYEES	% of USA
1	California	100,582	11.96%
2	New York	85,177	10.13%
3	Texas	64,247	7.64%
4	Florida	54,011	6.42%
5	Illinois	46,189	5.49%
6	New Jersey	32,785	3.90%
7	Ohio	29,718	3.53%
8	Pennsylvania	28,326	3.37%
9	Michigan	26,375	3.14%
10	Georgia	24,516	2.91%
11	Virginia	21,454	2.55%
12	Massachusetts	21,181	2.52%
13	North Carolina	19,633	2.33%
14	Louisiana	17,370	2.07%
15	Maryland	16,871	2.01%
16	Tennessee	16,349	1.94%
17	Missouri	15,370	1.83%
18	Wisconsin	15,279	1.82%
19	Indiana	14,935	1.78%
20	Arizona	13,243	1.57%
21	Washington	12,733	1.51%
22	Colorado	12,559	1.49%
23	Alabama	12,517	1.49%
24	Minnesota	10,171	1.21%
25	South Carolina	10,099	1.20%
26	Oklahoma	9,554	1.14%
27	Connecticut	9,276	1.10%
28	Oregon	8,310	0.99%
29	Kentucky	7,949	0.95%
30	Kansas	7,832	0.93%
31	Arkansas	6,823	0.81%
32	Mississippi	6,689	0.80%
33	Iowa	6,257	0.74%
34	Nevada	4,993	0.59%
35	New Mexico	4,957	0.59%
36	Utah	4,833	0.57%
37	Nebraska	4,194	0.50%
38	West Virginia	3,912	0.47%
39	Hawaii	3,478	0.41%
40	Maine	3,313	0.39%
41	Idaho	2,922	0.35%
42	New Hampshire	2,894	0.34%
43	Rhode Island	2,891	0.34%
44	Montana	2,121	0.25%
45	Wyoming	2,016	0.24%
46	Delaware	2,006	0.24%
47	Alaska	1,645	0.20%
48	South Dakota	1,592	0.19%
49	North Dakota	1,449	0.17%
50	Vermont	1,329	0.16%
	District of Columbia	6,174	0.73%

Source: U.S. Department of Justice, Bureau of Justice Statistics
   "Census of State and Local Law Enforcement Agencies, 1992" (Bulletin, July 1993, NCJ-142972)
*Includes state and local police, sheriffs' departments and special police agencies.

Full-Time Employees in Law Enforcement Agencies per 10,000 Population: 1992

National Rate = 32.97 Employees per 10,000 Population*

ALPHA ORDER				RANK ORDER		
RANK	STATE	RATE		RANK	STATE	RATE
20	Alabama	30.26		1	New York	47.01
30	Alaska	28.02		2	Wyoming	43.26
12	Arizona	34.56		3	New Jersey	42.09
27	Arkansas	28.44		4	Louisiana	40.52
15	California	32.59		5	Florida	40.04
10	Colorado	36.19		6	Illinois	39.71
28	Connecticut	28.27		7	Nevada	37.63
24	Delaware	29.11		8	Texas	36.39
5	Florida	40.04		9	Georgia	36.31
9	Georgia	36.31		10	Colorado	36.19
21	Hawaii	29.98		11	Massachusetts	35.31
33	Idaho	27.39		12	Arizona	34.56
6	Illinois	39.71		13	Maryland	34.37
37	Indiana	26.38		14	Virginia	33.64
48	Iowa	22.25		15	California	32.59
18	Kansas	31.04		16	Tennessee	32.54
50	Kentucky	21.17		17	New Mexico	31.35
4	Louisiana	40.52		18	Kansas	31.04
35	Maine	26.83		19	Wisconsin	30.52
13	Maryland	34.37		20	Alabama	30.26
11	Massachusetts	35.31		21	Hawaii	29.98
31	Michigan	27.95		22	Oklahoma	29.74
46	Minnesota	22.70		23	Missouri	29.60
41	Mississippi	25.59		24	Delaware	29.11
23	Missouri	29.60		25	Rhode Island	28.77
40	Montana	25.74		26	North Carolina	28.69
38	Nebraska	26.11		27	Arkansas	28.44
7	Nevada	37.63		28	Connecticut	28.27
39	New Hampshire	26.05		29	South Carolina	28.03
3	New Jersey	42.09		30	Alaska	28.02
17	New Mexico	31.35		31	Michigan	27.95
1	New York	47.01		32	Oregon	27.91
26	North Carolina	28.69		33	Idaho	27.39
45	North Dakota	22.78		34	Ohio	26.98
34	Ohio	26.98		35	Maine	26.83
22	Oklahoma	29.74		36	Utah	26.66
32	Oregon	27.91		37	Indiana	26.38
43	Pennsylvania	23.59		38	Nebraska	26.11
25	Rhode Island	28.77		39	New Hampshire	26.05
29	South Carolina	28.03		40	Montana	25.74
47	South Dakota	22.39		41	Mississippi	25.59
16	Tennessee	32.54		42	Washington	24.79
8	Texas	36.39		43	Pennsylvania	23.59
36	Utah	26.66		44	Vermont	23.32
44	Vermont	23.32		45	North Dakota	22.78
14	Virginia	33.64		46	Minnesota	22.70
42	Washington	24.79		47	South Dakota	22.39
49	West Virginia	21.59		48	Iowa	22.25
19	Wisconsin	30.52		49	West Virginia	21.59
2	Wyoming	43.26		50	Kentucky	21.17

District of Columbia   104.82

Source: Morgan Quitno Press using data from U.S. Department of Justice, Bureau of Justice Statistics
"Census of State and Local Law Enforcement Agencies, 1992" (Bulletin, July 1993, NCJ-142972)
*Includes state and local police, sheriffs' departments and special police agencies.

Full-Time Sworn Officers in State Police Departments in 1992

National Total = 52,980 Officers*

ALPHA ORDER

RANK ORDER

RANK	STATE	OFFICERS	% of USA
26	Alabama	629	1.19%
42	Alaska	260	0.49%
15	Arizona	1,100	2.08%
34	Arkansas	484	0.91%
1	California	6,062	11.44%
33	Colorado	493	0.93%
19	Connecticut	905	1.71%
28	Delaware	505	0.95%
11	Florida	1,605	3.03%
24	Georgia	777	1.47%
50	Hawaii	0	0.00%
45	Idaho	192	0.36%
8	Illinois	1,977	3.73%
16	Indiana	1,097	2.07%
37	Iowa	410	0.77%
27	Kansas	604	1.14%
18	Kentucky	960	1.81%
25	Louisiana	714	1.35%
39	Maine	332	0.63%
9	Maryland	1,700	3.21%
6	Massachusetts	2,070	3.91%
7	Michigan	2,019	3.81%
30	Minnesota	501	0.95%
31	Mississippi	499	0.94%
21	Missouri	883	1.67%
44	Montana	200	0.38%
29	Nebraska	502	0.95%
40	Nevada	306	0.58%
43	New Hampshire	250	0.47%
5	New Jersey	2,572	4.85%
36	New Mexico	425	0.80%
3	New York	4,013	7.57%
13	North Carolina	1,260	2.38%
49	North Dakota	125	0.24%
12	Ohio	1,292	2.44%
22	Oklahoma	786	1.48%
19	Oregon	905	1.71%
2	Pennsylvania	4,075	7.69%
46	Rhode Island	165	0.31%
14	South Carolina	1,193	2.25%
48	South Dakota	151	0.29%
23	Tennessee	782	1.48%
4	Texas	2,789	5.26%
38	Utah	365	0.69%
41	Vermont	285	0.54%
10	Virginia	1,606	3.03%
17	Washington	1,032	1.95%
35	West Virginia	468	0.88%
32	Wisconsin	498	0.94%
47	Wyoming	157	0.30%

RANK	STATE	OFFICERS	% of USA
1	California	6,062	11.44%
2	Pennsylvania	4,075	7.69%
3	New York	4,013	7.57%
4	Texas	2,789	5.26%
5	New Jersey	2,572	4.85%
6	Massachusetts	2,070	3.91%
7	Michigan	2,019	3.81%
8	Illinois	1,977	3.73%
9	Maryland	1,700	3.21%
10	Virginia	1,606	3.03%
11	Florida	1,605	3.03%
12	Ohio	1,292	2.44%
13	North Carolina	1,260	2.38%
14	South Carolina	1,193	2.25%
15	Arizona	1,100	2.08%
16	Indiana	1,097	2.07%
17	Washington	1,032	1.95%
18	Kentucky	960	1.81%
19	Connecticut	905	1.71%
19	Oregon	905	1.71%
21	Missouri	883	1.67%
22	Oklahoma	786	1.48%
23	Tennessee	782	1.48%
24	Georgia	777	1.47%
25	Louisiana	714	1.35%
26	Alabama	629	1.19%
27	Kansas	604	1.14%
28	Delaware	505	0.95%
29	Nebraska	502	0.95%
30	Minnesota	501	0.95%
31	Mississippi	499	0.94%
32	Wisconsin	498	0.94%
33	Colorado	493	0.93%
34	Arkansas	484	0.91%
35	West Virginia	468	0.88%
36	New Mexico	425	0.80%
37	Iowa	410	0.77%
38	Utah	365	0.69%
39	Maine	332	0.63%
40	Nevada	306	0.58%
41	Vermont	285	0.54%
42	Alaska	260	0.49%
43	New Hampshire	250	0.47%
44	Montana	200	0.38%
45	Idaho	192	0.36%
46	Rhode Island	165	0.31%
47	Wyoming	157	0.30%
48	South Dakota	151	0.29%
49	North Dakota	125	0.24%
50	Hawaii	0	0.00%
	District of Columbia	0	0.00%

Source: U.S. Department of Justice, Bureau of Justice Statistics
"Census of State and Local Law Enforcement Agencies, 1992" (Bulletin, July 1993, NCJ-142972)
All states except Hawaii and the District of Columbia have a state police department.

Percent of Full-Time State Police Department Employees
Who are Sworn Officers: 1992
National Rate = 67.43% of Employees*

ALPHA ORDER

RANK	STATE	PERCENT
47	Alabama	49.1
39	Alaska	59.2
30	Arizona	68.3
24	Arkansas	71.3
31	California	68.2
23	Colorado	71.7
29	Connecticut	68.5
19	Delaware	73.5
14	Florida	76.2
49	Georgia	40.9
NA	Hawaii**	NA
15	Idaho	75.6
37	Illinois	59.9
35	Indiana	62.9
4	Iowa	89.3
17	Kansas	73.6
40	Kentucky	58.0
28	Louisiana	68.5
22	Maine	72.2
25	Maryland	70.8
7	Massachusetts	80.3
26	Michigan	69.3
27	Minnesota	69.3
38	Mississippi	59.6
48	Missouri	48.2
13	Montana	76.3
10	Nebraska	78.1
33	Nevada	66.7
18	New Hampshire	73.5
21	New Jersey	72.5
12	New Mexico	77.0
5	New York	85.7
9	North Carolina	78.7
36	North Dakota	62.8
42	Ohio	55.0
41	Oklahoma	55.9
8	Oregon	79.0
11	Pennsylvania	77.9
6	Rhode Island	81.3
1	South Carolina	100.0
3	South Dakota	89.4
44	Tennessee	50.7
45	Texas	49.8
2	Utah	92.4
32	Vermont	66.9
20	Virginia	72.8
45	Washington	49.8
34	West Virginia	63.8
16	Wisconsin	74.9
43	Wyoming	51.0

RANK ORDER

RANK	STATE	PERCENT
1	South Carolina	100.0
2	Utah	92.4
3	South Dakota	89.4
4	Iowa	89.3
5	New York	85.7
6	Rhode Island	81.3
7	Massachusetts	80.3
8	Oregon	79.0
9	North Carolina	78.7
10	Nebraska	78.1
11	Pennsylvania	77.9
12	New Mexico	77.0
13	Montana	76.3
14	Florida	76.2
15	Idaho	75.6
16	Wisconsin	74.9
17	Kansas	73.6
18	New Hampshire	73.5
19	Delaware	73.5
20	Virginia	72.8
21	New Jersey	72.5
22	Maine	72.2
23	Colorado	71.7
24	Arkansas	71.3
25	Maryland	70.8
26	Michigan	69.3
27	Minnesota	69.3
28	Louisiana	68.5
29	Connecticut	68.5
30	Arizona	68.3
31	California	68.2
32	Vermont	66.9
33	Nevada	66.7
34	West Virginia	63.8
35	Indiana	62.9
36	North Dakota	62.8
37	Illinois	59.9
38	Mississippi	59.6
39	Alaska	59.2
40	Kentucky	58.0
41	Oklahoma	55.9
42	Ohio	55.0
43	Wyoming	51.0
44	Tennessee	50.7
45	Texas	49.8
45	Washington	49.8
47	Alabama	49.1
48	Missouri	48.2
49	Georgia	40.9
NA	Hawaii**	NA
	District of Columbia**	NA

Source: Morgan Quitno Press using data from U.S. Department of Justice, Bureau of Justice Statistics
   "Census of State and Local Law Enforcement Agencies, 1992" (Bulletin, July 1993, NCJ-142972)
*All states except Hawaii and the District of Columbia have a state police department.
**Not available.

Rate of Full-Time Sworn Officers in State Police Departments in 1992

National Rate = 2.08 Officers per 10,000 Population*

ALPHA ORDER

RANK	STATE	RATE
42	Alabama	1.52
3	Alaska	4.43
12	Arizona	2.87
27	Arkansas	2.02
31	California	1.96
44	Colorado	1.42
13	Connecticut	2.76
1	Delaware	7.33
45	Florida	1.19
47	Georgia	1.15
50	Hawaii	0.00
35	Idaho	1.80
36	Illinois	1.70
32	Indiana	1.94
43	Iowa	1.46
21	Kansas	2.39
17	Kentucky	2.56
38	Louisiana	1.67
14	Maine	2.69
4	Maryland	3.46
5	Massachusetts	3.45
25	Michigan	2.14
48	Minnesota	1.12
33	Mississippi	1.91
36	Missouri	1.70
20	Montana	2.43
10	Nebraska	3.13
22	Nevada	2.31
23	New Hampshire	2.25
9	New Jersey	3.30
14	New Mexico	2.69
24	New York	2.21
34	North Carolina	1.84
30	North Dakota	1.97
46	Ohio	1.17
19	Oklahoma	2.45
11	Oregon	3.04
6	Pennsylvania	3.39
39	Rhode Island	1.64
8	South Carolina	3.31
26	South Dakota	2.12
41	Tennessee	1.56
40	Texas	1.58
28	Utah	2.01
2	Vermont	5.00
18	Virginia	2.52
28	Washington	2.01
16	West Virginia	2.58
49	Wisconsin	0.99
7	Wyoming	3.37

RANK ORDER

RANK	STATE	RATE
1	Delaware	7.33
2	Vermont	5.00
3	Alaska	4.43
4	Maryland	3.46
5	Massachusetts	3.45
6	Pennsylvania	3.39
7	Wyoming	3.37
8	South Carolina	3.31
9	New Jersey	3.30
10	Nebraska	3.13
11	Oregon	3.04
12	Arizona	2.87
13	Connecticut	2.76
14	Maine	2.69
14	New Mexico	2.69
16	West Virginia	2.58
17	Kentucky	2.56
18	Virginia	2.52
19	Oklahoma	2.45
20	Montana	2.43
21	Kansas	2.39
22	Nevada	2.31
23	New Hampshire	2.25
24	New York	2.21
25	Michigan	2.14
26	South Dakota	2.12
27	Arkansas	2.02
28	Utah	2.01
28	Washington	2.01
30	North Dakota	1.97
31	California	1.96
32	Indiana	1.94
33	Mississippi	1.91
34	North Carolina	1.84
35	Idaho	1.80
36	Illinois	1.70
36	Missouri	1.70
38	Louisiana	1.67
39	Rhode Island	1.64
40	Texas	1.58
41	Tennessee	1.56
42	Alabama	1.52
43	Iowa	1.46
44	Colorado	1.42
45	Florida	1.19
46	Ohio	1.17
47	Georgia	1.15
48	Minnesota	1.12
49	Wisconsin	0.99
50	Hawaii	0.00
	District of Columbia	0.00

Source: Morgan Quitno Press using data from U.S. Department of Justice, Bureau of Justice Statistics
"Census of State and Local Law Enforcement Agencies, 1992" (Bulletin, July 1993, NCJ-142972)
*All states except Hawaii and the District of Columbia have a state police department.

State Government Law Enforcement Officers in 1994

National Total = 62,344 Officers*

ALPHA ORDER

RANK	STATE	OFFICERS	% of USA
24	Alabama	806	1.29%
41	Alaska	330	0.53%
20	Arizona	867	1.39%
34	Arkansas	476	0.76%
1	California	6,643	10.66%
23	Colorado	825	1.32%
18	Connecticut	977	1.57%
30	Delaware	658	1.06%
4	Florida	2,888	4.63%
12	Georgia	2,021	3.24%
49	Hawaii	0	0.00%
45	Idaho	213	0.34%
10	Illinois	2,320	3.72%
17	Indiana	1,059	1.70%
32	Iowa	608	0.98%
25	Kansas	802	1.29%
15	Kentucky	1,507	2.42%
28	Louisiana	723	1.16%
39	Maine	356	0.57%
5	Maryland	2,680	4.30%
9	Massachusetts	2,352	3.77%
13	Michigan	1,991	3.19%
NA	Minnesota**	NA	NA
33	Mississippi	508	0.81%
21	Missouri	865	1.39%
37	Montana	407	0.65%
35	Nebraska	453	0.73%
40	Nevada	349	0.56%
43	New Hampshire	248	0.40%
6	New Jersey	2,674	4.29%
36	New Mexico	412	0.66%
3	New York	4,371	7.01%
7	North Carolina	2,653	4.26%
48	North Dakota	118	0.19%
16	Ohio	1,435	2.30%
26	Oklahoma	768	1.23%
22	Oregon	850	1.36%
2	Pennsylvania	4,489	7.20%
43	Rhode Island	248	0.40%
14	South Carolina	1,707	2.74%
47	South Dakota	152	0.24%
27	Tennessee	744	1.19%
8	Texas	2,626	4.21%
38	Utah	379	0.61%
42	Vermont	280	0.45%
11	Virginia	2,035	3.26%
19	Washington	972	1.56%
31	West Virginia	652	1.05%
29	Wisconsin	694	1.11%
46	Wyoming	153	0.25%

RANK ORDER

RANK	STATE	OFFICERS	% of USA
1	California	6,643	10.66%
2	Pennsylvania	4,489	7.20%
3	New York	4,371	7.01%
4	Florida	2,888	4.63%
5	Maryland	2,680	4.30%
6	New Jersey	2,674	4.29%
7	North Carolina	2,653	4.26%
8	Texas	2,626	4.21%
9	Massachusetts	2,352	3.77%
10	Illinois	2,320	3.72%
11	Virginia	2,035	3.26%
12	Georgia	2,021	3.24%
13	Michigan	1,991	3.19%
14	South Carolina	1,707	2.74%
15	Kentucky	1,507	2.42%
16	Ohio	1,435	2.30%
17	Indiana	1,059	1.70%
18	Connecticut	977	1.57%
19	Washington	972	1.56%
20	Arizona	867	1.39%
21	Missouri	865	1.39%
22	Oregon	850	1.36%
23	Colorado	825	1.32%
24	Alabama	806	1.29%
25	Kansas	802	1.29%
26	Oklahoma	768	1.23%
27	Tennessee	744	1.19%
28	Louisiana	723	1.16%
29	Wisconsin	694	1.11%
30	Delaware	658	1.06%
31	West Virginia	652	1.05%
32	Iowa	608	0.98%
33	Mississippi	508	0.81%
34	Arkansas	476	0.76%
35	Nebraska	453	0.73%
36	New Mexico	412	0.66%
37	Montana	407	0.65%
38	Utah	379	0.61%
39	Maine	356	0.57%
40	Nevada	349	0.56%
41	Alaska	330	0.53%
42	Vermont	280	0.45%
43	New Hampshire	248	0.40%
43	Rhode Island	248	0.40%
45	Idaho	213	0.34%
46	Wyoming	153	0.25%
47	South Dakota	152	0.24%
48	North Dakota	118	0.19%
49	Hawaii	0	0.00%
NA	Minnesota**	NA	NA
	District of Columbia	0	0.00%

Source: Federal Bureau of Investigation
"Crime in the United States 1994" (Uniform Crime Reports, November 19, 1995)
*Total is of states shown separately. Includes state police agencies and other agencies with law enforcement powers. Hawaii and the District of Columbia do not have a state police agency.
**Not available.

Male State Government Law Enforcement Officers in 1994

National Total = 58,414 Male Officers*

RANK	STATE	OFFICERS	% of USA
23	Alabama	788	1.35%
41	Alaska	311	0.53%
21	Arizona	813	1.39%
34	Arkansas	456	0.78%
1	California	6,022	10.31%
24	Colorado	773	1.32%
19	Connecticut	912	1.56%
31	Delaware	613	1.05%
4	Florida	2,607	4.46%
12	Georgia	1,880	3.22%
49	Hawaii	0	0.00%
45	Idaho	204	0.35%
9	Illinois	2,139	3.66%
17	Indiana	1,012	1.73%
32	Iowa	577	0.99%
26	Kansas	731	1.25%
15	Kentucky	1,456	2.49%
27	Louisiana	713	1.22%
39	Maine	339	0.58%
8	Maryland	2,397	4.10%
10	Massachusetts	2,134	3.65%
13	Michigan	1,770	3.03%
NA	Minnesota**	NA	NA
33	Mississippi	500	0.86%
20	Missouri	838	1.43%
37	Montana	375	0.64%
35	Nebraska	433	0.74%
40	Nevada	327	0.56%
44	New Hampshire	225	0.39%
4	New Jersey	2,607	4.46%
36	New Mexico	402	0.69%
3	New York	4,046	6.93%
7	North Carolina	2,525	4.32%
48	North Dakota	115	0.20%
16	Ohio	1,338	2.29%
25	Oklahoma	761	1.30%
22	Oregon	799	1.37%
2	Pennsylvania	4,324	7.40%
43	Rhode Island	231	0.40%
14	South Carolina	1,605	2.75%
46	South Dakota	150	0.26%
28	Tennessee	708	1.21%
6	Texas	2,536	4.34%
38	Utah	360	0.62%
42	Vermont	268	0.46%
11	Virginia	1,960	3.36%
18	Washington	933	1.60%
29	West Virginia	631	1.08%
30	Wisconsin	620	1.06%
46	Wyoming	150	0.26%

RANK	STATE	OFFICERS	% of USA
1	California	6,022	10.31%
2	Pennsylvania	4,324	7.40%
3	New York	4,046	6.93%
4	Florida	2,607	4.46%
4	New Jersey	2,607	4.46%
6	Texas	2,536	4.34%
7	North Carolina	2,525	4.32%
8	Maryland	2,397	4.10%
9	Illinois	2,139	3.66%
10	Massachusetts	2,134	3.65%
11	Virginia	1,960	3.36%
12	Georgia	1,880	3.22%
13	Michigan	1,770	3.03%
14	South Carolina	1,605	2.75%
15	Kentucky	1,456	2.49%
16	Ohio	1,338	2.29%
17	Indiana	1,012	1.73%
18	Washington	933	1.60%
19	Connecticut	912	1.56%
20	Missouri	838	1.43%
21	Arizona	813	1.39%
22	Oregon	799	1.37%
23	Alabama	788	1.35%
24	Colorado	773	1.32%
25	Oklahoma	761	1.30%
26	Kansas	731	1.25%
27	Louisiana	713	1.22%
28	Tennessee	708	1.21%
29	West Virginia	631	1.08%
30	Wisconsin	620	1.06%
31	Delaware	613	1.05%
32	Iowa	577	0.99%
33	Mississippi	500	0.86%
34	Arkansas	456	0.78%
35	Nebraska	433	0.74%
36	New Mexico	402	0.69%
37	Montana	375	0.64%
38	Utah	360	0.62%
39	Maine	339	0.58%
40	Nevada	327	0.56%
41	Alaska	311	0.53%
42	Vermont	268	0.46%
43	Rhode Island	231	0.40%
44	New Hampshire	225	0.39%
45	Idaho	204	0.35%
46	South Dakota	150	0.26%
46	Wyoming	150	0.26%
48	North Dakota	115	0.20%
49	Hawaii	0	0.00%
NA	Minnesota**	NA	NA
	District of Columbia	0	0.00%

Source: Federal Bureau of Investigation
"Crime in the United States 1994" (Uniform Crime Reports, November 19, 1995)
*Total is of states shown separately. Includes state police agencies and other agencies with law enforcement powers. Hawaii and the District of Columbia do not have a state police agency.
**Not available.

Female State Government Law Enforcement Officers in 1994

National Total = 3,930 Female Officers*

ALPHA ORDER

RANK	STATE	OFFICERS	% of USA
37	Alabama	18	0.46%
35	Alaska	19	0.48%
19	Arizona	54	1.37%
33	Arkansas	20	0.51%
1	California	621	15.80%
20	Colorado	52	1.32%
18	Connecticut	65	1.65%
24	Delaware	45	1.15%
4	Florida	281	7.15%
9	Georgia	141	3.59%
49	Hawaii	0	0.00%
43	Idaho	9	0.23%
7	Illinois	181	4.61%
23	Indiana	47	1.20%
28	Iowa	31	0.79%
16	Kansas	71	1.81%
21	Kentucky	51	1.30%
41	Louisiana	10	0.25%
38	Maine	17	0.43%
3	Maryland	283	7.20%
6	Massachusetts	218	5.55%
5	Michigan	221	5.62%
NA	Minnesota**	NA	NA
44	Mississippi	8	0.20%
29	Missouri	27	0.69%
27	Montana	32	0.81%
33	Nebraska	20	0.51%
31	Nevada	22	0.56%
30	New Hampshire	23	0.59%
17	New Jersey	67	1.70%
41	New Mexico	10	0.25%
2	New York	325	8.27%
10	North Carolina	128	3.26%
46	North Dakota	3	0.08%
12	Ohio	97	2.47%
45	Oklahoma	7	0.18%
21	Oregon	51	1.30%
8	Pennsylvania	165	4.20%
38	Rhode Island	17	0.43%
11	South Carolina	102	2.60%
48	South Dakota	2	0.05%
26	Tennessee	36	0.92%
13	Texas	90	2.29%
35	Utah	19	0.48%
40	Vermont	12	0.31%
14	Virginia	75	1.91%
25	Washington	39	0.99%
32	West Virginia	21	0.53%
15	Wisconsin	74	1.88%
46	Wyoming	3	0.08%

RANK ORDER

RANK	STATE	OFFICERS	% of USA
1	California	621	15.80%
2	New York	325	8.27%
3	Maryland	283	7.20%
4	Florida	281	7.15%
5	Michigan	221	5.62%
6	Massachusetts	218	5.55%
7	Illinois	181	4.61%
8	Pennsylvania	165	4.20%
9	Georgia	141	3.59%
10	North Carolina	128	3.26%
11	South Carolina	102	2.60%
12	Ohio	97	2.47%
13	Texas	90	2.29%
14	Virginia	75	1.91%
15	Wisconsin	74	1.88%
16	Kansas	71	1.81%
17	New Jersey	67	1.70%
18	Connecticut	65	1.65%
19	Arizona	54	1.37%
20	Colorado	52	1.32%
21	Kentucky	51	1.30%
21	Oregon	51	1.30%
23	Indiana	47	1.20%
24	Delaware	45	1.15%
25	Washington	39	0.99%
26	Tennessee	36	0.92%
27	Montana	32	0.81%
28	Iowa	31	0.79%
29	Missouri	27	0.69%
30	New Hampshire	23	0.59%
31	Nevada	22	0.56%
32	West Virginia	21	0.53%
33	Arkansas	20	0.51%
33	Nebraska	20	0.51%
35	Alaska	19	0.48%
35	Utah	19	0.48%
37	Alabama	18	0.46%
38	Maine	17	0.43%
38	Rhode Island	17	0.43%
40	Vermont	12	0.31%
41	Louisiana	10	0.25%
41	New Mexico	10	0.25%
43	Idaho	9	0.23%
44	Mississippi	8	0.20%
45	Oklahoma	7	0.18%
46	North Dakota	3	0.08%
46	Wyoming	3	0.08%
48	South Dakota	2	0.05%
49	Hawaii	0	0.00%
NA	Minnesota**	NA	NA
	District of Columbia	0	0.00%

Source: Federal Bureau of Investigation
   "Crime in the United States 1994" (Uniform Crime Reports, November 19, 1995)
*Total is of states shown separately. Includes state police agencies and other agencies with law enforcement powers. Hawaii and the District of Columbia do not have a state police agency.
**Not available.

Female State Government Law Enforcement Officers
As a Percent of All Officers: 1994
National Percent = 6.30% of Officers*

RANK	STATE	PERCENT
43	Alabama	2.23
22	Alaska	5.76
19	Arizona	6.23
32	Arkansas	4.20
5	California	9.35
17	Colorado	6.30
16	Connecticut	6.65
14	Delaware	6.84
4	Florida	9.73
12	Georgia	6.98
NA	Hawaii**	NA
31	Idaho	4.23
10	Illinois	7.80
28	Indiana	4.44
23	Iowa	5.10
8	Kansas	8.85
37	Kentucky	3.38
46	Louisiana	1.38
27	Maine	4.78
3	Maryland	10.56
6	Massachusetts	9.27
1	Michigan	11.10
NA	Minnesota**	NA
45	Mississippi	1.57
39	Missouri	3.12
9	Montana	7.86
29	Nebraska	4.42
17	Nevada	6.30
6	New Hampshire	9.27
41	New Jersey	2.51
42	New Mexico	2.43
11	New York	7.44
26	North Carolina	4.82
40	North Dakota	2.54
15	Ohio	6.76
48	Oklahoma	0.91
20	Oregon	6.00
35	Pennsylvania	3.68
13	Rhode Island	6.85
21	South Carolina	5.98
47	South Dakota	1.32
25	Tennessee	4.84
36	Texas	3.43
24	Utah	5.01
30	Vermont	4.29
34	Virginia	3.69
33	Washington	4.01
38	West Virginia	3.22
2	Wisconsin	10.66
44	Wyoming	1.96

RANK	STATE	PERCENT
1	Michigan	11.10
2	Wisconsin	10.66
3	Maryland	10.56
4	Florida	9.73
5	California	9.35
6	Massachusetts	9.27
6	New Hampshire	9.27
8	Kansas	8.85
9	Montana	7.86
10	Illinois	7.80
11	New York	7.44
12	Georgia	6.98
13	Rhode Island	6.85
14	Delaware	6.84
15	Ohio	6.76
16	Connecticut	6.65
17	Colorado	6.30
17	Nevada	6.30
19	Arizona	6.23
20	Oregon	6.00
21	South Carolina	5.98
22	Alaska	5.76
23	Iowa	5.10
24	Utah	5.01
25	Tennessee	4.84
26	North Carolina	4.82
27	Maine	4.78
28	Indiana	4.44
29	Nebraska	4.42
30	Vermont	4.29
31	Idaho	4.23
32	Arkansas	4.20
33	Washington	4.01
34	Virginia	3.69
35	Pennsylvania	3.68
36	Texas	3.43
37	Kentucky	3.38
38	West Virginia	3.22
39	Missouri	3.12
40	North Dakota	2.54
41	New Jersey	2.51
42	New Mexico	2.43
43	Alabama	2.23
44	Wyoming	1.96
45	Mississippi	1.57
46	Louisiana	1.38
47	South Dakota	1.32
48	Oklahoma	0.91
NA	Hawaii**	NA
NA	Minnesota**	NA
	District of Columbia**	NA

Source: Morgan Quitno Press using data from Federal Bureau of Investigation
   "Crime in the United States 1994" (Uniform Crime Reports, November 19, 1995)
Total is of states shown separately. Includes state police agencies and other agencies with law enforcement powers.
**Hawaii and the District of Columbia do not have a state police agency. Minnesota data are not available.*

Local Police Departments in 1992

National Total = 12,502 Departments*

ALPHA ORDER

RANK	STATE	DEPARTMENTS	% of USA
18	Alabama	285	2.28%
46	Alaska	43	0.34%
40	Arizona	75	0.60%
28	Arkansas	185	1.48%
12	California	341	2.73%
32	Colorado	140	1.12%
35	Connecticut	108	0.86%
48	Delaware	33	0.26%
18	Florida	285	2.28%
11	Georgia	343	2.74%
50	Hawaii	4	0.03%
42	Idaho	66	0.53%
3	Illinois	748	5.98%
14	Indiana	336	2.69%
16	Iowa	321	2.57%
22	Kansas	221	1.77%
21	Kentucky	240	1.92%
20	Louisiana	256	2.05%
34	Maine	119	0.95%
38	Maryland	78	0.62%
12	Massachusetts	341	2.73%
6	Michigan	474	3.79%
10	Minnesota	359	2.87%
26	Mississippi	189	1.51%
7	Missouri	463	3.70%
43	Montana	59	0.47%
31	Nebraska	149	1.19%
49	Nevada	14	0.11%
23	New Hampshire	214	1.71%
5	New Jersey	488	3.90%
41	New Mexico	72	0.58%
7	New York	463	3.70%
15	North Carolina	332	2.66%
39	North Dakota	76	0.61%
2	Ohio	776	6.21%
17	Oklahoma	312	2.50%
33	Oregon	137	1.10%
1	Pennsylvania	1,049	8.39%
47	Rhode Island	39	0.31%
27	South Carolina	188	1.50%
36	South Dakota	102	0.82%
24	Tennessee	211	1.69%
4	Texas	632	5.06%
37	Utah	84	0.67%
44	Vermont	57	0.46%
29	Virginia	167	1.34%
25	Washington	202	1.62%
30	West Virginia	158	1.26%
9	Wisconsin	417	3.34%
45	Wyoming	50	0.40%

RANK ORDER

RANK	STATE	DEPARTMENTS	% of USA
1	Pennsylvania	1,049	8.39%
2	Ohio	776	6.21%
3	Illinois	748	5.98%
4	Texas	632	5.06%
5	New Jersey	488	3.90%
6	Michigan	474	3.79%
7	Missouri	463	3.70%
7	New York	463	3.70%
9	Wisconsin	417	3.34%
10	Minnesota	359	2.87%
11	Georgia	343	2.74%
12	California	341	2.73%
12	Massachusetts	341	2.73%
14	Indiana	336	2.69%
15	North Carolina	332	2.66%
16	Iowa	321	2.57%
17	Oklahoma	312	2.50%
18	Alabama	285	2.28%
18	Florida	285	2.28%
20	Louisiana	256	2.05%
21	Kentucky	240	1.92%
22	Kansas	221	1.77%
23	New Hampshire	214	1.71%
24	Tennessee	211	1.69%
25	Washington	202	1.62%
26	Mississippi	189	1.51%
27	South Carolina	188	1.50%
28	Arkansas	185	1.48%
29	Virginia	167	1.34%
30	West Virginia	158	1.26%
31	Nebraska	149	1.19%
32	Colorado	140	1.12%
33	Oregon	137	1.10%
34	Maine	119	0.95%
35	Connecticut	108	0.86%
36	South Dakota	102	0.82%
37	Utah	84	0.67%
38	Maryland	78	0.62%
39	North Dakota	76	0.61%
40	Arizona	75	0.60%
41	New Mexico	72	0.58%
42	Idaho	66	0.53%
43	Montana	59	0.47%
44	Vermont	57	0.46%
45	Wyoming	50	0.40%
46	Alaska	43	0.34%
47	Rhode Island	39	0.31%
48	Delaware	33	0.26%
49	Nevada	14	0.11%
50	Hawaii	4	0.03%
	District of Columbia	1	0.01%

Source: U.S. Department of Justice, Bureau of Justice Statistics
  "Census of State and Local Law Enforcement Agencies, 1992" (Bulletin, July 1993, NCJ-142972)
*Includes consolidated police-sheriffs' departments.

Full-Time Officers in Local Police Departments in 1992

National Total = 373,061 Officers*

ALPHA ORDER					RANK ORDER			
RANK	STATE		OFFICERS	% of USA	RANK	STATE	OFFICERS	% of USA
20	Alabama		5,640	1.51%	1	New York	45,822	12.28%
45	Alaska		677	0.18%	2	California	33,191	8.90%
22	Arizona		5,209	1.40%	3	Illinois	24,988	6.70%
34	Arkansas		2,494	0.67%	4	Texas	24,576	6.59%
2	California		33,191	8.90%	5	New Jersey	19,221	5.15%
23	Colorado		4,787	1.28%	6	Florida	18,037	4.83%
18	Connecticut		6,068	1.63%	7	Pennsylvania	17,256	4.63%
44	Delaware		887	0.24%	8	Ohio	14,668	3.93%
6	Florida		18,037	4.83%	9	Michigan	13,027	3.49%
11	Georgia		9,404	2.52%	10	Massachusetts	12,087	3.24%
33	Hawaii		2,690	0.72%	11	Georgia	9,404	2.52%
43	Idaho		921	0.25%	12	Maryland	8,273	2.22%
3	Illinois		24,988	6.70%	13	Virginia	8,205	2.20%
19	Indiana		5,992	1.61%	14	North Carolina	8,023	2.15%
30	Iowa		2,863	0.77%	15	Missouri	7,921	2.12%
29	Kansas		3,189	0.85%	16	Wisconsin	7,184	1.93%
27	Kentucky		3,804	1.02%	17	Tennessee	6,214	1.67%
21	Louisiana		5,548	1.49%	18	Connecticut	6,068	1.63%
41	Maine		1,399	0.38%	19	Indiana	5,992	1.61%
12	Maryland		8,273	2.22%	20	Alabama	5,640	1.51%
10	Massachusetts		12,087	3.24%	21	Louisiana	5,548	1.49%
9	Michigan		13,027	3.49%	22	Arizona	5,209	1.40%
25	Minnesota		4,580	1.23%	23	Colorado	4,787	1.28%
32	Mississippi		2,745	0.74%	24	Washington	4,704	1.26%
15	Missouri		7,921	2.12%	25	Minnesota	4,580	1.23%
49	Montana		568	0.15%	26	Oklahoma	4,529	1.21%
38	Nebraska		1,720	0.46%	27	Kentucky	3,804	1.02%
37	Nevada		1,795	0.48%	28	South Carolina	3,481	0.93%
39	New Hampshire		1,717	0.46%	29	Kansas	3,189	0.85%
5	New Jersey		19,221	5.15%	30	Iowa	2,863	0.77%
35	New Mexico		2,092	0.56%	31	Oregon	2,782	0.75%
1	New York		45,822	12.28%	32	Mississippi	2,745	0.74%
14	North Carolina		8,023	2.15%	33	Hawaii	2,690	0.72%
50	North Dakota		538	0.14%	34	Arkansas	2,494	0.67%
8	Ohio		14,668	3.93%	35	New Mexico	2,092	0.56%
26	Oklahoma		4,529	1.21%	36	Rhode Island	2,024	0.54%
31	Oregon		2,782	0.75%	37	Nevada	1,795	0.48%
7	Pennsylvania		17,256	4.63%	38	Nebraska	1,720	0.46%
36	Rhode Island		2,024	0.54%	39	New Hampshire	1,717	0.46%
28	South Carolina		3,481	0.93%	40	Utah	1,546	0.41%
46	South Dakota		648	0.17%	41	Maine	1,399	0.38%
17	Tennessee		6,214	1.67%	42	West Virginia	1,260	0.34%
4	Texas		24,576	6.59%	43	Idaho	921	0.25%
40	Utah		1,546	0.41%	44	Delaware	887	0.24%
47	Vermont		594	0.16%	45	Alaska	677	0.18%
13	Virginia		8,205	2.20%	46	South Dakota	648	0.17%
24	Washington		4,704	1.26%	47	Vermont	594	0.16%
42	West Virginia		1,260	0.34%	48	Wyoming	584	0.16%
16	Wisconsin		7,184	1.93%	49	Montana	568	0.15%
48	Wyoming		584	0.16%	50	North Dakota	538	0.14%
						District of Columbia	4,889	1.31%

Source: U.S. Department of Justice, Bureau of Justice Statistics
   "Census of State and Local Law Enforcement Agencies, 1992" (Bulletin, July 1993, NCJ-142972)
*Includes consolidated police-sheriffs' departments.

Percent of Full-Time Local Police Department Employees
Who Are Sworn Officers: 1992
National Percent = 78.33% of Employees*

ALPHA ORDER

RANK	STATE	PERCENT
31	Alabama	77.31
49	Alaska	63.21
44	Arizona	72.57
32	Arkansas	76.46
46	California	70.70
42	Colorado	74.27
5	Connecticut	83.86
3	Delaware	84.72
47	Florida	70.46
40	Georgia	75.09
25	Hawaii	79.49
23	Idaho	80.02
18	Illinois	80.68
33	Indiana	76.20
10	Iowa	82.36
36	Kansas	75.66
20	Kentucky	80.58
12	Louisiana	82.07
26	Maine	79.22
16	Maryland	81.46
2	Massachusetts	85.02
6	Michigan	83.31
7	Minnesota	83.18
37	Mississippi	75.56
33	Missouri	76.20
30	Montana	77.49
22	Nebraska	80.11
50	Nevada	56.54
28	New Hampshire	78.37
4	New Jersey	84.33
48	New Mexico	69.66
17	New York	81.24
13	North Carolina	81.83
24	North Dakota	79.82
14	Ohio	81.78
39	Oklahoma	75.13
45	Oregon	71.65
1	Pennsylvania	86.68
9	Rhode Island	82.41
21	South Carolina	80.52
19	South Dakota	80.60
35	Tennessee	75.74
41	Texas	74.34
11	Utah	82.15
27	Vermont	78.99
29	Virginia	77.93
38	Washington	75.31
8	West Virginia	82.51
15	Wisconsin	81.68
43	Wyoming	73.09

RANK ORDER

RANK	STATE	PERCENT
1	Pennsylvania	86.68
2	Massachusetts	85.02
3	Delaware	84.72
4	New Jersey	84.33
5	Connecticut	83.86
6	Michigan	83.31
7	Minnesota	83.18
8	West Virginia	82.51
9	Rhode Island	82.41
10	Iowa	82.36
11	Utah	82.15
12	Louisiana	82.07
13	North Carolina	81.83
14	Ohio	81.78
15	Wisconsin	81.68
16	Maryland	81.46
17	New York	81.24
18	Illinois	80.68
19	South Dakota	80.60
20	Kentucky	80.58
21	South Carolina	80.52
22	Nebraska	80.11
23	Idaho	80.02
24	North Dakota	79.82
25	Hawaii	79.49
26	Maine	79.22
27	Vermont	78.99
28	New Hampshire	78.37
29	Virginia	77.93
30	Montana	77.49
31	Alabama	77.31
32	Arkansas	76.46
33	Indiana	76.20
33	Missouri	76.20
35	Tennessee	75.74
36	Kansas	75.66
37	Mississippi	75.56
38	Washington	75.31
39	Oklahoma	75.13
40	Georgia	75.09
41	Texas	74.34
42	Colorado	74.27
43	Wyoming	73.09
44	Arizona	72.57
45	Oregon	71.65
46	California	70.70
47	Florida	70.46
48	New Mexico	69.66
49	Alaska	63.21
50	Nevada	56.54

District of Columbia	85.03

Source: Morgan Quitno Press using data from U.S. Department of Justice, Bureau of Justice Statistics
"Census of State and Local Law Enforcement Agencies, 1992" (Bulletin, July 1993, NCJ-142972)
*Includes consolidated police-sheriffs' departments.

Rate of Full-Time Officers in Local Police Departments in 1992

National Rate = 14.63 Officers per 10,000 Population*

ALPHA ORDER				RANK ORDER		
RANK	STATE	RATE		RANK	STATE	RATE
18	Alabama	13.64		1	New York	25.29
31	Alaska	11.53		2	New Jersey	24.68
19	Arizona	13.59		3	Hawaii	23.19
38	Arkansas	10.40		4	Illinois	21.48
33	California	10.75		5	Massachusetts	20.15
16	Colorado	13.80		6	Rhode Island	20.14
7	Connecticut	18.49		7	Connecticut	18.49
25	Delaware	12.87		8	Maryland	16.86
21	Florida	13.37		9	New Hampshire	15.45
14	Georgia	13.93		10	Missouri	15.25
3	Hawaii	23.19		11	Pennsylvania	14.37
46	Idaho	8.63		12	Wisconsin	14.35
4	Illinois	21.48		13	Oklahoma	14.10
35	Indiana	10.58		14	Georgia	13.93
40	Iowa	10.18		15	Texas	13.92
27	Kansas	12.64		16	Colorado	13.80
41	Kentucky	10.13		16	Michigan	13.80
24	Louisiana	12.94		18	Alabama	13.64
32	Maine	11.33		19	Arizona	13.59
8	Maryland	16.86		20	Nevada	13.53
5	Massachusetts	20.15		21	Florida	13.37
16	Michigan	13.80		22	Ohio	13.32
39	Minnesota	10.22		23	New Mexico	13.23
36	Mississippi	10.50		24	Louisiana	12.94
10	Missouri	15.25		25	Delaware	12.87
50	Montana	6.89		25	Virginia	12.87
34	Nebraska	10.71		27	Kansas	12.64
20	Nevada	13.53		28	Wyoming	12.53
9	New Hampshire	15.45		29	Tennessee	12.37
2	New Jersey	24.68		30	North Carolina	11.72
23	New Mexico	13.23		31	Alaska	11.53
1	New York	25.29		32	Maine	11.33
30	North Carolina	11.72		33	California	10.75
48	North Dakota	8.46		34	Nebraska	10.71
22	Ohio	13.32		35	Indiana	10.58
13	Oklahoma	14.10		36	Mississippi	10.50
43	Oregon	9.34		37	Vermont	10.42
11	Pennsylvania	14.37		38	Arkansas	10.40
6	Rhode Island	20.14		39	Minnesota	10.22
42	South Carolina	9.66		40	Iowa	10.18
45	South Dakota	9.11		41	Kentucky	10.13
29	Tennessee	12.37		42	South Carolina	9.66
15	Texas	13.92		43	Oregon	9.34
47	Utah	8.53		44	Washington	9.16
37	Vermont	10.42		45	South Dakota	9.11
25	Virginia	12.87		46	Idaho	8.63
44	Washington	9.16		47	Utah	8.53
49	West Virginia	6.95		48	North Dakota	8.46
12	Wisconsin	14.35		49	West Virginia	6.95
28	Wyoming	12.53		50	Montana	6.89
					District of Columbia	83.01

Source: Morgan Quitno Press using data from U.S. Department of Justice, Bureau of Justice Statistics
    "Census of State and Local Law Enforcement Agencies, 1992" (Bulletin, July 1993, NCJ-142972)
*Includes consolidated police-sheriffs' departments.

Full-Time Employees in Local Police Departments in 1992

National Total = 476,261 Employees*

	ALPHA ORDER					RANK ORDER		
RANK	STATE	EMPLOYEES	% of USA		RANK	STATE	EMPLOYEES	% of USA
19	Alabama	7,295	1.53%		1	New York	56,406	11.84%
44	Alaska	1,071	0.22%		2	California	46,947	9.86%
21	Arizona	7,178	1.51%		3	Texas	33,059	6.94%
34	Arkansas	3,262	0.68%		4	Illinois	30,971	6.50%
2	California	46,947	9.86%		5	Florida	25,598	5.37%
23	Colorado	6,445	1.35%		6	New Jersey	22,793	4.79%
20	Connecticut	7,236	1.52%		7	Pennsylvania	19,907	4.18%
45	Delaware	1,047	0.22%		8	Ohio	17,936	3.77%
5	Florida	25,598	5.37%		9	Michigan	15,636	3.28%
11	Georgia	12,524	2.63%		10	Massachusetts	14,217	2.99%
33	Hawaii	3,384	0.71%		11	Georgia	12,524	2.63%
43	Idaho	1,151	0.24%		12	Virginia	10,529	2.21%
4	Illinois	30,971	6.50%		13	Missouri	10,395	2.18%
18	Indiana	7,864	1.65%		14	Maryland	10,156	2.13%
32	Iowa	3,476	0.73%		15	North Carolina	9,805	2.06%
29	Kansas	4,215	0.89%		16	Wisconsin	8,795	1.85%
27	Kentucky	4,721	0.99%		17	Tennessee	8,204	1.72%
22	Louisiana	6,760	1.42%		18	Indiana	7,864	1.65%
41	Maine	1,766	0.37%		19	Alabama	7,295	1.53%
14	Maryland	10,156	2.13%		20	Connecticut	7,236	1.52%
10	Massachusetts	14,217	2.99%		21	Arizona	7,178	1.51%
9	Michigan	15,636	3.28%		22	Louisiana	6,760	1.42%
26	Minnesota	5,506	1.16%		23	Colorado	6,445	1.35%
31	Mississippi	3,633	0.76%		24	Washington	6,246	1.31%
13	Missouri	10,395	2.18%		25	Oklahoma	6,028	1.27%
49	Montana	733	0.15%		26	Minnesota	5,506	1.16%
39	Nebraska	2,147	0.45%		27	Kentucky	4,721	0.99%
35	Nevada	3,175	0.67%		28	South Carolina	4,323	0.91%
38	New Hampshire	2,191	0.46%		29	Kansas	4,215	0.89%
6	New Jersey	22,793	4.79%		30	Oregon	3,883	0.82%
36	New Mexico	3,003	0.63%		31	Mississippi	3,633	0.76%
1	New York	56,406	11.84%		32	Iowa	3,476	0.73%
15	North Carolina	9,805	2.06%		33	Hawaii	3,384	0.71%
50	North Dakota	674	0.14%		34	Arkansas	3,262	0.68%
8	Ohio	17,936	3.77%		35	Nevada	3,175	0.67%
25	Oklahoma	6,028	1.27%		36	New Mexico	3,003	0.63%
30	Oregon	3,883	0.82%		37	Rhode Island	2,456	0.52%
7	Pennsylvania	19,907	4.18%		38	New Hampshire	2,191	0.46%
37	Rhode Island	2,456	0.52%		39	Nebraska	2,147	0.45%
28	South Carolina	4,323	0.91%		40	Utah	1,882	0.40%
46	South Dakota	804	0.17%		41	Maine	1,766	0.37%
17	Tennessee	8,204	1.72%		42	West Virginia	1,527	0.32%
3	Texas	33,059	6.94%		43	Idaho	1,151	0.24%
40	Utah	1,882	0.40%		44	Alaska	1,071	0.22%
48	Vermont	752	0.16%		45	Delaware	1,047	0.22%
12	Virginia	10,529	2.21%		46	South Dakota	804	0.17%
24	Washington	6,246	1.31%		47	Wyoming	799	0.17%
42	West Virginia	1,527	0.32%		48	Vermont	752	0.16%
16	Wisconsin	8,795	1.85%		49	Montana	733	0.15%
47	Wyoming	799	0.17%		50	North Dakota	674	0.14%
						District of Columbia	5,750	1.21%

Source: U.S. Department of Justice, Bureau of Justice Statistics
"Census of State and Local Law Enforcement Agencies, 1992" (Bulletin, July 1993, NCJ-142972)
*Includes consolidated police-sheriffs' departments.

Sheriffs' Departments in 1992

National Total = 3,086 Departments*

<table>
<tr><td colspan="4">ALPHA ORDER</td><td colspan="4">RANK ORDER</td></tr>
<tr><td>RANK</td><td>STATE</td><td>DEPARTMENTS</td><td>% of USA</td><td>RANK</td><td>STATE</td><td>DEPARTMENTS</td><td>% of USA</td></tr>
<tr><td>20</td><td>Alabama</td><td>67</td><td>2.17%</td><td>1</td><td>Texas</td><td>255</td><td>8.26%</td></tr>
<tr><td>49</td><td>Alaska</td><td>0</td><td>0.00%</td><td>2</td><td>Georgia</td><td>159</td><td>5.15%</td></tr>
<tr><td>42</td><td>Arizona</td><td>15</td><td>0.49%</td><td>3</td><td>Virginia</td><td>125</td><td>4.05%</td></tr>
<tr><td>18</td><td>Arkansas</td><td>75</td><td>2.43%</td><td>4</td><td>Kentucky</td><td>120</td><td>3.89%</td></tr>
<tr><td>26</td><td>California</td><td>58</td><td>1.88%</td><td>5</td><td>Missouri</td><td>114</td><td>3.69%</td></tr>
<tr><td>25</td><td>Colorado</td><td>63</td><td>2.04%</td><td>6</td><td>Kansas</td><td>105</td><td>3.40%</td></tr>
<tr><td>46</td><td>Connecticut</td><td>8</td><td>0.26%</td><td>7</td><td>Illinois</td><td>102</td><td>3.31%</td></tr>
<tr><td>48</td><td>Delaware</td><td>3</td><td>0.10%</td><td>8</td><td>North Carolina</td><td>100</td><td>3.24%</td></tr>
<tr><td>23</td><td>Florida</td><td>65</td><td>2.11%</td><td>9</td><td>Iowa</td><td>99</td><td>3.21%</td></tr>
<tr><td>2</td><td>Georgia</td><td>159</td><td>5.15%</td><td>10</td><td>Tennessee</td><td>95</td><td>3.08%</td></tr>
<tr><td>49</td><td>Hawaii</td><td>0</td><td>0.00%</td><td>11</td><td>Nebraska</td><td>93</td><td>3.01%</td></tr>
<tr><td>32</td><td>Idaho</td><td>44</td><td>1.43%</td><td>12</td><td>Indiana</td><td>91</td><td>2.95%</td></tr>
<tr><td>7</td><td>Illinois</td><td>102</td><td>3.31%</td><td>13</td><td>Ohio</td><td>88</td><td>2.85%</td></tr>
<tr><td>12</td><td>Indiana</td><td>91</td><td>2.95%</td><td>14</td><td>Minnesota</td><td>87</td><td>2.82%</td></tr>
<tr><td>9</td><td>Iowa</td><td>99</td><td>3.21%</td><td>15</td><td>Michigan</td><td>83</td><td>2.69%</td></tr>
<tr><td>6</td><td>Kansas</td><td>105</td><td>3.40%</td><td>16</td><td>Mississippi</td><td>82</td><td>2.66%</td></tr>
<tr><td>4</td><td>Kentucky</td><td>120</td><td>3.89%</td><td>17</td><td>Oklahoma</td><td>77</td><td>2.50%</td></tr>
<tr><td>24</td><td>Louisiana</td><td>64</td><td>2.07%</td><td>18</td><td>Arkansas</td><td>75</td><td>2.43%</td></tr>
<tr><td>40</td><td>Maine</td><td>16</td><td>0.52%</td><td>19</td><td>Wisconsin</td><td>72</td><td>2.33%</td></tr>
<tr><td>37</td><td>Maryland</td><td>24</td><td>0.78%</td><td>20</td><td>Alabama</td><td>67</td><td>2.17%</td></tr>
<tr><td>43</td><td>Massachusetts</td><td>14</td><td>0.45%</td><td>21</td><td>Pennsylvania</td><td>66</td><td>2.14%</td></tr>
<tr><td>15</td><td>Michigan</td><td>83</td><td>2.69%</td><td>21</td><td>South Dakota</td><td>66</td><td>2.14%</td></tr>
<tr><td>14</td><td>Minnesota</td><td>87</td><td>2.82%</td><td>23</td><td>Florida</td><td>65</td><td>2.11%</td></tr>
<tr><td>16</td><td>Mississippi</td><td>82</td><td>2.66%</td><td>24</td><td>Louisiana</td><td>64</td><td>2.07%</td></tr>
<tr><td>5</td><td>Missouri</td><td>114</td><td>3.69%</td><td>25</td><td>Colorado</td><td>63</td><td>2.04%</td></tr>
<tr><td>28</td><td>Montana</td><td>55</td><td>1.78%</td><td>26</td><td>California</td><td>58</td><td>1.88%</td></tr>
<tr><td>11</td><td>Nebraska</td><td>93</td><td>3.01%</td><td>27</td><td>New York</td><td>57</td><td>1.85%</td></tr>
<tr><td>40</td><td>Nevada</td><td>16</td><td>0.52%</td><td>28</td><td>Montana</td><td>55</td><td>1.78%</td></tr>
<tr><td>45</td><td>New Hampshire</td><td>10</td><td>0.32%</td><td>28</td><td>West Virginia</td><td>55</td><td>1.78%</td></tr>
<tr><td>39</td><td>New Jersey</td><td>21</td><td>0.68%</td><td>30</td><td>North Dakota</td><td>53</td><td>1.72%</td></tr>
<tr><td>35</td><td>New Mexico</td><td>33</td><td>1.07%</td><td>31</td><td>South Carolina</td><td>46</td><td>1.49%</td></tr>
<tr><td>27</td><td>New York</td><td>57</td><td>1.85%</td><td>32</td><td>Idaho</td><td>44</td><td>1.43%</td></tr>
<tr><td>8</td><td>North Carolina</td><td>100</td><td>3.24%</td><td>33</td><td>Washington</td><td>39</td><td>1.26%</td></tr>
<tr><td>30</td><td>North Dakota</td><td>53</td><td>1.72%</td><td>34</td><td>Oregon</td><td>36</td><td>1.17%</td></tr>
<tr><td>13</td><td>Ohio</td><td>88</td><td>2.85%</td><td>35</td><td>New Mexico</td><td>33</td><td>1.07%</td></tr>
<tr><td>17</td><td>Oklahoma</td><td>77</td><td>2.50%</td><td>36</td><td>Utah</td><td>29</td><td>0.94%</td></tr>
<tr><td>34</td><td>Oregon</td><td>36</td><td>1.17%</td><td>37</td><td>Maryland</td><td>24</td><td>0.78%</td></tr>
<tr><td>21</td><td>Pennsylvania</td><td>66</td><td>2.14%</td><td>38</td><td>Wyoming</td><td>23</td><td>0.75%</td></tr>
<tr><td>47</td><td>Rhode Island</td><td>4</td><td>0.13%</td><td>39</td><td>New Jersey</td><td>21</td><td>0.68%</td></tr>
<tr><td>31</td><td>South Carolina</td><td>46</td><td>1.49%</td><td>40</td><td>Maine</td><td>16</td><td>0.52%</td></tr>
<tr><td>21</td><td>South Dakota</td><td>66</td><td>2.14%</td><td>40</td><td>Nevada</td><td>16</td><td>0.52%</td></tr>
<tr><td>10</td><td>Tennessee</td><td>95</td><td>3.08%</td><td>42</td><td>Arizona</td><td>15</td><td>0.49%</td></tr>
<tr><td>1</td><td>Texas</td><td>255</td><td>8.26%</td><td>43</td><td>Massachusetts</td><td>14</td><td>0.45%</td></tr>
<tr><td>36</td><td>Utah</td><td>29</td><td>0.94%</td><td>43</td><td>Vermont</td><td>14</td><td>0.45%</td></tr>
<tr><td>43</td><td>Vermont</td><td>14</td><td>0.45%</td><td>45</td><td>New Hampshire</td><td>10</td><td>0.32%</td></tr>
<tr><td>3</td><td>Virginia</td><td>125</td><td>4.05%</td><td>46</td><td>Connecticut</td><td>8</td><td>0.26%</td></tr>
<tr><td>33</td><td>Washington</td><td>39</td><td>1.26%</td><td>47</td><td>Rhode Island</td><td>4</td><td>0.13%</td></tr>
<tr><td>28</td><td>West Virginia</td><td>55</td><td>1.78%</td><td>48</td><td>Delaware</td><td>3</td><td>0.10%</td></tr>
<tr><td>19</td><td>Wisconsin</td><td>72</td><td>2.33%</td><td>49</td><td>Alaska</td><td>0</td><td>0.00%</td></tr>
<tr><td>38</td><td>Wyoming</td><td>23</td><td>0.75%</td><td>49</td><td>Hawaii</td><td>0</td><td>0.00%</td></tr>
<tr><td></td><td></td><td></td><td></td><td></td><td>District of Columbia</td><td>0</td><td>0.00%</td></tr>
</table>

Source: U.S. Department of Justice, Bureau of Justice Statistics
   "Census of State and Local Law Enforcement Agencies, 1992" (Bulletin, July 1993, NCJ-142972)
*Sheriffs' departments generally operate at the county level.

Full-Time Sworn Officers in Sheriffs' Departments in 1992

National Total = 136,542 Officers*

ALPHA ORDER

RANK	STATE	OFFICERS	% of USA
20	Alabama	1,902	1.39%
49	Alaska	0	0.00%
24	Arizona	1,427	1.05%
30	Arkansas	1,054	0.77%
1	California	22,552	16.52%
14	Colorado	3,042	2.23%
41	Connecticut	418	0.31%
48	Delaware	22	0.02%
2	Florida	11,805	8.65%
6	Georgia	5,852	4.29%
49	Hawaii	0	0.00%
32	Idaho	1,032	0.76%
5	Illinois	7,845	5.75%
17	Indiana	2,389	1.75%
27	Iowa	1,217	0.89%
23	Kansas	1,546	1.13%
31	Kentucky	1,041	0.76%
4	Louisiana	8,217	6.02%
42	Maine	367	0.27%
25	Maryland	1,348	0.99%
26	Massachusetts	1,264	0.93%
10	Michigan	3,954	2.90%
21	Minnesota	1,887	1.38%
28	Mississippi	1,107	0.81%
19	Missouri	2,071	1.52%
39	Montana	595	0.44%
37	Nebraska	769	0.56%
35	Nevada	808	0.59%
46	New Hampshire	104	0.08%
12	New Jersey	3,833	2.81%
36	New Mexico	792	0.58%
8	New York	5,039	3.69%
9	North Carolina	4,596	3.37%
43	North Dakota	348	0.25%
11	Ohio	3,870	2.83%
33	Oklahoma	842	0.62%
22	Oregon	1,691	1.24%
29	Pennsylvania	1,076	0.79%
45	Rhode Island	124	0.09%
16	South Carolina	2,494	1.83%
44	South Dakota	338	0.25%
15	Tennessee	2,866	2.10%
3	Texas	9,876	7.23%
34	Utah	818	0.60%
47	Vermont	78	0.06%
7	Virginia	5,590	4.09%
18	Washington	2,228	1.63%
38	West Virginia	651	0.48%
13	Wisconsin	3,309	2.42%
40	Wyoming	448	0.33%

RANK ORDER

RANK	STATE	OFFICERS	% of USA
1	California	22,552	16.52%
2	Florida	11,805	8.65%
3	Texas	9,876	7.23%
4	Louisiana	8,217	6.02%
5	Illinois	7,845	5.75%
6	Georgia	5,852	4.29%
7	Virginia	5,590	4.09%
8	New York	5,039	3.69%
9	North Carolina	4,596	3.37%
10	Michigan	3,954	2.90%
11	Ohio	3,870	2.83%
12	New Jersey	3,833	2.81%
13	Wisconsin	3,309	2.42%
14	Colorado	3,042	2.23%
15	Tennessee	2,866	2.10%
16	South Carolina	2,494	1.83%
17	Indiana	2,389	1.75%
18	Washington	2,228	1.63%
19	Missouri	2,071	1.52%
20	Alabama	1,902	1.39%
21	Minnesota	1,887	1.38%
22	Oregon	1,691	1.24%
23	Kansas	1,546	1.13%
24	Arizona	1,427	1.05%
25	Maryland	1,348	0.99%
26	Massachusetts	1,264	0.93%
27	Iowa	1,217	0.89%
28	Mississippi	1,107	0.81%
29	Pennsylvania	1,076	0.79%
30	Arkansas	1,054	0.77%
31	Kentucky	1,041	0.76%
32	Idaho	1,032	0.76%
33	Oklahoma	842	0.62%
34	Utah	818	0.60%
35	Nevada	808	0.59%
36	New Mexico	792	0.58%
37	Nebraska	769	0.56%
38	West Virginia	651	0.48%
39	Montana	595	0.44%
40	Wyoming	448	0.33%
41	Connecticut	418	0.31%
42	Maine	367	0.27%
43	North Dakota	348	0.25%
44	South Dakota	338	0.25%
45	Rhode Island	124	0.09%
46	New Hampshire	104	0.08%
47	Vermont	78	0.06%
48	Delaware	22	0.02%
49	Alaska	0	0.00%
49	Hawaii	0	0.00%
	District of Columbia	0	0.00%

Source: U.S. Department of Justice, Bureau of Justice Statistics
"Census of State and Local Law Enforcement Agencies, 1992" (Bulletin, July 1993, NCJ-142972)
*Sheriffs' departments generally operate at the county level.

Percent of Full-Time Sheriffs' Department Employees
Who Are Sworn Officers: 1992
National Percent = 60.59% of Employees*

ALPHA ORDER

RANK	STATE	PERCENT
24	Alabama	59.96
NA	Alaska**	NA
48	Arizona	34.01
29	Arkansas	57.00
23	California	62.22
16	Colorado	67.41
2	Connecticut	98.35
31	Delaware	55.00
43	Florida	48.33
12	Georgia	69.82
NA	Hawaii**	NA
15	Idaho	68.71
10	Illinois	72.52
37	Indiana	51.92
25	Iowa	59.14
20	Kansas	64.50
4	Kentucky	91.24
3	Louisiana	92.44
46	Maine	40.96
36	Maryland	52.95
47	Massachusetts	34.97
27	Michigan	57.63
33	Minnesota	54.44
22	Mississippi	62.61
7	Missouri	79.08
28	Montana	57.54
26	Nebraska	59.02
11	Nevada	70.75
17	New Hampshire	65.82
6	New Jersey	81.45
21	New Mexico	63.82
35	New York	54.28
19	North Carolina	64.65
14	North Dakota	69.18
39	Ohio	51.45
41	Oklahoma	48.50
34	Oregon	54.43
8	Pennsylvania	74.05
1	Rhode Island	99.20
9	South Carolina	72.86
30	South Dakota	56.05
42	Tennessee	48.35
38	Texas	51.77
44	Utah	47.86
18	Vermont	65.55
5	Virginia	85.34
32	Washington	54.47
45	West Virginia	47.41
13	Wisconsin	69.63
40	Wyoming	51.20

RANK ORDER

RANK	STATE	PERCENT
1	Rhode Island	99.20
2	Connecticut	98.35
3	Louisiana	92.44
4	Kentucky	91.24
5	Virginia	85.34
6	New Jersey	81.45
7	Missouri	79.08
8	Pennsylvania	74.05
9	South Carolina	72.86
10	Illinois	72.52
11	Nevada	70.75
12	Georgia	69.82
13	Wisconsin	69.63
14	North Dakota	69.18
15	Idaho	68.71
16	Colorado	67.41
17	New Hampshire	65.82
18	Vermont	65.55
19	North Carolina	64.65
20	Kansas	64.50
21	New Mexico	63.82
22	Mississippi	62.61
23	California	62.22
24	Alabama	59.96
25	Iowa	59.14
26	Nebraska	59.02
27	Michigan	57.63
28	Montana	57.54
29	Arkansas	57.00
30	South Dakota	56.05
31	Delaware	55.00
32	Washington	54.47
33	Minnesota	54.44
34	Oregon	54.43
35	New York	54.28
36	Maryland	52.95
37	Indiana	51.92
38	Texas	51.77
39	Ohio	51.45
40	Wyoming	51.20
41	Oklahoma	48.50
42	Tennessee	48.35
43	Florida	48.33
44	Utah	47.86
45	West Virginia	47.41
46	Maine	40.96
47	Massachusetts	34.97
48	Arizona	34.01
NA	Alaska**	NA
NA	Hawaii**	NA

District of Columbia**   NA

Source: Morgan Quitno Press using data from U.S. Department of Justice, Bureau of Justice Statistics
     "Census of State and Local Law Enforcement Agencies, 1992" (Bulletin, July 1993, NCJ-142972)
*Sheriffs' departments generally operate at the county level.
**Not applicable.

Rate of Full-Time Sworn Officers in Sheriffs' Departments in 1992

National Rate = 5.35 Officers per 10,000 Population*

ALPHA ORDER

RANK	STATE	RATE
24	Alabama	4.60
49	Alaska	0.00
34	Arizona	3.72
26	Arkansas	4.39
8	California	7.31
4	Colorado	8.77
44	Connecticut	1.27
48	Delaware	0.32
6	Florida	8.75
7	Georgia	8.67
49	Hawaii	0.00
2	Idaho	9.67
11	Illinois	6.74
30	Indiana	4.22
28	Iowa	4.33
14	Kansas	6.13
39	Kentucky	2.77
1	Louisiana	19.17
37	Maine	2.97
40	Maryland	2.75
42	Massachusetts	2.11
32	Michigan	4.19
31	Minnesota	4.21
29	Mississippi	4.23
33	Missouri	3.99
9	Montana	7.22
22	Nebraska	4.79
15	Nevada	6.09
46	New Hampshire	0.94
21	New Jersey	4.92
20	New Mexico	5.01
38	New York	2.78
12	North Carolina	6.72
19	North Dakota	5.47
36	Ohio	3.51
41	Oklahoma	2.62
17	Oregon	5.68
47	Pennsylvania	0.90
45	Rhode Island	1.23
10	South Carolina	6.92
23	South Dakota	4.75
16	Tennessee	5.70
18	Texas	5.59
25	Utah	4.51
43	Vermont	1.37
4	Virginia	8.77
27	Washington	4.34
35	West Virginia	3.59
13	Wisconsin	6.61
3	Wyoming	9.61

RANK ORDER

RANK	STATE	RATE
1	Louisiana	19.17
2	Idaho	9.67
3	Wyoming	9.61
4	Colorado	8.77
4	Virginia	8.77
6	Florida	8.75
7	Georgia	8.67
8	California	7.31
9	Montana	7.22
10	South Carolina	6.92
11	Illinois	6.74
12	North Carolina	6.72
13	Wisconsin	6.61
14	Kansas	6.13
15	Nevada	6.09
16	Tennessee	5.70
17	Oregon	5.68
18	Texas	5.59
19	North Dakota	5.47
20	New Mexico	5.01
21	New Jersey	4.92
22	Nebraska	4.79
23	South Dakota	4.75
24	Alabama	4.60
25	Utah	4.51
26	Arkansas	4.39
27	Washington	4.34
28	Iowa	4.33
29	Mississippi	4.23
30	Indiana	4.22
31	Minnesota	4.21
32	Michigan	4.19
33	Missouri	3.99
34	Arizona	3.72
35	West Virginia	3.59
36	Ohio	3.51
37	Maine	2.97
38	New York	2.78
39	Kentucky	2.77
40	Maryland	2.75
41	Oklahoma	2.62
42	Massachusetts	2.11
43	Vermont	1.37
44	Connecticut	1.27
45	Rhode Island	1.23
46	New Hampshire	0.94
47	Pennsylvania	0.90
48	Delaware	0.32
49	Alaska	0.00
49	Hawaii	0.00
	District of Columbia	0.00

Source: Morgan Quitno Press using data from U.S. Department of Justice, Bureau of Justice Statistics
"Census of State and Local Law Enforcement Agencies, 1992" (Bulletin, July 1993, NCJ-142972)
*Sheriffs' departments generally operate at the county level.

Full-Time Employees in Sheriffs' Departments in 1992

National Total = 225,342 Employees*

ALPHA ORDER

RANK	STATE	EMPLOYEES	% of USA
22	Alabama	3,172	1.41%
49	Alaska	0	0.00%
17	Arizona	4,196	1.86%
28	Arkansas	1,849	0.82%
1	California	36,243	16.08%
16	Colorado	4,513	2.00%
44	Connecticut	425	0.19%
48	Delaware	40	0.02%
2	Florida	24,426	10.84%
7	Georgia	8,381	3.72%
49	Hawaii	0	0.00%
32	Idaho	1,502	0.67%
4	Illinois	10,817	4.80%
15	Indiana	4,601	2.04%
27	Iowa	2,058	0.91%
26	Kansas	2,397	1.06%
38	Kentucky	1,141	0.51%
6	Louisiana	8,889	3.94%
40	Maine	896	0.40%
25	Maryland	2,546	1.13%
19	Massachusetts	3,615	1.60%
10	Michigan	6,861	3.04%
20	Minnesota	3,466	1.54%
29	Mississippi	1,768	0.78%
24	Missouri	2,619	1.16%
39	Montana	1,034	0.46%
35	Nebraska	1,303	0.58%
37	Nevada	1,142	0.51%
45	New Hampshire	158	0.07%
14	New Jersey	4,706	2.09%
36	New Mexico	1,241	0.55%
5	New York	9,284	4.12%
9	North Carolina	7,109	3.15%
43	North Dakota	503	0.22%
8	Ohio	7,522	3.34%
30	Oklahoma	1,736	0.77%
23	Oregon	3,107	1.38%
33	Pennsylvania	1,453	0.64%
46	Rhode Island	125	0.06%
21	South Carolina	3,423	1.52%
42	South Dakota	603	0.27%
12	Tennessee	5,927	2.63%
3	Texas	19,077	8.47%
31	Utah	1,709	0.76%
47	Vermont	119	0.05%
11	Virginia	6,550	2.91%
18	Washington	4,090	1.82%
34	West Virginia	1,373	0.61%
13	Wisconsin	4,752	2.11%
41	Wyoming	875	0.39%

RANK ORDER

RANK	STATE	EMPLOYEES	% of USA
1	California	36,243	16.08%
2	Florida	24,426	10.84%
3	Texas	19,077	8.47%
4	Illinois	10,817	4.80%
5	New York	9,284	4.12%
6	Louisiana	8,889	3.94%
7	Georgia	8,381	3.72%
8	Ohio	7,522	3.34%
9	North Carolina	7,109	3.15%
10	Michigan	6,861	3.04%
11	Virginia	6,550	2.91%
12	Tennessee	5,927	2.63%
13	Wisconsin	4,752	2.11%
14	New Jersey	4,706	2.09%
15	Indiana	4,601	2.04%
16	Colorado	4,513	2.00%
17	Arizona	4,196	1.86%
18	Washington	4,090	1.82%
19	Massachusetts	3,615	1.60%
20	Minnesota	3,466	1.54%
21	South Carolina	3,423	1.52%
22	Alabama	3,172	1.41%
23	Oregon	3,107	1.38%
24	Missouri	2,619	1.16%
25	Maryland	2,546	1.13%
26	Kansas	2,397	1.06%
27	Iowa	2,058	0.91%
28	Arkansas	1,849	0.82%
29	Mississippi	1,768	0.78%
30	Oklahoma	1,736	0.77%
31	Utah	1,709	0.76%
32	Idaho	1,502	0.67%
33	Pennsylvania	1,453	0.64%
34	West Virginia	1,373	0.61%
35	Nebraska	1,303	0.58%
36	New Mexico	1,241	0.55%
37	Nevada	1,142	0.51%
38	Kentucky	1,141	0.51%
39	Montana	1,034	0.46%
40	Maine	896	0.40%
41	Wyoming	875	0.39%
42	South Dakota	603	0.27%
43	North Dakota	503	0.22%
44	Connecticut	425	0.19%
45	New Hampshire	158	0.07%
46	Rhode Island	125	0.06%
47	Vermont	119	0.05%
48	Delaware	40	0.02%
49	Alaska	0	0.00%
49	Hawaii	0	0.00%
	District of Columbia	0	0.00%

Source: U.S. Department of Justice, Bureau of Justice Statistics
"Census of State and Local Law Enforcement Agencies, 1992" (Bulletin, July 1993, NCJ-142972)
*Sheriffs' departments generally operate at the county level.

Special Police Agencies in 1992

National Total = 1,721 Agencies*

<table>
<tr><td colspan="4">ALPHA ORDER</td><td colspan="4">RANK ORDER</td></tr>
<tr><td>RANK</td><td>STATE</td><td>AGENCIES</td><td>% of USA</td><td>RANK</td><td>STATE</td><td>AGENCIES</td><td>% of USA</td></tr>
<tr><td>13</td><td>Alabama</td><td>24</td><td>1.39%</td><td>1</td><td>Texas**</td><td>824</td><td>47.88%</td></tr>
<tr><td>39</td><td>Alaska</td><td>4</td><td>0.23%</td><td>2</td><td>California</td><td>93</td><td>5.40%</td></tr>
<tr><td>31</td><td>Arizona</td><td>11</td><td>0.64%</td><td>3</td><td>New York</td><td>57</td><td>3.31%</td></tr>
<tr><td>23</td><td>Arkansas</td><td>16</td><td>0.93%</td><td>4</td><td>Pennsylvania</td><td>51</td><td>2.96%</td></tr>
<tr><td>2</td><td>California</td><td>93</td><td>5.40%</td><td>5</td><td>Illinois</td><td>43</td><td>2.50%</td></tr>
<tr><td>28</td><td>Colorado</td><td>14</td><td>0.81%</td><td>5</td><td>Ohio</td><td>43</td><td>2.50%</td></tr>
<tr><td>23</td><td>Connecticut</td><td>16</td><td>0.93%</td><td>7</td><td>Georgia</td><td>37</td><td>2.15%</td></tr>
<tr><td>38</td><td>Delaware</td><td>5</td><td>0.29%</td><td>8</td><td>Virginia</td><td>34</td><td>1.98%</td></tr>
<tr><td>16</td><td>Florida</td><td>20</td><td>1.16%</td><td>9</td><td>Massachusetts</td><td>32</td><td>1.86%</td></tr>
<tr><td>7</td><td>Georgia</td><td>37</td><td>2.15%</td><td>10</td><td>Louisiana</td><td>27</td><td>1.57%</td></tr>
<tr><td>47</td><td>Hawaii</td><td>2</td><td>0.12%</td><td>11</td><td>Mississippi</td><td>25</td><td>1.45%</td></tr>
<tr><td>49</td><td>Idaho</td><td>1</td><td>0.06%</td><td>11</td><td>North Carolina</td><td>25</td><td>1.45%</td></tr>
<tr><td>5</td><td>Illinois</td><td>43</td><td>2.50%</td><td>13</td><td>Alabama</td><td>24</td><td>1.39%</td></tr>
<tr><td>16</td><td>Indiana</td><td>20</td><td>1.16%</td><td>13</td><td>New Jersey</td><td>24</td><td>1.39%</td></tr>
<tr><td>36</td><td>Iowa</td><td>6</td><td>0.35%</td><td>15</td><td>Maryland</td><td>21</td><td>1.22%</td></tr>
<tr><td>22</td><td>Kansas</td><td>18</td><td>1.05%</td><td>16</td><td>Florida</td><td>20</td><td>1.16%</td></tr>
<tr><td>23</td><td>Kentucky</td><td>16</td><td>0.93%</td><td>16</td><td>Indiana</td><td>20</td><td>1.16%</td></tr>
<tr><td>10</td><td>Louisiana</td><td>27</td><td>1.57%</td><td>16</td><td>Michigan</td><td>20</td><td>1.16%</td></tr>
<tr><td>36</td><td>Maine</td><td>6</td><td>0.35%</td><td>16</td><td>Oklahoma</td><td>20</td><td>1.16%</td></tr>
<tr><td>15</td><td>Maryland</td><td>21</td><td>1.22%</td><td>16</td><td>South Carolina</td><td>20</td><td>1.16%</td></tr>
<tr><td>9</td><td>Massachusetts</td><td>32</td><td>1.86%</td><td>21</td><td>Tennessee</td><td>19</td><td>1.10%</td></tr>
<tr><td>16</td><td>Michigan</td><td>20</td><td>1.16%</td><td>22</td><td>Kansas</td><td>18</td><td>1.05%</td></tr>
<tr><td>33</td><td>Minnesota</td><td>9</td><td>0.52%</td><td>23</td><td>Arkansas</td><td>16</td><td>0.93%</td></tr>
<tr><td>11</td><td>Mississippi</td><td>25</td><td>1.45%</td><td>23</td><td>Connecticut</td><td>16</td><td>0.93%</td></tr>
<tr><td>23</td><td>Missouri</td><td>16</td><td>0.93%</td><td>23</td><td>Kentucky</td><td>16</td><td>0.93%</td></tr>
<tr><td>39</td><td>Montana</td><td>4</td><td>0.23%</td><td>23</td><td>Missouri</td><td>16</td><td>0.93%</td></tr>
<tr><td>39</td><td>Nebraska</td><td>4</td><td>0.23%</td><td>23</td><td>Wisconsin</td><td>16</td><td>0.93%</td></tr>
<tr><td>39</td><td>Nevada</td><td>4</td><td>0.23%</td><td>28</td><td>Colorado</td><td>14</td><td>0.81%</td></tr>
<tr><td>45</td><td>New Hampshire</td><td>3</td><td>0.17%</td><td>28</td><td>West Virginia</td><td>14</td><td>0.81%</td></tr>
<tr><td>13</td><td>New Jersey</td><td>24</td><td>1.39%</td><td>30</td><td>Utah</td><td>13</td><td>0.76%</td></tr>
<tr><td>33</td><td>New Mexico</td><td>9</td><td>0.52%</td><td>31</td><td>Arizona</td><td>11</td><td>0.64%</td></tr>
<tr><td>3</td><td>New York</td><td>57</td><td>3.31%</td><td>32</td><td>Washington</td><td>10</td><td>0.58%</td></tr>
<tr><td>11</td><td>North Carolina</td><td>25</td><td>1.45%</td><td>33</td><td>Minnesota</td><td>9</td><td>0.52%</td></tr>
<tr><td>39</td><td>North Dakota</td><td>4</td><td>0.23%</td><td>33</td><td>New Mexico</td><td>9</td><td>0.52%</td></tr>
<tr><td>5</td><td>Ohio</td><td>43</td><td>2.50%</td><td>33</td><td>Oregon</td><td>9</td><td>0.52%</td></tr>
<tr><td>16</td><td>Oklahoma</td><td>20</td><td>1.16%</td><td>36</td><td>Iowa</td><td>6</td><td>0.35%</td></tr>
<tr><td>33</td><td>Oregon</td><td>9</td><td>0.52%</td><td>36</td><td>Maine</td><td>6</td><td>0.35%</td></tr>
<tr><td>4</td><td>Pennsylvania</td><td>51</td><td>2.96%</td><td>38</td><td>Delaware</td><td>5</td><td>0.29%</td></tr>
<tr><td>39</td><td>Rhode Island</td><td>4</td><td>0.23%</td><td>39</td><td>Alaska</td><td>4</td><td>0.23%</td></tr>
<tr><td>16</td><td>South Carolina</td><td>20</td><td>1.16%</td><td>39</td><td>Montana</td><td>4</td><td>0.23%</td></tr>
<tr><td>47</td><td>South Dakota</td><td>2</td><td>0.12%</td><td>39</td><td>Nebraska</td><td>4</td><td>0.23%</td></tr>
<tr><td>21</td><td>Tennessee</td><td>19</td><td>1.10%</td><td>39</td><td>Nevada</td><td>4</td><td>0.23%</td></tr>
<tr><td>1</td><td>Texas**</td><td>824</td><td>47.88%</td><td>39</td><td>North Dakota</td><td>4</td><td>0.23%</td></tr>
<tr><td>30</td><td>Utah</td><td>13</td><td>0.76%</td><td>39</td><td>Rhode Island</td><td>4</td><td>0.23%</td></tr>
<tr><td>49</td><td>Vermont</td><td>1</td><td>0.06%</td><td>45</td><td>New Hampshire</td><td>3</td><td>0.17%</td></tr>
<tr><td>8</td><td>Virginia</td><td>34</td><td>1.98%</td><td>45</td><td>Wyoming</td><td>3</td><td>0.17%</td></tr>
<tr><td>32</td><td>Washington</td><td>10</td><td>0.58%</td><td>47</td><td>Hawaii</td><td>2</td><td>0.12%</td></tr>
<tr><td>28</td><td>West Virginia</td><td>14</td><td>0.81%</td><td>47</td><td>South Dakota</td><td>2</td><td>0.12%</td></tr>
<tr><td>23</td><td>Wisconsin</td><td>16</td><td>0.93%</td><td>49</td><td>Idaho</td><td>1</td><td>0.06%</td></tr>
<tr><td>45</td><td>Wyoming</td><td>3</td><td>0.17%</td><td>49</td><td>Vermont</td><td>1</td><td>0.06%</td></tr>
<tr><td></td><td></td><td></td><td></td><td></td><td>District of Columbia</td><td>2</td><td>0.12%</td></tr>
</table>

Source: U.S. Department of Justice, Bureau of Justice Statistics
  "Census of State and Local Law Enforcement Agencies, 1992" (Bulletin, July 1993, NCJ-142972)
*Agencies with special jurisdictions or special enforcement responsibilities.
**Texas' total includes 751 county constable offices.

Full-Time Sworn Officers in Special Police Departments in 1992

National Total = 41,371 Officers*

ALPHA ORDER

RANK	STATE	OFFICERS	% of USA
15	Alabama	600	1.45%
38	Alaska	120	0.29%
35	Arizona	164	0.40%
21	Arkansas	443	1.07%
3	California	3,992	9.65%
22	Colorado	404	0.98%
30	Connecticut	248	0.60%
36	Delaware	158	0.38%
4	Florida	1,432	3.46%
11	Georgia	759	1.83%
41	Hawaii	93	0.22%
49	Idaho	12	0.03%
10	Illinois	864	2.09%
19	Indiana	560	1.35%
33	Iowa	213	0.51%
27	Kansas	292	0.71%
28	Kentucky	280	0.68%
18	Louisiana	570	1.38%
34	Maine	169	0.41%
6	Maryland	1,280	3.09%
16	Massachusetts	593	1.43%
13	Michigan	642	1.55%
23	Minnesota	397	0.96%
25	Mississippi	324	0.78%
24	Missouri	391	0.95%
46	Montana	47	0.11%
41	Nebraska	93	0.22%
37	Nevada	143	0.35%
44	New Hampshire	68	0.16%
8	New Jersey	1,062	2.57%
40	New Mexico	111	0.27%
1	New York	13,334	32.23%
12	North Carolina	707	1.71%
45	North Dakota	49	0.12%
7	Ohio	1,099	2.66%
26	Oklahoma	301	0.73%
39	Oregon	117	0.28%
5	Pennsylvania	1,293	3.13%
43	Rhode Island	76	0.18%
17	South Carolina	584	1.41%
50	South Dakota	8	0.02%
20	Tennessee	517	1.25%
2	Texas**	4,108	9.93%
29	Utah	250	0.60%
47	Vermont	21	0.05%
9	Virginia	964	2.33%
32	Washington	228	0.55%
31	West Virginia	243	0.59%
14	Wisconsin	603	1.46%
47	Wyoming	21	0.05%

RANK ORDER

RANK	STATE	OFFICERS	% of USA
1	New York	13,334	32.23%
2	Texas**	4,108	9.93%
3	California	3,992	9.65%
4	Florida	1,432	3.46%
5	Pennsylvania	1,293	3.13%
6	Maryland	1,280	3.09%
7	Ohio	1,099	2.66%
8	New Jersey	1,062	2.57%
9	Virginia	964	2.33%
10	Illinois	864	2.09%
11	Georgia	759	1.83%
12	North Carolina	707	1.71%
13	Michigan	642	1.55%
14	Wisconsin	603	1.46%
15	Alabama	600	1.45%
16	Massachusetts	593	1.43%
17	South Carolina	584	1.41%
18	Louisiana	570	1.38%
19	Indiana	560	1.35%
20	Tennessee	517	1.25%
21	Arkansas	443	1.07%
22	Colorado	404	0.98%
23	Minnesota	397	0.96%
24	Missouri	391	0.95%
25	Mississippi	324	0.78%
26	Oklahoma	301	0.73%
27	Kansas	292	0.71%
28	Kentucky	280	0.68%
29	Utah	250	0.60%
30	Connecticut	248	0.60%
31	West Virginia	243	0.59%
32	Washington	228	0.55%
33	Iowa	213	0.51%
34	Maine	169	0.41%
35	Arizona	164	0.40%
36	Delaware	158	0.38%
37	Nevada	143	0.35%
38	Alaska	120	0.29%
39	Oregon	117	0.28%
40	New Mexico	111	0.27%
41	Hawaii	93	0.22%
41	Nebraska	93	0.22%
43	Rhode Island	76	0.18%
44	New Hampshire	68	0.16%
45	North Dakota	49	0.12%
46	Montana	47	0.11%
47	Vermont	21	0.05%
47	Wyoming	21	0.05%
49	Idaho	12	0.03%
50	South Dakota	8	0.02%
	District of Columbia	324	0.78%

Source: U.S. Department of Justice, Bureau of Justice Statistics
"Census of State and Local Law Enforcement Agencies, 1992" (Bulletin, July 1993, NCJ-142972)
*Agencies with special jurisdictions or special enforcement responsibilities.
**Texas' total includes 751 county constable offices with 1,723 sworn constable office employees..

Percent of Full-Time Special Police Department Employees
Who Are Officers: 1992
National Percent = 67.90% of Employees*

ALPHA ORDER

RANK	STATE	PERCENT
14	Alabama	78.02
4	Alaska	88.89
34	Arizona	63.57
48	Arkansas	42.88
44	California	46.98
47	Colorado	44.25
7	Connecticut	84.35
27	Delaware	68.10
18	Florida	76.13
46	Georgia	44.36
1	Hawaii	98.94
11	Idaho	80.00
12	Illinois	78.47
15	Indiana	77.24
10	Iowa	80.68
21	Kansas	73.18
33	Kentucky	64.67
8	Louisiana	83.95
5	Maine	88.48
22	Maryland	72.36
16	Massachusetts	77.01
30	Michigan	66.53
9	Minnesota	83.40
23	Mississippi	72.00
19	Missouri	74.76
41	Montana	51.09
2	Nebraska	92.08
31	Nevada	65.90
49	New Hampshire	33.17
38	New Jersey	61.18
26	New Mexico	68.94
3	New York	90.08
35	North Carolina	63.29
28	North Dakota	67.12
39	Ohio	57.48
13	Oklahoma	78.39
29	Oregon	66.86
20	Pennsylvania	74.57
24	Rhode Island	71.03
42	South Carolina	50.34
43	South Dakota	50.00
17	Tennessee	76.59
36	Texas**	63.14
50	Utah	29.52
32	Vermont	65.63
45	Virginia	44.44
25	Washington	70.59
6	West Virginia	87.41
40	Wisconsin	56.51
37	Wyoming	61.76

RANK ORDER

RANK	STATE	PERCENT
1	Hawaii	98.94
2	Nebraska	92.08
3	New York	90.08
4	Alaska	88.89
5	Maine	88.48
6	West Virginia	87.41
7	Connecticut	84.35
8	Louisiana	83.95
9	Minnesota	83.40
10	Iowa	80.68
11	Idaho	80.00
12	Illinois	78.47
13	Oklahoma	78.39
14	Alabama	78.02
15	Indiana	77.24
16	Massachusetts	77.01
17	Tennessee	76.59
18	Florida	76.13
19	Missouri	74.76
20	Pennsylvania	74.57
21	Kansas	73.18
22	Maryland	72.36
23	Mississippi	72.00
24	Rhode Island	71.03
25	Washington	70.59
26	New Mexico	68.94
27	Delaware	68.10
28	North Dakota	67.12
29	Oregon	66.86
30	Michigan	66.53
31	Nevada	65.90
32	Vermont	65.63
33	Kentucky	64.67
34	Arizona	63.57
35	North Carolina	63.29
36	Texas**	63.14
37	Wyoming	61.76
38	New Jersey	61.18
39	Ohio	57.48
40	Wisconsin	56.51
41	Montana	51.09
42	South Carolina	50.34
43	South Dakota	50.00
44	California	46.98
45	Virginia	44.44
46	Georgia	44.36
47	Colorado	44.25
48	Arkansas	42.88
49	New Hampshire	33.17
50	Utah	29.52

| | District of Columbia | 76.42 |

Source: Morgan Quitno Press using data from U.S. Department of Justice, Bureau of Justice Statistics "Census of State and Local Law Enforcement Agencies, 1992" (Bulletin, July 1993, NCJ-142972)
Agencies with special jurisdictions or special enforcement responsibilities.
**Texas' total includes 751 county constable offices with 1,723 sworn constable office employees..*

Rate of Full-Time Sworn Officers in Special Police Departments in 1992

National Rate = 1.62 Officers per 10,000 Population*

ALPHA ORDER

RANK	STATE	RATE
9	Alabama	1.45
5	Alaska	2.04
46	Arizona	0.43
6	Arkansas	1.85
15	California	1.29
18	Colorado	1.16
33	Connecticut	0.76
4	Delaware	2.29
23	Florida	1.06
20	Georgia	1.12
31	Hawaii	0.80
49	Idaho	0.11
38	Illinois	0.74
27	Indiana	0.99
33	Iowa	0.76
18	Kansas	1.16
36	Kentucky	0.75
14	Louisiana	1.33
11	Maine	1.37
2	Maryland	2.61
27	Massachusetts	0.99
40	Michigan	0.68
30	Minnesota	0.89
16	Mississippi	1.24
36	Missouri	0.75
43	Montana	0.57
42	Nebraska	0.58
21	Nevada	1.08
41	New Hampshire	0.61
12	New Jersey	1.36
39	New Mexico	0.70
1	New York	7.36
24	North Carolina	1.03
32	North Dakota	0.77
26	Ohio	1.00
29	Oklahoma	0.94
47	Oregon	0.39
21	Pennsylvania	1.08
33	Rhode Island	0.76
7	South Carolina	1.62
49	South Dakota	0.11
24	Tennessee	1.03
3	Texas**	2.33
10	Utah	1.38
48	Vermont	0.37
8	Virginia	1.51
45	Washington	0.44
13	West Virginia	1.34
17	Wisconsin	1.20
44	Wyoming	0.45

RANK ORDER

RANK	STATE	RATE
1	New York	7.36
2	Maryland	2.61
3	Texas**	2.33
4	Delaware	2.29
5	Alaska	2.04
6	Arkansas	1.85
7	South Carolina	1.62
8	Virginia	1.51
9	Alabama	1.45
10	Utah	1.38
11	Maine	1.37
12	New Jersey	1.36
13	West Virginia	1.34
14	Louisiana	1.33
15	California	1.29
16	Mississippi	1.24
17	Wisconsin	1.20
18	Colorado	1.16
18	Kansas	1.16
20	Georgia	1.12
21	Nevada	1.08
21	Pennsylvania	1.08
23	Florida	1.06
24	North Carolina	1.03
24	Tennessee	1.03
26	Ohio	1.00
27	Indiana	0.99
27	Massachusetts	0.99
29	Oklahoma	0.94
30	Minnesota	0.89
31	Hawaii	0.80
32	North Dakota	0.77
33	Connecticut	0.76
33	Iowa	0.76
33	Rhode Island	0.76
36	Kentucky	0.75
36	Missouri	0.75
38	Illinois	0.74
39	New Mexico	0.70
40	Michigan	0.68
41	New Hampshire	0.61
42	Nebraska	0.58
43	Montana	0.57
44	Wyoming	0.45
45	Washington	0.44
46	Arizona	0.43
47	Oregon	0.39
48	Vermont	0.37
49	Idaho	0.11
49	South Dakota	0.11
	District of Columbia	5.50

Source: Morgan Quitno Press using data from U.S. Department of Justice, Bureau of Justice Statistics
"Census of State and Local Law Enforcement Agencies, 1992" (Bulletin, July 1993, NCJ-142972)
*Agencies with special jurisdictions or special enforcement responsibilities.
**Texas' total includes 751 county constable offices with 1,723 sworn constable office employees..

Full-Time Employees in Special Police Departments in 1992

National Total = 60,926 Employees*

ALPHA ORDER

RANK	STATE	EMPLOYEES	% of USA
20	Alabama	769	1.26%
41	Alaska	135	0.22%
34	Arizona	258	0.42%
15	Arkansas	1,033	1.70%
2	California	8,498	13.95%
17	Colorado	913	1.50%
31	Connecticut	294	0.48%
35	Delaware	232	0.38%
6	Florida	1,881	3.09%
10	Georgia	1,711	2.81%
44	Hawaii	94	0.15%
50	Idaho	15	0.02%
13	Illinois	1,101	1.81%
21	Indiana	725	1.19%
33	Iowa	264	0.43%
28	Kansas	399	0.65%
27	Kentucky	433	0.71%
22	Louisiana	679	1.11%
38	Maine	191	0.31%
7	Maryland	1,769	2.90%
19	Massachusetts	770	1.26%
16	Michigan	965	1.58%
25	Minnesota	476	0.78%
26	Mississippi	450	0.74%
24	Missouri	523	0.86%
45	Montana	92	0.15%
43	Nebraska	101	0.17%
36	Nevada	217	0.36%
37	New Hampshire	205	0.34%
8	New Jersey	1,736	2.85%
40	New Mexico	161	0.26%
1	New York	14,803	24.30%
12	North Carolina	1,117	1.83%
46	North Dakota	73	0.12%
5	Ohio	1,912	3.14%
29	Oklahoma	384	0.63%
39	Oregon	175	0.29%
9	Pennsylvania	1,734	2.85%
42	Rhode Island	107	0.18%
11	South Carolina	1,160	1.90%
49	South Dakota	16	0.03%
23	Tennessee	675	1.11%
3	Texas**	6,506	10.68%
18	Utah	847	1.39%
48	Vermont	32	0.05%
4	Virginia	2,169	3.56%
30	Washington	323	0.53%
32	West Virginia	278	0.46%
14	Wisconsin	1,067	1.75%
47	Wyoming	34	0.06%

RANK ORDER

RANK	STATE	EMPLOYEES	% of USA
1	New York	14,803	24.30%
2	California	8,498	13.95%
3	Texas**	6,506	10.68%
4	Virginia	2,169	3.56%
5	Ohio	1,912	3.14%
6	Florida	1,881	3.09%
7	Maryland	1,769	2.90%
8	New Jersey	1,736	2.85%
9	Pennsylvania	1,734	2.85%
10	Georgia	1,711	2.81%
11	South Carolina	1,160	1.90%
12	North Carolina	1,117	1.83%
13	Illinois	1,101	1.81%
14	Wisconsin	1,067	1.75%
15	Arkansas	1,033	1.70%
16	Michigan	965	1.58%
17	Colorado	913	1.50%
18	Utah	847	1.39%
19	Massachusetts	770	1.26%
20	Alabama	769	1.26%
21	Indiana	725	1.19%
22	Louisiana	679	1.11%
23	Tennessee	675	1.11%
24	Missouri	523	0.86%
25	Minnesota	476	0.78%
26	Mississippi	450	0.74%
27	Kentucky	433	0.71%
28	Kansas	399	0.65%
29	Oklahoma	384	0.63%
30	Washington	323	0.53%
31	Connecticut	294	0.48%
32	West Virginia	278	0.46%
33	Iowa	264	0.43%
34	Arizona	258	0.42%
35	Delaware	232	0.38%
36	Nevada	217	0.36%
37	New Hampshire	205	0.34%
38	Maine	191	0.31%
39	Oregon	175	0.29%
40	New Mexico	161	0.26%
41	Alaska	135	0.22%
42	Rhode Island	107	0.18%
43	Nebraska	101	0.17%
44	Hawaii	94	0.15%
45	Montana	92	0.15%
46	North Dakota	73	0.12%
47	Wyoming	34	0.06%
48	Vermont	32	0.05%
49	South Dakota	16	0.03%
50	Idaho	15	0.02%
	District of Columbia	424	0.70%

Source: U.S. Department of Justice, Bureau of Justice Statistics
    "Census of State and Local Law Enforcement Agencies, 1992" (Bulletin, July 1993, NCJ-142972)
*Agencies with special jurisdictions or special enforcement responsibilities.
**Texas' total includes 751 county constable offices with 1,723 sworn constable office employees..

Law Enforcement Officers Feloniously Killed in 1994

National Total = 70 Officers*

ALPHA ORDER

RANK	STATE	OFFICERS	% of USA
5	Alabama	3	4.29%
30	Alaska	0	0.00%
19	Arizona	1	1.43%
30	Arkansas	0	0.00%
1	California	8	11.43%
12	Colorado	2	2.86%
30	Connecticut	0	0.00%
30	Delaware	0	0.00%
30	Florida	0	0.00%
5	Georgia	3	4.29%
30	Hawaii	0	0.00%
19	Idaho	1	1.43%
19	Illinois	1	1.43%
19	Indiana	1	1.43%
30	Iowa	0	0.00%
30	Kansas	0	0.00%
30	Kentucky	0	0.00%
30	Louisiana	0	0.00%
30	Maine	0	0.00%
30	Maryland	0	0.00%
3	Massachusetts	4	5.71%
5	Michigan	3	4.29%
12	Minnesota	2	2.86%
5	Mississippi	3	4.29%
5	Missouri	3	4.29%
19	Montana	1	1.43%
30	Nebraska	0	0.00%
30	Nevada	0	0.00%
19	New Hampshire	1	1.43%
12	New Jersey	2	2.86%
12	New Mexico	2	2.86%
5	New York	3	4.29%
12	North Carolina	2	2.86%
30	North Dakota	0	0.00%
12	Ohio	2	2.86%
30	Oklahoma	0	0.00%
30	Oregon	0	0.00%
19	Pennsylvania	1	1.43%
19	Rhode Island	1	1.43%
19	South Carolina	1	1.43%
30	South Dakota	0	0.00%
19	Tennessee	1	1.43%
5	Texas	3	4.29%
19	Utah	1	1.43%
30	Vermont	0	0.00%
2	Virginia	5	7.14%
12	Washington	2	2.86%
30	West Virginia	0	0.00%
3	Wisconsin	4	5.71%
30	Wyoming	0	0.00%

RANK ORDER

RANK	STATE	OFFICERS	% of USA
1	California	8	11.43%
2	Virginia	5	7.14%
3	Massachusetts	4	5.71%
3	Wisconsin	4	5.71%
5	Alabama	3	4.29%
5	Georgia	3	4.29%
5	Michigan	3	4.29%
5	Mississippi	3	4.29%
5	Missouri	3	4.29%
5	New York	3	4.29%
5	Texas	3	4.29%
12	Colorado	2	2.86%
12	Minnesota	2	2.86%
12	New Jersey	2	2.86%
12	New Mexico	2	2.86%
12	North Carolina	2	2.86%
12	Ohio	2	2.86%
12	Washington	2	2.86%
19	Arizona	1	1.43%
19	Idaho	1	1.43%
19	Illinois	1	1.43%
19	Indiana	1	1.43%
19	Montana	1	1.43%
19	New Hampshire	1	1.43%
19	Pennsylvania	1	1.43%
19	Rhode Island	1	1.43%
19	South Carolina	1	1.43%
19	Tennessee	1	1.43%
19	Utah	1	1.43%
30	Alaska	0	0.00%
30	Arkansas	0	0.00%
30	Connecticut	0	0.00%
30	Delaware	0	0.00%
30	Florida	0	0.00%
30	Hawaii	0	0.00%
30	Iowa	0	0.00%
30	Kansas	0	0.00%
30	Kentucky	0	0.00%
30	Louisiana	0	0.00%
30	Maine	0	0.00%
30	Maryland	0	0.00%
30	Nebraska	0	0.00%
30	Nevada	0	0.00%
30	North Dakota	0	0.00%
30	Oklahoma	0	0.00%
30	Oregon	0	0.00%
30	South Dakota	0	0.00%
30	Vermont	0	0.00%
30	West Virginia	0	0.00%
30	Wyoming	0	0.00%
	District of Columbia	3	4.29%

Source: Federal Bureau of Investigation
   "Law Enforcement Officers Killed and Assaulted 1994"
*Total does not include six officers killed in Puerto Rico in 1994. Sixty-two additional officers were killed in accidents occurring while performing official duties.

Law Enforcement Officers Feloniously Killed: 1985 to 1994

National Total = 653 Officers*

ALPHA ORDER

RANK	STATE	OFFICERS	% of USA
15	Alabama	16	2.45%
31	Alaska	5	0.77%
13	Arizona	17	2.60%
29	Arkansas	7	1.07%
2	California	58	8.88%
22	Colorado	11	1.68%
35	Connecticut	3	0.46%
48	Delaware	0	0.00%
3	Florida	42	6.43%
5	Georgia	29	4.44%
35	Hawaii	3	0.46%
35	Idaho	3	0.46%
6	Illinois	27	4.13%
20	Indiana	12	1.84%
43	Iowa	1	0.15%
31	Kansas	5	0.77%
17	Kentucky	15	2.30%
15	Louisiana	16	2.45%
41	Maine	2	0.31%
25	Maryland	9	1.38%
18	Massachusetts	13	1.99%
7	Michigan	26	3.98%
23	Minnesota	10	1.53%
8	Mississippi	23	3.52%
10	Missouri	20	3.06%
31	Montana	5	0.77%
35	Nebraska	3	0.46%
35	Nevada	3	0.46%
43	New Hampshire	1	0.15%
25	New Jersey	9	1.38%
27	New Mexico	8	1.23%
4	New York	38	5.82%
11	North Carolina	19	2.91%
43	North Dakota	1	0.15%
18	Ohio	13	1.99%
27	Oklahoma	8	1.23%
41	Oregon	2	0.31%
9	Pennsylvania	21	3.22%
43	Rhode Island	1	0.15%
13	South Carolina	17	2.60%
43	South Dakota	1	0.15%
23	Tennessee	10	1.53%
1	Texas	69	10.57%
35	Utah	3	0.46%
48	Vermont	0	0.00%
12	Virginia	18	2.76%
29	Washington	7	1.07%
34	West Virginia	4	0.61%
20	Wisconsin	12	1.84%
48	Wyoming	0	0.00%

RANK ORDER

RANK	STATE	OFFICERS	% of USA
1	Texas	69	10.57%
2	California	58	8.88%
3	Florida	42	6.43%
4	New York	38	5.82%
5	Georgia	29	4.44%
6	Illinois	27	4.13%
7	Michigan	26	3.98%
8	Mississippi	23	3.52%
9	Pennsylvania	21	3.22%
10	Missouri	20	3.06%
11	North Carolina	19	2.91%
12	Virginia	18	2.76%
13	Arizona	17	2.60%
13	South Carolina	17	2.60%
15	Alabama	16	2.45%
15	Louisiana	16	2.45%
17	Kentucky	15	2.30%
18	Massachusetts	13	1.99%
18	Ohio	13	1.99%
20	Indiana	12	1.84%
20	Wisconsin	12	1.84%
22	Colorado	11	1.68%
23	Minnesota	10	1.53%
23	Tennessee	10	1.53%
25	Maryland	9	1.38%
25	New Jersey	9	1.38%
27	New Mexico	8	1.23%
27	Oklahoma	8	1.23%
29	Arkansas	7	1.07%
29	Washington	7	1.07%
31	Alaska	5	0.77%
31	Kansas	5	0.77%
31	Montana	5	0.77%
34	West Virginia	4	0.61%
35	Connecticut	3	0.46%
35	Hawaii	3	0.46%
35	Idaho	3	0.46%
35	Nebraska	3	0.46%
35	Nevada	3	0.46%
35	Utah	3	0.46%
41	Maine	2	0.31%
41	Oregon	2	0.31%
43	Iowa	1	0.15%
43	New Hampshire	1	0.15%
43	North Dakota	1	0.15%
43	Rhode Island	1	0.15%
43	South Dakota	1	0.15%
48	Delaware	0	0.00%
48	Vermont	0	0.00%
48	Wyoming	0	0.00%
	District of Columbia	7	1.07%

Source: Federal Bureau of Investigation
"Law Enforcement Officers Killed and Assaulted 1994"
Total does not include 55 officers killed in U.S. territories or abroad (52 officers killed in Puerto Rico, one in American Samoa, one in the U.S. Virgin Islands and one in Mexico).

U.S. District Judges in 1994

National Total = 649 Judges*

ALPHA ORDER

RANK	STATE	JUDGES	% of USA
12	Alabama	14	2.16%
41	Alaska	3	0.46%
25	Arizona	8	1.23%
25	Arkansas	8	1.23%
1	California	56	8.63%
29	Colorado	7	1.08%
25	Connecticut	8	1.23%
37	Delaware	4	0.62%
5	Florida	31	4.78%
10	Georgia	18	2.77%
37	Hawaii	4	0.62%
48	Idaho	2	0.31%
6	Illinois	30	4.62%
20	Indiana	10	1.54%
34	Iowa	5	0.77%
31	Kansas	6	0.92%
22	Kentucky	9	1.39%
7	Louisiana	22	3.39%
41	Maine	3	0.46%
20	Maryland	10	1.54%
16	Massachusetts	13	2.00%
8	Michigan	20	3.08%
29	Minnesota	7	1.08%
22	Mississippi	9	1.39%
12	Missouri	14	2.16%
41	Montana	3	0.46%
37	Nebraska	4	0.62%
37	Nevada	4	0.62%
41	New Hampshire	3	0.46%
11	New Jersey	17	2.62%
34	New Mexico	5	0.77%
2	New York	52	8.01%
17	North Carolina	11	1.69%
48	North Dakota	2	0.31%
8	Ohio	20	3.08%
17	Oklahoma	11	1.69%
31	Oregon	6	0.92%
4	Pennsylvania	39	6.01%
41	Rhode Island	3	0.46%
22	South Carolina	9	1.39%
41	South Dakota	3	0.46%
12	Tennessee	14	2.16%
3	Texas	47	7.24%
34	Utah	5	0.77%
48	Vermont	2	0.31%
12	Virginia	14	2.16%
17	Washington	11	1.69%
25	West Virginia	8	1.23%
31	Wisconsin	6	0.92%
41	Wyoming	3	0.46%

RANK ORDER

RANK	STATE	JUDGES	% of USA
1	California	56	8.63%
2	New York	52	8.01%
3	Texas	47	7.24%
4	Pennsylvania	39	6.01%
5	Florida	31	4.78%
6	Illinois	30	4.62%
7	Louisiana	22	3.39%
8	Michigan	20	3.08%
8	Ohio	20	3.08%
10	Georgia	18	2.77%
11	New Jersey	17	2.62%
12	Alabama	14	2.16%
12	Missouri	14	2.16%
12	Tennessee	14	2.16%
12	Virginia	14	2.16%
16	Massachusetts	13	2.00%
17	North Carolina	11	1.69%
17	Oklahoma	11	1.69%
17	Washington	11	1.69%
20	Indiana	10	1.54%
20	Maryland	10	1.54%
22	Kentucky	9	1.39%
22	Mississippi	9	1.39%
22	South Carolina	9	1.39%
25	Arizona	8	1.23%
25	Arkansas	8	1.23%
25	Connecticut	8	1.23%
25	West Virginia	8	1.23%
29	Colorado	7	1.08%
29	Minnesota	7	1.08%
31	Kansas	6	0.92%
31	Oregon	6	0.92%
31	Wisconsin	6	0.92%
34	Iowa	5	0.77%
34	New Mexico	5	0.77%
34	Utah	5	0.77%
37	Delaware	4	0.62%
37	Hawaii	4	0.62%
37	Nebraska	4	0.62%
37	Nevada	4	0.62%
41	Alaska	3	0.46%
41	Maine	3	0.46%
41	Montana	3	0.46%
41	New Hampshire	3	0.46%
41	Rhode Island	3	0.46%
41	South Dakota	3	0.46%
41	Wyoming	3	0.46%
48	Idaho	2	0.31%
48	North Dakota	2	0.31%
48	Vermont	2	0.31%
	District of Columbia	15	2.31%

Source: Administrative Office of the United States Courts
"1994 Federal Court Management Statistics" (June 1995)
Total includes 11 judgeships in U.S. territories.

Rate of U.S. District Judges in 1994

National Rate = 0.25 Judges per 100,000 Population*

ALPHA ORDER

RANK	STATE	RATE
12	Alabama	0.33
4	Alaska	0.50
39	Arizona	0.20
12	Arkansas	0.33
43	California	0.18
41	Colorado	0.19
29	Connecticut	0.24
2	Delaware	0.56
33	Florida	0.22
22	Georgia	0.26
8	Hawaii	0.34
43	Idaho	0.18
22	Illinois	0.26
47	Indiana	0.17
43	Iowa	0.18
29	Kansas	0.24
29	Kentucky	0.24
3	Louisiana	0.51
29	Maine	0.24
39	Maryland	0.20
33	Massachusetts	0.22
36	Michigan	0.21
49	Minnesota	0.15
8	Mississippi	0.34
19	Missouri	0.27
7	Montana	0.35
27	Nebraska	0.25
19	Nevada	0.27
22	New Hampshire	0.26
33	New Jersey	0.22
16	New Mexico	0.30
18	New York	0.29
48	North Carolina	0.16
15	North Dakota	0.31
43	Ohio	0.18
8	Oklahoma	0.34
41	Oregon	0.19
14	Pennsylvania	0.32
16	Rhode Island	0.30
27	South Carolina	0.25
6	South Dakota	0.41
19	Tennessee	0.27
22	Texas	0.26
22	Utah	0.26
8	Vermont	0.34
36	Virginia	0.21
36	Washington	0.21
5	West Virginia	0.44
50	Wisconsin	0.12
1	Wyoming	0.63

RANK ORDER

RANK	STATE	RATE
1	Wyoming	0.63
2	Delaware	0.56
3	Louisiana	0.51
4	Alaska	0.50
5	West Virginia	0.44
6	South Dakota	0.41
7	Montana	0.35
8	Hawaii	0.34
8	Mississippi	0.34
8	Oklahoma	0.34
8	Vermont	0.34
12	Alabama	0.33
12	Arkansas	0.33
14	Pennsylvania	0.32
15	North Dakota	0.31
16	New Mexico	0.30
16	Rhode Island	0.30
18	New York	0.29
19	Missouri	0.27
19	Nevada	0.27
19	Tennessee	0.27
22	Georgia	0.26
22	Illinois	0.26
22	New Hampshire	0.26
22	Texas	0.26
22	Utah	0.26
27	Nebraska	0.25
27	South Carolina	0.25
29	Connecticut	0.24
29	Kansas	0.24
29	Kentucky	0.24
29	Maine	0.24
33	Florida	0.22
33	Massachusetts	0.22
33	New Jersey	0.22
36	Michigan	0.21
36	Virginia	0.21
36	Washington	0.21
39	Arizona	0.20
39	Maryland	0.20
41	Colorado	0.19
41	Oregon	0.19
43	California	0.18
43	Idaho	0.18
43	Iowa	0.18
43	Ohio	0.18
47	Indiana	0.17
48	North Carolina	0.16
49	Minnesota	0.15
50	Wisconsin	0.12
	District of Columbia	2.65

Source: Morgan Quitno Press using data from Administrative Office of the United States Courts
"1994 Federal Court Management Statistics" (June 1995)
*Total includes 11 judgeships in U.S. territories.

Felony Criminal Cases Filed in U.S. District Court in 1994

National Total = 30,667 Felony Criminal Cases*

ALPHA ORDER

RANK	STATE	CASES	% of USA
16	Alabama	626	2.04%
47	Alaska	85	0.28%
10	Arizona	787	2.57%
25	Arkansas	384	1.25%
2	California	3,000	9.78%
29	Colorado	302	0.98%
37	Connecticut	199	0.65%
50	Delaware	70	0.23%
4	Florida	2,062	6.72%
13	Georgia	726	2.37%
42	Hawaii	142	0.46%
49	Idaho	71	0.23%
11	Illinois	775	2.53%
24	Indiana	394	1.28%
36	Iowa	209	0.68%
30	Kansas	290	0.95%
22	Kentucky	447	1.46%
21	Louisiana	476	1.55%
43	Maine	106	0.35%
26	Maryland	356	1.16%
32	Massachusetts	280	0.91%
9	Michigan	803	2.62%
33	Minnesota	277	0.90%
27	Mississippi	352	1.15%
17	Missouri	591	1.93%
39	Montana	187	0.61%
38	Nebraska	197	0.64%
28	Nevada	333	1.09%
43	New Hampshire	106	0.35%
18	New Jersey	552	1.80%
15	New Mexico	642	2.09%
3	New York	2,543	8.29%
7	North Carolina	869	2.83%
41	North Dakota	149	0.49%
12	Ohio	771	2.51%
23	Oklahoma	406	1.32%
20	Oregon	480	1.56%
6	Pennsylvania	973	3.17%
45	Rhode Island	102	0.33%
19	South Carolina	525	1.71%
35	South Dakota	240	0.78%
8	Tennessee	840	2.74%
1	Texas	3,143	10.25%
40	Utah	176	0.57%
48	Vermont	78	0.25%
5	Virginia	1,034	3.37%
14	Washington	709	2.31%
31	West Virginia	281	0.92%
34	Wisconsin	256	0.83%
46	Wyoming	86	0.28%

RANK ORDER

RANK	STATE	CASES	% of USA
1	Texas	3,143	10.25%
2	California	3,000	9.78%
3	New York	2,543	8.29%
4	Florida	2,062	6.72%
5	Virginia	1,034	3.37%
6	Pennsylvania	973	3.17%
7	North Carolina	869	2.83%
8	Tennessee	840	2.74%
9	Michigan	803	2.62%
10	Arizona	787	2.57%
11	Illinois	775	2.53%
12	Ohio	771	2.51%
13	Georgia	726	2.37%
14	Washington	709	2.31%
15	New Mexico	642	2.09%
16	Alabama	626	2.04%
17	Missouri	591	1.93%
18	New Jersey	552	1.80%
19	South Carolina	525	1.71%
20	Oregon	480	1.56%
21	Louisiana	476	1.55%
22	Kentucky	447	1.46%
23	Oklahoma	406	1.32%
24	Indiana	394	1.28%
25	Arkansas	384	1.25%
26	Maryland	356	1.16%
27	Mississippi	352	1.15%
28	Nevada	333	1.09%
29	Colorado	302	0.98%
30	Kansas	290	0.95%
31	West Virginia	281	0.92%
32	Massachusetts	280	0.91%
33	Minnesota	277	0.90%
34	Wisconsin	256	0.83%
35	South Dakota	240	0.78%
36	Iowa	209	0.68%
37	Connecticut	199	0.65%
38	Nebraska	197	0.64%
39	Montana	187	0.61%
40	Utah	176	0.57%
41	North Dakota	149	0.49%
42	Hawaii	142	0.46%
43	Maine	106	0.35%
43	New Hampshire	106	0.35%
45	Rhode Island	102	0.33%
46	Wyoming	86	0.28%
47	Alaska	85	0.28%
48	Vermont	78	0.25%
49	Idaho	71	0.23%
50	Delaware	70	0.23%
	District of Columbia	441	1.44%

Source: Morgan Quitno Press using data from Administrative Office of the United States Courts
"1994 Federal Court Management Statistics" (June 1995)
*National total includes 738 cases in U.S. territories. Does not include transfers from one district to another.

Felony Criminal Cases Filed per U.S. District Judge in 1994

National Rate = 49 Felony Criminal Cases per Judge*

ALPHA ORDER

RANK	STATE	RATE
21	Alabama	45
44	Alaska	29
2	Arizona	103
20	Arkansas	48
15	California	54
22	Colorado	43
45	Connecticut	26
50	Delaware	19
9	Florida	67
26	Georgia	40
34	Hawaii	36
34	Idaho	36
45	Illinois	26
30	Indiana	39
24	Iowa	42
18	Kansas	49
16	Kentucky	50
48	Louisiana	22
39	Maine	35
34	Maryland	36
48	Massachusetts	22
26	Michigan	40
26	Minnesota	40
30	Mississippi	39
24	Missouri	42
11	Montana	64
16	Nebraska	50
3	Nevada	85
34	New Hampshire	36
41	New Jersey	34
1	New Mexico	128
18	New York	49
6	North Carolina	79
7	North Dakota	76
30	Ohio	39
33	Oklahoma	37
4	Oregon	81
47	Pennsylvania	25
41	Rhode Island	34
13	South Carolina	61
4	South Dakota	81
14	Tennessee	60
9	Texas	67
34	Utah	36
26	Vermont	40
8	Virginia	74
11	Washington	64
39	West Virginia	35
22	Wisconsin	43
43	Wyoming	30

RANK ORDER

RANK	STATE	RATE
1	New Mexico	128
2	Arizona	103
3	Nevada	85
4	Oregon	81
4	South Dakota	81
6	North Carolina	79
7	North Dakota	76
8	Virginia	74
9	Florida	67
9	Texas	67
11	Montana	64
11	Washington	64
13	South Carolina	61
14	Tennessee	60
15	California	54
16	Kentucky	50
16	Nebraska	50
18	Kansas	49
18	New York	49
20	Arkansas	48
21	Alabama	45
22	Colorado	43
22	Wisconsin	43
24	Iowa	42
24	Missouri	42
26	Georgia	40
26	Michigan	40
26	Minnesota	40
26	Vermont	40
30	Indiana	39
30	Mississippi	39
30	Ohio	39
33	Oklahoma	37
34	Hawaii	36
34	Idaho	36
34	Maryland	36
34	New Hampshire	36
34	Utah	36
39	Maine	35
39	West Virginia	35
41	New Jersey	34
41	Rhode Island	34
43	Wyoming	30
44	Alaska	29
45	Connecticut	26
45	Illinois	26
47	Pennsylvania	25
48	Louisiana	22
48	Massachusetts	22
50	Delaware	19
	District of Columbia	29

Source: Morgan Quitno Press using data from Administrative Office of the United States Courts
"1994 Federal Court Management Statistics" (June 1995)
*National rate includes cases and judges in U.S. territories. Does not include transfers from one district to another.

Median Length of Federal Criminal Cases in 1994

National Median = 6.5 Months*

ALPHA ORDER

RANK	STATE	MONTHS
45	Alabama	5.0
38	Alaska	5.7
18	Arizona	7.0
40	Arkansas	5.5
22	California	6.7
43	Colorado	5.1
32	Connecticut	6.2
49	Delaware	4.3
22	Florida	6.7
4	Georgia	8.4
15	Hawaii	7.2
14	Idaho	7.3
6	Illinois	8.0
31	Indiana	6.3
22	Iowa	6.7
17	Kansas	7.1
37	Kentucky	5.9
43	Louisiana	5.1
28	Maine	6.5
10	Maryland	7.7
2	Massachusetts	10.2
12	Michigan	7.6
22	Minnesota	6.7
32	Mississippi	6.2
15	Missouri	7.2
20	Montana	6.8
4	Nebraska	8.4
9	Nevada	7.9
22	New Hampshire	6.7
6	New Jersey	8.0
40	New Mexico	5.5
3	New York	8.9
13	North Carolina	7.5
50	North Dakota	4.1
34	Ohio	6.1
47	Oklahoma	4.6
35	Oregon	6.0
20	Pennsylvania	6.8
19	Rhode Island	6.9
28	South Carolina	6.5
42	South Dakota	5.2
10	Tennessee	7.7
39	Texas	5.6
6	Utah	8.0
1	Vermont	11.2
28	Virginia	6.5
47	Washington	4.6
27	West Virginia	6.6
46	Wisconsin	4.8
35	Wyoming	6.0

RANK ORDER

RANK	STATE	MONTHS
1	Vermont	11.2
2	Massachusetts	10.2
3	New York	8.9
4	Georgia	8.4
4	Nebraska	8.4
6	Illinois	8.0
6	New Jersey	8.0
6	Utah	8.0
9	Nevada	7.9
10	Maryland	7.7
10	Tennessee	7.7
12	Michigan	7.6
13	North Carolina	7.5
14	Idaho	7.3
15	Hawaii	7.2
15	Missouri	7.2
17	Kansas	7.1
18	Arizona	7.0
19	Rhode Island	6.9
20	Montana	6.8
20	Pennsylvania	6.8
22	California	6.7
22	Florida	6.7
22	Iowa	6.7
22	Minnesota	6.7
22	New Hampshire	6.7
27	West Virginia	6.6
28	Maine	6.5
28	South Carolina	6.5
28	Virginia	6.5
31	Indiana	6.3
32	Connecticut	6.2
32	Mississippi	6.2
34	Ohio	6.1
35	Oregon	6.0
35	Wyoming	6.0
37	Kentucky	5.9
38	Alaska	5.7
39	Texas	5.6
40	Arkansas	5.5
40	New Mexico	5.5
42	South Dakota	5.2
43	Colorado	5.1
43	Louisiana	5.1
45	Alabama	5.0
46	Wisconsin	4.8
47	Oklahoma	4.6
47	Washington	4.6
49	Delaware	4.3
50	North Dakota	4.1

| District of Columbia | | 7.1 |

Source: Morgan Quitno Press using data from Administrative Office of the United States Courts
"1994 Federal Court Management Statistics" (June 1995)
*Felony criminal cases. National rate includes cases U.S. territories. Does not include transfers from one district to another.

State and Local Justice System Employment in 1992

National Total = 1,551,884 Employees*

ALPHA ORDER

RANK	STATE	EMPLOYEES	% of USA
23	Alabama	20,322	1.31%
46	Alaska	4,040	0.26%
17	Arizona	27,770	1.79%
33	Arkansas	10,882	0.70%
1	California	184,196	11.87%
24	Colorado	20,081	1.29%
27	Connecticut	17,959	1.16%
44	Delaware	4,952	0.32%
4	Florida	106,017	6.83%
10	Georgia	44,539	2.87%
36	Hawaii	8,173	0.53%
41	Idaho	5,587	0.36%
5	Illinois	74,763	4.82%
18	Indiana	27,663	1.78%
31	Iowa	11,660	0.75%
30	Kansas	14,680	0.95%
26	Kentucky	18,787	1.21%
19	Louisiana	27,606	1.78%
42	Maine	5,544	0.36%
14	Maryland	31,582	2.04%
13	Massachusetts	32,372	2.09%
9	Michigan	51,043	3.29%
25	Minnesota	19,234	1.24%
32	Mississippi	11,631	0.75%
15	Missouri	28,664	1.85%
45	Montana	4,053	0.26%
38	Nebraska	8,005	0.52%
35	Nevada	10,030	0.65%
43	New Hampshire	5,324	0.34%
6	New Jersey	64,941	4.18%
34	New Mexico	10,240	0.66%
2	New York	154,357	9.95%
11	North Carolina	38,362	2.47%
49	North Dakota	2,715	0.17%
8	Ohio	60,467	3.90%
28	Oklahoma	17,265	1.11%
29	Oregon	15,483	1.00%
7	Pennsylvania	62,620	4.04%
40	Rhode Island	5,855	0.38%
22	South Carolina	20,505	1.32%
47	South Dakota	3,089	0.20%
16	Tennessee	27,810	1.79%
3	Texas	113,336	7.30%
37	Utah	8,166	0.53%
50	Vermont	2,479	0.16%
12	Virginia	34,794	2.24%
20	Washington	26,222	1.69%
39	West Virginia	6,062	0.39%
21	Wisconsin	24,985	1.61%
48	Wyoming	3,036	0.20%

RANK ORDER

RANK	STATE	EMPLOYEES	% of USA
1	California	184,196	11.87%
2	New York	154,357	9.95%
3	Texas	113,336	7.30%
4	Florida	106,017	6.83%
5	Illinois	74,763	4.82%
6	New Jersey	64,941	4.18%
7	Pennsylvania	62,620	4.04%
8	Ohio	60,467	3.90%
9	Michigan	51,043	3.29%
10	Georgia	44,539	2.87%
11	North Carolina	38,362	2.47%
12	Virginia	34,794	2.24%
13	Massachusetts	32,372	2.09%
14	Maryland	31,582	2.04%
15	Missouri	28,664	1.85%
16	Tennessee	27,810	1.79%
17	Arizona	27,770	1.79%
18	Indiana	27,663	1.78%
19	Louisiana	27,606	1.78%
20	Washington	26,222	1.69%
21	Wisconsin	24,985	1.61%
22	South Carolina	20,505	1.32%
23	Alabama	20,322	1.31%
24	Colorado	20,081	1.29%
25	Minnesota	19,234	1.24%
26	Kentucky	18,787	1.21%
27	Connecticut	17,959	1.16%
28	Oklahoma	17,265	1.11%
29	Oregon	15,483	1.00%
30	Kansas	14,680	0.95%
31	Iowa	11,660	0.75%
32	Mississippi	11,631	0.75%
33	Arkansas	10,882	0.70%
34	New Mexico	10,240	0.66%
35	Nevada	10,030	0.65%
36	Hawaii	8,173	0.53%
37	Utah	8,166	0.53%
38	Nebraska	8,005	0.52%
39	West Virginia	6,062	0.39%
40	Rhode Island	5,855	0.38%
41	Idaho	5,587	0.36%
42	Maine	5,544	0.36%
43	New Hampshire	5,324	0.34%
44	Delaware	4,952	0.32%
45	Montana	4,053	0.26%
46	Alaska	4,040	0.26%
47	South Dakota	3,089	0.20%
48	Wyoming	3,036	0.20%
49	North Dakota	2,715	0.17%
50	Vermont	2,479	0.16%
	District of Columbia	11,936	0.77%

Source: Morgan Quitno Press using data from U.S. Bureau of the Census
    "Public Employment: 1992" (GE/92-1, September 1994)
*Full-time equivalent. Includes police, courts, prosecution, public defense and corrections.

Rate of State and Local Justice System Employees in 1992

National Rate = 60.8 Employees per 10,000 Population*

ALPHA ORDER

RANK	STATE	RATE
37	Alabama	49.2
8	Alaska	68.8
5	Arizona	72.5
41	Arkansas	45.4
16	California	59.7
19	Colorado	57.9
25	Connecticut	54.7
6	Delaware	71.8
3	Florida	78.6
9	Georgia	66.0
7	Hawaii	70.5
30	Idaho	52.3
14	Illinois	64.3
39	Indiana	48.8
49	Iowa	41.5
17	Kansas	58.2
34	Kentucky	50.0
12	Louisiana	64.5
43	Maine	44.9
13	Maryland	64.4
28	Massachusetts	54.0
27	Michigan	54.2
47	Minnesota	43.0
44	Mississippi	44.5
23	Missouri	55.3
37	Montana	49.2
35	Nebraska	49.9
4	Nevada	75.5
40	New Hampshire	48.0
2	New Jersey	83.4
11	New Mexico	64.7
1	New York	85.2
21	North Carolina	56.1
48	North Dakota	42.7
24	Ohio	54.9
29	Oklahoma	53.8
32	Oregon	52.0
31	Pennsylvania	52.1
17	Rhode Island	58.2
20	South Carolina	56.9
46	South Dakota	43.4
22	Tennessee	55.4
15	Texas	64.2
42	Utah	45.0
45	Vermont	43.5
26	Virginia	54.5
33	Washington	51.1
50	West Virginia	33.5
35	Wisconsin	49.9
10	Wyoming	65.1

RANK ORDER

RANK	STATE	RATE
1	New York	85.2
2	New Jersey	83.4
3	Florida	78.6
4	Nevada	75.5
5	Arizona	72.5
6	Delaware	71.8
7	Hawaii	70.5
8	Alaska	68.8
9	Georgia	66.0
10	Wyoming	65.1
11	New Mexico	64.7
12	Louisiana	64.5
13	Maryland	64.4
14	Illinois	64.3
15	Texas	64.2
16	California	59.7
17	Kansas	58.2
17	Rhode Island	58.2
19	Colorado	57.9
20	South Carolina	56.9
21	North Carolina	56.1
22	Tennessee	55.4
23	Missouri	55.3
24	Ohio	54.9
25	Connecticut	54.7
26	Virginia	54.5
27	Michigan	54.2
28	Massachusetts	54.0
29	Oklahoma	53.8
30	Idaho	52.3
31	Pennsylvania	52.1
32	Oregon	52.0
33	Washington	51.1
34	Kentucky	50.0
35	Nebraska	49.9
35	Wisconsin	49.9
37	Alabama	49.2
37	Montana	49.2
39	Indiana	48.8
40	New Hampshire	48.0
41	Arkansas	45.4
42	Utah	45.0
43	Maine	44.9
44	Mississippi	44.5
45	Vermont	43.5
46	South Dakota	43.4
47	Minnesota	43.0
48	North Dakota	42.7
49	Iowa	41.5
50	West Virginia	33.5

District of Columbia	202.6

Source: Morgan Quitno Press using data from U.S. Bureau of the Census
  "Public Employment: 1992" (GE/92-1, September 1994)
*Full-time equivalent. Includes police, courts, prosecution, public defense and corrections.

State and Local Judicial and Legal System Employment in 1992

National Total = 303,607 Employees*

ALPHA ORDER

RANK	STATE	EMPLOYEES	% of USA
25	Alabama	3,874	1.28%
42	Alaska	1,170	0.39%
11	Arizona	6,467	2.13%
36	Arkansas	1,703	0.56%
1	California	37,875	12.48%
22	Colorado	4,441	1.46%
27	Connecticut	3,292	1.08%
40	Delaware	1,331	0.44%
3	Florida	18,915	6.23%
10	Georgia	7,063	2.33%
32	Hawaii	2,711	0.89%
41	Idaho	1,197	0.39%
8	Illinois	14,474	4.77%
19	Indiana	5,035	1.66%
31	Iowa	2,805	0.92%
28	Kansas	2,903	0.96%
24	Kentucky	4,327	1.43%
16	Louisiana	5,553	1.83%
47	Maine	740	0.24%
12	Maryland	6,041	1.99%
14	Massachusetts	5,637	1.86%
9	Michigan	10,350	3.41%
23	Minnesota	4,335	1.43%
33	Mississippi	2,123	0.70%
18	Missouri	5,174	1.70%
45	Montana	783	0.26%
39	Nebraska	1,519	0.50%
34	Nevada	2,090	0.69%
44	New Hampshire	917	0.30%
6	New Jersey	15,880	5.23%
35	New Mexico	1,961	0.65%
2	New York	27,514	9.06%
15	North Carolina	5,601	1.84%
48	North Dakota	704	0.23%
5	Ohio	16,114	5.31%
30	Oklahoma	2,820	0.93%
26	Oregon	3,489	1.15%
7	Pennsylvania	15,064	4.96%
43	Rhode Island	1,030	0.34%
29	South Carolina	2,854	0.94%
46	South Dakota	747	0.25%
20	Tennessee	4,668	1.54%
4	Texas	18,202	6.00%
38	Utah	1,618	0.53%
50	Vermont	540	0.18%
17	Virginia	5,411	1.78%
13	Washington	5,834	1.92%
37	West Virginia	1,628	0.54%
21	Wisconsin	4,601	1.52%
49	Wyoming	690	0.23%

RANK ORDER

RANK	STATE	EMPLOYEES	% of USA
1	California	37,875	12.48%
2	New York	27,514	9.06%
3	Florida	18,915	6.23%
4	Texas	18,202	6.00%
5	Ohio	16,114	5.31%
6	New Jersey	15,880	5.23%
7	Pennsylvania	15,064	4.96%
8	Illinois	14,474	4.77%
9	Michigan	10,350	3.41%
10	Georgia	7,063	2.33%
11	Arizona	6,467	2.13%
12	Maryland	6,041	1.99%
13	Washington	5,834	1.92%
14	Massachusetts	5,637	1.86%
15	North Carolina	5,601	1.84%
16	Louisiana	5,553	1.83%
17	Virginia	5,411	1.78%
18	Missouri	5,174	1.70%
19	Indiana	5,035	1.66%
20	Tennessee	4,668	1.54%
21	Wisconsin	4,601	1.52%
22	Colorado	4,441	1.46%
23	Minnesota	4,335	1.43%
24	Kentucky	4,327	1.43%
25	Alabama	3,874	1.28%
26	Oregon	3,489	1.15%
27	Connecticut	3,292	1.08%
28	Kansas	2,903	0.96%
29	South Carolina	2,854	0.94%
30	Oklahoma	2,820	0.93%
31	Iowa	2,805	0.92%
32	Hawaii	2,711	0.89%
33	Mississippi	2,123	0.70%
34	Nevada	2,090	0.69%
35	New Mexico	1,961	0.65%
36	Arkansas	1,703	0.56%
37	West Virginia	1,628	0.54%
38	Utah	1,618	0.53%
39	Nebraska	1,519	0.50%
40	Delaware	1,331	0.44%
41	Idaho	1,197	0.39%
42	Alaska	1,170	0.39%
43	Rhode Island	1,030	0.34%
44	New Hampshire	917	0.30%
45	Montana	783	0.26%
46	South Dakota	747	0.25%
47	Maine	740	0.24%
48	North Dakota	704	0.23%
49	Wyoming	690	0.23%
50	Vermont	540	0.18%
	District of Columbia	1,792	0.59%

Source: U.S. Bureau of the Census
   "Public Employment: 1992" (GE/92-1, September 1994)
*Full-time equivalent. Includes courts, prosecution and public defense.

Rate of State and Local Judicial and Legal System Employment in 1992

National Rate = 11.9 Employees per 10,000 Population*

ALPHA ORDER

RANK	STATE	RATE
36	Alabama	9.4
3	Alaska	19.9
5	Arizona	16.9
49	Arkansas	7.1
16	California	12.3
12	Colorado	12.8
29	Connecticut	10.0
4	Delaware	19.3
10	Florida	14.0
25	Georgia	10.5
1	Hawaii	23.4
22	Idaho	11.2
14	Illinois	12.4
41	Indiana	8.9
29	Iowa	10.0
19	Kansas	11.5
19	Kentucky	11.5
11	Louisiana	13.0
50	Maine	6.0
16	Maryland	12.3
36	Massachusetts	9.4
24	Michigan	11.0
32	Minnesota	9.7
47	Mississippi	8.1
29	Missouri	10.0
33	Montana	9.5
33	Nebraska	9.5
6	Nevada	15.7
45	New Hampshire	8.3
2	New Jersey	20.4
14	New Mexico	12.4
7	New York	15.2
46	North Carolina	8.2
23	North Dakota	11.1
9	Ohio	14.6
43	Oklahoma	8.8
18	Oregon	11.7
13	Pennsylvania	12.5
28	Rhode Island	10.2
48	South Carolina	7.9
25	South Dakota	10.5
38	Tennessee	9.3
27	Texas	10.3
41	Utah	8.9
33	Vermont	9.5
44	Virginia	8.5
21	Washington	11.4
40	West Virginia	9.0
39	Wisconsin	9.2
8	Wyoming	14.8

RANK ORDER

RANK	STATE	RATE
1	Hawaii	23.4
2	New Jersey	20.4
3	Alaska	19.9
4	Delaware	19.3
5	Arizona	16.9
6	Nevada	15.7
7	New York	15.2
8	Wyoming	14.8
9	Ohio	14.6
10	Florida	14.0
11	Louisiana	13.0
12	Colorado	12.8
13	Pennsylvania	12.5
14	Illinois	12.4
14	New Mexico	12.4
16	California	12.3
16	Maryland	12.3
18	Oregon	11.7
19	Kansas	11.5
19	Kentucky	11.5
21	Washington	11.4
22	Idaho	11.2
23	North Dakota	11.1
24	Michigan	11.0
25	Georgia	10.5
25	South Dakota	10.5
27	Texas	10.3
28	Rhode Island	10.2
29	Connecticut	10.0
29	Iowa	10.0
29	Missouri	10.0
32	Minnesota	9.7
33	Montana	9.5
33	Nebraska	9.5
33	Vermont	9.5
36	Alabama	9.4
36	Massachusetts	9.4
38	Tennessee	9.3
39	Wisconsin	9.2
40	West Virginia	9.0
41	Indiana	8.9
41	Utah	8.9
43	Oklahoma	8.8
44	Virginia	8.5
45	New Hampshire	8.3
46	North Carolina	8.2
47	Mississippi	8.1
48	South Carolina	7.9
49	Arkansas	7.1
50	Maine	6.0

	District of Columbia	30.4

Source: U.S. Bureau of the Census
"Public Employment: 1992" (GE/92-1, September 1994)
Full-time equivalent. Includes courts, prosecution and public defense.

Authorized Wiretaps in 1994

National Total = 600 State Authorized Wiretaps*

ALPHA ORDER

RANK	STATE	WIRETAPS	% of USA
NA	Alabama**	NA	NA
NA	Alaska**	NA	NA
5	Arizona	11	1.83%
NA	Arkansas**	NA	NA
8	California	8	1.33%
11	Colorado	5	0.83%
8	Connecticut	8	1.33%
13	Delaware	3	0.50%
4	Florida	49	8.17%
6	Georgia	9	1.50%
18	Hawaii	0	0.00%
18	Idaho	0	0.00%
18	Illinois	0	0.00%
18	Indiana	0	0.00%
18	Iowa	0	0.00%
18	Kansas	0	0.00%
NA	Kentucky**	NA	NA
13	Louisiana	3	0.50%
NA	Maine**	NA	NA
6	Maryland	9	1.50%
18	Massachusetts	0	0.00%
NA	Michigan**	NA	NA
18	Minnesota	0	0.00%
15	Mississippi	2	0.33%
18	Missouri	0	0.00%
NA	Montana**	NA	NA
15	Nebraska	2	0.33%
11	Nevada	5	0.83%
18	New Hampshire	0	0.00%
2	New Jersey	59	9.83%
18	New Mexico	0	0.00%
1	New York	367	61.17%
NA	North Carolina**	NA	NA
18	North Dakota	0	0.00%
18	Ohio	0	0.00%
18	Oklahoma	0	0.00%
18	Oregon	0	0.00%
3	Pennsylvania	52	8.67%
18	Rhode Island	0	0.00%
NA	South Carolina**	NA	NA
18	South Dakota	0	0.00%
NA	Tennessee**	NA	NA
10	Texas	6	1.00%
15	Utah	2	0.33%
NA	Vermont**	NA	NA
18	Virginia	0	0.00%
18	Washington	0	0.00%
NA	West Virginia**	NA	NA
NA	Wisconsin**	NA	NA
18	Wyoming	0	0.00%

RANK ORDER

RANK	STATE	WIRETAPS	% of USA
1	New York	367	61.17%
2	New Jersey	59	9.83%
3	Pennsylvania	52	8.67%
4	Florida	49	8.17%
5	Arizona	11	1.83%
6	Georgia	9	1.50%
6	Maryland	9	1.50%
8	California	8	1.33%
8	Connecticut	8	1.33%
10	Texas	6	1.00%
11	Colorado	5	0.83%
11	Nevada	5	0.83%
13	Delaware	3	0.50%
13	Louisiana	3	0.50%
15	Mississippi	2	0.33%
15	Nebraska	2	0.33%
15	Utah	2	0.33%
18	Hawaii	0	0.00%
18	Idaho	0	0.00%
18	Illinois	0	0.00%
18	Indiana	0	0.00%
18	Iowa	0	0.00%
18	Kansas	0	0.00%
18	Massachusetts	0	0.00%
18	Minnesota	0	0.00%
18	Missouri	0	0.00%
18	New Hampshire	0	0.00%
18	New Mexico	0	0.00%
18	North Dakota	0	0.00%
18	Ohio	0	0.00%
18	Oklahoma	0	0.00%
18	Oregon	0	0.00%
18	Rhode Island	0	0.00%
18	South Dakota	0	0.00%
18	Virginia	0	0.00%
18	Washington	0	0.00%
18	Wyoming	0	0.00%
NA	Alabama**	NA	NA
NA	Alaska**	NA	NA
NA	Arkansas**	NA	NA
NA	Kentucky**	NA	NA
NA	Maine**	NA	NA
NA	Michigan**	NA	NA
NA	Montana**	NA	NA
NA	North Carolina**	NA	NA
NA	South Carolina**	NA	NA
NA	Tennessee**	NA	NA
NA	Vermont**	NA	NA
NA	West Virginia**	NA	NA
NA	Wisconsin**	NA	NA
	District of Columbia	0	0.00%

Source: Administrative Office of the United States Courts
    "Wiretap Reports 1994"
*Total does not include 554 wiretaps authorized under federal statute.
**No state statute authorizing wiretaps.

VI. OFFENSES

VI. OFFENSES (continued)

Urban/Rural Crime

VI. OFFENSES (continued)

1990 Crimes

VI. OFFENSES (continued)

Crimes in 1994

National Total = 13,991,675 Crimes*

ALPHA ORDER				RANK ORDER			
RANK	STATE	CRIMES	% of USA	RANK	STATE	CRIMES	% of USA
22	Alabama	206,859	1.48%	1	California	1,940,497	13.87%
44	Alaska	34,591	0.25%	2	Florida	1,151,121	8.23%
12	Arizona	322,926	2.31%	3	Texas	1,079,225	7.71%
32	Arkansas	117,713	0.84%	4	New York	921,278	6.58%
1	California	1,940,497	13.87%	5	Illinois	661,150	4.73%
25	Colorado	194,440	1.39%	6	Michigan	517,076	3.70%
28	Connecticut	148,946	1.06%	7	Ohio	495,310	3.54%
46	Delaware	29,282	0.21%	8	Georgia	424,029	3.03%
2	Florida	1,151,121	8.23%	9	North Carolina	397,705	2.84%
8	Georgia	424,029	3.03%	10	Pennsylvania	394,326	2.82%
37	Hawaii	78,763	0.56%	11	New Jersey	368,400	2.63%
39	Idaho	46,192	0.33%	12	Arizona	322,926	2.31%
5	Illinois	661,150	4.73%	13	Washington	322,051	2.30%
20	Indiana	264,180	1.89%	14	Maryland	306,496	2.19%
33	Iowa	103,389	0.74%	15	Louisiana	287,857	2.06%
31	Kansas	124,987	0.89%	16	Missouri	280,138	2.00%
29	Kentucky	133,890	0.96%	17	Massachusetts	268,281	1.92%
15	Louisiana	287,857	2.06%	18	Virginia	265,200	1.90%
43	Maine	40,582	0.29%	19	Tennessee	264,952	1.89%
14	Maryland	306,496	2.19%	20	Indiana	264,180	1.89%
17	Massachusetts	268,281	1.92%	21	South Carolina	219,870	1.57%
6	Michigan	517,076	3.70%	22	Alabama	206,859	1.48%
24	Minnesota	198,253	1.42%	23	Wisconsin	200,452	1.43%
30	Mississippi	129,101	0.92%	24	Minnesota	198,253	1.42%
16	Missouri	280,138	2.00%	25	Colorado	194,440	1.39%
41	Montana	42,961	0.31%	26	Oregon	194,307	1.39%
38	Nebraska	72,068	0.52%	27	Oklahoma	181,475	1.30%
36	Nevada	97,290	0.70%	28	Connecticut	148,946	1.06%
45	New Hampshire	31,165	0.22%	29	Kentucky	133,890	0.96%
11	New Jersey	368,400	2.63%	30	Mississippi	129,101	0.92%
34	New Mexico	102,346	0.73%	31	Kansas	124,987	0.89%
4	New York	921,278	6.58%	32	Arkansas	117,713	0.84%
9	North Carolina	397,705	2.84%	33	Iowa	103,389	0.74%
50	North Dakota	17,455	0.12%	34	New Mexico	102,346	0.73%
7	Ohio	495,310	3.54%	35	Utah	101,142	0.72%
27	Oklahoma	181,475	1.30%	36	Nevada	97,290	0.70%
26	Oregon	194,307	1.39%	37	Hawaii	78,763	0.56%
10	Pennsylvania	394,326	2.82%	38	Nebraska	72,068	0.52%
42	Rhode Island	41,067	0.29%	39	Idaho	46,192	0.33%
21	South Carolina	219,870	1.57%	40	West Virginia	46,067	0.33%
47	South Dakota	22,367	0.16%	41	Montana	42,961	0.31%
19	Tennessee	264,952	1.89%	42	Rhode Island	41,067	0.29%
3	Texas	1,079,225	7.71%	43	Maine	40,582	0.29%
35	Utah	101,142	0.72%	44	Alaska	34,591	0.25%
49	Vermont	18,852	0.13%	45	New Hampshire	31,165	0.22%
18	Virginia	265,200	1.90%	46	Delaware	29,282	0.21%
13	Washington	322,051	2.30%	47	South Dakota	22,367	0.16%
40	West Virginia	46,067	0.33%	48	Wyoming	20,419	0.15%
23	Wisconsin	200,452	1.43%	49	Vermont	18,852	0.13%
48	Wyoming	20,419	0.15%	50	North Dakota	17,455	0.12%
					District of Columbia	63,186	0.45%

Source: Federal Bureau of Investigation
"Crime in the United States 1994" (Uniform Crime Reports, November 19, 1995)
*Includes murder, rape, robbery, aggravated assault, burglary, larceny-theft and motor vehicle theft.

Average Time Between Crimes in 1994

National Rate = A Crime Occurs Every 2 Seconds*

ALPHA ORDER

RANK	STATE	MINUTES.SECONDS
29	Alabama	2.32
7	Alaska	15.11
38	Arizona	1.38
19	Arkansas	4.28
50	California	0.16
26	Colorado	2.42
23	Connecticut	3.32
5	Delaware	17.57
49	Florida	0.28
43	Georgia	1.14
14	Hawaii	6.40
12	Idaho	11.23
46	Illinois	0.48
31	Indiana	1.59
18	Iowa	5.05
20	Kansas	4.13
22	Kentucky	3.56
36	Louisiana	1.50
8	Maine	12.57
37	Maryland	1.43
34	Massachusetts	1.58
45	Michigan	1.01
27	Minnesota	2.39
21	Mississippi	4.04
35	Missouri	1.53
10	Montana	12.14
13	Nebraska	7.17
15	Nevada	5.24
6	New Hampshire	16.52
40	New Jersey	1.26
17	New Mexico	5.08
47	New York	0.34
42	North Carolina	1.19
1	North Dakota	30.07
44	Ohio	1.04
24	Oklahoma	2.54
25	Oregon	2.43
41	Pennsylvania	1.20
9	Rhode Island	12.48
30	South Carolina	2.23
4	South Dakota	23.30
31	Tennessee	1.59
48	Texas	0.29
16	Utah	5.12
2	Vermont	27.53
31	Virginia	1.59
38	Washington	1.38
11	West Virginia	11.25
28	Wisconsin	2.37
3	Wyoming	25.44

RANK ORDER

RANK	STATE	MINUTES.SECONDS
1	North Dakota	30.07
2	Vermont	27.53
3	Wyoming	25.44
4	South Dakota	23.30
5	Delaware	17.57
6	New Hampshire	16.52
7	Alaska	15.11
8	Maine	12.57
9	Rhode Island	12.48
10	Montana	12.14
11	West Virginia	11.25
12	Idaho	11.23
13	Nebraska	7.17
14	Hawaii	6.40
15	Nevada	5.24
16	Utah	5.12
17	New Mexico	5.08
18	Iowa	5.05
19	Arkansas	4.28
20	Kansas	4.13
21	Mississippi	4.04
22	Kentucky	3.56
23	Connecticut	3.32
24	Oklahoma	2.54
25	Oregon	2.43
26	Colorado	2.42
27	Minnesota	2.39
28	Wisconsin	2.37
29	Alabama	2.32
30	South Carolina	2.23
31	Indiana	1.59
31	Tennessee	1.59
31	Virginia	1.59
34	Massachusetts	1.58
35	Missouri	1.53
36	Louisiana	1.50
37	Maryland	1.43
38	Arizona	1.38
38	Washington	1.38
40	New Jersey	1.26
41	Pennsylvania	1.20
42	North Carolina	1.19
43	Georgia	1.14
44	Ohio	1.04
45	Michigan	1.01
46	Illinois	0.48
47	New York	0.34
48	Texas	0.29
49	Florida	0.28
50	California	0.16

District of Columbia   8.19

Source: Morgan Quitno Press using data from Federal Bureau of Investigation
"Crime in the United States 1994" (Uniform Crime Reports, November 19, 1995)
*Includes murder, rape, robbery, aggravated assault, burglary, larceny-theft and motor vehicle theft.

Crimes per Square Mile in 1994

National Rate = 3.76 Crimes per Square Mile*

ALPHA ORDER

RANK	STATE	RATE
25	Alabama	3.96
50	Alaska	0.06
29	Arizona	2.83
33	Arkansas	2.21
9	California	12.21
37	Colorado	1.87
4	Connecticut	26.87
8	Delaware	12.22
6	Florida	19.19
16	Georgia	7.19
10	Hawaii	12.19
45	Idaho	0.55
11	Illinois	11.42
15	Indiana	7.25
38	Iowa	1.84
39	Kansas	1.52
27	Kentucky	3.31
20	Louisiana	5.80
40	Maine	1.20
5	Maryland	24.92
3	Massachusetts	29.03
21	Michigan	5.35
32	Minnesota	2.28
30	Mississippi	2.67
24	Missouri	4.02
46	Montana	0.29
42	Nebraska	0.93
43	Nevada	0.88
26	New Hampshire	3.36
1	New Jersey	44.84
44	New Mexico	0.84
7	New York	17.06
14	North Carolina	7.55
48	North Dakota	0.25
12	Ohio	11.05
31	Oklahoma	2.60
34	Oregon	2.00
13	Pennsylvania	8.62
2	Rhode Island	33.36
17	South Carolina	7.05
46	South Dakota	0.29
18	Tennessee	6.29
23	Texas	4.04
41	Utah	1.19
35	Vermont	1.96
19	Virginia	6.27
22	Washington	4.56
36	West Virginia	1.90
28	Wisconsin	3.06
49	Wyoming	0.21

RANK ORDER

RANK	STATE	RATE
1	New Jersey	44.84
2	Rhode Island	33.36
3	Massachusetts	29.03
4	Connecticut	26.87
5	Maryland	24.92
6	Florida	19.19
7	New York	17.06
8	Delaware	12.22
9	California	12.21
10	Hawaii	12.19
11	Illinois	11.42
12	Ohio	11.05
13	Pennsylvania	8.62
14	North Carolina	7.55
15	Indiana	7.25
16	Georgia	7.19
17	South Carolina	7.05
18	Tennessee	6.29
19	Virginia	6.27
20	Louisiana	5.80
21	Michigan	5.35
22	Washington	4.56
23	Texas	4.04
24	Missouri	4.02
25	Alabama	3.96
26	New Hampshire	3.36
27	Kentucky	3.31
28	Wisconsin	3.06
29	Arizona	2.83
30	Mississippi	2.67
31	Oklahoma	2.60
32	Minnesota	2.28
33	Arkansas	2.21
34	Oregon	2.00
35	Vermont	1.96
36	West Virginia	1.90
37	Colorado	1.87
38	Iowa	1.84
39	Kansas	1.52
40	Maine	1.20
41	Utah	1.19
42	Nebraska	0.93
43	Nevada	0.88
44	New Mexico	0.84
45	Idaho	0.55
46	Montana	0.29
46	South Dakota	0.29
48	North Dakota	0.25
49	Wyoming	0.21
50	Alaska	0.06

District of Columbia	929.21

Source: Morgan Quitno Press using data from Federal Bureau of Investigation
"Crime in the United States 1994" (Uniform Crime Reports, November 19, 1995)
*Includes murder, rape, robbery, aggravated assault, burglary, larceny-theft and motor vehicle theft.

Percent Change in Number of Crimes: 1993 to 1994

National Percent Change = 1.1% Decrease*

ALPHA ORDER			RANK ORDER		
RANK	**STATE**	**PERCENT CHANGE**	**RANK**	**STATE**	**PERCENT CHANGE**
20	Alabama	1.3	1	Nevada	13.3
16	Alaska	3.7	2	Oregon	11.2
4	Arizona	10.4	3	Mississippi	10.6
24	Arkansas	0.9	4	Arizona	10.4
42	California	(3.7)	5	Idaho	9.3
36	Colorado	(1.3)	6	Kentucky	8.4
39	Connecticut	(2.3)	7	Hawaii	7.1
49	Delaware	(14.1)	8	Montana	6.9
25	Florida	0.8	9	Oklahoma	6.1
35	Georgia	(1.0)	10	South Dakota	5.7
7	Hawaii	7.1	11	Missouri	5.0
5	Idaho	9.3	12	Nebraska	4.8
26	Illinois	0.6	13	Wyoming	4.4
17	Indiana	3.6	14	Maine	3.9
43	Iowa	(4.5)	15	Utah	3.8
32	Kansas	(0.7)	16	Alaska	3.7
6	Kentucky	8.4	17	Indiana	3.6
38	Louisiana	(2.1)	18	Washington	3.0
14	Maine	3.9	19	South Carolina	2.2
22	Maryland	1.1	20	Alabama	1.3
47	Massachusetts	(8.8)	20	North Carolina	1.3
27	Michigan	0.1	22	Maryland	1.1
31	Minnesota	(0.5)	22	New Mexico	1.1
3	Mississippi	10.6	24	Arkansas	0.9
11	Missouri	5.0	25	Florida	0.8
8	Montana	6.9	26	Illinois	0.6
12	Nebraska	4.8	27	Michigan	0.1
1	Nevada	13.3	28	Pennsylvania	0.0
44	New Hampshire	(4.6)	29	West Virginia	(0.1)
41	New Jersey	(2.6)	30	Ohio	(0.4)
22	New Mexico	1.1	31	Minnesota	(0.5)
47	New York	(8.8)	32	Kansas	(0.7)
20	North Carolina	1.3	32	Virginia	(0.7)
40	North Dakota	(2.5)	34	Tennessee	(0.8)
30	Ohio	(0.4)	35	Georgia	(1.0)
9	Oklahoma	6.1	36	Colorado	(1.3)
2	Oregon	11.2	37	Wisconsin	(1.9)
28	Pennsylvania	0.0	38	Louisiana	(2.1)
46	Rhode Island	(8.7)	39	Connecticut	(2.3)
19	South Carolina	2.2	40	North Dakota	(2.5)
10	South Dakota	5.7	41	New Jersey	(2.6)
34	Tennessee	(0.8)	42	California	(3.7)
45	Texas	(7.0)	43	Iowa	(4.5)
15	Utah	3.8	44	New Hampshire	(4.6)
50	Vermont	(17.6)	45	Texas	(7.0)
32	Virginia	(0.7)	46	Rhode Island	(8.7)
18	Washington	3.0	47	Massachusetts	(8.8)
29	West Virginia	(0.1)	47	New York	(8.8)
37	Wisconsin	(1.9)	49	Delaware	(14.1)
13	Wyoming	4.4	50	Vermont	(17.6)
				District of Columbia	(7.1)

Source: Federal Bureau of Investigation
   "Crime in the United States 1994" (Uniform Crime Reports, November 19, 1995)
*Includes murder, rape, robbery, aggravated assault, burglary, larceny-theft and motor vehicle theft.

Crime Rate in 1994

National Rate = 5,374.4 Crimes per 100,000 Population*

ALPHA ORDER

RANK	STATE	RATE
25	Alabama	4,903.0
14	Alaska	5,708.1
2	Arizona	7,924.6
28	Arkansas	4,798.7
8	California	6,173.8
19	Colorado	5,318.4
31	Connecticut	4,548.0
37	Delaware	4,147.6
1	Florida	8,250.0
11	Georgia	6,010.3
3	Hawaii	6,680.5
39	Idaho	4,077.0
15	Illinois	5,625.9
30	Indiana	4,592.8
42	Iowa	3,654.6
26	Kansas	4,893.8
43	Kentucky	3,498.6
5	Louisiana	6,671.1
44	Maine	3,272.7
9	Maryland	6,122.6
33	Massachusetts	4,441.0
18	Michigan	5,445.2
35	Minnesota	4,341.0
27	Mississippi	4,837.1
20	Missouri	5,307.7
24	Montana	5,018.8
34	Nebraska	4,440.4
4	Nevada	6,677.4
48	New Hampshire	2,741.0
29	New Jersey	4,660.9
7	New Mexico	6,187.8
23	New York	5,070.6
16	North Carolina	5,625.2
49	North Dakota	2,735.9
32	Ohio	4,461.4
17	Oklahoma	5,570.1
6	Oregon	6,296.4
45	Pennsylvania	3,271.9
38	Rhode Island	4,119.1
12	South Carolina	6,000.8
47	South Dakota	3,102.2
22	Tennessee	5,119.8
13	Texas	5,872.4
21	Utah	5,300.9
46	Vermont	3,250.3
40	Virginia	4,047.6
10	Washington	6,027.5
50	West Virginia	2,528.4
41	Wisconsin	3,944.4
36	Wyoming	4,289.7

RANK ORDER

RANK	STATE	RATE
1	Florida	8,250.0
2	Arizona	7,924.6
3	Hawaii	6,680.5
4	Nevada	6,677.4
5	Louisiana	6,671.1
6	Oregon	6,296.4
7	New Mexico	6,187.8
8	California	6,173.8
9	Maryland	6,122.6
10	Washington	6,027.5
11	Georgia	6,010.3
12	South Carolina	6,000.8
13	Texas	5,872.4
14	Alaska	5,708.1
15	Illinois	5,625.9
16	North Carolina	5,625.2
17	Oklahoma	5,570.1
18	Michigan	5,445.2
19	Colorado	5,318.4
20	Missouri	5,307.7
21	Utah	5,300.9
22	Tennessee	5,119.8
23	New York	5,070.6
24	Montana	5,018.8
25	Alabama	4,903.0
26	Kansas	4,893.8
27	Mississippi	4,837.1
28	Arkansas	4,798.7
29	New Jersey	4,660.9
30	Indiana	4,592.8
31	Connecticut	4,548.0
32	Ohio	4,461.4
33	Massachusetts	4,441.0
34	Nebraska	4,440.4
35	Minnesota	4,341.0
36	Wyoming	4,289.7
37	Delaware	4,147.6
38	Rhode Island	4,119.1
39	Idaho	4,077.0
40	Virginia	4,047.6
41	Wisconsin	3,944.4
42	Iowa	3,654.6
43	Kentucky	3,498.6
44	Maine	3,272.7
45	Pennsylvania	3,271.9
46	Vermont	3,250.3
47	South Dakota	3,102.2
48	New Hampshire	2,741.0
49	North Dakota	2,735.9
50	West Virginia	2,528.4

District of Columbia   11,085.3

Source: Federal Bureau of Investigation
  "Crime in the United States 1994" (Uniform Crime Reports, November 19, 1995)
*Includes murder, rape, robbery, aggravated assault, burglary, larceny-theft and motor vehicle theft.

Percent Change in Crime Rate: 1993 to 1994

National Percent Change = 2.0% Decrease*

ALPHA ORDER				RANK ORDER		
RANK	STATE	PERCENT CHANGE		RANK	STATE	PERCENT CHANGE
20	Alabama	0.5		1	Mississippi	9.5
16	Alaska	2.5		2	Oregon	9.2
5	Arizona	6.6		3	Nevada	8.0
25	Arkansas	(0.2)		4	Kentucky	7.3
42	California	(4.4)		5	Arizona	6.6
41	Colorado	(3.8)		6	Hawaii	6.4
34	Connecticut	(2.2)		7	Idaho	6.0
49	Delaware	(14.9)		8	Oklahoma	5.2
29	Florida	(1.2)		9	South Dakota	4.9
39	Georgia	(3.0)		10	Montana	4.8
6	Hawaii	6.4		11	Missouri	4.2
7	Idaho	6.0		12	Maine	3.8
22	Illinois	0.1		13	Nebraska	3.7
15	Indiana	2.9		14	Wyoming	3.0
43	Iowa	(5.0)		15	Indiana	2.9
31	Kansas	(1.6)		16	Alaska	2.5
4	Kentucky	7.3		17	South Carolina	1.6
36	Louisiana	(2.6)		18	Washington	1.3
12	Maine	3.8		19	Utah	1.2
21	Maryland	0.3		20	Alabama	0.5
48	Massachusetts	(9.3)		21	Maryland	0.3
24	Michigan	(0.1)		22	Illinois	0.1
31	Minnesota	(1.6)		23	Pennsylvania	0.0
1	Mississippi	9.5		24	Michigan	(0.1)
11	Missouri	4.2		25	Arkansas	(0.2)
10	Montana	4.8		25	West Virginia	(0.2)
13	Nebraska	3.7		27	North Carolina	(0.5)
3	Nevada	8.0		27	Ohio	(0.5)
44	New Hampshire	(5.6)		29	Florida	(1.2)
38	New Jersey	(2.9)		29	New Mexico	(1.2)
29	New Mexico	(1.2)		31	Kansas	(1.6)
46	New York	(8.7)		31	Minnesota	(1.6)
27	North Carolina	(0.5)		31	Virginia	(1.6)
39	North Dakota	(3.0)		34	Connecticut	(2.2)
27	Ohio	(0.5)		35	Tennessee	(2.3)
8	Oklahoma	5.2		36	Louisiana	(2.6)
2	Oregon	9.2		37	Wisconsin	(2.7)
23	Pennsylvania	0.0		38	New Jersey	(2.9)
45	Rhode Island	(8.4)		39	Georgia	(3.0)
17	South Carolina	1.6		39	North Dakota	(3.0)
9	South Dakota	4.9		41	Colorado	(3.8)
35	Tennessee	(2.3)		42	California	(4.4)
47	Texas	(8.8)		43	Iowa	(5.0)
19	Utah	1.2		44	New Hampshire	(5.6)
50	Vermont	(18.2)		45	Rhode Island	(8.4)
31	Virginia	(1.6)		46	New York	(8.7)
18	Washington	1.3		47	Texas	(8.8)
25	West Virginia	(0.2)		48	Massachusetts	(9.3)
37	Wisconsin	(2.7)		49	Delaware	(14.9)
14	Wyoming	3.0		50	Vermont	(18.2)

District of Columbia   (5.7)

Source: Federal Bureau of Investigation
   "Crime in the United States 1994" (Uniform Crime Reports, November 19, 1995)
*Includes murder, rape, robbery, aggravated assault, burglary, larceny-theft and motor vehicle theft.

Violent Crimes in 1994

National Total = 1,864,168 Violent Crimes*

ALPHA ORDER

RANK	STATE	CRIMES	% of USA
19	Alabama	28,844	1.55%
38	Alaska	4,644	0.25%
20	Arizona	28,653	1.54%
30	Arkansas	14,598	0.78%
1	California	318,395	17.08%
25	Colorado	18,632	1.00%
28	Connecticut	14,916	0.80%
39	Delaware	3,961	0.21%
3	Florida	160,016	8.58%
11	Georgia	47,103	2.53%
43	Hawaii	3,091	0.17%
42	Idaho	3,238	0.17%
5	Illinois	112,928	6.06%
18	Indiana	30,205	1.62%
35	Iowa	8,914	0.48%
34	Kansas	12,226	0.66%
23	Kentucky	23,165	1.24%
14	Louisiana	42,369	2.27%
45	Maine	1,611	0.09%
10	Maryland	47,457	2.55%
13	Massachusetts	42,749	2.29%
6	Michigan	72,751	3.90%
26	Minnesota	16,397	0.88%
33	Mississippi	13,177	0.71%
15	Missouri	39,240	2.10%
46	Montana	1,516	0.08%
36	Nebraska	6,322	0.34%
31	Nevada	14,597	0.78%
47	New Hampshire	1,328	0.07%
9	New Jersey	48,544	2.60%
29	New Mexico	14,708	0.79%
2	New York	175,433	9.41%
12	North Carolina	46,308	2.48%
50	North Dakota	522	0.03%
7	Ohio	53,930	2.89%
24	Oklahoma	21,225	1.14%
27	Oregon	16,067	0.86%
8	Pennsylvania	51,425	2.76%
41	Rhode Island	3,744	0.20%
17	South Carolina	37,756	2.03%
44	South Dakota	1,641	0.09%
16	Tennessee	38,705	2.08%
4	Texas	129,838	6.96%
37	Utah	5,810	0.31%
49	Vermont	562	0.03%
22	Virginia	23,437	1.26%
21	Washington	27,317	1.47%
40	West Virginia	3,931	0.21%
32	Wisconsin	13,748	0.74%
48	Wyoming	1,297	0.07%

RANK ORDER

RANK	STATE	CRIMES	% of USA
1	California	318,395	17.08%
2	New York	175,433	9.41%
3	Florida	160,016	8.58%
4	Texas	129,838	6.96%
5	Illinois	112,928	6.06%
6	Michigan	72,751	3.90%
7	Ohio	53,930	2.89%
8	Pennsylvania	51,425	2.76%
9	New Jersey	48,544	2.60%
10	Maryland	47,457	2.55%
11	Georgia	47,103	2.53%
12	North Carolina	46,308	2.48%
13	Massachusetts	42,749	2.29%
14	Louisiana	42,369	2.27%
15	Missouri	39,240	2.10%
16	Tennessee	38,705	2.08%
17	South Carolina	37,756	2.03%
18	Indiana	30,205	1.62%
19	Alabama	28,844	1.55%
20	Arizona	28,653	1.54%
21	Washington	27,317	1.47%
22	Virginia	23,437	1.26%
23	Kentucky	23,165	1.24%
24	Oklahoma	21,225	1.14%
25	Colorado	18,632	1.00%
26	Minnesota	16,397	0.88%
27	Oregon	16,067	0.86%
28	Connecticut	14,916	0.80%
29	New Mexico	14,708	0.79%
30	Arkansas	14,598	0.78%
31	Nevada	14,597	0.78%
32	Wisconsin	13,748	0.74%
33	Mississippi	13,177	0.71%
34	Kansas	12,226	0.66%
35	Iowa	8,914	0.48%
36	Nebraska	6,322	0.34%
37	Utah	5,810	0.31%
38	Alaska	4,644	0.25%
39	Delaware	3,961	0.21%
40	West Virginia	3,931	0.21%
41	Rhode Island	3,744	0.20%
42	Idaho	3,238	0.17%
43	Hawaii	3,091	0.17%
44	South Dakota	1,641	0.09%
45	Maine	1,611	0.09%
46	Montana	1,516	0.08%
47	New Hampshire	1,328	0.07%
48	Wyoming	1,297	0.07%
49	Vermont	562	0.03%
50	North Dakota	522	0.03%
	District of Columbia	15,177	0.81%

Source: Federal Bureau of Investigation
   "Crime in the United States 1994" (Uniform Crime Reports, November 19, 1995)
*Violent crimes are offenses of murder, rape, robbery and aggravated assault.

Average Time Between Violent Crimes in 1994

National Rate = A Violent Crime Occurs Every 17 Seconds*

ALPHA ORDER

RANK	STATE	MINUTES.SECONDS
32	Alabama	18.13
13	Alaska	113.11
31	Arizona	18.20
20	Arkansas	36.01
50	California	1.39
26	Colorado	28.13
23	Connecticut	35.14
12	Delaware	132.41
48	Florida	3.17
40	Georgia	11.10
8	Hawaii	170.02
9	Idaho	162.19
46	Illinois	4.39
33	Indiana	17.24
16	Iowa	58.58
17	Kansas	42.59
28	Kentucky	22.41
37	Louisiana	12.25
6	Maine	326.16
41	Maryland	11.05
38	Massachusetts	12.18
45	Michigan	7.13
25	Minnesota	32.03
18	Mississippi	39.53
36	Missouri	13.23
5	Montana	346.42
15	Nebraska	83.08
20	Nevada	36.01
4	New Hampshire	395.47
42	New Jersey	10.50
22	New Mexico	35.44
49	New York	3.00
39	North Carolina	11.21
1	North Dakota	1,006.54
44	Ohio	9.45
27	Oklahoma	24.46
24	Oregon	32.43
43	Pennsylvania	10.13
10	Rhode Island	140.23
34	South Carolina	13.55
7	South Dakota	320.17
35	Tennessee	13.35
47	Texas	4.03
14	Utah	90.28
2	Vermont	935.14
29	Virginia	22.26
30	Washington	19.14
11	West Virginia	133.43
19	Wisconsin	38.14
3	Wyoming	405.14

RANK ORDER

RANK	STATE	MINUTES.SECONDS
1	North Dakota	1,006.54
2	Vermont	935.14
3	Wyoming	405.14
4	New Hampshire	395.47
5	Montana	346.42
6	Maine	326.16
7	South Dakota	320.17
8	Hawaii	170.02
9	Idaho	162.19
10	Rhode Island	140.23
11	West Virginia	133.43
12	Delaware	132.41
13	Alaska	113.11
14	Utah	90.28
15	Nebraska	83.08
16	Iowa	58.58
17	Kansas	42.59
18	Mississippi	39.53
19	Wisconsin	38.14
20	Arkansas	36.01
20	Nevada	36.01
22	New Mexico	35.44
23	Connecticut	35.14
24	Oregon	32.43
25	Minnesota	32.03
26	Colorado	28.13
27	Oklahoma	24.46
28	Kentucky	22.41
29	Virginia	22.26
30	Washington	19.14
31	Arizona	18.20
32	Alabama	18.13
33	Indiana	17.24
34	South Carolina	13.55
35	Tennessee	13.35
36	Missouri	13.23
37	Louisiana	12.25
38	Massachusetts	12.18
39	North Carolina	11.21
40	Georgia	11.10
41	Maryland	11.05
42	New Jersey	10.50
43	Pennsylvania	10.13
44	Ohio	9.45
45	Michigan	7.13
46	Illinois	4.39
47	Texas	4.03
48	Florida	3.17
49	New York	3.00
50	California	1.39
	District of Columbia	34.38

Source: Morgan Quitno Press using data from Federal Bureau of Investigation
   "Crime in the United States 1994" (Uniform Crime Reports, November 19, 1995)
*Violent crimes are offenses of murder, rape, robbery and aggravated assault.

Violent Crimes per Square Mile in 1994

National Rate = 0.50 Violent Crimes per Square Mile*

ALPHA ORDER

RANK	STATE	RATE
22	Alabama	0.55
47	Alaska	0.01
30	Arizona	0.25
28	Arkansas	0.27
8	California	2.00
33	Colorado	0.18
6	Connecticut	2.69
10	Delaware	1.65
7	Florida	2.67
18	Georgia	0.80
25	Hawaii	0.48
45	Idaho	0.04
9	Illinois	1.95
17	Indiana	0.83
35	Iowa	0.16
37	Kansas	0.15
20	Kentucky	0.57
16	Louisiana	0.85
44	Maine	0.05
3	Maryland	3.86
2	Massachusetts	4.63
19	Michigan	0.75
32	Minnesota	0.19
28	Mississippi	0.27
21	Missouri	0.56
47	Montana	0.01
41	Nebraska	0.08
39	Nevada	0.13
38	New Hampshire	0.14
1	New Jersey	5.91
40	New Mexico	0.12
4	New York	3.25
15	North Carolina	0.88
47	North Dakota	0.01
12	Ohio	1.20
27	Oklahoma	0.30
34	Oregon	0.17
13	Pennsylvania	1.12
5	Rhode Island	3.04
11	South Carolina	1.21
46	South Dakota	0.02
14	Tennessee	0.92
24	Texas	0.49
42	Utah	0.07
43	Vermont	0.06
22	Virginia	0.55
26	Washington	0.39
35	West Virginia	0.16
31	Wisconsin	0.21
47	Wyoming	0.01

RANK ORDER

RANK	STATE	RATE
1	New Jersey	5.91
2	Massachusetts	4.63
3	Maryland	3.86
4	New York	3.25
5	Rhode Island	3.04
6	Connecticut	2.69
7	Florida	2.67
8	California	2.00
9	Illinois	1.95
10	Delaware	1.65
11	South Carolina	1.21
12	Ohio	1.20
13	Pennsylvania	1.12
14	Tennessee	0.92
15	North Carolina	0.88
16	Louisiana	0.85
17	Indiana	0.83
18	Georgia	0.80
19	Michigan	0.75
20	Kentucky	0.57
21	Missouri	0.56
22	Alabama	0.55
22	Virginia	0.55
24	Texas	0.49
25	Hawaii	0.48
26	Washington	0.39
27	Oklahoma	0.30
28	Arkansas	0.27
28	Mississippi	0.27
30	Arizona	0.25
31	Wisconsin	0.21
32	Minnesota	0.19
33	Colorado	0.18
34	Oregon	0.17
35	Iowa	0.16
35	West Virginia	0.16
37	Kansas	0.15
38	New Hampshire	0.14
39	Nevada	0.13
40	New Mexico	0.12
41	Nebraska	0.08
42	Utah	0.07
43	Vermont	0.06
44	Maine	0.05
45	Idaho	0.04
46	South Dakota	0.02
47	Alaska	0.01
47	Montana	0.01
47	North Dakota	0.01
47	Wyoming	0.01
	District of Columbia	223.19

Source: Morgan Quitno Press using data from Federal Bureau of Investigation
    "Crime in the United States 1994" (Uniform Crime Reports, November 19, 1995)
*Includes murder, rape, robbery and aggravated assault.

Percent Change in Number of Violent Crimes: 1993 to 1994

National Percent Change = 3.2% Decrease*

ALPHA ORDER

RANK	STATE	PERCENT CHANGE
46	Alabama	(11.7)
16	Alaska	1.9
17	Arizona	1.8
19	Arkansas	1.5
39	California	(5.3)
44	Colorado	(7.9)
26	Connecticut	(0.2)
50	Delaware	(17.5)
33	Florida	(3.0)
41	Georgia	(5.8)
21	Hawaii	1.0
7	Idaho	4.6
24	Illinois	0.6
5	Indiana	8.1
31	Iowa	(2.7)
31	Kansas	(2.7)
1	Kentucky	32.1
43	Louisiana	(7.1)
12	Maine	3.4
38	Maryland	(4.2)
46	Massachusetts	(11.7)
33	Michigan	(3.0)
14	Minnesota	2.6
3	Mississippi	14.9
23	Missouri	0.7
17	Montana	1.8
8	Nebraska	4.1
2	Nevada	20.1
48	New Hampshire	(14.3)
28	New Jersey	(1.7)
30	New Mexico	(2.1)
45	New York	(10.2)
29	North Carolina	(1.8)
25	North Dakota	0.0
36	Ohio	(3.6)
11	Oklahoma	3.5
6	Oregon	5.3
15	Pennsylvania	2.2
42	Rhode Island	(6.8)
20	South Carolina	1.3
4	South Dakota	10.1
27	Tennessee	(0.9)
40	Texas	(5.5)
9	Utah	3.8
49	Vermont	(14.6)
33	Virginia	(3.0)
21	Washington	1.0
10	West Virginia	3.6
13	Wisconsin	3.2
36	Wyoming	(3.6)

RANK ORDER

RANK	STATE	PERCENT CHANGE
1	Kentucky	32.1
2	Nevada	20.1
3	Mississippi	14.9
4	South Dakota	10.1
5	Indiana	8.1
6	Oregon	5.3
7	Idaho	4.6
8	Nebraska	4.1
9	Utah	3.8
10	West Virginia	3.6
11	Oklahoma	3.5
12	Maine	3.4
13	Wisconsin	3.2
14	Minnesota	2.6
15	Pennsylvania	2.2
16	Alaska	1.9
17	Arizona	1.8
17	Montana	1.8
19	Arkansas	1.5
20	South Carolina	1.3
21	Hawaii	1.0
21	Washington	1.0
23	Missouri	0.7
24	Illinois	0.6
25	North Dakota	0.0
26	Connecticut	(0.2)
27	Tennessee	(0.9)
28	New Jersey	(1.7)
29	North Carolina	(1.8)
30	New Mexico	(2.1)
31	Iowa	(2.7)
31	Kansas	(2.7)
33	Florida	(3.0)
33	Michigan	(3.0)
33	Virginia	(3.0)
36	Ohio	(3.6)
36	Wyoming	(3.6)
38	Maryland	(4.2)
39	California	(5.3)
40	Texas	(5.5)
41	Georgia	(5.8)
42	Rhode Island	(6.8)
43	Louisiana	(7.1)
44	Colorado	(7.9)
45	New York	(10.2)
46	Alabama	(11.7)
46	Massachusetts	(11.7)
48	New Hampshire	(14.3)
49	Vermont	(14.6)
50	Delaware	(17.5)
	District of Columbia	(10.1)

Source: Federal Bureau of Investigation
   "Crime in the United States 1994" (Uniform Crime Reports, November 19, 1995)
*Violent crimes are offenses of murder, rape, robbery and aggravated assault.

Violent Crime Rate in 1994

National Rate = 716.0 Violent Crimes per 100,000 Population*

ALPHA ORDER

RANK	STATE	RATE
17	Alabama	683.7
10	Alaska	766.3
16	Arizona	703.1
23	Arkansas	595.1
3	California	1,013.0
28	Colorado	509.6
32	Connecticut	455.5
24	Delaware	561.0
1	Florida	1,146.8
18	Georgia	667.7
43	Hawaii	262.2
40	Idaho	285.8
7	Illinois	960.9
25	Indiana	525.1
38	Iowa	315.1
31	Kansas	478.7
22	Kentucky	605.3
5	Louisiana	981.9
47	Maine	129.9
8	Maryland	948.0
14	Massachusetts	707.6
11	Michigan	766.1
36	Minnesota	359.0
29	Mississippi	493.7
13	Missouri	743.5
46	Montana	177.1
34	Nebraska	389.5
4	Nevada	1,001.9
48	New Hampshire	116.8
21	New Jersey	614.2
9	New Mexico	889.2
6	New York	965.6
19	North Carolina	655.0
50	North Dakota	81.8
30	Ohio	485.8
20	Oklahoma	651.5
26	Oregon	520.6
33	Pennsylvania	426.7
35	Rhode Island	375.5
2	South Carolina	1,030.5
44	South Dakota	227.6
12	Tennessee	747.9
15	Texas	706.5
39	Utah	304.5
49	Vermont	96.9
37	Virginia	357.7
27	Washington	511.3
45	West Virginia	215.8
42	Wisconsin	270.5
41	Wyoming	272.5

RANK ORDER

RANK	STATE	RATE
1	Florida	1,146.8
2	South Carolina	1,030.5
3	California	1,013.0
4	Nevada	1,001.9
5	Louisiana	981.9
6	New York	965.6
7	Illinois	960.9
8	Maryland	948.0
9	New Mexico	889.2
10	Alaska	766.3
11	Michigan	766.1
12	Tennessee	747.9
13	Missouri	743.5
14	Massachusetts	707.6
15	Texas	706.5
16	Arizona	703.1
17	Alabama	683.7
18	Georgia	667.7
19	North Carolina	655.0
20	Oklahoma	651.5
21	New Jersey	614.2
22	Kentucky	605.3
23	Arkansas	595.1
24	Delaware	561.0
25	Indiana	525.1
26	Oregon	520.6
27	Washington	511.3
28	Colorado	509.6
29	Mississippi	493.7
30	Ohio	485.8
31	Kansas	478.7
32	Connecticut	455.5
33	Pennsylvania	426.7
34	Nebraska	389.5
35	Rhode Island	375.5
36	Minnesota	359.0
37	Virginia	357.7
38	Iowa	315.1
39	Utah	304.5
40	Idaho	285.8
41	Wyoming	272.5
42	Wisconsin	270.5
43	Hawaii	262.2
44	South Dakota	227.6
45	West Virginia	215.8
46	Montana	177.1
47	Maine	129.9
48	New Hampshire	116.8
49	Vermont	96.9
50	North Dakota	81.8
	District of Columbia	2,662.6

Source: Federal Bureau of Investigation
   "Crime in the United States 1994" (Uniform Crime Reports, November 19, 1995)
Violent crimes are offenses of murder, rape, robbery and aggravated assault.

Percent Change in Violent Crime Rate: 1993 to 1994

National Percent Change = 4.1% Decrease*

ALPHA ORDER

RANK	STATE	PERCENT CHANGE
47	Alabama	(12.4)
16	Alaska	0.7
26	Arizona	(1.7)
19	Arkansas	0.3
39	California	(6.0)
45	Colorado	(10.2)
22	Connecticut	(0.2)
50	Delaware	(18.2)
37	Florida	(4.9)
43	Georgia	(7.7)
18	Hawaii	0.4
13	Idaho	1.4
20	Illinois	0.1
5	Indiana	7.4
29	Iowa	(3.2)
31	Kansas	(3.6)
1	Kentucky	30.8
42	Louisiana	(7.5)
8	Maine	3.3
38	Maryland	(5.0)
46	Massachusetts	(12.1)
29	Michigan	(3.2)
13	Minnesota	1.4
3	Mississippi	13.8
21	Missouri	(0.1)
22	Montana	(0.2)
9	Nebraska	3.1
2	Nevada	14.5
49	New Hampshire	(15.2)
27	New Jersey	(2.0)
35	New Mexico	(4.4)
44	New York	(10.1)
31	North Carolina	(3.6)
24	North Dakota	(0.5)
31	Ohio	(3.6)
10	Oklahoma	2.6
7	Oregon	3.5
12	Pennsylvania	2.2
40	Rhode Island	(6.5)
16	South Carolina	0.7
4	South Dakota	9.2
28	Tennessee	(2.3)
41	Texas	(7.3)
15	Utah	1.2
48	Vermont	(15.1)
34	Virginia	(3.9)
25	Washington	(0.6)
6	West Virginia	3.6
11	Wisconsin	2.3
36	Wyoming	(4.8)

RANK ORDER

RANK	STATE	PERCENT CHANGE
1	Kentucky	30.8
2	Nevada	14.5
3	Mississippi	13.8
4	South Dakota	9.2
5	Indiana	7.4
6	West Virginia	3.6
7	Oregon	3.5
8	Maine	3.3
9	Nebraska	3.1
10	Oklahoma	2.6
11	Wisconsin	2.3
12	Pennsylvania	2.2
13	Idaho	1.4
13	Minnesota	1.4
15	Utah	1.2
16	Alaska	0.7
16	South Carolina	0.7
18	Hawaii	0.4
19	Arkansas	0.3
20	Illinois	0.1
21	Missouri	(0.1)
22	Connecticut	(0.2)
22	Montana	(0.2)
24	North Dakota	(0.5)
25	Washington	(0.6)
26	Arizona	(1.7)
27	New Jersey	(2.0)
28	Tennessee	(2.3)
29	Iowa	(3.2)
29	Michigan	(3.2)
31	Kansas	(3.6)
31	North Carolina	(3.6)
31	Ohio	(3.6)
34	Virginia	(3.9)
35	New Mexico	(4.4)
36	Wyoming	(4.8)
37	Florida	(4.9)
38	Maryland	(5.0)
39	California	(6.0)
40	Rhode Island	(6.5)
41	Texas	(7.3)
42	Louisiana	(7.5)
43	Georgia	(7.7)
44	New York	(10.1)
45	Colorado	(10.2)
46	Massachusetts	(12.1)
47	Alabama	(12.4)
48	Vermont	(15.1)
49	New Hampshire	(15.2)
50	Delaware	(18.2)

District of Columbia   (8.9)

Source: Federal Bureau of Investigation
  "Crime in the United States 1994" (Uniform Crime Reports, November 19, 1995)
Violent crimes are offenses of murder, rape, robbery and aggravated assault.

Violent Crimes with Firearms in 1994

National Total = 501,496 Violent Crimes*

ALPHA ORDER					RANK ORDER			
RANK	STATE	CRIMES	% of USA		RANK	STATE	CRIMES	% of USA
30	Alabama	3,367	0.67%		1	California	86,535	17.26%
34	Alaska	1,161	0.23%		2	New York	44,349	8.84%
17	Arizona	9,915	1.98%		3	Florida	43,416	8.66%
23	Arkansas	4,886	0.97%		4	Texas	42,392	8.45%
1	California	86,535	17.26%		5	Illinois	33,107	6.60%
27	Colorado	3,982	0.79%		6	Michigan	22,992	4.58%
28	Connecticut	3,560	0.71%		7	Maryland	16,900	3.37%
41	Delaware	261	0.05%		8	Louisiana	15,642	3.12%
3	Florida	43,416	8.66%		9	North Carolina	15,305	3.05%
10	Georgia	14,908	2.97%		10	Georgia	14,908	2.97%
40	Hawaii	423	0.08%		11	Ohio	14,371	2.87%
37	Idaho	862	0.17%		12	Missouri	14,229	2.84%
5	Illinois	33,107	6.60%		13	Pennsylvania	13,833	2.76%
20	Indiana	5,834	1.16%		14	New Jersey	12,423	2.48%
35	Iowa	1,135	0.23%		15	Tennessee	11,630	2.32%
NA	Kansas**	NA	NA		16	South Carolina	9,927	1.98%
NA	Kentucky**	NA	NA		17	Arizona	9,915	1.98%
8	Louisiana	15,642	3.12%		18	Washington	6,862	1.37%
44	Maine	126	0.03%		19	Virginia	6,594	1.31%
7	Maryland	16,900	3.37%		20	Indiana	5,834	1.16%
22	Massachusetts	4,945	0.99%		21	Oklahoma	5,577	1.11%
6	Michigan	22,992	4.58%		22	Massachusetts	4,945	0.99%
31	Minnesota	3,321	0.66%		23	Arkansas	4,886	0.97%
29	Mississippi	3,553	0.71%		24	Wisconsin	4,566	0.91%
12	Missouri	14,229	2.84%		25	Nevada	4,466	0.89%
NA	Montana**	NA	NA		26	Oregon	4,110	0.82%
32	Nebraska	1,517	0.30%		27	Colorado	3,982	0.79%
25	Nevada	4,466	0.89%		28	Connecticut	3,560	0.71%
45	New Hampshire	113	0.02%		29	Mississippi	3,553	0.71%
14	New Jersey	12,423	2.48%		30	Alabama	3,367	0.67%
36	New Mexico	986	0.20%		31	Minnesota	3,321	0.66%
2	New York	44,349	8.84%		32	Nebraska	1,517	0.30%
9	North Carolina	15,305	3.05%		33	Utah	1,168	0.23%
47	North Dakota	25	0.00%		34	Alaska	1,161	0.23%
11	Ohio	14,371	2.87%		35	Iowa	1,135	0.23%
21	Oklahoma	5,577	1.11%		36	New Mexico	986	0.20%
26	Oregon	4,110	0.82%		37	Idaho	862	0.17%
13	Pennsylvania	13,833	2.76%		38	West Virginia	758	0.15%
39	Rhode Island	591	0.12%		39	Rhode Island	591	0.12%
16	South Carolina	9,927	1.98%		40	Hawaii	423	0.08%
42	South Dakota	203	0.04%		41	Delaware	261	0.05%
15	Tennessee	11,630	2.32%		42	South Dakota	203	0.04%
4	Texas	42,392	8.45%		43	Wyoming	191	0.04%
33	Utah	1,168	0.23%		44	Maine	126	0.03%
46	Vermont	35	0.01%		45	New Hampshire	113	0.02%
19	Virginia	6,594	1.31%		46	Vermont	35	0.01%
18	Washington	6,862	1.37%		47	North Dakota	25	0.00%
38	West Virginia	758	0.15%		NA	Kansas**	NA	NA
24	Wisconsin	4,566	0.91%		NA	Kentucky**	NA	NA
43	Wyoming	191	0.04%		NA	Montana**	NA	NA
					District of Columbia**		NA	NA

Source: Morgan Quitno Press using data from Federal Bureau of Investigation
   "Crime in the United States 1994" (Uniform Crime Reports, November 19, 1995)
*Includes murder, robbery and aggravated assault. Does not include rape. National total reflects only those violent crimes for which the type of weapon was known and reported. There were an additional 128,091 violent crimes (excluding rape) for which the type of weapon was not reported to the F.B.I.
**Not available.

Violent Crime Rate with Firearms in 1994

National Rate = 225.7 Violent Crimes per 100,000 Population*

<u>ALPHA ORDER</u>

RANK	STATE	RATE
8	Alabama	320.5
19	Alaska	200.4
15	Arizona	253.2
18	Arkansas	201.6
11	California	275.5
25	Colorado	150.8
29	Connecticut	127.2
37	Delaware	67.9
6	Florida	322.9
14	Georgia	266.0
44	Hawaii	35.8
34	Idaho	78.1
1	Illinois	656.8
24	Indiana	155.2
40	Iowa	48.5
NA	Kansas**	NA
NA	Kentucky**	NA
2	Louisiana	418.9
46	Maine	10.4
3	Maryland	337.7
31	Massachusetts	98.3
10	Michigan	286.8
35	Minnesota	74.2
7	Mississippi	321.1
4	Missouri	337.5
NA	Montana**	NA
32	Nebraska	97.3
9	Nevada	312.4
45	New Hampshire	13.3
23	New Jersey	157.2
21	New Mexico	172.2
13	New York	269.5
17	North Carolina	223.2
47	North Dakota	4.1
20	Ohio	181.7
22	Oklahoma	171.5
27	Oregon	135.0
26	Pennsylvania	146.0
39	Rhode Island	59.3
12	South Carolina	272.9
41	South Dakota	45.0
5	Tennessee	333.2
16	Texas	231.2
38	Utah	64.9
36	Vermont	73.6
30	Virginia	101.4
28	Washington	132.3
42	West Virginia	41.6
33	Wisconsin	90.7
43	Wyoming	41.3

<u>RANK ORDER</u>

RANK	STATE	RATE
1	Illinois	656.8
2	Louisiana	418.9
3	Maryland	337.7
4	Missouri	337.5
5	Tennessee	333.2
6	Florida	322.9
7	Mississippi	321.1
8	Alabama	320.5
9	Nevada	312.4
10	Michigan	286.8
11	California	275.5
12	South Carolina	272.9
13	New York	269.5
14	Georgia	266.0
15	Arizona	253.2
16	Texas	231.2
17	North Carolina	223.2
18	Arkansas	201.6
19	Alaska	200.4
20	Ohio	181.7
21	New Mexico	172.2
22	Oklahoma	171.5
23	New Jersey	157.2
24	Indiana	155.2
25	Colorado	150.8
26	Pennsylvania	146.0
27	Oregon	135.0
28	Washington	132.3
29	Connecticut	127.2
30	Virginia	101.4
31	Massachusetts	98.3
32	Nebraska	97.3
33	Wisconsin	90.7
34	Idaho	78.1
35	Minnesota	74.2
36	Vermont	73.6
37	Delaware	67.9
38	Utah	64.9
39	Rhode Island	59.3
40	Iowa	48.5
41	South Dakota	45.0
42	West Virginia	41.6
43	Wyoming	41.3
44	Hawaii	35.8
45	New Hampshire	13.3
46	Maine	10.4
47	North Dakota	4.1
NA	Kansas**	NA
NA	Kentucky**	NA
NA	Montana**	NA
	District of Columbia**	NA

Source: Morgan Quitno Press using data from Federal Bureau of Investigation
"Crime in the United States 1994" (Uniform Crime Reports, November 19, 1995)
*Revised figures using only population of reporting jurisdictions. Includes murder, robbery and aggravated assault. Does not include rape. National rate reflects only those violent crimes for which the type of weapon was known and reported. There were an additional 128,091 violent crimes (excluding rape) for which the type of weapon was not reported to the F.B.I. Illinois' rate is especially affected by number of nonreporting jurisdictions. **Not available.

Percent of Violent Crimes Involving Firearms in 1994

National Percent = 30.69% of Violent Crimes*

ALPHA ORDER

ALPHA ORDER

RANK	STATE	PERCENT
29	Alabama	26.49
21	Alaska	28.97
6	Arizona	37.41
11	Arkansas	36.20
24	California	28.15
26	Colorado	27.92
33	Connecticut	25.23
37	Delaware	21.53
20	Florida	29.28
5	Georgia	38.36
44	Hawaii	15.48
19	Idaho	29.96
4	Illinois	38.97
32	Indiana	25.89
40	Iowa	17.18
NA	Kansas**	NA
NA	Kentucky**	NA
2	Louisiana	42.59
46	Maine	9.89
8	Maryland	37.21
45	Massachusetts	13.72
8	Michigan	37.21
34	Minnesota	24.55
1	Mississippi	48.91
3	Missouri	40.88
NA	Montana**	NA
30	Nebraska	26.40
15	Nevada	33.01
43	New Hampshire	16.19
28	New Jersey	26.68
17	New Mexico	31.58
31	New York	26.31
12	North Carolina	35.46
47	North Dakota	6.85
16	Ohio	32.94
23	Oklahoma	28.48
25	Oregon	28.05
14	Pennsylvania	33.27
41	Rhode Island	17.03
26	South Carolina	27.92
39	South Dakota	19.69
7	Tennessee	37.24
13	Texas	35.13
35	Utah	23.96
36	Vermont	21.88
18	Virginia	30.68
22	Washington	28.86
38	West Virginia	21.31
10	Wisconsin	36.61
42	Wyoming	16.95

RANK ORDER

RANK	STATE	PERCENT
1	Mississippi	48.91
2	Louisiana	42.59
3	Missouri	40.88
4	Illinois	38.97
5	Georgia	38.36
6	Arizona	37.41
7	Tennessee	37.24
8	Maryland	37.21
8	Michigan	37.21
10	Wisconsin	36.61
11	Arkansas	36.20
12	North Carolina	35.46
13	Texas	35.13
14	Pennsylvania	33.27
15	Nevada	33.01
16	Ohio	32.94
17	New Mexico	31.58
18	Virginia	30.68
19	Idaho	29.96
20	Florida	29.28
21	Alaska	28.97
22	Washington	28.86
23	Oklahoma	28.48
24	California	28.15
25	Oregon	28.05
26	Colorado	27.92
26	South Carolina	27.92
28	New Jersey	26.68
29	Alabama	26.49
30	Nebraska	26.40
31	New York	26.31
32	Indiana	25.89
33	Connecticut	25.23
34	Minnesota	24.55
35	Utah	23.96
36	Vermont	21.88
37	Delaware	21.53
38	West Virginia	21.31
39	South Dakota	19.69
40	Iowa	17.18
41	Rhode Island	17.03
42	Wyoming	16.95
43	New Hampshire	16.19
44	Hawaii	15.48
45	Massachusetts	13.72
46	Maine	9.89
47	North Dakota	6.85
NA	Kansas**	NA
NA	Kentucky**	NA
NA	Montana**	NA
	District of Columbia**	NA

Source: Morgan Quitno Press using data from Federal Bureau of Investigation
   "Crime in the United States 1994" (Uniform Crime Reports, November 19, 1995)
*Includes murder, robbery and aggravated assault. Does not include rape. National percent reflects only those violent crimes for which the type of weapon was known and reported. There were an additional 128,091 violent crimes (excluding rape) for which the type of weapon was not reported to the F.B.I.
**Not available.

Bombings in 1993

National Total = 2,394 Bombings*

ALPHA ORDER					RANK ORDER			
RANK	STATE		BOMBINGS	% of USA	RANK	STATE	BOMBINGS	% of USA
28	Alabama		17	0.71%	1	California	436	18.21%
42	Alaska		5	0.21%	2	Illinois	245	10.23%
5	Arizona		151	6.31%	3	Florida	205	8.56%
29	Arkansas		16	0.67%	4	Texas	166	6.93%
1	California		436	18.21%	5	Arizona	151	6.31%
8	Colorado		78	3.26%	6	New York	93	3.88%
37	Connecticut		11	0.46%	7	Michigan	84	3.51%
47	Delaware		3	0.13%	8	Colorado	78	3.26%
3	Florida		205	8.56%	8	Minnesota	78	3.26%
20	Georgia		26	1.09%	10	Ohio	73	3.05%
23	Hawaii		23	0.96%	11	Iowa	60	2.51%
45	Idaho		4	0.17%	12	Maryland	47	1.96%
2	Illinois		245	10.23%	13	Pennsylvania	46	1.92%
15	Indiana		44	1.84%	14	Washington	45	1.88%
11	Iowa		60	2.51%	15	Indiana	44	1.84%
33	Kansas		14	0.58%	16	Virginia	40	1.67%
34	Kentucky		13	0.54%	17	New Mexico	34	1.42%
18	Louisiana		33	1.38%	18	Louisiana	33	1.38%
50	Maine		1	0.04%	19	North Carolina	29	1.21%
12	Maryland		47	1.96%	20	Georgia	26	1.09%
37	Massachusetts		11	0.46%	20	New Jersey	26	1.09%
7	Michigan		84	3.51%	22	Missouri	25	1.04%
8	Minnesota		78	3.26%	23	Hawaii	23	0.96%
27	Mississippi		20	0.84%	23	Oregon	23	0.96%
22	Missouri		25	1.04%	23	Tennessee	23	0.96%
36	Montana		12	0.50%	26	Oklahoma	22	0.92%
30	Nebraska		15	0.63%	27	Mississippi	20	0.84%
30	Nevada		15	0.63%	28	Alabama	17	0.71%
42	New Hampshire		5	0.21%	29	Arkansas	16	0.67%
20	New Jersey		26	1.09%	30	Nebraska	15	0.63%
17	New Mexico		34	1.42%	30	Nevada	15	0.63%
6	New York		93	3.88%	30	Wisconsin	15	0.63%
19	North Carolina		29	1.21%	33	Kansas	14	0.58%
47	North Dakota		3	0.13%	34	Kentucky	13	0.54%
10	Ohio		73	3.05%	34	West Virginia	13	0.54%
26	Oklahoma		22	0.92%	36	Montana	12	0.50%
23	Oregon		23	0.96%	37	Connecticut	11	0.46%
13	Pennsylvania		46	1.92%	37	Massachusetts	11	0.46%
47	Rhode Island		3	0.13%	37	Wyoming	11	0.46%
41	South Carolina		9	0.38%	40	Utah	10	0.42%
42	South Dakota		5	0.21%	41	South Carolina	9	0.38%
23	Tennessee		23	0.96%	42	Alaska	5	0.21%
4	Texas		166	6.93%	42	New Hampshire	5	0.21%
40	Utah		10	0.42%	42	South Dakota	5	0.21%
45	Vermont		4	0.17%	45	Idaho	4	0.17%
16	Virginia		40	1.67%	45	Vermont	4	0.17%
14	Washington		45	1.88%	47	Delaware	3	0.13%
34	West Virginia		13	0.54%	47	North Dakota	3	0.13%
30	Wisconsin		15	0.63%	47	Rhode Island	3	0.13%
37	Wyoming		11	0.46%	50	Maine	1	0.04%
						District of Columbia	4	0.17%

Source: Federal Bureau of Investigation, Bomb Data Center
    "Bomb Summary 1993"
*Includes explosive and incendiary bombings and excludes bombing attempts. Total does not include 23 bombings
in Puerto Rico and 1 in Guam. There were 49 deaths and 1,323 injuries from bombings in 1993. Of this total, 6
deaths and 1,042 injuries were from the bombing of the World Trade Center in New York on February 26, 1993.

Murders in 1994

National Total = 23,305 Murders*

ALPHA ORDER				RANK ORDER			
RANK	STATE	MURDERS	% of USA	RANK	STATE	MURDERS	% of USA
15	Alabama	501	2.15%	1	California	3,703	15.89%
42	Alaska	38	0.16%	2	Texas	2,022	8.68%
18	Arizona	426	1.83%	3	New York	2,016	8.65%
22	Arkansas	294	1.26%	4	Illinois	1,378	5.91%
1	California	3,703	15.89%	5	Florida	1,165	5.00%
29	Colorado	199	0.85%	6	Michigan	927	3.98%
27	Connecticut	215	0.92%	7	Louisiana	856	3.67%
43	Delaware	33	0.14%	8	North Carolina	772	3.31%
5	Florida	1,165	5.00%	9	Pennsylvania	712	3.06%
10	Georgia	703	3.02%	10	Georgia	703	3.02%
38	Hawaii	50	0.21%	11	Ohio	662	2.84%
41	Idaho	40	0.17%	12	Maryland	579	2.48%
4	Illinois	1,378	5.91%	13	Virginia	571	2.45%
17	Indiana	453	1.94%	14	Missouri	554	2.38%
39	Iowa	47	0.20%	15	Alabama	501	2.15%
33	Kansas	149	0.64%	16	Tennessee	482	2.07%
24	Kentucky	244	1.05%	17	Indiana	453	1.94%
7	Louisiana	856	3.67%	18	Arizona	426	1.83%
44	Maine	28	0.12%	19	Mississippi	409	1.75%
12	Maryland	579	2.48%	20	New Jersey	396	1.70%
28	Massachusetts	214	0.92%	21	South Carolina	353	1.51%
6	Michigan	927	3.98%	22	Arkansas	294	1.26%
34	Minnesota	147	0.63%	22	Washington	294	1.26%
19	Mississippi	409	1.75%	24	Kentucky	244	1.05%
14	Missouri	554	2.38%	25	Wisconsin	227	0.97%
44	Montana	28	0.12%	26	Oklahoma	226	0.97%
37	Nebraska	51	0.22%	27	Connecticut	215	0.92%
31	Nevada	170	0.73%	28	Massachusetts	214	0.92%
46	New Hampshire	16	0.07%	29	Colorado	199	0.85%
20	New Jersey	396	1.70%	30	New Mexico	177	0.76%
30	New Mexico	177	0.76%	31	Nevada	170	0.73%
3	New York	2,016	8.65%	32	Oregon	150	0.64%
8	North Carolina	772	3.31%	33	Kansas	149	0.64%
50	North Dakota	1	0.00%	34	Minnesota	147	0.63%
11	Ohio	662	2.84%	35	West Virginia	99	0.42%
26	Oklahoma	226	0.97%	36	Utah	56	0.24%
32	Oregon	150	0.64%	37	Nebraska	51	0.22%
9	Pennsylvania	712	3.06%	38	Hawaii	50	0.21%
40	Rhode Island	41	0.18%	39	Iowa	47	0.20%
21	South Carolina	353	1.51%	40	Rhode Island	41	0.18%
48	South Dakota	10	0.04%	41	Idaho	40	0.17%
16	Tennessee	482	2.07%	42	Alaska	38	0.16%
2	Texas	2,022	8.68%	43	Delaware	33	0.14%
36	Utah	56	0.24%	44	Maine	28	0.12%
49	Vermont	6	0.03%	44	Montana	28	0.12%
13	Virginia	571	2.45%	46	New Hampshire	16	0.07%
22	Washington	294	1.26%	46	Wyoming	16	0.07%
35	West Virginia	99	0.42%	48	South Dakota	10	0.04%
25	Wisconsin	227	0.97%	49	Vermont	6	0.03%
46	Wyoming	16	0.07%	50	North Dakota	1	0.00%
					District of Columbia	399	1.71%

Source: Federal Bureau of Investigation
  "Crime in the United States 1994" (Uniform Crime Reports, November 19, 1995)
*Includes nonnegligent manslaughter.

Average Time Between Murders in 1994

National Rate = A Murder Occurs Every 23 Minutes*

<table>
<tr><td colspan="3"><u>ALPHA ORDER</u></td><td colspan="3"><u>RANK ORDER</u></td></tr>
<tr><td>RANK</td><td>STATE</td><td>HOURS.MINUTES</td><td>RANK</td><td>STATE</td><td>HOURS.MINUTES</td></tr>
<tr><td>36</td><td>Alabama</td><td>17.29</td><td>1</td><td>North Dakota</td><td>8,760.00</td></tr>
<tr><td>9</td><td>Alaska</td><td>230.32</td><td>2</td><td>Vermont</td><td>1,460.00</td></tr>
<tr><td>33</td><td>Arizona</td><td>20.34</td><td>3</td><td>South Dakota</td><td>876.00</td></tr>
<tr><td>28</td><td>Arkansas</td><td>29.48</td><td>4</td><td>New Hampshire</td><td>547.30</td></tr>
<tr><td>50</td><td>California</td><td>2.22</td><td>4</td><td>Wyoming</td><td>547.30</td></tr>
<tr><td>22</td><td>Colorado</td><td>44.01</td><td>6</td><td>Maine</td><td>312.52</td></tr>
<tr><td>24</td><td>Connecticut</td><td>40.44</td><td>6</td><td>Montana</td><td>312.52</td></tr>
<tr><td>8</td><td>Delaware</td><td>265.27</td><td>8</td><td>Delaware</td><td>265.27</td></tr>
<tr><td>46</td><td>Florida</td><td>7.31</td><td>9</td><td>Alaska</td><td>230.32</td></tr>
<tr><td>41</td><td>Georgia</td><td>12.28</td><td>10</td><td>Idaho</td><td>219.00</td></tr>
<tr><td>13</td><td>Hawaii</td><td>175.12</td><td>11</td><td>Rhode Island</td><td>213.40</td></tr>
<tr><td>10</td><td>Idaho</td><td>219.00</td><td>12</td><td>Iowa</td><td>186.23</td></tr>
<tr><td>47</td><td>Illinois</td><td>6.22</td><td>13</td><td>Hawaii</td><td>175.12</td></tr>
<tr><td>34</td><td>Indiana</td><td>19.20</td><td>14</td><td>Nebraska</td><td>171.46</td></tr>
<tr><td>12</td><td>Iowa</td><td>186.23</td><td>15</td><td>Utah</td><td>156.26</td></tr>
<tr><td>18</td><td>Kansas</td><td>58.47</td><td>16</td><td>West Virginia</td><td>88.29</td></tr>
<tr><td>27</td><td>Kentucky</td><td>35.54</td><td>17</td><td>Minnesota</td><td>59.35</td></tr>
<tr><td>44</td><td>Louisiana</td><td>10.14</td><td>18</td><td>Kansas</td><td>58.47</td></tr>
<tr><td>6</td><td>Maine</td><td>312.52</td><td>19</td><td>Oregon</td><td>58.24</td></tr>
<tr><td>39</td><td>Maryland</td><td>15.08</td><td>20</td><td>Nevada</td><td>51.32</td></tr>
<tr><td>23</td><td>Massachusetts</td><td>40.56</td><td>21</td><td>New Mexico</td><td>49.29</td></tr>
<tr><td>45</td><td>Michigan</td><td>9.27</td><td>22</td><td>Colorado</td><td>44.01</td></tr>
<tr><td>17</td><td>Minnesota</td><td>59.35</td><td>23</td><td>Massachusetts</td><td>40.56</td></tr>
<tr><td>32</td><td>Mississippi</td><td>21.25</td><td>24</td><td>Connecticut</td><td>40.44</td></tr>
<tr><td>37</td><td>Missouri</td><td>15.49</td><td>25</td><td>Oklahoma</td><td>38.46</td></tr>
<tr><td>6</td><td>Montana</td><td>312.52</td><td>26</td><td>Wisconsin</td><td>38.35</td></tr>
<tr><td>14</td><td>Nebraska</td><td>171.46</td><td>27</td><td>Kentucky</td><td>35.54</td></tr>
<tr><td>20</td><td>Nevada</td><td>51.32</td><td>28</td><td>Arkansas</td><td>29.48</td></tr>
<tr><td>4</td><td>New Hampshire</td><td>547.30</td><td>28</td><td>Washington</td><td>29.48</td></tr>
<tr><td>31</td><td>New Jersey</td><td>22.07</td><td>30</td><td>South Carolina</td><td>24.49</td></tr>
<tr><td>21</td><td>New Mexico</td><td>49.29</td><td>31</td><td>New Jersey</td><td>22.07</td></tr>
<tr><td>48</td><td>New York</td><td>4.21</td><td>32</td><td>Mississippi</td><td>21.25</td></tr>
<tr><td>43</td><td>North Carolina</td><td>11.21</td><td>33</td><td>Arizona</td><td>20.34</td></tr>
<tr><td>1</td><td>North Dakota</td><td>8,760.00</td><td>34</td><td>Indiana</td><td>19.20</td></tr>
<tr><td>40</td><td>Ohio</td><td>13.14</td><td>35</td><td>Tennessee</td><td>18.10</td></tr>
<tr><td>25</td><td>Oklahoma</td><td>38.46</td><td>36</td><td>Alabama</td><td>17.29</td></tr>
<tr><td>19</td><td>Oregon</td><td>58.24</td><td>37</td><td>Missouri</td><td>15.49</td></tr>
<tr><td>42</td><td>Pennsylvania</td><td>12.18</td><td>38</td><td>Virginia</td><td>15.20</td></tr>
<tr><td>11</td><td>Rhode Island</td><td>213.40</td><td>39</td><td>Maryland</td><td>15.08</td></tr>
<tr><td>30</td><td>South Carolina</td><td>24.49</td><td>40</td><td>Ohio</td><td>13.14</td></tr>
<tr><td>3</td><td>South Dakota</td><td>876.00</td><td>41</td><td>Georgia</td><td>12.28</td></tr>
<tr><td>35</td><td>Tennessee</td><td>18.10</td><td>42</td><td>Pennsylvania</td><td>12.18</td></tr>
<tr><td>49</td><td>Texas</td><td>4.20</td><td>43</td><td>North Carolina</td><td>11.21</td></tr>
<tr><td>15</td><td>Utah</td><td>156.26</td><td>44</td><td>Louisiana</td><td>10.14</td></tr>
<tr><td>2</td><td>Vermont</td><td>1,460.00</td><td>45</td><td>Michigan</td><td>9.27</td></tr>
<tr><td>38</td><td>Virginia</td><td>15.20</td><td>46</td><td>Florida</td><td>7.31</td></tr>
<tr><td>28</td><td>Washington</td><td>29.48</td><td>47</td><td>Illinois</td><td>6.22</td></tr>
<tr><td>16</td><td>West Virginia</td><td>88.29</td><td>48</td><td>New York</td><td>4.21</td></tr>
<tr><td>26</td><td>Wisconsin</td><td>38.35</td><td>49</td><td>Texas</td><td>4.20</td></tr>
<tr><td>4</td><td>Wyoming</td><td>547.30</td><td>50</td><td>California</td><td>2.22</td></tr>
<tr><td></td><td></td><td></td><td></td><td>District of Columbia</td><td>21.57</td></tr>
</table>

Source: Morgan Quitno Press using data from Federal Bureau of Investigation
"Crime in the United States 1994" (Uniform Crime Reports, November 19, 1995)
*Includes nonnegligent manslaughter.

Percent Change in Number of Murders: 1993 to 1994

National Percent Change = 5.0% Decrease*

ALPHA ORDER

RANK	STATE	PERCENT CHANGE
16	Alabama	3.5
46	Alaska	(29.6)
3	Arizona	25.7
5	Arkansas	19.0
38	California	(9.6)
25	Colorado	(3.4)
15	Connecticut	4.4
30	Delaware	(5.7)
27	Florida	(4.8)
39	Georgia	(10.9)
9	Hawaii	11.1
4	Idaho	25.0
16	Illinois	3.5
13	Indiana	5.3
45	Iowa	(28.8)
34	Kansas	(7.5)
23	Kentucky	(2.0)
24	Louisiana	(2.1)
1	Maine	40.0
37	Maryland	(8.4)
36	Massachusetts	(8.2)
20	Michigan	(0.6)
28	Minnesota	(5.2)
7	Mississippi	14.6
32	Missouri	(6.1)
8	Montana	12.0
43	Nebraska	(19.0)
6	Nevada	18.1
47	New Hampshire	(30.4)
29	New Jersey	(5.3)
2	New Mexico	36.2
41	New York	(16.7)
22	North Carolina	(1.7)
50	North Dakota	(90.9)
21	Ohio	(0.7)
42	Oklahoma	(17.2)
11	Oregon	7.1
40	Pennsylvania	(13.5)
14	Rhode Island	5.1
33	South Carolina	(6.4)
48	South Dakota	(58.3)
34	Tennessee	(7.5)
31	Texas	(5.8)
25	Utah	(3.4)
49	Vermont	(71.4)
12	Virginia	5.9
10	Washington	8.5
44	West Virginia	(21.4)
18	Wisconsin	2.3
19	Wyoming	0.0

RANK ORDER

RANK	STATE	PERCENT CHANGE
1	Maine	40.0
2	New Mexico	36.2
3	Arizona	25.7
4	Idaho	25.0
5	Arkansas	19.0
6	Nevada	18.1
7	Mississippi	14.6
8	Montana	12.0
9	Hawaii	11.1
10	Washington	8.5
11	Oregon	7.1
12	Virginia	5.9
13	Indiana	5.3
14	Rhode Island	5.1
15	Connecticut	4.4
16	Alabama	3.5
16	Illinois	3.5
18	Wisconsin	2.3
19	Wyoming	0.0
20	Michigan	(0.6)
21	Ohio	(0.7)
22	North Carolina	(1.7)
23	Kentucky	(2.0)
24	Louisiana	(2.1)
25	Colorado	(3.4)
25	Utah	(3.4)
27	Florida	(4.8)
28	Minnesota	(5.2)
29	New Jersey	(5.3)
30	Delaware	(5.7)
31	Texas	(5.8)
32	Missouri	(6.1)
33	South Carolina	(6.4)
34	Kansas	(7.5)
34	Tennessee	(7.5)
36	Massachusetts	(8.2)
37	Maryland	(8.4)
38	California	(9.6)
39	Georgia	(10.9)
40	Pennsylvania	(13.5)
41	New York	(16.7)
42	Oklahoma	(17.2)
43	Nebraska	(19.0)
44	West Virginia	(21.4)
45	Iowa	(28.8)
46	Alaska	(29.6)
47	New Hampshire	(30.4)
48	South Dakota	(58.3)
49	Vermont	(71.4)
50	North Dakota	(90.9)

| | District of Columbia | (12.1) |

Source: Federal Bureau of Investigation
"Crime in the United States 1994" (Uniform Crime Reports, November 19, 1995)
*Includes nonnegligent manslaughter.

Murder Rate in 1994

National Rate = 9.0 Murders per 100,000 Population*

<table>
<tr><td colspan="3">ALPHA ORDER</td><td colspan="3">RANK ORDER</td></tr>
<tr><td>RANK</td><td>STATE</td><td>RATE</td><td>RANK</td><td>STATE</td><td>RATE</td></tr>
<tr><td>4</td><td>Alabama</td><td>11.9</td><td>1</td><td>Louisiana</td><td>19.8</td></tr>
<tr><td>25</td><td>Alaska</td><td>6.3</td><td>2</td><td>Mississippi</td><td>15.3</td></tr>
<tr><td>13</td><td>Arizona</td><td>10.5</td><td>3</td><td>Arkansas</td><td>12.0</td></tr>
<tr><td>3</td><td>Arkansas</td><td>12.0</td><td>4</td><td>Alabama</td><td>11.9</td></tr>
<tr><td>5</td><td>California</td><td>11.8</td><td>5</td><td>California</td><td>11.8</td></tr>
<tr><td>30</td><td>Colorado</td><td>5.4</td><td>6</td><td>Illinois</td><td>11.7</td></tr>
<tr><td>23</td><td>Connecticut</td><td>6.6</td><td>6</td><td>Nevada</td><td>11.7</td></tr>
<tr><td>34</td><td>Delaware</td><td>4.7</td><td>8</td><td>Maryland</td><td>11.6</td></tr>
<tr><td>20</td><td>Florida</td><td>8.3</td><td>9</td><td>New York</td><td>11.1</td></tr>
<tr><td>15</td><td>Georgia</td><td>10.0</td><td>10</td><td>Texas</td><td>11.0</td></tr>
<tr><td>36</td><td>Hawaii</td><td>4.2</td><td>11</td><td>North Carolina</td><td>10.9</td></tr>
<tr><td>38</td><td>Idaho</td><td>3.5</td><td>12</td><td>New Mexico</td><td>10.7</td></tr>
<tr><td>6</td><td>Illinois</td><td>11.7</td><td>13</td><td>Arizona</td><td>10.5</td></tr>
<tr><td>21</td><td>Indiana</td><td>7.9</td><td>13</td><td>Missouri</td><td>10.5</td></tr>
<tr><td>46</td><td>Iowa</td><td>1.7</td><td>15</td><td>Georgia</td><td>10.0</td></tr>
<tr><td>28</td><td>Kansas</td><td>5.8</td><td>16</td><td>Michigan</td><td>9.8</td></tr>
<tr><td>24</td><td>Kentucky</td><td>6.4</td><td>17</td><td>South Carolina</td><td>9.6</td></tr>
<tr><td>1</td><td>Louisiana</td><td>19.8</td><td>18</td><td>Tennessee</td><td>9.3</td></tr>
<tr><td>45</td><td>Maine</td><td>2.3</td><td>19</td><td>Virginia</td><td>8.7</td></tr>
<tr><td>8</td><td>Maryland</td><td>11.6</td><td>20</td><td>Florida</td><td>8.3</td></tr>
<tr><td>38</td><td>Massachusetts</td><td>3.5</td><td>21</td><td>Indiana</td><td>7.9</td></tr>
<tr><td>16</td><td>Michigan</td><td>9.8</td><td>22</td><td>Oklahoma</td><td>6.9</td></tr>
<tr><td>42</td><td>Minnesota</td><td>3.2</td><td>23</td><td>Connecticut</td><td>6.6</td></tr>
<tr><td>2</td><td>Mississippi</td><td>15.3</td><td>24</td><td>Kentucky</td><td>6.4</td></tr>
<tr><td>13</td><td>Missouri</td><td>10.5</td><td>25</td><td>Alaska</td><td>6.3</td></tr>
<tr><td>41</td><td>Montana</td><td>3.3</td><td>26</td><td>Ohio</td><td>6.0</td></tr>
<tr><td>43</td><td>Nebraska</td><td>3.1</td><td>27</td><td>Pennsylvania</td><td>5.9</td></tr>
<tr><td>6</td><td>Nevada</td><td>11.7</td><td>28</td><td>Kansas</td><td>5.8</td></tr>
<tr><td>47</td><td>New Hampshire</td><td>1.4</td><td>29</td><td>Washington</td><td>5.5</td></tr>
<tr><td>32</td><td>New Jersey</td><td>5.0</td><td>30</td><td>Colorado</td><td>5.4</td></tr>
<tr><td>12</td><td>New Mexico</td><td>10.7</td><td>30</td><td>West Virginia</td><td>5.4</td></tr>
<tr><td>9</td><td>New York</td><td>11.1</td><td>32</td><td>New Jersey</td><td>5.0</td></tr>
<tr><td>11</td><td>North Carolina</td><td>10.9</td><td>33</td><td>Oregon</td><td>4.9</td></tr>
<tr><td>50</td><td>North Dakota</td><td>0.2</td><td>34</td><td>Delaware</td><td>4.7</td></tr>
<tr><td>26</td><td>Ohio</td><td>6.0</td><td>35</td><td>Wisconsin</td><td>4.5</td></tr>
<tr><td>22</td><td>Oklahoma</td><td>6.9</td><td>36</td><td>Hawaii</td><td>4.2</td></tr>
<tr><td>33</td><td>Oregon</td><td>4.9</td><td>37</td><td>Rhode Island</td><td>4.1</td></tr>
<tr><td>27</td><td>Pennsylvania</td><td>5.9</td><td>38</td><td>Idaho</td><td>3.5</td></tr>
<tr><td>37</td><td>Rhode Island</td><td>4.1</td><td>38</td><td>Massachusetts</td><td>3.5</td></tr>
<tr><td>17</td><td>South Carolina</td><td>9.6</td><td>40</td><td>Wyoming</td><td>3.4</td></tr>
<tr><td>47</td><td>South Dakota</td><td>1.4</td><td>41</td><td>Montana</td><td>3.3</td></tr>
<tr><td>18</td><td>Tennessee</td><td>9.3</td><td>42</td><td>Minnesota</td><td>3.2</td></tr>
<tr><td>10</td><td>Texas</td><td>11.0</td><td>43</td><td>Nebraska</td><td>3.1</td></tr>
<tr><td>44</td><td>Utah</td><td>2.9</td><td>44</td><td>Utah</td><td>2.9</td></tr>
<tr><td>49</td><td>Vermont</td><td>1.0</td><td>45</td><td>Maine</td><td>2.3</td></tr>
<tr><td>19</td><td>Virginia</td><td>8.7</td><td>46</td><td>Iowa</td><td>1.7</td></tr>
<tr><td>29</td><td>Washington</td><td>5.5</td><td>47</td><td>New Hampshire</td><td>1.4</td></tr>
<tr><td>30</td><td>West Virginia</td><td>5.4</td><td>47</td><td>South Dakota</td><td>1.4</td></tr>
<tr><td>35</td><td>Wisconsin</td><td>4.5</td><td>49</td><td>Vermont</td><td>1.0</td></tr>
<tr><td>40</td><td>Wyoming</td><td>3.4</td><td>50</td><td>North Dakota</td><td>0.2</td></tr>
<tr><td></td><td></td><td></td><td></td><td>District of Columbia</td><td>70.0</td></tr>
</table>

Source: Federal Bureau of Investigation
   "Crime in the United States 1994" (Uniform Crime Reports, November 19, 1995)
*Includes nonnegligent manslaughter.

Percent Change in Murder Rate: 1993 to 1994

National Percent Change = 5.3% Decrease*

ALPHA ORDER			RANK ORDER		
RANK	STATE	PERCENT CHANGE	RANK	STATE	PERCENT CHANGE
16	Alabama	2.6	1	Maine	43.8
46	Alaska	(30.0)	2	New Mexico	33.8
3	Arizona	22.1	3	Arizona	22.1
5	Arkansas	17.6	4	Idaho	20.7
37	California	(9.9)	5	Arkansas	17.6
31	Colorado	(6.9)	6	Mississippi	13.3
14	Connecticut	4.8	7	Nevada	12.5
27	Delaware	(6.0)	8	Hawaii	10.5
29	Florida	(6.7)	9	Montana	10.0
39	Georgia	(12.3)	10	Oregon	6.5
8	Hawaii	10.5	11	Washington	5.8
4	Idaho	20.7	12	Indiana	5.3
16	Illinois	2.6	13	Rhode Island	5.1
12	Indiana	5.3	14	Connecticut	4.8
45	Iowa	(26.1)	14	Virginia	4.8
36	Kansas	(9.4)	16	Alabama	2.6
23	Kentucky	(3.0)	16	Illinois	2.6
22	Louisiana	(2.5)	18	Wisconsin	2.3
1	Maine	43.8	19	Michigan	0.0
34	Maryland	(8.7)	19	Ohio	0.0
38	Massachusetts	(10.3)	19	Wyoming	0.0
19	Michigan	0.0	22	Louisiana	(2.5)
26	Minnesota	(5.9)	23	Kentucky	(3.0)
6	Mississippi	13.3	24	North Carolina	(3.5)
32	Missouri	(7.1)	25	New Jersey	(5.7)
9	Montana	10.0	26	Minnesota	(5.9)
43	Nebraska	(20.5)	27	Delaware	(6.0)
7	Nevada	12.5	28	Utah	(6.5)
46	New Hampshire	(30.0)	29	Florida	(6.7)
25	New Jersey	(5.7)	30	South Carolina	(6.8)
2	New Mexico	33.8	31	Colorado	(6.9)
41	New York	(16.5)	32	Missouri	(7.1)
24	North Carolina	(3.5)	33	Texas	(7.6)
50	North Dakota	(88.2)	34	Maryland	(8.7)
19	Ohio	0.0	35	Tennessee	(8.8)
42	Oklahoma	(17.9)	36	Kansas	(9.4)
10	Oregon	6.5	37	California	(9.9)
40	Pennsylvania	(13.2)	38	Massachusetts	(10.3)
13	Rhode Island	5.1	39	Georgia	(12.3)
30	South Carolina	(6.8)	40	Pennsylvania	(13.2)
48	South Dakota	(58.8)	41	New York	(16.5)
35	Tennessee	(8.8)	42	Oklahoma	(17.9)
33	Texas	(7.6)	43	Nebraska	(20.5)
28	Utah	(6.5)	44	West Virginia	(21.7)
49	Vermont	(72.2)	45	Iowa	(26.1)
14	Virginia	4.8	46	Alaska	(30.0)
11	Washington	5.8	46	New Hampshire	(30.0)
44	West Virginia	(21.7)	48	South Dakota	(58.8)
18	Wisconsin	2.3	49	Vermont	(72.2)
19	Wyoming	0.0	50	North Dakota	(88.2)
				District of Columbia	(10.8)

Source: Federal Bureau of Investigation
    "Crime in the United States 1994" (Uniform Crime Reports, November 19, 1995)
*Includes nonnegligent manslaughter.

Murders with Firearms in 1994

National Total = 15,397 Murders with Firearms*

ALPHA ORDER

RANK	STATE	MURDERS	% of USA
14	Alabama	372	2.42%
35	Alaska	24	0.16%
16	Arizona	304	1.97%
21	Arkansas	212	1.38%
1	California	2,790	18.12%
28	Colorado	113	0.73%
24	Connecticut	159	1.03%
44	Delaware	6	0.04%
6	Florida	647	4.20%
8	Georgia	492	3.20%
35	Hawaii	24	0.16%
35	Idaho	24	0.16%
4	Illinois	812	5.27%
18	Indiana	282	1.83%
38	Iowa	21	0.14%
NA	Kansas**	NA	NA
NA	Kentucky**	NA	NA
5	Louisiana	682	4.43%
40	Maine	11	0.07%
13	Maryland	407	2.64%
26	Massachusetts	132	0.86%
7	Michigan	646	4.20%
31	Minnesota	79	0.51%
23	Mississippi	181	1.18%
15	Missouri	342	2.22%
NA	Montana**	NA	NA
43	Nebraska	9	0.06%
29	Nevada	112	0.73%
41	New Hampshire	10	0.06%
20	New Jersey	214	1.39%
33	New Mexico	66	0.43%
3	New York	1,356	8.81%
9	North Carolina	483	3.14%
47	North Dakota	0	0.00%
11	Ohio	437	2.84%
24	Oklahoma	159	1.03%
30	Oregon	98	0.64%
10	Pennsylvania	465	3.02%
38	Rhode Island	21	0.14%
19	South Carolina	254	1.65%
45	South Dakota	4	0.03%
17	Tennessee	293	1.90%
2	Texas	1,485	9.64%
34	Utah	43	0.28%
46	Vermont	2	0.01%
12	Virginia	421	2.73%
22	Washington	184	1.20%
32	West Virginia	77	0.50%
27	Wisconsin	119	0.77%
41	Wyoming	10	0.06%

RANK ORDER

RANK	STATE	MURDERS	% of USA
1	California	2,790	18.12%
2	Texas	1,485	9.64%
3	New York	1,356	8.81%
4	Illinois	812	5.27%
5	Louisiana	682	4.43%
6	Florida	647	4.20%
7	Michigan	646	4.20%
8	Georgia	492	3.20%
9	North Carolina	483	3.14%
10	Pennsylvania	465	3.02%
11	Ohio	437	2.84%
12	Virginia	421	2.73%
13	Maryland	407	2.64%
14	Alabama	372	2.42%
15	Missouri	342	2.22%
16	Arizona	304	1.97%
17	Tennessee	293	1.90%
18	Indiana	282	1.83%
19	South Carolina	254	1.65%
20	New Jersey	214	1.39%
21	Arkansas	212	1.38%
22	Washington	184	1.20%
23	Mississippi	181	1.18%
24	Connecticut	159	1.03%
24	Oklahoma	159	1.03%
26	Massachusetts	132	0.86%
27	Wisconsin	119	0.77%
28	Colorado	113	0.73%
29	Nevada	112	0.73%
30	Oregon	98	0.64%
31	Minnesota	79	0.51%
32	West Virginia	77	0.50%
33	New Mexico	66	0.43%
34	Utah	43	0.28%
35	Alaska	24	0.16%
35	Hawaii	24	0.16%
35	Idaho	24	0.16%
38	Iowa	21	0.14%
38	Rhode Island	21	0.14%
40	Maine	11	0.07%
41	New Hampshire	10	0.06%
41	Wyoming	10	0.06%
43	Nebraska	9	0.06%
44	Delaware	6	0.04%
45	South Dakota	4	0.03%
46	Vermont	2	0.01%
47	North Dakota	0	0.00%
NA	Kansas**	NA	NA
NA	Kentucky**	NA	NA
NA	Montana**	NA	NA
	District of Columbia	313	2.03%

Source: Federal Bureau of Investigation
   "Crime in the United States 1994" (Uniform Crime Reports, November 19, 1995)
*Of the 21,992 murders in 1994 for which supplemental data were received by the F.B.I. There were an additional 1,313 murders for which the type of murder weapon was not reported to the F.B.I. Includes nonnegligent manslaughter.
**Not available.

Murder Rate with Firearms in 1994

National Rate = 6.1 Murders per 100,000 Population*

ALPHA ORDER				RANK ORDER		
RANK	STATE	RATE		RANK	STATE	RATE
3	Alabama	8.8		1	Louisiana	15.8
24	Alaska	4.0		2	California	8.9
8	Arizona	7.5		3	Alabama	8.8
4	Arkansas	8.6		4	Arkansas	8.6
2	California	8.9		5	Maryland	8.1
30	Colorado	3.1		5	Texas	8.1
19	Connecticut	4.9		7	Nevada	7.7
42	Delaware	0.8		8	Arizona	7.5
22	Florida	4.6		8	New York	7.5
10	Georgia	7.0		10	Georgia	7.0
38	Hawaii	2.0		11	Illinois	6.9
35	Idaho	2.1		11	South Carolina	6.9
11	Illinois	6.9		13	Michigan	6.8
19	Indiana	4.9		13	Mississippi	6.8
43	Iowa	0.7		13	North Carolina	6.8
NA	Kansas**	NA		16	Missouri	6.5
NA	Kentucky**	NA		17	Virginia	6.4
1	Louisiana	15.8		18	Tennessee	5.7
40	Maine	0.9		19	Connecticut	4.9
5	Maryland	8.1		19	Indiana	4.9
34	Massachusetts	2.2		19	Oklahoma	4.9
13	Michigan	6.8		22	Florida	4.6
39	Minnesota	1.7		23	West Virginia	4.2
13	Mississippi	6.8		24	Alaska	4.0
16	Missouri	6.5		24	New Mexico	4.0
NA	Montana**	NA		26	Ohio	3.9
44	Nebraska	0.6		26	Pennsylvania	3.9
7	Nevada	7.7		28	Washington	3.4
40	New Hampshire	0.9		29	Oregon	3.2
31	New Jersey	2.7		30	Colorado	3.1
24	New Mexico	4.0		31	New Jersey	2.7
8	New York	7.5		32	Utah	2.3
13	North Carolina	6.8		32	Wisconsin	2.3
47	North Dakota	0.0		34	Massachusetts	2.2
26	Ohio	3.9		35	Idaho	2.1
19	Oklahoma	4.9		35	Rhode Island	2.1
29	Oregon	3.2		35	Wyoming	2.1
26	Pennsylvania	3.9		38	Hawaii	2.0
35	Rhode Island	2.1		39	Minnesota	1.7
11	South Carolina	6.9		40	Maine	0.9
44	South Dakota	0.6		40	New Hampshire	0.9
18	Tennessee	5.7		42	Delaware	0.8
5	Texas	8.1		43	Iowa	0.7
32	Utah	2.3		44	Nebraska	0.6
46	Vermont	0.3		44	South Dakota	0.6
17	Virginia	6.4		46	Vermont	0.3
28	Washington	3.4		47	North Dakota	0.0
23	West Virginia	4.2		NA	Kansas**	NA
32	Wisconsin	2.3		NA	Kentucky**	NA
35	Wyoming	2.1		NA	Montana**	NA
					District of Columbia	54.9

Source: Morgan Quitno Press using data from Federal Bureau of Investigation
    "Crime in the United States 1994" (Uniform Crime Reports, November 19, 1995)
*Of the 21,992 murders in 1994 for which supplemental data were received by the F.B.I. There were an additional 1,313 murders for which the type of murder weapon was not reported to the F.B.I. Includes nonnegligent manslaughter. National rate based on population for reporting states.
**Not available.

Percent of Murders Involving Firearms in 1994

National Percent = 70.01% of Murders*

ALPHA ORDER				RANK ORDER		
RANK	STATE	PERCENT		RANK	STATE	PERCENT
5	Alabama	74.55		1	Louisiana	82.77
27	Alaska	64.86		2	Mississippi	79.04
12	Arizona	72.55		3	West Virginia	77.78
13	Arkansas	72.35		4	California	75.16
4	California	75.16		5	Alabama	74.55
30	Colorado	63.48		6	Indiana	74.02
7	Connecticut	73.61		7	Connecticut	73.61
43	Delaware	46.15		8	Virginia	73.34
37	Florida	54.78		9	Texas	73.26
11	Georgia	72.57		10	Ohio	72.83
41	Hawaii	48.00		11	Georgia	72.57
34	Idaho	60.00		12	Arizona	72.55
19	Illinois	68.99		13	Arkansas	72.35
6	Indiana	74.02		14	Michigan	72.34
42	Iowa	47.73		15	South Carolina	72.16
NA	Kansas**	NA		16	Maryland	70.29
NA	Kentucky**	NA		17	Tennessee	70.10
1	Louisiana	82.77		18	Oklahoma	70.04
45	Maine	40.74		19	Illinois	68.99
16	Maryland	70.29		20	Utah	68.25
26	Massachusetts	65.02		21	New York	68.07
14	Michigan	72.34		22	New Hampshire	66.67
36	Minnesota	57.25		23	Pennsylvania	66.52
2	Mississippi	79.04		24	Nevada	66.27
28	Missouri	64.29		25	Oregon	65.33
NA	Montana**	NA		26	Massachusetts	65.02
34	Nebraska	60.00		27	Alaska	64.86
24	Nevada	66.27		28	Missouri	64.29
22	New Hampshire	66.67		29	North Carolina	63.80
38	New Jersey	54.04		30	Colorado	63.48
33	New Mexico	61.68		31	Washington	62.80
21	New York	68.07		32	Wyoming	62.50
29	North Carolina	63.80		33	New Mexico	61.68
47	North Dakota	0.00		34	Idaho	60.00
10	Ohio	72.83		34	Nebraska	60.00
18	Oklahoma	70.04		36	Minnesota	57.25
25	Oregon	65.33		37	Florida	54.78
23	Pennsylvania	66.52		38	New Jersey	54.04
40	Rhode Island	51.22		39	Wisconsin	52.89
15	South Carolina	72.16		40	Rhode Island	51.22
44	South Dakota	44.44		41	Hawaii	48.00
17	Tennessee	70.10		42	Iowa	47.73
9	Texas	73.26		43	Delaware	46.15
20	Utah	68.25		44	South Dakota	44.44
46	Vermont	33.33		45	Maine	40.74
8	Virginia	73.34		46	Vermont	33.33
31	Washington	62.80		47	North Dakota	0.00
3	West Virginia	77.78		NA	Kansas**	NA
39	Wisconsin	52.89		NA	Kentucky**	NA
32	Wyoming	62.50		NA	Montana**	NA
					District of Columbia	78.64

Source: Morgan Quitno Press using data from Federal Bureau of Investigation
   "Crime in the United States 1994" (Uniform Crime Reports, November 19, 1995)
*Of the 21,992 murders in 1994 for which supplemental data were received by the F.B.I. There were an additional
1,313 murders for which the type of murder weapon was not reported to the F.B.I. Includes nonnegligent
manslaughter.
**Not available.

Murders with Handguns in 1994

National Total = 12,416 Murders*

ALPHA ORDER					RANK ORDER			
RANK	STATE		MURDERS	% of USA	RANK	STATE	MURDERS	% of USA
14	Alabama		314	2.53%	1	California	2,453	19.76%
36	Alaska		19	0.15%	2	New York	1,222	9.84%
18	Arizona		228	1.84%	3	Texas	1,098	8.84%
22	Arkansas		152	1.22%	4	Illinois	651	5.24%
1	California		2,453	19.76%	5	Louisiana	593	4.78%
27	Colorado		96	0.77%	6	Michigan	468	3.77%
24	Connecticut		140	1.13%	7	Florida	441	3.55%
44	Delaware		3	0.02%	8	Georgia	422	3.40%
7	Florida		441	3.55%	9	Pennsylvania	417	3.36%
8	Georgia		422	3.40%	10	North Carolina	389	3.13%
36	Hawaii		19	0.15%	11	Maryland	381	3.07%
35	Idaho		20	0.16%	12	Virginia	368	2.96%
4	Illinois		651	5.24%	13	Ohio	357	2.88%
17	Indiana		234	1.88%	14	Alabama	314	2.53%
39	Iowa		11	0.09%	15	Missouri	273	2.20%
NA	Kansas**		NA	NA	16	Tennessee	247	1.99%
NA	Kentucky**		NA	NA	17	Indiana	234	1.88%
5	Louisiana		593	4.78%	18	Arizona	228	1.84%
40	Maine		8	0.06%	19	New Jersey	196	1.58%
11	Maryland		381	3.07%	19	South Carolina	196	1.58%
30	Massachusetts		62	0.50%	21	Mississippi	165	1.33%
6	Michigan		468	3.77%	22	Arkansas	152	1.22%
31	Minnesota		59	0.48%	23	Washington	147	1.18%
21	Mississippi		165	1.33%	24	Connecticut	140	1.13%
15	Missouri		273	2.20%	25	Oklahoma	119	0.96%
NA	Montana**		NA	NA	26	Wisconsin	106	0.85%
43	Nebraska		5	0.04%	27	Colorado	96	0.77%
28	Nevada		94	0.76%	28	Nevada	94	0.76%
40	New Hampshire		8	0.06%	29	Oregon	69	0.56%
19	New Jersey		196	1.58%	30	Massachusetts	62	0.50%
33	New Mexico		49	0.39%	31	Minnesota	59	0.48%
2	New York		1,222	9.84%	32	West Virginia	57	0.46%
10	North Carolina		389	3.13%	33	New Mexico	49	0.39%
47	North Dakota		0	0.00%	34	Utah	33	0.27%
13	Ohio		357	2.88%	35	Idaho	20	0.16%
25	Oklahoma		119	0.96%	36	Alaska	19	0.15%
29	Oregon		69	0.56%	36	Hawaii	19	0.15%
9	Pennsylvania		417	3.36%	38	Rhode Island	17	0.14%
38	Rhode Island		17	0.14%	39	Iowa	11	0.09%
19	South Carolina		196	1.58%	40	Maine	8	0.06%
44	South Dakota		3	0.02%	40	New Hampshire	8	0.06%
16	Tennessee		247	1.99%	42	Wyoming	6	0.05%
3	Texas		1,098	8.84%	43	Nebraska	5	0.04%
34	Utah		33	0.27%	44	Delaware	3	0.02%
46	Vermont		1	0.01%	44	South Dakota	3	0.02%
12	Virginia		368	2.96%	46	Vermont	1	0.01%
23	Washington		147	1.18%	47	North Dakota	0	0.00%
32	West Virginia		57	0.46%	NA	Kansas**	NA	NA
26	Wisconsin		106	0.85%	NA	Kentucky**	NA	NA
42	Wyoming		6	0.05%	NA	Montana**	NA	NA
						District of Columbia**	NA	NA

Source: Federal Bureau of Investigation
   "Crime in the United States 1994" (Uniform Crime Reports, November 19, 1995)
*Of the 21,992 murders in 1994 for which supplemental data were received by the F.B.I. There were an additional 1,313 murders for which the type of murder weapon was not reported to the F.B.I. Includes nonnegligent manslaughter.
**Not available.

Murder Rate with Handguns in 1994

National Rate = 4.9 Murders per 100,000 Population*

ALPHA ORDER				RANK ORDER		
RANK	STATE	RATE		RANK	STATE	RATE
4	Alabama	7.4		1	Louisiana	13.7
25	Alaska	3.1		2	California	7.8
11	Arizona	5.6		3	Maryland	7.6
7	Arkansas	6.2		4	Alabama	7.4
2	California	7.8		5	New York	6.7
29	Colorado	2.6		6	Nevada	6.5
19	Connecticut	4.3		7	Arkansas	6.2
42	Delaware	0.4		7	Mississippi	6.2
23	Florida	3.2		9	Georgia	6.0
9	Georgia	6.0		9	Texas	6.0
36	Hawaii	1.6		11	Arizona	5.6
33	Idaho	1.8		11	Virginia	5.6
13	Illinois	5.5		13	Illinois	5.5
20	Indiana	4.1		13	North Carolina	5.5
42	Iowa	0.4		15	South Carolina	5.3
NA	Kansas**	NA		16	Missouri	5.2
NA	Kentucky**	NA		17	Michigan	4.9
1	Louisiana	13.7		18	Tennessee	4.8
41	Maine	0.6		19	Connecticut	4.3
3	Maryland	7.6		20	Indiana	4.1
39	Massachusetts	1.0		21	Oklahoma	3.7
17	Michigan	4.9		22	Pennsylvania	3.5
37	Minnesota	1.3		23	Florida	3.2
7	Mississippi	6.2		23	Ohio	3.2
16	Missouri	5.2		25	Alaska	3.1
NA	Montana**	NA		25	West Virginia	3.1
45	Nebraska	0.3		27	New Mexico	3.0
6	Nevada	6.5		28	Washington	2.8
40	New Hampshire	0.7		29	Colorado	2.6
30	New Jersey	2.5		30	New Jersey	2.5
27	New Mexico	3.0		31	Oregon	2.2
5	New York	6.7		32	Wisconsin	2.1
13	North Carolina	5.5		33	Idaho	1.8
47	North Dakota	0.0		34	Rhode Island	1.7
23	Ohio	3.2		34	Utah	1.7
21	Oklahoma	3.7		36	Hawaii	1.6
31	Oregon	2.2		37	Minnesota	1.3
22	Pennsylvania	3.5		37	Wyoming	1.3
34	Rhode Island	1.7		39	Massachusetts	1.0
15	South Carolina	5.3		40	New Hampshire	0.7
42	South Dakota	0.4		41	Maine	0.6
18	Tennessee	4.8		42	Delaware	0.4
9	Texas	6.0		42	Iowa	0.4
34	Utah	1.7		42	South Dakota	0.4
46	Vermont	0.2		45	Nebraska	0.3
11	Virginia	5.6		46	Vermont	0.2
28	Washington	2.8		47	North Dakota	0.0
25	West Virginia	3.1		NA	Kansas**	NA
32	Wisconsin	2.1		NA	Kentucky**	NA
37	Wyoming	1.3		NA	Montana**	NA
					District of Columbia**	NA

Source: Morgan Quitno Press using data from Federal Bureau of Investigation
   "Crime in the United States 1994" (Uniform Crime Reports, November 19, 1995)
*Of the 21,992 murders in 1994 for which supplemental data were received by the F.B.I. There were an additional
1,313 murders for which the type of murder weapon was not reported to the F.B.I. Includes nonnegligent
manslaughter. Revised figures using only population of reporting jurisdictions.
**Not available.

Percent of Murders Involving Handguns in 1994

National Percent = 57.50% of Murders*

ALPHA ORDER

RANK	STATE	PERCENT
7	Alabama	62.93
27	Alaska	51.35
18	Arizona	54.42
25	Arkansas	51.88
3	California	66.08
20	Colorado	53.93
5	Connecticut	64.81
45	Delaware	23.08
39	Florida	37.34
8	Georgia	62.24
37	Hawaii	38.00
30	Idaho	50.00
17	Illinois	55.31
9	Indiana	61.42
44	Iowa	25.00
NA	Kansas**	NA
NA	Kentucky**	NA
2	Louisiana	71.97
43	Maine	29.63
4	Maryland	65.80
42	Massachusetts	30.54
23	Michigan	52.41
35	Minnesota	42.75
1	Mississippi	72.05
28	Missouri	51.32
NA	Montana**	NA
40	Nebraska	33.33
16	Nevada	55.62
21	New Hampshire	53.33
31	New Jersey	49.49
34	New Mexico	45.79
10	New York	61.35
26	North Carolina	51.39
47	North Dakota	0.00
12	Ohio	59.50
22	Oklahoma	52.42
33	Oregon	46.00
11	Pennsylvania	59.66
36	Rhode Island	41.46
15	South Carolina	55.68
40	South Dakota	33.33
13	Tennessee	59.09
19	Texas	54.17
24	Utah	52.38
46	Vermont	16.67
6	Virginia	64.11
29	Washington	50.17
14	West Virginia	57.58
32	Wisconsin	47.11
38	Wyoming	37.50

RANK ORDER

RANK	STATE	PERCENT
1	Mississippi	72.05
2	Louisiana	71.97
3	California	66.08
4	Maryland	65.80
5	Connecticut	64.81
6	Virginia	64.11
7	Alabama	62.93
8	Georgia	62.24
9	Indiana	61.42
10	New York	61.35
11	Pennsylvania	59.66
12	Ohio	59.50
13	Tennessee	59.09
14	West Virginia	57.58
15	South Carolina	55.68
16	Nevada	55.62
17	Illinois	55.31
18	Arizona	54.42
19	Texas	54.17
20	Colorado	53.93
21	New Hampshire	53.33
22	Oklahoma	52.42
23	Michigan	52.41
24	Utah	52.38
25	Arkansas	51.88
26	North Carolina	51.39
27	Alaska	51.35
28	Missouri	51.32
29	Washington	50.17
30	Idaho	50.00
31	New Jersey	49.49
32	Wisconsin	47.11
33	Oregon	46.00
34	New Mexico	45.79
35	Minnesota	42.75
36	Rhode Island	41.46
37	Hawaii	38.00
38	Wyoming	37.50
39	Florida	37.34
40	Nebraska	33.33
40	South Dakota	33.33
42	Massachusetts	30.54
43	Maine	29.63
44	Iowa	25.00
45	Delaware	23.08
46	Vermont	16.67
47	North Dakota	0.00
NA	Kansas**	NA
NA	Kentucky**	NA
NA	Montana**	NA
	District of Columbia**	NA

Source: Morgan Quitno Press using data from Federal Bureau of Investigation
   "Crime in the United States 1994" (Uniform Crime Reports, November 19, 1995)
*Of the 21,992 murders in 1994 for which supplemental data were received by the F.B.I. There were an additional
1,313 murders for which the type of murder weapon was not reported to the F.B.I. Includes nonnegligent
manslaughter.
**Not available.

Murders with Rifles in 1994

National Total = 721 Murders*

ALPHA ORDER				RANK ORDER			
RANK	STATE	MURDERS	% of USA	RANK	STATE	MURDERS	% of USA
10	Alabama	21	2.91%	1	California	141	19.56%
37	Alaska	2	0.28%	2	Texas	81	11.23%
8	Arizona	23	3.19%	3	North Carolina	49	6.80%
12	Arkansas	18	2.50%	4	Louisiana	32	4.44%
1	California	141	19.56%	4	Michigan	32	4.44%
34	Colorado	3	0.42%	6	New York	28	3.88%
24	Connecticut	7	0.97%	7	Florida	27	3.74%
44	Delaware	0	0.00%	8	Arizona	23	3.19%
7	Florida	27	3.74%	8	Washington	23	3.19%
12	Georgia	18	2.50%	10	Alabama	21	2.91%
37	Hawaii	2	0.28%	11	South Carolina	20	2.77%
31	Idaho	4	0.55%	12	Arkansas	18	2.50%
19	Illinois	13	1.80%	12	Georgia	18	2.50%
27	Indiana	6	0.83%	12	Missouri	18	2.50%
42	Iowa	1	0.14%	15	Oklahoma	17	2.36%
NA	Kansas**	NA	NA	15	Virginia	17	2.36%
NA	Kentucky**	NA	NA	17	Pennsylvania	14	1.94%
4	Louisiana	32	4.44%	17	Tennessee	14	1.94%
44	Maine	0	0.00%	19	Illinois	13	1.80%
27	Maryland	6	0.83%	19	Oregon	13	1.80%
31	Massachusetts	4	0.55%	21	New Mexico	10	1.39%
4	Michigan	32	4.44%	22	Minnesota	8	1.11%
22	Minnesota	8	1.11%	22	West Virginia	8	1.11%
29	Mississippi	5	0.69%	24	Connecticut	7	0.97%
12	Missouri	18	2.50%	24	Nevada	7	0.97%
NA	Montana**	NA	NA	24	Ohio	7	0.97%
34	Nebraska	3	0.42%	27	Indiana	6	0.83%
24	Nevada	7	0.97%	27	Maryland	6	0.83%
37	New Hampshire	2	0.28%	29	Mississippi	5	0.69%
37	New Jersey	2	0.28%	29	Wisconsin	5	0.69%
21	New Mexico	10	1.39%	31	Idaho	4	0.55%
6	New York	28	3.88%	31	Massachusetts	4	0.55%
3	North Carolina	49	6.80%	31	Utah	4	0.55%
44	North Dakota	0	0.00%	34	Colorado	3	0.42%
24	Ohio	7	0.97%	34	Nebraska	3	0.42%
15	Oklahoma	17	2.36%	34	Wyoming	3	0.42%
19	Oregon	13	1.80%	37	Alaska	2	0.28%
17	Pennsylvania	14	1.94%	37	Hawaii	2	0.28%
37	Rhode Island	2	0.28%	37	New Hampshire	2	0.28%
11	South Carolina	20	2.77%	37	New Jersey	2	0.28%
42	South Dakota	1	0.14%	37	Rhode Island	2	0.28%
17	Tennessee	14	1.94%	42	Iowa	1	0.14%
2	Texas	81	11.23%	42	South Dakota	1	0.14%
31	Utah	4	0.55%	44	Delaware	0	0.00%
44	Vermont	0	0.00%	44	Maine	0	0.00%
15	Virginia	17	2.36%	44	North Dakota	0	0.00%
8	Washington	23	3.19%	44	Vermont	0	0.00%
22	West Virginia	8	1.11%	NA	Kansas**	NA	NA
29	Wisconsin	5	0.69%	NA	Kentucky**	NA	NA
34	Wyoming	3	0.42%	NA	Montana**	NA	NA
					District of Columbia**	NA	NA

Source: Federal Bureau of Investigation
   "Crime in the United States 1994" (Uniform Crime Reports, November 19, 1995)
*Of the 21,992 murders in 1994 for which supplemental data were received by the F.B.I. There were an additional 1,313 murders for which the type of murder weapon was not reported to the F.B.I. Includes nonnegligent manslaughter.
**Not available.

Percent of Murders Involving Rifles in 1994

National Percent = 3.34% of Murders*

ALPHA ORDER			RANK ORDER		
RANK	STATE	PERCENT	RANK	STATE	PERCENT
19	Alabama	4.21	1	Nebraska	20.00
17	Alaska	5.41	2	Wyoming	18.75
16	Arizona	5.49	3	New Hampshire	13.33
13	Arkansas	6.14	4	South Dakota	11.11
24	California	3.80	5	Idaho	10.00
37	Colorado	1.69	6	New Mexico	9.35
28	Connecticut	3.24	7	Oregon	8.67
44	Delaware	0.00	8	West Virginia	8.08
31	Florida	2.29	9	Washington	7.85
30	Georgia	2.65	10	Oklahoma	7.49
21	Hawaii	4.00	11	North Carolina	6.47
5	Idaho	10.00	12	Utah	6.35
41	Illinois	1.10	13	Arkansas	6.14
38	Indiana	1.57	14	Minnesota	5.80
32	Iowa	2.27	15	South Carolina	5.68
NA	Kansas**	NA	16	Arizona	5.49
NA	Kentucky**	NA	17	Alaska	5.41
23	Louisiana	3.88	18	Rhode Island	4.88
44	Maine	0.00	19	Alabama	4.21
42	Maryland	1.04	20	Nevada	4.14
36	Massachusetts	1.97	21	Hawaii	4.00
25	Michigan	3.58	21	Texas	4.00
14	Minnesota	5.80	23	Louisiana	3.88
34	Mississippi	2.18	24	California	3.80
26	Missouri	3.38	25	Michigan	3.58
NA	Montana**	NA	26	Missouri	3.38
1	Nebraska	20.00	27	Tennessee	3.35
20	Nevada	4.14	28	Connecticut	3.24
3	New Hampshire	13.33	29	Virginia	2.96
43	New Jersey	0.51	30	Georgia	2.65
6	New Mexico	9.35	31	Florida	2.29
39	New York	1.41	32	Iowa	2.27
11	North Carolina	6.47	33	Wisconsin	2.22
44	North Dakota	0.00	34	Mississippi	2.18
40	Ohio	1.17	35	Pennsylvania	2.00
10	Oklahoma	7.49	36	Massachusetts	1.97
7	Oregon	8.67	37	Colorado	1.69
35	Pennsylvania	2.00	38	Indiana	1.57
18	Rhode Island	4.88	39	New York	1.41
15	South Carolina	5.68	40	Ohio	1.17
4	South Dakota	11.11	41	Illinois	1.10
27	Tennessee	3.35	42	Maryland	1.04
21	Texas	4.00	43	New Jersey	0.51
12	Utah	6.35	44	Delaware	0.00
44	Vermont	0.00	44	Maine	0.00
29	Virginia	2.96	44	North Dakota	0.00
9	Washington	7.85	44	Vermont	0.00
8	West Virginia	8.08	NA	Kansas**	NA
33	Wisconsin	2.22	NA	Kentucky**	NA
2	Wyoming	18.75	NA	Montana**	NA
			District of Columbia**		NA

Source: Morgan Quitno Press using data from Federal Bureau of Investigation
"Crime in the United States 1994" (Uniform Crime Reports, November 19, 1995)
*Of the 21,992 murders in 1994 for which supplemental data were received by the F.B.I. There were an additional 1,313 murders for which the type of murder weapon was not reported to the F.B.I. Includes nonnegligent manslaughter.
**Not available.

Murders with Shotguns in 1994

National Total = 948 Murders*

ALPHA ORDER

RANK	STATE	MURDERS	% of USA
6	Alabama	37	3.90%
38	Alaska	2	0.21%
19	Arizona	17	1.79%
12	Arkansas	26	2.74%
1	California	165	17.41%
27	Colorado	7	0.74%
32	Connecticut	5	0.53%
43	Delaware	0	0.00%
7	Florida	33	3.48%
7	Georgia	33	3.48%
35	Hawaii	3	0.32%
43	Idaho	0	0.00%
21	Illinois	15	1.58%
16	Indiana	22	2.32%
30	Iowa	6	0.63%
NA	Kansas**	NA	NA
NA	Kentucky**	NA	NA
10	Louisiana	29	3.06%
35	Maine	3	0.32%
19	Maryland	17	1.79%
32	Massachusetts	5	0.53%
3	Michigan	65	6.86%
22	Minnesota	12	1.27%
27	Mississippi	7	0.74%
11	Missouri	28	2.95%
NA	Montana**	NA	NA
40	Nebraska	1	0.11%
24	Nevada	9	0.95%
43	New Hampshire	0	0.00%
25	New Jersey	8	0.84%
30	New Mexico	6	0.63%
5	New York	38	4.01%
4	North Carolina	41	4.32%
43	North Dakota	0	0.00%
7	Ohio	33	3.48%
18	Oklahoma	20	2.11%
25	Oregon	8	0.84%
16	Pennsylvania	22	2.32%
38	Rhode Island	2	0.21%
14	South Carolina	25	2.64%
43	South Dakota	0	0.00%
12	Tennessee	26	2.74%
2	Texas	120	12.66%
35	Utah	3	0.32%
40	Vermont	1	0.11%
14	Virginia	25	2.64%
34	Washington	4	0.42%
23	West Virginia	11	1.16%
27	Wisconsin	7	0.74%
40	Wyoming	1	0.11%

RANK ORDER

RANK	STATE	MURDERS	% of USA
1	California	165	17.41%
2	Texas	120	12.66%
3	Michigan	65	6.86%
4	North Carolina	41	4.32%
5	New York	38	4.01%
6	Alabama	37	3.90%
7	Florida	33	3.48%
7	Georgia	33	3.48%
7	Ohio	33	3.48%
10	Louisiana	29	3.06%
11	Missouri	28	2.95%
12	Arkansas	26	2.74%
12	Tennessee	26	2.74%
14	South Carolina	25	2.64%
14	Virginia	25	2.64%
16	Indiana	22	2.32%
16	Pennsylvania	22	2.32%
18	Oklahoma	20	2.11%
19	Arizona	17	1.79%
19	Maryland	17	1.79%
21	Illinois	15	1.58%
22	Minnesota	12	1.27%
23	West Virginia	11	1.16%
24	Nevada	9	0.95%
25	New Jersey	8	0.84%
25	Oregon	8	0.84%
27	Colorado	7	0.74%
27	Mississippi	7	0.74%
27	Wisconsin	7	0.74%
30	Iowa	6	0.63%
30	New Mexico	6	0.63%
32	Connecticut	5	0.53%
32	Massachusetts	5	0.53%
34	Washington	4	0.42%
35	Hawaii	3	0.32%
35	Maine	3	0.32%
35	Utah	3	0.32%
38	Alaska	2	0.21%
38	Rhode Island	2	0.21%
40	Nebraska	1	0.11%
40	Vermont	1	0.11%
40	Wyoming	1	0.11%
43	Delaware	0	0.00%
43	Idaho	0	0.00%
43	New Hampshire	0	0.00%
43	North Dakota	0	0.00%
43	South Dakota	0	0.00%
NA	Kansas**	NA	NA
NA	Kentucky**	NA	NA
NA	Montana**	NA	NA
	District of Columbia**	NA	NA

Source: Federal Bureau of Investigation
    "Crime in the United States 1994" (Uniform Crime Reports, November 19, 1995)
*Of the 21,992 murders in 1994 for which supplemental data were received by the F.B.I. There were an additional 1,313 murders for which the type of murder weapon was not reported to the F.B.I. Includes nonnegligent manslaughter.
**Not available.

Percent of Murders Involving Shotguns in 1994

National Percent = 4.39% of Murders*

ALPHA ORDER				RANK ORDER		
RANK	**STATE**	**PERCENT**		**RANK**	**STATE**	**PERCENT**
8	Alabama	7.41		1	Vermont	16.67
20	Alaska	5.41		2	Iowa	13.64
29	Arizona	4.06		3	Maine	11.11
5	Arkansas	8.87		3	West Virginia	11.11
27	California	4.45		5	Arkansas	8.87
30	Colorado	3.93		6	Oklahoma	8.81
38	Connecticut	2.31		7	Minnesota	8.70
43	Delaware	0.00		8	Alabama	7.41
36	Florida	2.79		9	Michigan	7.28
25	Georgia	4.87		10	South Carolina	7.10
14	Hawaii	6.00		11	Nebraska	6.67
43	Idaho	0.00		12	Wyoming	6.25
42	Illinois	1.27		13	Tennessee	6.22
16	Indiana	5.77		14	Hawaii	6.00
2	Iowa	13.64		15	Texas	5.92
NA	Kansas**	NA		16	Indiana	5.77
NA	Kentucky**	NA		17	New Mexico	5.61
31	Louisiana	3.52		18	Ohio	5.50
3	Maine	11.11		19	North Carolina	5.42
35	Maryland	2.94		20	Alaska	5.41
37	Massachusetts	2.46		21	Nevada	5.33
9	Michigan	7.28		21	Oregon	5.33
7	Minnesota	8.70		23	Missouri	5.26
34	Mississippi	3.06		24	Rhode Island	4.88
23	Missouri	5.26		25	Georgia	4.87
NA	Montana**	NA		26	Utah	4.76
11	Nebraska	6.67		27	California	4.45
21	Nevada	5.33		28	Virginia	4.36
43	New Hampshire	0.00		29	Arizona	4.06
39	New Jersey	2.02		30	Colorado	3.93
17	New Mexico	5.61		31	Louisiana	3.52
40	New York	1.91		32	Pennsylvania	3.15
19	North Carolina	5.42		33	Wisconsin	3.11
43	North Dakota	0.00		34	Mississippi	3.06
18	Ohio	5.50		35	Maryland	2.94
6	Oklahoma	8.81		36	Florida	2.79
21	Oregon	5.33		37	Massachusetts	2.46
32	Pennsylvania	3.15		38	Connecticut	2.31
24	Rhode Island	4.88		39	New Jersey	2.02
10	South Carolina	7.10		40	New York	1.91
43	South Dakota	0.00		41	Washington	1.37
13	Tennessee	6.22		42	Illinois	1.27
15	Texas	5.92		43	Delaware	0.00
26	Utah	4.76		43	Idaho	0.00
1	Vermont	16.67		43	New Hampshire	0.00
28	Virginia	4.36		43	North Dakota	0.00
41	Washington	1.37		43	South Dakota	0.00
3	West Virginia	11.11		NA	Kansas**	NA
33	Wisconsin	3.11		NA	Kentucky**	NA
12	Wyoming	6.25		NA	Montana**	NA
					District of Columbia**	NA

Source: Morgan Quitno Press using data from Federal Bureau of Investigation
"Crime in the United States 1994" (Uniform Crime Reports, November 19, 1995)
Of the 21,992 murders in 1994 for which supplemental data were received by the F.B.I. There were an additional 1,313 murders for which the type of murder weapon was not reported to the F.B.I. Includes nonnegligent manslaughter.
**Not available.*

Murders with Knives or Cutting Instruments in 1994

National Total = 2,790 Murders*

ALPHA ORDER

RANK	STATE	MURDERS	% of USA
16	Alabama	54	1.94%
36	Alaska	7	0.25%
18	Arizona	47	1.68%
27	Arkansas	29	1.04%
1	California	427	15.30%
27	Colorado	29	1.04%
25	Connecticut	30	1.08%
42	Delaware	2	0.07%
4	Florida	155	5.56%
9	Georgia	86	3.08%
38	Hawaii	6	0.22%
36	Idaho	7	0.25%
5	Illinois	147	5.27%
19	Indiana	46	1.65%
33	Iowa	10	0.36%
NA	Kansas**	NA	NA
NA	Kentucky**	NA	NA
15	Louisiana	60	2.15%
38	Maine	6	0.22%
10	Maryland	75	2.69%
23	Massachusetts	32	1.15%
7	Michigan	103	3.69%
29	Minnesota	28	1.00%
30	Mississippi	26	0.93%
13	Missouri	65	2.33%
NA	Montana**	NA	NA
45	Nebraska	1	0.04%
31	Nevada	18	0.65%
41	New Hampshire	3	0.11%
11	New Jersey	67	2.40%
32	New Mexico	17	0.61%
2	New York	291	10.43%
6	North Carolina	107	3.84%
47	North Dakota	0	0.00%
16	Ohio	54	1.94%
24	Oklahoma	31	1.11%
25	Oregon	30	1.08%
8	Pennsylvania	98	3.51%
35	Rhode Island	8	0.29%
22	South Carolina	40	1.43%
45	South Dakota	1	0.04%
14	Tennessee	62	2.22%
3	Texas	270	9.68%
34	Utah	9	0.32%
42	Vermont	2	0.07%
11	Virginia	67	2.40%
20	Washington	43	1.54%
40	West Virginia	4	0.14%
21	Wisconsin	41	1.47%
42	Wyoming	2	0.07%

RANK ORDER

RANK	STATE	MURDERS	% of USA
1	California	427	15.30%
2	New York	291	10.43%
3	Texas	270	9.68%
4	Florida	155	5.56%
5	Illinois	147	5.27%
6	North Carolina	107	3.84%
7	Michigan	103	3.69%
8	Pennsylvania	98	3.51%
9	Georgia	86	3.08%
10	Maryland	75	2.69%
11	New Jersey	67	2.40%
11	Virginia	67	2.40%
13	Missouri	65	2.33%
14	Tennessee	62	2.22%
15	Louisiana	60	2.15%
16	Alabama	54	1.94%
16	Ohio	54	1.94%
18	Arizona	47	1.68%
19	Indiana	46	1.65%
20	Washington	43	1.54%
21	Wisconsin	41	1.47%
22	South Carolina	40	1.43%
23	Massachusetts	32	1.15%
24	Oklahoma	31	1.11%
25	Connecticut	30	1.08%
25	Oregon	30	1.08%
27	Arkansas	29	1.04%
27	Colorado	29	1.04%
29	Minnesota	28	1.00%
30	Mississippi	26	0.93%
31	Nevada	18	0.65%
32	New Mexico	17	0.61%
33	Iowa	10	0.36%
34	Utah	9	0.32%
35	Rhode Island	8	0.29%
36	Alaska	7	0.25%
36	Idaho	7	0.25%
38	Hawaii	6	0.22%
38	Maine	6	0.22%
40	West Virginia	4	0.14%
41	New Hampshire	3	0.11%
42	Delaware	2	0.07%
42	Vermont	2	0.07%
42	Wyoming	2	0.07%
45	Nebraska	1	0.04%
45	South Dakota	1	0.04%
47	North Dakota	0	0.00%
NA	Kansas**	NA	NA
NA	Kentucky**	NA	NA
NA	Montana**	NA	NA
	District of Columbia	47	1.68%

Source: Federal Bureau of Investigation
  "Crime in the United States 1994" (Uniform Crime Reports, November 19, 1995)
Of the 21,992 murders in 1994 for which supplemental data were received by the F.B.I. There were an additional 1,313 murders for which the type of murder weapon was not reported to the F.B.I. Includes nonnegligent manslaughter.
**Not available.*

Percent of Murders Involving Knives or Cutting Instruments in 1994

National Percent = 12.92% of Murders*

ALPHA ORDER				RANK ORDER		
RANK	STATE	MURDERS		RANK	STATE	MURDERS
40	Alabama	10.82		1	Vermont	33.33
8	Alaska	18.92		2	Iowa	22.73
38	Arizona	11.22		3	Maine	22.22
42	Arkansas	9.90		4	Minnesota	20.29
35	California	11.50		5	New Hampshire	20.00
12	Colorado	16.29		5	Oregon	20.00
22	Connecticut	13.89		7	Rhode Island	19.51
15	Delaware	15.38		8	Alaska	18.92
25	Florida	13.12		9	Wisconsin	18.22
27	Georgia	12.68		10	Idaho	17.50
32	Hawaii	12.00		11	New Jersey	16.92
10	Idaho	17.50		12	Colorado	16.29
29	Illinois	12.49		13	New Mexico	15.89
31	Indiana	12.07		14	Massachusetts	15.76
2	Iowa	22.73		15	Delaware	15.38
NA	Kansas**	NA		16	Tennessee	14.83
NA	Kentucky**	NA		17	Washington	14.68
44	Louisiana	7.28		18	New York	14.61
3	Maine	22.22		19	Utah	14.29
26	Maryland	12.95		20	North Carolina	14.13
14	Massachusetts	15.76		21	Pennsylvania	14.02
34	Michigan	11.53		22	Connecticut	13.89
4	Minnesota	20.29		23	Oklahoma	13.66
37	Mississippi	11.35		24	Texas	13.32
30	Missouri	12.22		25	Florida	13.12
NA	Montana**	NA		26	Maryland	12.95
45	Nebraska	6.67		27	Georgia	12.68
41	Nevada	10.65		28	Wyoming	12.50
5	New Hampshire	20.00		29	Illinois	12.49
11	New Jersey	16.92		30	Missouri	12.22
13	New Mexico	15.89		31	Indiana	12.07
18	New York	14.61		32	Hawaii	12.00
20	North Carolina	14.13		33	Virginia	11.67
47	North Dakota	0.00		34	Michigan	11.53
43	Ohio	9.00		35	California	11.50
23	Oklahoma	13.66		36	South Carolina	11.36
5	Oregon	20.00		37	Mississippi	11.35
21	Pennsylvania	14.02		38	Arizona	11.22
7	Rhode Island	19.51		39	South Dakota	11.11
36	South Carolina	11.36		40	Alabama	10.82
39	South Dakota	11.11		41	Nevada	10.65
16	Tennessee	14.83		42	Arkansas	9.90
24	Texas	13.32		43	Ohio	9.00
19	Utah	14.29		44	Louisiana	7.28
1	Vermont	33.33		45	Nebraska	6.67
33	Virginia	11.67		46	West Virginia	4.04
17	Washington	14.68		47	North Dakota	0.00
46	West Virginia	4.04		NA	Kansas**	NA
9	Wisconsin	18.22		NA	Kentucky**	NA
28	Wyoming	12.50		NA	Montana**	NA

	District of Columbia	11.81

Source: Morgan Quitno Press using data from Federal Bureau of Investigation
"Crime in the United States 1994" (Uniform Crime Reports, November 19, 1995)
*Of the 21,992 murders in 1994 for which supplemental data were received by the F.B.I. There were an additional 1,313 murders for which the type of murder weapon was not reported to the F.B.I. Includes nonnegligent manslaughter.
**Not available.

Murders by Hands, Fists or Feet in 1994

National total = 1,164 Murders*

ALPHA ORDER

RANK	STATE	MURDERS	% of USA
13	Alabama	31	2.66%
34	Alaska	6	0.52%
16	Arizona	23	1.98%
27	Arkansas	9	0.77%
1	California	156	13.40%
26	Colorado	10	0.86%
24	Connecticut	14	1.20%
44	Delaware	1	0.09%
5	Florida	57	4.90%
11	Georgia	33	2.84%
30	Hawaii	7	0.60%
36	Idaho	4	0.34%
4	Illinois	64	5.50%
23	Indiana	16	1.37%
36	Iowa	4	0.34%
NA	Kansas**	NA	NA
NA	Kentucky**	NA	NA
13	Louisiana	31	2.66%
36	Maine	4	0.34%
11	Maryland	33	2.84%
30	Massachusetts	7	0.60%
9	Michigan	39	3.35%
29	Minnesota	8	0.69%
30	Mississippi	7	0.60%
19	Missouri	22	1.89%
NA	Montana**	NA	NA
41	Nebraska	2	0.17%
20	Nevada	20	1.72%
44	New Hampshire	1	0.09%
7	New Jersey	43	3.69%
30	New Mexico	7	0.60%
2	New York	119	10.22%
8	North Carolina	41	3.52%
47	North Dakota	0	0.00%
10	Ohio	37	3.18%
25	Oklahoma	13	1.12%
27	Oregon	9	0.77%
5	Pennsylvania	57	4.90%
41	Rhode Island	2	0.17%
22	South Carolina	19	1.63%
41	South Dakota	2	0.17%
16	Tennessee	23	1.98%
3	Texas	97	8.33%
39	Utah	3	0.26%
44	Vermont	1	0.09%
13	Virginia	31	2.66%
20	Washington	20	1.72%
35	West Virginia	5	0.43%
16	Wisconsin	23	1.98%
39	Wyoming	3	0.26%

RANK ORDER

RANK	STATE	MURDERS	% of USA
1	California	156	13.40%
2	New York	119	10.22%
3	Texas	97	8.33%
4	Illinois	64	5.50%
5	Florida	57	4.90%
5	Pennsylvania	57	4.90%
7	New Jersey	43	3.69%
8	North Carolina	41	3.52%
9	Michigan	39	3.35%
10	Ohio	37	3.18%
11	Georgia	33	2.84%
11	Maryland	33	2.84%
13	Alabama	31	2.66%
13	Louisiana	31	2.66%
13	Virginia	31	2.66%
16	Arizona	23	1.98%
16	Tennessee	23	1.98%
16	Wisconsin	23	1.98%
19	Missouri	22	1.89%
20	Nevada	20	1.72%
20	Washington	20	1.72%
22	South Carolina	19	1.63%
23	Indiana	16	1.37%
24	Connecticut	14	1.20%
25	Oklahoma	13	1.12%
26	Colorado	10	0.86%
27	Arkansas	9	0.77%
27	Oregon	9	0.77%
29	Minnesota	8	0.69%
30	Hawaii	7	0.60%
30	Massachusetts	7	0.60%
30	Mississippi	7	0.60%
30	New Mexico	7	0.60%
34	Alaska	6	0.52%
35	West Virginia	5	0.43%
36	Idaho	4	0.34%
36	Iowa	4	0.34%
36	Maine	4	0.34%
39	Utah	3	0.26%
39	Wyoming	3	0.26%
41	Nebraska	2	0.17%
41	Rhode Island	2	0.17%
41	South Dakota	2	0.17%
44	Delaware	1	0.09%
44	New Hampshire	1	0.09%
44	Vermont	1	0.09%
47	North Dakota	0	0.00%
NA	Kansas**	NA	NA
NA	Kentucky**	NA	NA
NA	Montana**	NA	NA
	District of Columbia	0	0.00%

Source: Federal Bureau of Investigation
    "Crime in the United States 1994" (Uniform Crime Reports, November 19, 1995)
*Of the 21,992 murders in 1994 for which supplemental data were received by the F.B.I. There were an additional
1,313 murders for which the type of murder weapon was not reported to the F.B.I. Includes nonnegligent
manslaughter.
**Not available.

Percent of Murders Involving Hands, Fists or Feet in 1994

National Percent = 5.39% of Murders*

ALPHA ORDER

RANK	STATE	MURDERS
19	Alabama	6.21
4	Alaska	16.22
28	Arizona	5.49
45	Arkansas	3.07
40	California	4.20
26	Colorado	5.62
18	Connecticut	6.48
14	Delaware	7.69
36	Florida	4.83
35	Georgia	4.87
6	Hawaii	14.00
11	Idaho	10.00
29	Illinois	5.44
40	Indiana	4.20
12	Iowa	9.09
NA	Kansas**	NA
NA	Kentucky**	NA
43	Louisiana	3.76
5	Maine	14.81
25	Maryland	5.70
44	Massachusetts	3.45
39	Michigan	4.37
23	Minnesota	5.80
46	Mississippi	3.06
42	Missouri	4.14
NA	Montana**	NA
7	Nebraska	13.33
8	Nevada	11.83
16	New Hampshire	6.67
9	New Jersey	10.86
17	New Mexico	6.54
22	New York	5.97
30	North Carolina	5.42
47	North Dakota	0.00
20	Ohio	6.17
24	Oklahoma	5.73
21	Oregon	6.00
13	Pennsylvania	8.15
34	Rhode Island	4.88
31	South Carolina	5.40
1	South Dakota	22.22
27	Tennessee	5.50
37	Texas	4.79
38	Utah	4.76
3	Vermont	16.67
31	Virginia	5.40
15	Washington	6.83
33	West Virginia	5.05
10	Wisconsin	10.22
2	Wyoming	18.75

RANK ORDER

RANK	STATE	MURDERS
1	South Dakota	22.22
2	Wyoming	18.75
3	Vermont	16.67
4	Alaska	16.22
5	Maine	14.81
6	Hawaii	14.00
7	Nebraska	13.33
8	Nevada	11.83
9	New Jersey	10.86
10	Wisconsin	10.22
11	Idaho	10.00
12	Iowa	9.09
13	Pennsylvania	8.15
14	Delaware	7.69
15	Washington	6.83
16	New Hampshire	6.67
17	New Mexico	6.54
18	Connecticut	6.48
19	Alabama	6.21
20	Ohio	6.17
21	Oregon	6.00
22	New York	5.97
23	Minnesota	5.80
24	Oklahoma	5.73
25	Maryland	5.70
26	Colorado	5.62
27	Tennessee	5.50
28	Arizona	5.49
29	Illinois	5.44
30	North Carolina	5.42
31	South Carolina	5.40
31	Virginia	5.40
33	West Virginia	5.05
34	Rhode Island	4.88
35	Georgia	4.87
36	Florida	4.83
37	Texas	4.79
38	Utah	4.76
39	Michigan	4.37
40	California	4.20
40	Indiana	4.20
42	Missouri	4.14
43	Louisiana	3.76
44	Massachusetts	3.45
45	Arkansas	3.07
46	Mississippi	3.06
47	North Dakota	0.00
NA	Kansas**	NA
NA	Kentucky**	NA
NA	Montana**	NA
	District of Columbia	0.00

Source: Morgan Quitno Press using data from Federal Bureau of Investigation
   "Crime in the United States 1994" (Uniform Crime Reports, November 19, 1995)
Of the 21,992 murders in 1994 for which supplemental data were received by the F.B.I. There were an additional 1,313 murders for which the type of murder weapon was not reported to the F.B.I. Includes nonnegligent manslaughter.
**Not available.*

Rapes in 1994

National Total = 102,096 Rapes*

ALPHA ORDER					RANK ORDER			

RANK	STATE	RAPES	% of USA
24	Alabama	1,487	1.46%
39	Alaska	418	0.41%
25	Arizona	1,465	1.43%
30	Arkansas	1,028	1.01%
1	California	10,984	10.76%
23	Colorado	1,579	1.55%
34	Connecticut	806	0.79%
37	Delaware	534	0.52%
3	Florida	7,301	7.15%
12	Georgia	2,448	2.40%
42	Hawaii	359	0.35%
44	Idaho	316	0.31%
7	Illinois	3,913	3.83%
14	Indiana	2,046	2.00%
36	Iowa	666	0.65%
32	Kansas	947	0.93%
26	Kentucky	1,350	1.32%
19	Louisiana	1,923	1.88%
43	Maine	318	0.31%
15	Maryland	2,035	1.99%
21	Massachusetts	1,825	1.79%
4	Michigan	6,720	6.58%
10	Minnesota	2,725	2.67%
28	Mississippi	1,212	1.19%
18	Missouri	1,955	1.91%
47	Montana	233	0.23%
38	Nebraska	500	0.49%
31	Nevada	1,001	0.98%
40	New Hampshire	407	0.40%
17	New Jersey	1,972	1.93%
33	New Mexico	866	0.85%
6	New York	4,700	4.60%
13	North Carolina	2,334	2.29%
50	North Dakota	149	0.15%
5	Ohio	5,231	5.12%
22	Oklahoma	1,616	1.58%
27	Oregon	1,333	1.31%
9	Pennsylvania	3,145	3.08%
46	Rhode Island	273	0.27%
16	South Carolina	1,991	1.95%
45	South Dakota	303	0.30%
11	Tennessee	2,545	2.49%
2	Texas	9,102	8.92%
34	Utah	806	0.79%
48	Vermont	160	0.16%
20	Virginia	1,868	1.83%
8	Washington	3,230	3.16%
41	West Virginia	370	0.36%
29	Wisconsin	1,192	1.17%
48	Wyoming	160	0.16%

RANK	STATE	RAPES	% of USA
1	California	10,984	10.76%
2	Texas	9,102	8.92%
3	Florida	7,301	7.15%
4	Michigan	6,720	6.58%
5	Ohio	5,231	5.12%
6	New York	4,700	4.60%
7	Illinois	3,913	3.83%
8	Washington	3,230	3.16%
9	Pennsylvania	3,145	3.08%
10	Minnesota	2,725	2.67%
11	Tennessee	2,545	2.49%
12	Georgia	2,448	2.40%
13	North Carolina	2,334	2.29%
14	Indiana	2,046	2.00%
15	Maryland	2,035	1.99%
16	South Carolina	1,991	1.95%
17	New Jersey	1,972	1.93%
18	Missouri	1,955	1.91%
19	Louisiana	1,923	1.88%
20	Virginia	1,868	1.83%
21	Massachusetts	1,825	1.79%
22	Oklahoma	1,616	1.58%
23	Colorado	1,579	1.55%
24	Alabama	1,487	1.46%
25	Arizona	1,465	1.43%
26	Kentucky	1,350	1.32%
27	Oregon	1,333	1.31%
28	Mississippi	1,212	1.19%
29	Wisconsin	1,192	1.17%
30	Arkansas	1,028	1.01%
31	Nevada	1,001	0.98%
32	Kansas	947	0.93%
33	New Mexico	866	0.85%
34	Connecticut	806	0.79%
34	Utah	806	0.79%
36	Iowa	666	0.65%
37	Delaware	534	0.52%
38	Nebraska	500	0.49%
39	Alaska	418	0.41%
40	New Hampshire	407	0.40%
41	West Virginia	370	0.36%
42	Hawaii	359	0.35%
43	Maine	318	0.31%
44	Idaho	316	0.31%
45	South Dakota	303	0.30%
46	Rhode Island	273	0.27%
47	Montana	233	0.23%
48	Vermont	160	0.16%
48	Wyoming	160	0.16%
50	North Dakota	149	0.15%
	District of Columbia	249	0.24%

Source: Federal Bureau of Investigation
    "Crime in the United States 1994" (Uniform Crime Reports, November 19, 1995)
*Forcible rape is the carnal knowledge of a female forcibly and against her will. Assaults or attempts to commit rape by force or threat of force are included. However, statutory rape without force and other sex offenses are excluded.

Average Time Between Rapes in 1994

National Rate = A Rape Occurs Every 5 Minutes*

ALPHA ORDER				RANK ORDER		
RANK	STATE	HOURS.MINUTES		RANK	STATE	HOURS.MINUTES
27	Alabama	5.53		1	North Dakota	58.47
12	Alaska	20.58		2	Vermont	54.45
26	Arizona	5.59		2	Wyoming	54.45
21	Arkansas	8.31		4	Montana	37.36
50	California	0.48		5	Rhode Island	32.05
28	Colorado	5.33		6	South Dakota	28.55
16	Connecticut	10.52		7	Idaho	27.43
14	Delaware	16.24		8	Maine	27.33
48	Florida	1.12		9	Hawaii	24.24
39	Georgia	3.35		10	West Virginia	23.41
9	Hawaii	24.24		11	New Hampshire	21.31
7	Idaho	27.43		12	Alaska	20.58
44	Illinois	2.14		13	Nebraska	17.31
37	Indiana	4.17		14	Delaware	16.24
15	Iowa	13.09		15	Iowa	13.09
19	Kansas	9.15		16	Connecticut	10.52
25	Kentucky	6.29		16	Utah	10.52
32	Louisiana	4.34		18	New Mexico	10.07
8	Maine	27.33		19	Kansas	9.15
36	Maryland	4.18		20	Nevada	8.45
30	Massachusetts	4.48		21	Arkansas	8.31
47	Michigan	1.18		22	Wisconsin	7.21
41	Minnesota	3.13		23	Mississippi	7.14
23	Mississippi	7.14		24	Oregon	6.34
33	Missouri	4.29		25	Kentucky	6.29
4	Montana	37.36		26	Arizona	5.59
13	Nebraska	17.31		27	Alabama	5.53
20	Nevada	8.45		28	Colorado	5.33
11	New Hampshire	21.31		29	Oklahoma	5.25
34	New Jersey	4.26		30	Massachusetts	4.48
18	New Mexico	10.07		31	Virginia	4.41
45	New York	1.52		32	Louisiana	4.34
38	North Carolina	3.45		33	Missouri	4.29
1	North Dakota	58.47		34	New Jersey	4.26
46	Ohio	1.40		35	South Carolina	4.24
29	Oklahoma	5.25		36	Maryland	4.18
24	Oregon	6.34		37	Indiana	4.17
42	Pennsylvania	2.47		38	North Carolina	3.45
5	Rhode Island	32.05		39	Georgia	3.35
35	South Carolina	4.24		40	Tennessee	3.26
6	South Dakota	28.55		41	Minnesota	3.13
40	Tennessee	3.26		42	Pennsylvania	2.47
49	Texas	0.58		43	Washington	2.43
16	Utah	10.52		44	Illinois	2.14
2	Vermont	54.45		45	New York	1.52
31	Virginia	4.41		46	Ohio	1.40
43	Washington	2.43		47	Michigan	1.18
10	West Virginia	23.41		48	Florida	1.12
22	Wisconsin	7.21		49	Texas	0.58
2	Wyoming	54.45		50	California	0.48
					District of Columbia	35.11

Source: Morgan Quitno Press using data from Federal Bureau of Investigation
"Crime in the United States 1994" (Uniform Crime Reports, November 19, 1995)
*Forcible rape is the carnal knowledge of a female forcibly and against her will. Assaults or attempts to commit rape by force or threat of force are included. However, statutory rape without force and other sex offenses are excluded.

Percent Change in Number of Rapes: 1993 to 1994

National Percent Change = 3.7% Decrease*

ALPHA ORDER				RANK ORDER		
RANK	STATE	PERCENT CHANGE		RANK	STATE	PERCENT CHANGE
11	Alabama	1.1		1	Nevada	18.3
47	Alaska	(16.7)		2	Nebraska	11.9
22	Arizona	(1.5)		3	Mississippi	7.7
13	Arkansas	0.0		4	Louisiana	5.8
37	California	(6.6)		5	South Carolina	4.5
28	Colorado	(3.3)		6	Kentucky	3.8
12	Connecticut	0.8		7	Missouri	3.2
21	Delaware	(0.9)		8	New Mexico	2.9
20	Florida	(0.8)		9	Oklahoma	1.5
13	Georgia	0.0		10	West Virginia	1.4
42	Hawaii	(8.9)		11	Alabama	1.1
49	Idaho	(18.6)		12	Connecticut	0.8
28	Illinois	(3.3)		13	Arkansas	0.0
41	Indiana	(8.4)		13	Georgia	0.0
27	Iowa	(2.9)		13	North Dakota	0.0
38	Kansas	(6.8)		13	Tennessee	0.0
6	Kentucky	3.8		17	Michigan	(0.3)
4	Louisiana	5.8		18	Montana	(0.4)
28	Maine	(3.3)		19	Wyoming	(0.6)
39	Maryland	(6.9)		20	Florida	(0.8)
43	Massachusetts	(9.0)		21	Delaware	(0.9)
17	Michigan	(0.3)		22	Arizona	(1.5)
25	Minnesota	(2.5)		23	Pennsylvania	(1.6)
3	Mississippi	7.7		24	North Carolina	(1.9)
7	Missouri	3.2		25	Minnesota	(2.5)
18	Montana	(0.4)		26	Utah	(2.8)
2	Nebraska	11.9		27	Iowa	(2.9)
1	Nevada	18.3		28	Colorado	(3.3)
48	New Hampshire	(18.4)		28	Illinois	(3.3)
45	New Jersey	(11.0)		28	Maine	(3.3)
8	New Mexico	2.9		31	Ohio	(3.9)
36	New York	(6.2)		32	Rhode Island	(4.5)
24	North Carolina	(1.9)		33	Washington	(4.6)
13	North Dakota	0.0		34	South Dakota	(4.7)
31	Ohio	(3.9)		35	Wisconsin	(6.1)
9	Oklahoma	1.5		36	New York	(6.2)
46	Oregon	(14.2)		37	California	(6.6)
23	Pennsylvania	(1.6)		38	Kansas	(6.8)
32	Rhode Island	(4.5)		39	Maryland	(6.9)
5	South Carolina	4.5		40	Texas	(8.3)
34	South Dakota	(4.7)		41	Indiana	(8.4)
13	Tennessee	0.0		42	Hawaii	(8.9)
40	Texas	(8.3)		43	Massachusetts	(9.0)
26	Utah	(2.8)		44	Virginia	(10.3)
50	Vermont	(30.1)		45	New Jersey	(11.0)
44	Virginia	(10.3)		46	Oregon	(14.2)
33	Washington	(4.6)		47	Alaska	(16.7)
10	West Virginia	1.4		48	New Hampshire	(18.4)
35	Wisconsin	(6.1)		49	Idaho	(18.6)
19	Wyoming	(0.6)		50	Vermont	(30.1)
					District of Columbia	(23.1)

Source: Federal Bureau of Investigation
   "Crime in the United States 1994" (Uniform Crime Reports, November 19, 1995)
*Forcible rape is the carnal knowledge of a female forcibly and against her will. Assaults or attempts to commit rape by force or threat of force are included. However, statutory rape without force and other sex offenses are excluded.

Rape Rate in 1994

National Rate = 39.2 Rapes per 100,000 Population*

ALPHA ORDER

RANK	STATE	RAPES
28	Alabama	35.2
3	Alaska	69.0
24	Arizona	36.0
20	Arkansas	41.9
29	California	34.9
16	Colorado	43.2
46	Connecticut	24.6
1	Delaware	75.6
9	Florida	52.3
30	Georgia	34.7
35	Hawaii	30.4
38	Idaho	27.9
32	Illinois	33.3
26	Indiana	35.6
47	Iowa	23.5
22	Kansas	37.1
27	Kentucky	35.3
15	Louisiana	44.6
44	Maine	25.6
21	Maryland	40.7
36	Massachusetts	30.2
2	Michigan	70.8
6	Minnesota	59.7
14	Mississippi	45.4
23	Missouri	37.0
41	Montana	27.2
34	Nebraska	30.8
4	Nevada	68.7
25	New Hampshire	35.8
45	New Jersey	24.9
8	New Mexico	52.4
43	New York	25.9
33	North Carolina	33.0
49	North Dakota	23.4
13	Ohio	47.1
10	Oklahoma	49.6
16	Oregon	43.2
42	Pennsylvania	26.1
40	Rhode Island	27.4
7	South Carolina	54.3
19	South Dakota	42.0
12	Tennessee	49.2
11	Texas	49.5
18	Utah	42.2
39	Vermont	27.6
37	Virginia	28.5
5	Washington	60.5
50	West Virginia	20.3
47	Wisconsin	23.5
31	Wyoming	33.6

RANK ORDER

RANK	STATE	RAPES
1	Delaware	75.6
2	Michigan	70.8
3	Alaska	69.0
4	Nevada	68.7
5	Washington	60.5
6	Minnesota	59.7
7	South Carolina	54.3
8	New Mexico	52.4
9	Florida	52.3
10	Oklahoma	49.6
11	Texas	49.5
12	Tennessee	49.2
13	Ohio	47.1
14	Mississippi	45.4
15	Louisiana	44.6
16	Colorado	43.2
16	Oregon	43.2
18	Utah	42.2
19	South Dakota	42.0
20	Arkansas	41.9
21	Maryland	40.7
22	Kansas	37.1
23	Missouri	37.0
24	Arizona	36.0
25	New Hampshire	35.8
26	Indiana	35.6
27	Kentucky	35.3
28	Alabama	35.2
29	California	34.9
30	Georgia	34.7
31	Wyoming	33.6
32	Illinois	33.3
33	North Carolina	33.0
34	Nebraska	30.8
35	Hawaii	30.4
36	Massachusetts	30.2
37	Virginia	28.5
38	Idaho	27.9
39	Vermont	27.6
40	Rhode Island	27.4
41	Montana	27.2
42	Pennsylvania	26.1
43	New York	25.9
44	Maine	25.6
45	New Jersey	24.9
46	Connecticut	24.6
47	Iowa	23.5
47	Wisconsin	23.5
49	North Dakota	23.4
50	West Virginia	20.3

District of Columbia   43.7

Source: Federal Bureau of Investigation
     "Crime in the United States 1994" (Uniform Crime Reports, November 19, 1995)
*Forcible rape is the carnal knowledge of a female forcibly and against her will. Assaults or attempts to commit rape by force or threat of force are included. However, statutory rape without force and other sex offenses are excluded.

Percent Change in Rape Rate: 1993 to 1994

National Percent Change = 4.6% Decrease*

ALPHA ORDER				RANK ORDER		
RANK	STATE	PERCENT CHANGE		RANK	STATE	PERCENT CHANGE
12	Alabama	0.3		1	Nevada	12.8
47	Alaska	(17.7)		2	Nebraska	10.8
30	Arizona	(4.8)		3	Mississippi	6.6
15	Arkansas	(1.2)		4	Louisiana	5.4
37	California	(7.4)		5	South Carolina	3.8
33	Colorado	(5.7)		6	Kentucky	2.9
9	Connecticut	0.8		7	Missouri	2.2
18	Delaware	(1.8)		8	West Virginia	1.0
22	Florida	(2.8)		9	Connecticut	0.8
19	Georgia	(2.0)		10	New Mexico	0.6
41	Hawaii	(9.5)		10	Oklahoma	0.6
49	Idaho	(21.0)		12	Alabama	0.3
25	Illinois	(3.8)		13	Michigan	(0.4)
40	Indiana	(9.0)		13	North Dakota	(0.4)
24	Iowa	(3.7)		15	Arkansas	(1.2)
38	Kansas	(7.5)		16	Tennessee	(1.4)
6	Kentucky	2.9		17	Pennsylvania	(1.5)
4	Louisiana	5.4		18	Delaware	(1.8)
25	Maine	(3.8)		19	Georgia	(2.0)
38	Maryland	(7.5)		19	Wyoming	(2.0)
42	Massachusetts	(9.6)		21	Montana	(2.5)
13	Michigan	(0.4)		22	Florida	(2.8)
23	Minnesota	(3.6)		23	Minnesota	(3.6)
3	Mississippi	6.6		24	Iowa	(3.7)
7	Missouri	2.2		25	Illinois	(3.8)
21	Montana	(2.5)		25	Maine	(3.8)
2	Nebraska	10.8		25	North Carolina	(3.8)
1	Nevada	12.8		28	Ohio	(4.1)
48	New Hampshire	(19.4)		29	Rhode Island	(4.2)
45	New Jersey	(11.4)		30	Arizona	(4.8)
10	New Mexico	0.6		31	Utah	(5.4)
34	New York	(5.8)		32	South Dakota	(5.6)
25	North Carolina	(3.8)		33	Colorado	(5.7)
13	North Dakota	(0.4)		34	New York	(5.8)
28	Ohio	(4.1)		35	Washington	(6.1)
10	Oklahoma	0.6		36	Wisconsin	(6.7)
46	Oregon	(15.8)		37	California	(7.4)
17	Pennsylvania	(1.5)		38	Kansas	(7.5)
29	Rhode Island	(4.2)		38	Maryland	(7.5)
5	South Carolina	3.8		40	Indiana	(9.0)
32	South Dakota	(5.6)		41	Hawaii	(9.5)
16	Tennessee	(1.4)		42	Massachusetts	(9.6)
43	Texas	(10.0)		43	Texas	(10.0)
31	Utah	(5.4)		44	Virginia	(11.2)
50	Vermont	(30.7)		45	New Jersey	(11.4)
44	Virginia	(11.2)		46	Oregon	(15.8)
35	Washington	(6.1)		47	Alaska	(17.7)
8	West Virginia	1.0		48	New Hampshire	(19.4)
36	Wisconsin	(6.7)		49	Idaho	(21.0)
19	Wyoming	(2.0)		50	Vermont	(30.7)
					District of Columbia	(22.1)

Source: Federal Bureau of Investigation
   "Crime in the United States 1994" (Uniform Crime Reports, November 19, 1995)
*Forcible rape is the carnal knowledge of a female forcibly and against her will. Assaults or attempts to commit rape by force or threat of force are included. However, statutory rape without force and other sex offenses are excluded.

345

Rape Rate per 100,000 Female Population in 1994

National Rate = 76.6 Rapes per 100,000 Females*

ALPHA ORDER				RANK ORDER		
RANK	STATE	RATE		RANK	STATE	RATE
29	Alabama	67.7		1	Delaware	147.2
2	Alaska	145.8		2	Alaska	145.8
24	Arizona	71.1		3	Nevada	139.9
20	Arkansas	81.0		4	Michigan	137.7
26	California	69.9		5	Washington	120.0
16	Colorado	85.6		6	Minnesota	117.4
46	Connecticut	47.7		7	South Carolina	105.1
1	Delaware	147.2		8	New Mexico	103.2
9	Florida	101.5		9	Florida	101.5
31	Georgia	67.5		10	Texas	97.7
34	Hawaii	61.7		11	Oklahoma	96.8
38	Idaho	55.6		12	Tennessee	94.9
32	Illinois	64.8		13	Ohio	91.1
27	Indiana	69.2		14	Mississippi	87.2
49	Iowa	45.8		15	Louisiana	85.9
22	Kansas	72.9		16	Colorado	85.6
28	Kentucky	68.5		17	Oregon	85.2
15	Louisiana	85.9		18	Utah	84.0
43	Maine	50.0		19	South Dakota	82.8
21	Maryland	79.0		20	Arkansas	81.0
36	Massachusetts	58.2		21	Maryland	79.0
4	Michigan	137.7		22	Kansas	72.9
6	Minnesota	117.4		23	Missouri	71.6
14	Mississippi	87.2		24	Arizona	71.1
23	Missouri	71.6		25	New Hampshire	70.3
40	Montana	54.1		26	California	69.9
35	Nebraska	60.2		27	Indiana	69.2
3	Nevada	139.9		28	Kentucky	68.5
25	New Hampshire	70.3		29	Alabama	67.7
45	New Jersey	48.3		30	Wyoming	67.6
8	New Mexico	103.2		31	Georgia	67.5
44	New York	49.8		32	Illinois	64.8
33	North Carolina	64.1		33	North Carolina	64.1
47	North Dakota	46.5		34	Hawaii	61.7
13	Ohio	91.1		35	Nebraska	60.2
11	Oklahoma	96.8		36	Massachusetts	58.2
17	Oregon	85.2		37	Virginia	55.9
42	Pennsylvania	50.2		38	Idaho	55.6
41	Rhode Island	52.7		39	Vermont	54.2
7	South Carolina	105.1		40	Montana	54.1
19	South Dakota	82.8		41	Rhode Island	52.7
12	Tennessee	94.9		42	Pennsylvania	50.2
10	Texas	97.7		43	Maine	50.0
18	Utah	84.0		44	New York	49.8
39	Vermont	54.2		45	New Jersey	48.3
37	Virginia	55.9		46	Connecticut	47.7
5	Washington	120.0		47	North Dakota	46.5
50	West Virginia	39.2		48	Wisconsin	46.0
48	Wisconsin	46.0		49	Iowa	45.8
30	Wyoming	67.6		50	West Virginia	39.2
					District of Columbia	81.9

Source: Morgan Quitno Press using data from Federal Bureau of Investigation
   "Crime in the United States 1994" (Uniform Crime Reports, November 19, 1995)
*Forcible rape is the carnal knowledge of a female forcibly and against her will. Assaults or attempts to commit rape by force or threat of force are included. However, statutory rape without force and other sex offenses are excluded.

Robberies in 1994

National Total = 618,817 Robberies*

ALPHA ORDER

RANK	STATE	ROBBERIES	% of USA
20	Alabama	7,223	1.17%
40	Alaska	886	0.14%
22	Arizona	6,601	1.07%
32	Arkansas	3,158	0.51%
1	California	112,160	18.12%
30	Colorado	3,910	0.63%
23	Connecticut	6,150	0.99%
39	Delaware	889	0.14%
3	Florida	45,871	7.41%
11	Georgia	15,703	2.54%
37	Hawaii	1,221	0.20%
46	Idaho	209	0.03%
4	Illinois	43,788	7.08%
18	Indiana	7,490	1.21%
35	Iowa	1,327	0.21%
33	Kansas	3,060	0.49%
31	Kentucky	3,595	0.58%
14	Louisiana	11,530	1.86%
45	Maine	278	0.04%
10	Maryland	20,147	3.26%
16	Massachusetts	10,160	1.64%
8	Michigan	21,733	3.51%
25	Minnesota	5,370	0.87%
27	Mississippi	4,336	0.70%
13	Missouri	12,178	1.97%
44	Montana	280	0.05%
36	Nebraska	1,223	0.20%
26	Nevada	5,134	0.83%
43	New Hampshire	308	0.05%
6	New Jersey	22,762	3.68%
34	New Mexico	2,329	0.38%
2	New York	86,617	14.00%
12	North Carolina	12,811	2.07%
49	North Dakota	71	0.01%
9	Ohio	20,821	3.36%
29	Oklahoma	4,174	0.67%
28	Oregon	4,264	0.69%
7	Pennsylvania	22,497	3.64%
41	Rhode Island	870	0.14%
21	South Carolina	6,817	1.10%
47	South Dakota	135	0.02%
15	Tennessee	10,735	1.73%
5	Texas	37,643	6.08%
38	Utah	1,213	0.20%
49	Vermont	71	0.01%
17	Virginia	8,704	1.41%
19	Washington	7,464	1.21%
42	West Virginia	772	0.12%
24	Wisconsin	5,739	0.93%
48	Wyoming	79	0.01%

RANK ORDER

RANK	STATE	ROBBERIES	% of USA
1	California	112,160	18.12%
2	New York	86,617	14.00%
3	Florida	45,871	7.41%
4	Illinois	43,788	7.08%
5	Texas	37,643	6.08%
6	New Jersey	22,762	3.68%
7	Pennsylvania	22,497	3.64%
8	Michigan	21,733	3.51%
9	Ohio	20,821	3.36%
10	Maryland	20,147	3.26%
11	Georgia	15,703	2.54%
12	North Carolina	12,811	2.07%
13	Missouri	12,178	1.97%
14	Louisiana	11,530	1.86%
15	Tennessee	10,735	1.73%
16	Massachusetts	10,160	1.64%
17	Virginia	8,704	1.41%
18	Indiana	7,490	1.21%
19	Washington	7,464	1.21%
20	Alabama	7,223	1.17%
21	South Carolina	6,817	1.10%
22	Arizona	6,601	1.07%
23	Connecticut	6,150	0.99%
24	Wisconsin	5,739	0.93%
25	Minnesota	5,370	0.87%
26	Nevada	5,134	0.83%
27	Mississippi	4,336	0.70%
28	Oregon	4,264	0.69%
29	Oklahoma	4,174	0.67%
30	Colorado	3,910	0.63%
31	Kentucky	3,595	0.58%
32	Arkansas	3,158	0.51%
33	Kansas	3,060	0.49%
34	New Mexico	2,329	0.38%
35	Iowa	1,327	0.21%
36	Nebraska	1,223	0.20%
37	Hawaii	1,221	0.20%
38	Utah	1,213	0.20%
39	Delaware	889	0.14%
40	Alaska	886	0.14%
41	Rhode Island	870	0.14%
42	West Virginia	772	0.12%
43	New Hampshire	308	0.05%
44	Montana	280	0.05%
45	Maine	278	0.04%
46	Idaho	209	0.03%
47	South Dakota	135	0.02%
48	Wyoming	79	0.01%
49	North Dakota	71	0.01%
49	Vermont	71	0.01%
	District of Columbia	6,311	1.02%

Source: Federal Bureau of Investigation
   "Crime in the United States 1994" (Uniform Crime Reports, November 19, 1995)
   *Robbery is the taking or attempting to take anything of value by force or threat of force.

Average Time Between Robberies in 1994

National Rate = A Robbery Occurs Every 51 Seconds*

ALPHA ORDER				RANK ORDER		
RANK	STATE	HOURS.MINUTES		RANK	STATE	HOURS.MINUTES
31	Alabama	1.13		1	North Dakota	123.23
11	Alaska	9.53		1	Vermont	123.23
29	Arizona	1.20		3	Wyoming	110.53
19	Arkansas	2.46		4	South Dakota	64.53
50	California	0.05		5	Idaho	41.55
21	Colorado	2.14		6	Maine	31.31
28	Connecticut	1.25		7	Montana	31.17
12	Delaware	9.51		8	New Hampshire	28.26
48	Florida	0.11		9	West Virginia	11.21
40	Georgia	0.34		10	Rhode Island	10.04
14	Hawaii	7.10		11	Alaska	9.53
5	Idaho	41.55		12	Delaware	9.51
47	Illinois	0.12		13	Utah	7.13
32	Indiana	1.10		14	Hawaii	7.10
16	Iowa	6.36		14	Nebraska	7.10
18	Kansas	2.52		16	Iowa	6.36
20	Kentucky	2.26		17	New Mexico	3.46
37	Louisiana	0.46		18	Kansas	2.52
6	Maine	31.31		19	Arkansas	2.46
41	Maryland	0.26		20	Kentucky	2.26
35	Massachusetts	0.52		21	Colorado	2.14
43	Michigan	0.24		22	Oklahoma	2.06
26	Minnesota	1.38		23	Oregon	2.03
24	Mississippi	2.01		24	Mississippi	2.01
38	Missouri	0.43		25	Nevada	1.43
7	Montana	31.17		26	Minnesota	1.38
14	Nebraska	7.10		27	Wisconsin	1.32
25	Nevada	1.43		28	Connecticut	1.25
8	New Hampshire	28.26		29	Arizona	1.20
44	New Jersey	0.23		30	South Carolina	1.17
17	New Mexico	3.46		31	Alabama	1.13
49	New York	0.06		32	Indiana	1.10
39	North Carolina	0.41		32	Washington	1.10
1	North Dakota	123.23		34	Virginia	1.01
42	Ohio	0.25		35	Massachusetts	0.52
22	Oklahoma	2.06		36	Tennessee	0.49
23	Oregon	2.03		37	Louisiana	0.46
44	Pennsylvania	0.23		38	Missouri	0.43
10	Rhode Island	10.04		39	North Carolina	0.41
30	South Carolina	1.17		40	Georgia	0.34
4	South Dakota	64.53		41	Maryland	0.26
36	Tennessee	0.49		42	Ohio	0.25
46	Texas	0.14		43	Michigan	0.24
13	Utah	7.13		44	New Jersey	0.23
1	Vermont	123.23		44	Pennsylvania	0.23
34	Virginia	1.01		46	Texas	0.14
32	Washington	1.10		47	Illinois	0.12
9	West Virginia	11.21		48	Florida	0.11
27	Wisconsin	1.32		49	New York	0.06
3	Wyoming	110.53		50	California	0.05
					District of Columbia	1.23

Source: Morgan Quitno Press using data from Federal Bureau of Investigation
   "Crime in the United States 1994" (Uniform Crime Reports, November 19, 1995)
*Robbery is the taking or attempting to take anything of value by force or threat of force.

Percent Change in Number of Robberies: 1993 to 1994

National Percent Change = 6.2% Decrease*

ALPHA ORDER

RANK	STATE	PERCENT CHANGE
12	Alabama	8.2
5	Alaska	20.9
21	Arizona	2.9
17	Arkansas	4.3
46	California	(11.3)
41	Colorado	(6.0)
38	Connecticut	(4.6)
50	Delaware	(32.0)
42	Florida	(6.2)
45	Georgia	(8.5)
23	Hawaii	0.6
7	Idaho	12.4
28	Illinois	(1.8)
9	Indiana	9.4
47	Iowa	(12.5)
29	Kansas	(2.2)
16	Kentucky	5.0
39	Louisiana	(5.4)
15	Maine	5.3
43	Maryland	(6.6)
33	Massachusetts	(3.8)
33	Michigan	(3.8)
14	Minnesota	5.5
6	Mississippi	17.7
33	Missouri	(3.8)
21	Montana	2.9
4	Nebraska	21.9
10	Nevada	8.7
25	New Hampshire	0.3
30	New Jersey	(2.4)
19	New Mexico	4.1
49	New York	(15.2)
36	North Carolina	(4.1)
2	North Dakota	34.0
32	Ohio	(2.6)
13	Oklahoma	6.1
11	Oregon	8.5
17	Pennsylvania	4.3
48	Rhode Island	(13.9)
26	South Carolina	(0.1)
3	South Dakota	26.2
37	Tennessee	(4.4)
44	Texas	(7.0)
8	Utah	11.3
1	Vermont	36.5
40	Virginia	(5.6)
20	Washington	3.6
27	West Virginia	(1.3)
24	Wisconsin	0.4
31	Wyoming	(2.5)

RANK ORDER

RANK	STATE	PERCENT CHANGE
1	Vermont	36.5
2	North Dakota	34.0
3	South Dakota	26.2
4	Nebraska	21.9
5	Alaska	20.9
6	Mississippi	17.7
7	Idaho	12.4
8	Utah	11.3
9	Indiana	9.4
10	Nevada	8.7
11	Oregon	8.5
12	Alabama	8.2
13	Oklahoma	6.1
14	Minnesota	5.5
15	Maine	5.3
16	Kentucky	5.0
17	Arkansas	4.3
17	Pennsylvania	4.3
19	New Mexico	4.1
20	Washington	3.6
21	Arizona	2.9
21	Montana	2.9
23	Hawaii	0.6
24	Wisconsin	0.4
25	New Hampshire	0.3
26	South Carolina	(0.1)
27	West Virginia	(1.3)
28	Illinois	(1.8)
29	Kansas	(2.2)
30	New Jersey	(2.4)
31	Wyoming	(2.5)
32	Ohio	(2.6)
33	Massachusetts	(3.8)
33	Michigan	(3.8)
33	Missouri	(3.8)
36	North Carolina	(4.1)
37	Tennessee	(4.4)
38	Connecticut	(4.6)
39	Louisiana	(5.4)
40	Virginia	(5.6)
41	Colorado	(6.0)
42	Florida	(6.2)
43	Maryland	(6.6)
44	Texas	(7.0)
45	Georgia	(8.5)
46	California	(11.3)
47	Iowa	(12.5)
48	Rhode Island	(13.9)
49	New York	(15.2)
50	Delaware	(32.0)
	District of Columbia	(11.2)

Source: Federal Bureau of Investigation
"Crime in the United States 1994" (Uniform Crime Reports, November 19, 1995)
Robbery is the taking or attempting to take anything of value by force or threat of force.

Robbery Rate in 1994

National Rate = 237.7 Robberies per 100,000 Population*

ALPHA ORDER

RANK	STATE	RATE
19	Alabama	171.2
23	Alaska	146.2
22	Arizona	162.0
29	Arkansas	128.7
4	California	356.8
35	Colorado	106.9
14	Connecticut	187.8
31	Delaware	125.9
6	Florida	328.8
11	Georgia	222.6
36	Hawaii	103.6
47	Idaho	18.4
3	Illinois	372.6
28	Indiana	130.2
41	Iowa	46.9
32	Kansas	119.8
37	Kentucky	93.9
8	Louisiana	267.2
45	Maine	22.4
2	Maryland	402.5
20	Massachusetts	168.2
10	Michigan	228.9
33	Minnesota	117.6
21	Mississippi	162.5
9	Missouri	230.7
43	Montana	32.7
39	Nebraska	75.4
5	Nevada	352.4
44	New Hampshire	27.1
7	New Jersey	288.0
24	New Mexico	140.8
1	New York	476.7
18	North Carolina	181.2
50	North Dakota	11.1
15	Ohio	187.5
30	Oklahoma	128.1
26	Oregon	138.2
16	Pennsylvania	186.7
38	Rhode Island	87.3
17	South Carolina	186.1
46	South Dakota	18.7
12	Tennessee	207.4
13	Texas	204.8
40	Utah	63.6
49	Vermont	12.2
27	Virginia	132.8
25	Washington	139.7
42	West Virginia	42.4
34	Wisconsin	112.9
48	Wyoming	16.6

RANK ORDER

RANK	STATE	RATE
1	New York	476.7
2	Maryland	402.5
3	Illinois	372.6
4	California	356.8
5	Nevada	352.4
6	Florida	328.8
7	New Jersey	288.0
8	Louisiana	267.2
9	Missouri	230.7
10	Michigan	228.9
11	Georgia	222.6
12	Tennessee	207.4
13	Texas	204.8
14	Connecticut	187.8
15	Ohio	187.5
16	Pennsylvania	186.7
17	South Carolina	186.1
18	North Carolina	181.2
19	Alabama	171.2
20	Massachusetts	168.2
21	Mississippi	162.5
22	Arizona	162.0
23	Alaska	146.2
24	New Mexico	140.8
25	Washington	139.7
26	Oregon	138.2
27	Virginia	132.8
28	Indiana	130.2
29	Arkansas	128.7
30	Oklahoma	128.1
31	Delaware	125.9
32	Kansas	119.8
33	Minnesota	117.6
34	Wisconsin	112.9
35	Colorado	106.9
36	Hawaii	103.6
37	Kentucky	93.9
38	Rhode Island	87.3
39	Nebraska	75.4
40	Utah	63.6
41	Iowa	46.9
42	West Virginia	42.4
43	Montana	32.7
44	New Hampshire	27.1
45	Maine	22.4
46	South Dakota	18.7
47	Idaho	18.4
48	Wyoming	16.6
49	Vermont	12.2
50	North Dakota	11.1
	District of Columbia	1,107.2

Source: Federal Bureau of Investigation
   "Crime in the United States 1994" (Uniform Crime Reports, November 19, 1995)
*Robbery is the taking or attempting to take anything of value by force or threat of force.

Percent Change in Robbery Rate: 1993 to 1994

National Percent Change = 7.1% Decrease*

ALPHA ORDER

RANK ORDER

RANK	STATE	PERCENT CHANGE		RANK	STATE	PERCENT CHANGE
10	Alabama	7.3		1	Vermont	35.6
5	Alaska	19.4		2	North Dakota	33.7
24	Arizona	(0.6)		3	South Dakota	24.7
18	Arkansas	3.0		4	Nebraska	20.8
46	California	(11.9)		5	Alaska	19.4
43	Colorado	(8.4)		6	Mississippi	16.7
35	Connecticut	(4.5)		7	Idaho	8.9
50	Delaware	(32.6)		8	Indiana	8.7
42	Florida	(8.1)		9	Utah	8.5
45	Georgia	(10.2)		10	Alabama	7.3
22	Hawaii	0.0		11	Oregon	6.6
7	Idaho	8.9		12	Maine	5.2
28	Illinois	(2.3)		12	Oklahoma	5.2
8	Indiana	8.7		14	Minnesota	4.3
47	Iowa	(13.0)		14	Pennsylvania	4.3
31	Kansas	(3.1)		16	Kentucky	3.9
16	Kentucky	3.9		17	Nevada	3.6
37	Louisiana	(5.8)		18	Arkansas	3.0
12	Maine	5.2		19	Washington	1.9
41	Maryland	(7.4)		20	New Mexico	1.7
34	Massachusetts	(4.3)		21	Montana	0.9
33	Michigan	(4.0)		22	Hawaii	0.0
14	Minnesota	4.3		23	Wisconsin	(0.4)
6	Mississippi	16.7		24	Arizona	(0.6)
36	Missouri	(4.6)		24	South Carolina	(0.6)
21	Montana	0.9		26	New Hampshire	(0.7)
4	Nebraska	20.8		27	West Virginia	(1.4)
17	Nevada	3.6		28	Illinois	(2.3)
26	New Hampshire	(0.7)		29	New Jersey	(2.7)
29	New Jersey	(2.7)		29	Ohio	(2.7)
20	New Mexico	1.7		31	Kansas	(3.1)
49	New York	(15.1)		32	Wyoming	(3.5)
37	North Carolina	(5.8)		33	Michigan	(4.0)
2	North Dakota	33.7		34	Massachusetts	(4.3)
29	Ohio	(2.7)		35	Connecticut	(4.5)
12	Oklahoma	5.2		36	Missouri	(4.6)
11	Oregon	6.6		37	Louisiana	(5.8)
14	Pennsylvania	4.3		37	North Carolina	(5.8)
48	Rhode Island	(13.6)		37	Tennessee	(5.8)
24	South Carolina	(0.6)		40	Virginia	(6.5)
3	South Dakota	24.7		41	Maryland	(7.4)
37	Tennessee	(5.8)		42	Florida	(8.1)
44	Texas	(8.7)		43	Colorado	(8.4)
9	Utah	8.5		44	Texas	(8.7)
1	Vermont	35.6		45	Georgia	(10.2)
40	Virginia	(6.5)		46	California	(11.9)
19	Washington	1.9		47	Iowa	(13.0)
27	West Virginia	(1.4)		48	Rhode Island	(13.6)
23	Wisconsin	(0.4)		49	New York	(15.1)
32	Wyoming	(3.5)		50	Delaware	(32.6)
					District of Columbia	(10.0)

Source: Federal Bureau of Investigation
   "Crime in the United States 1994" (Uniform Crime Reports, November 19, 1995)
*Robbery is the taking or attempting to take anything of value by force or threat of force.

Robberies with Firearms in 1994

National Total = 242,493 Robberies*

ALPHA ORDER

RANK	STATE	ROBBERIES	% of USA
32	Alabama	1,087	0.45%
35	Alaska	346	0.14%
20	Arizona	2,604	1.07%
27	Arkansas	1,623	0.67%
1	California	44,471	18.34%
30	Colorado	1,240	0.51%
24	Connecticut	2,359	0.97%
41	Delaware	79	0.03%
3	Florida	18,314	7.55%
11	Georgia	7,396	3.05%
39	Hawaii	161	0.07%
44	Idaho	62	0.03%
5	Illinois	16,188	6.68%
18	Indiana	3,026	1.25%
36	Iowa	295	0.12%
NA	Kansas**	NA	NA
29	Kentucky	1,373	0.57%
12	Louisiana	6,704	2.76%
42	Maine	72	0.03%
6	Maryland	10,865	4.48%
23	Massachusetts	2,425	1.00%
7	Michigan	10,667	4.40%
31	Minnesota	1,231	0.51%
26	Mississippi	1,665	0.69%
13	Missouri	5,766	2.38%
NA	Montana**	NA	NA
34	Nebraska	438	0.18%
19	Nevada	2,611	1.08%
43	New Hampshire	63	0.03%
10	New Jersey	7,675	3.17%
40	New Mexico	116	0.05%
2	New York	29,984	12.36%
14	North Carolina	5,470	2.26%
47	North Dakota	7	0.00%
9	Ohio	7,958	3.28%
25	Oklahoma	1,681	0.69%
28	Oregon	1,507	0.62%
8	Pennsylvania	9,066	3.74%
38	Rhode Island	232	0.10%
21	South Carolina	2,575	1.06%
45	South Dakota	36	0.01%
15	Tennessee	5,369	2.21%
4	Texas	17,400	7.18%
33	Utah	448	0.18%
48	Vermont	6	0.00%
16	Virginia	3,961	1.63%
22	Washington	2,475	1.02%
37	West Virginia	259	0.11%
17	Wisconsin	3,123	1.29%
46	Wyoming	14	0.01%

RANK ORDER

RANK	STATE	ROBBERIES	% of USA
1	California	44,471	18.34%
2	New York	29,984	12.36%
3	Florida	18,314	7.55%
4	Texas	17,400	7.18%
5	Illinois	16,188	6.68%
6	Maryland	10,865	4.48%
7	Michigan	10,667	4.40%
8	Pennsylvania	9,066	3.74%
9	Ohio	7,958	3.28%
10	New Jersey	7,675	3.17%
11	Georgia	7,396	3.05%
12	Louisiana	6,704	2.76%
13	Missouri	5,766	2.38%
14	North Carolina	5,470	2.26%
15	Tennessee	5,369	2.21%
16	Virginia	3,961	1.63%
17	Wisconsin	3,123	1.29%
18	Indiana	3,026	1.25%
19	Nevada	2,611	1.08%
20	Arizona	2,604	1.07%
21	South Carolina	2,575	1.06%
22	Washington	2,475	1.02%
23	Massachusetts	2,425	1.00%
24	Connecticut	2,359	0.97%
25	Oklahoma	1,681	0.69%
26	Mississippi	1,665	0.69%
27	Arkansas	1,623	0.67%
28	Oregon	1,507	0.62%
29	Kentucky	1,373	0.57%
30	Colorado	1,240	0.51%
31	Minnesota	1,231	0.51%
32	Alabama	1,087	0.45%
33	Utah	448	0.18%
34	Nebraska	438	0.18%
35	Alaska	346	0.14%
36	Iowa	295	0.12%
37	West Virginia	259	0.11%
38	Rhode Island	232	0.10%
39	Hawaii	161	0.07%
40	New Mexico	116	0.05%
41	Delaware	79	0.03%
42	Maine	72	0.03%
43	New Hampshire	63	0.03%
44	Idaho	62	0.03%
45	South Dakota	36	0.01%
46	Wyoming	14	0.01%
47	North Dakota	7	0.00%
48	Vermont	6	0.00%
NA	Kansas**	NA	NA
NA	Montana**	NA	NA
	District of Columbia**	NA	NA

Source: Federal Bureau of Investigation
   "Crime in the United States 1994" (Uniform Crime Reports, November 19, 1995)
*Of the 590,370 robberies in 1994 for which supplemental data were received by the F.B.I. There were an additional 28,447 robberies for which the type of weapon was not reported to the F.B.I. Robbery is the taking or attempting to take anything of value by force or threat of force.
**Not available.

Robbery Rate with Firearms in 1994

National Rate = 109.7 Robberies per 100,000 Population*

ALPHA ORDER			RANK ORDER		
RANK	STATE	RATE	RANK	STATE	RATE
13	Alabama	113.1	1	Illinois	325.8
26	Alaska	59.8	2	Maryland	217.1
23	Arizona	66.6	3	Nevada	182.7
22	Arkansas	67.0	3	New York	182.7
8	California	141.6	5	Louisiana	180.7
31	Colorado	47.3	6	Mississippi	155.2
18	Connecticut	84.8	7	Tennessee	155.1
38	Delaware	20.8	8	California	141.6
10	Florida	136.3	9	Missouri	137.4
12	Georgia	132.9	10	Florida	136.3
40	Hawaii	13.7	11	Michigan	133.7
46	Idaho	5.6	12	Georgia	132.9
1	Illinois	325.8	13	Alabama	113.1
19	Indiana	81.9	14	Ohio	101.6
42	Iowa	12.7	15	New Jersey	97.1
NA	Kansas**	NA	16	Pennsylvania	96.4
32	Kentucky	36.5	17	Texas	94.9
5	Louisiana	180.7	18	Connecticut	84.8
45	Maine	6.0	19	Indiana	81.9
2	Maryland	217.1	20	North Carolina	79.9
29	Massachusetts	48.4	21	South Carolina	70.8
11	Michigan	133.7	22	Arkansas	67.0
34	Minnesota	27.5	23	Arizona	66.6
6	Mississippi	155.2	24	Wisconsin	62.1
9	Missouri	137.4	25	Virginia	61.0
NA	Montana**	NA	26	Alaska	59.8
33	Nebraska	28.1	27	Oklahoma	51.7
3	Nevada	182.7	28	Oregon	49.5
44	New Hampshire	7.6	29	Massachusetts	48.4
15	New Jersey	97.1	30	Washington	47.8
37	New Mexico	21.2	31	Colorado	47.3
3	New York	182.7	32	Kentucky	36.5
20	North Carolina	79.9	33	Nebraska	28.1
48	North Dakota	1.2	34	Minnesota	27.5
14	Ohio	101.6	35	Utah	24.9
27	Oklahoma	51.7	36	Rhode Island	23.3
28	Oregon	49.5	37	New Mexico	21.2
16	Pennsylvania	96.4	38	Delaware	20.8
36	Rhode Island	23.3	39	West Virginia	14.2
21	South Carolina	70.8	40	Hawaii	13.7
43	South Dakota	8.0	41	Vermont	13.3
7	Tennessee	155.1	42	Iowa	12.7
17	Texas	94.9	43	South Dakota	8.0
35	Utah	24.9	44	New Hampshire	7.6
41	Vermont	13.3	45	Maine	6.0
25	Virginia	61.0	46	Idaho	5.6
30	Washington	47.8	47	Wyoming	3.0
39	West Virginia	14.2	48	North Dakota	1.2
24	Wisconsin	62.1	NA	Kansas**	NA
47	Wyoming	3.0	NA	Montana**	NA
				District of Columbia**	NA

Source: Morgan Quitno Press using data from Federal Bureau of Investigation
"Crime in the United States 1994" (Uniform Crime Reports, November 19, 1995)
*Of the 590,370 robberies in 1994 for which supplemental data were received by the F.B.I. There were an additional 28,447 robberies for which the type of weapon was not reported to the F.B.I. Robbery is the taking or attempting to take anything of value by force or threat of force. Revised figures using only population of reporting jurisdictions. Illinois' rate is especially affected by number of nonreporting jurisdictions. **Not available.

Percent of Robberies Involving Firearms in 1994

National Percent = 41.52% of Robberies*

ALPHA ORDER

RANK	STATE	PERCENT
43	Alabama	25.24
21	Alaska	39.95
20	Arizona	40.23
6	Arkansas	51.61
22	California	39.66
30	Colorado	35.26
24	Connecticut	38.36
32	Delaware	34.50
18	Florida	41.03
7	Georgia	51.50
47	Hawaii	13.19
36	Idaho	29.95
15	Illinois	43.85
11	Indiana	46.63
39	Iowa	27.80
NA	Kansas**	NA
23	Kentucky	38.75
1	Louisiana	60.54
41	Maine	25.99
3	Maryland	53.94
42	Massachusetts	25.37
8	Michigan	51.37
45	Minnesota	23.00
5	Mississippi	52.42
10	Missouri	48.21
NA	Montana**	NA
28	Nebraska	35.90
9	Nevada	51.06
44	New Hampshire	24.14
33	New Jersey	33.72
27	New Mexico	35.91
31	New York	34.67
16	North Carolina	43.34
48	North Dakota	10.00
17	Ohio	41.51
19	Oklahoma	40.30
29	Oregon	35.58
14	Pennsylvania	43.96
40	Rhode Island	26.67
25	South Carolina	37.97
37	South Dakota	29.51
4	Tennessee	52.96
12	Texas	46.23
26	Utah	36.93
38	Vermont	28.57
13	Virginia	45.65
35	Washington	33.39
34	West Virginia	33.59
2	Wisconsin	54.48
46	Wyoming	17.72

RANK ORDER

RANK	STATE	PERCENT
1	Louisiana	60.54
2	Wisconsin	54.48
3	Maryland	53.94
4	Tennessee	52.96
5	Mississippi	52.42
6	Arkansas	51.61
7	Georgia	51.50
8	Michigan	51.37
9	Nevada	51.06
10	Missouri	48.21
11	Indiana	46.63
12	Texas	46.23
13	Virginia	45.65
14	Pennsylvania	43.96
15	Illinois	43.85
16	North Carolina	43.34
17	Ohio	41.51
18	Florida	41.03
19	Oklahoma	40.30
20	Arizona	40.23
21	Alaska	39.95
22	California	39.66
23	Kentucky	38.75
24	Connecticut	38.36
25	South Carolina	37.97
26	Utah	36.93
27	New Mexico	35.91
28	Nebraska	35.90
29	Oregon	35.58
30	Colorado	35.26
31	New York	34.67
32	Delaware	34.50
33	New Jersey	33.72
34	West Virginia	33.59
35	Washington	33.39
36	Idaho	29.95
37	South Dakota	29.51
38	Vermont	28.57
39	Iowa	27.80
40	Rhode Island	26.67
41	Maine	25.99
42	Massachusetts	25.37
43	Alabama	25.24
44	New Hampshire	24.14
45	Minnesota	23.00
46	Wyoming	17.72
47	Hawaii	13.19
48	North Dakota	10.00
NA	Kansas**	NA
NA	Montana**	NA
	District of Columbia**	NA

*Source: Morgan Quitno Press using data from Federal Bureau of Investigation
"Crime in the United States 1994" (Uniform Crime Reports, November 19, 1995)*
Of the 590,370 robberies in 1994 for which supplemental data were received by the F.B.I. There were an additional 28,447 robberies for which the type of weapon was not reported to the F.B.I. Robbery is the taking or attempting to take anything of value by force or threat of force.
**Not available.*

Robberies with Knives or Cutting Instruments in 1994

National Total = 55,493 Robberies*

ALPHA ORDER					RANK ORDER			
RANK	STATE	ROBBERIES	% of USA		RANK	STATE	ROBBERIES	% of USA
12	Alabama	1,059	1.91%		1	New York	12,726	22.93%
34	Alaska	112	0.20%		2	California	11,006	19.83%
17	Arizona	675	1.22%		3	Texas	3,329	6.00%
32	Arkansas	218	0.39%		4	Illinois	3,036	5.47%
2	California	11,006	19.83%		5	Florida	2,961	5.34%
31	Colorado	324	0.58%		6	New Jersey	2,165	3.90%
22	Connecticut	618	1.11%		7	Massachusetts	1,839	3.31%
45	Delaware	10	0.02%		8	Maryland	1,498	2.70%
5	Florida	2,961	5.34%		9	Pennsylvania	1,441	2.60%
16	Georgia	792	1.43%		10	Michigan	1,271	2.29%
38	Hawaii	62	0.11%		11	Ohio	1,103	1.99%
40	Idaho	36	0.06%		12	Alabama	1,059	1.91%
4	Illinois	3,036	5.47%		13	North Carolina	981	1.77%
23	Indiana	512	0.92%		14	Louisiana	822	1.48%
37	Iowa	95	0.17%		15	Missouri	799	1.44%
NA	Kansas**	NA	NA		16	Georgia	792	1.43%
28	Kentucky	390	0.70%		17	Arizona	675	1.22%
14	Louisiana	822	1.48%		18	South Carolina	669	1.21%
43	Maine	24	0.04%		19	Washington	667	1.20%
8	Maryland	1,498	2.70%		20	Tennessee	645	1.16%
7	Massachusetts	1,839	3.31%		21	Virginia	637	1.15%
10	Michigan	1,271	2.29%		22	Connecticut	618	1.11%
27	Minnesota	396	0.71%		23	Indiana	512	0.92%
29	Mississippi	380	0.68%		24	Nevada	465	0.84%
15	Missouri	799	1.44%		25	Oregon	445	0.80%
NA	Montana**	NA	NA		26	Wisconsin	441	0.79%
33	Nebraska	132	0.24%		27	Minnesota	396	0.71%
24	Nevada	465	0.84%		28	Kentucky	390	0.70%
42	New Hampshire	25	0.05%		29	Mississippi	380	0.68%
6	New Jersey	2,165	3.90%		30	Oklahoma	358	0.65%
41	New Mexico	34	0.06%		31	Colorado	324	0.58%
1	New York	12,726	22.93%		32	Arkansas	218	0.39%
13	North Carolina	981	1.77%		33	Nebraska	132	0.24%
47	North Dakota	6	0.01%		34	Alaska	112	0.20%
11	Ohio	1,103	1.99%		35	Utah	105	0.19%
30	Oklahoma	358	0.65%		36	Rhode Island	100	0.18%
25	Oregon	445	0.80%		37	Iowa	95	0.17%
9	Pennsylvania	1,441	2.60%		38	Hawaii	62	0.11%
36	Rhode Island	100	0.18%		39	West Virginia	61	0.11%
18	South Carolina	669	1.21%		40	Idaho	36	0.06%
44	South Dakota	11	0.02%		41	New Mexico	34	0.06%
20	Tennessee	645	1.16%		42	New Hampshire	25	0.05%
3	Texas	3,329	6.00%		43	Maine	24	0.04%
35	Utah	105	0.19%		44	South Dakota	11	0.02%
48	Vermont	4	0.01%		45	Delaware	10	0.02%
21	Virginia	637	1.15%		46	Wyoming	8	0.01%
19	Washington	667	1.20%		47	North Dakota	6	0.01%
39	West Virginia	61	0.11%		48	Vermont	4	0.01%
26	Wisconsin	441	0.79%		NA	Kansas**	NA	NA
46	Wyoming	8	0.01%		NA	Montana**	NA	NA
						District of Columbia**	NA	NA

Source: Federal Bureau of Investigation
"Crime in the United States 1994" (Uniform Crime Reports, November 19, 1995)
Of the 590,370 robberies in 1994 for which supplemental data were received by the F.B.I. There were an additional 28,447 robberies for which the type of weapon was not reported to the F.B.I. Robbery is the taking or attempting to take anything of value by force or threat of force.
***Not available.*

Percent of Robberies Involving Knives or Cutting Instruments in 1994

National Percent = 9.50% of Robberies*

ALPHA ORDER

RANK	STATE	PERCENT
1	Alabama	24.59
6	Alaska	12.93
13	Arizona	10.43
40	Arkansas	6.93
17	California	9.81
20	Colorado	9.21
15	Connecticut	10.05
48	Delaware	4.37
42	Florida	6.63
46	Georgia	5.51
47	Hawaii	5.08
4	Idaho	17.39
30	Illinois	8.22
32	Indiana	7.89
24	Iowa	8.95
NA	Kansas**	NA
9	Kentucky	11.01
36	Louisiana	7.42
26	Maine	8.66
35	Maryland	7.44
2	Massachusetts	19.24
44	Michigan	6.12
37	Minnesota	7.40
7	Mississippi	11.96
41	Missouri	6.68
NA	Montana**	NA
10	Nebraska	10.82
21	Nevada	9.09
18	New Hampshire	9.58
19	New Jersey	9.51
11	New Mexico	10.53
5	New York	14.72
33	North Carolina	7.77
29	North Dakota	8.57
45	Ohio	5.75
28	Oklahoma	8.58
12	Oregon	10.51
39	Pennsylvania	6.99
8	Rhode Island	11.49
16	South Carolina	9.86
22	South Dakota	9.02
43	Tennessee	6.36
25	Texas	8.85
26	Utah	8.66
3	Vermont	19.05
38	Virginia	7.34
23	Washington	9.00
31	West Virginia	7.91
34	Wisconsin	7.69
14	Wyoming	10.13

RANK ORDER

RANK	STATE	PERCENT
1	Alabama	24.59
2	Massachusetts	19.24
3	Vermont	19.05
4	Idaho	17.39
5	New York	14.72
6	Alaska	12.93
7	Mississippi	11.96
8	Rhode Island	11.49
9	Kentucky	11.01
10	Nebraska	10.82
11	New Mexico	10.53
12	Oregon	10.51
13	Arizona	10.43
14	Wyoming	10.13
15	Connecticut	10.05
16	South Carolina	9.86
17	California	9.81
18	New Hampshire	9.58
19	New Jersey	9.51
20	Colorado	9.21
21	Nevada	9.09
22	South Dakota	9.02
23	Washington	9.00
24	Iowa	8.95
25	Texas	8.85
26	Maine	8.66
26	Utah	8.66
28	Oklahoma	8.58
29	North Dakota	8.57
30	Illinois	8.22
31	West Virginia	7.91
32	Indiana	7.89
33	North Carolina	7.77
34	Wisconsin	7.69
35	Maryland	7.44
36	Louisiana	7.42
37	Minnesota	7.40
38	Virginia	7.34
39	Pennsylvania	6.99
40	Arkansas	6.93
41	Missouri	6.68
42	Florida	6.63
43	Tennessee	6.36
44	Michigan	6.12
45	Ohio	5.75
46	Georgia	5.51
47	Hawaii	5.08
48	Delaware	4.37
NA	Kansas**	NA
NA	Montana**	NA
	District of Columbia**	NA

Source: Morgan Quitno Press using data from Federal Bureau of Investigation
   "Crime in the United States 1994" (Uniform Crime Reports, November 19, 1995)
*Of the 590,370 robberies in 1994 for which supplemental data were received by the F.B.I. There were an
additional 28,447 robberies for which the type of weapon was not reported to the F.B.I. Robbery is the taking or
attempting to take anything of value by force or threat of force.
**Not available.

Robberies with Blunt Objects and Other Dangerous Weapons in 1994

National Total = 56,711 Robberies*

ALPHA ORDER

RANK	STATE	ROBBERIES	% of USA
12	Alabama	1,056	1.86%
36	Alaska	72	0.13%
20	Arizona	637	1.12%
32	Arkansas	229	0.40%
1	California	13,829	24.39%
25	Colorado	452	0.80%
22	Connecticut	580	1.02%
43	Delaware	22	0.04%
3	Florida	3,448	6.08%
7	Georgia	1,788	3.15%
40	Hawaii	30	0.05%
40	Idaho	30	0.05%
6	Illinois	2,903	5.12%
23	Indiana	502	0.89%
34	Iowa	156	0.28%
NA	Kansas**	NA	NA
29	Kentucky	298	0.53%
18	Louisiana	748	1.32%
45	Maine	17	0.03%
10	Maryland	1,348	2.38%
13	Massachusetts	1,048	1.85%
5	Michigan	3,256	5.74%
24	Minnesota	488	0.86%
31	Mississippi	241	0.42%
15	Missouri	934	1.65%
NA	Montana**	NA	NA
35	Nebraska	85	0.15%
26	Nevada	388	0.68%
44	New Hampshire	19	0.03%
9	New Jersey	1,656	2.92%
42	New Mexico	23	0.04%
2	New York	8,921	15.73%
11	North Carolina	1,175	2.07%
38	North Dakota	44	0.08%
8	Ohio	1,782	3.14%
30	Oklahoma	249	0.44%
27	Oregon	378	0.67%
14	Pennsylvania	1,007	1.78%
37	Rhode Island	61	0.11%
17	South Carolina	754	1.33%
47	South Dakota	7	0.01%
19	Tennessee	718	1.27%
4	Texas	3,369	5.94%
33	Utah	173	0.31%
48	Vermont	5	0.01%
16	Virginia	780	1.38%
21	Washington	630	1.11%
39	West Virginia	40	0.07%
28	Wisconsin	325	0.57%
46	Wyoming	10	0.02%

RANK ORDER

RANK	STATE	ROBBERIES	% of USA
1	California	13,829	24.39%
2	New York	8,921	15.73%
3	Florida	3,448	6.08%
4	Texas	3,369	5.94%
5	Michigan	3,256	5.74%
6	Illinois	2,903	5.12%
7	Georgia	1,788	3.15%
8	Ohio	1,782	3.14%
9	New Jersey	1,656	2.92%
10	Maryland	1,348	2.38%
11	North Carolina	1,175	2.07%
12	Alabama	1,056	1.86%
13	Massachusetts	1,048	1.85%
14	Pennsylvania	1,007	1.78%
15	Missouri	934	1.65%
16	Virginia	780	1.38%
17	South Carolina	754	1.33%
18	Louisiana	748	1.32%
19	Tennessee	718	1.27%
20	Arizona	637	1.12%
21	Washington	630	1.11%
22	Connecticut	580	1.02%
23	Indiana	502	0.89%
24	Minnesota	488	0.86%
25	Colorado	452	0.80%
26	Nevada	388	0.68%
27	Oregon	378	0.67%
28	Wisconsin	325	0.57%
29	Kentucky	298	0.53%
30	Oklahoma	249	0.44%
31	Mississippi	241	0.42%
32	Arkansas	229	0.40%
33	Utah	173	0.31%
34	Iowa	156	0.28%
35	Nebraska	85	0.15%
36	Alaska	72	0.13%
37	Rhode Island	61	0.11%
38	North Dakota	44	0.08%
39	West Virginia	40	0.07%
40	Hawaii	30	0.05%
40	Idaho	30	0.05%
42	New Mexico	23	0.04%
43	Delaware	22	0.04%
44	New Hampshire	19	0.03%
45	Maine	17	0.03%
46	Wyoming	10	0.02%
47	South Dakota	7	0.01%
48	Vermont	5	0.01%
NA	Kansas**	NA	NA
NA	Montana**	NA	NA
	District of Columbia**	NA	NA

Source: Federal Bureau of Investigation
"Crime in the United States 1994" (Uniform Crime Reports, November 19, 1995)
Of the 590,370 robberies in 1994 for which supplemental data were received by the F.B.I. There were an additional 28,447 robberies for which the type of weapon was not reported to the F.B.I. Robbery is the taking or attempting to take anything of value by force or threat of force.
**Not available.

Percent of Robberies Involving Blunt Objects
And Other Dangerous Weapons in 1994
National Percent = 9.71% of Robberies*

ALPHA ORDER				RANK ORDER		
RANK	STATE	PERCENT		RANK	STATE	PERCENT
2	Alabama	24.52		1	North Dakota	62.86
26	Alaska	8.31		2	Alabama	24.52
15	Arizona	9.84		3	Vermont	23.81
33	Arkansas	7.28		4	Michigan	15.68
11	California	12.33		5	Iowa	14.70
8	Colorado	12.85		6	Idaho	14.49
17	Connecticut	9.43		7	Utah	14.26
16	Delaware	9.61		8	Colorado	12.85
30	Florida	7.72		9	Wyoming	12.66
10	Georgia	12.45		10	Georgia	12.45
48	Hawaii	2.46		11	California	12.33
6	Idaho	14.49		12	South Carolina	11.12
27	Illinois	7.86		13	Massachusetts	10.97
29	Indiana	7.74		14	New York	10.32
5	Iowa	14.70		15	Arizona	9.84
NA	Kansas**	NA		16	Delaware	9.61
25	Kentucky	8.41		17	Connecticut	9.43
40	Louisiana	6.75		18	North Carolina	9.31
42	Maine	6.14		19	Ohio	9.30
41	Maryland	6.69		20	Minnesota	9.12
13	Massachusetts	10.97		21	Virginia	8.99
4	Michigan	15.68		22	Texas	8.95
20	Minnesota	9.12		23	Oregon	8.92
31	Mississippi	7.59		24	Washington	8.50
28	Missouri	7.81		25	Kentucky	8.41
NA	Montana**	NA		26	Alaska	8.31
39	Nebraska	6.97		27	Illinois	7.86
31	Nevada	7.59		28	Missouri	7.81
33	New Hampshire	7.28		29	Indiana	7.74
33	New Jersey	7.28		30	Florida	7.72
36	New Mexico	7.12		31	Mississippi	7.59
14	New York	10.32		31	Nevada	7.59
18	North Carolina	9.31		33	Arkansas	7.28
1	North Dakota	62.86		33	New Hampshire	7.28
19	Ohio	9.30		33	New Jersey	7.28
43	Oklahoma	5.97		36	New Mexico	7.12
23	Oregon	8.92		37	Tennessee	7.08
47	Pennsylvania	4.88		38	Rhode Island	7.01
38	Rhode Island	7.01		39	Nebraska	6.97
12	South Carolina	11.12		40	Louisiana	6.75
44	South Dakota	5.74		41	Maryland	6.69
37	Tennessee	7.08		42	Maine	6.14
22	Texas	8.95		43	Oklahoma	5.97
7	Utah	14.26		44	South Dakota	5.74
3	Vermont	23.81		45	Wisconsin	5.67
21	Virginia	8.99		46	West Virginia	5.19
24	Washington	8.50		47	Pennsylvania	4.88
46	West Virginia	5.19		48	Hawaii	2.46
45	Wisconsin	5.67		NA	Kansas**	NA
9	Wyoming	12.66		NA	Montana**	NA
					District of Columbia**	NA

Source: Morgan Quitno Press using data from Federal Bureau of Investigation
"Crime in the United States 1994" (Uniform Crime Reports, November 19, 1995)
*Of the 590,370 robberies in 1994 for which supplemental data were received by the F.B.I. There were an additional 28,447 robberies for which the type of weapon was not reported to the F.B.I. Robbery is the taking or attempting to take anything of value by force or threat of force.
**Not available.

Robberies Committed with Hands, Fists or Feet in 1994

National Total = 229,362 Robberies*

ALPHA ORDER

RANK	STATE	ROBBERIES	% of USA
30	Alabama	1,104	0.48%
39	Alaska	336	0.15%
22	Arizona	2,557	1.11%
31	Arkansas	1,075	0.47%
1	California	42,835	18.68%
28	Colorado	1,501	0.65%
21	Connecticut	2,593	1.13%
43	Delaware	118	0.05%
3	Florida	19,912	8.68%
13	Georgia	4,386	1.91%
32	Hawaii	968	0.42%
44	Idaho	79	0.03%
4	Illinois	14,789	6.45%
23	Indiana	2,449	1.07%
35	Iowa	515	0.22%
NA	Kansas**	NA	NA
29	Kentucky	1,482	0.65%
19	Louisiana	2,800	1.22%
40	Maine	164	0.07%
9	Maryland	6,433	2.80%
14	Massachusetts	4,245	1.85%
10	Michigan	5,573	2.43%
18	Minnesota	3,238	1.41%
33	Mississippi	890	0.39%
12	Missouri	4,460	1.94%
NA	Montana**	NA	NA
34	Nebraska	565	0.25%
27	Nevada	1,650	0.72%
41	New Hampshire	154	0.07%
6	New Jersey	11,264	4.91%
42	New Mexico	150	0.07%
2	New York	34,842	15.19%
11	North Carolina	4,995	2.18%
47	North Dakota	13	0.01%
8	Ohio	8,326	3.63%
25	Oklahoma	1,883	0.82%
24	Oregon	1,906	0.83%
7	Pennsylvania	9,108	3.97%
37	Rhode Island	477	0.21%
20	South Carolina	2,784	1.21%
45	South Dakota	68	0.03%
16	Tennessee	3,406	1.48%
5	Texas	13,536	5.90%
36	Utah	487	0.21%
48	Vermont	6	0.00%
17	Virginia	3,298	1.44%
15	Washington	3,641	1.59%
38	West Virginia	411	0.18%
26	Wisconsin	1,843	0.80%
46	Wyoming	47	0.02%

RANK ORDER

RANK	STATE	ROBBERIES	% of USA
1	California	42,835	18.68%
2	New York	34,842	15.19%
3	Florida	19,912	8.68%
4	Illinois	14,789	6.45%
5	Texas	13,536	5.90%
6	New Jersey	11,264	4.91%
7	Pennsylvania	9,108	3.97%
8	Ohio	8,326	3.63%
9	Maryland	6,433	2.80%
10	Michigan	5,573	2.43%
11	North Carolina	4,995	2.18%
12	Missouri	4,460	1.94%
13	Georgia	4,386	1.91%
14	Massachusetts	4,245	1.85%
15	Washington	3,641	1.59%
16	Tennessee	3,406	1.48%
17	Virginia	3,298	1.44%
18	Minnesota	3,238	1.41%
19	Louisiana	2,800	1.22%
20	South Carolina	2,784	1.21%
21	Connecticut	2,593	1.13%
22	Arizona	2,557	1.11%
23	Indiana	2,449	1.07%
24	Oregon	1,906	0.83%
25	Oklahoma	1,883	0.82%
26	Wisconsin	1,843	0.80%
27	Nevada	1,650	0.72%
28	Colorado	1,501	0.65%
29	Kentucky	1,482	0.65%
30	Alabama	1,104	0.48%
31	Arkansas	1,075	0.47%
32	Hawaii	968	0.42%
33	Mississippi	890	0.39%
34	Nebraska	565	0.25%
35	Iowa	515	0.22%
36	Utah	487	0.21%
37	Rhode Island	477	0.21%
38	West Virginia	411	0.18%
39	Alaska	336	0.15%
40	Maine	164	0.07%
41	New Hampshire	154	0.07%
42	New Mexico	150	0.07%
43	Delaware	118	0.05%
44	Idaho	79	0.03%
45	South Dakota	68	0.03%
46	Wyoming	47	0.02%
47	North Dakota	13	0.01%
48	Vermont	6	0.00%
NA	Kansas**	NA	NA
NA	Montana**	NA	NA
	District of Columbia**	NA	NA

Source: Federal Bureau of Investigation
   "Crime in the United States 1994" (Uniform Crime Reports, November 19, 1995)
*Of the 590,370 robberies in 1994 for which supplemental data were received by the F.B.I. There were an additional 28,447 robberies for which the type of weapon was not reported to the F.B.I. Robbery is the taking or attempting to take anything of value by force or threat of force. Also called strong-armed robberies.
**Not available.

Percent of Robberies Committed with Hands, Fists or Feet in 1994

National Percent = 39.27% of Robberies*

<table>
<tr><th colspan="3">ALPHA ORDER</th><th colspan="3">RANK ORDER</th></tr>
<tr><th>RANK</th><th>STATE</th><th>PERCENT</th><th>RANK</th><th>STATE</th><th>PERCENT</th></tr>
<tr><td>46</td><td>Alabama</td><td>25.64</td><td>1</td><td>Hawaii</td><td>79.28</td></tr>
<tr><td>30</td><td>Alaska</td><td>38.80</td><td>2</td><td>Minnesota</td><td>60.49</td></tr>
<tr><td>29</td><td>Arizona</td><td>39.50</td><td>3</td><td>Wyoming</td><td>59.49</td></tr>
<tr><td>37</td><td>Arkansas</td><td>34.18</td><td>4</td><td>Maine</td><td>59.21</td></tr>
<tr><td>31</td><td>California</td><td>38.20</td><td>5</td><td>New Hampshire</td><td>59.00</td></tr>
<tr><td>21</td><td>Colorado</td><td>42.68</td><td>6</td><td>South Dakota</td><td>55.74</td></tr>
<tr><td>22</td><td>Connecticut</td><td>42.16</td><td>7</td><td>Rhode Island</td><td>54.83</td></tr>
<tr><td>9</td><td>Delaware</td><td>51.53</td><td>8</td><td>West Virginia</td><td>53.31</td></tr>
<tr><td>17</td><td>Florida</td><td>44.61</td><td>9</td><td>Delaware</td><td>51.53</td></tr>
<tr><td>42</td><td>Georgia</td><td>30.54</td><td>10</td><td>New Jersey</td><td>49.49</td></tr>
<tr><td>1</td><td>Hawaii</td><td>79.28</td><td>11</td><td>Washington</td><td>49.12</td></tr>
<tr><td>32</td><td>Idaho</td><td>38.16</td><td>12</td><td>Iowa</td><td>48.54</td></tr>
<tr><td>27</td><td>Illinois</td><td>40.06</td><td>13</td><td>New Mexico</td><td>46.44</td></tr>
<tr><td>34</td><td>Indiana</td><td>37.74</td><td>14</td><td>Nebraska</td><td>46.31</td></tr>
<tr><td>12</td><td>Iowa</td><td>48.54</td><td>15</td><td>Oklahoma</td><td>45.15</td></tr>
<tr><td>NA</td><td>Kansas**</td><td>NA</td><td>16</td><td>Oregon</td><td>45.00</td></tr>
<tr><td>23</td><td>Kentucky</td><td>41.83</td><td>17</td><td>Florida</td><td>44.61</td></tr>
<tr><td>47</td><td>Louisiana</td><td>25.28</td><td>18</td><td>Massachusetts</td><td>44.42</td></tr>
<tr><td>4</td><td>Maine</td><td>59.21</td><td>19</td><td>Pennsylvania</td><td>44.17</td></tr>
<tr><td>41</td><td>Maryland</td><td>31.94</td><td>20</td><td>Ohio</td><td>43.43</td></tr>
<tr><td>18</td><td>Massachusetts</td><td>44.42</td><td>21</td><td>Colorado</td><td>42.68</td></tr>
<tr><td>45</td><td>Michigan</td><td>26.84</td><td>22</td><td>Connecticut</td><td>42.16</td></tr>
<tr><td>2</td><td>Minnesota</td><td>60.49</td><td>23</td><td>Kentucky</td><td>41.83</td></tr>
<tr><td>44</td><td>Mississippi</td><td>28.02</td><td>24</td><td>South Carolina</td><td>41.05</td></tr>
<tr><td>35</td><td>Missouri</td><td>37.29</td><td>25</td><td>New York</td><td>40.29</td></tr>
<tr><td>NA</td><td>Montana**</td><td>NA</td><td>26</td><td>Utah</td><td>40.15</td></tr>
<tr><td>14</td><td>Nebraska</td><td>46.31</td><td>27</td><td>Illinois</td><td>40.06</td></tr>
<tr><td>39</td><td>Nevada</td><td>32.26</td><td>28</td><td>North Carolina</td><td>39.58</td></tr>
<tr><td>5</td><td>New Hampshire</td><td>59.00</td><td>29</td><td>Arizona</td><td>39.50</td></tr>
<tr><td>10</td><td>New Jersey</td><td>49.49</td><td>30</td><td>Alaska</td><td>38.80</td></tr>
<tr><td>13</td><td>New Mexico</td><td>46.44</td><td>31</td><td>California</td><td>38.20</td></tr>
<tr><td>25</td><td>New York</td><td>40.29</td><td>32</td><td>Idaho</td><td>38.16</td></tr>
<tr><td>28</td><td>North Carolina</td><td>39.58</td><td>33</td><td>Virginia</td><td>38.01</td></tr>
<tr><td>48</td><td>North Dakota</td><td>18.57</td><td>34</td><td>Indiana</td><td>37.74</td></tr>
<tr><td>20</td><td>Ohio</td><td>43.43</td><td>35</td><td>Missouri</td><td>37.29</td></tr>
<tr><td>15</td><td>Oklahoma</td><td>45.15</td><td>36</td><td>Texas</td><td>35.97</td></tr>
<tr><td>16</td><td>Oregon</td><td>45.00</td><td>37</td><td>Arkansas</td><td>34.18</td></tr>
<tr><td>19</td><td>Pennsylvania</td><td>44.17</td><td>38</td><td>Tennessee</td><td>33.60</td></tr>
<tr><td>7</td><td>Rhode Island</td><td>54.83</td><td>39</td><td>Nevada</td><td>32.26</td></tr>
<tr><td>24</td><td>South Carolina</td><td>41.05</td><td>40</td><td>Wisconsin</td><td>32.15</td></tr>
<tr><td>6</td><td>South Dakota</td><td>55.74</td><td>41</td><td>Maryland</td><td>31.94</td></tr>
<tr><td>38</td><td>Tennessee</td><td>33.60</td><td>42</td><td>Georgia</td><td>30.54</td></tr>
<tr><td>36</td><td>Texas</td><td>35.97</td><td>43</td><td>Vermont</td><td>28.57</td></tr>
<tr><td>26</td><td>Utah</td><td>40.15</td><td>44</td><td>Mississippi</td><td>28.02</td></tr>
<tr><td>43</td><td>Vermont</td><td>28.57</td><td>45</td><td>Michigan</td><td>26.84</td></tr>
<tr><td>33</td><td>Virginia</td><td>38.01</td><td>46</td><td>Alabama</td><td>25.64</td></tr>
<tr><td>11</td><td>Washington</td><td>49.12</td><td>47</td><td>Louisiana</td><td>25.28</td></tr>
<tr><td>8</td><td>West Virginia</td><td>53.31</td><td>48</td><td>North Dakota</td><td>18.57</td></tr>
<tr><td>40</td><td>Wisconsin</td><td>32.15</td><td>NA</td><td>Kansas**</td><td>NA</td></tr>
<tr><td>3</td><td>Wyoming</td><td>59.49</td><td>NA</td><td>Montana**</td><td>NA</td></tr>
<tr><td></td><td></td><td></td><td></td><td>District of Columbia**</td><td>NA</td></tr>
</table>

Source: Morgan Quitno Press using data from Federal Bureau of Investigation
"Crime in the United States 1994" (Uniform Crime Reports, November 19, 1995)
*Of the 590,370 robberies in 1994 for which supplemental data were received by the F.B.I. There were an additional 28,447 robberies for which the type of weapon was not reported to the F.B.I. Robbery is the taking or attempting to take anything of value by force or threat of force. Also called strong-armed robberies.
**Not available.

Bank Robberies in 1994

National Total = 7,011 Robberies*

ALPHA ORDER

RANK	STATE	ROBBERIES	% of USA
23	Alabama	73	1.04%
41	Alaska	12	0.17%
16	Arizona	115	1.64%
36	Arkansas	17	0.24%
1	California	2,215	31.59%
24	Colorado	67	0.96%
27	Connecticut	48	0.68%
40	Delaware	13	0.19%
2	Florida	662	9.44%
13	Georgia	152	2.17%
28	Hawaii	46	0.66%
45	Idaho	6	0.09%
14	Illinois	136	1.94%
15	Indiana	129	1.84%
38	Iowa	15	0.21%
31	Kansas	32	0.46%
29	Kentucky	42	0.60%
26	Louisiana	60	0.86%
44	Maine	7	0.10%
7	Maryland	252	3.59%
10	Massachusetts	180	2.57%
5	Michigan	261	3.72%
33	Minnesota	29	0.41%
32	Mississippi	30	0.43%
22	Missouri	74	1.06%
49	Montana	1	0.01%
37	Nebraska	16	0.23%
17	Nevada	101	1.44%
43	New Hampshire	8	0.11%
20	New Jersey	83	1.18%
29	New Mexico	42	0.60%
3	New York	329	4.69%
11	North Carolina	172	2.45%
50	North Dakota	0	0.00%
6	Ohio	253	3.61%
35	Oklahoma	21	0.30%
9	Oregon	215	3.07%
4	Pennsylvania	276	3.94%
39	Rhode Island	14	0.20%
25	South Carolina	65	0.93%
47	South Dakota	2	0.03%
21	Tennessee	82	1.17%
12	Texas	167	2.38%
34	Utah	26	0.37%
47	Vermont	2	0.03%
19	Virginia	94	1.34%
8	Washington	227	3.24%
42	West Virginia	10	0.14%
18	Wisconsin	100	1.43%
46	Wyoming	3	0.04%

RANK ORDER

RANK	STATE	ROBBERIES	% of USA
1	California	2,215	31.59%
2	Florida	662	9.44%
3	New York	329	4.69%
4	Pennsylvania	276	3.94%
5	Michigan	261	3.72%
6	Ohio	253	3.61%
7	Maryland	252	3.59%
8	Washington	227	3.24%
9	Oregon	215	3.07%
10	Massachusetts	180	2.57%
11	North Carolina	172	2.45%
12	Texas	167	2.38%
13	Georgia	152	2.17%
14	Illinois	136	1.94%
15	Indiana	129	1.84%
16	Arizona	115	1.64%
17	Nevada	101	1.44%
18	Wisconsin	100	1.43%
19	Virginia	94	1.34%
20	New Jersey	83	1.18%
21	Tennessee	82	1.17%
22	Missouri	74	1.06%
23	Alabama	73	1.04%
24	Colorado	67	0.96%
25	South Carolina	65	0.93%
26	Louisiana	60	0.86%
27	Connecticut	48	0.68%
28	Hawaii	46	0.66%
29	Kentucky	42	0.60%
29	New Mexico	42	0.60%
31	Kansas	32	0.46%
32	Mississippi	30	0.43%
33	Minnesota	29	0.41%
34	Utah	26	0.37%
35	Oklahoma	21	0.30%
36	Arkansas	17	0.24%
37	Nebraska	16	0.23%
38	Iowa	15	0.21%
39	Rhode Island	14	0.20%
40	Delaware	13	0.19%
41	Alaska	12	0.17%
42	West Virginia	10	0.14%
43	New Hampshire	8	0.11%
44	Maine	7	0.10%
45	Idaho	6	0.09%
46	Wyoming	3	0.04%
47	South Dakota	2	0.03%
47	Vermont	2	0.03%
49	Montana	1	0.01%
50	North Dakota	0	0.00%
	District of Columbia	29	0.41%

Source: Federal Bureau of Investigation
"Bank Crime Statistics, Federally Insured Financial Institutions, January 1, 1994 - December 31, 1994"
*Does not include 16 robberies in Puerto Rico and 2 in the Virgin Islands. In addition, there were 271 bank burglaries, 84 bank larcenies and 33 extortions. Of these 7,417 bank crimes, loot valued at $58,428,792 was taken in 6,804 cases. Of this, $14,261,800 was recovered.

Aggravated Assaults in 1994

National Total = 1,119,950 Aggravated Assaults*

ALPHA ORDER

RANK	STATE	ASSAULTS	% of USA
20	Alabama	19,633	1.75%
38	Alaska	3,302	0.29%
19	Arizona	20,161	1.80%
28	Arkansas	10,118	0.90%
1	California	191,548	17.10%
24	Colorado	12,944	1.16%
32	Connecticut	7,745	0.69%
42	Delaware	2,505	0.22%
2	Florida	105,679	9.44%
10	Georgia	28,249	2.52%
43	Hawaii	1,461	0.13%
40	Idaho	2,673	0.24%
5	Illinois	63,849	5.70%
18	Indiana	20,216	1.81%
34	Iowa	6,874	0.61%
31	Kansas	8,070	0.72%
21	Kentucky	17,976	1.61%
11	Louisiana	28,060	2.51%
46	Maine	987	0.09%
15	Maryland	24,696	2.21%
7	Massachusetts	30,550	2.73%
6	Michigan	43,371	3.87%
30	Minnesota	8,155	0.73%
33	Mississippi	7,220	0.64%
16	Missouri	24,553	2.19%
47	Montana	975	0.09%
36	Nebraska	4,548	0.41%
29	Nevada	8,292	0.74%
48	New Hampshire	597	0.05%
17	New Jersey	23,414	2.09%
26	New Mexico	11,336	1.01%
3	New York	82,100	7.33%
8	North Carolina	30,391	2.71%
50	North Dakota	301	0.03%
12	Ohio	27,216	2.43%
23	Oklahoma	15,209	1.36%
27	Oregon	10,320	0.92%
13	Pennsylvania	25,071	2.24%
41	Rhode Island	2,560	0.23%
9	South Carolina	28,595	2.55%
44	South Dakota	1,193	0.11%
14	Tennessee	24,943	2.23%
4	Texas	81,071	7.24%
37	Utah	3,735	0.33%
49	Vermont	325	0.03%
25	Virginia	12,294	1.10%
22	Washington	16,329	1.46%
39	West Virginia	2,690	0.24%
35	Wisconsin	6,590	0.59%
45	Wyoming	1,042	0.09%

RANK ORDER

RANK	STATE	ASSAULTS	% of USA
1	California	191,548	17.10%
2	Florida	105,679	9.44%
3	New York	82,100	7.33%
4	Texas	81,071	7.24%
5	Illinois	63,849	5.70%
6	Michigan	43,371	3.87%
7	Massachusetts	30,550	2.73%
8	North Carolina	30,391	2.71%
9	South Carolina	28,595	2.55%
10	Georgia	28,249	2.52%
11	Louisiana	28,060	2.51%
12	Ohio	27,216	2.43%
13	Pennsylvania	25,071	2.24%
14	Tennessee	24,943	2.23%
15	Maryland	24,696	2.21%
16	Missouri	24,553	2.19%
17	New Jersey	23,414	2.09%
18	Indiana	20,216	1.81%
19	Arizona	20,161	1.80%
20	Alabama	19,633	1.75%
21	Kentucky	17,976	1.61%
22	Washington	16,329	1.46%
23	Oklahoma	15,209	1.36%
24	Colorado	12,944	1.16%
25	Virginia	12,294	1.10%
26	New Mexico	11,336	1.01%
27	Oregon	10,320	0.92%
28	Arkansas	10,118	0.90%
29	Nevada	8,292	0.74%
30	Minnesota	8,155	0.73%
31	Kansas	8,070	0.72%
32	Connecticut	7,745	0.69%
33	Mississippi	7,220	0.64%
34	Iowa	6,874	0.61%
35	Wisconsin	6,590	0.59%
36	Nebraska	4,548	0.41%
37	Utah	3,735	0.33%
38	Alaska	3,302	0.29%
39	West Virginia	2,690	0.24%
40	Idaho	2,673	0.24%
41	Rhode Island	2,560	0.23%
42	Delaware	2,505	0.22%
43	Hawaii	1,461	0.13%
44	South Dakota	1,193	0.11%
45	Wyoming	1,042	0.09%
46	Maine	987	0.09%
47	Montana	975	0.09%
48	New Hampshire	597	0.05%
49	Vermont	325	0.03%
50	North Dakota	301	0.03%
	District of Columbia	8,218	0.73%

Source: Federal Bureau of Investigation
"Crime in the United States 1994" (Uniform Crime Reports, November 19, 1995)
*Aggravated assault is an attack for the purpose of inflicting severe bodily injury.

Average Time Between Aggravated Assaults in 1994

National Rate = An Aggravated Assault Occurs Every 28 Seconds*

ALPHA ORDER

RANK	STATE	MINUTES.SECONDS
31	Alabama	26.46
13	Alaska	159.11
32	Arizona	26.04
23	Arkansas	51.57
50	California	2.44
27	Colorado	40.37
19	Connecticut	67.52
9	Delaware	209.49
49	Florida	4.58
41	Georgia	18.37
8	Hawaii	359.45
11	Idaho	196.38
46	Illinois	8.14
33	Indiana	26.00
17	Iowa	76.28
20	Kansas	65.08
30	Kentucky	29.14
40	Louisiana	18.44
5	Maine	532.31
36	Maryland	21.17
44	Massachusetts	17.12
45	Michigan	12.07
21	Minnesota	64.27
18	Mississippi	72.48
35	Missouri	21.25
4	Montana	539.05
15	Nebraska	115.34
22	Nevada	63.23
3	New Hampshire	880.24
34	New Jersey	22.27
25	New Mexico	46.22
48	New York	6.24
43	North Carolina	17.17
1	North Dakota	1,746.11
39	Ohio	19.19
28	Oklahoma	34.34
24	Oregon	50.56
38	Pennsylvania	20.58
10	Rhode Island	205.19
42	South Carolina	18.23
7	South Dakota	440.34
37	Tennessee	21.04
47	Texas	6.29
14	Utah	140.43
2	Vermont	1,617.14
26	Virginia	42.45
29	Washington	32.11
12	West Virginia	195.23
16	Wisconsin	79.46
6	Wyoming	504.25

RANK ORDER

RANK	STATE	MINUTES.SECONDS
1	North Dakota	1,746.11
2	Vermont	1,617.14
3	New Hampshire	880.24
4	Montana	539.05
5	Maine	532.31
6	Wyoming	504.25
7	South Dakota	440.34
8	Hawaii	359.45
9	Delaware	209.49
10	Rhode Island	205.19
11	Idaho	196.38
12	West Virginia	195.23
13	Alaska	159.11
14	Utah	140.43
15	Nebraska	115.34
16	Wisconsin	79.46
17	Iowa	76.28
18	Mississippi	72.48
19	Connecticut	67.52
20	Kansas	65.08
21	Minnesota	64.27
22	Nevada	63.23
23	Arkansas	51.57
24	Oregon	50.56
25	New Mexico	46.22
26	Virginia	42.45
27	Colorado	40.37
28	Oklahoma	34.34
29	Washington	32.11
30	Kentucky	29.14
31	Alabama	26.46
32	Arizona	26.04
33	Indiana	26.00
34	New Jersey	22.27
35	Missouri	21.25
36	Maryland	21.17
37	Tennessee	21.04
38	Pennsylvania	20.58
39	Ohio	19.19
40	Louisiana	18.44
41	Georgia	18.37
42	South Carolina	18.23
43	North Carolina	17.17
44	Massachusetts	17.12
45	Michigan	12.07
46	Illinois	8.14
47	Texas	6.29
48	New York	6.24
49	Florida	4.58
50	California	2.44
	District of Columbia	63.58

Source: Morgan Quitno Press using data from Federal Bureau of Investigation
"Crime in the United States 1994" (Uniform Crime Reports, November 19, 1995)
*Aggravated assault is an attack for the purpose of inflicting severe bodily injury.

Percent Change in Number of Aggravated Assaults: 1993 to 1994

National Percent Change = 1.4% Decrease*

ALPHA ORDER			RANK ORDER		
RANK	STATE	PERCENT CHANGE	RANK	STATE	PERCENT CHANGE
50	Alabama	(18.3)	1	Kentucky	43.2
22	Alaska	1.0	2	Nevada	28.7
21	Arizona	1.3	3	Mississippi	14.6
25	Arkansas	0.4	3	South Dakota	14.6
31	California	(1.3)	5	Indiana	9.7
46	Colorado	(9.0)	6	Wisconsin	7.8
13	Connecticut	3.3	7	Idaho	7.3
47	Delaware	(14.2)	8	Oregon	7.2
32	Florida	(1.7)	9	West Virginia	6.7
43	Georgia	(4.7)	10	Maine	4.4
11	Hawaii	3.8	11	Hawaii	3.8
7	Idaho	7.3	12	Oklahoma	3.4
17	Illinois	2.5	13	Connecticut	3.3
5	Indiana	9.7	14	Missouri	3.1
27	Iowa	(0.2)	14	Utah	3.1
34	Kansas	(2.3)	16	Minnesota	2.7
1	Kentucky	43.2	17	Illinois	2.5
44	Louisiana	(8.7)	18	Montana	1.8
10	Maine	4.4	19	South Carolina	1.5
33	Maryland	(1.8)	20	Pennsylvania	1.4
47	Massachusetts	(14.2)	21	Arizona	1.3
36	Michigan	(3.1)	22	Alaska	1.0
16	Minnesota	2.7	23	Washington	0.9
3	Mississippi	14.6	24	Tennessee	0.7
14	Missouri	3.1	25	Arkansas	0.4
18	Montana	1.8	26	New Jersey	(0.1)
27	Nebraska	(0.2)	27	Iowa	(0.2)
2	Nevada	28.7	27	Nebraska	(0.2)
49	New Hampshire	(17.2)	27	Virginia	(0.2)
26	New Jersey	(0.1)	30	North Carolina	(0.8)
37	New Mexico	(4.1)	31	California	(1.3)
39	New York	(4.3)	32	Florida	(1.7)
30	North Carolina	(0.8)	33	Maryland	(1.8)
35	North Dakota	(2.6)	34	Kansas	(2.3)
39	Ohio	(4.3)	35	North Dakota	(2.6)
12	Oklahoma	3.4	36	Michigan	(3.1)
8	Oregon	7.2	37	New Mexico	(4.1)
20	Pennsylvania	1.4	37	Wyoming	(4.1)
41	Rhode Island	(4.5)	39	New York	(4.3)
19	South Carolina	1.5	39	Ohio	(4.3)
3	South Dakota	14.6	41	Rhode Island	(4.5)
24	Tennessee	0.7	41	Texas	(4.5)
41	Texas	(4.5)	43	Georgia	(4.7)
14	Utah	3.1	44	Louisiana	(8.7)
44	Vermont	(8.7)	44	Vermont	(8.7)
27	Virginia	(0.2)	46	Colorado	(9.0)
23	Washington	0.9	47	Delaware	(14.2)
9	West Virginia	6.7	47	Massachusetts	(14.2)
6	Wisconsin	7.8	49	New Hampshire	(17.2)
37	Wyoming	(4.1)	50	Alabama	(18.3)
				District of Columbia	(8.7)

Source: Federal Bureau of Investigation
   "Crime in the United States 1994" (Uniform Crime Reports, November 19, 1995)
*Aggravated assault is an attack for the purpose of inflicting severe bodily injury.

Aggravated Assault Rate in 1994

National Rate = 430.2 Aggravated Assaults per 100,000 Population*

ALPHA ORDER

RANK	STATE	RATE
15	Alabama	465.3
7	Alaska	544.9
10	Arizona	494.7
21	Arkansas	412.5
5	California	609.4
24	Colorado	354.0
35	Connecticut	236.5
23	Delaware	354.8
2	Florida	757.4
22	Georgia	400.4
45	Hawaii	123.9
36	Idaho	235.9
8	Illinois	543.3
25	Indiana	351.5
34	Iowa	243.0
27	Kansas	316.0
13	Kentucky	469.7
4	Louisiana	650.3
47	Maine	79.6
11	Maryland	493.3
9	Massachusetts	505.7
17	Michigan	456.7
41	Minnesota	178.6
31	Mississippi	270.5
16	Missouri	465.2
46	Montana	113.9
30	Nebraska	280.2
6	Nevada	569.1
49	New Hampshire	52.5
29	New Jersey	296.2
3	New Mexico	685.4
18	New York	451.9
20	North Carolina	429.9
50	North Dakota	47.2
33	Ohio	245.1
14	Oklahoma	466.8
26	Oregon	334.4
38	Pennsylvania	208.0
32	Rhode Island	256.8
1	South Carolina	780.4
42	South Dakota	165.5
12	Tennessee	482.0
19	Texas	441.1
39	Utah	195.8
48	Vermont	56.0
40	Virginia	187.6
28	Washington	305.6
43	West Virginia	147.6
44	Wisconsin	129.7
37	Wyoming	218.9

RANK ORDER

RANK	STATE	RATE
1	South Carolina	780.4
2	Florida	757.4
3	New Mexico	685.4
4	Louisiana	650.3
5	California	609.4
6	Nevada	569.1
7	Alaska	544.9
8	Illinois	543.3
9	Massachusetts	505.7
10	Arizona	494.7
11	Maryland	493.3
12	Tennessee	482.0
13	Kentucky	469.7
14	Oklahoma	466.8
15	Alabama	465.3
16	Missouri	465.2
17	Michigan	456.7
18	New York	451.9
19	Texas	441.1
20	North Carolina	429.9
21	Arkansas	412.5
22	Georgia	400.4
23	Delaware	354.8
24	Colorado	354.0
25	Indiana	351.5
26	Oregon	334.4
27	Kansas	316.0
28	Washington	305.6
29	New Jersey	296.2
30	Nebraska	280.2
31	Mississippi	270.5
32	Rhode Island	256.8
33	Ohio	245.1
34	Iowa	243.0
35	Connecticut	236.5
36	Idaho	235.9
37	Wyoming	218.9
38	Pennsylvania	208.0
39	Utah	195.8
40	Virginia	187.6
41	Minnesota	178.6
42	South Dakota	165.5
43	West Virginia	147.6
44	Wisconsin	129.7
45	Hawaii	123.9
46	Montana	113.9
47	Maine	79.6
48	Vermont	56.0
49	New Hampshire	52.5
50	North Dakota	47.2

District of Columbia   1,441.8

Source: Federal Bureau of Investigation
   "Crime in the United States 1994" (Uniform Crime Reports, November 19, 1995)
*Aggravated assault is an attack for the purpose of inflicting severe bodily injury.

Percent Change in Rate of Aggravated Assaults: 1993 to 1994

National Percent Change = 2.3% Decrease*

ALPHA ORDER				RANK ORDER		
RANK	STATE	PERCENT CHANGE		RANK	STATE	PERCENT CHANGE
50	Alabama	(19.0)		1	Kentucky	41.7
20	Alaska	(0.1)		2	Nevada	22.7
30	Arizona	(2.2)		3	South Dakota	13.7
26	Arkansas	(0.8)		4	Mississippi	13.5
29	California	(2.0)		5	Indiana	9.0
46	Colorado	(11.3)		6	Wisconsin	6.8
11	Connecticut	3.4		7	West Virginia	6.6
48	Delaware	(14.9)		8	Oregon	5.3
36	Florida	(3.6)		9	Maine	4.3
43	Georgia	(6.5)		10	Idaho	4.1
12	Hawaii	3.2		11	Connecticut	3.4
10	Idaho	4.1		12	Hawaii	3.2
15	Illinois	2.0		13	Oklahoma	2.5
5	Indiana	9.0		14	Missouri	2.2
23	Iowa	(0.7)		15	Illinois	2.0
34	Kansas	(3.2)		16	Minnesota	1.6
1	Kentucky	41.7		17	Pennsylvania	1.4
44	Louisiana	(9.1)		18	South Carolina	0.9
9	Maine	4.3		19	Utah	0.6
31	Maryland	(2.6)		20	Alaska	(0.1)
47	Massachusetts	(14.6)		21	Montana	(0.3)
35	Michigan	(3.3)		22	New Jersey	(0.4)
16	Minnesota	1.6		23	Iowa	(0.7)
4	Mississippi	13.5		23	Tennessee	(0.7)
14	Missouri	2.2		23	Washington	(0.7)
21	Montana	(0.3)		26	Arkansas	(0.8)
27	Nebraska	(1.2)		27	Nebraska	(1.2)
2	Nevada	22.7		27	Virginia	(1.2)
49	New Hampshire	(18.1)		29	California	(2.0)
22	New Jersey	(0.4)		30	Arizona	(2.2)
41	New Mexico	(6.3)		31	Maryland	(2.6)
37	New York	(4.2)		31	North Carolina	(2.6)
31	North Carolina	(2.6)		33	North Dakota	(3.1)
33	North Dakota	(3.1)		34	Kansas	(3.2)
39	Ohio	(4.4)		35	Michigan	(3.3)
13	Oklahoma	2.5		36	Florida	(3.6)
8	Oregon	5.3		37	New York	(4.2)
17	Pennsylvania	1.4		37	Rhode Island	(4.2)
37	Rhode Island	(4.2)		39	Ohio	(4.4)
18	South Carolina	0.9		40	Wyoming	(5.4)
3	South Dakota	13.7		41	New Mexico	(6.3)
23	Tennessee	(0.7)		41	Texas	(6.3)
41	Texas	(6.3)		43	Georgia	(6.5)
19	Utah	0.6		44	Louisiana	(9.1)
45	Vermont	(9.4)		45	Vermont	(9.4)
27	Virginia	(1.2)		46	Colorado	(11.3)
23	Washington	(0.7)		47	Massachusetts	(14.6)
7	West Virginia	6.6		48	Delaware	(14.9)
6	Wisconsin	6.8		49	New Hampshire	(18.1)
40	Wyoming	(5.4)		50	Alabama	(19.0)
					District of Columbia	(7.4)

Source: Federal Bureau of Investigation
"Crime in the United States 1994" (Uniform Crime Reports, November 19, 1995)
*Aggravated assault is an attack for the purpose of inflicting severe bodily injury.

Aggravated Assaults with Firearms in 1994

National Total = 243,606 Aggravated Assaults*

ALPHA ORDER

RANK	STATE	ASSAULTS	% of USA
28	Alabama	1,908	0.78%
36	Alaska	791	0.32%
12	Arizona	7,007	2.88%
20	Arkansas	3,051	1.25%
1	California	39,274	16.12%
22	Colorado	2,629	1.08%
33	Connecticut	1,042	0.43%
42	Delaware	176	0.07%
2	Florida	24,455	10.04%
11	Georgia	7,020	2.88%
41	Hawaii	238	0.10%
37	Idaho	776	0.32%
4	Illinois	16,107	6.61%
23	Indiana	2,526	1.04%
34	Iowa	819	0.34%
NA	Kansas**	NA	NA
21	Kentucky	2,758	1.13%
8	Louisiana	8,256	3.39%
45	Maine	43	0.02%
15	Maryland	5,628	2.31%
25	Massachusetts	2,388	0.98%
6	Michigan	11,679	4.79%
27	Minnesota	2,011	0.83%
30	Mississippi	1,707	0.70%
9	Missouri	8,121	3.33%
NA	Montana**	NA	NA
32	Nebraska	1,070	0.44%
29	Nevada	1,743	0.72%
46	New Hampshire	40	0.02%
16	New Jersey	4,534	1.86%
35	New Mexico	804	0.33%
5	New York	13,009	5.34%
7	North Carolina	9,352	3.84%
48	North Dakota	18	0.01%
13	Ohio	5,976	2.45%
19	Oklahoma	3,737	1.53%
24	Oregon	2,505	1.03%
17	Pennsylvania	4,302	1.77%
40	Rhode Island	338	0.14%
10	South Carolina	7,098	2.91%
44	South Dakota	163	0.07%
14	Tennessee	5,968	2.45%
3	Texas	23,507	9.65%
38	Utah	677	0.28%
47	Vermont	27	0.01%
26	Virginia	2,212	0.91%
18	Washington	4,203	1.73%
39	West Virginia	422	0.17%
31	Wisconsin	1,324	0.54%
43	Wyoming	167	0.07%

RANK ORDER

RANK	STATE	ASSAULTS	% of USA
1	California	39,274	16.12%
2	Florida	24,455	10.04%
3	Texas	23,507	9.65%
4	Illinois	16,107	6.61%
5	New York	13,009	5.34%
6	Michigan	11,679	4.79%
7	North Carolina	9,352	3.84%
8	Louisiana	8,256	3.39%
9	Missouri	8,121	3.33%
10	South Carolina	7,098	2.91%
11	Georgia	7,020	2.88%
12	Arizona	7,007	2.88%
13	Ohio	5,976	2.45%
14	Tennessee	5,968	2.45%
15	Maryland	5,628	2.31%
16	New Jersey	4,534	1.86%
17	Pennsylvania	4,302	1.77%
18	Washington	4,203	1.73%
19	Oklahoma	3,737	1.53%
20	Arkansas	3,051	1.25%
21	Kentucky	2,758	1.13%
22	Colorado	2,629	1.08%
23	Indiana	2,526	1.04%
24	Oregon	2,505	1.03%
25	Massachusetts	2,388	0.98%
26	Virginia	2,212	0.91%
27	Minnesota	2,011	0.83%
28	Alabama	1,908	0.78%
29	Nevada	1,743	0.72%
30	Mississippi	1,707	0.70%
31	Wisconsin	1,324	0.54%
32	Nebraska	1,070	0.44%
33	Connecticut	1,042	0.43%
34	Iowa	819	0.34%
35	New Mexico	804	0.33%
36	Alaska	791	0.32%
37	Idaho	776	0.32%
38	Utah	677	0.28%
39	West Virginia	422	0.17%
40	Rhode Island	338	0.14%
41	Hawaii	238	0.10%
42	Delaware	176	0.07%
43	Wyoming	167	0.07%
44	South Dakota	163	0.07%
45	Maine	43	0.02%
46	New Hampshire	40	0.02%
47	Vermont	27	0.01%
48	North Dakota	18	0.01%
NA	Kansas**	NA	NA
NA	Montana**	NA	NA
	District of Columbia**	NA	NA

Source: Federal Bureau of Investigation
   "Crime in the United States 1994" (Uniform Crime Reports, November 19, 1995)
*Of the 1,021,619 aggravated assaults in 1994 for which supplemental data were received by the F.B.I. There were an additional 98,331 aggravated assaults for which the type of weapon was not reported to the F.B.I. Aggravated assault is an attack for the purpose of inflicting severe bodily injury.
**Not available.

Aggravated Assault Rate with Firearms in 1994

National Rate = 110.2 Aggravated Assaults per 100,000 Population*

ALPHA ORDER			RANK ORDER		
RANK	STATE	RATE	RANK	STATE	RATE
3	Alabama	198.5	1	Illinois	324.1
12	Alaska	136.6	2	Louisiana	222.5
7	Arizona	179.1	3	Alabama	198.5
16	Arkansas	126.0	4	South Carolina	195.2
17	California	125.0	5	Missouri	193.6
21	Colorado	100.4	6	Florida	182.0
37	Connecticut	37.5	7	Arizona	179.1
33	Delaware	46.3	8	Tennessee	172.4
6	Florida	182.0	9	Mississippi	159.1
15	Georgia	126.1	10	New Mexico	147.0
45	Hawaii	20.2	11	Michigan	146.4
27	Idaho	70.4	12	Alaska	136.6
1	Illinois	324.1	12	North Carolina	136.6
29	Indiana	68.4	14	Texas	128.2
40	Iowa	35.2	15	Georgia	126.1
NA	Kansas**	NA	16	Arkansas	126.0
26	Kentucky	73.3	17	California	125.0
2	Louisiana	222.5	18	Nevada	122.0
47	Maine	3.6	19	Oklahoma	114.9
20	Maryland	112.5	20	Maryland	112.5
32	Massachusetts	47.7	21	Colorado	100.4
11	Michigan	146.4	22	Oregon	82.3
35	Minnesota	45.0	23	Washington	81.2
9	Mississippi	159.1	24	New York	79.3
5	Missouri	193.6	25	Ohio	76.3
NA	Montana**	NA	26	Kentucky	73.3
28	Nebraska	68.6	27	Idaho	70.4
18	Nevada	122.0	28	Nebraska	68.6
46	New Hampshire	4.8	29	Indiana	68.4
31	New Jersey	57.4	30	Vermont	60.0
10	New Mexico	147.0	31	New Jersey	57.4
24	New York	79.3	32	Massachusetts	47.7
12	North Carolina	136.6	33	Delaware	46.3
48	North Dakota	3.0	34	Pennsylvania	45.7
25	Ohio	76.3	35	Minnesota	45.0
19	Oklahoma	114.9	36	Utah	37.7
22	Oregon	82.3	37	Connecticut	37.5
34	Pennsylvania	45.7	38	South Dakota	36.4
42	Rhode Island	33.9	39	Wyoming	36.1
4	South Carolina	195.2	40	Iowa	35.2
38	South Dakota	36.4	41	Virginia	34.0
8	Tennessee	172.4	42	Rhode Island	33.9
14	Texas	128.2	43	Wisconsin	26.3
36	Utah	37.7	44	West Virginia	23.2
30	Vermont	60.0	45	Hawaii	20.2
41	Virginia	34.0	46	New Hampshire	4.8
23	Washington	81.2	47	Maine	3.6
44	West Virginia	23.2	48	North Dakota	3.0
43	Wisconsin	26.3	NA	Kansas**	NA
39	Wyoming	36.1	NA	Montana**	NA
				District of Columbia**	NA

Source: Morgan Quitno Press using data from Federal Bureau of Investigation
"Crime in the United States 1994" (Uniform Crime Reports, November 19, 1995)
*Of the 1,021,619 aggravated assaults in 1994 for which supplemental data were received by the F.B.I. There were an additional 98,331 aggravated assaults for which the type of weapon was not reported to the F.B.I. Aggravated assault is an attack for the purpose of inflicting severe bodily injury. Revised figures using only population of reporting jurisdictions. Illinois' rate is especially affected by number of nonreporting jurisdictions. **Not available.

Percent of Aggravated Assaults Involving Firearms in 1994

National Percent = 24.04% of Aggravated Assaults*

ALPHA ORDER

RANK ORDER

RANK	STATE	PERCENT		RANK	STATE	PERCENT
22	Alabama	24.14		1	Mississippi	44.23
15	Alaska	25.48		2	Missouri	36.39
3	Arizona	35.72		3	Arizona	35.72
7	Arkansas	30.33		4	Illinois	34.38
28	California	20.50		5	Louisiana	33.25
19	Colorado	24.87		6	North Carolina	31.40
43	Connecticut	13.45		7	Arkansas	30.33
33	Delaware	18.14		8	New Mexico	29.87
23	Florida	23.87		9	Idaho	29.51
10	Georgia	29.47		10	Georgia	29.47
36	Hawaii	16.29		11	Michigan	29.11
9	Idaho	29.51		12	Texas	29.02
4	Illinois	34.38		13	Tennessee	28.87
39	Indiana	16.13		14	Washington	26.16
42	Iowa	14.89		15	Alaska	25.48
NA	Kansas**	NA		16	Ohio	25.05
40	Kentucky	15.72		17	Minnesota	25.03
5	Louisiana	33.25		18	South Carolina	24.97
48	Maine	4.43		19	Colorado	24.87
25	Maryland	22.79		20	Oklahoma	24.61
46	Massachusetts	9.09		21	Oregon	24.39
11	Michigan	29.11		22	Alabama	24.14
17	Minnesota	25.03		23	Florida	23.87
1	Mississippi	44.23		24	Nebraska	23.72
2	Missouri	36.39		25	Maryland	22.79
NA	Montana**	NA		26	Pennsylvania	21.24
24	Nebraska	23.72		27	Nevada	21.14
27	Nevada	21.14		28	California	20.50
45	New Hampshire	9.48		29	Wisconsin	20.32
31	New Jersey	19.37		30	Vermont	20.30
8	New Mexico	29.87		31	New Jersey	19.37
37	New York	16.25		32	Utah	18.82
6	North Carolina	31.40		33	Delaware	18.14
47	North Dakota	6.12		34	South Dakota	18.11
16	Ohio	25.05		35	Virginia	18.06
20	Oklahoma	24.61		36	Hawaii	16.29
21	Oregon	24.39		37	New York	16.25
26	Pennsylvania	21.24		38	Wyoming	16.18
44	Rhode Island	13.20		39	Indiana	16.13
18	South Carolina	24.97		40	Kentucky	15.72
34	South Dakota	18.11		41	West Virginia	15.71
13	Tennessee	28.87		42	Iowa	14.89
12	Texas	29.02		43	Connecticut	13.45
32	Utah	18.82		44	Rhode Island	13.20
30	Vermont	20.30		45	New Hampshire	9.48
35	Virginia	18.06		46	Massachusetts	9.09
14	Washington	26.16		47	North Dakota	6.12
41	West Virginia	15.71		48	Maine	4.43
29	Wisconsin	20.32		NA	Kansas**	NA
38	Wyoming	16.18		NA	Montana**	NA
					District of Columbia**	NA

Source: Morgan Quitno Press using data from Federal Bureau of Investigation
   "Crime in the United States 1994" (Uniform Crime Reports, November 19, 1995)
*Of the 1,021,619 aggravated assaults in 1994 for which supplemental data were received by the F.B.I. There were an additional 98,331 aggravated assaults for which the type of weapon was not reported to the F.B.I. Aggravated assault is an attack for the purpose of inflicting severe bodily injury.
**Not available.

Aggravated Assaults with Knives or Cutting Instruments in 1994

National total = 180,053 Aggravated Assaults*

ALPHA ORDER

RANK	STATE	ASSAULTS	% of USA
23	Alabama	1,919	1.07%
37	Alaska	644	0.36%
17	Arizona	3,227	1.79%
27	Arkansas	1,392	0.77%
1	California	24,233	13.46%
24	Colorado	1,742	0.97%
29	Connecticut	1,220	0.68%
41	Delaware	251	0.14%
3	Florida	19,189	10.66%
10	Georgia	5,271	2.93%
44	Hawaii	173	0.10%
36	Idaho	647	0.36%
5	Illinois	10,477	5.82%
26	Indiana	1,593	0.88%
32	Iowa	806	0.45%
NA	Kansas**	NA	NA
28	Kentucky	1,361	0.76%
12	Louisiana	4,493	2.50%
45	Maine	144	0.08%
9	Maryland	5,282	2.93%
13	Massachusetts	4,276	2.37%
6	Michigan	7,140	3.97%
22	Minnesota	2,145	1.19%
33	Mississippi	754	0.42%
16	Missouri	3,355	1.86%
NA	Montana**	NA	NA
34	Nebraska	678	0.38%
31	Nevada	1,019	0.57%
46	New Hampshire	73	0.04%
11	New Jersey	4,972	2.76%
38	New Mexico	562	0.31%
2	New York	19,659	10.92%
8	North Carolina	5,843	3.25%
47	North Dakota	40	0.02%
14	Ohio	4,007	2.23%
21	Oklahoma	2,176	1.21%
25	Oregon	1,738	0.97%
18	Pennsylvania	3,048	1.69%
40	Rhode Island	422	0.23%
7	South Carolina	6,485	3.60%
42	South Dakota	231	0.13%
15	Tennessee	3,625	2.01%
4	Texas	16,064	8.92%
35	Utah	648	0.36%
48	Vermont	28	0.02%
20	Virginia	2,651	1.47%
19	Washington	2,664	1.48%
39	West Virginia	458	0.25%
30	Wisconsin	1,041	0.58%
43	Wyoming	187	0.10%

RANK ORDER

RANK	STATE	ASSAULTS	% of USA
1	California	24,233	13.46%
2	New York	19,659	10.92%
3	Florida	19,189	10.66%
4	Texas	16,064	8.92%
5	Illinois	10,477	5.82%
6	Michigan	7,140	3.97%
7	South Carolina	6,485	3.60%
8	North Carolina	5,843	3.25%
9	Maryland	5,282	2.93%
10	Georgia	5,271	2.93%
11	New Jersey	4,972	2.76%
12	Louisiana	4,493	2.50%
13	Massachusetts	4,276	2.37%
14	Ohio	4,007	2.23%
15	Tennessee	3,625	2.01%
16	Missouri	3,355	1.86%
17	Arizona	3,227	1.79%
18	Pennsylvania	3,048	1.69%
19	Washington	2,664	1.48%
20	Virginia	2,651	1.47%
21	Oklahoma	2,176	1.21%
22	Minnesota	2,145	1.19%
23	Alabama	1,919	1.07%
24	Colorado	1,742	0.97%
25	Oregon	1,738	0.97%
26	Indiana	1,593	0.88%
27	Arkansas	1,392	0.77%
28	Kentucky	1,361	0.76%
29	Connecticut	1,220	0.68%
30	Wisconsin	1,041	0.58%
31	Nevada	1,019	0.57%
32	Iowa	806	0.45%
33	Mississippi	754	0.42%
34	Nebraska	678	0.38%
35	Utah	648	0.36%
36	Idaho	647	0.36%
37	Alaska	644	0.36%
38	New Mexico	562	0.31%
39	West Virginia	458	0.25%
40	Rhode Island	422	0.23%
41	Delaware	251	0.14%
42	South Dakota	231	0.13%
43	Wyoming	187	0.10%
44	Hawaii	173	0.10%
45	Maine	144	0.08%
46	New Hampshire	73	0.04%
47	North Dakota	40	0.02%
48	Vermont	28	0.02%
NA	Kansas**	NA	NA
NA	Montana**	NA	NA
	District of Columbia**	NA	NA

Source: Federal Bureau of Investigation
    "Crime in the United States 1994" (Uniform Crime Reports, November 19, 1995)
Of the 1,021,619 aggravated assaults in 1994 for which supplemental data were received by the F.B.I. There were an additional 98,331 aggravated assaults for which the type of weapon was not reported to the F.B.I. Aggravated assault is an attack for the purpose of inflicting severe bodily injury.
***Not available.*

Percent of Aggravated Assaults Involving Knives or Cutting Instruments in 1994

National Percent = 17.77% of Aggravated Assaults*

ALPHA ORDER

RANK	STATE	PERCENT
6	Alabama	24.28
15	Alaska	20.74
32	Arizona	16.45
42	Arkansas	13.84
44	California	12.65
30	Colorado	16.48
35	Connecticut	15.75
2	Delaware	25.88
19	Florida	18.73
9	Georgia	22.13
46	Hawaii	11.84
4	Idaho	24.60
8	Illinois	22.36
47	Indiana	10.17
40	Iowa	14.65
NA	Kansas**	NA
48	Kentucky	7.76
21	Louisiana	18.09
39	Maine	14.85
11	Maryland	21.39
33	Massachusetts	16.27
23	Michigan	17.80
1	Minnesota	26.70
18	Mississippi	19.54
37	Missouri	15.03
NA	Montana**	NA
37	Nebraska	15.03
45	Nevada	12.36
25	New Hampshire	17.30
12	New Jersey	21.24
14	New Mexico	20.88
5	New York	24.55
17	North Carolina	19.62
43	North Dakota	13.61
28	Ohio	16.79
41	Oklahoma	14.33
27	Oregon	16.92
36	Pennsylvania	15.05
30	Rhode Island	16.48
7	South Carolina	22.81
3	South Dakota	25.67
24	Tennessee	17.54
16	Texas	19.83
22	Utah	18.01
13	Vermont	21.05
10	Virginia	21.65
29	Washington	16.58
26	West Virginia	17.05
34	Wisconsin	15.98
20	Wyoming	18.12

RANK ORDER

RANK	STATE	PERCENT
1	Minnesota	26.70
2	Delaware	25.88
3	South Dakota	25.67
4	Idaho	24.60
5	New York	24.55
6	Alabama	24.28
7	South Carolina	22.81
8	Illinois	22.36
9	Georgia	22.13
10	Virginia	21.65
11	Maryland	21.39
12	New Jersey	21.24
13	Vermont	21.05
14	New Mexico	20.88
15	Alaska	20.74
16	Texas	19.83
17	North Carolina	19.62
18	Mississippi	19.54
19	Florida	18.73
20	Wyoming	18.12
21	Louisiana	18.09
22	Utah	18.01
23	Michigan	17.80
24	Tennessee	17.54
25	New Hampshire	17.30
26	West Virginia	17.05
27	Oregon	16.92
28	Ohio	16.79
29	Washington	16.58
30	Colorado	16.48
30	Rhode Island	16.48
32	Arizona	16.45
33	Massachusetts	16.27
34	Wisconsin	15.98
35	Connecticut	15.75
36	Pennsylvania	15.05
37	Missouri	15.03
37	Nebraska	15.03
39	Maine	14.85
40	Iowa	14.65
41	Oklahoma	14.33
42	Arkansas	13.84
43	North Dakota	13.61
44	California	12.65
45	Nevada	12.36
46	Hawaii	11.84
47	Indiana	10.17
48	Kentucky	7.76
NA	Kansas**	NA
NA	Montana**	NA
	District of Columbia**	NA

Source: Morgan Quitno Press using data from Federal Bureau of Investigation
   "Crime in the United States 1994" (Uniform Crime Reports, November 19, 1995)
*Of the 1,021,619 aggravated assaults in 1994 for which supplemental data were received by the F.B.I. There
were an additional 98,331 aggravated assaults for which the type of weapon was not reported to the F.B.I.
Aggravated assault is an attack for the purpose of inflicting severe bodily injury.
**Not available.

Aggravated Assaults with Blunt Objects and Other Dangerous Weapons in 1994

National Total = 323,295 Aggravated Assaults*

ALPHA ORDER

RANK	STATE	ASSAULTS	% of USA
30	Alabama	1,973	0.61%
37	Alaska	743	0.23%
17	Arizona	5,165	1.60%
28	Arkansas	2,312	0.72%
1	California	53,657	16.60%
22	Colorado	3,883	1.20%
26	Connecticut	2,717	0.84%
41	Delaware	428	0.13%
2	Florida	43,139	13.34%
11	Georgia	7,484	2.31%
44	Hawaii	255	0.08%
36	Idaho	817	0.25%
5	Illinois	18,068	5.59%
23	Indiana	3,629	1.12%
32	Iowa	1,427	0.44%
NA	Kansas**	NA	NA
21	Kentucky	4,362	1.35%
15	Louisiana	6,808	2.11%
42	Maine	306	0.09%
9	Maryland	9,928	3.07%
8	Massachusetts	10,435	3.23%
6	Michigan	16,795	5.19%
27	Minnesota	2,323	0.72%
39	Mississippi	656	0.20%
14	Missouri	7,009	2.17%
NA	Montana**	NA	NA
31	Nebraska	1,440	0.45%
29	Nevada	2,064	0.64%
47	New Hampshire	96	0.03%
13	New Jersey	7,121	2.20%
38	New Mexico	663	0.21%
3	New York	28,071	8.68%
10	North Carolina	8,077	2.50%
46	North Dakota	100	0.03%
12	Ohio	7,266	2.25%
20	Oklahoma	4,393	1.36%
24	Oregon	3,396	1.05%
19	Pennsylvania	4,667	1.44%
35	Rhode Island	1,015	0.31%
7	South Carolina	10,927	3.38%
45	South Dakota	166	0.05%
16	Tennessee	6,720	2.08%
4	Texas	21,247	6.57%
33	Utah	1,343	0.42%
48	Vermont	60	0.02%
25	Virginia	3,300	1.02%
18	Washington	4,685	1.45%
40	West Virginia	541	0.17%
34	Wisconsin	1,342	0.42%
43	Wyoming	276	0.09%

RANK ORDER

RANK	STATE	ASSAULTS	% of USA
1	California	53,657	16.60%
2	Florida	43,139	13.34%
3	New York	28,071	8.68%
4	Texas	21,247	6.57%
5	Illinois	18,068	5.59%
6	Michigan	16,795	5.19%
7	South Carolina	10,927	3.38%
8	Massachusetts	10,435	3.23%
9	Maryland	9,928	3.07%
10	North Carolina	8,077	2.50%
11	Georgia	7,484	2.31%
12	Ohio	7,266	2.25%
13	New Jersey	7,121	2.20%
14	Missouri	7,009	2.17%
15	Louisiana	6,808	2.11%
16	Tennessee	6,720	2.08%
17	Arizona	5,165	1.60%
18	Washington	4,685	1.45%
19	Pennsylvania	4,667	1.44%
20	Oklahoma	4,393	1.36%
21	Kentucky	4,362	1.35%
22	Colorado	3,883	1.20%
23	Indiana	3,629	1.12%
24	Oregon	3,396	1.05%
25	Virginia	3,300	1.02%
26	Connecticut	2,717	0.84%
27	Minnesota	2,323	0.72%
28	Arkansas	2,312	0.72%
29	Nevada	2,064	0.64%
30	Alabama	1,973	0.61%
31	Nebraska	1,440	0.45%
32	Iowa	1,427	0.44%
33	Utah	1,343	0.42%
34	Wisconsin	1,342	0.42%
35	Rhode Island	1,015	0.31%
36	Idaho	817	0.25%
37	Alaska	743	0.23%
38	New Mexico	663	0.21%
39	Mississippi	656	0.20%
40	West Virginia	541	0.17%
41	Delaware	428	0.13%
42	Maine	306	0.09%
43	Wyoming	276	0.09%
44	Hawaii	255	0.08%
45	South Dakota	166	0.05%
46	North Dakota	100	0.03%
47	New Hampshire	96	0.03%
48	Vermont	60	0.02%
NA	Kansas**	NA	NA
NA	Montana**	NA	NA
	District of Columbia**	NA	NA

Source: Federal Bureau of Investigation
   "Crime in the United States 1994" (Uniform Crime Reports, November 19, 1995)
*Of the 1,021,619 aggravated assaults in 1994 for which supplemental data were received by the F.B.I. There were an additional 98,331 aggravated assaults for which the type of weapon was not reported to the F.B.I.
Aggravated assault is an attack for the purpose of inflicting severe bodily injury.
**Not available.

Percent of Aggravated Assaults Involving Blunt Objects
And Other Dangerous Weapons in 1994
National Percent = 31.90% of Aggravated Assaults*

ALPHA ORDER

RANK ORDER

RANK	STATE	PERCENT		RANK	STATE	PERCENT
36	Alabama	24.96		1	Vermont	45.11
39	Alaska	23.93		2	Delaware	44.12
32	Arizona	26.33		3	Florida	42.11
42	Arkansas	22.99		4	Michigan	41.86
27	California	28.01		5	Maryland	40.21
11	Colorado	36.74		6	Massachusetts	39.71
12	Connecticut	35.08		7	Rhode Island	39.65
2	Delaware	44.12		8	Illinois	38.56
3	Florida	42.11		9	South Carolina	38.44
19	Georgia	31.42		10	Utah	37.33
47	Hawaii	17.45		11	Colorado	36.74
21	Idaho	31.06		12	Connecticut	35.08
8	Illinois	38.56		13	New York	35.06
40	Indiana	23.17		14	North Dakota	34.01
34	Iowa	25.94		15	Oregon	33.07
NA	Kansas**	NA		16	Tennessee	32.51
37	Kentucky	24.86		17	Nebraska	31.92
28	Louisiana	27.42		18	Maine	31.55
18	Maine	31.55		19	Georgia	31.42
5	Maryland	40.21		20	Missouri	31.41
6	Massachusetts	39.71		21	Idaho	31.06
4	Michigan	41.86		22	Ohio	30.45
26	Minnesota	28.91		23	New Jersey	30.42
48	Mississippi	17.00		24	Washington	29.16
20	Missouri	31.41		25	Oklahoma	28.93
NA	Montana**	NA		26	Minnesota	28.91
17	Nebraska	31.92		27	California	28.01
35	Nevada	25.03		28	Louisiana	27.42
43	New Hampshire	22.75		29	North Carolina	27.12
23	New Jersey	30.42		30	Virginia	26.95
38	New Mexico	24.63		31	Wyoming	26.74
13	New York	35.06		32	Arizona	26.33
29	North Carolina	27.12		33	Texas	26.23
14	North Dakota	34.01		34	Iowa	25.94
22	Ohio	30.45		35	Nevada	25.03
25	Oklahoma	28.93		36	Alabama	24.96
15	Oregon	33.07		37	Kentucky	24.86
41	Pennsylvania	23.04		38	New Mexico	24.63
7	Rhode Island	39.65		39	Alaska	23.93
9	South Carolina	38.44		40	Indiana	23.17
46	South Dakota	18.44		41	Pennsylvania	23.04
16	Tennessee	32.51		42	Arkansas	22.99
33	Texas	26.23		43	New Hampshire	22.75
10	Utah	37.33		44	Wisconsin	20.60
1	Vermont	45.11		45	West Virginia	20.13
30	Virginia	26.95		46	South Dakota	18.44
24	Washington	29.16		47	Hawaii	17.45
45	West Virginia	20.13		48	Mississippi	17.00
44	Wisconsin	20.60		NA	Kansas**	NA
31	Wyoming	26.74		NA	Montana**	NA
					District of Columbia**	NA

Source: Morgan Quitno Press using data from Federal Bureau of Investigation
    "Crime in the United States 1994" (Uniform Crime Reports, November 19, 1995)
*Of the 1,021,619 aggravated assaults in 1994 for which supplemental data were received by the F.B.I. There
were an additional 98,331 aggravated assaults for which the type of weapon was not reported to the F.B.I.
Aggravated assault is an attack for the purpose of inflicting severe bodily injury.
**Not available.

Aggravated Assaults Committed with Hands, Fists or Feet in 1994

National Total = 266,447 Aggravated Assaults*

ALPHA ORDER

ALPHA ORDER

RANK	STATE	ASSAULTS	% of USA
31	Alabama	2,104	0.79%
36	Alaska	927	0.35%
17	Arizona	4,215	1.58%
24	Arkansas	3,303	1.24%
1	California	74,384	27.92%
29	Colorado	2,315	0.87%
26	Connecticut	2,766	1.04%
47	Delaware	115	0.04%
4	Florida	15,670	5.88%
19	Georgia	4,045	1.52%
37	Hawaii	795	0.30%
43	Idaho	390	0.15%
30	Illinois	2,204	0.83%
8	Indiana	7,916	2.97%
28	Iowa	2,450	0.92%
NA	Kansas**	NA	NA
6	Kentucky	9,067	3.40%
12	Louisiana	5,276	1.98%
41	Maine	477	0.18%
21	Maryland	3,852	1.45%
5	Massachusetts	9,181	3.45%
15	Michigan	4,509	1.69%
32	Minnesota	1,555	0.58%
39	Mississippi	742	0.28%
22	Missouri	3,832	1.44%
NA	Montana**	NA	NA
33	Nebraska	1,323	0.50%
23	Nevada	3,419	1.28%
45	New Hampshire	213	0.08%
9	New Jersey	6,783	2.55%
40	New Mexico	663	0.25%
3	New York	19,331	7.26%
11	North Carolina	6,510	2.44%
46	North Dakota	136	0.05%
10	Ohio	6,611	2.48%
13	Oklahoma	4,879	1.83%
27	Oregon	2,630	0.99%
7	Pennsylvania	8,239	3.09%
38	Rhode Island	785	0.29%
20	South Carolina	3,915	1.47%
44	South Dakota	340	0.13%
16	Tennessee	4,359	1.64%
2	Texas	20,196	7.58%
35	Utah	930	0.35%
48	Vermont	18	0.01%
18	Virginia	4,083	1.53%
14	Washington	4,517	1.70%
34	West Virginia	1,266	0.48%
25	Wisconsin	2,809	1.05%
42	Wyoming	402	0.15%

RANK ORDER

RANK	STATE	ASSAULTS	% of USA
1	California	74,384	27.92%
2	Texas	20,196	7.58%
3	New York	19,331	7.26%
4	Florida	15,670	5.88%
5	Massachusetts	9,181	3.45%
6	Kentucky	9,067	3.40%
7	Pennsylvania	8,239	3.09%
8	Indiana	7,916	2.97%
9	New Jersey	6,783	2.55%
10	Ohio	6,611	2.48%
11	North Carolina	6,510	2.44%
12	Louisiana	5,276	1.98%
13	Oklahoma	4,879	1.83%
14	Washington	4,517	1.70%
15	Michigan	4,509	1.69%
16	Tennessee	4,359	1.64%
17	Arizona	4,215	1.58%
18	Virginia	4,083	1.53%
19	Georgia	4,045	1.52%
20	South Carolina	3,915	1.47%
21	Maryland	3,852	1.45%
22	Missouri	3,832	1.44%
23	Nevada	3,419	1.28%
24	Arkansas	3,303	1.24%
25	Wisconsin	2,809	1.05%
26	Connecticut	2,766	1.04%
27	Oregon	2,630	0.99%
28	Iowa	2,450	0.92%
29	Colorado	2,315	0.87%
30	Illinois	2,204	0.83%
31	Alabama	2,104	0.79%
32	Minnesota	1,555	0.58%
33	Nebraska	1,323	0.50%
34	West Virginia	1,266	0.48%
35	Utah	930	0.35%
36	Alaska	927	0.35%
37	Hawaii	795	0.30%
38	Rhode Island	785	0.29%
39	Mississippi	742	0.28%
40	New Mexico	663	0.25%
41	Maine	477	0.18%
42	Wyoming	402	0.15%
43	Idaho	390	0.15%
44	South Dakota	340	0.13%
45	New Hampshire	213	0.08%
46	North Dakota	136	0.05%
47	Delaware	115	0.04%
48	Vermont	18	0.01%
NA	Kansas**	NA	NA
NA	Montana**	NA	NA
	District of Columbia**	NA	NA

Source: Federal Bureau of Investigation
   "Crime in the United States 1994" (Uniform Crime Reports, November 19, 1995)
*Of the 1,021,619 aggravated assaults in 1994 for which supplemental data were received by the F.B.I. There were an additional 98,331 aggravated assaults for which the type of weapon was not reported to the F.B.I. Aggravated assault is an attack for the purpose of inflicting severe bodily injury. Referred to as "personal weapons" by the F.B.I. **Not available.*

Percent of Aggravated Assaults Committed with Hands, Fists or Feet in 1994

National Percent = 26.29% of Aggravated Assaults*

ALPHA ORDER

RANK ORDER

RANK	STATE	PERCENT	RANK	STATE	PERCENT
26	Alabama	26.62	1	Hawaii	54.41
21	Alaska	29.86	2	Kentucky	51.67
34	Arizona	21.49	3	Indiana	50.54
18	Arkansas	32.84	4	New Hampshire	50.47
13	California	38.83	5	Maine	49.18
32	Colorado	21.90	6	West Virginia	47.12
15	Connecticut	35.71	7	North Dakota	46.26
46	Delaware	11.86	8	Iowa	44.53
42	Florida	15.29	9	Wisconsin	43.11
40	Georgia	16.98	10	Nevada	41.47
1	Hawaii	54.41	11	Pennsylvania	40.67
43	Idaho	14.83	12	Wyoming	38.95
48	Illinois	4.70	13	California	38.83
3	Indiana	50.54	14	South Dakota	37.78
8	Iowa	44.53	15	Connecticut	35.71
NA	Kansas**	NA	16	Massachusetts	34.94
2	Kentucky	51.67	17	Virginia	33.34
35	Louisiana	21.25	18	Arkansas	32.84
5	Maine	49.18	19	Oklahoma	32.13
41	Maryland	15.60	20	Rhode Island	30.66
16	Massachusetts	34.94	21	Alaska	29.86
47	Michigan	11.24	22	Nebraska	29.33
37	Minnesota	19.36	23	New Jersey	28.97
38	Mississippi	19.23	24	Washington	28.11
39	Missouri	17.17	25	Ohio	27.71
NA	Montana**	NA	26	Alabama	26.62
22	Nebraska	29.33	27	Utah	25.85
10	Nevada	41.47	28	Oregon	25.61
4	New Hampshire	50.47	29	Texas	24.93
23	New Jersey	28.97	30	New Mexico	24.63
30	New Mexico	24.63	31	New York	24.14
31	New York	24.14	32	Colorado	21.90
33	North Carolina	21.86	33	North Carolina	21.86
7	North Dakota	46.26	34	Arizona	21.49
25	Ohio	27.71	35	Louisiana	21.25
19	Oklahoma	32.13	36	Tennessee	21.09
28	Oregon	25.61	37	Minnesota	19.36
11	Pennsylvania	40.67	38	Mississippi	19.23
20	Rhode Island	30.66	39	Missouri	17.17
44	South Carolina	13.77	40	Georgia	16.98
14	South Dakota	37.78	41	Maryland	15.60
36	Tennessee	21.09	42	Florida	15.29
29	Texas	24.93	43	Idaho	14.83
27	Utah	25.85	44	South Carolina	13.77
45	Vermont	13.53	45	Vermont	13.53
17	Virginia	33.34	46	Delaware	11.86
24	Washington	28.11	47	Michigan	11.24
6	West Virginia	47.12	48	Illinois	4.70
9	Wisconsin	43.11	NA	Kansas**	NA
12	Wyoming	38.95	NA	Montana**	NA
				District of Columbia**	NA

Source: Morgan Quitno Press using data from Federal Bureau of Investigation
"Crime in the United States 1994" (Uniform Crime Reports, November 19, 1995)
*Of the 1,021,619 aggravated assaults in 1994 for which supplemental data were received by the F.B.I. There were an additional 98,331 aggravated assaults for which the type of weapon was not reported to the F.B.I. Aggravated assault is an attack for the purpose of inflicting severe bodily injury. Referred to as "personal weapons" by the F.B.I. **Not available.

Property Crimes in 1994

National Total = 12,127,507 Property Crimes*

ALPHA ORDER

ALPHA ORDER

RANK	STATE	CRIMES	% of USA
25	Alabama	178,015	1.47%
44	Alaska	29,947	0.25%
13	Arizona	294,273	2.43%
32	Arkansas	103,115	0.85%
1	California	1,622,102	13.38%
26	Colorado	175,808	1.45%
28	Connecticut	134,030	1.11%
46	Delaware	25,321	0.21%
2	Florida	991,105	8.17%
8	Georgia	376,926	3.11%
37	Hawaii	75,672	0.62%
39	Idaho	42,954	0.35%
5	Illinois	548,222	4.52%
18	Indiana	233,975	1.93%
34	Iowa	94,475	0.78%
30	Kansas	112,761	0.93%
31	Kentucky	110,725	0.91%
15	Louisiana	245,488	2.02%
42	Maine	38,971	0.32%
14	Maryland	259,039	2.14%
20	Massachusetts	225,532	1.86%
6	Michigan	444,325	3.66%
23	Minnesota	181,856	1.50%
29	Mississippi	115,924	0.96%
17	Missouri	240,898	1.99%
41	Montana	41,445	0.34%
38	Nebraska	65,746	0.54%
36	Nevada	82,693	0.68%
45	New Hampshire	29,837	0.25%
11	New Jersey	319,856	2.64%
35	New Mexico	87,638	0.72%
4	New York	745,845	6.15%
9	North Carolina	351,397	2.90%
50	North Dakota	16,933	0.14%
7	Ohio	441,380	3.64%
27	Oklahoma	160,250	1.32%
24	Oregon	178,240	1.47%
10	Pennsylvania	342,901	2.83%
43	Rhode Island	37,323	0.31%
22	South Carolina	182,114	1.50%
47	South Dakota	20,726	0.17%
19	Tennessee	226,247	1.87%
3	Texas	949,387	7.83%
33	Utah	95,332	0.79%
49	Vermont	18,290	0.15%
16	Virginia	241,763	1.99%
12	Washington	294,734	2.43%
40	West Virginia	42,136	0.35%
21	Wisconsin	186,704	1.54%
48	Wyoming	19,122	0.16%

RANK ORDER

RANK	STATE	CRIMES	% of USA
1	California	1,622,102	13.38%
2	Florida	991,105	8.17%
3	Texas	949,387	7.83%
4	New York	745,845	6.15%
5	Illinois	548,222	4.52%
6	Michigan	444,325	3.66%
7	Ohio	441,380	3.64%
8	Georgia	376,926	3.11%
9	North Carolina	351,397	2.90%
10	Pennsylvania	342,901	2.83%
11	New Jersey	319,856	2.64%
12	Washington	294,734	2.43%
13	Arizona	294,273	2.43%
14	Maryland	259,039	2.14%
15	Louisiana	245,488	2.02%
16	Virginia	241,763	1.99%
17	Missouri	240,898	1.99%
18	Indiana	233,975	1.93%
19	Tennessee	226,247	1.87%
20	Massachusetts	225,532	1.86%
21	Wisconsin	186,704	1.54%
22	South Carolina	182,114	1.50%
23	Minnesota	181,856	1.50%
24	Oregon	178,240	1.47%
25	Alabama	178,015	1.47%
26	Colorado	175,808	1.45%
27	Oklahoma	160,250	1.32%
28	Connecticut	134,030	1.11%
29	Mississippi	115,924	0.96%
30	Kansas	112,761	0.93%
31	Kentucky	110,725	0.91%
32	Arkansas	103,115	0.85%
33	Utah	95,332	0.79%
34	Iowa	94,475	0.78%
35	New Mexico	87,638	0.72%
36	Nevada	82,693	0.68%
37	Hawaii	75,672	0.62%
38	Nebraska	65,746	0.54%
39	Idaho	42,954	0.35%
40	West Virginia	42,136	0.35%
41	Montana	41,445	0.34%
42	Maine	38,971	0.32%
43	Rhode Island	37,323	0.31%
44	Alaska	29,947	0.25%
45	New Hampshire	29,837	0.25%
46	Delaware	25,321	0.21%
47	South Dakota	20,726	0.17%
48	Wyoming	19,122	0.16%
49	Vermont	18,290	0.15%
50	North Dakota	16,933	0.14%
	District of Columbia	48,009	0.40%

Source: Federal Bureau of Investigation
"Crime in the United States 1994" (Uniform Crime Reports, November 19, 1995)
*Property crimes are offenses of burglary, larceny-theft and motor vehicle theft.

Average Time Between Property Crimes in 1994

National Rate = A Property Crime Occurs Every 3 Seconds*

ALPHA ORDER				RANK ORDER		
RANK	STATE	MINUTES.SECONDS		RANK	STATE	MINUTES.SECONDS
26	Alabama	2.57		1	North Dakota	31.02
7	Alaska	17.33		2	Vermont	28.44
38	Arizona	1.47		3	Wyoming	27.29
19	Arkansas	5.06		4	South Dakota	25.22
50	California	0.19		5	Delaware	20.46
25	Colorado	2.59		6	New Hampshire	17.37
23	Connecticut	3.55		7	Alaska	17.33
5	Delaware	20.46		8	Rhode Island	14.05
49	Florida	0.32		9	Maine	13.29
43	Georgia	1.23		10	Montana	12.41
14	Hawaii	6.57		11	West Virginia	12.28
12	Idaho	12.14		12	Idaho	12.14
46	Illinois	0.58		13	Nebraska	7.59
33	Indiana	2.15		14	Hawaii	6.57
17	Iowa	5.34		15	Nevada	6.22
21	Kansas	4.40		16	New Mexico	6.00
20	Kentucky	4.45		17	Iowa	5.34
36	Louisiana	2.08		18	Utah	5.31
9	Maine	13.29		19	Arkansas	5.06
37	Maryland	2.02		20	Kentucky	4.45
31	Massachusetts	2.20		21	Kansas	4.40
44	Michigan	1.11		22	Mississippi	4.32
28	Minnesota	2.53		23	Connecticut	3.55
22	Mississippi	4.32		24	Oklahoma	3.17
34	Missouri	2.11		25	Colorado	2.59
10	Montana	12.41		26	Alabama	2.57
13	Nebraska	7.59		26	Oregon	2.57
15	Nevada	6.22		28	Minnesota	2.53
6	New Hampshire	17.37		28	South Carolina	2.53
40	New Jersey	1.38		30	Wisconsin	2.49
16	New Mexico	6.00		31	Massachusetts	2.20
47	New York	0.42		32	Tennessee	2.19
42	North Carolina	1.30		33	Indiana	2.15
1	North Dakota	31.02		34	Missouri	2.11
44	Ohio	1.11		35	Virginia	2.10
24	Oklahoma	3.17		36	Louisiana	2.08
26	Oregon	2.57		37	Maryland	2.02
41	Pennsylvania	1.32		38	Arizona	1.47
8	Rhode Island	14.05		38	Washington	1.47
28	South Carolina	2.53		40	New Jersey	1.38
4	South Dakota	25.22		41	Pennsylvania	1.32
32	Tennessee	2.19		42	North Carolina	1.30
48	Texas	0.33		43	Georgia	1.23
18	Utah	5.31		44	Michigan	1.11
2	Vermont	28.44		44	Ohio	1.11
35	Virginia	2.10		46	Illinois	0.58
38	Washington	1.47		47	New York	0.42
11	West Virginia	12.28		48	Texas	0.33
30	Wisconsin	2.49		49	Florida	0.32
3	Wyoming	27.29		50	California	0.19
					District of Columbia	10.57

Source: Morgan Quitno Press using data from Federal Bureau of Investigation
"Crime in the United States 1994" (Uniform Crime Reports, November 19, 1995)
*Property crimes are offenses of burglary, larceny-theft and motor vehicle theft.

Property Crimes per Square Mile in 1994

National Rate = 3.26 Property Crimes per Square Mile*

ALPHA ORDER			RANK ORDER		
RANK	STATE	RATE	RANK	STATE	RATE
25	Alabama	3.41	1	New Jersey	38.94
50	Alaska	0.05	2	Rhode Island	30.32
29	Arizona	2.58	3	Massachusetts	24.41
33	Arkansas	1.94	4	Connecticut	24.18
10	California	10.21	5	Maryland	21.07
37	Colorado	1.69	6	Florida	16.52
4	Connecticut	24.18	7	New York	13.81
9	Delaware	10.56	8	Hawaii	11.72
6	Florida	16.52	9	Delaware	10.56
16	Georgia	6.39	10	California	10.21
8	Hawaii	11.72	11	Ohio	9.85
45	Idaho	0.51	12	Illinois	9.47
12	Illinois	9.47	13	Pennsylvania	7.49
15	Indiana	6.42	14	North Carolina	6.67
38	Iowa	1.68	15	Indiana	6.42
39	Kansas	1.37	16	Georgia	6.39
28	Kentucky	2.74	17	South Carolina	5.84
20	Louisiana	4.94	18	Virginia	5.71
40	Maine	1.16	19	Tennessee	5.37
5	Maryland	21.07	20	Louisiana	4.94
3	Massachusetts	24.41	21	Michigan	4.59
21	Michigan	4.59	22	Washington	4.17
32	Minnesota	2.09	23	Texas	3.55
30	Mississippi	2.40	24	Missouri	3.46
24	Missouri	3.46	25	Alabama	3.41
46	Montana	0.28	26	New Hampshire	3.21
42	Nebraska	0.85	27	Wisconsin	2.85
43	Nevada	0.75	28	Kentucky	2.74
26	New Hampshire	3.21	29	Arizona	2.58
1	New Jersey	38.94	30	Mississippi	2.40
44	New Mexico	0.72	31	Oklahoma	2.29
7	New York	13.81	32	Minnesota	2.09
14	North Carolina	6.67	33	Arkansas	1.94
48	North Dakota	0.24	34	Vermont	1.90
11	Ohio	9.85	35	Oregon	1.84
31	Oklahoma	2.29	36	West Virginia	1.74
35	Oregon	1.84	37	Colorado	1.69
13	Pennsylvania	7.49	38	Iowa	1.68
2	Rhode Island	30.32	39	Kansas	1.37
17	South Carolina	5.84	40	Maine	1.16
47	South Dakota	0.27	41	Utah	1.12
19	Tennessee	5.37	42	Nebraska	0.85
23	Texas	3.55	43	Nevada	0.75
41	Utah	1.12	44	New Mexico	0.72
34	Vermont	1.90	45	Idaho	0.51
18	Virginia	5.71	46	Montana	0.28
22	Washington	4.17	47	South Dakota	0.27
36	West Virginia	1.74	48	North Dakota	0.24
27	Wisconsin	2.85	49	Wyoming	0.20
49	Wyoming	0.20	50	Alaska	0.05

District of Columbia 706.01

Source: Morgan Quitno Press using data from Federal Bureau of Investigation
    "Crime in the United States 1994" (Uniform Crime Reports, November 19, 1995)
*Property crimes are offenses of burglary, larceny-theft and motor vehicle theft.

Percent Change in Number of Property Crimes: 1993 to 1994

National Percent Change = 0.7% Decrease*

ALPHA ORDER

RANK	STATE	PERCENT CHANGE
17	Alabama	3.7
14	Alaska	4.0
3	Arizona	11.3
25	Arkansas	0.9
42	California	(3.4)
34	Colorado	(0.6)
39	Connecticut	(2.5)
49	Delaware	(13.6)
24	Florida	1.4
30	Georgia	(0.4)
6	Hawaii	7.3
5	Idaho	9.7
26	Illinois	0.6
19	Indiana	3.0
44	Iowa	(4.6)
32	Kansas	(0.5)
13	Kentucky	4.5
37	Louisiana	(1.2)
15	Maine	3.9
21	Maryland	2.1
46	Massachusetts	(8.3)
26	Michigan	0.6
35	Minnesota	(0.8)
4	Mississippi	10.1
9	Missouri	5.8
7	Montana	7.1
12	Nebraska	4.8
1	Nevada	12.2
43	New Hampshire	(4.2)
41	New Jersey	(2.7)
23	New Mexico	1.6
47	New York	(8.5)
22	North Carolina	1.7
40	North Dakota	(2.6)
28	Ohio	0.0
8	Oklahoma	6.4
2	Oregon	11.7
29	Pennsylvania	(0.3)
48	Rhode Island	(8.9)
20	South Carolina	2.4
10	South Dakota	5.4
35	Tennessee	(0.8)
45	Texas	(7.3)
16	Utah	3.8
50	Vermont	(17.7)
32	Virginia	(0.5)
18	Washington	3.1
30	West Virginia	(0.4)
38	Wisconsin	(2.2)
11	Wyoming	4.9

RANK ORDER

RANK	STATE	PERCENT CHANGE
1	Nevada	12.2
2	Oregon	11.7
3	Arizona	11.3
4	Mississippi	10.1
5	Idaho	9.7
6	Hawaii	7.3
7	Montana	7.1
8	Oklahoma	6.4
9	Missouri	5.8
10	South Dakota	5.4
11	Wyoming	4.9
12	Nebraska	4.8
13	Kentucky	4.5
14	Alaska	4.0
15	Maine	3.9
16	Utah	3.8
17	Alabama	3.7
18	Washington	3.1
19	Indiana	3.0
20	South Carolina	2.4
21	Maryland	2.1
22	North Carolina	1.7
23	New Mexico	1.6
24	Florida	1.4
25	Arkansas	0.9
26	Illinois	0.6
26	Michigan	0.6
28	Ohio	0.0
29	Pennsylvania	(0.3)
30	Georgia	(0.4)
30	West Virginia	(0.4)
32	Kansas	(0.5)
32	Virginia	(0.5)
34	Colorado	(0.6)
35	Minnesota	(0.8)
35	Tennessee	(0.8)
37	Louisiana	(1.2)
38	Wisconsin	(2.2)
39	Connecticut	(2.5)
40	North Dakota	(2.6)
41	New Jersey	(2.7)
42	California	(3.4)
43	New Hampshire	(4.2)
44	Iowa	(4.6)
45	Texas	(7.3)
46	Massachusetts	(8.3)
47	New York	(8.5)
48	Rhode Island	(8.9)
49	Delaware	(13.6)
50	Vermont	(17.7)

| | District of Columbia | (6.0) |

Source: Federal Bureau of Investigation
    "Crime in the United States 1994" (Uniform Crime Reports, November 19, 1995)
*Property crimes are offenses of burglary, larceny-theft and motor vehicle theft.

Property Crime Rate in 1994

National Rate = 4,658.3 Property Crimes per 100,000 Population*

ALPHA ORDER

RANK	STATE	RATE
26	Alabama	4,219.4
16	Alaska	4,941.7
1	Arizona	7,221.4
27	Arkansas	4,203.6
12	California	5,160.8
19	Colorado	4,808.8
29	Connecticut	4,092.5
41	Delaware	3,586.5
2	Florida	7,103.2
8	Georgia	5,342.7
3	Hawaii	6,418.3
36	Idaho	3,791.2
21	Illinois	4,664.9
30	Indiana	4,067.7
42	Iowa	3,339.5
23	Kansas	4,415.1
45	Kentucky	2,893.3
5	Louisiana	5,689.2
44	Maine	3,142.8
10	Maryland	5,174.6
38	Massachusetts	3,733.4
20	Michigan	4,679.1
34	Minnesota	3,982.0
25	Mississippi	4,343.3
22	Missouri	4,564.2
18	Montana	4,841.7
31	Nebraska	4,050.9
6	Nevada	5,675.6
49	New Hampshire	2,624.2
32	New Jersey	4,046.8
9	New Mexico	5,298.5
28	New York	4,105.0
15	North Carolina	4,970.3
48	North Dakota	2,654.1
35	Ohio	3,975.7
17	Oklahoma	4,918.7
4	Oregon	5,775.8
47	Pennsylvania	2,845.2
37	Rhode Island	3,743.5
14	South Carolina	4,970.4
46	South Dakota	2,874.6
24	Tennessee	4,371.9
11	Texas	5,165.9
13	Utah	4,996.4
43	Vermont	3,153.4
39	Virginia	3,689.9
7	Washington	5,516.3
50	West Virginia	2,312.6
40	Wisconsin	3,673.8
33	Wyoming	4,017.2

RANK ORDER

RANK	STATE	RATE
1	Arizona	7,221.4
2	Florida	7,103.2
3	Hawaii	6,418.3
4	Oregon	5,775.8
5	Louisiana	5,689.2
6	Nevada	5,675.6
7	Washington	5,516.3
8	Georgia	5,342.7
9	New Mexico	5,298.5
10	Maryland	5,174.6
11	Texas	5,165.9
12	California	5,160.8
13	Utah	4,996.4
14	South Carolina	4,970.4
15	North Carolina	4,970.3
16	Alaska	4,941.7
17	Oklahoma	4,918.7
18	Montana	4,841.7
19	Colorado	4,808.8
20	Michigan	4,679.1
21	Illinois	4,664.9
22	Missouri	4,564.2
23	Kansas	4,415.1
24	Tennessee	4,371.9
25	Mississippi	4,343.3
26	Alabama	4,219.4
27	Arkansas	4,203.6
28	New York	4,105.0
29	Connecticut	4,092.5
30	Indiana	4,067.7
31	Nebraska	4,050.9
32	New Jersey	4,046.8
33	Wyoming	4,017.2
34	Minnesota	3,982.0
35	Ohio	3,975.7
36	Idaho	3,791.2
37	Rhode Island	3,743.5
38	Massachusetts	3,733.4
39	Virginia	3,689.9
40	Wisconsin	3,673.8
41	Delaware	3,586.5
42	Iowa	3,339.5
43	Vermont	3,153.4
44	Maine	3,142.8
45	Kentucky	2,893.3
46	South Dakota	2,874.6
47	Pennsylvania	2,845.2
48	North Dakota	2,654.1
49	New Hampshire	2,624.2
50	West Virginia	2,312.6
	District of Columbia	8,422.6

Source: Federal Bureau of Investigation
"Crime in the United States 1994" (Uniform Crime Reports, November 19, 1995)
*Property crimes are offenses of burglary, larceny-theft and motor vehicle theft.

Percent Change in Property Crime Rate: 1993 to 1994

National Percent Change = 1.7% Decrease*

ALPHA ORDER

RANK	STATE	PERCENT CHANGE
15	Alabama	3.0
16	Alaska	2.8
3	Arizona	7.5
26	Arkansas	(0.3)
42	California	(4.1)
38	Colorado	(3.0)
37	Connecticut	(2.4)
49	Delaware	(14.3)
29	Florida	(0.6)
35	Georgia	(2.3)
5	Hawaii	6.7
6	Idaho	6.4
23	Illinois	0.1
17	Indiana	2.3
43	Iowa	(5.2)
31	Kansas	(1.4)
14	Kentucky	3.4
33	Louisiana	(1.7)
11	Maine	3.8
20	Maryland	1.3
47	Massachusetts	(8.7)
22	Michigan	0.4
34	Minnesota	(1.9)
2	Mississippi	9.0
9	Missouri	4.9
8	Montana	5.0
11	Nebraska	3.8
4	Nevada	7.0
43	New Hampshire	(5.2)
38	New Jersey	(3.0)
30	New Mexico	(0.7)
45	New York	(8.3)
24	North Carolina	(0.1)
40	North Dakota	(3.1)
24	Ohio	(0.1)
7	Oklahoma	5.6
1	Oregon	9.8
26	Pennsylvania	(0.3)
46	Rhode Island	(8.6)
18	South Carolina	1.9
10	South Dakota	4.5
35	Tennessee	(2.3)
48	Texas	(9.0)
21	Utah	1.2
50	Vermont	(18.3)
31	Virginia	(1.4)
19	Washington	1.4
28	West Virginia	(0.5)
40	Wisconsin	(3.1)
13	Wyoming	3.6

RANK ORDER

RANK	STATE	PERCENT CHANGE
1	Oregon	9.8
2	Mississippi	9.0
3	Arizona	7.5
4	Nevada	7.0
5	Hawaii	6.7
6	Idaho	6.4
7	Oklahoma	5.6
8	Montana	5.0
9	Missouri	4.9
10	South Dakota	4.5
11	Maine	3.8
11	Nebraska	3.8
13	Wyoming	3.6
14	Kentucky	3.4
15	Alabama	3.0
16	Alaska	2.8
17	Indiana	2.3
18	South Carolina	1.9
19	Washington	1.4
20	Maryland	1.3
21	Utah	1.2
22	Michigan	0.4
23	Illinois	0.1
24	North Carolina	(0.1)
24	Ohio	(0.1)
26	Arkansas	(0.3)
26	Pennsylvania	(0.3)
28	West Virginia	(0.5)
29	Florida	(0.6)
30	New Mexico	(0.7)
31	Kansas	(1.4)
31	Virginia	(1.4)
33	Louisiana	(1.7)
34	Minnesota	(1.9)
35	Georgia	(2.3)
35	Tennessee	(2.3)
37	Connecticut	(2.4)
38	Colorado	(3.0)
38	New Jersey	(3.0)
40	North Dakota	(3.1)
40	Wisconsin	(3.1)
42	California	(4.1)
43	Iowa	(5.2)
43	New Hampshire	(5.2)
45	New York	(8.3)
46	Rhode Island	(8.6)
47	Massachusetts	(8.7)
48	Texas	(9.0)
49	Delaware	(14.3)
50	Vermont	(18.3)
	District of Columbia	(4.7)

Source: Federal Bureau of Investigation
   "Crime in the United States 1994" (Uniform Crime Reports, November 19, 1995)
*Property crimes are offenses of burglary, larceny-theft and motor vehicle theft.

Burglaries in 1994

National Total = 2,712,156 Burglaries*

ALPHA ORDER

RANK	STATE	BURGLARIES	% of USA
21	Alabama	44,064	1.62%
46	Alaska	4,848	0.18%
12	Arizona	60,157	2.22%
32	Arkansas	26,911	0.99%
1	California	384,257	14.17%
27	Colorado	33,843	1.25%
29	Connecticut	29,142	1.07%
44	Delaware	5,580	0.21%
2	Florida	237,341	8.75%
9	Georgia	81,406	3.00%
37	Hawaii	14,029	0.52%
42	Idaho	8,147	0.30%
5	Illinois	118,116	4.36%
19	Indiana	48,921	1.80%
35	Iowa	18,872	0.70%
31	Kansas	28,635	1.06%
30	Kentucky	28,718	1.06%
16	Louisiana	55,188	2.03%
41	Maine	8,938	0.33%
18	Maryland	52,234	1.93%
17	Massachusetts	53,222	1.96%
8	Michigan	91,849	3.39%
24	Minnesota	36,157	1.33%
25	Mississippi	34,493	1.27%
15	Missouri	55,577	2.05%
43	Montana	6,178	0.23%
38	Nebraska	10,963	0.40%
34	Nevada	19,735	0.73%
45	New Hampshire	5,275	0.19%
10	New Jersey	72,074	2.66%
33	New Mexico	21,945	0.81%
4	New York	164,650	6.07%
6	North Carolina	104,118	3.84%
50	North Dakota	2,070	0.08%
7	Ohio	96,175	3.55%
23	Oklahoma	40,764	1.50%
26	Oregon	33,970	1.25%
11	Pennsylvania	66,468	2.45%
40	Rhode Island	9,101	0.34%
20	South Carolina	46,678	1.72%
48	South Dakota	3,938	0.15%
13	Tennessee	59,080	2.18%
3	Texas	214,687	7.92%
36	Utah	15,089	0.56%
47	Vermont	4,274	0.16%
22	Virginia	41,855	1.54%
14	Washington	55,793	2.06%
39	West Virginia	10,673	0.39%
28	Wisconsin	32,824	1.21%
49	Wyoming	3,097	0.11%

RANK ORDER

RANK	STATE	BURGLARIES	% of USA
1	California	384,257	14.17%
2	Florida	237,341	8.75%
3	Texas	214,687	7.92%
4	New York	164,650	6.07%
5	Illinois	118,116	4.36%
6	North Carolina	104,118	3.84%
7	Ohio	96,175	3.55%
8	Michigan	91,849	3.39%
9	Georgia	81,406	3.00%
10	New Jersey	72,074	2.66%
11	Pennsylvania	66,468	2.45%
12	Arizona	60,157	2.22%
13	Tennessee	59,080	2.18%
14	Washington	55,793	2.06%
15	Missouri	55,577	2.05%
16	Louisiana	55,188	2.03%
17	Massachusetts	53,222	1.96%
18	Maryland	52,234	1.93%
19	Indiana	48,921	1.80%
20	South Carolina	46,678	1.72%
21	Alabama	44,064	1.62%
22	Virginia	41,855	1.54%
23	Oklahoma	40,764	1.50%
24	Minnesota	36,157	1.33%
25	Mississippi	34,493	1.27%
26	Oregon	33,970	1.25%
27	Colorado	33,843	1.25%
28	Wisconsin	32,824	1.21%
29	Connecticut	29,142	1.07%
30	Kentucky	28,718	1.06%
31	Kansas	28,635	1.06%
32	Arkansas	26,911	0.99%
33	New Mexico	21,945	0.81%
34	Nevada	19,735	0.73%
35	Iowa	18,872	0.70%
36	Utah	15,089	0.56%
37	Hawaii	14,029	0.52%
38	Nebraska	10,963	0.40%
39	West Virginia	10,673	0.39%
40	Rhode Island	9,101	0.34%
41	Maine	8,938	0.33%
42	Idaho	8,147	0.30%
43	Montana	6,178	0.23%
44	Delaware	5,580	0.21%
45	New Hampshire	5,275	0.19%
46	Alaska	4,848	0.18%
47	Vermont	4,274	0.16%
48	South Dakota	3,938	0.15%
49	Wyoming	3,097	0.11%
50	North Dakota	2,070	0.08%
	District of Columbia	10,037	0.37%

Source: Federal Bureau of Investigation
"Crime in the United States 1994" (Uniform Crime Reports, November 19, 1995)
Burglary is the unlawful entry of a structure to commit a felony or theft. Attempts are included.

Average Time Between Burglaries in 1994

National Rate = A Burglary Occurs Every 12 Seconds*

ALPHA ORDER				RANK ORDER		
RANK	STATE	MINUTES.SECONDS		RANK	STATE	MINUTES.SECONDS
30	Alabama	11.56		1	North Dakota	253.55
5	Alaska	108.25		2	Wyoming	169.43
39	Arizona	8.44		3	South Dakota	133.28
19	Arkansas	19.32		4	Vermont	122.59
50	California	1.22		5	Alaska	108.25
24	Colorado	15.32		6	New Hampshire	99.38
22	Connecticut	18.02		7	Delaware	94.11
7	Delaware	94.11		8	Montana	85.05
49	Florida	2.13		9	Idaho	64.31
42	Georgia	6.28		10	Maine	58.49
14	Hawaii	37.28		11	Rhode Island	57.45
9	Idaho	64.31		12	West Virginia	49.15
46	Illinois	4.27		13	Nebraska	47.56
32	Indiana	10.44		14	Hawaii	37.28
16	Iowa	27.51		15	Utah	34.50
20	Kansas	18.22		16	Iowa	27.51
21	Kentucky	18.18		17	Nevada	26.38
35	Louisiana	9.31		18	New Mexico	23.57
10	Maine	58.49		19	Arkansas	19.32
33	Maryland	10.04		20	Kansas	18.22
34	Massachusetts	9.53		21	Kentucky	18.18
43	Michigan	5.43		22	Connecticut	18.02
27	Minnesota	14.32		23	Wisconsin	16.01
26	Mississippi	15.14		24	Colorado	15.32
36	Missouri	9.28		25	Oregon	15.28
8	Montana	85.05		26	Mississippi	15.14
13	Nebraska	47.56		27	Minnesota	14.32
17	Nevada	26.38		28	Oklahoma	12.53
6	New Hampshire	99.38		29	Virginia	12.34
41	New Jersey	7.17		30	Alabama	11.56
18	New Mexico	23.57		31	South Carolina	11.16
47	New York	3.11		32	Indiana	10.44
45	North Carolina	5.03		33	Maryland	10.04
1	North Dakota	253.55		34	Massachusetts	9.53
44	Ohio	5.28		35	Louisiana	9.31
28	Oklahoma	12.53		36	Missouri	9.28
25	Oregon	15.28		37	Washington	9.25
40	Pennsylvania	7.55		38	Tennessee	8.54
11	Rhode Island	57.45		39	Arizona	8.44
31	South Carolina	11.16		40	Pennsylvania	7.55
3	South Dakota	133.28		41	New Jersey	7.17
38	Tennessee	8.54		42	Georgia	6.28
48	Texas	2.27		43	Michigan	5.43
15	Utah	34.50		44	Ohio	5.28
4	Vermont	122.59		45	North Carolina	5.03
29	Virginia	12.34		46	Illinois	4.27
37	Washington	9.25		47	New York	3.11
12	West Virginia	49.15		48	Texas	2.27
23	Wisconsin	16.01		49	Florida	2.13
2	Wyoming	169.43		50	California	1.22
					District of Columbia	52.22

Source: Morgan Quitno Press using data from Federal Bureau of Investigation
    "Crime in the United States 1994" (Uniform Crime Reports, November 19, 1995)
Burglary is the unlawful entry of a structure to commit a felony or theft. Attempts are included.

Percent Change in Number of Burglaries: 1993 to 1994

National Percent Change = 4.3% Decrease*

ALPHA ORDER				RANK ORDER		
RANK	STATE	PERCENT CHANGE		RANK	STATE	PERCENT CHANGE
29	Alabama	(3.3)		1	Nevada	14.1
21	Alaska	(0.9)		2	Idaho	10.8
5	Arizona	4.3		3	Oregon	9.3
14	Arkansas	1.0		4	Hawaii	5.4
39	California	(7.2)		5	Arizona	4.3
35	Colorado	(6.0)		6	Missouri	3.5
43	Connecticut	(9.1)		7	Montana	3.1
46	Delaware	(10.6)		8	Nebraska	2.8
34	Florida	(5.5)		9	Utah	2.6
45	Georgia	(10.0)		10	Kentucky	2.4
4	Hawaii	5.4		10	Wyoming	2.4
2	Idaho	10.8		12	Oklahoma	2.2
20	Illinois	(0.6)		13	Mississippi	1.5
15	Indiana	0.5		14	Arkansas	1.0
40	Iowa	(8.2)		15	Indiana	0.5
18	Kansas	(0.1)		16	Maine	0.3
10	Kentucky	2.4		16	South Dakota	0.3
36	Louisiana	(6.1)		18	Kansas	(0.1)
16	Maine	0.3		19	Washington	(0.5)
38	Maryland	(7.1)		20	Illinois	(0.6)
47	Massachusetts	(11.6)		21	Alaska	(0.9)
24	Michigan	(1.4)		22	North Carolina	(1.1)
32	Minnesota	(5.2)		23	Ohio	(1.3)
13	Mississippi	1.5		24	Michigan	(1.4)
6	Missouri	3.5		25	Wisconsin	(1.7)
7	Montana	3.1		26	Tennessee	(2.0)
8	Nebraska	2.8		27	South Carolina	(2.1)
1	Nevada	14.1		27	West Virginia	(2.1)
42	New Hampshire	(9.0)		29	Alabama	(3.3)
36	New Jersey	(6.1)		30	Virginia	(3.4)
31	New Mexico	(4.4)		31	New Mexico	(4.4)
44	New York	(9.4)		32	Minnesota	(5.2)
22	North Carolina	(1.1)		32	Pennsylvania	(5.2)
49	North Dakota	(12.7)		34	Florida	(5.5)
23	Ohio	(1.3)		35	Colorado	(6.0)
12	Oklahoma	2.2		36	Louisiana	(6.1)
3	Oregon	9.3		36	New Jersey	(6.1)
32	Pennsylvania	(5.2)		38	Maryland	(7.1)
48	Rhode Island	(12.6)		39	California	(7.2)
27	South Carolina	(2.1)		40	Iowa	(8.2)
16	South Dakota	0.3		40	Texas	(8.2)
26	Tennessee	(2.0)		42	New Hampshire	(9.0)
40	Texas	(8.2)		43	Connecticut	(9.1)
9	Utah	2.6		44	New York	(9.4)
50	Vermont	(15.1)		45	Georgia	(10.0)
30	Virginia	(3.4)		46	Delaware	(10.6)
19	Washington	(0.5)		47	Massachusetts	(11.6)
27	West Virginia	(2.1)		48	Rhode Island	(12.6)
25	Wisconsin	(1.7)		49	North Dakota	(12.7)
10	Wyoming	2.4		50	Vermont	(15.1)
					District of Columbia	(13.0)

Source: Federal Bureau of Investigation
   "Crime in the United States 1994" (Uniform Crime Reports, November 19, 1995)
*Burglary is the unlawful entry of a structure to commit a felony or theft. Attempts are included.

Burglary Rate in 1994

National Rate = 1,041.8 Burglaries per 100,000 Population*

ALPHA ORDER

RANK ORDER

RANK	STATE	RATE	RANK	STATE	RATE
19	Alabama	1,044.4	1	Florida	1,701.0
32	Alaska	800.0	2	Arizona	1,476.2
2	Arizona	1,476.2	3	North Carolina	1,472.7
17	Arkansas	1,097.1	4	Nevada	1,354.5
10	California	1,222.5	5	New Mexico	1,326.8
24	Colorado	925.7	6	Mississippi	1,292.4
28	Connecticut	889.8	7	Louisiana	1,279.0
35	Delaware	790.4	8	South Carolina	1,274.0
1	Florida	1,701.0	9	Oklahoma	1,251.2
13	Georgia	1,153.9	10	California	1,222.5
11	Hawaii	1,189.9	11	Hawaii	1,189.9
40	Idaho	719.1	12	Texas	1,168.2
22	Illinois	1,005.1	13	Georgia	1,153.9
31	Indiana	850.5	14	Tennessee	1,141.6
42	Iowa	667.1	15	Kansas	1,121.2
15	Kansas	1,121.2	16	Oregon	1,100.8
36	Kentucky	750.4	17	Arkansas	1,097.1
7	Louisiana	1,279.0	18	Missouri	1,053.0
39	Maine	720.8	19	Alabama	1,044.4
21	Maryland	1,043.4	20	Washington	1,044.2
29	Massachusetts	881.0	21	Maryland	1,043.4
23	Michigan	967.2	22	Illinois	1,005.1
33	Minnesota	791.7	23	Michigan	967.2
6	Mississippi	1,292.4	24	Colorado	925.7
18	Missouri	1,053.0	25	Rhode Island	912.8
38	Montana	721.7	26	New Jersey	911.9
41	Nebraska	675.5	27	New York	906.2
4	Nevada	1,354.5	28	Connecticut	889.8
49	New Hampshire	463.9	29	Massachusetts	881.0
26	New Jersey	911.9	30	Ohio	866.3
5	New Mexico	1,326.8	31	Indiana	850.5
27	New York	906.2	32	Alaska	800.0
3	North Carolina	1,472.7	33	Minnesota	791.7
50	North Dakota	324.5	34	Utah	790.8
30	Ohio	866.3	35	Delaware	790.4
9	Oklahoma	1,251.2	36	Kentucky	750.4
16	Oregon	1,100.8	37	Vermont	736.9
47	Pennsylvania	551.5	38	Montana	721.7
25	Rhode Island	912.8	39	Maine	720.8
8	South Carolina	1,274.0	40	Idaho	719.1
48	South Dakota	546.2	41	Nebraska	675.5
14	Tennessee	1,141.6	42	Iowa	667.1
12	Texas	1,168.2	43	Wyoming	650.6
34	Utah	790.8	44	Wisconsin	645.9
37	Vermont	736.9	45	Virginia	638.8
45	Virginia	638.8	46	West Virginia	585.8
20	Washington	1,044.2	47	Pennsylvania	551.5
46	West Virginia	585.8	48	South Dakota	546.2
44	Wisconsin	645.9	49	New Hampshire	463.9
43	Wyoming	650.6	50	North Dakota	324.5

District of Columbia   1,760.9

Source: Federal Bureau of Investigation
   "Crime in the United States 1994" (Uniform Crime Reports, November 19, 1995)
*Burglary is the unlawful entry of a structure to commit a felony or theft. Attempts are included.

Percent Change in Rate of Burglaries: 1993 to 1994

National Percent Change = 5.2% Decrease*

RANK	STATE	PERCENT CHANGE
29	Alabama	(4.1)
22	Alaska	(2.1)
11	Arizona	0.7
15	Arkansas	(0.2)
37	California	(7.9)
39	Colorado	(8.3)
41	Connecticut	(9.0)
45	Delaware	(11.4)
36	Florida	(7.3)
46	Georgia	(11.7)
4	Hawaii	4.8
2	Idaho	7.5
18	Illinois	(1.0)
15	Indiana	(0.2)
40	Iowa	(8.7)
18	Kansas	(1.0)
7	Kentucky	1.4
34	Louisiana	(6.5)
13	Maine	0.3
37	Maryland	(7.9)
47	Massachusetts	(12.0)
21	Michigan	(1.6)
32	Minnesota	(6.3)
12	Mississippi	0.5
5	Missouri	2.7
10	Montana	1.1
6	Nebraska	1.8
1	Nevada	8.8
43	New Hampshire	(9.9)
33	New Jersey	(6.4)
35	New Mexico	(6.6)
42	New York	(9.3)
27	North Carolina	(2.8)
49	North Dakota	(13.0)
20	Ohio	(1.3)
8	Oklahoma	1.3
3	Oregon	7.4
31	Pennsylvania	(5.2)
48	Rhode Island	(12.3)
26	South Carolina	(2.7)
17	South Dakota	(0.5)
28	Tennessee	(3.5)
44	Texas	(10.0)
14	Utah	0.0
50	Vermont	(15.7)
30	Virginia	(4.3)
23	Washington	(2.2)
23	West Virginia	(2.2)
25	Wisconsin	(2.6)
9	Wyoming	1.2

RANK	STATE	PERCENT CHANGE
1	Nevada	8.8
2	Idaho	7.5
3	Oregon	7.4
4	Hawaii	4.8
5	Missouri	2.7
6	Nebraska	1.8
7	Kentucky	1.4
8	Oklahoma	1.3
9	Wyoming	1.2
10	Montana	1.1
11	Arizona	0.7
12	Mississippi	0.5
13	Maine	0.3
14	Utah	0.0
15	Arkansas	(0.2)
15	Indiana	(0.2)
17	South Dakota	(0.5)
18	Illinois	(1.0)
18	Kansas	(1.0)
20	Ohio	(1.3)
21	Michigan	(1.6)
22	Alaska	(2.1)
23	Washington	(2.2)
23	West Virginia	(2.2)
25	Wisconsin	(2.6)
26	South Carolina	(2.7)
27	North Carolina	(2.8)
28	Tennessee	(3.5)
29	Alabama	(4.1)
30	Virginia	(4.3)
31	Pennsylvania	(5.2)
32	Minnesota	(6.3)
33	New Jersey	(6.4)
34	Louisiana	(6.5)
35	New Mexico	(6.6)
36	Florida	(7.3)
37	California	(7.9)
37	Maryland	(7.9)
39	Colorado	(8.3)
40	Iowa	(8.7)
41	Connecticut	(9.0)
42	New York	(9.3)
43	New Hampshire	(9.9)
44	Texas	(10.0)
45	Delaware	(11.4)
46	Georgia	(11.7)
47	Massachusetts	(12.0)
48	Rhode Island	(12.3)
49	North Dakota	(13.0)
50	Vermont	(15.7)
	District of Columbia	(11.8)

Source: Federal Bureau of Investigation
"Crime in the United States 1994" (Uniform Crime Reports, November 19, 1995)
*Burglary is the unlawful entry of a structure to commit a felony or theft. Attempts are included.

Larceny and Theft in 1994

National Total = 7,876,254 Larcenies and Thefts*

ALPHA ORDER					RANK ORDER			
RANK	STATE		LARCENIES	% of USA	RANK	STATE	LARCENIES	% of USA
26	Alabama		119,951	1.52%	1	California	929,640	11.80%
45	Alaska		21,824	0.28%	2	Florida	626,578	7.96%
13	Arizona		190,649	2.42%	3	Texas	623,947	7.92%
34	Arkansas		68,478	0.87%	4	New York	452,322	5.74%
1	California		929,640	11.80%	5	Illinois	363,888	4.62%
23	Colorado		127,600	1.62%	6	Ohio	297,792	3.78%
28	Connecticut		84,721	1.08%	7	Michigan	290,172	3.68%
46	Delaware		17,270	0.22%	8	Georgia	256,208	3.25%
2	Florida		626,578	7.96%	9	North Carolina	225,937	2.87%
8	Georgia		256,208	3.25%	10	Pennsylvania	222,280	2.82%
36	Hawaii		55,260	0.70%	11	Washington	212,198	2.69%
40	Idaho		32,597	0.41%	12	New Jersey	195,618	2.48%
5	Illinois		363,888	4.62%	13	Arizona	190,649	2.42%
17	Indiana		160,043	2.03%	14	Virginia	181,619	2.31%
33	Iowa		70,507	0.90%	15	Maryland	168,608	2.14%
29	Kansas		75,459	0.96%	16	Louisiana	164,081	2.08%
31	Kentucky		73,449	0.93%	17	Indiana	160,043	2.03%
16	Louisiana		164,081	2.08%	18	Missouri	158,283	2.01%
41	Maine		28,257	0.36%	19	Tennessee	138,173	1.75%
15	Maryland		168,608	2.14%	20	Wisconsin	135,559	1.72%
22	Massachusetts		129,962	1.65%	21	Minnesota	131,344	1.67%
7	Michigan		290,172	3.68%	22	Massachusetts	129,962	1.65%
21	Minnesota		131,344	1.67%	23	Colorado	127,600	1.62%
32	Mississippi		70,621	0.90%	24	Oregon	122,506	1.56%
18	Missouri		158,283	2.01%	25	South Carolina	122,252	1.55%
39	Montana		32,817	0.42%	26	Alabama	119,951	1.52%
38	Nebraska		48,547	0.62%	27	Oklahoma	104,025	1.32%
37	Nevada		51,893	0.66%	28	Connecticut	84,721	1.08%
44	New Hampshire		22,260	0.28%	29	Kansas	75,459	0.96%
12	New Jersey		195,618	2.48%	30	Utah	74,554	0.95%
35	New Mexico		57,343	0.73%	31	Kentucky	73,449	0.93%
4	New York		452,322	5.74%	32	Mississippi	70,621	0.90%
9	North Carolina		225,937	2.87%	33	Iowa	70,507	0.90%
49	North Dakota		13,899	0.18%	34	Arkansas	68,478	0.87%
6	Ohio		297,792	3.78%	35	New Mexico	57,343	0.73%
27	Oklahoma		104,025	1.32%	36	Hawaii	55,260	0.70%
24	Oregon		122,506	1.56%	37	Nevada	51,893	0.66%
10	Pennsylvania		222,280	2.82%	38	Nebraska	48,547	0.62%
43	Rhode Island		23,039	0.29%	39	Montana	32,817	0.42%
25	South Carolina		122,252	1.55%	40	Idaho	32,597	0.41%
47	South Dakota		15,916	0.20%	41	Maine	28,257	0.36%
19	Tennessee		138,173	1.75%	42	West Virginia	28,189	0.36%
3	Texas		623,947	7.92%	43	Rhode Island	23,039	0.29%
30	Utah		74,554	0.95%	44	New Hampshire	22,260	0.28%
50	Vermont		13,154	0.17%	45	Alaska	21,824	0.28%
14	Virginia		181,619	2.31%	46	Delaware	17,270	0.22%
11	Washington		212,198	2.69%	47	South Dakota	15,916	0.20%
42	West Virginia		28,189	0.36%	48	Wyoming	15,254	0.19%
20	Wisconsin		135,559	1.72%	49	North Dakota	13,899	0.18%
48	Wyoming		15,254	0.19%	50	Vermont	13,154	0.17%
						District of Columbia	29,711	0.38%

Source: Federal Bureau of Investigation
"Crime in the United States 1994" (Uniform Crime Reports, November 19, 1995)
*Larceny and theft is the unlawful taking of property without use of force, violence or fraud. Attempts are included.
Motor vehicle thefts are excluded.

Average Time Between Larcenies-Thefts in 1994

National Rate = A Larceny-Theft Occurs Every 4 Seconds*

ALPHA ORDER				RANK ORDER		
RANK	**STATE**	**MINUTES.SECONDS**		**RANK**	**STATE**	**MINUTES.SECONDS**
25	Alabama	4.23		1	Vermont	39.58
6	Alaska	24.05		2	North Dakota	37.49
38	Arizona	2.46		3	Wyoming	34.28
17	Arkansas	7.41		4	South Dakota	33.01
50	California	0.34		5	Delaware	30.26
28	Colorado	4.07		6	Alaska	24.05
23	Connecticut	6.12		7	New Hampshire	23.37
5	Delaware	30.26		8	Rhode Island	22.49
48	Florida	0.50		9	West Virginia	18.39
43	Georgia	2.03		10	Maine	18.36
15	Hawaii	9.31		11	Idaho	16.07
11	Idaho	16.07		12	Montana	16.01
46	Illinois	1.26		13	Nebraska	10.50
34	Indiana	3.17		14	Nevada	10.08
18	Iowa	7.27		15	Hawaii	9.31
22	Kansas	6.58		16	New Mexico	9.10
20	Kentucky	7.10		17	Arkansas	7.41
35	Louisiana	3.12		18	Iowa	7.27
10	Maine	18.36		19	Mississippi	7.26
36	Maryland	3.07		20	Kentucky	7.10
29	Massachusetts	4.02		21	Utah	7.03
44	Michigan	1.49		22	Kansas	6.58
30	Minnesota	4.00		23	Connecticut	6.12
19	Mississippi	7.26		24	Oklahoma	5.03
33	Missouri	3.19		25	Alabama	4.23
12	Montana	16.01		26	South Carolina	4.18
13	Nebraska	10.50		27	Oregon	4.17
14	Nevada	10.08		28	Colorado	4.07
7	New Hampshire	23.37		29	Massachusetts	4.02
39	New Jersey	2.41		30	Minnesota	4.00
16	New Mexico	9.10		31	Wisconsin	3.53
47	New York	1.10		32	Tennessee	3.48
42	North Carolina	2.20		33	Missouri	3.19
2	North Dakota	37.49		34	Indiana	3.17
45	Ohio	1.46		35	Louisiana	3.12
24	Oklahoma	5.03		36	Maryland	3.07
27	Oregon	4.17		37	Virginia	2.53
41	Pennsylvania	2.22		38	Arizona	2.46
8	Rhode Island	22.49		39	New Jersey	2.41
26	South Carolina	4.18		40	Washington	2.29
4	South Dakota	33.01		41	Pennsylvania	2.22
32	Tennessee	3.48		42	North Carolina	2.20
48	Texas	0.50		43	Georgia	2.03
21	Utah	7.03		44	Michigan	1.49
1	Vermont	39.58		45	Ohio	1.46
37	Virginia	2.53		46	Illinois	1.26
40	Washington	2.29		47	New York	1.10
9	West Virginia	18.39		48	Florida	0.50
31	Wisconsin	3.53		48	Texas	0.50
3	Wyoming	34.28		50	California	0.34
					District of Columbia	17.41

Source: Morgan Quitno Press using data from Federal Bureau of Investigation
"Crime in the United States 1994" (Uniform Crime Reports, November 19, 1995)
*Larceny and theft is the unlawful taking of property without use of force, violence or fraud. Attempts are included.
Motor vehicle thefts are excluded.

Percent Change in Number of Larcenies and Thefts: 1993 to 1994

National Percent Change = 0.7% Increase*

RANK	STATE	PERCENT CHANGE
8	Alabama	7.2
22	Alaska	2.9
4	Arizona	10.4
28	Arkansas	1.0
41	California	(1.7)
25	Colorado	2.3
39	Connecticut	(1.3)
49	Delaware	(17.2)
17	Florida	3.8
17	Georgia	3.8
11	Hawaii	6.4
5	Idaho	9.4
29	Illinois	0.9
16	Indiana	3.9
43	Iowa	(3.6)
40	Kansas	(1.4)
13	Kentucky	5.3
32	Louisiana	0.5
14	Maine	4.9
21	Maryland	3.1
46	Massachusetts	(4.8)
35	Michigan	(0.1)
26	Minnesota	1.2
1	Mississippi	13.1
7	Missouri	8.9
9	Montana	7.1
19	Nebraska	3.7
2	Nevada	12.5
44	New Hampshire	(3.9)
35	New Jersey	(0.1)
27	New Mexico	1.1
47	New York	(6.0)
23	North Carolina	2.7
38	North Dakota	(1.2)
31	Ohio	0.6
5	Oklahoma	9.4
3	Oregon	10.5
30	Pennsylvania	0.7
45	Rhode Island	(4.4)
15	South Carolina	4.0
10	South Dakota	6.7
33	Tennessee	0.4
48	Texas	(6.2)
23	Utah	2.7
50	Vermont	(19.9)
34	Virginia	0.3
20	Washington	3.2
37	West Virginia	(0.9)
42	Wisconsin	(2.6)
12	Wyoming	5.4

RANK	STATE	PERCENT CHANGE
1	Mississippi	13.1
2	Nevada	12.5
3	Oregon	10.5
4	Arizona	10.4
5	Idaho	9.4
5	Oklahoma	9.4
7	Missouri	8.9
8	Alabama	7.2
9	Montana	7.1
10	South Dakota	6.7
11	Hawaii	6.4
12	Wyoming	5.4
13	Kentucky	5.3
14	Maine	4.9
15	South Carolina	4.0
16	Indiana	3.9
17	Florida	3.8
17	Georgia	3.8
19	Nebraska	3.7
20	Washington	3.2
21	Maryland	3.1
22	Alaska	2.9
23	North Carolina	2.7
23	Utah	2.7
25	Colorado	2.3
26	Minnesota	1.2
27	New Mexico	1.1
28	Arkansas	1.0
29	Illinois	0.9
30	Pennsylvania	0.7
31	Ohio	0.6
32	Louisiana	0.5
33	Tennessee	0.4
34	Virginia	0.3
35	Michigan	(0.1)
35	New Jersey	(0.1)
37	West Virginia	(0.9)
38	North Dakota	(1.2)
39	Connecticut	(1.3)
40	Kansas	(1.4)
41	California	(1.7)
42	Wisconsin	(2.6)
43	Iowa	(3.6)
44	New Hampshire	(3.9)
45	Rhode Island	(4.4)
46	Massachusetts	(4.8)
47	New York	(6.0)
48	Texas	(6.2)
49	Delaware	(17.2)
50	Vermont	(19.9)
	District of Columbia	(5.7)

Source: Federal Bureau of Investigation
    "Crime in the United States 1994" (Uniform Crime Reports, November 19, 1995)
*Larceny and theft is the unlawful taking of property without use of force, violence or fraud. Attempts are included.
Motor vehicle thefts are excluded.

Larceny and Theft Rate in 1994

National Rate = 3,025.4 Larcenies and Thefts per 100,000 Population*

ALPHA ORDER			RANK ORDER		
RANK	STATE	RATE	RANK	STATE	RATE
28	Alabama	2,843.1	1	Hawaii	4,687.0
10	Alaska	3,601.3	2	Arizona	4,678.5
2	Arizona	4,678.5	3	Florida	4,490.6
29	Arkansas	2,791.6	4	Washington	3,971.5
24	California	2,957.7	5	Oregon	3,969.7
12	Colorado	3,490.2	6	Utah	3,907.4
36	Connecticut	2,586.9	7	Montana	3,833.8
40	Delaware	2,446.2	8	Louisiana	3,802.6
3	Florida	4,490.6	9	Georgia	3,631.6
9	Georgia	3,631.6	10	Alaska	3,601.3
1	Hawaii	4,687.0	11	Nevada	3,561.6
26	Idaho	2,877.1	12	Colorado	3,490.2
20	Illinois	3,096.4	13	New Mexico	3,466.9
30	Indiana	2,782.4	14	Texas	3,395.1
37	Iowa	2,492.3	15	Maryland	3,368.1
25	Kansas	2,954.5	16	South Carolina	3,336.6
48	Kentucky	1,919.2	17	Wyoming	3,204.6
8	Louisiana	3,802.6	18	North Carolina	3,195.7
42	Maine	2,278.8	19	Oklahoma	3,192.9
15	Maryland	3,368.1	20	Illinois	3,096.4
46	Massachusetts	2,151.3	21	Michigan	3,055.7
21	Michigan	3,055.7	22	Missouri	2,998.9
27	Minnesota	2,875.9	23	Nebraska	2,991.2
35	Mississippi	2,646.0	24	California	2,957.7
22	Missouri	2,998.9	25	Kansas	2,954.5
7	Montana	3,833.8	26	Idaho	2,877.1
23	Nebraska	2,991.2	27	Minnesota	2,875.9
11	Nevada	3,561.6	28	Alabama	2,843.1
47	New Hampshire	1,957.8	29	Arkansas	2,791.6
39	New Jersey	2,474.9	30	Indiana	2,782.4
13	New Mexico	3,466.9	31	Virginia	2,772.0
38	New York	2,489.5	32	Ohio	2,682.3
18	North Carolina	3,195.7	33	Tennessee	2,670.0
45	North Dakota	2,178.5	34	Wisconsin	2,667.4
32	Ohio	2,682.3	35	Mississippi	2,646.0
19	Oklahoma	3,192.9	36	Connecticut	2,586.9
5	Oregon	3,969.7	37	Iowa	2,492.3
49	Pennsylvania	1,844.3	38	New York	2,489.5
41	Rhode Island	2,310.8	39	New Jersey	2,474.9
16	South Carolina	3,336.6	40	Delaware	2,446.2
44	South Dakota	2,207.5	41	Rhode Island	2,310.8
33	Tennessee	2,670.0	42	Maine	2,278.8
14	Texas	3,395.1	43	Vermont	2,267.9
6	Utah	3,907.4	44	South Dakota	2,207.5
43	Vermont	2,267.9	45	North Dakota	2,178.5
31	Virginia	2,772.0	46	Massachusetts	2,151.3
4	Washington	3,971.5	47	New Hampshire	1,957.8
50	West Virginia	1,547.1	48	Kentucky	1,919.2
34	Wisconsin	2,667.4	49	Pennsylvania	1,844.3
17	Wyoming	3,204.6	50	West Virginia	1,547.1
				District of Columbia	5,212.5

Source: Federal Bureau of Investigation
"Crime in the United States 1994" (Uniform Crime Reports, November 19, 1995)
*Larceny and theft is the unlawful taking of property without use of force, violence or fraud. Attempts are included. Motor vehicle thefts are excluded.

Percent Change in Rate of Larceny and Theft: 1993 to 1994

National Percent Change = 0.2% Decrease*

ALPHA ORDER

RANK	STATE	PERCENT CHANGE
7	Alabama	6.4
20	Alaska	1.7
6	Arizona	6.6
30	Arkansas	(0.1)
41	California	(2.4)
32	Colorado	(0.3)
38	Connecticut	(1.3)
49	Delaware	(17.9)
20	Florida	1.7
19	Georgia	1.8
9	Hawaii	5.8
8	Idaho	6.1
26	Illinois	0.4
16	Indiana	3.2
43	Iowa	(4.1)
40	Kansas	(2.3)
13	Kentucky	4.3
29	Louisiana	0.0
12	Maine	4.8
18	Maryland	2.3
46	Massachusetts	(5.3)
31	Michigan	(0.2)
27	Minnesota	0.1
1	Mississippi	12.0
4	Missouri	8.0
11	Montana	5.0
17	Nebraska	2.7
5	Nevada	7.2
45	New Hampshire	(4.9)
33	New Jersey	(0.5)
37	New Mexico	(1.2)
47	New York	(5.9)
23	North Carolina	0.8
39	North Dakota	(1.7)
25	Ohio	0.5
3	Oklahoma	8.5
2	Oregon	8.6
24	Pennsylvania	0.7
43	Rhode Island	(4.1)
15	South Carolina	3.4
9	South Dakota	5.8
36	Tennessee	(1.1)
48	Texas	(7.9)
27	Utah	0.1
50	Vermont	(20.5)
34	Virginia	(0.6)
22	Washington	1.5
35	West Virginia	(1.0)
42	Wisconsin	(3.4)
14	Wyoming	4.1

RANK ORDER

RANK	STATE	PERCENT CHANGE
1	Mississippi	12.0
2	Oregon	8.6
3	Oklahoma	8.5
4	Missouri	8.0
5	Nevada	7.2
6	Arizona	6.6
7	Alabama	6.4
8	Idaho	6.1
9	Hawaii	5.8
9	South Dakota	5.8
11	Montana	5.0
12	Maine	4.8
13	Kentucky	4.3
14	Wyoming	4.1
15	South Carolina	3.4
16	Indiana	3.2
17	Nebraska	2.7
18	Maryland	2.3
19	Georgia	1.8
20	Alaska	1.7
20	Florida	1.7
22	Washington	1.5
23	North Carolina	0.8
24	Pennsylvania	0.7
25	Ohio	0.5
26	Illinois	0.4
27	Minnesota	0.1
27	Utah	0.1
29	Louisiana	0.0
30	Arkansas	(0.1)
31	Michigan	(0.2)
32	Colorado	(0.3)
33	New Jersey	(0.5)
34	Virginia	(0.6)
35	West Virginia	(1.0)
36	Tennessee	(1.1)
37	New Mexico	(1.2)
38	Connecticut	(1.3)
39	North Dakota	(1.7)
40	Kansas	(2.3)
41	California	(2.4)
42	Wisconsin	(3.4)
43	Iowa	(4.1)
43	Rhode Island	(4.1)
45	New Hampshire	(4.9)
46	Massachusetts	(5.3)
47	New York	(5.9)
48	Texas	(7.9)
49	Delaware	(17.9)
50	Vermont	(20.5)
	District of Columbia	(4.3)

Source: Federal Bureau of Investigation
   "Crime in the United States 1994" (Uniform Crime Reports, November 19, 1995)
*Larceny and theft is the unlawful taking of property without use of force, violence or fraud. Attempts are included.
Motor vehicle thefts are excluded.

Motor Vehicle Thefts in 1994

National Total = 1,539,097 Motor Vehicle Thefts*

ALPHA ORDER				RANK ORDER			
RANK	STATE	THEFTS	% of USA	RANK	STATE	THEFTS	% of USA
27	Alabama	14,000	0.91%	1	California	308,205	20.03%
40	Alaska	3,275	0.21%	2	New York	128,873	8.37%
10	Arizona	43,467	2.82%	3	Florida	127,186	8.26%
34	Arkansas	7,726	0.50%	4	Texas	110,753	7.20%
1	California	308,205	20.03%	5	Illinois	66,218	4.30%
25	Colorado	14,365	0.93%	6	Michigan	62,304	4.05%
21	Connecticut	20,167	1.31%	7	Pennsylvania	54,153	3.52%
42	Delaware	2,471	0.16%	8	New Jersey	52,164	3.39%
3	Florida	127,186	8.26%	9	Ohio	47,413	3.08%
12	Georgia	39,312	2.55%	10	Arizona	43,467	2.82%
35	Hawaii	6,383	0.41%	11	Massachusetts	42,348	2.75%
45	Idaho	2,210	0.14%	12	Georgia	39,312	2.55%
5	Illinois	66,218	4.30%	13	Maryland	38,197	2.48%
18	Indiana	25,011	1.63%	14	Tennessee	28,994	1.88%
39	Iowa	5,096	0.33%	15	Missouri	27,038	1.76%
31	Kansas	8,667	0.56%	16	Washington	26,743	1.74%
32	Kentucky	8,558	0.56%	17	Louisiana	26,219	1.70%
17	Louisiana	26,219	1.70%	18	Indiana	25,011	1.63%
46	Maine	1,776	0.12%	19	Oregon	21,764	1.41%
13	Maryland	38,197	2.48%	20	North Carolina	21,342	1.39%
11	Massachusetts	42,348	2.75%	21	Connecticut	20,167	1.31%
6	Michigan	62,304	4.05%	22	Wisconsin	18,321	1.19%
26	Minnesota	14,355	0.93%	23	Virginia	18,289	1.19%
30	Mississippi	10,810	0.70%	24	Oklahoma	15,461	1.00%
15	Missouri	27,038	1.76%	25	Colorado	14,365	0.93%
43	Montana	2,450	0.16%	26	Minnesota	14,355	0.93%
36	Nebraska	6,236	0.41%	27	Alabama	14,000	0.91%
29	Nevada	11,065	0.72%	28	South Carolina	13,184	0.86%
44	New Hampshire	2,302	0.15%	29	Nevada	11,065	0.72%
8	New Jersey	52,164	3.39%	30	Mississippi	10,810	0.70%
33	New Mexico	8,350	0.54%	31	Kansas	8,667	0.56%
2	New York	128,873	8.37%	32	Kentucky	8,558	0.56%
20	North Carolina	21,342	1.39%	33	New Mexico	8,350	0.54%
47	North Dakota	964	0.06%	34	Arkansas	7,726	0.50%
9	Ohio	47,413	3.08%	35	Hawaii	6,383	0.41%
24	Oklahoma	15,461	1.00%	36	Nebraska	6,236	0.41%
19	Oregon	21,764	1.41%	37	Utah	5,689	0.37%
7	Pennsylvania	54,153	3.52%	38	Rhode Island	5,183	0.34%
38	Rhode Island	5,183	0.34%	39	Iowa	5,096	0.33%
28	South Carolina	13,184	0.86%	40	Alaska	3,275	0.21%
48	South Dakota	872	0.06%	41	West Virginia	3,274	0.21%
14	Tennessee	28,994	1.88%	42	Delaware	2,471	0.16%
4	Texas	110,753	7.20%	43	Montana	2,450	0.16%
37	Utah	5,689	0.37%	44	New Hampshire	2,302	0.15%
49	Vermont	862	0.06%	45	Idaho	2,210	0.14%
23	Virginia	18,289	1.19%	46	Maine	1,776	0.12%
16	Washington	26,743	1.74%	47	North Dakota	964	0.06%
41	West Virginia	3,274	0.21%	48	South Dakota	872	0.06%
22	Wisconsin	18,321	1.19%	49	Vermont	862	0.06%
50	Wyoming	771	0.05%	50	Wyoming	771	0.05%
					District of Columbia	8,261	0.54%

Source: Federal Bureau of Investigation
   "Crime in the United States 1994" (Uniform Crime Reports, November 19, 1995)
*Includes the theft or attempted theft of a self-propelled vehicle. Excludes motorboats, construction equipment, airplanes and farming equipment.

Average Time Between Motor Vehicle Thefts in 1994

National Rate = A Motor Vehicle Theft Occurs Every 20 Seconds*

RANK	STATE (ALPHA ORDER)	MINUTES.SECONDS		RANK	STATE (RANK ORDER)	MINUTES.SECONDS
24	Alabama	37.32		1	Wyoming	681.43
11	Alaska	160.29		2	Vermont	609.44
41	Arizona	12.05		3	South Dakota	602.45
17	Arkansas	68.02		4	North Dakota	545.14
50	California	1.43		5	Maine	295.57
26	Colorado	36.35		6	Idaho	237.50
30	Connecticut	26.04		7	New Hampshire	228.19
9	Delaware	212.43		8	Montana	214.32
48	Florida	4.08		9	Delaware	212.43
39	Georgia	13.22		10	West Virginia	160.32
16	Hawaii	82.20		11	Alaska	160.29
6	Idaho	237.50		12	Iowa	103.08
46	Illinois	7.56		13	Rhode Island	101.25
33	Indiana	21.01		14	Utah	92.23
12	Iowa	103.08		15	Nebraska	84.17
20	Kansas	60.38		16	Hawaii	82.20
19	Kentucky	61.25		17	Arkansas	68.02
34	Louisiana	20.03		18	New Mexico	62.57
5	Maine	295.57		19	Kentucky	61.25
38	Maryland	13.46		20	Kansas	60.38
40	Massachusetts	12.25		21	Mississippi	48.37
45	Michigan	8.26		22	Nevada	47.30
25	Minnesota	36.37		23	South Carolina	39.52
21	Mississippi	48.37		24	Alabama	37.32
36	Missouri	19.26		25	Minnesota	36.37
8	Montana	214.32		26	Colorado	36.35
15	Nebraska	84.17		27	Oklahoma	34.00
22	Nevada	47.30		28	Virginia	28.44
7	New Hampshire	228.19		29	Wisconsin	28.41
43	New Jersey	10.05		30	Connecticut	26.04
18	New Mexico	62.57		31	North Carolina	24.38
49	New York	4.05		32	Oregon	24.09
31	North Carolina	24.38		33	Indiana	21.01
4	North Dakota	545.14		34	Louisiana	20.03
42	Ohio	11.05		35	Washington	19.39
27	Oklahoma	34.00		36	Missouri	19.26
32	Oregon	24.09		37	Tennessee	18.08
44	Pennsylvania	9.43		38	Maryland	13.46
13	Rhode Island	101.25		39	Georgia	13.22
23	South Carolina	39.52		40	Massachusetts	12.25
3	South Dakota	602.45		41	Arizona	12.05
37	Tennessee	18.08		42	Ohio	11.05
47	Texas	4.45		43	New Jersey	10.05
14	Utah	92.23		44	Pennsylvania	9.43
2	Vermont	609.44		45	Michigan	8.26
28	Virginia	28.44		46	Illinois	7.56
35	Washington	19.39		47	Texas	4.45
10	West Virginia	160.32		48	Florida	4.08
29	Wisconsin	28.41		49	New York	4.05
1	Wyoming	681.43		50	California	1.43
					District of Columbia	63.37

Source: Morgan Quitno Press using data from Federal Bureau of Investigation
   "Crime in the United States 1994" (Uniform Crime Reports, November 19, 1995)
*Includes the theft or attempted theft of a self-propelled vehicle. Excludes motorboats, construction equipment, airplanes and farming equipment.

Percent Change in Number of Motor Vehicle Thefts: 1993 to 1994

National Percent Change = 1.5% Decrease*

ALPHA ORDER			RANK ORDER		
RANK	STATE	PERCENT CHANGE	RANK	STATE	PERCENT CHANGE
36	Alabama	(1.0)	1	Arizona	27.9
6	Alaska	21.3	2	New Mexico	27.5
1	Arizona	27.9	3	Utah	26.3
37	Arkansas	(1.2)	4	Oregon	23.6
40	California	(3.5)	5	Mississippi	22.1
15	Colorado	10.5	6	Alaska	21.3
28	Connecticut	3.3	7	Hawaii	20.8
12	Delaware	12.0	8	Nebraska	18.7
27	Florida	3.8	9	Montana	18.6
42	Georgia	(4.3)	10	Vermont	12.8
7	Hawaii	20.8	11	Maryland	12.6
16	Idaho	9.6	12	Delaware	12.0
32	Illinois	1.3	13	Washington	11.6
29	Indiana	2.3	14	West Virginia	11.4
43	Iowa	(5.1)	15	Colorado	10.5
22	Kansas	6.1	16	Idaho	9.6
26	Kentucky	4.5	17	Nevada	7.9
34	Louisiana	(0.5)	18	Michigan	6.9
19	Maine	6.7	19	Maine	6.7
11	Maryland	12.6	20	North Carolina	6.5
48	Massachusetts	(13.7)	20	South Dakota	6.5
18	Michigan	6.9	22	Kansas	6.1
45	Minnesota	(7.2)	23	Wyoming	5.9
5	Mississippi	22.1	24	New Hampshire	5.5
44	Missouri	(5.7)	25	South Carolina	5.2
9	Montana	18.6	26	Kentucky	4.5
8	Nebraska	18.7	27	Florida	3.8
17	Nevada	7.9	28	Connecticut	3.3
24	New Hampshire	5.5	29	Indiana	2.3
46	New Jersey	(7.3)	30	North Dakota	2.1
2	New Mexico	27.5	30	Pennsylvania	2.1
49	New York	(15.2)	32	Illinois	1.3
20	North Carolina	6.5	33	Wisconsin	(0.3)
30	North Dakota	2.1	34	Louisiana	(0.5)
39	Ohio	(1.8)	34	Oklahoma	(0.5)
34	Oklahoma	(0.5)	36	Alabama	(1.0)
4	Oregon	23.6	37	Arkansas	(1.2)
30	Pennsylvania	2.1	38	Virginia	(1.3)
50	Rhode Island	(19.8)	39	Ohio	(1.8)
25	South Carolina	5.2	40	California	(3.5)
20	South Dakota	6.5	41	Tennessee	(3.8)
41	Tennessee	(3.8)	42	Georgia	(4.3)
47	Texas	(11.3)	43	Iowa	(5.1)
3	Utah	26.3	44	Missouri	(5.7)
10	Vermont	12.8	45	Minnesota	(7.2)
38	Virginia	(1.3)	46	New Jersey	(7.3)
13	Washington	11.6	47	Texas	(11.3)
14	West Virginia	11.4	48	Massachusetts	(13.7)
33	Wisconsin	(0.3)	49	New York	(15.2)
23	Wyoming	5.9	50	Rhode Island	(19.8)
				District of Columbia	2.5

Source: Federal Bureau of Investigation
    "Crime in the United States 1994" (Uniform Crime Reports, November 19, 1995)
*Includes the theft or attempted theft of a self-propelled vehicle. Excludes motorboats, construction equipment, airplanes and farming equipment.

Motor Vehicle Theft Rate in 1994

National Rate = 591.2 Motor Vehicle Thefts per 100,000 Population*

ALPHA ORDER

RANK ORDER

RANK	STATE	RATE
34	Alabama	331.8
18	Alaska	540.4
1	Arizona	1,066.7
35	Arkansas	315.0
2	California	980.6
28	Colorado	392.9
11	Connecticut	615.8
32	Delaware	350.0
3	Florida	911.5
16	Georgia	557.2
17	Hawaii	541.4
43	Idaho	195.1
14	Illinois	563.5
25	Indiana	434.8
44	Iowa	180.1
33	Kansas	339.4
41	Kentucky	223.6
12	Louisiana	607.6
49	Maine	143.2
4	Maryland	763.0
8	Massachusetts	701.0
10	Michigan	656.1
36	Minnesota	314.3
27	Mississippi	405.0
20	Missouri	512.3
39	Montana	286.2
29	Nebraska	384.2
5	Nevada	759.4
42	New Hampshire	202.5
9	New Jersey	660.0
21	New Mexico	504.8
6	New York	709.3
37	North Carolina	301.9
47	North Dakota	151.1
26	Ohio	427.1
23	Oklahoma	474.6
7	Oregon	705.2
24	Pennsylvania	449.3
19	Rhode Island	519.9
31	South Carolina	359.8
50	South Dakota	120.9
15	Tennessee	560.3
13	Texas	602.6
38	Utah	298.2
48	Vermont	148.6
40	Virginia	279.1
22	Washington	500.5
45	West Virginia	179.7
30	Wisconsin	360.5
46	Wyoming	162.0

RANK	STATE	RATE
1	Arizona	1,066.7
2	California	980.6
3	Florida	911.5
4	Maryland	763.0
5	Nevada	759.4
6	New York	709.3
7	Oregon	705.2
8	Massachusetts	701.0
9	New Jersey	660.0
10	Michigan	656.1
11	Connecticut	615.8
12	Louisiana	607.6
13	Texas	602.6
14	Illinois	563.5
15	Tennessee	560.3
16	Georgia	557.2
17	Hawaii	541.4
18	Alaska	540.4
19	Rhode Island	519.9
20	Missouri	512.3
21	New Mexico	504.8
22	Washington	500.5
23	Oklahoma	474.6
24	Pennsylvania	449.3
25	Indiana	434.8
26	Ohio	427.1
27	Mississippi	405.0
28	Colorado	392.9
29	Nebraska	384.2
30	Wisconsin	360.5
31	South Carolina	359.8
32	Delaware	350.0
33	Kansas	339.4
34	Alabama	331.8
35	Arkansas	315.0
36	Minnesota	314.3
37	North Carolina	301.9
38	Utah	298.2
39	Montana	286.2
40	Virginia	279.1
41	Kentucky	223.6
42	New Hampshire	202.5
43	Idaho	195.1
44	Iowa	180.1
45	West Virginia	179.7
46	Wyoming	162.0
47	North Dakota	151.1
48	Vermont	148.6
49	Maine	143.2
50	South Dakota	120.9

District of Columbia — 1,449.3

Source: Federal Bureau of Investigation
"Crime in the United States 1994" (Uniform Crime Reports, November 19, 1995)
*Includes the theft or attempted theft of a self-propelled vehicle. Excludes motorboats, construction equipment, airplanes and farming equipment.

Percent Change in Rate of Motor Vehicle Thefts: 1993 to 1994

National Percent Change = 2.5% Decrease*

ALPHA ORDER

RANK ORDER

RANK	STATE	PERCENT CHANGE	RANK	STATE	PERCENT CHANGE
35	Alabama	(1.8)	1	New Mexico	24.6
7	Alaska	19.8	2	Arizona	23.5
2	Arizona	23.5	3	Utah	23.1
38	Arkansas	(2.3)	4	Oregon	21.4
39	California	(4.1)	5	Mississippi	20.9
46	Colorado	(12.7)	6	Hawaii	20.1
24	Connecticut	3.4	7	Alaska	19.8
13	Delaware	11.0	8	Nebraska	17.6
28	Florida	1.8	9	Montana	16.2
42	Georgia	(6.2)	10	Vermont	12.1
6	Hawaii	20.1	11	Maryland	11.6
17	Idaho	6.4	12	West Virginia	11.3
31	Illinois	0.9	13	Delaware	11.0
29	Indiana	1.6	14	Washington	9.7
41	Iowa	(5.6)	15	Michigan	6.7
19	Kansas	5.2	16	Maine	6.5
24	Kentucky	3.4	17	Idaho	6.4
32	Louisiana	(1.0)	18	South Dakota	5.6
16	Maine	6.5	19	Kansas	5.2
11	Maryland	11.6	20	North Carolina	4.6
48	Massachusetts	(14.1)	20	South Carolina	4.6
15	Michigan	6.7	20	Wyoming	4.6
45	Minnesota	(8.3)	23	New Hampshire	4.4
5	Mississippi	20.9	24	Connecticut	3.4
43	Missouri	(6.5)	24	Kentucky	3.4
9	Montana	16.2	26	Nevada	2.9
8	Nebraska	17.6	27	Pennsylvania	2.1
26	Nevada	2.9	28	Florida	1.8
23	New Hampshire	4.4	29	Indiana	1.6
44	New Jersey	(7.6)	29	North Dakota	1.6
1	New Mexico	24.6	31	Illinois	0.9
49	New York	(15.1)	32	Louisiana	(1.0)
20	North Carolina	4.6	33	Wisconsin	(1.2)
29	North Dakota	1.6	34	Oklahoma	(1.3)
36	Ohio	(1.9)	35	Alabama	(1.8)
34	Oklahoma	(1.3)	36	Ohio	(1.9)
4	Oregon	21.4	37	Virginia	(2.2)
27	Pennsylvania	2.1	38	Arkansas	(2.3)
50	Rhode Island	(19.6)	39	California	(4.1)
20	South Carolina	4.6	40	Tennessee	(5.2)
18	South Dakota	5.6	41	Iowa	(5.6)
40	Tennessee	(5.2)	42	Georgia	(6.2)
47	Texas	(13.0)	43	Missouri	(6.5)
3	Utah	23.1	44	New Jersey	(7.6)
10	Vermont	12.1	45	Minnesota	(8.3)
37	Virginia	(2.2)	46	Colorado	(12.7)
14	Washington	9.7	47	Texas	(13.0)
12	West Virginia	11.3	48	Massachusetts	(14.1)
33	Wisconsin	(1.2)	49	New York	(15.1)
20	Wyoming	4.6	50	Rhode Island	(19.6)
				District of Columbia	3.9

Source: Federal Bureau of Investigation
"Crime in the United States 1994" (Uniform Crime Reports, November 19, 1995)
*Includes the theft or attempted theft of a self-propelled vehicle. Excludes motorboats, construction equipment, airplanes and farming equipment.

Crime in Urban Areas in 1994

National Total = 13,343,319 Crimes*

ALPHA ORDER

RANK	STATE	CRIMES	% of USA
20	Alabama	197,850	1.48%
42	Alaska	28,542	0.21%
11	Arizona	315,677	2.37%
30	Arkansas	105,098	0.79%
1	California	1,919,454	14.39%
22	Colorado	185,221	1.39%
27	Connecticut	145,425	1.09%
43	Delaware	26,340	0.20%
2	Florida	1,121,159	8.40%
7	Georgia	388,161	2.91%
36	Hawaii	63,653	0.48%
38	Idaho	37,982	0.28%
NA	Illinois**	NA	NA
19	Indiana	244,604	1.83%
33	Iowa	93,243	0.70%
NA	Kansas**	NA	NA
28	Kentucky	114,057	0.85%
14	Louisiana	271,690	2.04%
40	Maine	34,161	0.26%
13	Maryland	299,887	2.25%
15	Massachusetts	268,172	2.01%
5	Michigan	490,225	3.67%
24	Minnesota	180,614	1.35%
29	Mississippi	112,914	0.85%
16	Missouri	264,381	1.98%
NA	Montana**	NA	NA
35	Nebraska	66,489	0.50%
34	Nevada	91,323	0.68%
41	New Hampshire	30,135	0.23%
9	New Jersey	368,400	2.76%
32	New Mexico	93,339	0.70%
4	New York	902,240	6.76%
10	North Carolina	356,095	2.67%
46	North Dakota	15,305	0.11%
6	Ohio	476,260	3.57%
26	Oklahoma	170,468	1.28%
25	Oregon	180,011	1.35%
8	Pennsylvania	378,676	2.84%
37	Rhode Island	41,044	0.31%
21	South Carolina	188,498	1.41%
44	South Dakota	19,378	0.15%
18	Tennessee	246,030	1.84%
3	Texas	1,046,694	7.84%
31	Utah	96,699	0.72%
47	Vermont	15,010	0.11%
17	Virginia	249,182	1.87%
12	Washington	307,753	2.31%
39	West Virginia	35,515	0.27%
23	Wisconsin	183,944	1.38%
45	Wyoming	17,710	0.13%

RANK ORDER

RANK	STATE	CRIMES	% of USA
1	California	1,919,454	14.39%
2	Florida	1,121,159	8.40%
3	Texas	1,046,694	7.84%
4	New York	902,240	6.76%
5	Michigan	490,225	3.67%
6	Ohio	476,260	3.57%
7	Georgia	388,161	2.91%
8	Pennsylvania	378,676	2.84%
9	New Jersey	368,400	2.76%
10	North Carolina	356,095	2.67%
11	Arizona	315,677	2.37%
12	Washington	307,753	2.31%
13	Maryland	299,887	2.25%
14	Louisiana	271,690	2.04%
15	Massachusetts	268,172	2.01%
16	Missouri	264,381	1.98%
17	Virginia	249,182	1.87%
18	Tennessee	246,030	1.84%
19	Indiana	244,604	1.83%
20	Alabama	197,850	1.48%
21	South Carolina	188,498	1.41%
22	Colorado	185,221	1.39%
23	Wisconsin	183,944	1.38%
24	Minnesota	180,614	1.35%
25	Oregon	180,011	1.35%
26	Oklahoma	170,468	1.28%
27	Connecticut	145,425	1.09%
28	Kentucky	114,057	0.85%
29	Mississippi	112,914	0.85%
30	Arkansas	105,098	0.79%
31	Utah	96,699	0.72%
32	New Mexico	93,339	0.70%
33	Iowa	93,243	0.70%
34	Nevada	91,323	0.68%
35	Nebraska	66,489	0.50%
36	Hawaii	63,653	0.48%
37	Rhode Island	41,044	0.31%
38	Idaho	37,982	0.28%
39	West Virginia	35,515	0.27%
40	Maine	34,161	0.26%
41	New Hampshire	30,135	0.23%
42	Alaska	28,542	0.21%
43	Delaware	26,340	0.20%
44	South Dakota	19,378	0.15%
45	Wyoming	17,710	0.13%
46	North Dakota	15,305	0.11%
47	Vermont	15,010	0.11%
NA	Illinois**	NA	NA
NA	Kansas**	NA	NA
NA	Montana**	NA	NA
	District of Columbia	63,186	0.47%

Source: Morgan Quitno Press using data from Federal Bureau of Investigation
   "Crime in the United States 1994" (Uniform Crime Reports, November 19, 1995)
*Estimated totals for urban areas, defined by the F.B.I. as Metropolitan Statistical Areas and other cities outside such areas. National total includes those states listed as not available. Includes murder, rape, robbery, aggravated assault, burglary, larceny-theft and motor vehicle theft.
**Not available.

Urban Crime Rate in 1994

National Rate = 5,840.4 Crimes per 100,000 Population*

ALPHA ORDER

RANK	STATE	RATE
22	Alabama	5,776.5
10	Alaska	6,871.0
2	Arizona	8,390.6
15	Arkansas	6,441.9
19	California	6,230.0
24	Colorado	5,627.8
34	Connecticut	4,715.2
41	Delaware	4,269.9
1	Florida	8,495.9
8	Georgia	6,888.6
7	Hawaii	6,917.0
28	Idaho	5,148.0
NA	Illinois**	NA
27	Indiana	5,209.2
32	Iowa	4,813.3
NA	Kansas**	NA
36	Kentucky	4,634.5
3	Louisiana	7,512.9
43	Maine	3,822.3
17	Maryland	6,329.7
40	Massachusetts	4,448.3
21	Michigan	5,797.0
30	Minnesota	4,893.9
4	Mississippi	7,250.2
14	Missouri	6,463.1
NA	Montana**	NA
25	Nebraska	5,507.5
5	Nevada	7,141.0
47	New Hampshire	3,028.7
35	New Jersey	4,660.9
9	New Mexico	6,888.0
26	New York	5,211.3
11	North Carolina	6,591.7
44	North Dakota	3,726.4
31	Ohio	4,866.8
13	Oklahoma	6,488.8
6	Oregon	6,956.7
45	Pennsylvania	3,444.6
42	Rhode Island	4,116.8
12	South Carolina	6,565.7
38	South Dakota	4,525.8
20	Tennessee	6,041.6
18	Texas	6,240.6
23	Utah	5,670.1
33	Vermont	4,767.0
37	Virginia	4,534.9
16	Washington	6,342.9
46	West Virginia	3,415.3
39	Wisconsin	4,483.7
29	Wyoming	5,049.9

RANK ORDER

RANK	STATE	RATE
1	Florida	8,495.9
2	Arizona	8,390.6
3	Louisiana	7,512.9
4	Mississippi	7,250.2
5	Nevada	7,141.0
6	Oregon	6,956.7
7	Hawaii	6,917.0
8	Georgia	6,888.6
9	New Mexico	6,888.0
10	Alaska	6,871.0
11	North Carolina	6,591.7
12	South Carolina	6,565.7
13	Oklahoma	6,488.8
14	Missouri	6,463.1
15	Arkansas	6,441.9
16	Washington	6,342.9
17	Maryland	6,329.7
18	Texas	6,240.6
19	California	6,230.0
20	Tennessee	6,041.6
21	Michigan	5,797.0
22	Alabama	5,776.5
23	Utah	5,670.1
24	Colorado	5,627.8
25	Nebraska	5,507.5
26	New York	5,211.3
27	Indiana	5,209.2
28	Idaho	5,148.0
29	Wyoming	5,049.9
30	Minnesota	4,893.9
31	Ohio	4,866.8
32	Iowa	4,813.3
33	Vermont	4,767.0
34	Connecticut	4,715.2
35	New Jersey	4,660.9
36	Kentucky	4,634.5
37	Virginia	4,534.9
38	South Dakota	4,525.8
39	Wisconsin	4,483.7
40	Massachusetts	4,448.3
41	Delaware	4,269.9
42	Rhode Island	4,116.8
43	Maine	3,822.3
44	North Dakota	3,726.4
45	Pennsylvania	3,444.6
46	West Virginia	3,415.3
47	New Hampshire	3,028.7
NA	Illinois**	NA
NA	Kansas**	NA
NA	Montana**	NA
	District of Columbia	11,085.3

Source: Morgan Quitno Press using data from Federal Bureau of Investigation
   "Crime in the United States 1994" (Uniform Crime Reports, November 19, 1995)
*Estimated rates for urban areas, defined by the F.B.I. as Metropolitan Statistical Areas and other cities outside
such areas. National rate includes those states listed as not available. Includes murder, rape, robbery,
aggravated assault, burglary, larceny-theft and motor vehicle theft.
**Not available.

Percent of Crimes Occurring in Urban Areas in 1994

National Percent = 95.37% of Crimes*

ALPHA ORDER

RANK	STATE	PERCENT
14	Alabama	95.64
43	Alaska	82.51
7	Arizona	97.76
35	Arkansas	89.28
4	California	98.92
17	Colorado	95.26
8	Connecticut	97.64
33	Delaware	89.95
9	Florida	97.40
29	Georgia	91.54
45	Hawaii	80.82
44	Idaho	82.23
NA	Illinois**	NA
26	Indiana	92.59
32	Iowa	90.19
NA	Kansas**	NA
41	Kentucky	85.19
19	Louisiana	94.38
42	Maine	84.18
6	Maryland	97.84
2	Massachusetts	99.96
18	Michigan	94.81
31	Minnesota	91.10
37	Mississippi	87.46
19	Missouri	94.38
NA	Montana**	NA
27	Nebraska	92.26
23	Nevada	93.87
11	New Hampshire	96.70
1	New Jersey	100.00
30	New Mexico	91.20
5	New York	97.93
34	North Carolina	89.54
36	North Dakota	87.68
12	Ohio	96.15
22	Oklahoma	93.93
25	Oregon	92.64
13	Pennsylvania	96.03
3	Rhode Island	99.94
40	South Carolina	85.73
39	South Dakota	86.64
24	Tennessee	92.86
10	Texas	96.99
15	Utah	95.61
46	Vermont	79.62
21	Virginia	93.96
16	Washington	95.56
47	West Virginia	77.09
28	Wisconsin	91.76
38	Wyoming	86.73

RANK ORDER

RANK	STATE	PERCENT
1	New Jersey	100.00
2	Massachusetts	99.96
3	Rhode Island	99.94
4	California	98.92
5	New York	97.93
6	Maryland	97.84
7	Arizona	97.76
8	Connecticut	97.64
9	Florida	97.40
10	Texas	96.99
11	New Hampshire	96.70
12	Ohio	96.15
13	Pennsylvania	96.03
14	Alabama	95.64
15	Utah	95.61
16	Washington	95.56
17	Colorado	95.26
18	Michigan	94.81
19	Louisiana	94.38
19	Missouri	94.38
21	Virginia	93.96
22	Oklahoma	93.93
23	Nevada	93.87
24	Tennessee	92.86
25	Oregon	92.64
26	Indiana	92.59
27	Nebraska	92.26
28	Wisconsin	91.76
29	Georgia	91.54
30	New Mexico	91.20
31	Minnesota	91.10
32	Iowa	90.19
33	Delaware	89.95
34	North Carolina	89.54
35	Arkansas	89.28
36	North Dakota	87.68
37	Mississippi	87.46
38	Wyoming	86.73
39	South Dakota	86.64
40	South Carolina	85.73
41	Kentucky	85.19
42	Maine	84.18
43	Alaska	82.51
44	Idaho	82.23
45	Hawaii	80.82
46	Vermont	79.62
47	West Virginia	77.09
NA	Illinois**	NA
NA	Kansas**	NA
NA	Montana**	NA

District of Columbia   100.00

Source: Morgan Quitno Press using data from Federal Bureau of Investigation
    "Crime in the United States 1994" (Uniform Crime Reports, November 19, 1995)
*Estimated percentages for urban areas, defined by the F.B.I. as Metropolitan Statistical Areas and other cities
outside such areas. National percent includes those states listed as not available. Includes murder, rape, robbery,
aggravated assault, burglary, larceny-theft and motor vehicle theft.
**Not available.

Crime in Rural Areas in 1994

National Total = 648,356 Crimes*

ALPHA ORDER					RANK ORDER			
RANK	STATE	CRIMES	% of USA		RANK	STATE	CRIMES	% of USA
28	Alabama	9,009	1.39%		1	North Carolina	41,610	6.42%
34	Alaska	6,049	0.93%		2	Georgia	35,868	5.53%
31	Arizona	7,249	1.12%		3	Texas	32,531	5.02%
23	Arkansas	12,615	1.95%		4	South Carolina	31,372	4.84%
7	California	21,043	3.25%		5	Florida	29,962	4.62%
27	Colorado	9,219	1.42%		6	Michigan	26,851	4.14%
39	Connecticut	3,521	0.54%		7	California	21,043	3.25%
41	Delaware	2,942	0.45%		8	Kentucky	19,833	3.06%
5	Florida	29,962	4.62%		9	Indiana	19,576	3.02%
2	Georgia	35,868	5.53%		10	Ohio	19,050	2.94%
20	Hawaii	15,110	2.33%		11	New York	19,038	2.94%
30	Idaho	8,210	1.27%		12	Tennessee	18,922	2.92%
NA	Illinois**	NA	NA		13	Minnesota	17,639	2.72%
9	Indiana	19,576	3.02%		14	Wisconsin	16,508	2.55%
26	Iowa	10,146	1.56%		15	Mississippi	16,187	2.50%
NA	Kansas**	NA	NA		16	Louisiana	16,167	2.49%
8	Kentucky	19,833	3.06%		17	Virginia	16,018	2.47%
16	Louisiana	16,167	2.49%		18	Missouri	15,757	2.43%
33	Maine	6,421	0.99%		19	Pennsylvania	15,650	2.41%
32	Maryland	6,609	1.02%		20	Hawaii	15,110	2.33%
45	Massachusetts	109	0.02%		21	Washington	14,298	2.21%
6	Michigan	26,851	4.14%		22	Oregon	14,296	2.20%
13	Minnesota	17,639	2.72%		23	Arkansas	12,615	1.95%
15	Mississippi	16,187	2.50%		24	Oklahoma	11,007	1.70%
18	Missouri	15,757	2.43%		25	West Virginia	10,552	1.63%
NA	Montana**	NA	NA		26	Iowa	10,146	1.56%
36	Nebraska	5,579	0.86%		27	Colorado	9,219	1.42%
35	Nevada	5,967	0.92%		28	Alabama	9,009	1.39%
44	New Hampshire	1,030	0.16%		29	New Mexico	9,007	1.39%
47	New Jersey	0	0.00%		30	Idaho	8,210	1.27%
29	New Mexico	9,007	1.39%		31	Arizona	7,249	1.12%
11	New York	19,038	2.94%		32	Maryland	6,609	1.02%
1	North Carolina	41,610	6.42%		33	Maine	6,421	0.99%
43	North Dakota	2,150	0.33%		34	Alaska	6,049	0.93%
10	Ohio	19,050	2.94%		35	Nevada	5,967	0.92%
24	Oklahoma	11,007	1.70%		36	Nebraska	5,579	0.86%
22	Oregon	14,296	2.20%		37	Utah	4,443	0.69%
19	Pennsylvania	15,650	2.41%		38	Vermont	3,842	0.59%
46	Rhode Island	23	0.00%		39	Connecticut	3,521	0.54%
4	South Carolina	31,372	4.84%		40	South Dakota	2,989	0.46%
40	South Dakota	2,989	0.46%		41	Delaware	2,942	0.45%
12	Tennessee	18,922	2.92%		42	Wyoming	2,709	0.42%
3	Texas	32,531	5.02%		43	North Dakota	2,150	0.33%
37	Utah	4,443	0.69%		44	New Hampshire	1,030	0.16%
38	Vermont	3,842	0.59%		45	Massachusetts	109	0.02%
17	Virginia	16,018	2.47%		46	Rhode Island	23	0.00%
21	Washington	14,298	2.21%		47	New Jersey	0	0.00%
25	West Virginia	10,552	1.63%		NA	Illinois**	NA	NA
14	Wisconsin	16,508	2.55%		NA	Kansas**	NA	NA
42	Wyoming	2,709	0.42%		NA	Montana**	NA	NA
						District of Columbia	0	0.00%

Source: Federal Bureau of Investigation
   "Crime in the United States 1994" (Uniform Crime Reports, November 19, 1995)
Estimated totals for rural areas, defined by the F.B.I. as other than Metropolitan Statistical Areas and other cities outside such areas. National total includes those states listed as not available. Includes murder, rape, robbery, aggravated assault, burglary, larceny-theft and motor vehicle theft.
**Not available.*

Rural Crime Rate in 1994

National Rate = 2,034.0 Crimes per 100,000 Population*

ALPHA ORDER

RANK	STATE	RATE
41	Alabama	1,134.7
7	Alaska	3,173.6
16	Arizona	2,318.0
30	Arkansas	1,535.5
4	California	3,387.4
12	Colorado	2,526.8
26	Connecticut	1,845.2
6	Delaware	3,300.8
2	Florida	3,960.8
13	Georgia	2,525.5
1	Hawaii	5,839.4
21	Idaho	2,077.4
NA	Illinois**	NA
25	Indiana	1,853.1
40	Iowa	1,137.7
NA	Kansas**	NA
34	Kentucky	1,451.9
17	Louisiana	2,313.9
24	Maine	1,854.3
15	Maryland	2,464.1
44	Massachusetts	885.0
11	Michigan	2,583.1
23	Minnesota	2,012.7
33	Mississippi	1,456.2
39	Missouri	1,327.0
NA	Montana**	NA
38	Nebraska	1,341.9
5	Nevada	3,349.5
45	New Hampshire	725.2
46	New Jersey	0.0
8	New Mexico	3,013.3
18	New York	2,224.4
14	North Carolina	2,494.8
43	North Dakota	945.9
36	Ohio	1,447.5
27	Oklahoma	1,744.7
10	Oregon	2,868.3
32	Pennsylvania	1,478.1
46	Rhode Island	0.0
3	South Carolina	3,955.8
42	South Dakota	1,020.7
28	Tennessee	1,715.9
22	Texas	2,025.9
19	Utah	2,193.2
35	Vermont	1,449.1
31	Virginia	1,515.1
9	Washington	2,911.4
37	West Virginia	1,349.2
29	Wisconsin	1,685.4
20	Wyoming	2,162.0

RANK ORDER

RANK	STATE	RATE
1	Hawaii	5,839.4
2	Florida	3,960.8
3	South Carolina	3,955.8
4	California	3,387.4
5	Nevada	3,349.5
6	Delaware	3,300.8
7	Alaska	3,173.6
8	New Mexico	3,013.3
9	Washington	2,911.4
10	Oregon	2,868.3
11	Michigan	2,583.1
12	Colorado	2,526.8
13	Georgia	2,525.5
14	North Carolina	2,494.8
15	Maryland	2,464.1
16	Arizona	2,318.0
17	Louisiana	2,313.9
18	New York	2,224.4
19	Utah	2,193.2
20	Wyoming	2,162.0
21	Idaho	2,077.4
22	Texas	2,025.9
23	Minnesota	2,012.7
24	Maine	1,854.3
25	Indiana	1,853.1
26	Connecticut	1,845.2
27	Oklahoma	1,744.7
28	Tennessee	1,715.9
29	Wisconsin	1,685.4
30	Arkansas	1,535.5
31	Virginia	1,515.1
32	Pennsylvania	1,478.1
33	Mississippi	1,456.2
34	Kentucky	1,451.9
35	Vermont	1,449.1
36	Ohio	1,447.5
37	West Virginia	1,349.2
38	Nebraska	1,341.9
39	Missouri	1,327.0
40	Iowa	1,137.7
41	Alabama	1,134.7
42	South Dakota	1,020.7
43	North Dakota	945.9
44	Massachusetts	885.0
45	New Hampshire	725.2
46	New Jersey	0.0
46	Rhode Island	0.0
NA	Illinois**	NA
NA	Kansas**	NA
NA	Montana**	NA
	District of Columbia	0.0

Source: Federal Bureau of Investigation
"Crime in the United States 1994" (Uniform Crime Reports, November 19, 1995)
Estimated rates for rural areas, defined by the F.B.I. as other than Metropolitan Statistical Areas and other cities outside such areas. National rate includes those states listed as not available. Includes murder, rape, robbery, aggravated assault, burglary, larceny-theft and motor vehicle theft.
**Not available.*

Percent of Crimes Occurring in Rural Areas in 1994

National Percent = 4.63% of Crimes*

ALPHA ORDER			RANK ORDER		
RANK	STATE	PERCENT	RANK	STATE	PERCENT
34	Alabama	4.36	1	West Virginia	22.91
5	Alaska	17.49	2	Vermont	20.38
41	Arizona	2.24	3	Hawaii	19.18
13	Arkansas	10.72	4	Idaho	17.77
44	California	1.08	5	Alaska	17.49
31	Colorado	4.74	6	Maine	15.82
40	Connecticut	2.36	7	Kentucky	14.81
15	Delaware	10.05	8	South Carolina	14.27
39	Florida	2.60	9	South Dakota	13.36
19	Georgia	8.46	10	Wyoming	13.27
3	Hawaii	19.18	11	Mississippi	12.54
4	Idaho	17.77	12	North Dakota	12.32
NA	Illinois**	NA	13	Arkansas	10.72
22	Indiana	7.41	14	North Carolina	10.46
16	Iowa	9.81	15	Delaware	10.05
NA	Kansas**	NA	16	Iowa	9.81
7	Kentucky	14.81	17	Minnesota	8.90
28	Louisiana	5.62	18	New Mexico	8.80
6	Maine	15.82	19	Georgia	8.46
42	Maryland	2.16	20	Wisconsin	8.24
46	Massachusetts	0.04	21	Nebraska	7.74
30	Michigan	5.19	22	Indiana	7.41
17	Minnesota	8.90	23	Oregon	7.36
11	Mississippi	12.54	24	Tennessee	7.14
28	Missouri	5.62	25	Nevada	6.13
NA	Montana**	NA	26	Oklahoma	6.07
21	Nebraska	7.74	27	Virginia	6.04
25	Nevada	6.13	28	Louisiana	5.62
37	New Hampshire	3.30	28	Missouri	5.62
47	New Jersey	0.00	30	Michigan	5.19
18	New Mexico	8.80	31	Colorado	4.74
43	New York	2.07	32	Washington	4.44
14	North Carolina	10.46	33	Utah	4.39
12	North Dakota	12.32	34	Alabama	4.36
36	Ohio	3.85	35	Pennsylvania	3.97
26	Oklahoma	6.07	36	Ohio	3.85
23	Oregon	7.36	37	New Hampshire	3.30
35	Pennsylvania	3.97	38	Texas	3.01
45	Rhode Island	0.06	39	Florida	2.60
8	South Carolina	14.27	40	Connecticut	2.36
9	South Dakota	13.36	41	Arizona	2.24
24	Tennessee	7.14	42	Maryland	2.16
38	Texas	3.01	43	New York	2.07
33	Utah	4.39	44	California	1.08
2	Vermont	20.38	45	Rhode Island	0.06
27	Virginia	6.04	46	Massachusetts	0.04
32	Washington	4.44	47	New Jersey	0.00
1	West Virginia	22.91	NA	Illinois**	NA
20	Wisconsin	8.24	NA	Kansas**	NA
10	Wyoming	13.27	NA	Montana**	NA
				District of Columbia	0.00

Source: Morgan Quitno Press using data from Federal Bureau of Investigation
   "Crime in the United States 1994" (Uniform Crime Reports, November 19, 1995)
*Estimated percentages for rural areas, defined by the F.B.I. as other than Metropolitan Statistical Areas and other cities outside such areas. National percent includes those states listed as not available. Includes murder, rape, robbery, aggravated assault, burglary, larceny-theft and motor vehicle theft.
**Not available.

Violent Crime in Urban Areas in 1994

National Total = 1,788,740 Violent Crimes*

ALPHA ORDER

ALPHA ORDER

RANK	STATE	CRIMES	% of USA
19	Alabama	27,526	1.54%
37	Alaska	3,606	0.20%
17	Arizona	27,566	1.54%
29	Arkansas	13,546	0.76%
1	California	315,847	17.66%
24	Colorado	17,935	1.00%
27	Connecticut	14,418	0.81%
38	Delaware	3,397	0.19%
3	Florida	155,560	8.70%
10	Georgia	43,134	2.41%
40	Hawaii	2,637	0.15%
41	Idaho	2,421	0.14%
NA	Illinois**	NA	NA
18	Indiana	27,547	1.54%
33	Iowa	8,360	0.47%
NA	Kansas**	NA	NA
23	Kentucky	18,163	1.02%
13	Louisiana	38,782	2.17%
42	Maine	1,394	0.08%
9	Maryland	46,489	2.60%
11	Massachusetts	42,694	2.39%
5	Michigan	69,744	3.90%
25	Minnesota	15,420	0.86%
32	Mississippi	11,002	0.62%
14	Missouri	36,883	2.06%
NA	Montana**	NA	NA
34	Nebraska	6,051	0.34%
28	Nevada	13,701	0.77%
44	New Hampshire	1,258	0.07%
8	New Jersey	48,544	2.71%
30	New Mexico	12,983	0.73%
2	New York	173,479	9.70%
12	North Carolina	42,134	2.36%
46	North Dakota	452	0.03%
6	Ohio	52,180	2.92%
22	Oklahoma	19,886	1.11%
26	Oregon	14,949	0.84%
7	Pennsylvania	50,120	2.80%
36	Rhode Island	3,742	0.21%
16	South Carolina	31,696	1.77%
43	South Dakota	1,393	0.08%
15	Tennessee	36,693	2.05%
4	Texas	125,440	7.01%
35	Utah	5,482	0.31%
47	Vermont	425	0.02%
21	Virginia	21,818	1.22%
20	Washington	26,393	1.48%
39	West Virginia	2,857	0.16%
31	Wisconsin	12,961	0.72%
45	Wyoming	1,040	0.06%

RANK ORDER

RANK	STATE	CRIMES	% of USA
1	California	315,847	17.66%
2	New York	173,479	9.70%
3	Florida	155,560	8.70%
4	Texas	125,440	7.01%
5	Michigan	69,744	3.90%
6	Ohio	52,180	2.92%
7	Pennsylvania	50,120	2.80%
8	New Jersey	48,544	2.71%
9	Maryland	46,489	2.60%
10	Georgia	43,134	2.41%
11	Massachusetts	42,694	2.39%
12	North Carolina	42,134	2.36%
13	Louisiana	38,782	2.17%
14	Missouri	36,883	2.06%
15	Tennessee	36,693	2.05%
16	South Carolina	31,696	1.77%
17	Arizona	27,566	1.54%
18	Indiana	27,547	1.54%
19	Alabama	27,526	1.54%
20	Washington	26,393	1.48%
21	Virginia	21,818	1.22%
22	Oklahoma	19,886	1.11%
23	Kentucky	18,163	1.02%
24	Colorado	17,935	1.00%
25	Minnesota	15,420	0.86%
26	Oregon	14,949	0.84%
27	Connecticut	14,418	0.81%
28	Nevada	13,701	0.77%
29	Arkansas	13,546	0.76%
30	New Mexico	12,983	0.73%
31	Wisconsin	12,961	0.72%
32	Mississippi	11,002	0.62%
33	Iowa	8,360	0.47%
34	Nebraska	6,051	0.34%
35	Utah	5,482	0.31%
36	Rhode Island	3,742	0.21%
37	Alaska	3,606	0.20%
38	Delaware	3,397	0.19%
39	West Virginia	2,857	0.16%
40	Hawaii	2,637	0.15%
41	Idaho	2,421	0.14%
42	Maine	1,394	0.08%
43	South Dakota	1,393	0.08%
44	New Hampshire	1,258	0.07%
45	Wyoming	1,040	0.06%
46	North Dakota	452	0.03%
47	Vermont	425	0.02%
NA	Illinois**	NA	NA
NA	Kansas**	NA	NA
NA	Montana**	NA	NA
	District of Columbia	15,177	0.85%

Source: Morgan Quitno Press using data from Federal Bureau of Investigation
"Crime in the United States 1994" (Uniform Crime Reports, November 19, 1995)
*Estimated totals for urban areas, defined by the F.B.I. as Metropolitan Statistical Areas and other cities outside such areas. National total includes those states listed as not available. Violent crimes are offenses of murder, forcible rape, robbery and aggravated assault.
**Not available.

Urban Violent Crime Rate in 1994

National Rate = 782.9 Violent Crimes per 100,000 Population*

RANK	STATE	RATE
14	Alabama	803.7
11	Alaska	868.1
20	Arizona	732.7
12	Arkansas	830.3
5	California	1,025.2
27	Colorado	544.9
31	Connecticut	467.5
26	Delaware	550.7
1	Florida	1,178.8
16	Georgia	765.5
42	Hawaii	286.6
37	Idaho	328.1
NA	Illinois**	NA
24	Indiana	586.7
33	Iowa	431.6
NA	Kansas**	NA
19	Kentucky	738.0
3	Louisiana	1,072.4
44	Maine	156.0
7	Maryland	981.2
21	Massachusetts	708.2
13	Michigan	824.7
34	Minnesota	417.8
22	Mississippi	706.4
9	Missouri	901.6
NA	Montana**	NA
30	Nebraska	501.2
4	Nevada	1,071.4
46	New Hampshire	126.4
23	New Jersey	614.2
8	New Mexico	958.1
6	New York	1,002.0
15	North Carolina	779.9
47	North Dakota	110.1
29	Ohio	533.2
17	Oklahoma	756.9
25	Oregon	577.7
32	Pennsylvania	455.9
36	Rhode Island	375.3
2	South Carolina	1,104.0
38	South Dakota	325.3
10	Tennessee	901.0
18	Texas	747.9
39	Utah	321.4
45	Vermont	135.0
35	Virginia	397.1
28	Washington	544.0
43	West Virginia	274.7
40	Wisconsin	315.9
41	Wyoming	296.5

RANK	STATE	RATE
1	Florida	1,178.8
2	South Carolina	1,104.0
3	Louisiana	1,072.4
4	Nevada	1,071.4
5	California	1,025.2
6	New York	1,002.0
7	Maryland	981.2
8	New Mexico	958.1
9	Missouri	901.6
10	Tennessee	901.0
11	Alaska	868.1
12	Arkansas	830.3
13	Michigan	824.7
14	Alabama	803.7
15	North Carolina	779.9
16	Georgia	765.5
17	Oklahoma	756.9
18	Texas	747.9
19	Kentucky	738.0
20	Arizona	732.7
21	Massachusetts	708.2
22	Mississippi	706.4
23	New Jersey	614.2
24	Indiana	586.7
25	Oregon	577.7
26	Delaware	550.7
27	Colorado	544.9
28	Washington	544.0
29	Ohio	533.2
30	Nebraska	501.2
31	Connecticut	467.5
32	Pennsylvania	455.9
33	Iowa	431.6
34	Minnesota	417.8
35	Virginia	397.1
36	Rhode Island	375.3
37	Idaho	328.1
38	South Dakota	325.3
39	Utah	321.4
40	Wisconsin	315.9
41	Wyoming	296.5
42	Hawaii	286.6
43	West Virginia	274.7
44	Maine	156.0
45	Vermont	135.0
46	New Hampshire	126.4
47	North Dakota	110.1
NA	Illinois**	NA
NA	Kansas**	NA
NA	Montana**	NA

District of Columbia — 2,662.6

Source: Morgan Quitno Press using data from Federal Bureau of Investigation
   "Crime in the United States 1994" (Uniform Crime Reports, November 19, 1995)
Estimated rates for urban areas, defined by the F.B.I. as Metropolitan Statistical Areas and other cities outside such areas. National rate includes those states listed as not available. Violent crimes are offenses of murder, forcible rape, robbery and aggravated assault.
***Not available.*

Percent of Violent Crimes Occurring in Urban Areas in 1994

National Percent = 95.95% of Violent Crimes*

ALPHA ORDER				RANK ORDER		
RANK	STATE	PERCENT		RANK	STATE	PERCENT
17	Alabama	95.43		1	New Jersey	100.00
44	Alaska	77.65		2	Rhode Island	99.95
14	Arizona	96.21		3	Massachusetts	99.87
29	Arkansas	92.79		4	California	99.20
4	California	99.20		5	New York	98.89
13	Colorado	96.26		6	Maryland	97.96
10	Connecticut	96.66		7	Pennsylvania	97.46
37	Delaware	85.76		8	Florida	97.22
8	Florida	97.22		9	Ohio	96.76
30	Georgia	91.57		10	Connecticut	96.66
38	Hawaii	85.31		11	Washington	96.62
46	Idaho	74.77		12	Texas	96.61
NA	Illinois**	NA		13	Colorado	96.26
32	Indiana	91.20		14	Arizona	96.21
25	Iowa	93.79		15	Michigan	95.87
NA	Kansas**	NA		16	Nebraska	95.71
43	Kentucky	78.41		17	Alabama	95.43
31	Louisiana	91.53		18	Tennessee	94.80
36	Maine	86.53		19	New Hampshire	94.73
6	Maryland	97.96		20	Utah	94.35
3	Massachusetts	99.87		21	Wisconsin	94.28
15	Michigan	95.87		22	Minnesota	94.04
22	Minnesota	94.04		23	Missouri	93.99
41	Mississippi	83.49		24	Nevada	93.86
23	Missouri	93.99		25	Iowa	93.79
NA	Montana**	NA		26	Oklahoma	93.69
16	Nebraska	95.71		27	Virginia	93.09
24	Nevada	93.86		28	Oregon	93.04
19	New Hampshire	94.73		29	Arkansas	92.79
1	New Jersey	100.00		30	Georgia	91.57
34	New Mexico	88.27		31	Louisiana	91.53
5	New York	98.89		32	Indiana	91.20
33	North Carolina	90.99		33	North Carolina	90.99
35	North Dakota	86.59		34	New Mexico	88.27
9	Ohio	96.76		35	North Dakota	86.59
26	Oklahoma	93.69		36	Maine	86.53
28	Oregon	93.04		37	Delaware	85.76
7	Pennsylvania	97.46		38	Hawaii	85.31
2	Rhode Island	99.95		39	South Dakota	84.89
40	South Carolina	83.95		40	South Carolina	83.95
39	South Dakota	84.89		41	Mississippi	83.49
18	Tennessee	94.80		42	Wyoming	80.19
12	Texas	96.61		43	Kentucky	78.41
20	Utah	94.35		44	Alaska	77.65
45	Vermont	75.62		45	Vermont	75.62
27	Virginia	93.09		46	Idaho	74.77
11	Washington	96.62		47	West Virginia	72.68
47	West Virginia	72.68		NA	Illinois**	NA
21	Wisconsin	94.28		NA	Kansas**	NA
42	Wyoming	80.19		NA	Montana**	NA
					District of Columbia	100.00

Source: Morgan Quitno Press using data from Federal Bureau of Investigation
     "Crime in the United States 1994" (Uniform Crime Reports, November 19, 1995)
*Estimated percentages for urban areas, defined by the F.B.I. as Metropolitan Statistical Areas and other cities outside such areas. National percent includes those states listed as not available. Violent crimes are offenses of murder, forcible rape, robbery and aggravated assault.
**Not available.

Violent Crime in Rural Areas in 1994

National Total = 75,428 Violent Crimes*

ALPHA ORDER

RANK	STATE	CRIMES	% of USA
19	Alabama	1,318	1.75%
25	Alaska	1,038	1.38%
22	Arizona	1,087	1.44%
24	Arkansas	1,052	1.39%
10	California	2,548	3.38%
32	Colorado	697	0.92%
35	Connecticut	498	0.66%
33	Delaware	564	0.75%
3	Florida	4,456	5.91%
6	Georgia	3,969	5.26%
36	Hawaii	454	0.60%
30	Idaho	817	1.08%
NA	Illinois**	NA	NA
9	Indiana	2,658	3.52%
34	Iowa	554	0.73%
NA	Kansas**	NA	NA
2	Kentucky	5,002	6.63%
7	Louisiana	3,587	4.76%
41	Maine	217	0.29%
27	Maryland	968	1.28%
45	Massachusetts	55	0.07%
8	Michigan	3,007	3.99%
26	Minnesota	977	1.30%
12	Mississippi	2,175	2.88%
11	Missouri	2,357	3.12%
NA	Montana**	NA	NA
38	Nebraska	271	0.36%
29	Nevada	896	1.19%
43	New Hampshire	70	0.09%
47	New Jersey	0	0.00%
16	New Mexico	1,725	2.29%
14	New York	1,954	2.59%
5	North Carolina	4,174	5.53%
43	North Dakota	70	0.09%
15	Ohio	1,750	2.32%
18	Oklahoma	1,339	1.78%
21	Oregon	1,118	1.48%
20	Pennsylvania	1,305	1.73%
46	Rhode Island	2	0.00%
1	South Carolina	6,060	8.03%
40	South Dakota	248	0.33%
13	Tennessee	2,012	2.67%
4	Texas	4,398	5.83%
37	Utah	328	0.43%
42	Vermont	137	0.18%
17	Virginia	1,619	2.15%
28	Washington	924	1.23%
23	West Virginia	1,074	1.42%
31	Wisconsin	787	1.04%
39	Wyoming	257	0.34%

RANK ORDER

RANK	STATE	CRIMES	% of USA
1	South Carolina	6,060	8.03%
2	Kentucky	5,002	6.63%
3	Florida	4,456	5.91%
4	Texas	4,398	5.83%
5	North Carolina	4,174	5.53%
6	Georgia	3,969	5.26%
7	Louisiana	3,587	4.76%
8	Michigan	3,007	3.99%
9	Indiana	2,658	3.52%
10	California	2,548	3.38%
11	Missouri	2,357	3.12%
12	Mississippi	2,175	2.88%
13	Tennessee	2,012	2.67%
14	New York	1,954	2.59%
15	Ohio	1,750	2.32%
16	New Mexico	1,725	2.29%
17	Virginia	1,619	2.15%
18	Oklahoma	1,339	1.78%
19	Alabama	1,318	1.75%
20	Pennsylvania	1,305	1.73%
21	Oregon	1,118	1.48%
22	Arizona	1,087	1.44%
23	West Virginia	1,074	1.42%
24	Arkansas	1,052	1.39%
25	Alaska	1,038	1.38%
26	Minnesota	977	1.30%
27	Maryland	968	1.28%
28	Washington	924	1.23%
29	Nevada	896	1.19%
30	Idaho	817	1.08%
31	Wisconsin	787	1.04%
32	Colorado	697	0.92%
33	Delaware	564	0.75%
34	Iowa	554	0.73%
35	Connecticut	498	0.66%
36	Hawaii	454	0.60%
37	Utah	328	0.43%
38	Nebraska	271	0.36%
39	Wyoming	257	0.34%
40	South Dakota	248	0.33%
41	Maine	217	0.29%
42	Vermont	137	0.18%
43	New Hampshire	70	0.09%
43	North Dakota	70	0.09%
45	Massachusetts	55	0.07%
46	Rhode Island	2	0.00%
47	New Jersey	0	0.00%
NA	Illinois**	NA	NA
NA	Kansas**	NA	NA
NA	Montana**	NA	NA
	District of Columbia	0	0.00%

Source: Federal Bureau of Investigation
   "Crime in the United States 1994" (Uniform Crime Reports, November 19, 1995)
*Estimated totals for rural areas, defined by the F.B.I. as other than Metropolitan Statistical Areas and other cities outside such areas. National total includes those states listed as not available. Violent crimes are offenses of murder, forcible rape, robbery and aggravated assault.
**Not available.

Rural Violent Crime Rate in 1994

National Rate = 236.6 Violent Crimes per 100,000 Population*

ALPHA ORDER

RANK	STATE	RATE
30	Alabama	166.0
5	Alaska	544.6
12	Arizona	347.6
35	Arkansas	128.1
9	California	410.2
26	Colorado	191.0
16	Connecticut	261.0
2	Delaware	632.8
3	Florida	589.1
14	Georgia	279.5
29	Hawaii	175.5
22	Idaho	206.7
NA	Illinois**	NA
17	Indiana	251.6
42	Iowa	62.1
NA	Kansas**	NA
10	Kentucky	366.2
6	Louisiana	513.4
41	Maine	62.7
11	Maryland	360.9
8	Massachusetts	446.6
13	Michigan	289.3
37	Minnesota	111.5
25	Mississippi	195.7
24	Missouri	198.5
NA	Montana**	NA
40	Nebraska	65.2
7	Nevada	503.0
44	New Hampshire	49.3
46	New Jersey	0.0
4	New Mexico	577.1
19	New York	228.3
18	North Carolina	250.3
45	North Dakota	30.8
34	Ohio	133.0
21	Oklahoma	212.2
20	Oregon	224.3
36	Pennsylvania	123.3
46	Rhode Island	0.0
1	South Carolina	764.1
38	South Dakota	84.7
28	Tennessee	182.5
15	Texas	273.9
31	Utah	161.9
43	Vermont	51.7
32	Virginia	153.1
27	Washington	188.1
33	West Virginia	137.3
39	Wisconsin	80.4
23	Wyoming	205.1

RANK ORDER

RANK	STATE	RATE
1	South Carolina	764.1
2	Delaware	632.8
3	Florida	589.1
4	New Mexico	577.1
5	Alaska	544.6
6	Louisiana	513.4
7	Nevada	503.0
8	Massachusetts	446.6
9	California	410.2
10	Kentucky	366.2
11	Maryland	360.9
12	Arizona	347.6
13	Michigan	289.3
14	Georgia	279.5
15	Texas	273.9
16	Connecticut	261.0
17	Indiana	251.6
18	North Carolina	250.3
19	New York	228.3
20	Oregon	224.3
21	Oklahoma	212.2
22	Idaho	206.7
23	Wyoming	205.1
24	Missouri	198.5
25	Mississippi	195.7
26	Colorado	191.0
27	Washington	188.1
28	Tennessee	182.5
29	Hawaii	175.5
30	Alabama	166.0
31	Utah	161.9
32	Virginia	153.1
33	West Virginia	137.3
34	Ohio	133.0
35	Arkansas	128.1
36	Pennsylvania	123.3
37	Minnesota	111.5
38	South Dakota	84.7
39	Wisconsin	80.4
40	Nebraska	65.2
41	Maine	62.7
42	Iowa	62.1
43	Vermont	51.7
44	New Hampshire	49.3
45	North Dakota	30.8
46	New Jersey	0.0
46	Rhode Island	0.0
NA	Illinois**	NA
NA	Kansas**	NA
NA	Montana**	NA
	District of Columbia	0.0

Source: Federal Bureau of Investigation
"Crime in the United States 1994" (Uniform Crime Reports, November 19, 1995)
*Estimated rates for rural areas, defined by the F.B.I. as other than Metropolitan Statistical Areas and other cities outside such areas. National rate includes those states listed as not available. Violent crimes are offenses of murder, forcible rape, robbery and aggravated assault.
**Not available.

Percent of Violent Crime Occurring in Rural Areas in 1994

National Percent = 4.05% of Violent Crimes*

ALPHA ORDER

RANK	STATE	PERCENT
31	Alabama	4.57
4	Alaska	22.35
34	Arizona	3.79
19	Arkansas	7.21
44	California	0.80
35	Colorado	3.74
38	Connecticut	3.34
11	Delaware	14.24
40	Florida	2.78
18	Georgia	8.43
10	Hawaii	14.69
2	Idaho	25.23
NA	Illinois**	NA
16	Indiana	8.80
23	Iowa	6.21
NA	Kansas**	NA
5	Kentucky	21.59
17	Louisiana	8.47
12	Maine	13.47
42	Maryland	2.04
45	Massachusetts	0.13
33	Michigan	4.13
26	Minnesota	5.96
7	Mississippi	16.51
25	Missouri	6.01
NA	Montana**	NA
32	Nebraska	4.29
24	Nevada	6.14
29	New Hampshire	5.27
47	New Jersey	0.00
14	New Mexico	11.73
43	New York	1.11
15	North Carolina	9.01
13	North Dakota	13.41
39	Ohio	3.24
22	Oklahoma	6.31
20	Oregon	6.96
41	Pennsylvania	2.54
46	Rhode Island	0.05
8	South Carolina	16.05
9	South Dakota	15.11
30	Tennessee	5.20
36	Texas	3.39
28	Utah	5.65
3	Vermont	24.38
21	Virginia	6.91
37	Washington	3.38
1	West Virginia	27.32
27	Wisconsin	5.72
6	Wyoming	19.81

RANK ORDER

RANK	STATE	PERCENT
1	West Virginia	27.32
2	Idaho	25.23
3	Vermont	24.38
4	Alaska	22.35
5	Kentucky	21.59
6	Wyoming	19.81
7	Mississippi	16.51
8	South Carolina	16.05
9	South Dakota	15.11
10	Hawaii	14.69
11	Delaware	14.24
12	Maine	13.47
13	North Dakota	13.41
14	New Mexico	11.73
15	North Carolina	9.01
16	Indiana	8.80
17	Louisiana	8.47
18	Georgia	8.43
19	Arkansas	7.21
20	Oregon	6.96
21	Virginia	6.91
22	Oklahoma	6.31
23	Iowa	6.21
24	Nevada	6.14
25	Missouri	6.01
26	Minnesota	5.96
27	Wisconsin	5.72
28	Utah	5.65
29	New Hampshire	5.27
30	Tennessee	5.20
31	Alabama	4.57
32	Nebraska	4.29
33	Michigan	4.13
34	Arizona	3.79
35	Colorado	3.74
36	Texas	3.39
37	Washington	3.38
38	Connecticut	3.34
39	Ohio	3.24
40	Florida	2.78
41	Pennsylvania	2.54
42	Maryland	2.04
43	New York	1.11
44	California	0.80
45	Massachusetts	0.13
46	Rhode Island	0.05
47	New Jersey	0.00
NA	Illinois**	NA
NA	Kansas**	NA
NA	Montana**	NA
	District of Columbia	0.00

Source: Morgan Quitno Press using data from Federal Bureau of Investigation
   "Crime in the United States 1994" (Uniform Crime Reports, November 19, 1995)
*Estimated percentages for rural areas, defined by the F.B.I. as other than Metropolitan Statistical Areas and other
cities outside such areas. National percent includes those states listed as not available. Violent crimes are
offenses of murder, forcible rape, robbery and aggravated assault.
**Not available.

Murder in Urban Areas in 1994

National Total = 21,713 Murders*

ALPHA ORDER					RANK ORDER			

RANK	STATE	MURDERS	% of USA		RANK	STATE	MURDERS	% of USA
14	Alabama	452	2.08%		1	California	3,675	16.93%
39	Alaska	28	0.13%		2	New York	1,988	9.16%
16	Arizona	399	1.84%		3	Texas	1,906	8.78%
22	Arkansas	227	1.05%		4	Florida	1,131	5.21%
1	California	3,675	16.93%		5	Michigan	902	4.15%
27	Colorado	183	0.84%		6	Louisiana	801	3.69%
24	Connecticut	210	0.97%		7	Pennsylvania	689	3.17%
40	Delaware	23	0.11%		8	North Carolina	648	2.98%
4	Florida	1,131	5.21%		9	Georgia	639	2.94%
9	Georgia	639	2.94%		10	Ohio	628	2.89%
38	Hawaii	39	0.18%		11	Maryland	571	2.63%
41	Idaho	21	0.10%		12	Missouri	518	2.39%
NA	Illinois**	NA	NA		13	Virginia	511	2.35%
18	Indiana	390	1.80%		14	Alabama	452	2.08%
36	Iowa	42	0.19%		15	Tennessee	441	2.03%
NA	Kansas**	NA	NA		16	Arizona	399	1.84%
29	Kentucky	151	0.70%		17	New Jersey	396	1.82%
6	Louisiana	801	3.69%		18	Indiana	390	1.80%
42	Maine	20	0.09%		19	Mississippi	277	1.28%
11	Maryland	571	2.63%		20	Washington	268	1.23%
23	Massachusetts	214	0.99%		21	South Carolina	266	1.23%
5	Michigan	902	4.15%		22	Arkansas	227	1.05%
30	Minnesota	131	0.60%		23	Massachusetts	214	0.99%
19	Mississippi	277	1.28%		24	Connecticut	210	0.97%
12	Missouri	518	2.39%		24	Wisconsin	210	0.97%
NA	Montana**	NA	NA		26	Oklahoma	188	0.87%
35	Nebraska	43	0.20%		27	Colorado	183	0.84%
28	Nevada	162	0.75%		28	Nevada	162	0.75%
43	New Hampshire	13	0.06%		29	Kentucky	151	0.70%
17	New Jersey	396	1.82%		30	Minnesota	131	0.60%
31	New Mexico	117	0.54%		31	New Mexico	117	0.54%
2	New York	1,988	9.16%		31	Oregon	117	0.54%
8	North Carolina	648	2.98%		33	Utah	52	0.24%
47	North Dakota	1	0.00%		34	West Virginia	48	0.22%
10	Ohio	628	2.89%		35	Nebraska	43	0.20%
26	Oklahoma	188	0.87%		36	Iowa	42	0.19%
31	Oregon	117	0.54%		37	Rhode Island	41	0.19%
7	Pennsylvania	689	3.17%		38	Hawaii	39	0.18%
37	Rhode Island	41	0.19%		39	Alaska	28	0.13%
21	South Carolina	266	1.23%		40	Delaware	23	0.11%
44	South Dakota	10	0.05%		41	Idaho	21	0.10%
15	Tennessee	441	2.03%		42	Maine	20	0.09%
3	Texas	1,906	8.78%		43	New Hampshire	13	0.06%
33	Utah	52	0.24%		44	South Dakota	10	0.05%
46	Vermont	5	0.02%		45	Wyoming	8	0.04%
13	Virginia	511	2.35%		46	Vermont	5	0.02%
20	Washington	268	1.23%		47	North Dakota	1	0.00%
34	West Virginia	48	0.22%		NA	Illinois**	NA	NA
24	Wisconsin	210	0.97%		NA	Kansas**	NA	NA
45	Wyoming	8	0.04%		NA	Montana**	NA	NA
						District of Columbia	399	1.84%

Source: Morgan Quitno Press using data from Federal Bureau of Investigation
"Crime in the United States 1994" (Uniform Crime Reports, November 19, 1995)
*Estimated totals for urban areas, defined by the F.B.I. as Metropolitan Statistical Areas and other cities outside such areas. National total includes those states listed as not available. Includes nonnegligent manslaughter.
**Not available.

Urban Murder Rate in 1994

National Rate = 9.5 Murders per 100,000 Population*

ALPHA ORDER

RANK	STATE	RATE
4	Alabama	13.2
23	Alaska	6.7
15	Arizona	10.6
3	Arkansas	13.9
9	California	11.9
27	Colorado	5.6
22	Connecticut	6.8
35	Delaware	3.7
18	Florida	8.6
12	Georgia	11.3
33	Hawaii	4.2
40	Idaho	2.8
NA	Illinois**	NA
20	Indiana	8.3
43	Iowa	2.2
NA	Kansas**	NA
26	Kentucky	6.1
1	Louisiana	22.1
43	Maine	2.2
7	Maryland	12.1
37	Massachusetts	3.5
14	Michigan	10.7
37	Minnesota	3.5
2	Mississippi	17.8
5	Missouri	12.7
NA	Montana**	NA
36	Nebraska	3.6
5	Nevada	12.7
46	New Hampshire	1.3
30	New Jersey	5.0
18	New Mexico	8.6
10	New York	11.5
8	North Carolina	12.0
47	North Dakota	0.2
24	Ohio	6.4
21	Oklahoma	7.2
32	Oregon	4.5
25	Pennsylvania	6.3
34	Rhode Island	4.1
16	South Carolina	9.3
41	South Dakota	2.3
13	Tennessee	10.8
11	Texas	11.4
39	Utah	3.0
45	Vermont	1.6
16	Virginia	9.3
28	Washington	5.5
31	West Virginia	4.6
29	Wisconsin	5.1
41	Wyoming	2.3

RANK ORDER

RANK	STATE	RATE
1	Louisiana	22.1
2	Mississippi	17.8
3	Arkansas	13.9
4	Alabama	13.2
5	Missouri	12.7
5	Nevada	12.7
7	Maryland	12.1
8	North Carolina	12.0
9	California	11.9
10	New York	11.5
11	Texas	11.4
12	Georgia	11.3
13	Tennessee	10.8
14	Michigan	10.7
15	Arizona	10.6
16	South Carolina	9.3
16	Virginia	9.3
18	Florida	8.6
18	New Mexico	8.6
20	Indiana	8.3
21	Oklahoma	7.2
22	Connecticut	6.8
23	Alaska	6.7
24	Ohio	6.4
25	Pennsylvania	6.3
26	Kentucky	6.1
27	Colorado	5.6
28	Washington	5.5
29	Wisconsin	5.1
30	New Jersey	5.0
31	West Virginia	4.6
32	Oregon	4.5
33	Hawaii	4.2
34	Rhode Island	4.1
35	Delaware	3.7
36	Nebraska	3.6
37	Massachusetts	3.5
37	Minnesota	3.5
39	Utah	3.0
40	Idaho	2.8
41	South Dakota	2.3
41	Wyoming	2.3
43	Iowa	2.2
43	Maine	2.2
45	Vermont	1.6
46	New Hampshire	1.3
47	North Dakota	0.2
NA	Illinois**	NA
NA	Kansas**	NA
NA	Montana**	NA
	District of Columbia	70.0

Source: Morgan Quitno Press using data from Federal Bureau of Investigation
"Crime in the United States 1994" (Uniform Crime Reports, November 19, 1995)
*Estimated rates for urban areas, defined by the F.B.I. as Metropolitan Statistical Areas and other cities outside such areas. National rate includes those states listed as not available. Includes nonnegligent manslaughter.
**Not available.

Percent of Murders Occurring in Urban Areas in 1994

National Percent = 93.17% of Murders*

RANK	STATE	PERCENT
25	Alabama	90.22
39	Alaska	73.68
16	Arizona	93.66
37	Arkansas	77.21
6	California	99.24
21	Colorado	91.96
9	Connecticut	97.67
41	Delaware	69.70
11	Florida	97.08
24	Georgia	90.90
35	Hawaii	78.00
45	Idaho	52.50
NA	Illinois**	NA
29	Indiana	86.09
27	Iowa	89.36
NA	Kansas**	NA
44	Kentucky	61.89
17	Louisiana	93.57
40	Maine	71.43
7	Maryland	98.62
1	Massachusetts	100.00
10	Michigan	97.30
28	Minnesota	89.12
42	Mississippi	67.73
18	Missouri	93.50
NA	Montana**	NA
30	Nebraska	84.31
13	Nevada	95.29
34	New Hampshire	81.25
1	New Jersey	100.00
43	New Mexico	66.10
8	New York	98.61
31	North Carolina	83.94
1	North Dakota	100.00
14	Ohio	94.86
33	Oklahoma	83.19
35	Oregon	78.00
12	Pennsylvania	96.77
1	Rhode Island	100.00
38	South Carolina	75.35
1	South Dakota	100.00
22	Tennessee	91.49
15	Texas	94.26
19	Utah	92.86
32	Vermont	83.33
26	Virginia	89.49
23	Washington	91.16
47	West Virginia	48.48
20	Wisconsin	92.51
46	Wyoming	50.00

RANK	STATE	PERCENT
1	Massachusetts	100.00
1	New Jersey	100.00
1	North Dakota	100.00
1	Rhode Island	100.00
1	South Dakota	100.00
6	California	99.24
7	Maryland	98.62
8	New York	98.61
9	Connecticut	97.67
10	Michigan	97.30
11	Florida	97.08
12	Pennsylvania	96.77
13	Nevada	95.29
14	Ohio	94.86
15	Texas	94.26
16	Arizona	93.66
17	Louisiana	93.57
18	Missouri	93.50
19	Utah	92.86
20	Wisconsin	92.51
21	Colorado	91.96
22	Tennessee	91.49
23	Washington	91.16
24	Georgia	90.90
25	Alabama	90.22
26	Virginia	89.49
27	Iowa	89.36
28	Minnesota	89.12
29	Indiana	86.09
30	Nebraska	84.31
31	North Carolina	83.94
32	Vermont	83.33
33	Oklahoma	83.19
34	New Hampshire	81.25
35	Hawaii	78.00
35	Oregon	78.00
37	Arkansas	77.21
38	South Carolina	75.35
39	Alaska	73.68
40	Maine	71.43
41	Delaware	69.70
42	Mississippi	67.73
43	New Mexico	66.10
44	Kentucky	61.89
45	Idaho	52.50
46	Wyoming	50.00
47	West Virginia	48.48
NA	Illinois**	NA
NA	Kansas**	NA
NA	Montana**	NA
	District of Columbia	100.00

Source: Morgan Quitno Press using data from Federal Bureau of Investigation
"Crime in the United States 1994" (Uniform Crime Reports, November 19, 1995)
*Estimated percentages for urban areas, defined by the F.B.I. as Metropolitan Statistical Areas and other cities outside such areas. National percent includes those states listed as not available. Includes nonnegligent manslaughter.
**Not available.

Murder in Rural Areas in 1994

National Total = 1,592 Murders*

RANK	STATE	MURDERS	% of USA
13	Alabama	49	3.08%
31	Alaska	10	0.63%
22	Arizona	27	1.70%
6	Arkansas	67	4.21%
20	California	28	1.76%
28	Colorado	16	1.01%
38	Connecticut	5	0.31%
31	Delaware	10	0.63%
17	Florida	34	2.14%
7	Georgia	64	4.02%
30	Hawaii	11	0.69%
26	Idaho	19	1.19%
NA	Illinois**	NA	NA
8	Indiana	63	3.96%
38	Iowa	5	0.31%
NA	Kansas**	NA	NA
4	Kentucky	93	5.84%
11	Louisiana	55	3.45%
33	Maine	8	0.50%
33	Maryland	8	0.50%
43	Massachusetts	0	0.00%
24	Michigan	25	1.57%
28	Minnesota	16	1.01%
1	Mississippi	132	8.29%
16	Missouri	36	2.26%
NA	Montana**	NA	NA
33	Nebraska	8	0.50%
33	Nevada	8	0.50%
41	New Hampshire	3	0.19%
43	New Jersey	0	0.00%
9	New Mexico	60	3.77%
20	New York	28	1.76%
2	North Carolina	124	7.79%
43	North Dakota	0	0.00%
17	Ohio	34	2.14%
15	Oklahoma	38	2.39%
19	Oregon	33	2.07%
25	Pennsylvania	23	1.44%
43	Rhode Island	0	0.00%
5	South Carolina	87	5.46%
43	South Dakota	0	0.00%
14	Tennessee	41	2.58%
3	Texas	116	7.29%
40	Utah	4	0.25%
42	Vermont	1	0.06%
9	Virginia	60	3.77%
23	Washington	26	1.63%
12	West Virginia	51	3.20%
27	Wisconsin	17	1.07%
33	Wyoming	8	0.50%

RANK	STATE	MURDERS	% of USA
1	Mississippi	132	8.29%
2	North Carolina	124	7.79%
3	Texas	116	7.29%
4	Kentucky	93	5.84%
5	South Carolina	87	5.46%
6	Arkansas	67	4.21%
7	Georgia	64	4.02%
8	Indiana	63	3.96%
9	New Mexico	60	3.77%
9	Virginia	60	3.77%
11	Louisiana	55	3.45%
12	West Virginia	51	3.20%
13	Alabama	49	3.08%
14	Tennessee	41	2.58%
15	Oklahoma	38	2.39%
16	Missouri	36	2.26%
17	Florida	34	2.14%
17	Ohio	34	2.14%
19	Oregon	33	2.07%
20	California	28	1.76%
20	New York	28	1.76%
22	Arizona	27	1.70%
23	Washington	26	1.63%
24	Michigan	25	1.57%
25	Pennsylvania	23	1.44%
26	Idaho	19	1.19%
27	Wisconsin	17	1.07%
28	Colorado	16	1.01%
28	Minnesota	16	1.01%
30	Hawaii	11	0.69%
31	Alaska	10	0.63%
31	Delaware	10	0.63%
33	Maine	8	0.50%
33	Maryland	8	0.50%
33	Nebraska	8	0.50%
33	Nevada	8	0.50%
33	Wyoming	8	0.50%
38	Connecticut	5	0.31%
38	Iowa	5	0.31%
40	Utah	4	0.25%
41	New Hampshire	3	0.19%
42	Vermont	1	0.06%
43	Massachusetts	0	0.00%
43	New Jersey	0	0.00%
43	North Dakota	0	0.00%
43	Rhode Island	0	0.00%
43	South Dakota	0	0.00%
NA	Illinois**	NA	NA
NA	Kansas**	NA	NA
NA	Montana**	NA	NA
	District of Columbia	0	0.00%

Source: Federal Bureau of Investigation
   "Crime in the United States 1994" (Uniform Crime Reports, November 19, 1995)
*Estimated totals for rural areas, defined by the F.B.I. as other than Metropolitan Statistical Areas and other cities outside such areas. National total includes those states listed as not available. Includes nonnegligent manslaughter.
**Not available.

Rural Murder Rate in 1994

National Rate = 5.0 Murders per 100,000 Population*

RANK	STATE	RATE
14	Alabama	6.2
19	Alaska	5.2
5	Arizona	8.6
6	Arkansas	8.2
21	California	4.5
25	Colorado	4.4
31	Connecticut	2.6
3	Delaware	11.2
21	Florida	4.5
21	Georgia	4.5
26	Hawaii	4.3
20	Idaho	4.8
NA	Illinois**	NA
15	Indiana	6.0
41	Iowa	0.6
NA	Kansas**	NA
10	Kentucky	6.8
7	Louisiana	7.9
34	Maine	2.3
29	Maryland	3.0
43	Massachusetts	0.0
33	Michigan	2.4
39	Minnesota	1.8
2	Mississippi	11.9
29	Missouri	3.0
NA	Montana**	NA
38	Nebraska	1.9
21	Nevada	4.5
36	New Hampshire	2.1
43	New Jersey	0.0
1	New Mexico	20.1
28	New York	3.3
8	North Carolina	7.4
43	North Dakota	0.0
31	Ohio	2.6
15	Oklahoma	6.0
11	Oregon	6.6
35	Pennsylvania	2.2
43	Rhode Island	0.0
4	South Carolina	11.0
43	South Dakota	0.0
27	Tennessee	3.7
9	Texas	7.2
37	Utah	2.0
42	Vermont	0.4
17	Virginia	5.7
18	Washington	5.3
12	West Virginia	6.5
40	Wisconsin	1.7
13	Wyoming	6.4

RANK	STATE	RATE
1	New Mexico	20.1
2	Mississippi	11.9
3	Delaware	11.2
4	South Carolina	11.0
5	Arizona	8.6
6	Arkansas	8.2
7	Louisiana	7.9
8	North Carolina	7.4
9	Texas	7.2
10	Kentucky	6.8
11	Oregon	6.6
12	West Virginia	6.5
13	Wyoming	6.4
14	Alabama	6.2
15	Indiana	6.0
15	Oklahoma	6.0
17	Virginia	5.7
18	Washington	5.3
19	Alaska	5.2
20	Idaho	4.8
21	California	4.5
21	Florida	4.5
21	Georgia	4.5
21	Nevada	4.5
25	Colorado	4.4
26	Hawaii	4.3
27	Tennessee	3.7
28	New York	3.3
29	Maryland	3.0
29	Missouri	3.0
31	Connecticut	2.6
31	Ohio	2.6
33	Michigan	2.4
34	Maine	2.3
35	Pennsylvania	2.2
36	New Hampshire	2.1
37	Utah	2.0
38	Nebraska	1.9
39	Minnesota	1.8
40	Wisconsin	1.7
41	Iowa	0.6
42	Vermont	0.4
43	Massachusetts	0.0
43	New Jersey	0.0
43	North Dakota	0.0
43	Rhode Island	0.0
43	South Dakota	0.0
NA	Illinois**	NA
NA	Kansas**	NA
NA	Montana**	NA
	District of Columbia	0.0

Source: Federal Bureau of Investigation
"Crime in the United States 1994" (Uniform Crime Reports, November 19, 1995)
*Estimated rates for rural areas, defined by the F.B.I. as other than Metropolitan Statistical Areas and other cities outside such areas. National rate includes those states listed as not available. Includes nonnegligent manslaughter.
**Not available.

Percent of Murders Occurring in Rural Areas in 1994

National Percent = 6.83% of Murders*

ALPHA ORDER

RANK	STATE	PERCENT
23	Alabama	9.78
9	Alaska	26.32
32	Arizona	6.34
11	Arkansas	22.79
42	California	0.76
27	Colorado	8.04
39	Connecticut	2.33
7	Delaware	30.30
37	Florida	2.92
24	Georgia	9.10
12	Hawaii	22.00
3	Idaho	47.50
NA	Illinois**	NA
19	Indiana	13.91
21	Iowa	10.64
NA	Kansas**	NA
4	Kentucky	38.11
31	Louisiana	6.43
8	Maine	28.57
41	Maryland	1.38
43	Massachusetts	0.00
38	Michigan	2.70
20	Minnesota	10.88
6	Mississippi	32.27
30	Missouri	6.50
NA	Montana**	NA
18	Nebraska	15.69
35	Nevada	4.71
14	New Hampshire	18.75
43	New Jersey	0.00
5	New Mexico	33.90
40	New York	1.39
17	North Carolina	16.06
43	North Dakota	0.00
34	Ohio	5.14
15	Oklahoma	16.81
12	Oregon	22.00
36	Pennsylvania	3.23
43	Rhode Island	0.00
10	South Carolina	24.65
43	South Dakota	0.00
26	Tennessee	8.51
33	Texas	5.74
29	Utah	7.14
16	Vermont	16.67
22	Virginia	10.51
25	Washington	8.84
1	West Virginia	51.52
28	Wisconsin	7.49
2	Wyoming	50.00

RANK ORDER

RANK	STATE	PERCENT
1	West Virginia	51.52
2	Wyoming	50.00
3	Idaho	47.50
4	Kentucky	38.11
5	New Mexico	33.90
6	Mississippi	32.27
7	Delaware	30.30
8	Maine	28.57
9	Alaska	26.32
10	South Carolina	24.65
11	Arkansas	22.79
12	Hawaii	22.00
12	Oregon	22.00
14	New Hampshire	18.75
15	Oklahoma	16.81
16	Vermont	16.67
17	North Carolina	16.06
18	Nebraska	15.69
19	Indiana	13.91
20	Minnesota	10.88
21	Iowa	10.64
22	Virginia	10.51
23	Alabama	9.78
24	Georgia	9.10
25	Washington	8.84
26	Tennessee	8.51
27	Colorado	8.04
28	Wisconsin	7.49
29	Utah	7.14
30	Missouri	6.50
31	Louisiana	6.43
32	Arizona	6.34
33	Texas	5.74
34	Ohio	5.14
35	Nevada	4.71
36	Pennsylvania	3.23
37	Florida	2.92
38	Michigan	2.70
39	Connecticut	2.33
40	New York	1.39
41	Maryland	1.38
42	California	0.76
43	Massachusetts	0.00
43	New Jersey	0.00
43	North Dakota	0.00
43	Rhode Island	0.00
43	South Dakota	0.00
NA	Illinois**	NA
NA	Kansas**	NA
NA	Montana**	NA
	District of Columbia	0.00

Source: Morgan Quitno Press using data from Federal Bureau of Investigation
"Crime in the United States 1994" (Uniform Crime Reports, November 19, 1995)
*Estimated percentages for rural areas, defined by the F.B.I. as other than Metropolitan Statistical Areas and other cities outside such areas. National percent includes those states listed as not available. Includes nonnegligent manslaughter.
**Not available.

Rape in Urban Areas in 1994

National Total = 93,711 Rapes*

ALPHA ORDER

RANK	STATE	RAPES	% of USA
24	Alabama	1,388	1.48%
39	Alaska	272	0.29%
23	Arizona	1,410	1.50%
30	Arkansas	888	0.95%
1	California	10,816	11.54%
21	Colorado	1,523	1.63%
31	Connecticut	756	0.81%
36	Delaware	430	0.46%
3	Florida	6,907	7.37%
11	Georgia	2,178	2.32%
38	Hawaii	283	0.30%
43	Idaho	240	0.26%
NA	Illinois**	NA	NA
15	Indiana	1,851	1.98%
34	Iowa	615	0.66%
NA	Kansas**	NA	NA
29	Kentucky	891	0.95%
18	Louisiana	1,739	1.86%
44	Maine	228	0.24%
14	Maryland	1,950	2.08%
16	Massachusetts	1,823	1.95%
4	Michigan	5,594	5.97%
10	Minnesota	2,332	2.49%
27	Mississippi	955	1.02%
17	Missouri	1,741	1.86%
NA	Montana**	NA	NA
35	Nebraska	462	0.49%
28	Nevada	951	1.01%
37	New Hampshire	389	0.42%
13	New Jersey	1,972	2.10%
33	New Mexico	720	0.77%
6	New York	4,529	4.83%
12	North Carolina	2,026	2.16%
45	North Dakota	123	0.13%
5	Ohio	5,015	5.35%
22	Oklahoma	1,492	1.59%
25	Oregon	1,145	1.22%
8	Pennsylvania	2,908	3.10%
40	Rhode Island	271	0.29%
20	South Carolina	1,635	1.74%
41	South Dakota	259	0.28%
9	Tennessee	2,401	2.56%
2	Texas	8,701	9.28%
32	Utah	743	0.79%
46	Vermont	120	0.13%
19	Virginia	1,687	1.80%
7	Washington	3,070	3.28%
42	West Virginia	258	0.28%
26	Wisconsin	1,087	1.16%
46	Wyoming	120	0.13%

RANK ORDER

RANK	STATE	RAPES	% of USA
1	California	10,816	11.54%
2	Texas	8,701	9.28%
3	Florida	6,907	7.37%
4	Michigan	5,594	5.97%
5	Ohio	5,015	5.35%
6	New York	4,529	4.83%
7	Washington	3,070	3.28%
8	Pennsylvania	2,908	3.10%
9	Tennessee	2,401	2.56%
10	Minnesota	2,332	2.49%
11	Georgia	2,178	2.32%
12	North Carolina	2,026	2.16%
13	New Jersey	1,972	2.10%
14	Maryland	1,950	2.08%
15	Indiana	1,851	1.98%
16	Massachusetts	1,823	1.95%
17	Missouri	1,741	1.86%
18	Louisiana	1,739	1.86%
19	Virginia	1,687	1.80%
20	South Carolina	1,635	1.74%
21	Colorado	1,523	1.63%
22	Oklahoma	1,492	1.59%
23	Arizona	1,410	1.50%
24	Alabama	1,388	1.48%
25	Oregon	1,145	1.22%
26	Wisconsin	1,087	1.16%
27	Mississippi	955	1.02%
28	Nevada	951	1.01%
29	Kentucky	891	0.95%
30	Arkansas	888	0.95%
31	Connecticut	756	0.81%
32	Utah	743	0.79%
33	New Mexico	720	0.77%
34	Iowa	615	0.66%
35	Nebraska	462	0.49%
36	Delaware	430	0.46%
37	New Hampshire	389	0.42%
38	Hawaii	283	0.30%
39	Alaska	272	0.29%
40	Rhode Island	271	0.29%
41	South Dakota	259	0.28%
42	West Virginia	258	0.28%
43	Idaho	240	0.26%
44	Maine	228	0.24%
45	North Dakota	123	0.13%
46	Vermont	120	0.13%
46	Wyoming	120	0.13%
NA	Illinois**	NA	NA
NA	Kansas**	NA	NA
NA	Montana**	NA	NA
	District of Columbia	249	0.27%

Source: Morgan Quitno Press using data from Federal Bureau of Investigation
   "Crime in the United States 1994" (Uniform Crime Reports, November 19, 1995)
*Estimated totals for urban areas, defined by the F.B.I. as Metropolitan Statistical Areas and other cities outside
such areas. National total includes those states listed as not available. Forcible rape is the carnal knowledge of
a female forcibly and against her will. Attempts are included. However, statutory rape without force and other sex
offenses are excluded. **Not available.

Urban Rape Rate in 1994

National Urban Rate = 41.0 Rapes per 100,000 Population*

ALPHA ORDER

RANK	STATE	RATE
23	Alabama	40.5
4	Alaska	65.5
29	Arizona	37.5
12	Arkansas	54.4
32	California	35.1
18	Colorado	46.3
47	Connecticut	24.5
2	Delaware	69.7
14	Florida	52.3
26	Georgia	38.7
36	Hawaii	30.8
34	Idaho	32.5
NA	Illinois**	NA
24	Indiana	39.4
35	Iowa	31.7
NA	Kansas**	NA
31	Kentucky	36.2
17	Louisiana	48.1
44	Maine	25.5
22	Maryland	41.2
38	Massachusetts	30.2
3	Michigan	66.2
6	Minnesota	63.2
7	Mississippi	61.3
21	Missouri	42.6
NA	Montana**	NA
27	Nebraska	38.3
1	Nevada	74.4
25	New Hampshire	39.1
45	New Jersey	24.9
13	New Mexico	53.1
43	New York	26.2
29	North Carolina	37.5
39	North Dakota	29.9
16	Ohio	51.2
11	Oklahoma	56.8
19	Oregon	44.2
41	Pennsylvania	26.5
40	Rhode Island	27.2
10	South Carolina	57.0
8	South Dakota	60.5
9	Tennessee	59.0
15	Texas	51.9
20	Utah	43.6
28	Vermont	38.1
37	Virginia	30.7
5	Washington	63.3
46	West Virginia	24.8
41	Wisconsin	26.5
33	Wyoming	34.2

RANK ORDER

RANK	STATE	RATE
1	Nevada	74.4
2	Delaware	69.7
3	Michigan	66.2
4	Alaska	65.5
5	Washington	63.3
6	Minnesota	63.2
7	Mississippi	61.3
8	South Dakota	60.5
9	Tennessee	59.0
10	South Carolina	57.0
11	Oklahoma	56.8
12	Arkansas	54.4
13	New Mexico	53.1
14	Florida	52.3
15	Texas	51.9
16	Ohio	51.2
17	Louisiana	48.1
18	Colorado	46.3
19	Oregon	44.2
20	Utah	43.6
21	Missouri	42.6
22	Maryland	41.2
23	Alabama	40.5
24	Indiana	39.4
25	New Hampshire	39.1
26	Georgia	38.7
27	Nebraska	38.3
28	Vermont	38.1
29	Arizona	37.5
29	North Carolina	37.5
31	Kentucky	36.2
32	California	35.1
33	Wyoming	34.2
34	Idaho	32.5
35	Iowa	31.7
36	Hawaii	30.8
37	Virginia	30.7
38	Massachusetts	30.2
39	North Dakota	29.9
40	Rhode Island	27.2
41	Pennsylvania	26.5
41	Wisconsin	26.5
43	New York	26.2
44	Maine	25.5
45	New Jersey	24.9
46	West Virginia	24.8
47	Connecticut	24.5
NA	Illinois**	NA
NA	Kansas**	NA
NA	Montana**	NA
	District of Columbia	43.7

Source: Morgan Quitno Press using data from Federal Bureau of Investigation
"Crime in the United States 1994" (Uniform Crime Reports, November 19, 1995)
*Estimated rates for urban areas, defined by the F.B.I. as Metropolitan Statistical Areas and other cities outside such areas. National rate includes those states listed as not available. Forcible rape is the carnal knowledge of a female forcibly and against her will. Attempts are included. However, statutory rape without force and other sex offenses are excluded. **Not available.

Percent of Rapes Occurring in Urban Areas in 1994

National Percent = 91.79% of Rapes*

ALPHA ORDER				RANK ORDER		
RANK	STATE	PERCENT		RANK	STATE	PERCENT
17	Alabama	93.34		1	New Jersey	100.00
47	Alaska	65.07		2	Massachusetts	99.89
7	Arizona	96.25		3	Rhode Island	99.27
30	Arkansas	86.38		4	California	98.47
4	California	98.47		5	Colorado	96.45
5	Colorado	96.45		6	New York	96.36
16	Connecticut	93.80		7	Arizona	96.25
38	Delaware	80.52		8	Ohio	95.87
14	Florida	94.60		9	Maryland	95.82
28	Georgia	88.97		10	Texas	95.59
39	Hawaii	78.83		11	New Hampshire	95.58
41	Idaho	75.95		12	Washington	95.05
NA	Illinois**	NA		13	Nevada	95.00
24	Indiana	90.47		14	Florida	94.60
20	Iowa	92.34		15	Tennessee	94.34
NA	Kansas**	NA		16	Connecticut	93.80
46	Kentucky	66.00		17	Alabama	93.34
25	Louisiana	90.43		18	Pennsylvania	92.46
44	Maine	71.70		19	Nebraska	92.40
9	Maryland	95.82		20	Iowa	92.34
2	Massachusetts	99.89		21	Oklahoma	92.33
34	Michigan	83.24		22	Utah	92.18
32	Minnesota	85.58		23	Wisconsin	91.19
40	Mississippi	78.80		24	Indiana	90.47
27	Missouri	89.05		25	Louisiana	90.43
NA	Montana**	NA		26	Virginia	90.31
19	Nebraska	92.40		27	Missouri	89.05
13	Nevada	95.00		28	Georgia	88.97
11	New Hampshire	95.58		29	North Carolina	86.80
1	New Jersey	100.00		30	Arkansas	86.38
35	New Mexico	83.14		31	Oregon	85.90
6	New York	96.36		32	Minnesota	85.58
29	North Carolina	86.80		33	South Dakota	85.48
36	North Dakota	82.55		34	Michigan	83.24
8	Ohio	95.87		35	New Mexico	83.14
21	Oklahoma	92.33		36	North Dakota	82.55
31	Oregon	85.90		37	South Carolina	82.12
18	Pennsylvania	92.46		38	Delaware	80.52
3	Rhode Island	99.27		39	Hawaii	78.83
37	South Carolina	82.12		40	Mississippi	78.80
33	South Dakota	85.48		41	Idaho	75.95
15	Tennessee	94.34		42	Vermont	75.00
10	Texas	95.59		42	Wyoming	75.00
22	Utah	92.18		44	Maine	71.70
42	Vermont	75.00		45	West Virginia	69.73
26	Virginia	90.31		46	Kentucky	66.00
12	Washington	95.05		47	Alaska	65.07
45	West Virginia	69.73		NA	Illinois**	NA
23	Wisconsin	91.19		NA	Kansas**	NA
42	Wyoming	75.00		NA	Montana**	NA
					District of Columbia	100.00

Source: Morgan Quitno Press using data from Federal Bureau of Investigation
    "Crime in the United States 1994" (Uniform Crime Reports, November 19, 1995)
*Estimated percentages for urban areas, defined by the F.B.I. as Metropolitan Statistical Areas and other cities outside such areas. National percent includes those states listed as not available. Forcible rape is the carnal knowledge of a female forcibly and against her will. Attempts are included. However, statutory rape without force and other sex offenses are excluded. **Not available.

Rape in Rural Areas in 1994

National Total = 8,385 Rapes*

ALPHA ORDER

RANK	STATE	RAPES	% of USA
28	Alabama	99	1.18%
20	Alaska	146	1.74%
35	Arizona	55	0.66%
23	Arkansas	140	1.67%
18	California	168	2.00%
34	Colorado	56	0.67%
37	Connecticut	50	0.60%
27	Delaware	104	1.24%
4	Florida	394	4.70%
8	Georgia	270	3.22%
31	Hawaii	76	0.91%
31	Idaho	76	0.91%
NA	Illinois**	NA	NA
13	Indiana	195	2.33%
36	Iowa	51	0.61%
NA	Kansas**	NA	NA
2	Kentucky	459	5.47%
15	Louisiana	184	2.19%
29	Maine	90	1.07%
30	Maryland	85	1.01%
45	Massachusetts	2	0.02%
1	Michigan	1,126	13.43%
5	Minnesota	393	4.69%
9	Mississippi	257	3.06%
12	Missouri	214	2.55%
NA	Montana**	NA	NA
42	Nebraska	38	0.45%
37	Nevada	50	0.60%
44	New Hampshire	18	0.21%
47	New Jersey	0	0.00%
20	New Mexico	146	1.74%
17	New York	171	2.04%
7	North Carolina	308	3.67%
43	North Dakota	26	0.31%
11	Ohio	216	2.58%
24	Oklahoma	124	1.48%
14	Oregon	188	2.24%
10	Pennsylvania	237	2.83%
45	Rhode Island	2	0.02%
6	South Carolina	356	4.25%
39	South Dakota	44	0.52%
22	Tennessee	144	1.72%
3	Texas	401	4.78%
33	Utah	63	0.75%
40	Vermont	40	0.48%
16	Virginia	181	2.16%
19	Washington	160	1.91%
25	West Virginia	112	1.34%
26	Wisconsin	105	1.25%
40	Wyoming	40	0.48%

RANK ORDER

RANK	STATE	RAPES	% of USA
1	Michigan	1,126	13.43%
2	Kentucky	459	5.47%
3	Texas	401	4.78%
4	Florida	394	4.70%
5	Minnesota	393	4.69%
6	South Carolina	356	4.25%
7	North Carolina	308	3.67%
8	Georgia	270	3.22%
9	Mississippi	257	3.06%
10	Pennsylvania	237	2.83%
11	Ohio	216	2.58%
12	Missouri	214	2.55%
13	Indiana	195	2.33%
14	Oregon	188	2.24%
15	Louisiana	184	2.19%
16	Virginia	181	2.16%
17	New York	171	2.04%
18	California	168	2.00%
19	Washington	160	1.91%
20	Alaska	146	1.74%
20	New Mexico	146	1.74%
22	Tennessee	144	1.72%
23	Arkansas	140	1.67%
24	Oklahoma	124	1.48%
25	West Virginia	112	1.34%
26	Wisconsin	105	1.25%
27	Delaware	104	1.24%
28	Alabama	99	1.18%
29	Maine	90	1.07%
30	Maryland	85	1.01%
31	Hawaii	76	0.91%
31	Idaho	76	0.91%
33	Utah	63	0.75%
34	Colorado	56	0.67%
35	Arizona	55	0.66%
36	Iowa	51	0.61%
37	Connecticut	50	0.60%
37	Nevada	50	0.60%
39	South Dakota	44	0.52%
40	Vermont	40	0.48%
40	Wyoming	40	0.48%
42	Nebraska	38	0.45%
43	North Dakota	26	0.31%
44	New Hampshire	18	0.21%
45	Massachusetts	2	0.02%
45	Rhode Island	2	0.02%
47	New Jersey	0	0.00%
NA	Illinois**	NA	NA
NA	Kansas**	NA	NA
NA	Montana**	NA	NA
	District of Columbia	0	0.00%

Source: Federal Bureau of Investigation
"Crime in the United States 1994" (Uniform Crime Reports, November 19, 1995)

*Estimated totals for rural areas, defined by the F.B.I. as other than Metropolitan Statistical Areas and other cities outside such areas. National total includes those states listed as not available. Forcible rape is the carnal knowledge of a female forcibly and against her will. Attempts are included. However, statutory rape without force and other sex offenses are excluded. **Not available.*

Rural Rape Rate in 1994

National Rural Rate = 26.3 Rapes per 100,000 Population*

ALPHA ORDER				RANK ORDER		
RANK	STATE	RATE		RANK	STATE	RATE
41	Alabama	12.5		1	Delaware	116.7
3	Alaska	76.6		2	Michigan	108.3
30	Arizona	17.6		3	Alaska	76.6
32	Arkansas	17.0		4	Florida	52.1
16	California	27.0		5	New Mexico	48.8
35	Colorado	15.3		6	South Carolina	44.9
18	Connecticut	26.2		7	Minnesota	44.8
1	Delaware	116.7		8	Oregon	37.7
4	Florida	52.1		9	Kentucky	33.6
26	Georgia	19.0		10	Washington	32.6
14	Hawaii	29.4		11	Wyoming	31.9
25	Idaho	19.2		12	Maryland	31.7
NA	Illinois**	NA		13	Utah	31.1
27	Indiana	18.5		14	Hawaii	29.4
45	Iowa	5.7		15	Nevada	28.1
NA	Kansas**	NA		16	California	27.0
9	Kentucky	33.6		17	Louisiana	26.3
17	Louisiana	26.3		18	Connecticut	26.2
19	Maine	26.0		19	Maine	26.0
12	Maryland	31.7		20	Texas	25.0
34	Massachusetts	16.2		21	Mississippi	23.1
2	Michigan	108.3		22	Pennsylvania	22.4
7	Minnesota	44.8		23	New York	20.0
21	Mississippi	23.1		24	Oklahoma	19.7
29	Missouri	18.0		25	Idaho	19.2
NA	Montana**	NA		26	Georgia	19.0
44	Nebraska	9.1		27	Indiana	18.5
15	Nevada	28.1		27	North Carolina	18.5
40	New Hampshire	12.7		29	Missouri	18.0
46	New Jersey	0.0		30	Arizona	17.6
5	New Mexico	48.8		31	Virginia	17.1
23	New York	20.0		32	Arkansas	17.0
27	North Carolina	18.5		33	Ohio	16.4
42	North Dakota	11.4		34	Massachusetts	16.2
33	Ohio	16.4		35	Colorado	15.3
24	Oklahoma	19.7		36	Vermont	15.1
8	Oregon	37.7		37	South Dakota	15.0
22	Pennsylvania	22.4		38	West Virginia	14.3
46	Rhode Island	0.0		39	Tennessee	13.1
6	South Carolina	44.9		40	New Hampshire	12.7
37	South Dakota	15.0		41	Alabama	12.5
39	Tennessee	13.1		42	North Dakota	11.4
20	Texas	25.0		43	Wisconsin	10.7
13	Utah	31.1		44	Nebraska	9.1
36	Vermont	15.1		45	Iowa	5.7
31	Virginia	17.1		46	New Jersey	0.0
10	Washington	32.6		46	Rhode Island	0.0
38	West Virginia	14.3		NA	Illinois**	NA
43	Wisconsin	10.7		NA	Kansas**	NA
11	Wyoming	31.9		NA	Montana**	NA
					District of Columbia	0.0

Source: Federal Bureau of Investigation
     "Crime in the United States 1994" (Uniform Crime Reports, November 19, 1995)
*Estimated rates for rural areas, defined by the F.B.I. as other than Metropolitan Statistical Areas and other cities outside such areas. National rate includes those states listed as not available. Forcible rape is the carnal knowledge of a female forcibly and against her will. Attempts are included. However, statutory rape without force and other sex offenses are excluded. **Not available.

419

Percent of Rapes Occurring in Rural Areas in 1994

National Percent = 8.21% of Rapes*

ALPHA ORDER

RANK	STATE	PERCENT
31	Alabama	6.66
1	Alaska	34.93
41	Arizona	3.75
18	Arkansas	13.62
44	California	1.53
43	Colorado	3.55
32	Connecticut	6.20
10	Delaware	19.48
34	Florida	5.40
20	Georgia	11.03
9	Hawaii	21.17
7	Idaho	24.05
NA	Illinois**	NA
24	Indiana	9.53
28	Iowa	7.66
NA	Kansas**	NA
2	Kentucky	34.00
23	Louisiana	9.57
4	Maine	28.30
39	Maryland	4.18
46	Massachusetts	0.11
14	Michigan	16.76
16	Minnesota	14.42
8	Mississippi	21.20
21	Missouri	10.95
NA	Montana**	NA
29	Nebraska	7.60
35	Nevada	5.00
37	New Hampshire	4.42
47	New Jersey	0.00
13	New Mexico	16.86
42	New York	3.64
19	North Carolina	13.20
12	North Dakota	17.45
40	Ohio	4.13
27	Oklahoma	7.67
17	Oregon	14.10
30	Pennsylvania	7.54
45	Rhode Island	0.73
11	South Carolina	17.88
15	South Dakota	14.52
33	Tennessee	5.66
38	Texas	4.41
26	Utah	7.82
5	Vermont	25.00
22	Virginia	9.69
36	Washington	4.95
3	West Virginia	30.27
25	Wisconsin	8.81
5	Wyoming	25.00

RANK ORDER

RANK	STATE	PERCENT
1	Alaska	34.93
2	Kentucky	34.00
3	West Virginia	30.27
4	Maine	28.30
5	Vermont	25.00
5	Wyoming	25.00
7	Idaho	24.05
8	Mississippi	21.20
9	Hawaii	21.17
10	Delaware	19.48
11	South Carolina	17.88
12	North Dakota	17.45
13	New Mexico	16.86
14	Michigan	16.76
15	South Dakota	14.52
16	Minnesota	14.42
17	Oregon	14.10
18	Arkansas	13.62
19	North Carolina	13.20
20	Georgia	11.03
21	Missouri	10.95
22	Virginia	9.69
23	Louisiana	9.57
24	Indiana	9.53
25	Wisconsin	8.81
26	Utah	7.82
27	Oklahoma	7.67
28	Iowa	7.66
29	Nebraska	7.60
30	Pennsylvania	7.54
31	Alabama	6.66
32	Connecticut	6.20
33	Tennessee	5.66
34	Florida	5.40
35	Nevada	5.00
36	Washington	4.95
37	New Hampshire	4.42
38	Texas	4.41
39	Maryland	4.18
40	Ohio	4.13
41	Arizona	3.75
42	New York	3.64
43	Colorado	3.55
44	California	1.53
45	Rhode Island	0.73
46	Massachusetts	0.11
47	New Jersey	0.00
NA	Illinois**	NA
NA	Kansas**	NA
NA	Montana**	NA
	District of Columbia	0.00

Source: Morgan Quitno Press using data from Federal Bureau of Investigation
  "Crime in the United States 1994" (Uniform Crime Reports, November 19, 1995)
*Estimated percentages for rural areas, defined by the F.B.I. as other than Metropolitan Statistical Areas and other cities outside such areas. National percent includes those states listed as not available. Forcible rape is the carnal knowledge of a female forcibly and against her will. Attempts are included. However, statutory rape without force and other sex offenses are excluded. **Not available.

Robbery in Urban Areas in 1994

National Total = 613,470 Robberies*

ALPHA ORDER

RANK	STATE	ROBBERIES	% of USA
19	Alabama	7,118	1.16%
38	Alaska	855	0.14%
20	Arizona	6,561	1.07%
31	Arkansas	3,053	0.50%
1	California	112,028	18.26%
29	Colorado	3,887	0.63%
21	Connecticut	6,117	1.00%
39	Delaware	837	0.14%
3	Florida	45,410	7.40%
10	Georgia	15,271	2.49%
36	Hawaii	1,092	0.18%
43	Idaho	186	0.03%
NA	Illinois**	NA	NA
18	Indiana	7,354	1.20%
33	Iowa	1,303	0.21%
NA	Kansas**	NA	NA
30	Kentucky	3,434	0.56%
13	Louisiana	11,350	1.85%
42	Maine	255	0.04%
9	Maryland	20,021	3.26%
15	Massachusetts	10,160	1.66%
7	Michigan	21,634	3.53%
24	Minnesota	5,340	0.87%
28	Mississippi	4,071	0.66%
12	Missouri	12,097	1.97%
NA	Montana**	NA	NA
34	Nebraska	1,210	0.20%
25	Nevada	5,087	0.83%
41	New Hampshire	304	0.05%
5	New Jersey	22,762	3.71%
32	New Mexico	2,234	0.36%
2	New York	86,521	14.10%
11	North Carolina	12,340	2.01%
46	North Dakota	71	0.01%
8	Ohio	20,740	3.38%
27	Oklahoma	4,110	0.67%
26	Oregon	4,173	0.68%
6	Pennsylvania	22,392	3.65%
37	Rhode Island	870	0.14%
22	South Carolina	6,111	1.00%
44	South Dakota	123	0.02%
14	Tennessee	10,595	1.73%
4	Texas	37,422	6.10%
35	Utah	1,195	0.19%
47	Vermont	59	0.01%
16	Virginia	8,533	1.39%
17	Washington	7,407	1.21%
40	West Virginia	698	0.11%
23	Wisconsin	5,719	0.93%
45	Wyoming	77	0.01%

RANK ORDER

RANK	STATE	ROBBERIES	% of USA
1	California	112,028	18.26%
2	New York	86,521	14.10%
3	Florida	45,410	7.40%
4	Texas	37,422	6.10%
5	New Jersey	22,762	3.71%
6	Pennsylvania	22,392	3.65%
7	Michigan	21,634	3.53%
8	Ohio	20,740	3.38%
9	Maryland	20,021	3.26%
10	Georgia	15,271	2.49%
11	North Carolina	12,340	2.01%
12	Missouri	12,097	1.97%
13	Louisiana	11,350	1.85%
14	Tennessee	10,595	1.73%
15	Massachusetts	10,160	1.66%
16	Virginia	8,533	1.39%
17	Washington	7,407	1.21%
18	Indiana	7,354	1.20%
19	Alabama	7,118	1.16%
20	Arizona	6,561	1.07%
21	Connecticut	6,117	1.00%
22	South Carolina	6,111	1.00%
23	Wisconsin	5,719	0.93%
24	Minnesota	5,340	0.87%
25	Nevada	5,087	0.83%
26	Oregon	4,173	0.68%
27	Oklahoma	4,110	0.67%
28	Mississippi	4,071	0.66%
29	Colorado	3,887	0.63%
30	Kentucky	3,434	0.56%
31	Arkansas	3,053	0.50%
32	New Mexico	2,234	0.36%
33	Iowa	1,303	0.21%
34	Nebraska	1,210	0.20%
35	Utah	1,195	0.19%
36	Hawaii	1,092	0.18%
37	Rhode Island	870	0.14%
38	Alaska	855	0.14%
39	Delaware	837	0.14%
40	West Virginia	698	0.11%
41	New Hampshire	304	0.05%
42	Maine	255	0.04%
43	Idaho	186	0.03%
44	South Dakota	123	0.02%
45	Wyoming	77	0.01%
46	North Dakota	71	0.01%
47	Vermont	59	0.01%
NA	Illinois**	NA	NA
NA	Kansas**	NA	NA
NA	Montana**	NA	NA
	District of Columbia	6,311	1.03%

Source: Morgan Quitno Press using data from Federal Bureau of Investigation
   "Crime in the United States 1994" (Uniform Crime Reports, November 19, 1995)
*Estimated totals for urban areas, defined by the F.B.I. as Metropolitan Statistical Areas and other cities outside such areas. National total includes those states listed as not available. Robbery is the taking or attempting to take anything of value by force or threat of force.
**Not available.

Urban Robbery Rate in 1994

National Urban Rate = 268.5 Robberies per 100,000 Population*

ALPHA ORDER

RANK	STATE	RATE
17	Alabama	207.8
18	Alaska	205.8
22	Arizona	174.4
21	Arkansas	187.1
4	California	363.6
35	Colorado	118.1
20	Connecticut	198.3
33	Delaware	135.7
5	Florida	344.1
9	Georgia	271.0
34	Hawaii	118.7
44	Idaho	25.2
NA	Illinois**	NA
26	Indiana	156.6
39	Iowa	67.3
NA	Kansas**	NA
31	Kentucky	139.5
6	Louisiana	313.9
43	Maine	28.5
2	Maryland	422.6
23	Massachusetts	168.5
12	Michigan	255.8
30	Minnesota	144.7
10	Mississippi	261.4
7	Missouri	295.7
NA	Montana**	NA
36	Nebraska	100.2
3	Nevada	397.8
41	New Hampshire	30.6
8	New Jersey	288.0
24	New Mexico	164.9
1	New York	499.7
13	North Carolina	228.4
47	North Dakota	17.3
16	Ohio	211.9
27	Oklahoma	156.4
25	Oregon	161.3
19	Pennsylvania	203.7
37	Rhode Island	87.3
15	South Carolina	212.9
42	South Dakota	28.7
11	Tennessee	260.2
14	Texas	223.1
38	Utah	70.1
46	Vermont	18.7
28	Virginia	155.3
29	Washington	152.7
40	West Virginia	67.1
32	Wisconsin	139.4
45	Wyoming	22.0

RANK ORDER

RANK	STATE	RATE
1	New York	499.7
2	Maryland	422.6
3	Nevada	397.8
4	California	363.6
5	Florida	344.1
6	Louisiana	313.9
7	Missouri	295.7
8	New Jersey	288.0
9	Georgia	271.0
10	Mississippi	261.4
11	Tennessee	260.2
12	Michigan	255.8
13	North Carolina	228.4
14	Texas	223.1
15	South Carolina	212.9
16	Ohio	211.9
17	Alabama	207.8
18	Alaska	205.8
19	Pennsylvania	203.7
20	Connecticut	198.3
21	Arkansas	187.1
22	Arizona	174.4
23	Massachusetts	168.5
24	New Mexico	164.9
25	Oregon	161.3
26	Indiana	156.6
27	Oklahoma	156.4
28	Virginia	155.3
29	Washington	152.7
30	Minnesota	144.7
31	Kentucky	139.5
32	Wisconsin	139.4
33	Delaware	135.7
34	Hawaii	118.7
35	Colorado	118.1
36	Nebraska	100.2
37	Rhode Island	87.3
38	Utah	70.1
39	Iowa	67.3
40	West Virginia	67.1
41	New Hampshire	30.6
42	South Dakota	28.7
43	Maine	28.5
44	Idaho	25.2
45	Wyoming	22.0
46	Vermont	18.7
47	North Dakota	17.3
NA	Illinois**	NA
NA	Kansas**	NA
NA	Montana**	NA

District of Columbia 1,107.2

Source: Morgan Quitno Press using data from Federal Bureau of Investigation
   "Crime in the United States 1994" (Uniform Crime Reports, November 19, 1995)
*Estimated rates for urban areas, defined by the F.B.I. as Metropolitan Statistical Areas and other cities outside
such areas. National rate includes those states listed as not available. Robbery is the taking or attempting to take
anything of value by force or threat of force.
**Not available.

Percent of Robberies Occurring in Urban Areas in 1994

National Percent = 99.14% of Robberies*

<table>
<tr><td colspan="3">ALPHA ORDER</td><td colspan="3">RANK ORDER</td></tr>
<tr><td>RANK</td><td>STATE</td><td>PERCENT</td><td>RANK</td><td>STATE</td><td>PERCENT</td></tr>
<tr><td>24</td><td>Alabama</td><td>98.55</td><td>1</td><td>Massachusetts</td><td>100.00</td></tr>
<tr><td>35</td><td>Alaska</td><td>96.50</td><td>1</td><td>New Jersey</td><td>100.00</td></tr>
<tr><td>15</td><td>Arizona</td><td>99.39</td><td>1</td><td>North Dakota</td><td>100.00</td></tr>
<tr><td>34</td><td>Arkansas</td><td>96.68</td><td>1</td><td>Rhode Island</td><td>100.00</td></tr>
<tr><td>6</td><td>California</td><td>99.88</td><td>5</td><td>New York</td><td>99.89</td></tr>
<tr><td>13</td><td>Colorado</td><td>99.41</td><td>6</td><td>California</td><td>99.88</td></tr>
<tr><td>11</td><td>Connecticut</td><td>99.46</td><td>7</td><td>Wisconsin</td><td>99.65</td></tr>
<tr><td>39</td><td>Delaware</td><td>94.15</td><td>8</td><td>Ohio</td><td>99.61</td></tr>
<tr><td>20</td><td>Florida</td><td>99.00</td><td>9</td><td>Michigan</td><td>99.54</td></tr>
<tr><td>33</td><td>Georgia</td><td>97.25</td><td>10</td><td>Pennsylvania</td><td>99.53</td></tr>
<tr><td>45</td><td>Hawaii</td><td>89.43</td><td>11</td><td>Connecticut</td><td>99.46</td></tr>
<tr><td>46</td><td>Idaho</td><td>89.00</td><td>12</td><td>Minnesota</td><td>99.44</td></tr>
<tr><td>NA</td><td>Illinois**</td><td>NA</td><td>13</td><td>Colorado</td><td>99.41</td></tr>
<tr><td>29</td><td>Indiana</td><td>98.18</td><td>13</td><td>Texas</td><td>99.41</td></tr>
<tr><td>28</td><td>Iowa</td><td>98.19</td><td>15</td><td>Arizona</td><td>99.39</td></tr>
<tr><td>NA</td><td>Kansas**</td><td>NA</td><td>16</td><td>Maryland</td><td>99.37</td></tr>
<tr><td>38</td><td>Kentucky</td><td>95.52</td><td>17</td><td>Missouri</td><td>99.33</td></tr>
<tr><td>27</td><td>Louisiana</td><td>98.44</td><td>18</td><td>Washington</td><td>99.24</td></tr>
<tr><td>41</td><td>Maine</td><td>91.73</td><td>19</td><td>Nevada</td><td>99.08</td></tr>
<tr><td>16</td><td>Maryland</td><td>99.37</td><td>20</td><td>Florida</td><td>99.00</td></tr>
<tr><td>1</td><td>Massachusetts</td><td>100.00</td><td>21</td><td>Nebraska</td><td>98.94</td></tr>
<tr><td>9</td><td>Michigan</td><td>99.54</td><td>22</td><td>New Hampshire</td><td>98.70</td></tr>
<tr><td>12</td><td>Minnesota</td><td>99.44</td><td>22</td><td>Tennessee</td><td>98.70</td></tr>
<tr><td>40</td><td>Mississippi</td><td>93.89</td><td>24</td><td>Alabama</td><td>98.55</td></tr>
<tr><td>17</td><td>Missouri</td><td>99.33</td><td>25</td><td>Utah</td><td>98.52</td></tr>
<tr><td>NA</td><td>Montana**</td><td>NA</td><td>26</td><td>Oklahoma</td><td>98.47</td></tr>
<tr><td>21</td><td>Nebraska</td><td>98.94</td><td>27</td><td>Louisiana</td><td>98.44</td></tr>
<tr><td>19</td><td>Nevada</td><td>99.08</td><td>28</td><td>Iowa</td><td>98.19</td></tr>
<tr><td>22</td><td>New Hampshire</td><td>98.70</td><td>29</td><td>Indiana</td><td>98.18</td></tr>
<tr><td>1</td><td>New Jersey</td><td>100.00</td><td>30</td><td>Virginia</td><td>98.04</td></tr>
<tr><td>37</td><td>New Mexico</td><td>95.92</td><td>31</td><td>Oregon</td><td>97.87</td></tr>
<tr><td>5</td><td>New York</td><td>99.89</td><td>32</td><td>Wyoming</td><td>97.47</td></tr>
<tr><td>36</td><td>North Carolina</td><td>96.32</td><td>33</td><td>Georgia</td><td>97.25</td></tr>
<tr><td>1</td><td>North Dakota</td><td>100.00</td><td>34</td><td>Arkansas</td><td>96.68</td></tr>
<tr><td>8</td><td>Ohio</td><td>99.61</td><td>35</td><td>Alaska</td><td>96.50</td></tr>
<tr><td>26</td><td>Oklahoma</td><td>98.47</td><td>36</td><td>North Carolina</td><td>96.32</td></tr>
<tr><td>31</td><td>Oregon</td><td>97.87</td><td>37</td><td>New Mexico</td><td>95.92</td></tr>
<tr><td>10</td><td>Pennsylvania</td><td>99.53</td><td>38</td><td>Kentucky</td><td>95.52</td></tr>
<tr><td>1</td><td>Rhode Island</td><td>100.00</td><td>39</td><td>Delaware</td><td>94.15</td></tr>
<tr><td>44</td><td>South Carolina</td><td>89.64</td><td>40</td><td>Mississippi</td><td>93.89</td></tr>
<tr><td>42</td><td>South Dakota</td><td>91.11</td><td>41</td><td>Maine</td><td>91.73</td></tr>
<tr><td>22</td><td>Tennessee</td><td>98.70</td><td>42</td><td>South Dakota</td><td>91.11</td></tr>
<tr><td>13</td><td>Texas</td><td>99.41</td><td>43</td><td>West Virginia</td><td>90.41</td></tr>
<tr><td>25</td><td>Utah</td><td>98.52</td><td>44</td><td>South Carolina</td><td>89.64</td></tr>
<tr><td>47</td><td>Vermont</td><td>83.10</td><td>45</td><td>Hawaii</td><td>89.43</td></tr>
<tr><td>30</td><td>Virginia</td><td>98.04</td><td>46</td><td>Idaho</td><td>89.00</td></tr>
<tr><td>18</td><td>Washington</td><td>99.24</td><td>47</td><td>Vermont</td><td>83.10</td></tr>
<tr><td>43</td><td>West Virginia</td><td>90.41</td><td>NA</td><td>Illinois**</td><td>NA</td></tr>
<tr><td>7</td><td>Wisconsin</td><td>99.65</td><td>NA</td><td>Kansas**</td><td>NA</td></tr>
<tr><td>32</td><td>Wyoming</td><td>97.47</td><td>NA</td><td>Montana**</td><td>NA</td></tr>
<tr><td></td><td></td><td></td><td></td><td>District of Columbia</td><td>100.00</td></tr>
</table>

Source: Morgan Quitno Press using data from Federal Bureau of Investigation
   "Crime in the United States 1994" (Uniform Crime Reports, November 19, 1995)
Estimated percentages for urban areas, defined by the F.B.I. as Metropolitan Statistical Areas and other cities outside such areas. National percent includes those states listed as not available. Robbery is the taking or attempting to take anything of value by force or threat of force.
**Not available.*

Robbery in Rural Areas in 1994

National Total = 5,347 Robberies*

ALPHA ORDER

RANK	STATE	ROBBERIES	% of USA
15	Alabama	105	1.96%
31	Alaska	31	0.58%
29	Arizona	40	0.75%
15	Arkansas	105	1.96%
12	California	132	2.47%
34	Colorado	23	0.43%
30	Connecticut	33	0.62%
27	Delaware	52	0.97%
3	Florida	461	8.62%
4	Georgia	432	8.08%
13	Hawaii	129	2.41%
34	Idaho	23	0.43%
NA	Illinois**	NA	NA
11	Indiana	136	2.54%
33	Iowa	24	0.45%
NA	Kansas**	NA	NA
9	Kentucky	161	3.01%
7	Louisiana	180	3.37%
34	Maine	23	0.43%
14	Maryland	126	2.36%
44	Massachusetts	0	0.00%
18	Michigan	99	1.85%
32	Minnesota	30	0.56%
5	Mississippi	265	4.96%
22	Missouri	81	1.51%
NA	Montana**	NA	NA
39	Nebraska	13	0.24%
28	Nevada	47	0.88%
42	New Hampshire	4	0.07%
44	New Jersey	0	0.00%
20	New Mexico	95	1.78%
19	New York	96	1.80%
2	North Carolina	471	8.81%
44	North Dakota	0	0.00%
22	Ohio	81	1.51%
25	Oklahoma	64	1.20%
21	Oregon	91	1.70%
15	Pennsylvania	105	1.96%
44	Rhode Island	0	0.00%
1	South Carolina	706	13.20%
40	South Dakota	12	0.22%
10	Tennessee	140	2.62%
6	Texas	221	4.13%
38	Utah	18	0.34%
40	Vermont	12	0.22%
8	Virginia	171	3.20%
26	Washington	57	1.07%
24	West Virginia	74	1.38%
37	Wisconsin	20	0.37%
43	Wyoming	2	0.04%

RANK ORDER

RANK	STATE	ROBBERIES	% of USA
1	South Carolina	706	13.20%
2	North Carolina	471	8.81%
3	Florida	461	8.62%
4	Georgia	432	8.08%
5	Mississippi	265	4.96%
6	Texas	221	4.13%
7	Louisiana	180	3.37%
8	Virginia	171	3.20%
9	Kentucky	161	3.01%
10	Tennessee	140	2.62%
11	Indiana	136	2.54%
12	California	132	2.47%
13	Hawaii	129	2.41%
14	Maryland	126	2.36%
15	Alabama	105	1.96%
15	Arkansas	105	1.96%
15	Pennsylvania	105	1.96%
18	Michigan	99	1.85%
19	New York	96	1.80%
20	New Mexico	95	1.78%
21	Oregon	91	1.70%
22	Missouri	81	1.51%
22	Ohio	81	1.51%
24	West Virginia	74	1.38%
25	Oklahoma	64	1.20%
26	Washington	57	1.07%
27	Delaware	52	0.97%
28	Nevada	47	0.88%
29	Arizona	40	0.75%
30	Connecticut	33	0.62%
31	Alaska	31	0.58%
32	Minnesota	30	0.56%
33	Iowa	24	0.45%
34	Colorado	23	0.43%
34	Idaho	23	0.43%
34	Maine	23	0.43%
37	Wisconsin	20	0.37%
38	Utah	18	0.34%
39	Nebraska	13	0.24%
40	South Dakota	12	0.22%
40	Vermont	12	0.22%
42	New Hampshire	4	0.07%
43	Wyoming	2	0.04%
44	Massachusetts	0	0.00%
44	New Jersey	0	0.00%
44	North Dakota	0	0.00%
44	Rhode Island	0	0.00%
NA	Illinois**	NA	NA
NA	Kansas**	NA	NA
NA	Montana**	NA	NA
	District of Columbia	0	0.00%

Source: Federal Bureau of Investigation
   "Crime in the United States 1994" (Uniform Crime Reports, November 19, 1995)
*Estimated totals for rural areas, defined by the F.B.I. as other than Metropolitan Statistical Areas and other cities outside such areas. National total includes those states listed as not available. Robbery is the taking or attempting to take anything of value by force or threat of force.
**Not available.

Rural Robbery Rate in 1994

National Rural Rate = 16.8 Robberies per 100,000 Population*

ALPHA ORDER

RANK	STATE	RATE
18	Alabama	13.2
15	Alaska	16.3
20	Arizona	12.8
20	Arkansas	12.8
12	California	21.2
33	Colorado	6.3
14	Connecticut	17.3
3	Delaware	58.3
2	Florida	60.9
7	Georgia	30.4
4	Hawaii	49.9
35	Idaho	5.8
NA	Illinois**	NA
19	Indiana	12.9
41	Iowa	2.7
NA	Kansas**	NA
23	Kentucky	11.8
10	Louisiana	25.8
32	Maine	6.6
5	Maryland	47.0
44	Massachusetts	0.0
28	Michigan	9.5
38	Minnesota	3.4
11	Mississippi	23.8
31	Missouri	6.8
NA	Montana**	NA
39	Nebraska	3.1
9	Nevada	26.4
40	New Hampshire	2.8
44	New Jersey	0.0
6	New Mexico	31.8
25	New York	11.2
8	North Carolina	28.2
44	North Dakota	0.0
34	Ohio	6.2
26	Oklahoma	10.1
13	Oregon	18.3
27	Pennsylvania	9.9
44	Rhode Island	0.0
1	South Carolina	89.0
37	South Dakota	4.1
22	Tennessee	12.7
17	Texas	13.8
30	Utah	8.9
36	Vermont	4.5
16	Virginia	16.2
24	Washington	11.6
28	West Virginia	9.5
42	Wisconsin	2.0
43	Wyoming	1.6

RANK ORDER

RANK	STATE	RATE
1	South Carolina	89.0
2	Florida	60.9
3	Delaware	58.3
4	Hawaii	49.9
5	Maryland	47.0
6	New Mexico	31.8
7	Georgia	30.4
8	North Carolina	28.2
9	Nevada	26.4
10	Louisiana	25.8
11	Mississippi	23.8
12	California	21.2
13	Oregon	18.3
14	Connecticut	17.3
15	Alaska	16.3
16	Virginia	16.2
17	Texas	13.8
18	Alabama	13.2
19	Indiana	12.9
20	Arizona	12.8
20	Arkansas	12.8
22	Tennessee	12.7
23	Kentucky	11.8
24	Washington	11.6
25	New York	11.2
26	Oklahoma	10.1
27	Pennsylvania	9.9
28	Michigan	9.5
28	West Virginia	9.5
30	Utah	8.9
31	Missouri	6.8
32	Maine	6.6
33	Colorado	6.3
34	Ohio	6.2
35	Idaho	5.8
36	Vermont	4.5
37	South Dakota	4.1
38	Minnesota	3.4
39	Nebraska	3.1
40	New Hampshire	2.8
41	Iowa	2.7
42	Wisconsin	2.0
43	Wyoming	1.6
44	Massachusetts	0.0
44	New Jersey	0.0
44	North Dakota	0.0
44	Rhode Island	0.0
NA	Illinois**	NA
NA	Kansas**	NA
NA	Montana**	NA
	District of Columbia	0.0

Source: Federal Bureau of Investigation
"Crime in the United States 1994" (Uniform Crime Reports, November 19, 1995)
*Estimated rates for rural areas, defined by the F.B.I. as other than Metropolitan Statistical Areas and other cities outside such areas. National rate includes those states listed as not available. Robbery is the taking or attempting to take anything of value by force or threat of force.
**Not available.*

Percent of Robberies Occurring in Rural Areas in 1994

National Percent = 0.86% of Robberies*

ALPHA ORDER		
RANK	STATE	PERCENT
24	Alabama	1.45
13	Alaska	3.50
33	Arizona	0.61
14	Arkansas	3.32
42	California	0.12
34	Colorado	0.59
37	Connecticut	0.54
9	Delaware	5.85
28	Florida	1.00
15	Georgia	2.75
3	Hawaii	10.57
2	Idaho	11.00
NA	Illinois**	NA
19	Indiana	1.82
20	Iowa	1.81
NA	Kansas**	NA
10	Kentucky	4.48
21	Louisiana	1.56
7	Maine	8.27
32	Maryland	0.63
44	Massachusetts	0.00
39	Michigan	0.46
36	Minnesota	0.56
8	Mississippi	6.11
31	Missouri	0.67
NA	Montana**	NA
27	Nebraska	1.06
29	Nevada	0.92
25	New Hampshire	1.30
44	New Jersey	0.00
11	New Mexico	4.08
43	New York	0.11
12	North Carolina	3.68
44	North Dakota	0.00
40	Ohio	0.39
22	Oklahoma	1.53
17	Oregon	2.13
38	Pennsylvania	0.47
44	Rhode Island	0.00
4	South Carolina	10.36
6	South Dakota	8.89
25	Tennessee	1.30
34	Texas	0.59
23	Utah	1.48
1	Vermont	16.90
18	Virginia	1.96
30	Washington	0.76
5	West Virginia	9.59
41	Wisconsin	0.35
16	Wyoming	2.53

RANK ORDER		
RANK	STATE	PERCENT
1	Vermont	16.90
2	Idaho	11.00
3	Hawaii	10.57
4	South Carolina	10.36
5	West Virginia	9.59
6	South Dakota	8.89
7	Maine	8.27
8	Mississippi	6.11
9	Delaware	5.85
10	Kentucky	4.48
11	New Mexico	4.08
12	North Carolina	3.68
13	Alaska	3.50
14	Arkansas	3.32
15	Georgia	2.75
16	Wyoming	2.53
17	Oregon	2.13
18	Virginia	1.96
19	Indiana	1.82
20	Iowa	1.81
21	Louisiana	1.56
22	Oklahoma	1.53
23	Utah	1.48
24	Alabama	1.45
25	New Hampshire	1.30
25	Tennessee	1.30
27	Nebraska	1.06
28	Florida	1.00
29	Nevada	0.92
30	Washington	0.76
31	Missouri	0.67
32	Maryland	0.63
33	Arizona	0.61
34	Colorado	0.59
34	Texas	0.59
36	Minnesota	0.56
37	Connecticut	0.54
38	Pennsylvania	0.47
39	Michigan	0.46
40	Ohio	0.39
41	Wisconsin	0.35
42	California	0.12
43	New York	0.11
44	Massachusetts	0.00
44	New Jersey	0.00
44	North Dakota	0.00
44	Rhode Island	0.00
NA	Illinois**	NA
NA	Kansas**	NA
NA	Montana**	NA
	District of Columbia	0.00

Source: Morgan Quitno Press using data from Federal Bureau of Investigation
"Crime in the United States 1994" (Uniform Crime Reports, November 19, 1995)
*Estimated percentages for rural areas, defined by the F.B.I. as other than Metropolitan Statistical Areas and other cities outside such areas. National percent includes those states listed as not available. Robbery is the taking or attempting to take anything of value by force or threat of force.
**Not available.

Aggravated Assault in Urban Areas in 1994

National Total = 1,059,846 Aggravated Assaults*

ALPHA ORDER

RANK	STATE	ASSAULTS	% of USA
18	Alabama	18,568	1.75%
37	Alaska	2,451	0.23%
17	Arizona	19,196	1.81%
27	Arkansas	9,378	0.88%
1	California	189,328	17.86%
23	Colorado	12,342	1.16%
30	Connecticut	7,335	0.69%
38	Delaware	2,107	0.20%
2	Florida	102,112	9.63%
9	Georgia	25,046	2.36%
41	Hawaii	1,223	0.12%
39	Idaho	1,974	0.19%
NA	Illinois**	NA	NA
19	Indiana	17,952	1.69%
31	Iowa	6,400	0.60%
NA	Kansas**	NA	NA
22	Kentucky	13,687	1.29%
10	Louisiana	24,892	2.35%
43	Maine	891	0.08%
12	Maryland	23,947	2.26%
6	Massachusetts	30,497	2.88%
5	Michigan	41,614	3.93%
28	Minnesota	7,617	0.72%
33	Mississippi	5,699	0.54%
16	Missouri	22,527	2.13%
NA	Montana**	NA	NA
34	Nebraska	4,336	0.41%
29	Nevada	7,501	0.71%
45	New Hampshire	552	0.05%
14	New Jersey	23,414	2.21%
25	New Mexico	9,912	0.94%
3	New York	80,441	7.59%
7	North Carolina	27,120	2.56%
46	North Dakota	257	0.02%
8	Ohio	25,797	2.43%
21	Oklahoma	14,096	1.33%
26	Oregon	9,514	0.90%
11	Pennsylvania	24,131	2.28%
36	Rhode Island	2,560	0.24%
13	South Carolina	23,684	2.23%
42	South Dakota	1,001	0.09%
15	Tennessee	23,256	2.19%
4	Texas	77,411	7.30%
35	Utah	3,492	0.33%
47	Vermont	241	0.02%
24	Virginia	11,087	1.05%
20	Washington	15,648	1.48%
40	West Virginia	1,853	0.17%
32	Wisconsin	5,945	0.56%
44	Wyoming	835	0.08%

RANK ORDER

RANK	STATE	ASSAULTS	% of USA
1	California	189,328	17.86%
2	Florida	102,112	9.63%
3	New York	80,441	7.59%
4	Texas	77,411	7.30%
5	Michigan	41,614	3.93%
6	Massachusetts	30,497	2.88%
7	North Carolina	27,120	2.56%
8	Ohio	25,797	2.43%
9	Georgia	25,046	2.36%
10	Louisiana	24,892	2.35%
11	Pennsylvania	24,131	2.28%
12	Maryland	23,947	2.26%
13	South Carolina	23,684	2.23%
14	New Jersey	23,414	2.21%
15	Tennessee	23,256	2.19%
16	Missouri	22,527	2.13%
17	Arizona	19,196	1.81%
18	Alabama	18,568	1.75%
19	Indiana	17,952	1.69%
20	Washington	15,648	1.48%
21	Oklahoma	14,096	1.33%
22	Kentucky	13,687	1.29%
23	Colorado	12,342	1.16%
24	Virginia	11,087	1.05%
25	New Mexico	9,912	0.94%
26	Oregon	9,514	0.90%
27	Arkansas	9,378	0.88%
28	Minnesota	7,617	0.72%
29	Nevada	7,501	0.71%
30	Connecticut	7,335	0.69%
31	Iowa	6,400	0.60%
32	Wisconsin	5,945	0.56%
33	Mississippi	5,699	0.54%
34	Nebraska	4,336	0.41%
35	Utah	3,492	0.33%
36	Rhode Island	2,560	0.24%
37	Alaska	2,451	0.23%
38	Delaware	2,107	0.20%
39	Idaho	1,974	0.19%
40	West Virginia	1,853	0.17%
41	Hawaii	1,223	0.12%
42	South Dakota	1,001	0.09%
43	Maine	891	0.08%
44	Wyoming	835	0.08%
45	New Hampshire	552	0.05%
46	North Dakota	257	0.02%
47	Vermont	241	0.02%
NA	Illinois**	NA	NA
NA	Kansas**	NA	NA
NA	Montana**	NA	NA
	District of Columbia	8,218	0.78%

Source: Morgan Quitno Press using data from Federal Bureau of Investigation
"Crime in the United States 1994" (Uniform Crime Reports, November 19, 1995)
*Estimated totals for urban areas, defined by the F.B.I. as Metropolitan Statistical Areas and other cities outside such areas. National total includes those states listed as not available. Aggravated assault is an attack for the purpose of inflicting severe bodily injury.
**Not available.

Urban Aggravated Assault Rate in 1994

National Urban Rate = 463.9 Aggravated Assaults per 100,000 Population*

ALPHA ORDER

RANK	STATE	RATE
12	Alabama	542.1
6	Alaska	590.0
14	Arizona	510.2
8	Arkansas	574.8
5	California	614.5
23	Colorado	375.0
35	Connecticut	237.8
27	Delaware	341.6
2	Florida	773.8
21	Georgia	444.5
43	Hawaii	132.9
31	Idaho	267.6
NA	Illinois**	NA
22	Indiana	382.3
28	Iowa	330.4
NA	Kansas**	NA
10	Kentucky	556.1
4	Louisiana	688.3
44	Maine	99.7
16	Maryland	505.4
15	Massachusetts	505.9
18	Michigan	492.1
38	Minnesota	206.4
25	Mississippi	365.9
11	Missouri	550.7
NA	Montana**	NA
26	Nebraska	359.2
7	Nevada	586.5
47	New Hampshire	55.5
30	New Jersey	296.2
3	New Mexico	731.5
19	New York	464.6
17	North Carolina	502.0
46	North Dakota	62.6
32	Ohio	263.6
13	Oklahoma	536.6
24	Oregon	367.7
37	Pennsylvania	219.5
33	Rhode Island	256.8
1	South Carolina	825.0
36	South Dakota	233.8
9	Tennessee	571.1
20	Texas	461.5
39	Utah	204.8
45	Vermont	76.5
40	Virginia	201.8
29	Washington	322.5
41	West Virginia	178.2
42	Wisconsin	144.9
34	Wyoming	238.1

RANK ORDER

RANK	STATE	RATE
1	South Carolina	825.0
2	Florida	773.8
3	New Mexico	731.5
4	Louisiana	688.3
5	California	614.5
6	Alaska	590.0
7	Nevada	586.5
8	Arkansas	574.8
9	Tennessee	571.1
10	Kentucky	556.1
11	Missouri	550.7
12	Alabama	542.1
13	Oklahoma	536.6
14	Arizona	510.2
15	Massachusetts	505.9
16	Maryland	505.4
17	North Carolina	502.0
18	Michigan	492.1
19	New York	464.6
20	Texas	461.5
21	Georgia	444.5
22	Indiana	382.3
23	Colorado	375.0
24	Oregon	367.7
25	Mississippi	365.9
26	Nebraska	359.2
27	Delaware	341.6
28	Iowa	330.4
29	Washington	322.5
30	New Jersey	296.2
31	Idaho	267.6
32	Ohio	263.6
33	Rhode Island	256.8
34	Wyoming	238.1
35	Connecticut	237.8
36	South Dakota	233.8
37	Pennsylvania	219.5
38	Minnesota	206.4
39	Utah	204.8
40	Virginia	201.8
41	West Virginia	178.2
42	Wisconsin	144.9
43	Hawaii	132.9
44	Maine	99.7
45	Vermont	76.5
46	North Dakota	62.6
47	New Hampshire	55.5
NA	Illinois**	NA
NA	Kansas**	NA
NA	Montana**	NA

District of Columbia	1,441.8

Source: Morgan Quitno Press using data from Federal Bureau of Investigation
  "Crime in the United States 1994" (Uniform Crime Reports, November 19, 1995)
*Estimated rates for urban areas, defined by the F.B.I. as Metropolitan Statistical Areas and other cities outside such areas. National rate includes those states listed as not available. Aggravated assault is an attack for the purpose of inflicting severe bodily injury.
**Not available.

Percent of Aggravated Assaults Occurring in Urban Areas in 1994

National Percent = 94.63% of Aggravated Assaults*

ALPHA ORDER

RANK	STATE	PERCENT
17	Alabama	94.58
44	Alaska	74.23
14	Arizona	95.21
22	Arkansas	92.69
4	California	98.84
12	Colorado	95.35
16	Connecticut	94.71
37	Delaware	84.11
7	Florida	96.62
34	Georgia	88.66
39	Hawaii	83.71
46	Idaho	73.85
NA	Illinois**	NA
32	Indiana	88.80
21	Iowa	93.10
NA	Kansas**	NA
43	Kentucky	76.14
33	Louisiana	88.71
28	Maine	90.27
6	Maryland	96.97
3	Massachusetts	99.83
9	Michigan	95.95
19	Minnesota	93.40
42	Mississippi	78.93
26	Missouri	91.75
NA	Montana**	NA
13	Nebraska	95.34
27	Nevada	90.46
24	New Hampshire	92.46
1	New Jersey	100.00
35	New Mexico	87.44
5	New York	97.98
31	North Carolina	89.24
36	North Dakota	85.38
15	Ohio	94.79
23	Oklahoma	92.68
25	Oregon	92.19
8	Pennsylvania	96.25
1	Rhode Island	100.00
40	South Carolina	82.83
38	South Dakota	83.91
20	Tennessee	93.24
11	Texas	95.49
18	Utah	93.49
45	Vermont	74.15
30	Virginia	90.18
10	Washington	95.83
47	West Virginia	68.88
29	Wisconsin	90.21
41	Wyoming	80.13

RANK ORDER

RANK	STATE	PERCENT
1	New Jersey	100.00
1	Rhode Island	100.00
3	Massachusetts	99.83
4	California	98.84
5	New York	97.98
6	Maryland	96.97
7	Florida	96.62
8	Pennsylvania	96.25
9	Michigan	95.95
10	Washington	95.83
11	Texas	95.49
12	Colorado	95.35
13	Nebraska	95.34
14	Arizona	95.21
15	Ohio	94.79
16	Connecticut	94.71
17	Alabama	94.58
18	Utah	93.49
19	Minnesota	93.40
20	Tennessee	93.24
21	Iowa	93.10
22	Arkansas	92.69
23	Oklahoma	92.68
24	New Hampshire	92.46
25	Oregon	92.19
26	Missouri	91.75
27	Nevada	90.46
28	Maine	90.27
29	Wisconsin	90.21
30	Virginia	90.18
31	North Carolina	89.24
32	Indiana	88.80
33	Louisiana	88.71
34	Georgia	88.66
35	New Mexico	87.44
36	North Dakota	85.38
37	Delaware	84.11
38	South Dakota	83.91
39	Hawaii	83.71
40	South Carolina	82.83
41	Wyoming	80.13
42	Mississippi	78.93
43	Kentucky	76.14
44	Alaska	74.23
45	Vermont	74.15
46	Idaho	73.85
47	West Virginia	68.88
NA	Illinois**	NA
NA	Kansas**	NA
NA	Montana**	NA
	District of Columbia	100.00

Source: Morgan Quitno Press using data from Federal Bureau of Investigation
"Crime in the United States 1994" (Uniform Crime Reports, November 19, 1995)
*Estimated percentages for urban areas, defined by the F.B.I. as Metropolitan Statistical Areas and other cities outside such areas. National percent includes those states listed as not available. Aggravated assault is an attack for the purpose of inflicting severe bodily injury.
**Not available.

Aggravated Assault in Rural Areas in 1994

National Total = 60,104 Aggravated Assaults*

ALPHA ORDER

RANK	STATE	ASSAULTS	% of USA
19	Alabama	1,065	1.77%
22	Alaska	851	1.42%
20	Arizona	965	1.61%
27	Arkansas	740	1.23%
9	California	2,220	3.69%
31	Colorado	602	1.00%
34	Connecticut	410	0.68%
35	Delaware	398	0.66%
4	Florida	3,567	5.93%
6	Georgia	3,203	5.33%
37	Hawaii	238	0.40%
28	Idaho	699	1.16%
NA	Illinois**	NA	NA
8	Indiana	2,264	3.77%
33	Iowa	474	0.79%
NA	Kansas**	NA	NA
2	Kentucky	4,289	7.14%
7	Louisiana	3,168	5.27%
41	Maine	96	0.16%
26	Maryland	749	1.25%
43	Massachusetts	53	0.09%
11	Michigan	1,757	2.92%
32	Minnesota	538	0.90%
14	Mississippi	1,521	2.53%
10	Missouri	2,026	3.37%
NA	Montana**	NA	NA
38	Nebraska	212	0.35%
25	Nevada	791	1.32%
44	New Hampshire	45	0.07%
46	New Jersey	0	0.00%
15	New Mexico	1,424	2.37%
13	New York	1,659	2.76%
5	North Carolina	3,271	5.44%
45	North Dakota	44	0.07%
16	Ohio	1,419	2.36%
18	Oklahoma	1,113	1.85%
24	Oregon	806	1.34%
21	Pennsylvania	940	1.56%
46	Rhode Island	0	0.00%
1	South Carolina	4,911	8.17%
40	South Dakota	192	0.32%
12	Tennessee	1,687	2.81%
3	Texas	3,660	6.09%
36	Utah	243	0.40%
42	Vermont	84	0.14%
17	Virginia	1,207	2.01%
29	Washington	681	1.13%
23	West Virginia	837	1.39%
30	Wisconsin	645	1.07%
39	Wyoming	207	0.34%

RANK ORDER

RANK	STATE	ASSAULTS	% of USA
1	South Carolina	4,911	8.17%
2	Kentucky	4,289	7.14%
3	Texas	3,660	6.09%
4	Florida	3,567	5.93%
5	North Carolina	3,271	5.44%
6	Georgia	3,203	5.33%
7	Louisiana	3,168	5.27%
8	Indiana	2,264	3.77%
9	California	2,220	3.69%
10	Missouri	2,026	3.37%
11	Michigan	1,757	2.92%
12	Tennessee	1,687	2.81%
13	New York	1,659	2.76%
14	Mississippi	1,521	2.53%
15	New Mexico	1,424	2.37%
16	Ohio	1,419	2.36%
17	Virginia	1,207	2.01%
18	Oklahoma	1,113	1.85%
19	Alabama	1,065	1.77%
20	Arizona	965	1.61%
21	Pennsylvania	940	1.56%
22	Alaska	851	1.42%
23	West Virginia	837	1.39%
24	Oregon	806	1.34%
25	Nevada	791	1.32%
26	Maryland	749	1.25%
27	Arkansas	740	1.23%
28	Idaho	699	1.16%
29	Washington	681	1.13%
30	Wisconsin	645	1.07%
31	Colorado	602	1.00%
32	Minnesota	538	0.90%
33	Iowa	474	0.79%
34	Connecticut	410	0.68%
35	Delaware	398	0.66%
36	Utah	243	0.40%
37	Hawaii	238	0.40%
38	Nebraska	212	0.35%
39	Wyoming	207	0.34%
40	South Dakota	192	0.32%
41	Maine	96	0.16%
42	Vermont	84	0.14%
43	Massachusetts	53	0.09%
44	New Hampshire	45	0.07%
45	North Dakota	44	0.07%
46	New Jersey	0	0.00%
46	Rhode Island	0	0.00%
NA	Illinois**	NA	NA
NA	Kansas**	NA	NA
NA	Montana**	NA	NA
	District of Columbia	0	0.00%

Source: Federal Bureau of Investigation
  "Crime in the United States 1994" (Uniform Crime Reports, November 19, 1995)
*Estimated totals for rural areas, defined by the F.B.I. as other than Metropolitan Statistical Areas and other cities outside such areas. National total includes those states listed as not available. Aggravated assault is an attack for the purpose of inflicting severe bodily injury.
**Not available.

Rural Aggravated Assault Rate in 1994

National Rural Rate = 188.6 Aggravated Assaults per 100,000 Population*

ALPHA ORDER

RANK	STATE	RATE
29	Alabama	134.1
5	Alaska	446.5
11	Arizona	308.6
35	Arkansas	90.1
9	California	357.4
24	Colorado	165.0
15	Connecticut	214.9
5	Delaware	446.5
3	Florida	471.5
14	Georgia	225.5
34	Hawaii	92.0
19	Idaho	176.9
NA	Illinois**	NA
16	Indiana	214.3
40	Iowa	53.2
NA	Kansas**	NA
10	Kentucky	314.0
4	Louisiana	453.4
44	Maine	27.7
12	Maryland	279.3
8	Massachusetts	430.3
22	Michigan	169.0
39	Minnesota	61.4
28	Mississippi	136.8
21	Missouri	170.6
NA	Montana**	NA
41	Nebraska	51.0
7	Nevada	444.0
42	New Hampshire	31.7
46	New Jersey	0.0
2	New Mexico	476.4
18	New York	193.8
17	North Carolina	196.1
45	North Dakota	19.4
32	Ohio	107.8
20	Oklahoma	176.4
25	Oregon	161.7
36	Pennsylvania	88.8
46	Rhode Island	0.0
1	South Carolina	619.2
38	South Dakota	65.6
26	Tennessee	153.0
13	Texas	227.9
30	Utah	120.0
42	Vermont	31.7
31	Virginia	114.2
27	Washington	138.7
33	West Virginia	107.0
37	Wisconsin	65.9
23	Wyoming	165.2

RANK ORDER

RANK	STATE	RATE
1	South Carolina	619.2
2	New Mexico	476.4
3	Florida	471.5
4	Louisiana	453.4
5	Alaska	446.5
5	Delaware	446.5
7	Nevada	444.0
8	Massachusetts	430.3
9	California	357.4
10	Kentucky	314.0
11	Arizona	308.6
12	Maryland	279.3
13	Texas	227.9
14	Georgia	225.5
15	Connecticut	214.9
16	Indiana	214.3
17	North Carolina	196.1
18	New York	193.8
19	Idaho	176.9
20	Oklahoma	176.4
21	Missouri	170.6
22	Michigan	169.0
23	Wyoming	165.2
24	Colorado	165.0
25	Oregon	161.7
26	Tennessee	153.0
27	Washington	138.7
28	Mississippi	136.8
29	Alabama	134.1
30	Utah	120.0
31	Virginia	114.2
32	Ohio	107.8
33	West Virginia	107.0
34	Hawaii	92.0
35	Arkansas	90.1
36	Pennsylvania	88.8
37	Wisconsin	65.9
38	South Dakota	65.6
39	Minnesota	61.4
40	Iowa	53.2
41	Nebraska	51.0
42	New Hampshire	31.7
42	Vermont	31.7
44	Maine	27.7
45	North Dakota	19.4
46	New Jersey	0.0
46	Rhode Island	0.0
NA	Illinois**	NA
NA	Kansas**	NA
NA	Montana**	NA
	District of Columbia	0.0

Source: Federal Bureau of Investigation
"Crime in the United States 1994" (Uniform Crime Reports, November 19, 1995)
*Estimated rates for rural areas, defined by the F.B.I. as other than Metropolitan Statistical Areas and other cities outside such areas. National rate includes those states listed as not available. Aggravated assault is an attack for the purpose of inflicting severe bodily injury.
**Not available.

Percent of Aggravated Assaults Occurring in Rural Areas in 1994

National Percent = 5.37% of Aggravated Assaults*

ALPHA ORDER

RANK ORDER

RANK	STATE	PERCENT		RANK	STATE	PERCENT
31	Alabama	5.42		1	West Virginia	31.12
4	Alaska	25.77		2	Idaho	26.15
34	Arizona	4.79		3	Vermont	25.85
26	Arkansas	7.31		4	Alaska	25.77
44	California	1.16		5	Kentucky	23.86
36	Colorado	4.65		6	Mississippi	21.07
32	Connecticut	5.29		7	Wyoming	19.87
11	Delaware	15.89		8	South Carolina	17.17
41	Florida	3.38		9	Hawaii	16.29
14	Georgia	11.34		10	South Dakota	16.09
9	Hawaii	16.29		11	Delaware	15.89
2	Idaho	26.15		12	North Dakota	14.62
NA	Illinois**	NA		13	New Mexico	12.56
16	Indiana	11.20		14	Georgia	11.34
27	Iowa	6.90		15	Louisiana	11.29
NA	Kansas**	NA		16	Indiana	11.20
5	Kentucky	23.86		17	North Carolina	10.76
15	Louisiana	11.29		18	Virginia	9.82
20	Maine	9.73		19	Wisconsin	9.79
42	Maryland	3.03		20	Maine	9.73
45	Massachusetts	0.17		21	Nevada	9.54
39	Michigan	4.05		22	Missouri	8.25
29	Minnesota	6.60		23	Oregon	7.81
6	Mississippi	21.07		24	New Hampshire	7.54
22	Missouri	8.25		25	Oklahoma	7.32
NA	Montana**	NA		26	Arkansas	7.31
35	Nebraska	4.66		27	Iowa	6.90
21	Nevada	9.54		28	Tennessee	6.76
24	New Hampshire	7.54		29	Minnesota	6.60
46	New Jersey	0.00		30	Utah	6.51
13	New Mexico	12.56		31	Alabama	5.42
43	New York	2.02		32	Connecticut	5.29
17	North Carolina	10.76		33	Ohio	5.21
12	North Dakota	14.62		34	Arizona	4.79
33	Ohio	5.21		35	Nebraska	4.66
25	Oklahoma	7.32		36	Colorado	4.65
23	Oregon	7.81		37	Texas	4.51
40	Pennsylvania	3.75		38	Washington	4.17
46	Rhode Island	0.00		39	Michigan	4.05
8	South Carolina	17.17		40	Pennsylvania	3.75
10	South Dakota	16.09		41	Florida	3.38
28	Tennessee	6.76		42	Maryland	3.03
37	Texas	4.51		43	New York	2.02
30	Utah	6.51		44	California	1.16
3	Vermont	25.85		45	Massachusetts	0.17
18	Virginia	9.82		46	New Jersey	0.00
38	Washington	4.17		46	Rhode Island	0.00
1	West Virginia	31.12		NA	Illinois**	NA
19	Wisconsin	9.79		NA	Kansas**	NA
7	Wyoming	19.87		NA	Montana**	NA
					District of Columbia	0.00

Source: Morgan Quitno Press using data from Federal Bureau of Investigation
    "Crime in the United States 1994" (Uniform Crime Reports, November 19, 1995)
*Estimated percentages for rural areas, defined by the F.B.I. as other than Metropolitan Statistical Areas and other cities outside such areas. National percent includes those states listed as not available. Aggravated assault is an attack for the purpose of inflicting severe bodily injury.
**Not available.

Property Crime in Urban Areas in 1994

National Total = 11,554,579 Property Crimes*

RANK	STATE	CRIMES	% of USA	RANK	STATE	CRIMES	% of USA
21	Alabama	170,324	1.47%	1	California	1,603,607	13.88%
42	Alaska	24,936	0.22%	2	Florida	965,599	8.36%
11	Arizona	288,111	2.49%	3	Texas	921,254	7.97%
30	Arkansas	91,552	0.79%	4	New York	728,761	6.31%
1	California	1,603,607	13.88%	5	Ohio	424,080	3.67%
22	Colorado	167,286	1.45%	6	Michigan	420,481	3.64%
27	Connecticut	131,007	1.13%	7	Georgia	345,027	2.99%
43	Delaware	22,943	0.20%	8	Pennsylvania	328,556	2.84%
2	Florida	965,599	8.36%	9	New Jersey	319,856	2.77%
7	Georgia	345,027	2.99%	10	North Carolina	313,961	2.72%
35	Hawaii	61,016	0.53%	11	Arizona	288,111	2.49%
38	Idaho	35,561	0.31%	12	Washington	281,360	2.44%
NA	Illinois**	NA	NA	13	Maryland	253,398	2.19%
18	Indiana	217,057	1.88%	14	Louisiana	232,908	2.02%
32	Iowa	84,883	0.73%	15	Missouri	227,498	1.97%
NA	Kansas**	NA	NA	16	Virginia	227,364	1.97%
29	Kentucky	95,894	0.83%	17	Massachusetts	225,478	1.95%
14	Louisiana	232,908	2.02%	18	Indiana	217,057	1.88%
39	Maine	32,767	0.28%	19	Tennessee	209,337	1.81%
13	Maryland	253,398	2.19%	20	Wisconsin	170,983	1.48%
17	Massachusetts	225,478	1.95%	21	Alabama	170,324	1.47%
6	Michigan	420,481	3.64%	22	Colorado	167,286	1.45%
23	Minnesota	165,194	1.43%	23	Minnesota	165,194	1.43%
28	Mississippi	101,912	0.88%	24	Oregon	165,062	1.43%
15	Missouri	227,498	1.97%	25	South Carolina	156,802	1.36%
NA	Montana**	NA	NA	26	Oklahoma	150,582	1.30%
36	Nebraska	60,438	0.52%	27	Connecticut	131,007	1.13%
34	Nevada	77,622	0.67%	28	Mississippi	101,912	0.88%
41	New Hampshire	28,877	0.25%	29	Kentucky	95,894	0.83%
9	New Jersey	319,856	2.77%	30	Arkansas	91,552	0.79%
33	New Mexico	80,356	0.70%	31	Utah	91,217	0.79%
4	New York	728,761	6.31%	32	Iowa	84,883	0.73%
10	North Carolina	313,961	2.72%	33	New Mexico	80,356	0.70%
46	North Dakota	14,853	0.13%	34	Nevada	77,622	0.67%
5	Ohio	424,080	3.67%	35	Hawaii	61,016	0.53%
26	Oklahoma	150,582	1.30%	36	Nebraska	60,438	0.52%
24	Oregon	165,062	1.43%	37	Rhode Island	37,302	0.32%
8	Pennsylvania	328,556	2.84%	38	Idaho	35,561	0.31%
37	Rhode Island	37,302	0.32%	39	Maine	32,767	0.28%
25	South Carolina	156,802	1.36%	40	West Virginia	32,658	0.28%
44	South Dakota	17,985	0.16%	41	New Hampshire	28,877	0.25%
19	Tennessee	209,337	1.81%	42	Alaska	24,936	0.22%
3	Texas	921,254	7.97%	43	Delaware	22,943	0.20%
31	Utah	91,217	0.79%	44	South Dakota	17,985	0.16%
47	Vermont	14,585	0.13%	45	Wyoming	16,670	0.14%
16	Virginia	227,364	1.97%	46	North Dakota	14,853	0.13%
12	Washington	281,360	2.44%	47	Vermont	14,585	0.13%
40	West Virginia	32,658	0.28%	NA	Illinois**	NA	NA
20	Wisconsin	170,983	1.48%	NA	Kansas**	NA	NA
45	Wyoming	16,670	0.14%	NA	Montana**	NA	NA
					District of Columbia	48,009	0.42%

ALPHA ORDER / RANK ORDER

Source: Morgan Quitno Press using data from Federal Bureau of Investigation
"Crime in the United States 1994" (Uniform Crime Reports, November 19, 1995)
Estimated totals for urban areas, defined by the F.B.I. as Metropolitan Statistical Areas and other cities outside such areas. National total includes those states listed as not available. Property crimes are offenses of burglary, larceny-theft and motor vehicle theft.
**Not available.*

433

Urban Property Crime Rate in 1994

National Urban Rate = 5,057.5 Property Crimes per 100,000 Population*

ALPHA ORDER

RANK ORDER

RANK	STATE	RATE		RANK	STATE	RATE
24	Alabama	4,972.9		1	Arizona	7,657.9
9	Alaska	6,002.9		2	Florida	7,317.1
1	Arizona	7,657.9		3	Hawaii	6,630.4
14	Arkansas	5,611.7		4	Mississippi	6,543.7
20	California	5,204.9		5	Louisiana	6,440.5
22	Colorado	5,082.9		6	Oregon	6,379.0
33	Connecticut	4,247.7		7	Georgia	6,123.2
42	Delaware	3,719.3		8	Nevada	6,069.7
2	Florida	7,317.1		9	Alaska	6,002.9
7	Georgia	6,123.2		10	New Mexico	5,929.9
3	Hawaii	6,630.4		11	North Carolina	5,811.8
26	Idaho	4,819.9		12	Washington	5,799.0
NA	Illinois**	NA		13	Oklahoma	5,731.8
29	Indiana	4,622.6		14	Arkansas	5,611.7
31	Iowa	4,381.7		15	Missouri	5,561.5
NA	Kansas**	NA		16	Texas	5,492.7
39	Kentucky	3,896.5		17	South Carolina	5,461.7
5	Louisiana	6,440.5		18	Utah	5,348.7
43	Maine	3,666.3		19	Maryland	5,348.4
19	Maryland	5,348.4		20	California	5,204.9
41	Massachusetts	3,740.1		21	Tennessee	5,140.6
25	Michigan	4,972.3		22	Colorado	5,082.9
30	Minnesota	4,476.0		23	Nebraska	5,006.2
4	Mississippi	6,543.7		24	Alabama	4,972.9
15	Missouri	5,561.5		25	Michigan	4,972.3
NA	Montana**	NA		26	Idaho	4,819.9
23	Nebraska	5,006.2		27	Wyoming	4,753.4
8	Nevada	6,069.7		28	Vermont	4,632.0
47	New Hampshire	2,902.3		29	Indiana	4,622.6
38	New Jersey	4,046.8		30	Minnesota	4,476.0
10	New Mexico	5,929.9		31	Iowa	4,381.7
34	New York	4,209.3		32	Ohio	4,333.6
11	North Carolina	5,811.8		33	Connecticut	4,247.7
44	North Dakota	3,616.4		34	New York	4,209.3
32	Ohio	4,333.6		35	South Dakota	4,200.4
13	Oklahoma	5,731.8		36	Wisconsin	4,167.7
6	Oregon	6,379.0		37	Virginia	4,137.8
46	Pennsylvania	2,988.7		38	New Jersey	4,046.8
40	Rhode Island	3,741.4		39	Kentucky	3,896.5
17	South Carolina	5,461.7		40	Rhode Island	3,741.4
35	South Dakota	4,200.4		41	Massachusetts	3,740.1
21	Tennessee	5,140.6		42	Delaware	3,719.3
16	Texas	5,492.7		43	Maine	3,666.3
18	Utah	5,348.7		44	North Dakota	3,616.4
28	Vermont	4,632.0		45	West Virginia	3,140.5
37	Virginia	4,137.8		46	Pennsylvania	2,988.7
12	Washington	5,799.0		47	New Hampshire	2,902.3
45	West Virginia	3,140.5		NA	Illinois**	NA
36	Wisconsin	4,167.7		NA	Kansas**	NA
27	Wyoming	4,753.4		NA	Montana**	NA
					District of Columbia	8,422.6

Source: Morgan Quitno Press using data from Federal Bureau of Investigation
"Crime in the United States 1994" (Uniform Crime Reports, November 19, 1995)
*Estimated rates for urban areas, defined by the F.B.I. as Metropolitan Statistical Areas and other cities outside such areas. National rate includes those states listed as not available. Property crimes are offenses of burglary, larceny-theft and motor vehicle theft.
**Not available.

434

Percent of Property Crimes Occurring in Urban Areas in 1994

National Percent = 95.28% of Property Crimes*

ALPHA ORDER				RANK ORDER		
RANK	STATE	PERCENT		RANK	STATE	PERCENT
14	Alabama	95.68		1	New Jersey	100.00
43	Alaska	83.27		2	Massachusetts	99.98
5	Arizona	97.91		3	Rhode Island	99.94
35	Arkansas	88.79		4	California	98.86
4	California	98.86		5	Arizona	97.91
17	Colorado	95.15		6	Maryland	97.82
7	Connecticut	97.74		7	Connecticut	97.74
32	Delaware	90.61		8	New York	97.71
9	Florida	97.43		9	Florida	97.43
30	Georgia	91.54		10	Texas	97.04
45	Hawaii	80.63		11	New Hampshire	96.78
44	Idaho	82.79		12	Ohio	96.08
NA	Illinois**	NA		13	Pennsylvania	95.82
24	Indiana	92.77		14	Alabama	95.68
33	Iowa	89.85		14	Utah	95.68
NA	Kansas**	NA		16	Washington	95.46
40	Kentucky	86.61		17	Colorado	95.15
18	Louisiana	94.88		18	Louisiana	94.88
42	Maine	84.08		19	Michigan	94.63
6	Maryland	97.82		20	Missouri	94.44
2	Massachusetts	99.98		21	Virginia	94.04
19	Michigan	94.63		22	Oklahoma	93.97
31	Minnesota	90.84		23	Nevada	93.87
36	Mississippi	87.91		24	Indiana	92.77
20	Missouri	94.44		25	Oregon	92.61
NA	Montana**	NA		26	Tennessee	92.53
27	Nebraska	91.93		27	Nebraska	91.93
23	Nevada	93.87		28	New Mexico	91.69
11	New Hampshire	96.78		29	Wisconsin	91.58
1	New Jersey	100.00		30	Georgia	91.54
28	New Mexico	91.69		31	Minnesota	90.84
8	New York	97.71		32	Delaware	90.61
34	North Carolina	89.35		33	Iowa	89.85
37	North Dakota	87.72		34	North Carolina	89.35
12	Ohio	96.08		35	Arkansas	88.79
22	Oklahoma	93.97		36	Mississippi	87.91
25	Oregon	92.61		37	North Dakota	87.72
13	Pennsylvania	95.82		38	Wyoming	87.18
3	Rhode Island	99.94		39	South Dakota	86.78
41	South Carolina	86.10		40	Kentucky	86.61
39	South Dakota	86.78		41	South Carolina	86.10
26	Tennessee	92.53		42	Maine	84.08
10	Texas	97.04		43	Alaska	83.27
14	Utah	95.68		44	Idaho	82.79
46	Vermont	79.74		45	Hawaii	80.63
21	Virginia	94.04		46	Vermont	79.74
16	Washington	95.46		47	West Virginia	77.51
47	West Virginia	77.51		NA	Illinois**	NA
29	Wisconsin	91.58		NA	Kansas**	NA
38	Wyoming	87.18		NA	Montana**	NA
				District of Columbia		100.00

Source: Morgan Quitno Press using data from Federal Bureau of Investigation
"Crime in the United States 1994" (Uniform Crime Reports, November 19, 1995)
*Estimated percentages for urban areas, defined by the F.B.I. as Metropolitan Statistical Areas and other cities outside such areas. National percent includes those states listed as not available. Property crimes are offenses of burglary, larceny-theft and motor vehicle theft.
**Not available.

Property Crime in Rural Areas in 1994

National Total = 572,928 Property Crimes*

RANK	STATE	CRIMES	% of USA
28	Alabama	7,691	1.34%
36	Alaska	5,011	0.87%
32	Arizona	6,162	1.08%
23	Arkansas	11,563	2.02%
7	California	18,495	3.23%
27	Colorado	8,522	1.49%
39	Connecticut	3,023	0.53%
42	Delaware	2,378	0.42%
4	Florida	25,506	4.45%
2	Georgia	31,899	5.57%
15	Hawaii	14,656	2.56%
29	Idaho	7,393	1.29%
NA	Illinois**	NA	NA
10	Indiana	16,918	2.95%
25	Iowa	9,592	1.67%
NA	Kansas**	NA	NA
14	Kentucky	14,831	2.59%
22	Louisiana	12,580	2.20%
31	Maine	6,204	1.08%
33	Maryland	5,641	0.98%
45	Massachusetts	54	0.01%
6	Michigan	23,844	4.16%
12	Minnesota	16,662	2.91%
18	Mississippi	14,012	2.45%
19	Missouri	13,400	2.34%
NA	Montana**	NA	NA
34	Nebraska	5,308	0.93%
35	Nevada	5,071	0.89%
44	New Hampshire	960	0.17%
47	New Jersey	0	0.00%
30	New Mexico	7,282	1.27%
9	New York	17,084	2.98%
1	North Carolina	37,436	6.53%
43	North Dakota	2,080	0.36%
8	Ohio	17,300	3.02%
24	Oklahoma	9,668	1.69%
21	Oregon	13,178	2.30%
17	Pennsylvania	14,345	2.50%
46	Rhode Island	21	0.00%
5	South Carolina	25,312	4.42%
40	South Dakota	2,741	0.48%
11	Tennessee	16,910	2.95%
3	Texas	28,133	4.91%
37	Utah	4,115	0.72%
38	Vermont	3,705	0.65%
16	Virginia	14,399	2.51%
20	Washington	13,374	2.33%
26	West Virginia	9,478	1.65%
13	Wisconsin	15,721	2.74%
41	Wyoming	2,452	0.43%

RANK	STATE	CRIMES	% of USA
1	North Carolina	37,436	6.53%
2	Georgia	31,899	5.57%
3	Texas	28,133	4.91%
4	Florida	25,506	4.45%
5	South Carolina	25,312	4.42%
6	Michigan	23,844	4.16%
7	California	18,495	3.23%
8	Ohio	17,300	3.02%
9	New York	17,084	2.98%
10	Indiana	16,918	2.95%
11	Tennessee	16,910	2.95%
12	Minnesota	16,662	2.91%
13	Wisconsin	15,721	2.74%
14	Kentucky	14,831	2.59%
15	Hawaii	14,656	2.56%
16	Virginia	14,399	2.51%
17	Pennsylvania	14,345	2.50%
18	Mississippi	14,012	2.45%
19	Missouri	13,400	2.34%
20	Washington	13,374	2.33%
21	Oregon	13,178	2.30%
22	Louisiana	12,580	2.20%
23	Arkansas	11,563	2.02%
24	Oklahoma	9,668	1.69%
25	Iowa	9,592	1.67%
26	West Virginia	9,478	1.65%
27	Colorado	8,522	1.49%
28	Alabama	7,691	1.34%
29	Idaho	7,393	1.29%
30	New Mexico	7,282	1.27%
31	Maine	6,204	1.08%
32	Arizona	6,162	1.08%
33	Maryland	5,641	0.98%
34	Nebraska	5,308	0.93%
35	Nevada	5,071	0.89%
36	Alaska	5,011	0.87%
37	Utah	4,115	0.72%
38	Vermont	3,705	0.65%
39	Connecticut	3,023	0.53%
40	South Dakota	2,741	0.48%
41	Wyoming	2,452	0.43%
42	Delaware	2,378	0.42%
43	North Dakota	2,080	0.36%
44	New Hampshire	960	0.17%
45	Massachusetts	54	0.01%
46	Rhode Island	21	0.00%
47	New Jersey	0	0.00%
NA	Illinois**	NA	NA
NA	Kansas**	NA	NA
NA	Montana**	NA	NA
	District of Columbia	0	0.00%

Source: Federal Bureau of Investigation
  "Crime in the United States 1994" (Uniform Crime Reports, November 19, 1995)
*Estimated totals for rural areas, defined by the F.B.I. as other than Metropolitan Statistical Areas and other cities outside such areas. National total includes those states listed as not available. Property crimes are offenses of burglary, larceny-theft and motor vehicle theft.
**Not available.

Rural Property Crime Rate in 1994

National Rural Rate = 1,797.4 Property Crimes per 100,000 Population*

ALPHA ORDER			RANK ORDER		
RANK	**STATE**	**RATE**	**RANK**	**STATE**	**RATE**
41	Alabama	968.7	1	Hawaii	5,664.0
9	Alaska	2,629.0	2	Florida	3,371.7
18	Arizona	1,970.4	3	South Carolina	3,191.7
30	Arkansas	1,407.5	4	California	2,977.2
4	California	2,977.2	5	Nevada	2,846.5
11	Colorado	2,335.8	6	Washington	2,723.3
27	Connecticut	1,584.2	7	Delaware	2,668.0
7	Delaware	2,668.0	8	Oregon	2,644.0
2	Florida	3,371.7	9	Alaska	2,629.0
13	Georgia	2,246.1	10	New Mexico	2,436.2
1	Hawaii	5,664.0	11	Colorado	2,335.8
21	Idaho	1,870.7	12	Michigan	2,293.8
NA	Illinois**	NA	13	Georgia	2,246.1
26	Indiana	1,601.5	14	North Carolina	2,244.6
40	Iowa	1,075.6	15	Maryland	2,103.2
NA	Kansas**	NA	16	Utah	2,031.3
39	Kentucky	1,085.8	17	New York	1,996.1
22	Louisiana	1,800.5	18	Arizona	1,970.4
23	Maine	1,791.6	19	Wyoming	1,956.9
15	Maryland	2,103.2	20	Minnesota	1,901.2
45	Massachusetts	438.5	21	Idaho	1,870.7
12	Michigan	2,293.8	22	Louisiana	1,800.5
20	Minnesota	1,901.2	23	Maine	1,791.6
36	Mississippi	1,260.5	24	Texas	1,752.0
38	Missouri	1,128.5	25	Wisconsin	1,605.1
NA	Montana**	NA	26	Indiana	1,601.5
35	Nebraska	1,276.7	27	Connecticut	1,584.2
5	Nevada	2,846.5	28	Tennessee	1,533.4
44	New Hampshire	676.0	29	Oklahoma	1,532.5
46	New Jersey	0.0	30	Arkansas	1,407.5
10	New Mexico	2,436.2	31	Vermont	1,397.4
17	New York	1,996.1	32	Virginia	1,361.9
14	North Carolina	2,244.6	33	Pennsylvania	1,354.8
43	North Dakota	915.1	34	Ohio	1,314.6
34	Ohio	1,314.6	35	Nebraska	1,276.7
29	Oklahoma	1,532.5	36	Mississippi	1,260.5
8	Oregon	2,644.0	37	West Virginia	1,211.9
33	Pennsylvania	1,354.8	38	Missouri	1,128.5
46	Rhode Island	0.0	39	Kentucky	1,085.8
3	South Carolina	3,191.7	40	Iowa	1,075.6
42	South Dakota	936.0	41	Alabama	968.7
28	Tennessee	1,533.4	42	South Dakota	936.0
24	Texas	1,752.0	43	North Dakota	915.1
16	Utah	2,031.3	44	New Hampshire	676.0
31	Vermont	1,397.4	45	Massachusetts	438.5
32	Virginia	1,361.9	46	New Jersey	0.0
6	Washington	2,723.3	46	Rhode Island	0.0
37	West Virginia	1,211.9	NA	Illinois**	NA
25	Wisconsin	1,605.1	NA	Kansas**	NA
19	Wyoming	1,956.9	NA	Montana**	NA
				District of Columbia	0.0

Source: Federal Bureau of Investigation
 "Crime in the United States 1994" (Uniform Crime Reports, November 19, 1995)
*Estimated rates for rural areas, defined by the F.B.I. as other than Metropolitan Statistical Areas and other cities outside such areas. National rate includes those states listed as not available. Property crimes are offenses of burglary, larceny-theft and motor vehicle theft.
**Not available.

Percent of Property Crime Occurring in Rural Areas in 1994

National Percent = 4.72% of Property Crimes*

ALPHA ORDER

RANK	STATE	PERCENT
33	Alabama	4.32
5	Alaska	16.73
43	Arizona	2.09
13	Arkansas	11.21
44	California	1.14
31	Colorado	4.85
41	Connecticut	2.26
16	Delaware	9.39
39	Florida	2.57
18	Georgia	8.46
3	Hawaii	19.37
4	Idaho	17.21
NA	Illinois**	NA
24	Indiana	7.23
15	Iowa	10.15
NA	Kansas**	NA
8	Kentucky	13.39
30	Louisiana	5.12
6	Maine	15.92
42	Maryland	2.18
46	Massachusetts	0.02
29	Michigan	5.37
17	Minnesota	9.16
12	Mississippi	12.09
28	Missouri	5.56
NA	Montana**	NA
21	Nebraska	8.07
25	Nevada	6.13
37	New Hampshire	3.22
47	New Jersey	0.00
20	New Mexico	8.31
40	New York	2.29
14	North Carolina	10.65
11	North Dakota	12.28
36	Ohio	3.92
26	Oklahoma	6.03
23	Oregon	7.39
35	Pennsylvania	4.18
45	Rhode Island	0.06
7	South Carolina	13.90
9	South Dakota	13.22
22	Tennessee	7.47
38	Texas	2.96
33	Utah	4.32
2	Vermont	20.26
27	Virginia	5.96
32	Washington	4.54
1	West Virginia	22.49
19	Wisconsin	8.42
10	Wyoming	12.82

RANK ORDER

RANK	STATE	PERCENT
1	West Virginia	22.49
2	Vermont	20.26
3	Hawaii	19.37
4	Idaho	17.21
5	Alaska	16.73
6	Maine	15.92
7	South Carolina	13.90
8	Kentucky	13.39
9	South Dakota	13.22
10	Wyoming	12.82
11	North Dakota	12.28
12	Mississippi	12.09
13	Arkansas	11.21
14	North Carolina	10.65
15	Iowa	10.15
16	Delaware	9.39
17	Minnesota	9.16
18	Georgia	8.46
19	Wisconsin	8.42
20	New Mexico	8.31
21	Nebraska	8.07
22	Tennessee	7.47
23	Oregon	7.39
24	Indiana	7.23
25	Nevada	6.13
26	Oklahoma	6.03
27	Virginia	5.96
28	Missouri	5.56
29	Michigan	5.37
30	Louisiana	5.12
31	Colorado	4.85
32	Washington	4.54
33	Alabama	4.32
33	Utah	4.32
35	Pennsylvania	4.18
36	Ohio	3.92
37	New Hampshire	3.22
38	Texas	2.96
39	Florida	2.57
40	New York	2.29
41	Connecticut	2.26
42	Maryland	2.18
43	Arizona	2.09
44	California	1.14
45	Rhode Island	0.06
46	Massachusetts	0.02
47	New Jersey	0.00
NA	Illinois**	NA
NA	Kansas**	NA
NA	Montana**	NA
	District of Columbia	0.00

Source: Morgan Quitno Press using data from Federal Bureau of Investigation
  "Crime in the United States 1994" (Uniform Crime Reports, November 19, 1995)
*Estimated percentages for rural areas, defined by the F.B.I. as other than Metropolitan Statistical Areas and other cities outside such areas. National percent includes those states listed as not available. Property crimes are offenses of burglary, larceny-theft and motor vehicle theft.
**Not available.

Burglary in Urban Areas in 1994

National Total = 2,510,583 Burglaries*

ALPHA ORDER

ALPHA ORDER

RANK ORDER

RANK	STATE	BURGLARIES	% of USA		RANK	STATE	BURGLARIES	% of USA
19	Alabama	40,677	1.62%		1	California	377,328	15.03%
43	Alaska	3,363	0.13%		2	Florida	228,298	9.09%
11	Arizona	58,132	2.32%		3	Texas	203,154	8.09%
30	Arkansas	22,596	0.90%		4	New York	158,383	6.31%
1	California	377,328	15.03%		5	Ohio	91,166	3.63%
23	Colorado	31,886	1.27%		6	North Carolina	87,350	3.48%
27	Connecticut	28,157	1.12%		7	Michigan	83,192	3.31%
42	Delaware	4,616	0.18%		8	New Jersey	72,074	2.87%
2	Florida	228,298	9.09%		9	Georgia	71,101	2.83%
9	Georgia	71,101	2.83%		10	Pennsylvania	60,758	2.42%
35	Hawaii	10,623	0.42%		11	Arizona	58,132	2.32%
40	Idaho	6,067	0.24%		12	Massachusetts	53,215	2.12%
NA	Illinois**	NA	NA		13	Tennessee	51,675	2.06%
18	Indiana	43,450	1.73%		14	Washington	51,620	2.06%
33	Iowa	15,981	0.64%		15	Louisiana	51,459	2.05%
NA	Kansas**	NA	NA		16	Maryland	50,470	2.01%
29	Kentucky	22,712	0.90%		17	Missouri	50,122	2.00%
15	Louisiana	51,459	2.05%		18	Indiana	43,450	1.73%
39	Maine	6,385	0.25%		19	Alabama	40,677	1.62%
16	Maryland	50,470	2.01%		20	South Carolina	38,510	1.53%
12	Massachusetts	53,215	2.12%		21	Virginia	37,552	1.50%
7	Michigan	83,192	3.31%		22	Oklahoma	36,550	1.46%
24	Minnesota	30,686	1.22%		23	Colorado	31,886	1.27%
26	Mississippi	28,218	1.12%		24	Minnesota	30,686	1.22%
17	Missouri	50,122	2.00%		25	Oregon	29,908	1.19%
NA	Montana**	NA	NA		26	Mississippi	28,218	1.12%
36	Nebraska	9,664	0.38%		27	Connecticut	28,157	1.12%
32	Nevada	18,317	0.73%		28	Wisconsin	27,220	1.08%
41	New Hampshire	4,988	0.20%		29	Kentucky	22,712	0.90%
8	New Jersey	72,074	2.87%		30	Arkansas	22,596	0.90%
31	New Mexico	18,823	0.75%		31	New Mexico	18,823	0.75%
4	New York	158,383	6.31%		32	Nevada	18,317	0.73%
6	North Carolina	87,350	3.48%		33	Iowa	15,981	0.64%
47	North Dakota	1,530	0.06%		34	Utah	14,110	0.56%
5	Ohio	91,166	3.63%		35	Hawaii	10,623	0.42%
22	Oklahoma	36,550	1.46%		36	Nebraska	9,664	0.38%
25	Oregon	29,908	1.19%		37	Rhode Island	9,099	0.36%
10	Pennsylvania	60,758	2.42%		38	West Virginia	7,348	0.29%
37	Rhode Island	9,099	0.36%		39	Maine	6,385	0.25%
20	South Carolina	38,510	1.53%		40	Idaho	6,067	0.24%
44	South Dakota	3,189	0.13%		41	New Hampshire	4,988	0.20%
13	Tennessee	51,675	2.06%		42	Delaware	4,616	0.18%
3	Texas	203,154	8.09%		43	Alaska	3,363	0.13%
34	Utah	14,110	0.56%		44	South Dakota	3,189	0.13%
45	Vermont	2,666	0.11%		45	Vermont	2,666	0.11%
21	Virginia	37,552	1.50%		46	Wyoming	2,416	0.10%
14	Washington	51,620	2.06%		47	North Dakota	1,530	0.06%
38	West Virginia	7,348	0.29%		NA	Illinois**	NA	NA
28	Wisconsin	27,220	1.08%		NA	Kansas**	NA	NA
46	Wyoming	2,416	0.10%		NA	Montana**	NA	NA
						District of Columbia	10,037	0.40%

Source: Morgan Quitno Press using data from Federal Bureau of Investigation
   "Crime in the United States 1994" (Uniform Crime Reports, November 19, 1995)
*Estimated totals for urban areas, defined by the F.B.I. as Metropolitan Statistical Areas and other cities outside
such areas. National total includes those states listed as not available. Burglary is the unlawful entry of a
structure to commit a felony or theft. Attempts are included.
**Not available.

Urban Burglary Rate in 1994

National Urban Rate = 1,098.9 Burglaries per 100,000 Population*

ALPHA ORDER

RANK	STATE	RATE
16	Alabama	1,187.6
36	Alaska	809.6
4	Arizona	1,545.1
9	Arkansas	1,385.0
14	California	1,224.7
22	Colorado	968.8
27	Connecticut	912.9
38	Delaware	748.3
2	Florida	1,730.0
12	Georgia	1,261.8
18	Hawaii	1,154.4
35	Idaho	822.3
NA	Illinois**	NA
24	Indiana	925.3
34	Iowa	825.0
NA	Kansas**	NA
25	Kentucky	922.9
6	Louisiana	1,423.0
40	Maine	714.4
19	Maryland	1,065.3
30	Massachusetts	882.7
21	Michigan	983.8
32	Minnesota	831.5
1	Mississippi	1,811.9
13	Missouri	1,225.3
NA	Montana**	NA
37	Nebraska	800.5
5	Nevada	1,432.3
46	New Hampshire	501.3
29	New Jersey	911.9
8	New Mexico	1,389.1
26	New York	914.8
3	North Carolina	1,616.9
47	North Dakota	372.5
23	Ohio	931.6
7	Oklahoma	1,391.3
17	Oregon	1,155.8
45	Pennsylvania	552.7
28	Rhode Island	912.6
10	South Carolina	1,341.4
39	South Dakota	744.8
11	Tennessee	1,269.0
15	Texas	1,211.3
33	Utah	827.4
31	Vermont	846.7
43	Virginia	683.4
20	Washington	1,063.9
41	West Virginia	706.6
44	Wisconsin	663.5
42	Wyoming	688.9

RANK ORDER

RANK	STATE	RATE
1	Mississippi	1,811.9
2	Florida	1,730.0
3	North Carolina	1,616.9
4	Arizona	1,545.1
5	Nevada	1,432.3
6	Louisiana	1,423.0
7	Oklahoma	1,391.3
8	New Mexico	1,389.1
9	Arkansas	1,385.0
10	South Carolina	1,341.4
11	Tennessee	1,269.0
12	Georgia	1,261.8
13	Missouri	1,225.3
14	California	1,224.7
15	Texas	1,211.3
16	Alabama	1,187.6
17	Oregon	1,155.8
18	Hawaii	1,154.4
19	Maryland	1,065.3
20	Washington	1,063.9
21	Michigan	983.8
22	Colorado	968.8
23	Ohio	931.6
24	Indiana	925.3
25	Kentucky	922.9
26	New York	914.8
27	Connecticut	912.9
28	Rhode Island	912.6
29	New Jersey	911.9
30	Massachusetts	882.7
31	Vermont	846.7
32	Minnesota	831.5
33	Utah	827.4
34	Iowa	825.0
35	Idaho	822.3
36	Alaska	809.6
37	Nebraska	800.5
38	Delaware	748.3
39	South Dakota	744.8
40	Maine	714.4
41	West Virginia	706.6
42	Wyoming	688.9
43	Virginia	683.4
44	Wisconsin	663.5
45	Pennsylvania	552.7
46	New Hampshire	501.3
47	North Dakota	372.5
NA	Illinois**	NA
NA	Kansas**	NA
NA	Montana**	NA

District of Columbia   1,760.9

Source: Morgan Quitno Press using data from Federal Bureau of Investigation
   "Crime in the United States 1994" (Uniform Crime Reports, November 19, 1995)
*Estimated rates for urban areas, defined by the F.B.I. as Metropolitan Statistical Areas and other cities outside
such areas. National rate includes those states listed as not available. Burglary is the unlawful entry of a
structure to commit a felony or theft. Attempts are included.
**Not available.

Percent of Burglaries Occurring in Urban Areas in 1994

National Percent = 92.57% of Burglaries*

ALPHA ORDER				RANK ORDER		
RANK	STATE	PERCENT		RANK	STATE	PERCENT
18	Alabama	92.31		1	New Jersey	100.00
45	Alaska	69.37		2	Massachusetts	99.99
5	Arizona	96.63		3	Rhode Island	99.98
32	Arkansas	83.97		4	California	98.20
4	California	98.20		5	Arizona	96.63
13	Colorado	94.22		6	Connecticut	96.62
6	Connecticut	96.62		6	Maryland	96.62
35	Delaware	82.72		8	Florida	96.19
8	Florida	96.19		8	New York	96.19
28	Georgia	87.34		10	Ohio	94.79
41	Hawaii	75.72		11	Texas	94.63
42	Idaho	74.47		12	New Hampshire	94.56
NA	Illinois**	NA		13	Colorado	94.22
24	Indiana	88.82		14	Utah	93.51
31	Iowa	84.68		15	Louisiana	93.24
NA	Kansas**	NA		16	Nevada	92.81
39	Kentucky	79.09		17	Washington	92.52
15	Louisiana	93.24		18	Alabama	92.31
44	Maine	71.44		19	Pennsylvania	91.41
6	Maryland	96.62		20	Michigan	90.57
2	Massachusetts	99.99		21	Missouri	90.18
20	Michigan	90.57		22	Virginia	89.72
30	Minnesota	84.87		23	Oklahoma	89.66
37	Mississippi	81.81		24	Indiana	88.82
21	Missouri	90.18		25	Nebraska	88.15
NA	Montana**	NA		26	Oregon	88.04
25	Nebraska	88.15		27	Tennessee	87.47
16	Nevada	92.81		28	Georgia	87.34
12	New Hampshire	94.56		29	New Mexico	85.77
1	New Jersey	100.00		30	Minnesota	84.87
29	New Mexico	85.77		31	Iowa	84.68
8	New York	96.19		32	Arkansas	83.97
33	North Carolina	83.90		33	North Carolina	83.90
43	North Dakota	73.91		34	Wisconsin	82.93
10	Ohio	94.79		35	Delaware	82.72
23	Oklahoma	89.66		36	South Carolina	82.50
26	Oregon	88.04		37	Mississippi	81.81
19	Pennsylvania	91.41		38	South Dakota	80.98
3	Rhode Island	99.98		39	Kentucky	79.09
36	South Carolina	82.50		40	Wyoming	78.01
38	South Dakota	80.98		41	Hawaii	75.72
27	Tennessee	87.47		42	Idaho	74.47
11	Texas	94.63		43	North Dakota	73.91
14	Utah	93.51		44	Maine	71.44
47	Vermont	62.38		45	Alaska	69.37
22	Virginia	89.72		46	West Virginia	68.85
17	Washington	92.52		47	Vermont	62.38
46	West Virginia	68.85		NA	Illinois**	NA
34	Wisconsin	82.93		NA	Kansas**	NA
40	Wyoming	78.01		NA	Montana**	NA
					District of Columbia	100.00

Source: Morgan Quitno Press using data from Federal Bureau of Investigation
   "Crime in the United States 1994" (Uniform Crime Reports, November 19, 1995)
*Estimated percentages for urban areas, defined by the F.B.I. as Metropolitan Statistical Areas and other cities outside such areas. National percent includes those states listed as not available. Burglary is the unlawful entry of a structure to commit a felony or theft. Attempts are included.
**Not available.

Burglary in Rural Areas in 1994

National Total = 201,573 Burglaries*

ALPHA ORDER				RANK ORDER			
RANK	STATE	PERCENT	% of USA	RANK	STATE	PERCENT	% of USA
25	Alabama	3,387	1.68%	1	North Carolina	16,768	8.32%
35	Alaska	1,485	0.74%	2	Texas	11,533	5.72%
31	Arizona	2,025	1.00%	3	Georgia	10,305	5.11%
18	Arkansas	4,315	2.14%	4	Florida	9,043	4.49%
8	California	6,929	3.44%	5	Michigan	8,657	4.29%
32	Colorado	1,957	0.97%	6	South Carolina	8,168	4.05%
38	Connecticut	985	0.49%	7	Tennessee	7,405	3.67%
40	Delaware	964	0.48%	8	California	6,929	3.44%
4	Florida	9,043	4.49%	9	Mississippi	6,275	3.11%
3	Georgia	10,305	5.11%	10	New York	6,267	3.11%
24	Hawaii	3,406	1.69%	11	Kentucky	6,006	2.98%
30	Idaho	2,080	1.03%	12	Pennsylvania	5,710	2.83%
NA	Illinois**	NA	NA	13	Wisconsin	5,604	2.78%
14	Indiana	5,471	2.71%	14	Indiana	5,471	2.71%
28	Iowa	2,891	1.43%	14	Minnesota	5,471	2.71%
NA	Kansas**	NA	NA	16	Missouri	5,455	2.71%
11	Kentucky	6,006	2.98%	17	Ohio	5,009	2.48%
23	Louisiana	3,729	1.85%	18	Arkansas	4,315	2.14%
29	Maine	2,553	1.27%	19	Virginia	4,303	2.13%
33	Maryland	1,764	0.88%	20	Oklahoma	4,214	2.09%
45	Massachusetts	7	0.00%	21	Washington	4,173	2.07%
5	Michigan	8,657	4.29%	22	Oregon	4,062	2.02%
14	Minnesota	5,471	2.71%	23	Louisiana	3,729	1.85%
9	Mississippi	6,275	3.11%	24	Hawaii	3,406	1.69%
16	Missouri	5,455	2.71%	25	Alabama	3,387	1.68%
NA	Montana**	NA	NA	26	West Virginia	3,325	1.65%
37	Nebraska	1,299	0.64%	27	New Mexico	3,122	1.55%
36	Nevada	1,418	0.70%	28	Iowa	2,891	1.43%
44	New Hampshire	287	0.14%	29	Maine	2,553	1.27%
47	New Jersey	0	0.00%	30	Idaho	2,080	1.03%
27	New Mexico	3,122	1.55%	31	Arizona	2,025	1.00%
10	New York	6,267	3.11%	32	Colorado	1,957	0.97%
1	North Carolina	16,768	8.32%	33	Maryland	1,764	0.88%
43	North Dakota	540	0.27%	34	Vermont	1,608	0.80%
17	Ohio	5,009	2.48%	35	Alaska	1,485	0.74%
20	Oklahoma	4,214	2.09%	36	Nevada	1,418	0.70%
22	Oregon	4,062	2.02%	37	Nebraska	1,299	0.64%
12	Pennsylvania	5,710	2.83%	38	Connecticut	985	0.49%
46	Rhode Island	2	0.00%	39	Utah	979	0.49%
6	South Carolina	8,168	4.05%	40	Delaware	964	0.48%
41	South Dakota	749	0.37%	41	South Dakota	749	0.37%
7	Tennessee	7,405	3.67%	42	Wyoming	681	0.34%
2	Texas	11,533	5.72%	43	North Dakota	540	0.27%
39	Utah	979	0.49%	44	New Hampshire	287	0.14%
34	Vermont	1,608	0.80%	45	Massachusetts	7	0.00%
19	Virginia	4,303	2.13%	46	Rhode Island	2	0.00%
21	Washington	4,173	2.07%	47	New Jersey	0	0.00%
26	West Virginia	3,325	1.65%	NA	Illinois**	NA	NA
13	Wisconsin	5,604	2.78%	NA	Kansas**	NA	NA
42	Wyoming	681	0.34%	NA	Montana**	NA	NA
					District of Columbia	0	0.00%

Source: Federal Bureau of Investigation
    "Crime in the United States 1994" (Uniform Crime Reports, November 19, 1995)
*Estimated totals for rural areas, defined by the F.B.I. as other than Metropolitan Statistical Areas and other cities outside such areas. National total includes those states listed as not available. Burglary is the unlawful entry of a structure to commit a felony or theft. Attempts are included.
**Not available.

Rural Burglary Rate in 1994

National Rural Rate = 632.4 Burglaries per 100,000 Population*

ALPHA ORDER

RANK	STATE	RATE
36	Alabama	426.6
12	Alaska	779.1
20	Arizona	647.5
30	Arkansas	525.2
3	California	1,115.4
27	Colorado	536.4
32	Connecticut	516.2
4	Delaware	1,081.6
2	Florida	1,195.4
15	Georgia	725.6
1	Hawaii	1,316.3
29	Idaho	526.3
NA	Illinois**	NA
31	Indiana	517.9
40	Iowa	324.2
NA	Kansas**	NA
35	Kentucky	439.7
28	Louisiana	533.7
13	Maine	737.3
19	Maryland	657.7
45	Massachusetts	56.8
9	Michigan	832.8
21	Minnesota	624.3
24	Mississippi	564.5
34	Missouri	459.4
NA	Montana**	NA
41	Nebraska	312.4
11	Nevada	796.0
44	New Hampshire	202.1
46	New Jersey	0.0
5	New Mexico	1,044.5
14	New York	732.2
7	North Carolina	1,005.4
43	North Dakota	237.6
39	Ohio	380.6
18	Oklahoma	668.0
10	Oregon	815.0
26	Pennsylvania	539.3
46	Rhode Island	0.0
6	South Carolina	1,029.9
42	South Dakota	255.8
17	Tennessee	671.5
16	Texas	718.2
33	Utah	483.3
22	Vermont	606.5
38	Virginia	407.0
8	Washington	849.7
37	West Virginia	425.1
23	Wisconsin	572.2
25	Wyoming	543.5

RANK ORDER

RANK	STATE	RATE
1	Hawaii	1,316.3
2	Florida	1,195.4
3	California	1,115.4
4	Delaware	1,081.6
5	New Mexico	1,044.5
6	South Carolina	1,029.9
7	North Carolina	1,005.4
8	Washington	849.7
9	Michigan	832.8
10	Oregon	815.0
11	Nevada	796.0
12	Alaska	779.1
13	Maine	737.3
14	New York	732.2
15	Georgia	725.6
16	Texas	718.2
17	Tennessee	671.5
18	Oklahoma	668.0
19	Maryland	657.7
20	Arizona	647.5
21	Minnesota	624.3
22	Vermont	606.5
23	Wisconsin	572.2
24	Mississippi	564.5
25	Wyoming	543.5
26	Pennsylvania	539.3
27	Colorado	536.4
28	Louisiana	533.7
29	Idaho	526.3
30	Arkansas	525.2
31	Indiana	517.9
32	Connecticut	516.2
33	Utah	483.3
34	Missouri	459.4
35	Kentucky	439.7
36	Alabama	426.6
37	West Virginia	425.1
38	Virginia	407.0
39	Ohio	380.6
40	Iowa	324.2
41	Nebraska	312.4
42	South Dakota	255.8
43	North Dakota	237.6
44	New Hampshire	202.1
45	Massachusetts	56.8
46	New Jersey	0.0
46	Rhode Island	0.0
NA	Illinois**	NA
NA	Kansas**	NA
NA	Montana**	NA
	District of Columbia	0.0

Source: Federal Bureau of Investigation
   "Crime in the United States 1994" (Uniform Crime Reports, November 19, 1995)
*Estimated rates for rural areas, defined by the F.B.I. as other than Metropolitan Statistical Areas and other cities outside such areas. National rate includes those states listed as not available. Burglary is the unlawful entry of a structure to commit a felony or theft. Attempts are included.
**Not available.

Percent of Burglaries Occurring in Rural Areas in 1994

National Percent = 7.43% of Burglaries*

ALPHA ORDER			RANK ORDER		
RANK	STATE	PERCENT	RANK	STATE	PERCENT
30	Alabama	7.69	1	Vermont	37.62
3	Alaska	30.63	2	West Virginia	31.15
43	Arizona	3.37	3	Alaska	30.63
16	Arkansas	16.03	4	Maine	28.56
44	California	1.80	5	North Dakota	26.09
35	Colorado	5.78	6	Idaho	25.53
41	Connecticut	3.38	7	Hawaii	24.28
13	Delaware	17.28	8	Wyoming	21.99
39	Florida	3.81	9	Kentucky	20.91
20	Georgia	12.66	10	South Dakota	19.02
7	Hawaii	24.28	11	Mississippi	18.19
6	Idaho	25.53	12	South Carolina	17.50
NA	Illinois**	NA	13	Delaware	17.28
24	Indiana	11.18	14	Wisconsin	17.07
17	Iowa	15.32	15	North Carolina	16.10
NA	Kansas**	NA	16	Arkansas	16.03
9	Kentucky	20.91	17	Iowa	15.32
33	Louisiana	6.76	18	Minnesota	15.13
4	Maine	28.56	19	New Mexico	14.23
41	Maryland	3.38	20	Georgia	12.66
46	Massachusetts	0.01	21	Tennessee	12.53
28	Michigan	9.43	22	Oregon	11.96
18	Minnesota	15.13	23	Nebraska	11.85
11	Mississippi	18.19	24	Indiana	11.18
27	Missouri	9.82	25	Oklahoma	10.34
NA	Montana**	NA	26	Virginia	10.28
23	Nebraska	11.85	27	Missouri	9.82
32	Nevada	7.19	28	Michigan	9.43
36	New Hampshire	5.44	29	Pennsylvania	8.59
47	New Jersey	0.00	30	Alabama	7.69
19	New Mexico	14.23	31	Washington	7.48
39	New York	3.81	32	Nevada	7.19
15	North Carolina	16.10	33	Louisiana	6.76
5	North Dakota	26.09	34	Utah	6.49
38	Ohio	5.21	35	Colorado	5.78
25	Oklahoma	10.34	36	New Hampshire	5.44
22	Oregon	11.96	37	Texas	5.37
29	Pennsylvania	8.59	38	Ohio	5.21
45	Rhode Island	0.02	39	Florida	3.81
12	South Carolina	17.50	39	New York	3.81
10	South Dakota	19.02	41	Connecticut	3.38
21	Tennessee	12.53	41	Maryland	3.38
37	Texas	5.37	43	Arizona	3.37
34	Utah	6.49	44	California	1.80
1	Vermont	37.62	45	Rhode Island	0.02
26	Virginia	10.28	46	Massachusetts	0.01
31	Washington	7.48	47	New Jersey	0.00
2	West Virginia	31.15	NA	Illinois**	NA
14	Wisconsin	17.07	NA	Kansas**	NA
8	Wyoming	21.99	NA	Montana**	NA
				District of Columbia	0.00

Source: Morgan Quitno Press using data from Federal Bureau of Investigation
    "Crime in the United States 1994" (Uniform Crime Reports, November 19, 1995)
*Estimated percentages for rural areas, defined by the F.B.I. as other than Metropolitan Statistical Areas and other cities outside such areas. National percent includes those states listed as not available. Burglary is the unlawful entry of a structure to commit a felony or theft. Attempts are included.
**Not available.

Larceny and Theft in Urban Areas in 1994

National Total = 7,542,982 Larcenies and Thefts*

ALPHA ORDER

RANK	STATE	THEFTS	% of USA
23	Alabama	116,118	1.54%
42	Alaska	18,717	0.25%
12	Arizona	186,905	2.48%
32	Arkansas	62,112	0.82%
1	California	920,101	12.20%
21	Colorado	121,455	1.61%
27	Connecticut	82,941	1.10%
43	Delaware	15,920	0.21%
2	Florida	611,893	8.11%
7	Georgia	237,060	3.14%
36	Hawaii	44,590	0.59%
37	Idaho	27,785	0.37%
NA	Illinois**	NA	NA
17	Indiana	149,814	1.99%
30	Iowa	64,326	0.85%
NA	Kansas**	NA	NA
29	Kentucky	65,950	0.87%
15	Louisiana	155,733	2.06%
38	Maine	24,975	0.33%
14	Maryland	165,004	2.19%
19	Massachusetts	129,925	1.72%
6	Michigan	276,054	3.66%
22	Minnesota	121,314	1.61%
31	Mississippi	63,973	0.85%
16	Missouri	151,206	2.00%
NA	Montana**	NA	NA
35	Nebraska	44,834	0.59%
34	Nevada	48,542	0.64%
41	New Hampshire	21,631	0.29%
11	New Jersey	195,618	2.59%
33	New Mexico	53,872	0.71%
4	New York	442,083	5.86%
9	North Carolina	207,742	2.75%
46	North Dakota	12,504	0.17%
5	Ohio	286,527	3.80%
26	Oklahoma	99,277	1.32%
24	Oregon	114,500	1.52%
8	Pennsylvania	214,770	2.85%
39	Rhode Island	23,021	0.31%
25	South Carolina	106,814	1.42%
44	South Dakota	14,039	0.19%
18	Tennessee	130,201	1.73%
3	Texas	608,907	8.07%
28	Utah	71,659	0.95%
47	Vermont	11,246	0.15%
13	Virginia	172,539	2.29%
10	Washington	203,775	2.70%
40	West Virginia	23,015	0.31%
20	Wisconsin	126,401	1.68%
45	Wyoming	13,574	0.18%

RANK ORDER

RANK	STATE	THEFTS	% of USA
1	California	920,101	12.20%
2	Florida	611,893	8.11%
3	Texas	608,907	8.07%
4	New York	442,083	5.86%
5	Ohio	286,527	3.80%
6	Michigan	276,054	3.66%
7	Georgia	237,060	3.14%
8	Pennsylvania	214,770	2.85%
9	North Carolina	207,742	2.75%
10	Washington	203,775	2.70%
11	New Jersey	195,618	2.59%
12	Arizona	186,905	2.48%
13	Virginia	172,539	2.29%
14	Maryland	165,004	2.19%
15	Louisiana	155,733	2.06%
16	Missouri	151,206	2.00%
17	Indiana	149,814	1.99%
18	Tennessee	130,201	1.73%
19	Massachusetts	129,925	1.72%
20	Wisconsin	126,401	1.68%
21	Colorado	121,455	1.61%
22	Minnesota	121,314	1.61%
23	Alabama	116,118	1.54%
24	Oregon	114,500	1.52%
25	South Carolina	106,814	1.42%
26	Oklahoma	99,277	1.32%
27	Connecticut	82,941	1.10%
28	Utah	71,659	0.95%
29	Kentucky	65,950	0.87%
30	Iowa	64,326	0.85%
31	Mississippi	63,973	0.85%
32	Arkansas	62,112	0.82%
33	New Mexico	53,872	0.71%
34	Nevada	48,542	0.64%
35	Nebraska	44,834	0.59%
36	Hawaii	44,590	0.59%
37	Idaho	27,785	0.37%
38	Maine	24,975	0.33%
39	Rhode Island	23,021	0.31%
40	West Virginia	23,015	0.31%
41	New Hampshire	21,631	0.29%
42	Alaska	18,717	0.25%
43	Delaware	15,920	0.21%
44	South Dakota	14,039	0.19%
45	Wyoming	13,574	0.18%
46	North Dakota	12,504	0.17%
47	Vermont	11,246	0.15%
NA	Illinois**	NA	NA
NA	Kansas**	NA	NA
NA	Montana**	NA	NA
	District of Columbia	29,711	0.39%

Source: Morgan Quitno Press using data from Federal Bureau of Investigation
  "Crime in the United States 1994" (Uniform Crime Reports, November 19, 1995)
*Estimated totals for urban areas, defined by the F.B.I. as Metropolitan Statistical Areas and other cities outside such areas. National total includes those states listed as not available. Larceny and theft is the unlawful taking of property without use of force, violence or fraud. Attempts are included. Motor vehicle thefts are excluded.
**Not available.

Urban Larceny and Theft Rate in 1994

National Urban Rate = 3,301.6 Larcenies and Thefts per 100,000 Population*

ALPHA ORDER			RANK ORDER		
RANK	STATE	RATE	RANK	STATE	RATE
25	Alabama	3,390.2	1	Arizona	4,967.9
4	Alaska	4,505.8	2	Hawaii	4,845.5
1	Arizona	4,967.9	3	Florida	4,636.8
14	Arkansas	3,807.1	4	Alaska	4,505.8
35	California	2,986.4	5	Oregon	4,425.0
21	Colorado	3,690.3	6	Louisiana	4,306.4
38	Connecticut	2,689.2	7	Georgia	4,207.1
40	Delaware	2,580.8	8	Utah	4,201.8
3	Florida	4,636.8	9	Washington	4,199.9
7	Georgia	4,207.1	10	Mississippi	4,107.7
2	Hawaii	4,845.5	11	New Mexico	3,975.5
17	Idaho	3,765.9	12	Wyoming	3,870.5
NA	Illinois**	NA	13	North Carolina	3,845.5
31	Indiana	3,190.5	14	Arkansas	3,807.1
26	Iowa	3,320.6	15	Nevada	3,795.7
NA	Kansas**	NA	16	Oklahoma	3,778.9
39	Kentucky	2,679.8	17	Idaho	3,765.9
6	Louisiana	4,306.4	18	South Carolina	3,720.5
37	Maine	2,794.5	19	Nebraska	3,713.7
24	Maryland	3,482.7	20	Missouri	3,696.4
46	Massachusetts	2,155.1	21	Colorado	3,690.3
29	Michigan	3,264.4	22	Texas	3,630.5
27	Minnesota	3,287.1	23	Vermont	3,571.6
10	Mississippi	4,107.7	24	Maryland	3,482.7
20	Missouri	3,696.4	25	Alabama	3,390.2
NA	Montana**	NA	26	Iowa	3,320.6
19	Nebraska	3,713.7	27	Minnesota	3,287.1
15	Nevada	3,795.7	28	South Dakota	3,278.8
45	New Hampshire	2,174.0	29	Michigan	3,264.4
42	New Jersey	2,474.9	30	Tennessee	3,197.3
11	New Mexico	3,975.5	31	Indiana	3,190.5
41	New York	2,553.5	32	Virginia	3,140.1
13	North Carolina	3,845.5	33	Wisconsin	3,081.0
34	North Dakota	3,044.5	34	North Dakota	3,044.5
36	Ohio	2,927.9	35	California	2,986.4
16	Oklahoma	3,778.9	36	Ohio	2,927.9
5	Oregon	4,425.0	37	Maine	2,794.5
47	Pennsylvania	1,953.7	38	Connecticut	2,689.2
43	Rhode Island	2,309.0	39	Kentucky	2,679.8
18	South Carolina	3,720.5	40	Delaware	2,580.8
28	South Dakota	3,278.8	41	New York	2,553.5
30	Tennessee	3,197.3	42	New Jersey	2,474.9
22	Texas	3,630.5	43	Rhode Island	2,309.0
8	Utah	4,201.8	44	West Virginia	2,213.2
23	Vermont	3,571.6	45	New Hampshire	2,174.0
32	Virginia	3,140.1	46	Massachusetts	2,155.1
9	Washington	4,199.9	47	Pennsylvania	1,953.7
44	West Virginia	2,213.2	NA	Illinois**	NA
33	Wisconsin	3,081.0	NA	Kansas**	NA
12	Wyoming	3,870.5	NA	Montana**	NA
				District of Columbia	5,212.5

Source: Morgan Quitno Press using data from Federal Bureau of Investigation
    "Crime in the United States 1994" (Uniform Crime Reports, November 19, 1995)
*Estimated rates for urban areas, defined by the F.B.I. as Metropolitan Statistical Areas and other cities outside
such areas. National rate includes those states listed as not available. Larceny and theft is the unlawful taking of
property without use of force, violence or fraud. Attempts are included. Motor vehicle thefts are excluded.
**Not available.

Percent of Larcenies and Thefts Occurring in Urban Areas in 1994

National Percent = 95.77% of Larcenies and Thefts*

RANK	STATE	PERCENT
12	Alabama	96.80
43	Alaska	85.76
5	Arizona	98.04
35	Arkansas	90.70
4	California	98.97
19	Colorado	95.18
6	Connecticut	97.90
32	Delaware	92.18
9	Florida	97.66
29	Georgia	92.53
47	Hawaii	80.69
45	Idaho	85.24
NA	Illinois**	NA
25	Indiana	93.61
34	Iowa	91.23
NA	Kansas**	NA
38	Kentucky	89.79
22	Louisiana	94.91
40	Maine	88.39
7	Maryland	97.86
2	Massachusetts	99.97
20	Michigan	95.13
30	Minnesota	92.36
36	Mississippi	90.59
17	Missouri	95.53
NA	Montana**	NA
31	Nebraska	92.35
26	Nevada	93.54
11	New Hampshire	97.17
1	New Jersey	100.00
24	New Mexico	93.95
8	New York	97.74
33	North Carolina	91.95
37	North Dakota	89.96
14	Ohio	96.22
18	Oklahoma	95.44
27	Oregon	93.46
13	Pennsylvania	96.62
3	Rhode Island	99.92
42	South Carolina	87.37
41	South Dakota	88.21
23	Tennessee	94.23
10	Texas	97.59
15	Utah	96.12
44	Vermont	85.49
21	Virginia	95.00
16	Washington	96.03
46	West Virginia	81.65
28	Wisconsin	93.24
39	Wyoming	88.99

RANK	STATE	PERCENT
1	New Jersey	100.00
2	Massachusetts	99.97
3	Rhode Island	99.92
4	California	98.97
5	Arizona	98.04
6	Connecticut	97.90
7	Maryland	97.86
8	New York	97.74
9	Florida	97.66
10	Texas	97.59
11	New Hampshire	97.17
12	Alabama	96.80
13	Pennsylvania	96.62
14	Ohio	96.22
15	Utah	96.12
16	Washington	96.03
17	Missouri	95.53
18	Oklahoma	95.44
19	Colorado	95.18
20	Michigan	95.13
21	Virginia	95.00
22	Louisiana	94.91
23	Tennessee	94.23
24	New Mexico	93.95
25	Indiana	93.61
26	Nevada	93.54
27	Oregon	93.46
28	Wisconsin	93.24
29	Georgia	92.53
30	Minnesota	92.36
31	Nebraska	92.35
32	Delaware	92.18
33	North Carolina	91.95
34	Iowa	91.23
35	Arkansas	90.70
36	Mississippi	90.59
37	North Dakota	89.96
38	Kentucky	89.79
39	Wyoming	88.99
40	Maine	88.39
41	South Dakota	88.21
42	South Carolina	87.37
43	Alaska	85.76
44	Vermont	85.49
45	Idaho	85.24
46	West Virginia	81.65
47	Hawaii	80.69
NA	Illinois**	NA
NA	Kansas**	NA
NA	Montana**	NA
	District of Columbia	100.00

Source: Morgan Quitno Press using data from Federal Bureau of Investigation
    "Crime in the United States 1994" (Uniform Crime Reports, November 19, 1995)
*Estimated percentages for urban areas, defined by the F.B.I. as Metropolitan Statistical Areas and other cities outside such areas. National percent includes those states listed as not available. Larceny and theft is the unlawful taking of property without use of force, violence or fraud. Attempts are included. Motor vehicle thefts are excluded.
**Not available.

Larceny and Theft in Rural Areas in 1994

National Total = 333,272 Larcenies and Thefts*

ALPHA ORDER

RANK	STATE	THEFTS	% of USA
29	Alabama	3,833	1.15%
36	Alaska	3,107	0.93%
30	Arizona	3,744	1.12%
23	Arkansas	6,366	1.91%
12	California	9,539	2.86%
25	Colorado	6,145	1.84%
40	Connecticut	1,780	0.53%
43	Delaware	1,350	0.41%
5	Florida	14,685	4.41%
1	Georgia	19,148	5.75%
8	Hawaii	10,670	3.20%
27	Idaho	4,812	1.44%
NA	Illinois**	NA	NA
10	Indiana	10,229	3.07%
24	Iowa	6,181	1.85%
NA	Kansas**	NA	NA
20	Kentucky	7,499	2.25%
16	Louisiana	8,348	2.50%
35	Maine	3,282	0.98%
32	Maryland	3,604	1.08%
45	Massachusetts	37	0.01%
6	Michigan	14,118	4.24%
11	Minnesota	10,030	3.01%
22	Mississippi	6,648	1.99%
21	Missouri	7,077	2.12%
NA	Montana**	NA	NA
31	Nebraska	3,713	1.11%
34	Nevada	3,351	1.01%
44	New Hampshire	629	0.19%
47	New Jersey	0	0.00%
33	New Mexico	3,471	1.04%
9	New York	10,239	3.07%
2	North Carolina	18,195	5.46%
42	North Dakota	1,395	0.42%
7	Ohio	11,265	3.38%
28	Oklahoma	4,748	1.42%
17	Oregon	8,006	2.40%
19	Pennsylvania	7,510	2.25%
46	Rhode Island	18	0.01%
3	South Carolina	15,438	4.63%
39	South Dakota	1,877	0.56%
18	Tennessee	7,972	2.39%
4	Texas	15,040	4.51%
37	Utah	2,895	0.87%
38	Vermont	1,908	0.57%
14	Virginia	9,080	2.72%
15	Washington	8,423	2.53%
26	West Virginia	5,174	1.55%
13	Wisconsin	9,158	2.75%
41	Wyoming	1,680	0.50%

RANK ORDER

RANK	STATE	THEFTS	% of USA
1	Georgia	19,148	5.75%
2	North Carolina	18,195	5.46%
3	South Carolina	15,438	4.63%
4	Texas	15,040	4.51%
5	Florida	14,685	4.41%
6	Michigan	14,118	4.24%
7	Ohio	11,265	3.38%
8	Hawaii	10,670	3.20%
9	New York	10,239	3.07%
10	Indiana	10,229	3.07%
11	Minnesota	10,030	3.01%
12	California	9,539	2.86%
13	Wisconsin	9,158	2.75%
14	Virginia	9,080	2.72%
15	Washington	8,423	2.53%
16	Louisiana	8,348	2.50%
17	Oregon	8,006	2.40%
18	Tennessee	7,972	2.39%
19	Pennsylvania	7,510	2.25%
20	Kentucky	7,499	2.25%
21	Missouri	7,077	2.12%
22	Mississippi	6,648	1.99%
23	Arkansas	6,366	1.91%
24	Iowa	6,181	1.85%
25	Colorado	6,145	1.84%
26	West Virginia	5,174	1.55%
27	Idaho	4,812	1.44%
28	Oklahoma	4,748	1.42%
29	Alabama	3,833	1.15%
30	Arizona	3,744	1.12%
31	Nebraska	3,713	1.11%
32	Maryland	3,604	1.08%
33	New Mexico	3,471	1.04%
34	Nevada	3,351	1.01%
35	Maine	3,282	0.98%
36	Alaska	3,107	0.93%
37	Utah	2,895	0.87%
38	Vermont	1,908	0.57%
39	South Dakota	1,877	0.56%
40	Connecticut	1,780	0.53%
41	Wyoming	1,680	0.50%
42	North Dakota	1,395	0.42%
43	Delaware	1,350	0.41%
44	New Hampshire	629	0.19%
45	Massachusetts	37	0.01%
46	Rhode Island	18	0.01%
47	New Jersey	0	0.00%
NA	Illinois**	NA	NA
NA	Kansas**	NA	NA
NA	Montana**	NA	NA
	District of Columbia	0	0.00%

Source: Federal Bureau of Investigation
    "Crime in the United States 1994" (Uniform Crime Reports, November 19, 1995)
Estimated totals for rural areas, defined by the F.B.I. as other than Metropolitan Statistical Areas and other cities outside such areas. National total includes those states listed as not available. Larceny and theft is the unlawful taking of property without use of force, violence or fraud. Attempts are included. Motor vehicle thefts are excluded.
***Not available.**

Rural Larceny and Theft Rate in 1994

National Rural Rate = 1,045.6 Larcenies and Thefts per 100,000 Population*

ALPHA ORDER		
RANK	STATE	RATE
43	Alabama	482.8
7	Alaska	1,630.1
17	Arizona	1,197.2
31	Arkansas	774.9
9	California	1,535.5
6	Colorado	1,684.3
27	Connecticut	932.8
10	Delaware	1,514.7
3	Florida	1,941.3
13	Georgia	1,348.3
1	Hawaii	4,123.5
16	Idaho	1,217.6
NA	Illinois**	NA
23	Indiana	968.3
36	Iowa	693.1
NA	Kansas**	NA
42	Kentucky	549.0
19	Louisiana	1,194.8
24	Maine	947.8
14	Maryland	1,343.7
45	Massachusetts	300.4
12	Michigan	1,358.2
21	Minnesota	1,144.5
40	Mississippi	598.1
41	Missouri	596.0
NA	Montana**	NA
28	Nebraska	893.1
4	Nevada	1,881.0
44	New Hampshire	442.9
46	New Jersey	0.0
20	New Mexico	1,161.2
18	New York	1,196.3
22	North Carolina	1,090.9
39	North Dakota	613.8
30	Ohio	856.0
32	Oklahoma	752.6
8	Oregon	1,606.3
35	Pennsylvania	709.3
46	Rhode Island	0.0
2	South Carolina	1,946.6
38	South Dakota	641.0
33	Tennessee	722.9
25	Texas	936.6
11	Utah	1,429.1
34	Vermont	719.7
29	Virginia	858.8
5	Washington	1,715.1
37	West Virginia	661.5
26	Wisconsin	935.0
15	Wyoming	1,340.8

RANK ORDER		
RANK	STATE	RATE
1	Hawaii	4,123.5
2	South Carolina	1,946.6
3	Florida	1,941.3
4	Nevada	1,881.0
5	Washington	1,715.1
6	Colorado	1,684.3
7	Alaska	1,630.1
8	Oregon	1,606.3
9	California	1,535.5
10	Delaware	1,514.7
11	Utah	1,429.1
12	Michigan	1,358.2
13	Georgia	1,348.3
14	Maryland	1,343.7
15	Wyoming	1,340.8
16	Idaho	1,217.6
17	Arizona	1,197.2
18	New York	1,196.3
19	Louisiana	1,194.8
20	New Mexico	1,161.2
21	Minnesota	1,144.5
22	North Carolina	1,090.9
23	Indiana	968.3
24	Maine	947.8
25	Texas	936.6
26	Wisconsin	935.0
27	Connecticut	932.8
28	Nebraska	893.1
29	Virginia	858.8
30	Ohio	856.0
31	Arkansas	774.9
32	Oklahoma	752.6
33	Tennessee	722.9
34	Vermont	719.7
35	Pennsylvania	709.3
36	Iowa	693.1
37	West Virginia	661.5
38	South Dakota	641.0
39	North Dakota	613.8
40	Mississippi	598.1
41	Missouri	596.0
42	Kentucky	549.0
43	Alabama	482.8
44	New Hampshire	442.9
45	Massachusetts	300.4
46	New Jersey	0.0
46	Rhode Island	0.0
NA	Illinois**	NA
NA	Kansas**	NA
NA	Montana**	NA
	District of Columbia	0.0

Source: Federal Bureau of Investigation
    "Crime in the United States 1994" (Uniform Crime Reports, November 19, 1995)
*Estimated rates for rural areas, defined by the F.B.I. as other than Metropolitan Statistical Areas and other cities outside such areas. National rate includes those states listed as not available. Larceny and theft is the unlawful taking of property without use of force, violence or fraud. Attempts are included. Motor vehicle thefts are excluded.
**Not available.

Percent of Larcenies and Thefts Occurring in Rural Areas in 1994

National Percent = 4.23% of Larcenies and Thefts*

ALPHA ORDER

RANK ORDER

RANK	STATE	PERCENT
36	Alabama	3.20
5	Alaska	14.24
43	Arizona	1.96
13	Arkansas	9.30
44	California	1.03
29	Colorado	4.82
42	Connecticut	2.10
16	Delaware	7.82
39	Florida	2.34
19	Georgia	7.47
1	Hawaii	19.31
3	Idaho	14.76
NA	Illinois**	NA
23	Indiana	6.39
14	Iowa	8.77
NA	Kansas**	NA
10	Kentucky	10.21
26	Louisiana	5.09
8	Maine	11.61
41	Maryland	2.14
46	Massachusetts	0.03
28	Michigan	4.87
18	Minnesota	7.64
12	Mississippi	9.41
31	Missouri	4.47
NA	Montana**	NA
17	Nebraska	7.65
22	Nevada	6.46
37	New Hampshire	2.83
47	New Jersey	0.00
24	New Mexico	6.05
40	New York	2.26
15	North Carolina	8.05
11	North Dakota	10.04
34	Ohio	3.78
30	Oklahoma	4.56
21	Oregon	6.54
35	Pennsylvania	3.38
45	Rhode Island	0.08
6	South Carolina	12.63
7	South Dakota	11.79
25	Tennessee	5.77
38	Texas	2.41
33	Utah	3.88
4	Vermont	14.51
27	Virginia	5.00
32	Washington	3.97
2	West Virginia	18.35
20	Wisconsin	6.76
9	Wyoming	11.01

RANK	STATE	PERCENT
1	Hawaii	19.31
2	West Virginia	18.35
3	Idaho	14.76
4	Vermont	14.51
5	Alaska	14.24
6	South Carolina	12.63
7	South Dakota	11.79
8	Maine	11.61
9	Wyoming	11.01
10	Kentucky	10.21
11	North Dakota	10.04
12	Mississippi	9.41
13	Arkansas	9.30
14	Iowa	8.77
15	North Carolina	8.05
16	Delaware	7.82
17	Nebraska	7.65
18	Minnesota	7.64
19	Georgia	7.47
20	Wisconsin	6.76
21	Oregon	6.54
22	Nevada	6.46
23	Indiana	6.39
24	New Mexico	6.05
25	Tennessee	5.77
26	Louisiana	5.09
27	Virginia	5.00
28	Michigan	4.87
29	Colorado	4.82
30	Oklahoma	4.56
31	Missouri	4.47
32	Washington	3.97
33	Utah	3.88
34	Ohio	3.78
35	Pennsylvania	3.38
36	Alabama	3.20
37	New Hampshire	2.83
38	Texas	2.41
39	Florida	2.34
40	New York	2.26
41	Maryland	2.14
42	Connecticut	2.10
43	Arizona	1.96
44	California	1.03
45	Rhode Island	0.08
46	Massachusetts	0.03
47	New Jersey	0.00
NA	Illinois**	NA
NA	Kansas**	NA
NA	Montana**	NA
	District of Columbia	0.00

Source: Morgan Quitno Press using data from Federal Bureau of Investigation
"Crime in the United States 1994" (Uniform Crime Reports, November 19, 1995)
*Estimated percentages for rural areas, defined by the F.B.I. as other than Metropolitan Statistical Areas and other cities outside such areas. National percent includes those states listed as not available. Larceny and theft is the unlawful taking of property without use of force, violence or fraud. Attempts are included. Motor vehicle thefts are excluded. **Not available.*

Motor Vehicle Thefts in Urban Areas in 1994

National Total = 1,501,014 Motor Vehicle Thefts*

ALPHA ORDER					RANK ORDER			
RANK	STATE		THEFTS	% of USA	RANK	STATE	THEFTS	% of USA
25	Alabama		13,529	0.90%	1	California	306,178	20.40%
38	Alaska		2,856	0.19%	2	New York	128,295	8.55%
9	Arizona		43,074	2.87%	3	Florida	125,408	8.35%
32	Arkansas		6,844	0.46%	4	Texas	109,193	7.27%
1	California		306,178	20.40%	5	Michigan	61,235	4.08%
24	Colorado		13,945	0.93%	6	Pennsylvania	53,028	3.53%
19	Connecticut		19,909	1.33%	7	New Jersey	52,164	3.48%
39	Delaware		2,407	0.16%	8	Ohio	46,387	3.09%
3	Florida		125,408	8.35%	9	Arizona	43,074	2.87%
12	Georgia		36,866	2.46%	10	Massachusetts	42,338	2.82%
34	Hawaii		5,803	0.39%	11	Maryland	37,924	2.53%
42	Idaho		1,709	0.11%	12	Georgia	36,866	2.46%
NA	Illinois**		NA	NA	13	Tennessee	27,461	1.83%
17	Indiana		23,793	1.59%	14	Missouri	26,170	1.74%
37	Iowa		4,576	0.30%	15	Washington	25,965	1.73%
NA	Kansas**		NA	NA	16	Louisiana	25,716	1.71%
31	Kentucky		7,232	0.48%	17	Indiana	23,793	1.59%
16	Louisiana		25,716	1.71%	18	Oregon	20,654	1.38%
43	Maine		1,407	0.09%	19	Connecticut	19,909	1.33%
11	Maryland		37,924	2.53%	20	North Carolina	18,869	1.26%
10	Massachusetts		42,338	2.82%	21	Wisconsin	17,362	1.16%
5	Michigan		61,235	4.08%	22	Virginia	17,273	1.15%
26	Minnesota		13,194	0.88%	23	Oklahoma	14,755	0.98%
29	Mississippi		9,721	0.65%	24	Colorado	13,945	0.93%
14	Missouri		26,170	1.74%	25	Alabama	13,529	0.90%
NA	Montana**		NA	NA	26	Minnesota	13,194	0.88%
33	Nebraska		5,940	0.40%	27	South Carolina	11,478	0.76%
28	Nevada		10,763	0.72%	28	Nevada	10,763	0.72%
41	New Hampshire		2,258	0.15%	29	Mississippi	9,721	0.65%
7	New Jersey		52,164	3.48%	30	New Mexico	7,661	0.51%
30	New Mexico		7,661	0.51%	31	Kentucky	7,232	0.48%
2	New York		128,295	8.55%	32	Arkansas	6,844	0.46%
20	North Carolina		18,869	1.26%	33	Nebraska	5,940	0.40%
44	North Dakota		819	0.05%	34	Hawaii	5,803	0.39%
8	Ohio		46,387	3.09%	35	Utah	5,448	0.36%
23	Oklahoma		14,755	0.98%	36	Rhode Island	5,182	0.35%
18	Oregon		20,654	1.38%	37	Iowa	4,576	0.30%
6	Pennsylvania		53,028	3.53%	38	Alaska	2,856	0.19%
36	Rhode Island		5,182	0.35%	39	Delaware	2,407	0.16%
27	South Carolina		11,478	0.76%	40	West Virginia	2,295	0.15%
45	South Dakota		757	0.05%	41	New Hampshire	2,258	0.15%
13	Tennessee		27,461	1.83%	42	Idaho	1,709	0.11%
4	Texas		109,193	7.27%	43	Maine	1,407	0.09%
35	Utah		5,448	0.36%	44	North Dakota	819	0.05%
47	Vermont		673	0.04%	45	South Dakota	757	0.05%
22	Virginia		17,273	1.15%	46	Wyoming	680	0.05%
15	Washington		25,965	1.73%	47	Vermont	673	0.04%
40	West Virginia		2,295	0.15%	NA	Illinois**	NA	NA
21	Wisconsin		17,362	1.16%	NA	Kansas**	NA	NA
46	Wyoming		680	0.05%	NA	Montana**	NA	NA
						District of Columbia	8,261	0.55%

Source: Morgan Quitno Press using data from Federal Bureau of Investigation
"Crime in the United States 1994" (Uniform Crime Reports, November 19, 1995)
*Estimated totals for urban areas, defined by the F.B.I. as Metropolitan Statistical Areas and other cities outside such areas. National total includes those states listed as not available. Motor vehicle theft includes the theft or attempted theft of a self-propelled vehicle. Excludes motorboats, construction equipment, airplanes and farming equipment. **Not available.

Urban Motor Vehicle Theft Rate in 1994

National Urban Rate = 657.0 Motor Vehicle Thefts per 100,000 Population*

ALPHA ORDER

RANK	STATE	RATE
32	Alabama	395.0
11	Alaska	687.5
1	Arizona	1,144.9
30	Arkansas	419.5
2	California	993.8
28	Colorado	423.7
16	Connecticut	645.5
33	Delaware	390.2
3	Florida	950.3
14	Georgia	654.3
18	Hawaii	630.6
40	Idaho	231.6
NA	Illinois**	NA
24	Indiana	506.7
39	Iowa	236.2
NA	Kansas**	NA
38	Kentucky	293.9
9	Louisiana	711.1
47	Maine	157.4
5	Maryland	800.5
10	Massachusetts	702.3
8	Michigan	724.1
34	Minnesota	357.5
19	Mississippi	624.2
17	Missouri	639.8
NA	Montana**	NA
25	Nebraska	492.0
4	Nevada	841.6
41	New Hampshire	226.9
13	New Jersey	660.0
20	New Mexico	565.3
7	New York	741.0
35	North Carolina	349.3
44	North Dakota	199.4
27	Ohio	474.0
21	Oklahoma	561.6
6	Oregon	798.2
26	Pennsylvania	482.4
23	Rhode Island	519.8
31	South Carolina	399.8
46	South Dakota	176.8
12	Tennessee	674.3
15	Texas	651.0
36	Utah	319.5
43	Vermont	213.7
37	Virginia	314.4
22	Washington	535.2
42	West Virginia	220.7
29	Wisconsin	423.2
45	Wyoming	193.9

RANK ORDER

RANK	STATE	RATE
1	Arizona	1,144.9
2	California	993.8
3	Florida	950.3
4	Nevada	841.6
5	Maryland	800.5
6	Oregon	798.2
7	New York	741.0
8	Michigan	724.1
9	Louisiana	711.1
10	Massachusetts	702.3
11	Alaska	687.5
12	Tennessee	674.3
13	New Jersey	660.0
14	Georgia	654.3
15	Texas	651.0
16	Connecticut	645.5
17	Missouri	639.8
18	Hawaii	630.6
19	Mississippi	624.2
20	New Mexico	565.3
21	Oklahoma	561.6
22	Washington	535.2
23	Rhode Island	519.8
24	Indiana	506.7
25	Nebraska	492.0
26	Pennsylvania	482.4
27	Ohio	474.0
28	Colorado	423.7
29	Wisconsin	423.2
30	Arkansas	419.5
31	South Carolina	399.8
32	Alabama	395.0
33	Delaware	390.2
34	Minnesota	357.5
35	North Carolina	349.3
36	Utah	319.5
37	Virginia	314.4
38	Kentucky	293.9
39	Iowa	236.2
40	Idaho	231.6
41	New Hampshire	226.9
42	West Virginia	220.7
43	Vermont	213.7
44	North Dakota	199.4
45	Wyoming	193.9
46	South Dakota	176.8
47	Maine	157.4
NA	Illinois**	NA
NA	Kansas**	NA
NA	Montana**	NA
	District of Columbia	1,449.3

Source: Morgan Quitno Press using data from Federal Bureau of Investigation
"Crime in the United States 1994" (Uniform Crime Reports, November 19, 1995)
*Estimated rates for urban areas, defined by the F.B.I. as Metropolitan Statistical Areas and other cities outside such areas. National rate includes those states listed as not available. Motor vehicle theft includes the theft or attempted theft of a self-propelled vehicle. Excludes motorboats, construction equipment, airplanes and farming equipment. **Not available.*

Percent of Motor Vehicle Thefts Occurring in Urban Areas in 1994

National Percent = 97.53% of Motor Vehicle Thefts*

ALPHA ORDER

RANK ORDER

RANK	STATE	PERCENT		RANK	STATE	PERCENT
21	Alabama	96.64		1	New Jersey	100.00
39	Alaska	87.21		2	Massachusetts	99.98
7	Arizona	99.10		2	Rhode Island	99.98
36	Arkansas	88.58		4	New York	99.55
5	California	99.34		5	California	99.34
19	Colorado	97.08		6	Maryland	99.29
8	Connecticut	98.72		7	Arizona	99.10
16	Delaware	97.41		8	Connecticut	98.72
9	Florida	98.60		9	Florida	98.60
30	Georgia	93.78		10	Texas	98.59
33	Hawaii	90.91		11	Michigan	98.28
46	Idaho	77.33		12	New Hampshire	98.09
NA	Illinois**	NA		13	Louisiana	98.08
25	Indiana	95.13		14	Pennsylvania	97.92
35	Iowa	89.80		15	Ohio	97.84
NA	Kansas**	NA		16	Delaware	97.41
43	Kentucky	84.51		17	Nevada	97.27
13	Louisiana	98.08		18	Washington	97.09
44	Maine	79.22		19	Colorado	97.08
6	Maryland	99.29		20	Missouri	96.79
2	Massachusetts	99.98		21	Alabama	96.64
11	Michigan	98.28		22	Utah	95.76
31	Minnesota	91.91		23	Oklahoma	95.43
34	Mississippi	89.93		24	Nebraska	95.25
20	Missouri	96.79		25	Indiana	95.13
NA	Montana**	NA		26	Oregon	94.90
24	Nebraska	95.25		27	Wisconsin	94.77
17	Nevada	97.27		28	Tennessee	94.71
12	New Hampshire	98.09		29	Virginia	94.44
1	New Jersey	100.00		30	Georgia	93.78
32	New Mexico	91.75		31	Minnesota	91.91
4	New York	99.55		32	New Mexico	91.75
37	North Carolina	88.41		33	Hawaii	90.91
42	North Dakota	84.96		34	Mississippi	89.93
15	Ohio	97.84		35	Iowa	89.80
23	Oklahoma	95.43		36	Arkansas	88.58
26	Oregon	94.90		37	North Carolina	88.41
14	Pennsylvania	97.92		38	Wyoming	88.20
2	Rhode Island	99.98		39	Alaska	87.21
40	South Carolina	87.06		40	South Carolina	87.06
41	South Dakota	86.81		41	South Dakota	86.81
28	Tennessee	94.71		42	North Dakota	84.96
10	Texas	98.59		43	Kentucky	84.51
22	Utah	95.76		44	Maine	79.22
45	Vermont	78.07		45	Vermont	78.07
29	Virginia	94.44		46	Idaho	77.33
18	Washington	97.09		47	West Virginia	70.10
47	West Virginia	70.10		NA	Illinois**	NA
27	Wisconsin	94.77		NA	Kansas**	NA
38	Wyoming	88.20		NA	Montana**	NA

District of Columbia   100.00

Source: Morgan Quitno Press using data from Federal Bureau of Investigation
   "Crime in the United States 1994" (Uniform Crime Reports, November 19, 1995)
*Estimated percentages for urban areas, defined by the F.B.I. as Metropolitan Statistical Areas and other cities outside such areas. National percent includes those states listed as not available. Motor vehicle theft includes the theft or attempted theft of a self-propelled vehicle. Excludes motorboats, construction equipment, airplanes and farming equipment. **Not available.

Motor Vehicle Theft in Rural Areas in 1994

National Total = 38,083 Motor Vehicle Thefts*

ALPHA ORDER

RANK	STATE	THEFTS	% of USA
29	Alabama	471	1.24%
31	Alaska	419	1.10%
32	Arizona	393	1.03%
19	Arkansas	882	2.32%
3	California	2,027	5.32%
30	Colorado	420	1.10%
37	Connecticut	258	0.68%
43	Delaware	64	0.17%
4	Florida	1,778	4.67%
2	Georgia	2,446	6.42%
24	Hawaii	580	1.52%
28	Idaho	501	1.32%
NA	Illinois**	NA	NA
9	Indiana	1,218	3.20%
26	Iowa	520	1.37%
NA	Kansas**	NA	NA
8	Kentucky	1,326	3.48%
27	Louisiana	503	1.32%
33	Maine	369	0.97%
36	Maryland	273	0.72%
45	Massachusetts	10	0.03%
14	Michigan	1,069	2.81%
10	Minnesota	1,161	3.05%
13	Mississippi	1,089	2.86%
20	Missouri	868	2.28%
NA	Montana**	NA	NA
35	Nebraska	296	0.78%
34	Nevada	302	0.79%
44	New Hampshire	44	0.12%
47	New Jersey	0	0.00%
23	New Mexico	689	1.81%
25	New York	578	1.52%
1	North Carolina	2,473	6.49%
40	North Dakota	145	0.38%
15	Ohio	1,026	2.69%
22	Oklahoma	706	1.85%
12	Oregon	1,110	2.91%
11	Pennsylvania	1,125	2.95%
46	Rhode Island	1	0.00%
5	South Carolina	1,706	4.48%
41	South Dakota	115	0.30%
7	Tennessee	1,533	4.03%
6	Texas	1,560	4.10%
38	Utah	241	0.63%
39	Vermont	189	0.50%
16	Virginia	1,016	2.67%
21	Washington	778	2.04%
17	West Virginia	979	2.57%
18	Wisconsin	959	2.52%
42	Wyoming	91	0.24%

RANK ORDER

RANK	STATE	THEFTS	% of USA
1	North Carolina	2,473	6.49%
2	Georgia	2,446	6.42%
3	California	2,027	5.32%
4	Florida	1,778	4.67%
5	South Carolina	1,706	4.48%
6	Texas	1,560	4.10%
7	Tennessee	1,533	4.03%
8	Kentucky	1,326	3.48%
9	Indiana	1,218	3.20%
10	Minnesota	1,161	3.05%
11	Pennsylvania	1,125	2.95%
12	Oregon	1,110	2.91%
13	Mississippi	1,089	2.86%
14	Michigan	1,069	2.81%
15	Ohio	1,026	2.69%
16	Virginia	1,016	2.67%
17	West Virginia	979	2.57%
18	Wisconsin	959	2.52%
19	Arkansas	882	2.32%
20	Missouri	868	2.28%
21	Washington	778	2.04%
22	Oklahoma	706	1.85%
23	New Mexico	689	1.81%
24	Hawaii	580	1.52%
25	New York	578	1.52%
26	Iowa	520	1.37%
27	Louisiana	503	1.32%
28	Idaho	501	1.32%
29	Alabama	471	1.24%
30	Colorado	420	1.10%
31	Alaska	419	1.10%
32	Arizona	393	1.03%
33	Maine	369	0.97%
34	Nevada	302	0.79%
35	Nebraska	296	0.78%
36	Maryland	273	0.72%
37	Connecticut	258	0.68%
38	Utah	241	0.63%
39	Vermont	189	0.50%
40	North Dakota	145	0.38%
41	South Dakota	115	0.30%
42	Wyoming	91	0.24%
43	Delaware	64	0.17%
44	New Hampshire	44	0.12%
45	Massachusetts	10	0.03%
46	Rhode Island	1	0.00%
47	New Jersey	0	0.00%
NA	Illinois**	NA	NA
NA	Kansas**	NA	NA
NA	Montana**	NA	NA
	District of Columbia	0	0.00%

Source: Federal Bureau of Investigation
    "Crime in the United States 1994" (Uniform Crime Reports, November 19, 1995)
*Estimated totals for rural areas, defined by the F.B.I. as other than Metropolitan Statistical Areas and other cities outside such areas. National total includes those states listed as not available. Motor vehicle theft includes the theft or attempted theft of a self-propelled vehicle. Excludes motorboats, construction equipment, airplanes and farming equipment. **Not available.

Rural Motor Vehicle Theft Rate in 1994

National Rural Rate = 119.5 Motor Vehicle Thefts per 100,000 Population*

ALPHA ORDER			RANK ORDER		
RANK	STATE	RATE	RANK	STATE	RATE
42	Alabama	59.3	1	California	326.3
6	Alaska	219.8	2	Florida	235.0
16	Arizona	125.7	3	New Mexico	230.5
22	Arkansas	107.4	4	Hawaii	224.1
1	California	326.3	5	Oregon	222.7
20	Colorado	115.1	6	Alaska	219.8
13	Connecticut	135.2	7	South Carolina	215.1
37	Delaware	71.8	8	Georgia	172.2
2	Florida	235.0	9	Nevada	169.5
8	Georgia	172.2	10	Washington	158.4
4	Hawaii	224.1	11	North Carolina	148.3
15	Idaho	126.8	12	Tennessee	139.0
NA	Illinois**	NA	13	Connecticut	135.2
19	Indiana	115.3	14	Minnesota	132.5
43	Iowa	58.3	15	Idaho	126.8
NA	Kansas**	NA	16	Arizona	125.7
29	Kentucky	97.1	17	West Virginia	125.2
36	Louisiana	72.0	18	Utah	119.0
23	Maine	106.6	19	Indiana	115.3
26	Maryland	101.8	20	Colorado	115.1
32	Massachusetts	81.2	21	Oklahoma	111.9
25	Michigan	102.8	22	Arkansas	107.4
14	Minnesota	132.5	23	Maine	106.6
27	Mississippi	98.0	24	Pennsylvania	106.3
34	Missouri	73.1	25	Michigan	102.8
NA	Montana**	NA	26	Maryland	101.8
39	Nebraska	71.2	27	Mississippi	98.0
9	Nevada	169.5	28	Wisconsin	97.9
45	New Hampshire	31.0	29	Kentucky	97.1
46	New Jersey	0.0	29	Texas	97.1
3	New Mexico	230.5	31	Virginia	96.1
40	New York	67.5	32	Massachusetts	81.2
11	North Carolina	148.3	33	Ohio	78.0
41	North Dakota	63.8	34	Missouri	73.1
33	Ohio	78.0	35	Wyoming	72.6
21	Oklahoma	111.9	36	Louisiana	72.0
5	Oregon	222.7	37	Delaware	71.8
24	Pennsylvania	106.3	38	Vermont	71.3
46	Rhode Island	0.0	39	Nebraska	71.2
7	South Carolina	215.1	40	New York	67.5
44	South Dakota	39.3	41	North Dakota	63.8
12	Tennessee	139.0	42	Alabama	59.3
29	Texas	97.1	43	Iowa	58.3
18	Utah	119.0	44	South Dakota	39.3
38	Vermont	71.3	45	New Hampshire	31.0
31	Virginia	96.1	46	New Jersey	0.0
10	Washington	158.4	46	Rhode Island	0.0
17	West Virginia	125.2	NA	Illinois**	NA
28	Wisconsin	97.9	NA	Kansas**	NA
35	Wyoming	72.6	NA	Montana**	NA

District of Columbia   0.0

Source: Federal Bureau of Investigation
"Crime in the United States 1994" (Uniform Crime Reports, November 19, 1995)
*Estimated rates for rural areas, defined by the F.B.I. as other than Metropolitan Statistical Areas and other cities outside such areas. National rate includes those states listed as not available. Motor vehicle theft includes the theft or attempted theft of a self-propelled vehicle. Excludes motorboats, construction equipment, airplanes and farming equipment. **Not available.

Percent of Motor Vehicle Thefts Occurring in Rural Areas in 1994

National Percent = 2.47% of Motor Vehicle Thefts*

RANK	STATE	PERCENT		RANK	STATE	PERCENT
27	Alabama	3.36		1	West Virginia	29.90
9	Alaska	12.79		2	Idaho	22.67
41	Arizona	0.90		3	Vermont	21.93
12	Arkansas	11.42		4	Maine	20.78
43	California	0.66		5	Kentucky	15.49
29	Colorado	2.92		6	North Dakota	15.04
40	Connecticut	1.28		7	South Dakota	13.19
32	Delaware	2.59		8	South Carolina	12.94
39	Florida	1.40		9	Alaska	12.79
18	Georgia	6.22		10	Wyoming	11.80
15	Hawaii	9.09		11	North Carolina	11.59
2	Idaho	22.67		12	Arkansas	11.42
NA	Illinois**	NA		13	Iowa	10.20
23	Indiana	4.87		14	Mississippi	10.07
13	Iowa	10.20		15	Hawaii	9.09
NA	Kansas**	NA		16	New Mexico	8.25
5	Kentucky	15.49		17	Minnesota	8.09
35	Louisiana	1.92		18	Georgia	6.22
4	Maine	20.78		19	Virginia	5.56
42	Maryland	0.71		20	Tennessee	5.29
45	Massachusetts	0.02		21	Wisconsin	5.23
37	Michigan	1.72		22	Oregon	5.10
17	Minnesota	8.09		23	Indiana	4.87
14	Mississippi	10.07		24	Nebraska	4.75
28	Missouri	3.21		25	Oklahoma	4.57
NA	Montana**	NA		26	Utah	4.24
24	Nebraska	4.75		27	Alabama	3.36
31	Nevada	2.73		28	Missouri	3.21
36	New Hampshire	1.91		29	Colorado	2.92
47	New Jersey	0.00		30	Washington	2.91
16	New Mexico	8.25		31	Nevada	2.73
44	New York	0.45		32	Delaware	2.59
11	North Carolina	11.59		33	Ohio	2.16
6	North Dakota	15.04		34	Pennsylvania	2.08
33	Ohio	2.16		35	Louisiana	1.92
25	Oklahoma	4.57		36	New Hampshire	1.91
22	Oregon	5.10		37	Michigan	1.72
34	Pennsylvania	2.08		38	Texas	1.41
45	Rhode Island	0.02		39	Florida	1.40
8	South Carolina	12.94		40	Connecticut	1.28
7	South Dakota	13.19		41	Arizona	0.90
20	Tennessee	5.29		42	Maryland	0.71
38	Texas	1.41		43	California	0.66
26	Utah	4.24		44	New York	0.45
3	Vermont	21.93		45	Massachusetts	0.02
19	Virginia	5.56		45	Rhode Island	0.02
30	Washington	2.91		47	New Jersey	0.00
1	West Virginia	29.90		NA	Illinois**	NA
21	Wisconsin	5.23		NA	Kansas**	NA
10	Wyoming	11.80		NA	Montana**	NA
					District of Columbia	0.00

Source: Morgan Quitno Press using data from Federal Bureau of Investigation
"Crime in the United States 1994" (Uniform Crime Reports, November 19, 1995)
*Estimated percentages for rural areas, defined by the F.B.I. as other than Metropolitan Statistical Areas and other cities outside such areas. National percent includes those states listed as not available. Motor vehicle theft includes the theft or attempted theft of a self-propelled vehicle. Excludes motorboats, construction equipment, airplanes and farming equipment. **Not available.

Crimes Reported at Universities and Colleges in 1994

National Total = 119,807 Reported Crimes*

ALPHA ORDER

RANK	STATE	CRIMES	% of USA
24	Alabama	1,471	1.23%
39	Alaska	274	0.23%
14	Arizona	2,892	2.41%
28	Arkansas	1,269	1.06%
1	California	17,720	14.79%
19	Colorado	2,266	1.89%
21	Connecticut	2,189	1.83%
NA	Delaware**	NA	NA
9	Florida	4,243	3.54%
7	Georgia	5,143	4.29%
NA	Hawaii**	NA	NA
NA	Idaho**	NA	NA
NA	Illinois**	NA	NA
10	Indiana	3,897	3.25%
30	Iowa	850	0.71%
NA	Kansas**	NA	NA
20	Kentucky	2,229	1.86%
16	Louisiana	2,451	2.05%
37	Maine	411	0.34%
12	Maryland	3,658	3.05%
11	Massachusetts	3,763	3.14%
6	Michigan	5,426	4.53%
26	Minnesota	1,371	1.14%
31	Mississippi	847	0.71%
29	Missouri	1,228	1.02%
NA	Montana**	NA	NA
33	Nebraska	782	0.65%
34	Nevada	730	0.61%
38	New Hampshire	312	0.26%
13	New Jersey	3,538	2.95%
36	New Mexico	694	0.58%
3	New York	6,801	5.68%
5	North Carolina	5,834	4.87%
41	North Dakota	248	0.21%
4	Ohio	6,361	5.31%
25	Oklahoma	1,388	1.16%
NA	Oregon**	NA	NA
15	Pennsylvania	2,555	2.13%
32	Rhode Island	841	0.70%
22	South Carolina	1,989	1.66%
43	South Dakota	210	0.18%
27	Tennessee	1,369	1.14%
2	Texas	10,231	8.54%
23	Utah	1,972	1.65%
42	Vermont	237	0.20%
8	Virginia	4,465	3.73%
18	Washington	2,282	1.90%
35	West Virginia	713	0.60%
17	Wisconsin	2,391	2.00%
40	Wyoming	266	0.22%

RANK ORDER

RANK	STATE	CRIMES	% of USA
1	California	17,720	14.79%
2	Texas	10,231	8.54%
3	New York	6,801	5.68%
4	Ohio	6,361	5.31%
5	North Carolina	5,834	4.87%
6	Michigan	5,426	4.53%
7	Georgia	5,143	4.29%
8	Virginia	4,465	3.73%
9	Florida	4,243	3.54%
10	Indiana	3,897	3.25%
11	Massachusetts	3,763	3.14%
12	Maryland	3,658	3.05%
13	New Jersey	3,538	2.95%
14	Arizona	2,892	2.41%
15	Pennsylvania	2,555	2.13%
16	Louisiana	2,451	2.05%
17	Wisconsin	2,391	2.00%
18	Washington	2,282	1.90%
19	Colorado	2,266	1.89%
20	Kentucky	2,229	1.86%
21	Connecticut	2,189	1.83%
22	South Carolina	1,989	1.66%
23	Utah	1,972	1.65%
24	Alabama	1,471	1.23%
25	Oklahoma	1,388	1.16%
26	Minnesota	1,371	1.14%
27	Tennessee	1,369	1.14%
28	Arkansas	1,269	1.06%
29	Missouri	1,228	1.02%
30	Iowa	850	0.71%
31	Mississippi	847	0.71%
32	Rhode Island	841	0.70%
33	Nebraska	782	0.65%
34	Nevada	730	0.61%
35	West Virginia	713	0.60%
36	New Mexico	694	0.58%
37	Maine	411	0.34%
38	New Hampshire	312	0.26%
39	Alaska	274	0.23%
40	Wyoming	266	0.22%
41	North Dakota	248	0.21%
42	Vermont	237	0.20%
43	South Dakota	210	0.18%
NA	Delaware**	NA	NA
NA	Hawaii**	NA	NA
NA	Idaho**	NA	NA
NA	Illinois**	NA	NA
NA	Kansas**	NA	NA
NA	Montana**	NA	NA
NA	Oregon**	NA	NA
	District of Columbia**	NA	NA

Source: Federal Bureau of Investigation
   "Crime in the United States 1994" (Uniform Crime Reports, November 19, 1995)
Includes murder, rape, robbery, aggravated assault, burglary, larceny-theft and motor vehicle theft. Total is only for states shown separately. Many states had incomplete reports.
**Not available.*

Crimes Reported at Universities and Colleges as a Percent of All Crimes in 1994

National Percent = 0.86% of Crimes*

RANK	STATE	PERCENT
35	Alabama	0.71
31	Alaska	0.79
27	Arizona	0.90
19	Arkansas	1.08
26	California	0.91
17	Colorado	1.17
7	Connecticut	1.47
NA	Delaware**	NA
43	Florida	0.37
14	Georgia	1.21
NA	Hawaii**	NA
NA	Idaho**	NA
NA	Illinois**	NA
6	Indiana	1.48
30	Iowa	0.82
NA	Kansas**	NA
4	Kentucky	1.66
29	Louisiana	0.85
21	Maine	1.01
15	Maryland	1.19
10	Massachusetts	1.40
20	Michigan	1.05
37	Minnesota	0.69
39	Mississippi	0.66
42	Missouri	0.44
NA	Montana**	NA
18	Nebraska	1.09
33	Nevada	0.75
22	New Hampshire	1.00
23	New Jersey	0.96
38	New Mexico	0.68
34	New York	0.74
7	North Carolina	1.47
9	North Dakota	1.42
12	Ohio	1.28
32	Oklahoma	0.76
NA	Oregon**	NA
40	Pennsylvania	0.65
1	Rhode Island	2.05
27	South Carolina	0.90
25	South Dakota	0.94
41	Tennessee	0.52
24	Texas	0.95
2	Utah	1.95
13	Vermont	1.26
3	Virginia	1.68
35	Washington	0.71
5	West Virginia	1.55
15	Wisconsin	1.19
11	Wyoming	1.30

RANK	STATE	PERCENT
1	Rhode Island	2.05
2	Utah	1.95
3	Virginia	1.68
4	Kentucky	1.66
5	West Virginia	1.55
6	Indiana	1.48
7	Connecticut	1.47
7	North Carolina	1.47
9	North Dakota	1.42
10	Massachusetts	1.40
11	Wyoming	1.30
12	Ohio	1.28
13	Vermont	1.26
14	Georgia	1.21
15	Maryland	1.19
15	Wisconsin	1.19
17	Colorado	1.17
18	Nebraska	1.09
19	Arkansas	1.08
20	Michigan	1.05
21	Maine	1.01
22	New Hampshire	1.00
23	New Jersey	0.96
24	Texas	0.95
25	South Dakota	0.94
26	California	0.91
27	Arizona	0.90
27	South Carolina	0.90
29	Louisiana	0.85
30	Iowa	0.82
31	Alaska	0.79
32	Oklahoma	0.76
33	Nevada	0.75
34	New York	0.74
35	Alabama	0.71
35	Washington	0.71
37	Minnesota	0.69
38	New Mexico	0.68
39	Mississippi	0.66
40	Pennsylvania	0.65
41	Tennessee	0.52
42	Missouri	0.44
43	Florida	0.37
NA	Delaware**	NA
NA	Hawaii**	NA
NA	Idaho**	NA
NA	Illinois**	NA
NA	Kansas**	NA
NA	Montana**	NA
NA	Oregon**	NA
	District of Columbia**	NA

Source: Morgan Quitno Press using data from Federal Bureau of Investigation
"Crime in the United States 1994" (Uniform Crime Reports, November 19, 1995)
*Includes murder, rape, robbery and aggravated assault. Total is only for states shown separately. Many states had incomplete reports.
**Not available.

Violent Crimes Reported at Universities and Colleges in 1994

National Total = 3,095 Reported Violent Crimes*

RANK	STATE	CRIMES	% of USA
17	Alabama	75	2.42%
33	Alaska	15	0.48%
18	Arizona	71	2.29%
19	Arkansas	69	2.23%
1	California	382	12.34%
26	Colorado	30	0.97%
24	Connecticut	36	1.16%
NA	Delaware**	NA	NA
6	Florida	125	4.04%
13	Georgia	109	3.52%
NA	Hawaii**	NA	NA
NA	Idaho**	NA	NA
NA	Illinois**	NA	NA
9	Indiana	114	3.68%
37	Iowa	6	0.19%
NA	Kansas**	NA	NA
12	Kentucky	110	3.55%
10	Louisiana	113	3.65%
43	Maine	0	0.00%
11	Maryland	111	3.59%
14	Massachusetts	107	3.46%
6	Michigan	125	4.04%
30	Minnesota	21	0.68%
21	Mississippi	43	1.39%
29	Missouri	22	0.71%
NA	Montana**	NA	NA
37	Nebraska	6	0.19%
31	Nevada	18	0.58%
35	New Hampshire	8	0.26%
8	New Jersey	121	3.91%
35	New Mexico	8	0.26%
15	New York	105	3.39%
3	North Carolina	221	7.14%
39	North Dakota	4	0.13%
5	Ohio	138	4.46%
25	Oklahoma	34	1.10%
NA	Oregon**	NA	NA
16	Pennsylvania	85	2.75%
34	Rhode Island	12	0.39%
20	South Carolina	64	2.07%
39	South Dakota	4	0.13%
22	Tennessee	41	1.32%
2	Texas	273	8.82%
28	Utah	27	0.87%
42	Vermont	2	0.06%
4	Virginia	151	4.88%
23	Washington	39	1.26%
32	West Virginia	17	0.55%
26	Wisconsin	30	0.97%
41	Wyoming	3	0.10%

RANK	STATE	CRIMES	% of USA
1	California	382	12.34%
2	Texas	273	8.82%
3	North Carolina	221	7.14%
4	Virginia	151	4.88%
5	Ohio	138	4.46%
6	Florida	125	4.04%
6	Michigan	125	4.04%
8	New Jersey	121	3.91%
9	Indiana	114	3.68%
10	Louisiana	113	3.65%
11	Maryland	111	3.59%
12	Kentucky	110	3.55%
13	Georgia	109	3.52%
14	Massachusetts	107	3.46%
15	New York	105	3.39%
16	Pennsylvania	85	2.75%
17	Alabama	75	2.42%
18	Arizona	71	2.29%
19	Arkansas	69	2.23%
20	South Carolina	64	2.07%
21	Mississippi	43	1.39%
22	Tennessee	41	1.32%
23	Washington	39	1.26%
24	Connecticut	36	1.16%
25	Oklahoma	34	1.10%
26	Colorado	30	0.97%
26	Wisconsin	30	0.97%
28	Utah	27	0.87%
29	Missouri	22	0.71%
30	Minnesota	21	0.68%
31	Nevada	18	0.58%
32	West Virginia	17	0.55%
33	Alaska	15	0.48%
34	Rhode Island	12	0.39%
35	New Hampshire	8	0.26%
35	New Mexico	8	0.26%
37	Iowa	6	0.19%
37	Nebraska	6	0.19%
39	North Dakota	4	0.13%
39	South Dakota	4	0.13%
41	Wyoming	3	0.10%
42	Vermont	2	0.06%
43	Maine	0	0.00%
NA	Delaware**	NA	NA
NA	Hawaii**	NA	NA
NA	Idaho**	NA	NA
NA	Illinois**	NA	NA
NA	Kansas**	NA	NA
NA	Montana**	NA	NA
NA	Oregon**	NA	NA
	District of Columbia**	NA	NA

Source: Federal Bureau of Investigation
"Crime in the United States 1994" (Uniform Crime Reports, November 19, 1995)
*Includes murder, rape, robbery and aggravated assault. Total is only for states shown separately. Many states had incomplete reports.
**Not available.

Violent Crimes Reported at Universities and Colleges
As a Percent of All Violent Crimes in 1994
National Percent = 0.17% of Violent Crimes*

ALPHA ORDER				RANK ORDER		
RANK	STATE	PERCENT		RANK	STATE	PERCENT
15	Alabama	0.26		1	North Dakota	0.77
12	Alaska	0.32		2	Virginia	0.64
17	Arizona	0.25		3	New Hampshire	0.60
5	Arkansas	0.47		4	North Carolina	0.48
34	California	0.12		5	Arkansas	0.47
30	Colorado	0.16		5	Kentucky	0.47
20	Connecticut	0.24		7	Utah	0.46
NA	Delaware**	NA		8	West Virginia	0.43
38	Florida	0.08		9	Indiana	0.38
22	Georgia	0.23		10	Vermont	0.36
NA	Hawaii**	NA		11	Mississippi	0.33
NA	Idaho**	NA		12	Alaska	0.32
NA	Illinois**	NA		12	Rhode Island	0.32
9	Indiana	0.38		14	Louisiana	0.27
39	Iowa	0.07		15	Alabama	0.26
NA	Kansas**	NA		15	Ohio	0.26
5	Kentucky	0.47		17	Arizona	0.25
14	Louisiana	0.27		17	Massachusetts	0.25
43	Maine	0.00		17	New Jersey	0.25
22	Maryland	0.23		20	Connecticut	0.24
17	Massachusetts	0.25		20	South Dakota	0.24
27	Michigan	0.17		22	Georgia	0.23
33	Minnesota	0.13		22	Maryland	0.23
11	Mississippi	0.33		22	Wyoming	0.23
40	Missouri	0.06		25	Wisconsin	0.22
NA	Montana**	NA		26	Texas	0.21
37	Nebraska	0.09		27	Michigan	0.17
34	Nevada	0.12		27	Pennsylvania	0.17
3	New Hampshire	0.60		27	South Carolina	0.17
17	New Jersey	0.25		30	Colorado	0.16
42	New Mexico	0.05		30	Oklahoma	0.16
40	New York	0.06		32	Washington	0.14
4	North Carolina	0.48		33	Minnesota	0.13
1	North Dakota	0.77		34	California	0.12
15	Ohio	0.26		34	Nevada	0.12
30	Oklahoma	0.16		36	Tennessee	0.11
NA	Oregon**	NA		37	Nebraska	0.09
27	Pennsylvania	0.17		38	Florida	0.08
12	Rhode Island	0.32		39	Iowa	0.07
27	South Carolina	0.17		40	Missouri	0.06
20	South Dakota	0.24		40	New York	0.06
36	Tennessee	0.11		42	New Mexico	0.05
26	Texas	0.21		43	Maine	0.00
7	Utah	0.46		NA	Delaware**	NA
10	Vermont	0.36		NA	Hawaii**	NA
2	Virginia	0.64		NA	Idaho**	NA
32	Washington	0.14		NA	Illinois**	NA
8	West Virginia	0.43		NA	Kansas**	NA
25	Wisconsin	0.22		NA	Montana**	NA
22	Wyoming	0.23		NA	Oregon**	NA
					District of Columbia**	NA

Source: Morgan Quitno Press using data from Federal Bureau of Investigation
   "Crime in the United States 1994" (Uniform Crime Reports, November 19, 1995)
*Includes murder, rape, robbery and aggravated assault. Total is only for states shown separately. Many states had incomplete reports.
**Not available.

Property Crimes Reported at Universities and Colleges in 1994

National Total = 116,712 Reported Property Crimes*

ALPHA ORDER						RANK ORDER			
RANK	STATE		CRIMES	% of USA		RANK	STATE	CRIMES	% of USA
24	Alabama		1,396	1.20%		1	California	17,338	14.86%
40	Alaska		259	0.22%		2	Texas	9,958	8.53%
14	Arizona		2,821	2.42%		3	New York	6,696	5.74%
29	Arkansas		1,200	1.03%		4	Ohio	6,223	5.33%
1	California		17,338	14.86%		5	North Carolina	5,613	4.81%
19	Colorado		2,236	1.92%		6	Michigan	5,301	4.54%
20	Connecticut		2,153	1.84%		7	Georgia	5,034	4.31%
NA	Delaware**		NA	NA		8	Virginia	4,314	3.70%
9	Florida		4,118	3.53%		9	Florida	4,118	3.53%
7	Georgia		5,034	4.31%		10	Indiana	3,783	3.24%
NA	Hawaii**		NA	NA		11	Massachusetts	3,656	3.13%
NA	Idaho**		NA	NA		12	Maryland	3,547	3.04%
NA	Illinois**		NA	NA		13	New Jersey	3,417	2.93%
10	Indiana		3,783	3.24%		14	Arizona	2,821	2.42%
30	Iowa		844	0.72%		15	Pennsylvania	2,470	2.12%
NA	Kansas**		NA	NA		16	Wisconsin	2,361	2.02%
21	Kentucky		2,119	1.82%		17	Louisiana	2,338	2.00%
17	Louisiana		2,338	2.00%		18	Washington	2,243	1.92%
37	Maine		411	0.35%		19	Colorado	2,236	1.92%
12	Maryland		3,547	3.04%		20	Connecticut	2,153	1.84%
11	Massachusetts		3,656	3.13%		21	Kentucky	2,119	1.82%
6	Michigan		5,301	4.54%		22	Utah	1,945	1.67%
26	Minnesota		1,350	1.16%		23	South Carolina	1,925	1.65%
32	Mississippi		804	0.69%		24	Alabama	1,396	1.20%
28	Missouri		1,206	1.03%		25	Oklahoma	1,354	1.16%
NA	Montana**		NA	NA		26	Minnesota	1,350	1.16%
33	Nebraska		776	0.66%		27	Tennessee	1,328	1.14%
34	Nevada		712	0.61%		28	Missouri	1,206	1.03%
38	New Hampshire		304	0.26%		29	Arkansas	1,200	1.03%
13	New Jersey		3,417	2.93%		30	Iowa	844	0.72%
36	New Mexico		686	0.59%		31	Rhode Island	829	0.71%
3	New York		6,696	5.74%		32	Mississippi	804	0.69%
5	North Carolina		5,613	4.81%		33	Nebraska	776	0.66%
41	North Dakota		244	0.21%		34	Nevada	712	0.61%
4	Ohio		6,223	5.33%		35	West Virginia	696	0.60%
25	Oklahoma		1,354	1.16%		36	New Mexico	686	0.59%
NA	Oregon**		NA	NA		37	Maine	411	0.35%
15	Pennsylvania		2,470	2.12%		38	New Hampshire	304	0.26%
31	Rhode Island		829	0.71%		39	Wyoming	263	0.23%
23	South Carolina		1,925	1.65%		40	Alaska	259	0.22%
43	South Dakota		206	0.18%		41	North Dakota	244	0.21%
27	Tennessee		1,328	1.14%		42	Vermont	235	0.20%
2	Texas		9,958	8.53%		43	South Dakota	206	0.18%
22	Utah		1,945	1.67%		NA	Delaware**	NA	NA
42	Vermont		235	0.20%		NA	Hawaii**	NA	NA
8	Virginia		4,314	3.70%		NA	Idaho**	NA	NA
18	Washington		2,243	1.92%		NA	Illinois**	NA	NA
35	West Virginia		696	0.60%		NA	Kansas**	NA	NA
16	Wisconsin		2,361	2.02%		NA	Montana**	NA	NA
39	Wyoming		263	0.23%		NA	Oregon**	NA	NA
							District of Columbia**	NA	NA

Source: Federal Bureau of Investigation

"Crime in the United States 1994" (Uniform Crime Reports, November 19, 1995)

*Includes burglary, larceny-theft and motor vehicle theft. Total is only for states shown separately. Many states had incomplete reports.

**Not available.

Property Crimes at Universities and Colleges
As a Percent of All Property Crimes in 1994
National Percent = 0.96% of Property Crimes*

ALPHA ORDER

RANK	STATE	PERCENT
35	Alabama	0.78
32	Alaska	0.86
28	Arizona	0.96
20	Arkansas	1.16
21	California	1.07
16	Colorado	1.27
8	Connecticut	1.61
NA	Delaware**	NA
43	Florida	0.42
14	Georgia	1.34
NA	Hawaii**	NA
NA	Idaho**	NA
NA	Illinois**	NA
6	Indiana	1.62
31	Iowa	0.89
NA	Kansas**	NA
3	Kentucky	1.91
29	Louisiana	0.95
24	Maine	1.05
13	Maryland	1.37
6	Massachusetts	1.62
18	Michigan	1.19
38	Minnesota	0.74
40	Mississippi	0.69
42	Missouri	0.50
NA	Montana**	NA
19	Nebraska	1.18
32	Nevada	0.86
26	New Hampshire	1.02
21	New Jersey	1.07
35	New Mexico	0.78
30	New York	0.90
9	North Carolina	1.60
10	North Dakota	1.44
11	Ohio	1.41
34	Oklahoma	0.84
NA	Oregon**	NA
39	Pennsylvania	0.72
1	Rhode Island	2.22
23	South Carolina	1.06
27	South Dakota	0.99
41	Tennessee	0.59
24	Texas	1.05
2	Utah	2.04
15	Vermont	1.28
4	Virginia	1.78
37	Washington	0.76
5	West Virginia	1.65
17	Wisconsin	1.26
12	Wyoming	1.38

RANK ORDER

RANK	STATE	PERCENT
1	Rhode Island	2.22
2	Utah	2.04
3	Kentucky	1.91
4	Virginia	1.78
5	West Virginia	1.65
6	Indiana	1.62
6	Massachusetts	1.62
8	Connecticut	1.61
9	North Carolina	1.60
10	North Dakota	1.44
11	Ohio	1.41
12	Wyoming	1.38
13	Maryland	1.37
14	Georgia	1.34
15	Vermont	1.28
16	Colorado	1.27
17	Wisconsin	1.26
18	Michigan	1.19
19	Nebraska	1.18
20	Arkansas	1.16
21	California	1.07
21	New Jersey	1.07
23	South Carolina	1.06
24	Maine	1.05
24	Texas	1.05
26	New Hampshire	1.02
27	South Dakota	0.99
28	Arizona	0.96
29	Louisiana	0.95
30	New York	0.90
31	Iowa	0.89
32	Alaska	0.86
32	Nevada	0.86
34	Oklahoma	0.84
35	Alabama	0.78
35	New Mexico	0.78
37	Washington	0.76
38	Minnesota	0.74
39	Pennsylvania	0.72
40	Mississippi	0.69
41	Tennessee	0.59
42	Missouri	0.50
43	Florida	0.42
NA	Delaware**	NA
NA	Hawaii**	NA
NA	Idaho**	NA
NA	Illinois**	NA
NA	Kansas**	NA
NA	Montana**	NA
NA	Oregon**	NA
	District of Columbia**	NA

Source: Morgan Quitno Press using data from Federal Bureau of Investigation
"Crime in the United States 1994" (Uniform Crime Reports, November 19, 1995)
*Includes burglary, larceny-theft and motor vehicle theft. Total is only for states shown separately. Many states had incomplete reports.
**Not available.

Crimes in 1990

National Total = 14,475,613 Crimes*

ALPHA ORDER

RANK	STATE	CRIMES	% of USA
24	Alabama	198,604	1.37%
46	Alaska	28,342	0.20%
14	Arizona	289,140	2.00%
31	Arkansas	114,408	0.79%
1	California	1,965,237	13.58%
23	Colorado	199,434	1.38%
26	Connecticut	177,068	1.22%
45	Delaware	35,709	0.25%
4	Florida	1,139,934	7.87%
8	Georgia	438,161	3.03%
37	Hawaii	67,676	0.47%
42	Idaho	40,845	0.28%
5	Illinois	678,416	4.69%
19	Indiana	259,651	1.79%
32	Iowa	113,871	0.79%
29	Kansas	128,664	0.89%
30	Kentucky	121,594	0.84%
17	Louisiana	273,736	1.89%
40	Maine	45,406	0.31%
15	Maryland	278,782	1.93%
12	Massachusetts	318,742	2.20%
6	Michigan	557,232	3.85%
25	Minnesota	198,577	1.37%
34	Mississippi	99,561	0.69%
18	Missouri	262,024	1.81%
44	Montana	35,975	0.25%
38	Nebraska	66,499	0.46%
36	Nevada	72,874	0.50%
43	New Hampshire	40,435	0.28%
9	New Jersey	421,080	2.91%
33	New Mexico	101,269	0.70%
3	New York	1,144,874	7.91%
11	North Carolina	363,638	2.51%
50	North Dakota	18,668	0.13%
7	Ohio	525,373	3.63%
27	Oklahoma	176,111	1.22%
28	Oregon	160,478	1.11%
10	Pennsylvania	413,018	2.85%
39	Rhode Island	53,712	0.37%
22	South Carolina	210,779	1.46%
48	South Dakota	20,249	0.14%
20	Tennessee	246,346	1.70%
2	Texas	1,329,494	9.18%
35	Utah	97,512	0.67%
47	Vermont	24,429	0.17%
16	Virginia	274,757	1.90%
13	Washington	302,850	2.09%
41	West Virginia	44,891	0.31%
21	Wisconsin	215,000	1.49%
49	Wyoming	19,099	0.13%

RANK ORDER

RANK	STATE	CRIMES	% of USA
1	California	1,965,237	13.58%
2	Texas	1,329,494	9.18%
3	New York	1,144,874	7.91%
4	Florida	1,139,934	7.87%
5	Illinois	678,416	4.69%
6	Michigan	557,232	3.85%
7	Ohio	525,373	3.63%
8	Georgia	438,161	3.03%
9	New Jersey	421,080	2.91%
10	Pennsylvania	413,018	2.85%
11	North Carolina	363,638	2.51%
12	Massachusetts	318,742	2.20%
13	Washington	302,850	2.09%
14	Arizona	289,140	2.00%
15	Maryland	278,782	1.93%
16	Virginia	274,757	1.90%
17	Louisiana	273,736	1.89%
18	Missouri	262,024	1.81%
19	Indiana	259,651	1.79%
20	Tennessee	246,346	1.70%
21	Wisconsin	215,000	1.49%
22	South Carolina	210,779	1.46%
23	Colorado	199,434	1.38%
24	Alabama	198,604	1.37%
25	Minnesota	198,577	1.37%
26	Connecticut	177,068	1.22%
27	Oklahoma	176,111	1.22%
28	Oregon	160,478	1.11%
29	Kansas	128,664	0.89%
30	Kentucky	121,594	0.84%
31	Arkansas	114,408	0.79%
32	Iowa	113,871	0.79%
33	New Mexico	101,269	0.70%
34	Mississippi	99,561	0.69%
35	Utah	97,512	0.67%
36	Nevada	72,874	0.50%
37	Hawaii	67,676	0.47%
38	Nebraska	66,499	0.46%
39	Rhode Island	53,712	0.37%
40	Maine	45,406	0.31%
41	West Virginia	44,891	0.31%
42	Idaho	40,845	0.28%
43	New Hampshire	40,435	0.28%
44	Montana	35,975	0.25%
45	Delaware	35,709	0.25%
46	Alaska	28,342	0.20%
47	Vermont	24,429	0.17%
48	South Dakota	20,249	0.14%
49	Wyoming	19,099	0.13%
50	North Dakota	18,668	0.13%
	District of Columbia	65,389	0.45%

Source: Federal Bureau of Investigation
  "Crime in the United States 1990" (Uniform Crime Reports, August 11, 1991)
*Includes murder, rape, robbery, aggravated assault, burglary, larceny-theft and motor vehicle theft.

Percent Change in Number of Crimes: 1990 to 1994

National Percent Change = 3.3% Decrease*

ALPHA ORDER			RANK ORDER		
RANK	STATE	PERCENT CHANGE	RANK	STATE	PERCENT CHANGE
20	Alabama	4.2	1	Nevada	33.5
3	Alaska	22.1	2	Mississippi	29.7
8	Arizona	11.7	3	Alaska	22.1
23	Arkansas	2.9	4	Oregon	21.1
29	California	(1.3)	5	Montana	19.4
30	Colorado	(2.5)	6	Hawaii	16.4
44	Connecticut	(15.9)	7	Idaho	13.1
45	Delaware	(18.0)	8	Arizona	11.7
27	Florida	1.0	9	South Dakota	10.5
33	Georgia	(3.2)	10	Kentucky	10.1
6	Hawaii	16.4	11	Maryland	9.9
7	Idaho	13.1	12	North Carolina	9.4
31	Illinois	(2.6)	13	Nebraska	8.4
25	Indiana	1.7	14	Tennessee	7.6
40	Iowa	(9.2)	15	Missouri	6.9
32	Kansas	(2.9)	15	Wyoming	6.9
10	Kentucky	10.1	17	Washington	6.3
18	Louisiana	5.2	18	Louisiana	5.2
41	Maine	(10.6)	19	South Carolina	4.3
11	Maryland	9.9	20	Alabama	4.2
43	Massachusetts	(15.8)	21	Utah	3.7
39	Michigan	(7.2)	22	Oklahoma	3.1
28	Minnesota	(0.2)	23	Arkansas	2.9
2	Mississippi	29.7	24	West Virginia	2.6
15	Missouri	6.9	25	Indiana	1.7
5	Montana	19.4	26	New Mexico	1.1
13	Nebraska	8.4	27	Florida	1.0
1	Nevada	33.5	28	Minnesota	(0.2)
49	New Hampshire	(22.9)	29	California	(1.3)
42	New Jersey	(12.5)	30	Colorado	(2.5)
26	New Mexico	1.1	31	Illinois	(2.6)
47	New York	(19.5)	32	Kansas	(2.9)
12	North Carolina	9.4	33	Georgia	(3.2)
37	North Dakota	(6.5)	34	Virginia	(3.5)
36	Ohio	(5.7)	35	Pennsylvania	(4.5)
22	Oklahoma	3.1	36	Ohio	(5.7)
4	Oregon	21.1	37	North Dakota	(6.5)
35	Pennsylvania	(4.5)	38	Wisconsin	(6.8)
50	Rhode Island	(23.5)	39	Michigan	(7.2)
19	South Carolina	4.3	40	Iowa	(9.2)
9	South Dakota	10.5	41	Maine	(10.6)
14	Tennessee	7.6	42	New Jersey	(12.5)
46	Texas	(18.8)	43	Massachusetts	(15.8)
21	Utah	3.7	44	Connecticut	(15.9)
48	Vermont	(22.8)	45	Delaware	(18.0)
34	Virginia	(3.5)	46	Texas	(18.8)
17	Washington	6.3	47	New York	(19.5)
24	West Virginia	2.6	48	Vermont	(22.8)
38	Wisconsin	(6.8)	49	New Hampshire	(22.9)
15	Wyoming	6.9	50	Rhode Island	(23.5)
				District of Columbia	(3.4)

Source: Morgan Quitno Press using data from Federal Bureau of Investigation
"Crime in the United States" (Uniform Crime Reports, 1990 and 1994 editions)
*Includes murder, rape, robbery, aggravated assault, burglary, larceny-theft and motor vehicle theft.

Crime Rate in 1990

National Rate = 5,820.3 Crimes per 100,000 Population*

<table>
<tr><td colspan="3">ALPHA ORDER</td><td colspan="3">RANK ORDER</td></tr>
<tr><th>RANK</th><th>STATE</th><th>RATE</th><th>RANK</th><th>STATE</th><th>RATE</th></tr>
<tr><td>30</td><td>Alabama</td><td>4,915.2</td><td>1</td><td>Florida</td><td>8,810.8</td></tr>
<tr><td>27</td><td>Alaska</td><td>5,152.7</td><td>2</td><td>Arizona</td><td>7,888.7</td></tr>
<tr><td>2</td><td>Arizona</td><td>7,888.7</td><td>3</td><td>Texas</td><td>7,826.8</td></tr>
<tr><td>31</td><td>Arkansas</td><td>4,866.9</td><td>4</td><td>Georgia</td><td>6,763.6</td></tr>
<tr><td>6</td><td>California</td><td>6,603.6</td><td>5</td><td>New Mexico</td><td>6,684.1</td></tr>
<tr><td>12</td><td>Colorado</td><td>6,053.7</td><td>6</td><td>California</td><td>6,603.6</td></tr>
<tr><td>22</td><td>Connecticut</td><td>5,386.7</td><td>7</td><td>Louisiana</td><td>6,486.7</td></tr>
<tr><td>23</td><td>Delaware</td><td>5,360.4</td><td>8</td><td>New York</td><td>6,363.8</td></tr>
<tr><td>1</td><td>Florida</td><td>8,810.8</td><td>9</td><td>Washington</td><td>6,222.9</td></tr>
<tr><td>4</td><td>Georgia</td><td>6,763.6</td><td>10</td><td>Hawaii</td><td>6,106.7</td></tr>
<tr><td>10</td><td>Hawaii</td><td>6,106.7</td><td>11</td><td>Nevada</td><td>6,063.6</td></tr>
<tr><td>42</td><td>Idaho</td><td>4,057.1</td><td>12</td><td>Colorado</td><td>6,053.7</td></tr>
<tr><td>15</td><td>Illinois</td><td>5,935.1</td><td>13</td><td>South Carolina</td><td>6,045.2</td></tr>
<tr><td>33</td><td>Indiana</td><td>4,683.3</td><td>14</td><td>Michigan</td><td>5,994.8</td></tr>
<tr><td>41</td><td>Iowa</td><td>4,100.9</td><td>15</td><td>Illinois</td><td>5,935.1</td></tr>
<tr><td>26</td><td>Kansas</td><td>5,193.1</td><td>16</td><td>Maryland</td><td>5,830.5</td></tr>
<tr><td>47</td><td>Kentucky</td><td>3,299.4</td><td>17</td><td>Utah</td><td>5,659.9</td></tr>
<tr><td>7</td><td>Louisiana</td><td>6,486.7</td><td>18</td><td>Oregon</td><td>5,646.0</td></tr>
<tr><td>44</td><td>Maine</td><td>3,697.8</td><td>19</td><td>Oklahoma</td><td>5,598.7</td></tr>
<tr><td>16</td><td>Maryland</td><td>5,830.5</td><td>20</td><td>North Carolina</td><td>5,485.9</td></tr>
<tr><td>25</td><td>Massachusetts</td><td>5,297.9</td><td>21</td><td>New Jersey</td><td>5,447.2</td></tr>
<tr><td>14</td><td>Michigan</td><td>5,994.8</td><td>22</td><td>Connecticut</td><td>5,386.7</td></tr>
<tr><td>34</td><td>Minnesota</td><td>4,538.8</td><td>23</td><td>Delaware</td><td>5,360.4</td></tr>
<tr><td>43</td><td>Mississippi</td><td>3,869.1</td><td>24</td><td>Rhode Island</td><td>5,352.7</td></tr>
<tr><td>28</td><td>Missouri</td><td>5,120.6</td><td>25</td><td>Massachusetts</td><td>5,297.9</td></tr>
<tr><td>35</td><td>Montana</td><td>4,502.1</td><td>26</td><td>Kansas</td><td>5,193.1</td></tr>
<tr><td>39</td><td>Nebraska</td><td>4,213.1</td><td>27</td><td>Alaska</td><td>5,152.7</td></tr>
<tr><td>11</td><td>Nevada</td><td>6,063.6</td><td>28</td><td>Missouri</td><td>5,120.6</td></tr>
<tr><td>45</td><td>New Hampshire</td><td>3,645.2</td><td>29</td><td>Tennessee</td><td>5,051.0</td></tr>
<tr><td>21</td><td>New Jersey</td><td>5,447.2</td><td>30</td><td>Alabama</td><td>4,915.2</td></tr>
<tr><td>5</td><td>New Mexico</td><td>6,684.1</td><td>31</td><td>Arkansas</td><td>4,866.9</td></tr>
<tr><td>8</td><td>New York</td><td>6,363.8</td><td>32</td><td>Ohio</td><td>4,843.4</td></tr>
<tr><td>20</td><td>North Carolina</td><td>5,485.9</td><td>33</td><td>Indiana</td><td>4,683.3</td></tr>
<tr><td>48</td><td>North Dakota</td><td>2,922.4</td><td>34</td><td>Minnesota</td><td>4,538.8</td></tr>
<tr><td>32</td><td>Ohio</td><td>4,843.4</td><td>35</td><td>Montana</td><td>4,502.1</td></tr>
<tr><td>19</td><td>Oklahoma</td><td>5,598.7</td><td>36</td><td>Virginia</td><td>4,440.6</td></tr>
<tr><td>18</td><td>Oregon</td><td>5,646.0</td><td>37</td><td>Wisconsin</td><td>4,395.1</td></tr>
<tr><td>46</td><td>Pennsylvania</td><td>3,476.1</td><td>38</td><td>Vermont</td><td>4,340.9</td></tr>
<tr><td>24</td><td>Rhode Island</td><td>5,352.7</td><td>39</td><td>Nebraska</td><td>4,213.1</td></tr>
<tr><td>13</td><td>South Carolina</td><td>6,045.2</td><td>40</td><td>Wyoming</td><td>4,210.6</td></tr>
<tr><td>49</td><td>South Dakota</td><td>2,909.3</td><td>41</td><td>Iowa</td><td>4,100.9</td></tr>
<tr><td>29</td><td>Tennessee</td><td>5,051.0</td><td>42</td><td>Idaho</td><td>4,057.1</td></tr>
<tr><td>3</td><td>Texas</td><td>7,826.8</td><td>43</td><td>Mississippi</td><td>3,869.1</td></tr>
<tr><td>17</td><td>Utah</td><td>5,659.9</td><td>44</td><td>Maine</td><td>3,697.8</td></tr>
<tr><td>38</td><td>Vermont</td><td>4,340.9</td><td>45</td><td>New Hampshire</td><td>3,645.2</td></tr>
<tr><td>36</td><td>Virginia</td><td>4,440.6</td><td>46</td><td>Pennsylvania</td><td>3,476.1</td></tr>
<tr><td>9</td><td>Washington</td><td>6,222.9</td><td>47</td><td>Kentucky</td><td>3,299.4</td></tr>
<tr><td>50</td><td>West Virginia</td><td>2,503.0</td><td>48</td><td>North Dakota</td><td>2,922.4</td></tr>
<tr><td>37</td><td>Wisconsin</td><td>4,395.1</td><td>49</td><td>South Dakota</td><td>2,909.3</td></tr>
<tr><td>40</td><td>Wyoming</td><td>4,210.6</td><td>50</td><td>West Virginia</td><td>2,503.0</td></tr>
<tr><td></td><td></td><td></td><td></td><td>District of Columbia</td><td>10,774.3</td></tr>
</table>

Source: Federal Bureau of Investigation
  "Crime in the United States 1990" (Uniform Crime Reports, August 11, 1991)
*Includes murder, rape, robbery, aggravated assault, burglary, larceny-theft and motor vehicle theft.

Percent Change in Crime Rate: 1990 to 1994

National Percent Change = 7.7% Decrease*

RANK	STATE	PERCENT CHANGE
19	Alabama	(0.3)
4	Alaska	10.8
17	Arizona	0.5
22	Arkansas	(1.4)
32	California	(6.5)
41	Colorado	(12.2)
43	Connecticut	(15.6)
46	Delaware	(22.6)
30	Florida	(6.4)
39	Georgia	(11.1)
6	Hawaii	9.4
17	Idaho	0.5
26	Illinois	(5.2)
23	Indiana	(1.9)
38	Iowa	(10.9)
27	Kansas	(5.8)
8	Kentucky	6.0
12	Louisiana	2.8
40	Maine	(11.5)
10	Maryland	5.0
44	Massachusetts	(16.2)
36	Michigan	(9.2)
25	Minnesota	(4.4)
1	Mississippi	25.0
11	Missouri	3.7
2	Montana	11.5
9	Nebraska	5.4
5	Nevada	10.1
48	New Hampshire	(24.8)
42	New Jersey	(14.4)
33	New Mexico	(7.4)
45	New York	(20.3)
13	North Carolina	2.5
30	North Dakota	(6.4)
34	Ohio	(7.9)
20	Oklahoma	(0.5)
2	Oregon	11.5
28	Pennsylvania	(5.9)
47	Rhode Island	(23.1)
21	South Carolina	(0.7)
7	South Dakota	6.6
15	Tennessee	1.4
49	Texas	(25.0)
29	Utah	(6.3)
50	Vermont	(25.1)
35	Virginia	(8.9)
24	Washington	(3.1)
16	West Virginia	1.0
37	Wisconsin	(10.3)
14	Wyoming	1.9

RANK	STATE	PERCENT CHANGE
1	Mississippi	25.0
2	Montana	11.5
2	Oregon	11.5
4	Alaska	10.8
5	Nevada	10.1
6	Hawaii	9.4
7	South Dakota	6.6
8	Kentucky	6.0
9	Nebraska	5.4
10	Maryland	5.0
11	Missouri	3.7
12	Louisiana	2.8
13	North Carolina	2.5
14	Wyoming	1.9
15	Tennessee	1.4
16	West Virginia	1.0
17	Arizona	0.5
17	Idaho	0.5
19	Alabama	(0.3)
20	Oklahoma	(0.5)
21	South Carolina	(0.7)
22	Arkansas	(1.4)
23	Indiana	(1.9)
24	Washington	(3.1)
25	Minnesota	(4.4)
26	Illinois	(5.2)
27	Kansas	(5.8)
28	Pennsylvania	(5.9)
29	Utah	(6.3)
30	Florida	(6.4)
30	North Dakota	(6.4)
32	California	(6.5)
33	New Mexico	(7.4)
34	Ohio	(7.9)
35	Virginia	(8.9)
36	Michigan	(9.2)
37	Wisconsin	(10.3)
38	Iowa	(10.9)
39	Georgia	(11.1)
40	Maine	(11.5)
41	Colorado	(12.2)
42	New Jersey	(14.4)
43	Connecticut	(15.6)
44	Massachusetts	(16.2)
45	New York	(20.3)
46	Delaware	(22.6)
47	Rhode Island	(23.1)
48	New Hampshire	(24.8)
49	Texas	(25.0)
50	Vermont	(25.1)

District of Columbia   2.9

Source: Morgan Quitno Press using data from Federal Bureau of Investigation
"Crime in the United States" (Uniform Crime Reports, 1990 and 1994 editions)
*Includes murder, rape, robbery, aggravated assault, burglary, larceny-theft and motor vehicle theft.

Violent Crimes in 1990

National Total = 1,820,127 Violent Crimes*

ALPHA ORDER

RANK	STATE	CRIMES	% of USA
18	Alabama	28,630	1.57%
42	Alaska	2,885	0.16%
21	Arizona	23,911	1.31%
30	Arkansas	12,511	0.69%
1	California	311,051	17.09%
24	Colorado	17,328	0.95%
23	Connecticut	18,201	1.00%
38	Delaware	4,365	0.24%
3	Florida	160,990	8.84%
10	Georgia	48,996	2.69%
40	Hawaii	3,113	0.17%
43	Idaho	2,776	0.15%
5	Illinois	110,575	6.08%
19	Indiana	26,275	1.44%
34	Iowa	8,321	0.46%
32	Kansas	11,093	0.61%
27	Kentucky	14,386	0.79%
14	Louisiana	37,914	2.08%
44	Maine	1,759	0.10%
12	Maryland	43,940	2.41%
11	Massachusetts	44,300	2.43%
6	Michigan	73,468	4.04%
28	Minnesota	13,392	0.74%
33	Mississippi	8,758	0.48%
15	Missouri	36,602	2.01%
47	Montana	1,273	0.07%
36	Nebraska	5,209	0.29%
35	Nevada	7,222	0.40%
45	New Hampshire	1,459	0.08%
9	New Jersey	50,057	2.75%
31	New Mexico	11,821	0.65%
2	New York	212,458	11.67%
13	North Carolina	41,332	2.27%
50	North Dakota	472	0.03%
7	Ohio	54,904	3.02%
25	Oklahoma	17,222	0.95%
26	Oregon	14,405	0.79%
8	Pennsylvania	51,213	2.81%
39	Rhode Island	4,334	0.24%
16	South Carolina	34,050	1.87%
48	South Dakota	1,133	0.06%
17	Tennessee	32,698	1.80%
4	Texas	129,343	7.11%
37	Utah	4,892	0.27%
49	Vermont	716	0.04%
22	Virginia	21,694	1.19%
20	Washington	24,410	1.34%
41	West Virginia	3,036	0.17%
29	Wisconsin	12,948	0.71%
46	Wyoming	1,367	0.08%

RANK ORDER

RANK	STATE	CRIMES	% of USA
1	California	311,051	17.09%
2	New York	212,458	11.67%
3	Florida	160,990	8.84%
4	Texas	129,343	7.11%
5	Illinois	110,575	6.08%
6	Michigan	73,468	4.04%
7	Ohio	54,904	3.02%
8	Pennsylvania	51,213	2.81%
9	New Jersey	50,057	2.75%
10	Georgia	48,996	2.69%
11	Massachusetts	44,300	2.43%
12	Maryland	43,940	2.41%
13	North Carolina	41,332	2.27%
14	Louisiana	37,914	2.08%
15	Missouri	36,602	2.01%
16	South Carolina	34,050	1.87%
17	Tennessee	32,698	1.80%
18	Alabama	28,630	1.57%
19	Indiana	26,275	1.44%
20	Washington	24,410	1.34%
21	Arizona	23,911	1.31%
22	Virginia	21,694	1.19%
23	Connecticut	18,201	1.00%
24	Colorado	17,328	0.95%
25	Oklahoma	17,222	0.95%
26	Oregon	14,405	0.79%
27	Kentucky	14,386	0.79%
28	Minnesota	13,392	0.74%
29	Wisconsin	12,948	0.71%
30	Arkansas	12,511	0.69%
31	New Mexico	11,821	0.65%
32	Kansas	11,093	0.61%
33	Mississippi	8,758	0.48%
34	Iowa	8,321	0.46%
35	Nevada	7,222	0.40%
36	Nebraska	5,209	0.29%
37	Utah	4,892	0.27%
38	Delaware	4,365	0.24%
39	Rhode Island	4,334	0.24%
40	Hawaii	3,113	0.17%
41	West Virginia	3,036	0.17%
42	Alaska	2,885	0.16%
43	Idaho	2,776	0.15%
44	Maine	1,759	0.10%
45	New Hampshire	1,459	0.08%
46	Wyoming	1,367	0.08%
47	Montana	1,273	0.07%
48	South Dakota	1,133	0.06%
49	Vermont	716	0.04%
50	North Dakota	472	0.03%
	District of Columbia	14,919	0.82%

Source: Federal Bureau of Investigation
"Crime in the United States 1990" (Uniform Crime Reports, August 11, 1991)
Violent crimes are offenses of murder, rape, robbery and aggravated assault.

Percent Change in Number of Violent Crimes: 1990 to 1994

National Percent Change = 2.4% Increase*

ALPHA ORDER

RANK	STATE	PERCENT CHANGE
33	Alabama	0.8
2	Alaska	61.0
11	Arizona	19.8
15	Arkansas	16.7
31	California	2.4
27	Colorado	7.5
49	Connecticut	(18.1)
46	Delaware	(9.3)
36	Florida	(0.6)
42	Georgia	(3.9)
37	Hawaii	(0.7)
16	Idaho	16.6
32	Illinois	2.1
17	Indiana	15.0
29	Iowa	7.1
24	Kansas	10.2
2	Kentucky	61.0
20	Louisiana	11.8
44	Maine	(8.4)
25	Maryland	8.0
41	Massachusetts	(3.5)
38	Michigan	(1.0)
9	Minnesota	22.4
4	Mississippi	50.5
28	Missouri	7.2
12	Montana	19.1
10	Nebraska	21.4
1	Nevada	102.1
45	New Hampshire	(9.0)
40	New Jersey	(3.0)
7	New Mexico	24.4
48	New York	(17.4)
18	North Carolina	12.0
23	North Dakota	10.6
39	Ohio	(1.8)
8	Oklahoma	23.2
21	Oregon	11.5
34	Pennsylvania	0.4
47	Rhode Island	(13.6)
22	South Carolina	10.9
5	South Dakota	44.8
14	Tennessee	18.4
34	Texas	0.4
13	Utah	18.8
50	Vermont	(21.5)
25	Virginia	8.0
19	Washington	11.9
6	West Virginia	29.5
30	Wisconsin	6.2
43	Wyoming	(5.1)

RANK ORDER

RANK	STATE	PERCENT CHANGE
1	Nevada	102.1
2	Alaska	61.0
2	Kentucky	61.0
4	Mississippi	50.5
5	South Dakota	44.8
6	West Virginia	29.5
7	New Mexico	24.4
8	Oklahoma	23.2
9	Minnesota	22.4
10	Nebraska	21.4
11	Arizona	19.8
12	Montana	19.1
13	Utah	18.8
14	Tennessee	18.4
15	Arkansas	16.7
16	Idaho	16.6
17	Indiana	15.0
18	North Carolina	12.0
19	Washington	11.9
20	Louisiana	11.8
21	Oregon	11.5
22	South Carolina	10.9
23	North Dakota	10.6
24	Kansas	10.2
25	Maryland	8.0
25	Virginia	8.0
27	Colorado	7.5
28	Missouri	7.2
29	Iowa	7.1
30	Wisconsin	6.2
31	California	2.4
32	Illinois	2.1
33	Alabama	0.8
34	Pennsylvania	0.4
34	Texas	0.4
36	Florida	(0.6)
37	Hawaii	(0.7)
38	Michigan	(1.0)
39	Ohio	(1.8)
40	New Jersey	(3.0)
41	Massachusetts	(3.5)
42	Georgia	(3.9)
43	Wyoming	(5.1)
44	Maine	(8.4)
45	New Hampshire	(9.0)
46	Delaware	(9.3)
47	Rhode Island	(13.6)
48	New York	(17.4)
49	Connecticut	(18.1)
50	Vermont	(21.5)

District of Columbia	1.7

Source: Morgan Quitno Press using data from Federal Bureau of Investigation
   "Crime in the United States" (Uniform Crime Reports, 1990 and 1994 editions)
Violent crimes are offenses of murder, rape, robbery and aggravated assault.

Violent Crime Rate in 1990

National Rate = 731.8 Violent Crimes per 100,000 Population*

ALPHA ORDER			RANK ORDER		
RANK	STATE	RATE	RANK	STATE	RATE
14	Alabama	708.6	1	Florida	1,244.3
25	Alaska	524.5	2	New York	1,180.9
17	Arizona	652.4	3	California	1,045.2
23	Arkansas	532.2	4	South Carolina	976.6
3	California	1,045.2	5	Illinois	967.4
24	Colorado	526.0	6	Maryland	919.0
21	Connecticut	553.7	7	Louisiana	898.4
16	Delaware	655.2	8	Michigan	790.4
1	Florida	1,244.3	9	New Mexico	780.2
11	Georgia	756.3	10	Texas	761.4
41	Hawaii	280.9	11	Georgia	756.3
42	Idaho	275.7	12	Massachusetts	736.3
5	Illinois	967.4	13	Missouri	715.3
29	Indiana	473.9	14	Alabama	708.6
39	Iowa	299.7	15	Tennessee	670.4
30	Kansas	447.7	16	Delaware	655.2
33	Kentucky	390.4	17	Arizona	652.4
7	Louisiana	898.4	18	New Jersey	647.6
47	Maine	143.2	19	North Carolina	623.5
6	Maryland	919.0	20	Nevada	600.9
12	Massachusetts	736.3	21	Connecticut	553.7
8	Michigan	790.4	22	Oklahoma	547.5
37	Minnesota	306.1	23	Arkansas	532.2
35	Mississippi	340.4	24	Colorado	526.0
13	Missouri	715.3	25	Alaska	524.5
46	Montana	159.3	26	Oregon	506.8
36	Nebraska	330.0	27	Ohio	506.2
20	Nevada	600.9	28	Washington	501.6
48	New Hampshire	131.5	29	Indiana	473.9
18	New Jersey	647.6	30	Kansas	447.7
9	New Mexico	780.2	31	Rhode Island	431.9
2	New York	1,180.9	32	Pennsylvania	431.0
19	North Carolina	623.5	33	Kentucky	390.4
50	North Dakota	73.9	34	Virginia	350.6
27	Ohio	506.2	35	Mississippi	340.4
22	Oklahoma	547.5	36	Nebraska	330.0
26	Oregon	506.8	37	Minnesota	306.1
32	Pennsylvania	431.0	38	Wyoming	301.4
31	Rhode Island	431.9	39	Iowa	299.7
4	South Carolina	976.6	40	Utah	283.9
45	South Dakota	162.8	41	Hawaii	280.9
15	Tennessee	670.4	42	Idaho	275.7
10	Texas	761.4	43	Wisconsin	264.7
40	Utah	283.9	44	West Virginia	169.3
49	Vermont	127.2	45	South Dakota	162.8
34	Virginia	350.6	46	Montana	159.3
28	Washington	501.6	47	Maine	143.2
44	West Virginia	169.3	48	New Hampshire	131.5
43	Wisconsin	264.7	49	Vermont	127.2
38	Wyoming	301.4	50	North Dakota	73.9
				District of Columbia	2,458.2

Source: Federal Bureau of Investigation
"Crime in the United States 1990" (Uniform Crime Reports, August 11, 1991)
Violent crimes are offenses of murder, rape, robbery and aggravated assault.

Percent Change in Violent Crime Rate: 1990 to 1994

National Percent Change = 2.2% Decrease*

ALPHA ORDER

RANK	STATE	PERCENT CHANGE	RANK	STATE	PERCENT CHANGE
35	Alabama	(3.5)	1	Nevada	66.7
3	Alaska	46.1	2	Kentucky	55.1
17	Arizona	7.8	3	Alaska	46.1
11	Arkansas	11.8	4	Mississippi	45.0
32	California	(3.1)	5	South Dakota	39.8
32	Colorado	(3.1)	6	West Virginia	27.5
48	Connecticut	(17.7)	7	Oklahoma	19.0
47	Delaware	(14.4)	8	Nebraska	18.0
41	Florida	(7.8)	9	Minnesota	17.3
45	Georgia	(11.7)	10	New Mexico	14.0
39	Hawaii	(6.7)	11	Arkansas	11.8
24	Idaho	3.7	12	Tennessee	11.6
30	Illinois	(0.7)	13	Montana	11.2
14	Indiana	10.8	14	Indiana	10.8
21	Iowa	5.1	15	North Dakota	10.7
19	Kansas	6.9	16	Louisiana	9.3
2	Kentucky	55.1	17	Arizona	7.8
16	Louisiana	9.3	18	Utah	7.3
42	Maine	(9.3)	19	Kansas	6.9
25	Maryland	3.2	20	South Carolina	5.5
36	Massachusetts	(3.9)	21	Iowa	5.1
32	Michigan	(3.1)	21	North Carolina	5.1
9	Minnesota	17.3	23	Missouri	3.9
4	Mississippi	45.0	24	Idaho	3.7
23	Missouri	3.9	25	Maryland	3.2
13	Montana	11.2	26	Oregon	2.7
8	Nebraska	18.0	27	Wisconsin	2.2
1	Nevada	66.7	28	Virginia	2.0
44	New Hampshire	(11.2)	29	Washington	1.9
38	New Jersey	(5.2)	30	Illinois	(0.7)
10	New Mexico	14.0	31	Pennsylvania	(1.0)
49	New York	(18.2)	32	California	(3.1)
21	North Carolina	5.1	32	Colorado	(3.1)
15	North Dakota	10.7	32	Michigan	(3.1)
37	Ohio	(4.0)	35	Alabama	(3.5)
7	Oklahoma	19.0	36	Massachusetts	(3.9)
26	Oregon	2.7	37	Ohio	(4.0)
31	Pennsylvania	(1.0)	38	New Jersey	(5.2)
46	Rhode Island	(13.1)	39	Hawaii	(6.7)
20	South Carolina	5.5	40	Texas	(7.2)
5	South Dakota	39.8	41	Florida	(7.8)
12	Tennessee	11.6	42	Maine	(9.3)
40	Texas	(7.2)	43	Wyoming	(9.6)
18	Utah	7.3	44	New Hampshire	(11.2)
50	Vermont	(23.8)	45	Georgia	(11.7)
28	Virginia	2.0	46	Rhode Island	(13.1)
29	Washington	1.9	47	Delaware	(14.4)
6	West Virginia	27.5	48	Connecticut	(17.7)
27	Wisconsin	2.2	49	New York	(18.2)
43	Wyoming	(9.6)	50	Vermont	(23.8)

RANK ORDER

District of Columbia   8.3

Source: Morgan Quitno Press using data from Federal Bureau of Investigation
"Crime in the United States" (Uniform Crime Reports, 1990 and 1994 editions)
*Violent crimes are offenses of murder, rape, robbery and aggravated assault.

Murders in 1990

National Total = 23,438 Murders*

ALPHA ORDER					RANK ORDER			
RANK	STATE	MURDERS	% of USA		RANK	STATE	MURDERS	% of USA
15	Alabama	467	1.99%		1	California	3,553	15.16%
41	Alaska	41	0.17%		2	New York	2,605	11.11%
21	Arizona	284	1.21%		3	Texas	2,389	10.19%
25	Arkansas	241	1.03%		4	Florida	1,379	5.88%
1	California	3,553	15.16%		5	Illinois	1,182	5.04%
30	Colorado	138	0.59%		6	Michigan	971	4.14%
28	Connecticut	166	0.71%		7	Pennsylvania	801	3.42%
43	Delaware	33	0.14%		8	Georgia	767	3.27%
4	Florida	1,379	5.88%		9	Louisiana	724	3.09%
8	Georgia	767	3.27%		10	North Carolina	711	3.03%
39	Hawaii	44	0.19%		11	Ohio	663	2.83%
45	Idaho	27	0.12%		12	Maryland	552	2.36%
5	Illinois	1,182	5.04%		13	Virginia	545	2.33%
19	Indiana	344	1.47%		14	Tennessee	511	2.18%
36	Iowa	54	0.23%		15	Alabama	467	1.99%
35	Kansas	98	0.42%		16	Missouri	449	1.92%
22	Kentucky	264	1.13%		17	New Jersey	432	1.84%
9	Louisiana	724	3.09%		18	South Carolina	390	1.66%
44	Maine	30	0.13%		19	Indiana	344	1.47%
12	Maryland	552	2.36%		20	Mississippi	313	1.34%
24	Massachusetts	243	1.04%		21	Arizona	284	1.21%
6	Michigan	971	4.14%		22	Kentucky	264	1.13%
31	Minnesota	117	0.50%		23	Oklahoma	253	1.08%
20	Mississippi	313	1.34%		24	Massachusetts	243	1.04%
16	Missouri	449	1.92%		25	Arkansas	241	1.03%
42	Montana	39	0.17%		26	Washington	238	1.02%
40	Nebraska	43	0.18%		27	Wisconsin	225	0.96%
32	Nevada	116	0.49%		28	Connecticut	166	0.71%
47	New Hampshire	21	0.09%		29	New Mexico	139	0.59%
17	New Jersey	432	1.84%		30	Colorado	138	0.59%
29	New Mexico	139	0.59%		31	Minnesota	117	0.50%
2	New York	2,605	11.11%		32	Nevada	116	0.49%
10	North Carolina	711	3.03%		33	Oregon	108	0.46%
50	North Dakota	5	0.02%		34	West Virginia	102	0.44%
11	Ohio	663	2.83%		35	Kansas	98	0.42%
23	Oklahoma	253	1.08%		36	Iowa	54	0.23%
33	Oregon	108	0.46%		37	Utah	52	0.22%
7	Pennsylvania	801	3.42%		38	Rhode Island	48	0.20%
38	Rhode Island	48	0.20%		39	Hawaii	44	0.19%
18	South Carolina	390	1.66%		40	Nebraska	43	0.18%
48	South Dakota	14	0.06%		41	Alaska	41	0.17%
14	Tennessee	511	2.18%		42	Montana	39	0.17%
3	Texas	2,389	10.19%		43	Delaware	33	0.14%
37	Utah	52	0.22%		44	Maine	30	0.13%
49	Vermont	13	0.06%		45	Idaho	27	0.12%
13	Virginia	545	2.33%		46	Wyoming	22	0.09%
26	Washington	238	1.02%		47	New Hampshire	21	0.09%
34	West Virginia	102	0.44%		48	South Dakota	14	0.06%
27	Wisconsin	225	0.96%		49	Vermont	13	0.06%
46	Wyoming	22	0.09%		50	North Dakota	5	0.02%
						District of Columbia	472	2.01%

Source: Federal Bureau of Investigation
"Crime in the United States 1990" (Uniform Crime Reports, August 11, 1991)
*Includes nonnegligent manslaughter.

Percent Change in Number of Murders: 1990 to 1994

National Percent Change = 0.6% Decrease*

	ALPHA ORDER			RANK ORDER	
RANK	STATE	PERCENT CHANGE	RANK	STATE	PERCENT CHANGE
21	Alabama	7.3	1	Kansas	52.0
32	Alaska	(7.3)	2	Arizona	50.0
2	Arizona	50.0	3	Idaho	48.2
14	Arkansas	22.0	4	Nevada	46.6
24	California	4.2	5	Colorado	44.2
5	Colorado	44.2	6	Oregon	38.9
9	Connecticut	29.5	7	Indiana	31.7
26	Delaware	0.0	8	Mississippi	30.7
43	Florida	(15.5)	9	Connecticut	29.5
34	Georgia	(8.3)	10	New Mexico	27.3
18	Hawaii	13.6	11	Minnesota	25.6
3	Idaho	48.2	12	Washington	23.5
17	Illinois	16.6	13	Missouri	23.4
7	Indiana	31.7	14	Arkansas	22.0
40	Iowa	(13.0)	15	Nebraska	18.6
1	Kansas	52.0	16	Louisiana	18.2
33	Kentucky	(7.6)	17	Illinois	16.6
16	Louisiana	18.2	18	Hawaii	13.6
31	Maine	(6.7)	19	North Carolina	8.6
22	Maryland	4.9	20	Utah	7.7
39	Massachusetts	(11.9)	21	Alabama	7.3
29	Michigan	(4.5)	22	Maryland	4.9
11	Minnesota	25.6	23	Virginia	4.8
8	Mississippi	30.7	24	California	4.2
13	Missouri	23.4	25	Wisconsin	0.9
47	Montana	(28.2)	26	Delaware	0.0
15	Nebraska	18.6	27	Ohio	(0.2)
4	Nevada	46.6	28	West Virginia	(2.9)
45	New Hampshire	(23.8)	29	Michigan	(4.5)
34	New Jersey	(8.3)	30	Tennessee	(5.7)
10	New Mexico	27.3	31	Maine	(6.7)
44	New York	(22.6)	32	Alaska	(7.3)
19	North Carolina	8.6	33	Kentucky	(7.6)
50	North Dakota	(80.0)	34	Georgia	(8.3)
27	Ohio	(0.2)	34	New Jersey	(8.3)
37	Oklahoma	(10.7)	36	South Carolina	(9.5)
6	Oregon	38.9	37	Oklahoma	(10.7)
38	Pennsylvania	(11.1)	38	Pennsylvania	(11.1)
41	Rhode Island	(14.6)	39	Massachusetts	(11.9)
36	South Carolina	(9.5)	40	Iowa	(13.0)
48	South Dakota	(28.6)	41	Rhode Island	(14.6)
30	Tennessee	(5.7)	42	Texas	(15.4)
42	Texas	(15.4)	43	Florida	(15.5)
20	Utah	7.7	44	New York	(22.6)
49	Vermont	(53.9)	45	New Hampshire	(23.8)
23	Virginia	4.8	46	Wyoming	(27.3)
12	Washington	23.5	47	Montana	(28.2)
28	West Virginia	(2.9)	48	South Dakota	(28.6)
25	Wisconsin	0.9	49	Vermont	(53.9)
46	Wyoming	(27.3)	50	North Dakota	(80.0)
				District of Columbia	(15.5)

Source: Morgan Quitno Press using data from Federal Bureau of Investigation
    "Crime in the United States" (Uniform Crime Reports, 1990 and 1994 editions)
*Includes nonnegligent manslaughter.

Murder Rate in 1990

National Rate = 9.4 Murders per 100,000 Population*

ALPHA ORDER

RANK	STATE	RATE
7	Alabama	11.6
22	Alaska	7.5
21	Arizona	7.7
14	Arkansas	10.3
5	California	11.9
36	Colorado	4.2
29	Connecticut	5.1
30	Delaware	5.0
10	Florida	10.7
6	Georgia	11.8
37	Hawaii	4.0
42	Idaho	2.7
14	Illinois	10.3
25	Indiana	6.2
48	Iowa	1.9
37	Kansas	4.0
23	Kentucky	7.2
1	Louisiana	17.2
45	Maine	2.4
8	Maryland	11.5
37	Massachusetts	4.0
13	Michigan	10.4
42	Minnesota	2.7
4	Mississippi	12.2
18	Missouri	8.8
31	Montana	4.9
42	Nebraska	2.7
16	Nevada	9.7
48	New Hampshire	1.9
28	New Jersey	5.6
17	New Mexico	9.2
2	New York	14.5
10	North Carolina	10.7
50	North Dakota	0.8
26	Ohio	6.1
20	Oklahoma	8.0
40	Oregon	3.8
24	Pennsylvania	6.7
34	Rhode Island	4.8
9	South Carolina	11.2
47	South Dakota	2.0
12	Tennessee	10.5
3	Texas	14.1
41	Utah	3.0
46	Vermont	2.3
18	Virginia	8.8
31	Washington	4.9
27	West Virginia	5.7
35	Wisconsin	4.6
31	Wyoming	4.9

RANK ORDER

RANK	STATE	RATE
1	Louisiana	17.2
2	New York	14.5
3	Texas	14.1
4	Mississippi	12.2
5	California	11.9
6	Georgia	11.8
7	Alabama	11.6
8	Maryland	11.5
9	South Carolina	11.2
10	Florida	10.7
10	North Carolina	10.7
12	Tennessee	10.5
13	Michigan	10.4
14	Arkansas	10.3
14	Illinois	10.3
16	Nevada	9.7
17	New Mexico	9.2
18	Missouri	8.8
18	Virginia	8.8
20	Oklahoma	8.0
21	Arizona	7.7
22	Alaska	7.5
23	Kentucky	7.2
24	Pennsylvania	6.7
25	Indiana	6.2
26	Ohio	6.1
27	West Virginia	5.7
28	New Jersey	5.6
29	Connecticut	5.1
30	Delaware	5.0
31	Montana	4.9
31	Washington	4.9
31	Wyoming	4.9
34	Rhode Island	4.8
35	Wisconsin	4.6
36	Colorado	4.2
37	Hawaii	4.0
37	Kansas	4.0
37	Massachusetts	4.0
40	Oregon	3.8
41	Utah	3.0
42	Idaho	2.7
42	Minnesota	2.7
42	Nebraska	2.7
45	Maine	2.4
46	Vermont	2.3
47	South Dakota	2.0
48	Iowa	1.9
48	New Hampshire	1.9
50	North Dakota	0.8
	District of Columbia	77.8

Source: Federal Bureau of Investigation
  "Crime in the United States 1990" (Uniform Crime Reports, August 11, 1991)
*Includes nonnegligent manslaughter.

Percent Change in Murder Rate: 1990 to 1994

National Percent Change = 4.3% Decrease*

ALPHA ORDER			RANK ORDER		
RANK	**STATE**	**PERCENT CHANGE**	**RANK**	**STATE**	**PERCENT CHANGE**
19	Alabama	2.6	1	Kansas	45.0
41	Alaska	(16.0)	2	Arizona	36.4
2	Arizona	36.4	3	Idaho	29.6
12	Arkansas	16.5	4	Connecticut	29.4
22	California	(0.8)	5	Oregon	29.0
6	Colorado	28.6	6	Colorado	28.6
4	Connecticut	29.4	7	Indiana	27.4
30	Delaware	(6.0)	8	Mississippi	25.4
43	Florida	(22.4)	9	Nevada	20.6
40	Georgia	(15.3)	10	Missouri	19.3
18	Hawaii	5.0	11	Minnesota	18.5
3	Idaho	29.6	12	Arkansas	16.5
16	Illinois	13.6	13	New Mexico	16.3
7	Indiana	27.4	14	Louisiana	15.1
31	Iowa	(10.5)	15	Nebraska	14.8
1	Kansas	45.0	16	Illinois	13.6
33	Kentucky	(11.1)	17	Washington	12.2
14	Louisiana	15.1	18	Hawaii	5.0
27	Maine	(4.2)	19	Alabama	2.6
21	Maryland	0.9	20	North Carolina	1.9
36	Massachusetts	(12.5)	21	Maryland	0.9
29	Michigan	(5.8)	22	California	(0.8)
11	Minnesota	18.5	23	Virginia	(1.1)
8	Mississippi	25.4	24	Ohio	(1.6)
10	Missouri	19.3	25	Wisconsin	(2.2)
48	Montana	(32.7)	26	Utah	(3.3)
15	Nebraska	14.8	27	Maine	(4.2)
9	Nevada	20.6	28	West Virginia	(5.3)
45	New Hampshire	(26.3)	29	Michigan	(5.8)
32	New Jersey	(10.7)	30	Delaware	(6.0)
13	New Mexico	16.3	31	Iowa	(10.5)
44	New York	(23.5)	32	New Jersey	(10.7)
20	North Carolina	1.9	33	Kentucky	(11.1)
50	North Dakota	(75.0)	34	Tennessee	(11.4)
24	Ohio	(1.6)	35	Pennsylvania	(11.9)
37	Oklahoma	(13.8)	36	Massachusetts	(12.5)
5	Oregon	29.0	37	Oklahoma	(13.8)
35	Pennsylvania	(11.9)	38	South Carolina	(14.3)
39	Rhode Island	(14.6)	39	Rhode Island	(14.6)
38	South Carolina	(14.3)	40	Georgia	(15.3)
46	South Dakota	(30.0)	41	Alaska	(16.0)
34	Tennessee	(11.4)	42	Texas	(22.0)
42	Texas	(22.0)	43	Florida	(22.4)
26	Utah	(3.3)	44	New York	(23.5)
49	Vermont	(56.5)	45	New Hampshire	(26.3)
23	Virginia	(1.1)	46	South Dakota	(30.0)
17	Washington	12.2	47	Wyoming	(30.6)
28	West Virginia	(5.3)	48	Montana	(32.7)
25	Wisconsin	(2.2)	49	Vermont	(56.5)
47	Wyoming	(30.6)	50	North Dakota	(75.0)
				District of Columbia	(10.0)

Source: Morgan Quitno Press using data from Federal Bureau of Investigation
"Crime in the United States" (Uniform Crime Reports, 1990 and 1994 editions)
*Includes nonnegligent manslaughter.

Rapes in 1990

National Total = 102,555 Rapes*

ALPHA ORDER

RANK	STATE	RAPE	% of USA
26	Alabama	1,319	1.29%
40	Alaska	401	0.39%
22	Arizona	1,500	1.46%
29	Arkansas	1,019	0.99%
1	California	12,688	12.37%
21	Colorado	1,521	1.48%
32	Connecticut	918	0.90%
36	Delaware	587	0.57%
4	Florida	6,781	6.61%
8	Georgia	3,472	3.39%
42	Hawaii	360	0.35%
43	Idaho	275	0.27%
7	Illinois	4,505	4.39%
15	Indiana	2,103	2.05%
37	Iowa	510	0.50%
31	Kansas	1,002	0.98%
28	Kentucky	1,068	1.04%
19	Louisiana	1,781	1.74%
45	Maine	242	0.24%
14	Maryland	2,185	2.13%
16	Massachusetts	2,030	1.98%
3	Michigan	7,209	7.03%
23	Minnesota	1,487	1.45%
27	Mississippi	1,134	1.11%
20	Missouri	1,663	1.62%
47	Montana	195	0.19%
38	Nebraska	473	0.46%
34	Nevada	748	0.73%
41	New Hampshire	386	0.38%
12	New Jersey	2,307	2.25%
33	New Mexico	753	0.73%
5	New York	5,368	5.23%
13	North Carolina	2,272	2.22%
50	North Dakota	114	0.11%
6	Ohio	5,075	4.95%
24	Oklahoma	1,479	1.44%
25	Oregon	1,332	1.30%
10	Pennsylvania	3,068	2.99%
44	Rhode Island	248	0.24%
18	South Carolina	1,873	1.83%
46	South Dakota	239	0.23%
11	Tennessee	2,415	2.35%
2	Texas	8,750	8.53%
35	Utah	651	0.63%
48	Vermont	146	0.14%
17	Virginia	1,915	1.87%
9	Washington	3,115	3.04%
39	West Virginia	423	0.41%
30	Wisconsin	1,013	0.99%
49	Wyoming	134	0.13%

RANK ORDER

RANK	STATE	RAPE	% of USA
1	California	12,688	12.37%
2	Texas	8,750	8.53%
3	Michigan	7,209	7.03%
4	Florida	6,781	6.61%
5	New York	5,368	5.23%
6	Ohio	5,075	4.95%
7	Illinois	4,505	4.39%
8	Georgia	3,472	3.39%
9	Washington	3,115	3.04%
10	Pennsylvania	3,068	2.99%
11	Tennessee	2,415	2.35%
12	New Jersey	2,307	2.25%
13	North Carolina	2,272	2.22%
14	Maryland	2,185	2.13%
15	Indiana	2,103	2.05%
16	Massachusetts	2,030	1.98%
17	Virginia	1,915	1.87%
18	South Carolina	1,873	1.83%
19	Louisiana	1,781	1.74%
20	Missouri	1,663	1.62%
21	Colorado	1,521	1.48%
22	Arizona	1,500	1.46%
23	Minnesota	1,487	1.45%
24	Oklahoma	1,479	1.44%
25	Oregon	1,332	1.30%
26	Alabama	1,319	1.29%
27	Mississippi	1,134	1.11%
28	Kentucky	1,068	1.04%
29	Arkansas	1,019	0.99%
30	Wisconsin	1,013	0.99%
31	Kansas	1,002	0.98%
32	Connecticut	918	0.90%
33	New Mexico	753	0.73%
34	Nevada	748	0.73%
35	Utah	651	0.63%
36	Delaware	587	0.57%
37	Iowa	510	0.50%
38	Nebraska	473	0.46%
39	West Virginia	423	0.41%
40	Alaska	401	0.39%
41	New Hampshire	386	0.38%
42	Hawaii	360	0.35%
43	Idaho	275	0.27%
44	Rhode Island	248	0.24%
45	Maine	242	0.24%
46	South Dakota	239	0.23%
47	Montana	195	0.19%
48	Vermont	146	0.14%
49	Wyoming	134	0.13%
50	North Dakota	114	0.11%
	District of Columbia	303	0.30%

Source: Federal Bureau of Investigation
"Crime in the United States 1990" (Uniform Crime Reports, August 11, 1991)
*Forcible rape is the carnal knowledge of a female forcibly and against her will. Assaults or attempts to commit rape by force or threat of force are included. However, statutory rape without force and other sex offenses are excluded.

Percent Change in Number of Rapes: 1990 to 1994

National Percent Change = 0.5% Decrease*

ALPHA ORDER			RANK ORDER		
RANK	STATE	PERCENT CHANGE	RANK	STATE	PERCENT CHANGE
15	Alabama	12.7	1	Minnesota	83.3
26	Alaska	4.2	2	Nevada	33.8
36	Arizona	(2.3)	3	Maine	31.4
33	Arkansas	0.9	4	North Dakota	30.7
48	California	(13.4)	5	Iowa	30.6
28	Colorado	3.8	6	South Dakota	26.8
44	Connecticut	(12.2)	7	Kentucky	26.4
42	Delaware	(9.0)	8	Utah	23.8
20	Florida	7.7	9	Montana	19.5
50	Georgia	(29.5)	10	Wyoming	19.4
35	Hawaii	(0.3)	11	Wisconsin	17.7
14	Idaho	14.9	12	Missouri	17.6
47	Illinois	(13.1)	13	New Mexico	15.0
38	Indiana	(2.7)	14	Idaho	14.9
5	Iowa	30.6	15	Alabama	12.7
39	Kansas	(5.5)	16	Rhode Island	10.1
7	Kentucky	26.4	17	Vermont	9.6
19	Louisiana	8.0	18	Oklahoma	9.3
3	Maine	31.4	19	Louisiana	8.0
41	Maryland	(6.9)	20	Florida	7.7
43	Massachusetts	(10.1)	21	Mississippi	6.9
40	Michigan	(6.8)	22	South Carolina	6.3
1	Minnesota	83.3	23	Nebraska	5.7
21	Mississippi	6.9	24	New Hampshire	5.4
12	Missouri	17.6	24	Tennessee	5.4
9	Montana	19.5	26	Alaska	4.2
23	Nebraska	5.7	27	Texas	4.0
2	Nevada	33.8	28	Colorado	3.8
24	New Hampshire	5.4	29	Washington	3.7
49	New Jersey	(14.5)	30	Ohio	3.1
13	New Mexico	15.0	31	North Carolina	2.7
45	New York	(12.4)	32	Pennsylvania	2.5
31	North Carolina	2.7	33	Arkansas	0.9
4	North Dakota	30.7	34	Oregon	0.1
30	Ohio	3.1	35	Hawaii	(0.3)
18	Oklahoma	9.3	36	Arizona	(2.3)
34	Oregon	0.1	37	Virginia	(2.5)
32	Pennsylvania	2.5	38	Indiana	(2.7)
16	Rhode Island	10.1	39	Kansas	(5.5)
22	South Carolina	6.3	40	Michigan	(6.8)
6	South Dakota	26.8	41	Maryland	(6.9)
24	Tennessee	5.4	42	Delaware	(9.0)
27	Texas	4.0	43	Massachusetts	(10.1)
8	Utah	23.8	44	Connecticut	(12.2)
17	Vermont	9.6	45	New York	(12.4)
37	Virginia	(2.5)	46	West Virginia	(12.5)
29	Washington	3.7	47	Illinois	(13.1)
46	West Virginia	(12.5)	48	California	(13.4)
11	Wisconsin	17.7	49	New Jersey	(14.5)
10	Wyoming	19.4	50	Georgia	(29.5)
				District of Columbia	(17.8)

Source: Morgan Quitno Press using data from Federal Bureau of Investigation
    "Crime in the United States" (Uniform Crime Reports, 1990 and 1994 editions)
*Forcible rape is the carnal knowledge of a female forcibly and against her will. Assaults or attempts to commit rape by force or threat of force are included. However, statutory rape without force and other sex offenses are excluded.

Rape Rate in 1990

National Rate = 41.2 Rapes per 100,000 Population*

<table>
<tr><td colspan="3">ALPHA ORDER</td><td colspan="3">RANK ORDER</td></tr>
<tr><td>RANK</td><td>STATE</td><td>RATE</td><td>RANK</td><td>STATE</td><td>RATE</td></tr>
<tr><td>31</td><td>Alabama</td><td>32.6</td><td>1</td><td>Delaware</td><td>88.1</td></tr>
<tr><td>3</td><td>Alaska</td><td>72.9</td><td>2</td><td>Michigan</td><td>77.6</td></tr>
<tr><td>21</td><td>Arizona</td><td>40.9</td><td>3</td><td>Alaska</td><td>72.9</td></tr>
<tr><td>18</td><td>Arkansas</td><td>43.3</td><td>4</td><td>Washington</td><td>64.0</td></tr>
<tr><td>19</td><td>California</td><td>42.6</td><td>5</td><td>Nevada</td><td>62.2</td></tr>
<tr><td>15</td><td>Colorado</td><td>46.2</td><td>6</td><td>South Carolina</td><td>53.7</td></tr>
<tr><td>40</td><td>Connecticut</td><td>27.9</td><td>7</td><td>Georgia</td><td>53.6</td></tr>
<tr><td>1</td><td>Delaware</td><td>88.1</td><td>8</td><td>Florida</td><td>52.4</td></tr>
<tr><td>8</td><td>Florida</td><td>52.4</td><td>9</td><td>Texas</td><td>51.5</td></tr>
<tr><td>7</td><td>Georgia</td><td>53.6</td><td>10</td><td>New Mexico</td><td>49.7</td></tr>
<tr><td>32</td><td>Hawaii</td><td>32.5</td><td>11</td><td>Tennessee</td><td>49.5</td></tr>
<tr><td>41</td><td>Idaho</td><td>27.3</td><td>12</td><td>Oklahoma</td><td>47.0</td></tr>
<tr><td>23</td><td>Illinois</td><td>39.4</td><td>13</td><td>Oregon</td><td>46.9</td></tr>
<tr><td>24</td><td>Indiana</td><td>37.9</td><td>14</td><td>Ohio</td><td>46.8</td></tr>
<tr><td>49</td><td>Iowa</td><td>18.4</td><td>15</td><td>Colorado</td><td>46.2</td></tr>
<tr><td>22</td><td>Kansas</td><td>40.4</td><td>16</td><td>Maryland</td><td>45.7</td></tr>
<tr><td>39</td><td>Kentucky</td><td>29.0</td><td>17</td><td>Mississippi</td><td>44.1</td></tr>
<tr><td>20</td><td>Louisiana</td><td>42.2</td><td>18</td><td>Arkansas</td><td>43.3</td></tr>
<tr><td>48</td><td>Maine</td><td>19.7</td><td>19</td><td>California</td><td>42.6</td></tr>
<tr><td>16</td><td>Maryland</td><td>45.7</td><td>20</td><td>Louisiana</td><td>42.2</td></tr>
<tr><td>30</td><td>Massachusetts</td><td>33.7</td><td>21</td><td>Arizona</td><td>40.9</td></tr>
<tr><td>2</td><td>Michigan</td><td>77.6</td><td>22</td><td>Kansas</td><td>40.4</td></tr>
<tr><td>28</td><td>Minnesota</td><td>34.0</td><td>23</td><td>Illinois</td><td>39.4</td></tr>
<tr><td>17</td><td>Mississippi</td><td>44.1</td><td>24</td><td>Indiana</td><td>37.9</td></tr>
<tr><td>32</td><td>Missouri</td><td>32.5</td><td>25</td><td>Utah</td><td>37.8</td></tr>
<tr><td>45</td><td>Montana</td><td>24.4</td><td>26</td><td>New Hampshire</td><td>34.8</td></tr>
<tr><td>35</td><td>Nebraska</td><td>30.0</td><td>27</td><td>North Carolina</td><td>34.3</td></tr>
<tr><td>5</td><td>Nevada</td><td>62.2</td><td>28</td><td>Minnesota</td><td>34.0</td></tr>
<tr><td>26</td><td>New Hampshire</td><td>34.8</td><td>28</td><td>South Dakota</td><td>34.0</td></tr>
<tr><td>36</td><td>New Jersey</td><td>29.8</td><td>30</td><td>Massachusetts</td><td>33.7</td></tr>
<tr><td>10</td><td>New Mexico</td><td>49.7</td><td>31</td><td>Alabama</td><td>32.6</td></tr>
<tr><td>36</td><td>New York</td><td>29.8</td><td>32</td><td>Hawaii</td><td>32.5</td></tr>
<tr><td>27</td><td>North Carolina</td><td>34.3</td><td>32</td><td>Missouri</td><td>32.5</td></tr>
<tr><td>50</td><td>North Dakota</td><td>17.8</td><td>34</td><td>Virginia</td><td>31.0</td></tr>
<tr><td>14</td><td>Ohio</td><td>46.8</td><td>35</td><td>Nebraska</td><td>30.0</td></tr>
<tr><td>12</td><td>Oklahoma</td><td>47.0</td><td>36</td><td>New Jersey</td><td>29.8</td></tr>
<tr><td>13</td><td>Oregon</td><td>46.9</td><td>36</td><td>New York</td><td>29.8</td></tr>
<tr><td>43</td><td>Pennsylvania</td><td>25.8</td><td>38</td><td>Wyoming</td><td>29.5</td></tr>
<tr><td>44</td><td>Rhode Island</td><td>24.7</td><td>39</td><td>Kentucky</td><td>29.0</td></tr>
<tr><td>6</td><td>South Carolina</td><td>53.7</td><td>40</td><td>Connecticut</td><td>27.9</td></tr>
<tr><td>28</td><td>South Dakota</td><td>34.0</td><td>41</td><td>Idaho</td><td>27.3</td></tr>
<tr><td>11</td><td>Tennessee</td><td>49.5</td><td>42</td><td>Vermont</td><td>25.9</td></tr>
<tr><td>9</td><td>Texas</td><td>51.5</td><td>43</td><td>Pennsylvania</td><td>25.8</td></tr>
<tr><td>25</td><td>Utah</td><td>37.8</td><td>44</td><td>Rhode Island</td><td>24.7</td></tr>
<tr><td>42</td><td>Vermont</td><td>25.9</td><td>45</td><td>Montana</td><td>24.4</td></tr>
<tr><td>34</td><td>Virginia</td><td>31.0</td><td>46</td><td>West Virginia</td><td>23.6</td></tr>
<tr><td>4</td><td>Washington</td><td>64.0</td><td>47</td><td>Wisconsin</td><td>20.7</td></tr>
<tr><td>46</td><td>West Virginia</td><td>23.6</td><td>48</td><td>Maine</td><td>19.7</td></tr>
<tr><td>47</td><td>Wisconsin</td><td>20.7</td><td>49</td><td>Iowa</td><td>18.4</td></tr>
<tr><td>38</td><td>Wyoming</td><td>29.5</td><td>50</td><td>North Dakota</td><td>17.8</td></tr>
<tr><td></td><td></td><td></td><td></td><td>District of Columbia</td><td>49.9</td></tr>
</table>

Source: Federal Bureau of Investigation
      "Crime in the United States 1990" (Uniform Crime Reports, August 11, 1991)
*Forcible rape is the carnal knowledge of a female forcibly and against her will. Assaults or attempts to commit rape by force or threat of force are included. However, statutory rape without force and other sex offenses are excluded.

Percent Change in Rape Rate: 1990 to 1994

National Percent Change = 4.9% Decrease*

ALPHA ORDER

RANK	STATE	PERCENT CHANGE	RANK	STATE	PERCENT CHANGE
14	Alabama	8.0	1	Minnesota	75.6
31	Alaska	(5.4)	2	North Dakota	31.5
43	Arizona	(12.0)	3	Maine	30.0
28	Arkansas	(3.2)	4	Iowa	27.7
49	California	(18.1)	5	South Dakota	23.5
34	Colorado	(6.5)	6	Kentucky	21.7
42	Connecticut	(11.8)	7	Missouri	13.9
46	Delaware	(14.2)	7	Wyoming	13.9
26	Florida	(0.2)	9	Wisconsin	13.5
50	Georgia	(35.3)	10	Utah	11.6
34	Hawaii	(6.5)	11	Montana	11.5
22	Idaho	2.2	12	Rhode Island	10.9
47	Illinois	(15.5)	13	Nevada	10.5
33	Indiana	(6.1)	14	Alabama	8.0
4	Iowa	27.7	15	Vermont	6.6
38	Kansas	(8.2)	16	Louisiana	5.7
6	Kentucky	21.7	17	Oklahoma	5.5
16	Louisiana	5.7	18	New Mexico	5.4
3	Maine	30.0	19	Mississippi	3.0
41	Maryland	(10.9)	20	New Hampshire	2.9
40	Massachusetts	(10.4)	21	Nebraska	2.7
39	Michigan	(8.8)	22	Idaho	2.2
1	Minnesota	75.6	23	Pennsylvania	1.2
19	Mississippi	3.0	24	South Carolina	1.1
7	Missouri	13.9	25	Ohio	0.6
11	Montana	11.5	26	Florida	(0.2)
21	Nebraska	2.7	27	Tennessee	(0.6)
13	Nevada	10.5	28	Arkansas	(3.2)
20	New Hampshire	2.9	29	North Carolina	(3.8)
48	New Jersey	(16.4)	30	Texas	(3.9)
18	New Mexico	5.4	31	Alaska	(5.4)
44	New York	(13.1)	32	Washington	(5.5)
29	North Carolina	(3.8)	33	Indiana	(6.1)
2	North Dakota	31.5	34	Colorado	(6.5)
25	Ohio	0.6	34	Hawaii	(6.5)
17	Oklahoma	5.5	36	Oregon	(7.9)
36	Oregon	(7.9)	37	Virginia	(8.1)
23	Pennsylvania	1.2	38	Kansas	(8.2)
12	Rhode Island	10.9	39	Michigan	(8.8)
24	South Carolina	1.1	40	Massachusetts	(10.4)
5	South Dakota	23.5	41	Maryland	(10.9)
27	Tennessee	(0.6)	42	Connecticut	(11.8)
30	Texas	(3.9)	43	Arizona	(12.0)
10	Utah	11.6	44	New York	(13.1)
15	Vermont	6.6	45	West Virginia	(14.0)
37	Virginia	(8.1)	46	Delaware	(14.2)
32	Washington	(5.5)	47	Illinois	(15.5)
45	West Virginia	(14.0)	48	New Jersey	(16.4)
9	Wisconsin	13.5	49	California	(18.1)
7	Wyoming	13.9	50	Georgia	(35.3)

	District of Columbia	(12.4)

Source: Morgan Quitno Press using data from Federal Bureau of Investigation
    "Crime in the United States" (Uniform Crime Reports, 1990 and 1994 editions)
*Forcible rape is the carnal knowledge of a female forcibly and against her will. Assaults or attempts to commit rape by force or threat of force are included. However, statutory rape without force and other sex offenses are excluded.

Robberies in 1990

National Total = 639,271 Robberies*

ALPHA ORDER				RANK ORDER			
RANK	STATE	ROBBERIES	% of USA	RANK	STATE	ROBBERIES	% of USA
21	Alabama	5,805	0.91%	1	New York	112,380	17.58%
42	Alaska	422	0.07%	2	California	112,208	17.55%
20	Arizona	5,897	0.92%	3	Florida	53,928	8.44%
31	Arkansas	2,661	0.42%	4	Illinois	45,038	7.05%
2	California	112,208	17.55%	5	Texas	44,297	6.93%
28	Colorado	2,985	0.47%	6	New Jersey	23,269	3.64%
17	Connecticut	7,717	1.21%	7	Michigan	21,752	3.40%
36	Delaware	1,098	0.17%	8	Pennsylvania	20,930	3.27%
3	Florida	53,928	8.44%	9	Ohio	20,451	3.20%
11	Georgia	17,067	2.67%	10	Maryland	17,394	2.72%
38	Hawaii	1,013	0.16%	11	Georgia	17,067	2.67%
46	Idaho	151	0.02%	12	Massachusetts	13,062	2.04%
4	Illinois	45,038	7.05%	13	Louisiana	11,387	1.78%
22	Indiana	5,619	0.88%	14	Missouri	11,073	1.73%
37	Iowa	1,089	0.17%	15	North Carolina	10,082	1.58%
29	Kansas	2,914	0.46%	16	Tennessee	9,325	1.46%
32	Kentucky	2,545	0.40%	17	Connecticut	7,717	1.21%
13	Louisiana	11,387	1.78%	18	Virginia	7,626	1.19%
43	Maine	308	0.05%	19	Washington	6,326	0.99%
10	Maryland	17,394	2.72%	20	Arizona	5,897	0.92%
12	Massachusetts	13,062	2.04%	21	Alabama	5,805	0.91%
7	Michigan	21,752	3.40%	22	Indiana	5,619	0.88%
26	Minnesota	4,057	0.63%	23	Wisconsin	5,514	0.86%
33	Mississippi	2,217	0.35%	24	South Carolina	5,313	0.83%
14	Missouri	11,073	1.73%	25	Oregon	4,102	0.64%
45	Montana	173	0.03%	26	Minnesota	4,057	0.63%
40	Nebraska	807	0.13%	27	Oklahoma	3,836	0.60%
30	Nevada	2,864	0.45%	28	Colorado	2,985	0.47%
44	New Hampshire	302	0.05%	29	Kansas	2,914	0.46%
6	New Jersey	23,269	3.64%	30	Nevada	2,864	0.45%
34	New Mexico	1,744	0.27%	31	Arkansas	2,661	0.42%
1	New York	112,380	17.58%	32	Kentucky	2,545	0.40%
15	North Carolina	10,082	1.58%	33	Mississippi	2,217	0.35%
50	North Dakota	50	0.01%	34	New Mexico	1,744	0.27%
9	Ohio	20,451	3.20%	35	Rhode Island	1,224	0.19%
27	Oklahoma	3,836	0.60%	36	Delaware	1,098	0.17%
25	Oregon	4,102	0.64%	37	Iowa	1,089	0.17%
8	Pennsylvania	20,930	3.27%	38	Hawaii	1,013	0.16%
35	Rhode Island	1,224	0.19%	39	Utah	980	0.15%
24	South Carolina	5,313	0.83%	40	Nebraska	807	0.13%
47	South Dakota	86	0.01%	41	West Virginia	680	0.11%
16	Tennessee	9,325	1.46%	42	Alaska	422	0.07%
5	Texas	44,297	6.93%	43	Maine	308	0.05%
39	Utah	980	0.15%	44	New Hampshire	302	0.05%
49	Vermont	66	0.01%	45	Montana	173	0.03%
18	Virginia	7,626	1.19%	46	Idaho	151	0.02%
19	Washington	6,326	0.99%	47	South Dakota	86	0.01%
41	West Virginia	680	0.11%	48	Wyoming	72	0.01%
23	Wisconsin	5,514	0.86%	49	Vermont	66	0.01%
48	Wyoming	72	0.01%	50	North Dakota	50	0.01%
					District of Columbia	7,365	1.15%

Source: Federal Bureau of Investigation
"Crime in the United States 1990" (Uniform Crime Reports, August 11, 1991)
*Robbery is the taking or attempting to take anything of value by force or threat of force.

Percent Change in Number of Robberies: 1990 to 1994

National Percent Change = 3.2% Decrease*

RANK	STATE	PERCENT CHANGE		RANK	STATE	PERCENT CHANGE
16	Alabama	24.4		1	Alaska	110.0
1	Alaska	110.0		2	Mississippi	95.6
26	Arizona	11.9		3	Nevada	79.3
20	Arkansas	18.7		4	Montana	61.9
38	California	0.0		5	South Dakota	57.0
13	Colorado	31.0		6	Nebraska	51.6
47	Connecticut	(20.3)		7	North Dakota	42.0
46	Delaware	(19.0)		8	Kentucky	41.3
44	Florida	(14.9)		9	Idaho	38.4
42	Georgia	(8.0)		10	New Mexico	33.5
19	Hawaii	20.5		11	Indiana	33.3
9	Idaho	38.4		12	Minnesota	32.4
41	Illinois	(2.8)		13	Colorado	31.0
11	Indiana	33.3		14	South Carolina	28.3
18	Iowa	21.9		15	North Carolina	27.1
32	Kansas	5.0		16	Alabama	24.4
8	Kentucky	41.3		17	Utah	23.8
37	Louisiana	1.3		18	Iowa	21.9
43	Maine	(9.7)		19	Hawaii	20.5
22	Maryland	15.8		20	Arkansas	18.7
48	Massachusetts	(22.2)		21	Washington	18.0
39	Michigan	(0.1)		22	Maryland	15.8
12	Minnesota	32.4		23	Tennessee	15.1
2	Mississippi	95.6		24	Virginia	14.1
27	Missouri	10.0		25	West Virginia	13.5
4	Montana	61.9		26	Arizona	11.9
6	Nebraska	51.6		27	Missouri	10.0
3	Nevada	79.3		28	Wyoming	9.7
35	New Hampshire	2.0		29	Oklahoma	8.8
40	New Jersey	(2.2)		30	Vermont	7.6
10	New Mexico	33.5		31	Pennsylvania	7.5
49	New York	(22.9)		32	Kansas	5.0
15	North Carolina	27.1		33	Wisconsin	4.1
7	North Dakota	42.0		34	Oregon	4.0
36	Ohio	1.8		35	New Hampshire	2.0
29	Oklahoma	8.8		36	Ohio	1.8
34	Oregon	4.0		37	Louisiana	1.3
31	Pennsylvania	7.5		38	California	0.0
50	Rhode Island	(28.9)		39	Michigan	(0.1)
14	South Carolina	28.3		40	New Jersey	(2.2)
5	South Dakota	57.0		41	Illinois	(2.8)
23	Tennessee	15.1		42	Georgia	(8.0)
45	Texas	(15.0)		43	Maine	(9.7)
17	Utah	23.8		44	Florida	(14.9)
30	Vermont	7.6		45	Texas	(15.0)
24	Virginia	14.1		46	Delaware	(19.0)
21	Washington	18.0		47	Connecticut	(20.3)
25	West Virginia	13.5		48	Massachusetts	(22.2)
33	Wisconsin	4.1		49	New York	(22.9)
28	Wyoming	9.7		50	Rhode Island	(28.9)
					District of Columbia	(14.3)

ALPHA ORDER — RANK ORDER

Source: Morgan Quitno Press using data from Federal Bureau of Investigation
   "Crime in the United States" (Uniform Crime Reports, 1990 and 1994 editions)
*Robbery is the taking or attempting to take anything of value by force or threat of force.

Robbery Rate in 1990

National Rate = 257.0 Robberies per 100,000 Population*

ALPHA ORDER

RANK ORDER

RANK	STATE	RATE		RANK	STATE	RATE
23	Alabama	143.7		1	New York	624.7
37	Alaska	76.7		2	Florida	416.8
19	Arizona	160.9		3	Illinois	394.0
30	Arkansas	113.2		4	California	377.0
4	California	377.0		5	Maryland	363.8
35	Colorado	90.6		6	New Jersey	301.0
11	Connecticut	234.8		7	Louisiana	269.8
18	Delaware	164.8		8	Georgia	263.5
2	Florida	416.8		9	Texas	260.8
8	Georgia	263.5		10	Nevada	238.3
34	Hawaii	91.4		11	Connecticut	234.8
47	Idaho	15.0		12	Michigan	234.0
3	Illinois	394.0		13	Massachusetts	217.1
32	Indiana	101.3		14	Missouri	216.4
41	Iowa	39.2		15	Tennessee	191.2
28	Kansas	117.6		16	Ohio	188.5
38	Kentucky	69.1		17	Pennsylvania	176.2
7	Louisiana	269.8		18	Delaware	164.8
44	Maine	25.1		19	Arizona	160.9
5	Maryland	363.8		20	South Carolina	152.4
13	Massachusetts	217.1		21	North Carolina	152.1
12	Michigan	234.0		22	Oregon	144.3
33	Minnesota	92.7		23	Alabama	143.7
36	Mississippi	86.2		24	Washington	130.0
14	Missouri	216.4		25	Virginia	123.3
45	Montana	21.7		26	Rhode Island	122.0
40	Nebraska	51.1		27	Oklahoma	121.9
10	Nevada	238.3		28	Kansas	117.6
43	New Hampshire	27.2		29	New Mexico	115.1
6	New Jersey	301.0		30	Arkansas	113.2
29	New Mexico	115.1		31	Wisconsin	112.7
1	New York	624.7		32	Indiana	101.3
21	North Carolina	152.1		33	Minnesota	92.7
50	North Dakota	7.8		34	Hawaii	91.4
16	Ohio	188.5		35	Colorado	90.6
27	Oklahoma	121.9		36	Mississippi	86.2
22	Oregon	144.3		37	Alaska	76.7
17	Pennsylvania	176.2		38	Kentucky	69.1
26	Rhode Island	122.0		39	Utah	56.9
20	South Carolina	152.4		40	Nebraska	51.1
48	South Dakota	12.4		41	Iowa	39.2
15	Tennessee	191.2		42	West Virginia	37.9
9	Texas	260.8		43	New Hampshire	27.2
39	Utah	56.9		44	Maine	25.1
49	Vermont	11.7		45	Montana	21.7
25	Virginia	123.3		46	Wyoming	15.9
24	Washington	130.0		47	Idaho	15.0
42	West Virginia	37.9		48	South Dakota	12.4
31	Wisconsin	112.7		49	Vermont	11.7
46	Wyoming	15.9		50	North Dakota	7.8
					District of Columbia	1,213.5

Source: Federal Bureau of Investigation
    "Crime in the United States 1990" (Uniform Crime Reports, August 11, 1991)
*Robbery is the taking or attempting to take anything of value by force or threat of force.

Percent Change in Robbery Rate: 1990 to 1994

National Percent Change = 7.5% Decrease*

<table>
<tr><th colspan="3">ALPHA ORDER</th><th colspan="3">RANK ORDER</th></tr>
<tr><th>RANK</th><th>STATE</th><th>PERCENT CHANGE</th><th>RANK</th><th>STATE</th><th>PERCENT CHANGE</th></tr>
<tr><td>15</td><td>Alabama</td><td>19.1</td><td>1</td><td>Alaska</td><td>90.6</td></tr>
<tr><td>1</td><td>Alaska</td><td>90.6</td><td>2</td><td>Mississippi</td><td>88.5</td></tr>
<tr><td>32</td><td>Arizona</td><td>0.7</td><td>3</td><td>South Dakota</td><td>50.8</td></tr>
<tr><td>18</td><td>Arkansas</td><td>13.7</td><td>4</td><td>Montana</td><td>50.7</td></tr>
<tr><td>40</td><td>California</td><td>(5.4)</td><td>5</td><td>Nevada</td><td>47.9</td></tr>
<tr><td>17</td><td>Colorado</td><td>18.0</td><td>6</td><td>Nebraska</td><td>47.6</td></tr>
<tr><td>44</td><td>Connecticut</td><td>(20.0)</td><td>7</td><td>North Dakota</td><td>42.3</td></tr>
<tr><td>48</td><td>Delaware</td><td>(23.6)</td><td>8</td><td>Kentucky</td><td>35.9</td></tr>
<tr><td>45</td><td>Florida</td><td>(21.1)</td><td>9</td><td>Indiana</td><td>28.5</td></tr>
<tr><td>43</td><td>Georgia</td><td>(15.5)</td><td>10</td><td>Minnesota</td><td>26.9</td></tr>
<tr><td>19</td><td>Hawaii</td><td>13.4</td><td>11</td><td>Idaho</td><td>22.7</td></tr>
<tr><td>11</td><td>Idaho</td><td>22.7</td><td>12</td><td>New Mexico</td><td>22.3</td></tr>
<tr><td>40</td><td>Illinois</td><td>(5.4)</td><td>13</td><td>South Carolina</td><td>22.1</td></tr>
<tr><td>9</td><td>Indiana</td><td>28.5</td><td>14</td><td>Iowa</td><td>19.6</td></tr>
<tr><td>14</td><td>Iowa</td><td>19.6</td><td>15</td><td>Alabama</td><td>19.1</td></tr>
<tr><td>31</td><td>Kansas</td><td>1.9</td><td>15</td><td>North Carolina</td><td>19.1</td></tr>
<tr><td>8</td><td>Kentucky</td><td>35.9</td><td>17</td><td>Colorado</td><td>18.0</td></tr>
<tr><td>36</td><td>Louisiana</td><td>(1.0)</td><td>18</td><td>Arkansas</td><td>13.7</td></tr>
<tr><td>42</td><td>Maine</td><td>(10.8)</td><td>19</td><td>Hawaii</td><td>13.4</td></tr>
<tr><td>22</td><td>Maryland</td><td>10.6</td><td>20</td><td>West Virginia</td><td>11.9</td></tr>
<tr><td>47</td><td>Massachusetts</td><td>(22.5)</td><td>21</td><td>Utah</td><td>11.8</td></tr>
<tr><td>37</td><td>Michigan</td><td>(2.2)</td><td>22</td><td>Maryland</td><td>10.6</td></tr>
<tr><td>10</td><td>Minnesota</td><td>26.9</td><td>23</td><td>Tennessee</td><td>8.5</td></tr>
<tr><td>2</td><td>Mississippi</td><td>88.5</td><td>24</td><td>Virginia</td><td>7.7</td></tr>
<tr><td>26</td><td>Missouri</td><td>6.6</td><td>25</td><td>Washington</td><td>7.5</td></tr>
<tr><td>4</td><td>Montana</td><td>50.7</td><td>26</td><td>Missouri</td><td>6.6</td></tr>
<tr><td>6</td><td>Nebraska</td><td>47.6</td><td>27</td><td>Pennsylvania</td><td>6.0</td></tr>
<tr><td>5</td><td>Nevada</td><td>47.9</td><td>28</td><td>Oklahoma</td><td>5.1</td></tr>
<tr><td>34</td><td>New Hampshire</td><td>(0.4)</td><td>29</td><td>Wyoming</td><td>4.4</td></tr>
<tr><td>39</td><td>New Jersey</td><td>(4.3)</td><td>30</td><td>Vermont</td><td>4.3</td></tr>
<tr><td>12</td><td>New Mexico</td><td>22.3</td><td>31</td><td>Kansas</td><td>1.9</td></tr>
<tr><td>49</td><td>New York</td><td>(23.7)</td><td>32</td><td>Arizona</td><td>0.7</td></tr>
<tr><td>15</td><td>North Carolina</td><td>19.1</td><td>33</td><td>Wisconsin</td><td>0.2</td></tr>
<tr><td>7</td><td>North Dakota</td><td>42.3</td><td>34</td><td>New Hampshire</td><td>(0.4)</td></tr>
<tr><td>35</td><td>Ohio</td><td>(0.5)</td><td>35</td><td>Ohio</td><td>(0.5)</td></tr>
<tr><td>28</td><td>Oklahoma</td><td>5.1</td><td>36</td><td>Louisiana</td><td>(1.0)</td></tr>
<tr><td>38</td><td>Oregon</td><td>(4.2)</td><td>37</td><td>Michigan</td><td>(2.2)</td></tr>
<tr><td>27</td><td>Pennsylvania</td><td>6.0</td><td>38</td><td>Oregon</td><td>(4.2)</td></tr>
<tr><td>50</td><td>Rhode Island</td><td>(28.4)</td><td>39</td><td>New Jersey</td><td>(4.3)</td></tr>
<tr><td>13</td><td>South Carolina</td><td>22.1</td><td>40</td><td>California</td><td>(5.4)</td></tr>
<tr><td>3</td><td>South Dakota</td><td>50.8</td><td>40</td><td>Illinois</td><td>(5.4)</td></tr>
<tr><td>23</td><td>Tennessee</td><td>8.5</td><td>42</td><td>Maine</td><td>(10.8)</td></tr>
<tr><td>46</td><td>Texas</td><td>(21.5)</td><td>43</td><td>Georgia</td><td>(15.5)</td></tr>
<tr><td>21</td><td>Utah</td><td>11.8</td><td>44</td><td>Connecticut</td><td>(20.0)</td></tr>
<tr><td>30</td><td>Vermont</td><td>4.3</td><td>45</td><td>Florida</td><td>(21.1)</td></tr>
<tr><td>24</td><td>Virginia</td><td>7.7</td><td>46</td><td>Texas</td><td>(21.5)</td></tr>
<tr><td>25</td><td>Washington</td><td>7.5</td><td>47</td><td>Massachusetts</td><td>(22.5)</td></tr>
<tr><td>20</td><td>West Virginia</td><td>11.9</td><td>48</td><td>Delaware</td><td>(23.6)</td></tr>
<tr><td>33</td><td>Wisconsin</td><td>0.2</td><td>49</td><td>New York</td><td>(23.7)</td></tr>
<tr><td>29</td><td>Wyoming</td><td>4.4</td><td>50</td><td>Rhode Island</td><td>(28.4)</td></tr>
<tr><td></td><td></td><td></td><td></td><td>District of Columbia</td><td>(8.8)</td></tr>
</table>

Source: Morgan Quitno Press using data from Federal Bureau of Investigation
"Crime in the United States" (Uniform Crime Reports, 1990 and 1994 editions)
*Robbery is the taking or attempting to take anything of value by force or threat of force.

Aggravated Assaults in 1990

National Total = 1,054,863 Aggravated Assaults*

ALPHA ORDER

RANK	STATE	ASSAULTS	% of USA
17	Alabama	21,039	1.99%
41	Alaska	2,021	0.19%
20	Arizona	16,230	1.54%
29	Arkansas	8,590	0.81%
1	California	182,602	17.31%
22	Colorado	12,684	1.20%
26	Connecticut	9,400	0.89%
39	Delaware	2,647	0.25%
2	Florida	98,902	9.38%
10	Georgia	27,690	2.62%
43	Hawaii	1,696	0.16%
40	Idaho	2,323	0.22%
5	Illinois	59,850	5.67%
19	Indiana	18,209	1.73%
32	Iowa	6,668	0.63%
31	Kansas	7,079	0.67%
25	Kentucky	10,509	1.00%
14	Louisiana	24,022	2.28%
44	Maine	1,179	0.11%
15	Maryland	23,809	2.26%
7	Massachusetts	28,965	2.75%
6	Michigan	43,536	4.13%
30	Minnesota	7,731	0.73%
34	Mississippi	5,094	0.48%
16	Missouri	23,417	2.22%
46	Montana	866	0.08%
35	Nebraska	3,886	0.37%
36	Nevada	3,494	0.33%
48	New Hampshire	750	0.07%
13	New Jersey	24,049	2.28%
27	New Mexico	9,185	0.87%
3	New York	92,105	8.73%
9	North Carolina	28,267	2.68%
50	North Dakota	303	0.03%
8	Ohio	28,715	2.72%
23	Oklahoma	11,654	1.10%
28	Oregon	8,863	0.84%
12	Pennsylvania	26,414	2.50%
38	Rhode Island	2,814	0.27%
11	South Carolina	26,474	2.51%
47	South Dakota	794	0.08%
18	Tennessee	20,447	1.94%
4	Texas	73,907	7.01%
37	Utah	3,209	0.30%
49	Vermont	491	0.05%
24	Virginia	11,608	1.10%
21	Washington	14,731	1.40%
42	West Virginia	1,831	0.17%
33	Wisconsin	6,196	0.59%
45	Wyoming	1,139	0.11%

RANK ORDER

RANK	STATE	ASSAULTS	% of USA
1	California	182,602	17.31%
2	Florida	98,902	9.38%
3	New York	92,105	8.73%
4	Texas	73,907	7.01%
5	Illinois	59,850	5.67%
6	Michigan	43,536	4.13%
7	Massachusetts	28,965	2.75%
8	Ohio	28,715	2.72%
9	North Carolina	28,267	2.68%
10	Georgia	27,690	2.62%
11	South Carolina	26,474	2.51%
12	Pennsylvania	26,414	2.50%
13	New Jersey	24,049	2.28%
14	Louisiana	24,022	2.28%
15	Maryland	23,809	2.26%
16	Missouri	23,417	2.22%
17	Alabama	21,039	1.99%
18	Tennessee	20,447	1.94%
19	Indiana	18,209	1.73%
20	Arizona	16,230	1.54%
21	Washington	14,731	1.40%
22	Colorado	12,684	1.20%
23	Oklahoma	11,654	1.10%
24	Virginia	11,608	1.10%
25	Kentucky	10,509	1.00%
26	Connecticut	9,400	0.89%
27	New Mexico	9,185	0.87%
28	Oregon	8,863	0.84%
29	Arkansas	8,590	0.81%
30	Minnesota	7,731	0.73%
31	Kansas	7,079	0.67%
32	Iowa	6,668	0.63%
33	Wisconsin	6,196	0.59%
34	Mississippi	5,094	0.48%
35	Nebraska	3,886	0.37%
36	Nevada	3,494	0.33%
37	Utah	3,209	0.30%
38	Rhode Island	2,814	0.27%
39	Delaware	2,647	0.25%
40	Idaho	2,323	0.22%
41	Alaska	2,021	0.19%
42	West Virginia	1,831	0.17%
43	Hawaii	1,696	0.16%
44	Maine	1,179	0.11%
45	Wyoming	1,139	0.11%
46	Montana	866	0.08%
47	South Dakota	794	0.08%
48	New Hampshire	750	0.07%
49	Vermont	491	0.05%
50	North Dakota	303	0.03%
	District of Columbia	6,779	0.64%

Source: Federal Bureau of Investigation
"Crime in the United States 1990" (Uniform Crime Reports, August 11, 1991)
*Aggravated assault is an attack for the purpose of inflicting severe bodily injury.

Percent Change in Number of Aggravated Assaults: 1990 to 1994

National Percent Change = 6.2% Increase*

ALPHA ORDER

RANK	STATE	PERCENT CHANGE
42	Alabama	(6.7)
3	Alaska	63.4
8	Arizona	24.2
11	Arkansas	17.8
30	California	4.9
34	Colorado	2.1
48	Connecticut	(17.6)
41	Delaware	(5.4)
24	Florida	6.9
35	Georgia	2.0
46	Hawaii	(13.9)
16	Idaho	15.1
25	Illinois	6.7
19	Indiana	11.0
33	Iowa	3.1
17	Kansas	14.0
2	Kentucky	71.1
13	Louisiana	16.8
47	Maine	(16.3)
32	Maryland	3.7
28	Massachusetts	5.5
36	Michigan	(0.4)
28	Minnesota	5.5
6	Mississippi	41.7
30	Missouri	4.9
18	Montana	12.6
12	Nebraska	17.0
1	Nevada	137.3
49	New Hampshire	(20.4)
38	New Jersey	(2.6)
9	New Mexico	23.4
45	New York	(10.9)
23	North Carolina	7.5
37	North Dakota	(0.7)
40	Ohio	(5.2)
7	Oklahoma	30.5
14	Oregon	16.4
39	Pennsylvania	(5.1)
44	Rhode Island	(9.0)
22	South Carolina	8.0
4	South Dakota	50.3
10	Tennessee	22.0
21	Texas	9.7
14	Utah	16.4
50	Vermont	(33.8)
27	Virginia	5.9
20	Washington	10.9
5	West Virginia	46.9
26	Wisconsin	6.4
43	Wyoming	(8.5)

RANK ORDER

RANK	STATE	PERCENT CHANGE
1	Nevada	137.3
2	Kentucky	71.1
3	Alaska	63.4
4	South Dakota	50.3
5	West Virginia	46.9
6	Mississippi	41.7
7	Oklahoma	30.5
8	Arizona	24.2
9	New Mexico	23.4
10	Tennessee	22.0
11	Arkansas	17.8
12	Nebraska	17.0
13	Louisiana	16.8
14	Oregon	16.4
14	Utah	16.4
16	Idaho	15.1
17	Kansas	14.0
18	Montana	12.6
19	Indiana	11.0
20	Washington	10.9
21	Texas	9.7
22	South Carolina	8.0
23	North Carolina	7.5
24	Florida	6.9
25	Illinois	6.7
26	Wisconsin	6.4
27	Virginia	5.9
28	Massachusetts	5.5
28	Minnesota	5.5
30	California	4.9
30	Missouri	4.9
32	Maryland	3.7
33	Iowa	3.1
34	Colorado	2.1
35	Georgia	2.0
36	Michigan	(0.4)
37	North Dakota	(0.7)
38	New Jersey	(2.6)
39	Pennsylvania	(5.1)
40	Ohio	(5.2)
41	Delaware	(5.4)
42	Alabama	(6.7)
43	Wyoming	(8.5)
44	Rhode Island	(9.0)
45	New York	(10.9)
46	Hawaii	(13.9)
47	Maine	(16.3)
48	Connecticut	(17.6)
49	New Hampshire	(20.4)
50	Vermont	(33.8)

| | District of Columbia | 21.2 |

Source: Morgan Quitno Press using data from Federal Bureau of Investigation
"Crime in the United States" (Uniform Crime Reports, 1990 and 1994 editions)
*Aggravated assault is an attack for the purpose of inflicting severe bodily injury.

Aggravated Assault Rate in 1990

National Rate = 424.1 Aggravated Assaulted per 100,000 Population*

ALPHA ORDER

RANK	STATE	RATE
7	Alabama	520.7
21	Alaska	367.4
13	Arizona	442.8
22	Arkansas	365.4
3	California	613.6
19	Colorado	385.0
28	Connecticut	286.0
18	Delaware	397.3
1	Florida	764.4
15	Georgia	427.4
42	Hawaii	153.0
36	Idaho	230.7
6	Illinois	523.6
23	Indiana	328.4
35	Iowa	240.1
29	Kansas	285.7
30	Kentucky	285.2
5	Louisiana	569.2
47	Maine	96.0
9	Maryland	497.9
10	Massachusetts	481.4
11	Michigan	468.4
41	Minnesota	176.7
38	Mississippi	198.0
12	Missouri	457.6
45	Montana	108.4
34	Nebraska	246.2
27	Nevada	290.7
49	New Hampshire	67.6
25	New Jersey	311.1
4	New Mexico	606.2
8	New York	512.0
16	North Carolina	426.4
50	North Dakota	47.4
32	Ohio	264.7
20	Oklahoma	370.5
24	Oregon	311.8
37	Pennsylvania	222.3
31	Rhode Island	280.4
2	South Carolina	759.3
44	South Dakota	114.1
17	Tennessee	419.2
14	Texas	435.1
40	Utah	186.3
48	Vermont	87.2
39	Virginia	187.6
26	Washington	302.7
46	West Virginia	102.1
43	Wisconsin	126.7
33	Wyoming	251.1

RANK ORDER

RANK	STATE	RATE
1	Florida	764.4
2	South Carolina	759.3
3	California	613.6
4	New Mexico	606.2
5	Louisiana	569.2
6	Illinois	523.6
7	Alabama	520.7
8	New York	512.0
9	Maryland	497.9
10	Massachusetts	481.4
11	Michigan	468.4
12	Missouri	457.6
13	Arizona	442.8
14	Texas	435.1
15	Georgia	427.4
16	North Carolina	426.4
17	Tennessee	419.2
18	Delaware	397.3
19	Colorado	385.0
20	Oklahoma	370.5
21	Alaska	367.4
22	Arkansas	365.4
23	Indiana	328.4
24	Oregon	311.8
25	New Jersey	311.1
26	Washington	302.7
27	Nevada	290.7
28	Connecticut	286.0
29	Kansas	285.7
30	Kentucky	285.2
31	Rhode Island	280.4
32	Ohio	264.7
33	Wyoming	251.1
34	Nebraska	246.2
35	Iowa	240.1
36	Idaho	230.7
37	Pennsylvania	222.3
38	Mississippi	198.0
39	Virginia	187.6
40	Utah	186.3
41	Minnesota	176.7
42	Hawaii	153.0
43	Wisconsin	126.7
44	South Dakota	114.1
45	Montana	108.4
46	West Virginia	102.1
47	Maine	96.0
48	Vermont	87.2
49	New Hampshire	67.6
50	North Dakota	47.4

District of Columbia   1,117.0

Source: Federal Bureau of Investigation
"Crime in the United States 1990" (Uniform Crime Reports, August 11, 1991)
*Aggravated assault is an attack for the purpose of inflicting severe bodily injury.

Percent Change in Rate of Aggravated Assaults: 1990 to 1994

National Percent Change = 1.4% Increase*

ALPHA ORDER			RANK ORDER		
RANK	STATE	PERCENT CHANGE	RANK	STATE	PERCENT CHANGE
42	Alabama	(10.6)	1	Nevada	95.8
3	Alaska	48.3	2	Kentucky	64.7
13	Arizona	11.7	3	Alaska	48.3
12	Arkansas	12.9	4	South Dakota	45.1
32	California	(0.7)	5	West Virginia	44.6
40	Colorado	(8.1)	6	Mississippi	36.6
47	Connecticut	(17.3)	7	Oklahoma	26.0
43	Delaware	(10.7)	8	Tennessee	15.0
33	Florida	(0.9)	9	Louisiana	14.3
37	Georgia	(6.3)	10	Nebraska	13.8
48	Hawaii	(19.0)	11	New Mexico	13.1
23	Idaho	2.3	12	Arkansas	12.9
20	Illinois	3.8	13	Arizona	11.7
16	Indiana	7.0	14	Kansas	10.6
26	Iowa	1.2	15	Oregon	7.3
14	Kansas	10.6	16	Indiana	7.0
2	Kentucky	64.7	17	Massachusetts	5.1
9	Louisiana	14.3	17	Montana	5.1
46	Maine	(17.1)	17	Utah	5.1
33	Maryland	(0.9)	20	Illinois	3.8
17	Massachusetts	5.1	21	South Carolina	2.8
35	Michigan	(2.5)	22	Wisconsin	2.4
27	Minnesota	1.1	23	Idaho	2.3
6	Mississippi	36.6	24	Missouri	1.7
24	Missouri	1.7	25	Texas	1.4
17	Montana	5.1	26	Iowa	1.2
10	Nebraska	13.8	27	Minnesota	1.1
1	Nevada	95.8	28	Washington	1.0
49	New Hampshire	(22.3)	29	North Carolina	0.8
36	New Jersey	(4.8)	30	Virginia	0.0
11	New Mexico	13.1	31	North Dakota	(0.4)
44	New York	(11.7)	32	California	(0.7)
29	North Carolina	0.8	33	Florida	(0.9)
31	North Dakota	(0.4)	33	Maryland	(0.9)
39	Ohio	(7.4)	35	Michigan	(2.5)
7	Oklahoma	26.0	36	New Jersey	(4.8)
15	Oregon	7.3	37	Georgia	(6.3)
38	Pennsylvania	(6.4)	38	Pennsylvania	(6.4)
41	Rhode Island	(8.4)	39	Ohio	(7.4)
21	South Carolina	2.8	40	Colorado	(8.1)
4	South Dakota	45.1	41	Rhode Island	(8.4)
8	Tennessee	15.0	42	Alabama	(10.6)
25	Texas	1.4	43	Delaware	(10.7)
17	Utah	5.1	44	New York	(11.7)
50	Vermont	(35.8)	45	Wyoming	(12.8)
30	Virginia	0.0	46	Maine	(17.1)
28	Washington	1.0	47	Connecticut	(17.3)
5	West Virginia	44.6	48	Hawaii	(19.0)
22	Wisconsin	2.4	49	New Hampshire	(22.3)
45	Wyoming	(12.8)	50	Vermont	(35.8)

	District of Columbia	29.1

Source: Morgan Quitno Press using data from Federal Bureau of Investigation
"Crime in the United States" (Uniform Crime Reports, 1990 and 1994 editions)
*Aggravated assault is an attack for the purpose of inflicting severe bodily injury.

Property Crimes in 1990

National Total = 12,655,486 Property Crimes*

<table>
<tr><td colspan="4">ALPHA ORDER</td><td colspan="4">RANK ORDER</td></tr>
<tr><td>RANK</td><td>STATE</td><td>CRIMES</td><td>% of USA</td><td>RANK</td><td>STATE</td><td>CRIMES</td><td>% of USA</td></tr>
<tr><td>25</td><td>Alabama</td><td>169,974</td><td>1.34%</td><td>1</td><td>California</td><td>1,654,186</td><td>13.07%</td></tr>
<tr><td>46</td><td>Alaska</td><td>25,457</td><td>0.20%</td><td>2</td><td>Texas</td><td>1,200,151</td><td>9.48%</td></tr>
<tr><td>14</td><td>Arizona</td><td>265,229</td><td>2.10%</td><td>3</td><td>Florida</td><td>978,944</td><td>7.74%</td></tr>
<tr><td>32</td><td>Arkansas</td><td>101,897</td><td>0.81%</td><td>4</td><td>New York</td><td>932,416</td><td>7.37%</td></tr>
<tr><td>1</td><td>California</td><td>1,654,186</td><td>13.07%</td><td>5</td><td>Illinois</td><td>567,841</td><td>4.49%</td></tr>
<tr><td>23</td><td>Colorado</td><td>182,106</td><td>1.44%</td><td>6</td><td>Michigan</td><td>483,764</td><td>3.82%</td></tr>
<tr><td>27</td><td>Connecticut</td><td>158,867</td><td>1.26%</td><td>7</td><td>Ohio</td><td>470,469</td><td>3.72%</td></tr>
<tr><td>45</td><td>Delaware</td><td>31,344</td><td>0.25%</td><td>8</td><td>Georgia</td><td>389,165</td><td>3.08%</td></tr>
<tr><td>3</td><td>Florida</td><td>978,944</td><td>7.74%</td><td>9</td><td>New Jersey</td><td>371,023</td><td>2.93%</td></tr>
<tr><td>8</td><td>Georgia</td><td>389,165</td><td>3.08%</td><td>10</td><td>Pennsylvania</td><td>361,805</td><td>2.86%</td></tr>
<tr><td>37</td><td>Hawaii</td><td>64,563</td><td>0.51%</td><td>11</td><td>North Carolina</td><td>322,306</td><td>2.55%</td></tr>
<tr><td>43</td><td>Idaho</td><td>38,069</td><td>0.30%</td><td>12</td><td>Washington</td><td>278,440</td><td>2.20%</td></tr>
<tr><td>5</td><td>Illinois</td><td>567,841</td><td>4.49%</td><td>13</td><td>Massachusetts</td><td>274,442</td><td>2.17%</td></tr>
<tr><td>18</td><td>Indiana</td><td>233,376</td><td>1.84%</td><td>14</td><td>Arizona</td><td>265,229</td><td>2.10%</td></tr>
<tr><td>31</td><td>Iowa</td><td>105,550</td><td>0.83%</td><td>15</td><td>Virginia</td><td>253,063</td><td>2.00%</td></tr>
<tr><td>29</td><td>Kansas</td><td>117,571</td><td>0.93%</td><td>16</td><td>Louisiana</td><td>235,822</td><td>1.86%</td></tr>
<tr><td>30</td><td>Kentucky</td><td>107,208</td><td>0.85%</td><td>17</td><td>Maryland</td><td>234,842</td><td>1.86%</td></tr>
<tr><td>16</td><td>Louisiana</td><td>235,822</td><td>1.86%</td><td>18</td><td>Indiana</td><td>233,376</td><td>1.84%</td></tr>
<tr><td>40</td><td>Maine</td><td>43,647</td><td>0.34%</td><td>19</td><td>Missouri</td><td>225,422</td><td>1.78%</td></tr>
<tr><td>17</td><td>Maryland</td><td>234,842</td><td>1.86%</td><td>20</td><td>Tennessee</td><td>213,648</td><td>1.69%</td></tr>
<tr><td>13</td><td>Massachusetts</td><td>274,442</td><td>2.17%</td><td>21</td><td>Wisconsin</td><td>202,052</td><td>1.60%</td></tr>
<tr><td>6</td><td>Michigan</td><td>483,764</td><td>3.82%</td><td>22</td><td>Minnesota</td><td>185,185</td><td>1.46%</td></tr>
<tr><td>22</td><td>Minnesota</td><td>185,185</td><td>1.46%</td><td>23</td><td>Colorado</td><td>182,106</td><td>1.44%</td></tr>
<tr><td>34</td><td>Mississippi</td><td>90,803</td><td>0.72%</td><td>24</td><td>South Carolina</td><td>176,729</td><td>1.40%</td></tr>
<tr><td>19</td><td>Missouri</td><td>225,422</td><td>1.78%</td><td>25</td><td>Alabama</td><td>169,974</td><td>1.34%</td></tr>
<tr><td>44</td><td>Montana</td><td>34,702</td><td>0.27%</td><td>26</td><td>Oklahoma</td><td>158,889</td><td>1.26%</td></tr>
<tr><td>38</td><td>Nebraska</td><td>61,290</td><td>0.48%</td><td>27</td><td>Connecticut</td><td>158,867</td><td>1.26%</td></tr>
<tr><td>36</td><td>Nevada</td><td>65,652</td><td>0.52%</td><td>28</td><td>Oregon</td><td>146,073</td><td>1.15%</td></tr>
<tr><td>42</td><td>New Hampshire</td><td>38,976</td><td>0.31%</td><td>29</td><td>Kansas</td><td>117,571</td><td>0.93%</td></tr>
<tr><td>9</td><td>New Jersey</td><td>371,023</td><td>2.93%</td><td>30</td><td>Kentucky</td><td>107,208</td><td>0.85%</td></tr>
<tr><td>35</td><td>New Mexico</td><td>89,448</td><td>0.71%</td><td>31</td><td>Iowa</td><td>105,550</td><td>0.83%</td></tr>
<tr><td>4</td><td>New York</td><td>932,416</td><td>7.37%</td><td>32</td><td>Arkansas</td><td>101,897</td><td>0.81%</td></tr>
<tr><td>11</td><td>North Carolina</td><td>322,306</td><td>2.55%</td><td>33</td><td>Utah</td><td>92,620</td><td>0.73%</td></tr>
<tr><td>49</td><td>North Dakota</td><td>18,196</td><td>0.14%</td><td>34</td><td>Mississippi</td><td>90,803</td><td>0.72%</td></tr>
<tr><td>7</td><td>Ohio</td><td>470,469</td><td>3.72%</td><td>35</td><td>New Mexico</td><td>89,448</td><td>0.71%</td></tr>
<tr><td>26</td><td>Oklahoma</td><td>158,889</td><td>1.26%</td><td>36</td><td>Nevada</td><td>65,652</td><td>0.52%</td></tr>
<tr><td>28</td><td>Oregon</td><td>146,073</td><td>1.15%</td><td>37</td><td>Hawaii</td><td>64,563</td><td>0.51%</td></tr>
<tr><td>10</td><td>Pennsylvania</td><td>361,805</td><td>2.86%</td><td>38</td><td>Nebraska</td><td>61,290</td><td>0.48%</td></tr>
<tr><td>39</td><td>Rhode Island</td><td>49,378</td><td>0.39%</td><td>39</td><td>Rhode Island</td><td>49,378</td><td>0.39%</td></tr>
<tr><td>24</td><td>South Carolina</td><td>176,729</td><td>1.40%</td><td>40</td><td>Maine</td><td>43,647</td><td>0.34%</td></tr>
<tr><td>48</td><td>South Dakota</td><td>19,116</td><td>0.15%</td><td>41</td><td>West Virginia</td><td>41,855</td><td>0.33%</td></tr>
<tr><td>20</td><td>Tennessee</td><td>213,648</td><td>1.69%</td><td>42</td><td>New Hampshire</td><td>38,976</td><td>0.31%</td></tr>
<tr><td>2</td><td>Texas</td><td>1,200,151</td><td>9.48%</td><td>43</td><td>Idaho</td><td>38,069</td><td>0.30%</td></tr>
<tr><td>33</td><td>Utah</td><td>92,620</td><td>0.73%</td><td>44</td><td>Montana</td><td>34,702</td><td>0.27%</td></tr>
<tr><td>47</td><td>Vermont</td><td>23,713</td><td>0.19%</td><td>45</td><td>Delaware</td><td>31,344</td><td>0.25%</td></tr>
<tr><td>15</td><td>Virginia</td><td>253,063</td><td>2.00%</td><td>46</td><td>Alaska</td><td>25,457</td><td>0.20%</td></tr>
<tr><td>12</td><td>Washington</td><td>278,440</td><td>2.20%</td><td>47</td><td>Vermont</td><td>23,713</td><td>0.19%</td></tr>
<tr><td>41</td><td>West Virginia</td><td>41,855</td><td>0.33%</td><td>48</td><td>South Dakota</td><td>19,116</td><td>0.15%</td></tr>
<tr><td>21</td><td>Wisconsin</td><td>202,052</td><td>1.60%</td><td>49</td><td>North Dakota</td><td>18,196</td><td>0.14%</td></tr>
<tr><td>50</td><td>Wyoming</td><td>17,732</td><td>0.14%</td><td>50</td><td>Wyoming</td><td>17,732</td><td>0.14%</td></tr>
<tr><td></td><td></td><td></td><td></td><td></td><td>District of Columbia</td><td>50,470</td><td>0.40%</td></tr>
</table>

Source: Federal Bureau of Investigation
"Crime in the United States 1990" (Uniform Crime Reports, August 11, 1991)
*Property crimes are offenses of burglary, larceny-theft and motor vehicle theft.

Percent Change in Number of Property Crimes: 1990 to 1994

National Percent Change = 4.2% Decrease*

ALPHA ORDER			RANK ORDER		
RANK	STATE	PERCENT CHANGE	RANK	STATE	PERCENT CHANGE
17	Alabama	4.7	1	Mississippi	27.7
5	Alaska	17.6	2	Nevada	26.0
8	Arizona	11.0	3	Oregon	22.0
22	Arkansas	1.2	4	Montana	19.4
28	California	(1.9)	5	Alaska	17.6
31	Colorado	(3.5)	6	Hawaii	17.2
43	Connecticut	(15.6)	7	Idaho	12.8
45	Delaware	(19.2)	8	Arizona	11.0
22	Florida	1.2	9	Maryland	10.3
30	Georgia	(3.1)	10	North Carolina	9.0
6	Hawaii	17.2	11	South Dakota	8.4
7	Idaho	12.8	12	Wyoming	7.8
31	Illinois	(3.5)	13	Nebraska	7.3
26	Indiana	0.3	14	Missouri	6.9
40	Iowa	(10.5)	15	Tennessee	5.9
33	Kansas	(4.1)	15	Washington	5.9
19	Kentucky	3.3	17	Alabama	4.7
18	Louisiana	4.1	18	Louisiana	4.1
41	Maine	(10.7)	19	Kentucky	3.3
9	Maryland	10.3	20	South Carolina	3.1
44	Massachusetts	(17.8)	21	Utah	2.9
39	Michigan	(8.2)	22	Arkansas	1.2
27	Minnesota	(1.8)	22	Florida	1.2
1	Mississippi	27.7	24	Oklahoma	0.9
14	Missouri	6.9	25	West Virginia	0.7
4	Montana	19.4	26	Indiana	0.3
13	Nebraska	7.3	27	Minnesota	(1.8)
2	Nevada	26.0	28	California	(1.9)
49	New Hampshire	(23.5)	29	New Mexico	(2.0)
42	New Jersey	(13.8)	30	Georgia	(3.1)
29	New Mexico	(2.0)	31	Colorado	(3.5)
46	New York	(20.0)	31	Illinois	(3.5)
10	North Carolina	9.0	33	Kansas	(4.1)
37	North Dakota	(6.9)	34	Virginia	(4.5)
36	Ohio	(6.2)	35	Pennsylvania	(5.2)
24	Oklahoma	0.9	36	Ohio	(6.2)
3	Oregon	22.0	37	North Dakota	(6.9)
35	Pennsylvania	(5.2)	38	Wisconsin	(7.6)
50	Rhode Island	(24.4)	39	Michigan	(8.2)
20	South Carolina	3.1	40	Iowa	(10.5)
11	South Dakota	8.4	41	Maine	(10.7)
15	Tennessee	5.9	42	New Jersey	(13.8)
47	Texas	(20.9)	43	Connecticut	(15.6)
21	Utah	2.9	44	Massachusetts	(17.8)
48	Vermont	(22.9)	45	Delaware	(19.2)
34	Virginia	(4.5)	46	New York	(20.0)
15	Washington	5.9	47	Texas	(20.9)
25	West Virginia	0.7	48	Vermont	(22.9)
38	Wisconsin	(7.6)	49	New Hampshire	(23.5)
12	Wyoming	7.8	50	Rhode Island	(24.4)
				District of Columbia	(4.9)

Source: Morgan Quitno Press using data from Federal Bureau of Investigation
"Crime in the United States" (Uniform Crime Reports, 1990 and 1994 editions)
*Property crimes are offenses of burglary, larceny-theft and motor vehicle theft.

Property Crime Rate in 1990

National Rate = 5,088.5 Property Crimes per 100,000 Population*

ALPHA ORDER				RANK ORDER		
RANK	STATE	RATE		RANK	STATE	RATE
36	Alabama	4,206.7		1	Florida	7,566.5
26	Alaska	4,628.2		2	Arizona	7,236.4
2	Arizona	7,236.4		3	Texas	7,065.3
32	Arkansas	4,334.7		4	Georgia	6,007.3
9	California	5,558.4		5	New Mexico	5,903.9
10	Colorado	5,527.8		6	Hawaii	5,825.8
22	Connecticut	4,833.0		7	Washington	5,721.3
25	Delaware	4,705.1		8	Louisiana	5,588.2
1	Florida	7,566.5		9	California	5,558.4
4	Georgia	6,007.3		10	Colorado	5,527.8
6	Hawaii	5,825.8		11	Nevada	5,462.7
42	Idaho	3,781.4		12	Utah	5,376.0
18	Illinois	4,967.7		13	Michigan	5,204.4
35	Indiana	4,209.4		14	New York	5,182.8
41	Iowa	3,801.2		15	Oregon	5,139.2
24	Kansas	4,745.4		16	South Carolina	5,068.7
47	Kentucky	2,909.1		17	Oklahoma	5,051.2
8	Louisiana	5,588.2		18	Illinois	4,967.7
43	Maine	3,554.5		19	Rhode Island	4,920.8
20	Maryland	4,911.5		20	Maryland	4,911.5
27	Massachusetts	4,561.5		21	North Carolina	4,862.3
13	Michigan	5,204.4		22	Connecticut	4,833.0
33	Minnesota	4,232.7		23	New Jersey	4,799.7
44	Mississippi	3,528.8		24	Kansas	4,745.4
28	Missouri	4,405.3		25	Delaware	4,705.1
30	Montana	4,342.8		26	Alaska	4,628.2
40	Nebraska	3,883.1		27	Massachusetts	4,561.5
11	Nevada	5,462.7		28	Missouri	4,405.3
45	New Hampshire	3,513.7		29	Tennessee	4,380.6
23	New Jersey	4,799.7		30	Montana	4,342.8
5	New Mexico	5,903.9		31	Ohio	4,337.3
14	New York	5,182.8		32	Arkansas	4,334.7
21	North Carolina	4,862.3		33	Minnesota	4,232.7
48	North Dakota	2,848.5		34	Vermont	4,213.7
31	Ohio	4,337.3		35	Indiana	4,209.4
17	Oklahoma	5,051.2		36	Alabama	4,206.7
15	Oregon	5,139.2		37	Wisconsin	4,130.4
46	Pennsylvania	3,045.1		38	Virginia	4,090.0
19	Rhode Island	4,920.8		39	Wyoming	3,909.3
16	South Carolina	5,068.7		40	Nebraska	3,883.1
49	South Dakota	2,746.5		41	Iowa	3,801.2
29	Tennessee	4,380.6		42	Idaho	3,781.4
3	Texas	7,065.3		43	Maine	3,554.5
12	Utah	5,376.0		44	Mississippi	3,528.8
34	Vermont	4,213.7		45	New Hampshire	3,513.7
38	Virginia	4,090.0		46	Pennsylvania	3,045.1
7	Washington	5,721.3		47	Kentucky	2,909.1
50	West Virginia	2,333.7		48	North Dakota	2,848.5
37	Wisconsin	4,130.4		49	South Dakota	2,746.5
39	Wyoming	3,909.3		50	West Virginia	2,333.7
					District of Columbia	8,316.0

Source: Federal Bureau of Investigation
   "Crime in the United States 1990" (Uniform Crime Reports, August 11, 1991)
*Property crimes are offenses of burglary, larceny-theft and motor vehicle theft.

Percent Change in Property Crime Rate: 1990 to 1994

National Percent Change = 8.5% Decrease*

ALPHA ORDER			RANK ORDER		
RANK	STATE	PERCENT CHANGE	RANK	STATE	PERCENT CHANGE
14	Alabama	0.3	1	Mississippi	23.1
5	Alaska	6.8	2	Oregon	12.4
16	Arizona	(0.2)	3	Montana	11.5
22	Arkansas	(3.0)	4	Hawaii	10.2
32	California	(7.2)	5	Alaska	6.8
41	Colorado	(13.0)	6	Maryland	5.4
42	Connecticut	(15.3)	7	South Dakota	4.7
46	Delaware	(23.8)	8	Nebraska	4.3
26	Florida	(6.1)	9	Nevada	3.9
37	Georgia	(11.1)	10	Missouri	3.6
4	Hawaii	10.2	11	Wyoming	2.8
14	Idaho	0.3	12	North Carolina	2.2
26	Illinois	(6.1)	13	Louisiana	1.8
23	Indiana	(3.4)	14	Alabama	0.3
40	Iowa	(12.2)	14	Idaho	0.3
30	Kansas	(7.0)	16	Arizona	(0.2)
18	Kentucky	(0.5)	16	Tennessee	(0.2)
13	Louisiana	1.8	18	Kentucky	(0.5)
39	Maine	(11.6)	19	West Virginia	(0.9)
6	Maryland	5.4	20	South Carolina	(1.9)
44	Massachusetts	(18.2)	21	Oklahoma	(2.6)
35	Michigan	(10.1)	22	Arkansas	(3.0)
25	Minnesota	(5.9)	23	Indiana	(3.4)
1	Mississippi	23.1	24	Washington	(3.6)
10	Missouri	3.6	25	Minnesota	(5.9)
3	Montana	11.5	26	Florida	(6.1)
8	Nebraska	4.3	26	Illinois	(6.1)
9	Nevada	3.9	28	Pennsylvania	(6.6)
49	New Hampshire	(25.3)	29	North Dakota	(6.8)
43	New Jersey	(15.7)	30	Kansas	(7.0)
36	New Mexico	(10.3)	31	Utah	(7.1)
45	New York	(20.8)	32	California	(7.2)
12	North Carolina	2.2	33	Ohio	(8.3)
29	North Dakota	(6.8)	34	Virginia	(9.8)
33	Ohio	(8.3)	35	Michigan	(10.1)
21	Oklahoma	(2.6)	36	New Mexico	(10.3)
2	Oregon	12.4	37	Georgia	(11.1)
28	Pennsylvania	(6.6)	37	Wisconsin	(11.1)
47	Rhode Island	(23.9)	39	Maine	(11.6)
20	South Carolina	(1.9)	40	Iowa	(12.2)
7	South Dakota	4.7	41	Colorado	(13.0)
16	Tennessee	(0.2)	42	Connecticut	(15.3)
50	Texas	(26.9)	43	New Jersey	(15.7)
31	Utah	(7.1)	44	Massachusetts	(18.2)
48	Vermont	(25.2)	45	New York	(20.8)
34	Virginia	(9.8)	46	Delaware	(23.8)
24	Washington	(3.6)	47	Rhode Island	(23.9)
19	West Virginia	(0.9)	48	Vermont	(25.2)
37	Wisconsin	(11.1)	49	New Hampshire	(25.3)
11	Wyoming	2.8	50	Texas	(26.9)

District of Columbia   1.3

Source: Morgan Quitno Press using data from Federal Bureau of Investigation
"Crime in the United States" (Uniform Crime Reports, 1990 and 1994 editions)
*Property crimes are offenses of burglary, larceny-theft and motor vehicle theft.

Burglaries in 1990

National Total = 3,073,909 Burglaries*

ALPHA ORDER					RANK ORDER			
RANK	STATE	BURGLARIES	% of USA		RANK	STATE	BURGLARIES	% of USA
23	Alabama	44,585	1.45%		1	California	400,392	13.03%
47	Alaska	4,919	0.16%		2	Texas	314,512	10.23%
15	Arizona	61,206	1.99%		3	Florida	280,832	9.14%
31	Arkansas	28,464	0.93%		4	New York	208,813	6.79%
1	California	400,392	13.03%		5	Illinois	121,506	3.95%
25	Colorado	39,822	1.30%		6	Ohio	106,575	3.47%
24	Connecticut	40,355	1.31%		7	Michigan	106,275	3.46%
44	Delaware	6,465	0.21%		8	Georgia	104,905	3.41%
3	Florida	280,832	9.14%		9	North Carolina	101,444	3.30%
8	Georgia	104,905	3.41%		10	Pennsylvania	86,624	2.82%
37	Hawaii	13,611	0.44%		11	New Jersey	78,628	2.56%
42	Idaho	8,187	0.27%		12	Massachusetts	66,942	2.18%
5	Illinois	121,506	3.95%		13	Tennessee	61,646	2.01%
19	Indiana	52,297	1.70%		14	Washington	61,460	2.00%
34	Iowa	22,448	0.73%		15	Arizona	61,206	1.99%
30	Kansas	28,901	0.94%		16	Louisiana	60,677	1.97%
32	Kentucky	28,264	0.92%		17	Missouri	54,536	1.77%
16	Louisiana	60,677	1.97%		18	Maryland	53,549	1.74%
41	Maine	10,106	0.33%		19	Indiana	52,297	1.70%
18	Maryland	53,549	1.74%		20	South Carolina	48,132	1.57%
12	Massachusetts	66,942	2.18%		21	Oklahoma	45,531	1.48%
7	Michigan	106,275	3.46%		22	Virginia	45,236	1.47%
26	Minnesota	39,691	1.29%		23	Alabama	44,585	1.45%
29	Mississippi	32,196	1.05%		24	Connecticut	40,355	1.31%
17	Missouri	54,536	1.77%		25	Colorado	39,822	1.30%
46	Montana	5,666	0.18%		26	Minnesota	39,691	1.29%
40	Nebraska	11,424	0.37%		27	Wisconsin	36,755	1.20%
35	Nevada	16,434	0.53%		28	Oregon	32,273	1.05%
43	New Hampshire	8,158	0.27%		29	Mississippi	32,196	1.05%
11	New Jersey	78,628	2.56%		30	Kansas	28,901	0.94%
33	New Mexico	26,343	0.86%		31	Arkansas	28,464	0.93%
4	New York	208,813	6.79%		32	Kentucky	28,264	0.92%
9	North Carolina	101,444	3.30%		33	New Mexico	26,343	0.86%
50	North Dakota	2,725	0.09%		34	Iowa	22,448	0.73%
6	Ohio	106,575	3.47%		35	Nevada	16,434	0.53%
21	Oklahoma	45,531	1.48%		36	Utah	15,172	0.49%
28	Oregon	32,273	1.05%		37	Hawaii	13,611	0.44%
10	Pennsylvania	86,624	2.82%		38	Rhode Island	12,755	0.41%
38	Rhode Island	12,755	0.41%		39	West Virginia	11,785	0.38%
20	South Carolina	48,132	1.57%		40	Nebraska	11,424	0.37%
48	South Dakota	3,671	0.12%		41	Maine	10,106	0.33%
13	Tennessee	61,646	2.01%		42	Idaho	8,187	0.27%
2	Texas	314,512	10.23%		43	New Hampshire	8,158	0.27%
36	Utah	15,172	0.49%		44	Delaware	6,465	0.21%
45	Vermont	6,119	0.20%		45	Vermont	6,119	0.20%
22	Virginia	45,236	1.47%		46	Montana	5,666	0.18%
14	Washington	61,460	2.00%		47	Alaska	4,919	0.16%
39	West Virginia	11,785	0.38%		48	South Dakota	3,671	0.12%
27	Wisconsin	36,755	1.20%		49	Wyoming	2,862	0.09%
49	Wyoming	2,862	0.09%		50	North Dakota	2,725	0.09%
						District of Columbia	12,035	0.39%

Source: Federal Bureau of Investigation
   "Crime in the United States 1990" (Uniform Crime Reports, August 11, 1991)
*Burglary is the unlawful entry of a structure to commit a felony or theft. Attempts are included.

Percent Change in Number of Burglaries: 1990 to 1994

National Percent Change = 11.8% Decrease*

ALPHA ORDER			RANK ORDER		
RANK	STATE	PERCENT CHANGE	RANK	STATE	PERCENT CHANGE
14	Alabama	(1.2)	1	Nevada	20.1
15	Alaska	(1.4)	2	Montana	9.0
16	Arizona	(1.7)	3	Wyoming	8.2
23	Arkansas	(5.5)	4	South Dakota	7.3
20	California	(4.0)	5	Mississippi	7.1
37	Colorado	(15.0)	6	Oregon	5.3
46	Connecticut	(27.8)	7	Hawaii	3.1
36	Delaware	(13.7)	8	North Carolina	2.6
38	Florida	(15.5)	9	Missouri	1.9
43	Georgia	(22.4)	10	Kentucky	1.6
7	Hawaii	3.1	11	Idaho	(0.5)
11	Idaho	(0.5)	12	Utah	(0.6)
18	Illinois	(2.8)	13	Kansas	(0.9)
24	Indiana	(6.5)	14	Alabama	(1.2)
39	Iowa	(15.9)	15	Alaska	(1.4)
13	Kansas	(0.9)	16	Arizona	(1.7)
10	Kentucky	1.6	17	Maryland	(2.5)
28	Louisiana	(9.1)	18	Illinois	(2.8)
34	Maine	(11.6)	19	South Carolina	(3.0)
17	Maryland	(2.5)	20	California	(4.0)
41	Massachusetts	(20.5)	20	Nebraska	(4.0)
35	Michigan	(13.6)	22	Tennessee	(4.2)
27	Minnesota	(8.9)	23	Arkansas	(5.5)
5	Mississippi	7.1	24	Indiana	(6.5)
9	Missouri	1.9	25	Virginia	(7.5)
2	Montana	9.0	26	New Jersey	(8.3)
20	Nebraska	(4.0)	27	Minnesota	(8.9)
1	Nevada	20.1	28	Louisiana	(9.1)
50	New Hampshire	(35.3)	29	Washington	(9.2)
26	New Jersey	(8.3)	30	West Virginia	(9.4)
40	New Mexico	(16.7)	31	Ohio	(9.8)
42	New York	(21.2)	32	Oklahoma	(10.5)
8	North Carolina	2.6	33	Wisconsin	(10.7)
45	North Dakota	(24.0)	34	Maine	(11.6)
31	Ohio	(9.8)	35	Michigan	(13.6)
32	Oklahoma	(10.5)	36	Delaware	(13.7)
6	Oregon	5.3	37	Colorado	(15.0)
44	Pennsylvania	(23.3)	38	Florida	(15.5)
47	Rhode Island	(28.7)	39	Iowa	(15.9)
19	South Carolina	(3.0)	40	New Mexico	(16.7)
4	South Dakota	7.3	41	Massachusetts	(20.5)
22	Tennessee	(4.2)	42	New York	(21.2)
49	Texas	(31.7)	43	Georgia	(22.4)
12	Utah	(0.6)	44	Pennsylvania	(23.3)
48	Vermont	(30.2)	45	North Dakota	(24.0)
25	Virginia	(7.5)	46	Connecticut	(27.8)
29	Washington	(9.2)	47	Rhode Island	(28.7)
30	West Virginia	(9.4)	48	Vermont	(30.2)
33	Wisconsin	(10.7)	49	Texas	(31.7)
3	Wyoming	8.2	50	New Hampshire	(35.3)
				District of Columbia	(16.6)

Source: Morgan Quitno Press using data from Federal Bureau of Investigation
   "Crime in the United States" (Uniform Crime Reports, 1990 and 1994 editions)
*Burglary is the unlawful entry of a structure to commit a felony or theft. Attempts are included.

Burglary Rate in 1990

National Rate = 1,235.9 Burglaries per 100,000 Population*

ALPHA ORDER

RANK	STATE	RATE
26	Alabama	1,103.4
35	Alaska	894.3
4	Arizona	1,669.9
18	Arkansas	1,210.9
11	California	1,345.4
19	Colorado	1,208.8
17	Connecticut	1,227.7
32	Delaware	970.5
1	Florida	2,170.6
5	Georgia	1,619.4
16	Hawaii	1,228.2
38	Idaho	813.2
29	Illinois	1,063.0
33	Indiana	943.3
39	Iowa	808.4
20	Kansas	1,166.5
40	Kentucky	766.9
8	Louisiana	1,437.9
37	Maine	823.0
24	Maryland	1,119.9
25	Massachusetts	1,112.7
22	Michigan	1,143.3
34	Minnesota	907.2
15	Mississippi	1,251.2
28	Missouri	1,065.8
46	Montana	709.1
45	Nebraska	723.8
10	Nevada	1,367.4
42	New Hampshire	735.5
30	New Jersey	1,017.2
3	New Mexico	1,738.7
21	New York	1,160.7
6	North Carolina	1,530.4
50	North Dakota	426.6
31	Ohio	982.5
7	Oklahoma	1,447.5
23	Oregon	1,135.4
44	Pennsylvania	729.1
12	Rhode Island	1,271.1
9	South Carolina	1,380.4
49	South Dakota	527.4
13	Tennessee	1,264.0
2	Texas	1,851.5
36	Utah	880.6
27	Vermont	1,087.3
43	Virginia	731.1
14	Washington	1,262.9
47	West Virginia	657.1
41	Wisconsin	751.4
48	Wyoming	631.0

RANK ORDER

RANK	STATE	RATE
1	Florida	2,170.6
2	Texas	1,851.5
3	New Mexico	1,738.7
4	Arizona	1,669.9
5	Georgia	1,619.4
6	North Carolina	1,530.4
7	Oklahoma	1,447.5
8	Louisiana	1,437.9
9	South Carolina	1,380.4
10	Nevada	1,367.4
11	California	1,345.4
12	Rhode Island	1,271.1
13	Tennessee	1,264.0
14	Washington	1,262.9
15	Mississippi	1,251.2
16	Hawaii	1,228.2
17	Connecticut	1,227.7
18	Arkansas	1,210.9
19	Colorado	1,208.8
20	Kansas	1,166.5
21	New York	1,160.7
22	Michigan	1,143.3
23	Oregon	1,135.4
24	Maryland	1,119.9
25	Massachusetts	1,112.7
26	Alabama	1,103.4
27	Vermont	1,087.3
28	Missouri	1,065.8
29	Illinois	1,063.0
30	New Jersey	1,017.2
31	Ohio	982.5
32	Delaware	970.5
33	Indiana	943.3
34	Minnesota	907.2
35	Alaska	894.3
36	Utah	880.6
37	Maine	823.0
38	Idaho	813.2
39	Iowa	808.4
40	Kentucky	766.9
41	Wisconsin	751.4
42	New Hampshire	735.5
43	Virginia	731.1
44	Pennsylvania	729.1
45	Nebraska	723.8
46	Montana	709.1
47	West Virginia	657.1
48	Wyoming	631.0
49	South Dakota	527.4
50	North Dakota	426.6

District of Columbia	1,983.0

Source: Federal Bureau of Investigation
   "Crime in the United States 1990" (Uniform Crime Reports, August 11, 1991)
*Burglary is the unlawful entry of a structure to commit a felony or theft. Attempts are included.

Percent Change in Burglary Rate: 1990 to 1994

National Percent Change = 15.7% Decrease*

ALPHA ORDER			RANK ORDER		
RANK	STATE	PERCENT CHANGE	RANK	STATE	PERCENT CHANGE
12	Alabama	(5.4)	1	South Dakota	3.6
23	Alaska	(10.5)	2	Mississippi	3.3
26	Arizona	(11.6)	3	Wyoming	3.1
18	Arkansas	(9.4)	4	Montana	1.8
17	California	(9.1)	5	Nevada	(0.9)
41	Colorado	(23.4)	6	Missouri	(1.2)
45	Connecticut	(27.5)	7	Kentucky	(2.2)
37	Delaware	(18.6)	8	Hawaii	(3.1)
39	Florida	(21.6)	8	Oregon	(3.1)
47	Georgia	(28.8)	10	North Carolina	(3.8)
8	Hawaii	(3.1)	11	Kansas	(3.9)
26	Idaho	(11.6)	12	Alabama	(5.4)
13	Illinois	(5.5)	13	Illinois	(5.5)
20	Indiana	(9.8)	14	Nebraska	(6.7)
36	Iowa	(17.5)	15	Maryland	(6.8)
11	Kansas	(3.9)	16	South Carolina	(7.7)
7	Kentucky	(2.2)	17	California	(9.1)
25	Louisiana	(11.1)	18	Arkansas	(9.4)
29	Maine	(12.4)	19	Tennessee	(9.7)
15	Maryland	(6.8)	20	Indiana	(9.8)
38	Massachusetts	(20.8)	21	Utah	(10.2)
34	Michigan	(15.4)	22	New Jersey	(10.4)
31	Minnesota	(12.7)	23	Alaska	(10.5)
2	Mississippi	3.3	24	West Virginia	(10.9)
6	Missouri	(1.2)	25	Louisiana	(11.1)
4	Montana	1.8	26	Arizona	(11.6)
14	Nebraska	(6.7)	26	Idaho	(11.6)
5	Nevada	(0.9)	28	Ohio	(11.8)
49	New Hampshire	(36.9)	29	Maine	(12.4)
22	New Jersey	(10.4)	30	Virginia	(12.6)
42	New Mexico	(23.7)	31	Minnesota	(12.7)
40	New York	(21.9)	32	Oklahoma	(13.6)
10	North Carolina	(3.8)	33	Wisconsin	(14.0)
43	North Dakota	(23.9)	34	Michigan	(15.4)
28	Ohio	(11.8)	35	Washington	(17.3)
32	Oklahoma	(13.6)	36	Iowa	(17.5)
8	Oregon	(3.1)	37	Delaware	(18.6)
44	Pennsylvania	(24.4)	38	Massachusetts	(20.8)
46	Rhode Island	(28.2)	39	Florida	(21.6)
16	South Carolina	(7.7)	40	New York	(21.9)
1	South Dakota	3.6	41	Colorado	(23.4)
19	Tennessee	(9.7)	42	New Mexico	(23.7)
49	Texas	(36.9)	43	North Dakota	(23.9)
21	Utah	(10.2)	44	Pennsylvania	(24.4)
48	Vermont	(32.2)	45	Connecticut	(27.5)
30	Virginia	(12.6)	46	Rhode Island	(28.2)
35	Washington	(17.3)	47	Georgia	(28.8)
24	West Virginia	(10.9)	48	Vermont	(32.2)
33	Wisconsin	(14.0)	49	New Hampshire	(36.9)
3	Wyoming	3.1	49	Texas	(36.9)
				District of Columbia	(11.2)

Source: Morgan Quitno Press using data from Federal Bureau of Investigation
"Crime in the United States" (Uniform Crime Reports, 1990 and 1994 editions)
*Burglary is the unlawful entry of a structure to commit a felony or theft. Attempts are included.

Larceny and Theft in 1990

National Total = 7,945,670 Larcenies and Thefts*

ALPHA ORDER

RANK	STATE	THEFTS	% of USA
25	Alabama	111,336	1.40%
46	Alaska	17,428	0.22%
14	Arizona	172,375	2.17%
33	Arkansas	66,630	0.84%
1	California	951,580	11.98%
22	Colorado	128,172	1.61%
27	Connecticut	94,485	1.19%
45	Delaware	21,922	0.28%
3	Florida	591,210	7.44%
8	Georgia	240,623	3.03%
37	Hawaii	46,735	0.59%
40	Idaho	28,216	0.36%
5	Illinois	372,862	4.69%
15	Indiana	156,741	1.97%
30	Iowa	78,384	0.99%
29	Kansas	80,361	1.01%
32	Kentucky	71,594	0.90%
17	Louisiana	149,752	1.88%
39	Maine	31,372	0.39%
18	Maryland	147,407	1.86%
16	Massachusetts	151,933	1.91%
6	Michigan	311,153	3.92%
21	Minnesota	129,500	1.63%
35	Mississippi	53,266	0.67%
20	Missouri	143,287	1.80%
43	Montana	27,098	0.34%
36	Nebraska	47,054	0.59%
38	Nevada	42,097	0.53%
41	New Hampshire	28,111	0.35%
9	New Jersey	219,767	2.77%
34	New Mexico	58,004	0.73%
4	New York	536,012	6.75%
11	North Carolina	202,059	2.54%
49	North Dakota	14,621	0.18%
7	Ohio	310,673	3.91%
28	Oklahoma	94,432	1.19%
26	Oregon	100,765	1.27%
10	Pennsylvania	215,119	2.71%
44	Rhode Island	27,046	0.34%
24	South Carolina	115,144	1.45%
48	South Dakota	14,678	0.18%
23	Tennessee	124,127	1.56%
2	Texas	731,224	9.20%
31	Utah	73,352	0.92%
47	Vermont	16,424	0.21%
13	Virginia	187,564	2.36%
12	Washington	195,221	2.46%
42	West Virginia	27,310	0.34%
19	Wisconsin	144,924	1.82%
50	Wyoming	14,194	0.18%

RANK ORDER

RANK	STATE	THEFTS	% of USA
1	California	951,580	11.98%
2	Texas	731,224	9.20%
3	Florida	591,210	7.44%
4	New York	536,012	6.75%
5	Illinois	372,862	4.69%
6	Michigan	311,153	3.92%
7	Ohio	310,673	3.91%
8	Georgia	240,623	3.03%
9	New Jersey	219,767	2.77%
10	Pennsylvania	215,119	2.71%
11	North Carolina	202,059	2.54%
12	Washington	195,221	2.46%
13	Virginia	187,564	2.36%
14	Arizona	172,375	2.17%
15	Indiana	156,741	1.97%
16	Massachusetts	151,933	1.91%
17	Louisiana	149,752	1.88%
18	Maryland	147,407	1.86%
19	Wisconsin	144,924	1.82%
20	Missouri	143,287	1.80%
21	Minnesota	129,500	1.63%
22	Colorado	128,172	1.61%
23	Tennessee	124,127	1.56%
24	South Carolina	115,144	1.45%
25	Alabama	111,336	1.40%
26	Oregon	100,765	1.27%
27	Connecticut	94,485	1.19%
28	Oklahoma	94,432	1.19%
29	Kansas	80,361	1.01%
30	Iowa	78,384	0.99%
31	Utah	73,352	0.92%
32	Kentucky	71,594	0.90%
33	Arkansas	66,630	0.84%
34	New Mexico	58,004	0.73%
35	Mississippi	53,266	0.67%
36	Nebraska	47,054	0.59%
37	Hawaii	46,735	0.59%
38	Nevada	42,097	0.53%
39	Maine	31,372	0.39%
40	Idaho	28,216	0.36%
41	New Hampshire	28,111	0.35%
42	West Virginia	27,310	0.34%
43	Montana	27,098	0.34%
44	Rhode Island	27,046	0.34%
45	Delaware	21,922	0.28%
46	Alaska	17,428	0.22%
47	Vermont	16,424	0.21%
48	South Dakota	14,678	0.18%
49	North Dakota	14,621	0.18%
50	Wyoming	14,194	0.18%
	District of Columbia	30,326	0.38%

Source: Federal Bureau of Investigation
"Crime in the United States 1990" (Uniform Crime Reports, August 11, 1991)
*Larceny and theft is the unlawful taking of property without use of force, violence or fraud. Attempts are included. Motor vehicle thefts are excluded.

Percent Change in Number of Larcenies and Thefts: 1990 to 1994

National Percent Change = 0.9% Decrease*

ALPHA ORDER			RANK ORDER		
RANK	STATE	PERCENT CHANGE	RANK	STATE	PERCENT CHANGE
17	Alabama	7.7	1	Mississippi	32.6
2	Alaska	25.2	2	Alaska	25.2
11	Arizona	10.6	3	Nevada	23.3
25	Arkansas	2.8	4	Oregon	21.6
32	California	(2.3)	5	Montana	21.1
30	Colorado	(0.5)	6	Hawaii	18.2
42	Connecticut	(10.3)	7	Idaho	15.5
50	Delaware	(21.2)	8	Maryland	14.4
21	Florida	6.0	9	North Carolina	11.8
19	Georgia	6.5	10	Tennessee	11.3
6	Hawaii	18.2	11	Arizona	10.6
7	Idaho	15.5	12	Missouri	10.5
33	Illinois	(2.4)	13	Oklahoma	10.2
27	Indiana	2.1	14	Louisiana	9.6
41	Iowa	(10.1)	15	Washington	8.7
37	Kansas	(6.1)	16	South Dakota	8.4
26	Kentucky	2.6	17	Alabama	7.7
14	Louisiana	9.6	18	Wyoming	7.5
40	Maine	(9.9)	19	Georgia	6.5
8	Maryland	14.4	20	South Carolina	6.2
44	Massachusetts	(14.5)	21	Florida	6.0
39	Michigan	(6.7)	22	Pennsylvania	3.3
29	Minnesota	1.4	23	Nebraska	3.2
1	Mississippi	32.6	23	West Virginia	3.2
12	Missouri	10.5	25	Arkansas	2.8
5	Montana	21.1	26	Kentucky	2.6
23	Nebraska	3.2	27	Indiana	2.1
3	Nevada	23.3	28	Utah	1.6
49	New Hampshire	(20.8)	29	Minnesota	1.4
43	New Jersey	(11.0)	30	Colorado	(0.5)
31	New Mexico	(1.1)	31	New Mexico	(1.1)
47	New York	(15.6)	32	California	(2.3)
9	North Carolina	11.8	33	Illinois	(2.4)
36	North Dakota	(4.9)	34	Virginia	(3.2)
35	Ohio	(4.2)	35	Ohio	(4.2)
13	Oklahoma	10.2	36	North Dakota	(4.9)
4	Oregon	21.6	37	Kansas	(6.1)
22	Pennsylvania	3.3	38	Wisconsin	(6.5)
46	Rhode Island	(14.8)	39	Michigan	(6.7)
20	South Carolina	6.2	40	Maine	(9.9)
16	South Dakota	8.4	41	Iowa	(10.1)
10	Tennessee	11.3	42	Connecticut	(10.3)
45	Texas	(14.7)	43	New Jersey	(11.0)
28	Utah	1.6	44	Massachusetts	(14.5)
48	Vermont	(19.9)	45	Texas	(14.7)
34	Virginia	(3.2)	46	Rhode Island	(14.8)
15	Washington	8.7	47	New York	(15.6)
23	West Virginia	3.2	48	Vermont	(19.9)
38	Wisconsin	(6.5)	49	New Hampshire	(20.8)
18	Wyoming	7.5	50	Delaware	(21.2)
				District of Columbia	(2.0)

Source: Morgan Quitno Press using data from Federal Bureau of Investigation
   "Crime in the United States" (Uniform Crime Reports, 1990 and 1994 editions)
*Larceny and theft is the unlawful taking of property without use of force, violence or fraud. Attempts are included.
Motor vehicle thefts are excluded.

Larceny and Theft Rate in 1990

National Rate = 3,194.8 Larcenies and Thefts per 100,000 Population*

ALPHA ORDER			RANK ORDER		
RANK	**STATE**	**RATE**	**RANK**	**STATE**	**RATE**
39	Alabama	2,755.4	1	Arizona	4,703.0
20	Alaska	3,168.5	2	Florida	4,569.6
1	Arizona	4,703.0	3	Texas	4,304.7
34	Arkansas	2,834.4	4	Utah	4,257.6
19	California	3,197.5	5	Hawaii	4,217.1
7	Colorado	3,890.6	6	Washington	4,011.4
31	Connecticut	2,874.4	7	Colorado	3,890.6
16	Delaware	3,290.8	8	New Mexico	3,828.5
2	Florida	4,569.6	9	Georgia	3,714.3
9	Georgia	3,714.3	10	Louisiana	3,548.6
5	Hawaii	4,217.1	11	Oregon	3,545.2
37	Idaho	2,802.7	12	Nevada	3,502.7
17	Illinois	3,262.0	13	Montana	3,391.2
35	Indiana	2,827.1	14	Michigan	3,347.4
36	Iowa	2,822.9	15	South Carolina	3,302.4
18	Kansas	3,243.5	16	Delaware	3,290.8
48	Kentucky	1,942.7	17	Illinois	3,262.0
10	Louisiana	3,548.6	18	Kansas	3,243.5
41	Maine	2,554.9	19	California	3,197.5
22	Maryland	3,082.9	20	Alaska	3,168.5
44	Massachusetts	2,525.3	21	Wyoming	3,129.3
14	Michigan	3,347.4	22	Maryland	3,082.9
29	Minnesota	2,959.9	23	North Carolina	3,048.3
47	Mississippi	2,070.0	24	Virginia	3,031.4
38	Missouri	2,800.2	25	Oklahoma	3,002.0
13	Montana	3,391.2	26	Nebraska	2,981.1
26	Nebraska	2,981.1	27	New York	2,979.4
12	Nevada	3,502.7	28	Wisconsin	2,962.6
43	New Hampshire	2,534.2	29	Minnesota	2,959.9
33	New Jersey	2,843.0	30	Vermont	2,918.5
8	New Mexico	3,828.5	31	Connecticut	2,874.4
27	New York	2,979.4	32	Ohio	2,864.1
23	North Carolina	3,048.3	33	New Jersey	2,843.0
45	North Dakota	2,288.8	34	Arkansas	2,834.4
32	Ohio	2,864.1	35	Indiana	2,827.1
25	Oklahoma	3,002.0	36	Iowa	2,822.9
11	Oregon	3,545.2	37	Idaho	2,802.7
49	Pennsylvania	1,810.5	38	Missouri	2,800.2
40	Rhode Island	2,695.3	39	Alabama	2,755.4
15	South Carolina	3,302.4	40	Rhode Island	2,695.3
46	South Dakota	2,108.9	41	Maine	2,554.9
42	Tennessee	2,545.1	42	Tennessee	2,545.1
3	Texas	4,304.7	43	New Hampshire	2,534.2
4	Utah	4,257.6	44	Massachusetts	2,525.3
30	Vermont	2,918.5	45	North Dakota	2,288.8
24	Virginia	3,031.4	46	South Dakota	2,108.9
6	Washington	4,011.4	47	Mississippi	2,070.0
50	West Virginia	1,522.7	48	Kentucky	1,942.7
28	Wisconsin	2,962.6	49	Pennsylvania	1,810.5
21	Wyoming	3,129.3	50	West Virginia	1,522.7
				District of Columbia	4,996.9

Source: Federal Bureau of Investigation
"Crime in the United States 1990" (Uniform Crime Reports, August 11, 1991)
*Larceny and theft is the unlawful taking of property without use of force, violence or fraud. Attempts are included.
Motor vehicle thefts are excluded.

Percent Change in Rate of Larcenies and Thefts: 1990 to 1994

National Percent Change = 5.3% Decrease*

ALPHA ORDER

RANK ORDER

RANK	STATE	PERCENT CHANGE
13	Alabama	3.2
2	Alaska	13.7
21	Arizona	(0.5)
24	Arkansas	(1.5)
32	California	(7.5)
40	Colorado	(10.3)
38	Connecticut	(10.0)
50	Delaware	(25.7)
26	Florida	(1.7)
27	Georgia	(2.2)
5	Hawaii	11.1
14	Idaho	2.7
30	Illinois	(5.1)
25	Indiana	(1.6)
42	Iowa	(11.7)
36	Kansas	(8.9)
23	Kentucky	(1.2)
7	Louisiana	7.2
41	Maine	(10.8)
6	Maryland	9.3
45	Massachusetts	(14.8)
35	Michigan	(8.7)
28	Minnesota	(2.8)
1	Mississippi	27.8
8	Missouri	7.1
3	Montana	13.1
20	Nebraska	0.3
17	Nevada	1.7
49	New Hampshire	(22.7)
43	New Jersey	(13.0)
37	New Mexico	(9.4)
46	New York	(16.4)
11	North Carolina	4.8
29	North Dakota	(4.8)
31	Ohio	(6.4)
9	Oklahoma	6.4
4	Oregon	12.0
16	Pennsylvania	1.9
44	Rhode Island	(14.3)
19	South Carolina	1.0
12	South Dakota	4.7
10	Tennessee	4.9
47	Texas	(21.1)
33	Utah	(8.2)
48	Vermont	(22.3)
34	Virginia	(8.6)
22	Washington	(1.0)
18	West Virginia	1.6
38	Wisconsin	(10.0)
15	Wyoming	2.4

RANK	STATE	PERCENT CHANGE
1	Mississippi	27.8
2	Alaska	13.7
3	Montana	13.1
4	Oregon	12.0
5	Hawaii	11.1
6	Maryland	9.3
7	Louisiana	7.2
8	Missouri	7.1
9	Oklahoma	6.4
10	Tennessee	4.9
11	North Carolina	4.8
12	South Dakota	4.7
13	Alabama	3.2
14	Idaho	2.7
15	Wyoming	2.4
16	Pennsylvania	1.9
17	Nevada	1.7
18	West Virginia	1.6
19	South Carolina	1.0
20	Nebraska	0.3
21	Arizona	(0.5)
22	Washington	(1.0)
23	Kentucky	(1.2)
24	Arkansas	(1.5)
25	Indiana	(1.6)
26	Florida	(1.7)
27	Georgia	(2.2)
28	Minnesota	(2.8)
29	North Dakota	(4.8)
30	Illinois	(5.1)
31	Ohio	(6.4)
32	California	(7.5)
33	Utah	(8.2)
34	Virginia	(8.6)
35	Michigan	(8.7)
36	Kansas	(8.9)
37	New Mexico	(9.4)
38	Connecticut	(10.0)
38	Wisconsin	(10.0)
40	Colorado	(10.3)
41	Maine	(10.8)
42	Iowa	(11.7)
43	New Jersey	(13.0)
44	Rhode Island	(14.3)
45	Massachusetts	(14.8)
46	New York	(16.4)
47	Texas	(21.1)
48	Vermont	(22.3)
49	New Hampshire	(22.7)
50	Delaware	(25.7)

District of Columbia 4.3

Source: Morgan Quitno Press using data from Federal Bureau of Investigation
   "Crime in the United States" (Uniform Crime Reports, 1990 and 1994 editions)
*Larceny and theft is the unlawful taking of property without use of force, violence or fraud. Attempts are included. Motor vehicle thefts are excluded.

Motor Vehicle Thefts in 1990

National Total = 1,635,907 Motor Vehicle Thefts*

ALPHA ORDER

RANK	STATE	THEFTS	% of USA
26	Alabama	14,053	0.86%
39	Alaska	3,110	0.19%
13	Arizona	31,648	1.93%
33	Arkansas	6,803	0.42%
1	California	302,214	18.47%
25	Colorado	14,112	0.86%
18	Connecticut	24,027	1.47%
40	Delaware	2,957	0.18%
4	Florida	106,902	6.53%
11	Georgia	43,637	2.67%
37	Hawaii	4,217	0.26%
46	Idaho	1,666	0.10%
5	Illinois	73,473	4.49%
17	Indiana	24,338	1.49%
36	Iowa	4,718	0.29%
30	Kansas	8,309	0.51%
31	Kentucky	7,350	0.45%
16	Louisiana	25,393	1.55%
44	Maine	2,169	0.13%
12	Maryland	33,886	2.07%
9	Massachusetts	55,567	3.40%
7	Michigan	66,336	4.05%
24	Minnesota	15,994	0.98%
34	Mississippi	5,341	0.33%
15	Missouri	27,599	1.69%
45	Montana	1,938	0.12%
41	Nebraska	2,812	0.17%
32	Nevada	7,121	0.44%
43	New Hampshire	2,707	0.17%
6	New Jersey	72,628	4.44%
35	New Mexico	5,101	0.31%
2	New York	187,591	11.47%
23	North Carolina	18,803	1.15%
48	North Dakota	850	0.05%
10	Ohio	53,221	3.25%
22	Oklahoma	18,926	1.16%
28	Oregon	13,035	0.80%
8	Pennsylvania	60,062	3.67%
29	Rhode Island	9,577	0.59%
27	South Carolina	13,453	0.82%
49	South Dakota	767	0.05%
14	Tennessee	27,875	1.70%
3	Texas	154,415	9.44%
38	Utah	4,096	0.25%
47	Vermont	1,170	0.07%
21	Virginia	20,263	1.24%
19	Washington	21,759	1.33%
42	West Virginia	2,760	0.17%
20	Wisconsin	20,373	1.25%
50	Wyoming	676	0.04%

RANK ORDER

RANK	STATE	THEFTS	% of USA
1	California	302,214	18.47%
2	New York	187,591	11.47%
3	Texas	154,415	9.44%
4	Florida	106,902	6.53%
5	Illinois	73,473	4.49%
6	New Jersey	72,628	4.44%
7	Michigan	66,336	4.05%
8	Pennsylvania	60,062	3.67%
9	Massachusetts	55,567	3.40%
10	Ohio	53,221	3.25%
11	Georgia	43,637	2.67%
12	Maryland	33,886	2.07%
13	Arizona	31,648	1.93%
14	Tennessee	27,875	1.70%
15	Missouri	27,599	1.69%
16	Louisiana	25,393	1.55%
17	Indiana	24,338	1.49%
18	Connecticut	24,027	1.47%
19	Washington	21,759	1.33%
20	Wisconsin	20,373	1.25%
21	Virginia	20,263	1.24%
22	Oklahoma	18,926	1.16%
23	North Carolina	18,803	1.15%
24	Minnesota	15,994	0.98%
25	Colorado	14,112	0.86%
26	Alabama	14,053	0.86%
27	South Carolina	13,453	0.82%
28	Oregon	13,035	0.80%
29	Rhode Island	9,577	0.59%
30	Kansas	8,309	0.51%
31	Kentucky	7,350	0.45%
32	Nevada	7,121	0.44%
33	Arkansas	6,803	0.42%
34	Mississippi	5,341	0.33%
35	New Mexico	5,101	0.31%
36	Iowa	4,718	0.29%
37	Hawaii	4,217	0.26%
38	Utah	4,096	0.25%
39	Alaska	3,110	0.19%
40	Delaware	2,957	0.18%
41	Nebraska	2,812	0.17%
42	West Virginia	2,760	0.17%
43	New Hampshire	2,707	0.17%
44	Maine	2,169	0.13%
45	Montana	1,938	0.12%
46	Idaho	1,666	0.10%
47	Vermont	1,170	0.07%
48	North Dakota	850	0.05%
49	South Dakota	767	0.05%
50	Wyoming	676	0.04%
	District of Columbia	8,109	0.50%

Source: Federal Bureau of Investigation
"Crime in the United States 1990" (Uniform Crime Reports, August 11, 1991)
Includes the theft or attempted theft of a self-propelled vehicle. Excludes motorboats, construction equipment, airplanes and farming equipment.

Percent Change in Number of Motor Vehicle Thefts: 1990 to 1994

National Percent Change = 5.9% Decrease*

ALPHA ORDER				RANK ORDER		
RANK	STATE	PERCENT CHANGE		RANK	STATE	PERCENT CHANGE
29	Alabama	(0.4)		1	Nebraska	121.8
22	Alaska	5.3		2	Mississippi	102.4
8	Arizona	37.4		3	Oregon	67.0
17	Arkansas	13.6		4	New Mexico	63.7
27	California	2.0		5	Nevada	55.4
28	Colorado	1.8		6	Hawaii	51.4
41	Connecticut	(16.1)		7	Utah	38.9
42	Delaware	(16.4)		8	Arizona	37.4
12	Florida	19.0		9	Idaho	32.7
35	Georgia	(9.9)		10	Montana	26.4
6	Hawaii	51.4		11	Washington	22.9
9	Idaho	32.7		12	Florida	19.0
35	Illinois	(9.9)		13	West Virginia	18.6
26	Indiana	2.8		14	Kentucky	16.4
21	Iowa	8.0		15	Wyoming	14.1
23	Kansas	4.3		16	South Dakota	13.7
14	Kentucky	16.4		17	Arkansas	13.6
25	Louisiana	3.3		18	North Carolina	13.5
43	Maine	(18.1)		19	North Dakota	13.4
20	Maryland	12.7		20	Maryland	12.7
45	Massachusetts	(23.8)		21	Iowa	8.0
32	Michigan	(6.1)		22	Alaska	5.3
38	Minnesota	(10.3)		23	Kansas	4.3
2	Mississippi	102.4		24	Tennessee	4.0
30	Missouri	(2.0)		25	Louisiana	3.3
10	Montana	26.4		26	Indiana	2.8
1	Nebraska	121.8		27	California	2.0
5	Nevada	55.4		28	Colorado	1.8
40	New Hampshire	(15.0)		29	Alabama	(0.4)
47	New Jersey	(28.2)		30	Missouri	(2.0)
4	New Mexico	63.7		30	South Carolina	(2.0)
49	New York	(31.3)		32	Michigan	(6.1)
18	North Carolina	13.5		33	Virginia	(9.7)
19	North Dakota	13.4		34	Pennsylvania	(9.8)
39	Ohio	(10.9)		35	Georgia	(9.9)
44	Oklahoma	(18.3)		35	Illinois	(9.9)
3	Oregon	67.0		37	Wisconsin	(10.1)
34	Pennsylvania	(9.8)		38	Minnesota	(10.3)
50	Rhode Island	(45.9)		39	Ohio	(10.9)
30	South Carolina	(2.0)		40	New Hampshire	(15.0)
16	South Dakota	13.7		41	Connecticut	(16.1)
24	Tennessee	4.0		42	Delaware	(16.4)
48	Texas	(28.3)		43	Maine	(18.1)
7	Utah	38.9		44	Oklahoma	(18.3)
46	Vermont	(26.3)		45	Massachusetts	(23.8)
33	Virginia	(9.7)		46	Vermont	(26.3)
11	Washington	22.9		47	New Jersey	(28.2)
13	West Virginia	18.6		48	Texas	(28.3)
37	Wisconsin	(10.1)		49	New York	(31.3)
15	Wyoming	14.1		50	Rhode Island	(45.9)

District of Columbia   1.9

Source: Morgan Quitno Press using data from Federal Bureau of Investigation
"Crime in the United States" (Uniform Crime Reports, 1990 and 1994 editions)
*Includes the theft or attempted theft of a self-propelled vehicle. Excludes motorboats, construction equipment, airplanes and farming equipment.

Motor Vehicle Theft Rate in 1990

National Rate = 657.8 Motor Vehicle Thefts per 100,000 Population*

ALPHA ORDER

RANK ORDER

RANK	STATE	RATE		RANK	STATE	RATE
31	Alabama	347.8		1	New York	1,042.7
18	Alaska	565.4		2	California	1,015.5
7	Arizona	863.5		3	Rhode Island	954.4
35	Arkansas	289.4		4	New Jersey	939.5
2	California	1,015.5		5	Massachusetts	923.6
26	Colorado	428.4		6	Texas	909.0
9	Connecticut	730.9		7	Arizona	863.5
24	Delaware	443.9		8	Florida	826.3
8	Florida	826.3		9	Connecticut	730.9
12	Georgia	673.6		10	Michigan	713.7
29	Hawaii	380.5		11	Maryland	708.7
46	Idaho	165.5		12	Georgia	673.6
13	Illinois	642.8		13	Illinois	642.8
25	Indiana	439.0		14	Louisiana	601.7
45	Iowa	169.9		14	Oklahoma	601.7
33	Kansas	335.4		16	Nevada	592.5
42	Kentucky	199.4		17	Tennessee	571.5
14	Louisiana	601.7		18	Alaska	565.4
44	Maine	176.6		19	Missouri	539.4
11	Maryland	708.7		20	Pennsylvania	505.5
5	Massachusetts	923.6		21	Ohio	490.6
10	Michigan	713.7		22	Oregon	458.6
30	Minnesota	365.6		23	Washington	447.1
41	Mississippi	207.6		24	Delaware	443.9
19	Missouri	539.4		25	Indiana	439.0
38	Montana	242.5		26	Colorado	428.4
43	Nebraska	178.2		27	Wisconsin	416.5
16	Nevada	592.5		28	South Carolina	385.8
37	New Hampshire	244.0		29	Hawaii	380.5
4	New Jersey	939.5		30	Minnesota	365.6
32	New Mexico	336.7		31	Alabama	347.8
1	New York	1,042.7		32	New Mexico	336.7
36	North Carolina	283.7		33	Kansas	335.4
49	North Dakota	133.1		34	Virginia	327.5
21	Ohio	490.6		35	Arkansas	289.4
14	Oklahoma	601.7		36	North Carolina	283.7
22	Oregon	458.6		37	New Hampshire	244.0
20	Pennsylvania	505.5		38	Montana	242.5
3	Rhode Island	954.4		39	Utah	237.7
28	South Carolina	385.8		40	Vermont	207.9
50	South Dakota	110.2		41	Mississippi	207.6
17	Tennessee	571.5		42	Kentucky	199.4
6	Texas	909.0		43	Nebraska	178.2
39	Utah	237.7		44	Maine	176.6
40	Vermont	207.9		45	Iowa	169.9
34	Virginia	327.5		46	Idaho	165.5
23	Washington	447.1		47	West Virginia	153.9
47	West Virginia	153.9		48	Wyoming	149.0
27	Wisconsin	416.5		49	North Dakota	133.1
48	Wyoming	149.0		50	South Dakota	110.2

District of Columbia   1,336.1

Source: Federal Bureau of Investigation
    "Crime in the United States 1990" (Uniform Crime Reports, August 11, 1991)
*Includes the theft or attempted theft of a self-propelled vehicle. Excludes motorboats, construction equipment, airplanes and farming equipment.

Percent Change in Rate of Motor Vehicle Thefts: 1990 to 1994

National Percent Change = 10.1% Decrease*

ALPHA ORDER				RANK ORDER		
RANK	STATE	PERCENT CHANGE		RANK	STATE	PERCENT CHANGE
28	Alabama	(4.6)		1	Nebraska	115.6
27	Alaska	(4.4)		2	Mississippi	95.1
8	Arizona	23.5		3	Oregon	53.8
17	Arkansas	8.9		4	New Mexico	49.9
26	California	(3.4)		5	Hawaii	42.3
32	Colorado	(8.3)		6	Nevada	28.2
39	Connecticut	(15.8)		7	Utah	25.5
44	Delaware	(21.2)		8	Arizona	23.5
15	Florida	10.3		9	Montana	18.0
41	Georgia	(17.3)		10	Idaho	17.9
5	Hawaii	42.3		11	West Virginia	16.8
10	Idaho	17.9		12	North Dakota	13.5
34	Illinois	(12.3)		13	Kentucky	12.1
24	Indiana	(1.0)		14	Washington	11.9
21	Iowa	6.0		15	Florida	10.3
22	Kansas	1.2		16	South Dakota	9.7
13	Kentucky	12.1		17	Arkansas	8.9
23	Louisiana	1.0		18	Wyoming	8.7
42	Maine	(18.9)		19	Maryland	7.7
19	Maryland	7.7		20	North Carolina	6.4
45	Massachusetts	(24.1)		21	Iowa	6.0
31	Michigan	(8.1)		22	Kansas	1.2
37	Minnesota	(14.0)		23	Louisiana	1.0
2	Mississippi	95.1		24	Indiana	(1.0)
29	Missouri	(5.0)		25	Tennessee	(2.0)
9	Montana	18.0		26	California	(3.4)
1	Nebraska	115.6		27	Alaska	(4.4)
6	Nevada	28.2		28	Alabama	(4.6)
40	New Hampshire	(17.0)		29	Missouri	(5.0)
47	New Jersey	(29.8)		30	South Carolina	(6.7)
4	New Mexico	49.9		31	Michigan	(8.1)
48	New York	(32.0)		32	Colorado	(8.3)
20	North Carolina	6.4		33	Pennsylvania	(11.1)
12	North Dakota	13.5		34	Illinois	(12.3)
35	Ohio	(12.9)		35	Ohio	(12.9)
43	Oklahoma	(21.1)		36	Wisconsin	(13.5)
3	Oregon	53.8		37	Minnesota	(14.0)
33	Pennsylvania	(11.1)		38	Virginia	(14.8)
50	Rhode Island	(45.5)		39	Connecticut	(15.8)
30	South Carolina	(6.7)		40	New Hampshire	(17.0)
16	South Dakota	9.7		41	Georgia	(17.3)
25	Tennessee	(2.0)		42	Maine	(18.9)
49	Texas	(33.7)		43	Oklahoma	(21.1)
7	Utah	25.5		44	Delaware	(21.2)
46	Vermont	(28.5)		45	Massachusetts	(24.1)
38	Virginia	(14.8)		46	Vermont	(28.5)
14	Washington	11.9		47	New Jersey	(29.8)
11	West Virginia	16.8		48	New York	(32.0)
36	Wisconsin	(13.5)		49	Texas	(33.7)
18	Wyoming	8.7		50	Rhode Island	(45.5)
					District of Columbia	8.5

Source: Morgan Quitno Press using data from Federal Bureau of Investigation
     "Crime in the United States" (Uniform Crime Reports, 1990 and 1994 editions)
*Includes the theft or attempted theft of a self-propelled vehicle. Excludes motorboats, construction equipment, airplanes and farming equipment.

VII. APPENDIX

Population in 1995

National Total = 262,755,000*

<table>
<tr><th colspan="4">ALPHA ORDER</th><th colspan="4">RANK ORDER</th></tr>
<tr><th>RANK</th><th>STATE</th><th>POPULATION</th><th>% of USA</th><th>RANK</th><th>STATE</th><th>POPULATION</th><th>% of USA</th></tr>
<tr><td>22</td><td>Alabama</td><td>4,253,000</td><td>1.62%</td><td>1</td><td>California</td><td>31,589,000</td><td>12.02%</td></tr>
<tr><td>48</td><td>Alaska</td><td>604,000</td><td>0.23%</td><td>2</td><td>Texas</td><td>18,724,000</td><td>7.13%</td></tr>
<tr><td>23</td><td>Arizona</td><td>4,218,000</td><td>1.61%</td><td>3</td><td>New York</td><td>18,136,000</td><td>6.90%</td></tr>
<tr><td>33</td><td>Arkansas</td><td>2,484,000</td><td>0.95%</td><td>4</td><td>Florida</td><td>14,166,000</td><td>5.39%</td></tr>
<tr><td>1</td><td>California</td><td>31,589,000</td><td>12.02%</td><td>5</td><td>Pennsylvania</td><td>12,072,000</td><td>4.59%</td></tr>
<tr><td>25</td><td>Colorado</td><td>3,747,000</td><td>1.43%</td><td>6</td><td>Illinois</td><td>11,830,000</td><td>4.50%</td></tr>
<tr><td>28</td><td>Connecticut</td><td>3,275,000</td><td>1.25%</td><td>7</td><td>Ohio</td><td>11,151,000</td><td>4.24%</td></tr>
<tr><td>46</td><td>Delaware</td><td>717,000</td><td>0.27%</td><td>8</td><td>Michigan</td><td>9,549,000</td><td>3.63%</td></tr>
<tr><td>4</td><td>Florida</td><td>14,166,000</td><td>5.39%</td><td>9</td><td>New Jersey</td><td>7,945,000</td><td>3.02%</td></tr>
<tr><td>10</td><td>Georgia</td><td>7,201,000</td><td>2.74%</td><td>10</td><td>Georgia</td><td>7,201,000</td><td>2.74%</td></tr>
<tr><td>40</td><td>Hawaii</td><td>1,187,000</td><td>0.45%</td><td>11</td><td>North Carolina</td><td>7,195,000</td><td>2.74%</td></tr>
<tr><td>41</td><td>Idaho</td><td>1,163,000</td><td>0.44%</td><td>12</td><td>Virginia</td><td>6,618,000</td><td>2.52%</td></tr>
<tr><td>6</td><td>Illinois</td><td>11,830,000</td><td>4.50%</td><td>13</td><td>Massachusetts</td><td>6,074,000</td><td>2.31%</td></tr>
<tr><td>14</td><td>Indiana</td><td>5,803,000</td><td>2.21%</td><td>14</td><td>Indiana</td><td>5,803,000</td><td>2.21%</td></tr>
<tr><td>30</td><td>Iowa</td><td>2,842,000</td><td>1.08%</td><td>15</td><td>Washington</td><td>5,431,000</td><td>2.07%</td></tr>
<tr><td>32</td><td>Kansas</td><td>2,565,000</td><td>0.98%</td><td>16</td><td>Missouri</td><td>5,324,000</td><td>2.03%</td></tr>
<tr><td>24</td><td>Kentucky</td><td>3,860,000</td><td>1.47%</td><td>17</td><td>Tennessee</td><td>5,256,000</td><td>2.00%</td></tr>
<tr><td>21</td><td>Louisiana</td><td>4,342,000</td><td>1.65%</td><td>18</td><td>Wisconsin</td><td>5,123,000</td><td>1.95%</td></tr>
<tr><td>39</td><td>Maine</td><td>1,241,000</td><td>0.47%</td><td>19</td><td>Maryland</td><td>5,042,000</td><td>1.92%</td></tr>
<tr><td>19</td><td>Maryland</td><td>5,042,000</td><td>1.92%</td><td>20</td><td>Minnesota</td><td>4,610,000</td><td>1.75%</td></tr>
<tr><td>13</td><td>Massachusetts</td><td>6,074,000</td><td>2.31%</td><td>21</td><td>Louisiana</td><td>4,342,000</td><td>1.65%</td></tr>
<tr><td>8</td><td>Michigan</td><td>9,549,000</td><td>3.63%</td><td>22</td><td>Alabama</td><td>4,253,000</td><td>1.62%</td></tr>
<tr><td>20</td><td>Minnesota</td><td>4,610,000</td><td>1.75%</td><td>23</td><td>Arizona</td><td>4,218,000</td><td>1.61%</td></tr>
<tr><td>31</td><td>Mississippi</td><td>2,697,000</td><td>1.03%</td><td>24</td><td>Kentucky</td><td>3,860,000</td><td>1.47%</td></tr>
<tr><td>16</td><td>Missouri</td><td>5,324,000</td><td>2.03%</td><td>25</td><td>Colorado</td><td>3,747,000</td><td>1.43%</td></tr>
<tr><td>44</td><td>Montana</td><td>870,000</td><td>0.33%</td><td>26</td><td>South Carolina</td><td>3,673,000</td><td>1.40%</td></tr>
<tr><td>37</td><td>Nebraska</td><td>1,637,000</td><td>0.62%</td><td>27</td><td>Oklahoma</td><td>3,278,000</td><td>1.25%</td></tr>
<tr><td>38</td><td>Nevada</td><td>1,530,000</td><td>0.58%</td><td>28</td><td>Connecticut</td><td>3,275,000</td><td>1.25%</td></tr>
<tr><td>42</td><td>New Hampshire</td><td>1,148,000</td><td>0.44%</td><td>29</td><td>Oregon</td><td>3,141,000</td><td>1.20%</td></tr>
<tr><td>9</td><td>New Jersey</td><td>7,945,000</td><td>3.02%</td><td>30</td><td>Iowa</td><td>2,842,000</td><td>1.08%</td></tr>
<tr><td>36</td><td>New Mexico</td><td>1,685,000</td><td>0.64%</td><td>31</td><td>Mississippi</td><td>2,697,000</td><td>1.03%</td></tr>
<tr><td>3</td><td>New York</td><td>18,136,000</td><td>6.90%</td><td>32</td><td>Kansas</td><td>2,565,000</td><td>0.98%</td></tr>
<tr><td>11</td><td>North Carolina</td><td>7,195,000</td><td>2.74%</td><td>33</td><td>Arkansas</td><td>2,484,000</td><td>0.95%</td></tr>
<tr><td>47</td><td>North Dakota</td><td>641,000</td><td>0.24%</td><td>34</td><td>Utah</td><td>1,951,000</td><td>0.74%</td></tr>
<tr><td>7</td><td>Ohio</td><td>11,151,000</td><td>4.24%</td><td>35</td><td>West Virginia</td><td>1,828,000</td><td>0.70%</td></tr>
<tr><td>27</td><td>Oklahoma</td><td>3,278,000</td><td>1.25%</td><td>36</td><td>New Mexico</td><td>1,685,000</td><td>0.64%</td></tr>
<tr><td>29</td><td>Oregon</td><td>3,141,000</td><td>1.20%</td><td>37</td><td>Nebraska</td><td>1,637,000</td><td>0.62%</td></tr>
<tr><td>5</td><td>Pennsylvania</td><td>12,072,000</td><td>4.59%</td><td>38</td><td>Nevada</td><td>1,530,000</td><td>0.58%</td></tr>
<tr><td>43</td><td>Rhode Island</td><td>990,000</td><td>0.38%</td><td>39</td><td>Maine</td><td>1,241,000</td><td>0.47%</td></tr>
<tr><td>26</td><td>South Carolina</td><td>3,673,000</td><td>1.40%</td><td>40</td><td>Hawaii</td><td>1,187,000</td><td>0.45%</td></tr>
<tr><td>45</td><td>South Dakota</td><td>729,000</td><td>0.28%</td><td>41</td><td>Idaho</td><td>1,163,000</td><td>0.44%</td></tr>
<tr><td>17</td><td>Tennessee</td><td>5,256,000</td><td>2.00%</td><td>42</td><td>New Hampshire</td><td>1,148,000</td><td>0.44%</td></tr>
<tr><td>2</td><td>Texas</td><td>18,724,000</td><td>7.13%</td><td>43</td><td>Rhode Island</td><td>990,000</td><td>0.38%</td></tr>
<tr><td>34</td><td>Utah</td><td>1,951,000</td><td>0.74%</td><td>44</td><td>Montana</td><td>870,000</td><td>0.33%</td></tr>
<tr><td>49</td><td>Vermont</td><td>585,000</td><td>0.22%</td><td>45</td><td>South Dakota</td><td>729,000</td><td>0.28%</td></tr>
<tr><td>12</td><td>Virginia</td><td>6,618,000</td><td>2.52%</td><td>46</td><td>Delaware</td><td>717,000</td><td>0.27%</td></tr>
<tr><td>15</td><td>Washington</td><td>5,431,000</td><td>2.07%</td><td>47</td><td>North Dakota</td><td>641,000</td><td>0.24%</td></tr>
<tr><td>35</td><td>West Virginia</td><td>1,828,000</td><td>0.70%</td><td>48</td><td>Alaska</td><td>604,000</td><td>0.23%</td></tr>
<tr><td>18</td><td>Wisconsin</td><td>5,123,000</td><td>1.95%</td><td>49</td><td>Vermont</td><td>585,000</td><td>0.22%</td></tr>
<tr><td>50</td><td>Wyoming</td><td>480,000</td><td>0.18%</td><td>50</td><td>Wyoming</td><td>480,000</td><td>0.18%</td></tr>
<tr><td></td><td></td><td></td><td></td><td></td><td>District of Columbia</td><td>554,000</td><td>0.21%</td></tr>
</table>

Source: U.S. Bureau of the Census
   Press Release (CB96-10, January 26, 1996)
As of July 1, 1995. Includes armed forces residing in each state.

Population in 1994

National Total = 260,350,000*

ALPHA ORDER

ALPHA ORDER

RANK	STATE	POPULATION	% of USA
22	Alabama	4,220,000	1.62%
48	Alaska	603,000	0.23%
23	Arizona	4,079,000	1.57%
33	Arkansas	2,453,000	0.94%
1	California	31,408,000	12.06%
25	Colorado	3,662,000	1.41%
27	Connecticut	3,275,000	1.26%
46	Delaware	708,000	0.27%
4	Florida	13,958,000	5.36%
11	Georgia	7,058,000	2.71%
40	Hawaii	1,178,000	0.45%
42	Idaho	1,134,000	0.44%
6	Illinois	11,759,000	4.52%
14	Indiana	5,755,000	2.21%
30	Iowa	2,831,000	1.09%
32	Kansas	2,551,000	0.98%
24	Kentucky	3,828,000	1.47%
21	Louisiana	4,316,000	1.66%
39	Maine	1,239,000	0.48%
19	Maryland	5,000,000	1.92%
13	Massachusetts	6,041,000	2.32%
8	Michigan	9,492,000	3.65%
20	Minnesota	4,568,000	1.75%
31	Mississippi	2,670,000	1.03%
16	Missouri	5,279,000	2.03%
44	Montana	856,000	0.33%
37	Nebraska	1,624,000	0.62%
38	Nevada	1,462,000	0.56%
41	New Hampshire	1,135,000	0.44%
9	New Jersey	7,903,000	3.04%
36	New Mexico	1,655,000	0.64%
3	New York	18,153,000	6.97%
10	North Carolina	7,070,000	2.72%
47	North Dakota	639,000	0.25%
7	Ohio	11,104,000	4.27%
28	Oklahoma	3,257,000	1.25%
29	Oregon	3,087,000	1.19%
5	Pennsylvania	12,062,000	4.63%
43	Rhode Island	994,000	0.38%
26	South Carolina	3,643,000	1.40%
45	South Dakota	723,000	0.28%
17	Tennessee	5,176,000	1.99%
2	Texas	18,413,000	7.07%
34	Utah	1,909,000	0.73%
49	Vermont	580,000	0.22%
12	Virginia	6,551,000	2.52%
15	Washington	5,338,000	2.05%
35	West Virginia	1,824,000	0.70%
18	Wisconsin	5,083,000	1.95%
50	Wyoming	476,000	0.18%

RANK ORDER

RANK	STATE	POPULATION	% of USA
1	California	31,408,000	12.06%
2	Texas	18,413,000	7.07%
3	New York	18,153,000	6.97%
4	Florida	13,958,000	5.36%
5	Pennsylvania	12,062,000	4.63%
6	Illinois	11,759,000	4.52%
7	Ohio	11,104,000	4.27%
8	Michigan	9,492,000	3.65%
9	New Jersey	7,903,000	3.04%
10	North Carolina	7,070,000	2.72%
11	Georgia	7,058,000	2.71%
12	Virginia	6,551,000	2.52%
13	Massachusetts	6,041,000	2.32%
14	Indiana	5,755,000	2.21%
15	Washington	5,338,000	2.05%
16	Missouri	5,279,000	2.03%
17	Tennessee	5,176,000	1.99%
18	Wisconsin	5,083,000	1.95%
19	Maryland	5,000,000	1.92%
20	Minnesota	4,568,000	1.75%
21	Louisiana	4,316,000	1.66%
22	Alabama	4,220,000	1.62%
23	Arizona	4,079,000	1.57%
24	Kentucky	3,828,000	1.47%
25	Colorado	3,662,000	1.41%
26	South Carolina	3,643,000	1.40%
27	Connecticut	3,275,000	1.26%
28	Oklahoma	3,257,000	1.25%
29	Oregon	3,087,000	1.19%
30	Iowa	2,831,000	1.09%
31	Mississippi	2,670,000	1.03%
32	Kansas	2,551,000	0.98%
33	Arkansas	2,453,000	0.94%
34	Utah	1,909,000	0.73%
35	West Virginia	1,824,000	0.70%
36	New Mexico	1,655,000	0.64%
37	Nebraska	1,624,000	0.62%
38	Nevada	1,462,000	0.56%
39	Maine	1,239,000	0.48%
40	Hawaii	1,178,000	0.45%
41	New Hampshire	1,135,000	0.44%
42	Idaho	1,134,000	0.44%
43	Rhode Island	994,000	0.38%
44	Montana	856,000	0.33%
45	South Dakota	723,000	0.28%
46	Delaware	708,000	0.27%
47	North Dakota	639,000	0.25%
48	Alaska	603,000	0.23%
49	Vermont	580,000	0.22%
50	Wyoming	476,000	0.18%
	District of Columbia	567,000	0.22%

Source: U.S. Bureau of the Census
    Press Release (CB96-10, January 26, 1996)
*Includes armed forces residing in each state. This updates earlier 1994 population estimates.

Population in 1993

National Total = 257,800,000*

ALPHA ORDER

RANK	STATE	POPULATION	% of USA
22	Alabama	4,181,000	1.62%
48	Alaska	598,000	0.23%
23	Arizona	3,944,000	1.53%
33	Arkansas	2,425,000	0.94%
1	California	31,220,000	12.11%
26	Colorado	3,568,000	1.38%
27	Connecticut	3,278,000	1.27%
46	Delaware	699,000	0.27%
4	Florida	13,722,000	5.32%
11	Georgia	6,901,000	2.68%
40	Hawaii	1,166,000	0.45%
42	Idaho	1,101,000	0.43%
6	Illinois	11,690,000	4.53%
14	Indiana	5,707,000	2.21%
30	Iowa	2,822,000	1.09%
32	Kansas	2,532,000	0.98%
24	Kentucky	3,793,000	1.47%
21	Louisiana	4,289,000	1.66%
39	Maine	1,239,000	0.48%
19	Maryland	4,952,000	1.92%
13	Massachusetts	6,018,000	2.33%
8	Michigan	9,457,000	3.67%
20	Minnesota	4,524,000	1.75%
31	Mississippi	2,639,000	1.02%
16	Missouri	5,235,000	2.03%
44	Montana	841,000	0.33%
37	Nebraska	1,614,000	0.63%
38	Nevada	1,385,000	0.54%
41	New Hampshire	1,123,000	0.44%
9	New Jersey	7,859,000	3.05%
36	New Mexico	1,616,000	0.63%
2	New York	18,153,000	7.04%
10	North Carolina	6,953,000	2.70%
47	North Dakota	637,000	0.25%
7	Ohio	11,061,000	4.29%
28	Oklahoma	3,232,000	1.25%
29	Oregon	3,035,000	1.18%
5	Pennsylvania	12,031,000	4.67%
43	Rhode Island	999,000	0.39%
25	South Carolina	3,627,000	1.41%
45	South Dakota	717,000	0.28%
17	Tennessee	5,093,000	1.98%
3	Texas	18,049,000	7.00%
34	Utah	1,860,000	0.72%
49	Vermont	576,000	0.22%
12	Virginia	6,475,000	2.51%
15	Washington	5,255,000	2.04%
35	West Virginia	1,818,000	0.71%
18	Wisconsin	5,044,000	1.96%
50	Wyoming	470,000	0.18%

RANK ORDER

RANK	STATE	POPULATION	% of USA
1	California	31,220,000	12.11%
2	New York	18,153,000	7.04%
3	Texas	18,049,000	7.00%
4	Florida	13,722,000	5.32%
5	Pennsylvania	12,031,000	4.67%
6	Illinois	11,690,000	4.53%
7	Ohio	11,061,000	4.29%
8	Michigan	9,457,000	3.67%
9	New Jersey	7,859,000	3.05%
10	North Carolina	6,953,000	2.70%
11	Georgia	6,901,000	2.68%
12	Virginia	6,475,000	2.51%
13	Massachusetts	6,018,000	2.33%
14	Indiana	5,707,000	2.21%
15	Washington	5,255,000	2.04%
16	Missouri	5,235,000	2.03%
17	Tennessee	5,093,000	1.98%
18	Wisconsin	5,044,000	1.96%
19	Maryland	4,952,000	1.92%
20	Minnesota	4,524,000	1.75%
21	Louisiana	4,289,000	1.66%
22	Alabama	4,181,000	1.62%
23	Arizona	3,944,000	1.53%
24	Kentucky	3,793,000	1.47%
25	South Carolina	3,627,000	1.41%
26	Colorado	3,568,000	1.38%
27	Connecticut	3,278,000	1.27%
28	Oklahoma	3,232,000	1.25%
29	Oregon	3,035,000	1.18%
30	Iowa	2,822,000	1.09%
31	Mississippi	2,639,000	1.02%
32	Kansas	2,532,000	0.98%
33	Arkansas	2,425,000	0.94%
34	Utah	1,860,000	0.72%
35	West Virginia	1,818,000	0.71%
36	New Mexico	1,616,000	0.63%
37	Nebraska	1,614,000	0.63%
38	Nevada	1,385,000	0.54%
39	Maine	1,239,000	0.48%
40	Hawaii	1,166,000	0.45%
41	New Hampshire	1,123,000	0.44%
42	Idaho	1,101,000	0.43%
43	Rhode Island	999,000	0.39%
44	Montana	841,000	0.33%
45	South Dakota	717,000	0.28%
46	Delaware	699,000	0.27%
47	North Dakota	637,000	0.25%
48	Alaska	598,000	0.23%
49	Vermont	576,000	0.22%
50	Wyoming	470,000	0.18%
	District of Columbia	578,000	0.22%

Source: U.S. Bureau of the Census
      Press Release (CB96-10, January 26, 1996)
*Includes armed forces residing in each state. This updates earlier 1993 population estimates.

Population in 1990

National Total = 248,718,000*

ALPHA ORDER

RANK	STATE	Population	% of USA
22	Alabama	4,040,000	1.62%
49	Alaska	550,000	0.22%
24	Arizona	3,665,000	1.47%
33	Arkansas	2,351,000	0.95%
1	California	29,758,000	11.96%
26	Colorado	3,294,000	1.32%
27	Connecticut	3,287,000	1.32%
46	Delaware	666,000	0.27%
4	Florida	12,938,000	5.20%
11	Georgia	6,478,000	2.60%
41	Hawaii	1,108,000	0.45%
42	Idaho	1,007,000	0.40%
6	Illinois	11,431,000	4.60%
14	Indiana	5,544,000	2.23%
30	Iowa	2,777,000	1.12%
32	Kansas	2,478,000	1.00%
23	Kentucky	3,687,000	1.48%
21	Louisiana	4,220,000	1.70%
38	Maine	1,228,000	0.49%
19	Maryland	4,781,000	1.92%
13	Massachusetts	6,016,000	2.42%
8	Michigan	9,295,000	3.74%
20	Minnesota	4,376,000	1.76%
31	Mississippi	2,575,000	1.04%
15	Missouri	5,117,000	2.06%
44	Montana	799,000	0.32%
36	Nebraska	1,578,000	0.63%
39	Nevada	1,202,000	0.48%
40	New Hampshire	1,109,000	0.45%
9	New Jersey	7,730,000	3.11%
37	New Mexico	1,515,000	0.61%
2	New York	17,991,000	7.23%
10	North Carolina	6,632,000	2.67%
47	North Dakota	639,000	0.26%
7	Ohio	10,847,000	4.36%
28	Oklahoma	3,146,000	1.26%
29	Oregon	2,842,000	1.14%
5	Pennsylvania	11,883,000	4.78%
43	Rhode Island	1,003,000	0.40%
25	South Carolina	3,486,000	1.40%
45	South Dakota	696,000	0.28%
17	Tennessee	4,877,000	1.96%
3	Texas	16,986,000	6.83%
35	Utah	1,723,000	0.69%
48	Vermont	563,000	0.23%
12	Virginia	6,189,000	2.49%
18	Washington	4,867,000	1.96%
34	West Virginia	1,793,000	0.72%
16	Wisconsin	4,892,000	1.97%
50	Wyoming	454,000	0.18%

RANK ORDER

RANK	STATE	Population	% of USA
1	California	29,758,000	11.96%
2	New York	17,991,000	7.23%
3	Texas	16,986,000	6.83%
4	Florida	12,938,000	5.20%
5	Pennsylvania	11,883,000	4.78%
6	Illinois	11,431,000	4.60%
7	Ohio	10,847,000	4.36%
8	Michigan	9,295,000	3.74%
9	New Jersey	7,730,000	3.11%
10	North Carolina	6,632,000	2.67%
11	Georgia	6,478,000	2.60%
12	Virginia	6,189,000	2.49%
13	Massachusetts	6,016,000	2.42%
14	Indiana	5,544,000	2.23%
15	Missouri	5,117,000	2.06%
16	Wisconsin	4,892,000	1.97%
17	Tennessee	4,877,000	1.96%
18	Washington	4,867,000	1.96%
19	Maryland	4,781,000	1.92%
20	Minnesota	4,376,000	1.76%
21	Louisiana	4,220,000	1.70%
22	Alabama	4,040,000	1.62%
23	Kentucky	3,687,000	1.48%
24	Arizona	3,665,000	1.47%
25	South Carolina	3,486,000	1.40%
26	Colorado	3,294,000	1.32%
27	Connecticut	3,287,000	1.32%
28	Oklahoma	3,146,000	1.26%
29	Oregon	2,842,000	1.14%
30	Iowa	2,777,000	1.12%
31	Mississippi	2,575,000	1.04%
32	Kansas	2,478,000	1.00%
33	Arkansas	2,351,000	0.95%
34	West Virginia	1,793,000	0.72%
35	Utah	1,723,000	0.69%
36	Nebraska	1,578,000	0.63%
37	New Mexico	1,515,000	0.61%
38	Maine	1,228,000	0.49%
39	Nevada	1,202,000	0.48%
40	New Hampshire	1,109,000	0.45%
41	Hawaii	1,108,000	0.45%
42	Idaho	1,007,000	0.40%
43	Rhode Island	1,003,000	0.40%
44	Montana	799,000	0.32%
45	South Dakota	696,000	0.28%
46	Delaware	666,000	0.27%
47	North Dakota	639,000	0.26%
48	Vermont	563,000	0.23%
49	Alaska	550,000	0.22%
50	Wyoming	454,000	0.18%
	District of Columbia	607,000	0.24%

Source: U.S. Bureau of the Census
   Press Release (CB96-10, January 26, 1996)
*Includes armed forces residing in each state. As of April 1, 1990.

Urban Population in 1994

National Total = 228,465,728 Urban Population*

ALPHA ORDER					RANK ORDER			
RANK	STATE	POPULATION	% of USA		RANK	STATE	POPULATION	% of USA
22	Alabama	3,425,069	1.50%		1	California	30,809,789	13.49%
44	Alaska	415,397	0.18%		2	New York	17,313,115	7.58%
19	Arizona	3,762,274	1.65%		3	Texas	16,772,207	7.34%
31	Arkansas	1,631,463	0.71%		4	Florida	13,196,529	5.78%
1	California	30,809,789	13.49%		5	Pennsylvania	10,993,178	4.81%
23	Colorado	3,291,155	1.44%		6	Ohio	9,785,964	4.28%
24	Connecticut	3,084,183	1.35%		7	Michigan	8,456,516	3.70%
42	Delaware	616,871	0.27%		8	New Jersey	7,904,000	3.46%
4	Florida	13,196,529	5.78%		9	Massachusetts	6,028,684	2.64%
10	Georgia	5,634,794	2.47%		10	Georgia	5,634,794	2.47%
39	Hawaii	920,242	0.40%		11	Virginia	5,494,751	2.41%
41	Idaho	737,800	0.32%		12	North Carolina	5,402,154	2.36%
NA	Illinois**	NA	NA		13	Washington	4,851,896	2.12%
15	Indiana	4,695,602	2.06%		14	Maryland	4,737,790	2.07%
29	Iowa	1,937,199	0.85%		15	Indiana	4,695,602	2.06%
NA	Kansas**	NA	NA		16	Wisconsin	4,102,543	1.80%
28	Kentucky	2,461,034	1.08%		17	Missouri	4,090,612	1.79%
21	Louisiana	3,616,324	1.58%		18	Tennessee	4,072,251	1.78%
40	Maine	893,725	0.39%		19	Arizona	3,762,274	1.65%
14	Maryland	4,737,790	2.07%		20	Minnesota	3,690,626	1.62%
9	Massachusetts	6,028,684	2.64%		21	Louisiana	3,616,324	1.58%
7	Michigan	8,456,516	3.70%		22	Alabama	3,425,069	1.50%
20	Minnesota	3,690,626	1.62%		23	Colorado	3,291,155	1.44%
32	Mississippi	1,557,396	0.68%		24	Connecticut	3,084,183	1.35%
17	Missouri	4,090,612	1.79%		25	South Carolina	2,870,939	1.26%
NA	Montana**	NA	NA		26	Oklahoma	2,627,128	1.15%
35	Nebraska	1,207,251	0.53%		27	Oregon	2,587,581	1.13%
34	Nevada	1,278,853	0.56%		28	Kentucky	2,461,034	1.08%
38	New Hampshire	994,980	0.44%		29	Iowa	1,937,199	0.85%
8	New Jersey	7,904,000	3.46%		30	Utah	1,705,418	0.75%
33	New Mexico	1,355,091	0.59%		31	Arkansas	1,631,463	0.71%
2	New York	17,313,115	7.58%		32	Mississippi	1,557,396	0.68%
12	North Carolina	5,402,154	2.36%		33	New Mexico	1,355,091	0.59%
45	North Dakota	410,713	0.18%		34	Nevada	1,278,853	0.56%
6	Ohio	9,785,964	4.28%		35	Nebraska	1,207,251	0.53%
26	Oklahoma	2,627,128	1.15%		36	West Virginia	1,039,894	0.46%
27	Oregon	2,587,581	1.13%		37	Rhode Island	997,000	0.44%
5	Pennsylvania	10,993,178	4.81%		38	New Hampshire	994,980	0.44%
37	Rhode Island	997,000	0.44%		39	Hawaii	920,242	0.40%
25	South Carolina	2,870,939	1.26%		40	Maine	893,725	0.39%
43	South Dakota	428,171	0.19%		41	Idaho	737,800	0.32%
18	Tennessee	4,072,251	1.78%		42	Delaware	616,871	0.27%
3	Texas	16,772,207	7.34%		43	South Dakota	428,171	0.19%
30	Utah	1,705,418	0.75%		44	Alaska	415,397	0.18%
47	Vermont	314,873	0.14%		45	North Dakota	410,713	0.18%
11	Virginia	5,494,751	2.41%		46	Wyoming	350,700	0.15%
13	Washington	4,851,896	2.12%		47	Vermont	314,873	0.14%
36	West Virginia	1,039,894	0.46%		NA	Illinois**	NA	NA
16	Wisconsin	4,102,543	1.80%		NA	Kansas**	NA	NA
46	Wyoming	350,700	0.15%		NA	Montana**	NA	NA
						District of Columbia	570,000	0.25%

Source: Morgan Quitno Press using data from Federal Bureau of Investigation
  "Crime in the United States 1994" (Uniform Crime Reports, November 19, 1995)
*Estimated totals for urban areas, defined by the F.B.I. as Metropolitan Statistical Areas and other cities outside
such areas. National total includes states not shown separately.
**Not available.

Rural Population in 1994

National Total = 31,875,272 Rural Population*

ALPHA ORDER

RANK	STATE	POPULATION	% of USA
18	Alabama	793,931	2.49%
40	Alaska	190,603	0.60%
31	Arizona	312,726	0.98%
17	Arkansas	821,537	2.58%
24	California	621,211	1.95%
29	Colorado	364,845	1.14%
39	Connecticut	190,817	0.60%
44	Delaware	89,129	0.28%
21	Florida	756,471	2.37%
3	Georgia	1,420,206	4.46%
36	Hawaii	258,758	0.81%
28	Idaho	395,200	1.24%
NA	Illinois**	NA	NA
11	Indiana	1,056,398	3.31%
14	Iowa	891,801	2.80%
NA	Kansas**	NA	NA
4	Kentucky	1,365,966	4.29%
22	Louisiana	698,676	2.19%
30	Maine	346,275	1.09%
34	Maryland	268,210	0.84%
45	Massachusetts	12,316	0.04%
12	Michigan	1,039,484	3.26%
15	Minnesota	876,374	2.75%
7	Mississippi	1,111,604	3.49%
6	Missouri	1,187,388	3.73%
NA	Montana**	NA	NA
27	Nebraska	415,749	1.30%
41	Nevada	178,147	0.56%
42	New Hampshire	142,020	0.45%
46	New Jersey	0	0.00%
32	New Mexico	298,909	0.94%
16	New York	855,885	2.69%
1	North Carolina	1,667,846	5.23%
37	North Dakota	227,287	0.71%
5	Ohio	1,316,036	4.13%
23	Oklahoma	630,872	1.98%
25	Oregon	498,419	1.56%
9	Pennsylvania	1,058,822	3.32%
46	Rhode Island	0	0.00%
19	South Carolina	793,061	2.49%
33	South Dakota	292,829	0.92%
8	Tennessee	1,102,749	3.46%
2	Texas	1,605,793	5.04%
38	Utah	202,582	0.64%
35	Vermont	265,127	0.83%
10	Virginia	1,057,249	3.32%
26	Washington	491,104	1.54%
20	West Virginia	782,106	2.45%
13	Wisconsin	979,457	3.07%
43	Wyoming	125,300	0.39%

RANK ORDER

RANK	STATE	POPULATION	% of USA
1	North Carolina	1,667,846	5.23%
2	Texas	1,605,793	5.04%
3	Georgia	1,420,206	4.46%
4	Kentucky	1,365,966	4.29%
5	Ohio	1,316,036	4.13%
6	Missouri	1,187,388	3.73%
7	Mississippi	1,111,604	3.49%
8	Tennessee	1,102,749	3.46%
9	Pennsylvania	1,058,822	3.32%
10	Virginia	1,057,249	3.32%
11	Indiana	1,056,398	3.31%
12	Michigan	1,039,484	3.26%
13	Wisconsin	979,457	3.07%
14	Iowa	891,801	2.80%
15	Minnesota	876,374	2.75%
16	New York	855,885	2.69%
17	Arkansas	821,537	2.58%
18	Alabama	793,931	2.49%
19	South Carolina	793,061	2.49%
20	West Virginia	782,106	2.45%
21	Florida	756,471	2.37%
22	Louisiana	698,676	2.19%
23	Oklahoma	630,872	1.98%
24	California	621,211	1.95%
25	Oregon	498,419	1.56%
26	Washington	491,104	1.54%
27	Nebraska	415,749	1.30%
28	Idaho	395,200	1.24%
29	Colorado	364,845	1.14%
30	Maine	346,275	1.09%
31	Arizona	312,726	0.98%
32	New Mexico	298,909	0.94%
33	South Dakota	292,829	0.92%
34	Maryland	268,210	0.84%
35	Vermont	265,127	0.83%
36	Hawaii	258,758	0.81%
37	North Dakota	227,287	0.71%
38	Utah	202,582	0.64%
39	Connecticut	190,817	0.60%
40	Alaska	190,603	0.60%
41	Nevada	178,147	0.56%
42	New Hampshire	142,020	0.45%
43	Wyoming	125,300	0.39%
44	Delaware	89,129	0.28%
45	Massachusetts	12,316	0.04%
46	New Jersey	0	0.00%
46	Rhode Island	0	0.00%
NA	Illinois**	NA	NA
NA	Kansas**	NA	NA
NA	Montana**	NA	NA
	District of Columbia	0	0.00%

Source: Morgan Quitno Press using data from Federal Bureau of Investigation
"Crime in the United States 1994" (Uniform Crime Reports, November 19, 1995)
*Estimated totals for rural areas, defined by the F.B.I. as other than Metropolitan Statistical Areas and other cities outside such areas. National total includes states not shown separately.
**Not available.

VIII. SOURCES

Administrative Office of the U.S. Courts
Statistics Division
One Columbus Circle
Washington, DC   20544
202-273-2290

American Correctional Association
4380 Forbes Blvd.
Lanham, MD   20706-4322
301-918-1800

Bureau of the Census
3 Silver Hill & Suitland Roads
Suitland, MD   20746
301-457-2794
Internet: http://www.census.gov

Bureau of Justice Assistance Clearinghouse
Box 6000
Rockville, MD   20850
800-688-4252

Bureau of Justice Statistics Clearinghouse
Box 6000
Rockville, MD   20850
800-732-3277
Internet: http://www.ojp.jsdoj.gov/bjs/

Corrections Compendium
CEGA Publishing
P.O. Box 81826
Lincoln, NE   68501-1826
402-464-0602

Drugs and Crime Data Center & Clearinghouse
1600 Research Boulevard
Rockville, MD   20850
800-666-3332

Federal Bureau of Investigation
J. Edgar Hoover FBI Building
935 Pennsylvania Avenue, NW
Washington, DC   20535
202-324-3000
Internet: http://www.fbi.gov

Juvenile Justice Clearinghouse
Box 6000
Rockville, MD   20850
800-638-8736

National Archive of Criminal Justice Data
Inter-University Consortium for Political
  and Social Research
P.O. Box 1248
Ann Arbor, MI   48106
800-999-0960

National Association of State Alcohol and Drug Abuse Directors, Inc.
444 North Capitol Street, NW
Suite 642
Washington, DC   20001
202-783-6868

National Center for State Courts
300 Newport Avenue
Williamsburg, VA   23185
804-253-2000

National Institute of Justice
**National Criminal Justice Reference
  Service (NCJRS)**
Box 6000
Rockville, MD   20850
800-851-3420

Substance Abuse and Mental Health Services Administration
U.S. Department of Health
  and Human Services
5600 Fishers Lane
Rockville, MD   20857
301-468-2600

Victims of Crime Resource Center
Box 6000
Rockville, MD   20850
800-627-6872

IX. INDEX

IX. INDEX (continued)

IX. INDEX (continued)

IX. INDEX (continued)

CHAPTER INDEX

Arrests

Corrections

Drugs and Alcohol

Finance

Law Enforcement

Offenses

HOW TO USE THIS INDEX

Place left thumb on the outer edge of this page. To locate the desired entry, fold back the remaining page edges and align the index edge mark with the appropriate page edge mark.

Other books by Morgan Quitno Press:
- *State Rankings 1996*
- *City Crime Rankings, 2nd Edition*
- *Health Care State Rankings 1996*

Call toll free: 1-800-457-0742